INTERNATIONAL BIBLIOGRAPHY
OF THE SOCIAL SCIENCES

BIBLIOGRAPHIE INTERNATIONALE
DES SCIENCES SOCIALES

Publications of the ICSSD / Publications du CIDSS

INTERNATIONAL BIBLIOGRAPHY OF THE SOCIAL SCIENCES / BIBLIOGRAPHIE INTERNATIONALE DES SCIENCES SOCIALES

[published annually in four parts / paraissant chaque année en quatre parties, until 1961 / Jusqu'en 1961: UNESCO, Paris].

International bibliography of sociology / Bibliographie internationale de sociologie [red cover/couverture rouge.] Vol. 1: 1951 (Publ. 1952).
International bibliography of political science / Bibliographie internationale de science politique [grey cover/couverture grise]. Vol. 1: 1952 (Publ. 1954).
International bibliography of economics / Bibliographie internationale de science économique [yellow cover/couverture jaune]. Vol. 1: 1952 (Publ. 1955).
International bibliography of social and cultural anthropology / Bibliographie internationale d'anthropologie sociale et culturelle [green cover/couverture verte]. Vol. 1: 1955 Publ. 1958).

EDITORIAL BOARD
COMITÉ DE RÉDACATION

THE INTERNATIONAL COMMITTEE FOR SOCIAL SCIENCE INFORMATION AND DOCUMENTATION
LE COMITÉ INTERNATIONAL POUR L'INFORMATION ET LA DOCUMENTATION EN SCIENCES SOCIALES

27, rue Saint-Guillaume, 75007 Paris

Michel Bassand, Université de Lausanne
Abdelwahab Bouhdiba, Université de Tunis
Isac Chiva, Ecole des Hautes Etudes en Sciences Sociales, Paris
Derek Clarke, British Library of Political and Economic Science, London
Robert L. Cliquet, Centrum voor Bevolkings — en Gezinsstudien, Bruxelles
Tamás Földi, Bureau d'information économique, académie des Sciences de Hongrie, Budapest
Herbert Giersch, Institut für Weltwirtschaft, Kiel
Jean Laponce, University of British Columbia, Vancouver
Kéba M'Baye, Cour suprême, Dakar
Robert Mdivani, Institut d'information scientifique des sciences sociales, Moscou
Luis Ramallo, Facultad latinoamericana de ciencias sociales, Santiago de Chile
Gerhard J.A. Riesthuis, International Instituut voor Sociale Geschiedenis, Amsterdam
Janusz Šach, Centre d'information scientifique de l'Académie polonaise des Sciences, Varsovie
Géry d'Ydevalle, Universiteit te Leuven

General Secretary / Secrétaire général
JEAN MEYRIAT
Ecole des hautes études en sciences sociales, Paris

Assistant General Secretary and Managing Editor
JEAN VIET
Maison des sciences de l'homme, Paris

Associate Editor / Co-rédacteur
JOHN B. BLACK
University of Guelph

INTERNATIONAL BIBLIOGRAPHY OF THE SOCIAL SCIENCES

BIBLIOGRAPHIE INTERNATIONALE DES SCIENCES SOCIALES

1980

International Bibliography of SOCIOLOGY

Bibliographie internationale de SOCIOLOGIE

VOL. XXX

Prepared by the
International Committee for Social Science Information and Documentation

Établie par le
Comité international pour l'information et la documentation en sciences sociales

TAVISTOCK PUBLICATIONS
LONDON AND NEW YORK

*Manuscript prepared under the auspices of the International Sociological Association
by the ICSSD with the financial support of Unesco
(Subvention — 1981-1983 BG/7.6.2/SUB.16 (SS)*

*Manuscrit préparé sous les auspices de l'Association International de Sociologie
par le CIDSS avec le concours financier de l'Unesco
(Subvention — 1981-1983 DG/7.6.2/SUB.16 (SS)*

Published in 1982 by
Tavistock Publications Ltd.
11 New Fetter Lane,
London EC4P 4EE

Published in the USA by
Tavistock Publications
in association with Methuen, Inc.
733 Third Avenue, New York, NY 10017

All rights reserved. No part of this book may be reprinted or reproduced or utilized in any form or by any electronic, mechanical, or other means, now known or hereafter invented, including photocopying and recording, or in any information storage or retrieval system, without permission in writing from the publishers.

British Library Cataloguing in Publication Data

International bibliography of sociology. —
Vol. 30 (1980). — (International bibliography of the social sciences)
1. Sociology — Bibliography
I. International Committee for Social Science Information and Documentation
II. Series
016.310   Z7164.S68

ISBN 0-422-80970-5
ISSN 0085-2066

©ICSSD/CIDSS 1982

Printed in Great Britain
by Richard Clay & Co. Ltd.
Bungay, Suffolk

TABLE OF CONTENTS
TABLE DES MATIERES

Preface VII
Préface XII
List of Periodicals consulted / Liste des périodiques consultés XVII
Classification scheme / Plan de classification XXIX

Bibliography for 1980 / Bibliographie pour 1980 1
Author Index / Index des auteurs 271
Subject Index 331
Index des matières 366

PREFACE

This *International Bibliography of Sociology* is one of four annual volumes of the *International Bibliography of the Social Sciences,* publication of which was started by the International Committee for Social Science Information and Documentation in 1952 and had continued since then.

Over the years, a number of other, more or less specialized bibliographies have been published. Automated data bases have been put at the disposal of researchers. All these other means of information usefully complement our *International Bibliography of the Social Sciences,* yet they do not substitute for it. We are convinced that this Bibliography plays an indispensable role, as the large number of its subscribers continues to testify year after year.

The *International Bibliography of Sociology,* like its three sister bibliographies, constitutes in fact the most complete means to obtain global information about the previous year's publications in this domain from the entire world, and this by a simple, fast search, made easy by its indexes. This information is not "current" in the sense that it comes to the user shortly after publication of the cited documents; there is a twelve to twenty months' delay between the publication of a document and its subsequent signalling in the next annual volume of the Bibliography. Obviously, an annual bibliography is not the same as a monthly bulletin or a selective dissemination of information. It is the only place to collect in a definite and uniform manner the result of twelve months' scientific activity, the only place to find easily recent publications of all the authors from all countries about all the subjects in this field, and above all, the only place allowing the search of a period of thirty years as a whole.

Sociology now possesses — together with three other main branches of social sciences — a central bibliographic memory, cumulative and easily accessible, as in other fields of humanities, such as history, geography, classical philology, linguistics, etc., where the bibliographical references constitute a fundamental source. The parallel publication of four bibliographies, each in a different scientific field, is justified by two reasons: on the one hand, the purpose of giving to each scientific community a work tool responding best to its requirements, and on the other the desire to offer volumes of manageable size.

Such a venture is necessarily arbitrary: the lines between fields of social sciences have never been clearly defined, and contemporary evolution of these sciences further complicates the matter by emphasizing interdisciplinarity. Inside the domain of what we are used to call "social sciences", it is sometimes difficult to assign a publication to one of the branches while the same subject can be studied by different specialists. So we had to decide in some cases to repeat some of the notices in two or even three volumes of our *International Bibliography of the Social Sciences* in order to put at the user's disposal a sufficiently complete view of his discipline in each volume.

We should, nevertheless, emphasize that our four volumes are complementary to each other and that the scientist will sometimes need to consult another branch's volume. Also, it may be necessary to complete the information found in this Bibliography by information from bibliographies of other disciplines such as history, philosophy, psychology or medical sciences. The **Annex** on p. XIII lists the most important from these other bibliographical journals.

****

The design of presenting "sufficiently complete" volumes does not imply necessarily that they are also comprehensive. We need to emphasize the fact that the *International Bibliography of the Social Sciences* is *selective* and that this selection has the tendency of being more and more rigorous. In fact, all calculations indicate that for twenty-five years the number of primary publications in the social sciences increased at least threefold, while we maintained the quantitative increase of our Bibliography at a much lower level.

This voluntary selection is based partially on the already stated purpose of keeping these volumes manageable, and principally on the conviction that the user will not want to be submerged by an increasing mass of indiscriminate information, but on the contrary, appreciates having only useful references. He can, in this case, see a more specialized source later on, and eventually find complementary information.

The decision we made to collect in each volume only the information relevant to the field in question — sociology in this case — as it is defined pragmatically in the classification table following this foreword, represents a first selection. Further selection was made by applying the following principles:

a) We cite scientific studies, rather than simply informative documents: we give priority to books, articles from scientific journals, and research reports while we eliminate the presentation of primary data, purely administrative reports, legislative or judicial texts as well as popular articles.

b) The use of some secondary criteria of objective character also helped our choice: we only include signed articles, those published in monthly journals or in journals with less than monthly periodicity and non-polemical non-biased articles.

c) We search all of the most important publishers' catalogues and the most representative periodicals in each domain or speciality. We pick out from these periodicals also critical reviews and we cite them after the citation of the work itself. (If this latter was already cited in a previous volume, its bibliographical description after the title is replaced by the word: Bibl., then the number of the previous citation followed by the reference to the review.)

d) We pay particular attention to articles having a subject in one of our fields but published in a journal of some other speciality; this kind of material can be particularly difficult to identify.

e) We exclude, on the contrary, translations of a work already included in a well known original language but we include translations from a less known language. We also exclude new editions (except of course, when a new edition is entirely revised and becomes in fact an original work.)

f) We use all possible means to limit the number of redundant works, such as multiple articles of the same author about the same subject, while we keep preferentially a work covering a subject already discussed by several articles.

g) We give reference to studies of general interest, even when based on a definite case. We exclude those treating such a narrow speciality in a country that they have no real interest to foreign readers.

h) Studies produced in developing countries or in those originating books with poor foreign circulation, and thus generally least mentioned by bibliographies, are preferentially included in our Bibliography and our exclusion criteria are less strictly applied to them.

****

To keep an openness, the selection should be based on the largest possible knowledge of primary publications which are susceptible to be included as references. Our efforts aim to give first a comprehensive bibliographic information to ourselves. We try to reach this goal by combining the work of our editorial office, which uses all possible sources for its work, and the communications of our foreign contributors who give us firsthand knowledge of their country's publications.

We must thank here the institutions and specialists of several countries who kept us informed of their publications thus specially helping the compilation of this volume. Increasing the network of our contributors and benevolent collaborators is the only mean of a useful continuation of our work. We would like to ask, however, that the bibliographic lists arrive to us before March 1st of each year concerning publications of the previous year.

Special thanks are due to persons and institutions whose collaboration helped so greatly in the realization of this volume, especially to our contributors who were kind enough to send us information for the following countries: *Hungary,* Mr. László Remete and Mrs. Mária Vágh (Fövárosi Szabó Ervin Könyvtár, Budapest); *India,* Mr. S. P. Agrawal (Social Science Documentation Centre, Indian Council of Social Science Research, New Delhi); *Japan,* (Japan Sociological Society, Tokyo); *Netherlands,* (Sociologisch Instituut van de Rijksuniversiteit, Utrecht); *Poland,* Professor Władisław Adamski (Instytut Filozofii i Socjologii, Warszawa); *Spain,* Mrs. Valentina Fernandez Vargas (Instituto Balmes de Sociología, Madrid); *Union of Soviet Socialist Republics,* Professor Vladimir A. Vinogradov and Mr. Robert Mdivani (Institut Naučnoj Informacii no Obščestvennym Naukam, Moskva).

Preface

The present volume is the second one in our series to have been computerized, after the volume for **Economics** 1979. The bibliographical data were, as usual, collected, sorted out, standardized, classified and indexed by the editorial office in Paris. We express our grateful thanks to Agnès Majoros who has once again helped the editor.

The data so prepared were periodically sent to the office of the associate editor in Guelph, Ontario, where they were fed into a microcomputer, then processed and rearranged using the computer of Guelph University. We wish to thank in particular the Library of that University and the three system analysts, Don Hamilton, George Loney and Kathie McLaughlin whose efforts in developing the automated system were invaluable.

Thus was initiated a bibliographical data base which may now be retrieved on-line and will be offered for wider use when sufficiently enlarged by entires referring to post 1980 publications. At the same time a special programme was prepared in order to allow for the phototypesetting of the base. The present volume was produced using this procedure, which will be now applied to the other volumes of our International Bibliography.

PRÉFACE

Cette *Bibliographie internationale de sociologie* est un des quatre volumes annuels de la *Bibliographie internationale des sciences sociales,* dont la publication a été commencée en 1952 par le Comité international pour l'information et la documentation en sciences sociales et se poursuit régulièrement depuis lors.

Avec les années, beaucoup d'autres répertoires bibliographiques, plus ou moins spécialisés, sont parus. Des bases de données automatisées ont également été mises à la disposition des chercheurs. Tous ces moyens d'information complètent utilement notre *Bibliographie internationale des sciences sociales,* mais ne la remplacent pas. Nous sommes au contraire convaincus que celle-ci exerce une fonction qui lui est propre et qu'elle joue un rôle indispensable, comme en témoigne le fait que les années passant, le nombre de ses souscripteurs reste aussi élevé.

La *Bibliographie internationale de sociologie,* comme ses trois sœurs, constitue en effet le moyen le plus global d'obtenir, en une recherche simple et rapide facilitée par ses index, une information d'ensemble sur les publications relevant de la discipline pendant une année écoulée, et ce au niveau mondial. Cette information n'est pas "courante" en ce sens qu'elle parvient au lecteur un certain temps après l'apparition des documents signalés: le délai qui s'écoule entre la parution d'une publication primaire et celle du volume bibliographique qui la signale se situe normalement entre douze et vingt mois. Une bibliographie annuelle ne rend pas les mêmes services qu'un bulletin mensuel ou un service de diffusion sélective de l'information. Mais elle est seule à rassembler définitivement dans un cadre uniforme les résultats de douze mois d'activité scientifique, la seule à permettre de retrouver facilement les publications récentes de n'importe quel auteur en n'importe quel pays, sur n'importe quel sujet relevant de la discipline couverte, et a fortiori seule à autoriser une telle recherche sur l'ensemble d'une période qui, maintenant, couvre trente années.

La sociologie (parallèlement à trois autres des principes sciences sociales) dispose ainsi d'une mémoire bibliographique centrale, cumulative et facilement consultable, au même titre que bien d'autres sciences humaines pour lesquelles les références bibliographiques sont des sources fondamentales: histoire, géographie, philologie classique, linguistique, etc. Cette publication parallèle de quatre volumes bibliographiques consacrés chacun à une discipline se justifie par deux raisons: la volonté de fournir à chaque communauté scientifique bien identifiée un instrument de travail qui réponde le plus directement possible à ses préoccupations les plus fréquentes; et celle d'offrir des volumes d'une dimension non excessive et qui restent facilement maniables.

Elle entraîne nécessairement un certain arbitraire: les frontières entre les disciplines n'ont jamais été très nettement délimitées, et l'évolution contemporaine des sciences tend à les compliquer encore en mettant l'accent sur l'interdisciplinarité. A l'intérieur de ce qu'on est convenu d'appeler "sciences sociales", l'attribution d'une publication à une discipline déterminée est parfois difficile, et le même sujet peut souvent être étudié par des spécialistes différents. Aussi avons-nous décidé de répéter certaines références dans deux ou même trois volumes de notre *Bibliographie internationale des sciences sociales*, afin de mettre à la disposition de l'utilisateur de chaque volume un ensemble suffisamment complet du point de vue de sa discipline.

Il faut néanmoins insister sur le fait que nos quatre volumes sont complémentaires les uns des autres, et que le spécialiste de sociologie aura parfois intérêt à consulter un volume relevant d'une autre discipline. Il devra sans doute aussi, pour certains sujets, compléter les informations fournies par celles qu'il trouvera dans d'autres bibliographies n'appartenant pas à notre série mais relevant par exemple de l'histoire, de la philosophie, de la psychologie, de la médecine, etc. Une **Annexe,** p. XIII, donne une liste des plus importantes de ces autres revues bibliographiques.

****

Le dessein de présenter des volumes "suffisament complets" n'implique pas que ceux-ci soient exhaustifs. Il faut insister sur le fait que la *Bibliographie internationale des sciences sociales* est *sélective* et que cette sélection tend à être de plus en plus rigoureuse. En effet, depuis vingt-cinq ans, tous les calculs indiquent que le nombre des publications primaires de sciences sociales a au moins triplé; c'est délibérément que nous avons maintenu à un niveau beaucoup plus bas la croissance quantitative de notre Bibliographie.

Ce parti-pris de sélection se fonde, en partie, sur la volonté affirmée plus haut de préserver la maniabilité des quatre volumes; mais surtout sur la conviction que l'utilisateur n'a pas envie d'être submergé sous une masse croissante d'informations non discriminées, mais qu'il aspire à recevoir plutôt les seules références qui peuvent lui être utiles. Il pourra dans un deuxième temps, s'il le désire, recourir à une source bibliographique plus spécialisée pour y trouver des références complémentaires.

Le tri que nous opérons pour regrouper dans chaque volume les seules références pertinentes à la discipline couverte, ici la sociologie, telle qu'elle est pragmatiquement définie par le plan de classification reproduit à la suite de cette préface, représente une première sélection. Mais nous allons plus loin, en appliquant de notre mieux les principes suivants:

Preface

a) nous entendons signaler les études scientifiques plutôt que les documents purement informatifs; nous retenons donc de façon privilégiée les livres, articles de revues, rapports de recherche, pour éliminer les présentations de données brutes, les rapports purement administratifs, les textes législatifs ou juridiques, aussi bien que les articles de vulgarisation;

b) nous sommes aidés dans ce choix par l'utilisation de critères secondaires de nature objective: nous retenons en principe seulement les articles signés, ceux qui paraissent dans des revues à périodicité mensuelle ou moins fréquente, ceux qui ne présentent pas un caractère polémique ou partisan;

c) nous dépouillons entièrement les catalogues des éditeurs les plus importants et les périodiques généralement considérés comme les plus représentatifs de chaque discipline ou spécialité. Dans ces périodiques nous relevons aussi les comptes-rendus critiques et nous les signalons après la référence de l'ouvrage concerné. (Si celui-ci a été déjà cité dans un volume précédent, les données bibliographiques autres que son titre sont remplacées par le mot Bibl. suivi du n° d'ordre de la référence précédente, puis de la référence au compterendu.)

d) nous attachons une particulière importance aux articles qui concernent l'une de nos disciplines lorsqu'ils paraissent dans des revues généralement consacrées à un autre champ scientifique, car il s'agit là d'un matériel souvent le plus difficile à indentifier;

e) en revanche, nous excluons les traductions d'une publication dont nous avons signalé l'édition originale dans une langue de grande diffusion, mais nous retenons les traductions d'une langue moins connue à une langue de diffusion mondiale. Nous excluons aussi les rééditions (sauf lorsqu'une nouvelle édition entièrement revue constitue en fait un ouvrage original);

f) dans la mesure du possible, nous limitons le nombre des publications redondantes, les articles multiples d'un même auteur traitant le même sujet, etc.; et nous retenons de préférence un ouvrage lorsque, comme il arrive souvent, il couvre un sujet qui vient d'être abordé par de nombreux articles;

g) nous préférons les études de portée générale, même si elles reposent sur l'analyse d'un cas précis, mais nous négligeons celles qui, dans un pays, ont trait à des particularités si spécifiques qu'elles n'ont pas de réel intérêt pour des lecteurs étrangers;

h) nous privilégions relativement les études produites dans les pays en voie de développement ou dans les pays dont la production écrite est peu diffusée et de ce fait mal signalée par les services bibliographiques, en leur appliquant moins strictement les critères d'exclusion exposés ci-dessus.

****

Pour être légitime, la sélection opérée doit, bien entendu, se fonder sur la connaissance la plus large possible des publications primaires candidates à référence. Aussi nos efforts tendent-ils à l'exhaustivité de notre propre information bibliographique. Nous essayons d'y parvenir en combinant le travail de notre Bureau de rédaction, qui exploite toutes les sources possibles, et les contributions de divers correspondants étrangers qui nous font connaître de première main les publications de leur pays respectif.

Aussi nous est-il agréable de remercier ici les institutions et les spécialistes de nombreux pays qui nous ont informés de leurs publications et ont ainsi facilité la rédaction de ce volume. C'est seulement, en effet, en étendant toujours davantage le réseau de nos correspondants et collaborateurs bénévoles que nous pourrons poursuivre utilement notre tâche. Nous demandons cependant que les indications bibliographiques nous parviennent au plus tard le premier mars de chaque année, pour toute publication parue l'année précédente.

Des remerciements tout particuliers vont aux personnalités et aux institutions dont le concours a permis la réalisation de ce volume, notamment aux correspondants qui ont bien voulu nous envoyer des informations pour les pays suivants: *Espagne:* Mme Valentina Fernandez Vargas (Instituto Balmes de Sociología, Madrid); *Hongrie:* M. László Remete et Mme Mária Vágh (Fövárosi Szabó Ervin Könyvtar, Budapest); *Inde:* M. S. P. Agarwal (Social Science Documentation Centre, Indian Council of Social Science Research, New Delhi); *Japon:* (Japan Sociological Society, Tokyo); *Pays-Bas:* (Sociologisch Instituut van de Rijksuniversiteit, Utrecht); *Pologne:* Professeur Władysław Adamski (Instytut Filozofii i Sociologii, Warszawa); *Union des Républiques Socialistes Soviétiques:* Professeur Vladimir A. Vinogradov et M. Robert Mdivani (Institut Naučnoj Informacii no Obščestvennym Naukam, Moskova).

****

Nous voudrions enfin mentionner la façon dont le présent volume a été établi. Après celui de **Science économique** pour 1979, sa préparation a en effet été informatisée. Les données bibliographiques ont été, comme à l'habitude collectées, triées, normalisées, classées et indexées par le Bureau de rédaction à Paris. Nous devons remercier ici Agnès Majoros qui, cette année encore, a aidé le Rédacteur dans ce travail.

Les données ainsi préparées étaient au fur et à mesure envoyées au Bureau du co-rédacteur à Guelph, Ontario : c'est là qu'elles étaient saisies d'abord sur un micro-ordinateur, puis traitées et ordonnées sur le calculateur de l'Université de Guelph. Nous remercions tout particulièrement la Bibliothèque de cette Université, et les trois analystes, Don Hamilton, George Loney et Kathie McLaughlin, dont l'importante contribution a permis de maner à bien cette expérience d'automatisation.

Ainsi a été commencée une base de données bibliographiques qui d'ores et déjà est interrogeable en ligne, et qui sera offerte à l'utilisation lorsqu'elle aura été suffisamment enrichie par les références aux publications postérieures à 1980. En même temps un programme spécial a permis d'obtenir une version de la base préparée pour la photocomposition, et c'est par cette technique que le présent volume a été composé. Cette même procédure va être progressivement appliquée aux autres volumes de notre Bibliographie internationale.

ANNEX / ANNEXE
OTHER BIBLIOGRAPHICAL JOURNALS /
AUTRES REVUES BIBLIOGRAPHIQUES

I. ABSTRACTING JOURNALS (covering the same fields as the *International Bibliography of the Social Sciences*)
RECUEILS DE RÉSUMÉS ANALYTIQUES (couvrant les mêmes disciplines que la *Bibliographie internationale des sciences sociales*)

Economics / Science économique:
Economic Titles / Abstracts. The Hague, Nijhoff, 1974 — . 24 x (per year / par an)
Journal of Economic Literature. Pittsburgh, American Economic Association, 1962 — . 4 x (per year / per an)

Political Science / Science politique:
International Political Science Abstracts / Documentation politique internationale. Paris, International Political Science Association, 1951 — . 6 x (per year / per an)

Social and Cultural Anthropology / Anthropologie sociale et culturelle:
Abstracts in Anthropology. New York, Baywood Publishing Co., 1970 — . 4 x (per year / per an)

Sociology / Sociologie:
Sociological Abstracts. San Diego, CA, Sociological Abstracts Inc., 1952 — . 8 x (per year / per an)

II. CURRENT BIBLIOGRAPHIES (in related fields)
BIBLIOGRAPHIES COURANTES (dans des disciplines voisines)

Social Sciences in general / Sciences sociales en général:
London Bibliography of the Social Sciences. London, Mansell, 1975 — . 1 x (per year / per an)
Novaja Inostrannaja Literatura po Obscestvennym Naukam. Moskva, INION, 1947 — . (7 series) 12 x (per year / per an)
Social Sciences Citation Index. Philadelphia, Institute for Scientific Information, 1973 — . 2 x (per year / per an)
Social Sciences Index. New York, Wilson Co., 1974 — . 4 x (per year / per an)

Biological Sciences / Sciences biologiques:
Biological Abstracts. Philadelphia, BioSciences Information Service of Biological Abstracts, 1927 — . 24 x (per year / per an)

Business Economics / Économie d'entreprise:
Business Periodicals Index. New York, Wilson, Co., 1958 — . 12 x (per year per an)

Demography / Démographie:
Population Index. Princeton, Office of Population Research, 1935 — . 4 x (per year / per an)

Geography / Géographie:
Bibliographie géographique internationale. Paris, Centre National de la Recherche Scientifique, 1891 — 1976 : 1 x (per year / per an); 1977 — . 4 x (per year / per an)
Geo-abstracts. Norwich, University of East Anglia, 1960 — . (7 series) 6 x (per year / per an)

Annex

History / Histoire:
Bibliographie internationale des sciences historiques. Paris, Colin, 1926 — . 1 x (per year / per an)
Historical Abstracts. Santa Barbara, CA, American Bibliographical Center-Clio Press, 1955 — . 4 x (per year / per an)

Law / Droit:
Index to Foreign Legal Periodicals. London, Institute of Advanced Legal Studies, 1960 — . 4 x (per year / per an)

Linguistics / Linguistique:
Bibliographie linguistique. Utrecht, Spectrum 1949 — . 1 x (per year / per an)

Philosophy / Philosophie:
Bibliographie de la philosophie. Paris, Vrin, 1937 — . 4 x (per year / per an)

Psychology / Psychologie:
Psychological Abstracts. Washington, DC, American Psychological Association, 1927 — . 12 x (per year / per an)

LIST OF PERIODICALS CONSULTED
LISTE DES PÉRIODIQUES CONSULTÉS

Acta juridica (Budapest)	Budapest
Acta Sociologica	København
Actes de la Recherche en Sciences Sociales	Paris
Administration (Dublin)	Dublin
Administrative Change	Jaipur
Administrative Science Quarterly	Ithaca, NY
Affari sociali internazionale	Milano
Africa Development	Dakar
African Perspectives	Leyden
African Studies Review	East Lansing, MI
Afrika Spectrum	Hamburg
Aggiornamenti sociali	Milano
Agricultura y Sociedad	Madrid
Aichi kyoiku daigaku kenpo	&Nihoné
Aichi kyoiku daigaku shakai-kagaku ronshu	&Nihoné
Alternatives	Amsterdam
América indígena	Mexico
American behavioral Scientist	Princeton, NJ
American Journal of Economics and Sociology	New York, NY
American Journal of political Science	Detroit, MI
American Journal of Sociology	Chicago, IL
American political Science Review	Washington, DC
American Politics Quarterly	Riverside, CA
American Psychologist	Lancaster, PA
American sociological Review	New York, NY
American Sociologist	Washington, DC
Amérique latine	Paris
Análise Social	Lisbõa
Analyse und Kritik	Opladen
Annales de Géographie	Paris
Annales de l'Économie publique, sociale et coopérative	Liège
Annales de l'Université des Sciences sociales de Toulouse	Toulouse
Annales de la Faculté de Droit d'Istanbul	Istanbul
Annales de Sciences économiques appliquées	Louvain
Annales de Vaucresson	Vaucresson
Annales économiques	Clermont-Ferrand
Annales Universitatis Scientiarum budapestinensis de Rolando Eötvös nominatae. Sectio iuridica	Budapest
Annales-Économies-Sociétés-Civilisations	Paris
Annals of the American Academy of political and social Science	Philadelphia, PA
Année africaine	Paris
Annuaire de l'URSS et des Pays socialistes européens	Strasbourg
Annuaire des Pays de l'Océan indien	Aix-en-Provence
Annual Review of Sociology	Palo Alto, CA
Aoi umi	[Nihon]
Aperçus sur l'Économie tchécoslovaque	Prague
Arab Studies Quarterly	Detroit, MI
Arbeitsrecht der Gegenwart	Berlin
Archiv des öffentlichen Rechts	Tübingen
Archiv für Kommunalwissenschaften	Berlin
Archiv für Rechts- und Sozialphilosophie	Wiesbaden
Archiv für Sozialgeschichte	Bonn
Archiv für Wissenschaft und Praxis der sozialen Arbeit	Frankfurt a./M
Archives de Sciences sociales des Religions	Paris

XVII

List of periodicals consulted

Archives européennes de Sociologie	Paris
Argument (Berlin)	Berlin
Armed Forces and Society	Chicago, IL
Asahakawa daigaku kiyo	[Nihon]
Asahi Journal	[Nihon]
Asia Quarterly	Brussels
Asian Affairs (London)	London
Asian Economies	Seoul
Asian Profile	Hong Kong
Asian Survey	Berkeley, CA
Atarashii shakaigaku no tameni	[Nihoné
Aus Politik und Zeitgeschichte	Bonn
Australian and New Zealand Journal of Sociology	Melbourne
Australian Outlook	Melbourne
Australian Quarterly	Sydney
Baika tanki daigaku kenkyû kiyô	[Nihon]
Bangladesh Development Studies	Dacca
Behavior Science Research	New Haven, CT
Beiträge zur Konfliktforschung	Köln
Berkeley Journal of Sociology	Berkeley, CA
Betriebswirtschaft	Stuttgart
Bevolking en Gezin	Voorburg
Blätter für deutsche und internationale Politik	Köln
Boletín de Ciencias políticas y sociales	Mendoza
Boletín de Estudios latinoamericanos y del Caribe	Amsterdam
British Journal of industrial Relations	London
British Journal of international Studies	Leicester
British Journal of political Science	London
British Journal of Sociology	London
Bukkyô daigaku shakaigaku kenkyûjo kiyô	[Nihon]
Bukkyo bunka kenkyujo kiyo	Kyoto
Bukkyo-daigaku daigakuin kenkyu kiyo	[Nihon]
Bukkyo daigaku shakaigakubu ronso	Kyoto
Bulletin démographique des Nations-Unies	Genève
Bulletin de l'Institut fondamental d'Afrique noire	Dakar
Bulletin des Stupéfiants	New York
Bulletin of concerned American Scholars	San Francisco, CA
Byôin	[Nihon]
Cahiers d'Études africaines	Paris
Cahiers d'Outre-Mer	Bordeaux
Cahiers de Sociologie et de Démographie médicales	Paris
Cahiers des Amériques latines. Série Sciences de l'Homme	Paris
Cahiers internationaux de Sociologie	Paris
Cahiers québécois de Démographie	Québec
Canadian Journal of African Studies	Ottawa
Canadian Journal of political Science	Toronto
Canadian Journal of Sociology	Edmonton, Alberta
Canadian Review of Sociology and Anthropology	Calgary
Canadian Slavonic Papers	Ottawa
Canadian Studies in Population	Edmonton, Alberta
Chukyo shogaku ronso	[Nihon]
Columbia Law Review	New York, NY
Commentaire	Paris
Communantés	Paris
Communications (Paris)	Paris
Community Development Journal	Manchester
Comparative Education Review	Los Angeles, CA
Comparative political Studies	Beverly Hills, CA
Comparative Politics	Chicago, IL
Comparative Studies in Society and History	Ann Arbor, MI
Connexions	Paris
Consommation	Paris

Liste des périodiques consultés

Contemporary Sociology	Albany
Contributions to Indian Sociology. New Series	Delhi
Cornell Journal of social Relations	Ithaca, NY
Courrier des Pays de l'Est	Paris
Critica sociologica	Roma
Cuadernos de Realidades sociales	Madrid
Cultures	Paris
Current History	Philadelphia, PA
Dados	Rio de Janeiro
Daedalus	Cambridge, MA
Demográfia	Budapest
Demografía y Economía	México
Demografie	Praha
Demography	Ann Arbor, MI
Demosta	Praha
Desarrollo económico (Buenos Aires)	Buenos Aires
Deutsche Zeitschrift für Philosophie	Berlin
Developing Economies	Tokyo
Development and Change	The Hague
Développement et Progrès socio-économique	Le Caire
Déviance et Société	Genève
Diogène	Paris
Ditchley Journal	Enstone
Documentación social	Madrid
Dritte Welt	Meisenheim am Glan
Droit social	Paris
Economic and industrial Democracy	London
Economic Bulletin for Asia and the Pacific	New York, NY
Economic Development and cultural Change	Chicago, IL
Economic Geography	Worcester, MA
Économie et humanisme	Caluire
Économies et Sociétés. Cahiers de l'ISÉA	Paris
Economisch en sociaal Tijdschrift	Antwerpen
Economy and Society	London
Education (Tübingen)	Tübingen
Ekonomičeskie Nauki	Moskva
Ekonomika i matematičeskie Metody	Moskva
Espaces et Sociétes	Paris
Esprit	Paris
Ethnic and racial Studies	Henley-on-Thames
Études rurales	Paris
European Journal of social Psychology	The Hague
Family Planning Perspectives	New York
Family Process	Baltimore, MD
Filosofie Nauki	Moskva
Forum DS	Karlsruhe
Fudai keizai ronshû	Toyama
Futures	Guildford
Gegenwartskunde	Opladen
Gekkan rôdô mondai	Tokyo
Gendai nihon keizai shakai kenkyu	[Nihon]
Gendai no esupuri bessatsu hendo suru shakai to ningen	[Nihon]
Gendai shakaigaku	[Nihon]
Gendai shakaigaku no chihei to shôten	[Nihon]
Genus	Roma
Geographical Review	New York, NY
Geographische Rundschau	Braunschweig
Geographische Zeitschrift	Wiesbaden
Gérontologie et Société	Paris
Geschichte und Gesellschaft	Göttingen
Gewerkschaftliche Monatshefte	Köln
Gledišta	Beograd

XIX

List of periodicals consulted

GPSA Journal	Atlanta GA
Growth and Change	Lexington, KY
Harvard educational Review	Cambridge, MA
Hauswirtschaft und Wissenschaft	Bad Godesberg
Hérodote	Paris
Higher Education	Amsterdam
Hiroshima daigaku gakuko kyoikugakubu kiyo	Hiroshima
Hokkaido daigaku bungakubu kiyo	Sapporo
Hommes et Migrations	Paris
Human Organization	New York, NY
Human Relations	London
Ibaragi daigaku jinbun-gakubu kiyo shakai-kagaku	[Nihon]
Iberoamericana	[Nihon]
IFO-Studien	München
Impact. Science et Société	Paris
India international Centre Quarterly	New Delhi
India Quarterly	New Delhi
Indian Journal of social Research	Baraut
Indian Labour Journal	Simla
Indian political Science Review	Delhi
Industrial and Labor Relations Review	Ithaca, NY
Industrial Relations	Berkeley, CA
Informations sociales	Paris
Inquiry	Oslo
Insurgent Sociologist	Eugene, OR
International and comparative Law Quarterly	London
International Journal of comparative Sociology	Leiden
International Journal of contemporary Sociology	Ghaziabad
International Journal of Group Tensions	London
International Journal of Middle East Studies	London
International Journal of Politics	New York NY
International Journal of social Economics	Bradford
International Journal of Sociology	New York, NY
International Journal of Sociology of the Family	Lucknow
International Journal of the Sociology of Language	The Hague
International Journal of the Sociology of Law	London
International Journal of urban and regional Research	London
International Journal of Women's Studies	[Japan]
International Migration Review	New York
International political Science Review	
International Review of modern Sociology	Lucknow
International Studies Quarterly	Detroit, MI
Internationale wissenschaftliche Korrespondenz zur Geschichte der deutschen Arbeiterbewegung	Berlin
Irish Banking Review	Dublin
Israel Law Review	Jerusalem
Issue. A quarterly Journal of Opinion	Waltham, MA
Issues	Paris
Izvestija Akademii Nauk latvijskoj SSR	Riga
Izvestija Akademii Nauk moldavskoj SSR. Serija obščestvennyh Nauk	Kišinev
Izvestija Akademii Nauk turkmenskoj SSR. Serija obščestvennaja Nauk	Achkabad
Jahrbuch für Geschichte von Staat, Wirtschaft und Gesellschaft Lateinamerikas	Köln
Jahrbuch für Sozialwissenschaft	Göttingen
Japan Quarterly	Tokyo
Japanese Journal of religious Studies Japan]	
Jerusalem Quarterly	Jerusalem
Jewish Journal of Sociology	London
Jido shinri	[Nihon]
Jinbun kenkyu	Osaka

Jinko mondai kenkyû	Tokyo
Jochi daigaku kokusaigaku ronshu	[Nihon]
Journal for the Theory of social Behaviour	Oxford
Journal of Administration Overseas	London
Journal of African Studies	Berkeley, CA
Journal of applied behavioral Science	New York
Journal of Biosocial Science	Cambridge
Journal of Black Studies	Los Angeles, CA
Journal of Broadcasting	Philadelphia, PA
Journal of Communication	Austin, TX
Journal of Conflict Resolution	Ann Arbor, MI
Journal of contemporary Asia	Stockholm
Journal of contemporary History	London
Journal of developing Areas	Macomb, IL
Journal of Development Studies	London
Journal of Family History	Minneapolis, MN
Journal of general Management	London
Journal of human Resources	Madison, WI
Journal of Jewish communal Service	Albany, NY
Journal of Latin American Studies	Cambridge
Journal of legal Studies	Chicago, IL
Journal of Management Studies	Oxford
Journal of Marriage and Family	Minneapolis, MN
Journal of mathematical Sociology	London
Journal of modern African Studies	Cambridge
Journal of Peace Research	Oslo
Journal of Peasant Studies	London
Journal of Personality and social Psychology	Washington, DC
Journal of political and military Sociology	Dekalb, IL
Journal of Population	Chapel Hill, NC
Journal of social and political Studies	Washington, DC
Journal of social Issues	New York, NY
Journal of social Policy	London
Journal of social Psychology	Provincetown, MA
Journal of Southeast Asian Studies	Singapore
Journal of Southern African Affairs	College Park, MD
Journal of Southern African Studies	London
Journal of the American statistical Association	Washington, DC
Journal of the History of Sociology	Boston, MA
Journal of the social Sciences	Kuwait
Journal of vocational Bahavior	Ann Arbor, MI
Journalism Quarterly	Minneapolis, MN
Jugoslovenski Pregled	Beograd
Julist zokan	[Nihon]
Jurisuto zokan sogo tokushu	[Nihon]
Kabar Seberang	Townsville
Kagaku tetsugaku	[Nihon]
Kasvatus	Iyvaskyla
Kategorii Dialektiki	Sverdlovsk
Keio daigaku hogaku kenkyu	[Nihon]
Keio gijuku daigaku daigaku'in shakaigaku kenkyuka kiyo	[Nihon]
Khamsin	Paris
Kikan rôdôho bessatsu	[Nihon]
Kikan rodoho bessatsu gendai shakaigaku	[Nihon]
Kobe University Law Review	Kobe
Kokumin keizai zasshi	Kobe
Kokusai seiji	Tokyo-Yûhikaku
Kokusai shika daigaku ronso	[Nihon]
Kokusaigaku kenkyu	[Nihon]
Kölner Zeitschrift für Soziologie und sozial-Psychologie	Köln-Opladen
Kommunist Moldavii	Kišinev
Kommunist Tatarii	Kazan'

Kommunist vooružennyh Sil	Moskva
Kommunističeskoe Vospitanie	Moskva
Kwansei gakuin daigaku shakaigakubu kiyo	Nishinomiya
Kyoiku shakaigaku kenkyu	Tokyo
Kyoiku shakaigaku kiyo	[Nihon]
Kyoikugaku kenkyu	Tokyo
Kyosan-shugi to kokusai seiji	[Nihon]
Langages	Paris
Laru Studies	Toronto
Latin American Perspectives	Riverside, CA
Latin American Research Review	Austin, TX
Law and Society Review	New York
Leviathan	Bonn
Liberal (Bonn)	Bonn
Ličnost' i Obščestvo	Kaliningrad
Loisir et Société	Québec
Maghreb-Machrek	Paris
Majalah Demografi Indonesia	Djakarta
Management international Review	Wiesbaden
Masses ouvrières	Paris
Méditerranée	Aix-en-Provence
Meijigakuin ronsô	Tokyo
Mens en Maatschappij	Amsterdam
Metodologičeskie Voprosy Nauki	Saratov
Meždunarodnaja Žizn'	Moskva
Middle East Journal	Washington, DC
Middle East Review	New York
Middle Eastern Studies	London
Migrations internationales	La Haye
Milbank Memorial Fund Quarterly	New York
Minerva	London
Mitteilungen aus der Arbeitsmarkt- und Berufsforschung	Stuttgart
Mois en Afrique	Paris
Mondes en Développement	Paris
Monthly Review	New York
Mulino	Bologna
Muslim World	Hartford, CT
Nagoya daigaku shakaigaku ronshu	Nagoya
Naučnye Doklady vysšej Školy. Naučnyj Kommunizma	Moskva
Naučnye Trudy Azerbajdžanskogo Universiteta. Serija istoričeskih i filosofskih Nauk	Baku
Naučnye Trudy Azerbajdžanskogo Universiteta. Serija juridičeskij Nauk	Baku
Naučnye Trudy Kujbyševskogo pedagogičeskogo Instituta	Kujbyšev
Naučnye Trudy po Istorii KPSS	Kiev
Naučnye Trudy. Moskovskij zaočnyj pedagogičeskij Institut	Moskva
Naučnyj Kommunizm	Moskva
Nekotorye filosovskie Problemy Gosudarstva i Prava	Saratov
Nenpo ningen kagaku	[Nihon]
Nenpo shakai shinrigaku	Tokyo
Netherlands Journal of Sociology	Amsterdam
Neue Gesellschaft	Bielefeld
Neue Praxis	Neuwied
New Left Review	London
NHK hoso bunka kenkyu nenpo	Tokyo
Nigerian Journal of economic and social Studies	Ibadan
Nihon shakai-kyôiku gakukai kiyô	[Nihon]
Nihon shogai kyoiku gakukai nenpo	[Nihon]
Nihon toshigakukai nenpo	[Nihon]
Notas de Población	San José
Novaja i novejšaja Istorija	Moskva
Nueva Sociedad	Caracas

Liste des périodiques consultés

Obščestvennye Nauki (Moskva)	Moskva
Obščestvennye Nauki v Uzbekistane	Taškent
Oitemon gakuin daigaku bungakubu kiyo	[Nihon]
Okinawa kokusai daigaku bungakubu kiyo	[Nihon]
Organization Studies	New York- Berlin
Organizational studies	[Nihon]
Orient (Opladen)	Opladen
Orientation scolaire et professionnelle	Paris
Osaka daigaku nenpo ningen kagaku	Osaka
Osaka kyoiku daigaku kyikagaku ronshu	Osaka
Österreichische Monatshefte	Wien
Österreichische Osthefte	Wien
Österreichische Zeitschrift für Politikwissenschaft	Wien
Otsuma joshidaigaku kaseigakubu kiyo	[Nihon]
Pacific Affairs	New York
Pacific sociological Review	San Diego, CA
Pacific Viewpoint	Wellington
Peasant Studies	Pittsburg, PA
Pensée	Paris
Personnel Psychology	Baltimore, MD
Perspectives (Unesco)	Paris
Peuples méditerranéens/ Mediterranean Peoples	Paris
Peuples noirs — Peuples africains	Paris
Philosophical Forum	Boston, MA
Philosophy of the social Sciences	Aberdeen
Planning and Development in the Netherlands	Assen
Plannning and Administration	The Hague
Plural Societies	The Hague
Pluriel	Paris
Pod Znamenem Leninizma	Kiev
Policy and Politics	London
Policy Sciences	Santa Monica, NY
Policy Studies Review Annual	
Politićka Misao	Beograd
Političeskaja Organizacija Obščestva i Upravlenija pri Socializme	Leningrad
Political Behavior	New York
Political Psychology	Los Angeles, CA
Political Quarterly	London
Political Science Quarterly	New York
Political Studies (Oxford)	Oxford
Politico	Pavia
Politique aujourd'hui	Paris
Politische Vierteljahresschrift	Heidelberg-Köln-Opladen
Ponte	Firenze
Populacni Zpravy	Praha
Population	Paris
Population and Development Review	New York
Population et Famille	Bruxelles
Population Studies	London
Populi	New York
Pouvoirs	Paris
Présence africaine	Paris
Problemas del Desarrollo	México
Problemi del Socialismo	Milano
Problemy Filosofii	Kiev
Problemy naučnogo Kommunizma	Moskva
Problemy Pravovedenija	Kiev
Problemy social'nogo Prognozirovanija	Krasnojarsk
Problemy social'noj Aktivnosti	Čeljabinsk
Proceedings of the Academy of political Science	New York
Proceedings of the annual Symposium of the Eugenics Society	London

XXIII

List of periodicals consulted

Projet	Paris
Prospettive settanta	Roma
Psychologie française	Paris
Psykologia	Helsinki
Public Choice	Blacksburg, VA
Public Interest	New York
Public Opinion Quarterly	Princeton, NJ
Publizistik	Münster-in-Westfalen
Quaderni di Sociologia	Torino
Quality and Quantity	Padova
Queen's Quarterly	Kingston, Ont.
Questions actuelles du Socialisme	Paris-Belgrade
Rabels Zeitschrift für ausländisches und internationales Privatrecht	Berlin
Rabočij Klass i sovremennyj Mir	Moskva
Radical Humanist	New Delhi
Raison présente	Paris
Rassegna italiana di Sociologia	Firenze
Rassegna sindacale Quaderni	Roma
Razón y Fe	Madrid
Recherche	Paris
Recherche sociale (Paris)	Paris
Recherches internationales à la Lumière du Marxisme	Paris
Recherches sociographiques	Québec
Recherches sociologiques	Louvain
Recht der Arbeit	München
Recht der Jugend und des Bildungswesens	Berlin-Neuwied
Regional Studies	Oxford
Relations industrielles	Québec
Research in Labor Economics	Greenwich, CT
Research in Law and Sociology	Greenwich, CT
Research in organizational Behavior	Greenwich, CT
Research in Population Economics	Greenwich, CT
Research in Race and ethnic Relations	Greenwich, CT
Research in social Movements, Conflicts and Changes	Greenwich, CT
Research in social Problems and public Policy	Greenwich, CT
Revija za Sociologiju	Zagreb
Revista brasileira de Estudos políticos	Belo Horizonte
Revista de Administração de Emprêsas	Rio de Janeiro
Revista de Ciências sociais	Fortaleza
Revista de Economía latinoamericana	Caracas
Revista de Estudios agro-sociales	Madrid
Revista de Estudios de la Vida local	Madrid
Revista de Estudios políticos	Madrid
Revista de Filozofie	București
Revista de Fomento social	Madrid
Revista de la Universidad Externado de Colombia	Bogotá
Revista de Política social	Madrid
Revista española de Investigaciones sociológicas	Madrid
Revista internacional de Sociología	Madrid
Revista javeriana	Bogotá
Revista latinoamericana de Psicología	Bogotá
Revista mexicana de Ciencias políticas y sociales	México
Revista mexicana de Sociología	México
Révoltes logiques	Paris
Revue algérienne des Sciences juridiques, économiques et politiques	Alger
Revue belge de Sécurité sociale	Bruxelles
Revue d'Intégration européenne	Montréal
Revue de Géographie alpine	Grenoble
Revue de Géographie de Lyon	Lyon
Revue de l'AUPELF	Montréal
Revue de l'Institut de Sociologie	Bruxelles

Revue de l'Occident musulman et de la Méditerranée	Aix-en-Provence
Revue de la Coopération internationale	Londres
Revue des Études coopératives	Paris
Revue des Sciences humaines	Paris
Revue des Travaux de l'Académie des Sciences morales et politiques	Paris
Revue économique et sociale	Lausanne
Revue européenne des Sciences sociales. Cahiers Vilfredo Pareto	Genève
Revue française d'Administration publique	Paris
Revue française de Gestion	Paris
Revue française de Pédagogie	Paris
Revue française de Science politique	Paris
Revue française de Sociologie	Paris
Revue française des Affaires sociales	Paris
Revue géographique des Pyrénées et du Sud-Ouest	Toulouse
Revue interdisciplinaire d'Études juridiques	Bruxelles
Revue internationale de la Sécurité sociale	Genève
Revue internationale de sociologie/International Review of Sociology	Rome
Revue internationale des Sciences administratives	Bruxelles
Revue internationale des Sciences sociales	Paris
Revue internationale du Travail	Genève
Revue juridique et politique — Indépendance et Coopération	Paris
Revue nouvelle	Tournai
Revue trimestrielle de Droit sanitaire et social	Paris
Revue tunisienne de Géographie	Tunis
Revue tunisienne des Sciences sociales	Tunis
Rice University	[Nihon]
Risshô daigaku shakaigaku-shakaifukushigakukai ronsô	Tokyo
Risshô daigaku tanki daigakubu kiyo	[Nihon]
Ritsumeikan sangyo-shakai ronshû	Kyoto
Rivista geografica italiana	Firenze
Rivista italiana de Scienza politica	Bologna
Rundfunk und Fernsehen	Hamburg
Rural Demography	Dacca
Rural Sociology	Lexington, KY
Rural sociology in an international context	[Nihon]
Sage Yearbooks in Politics and public Policy	Beverly Hills, CA
Sage Yearbooks in Women's Policy Studies	Beverly Hills, CA
Sapienchia	[Nihon]
Sbornik naučnyh Trudov (Sverdlovskij pedagogičeskij Institut)	Sverdlovsk
Sbornik naučnyh Trudov Taškentskogo Universiteta	Taškent
Scandinavian political Studies	Helsinki
Schweizerische Zeitschrift für Soziologie/ Revue suisse de Sociologie	Genf/Genève
Science and public Policy	London
Sciences sociales. Académie des Sciences de l'URSS	Moscou
Scottish Journal of Sociology	Stirling
Seinen shinri	[Nihon]
Senshû keieigaku ronshû	Tokyo
Shakaigaku hyoron	Tokyo
Shakaigaku kenkyu	[Nihon]
Shakaigaku nenpo	Tokyo
Shakaigaku ronso	Tokyo
Shakaigaku tsushin	[Nihon]
Shinri to sozo	[Nihon]
Shukugawa gakuin tanki daigaku kenkyu kiyo	[Nihon]
Signs	New York
Sistema. Revista de Ciencias sociales	Madrid
Slavic Review	New York
Sloan Management Review	Cambridge
Sociaal Maandblad Arbeid	Alphen-an-den-Rijn- Rotterdam
Social Action	New Delhi

Social Biology	New York
Social Compass	The Hague
Social Forces	Chapel Hill, NC
Social Indicators Research	Dordrecht
Social Networks	Lausanne
Social Policy	New York
Social praxis	[Nihon]
Social Praxis	Paris
Social Problems	New York, Rochester, MI
Social Psychology Quarterly	Albany, NY
Social Research	New York
Social Science	Winfield
Social Science Information	Paris
Social Science Journal	Fort Collins, CO
Social Science Quarterly	Austin, TX
Social Science Research	Ann Arbor, MI
Social Sciences Information Studies	Borough Green
Social Service Delivery Systems	Beverly Hills, CA
Social Service Review	Chicago, IL
Social Welfare	New Delhi
Socialism in Yugoslav Theory and Practice	Belgrade
Socialist Register	London
Socialist Review	London
Society	Washington, DC
Socijalizam	Beograd
Socio-economic planning Sciences	New York
Sociologičeskie Issledovanija	Moskva
Sociologia (Roma)	Roma
Sociologia ruralis	Assen
Sociological Analysis	San Antonio, TX
Sociological Focus	Akron, OH
Sociological Inquiry	Toronto
Sociological Methods and Research	Beverly Hills, CA
Sociological Quarterly	Carbondale, IL
Sociological Review	Keele
Sociologický Časopis	Praha
Sociologie contemporaine/ Current Sociology	Oxford
Sociologie du Travail	Paris
Sociologie et Sociétés	Montréal
Sociologija	Beograd
Sociologija sela	Zagreb
Sociologische Gids	Meppel
Sociologos	[Nihon]
Sociologus	Berlin
Sociology	London
Sociology and social Research	Los Angeles, CA
Sociology of Education	Washington, DC
Sociology of the Sciences. A Yearbook	Dordrecht
Sociology of Work and Occupations	Beverly Hills, CA, London
Soka daigaku daigakuin kiyo	[Nihon]
Soka daigaku sociologica	[Nihon]
Soka daigaku soritsu 10-shunen kinen ronbunshu	[Nihon]
Soshiki kagaku	[Nihon]
Soshiorogosu	[Nihon]
Soshioroji	Kyoto
Sosaalivakuutus	Helsinki
Sosiologia	Helsinki
South Africa International	Johannesburg
Southeast Asian Affairs	Singapore
Sovetskoe Gosudarstvo i Pravo	Moskva

Liste des périodiques consultés

Soviet Geography	New York
Soviet Jewish Affairs	London
Soviet Studies	Glasgow
Soziale Welt	Göttingen
Sozialer Fortschritt	Bonn
Soziologische Revue	München
Sri Lanka Labour Gazette	Sri Lanka
Staat und Recht	Potsdam
Stamp Memorial Lecture	London
Statistiques du Travail. Supplément au Bulletin mensuel	Paris
Studi di Sociologia	Milano
Studi Emigrazione	Roma
Studi italiani di Linguistica teorica ed applicata	Padova
Studia islamica	Paris
Studies in comparative Communism	
Studies in Family Planning	Greenwich, CT
Studies of Broadcasting	Tokyo
Supreme Court Review	Chicago, IL
Tôhoku kôgyô daigaku kiyô bunkakei-hen	Fukuoka
Takachiho ronsô	[Nihon]
Teaching Sociology	Beverly Hills, CA
Technological Forecasting and social Change	New York
Teikyo tanki daigaku kiyo	[Nihon]
Teorija in Praksa	Ljubljana
Textes et Documents	Bruxelles
Theorie und Praxis der sozialen Arbeit	Bonn
Theory and Society	Amsterdam
Third World Quarterly	London
Tocqueville Review	Charlottesville, Va.
Tohoku shakaigaku kenkyukai shakaigaku kenkyu	Fukuoka
Tokushima daigaku gakugei kiyo shakai-kagaku	Tokushima
Tokyo daigaku shakaigaku kenkyujo nenpo	Tokyo
Tokyo kogei daigaku kogakubu kiyo	Tokyo
Tokyo toritsu daigaku jinbungaku-ho	Tokyo
Tokyo toritsu daigaku shakaigaku ronko	Tokyo
Tokyo toritsu daigaku sogo toshi kenkyu	Tokyo
Toxicomanies	Québec
Toyamadaigaku Nihonkai kankyujo kenkyu nenpo	Toyama
Travail et Emploi	Paris
Travail et Méthodes	Paris
Travail et Société	Genève
Trudy Omskogo vysšej Školy Milicii	Omsk
Trudy Samarkandskogo Universiteta	Samarkand
Tsukuba daigaku Latin America tokubetsu project nenji hokokusho	[Nihon]
Universitas. Zeitschrift für Wissenschaft, Kunst und Literatur	Stuttgart
Urban Affairs annual Review	Beverly Hills, CA
Urban Affairs Quarterly	Beverly Hills, CA
Urban Studies	Edinburgh
Uzbekistonda iżtimoii Fanlar	Taškent
Verfassung und Recht in Übersee	Hamburg
Vestnik Akademii Nauk SSSR	Moskva
Vestnik Moskovskogo Universiteta. Teorija naučnogo Kommunizma	Moskva
Vestnik Moskovskogo Universiteta. Serija Filosofija	Moskva
Voprosy Filosofii	Moskva
Voprosy Istorii	Moskva
Voprosy naučnogo Kommunizma	Kiev
Voprosy naučnogo Kommunizma	Erevan
Voprosy obščestvennyh Nauk	Kiev
Voprosy Teorii i Metodov ideologičeskoj Raboty	Moskva
Waseda daigaku keizaigaku kenkyu nenpô	Tokyo
Waseda daigaku shakai-kagaku tokyu	Tokyo

West European Politics	London
Western political Quarterly	Salt Lake City, UT
Yearbook of agricultural Cooperation	Oxford
Yearbook of Population Research in Finland	Helsinki
Youth and Society	Los Angeles, CA
Yugoslav Survey	Belgrade
Zaïre-Afrique	Kinshasa
Zaiseigaku kenkyu	[Nihon]
Zbornik pravnog Fakulteta u Zagrebu	Zagreb
Zeitschrift für Arbeitswissenschaft	Dortmund
Zeitschrift für Bevölkerungswissenschaft	Wiesbaden
Zeitschrift für das gesamte Genossenschaftswesen	Göttingen
Zeitschrift für Politik	Berlin
Zeitschrift für Soziologie	Stuttgart
Zeitschrift für Unternehmensgeschichte	Wiesbaden R

CLASSIFICATION SCHEME
PLAN DE CLASSIFICATION

10	Social Sciences. Research. Documentation Sciences sociales. Recherche. Documentation	
10100	Social sciences. Sociology / Sciences sociales. Sociologie	1-75
10200	Research worker. Sociologist / Chercheur. Sociologue	76-111
10300	Organization of research. Research policy / Organisation de la recherche. Politique de recherche	
10310	Current research / Recherche en cours	112-137
10320	Applied research. Interdisciplinary research / Recherche appliquée. Recherche interdisciplinaire	138-144
10330	Research centre / Centre de recherche	145-146
10340	Organization of research. Research policy / Organisation de la recherche. Politique de la recherche	147-164
10350	Research equipment / Équipement de la recherche	165-169
10360	Sociological association / Association de sociologie	170-171
10400	Congres. Meeting / Congrès. Réunion	172-177
10500	Document. Information processing / Document. Traitement de l'information	
10510	Documentation / Documentation	178-196
10520	Document analysis. Reference book / Analyse documentaire. Ouvrage de référence	197-199
10530	Documentation centre / Centre de documentation	200-202
10540	Documentalist / Documentaliste.............................	203
10550	Terminology / Terminologie................................	204-208
10560	Biography / Biographie	209-226
10570	Article. Periodical / Article. Périodique	227-232
10580	Proceedings. Report / Actes. Rapport	
10590	Textbook. Thesis Manuel. Thèse	233-241
11	Methodology. Theory Méthodologie. Théorie	
11100	Epistemology. Research method. Theory / Epistémologie. Méthode de recherche. Théorie	
11110	Philosophy. Theory / Philosophie. Théorie	242-338
11120	Epistemology. Explanation. Understanding / Epistémologie. Explication. Compréhension	339-385
11130	Research method. Sociological analysis / Méthode de recherche. Analyse sociologique	403-471
11200	Data collection. Experiment / Rassemblement des données. Expérience	
11210	Experimentation. Observation / Expérimentation. Observation....	472-493
11220	Sampling. Survey / Échantillonnage. Enquête	495-494
11230	Interview. Questionnaire / Entretien. Questionnaire	503-515
11240	Personality measurement. Test / Mesure de la personnalité. Test...	516-517
11250	Sociodrama / Sociodrame	
11300	Mathematical analysis. Statistical analysis / Analyse mathématique. Analyse statistique	
11310	Algebra. Calculus. Logic / Algèbre. Calcul. Logique	518-525
11320	Statistical analysis / Analyse statistique	526-597
11330	Cybernetics. Information theory / Cybernétique. Théorie de l'information...	598-601

XXIX

11340	Graph theory / Théorie des graphes	604-609
11350	Stochastic processes. Statistical decision. Game theory / Processus stochastiques. Décision statistique. Théorie des jeux	610-615
11360	Attitude scale / Échelle d'attitude	617-6

12	**Individual. Group. Organization** **Individu. Groupe. Organisation**	
12100	Psychology. Social psychology. Sociometry / Psychologie. Psychologie sociale. Sociométrie	
12110	Psychoanalysis. Social psychology / Psychanalyse. Psychologie sociale	625-657
12120	Psychological factor / Facteur psychologique	
12200	Individual. Personality / Individu. Personnalité	
12210	Ego. Identity / Ego. Identité	658-666
12220	Egocentrism. Self concept / Égocentrisme. Conception de soi	667-712
12230	Personality / Personnalité	713-770
12240	Cognition. Emotion. Motivation / Cognition. Émotion. Motivation	772-875
12300	Interpersonal relations / Relations interpersonnelles	
12310	Human relations. Sociability / Relations humaines. Sociabilité	883-900
12320	Social perception / Perception sociale	901-915
12330	Interpersonal attraction / Attraction interpersonnelle	916-934
12340	Interpersonal influence / Influence interpersonnelle	935-940
12350	Interpersonal conflict / Conflit interpersonnel	941-957
12360	Intergroup relations / Relations intergroupes	960-978
12400	Group / Groupe	
12410	Group dynamics / Dynamique de groupe	983-999
12420	Primary group. Training group / Groupe primaire. Groupe de formation	1000-1016
12430	Group size / Dimension du groupe	1017-1026
12440	Group integration / Intégration du groupe	1027-1036
12450	Group membership / Appartenance au groupe	1037-1045
12460	Group performance / Performance du groupe	1046-1049
12500	Bureaucracy. Organization / Bureaucratie. Organisation	
12510	Sociology of organization / Sociologie des organisations	1050-1066
12520	Complex organization / Organisation complexe	1067-1072
12530	Bureaucracy / Bureaucratie	1073-1133
12600	Leadership. Role / Commandement. Rôle	
12610	Authority / Autorité	1134-1142
12620	Leadership / Commandement	1143-1155
12630	Role / Rôle	1156-1171
12700	Attitude. Opinion / Attitude. Opinion	
12710	Behaviour / Comportement	1172-1199
12720	Cognitive dissonance. Prejudice / Dissonance cognitive. Préjugé	1200-1210
12730	Dogmatism. F scale / Dogmatisme. Échelle F	1211-1218
12740	Opinion / Opinion	1219-1241
12750	Ideology / Idéologie	1242-1266
12760	Collective behaviour / Comportement collectif	1267-1275

13	**Culture. Socialization. Social life** **Culture. Socialisation. Vie sociale**	
13100	Culture. Social environment. Value / Culture. Milieu social. Valeur	
13110	Social and cultural anthropology / Ethnologie	1276-1279
13120	Civilization. Culture. Society / Civilisation. Culture. Société	1280-1398
13130	Cultural dynamics. Cultural relations / Dynamique culturelle. Relations culturelles	1407-1440
13140	Norm. Social control. Value / Norme. Régulation sociale. Valeur	1442-1492
13150	Alienation. Socialization. Social conformity / Aliénation. Socialisation. Conformité sociale	1497-1594

13200	Custom. Tradition / Coutume. Tradition.....................	1595-1601
13300	Ethics. Morals / Éthique. Morale...........................	1602-1635
13400	Law. Regulation / Loi. Réglementation.....................	1636-1672
13500	Magic. Mythology. Religion / Magie. Mythologie. Religion	
13510	Religion. Sociology of religion / Religion. Sociologie religieuse.....	1673-1690
13520	Magic. Primitive religion / Magie. Religion primitive............	1691-1702
13530	Buddhism. Christianity / Bouddhisme. Christianisme............	1703-1795
13540	Church. Religious community. Sect / Église. Communauté religieuse. Secte...	1799-1823
13550	Clergy. Religious authority / Clergé. Autorité religieuse..........	1833-1834
13560	Cult. Rite / Culte. Rite....................................	1839-1854
13570	Myth. Religious doctrine / Mythe. Doctrine religieuse..........	1855-1879
13580	Religious behaviour / Comportement religieux..................	1883-1905
13590	Church and State. Religious practice / Église et État. Pratique religieuse..	1906-1944
13600	Science. Sociology of knowledge / Science. Sociologie de la connaissance..	1945-2006
13700	Communication. Language / Communication. Langage	
13710	Linguistics. Semiotics / Linguistique. Sémiotique	2007-2033
13720	Communication. Sign / Communication. Signe.................	2034-2069
13730	Language / Langage.......................................	2070-2122
13740	Audience / Audience	
13750	Advertising. Propaganda / Publicité. Propagande...............	2123-2131
13760	Mass communication / Communication de masse...............	2135-2214
13800	Art / Art	
13810	Aesthetics. Artist. Museum / Esthétique. Artiste. Musée.........	2215-2239
13820	Literature / Littérature.....................................	2240-2263
13830	Fine arts / Beaux-arts......................................	2264-2265
13840	Music / Musique..	2266-2272
13850	Dramatic art / Art dramatique..............................	2273-2276
13860	Folk art / Art populaire....................................	2277-2281
13900	Education / Éducation	
13910	Educational sociology / Sociologie de l'éducation	2282-2315
13920	Educational system. Educational policy / Système d'enseignement. Politique de l'enseignement	2316-2391
13930	Primary education. Secondary education / Enseignement primaire. Enseignement secondaire	2403-2419
13940	School environment / Milieu scolaire	2420-2422
13950	Higher education / Enseignement supérieur....................	2423-2487
13960	Adult education / Éducation des adultes	2488-2520
13970	Civic education. Technical education / Instruction civique. Enseignement technique	2521-2528
13980	Academic achievement. School failure / Réussite des études. Échec scolaire	2529-2533
13990	Pedagogy. Teaching. Teacher / Pédagogie. Enseignement. Enseignant	2535-2545
14	**Social structure** **Structure sociale**	
14100	Social system / Système social...............................	2560-2591
14200	Social stratification / Stratification sociale	
14210	Social differentiation / Différenciation sociale	2592-2630
14220	Caste. Slavery / Caste. Esclavage	2631-2647
14230	Social class / Classe sociale	2648-2722
14240	Status / Status..	2723-2730
14250	Elite. Intellectual / Élite. Intellectuel	2731-2774
14260	Social mobility / Mobilité sociale	2775-2787
14300	Social change / Changement social	

XXXI

14310	History / Histoire	2788-2810
14320	Future / Futur	2811-2814
14330	Social change / Changement social	2815-2872
14340	Changing society / Société en transformation	2873-2893

15	**Population. Family. Ethnic group**
	Population. Famille. Groupe ethnique

15100	Demography. Genetics / Démographie. Génétique	
15110	Population research / Recherche démographique	2894-2913
15120	Household. Man. Woman / Ménage. Homme. Femme	2914-2994
15130	Eugenism. Heredity / Eugénisme. Hérédité	2995-3003

15200	Age group / Groupe d'âge	
15210	Age. Cohort. Generation / Âge. Cohorte. Génération	3004-3006
15220	Childhood / Enfance	3007-3029
15230	Youth / Jeunesse	3030-3065
15240	Adult / Adulte	3066-3067
15250	Old age / Vieillesse	3068-3112

15300	Population evolution. Population policy / Évolution de la population. Politique démographique	
15310	Population growth / Accroissement de la population	3113-3178
15320	Morbidity / Morbidité	3180-3204
15330	Mortality / Mortalité	3205-3229
15340	Fertility. Natality / Fécondité. Natalité	3230-3282
15350	Family planning / Planification de la famille	3283-3351

15400	Marriage. Family / Mariage. Famille	
15410	Sexual behaviour / Comportement sexuel	3352-3388
15420	Marriage. Nuptiality / Mariage. Nuptialité	3389-3451
15430	Family / Famille	3455-3573
15440	Woman's status / Condition de la femme	3574-3647

15500	Ethnic group / Groupe ethnique	
15510	Ethnicity. Tribe / Ethnicité. Tribu	3648-3701
15520	Interethnic relations. Racism / Relations interethniques. Racisme	3746-3793

15600	Migration / Migration	
15610	Migrant. Migration policy / Migrant. Politique migratoire	3794-3811
15620	External migration / Migration externe	3815-3881
15630	Internal migration / Migration interne	3883-3937

16	**Environment. Community. Rural. Urban**
	Environnement. Communauté. Rural. Urbain

16100	Ecology. Geography. Population settlement / Écologie. Géographie. Habitat	
16110	Human geography / Géographie humaine	3938-3965
16120	Nature. Soil. Water / Nature. Sol. Eau	3966-3971
16130	Citizen. Inhabitant / Citoyen. Habitant	3972-3983

16200	Community / Communauté	3984-4012

16300	Rural. Urban / Rural. Urbain	
16310	Rural sociology / Sociologie rurale	4033-4191
16320	Urban sociology / Sociologie urbaine	4215-4403

17	**Economics / Science économique**

17100	Economic sociology / Sociologie économique	4410-4414

17200	Economic system / Système économique	
17210	Economic doctrine / Doctrine éco	4415-4420
17220	Capitalism. Collectivism / Capitalisme. Collectivisme	4446-4461

17300	Economic situation. Standard of living / Situation économique. Niveau de vie	

17310	Economy. Economic development / Économie. Développement économique	4464-4468
17320	Income. Living conditions / Revenu. Conditions de vie	4469-4518
17400	Enterprise. Production / Entreprise. Production	
17410	Business economics. Management / Économie de l'entreprise. Gestion	4519-4568
17420	Productivity. Technology / Productivité. Technologie	4569-4584
17430	Agriculture. Commerce. Industry / Agriculture. Commerce. Industrie	4615-4619
17500	Consumption. Market. Price / Consommation. Marché. Prix	
17510	Consumer behaviour / Comportement du consommateur	4651-4661
17520	Demand. Supply / Demande. Offre	4662-4665
17600	Credit. Financing. Money / Crédit. Financement. Monnaie	4666-4670
17700	Economic policy. Planning / Politique économique. Planification ..	4671-4675
18	**Labour** **Travail**	
18100	Industrial sociology. Sociology of work / Sociologie industrielle. Sociologie du travail	4676-4692
18200	Employment. Labour market / Emploi. Marché du travail	
18210	Labour. Manpower / Travail. Main-d'œuvre	4693-4730
18220	Employment. Unemployment / Emploi. Chômage	4731-4763
18230	Employment service. Job evaluation / Service d'emploi. Évaluation d'emploi	4764-4784
18240	Woman worker. Young / Travailleur féminin. Jeune travailleur ...	4785-4871
18300	Personnel management. Working conditions / Administration du personnel. Conditions de travail	
18310	Labour standard. Work study / Norme de travail. Étude du travail .	4874-4906
18320	Working conditions / Conditions de travail	4953-4957
18330	Labour turnover / Renouvellement de la main-d'œuvre	4993-5011
18400	Occupation. Vocational training / Profession. Formation professionnelle	
18410	Occupational sociology / Sociologie de la profession	5012-5027
18420	Occupational life. Vocational guidance / Vie professionnelle. Orientation professionnelle	5028-5080
18500	Employee. Technician. Worker / Employé. Technicien. Travailleur	
18510	Worker / Travailleur	5081-5101
18520	Employee / Employé	5102-5106
18530	Manager. Technician / Cadre. Technicien	5107-5124
18540	Liberal profession / Profession libérale........................	5125
18600	Labour management relations / Relations du travail	5126-5158
18610	Labour law / Droit du travail	5159-5164
18620	Employers' organization / Organisation patronale	5165
18630	Trade union / Syndicat	5166-5252
18640	Labour conflict / Conflit du travail	5253-5286
18650	Arbitration. Mediation / Arbitrage. Médiation	5287-5306
18660	Collective agreement. Joint management / Convention collective. Cogestion	5307-5336
18700	Leisure / Loisir	5337-5345
18710	Leisure time / Temps de loisir...............................	5346-5357
18720	Leisure utilization / Utilisation des loisirs	5358-5395
19	**Politics. State. International relations** **Politique. État. Relations internationales**	
19100	Political science. Political sociology / Science politique. Sociologie politique	5396-5406
19200	Political doctrine. Political thought / Doctrine politique. Pensée politique	

19210	Political philosophy / Philosophie politique	5407-5417
19220	Power / Pouvoir	5418-5421
19230	Communism. Nationalism / Communisme. Nationalisme	5422-5462
19240	Democracy. Dictatorship / Démocratie. Dictature	5463-5475
19300	Constitution. State / Constitution. État	
19310	Political system / Système politique	5476-5516
19320	Human rights / Droits de l'homme	5517-5526
19330	Political representation / Représentation politique	5527
19340	Government / Gouvernement	5528-5543
19350	Parliament / Parlement	
19360	Judiciary power / Pouvoir judiciaire	5544-5548
19400	Public administration / Administration publique	
19410	Civil service. Technocracy / Fonction publique. Technocratie	5549-5559
19420	Central government. Local government / Administration centrale. Administration locale	5560-5568
19500	Political party. Pressure group / Parti politique. Groupe de pression	
19510	Party system. Political party / Système de parti. Parti politique	5569-5595
19520	Pressure group. Protest movement / Groupe de pression. Mouvement contesta	5596-5614
19530	Political majority. Political opposition / Majorité politique. Opposition politique	
19600	Political behaviour. Elections. Politics / Comportement politique. Élections. Politique	
19610	Political leader. Political society / Leader politique. Société politique	5615-5618
19620	Political attitude. Political participation / Attitude politique. Participation politique	5619-5669
19630	Elections / Élections	5670-5685
19640	Politics / Politique	5686-5694
19700	Army. Military sociology / Armée. Sociologie militaire	5695-5720
19800	International relations / Relations internationales	
19810	International law. International organization / Droit international. Organisation internationale	5721-5730
19820	Foreign policy. Sovereignty / Politique étrangère. Souveraineté	5731-5735
19830	International cooperation. War / Coopération internationale. Guerre	5736-5741
19840	Disarmament. Weapon / Désarmement. Arme	
20	**Social problem. Social service. Social work** **Problème social. Service social. Travail social**	
20100	Social problem / Problème social	
20110	Applied sociology / Sociologie appliquée	5742-5753
20120	Social pathology / Pathologie sociale	5754-5757
20130	Disaster / Catastrophe	
20140	Poverty / Pauvreté	5758-5793
20150	Alcoholism. Drug / Alcoolisme. Stupéfiants	5794-5826
20160	Crime. Delinquency / Délit. Délinquance	584-5832
20200	Social policy / Politique sociale	
20210	Social action. Social planning / Action sociale. Planification sociale	5995-6105
20220	Social security / Sécurité sociale	6106-6137
20300	Social work / Travail social	6138-6159
20400	Social service / Service social	
20410	Medical sociology. Medicine / Sociologie médicale. Médecine	6160-6178
20420	Public health / Santé publique	6179-6207
20430	Hospital / Hôpital	6208-6233
20440	Social worker / Travailleur social	6234-6259

10. SOCIAL SCIENCES. RESEARCH. DOCUMENTATION
SCIENCES SOCIALES. RECHERCHE. DOCUMENTATION

10100. SOCIAL SCIENCES. SOCIOLOGY
SCIENCES SOCIALES. SOCIOLOGIE

[See also / voir aussi: 95, 164, 236, 241, 330, 370, 480, 492, 701, 1628, 1972, 2281, 3692, 4375, 4537, 4552, 5406, 5438, 6000, 6077]

1. "Ideals and realities: some problem areas of professional social science", *International Journal of contemporary Sociology* 16(1-2), jan-apr 79 : 1-242.
2. "Entretien avec Pierre Bourdieu: la sociologie est-elle une science?", *Recherche* 112, jun 80 : 738-743.
3. "Autour de la sociologie", *Revue de l'Institut de Sociologie* 80 : 7-142.
4. "Važnaja problema sovetskoj sociologičeskoj nauki" (An essential problem of the Soviet sociological science), *Sociologičeskie Issledovanija* 79 : 3-10.
5. AIDA, Akira; TAKASHIMA, Shōji; [eds.]. *Tenkanki no gendai shakaigaku* (Modern sociology in transition). Kyōto, Akademia shuppankai, 80, 253 p.
6. BOGDÁNY, Franz Josef. "Soziobiologie, Möglichkeiten und Grenzen der "neuen Synthesis"" (Social biology: possibilities and bases of a new synthesis), *Kölner Zeitschrift für Soziologie und Sozialpsychologie* 32, 80 : 312-324.
7. Bibl.XXIX-6. BORENSTEIN, Audrey. *Redeeming the sin: social science and literature.* CR: Alan SWINGEWOOD, *American Journal of Sociology* 58(6), mai 80: 1465-1467. [also CR: Howard L. KAYE, Contemporary Sociology (Albany), 9(4), jul 80: 528.]
8. CHARON, Joel M. *The meaning of sociology.* Sherman Oaks, CA, Alfred Pub. Co., 80, xii-219 p.
9. ČIMIČ, Esad. "O socijalnom kontekstu sociološkog poziva" (On the social context of the sociological calling), *Revija za Sociologiju* (3-4), 78 : 21-30.
10. CLARK, S. D. "The changing image of sociology in English-speaking Canada", *Canadian Journal of Sociology* 79 : 393-403.
11. CLAVAL, Paul. *Les mythes fondateurs des sciences sociales.* Paris, Presses universitaires de France, 80, 261 p.
12. COHEN, Bernard P. *Developing sociological knowledge: theory and method.* Englewood Cliffs, NJ, Prentice-Hall, 80, viii-279 p.
13. DEBRIZZI, John. "Ideology and early American theory: the contributions of Henry Carter Adams", *Journal of the History of Sociology* 79 : 63-75.
14. DEEGAN, Mary Jo; [ed.]. "Sociology at Nebraska: 1884-1929", *Journal of the History of Sociology* 79 : 40-41.
15. DUBERMAN, Lucile; HARTJEN, Clayton A. *Sociology: focus on society.* Glenview, IL, Scott, Foresman, 79, xix-601 p.
16. EHARA, Yumiko. "Shakai-kagaku to seikatsu sekai"(Social sciences and the life-world), *Tokyo toritsu daigaku jinbungaku-ho* 143, 80 : 89-115.
17. FABIANO, Mauro Antonio. "Alle origini della sociologia empirica in Francia" (At the beginnings of empirical sociology in France), *Sociologia (Roma)* 13(2-3), mai-dec 79 : 139-169.
18. FEDOSEEV, P. N. "Obščestvennye nauki i social'nyj progress" (Social sciences and social progress), *IN: Konstitucija SSSR i dal'nejsee razvitie gosudarstvovedenija i teorii prava.* Moskva, 79 : 5-8.
19. FLERE, Sergej. "O nekim pojavama u razvoju savremene (buržoaske) sociologije" (On some phenomena in the development of contemporary sociology), *Sociologija* 22(1-2), 80 : 93-110.
20. GARMENDIA, Jose Antonio. *Sociología: claves para el estudio y transformación de la estructura social* (Sociology: keys for the study and transformation of social structure). Madrid, Centro de Investigaciones Sociológicas, 79, 179 p.
21. GLASER, Edward M. "Using behavioral science strategies for defining the state-of-the-art", *Journal of applied behavioral Science* 16, jan-mar 80 : 79-92.
22. GORDON, Howard Scott. *A critique of sociobiology.* Kingston, Ont., Institute for Economic Research, Queen's University, 79, 70 p.

23   HERTZLER, J. O. "A history of sociology at the University of Nebraska", *Journal of the History of Sociology* 79 : 42-62.
24   HINKLE, Roscoe C. *Founding theory of American sociology, 1881-1915.* Boston, Routledge & Kegan Paul, 80, xiv-376 p.
25   HUSZÁR, Tibor. *Történelem és szocioloógia*(History and sociology). Budapest, Magvető, 79, 574 p. [Studies on the history of Hungarian sociology.]
26   ISOMURA, Eiichi. "Shakaigaku kenkyu no kokusai-teki, gakusai-teki kadai" (International aspects of sociological studies), *Shakaigaku hyoron* 31, 80 : 45-54.
27   JEREZ MIR, Rafael. *La introducción de la Sociología en España. Manuel Sales y Ferré: Una experiencia frustrada* (The introduction of sociology in Spain. Manuel Sales y Ferré: a missed experience). Madrid, Editorial Ayuso, 80, 495 p.
28   JUNHO PENA, Maria Valéria. "Uma nova sociologia?" (A new sociology?), *Dados* 23, 80 : 93-107.
29   KOVAČIĆ, Ivan. "O humanističkoj perspektivi sociologije — teze za diskusiju"(On the humanistic perspective of sociology: theses for discussion), *Revija za Sociologiju* (3-4), 78 : 15-20.
30   KRAUSE, Elliott A. *Why study sociology.* New York, Random House, 80, xi-187 p.
31   KUVAČIČ, Ivan. "Šta je sociologija, čime se ona bavi" (What is sociology), *Sociologija* 21, 79 : 215-230.
32   KUVAČIČ, Ivan. "Šta je sociologija, čime se ona bavi" (What is sociology), *Sociologija* 21, 79 : 215-230.
33   Bibl.XXIX-21. LEMERT, Charles. *Sociology and the twilight of man: homocentrism and discourse in sociological theory.* CR: Don MARTINDALE, *American Journal of Sociology* 86(1), jul 80: 198-199. [also CR: Leon H. WARSHAY, *Contemporary Sociology* (Albany), 9(2), mar 80: 305-306.]
34   LOJKINE, Jean. "La spécialisation des champs en sociologie", *Cahiers internationaux de Sociologie* 68, jul-dec 79 : 47-67.
35   LUCAS, Marín, Antonio. *Introducción a la sociología.* Pamplona, EUNSA, 79, 221 p.
36   LUCCHINI, Riccardo; RIDORÉ, Charles. *Culture et société: une introduction à la sociologie générale.* Fribourg, Éditions universitaires, 79, 310 p.
37   MADAN, Gurmukh Ram. *Western sociologists on Indian society: Marx, Spencer, Weber, Durkheim, Pareto.* London, Boston, Routledge & Kegan Paul, 79, vii-398 p.
38   MARTINDALE, Don. "The golden age of Minnesota sociology, 1921-1930", *Journal of the History of Sociology* 80 : 35-60.
39   MINAMI, Hiroshi. *Ningen kodogaku* (Science of human behavior). Tokyo, Iwanami shoten, 80, 586 p.
40   MUCCHIELLI, Roger. *Histoire de la philosophie et des sciences humaines.* Paris, Bordas, 79, 304 p.
41   MÜLLER, Ursula. *Reflexive Soziologie und empirische Sozialforschung* (Reflexive sociology and empirical social research). Frankfurt/Main, New York, Campus Verlag, 79, 162 p.
42   MURRAY, Stephen. "Resistance to sociology at Berkeley", *Journal of the History of Sociology* 80 : 61-84. [1900-1978.]
43   NAITŌ, Kanji. *Shakaigaku ronkō* (Essays in sociology). Tokyo, Ochanomizu shobo, 80, 398 p.
44   NAKAJIMA, Akinori. "L'Année sociologique and Durkheim", *Aichi kyoiku daigaku kenpo* 29, 80 : 29-48.
45   NIZEK, William E.; FUHRMAN, Ellsworth R.; HALL, Richard H. "Theoretical observations on applied behavioral science. Effectiveness theory and organizational effectiveness", *Journal of applied behavioral Science* 16, oct-dec 80 : 535-545.
46   OPP, Karl-Dieter. *Individualistische Sozialwissenschaft* (Individualist social science). Stuttgart, Enke, 79, xi-163 p.
47   Organization for Economic Cooperation and Development. *Social sciences in policy making.* Paris, OECD, 79, 56 p.
48   PAPP, Zsolt. *A válság filozófiájától a "konszenzus" szociológiájáig. Útvesztők és útelágazások a huszadik századi német polgári filozófia és szociológia történetében* (From the philosophy of crisis to the sociology of "consent". Labyrinths and crossroads in the history of the German bourgeois philosophy and sociology of the 20th century). Budapest, Kossuth Kiadó, 80, 370 p.
49   PELLIZZI, Camillo. "Per una deontologia nelle scienze dell'Iuomo" (For a deontology in the human sciences), *Rassegna italiana di Sociologia* 20, oct-dec 79 : 557-564.
50   PODGÓRECKI, Adam; ŁOŚ, Maria. *Multi-dimensional sociology.* London, Boston, Routledge & Kegan Paul, 79, vii-344 p.

51 Bibl.XXIX-25. POLOMA, Margaret M. *Contemporary sociological theory.* CR: John HOUGHTON, *Contemporary Sociology (Albany)* 9(4), jul 80: 584-585.
52 POMFRET, Alan. "Comparative historical school change: Newfoundland, Southern Ontario and New England", *Canadian Journal of Sociology* 79 : 241-255.
53 Bibl.XXIX-26. PRATT, Vernon. *The philosophy of the social sciences.* CR: Ted BENTON, *British Journal of Sociology* 31(2), jun 80: 302-304.
54 RABINOW, Paul; SULLIVAN, William M.; [eds.]. *Interpretive social science: a reader.* Berkeley, University of California Press, 79, viii-367 p. CR: R. J. ANDERSON, *British Journal of Sociology* 31(4), dec 80: 586-588.
55 RABOW, Jerome; ZUCKER, Lynne G. "Whither sociology", *Sociology and social Research* 65, oct 80 : 10-22.
56 RAISON, Timothy; [comp.]. *The founding fathers of social science: a series from New society.* London, Scolar Press, 79, 319 p. [A series of articles first published in the New society, chiefly between 1963 and 1967.]
57 SCHELSKY, Helmut. "Zur Entstehungsgeschichte der Bundesdeutschen Soziologie. Ein Brief an Rainer Leipsius" (On the history of the origins of the federal German sociology. A letter to Rainer Leipsius), *Kölner Zeitschrift für Soziologie und Sozialpsychologie* 32, 80 : 417-456.
58 SCHULTER, David B. "Economics and the sociology of consumption: Simon Patten and early academic sociology of America, 1894-1904", *Journal of the History of Sociology* 79-80 : 133-162.
59 SHERMAN, Howard; WOOD, James L. *Sociology, traditional and radical perspectives.* New York, Harper & Row, 79, xv-413 p.
60 SHLIAPENTOKH, Vladimir E. "Essays on sociology", *International Journal of Sociology* 10, 80 : 3-105.
61 SICA, Alan M. "Received wisdom versus historical fact: on the mutual awareness of Weber and Pareto", *Journal of the History of Sociology* 79 : 17-38.
62 SIGNORELLI, Adriana. "Utilizzazione delle scienze sociali da parte della pubblica amministrazione" (The utilization of social sciences by public administrators), *Critica sociologica* 50, 79 : 209-227.
63 SNIZEK, William E.; FUHRMAN, Ellsworth R. "Theoretical observations on applied behavioral science", *Journal of applied behavioral Science* 16, jan-mar 80 : 93-103.
64 SNIZEK, William E.; FUHRMAN, Ellsworth R. "Theoretical observations on applied behavioral science", *Journal of applied behavioral Science* 16, apr-jun 80 : 228-236.
65 STAVROV, Boris Dimov. *Burzhoaznata sotsiologiia v Bŭlgariia mezhdu dvete svetovni voĭni* (Bourgeois sociology in Bulgaria between the two world wars). Sofiia, BAN, 79, 243 p.
66 SUPEK, Rudi. "Situacija sociologije u svijetu danas" (The state of sociology in the world today), *Revija za Sociologiju* (3-4), 78 : 5-14.
67 SUPEK, Rudi. "Sociologija i humanističke znanosti — od strukturalizma do dijalektič holizma" (Sociology and humanist sciences: from structuralism to dialectic wholism), *Sociologija* 22(1-2), 80 : 85-92.
68 SUPEK, Rudi. "Sociologija i humanističke znanostiod strukturalizma do dijalektičkog holizma" (Sociology and humanist sciences — from structuralism to dialectic wholism), *Sociologija* 22(1-2), 80 : 85-92.
69 SZACKI, Jerzy. *History of sociological thought.* Westport, CT, Greenwood Press, 79, xxi-581 p.
70 SZYMANSKI, Albert; GOERTZEL, Ted George. *Sociology: class, consciousness, and contradictions.* New York, Van Nostrand, 79, vii-344 p.
71 THOMAS, David. *Naturalism and social science: a post-empiricist philosophy of social science.* Cambridge, Eng., New York, Cambridge University Press, 79, vii-213 p.
72 WENDT, Bruno. *Ökonomie und Soziologie als geographische Hilfswissenschaften: Grundbegriffe u. Anwendungsbereiche* (Economics and sociology as geographic aid sciences). Freiburg/Breisgau, Würzburg, Ploetz, 79, 123 p.
73 WILSON, Kenneth L. "Methodological observations on applied behavioral science", *Journal of applied behavioral Science* 16, jan-mar 80 : 105-114.
74 WILSON, Kenneth L.; SMITH-LOVIN, Lynn. "Methodological observations on applied behavioral science. On the practical value of causal modeling. II. Educational attainment and the measurement of conceptual variables", *Journal of applied behavioral Science* 16, oct-dec 80 : 546-565.
75 ŽUPANOV, Josip. "Sociologija, marksizma i industrijska sociologija" (Sociology, Marxism and industrial sociology), *Sociologija* 22(1-2), 80 : 15-25.

**10200. RESEARCH WORKER. SOCIOLOGIST
CHERCHEUR. SOCIOLOGUE**

[See also / voir aussi: 49, 178, 445, 1013, 1297, 1871, 2286, 3673, 5027]

76 Bibl.XXIX-35. BARRY, Brian. *Sociologists, economists and democracy.* CR: Christopher K. VANDERPOOL, *Contemporary Sociology (Albany)* 9(3), mai 80: 422-423.
77 BERNSDORF, Wilhelm; KNOSPE, Horst; [eds.]. *Internationales Soziologenlexikon* (International directory of sociologists). Stuttgart, Enke, 80, v-24 p.
78 BISOGNO, Paolo; [ed.]. *Il ricercatore oggi in Italia: indagini e studi sul profilo del ricercatore dei grandi enti pubblici* (The research worker in Italy today: studies on the research worker's profile in the big public organizations). Milano, F. Angeli, 79, 408 p.
79 BRADSHAW, Ted R.; MCPHERRON, Sharon M. "Issues and resources in undergraduate sociology curriculum", *American Sociologist* 15, feb 80 : 6-21.
80 COAN, Richard W. *Psychologists: personal and theoretical pathways.* New York, Irvington Publishers, distributed by Halsted Press, 79, viii-196 p.
81 ENDRUWEIT, Günter. "Soziologiestudium und Soziologenpraxis" (Sociological studies and sociologists' practice), *Soziologische Revue* 80 : 22-27. [review article.]
82 GOLDSMID, Charles A.; GOLDSMID, Paula L. "The great leap forward? The teaching of sociology 1975-1979, and beyond", *Teaching Sociology* jul 80 : 373-395.
83 GONZALEZ BLASCO, Pedro. "Motivación y productividad en la investigación científica española" (Motivation and productivity in Spanish scientific research), *Revista española de Investigaciones sociológicas* jul-sep 79 : 63-75.
84 GREEN, Charles S. III; [et al.]. "Careers and the undergraduate curriculum: an integrated program", *American Sociologist* 15, feb 80 : 30-39.
85 HEILMAN, Samuel C. "Jewish sociologist: native-as-stranger", *American Sociologist* 15, mai 80 : 100-108.
86 HOOGSTRATEN, Johan. *De machteloze onderzoeker: voetangels en klemmen van sociaal-wetenschappelijk onderzoek* (The weak research worker- traps of social science research). Meppel, Boom, 79.
87 HOSHI, Akira. "Daigaku kyoju no recruitment ni tsuite -tokuni shakaigaku kankei no kyoju no baai" (A study on recruitment in faculties of sociology), *Bukkyo daigaku daigakuin kenkyu kiyo* 80 : 107-126.
88 JAMIN, Jean. "Un sacré collège ou les apprentis-sorciers de la sociologie", *Cahiers internationaux de Sociologie* 68, jan-jun 80 : 5-30.
89 KING, Kathleen Piker. "The reward system in sociology departments: what we always knew — or did we?", *Sociological Focus* 13, apr 80 : 155-171.
90 KUGEL', S. A.; [ed.]. *Naučnye kadry v socialističeskom obščestve: struktura i dinamika* (The scientific managers in the socialist society: structure and dynamics). Moskva, Sekretariat SĖV, 79, 178 p.
91 LAPASSADE, Georges. "Psychosociologue à temps plein, 1959-1979", *Connexions* 29, 80 : 95-125.
92 LENA, Hugh F.; LONDON, Bruce. "An introduction to sociology through fiction using Kesey's "One Flew over the Cuckoo's Nest"", *Teaching Sociology* jan 79 : 123-131. [published in 1962.]
93 LUTZ, Gene M. "Employment and a liberal arts undergraduate education in sociology", *Teaching Sociology* jul 79 : 373-390.
94 MEIGNANT, Alain. "Le métier de psychosociologue et la demande sociale", *Connexions* 29, 80 : 81-94.
95 MORGAN, J. Graham. "Women in American sociology in the 19th century", *Journal of the History of Sociology* 80 : 1-34.
96 NAWTON, Rae R.; GUTMANN, Gail. "The other side of teaching: a student-generated look at faculty commitment to office hours", *Teaching Sociology* jan 79 : 107-120.
97 NETTLER, Gwynn. "Sociologist as advocate", *Canadian Journal of Sociology* 80 : 31-53.
98 OROMANER, Mark. "The American sociological community and the works of Talcott Parsons: 1936-1950", *Journal of the History of Sociology* 79 : 76-92.
99 PAIRAULT, Claude. "L'économiste et l'anthropologue", *Cahiers internationaux de Sociologie* 66, jan-jun 79 : 161-171.
100 PERRUCCI, Robert. "Sociology and the introductory textbook", *American Sociologist* 15, feb 80 : 39-49.
101 REYNOLDS, Paul D. *Ethical #5 dilemmas and social science research:* [an analysis of moral issues confronting investigators in research using human participants]. San Francisco,

Jossey-Bass Publishers, 79, xx-505 p. CR: Bernard BARBER, *Contemporary Sociology (Albany)* 9(5), sep 80: 665-666.

102 RHOADES, Lawrence J. "Undergraduate sociology curriculum: a proposal", *American Sociologist* 15, feb 80 : 21-29.

103 SATARIANO, William A.; ROGERS, Sharon J. "Undergraduate internships: problems and prospects", *Teaching Sociology* jul 79 : 355-372.

104 SCHULTZ, Clarence C. "A comparative study in the identification of major family theorists: polling versus textbook recognition", *International Journal of the Sociology of the Family* jan-jun 79 : 35-46.

105 SILVA, Edward T.; SLAUGHTER, Sheila. "Prometheus Bound: the limits of social science professionalization in the progressive period", *Theory and Society* nov 80 : 781-819.

106 VAUGHAN, Charlotte A. "Career information for sociology undergraduates", *Teaching Sociology* oct 79 : 55-64.

107 Bibl.XXIX-53. WEBER, George H.; MCCALL, George J.; [eds.]. *Social scientists and advocates: views from the applied disciplines.* CR: C. Paul MARSH, *Contemporary Sociology (Washington)* 9(4), jul 80: 580-581.

108 WELCH, Michael; LEWIS, Stephen. "A mid-decade assessment of sex biases in placement of sociology Ph. D.s: evidence for contextual variation", *American Sociologist* 15, aug 80 : 120-127.

109 WESTIE, Frank R.; KICK, Edward L. "Retired sociologists' expectations for professional immortality: further demonstrations of the constructed nature of reality", *American Sociologist* 15, mai 80 : 93-99.

110 WOOLF, William J. Jr.; BISHOP, James M. "Implications of competency-base education for undergraduate sociology", *American Sociologist* 15, feb 80 : 50-58.

111 YZERMAN, Thomas J. "The Dutch labour-market for sociologists", *Netherlands' Journal of Sociology* 15, jul 79 : 83-86.

10300. ORGANIZATION OF RESEARCH. RESEARCH POLICY.
ORGANISATION DE LA RECHERCHE. POLITIQUE DE RECHERCHE.

10310. Current research
Recherche en cours

[See also / voir aussi: 172, 382, 1454, 4075, 5584]

112 *Ciencias sociales en México: desarrollo y perspectiva* (Social sciences in Mexico: development and prospects). México, Colegio de México, 79, 332 p.

113 BENDIX, Reinhard. "Western Europe as the object and source of social science research", *Social Research* 46, 79 : 787-804.

114 CAMACHO, Daniel; [ed.]. *Debates sobre la teoría de la dependencia y la sociología latinoamericana: ponencias del XI Congreso Latinoamericano de Sociología.* San José, Editorial Universitaria Centroamericana, 79, 767 p.

115 CHENG-FANG, Yang. "Les sciences sociales en Chine", *Revue internationale des Sciences sociales* 32, 80 : 613-615.

116 COURT, David. "The idea of social science in East Africa: an aspect of the development of higher education", *Minerva* 17, sum 79 : 244-282.

117 CVJETIČANTIN, Veljko. "Petnaest godina sociologije na Filozofskom fakultetu u Zabrebu" (Fifteen years of sociology at the Faculty of Philosophy in Zagreb), *Revija za Sociologiju* (3-4), 78 : 73-79.

118 ERBE, Michel. *Zur neueren französischen Sozialgeschichtsforschung. Die Gruppe um die "Annales"* (The new French social history research. The group of the "Annales"). Darmstadt, Wissenschaftliche Buchgesellschaft, 79, 159 p.

119 FRASSINETTI, Antonio Murga; BOILS MORALES, Guillermo. *La Ciencias sociales en América Latina* (Social sciences in Latin America). México, Universidad Nacional Autónoma de México, Facultad de Ciencias Políticas y Sociales, 79, 245 p.

120 GEORGIEVSKI, Petre. "Razvoj sociologije na Filozofskom fakultetu u Skopju" (The development of sociology at the Faculty of Philosophy in Skopje), *Revija za Sociologiju* (3-4), 78 : 100-108.

121 HILLER, Harry H. "The Canadian sociology movement: analysis and assessment", *Canadian Journal of Sociology* 79 : 125-150.

122 IGUÍÑIZ, Javier; [et al.]. *La investigación en ciencias sociales en el Perú* (Social science research in Peru). Lima, Tarea, Centro de Publicaciones Educativas, 79, iv-268 p.

123 JAMES, Dilmus D.; STREET, James H.; JEDLICKA, Allen D. "Indigenous research development in the Third World countries", *Social Science Quarterly* 60, mar 80 : 588-603.

124 JOSIFOVSKI, Ilija; KEPEVSKA, Jovanka. "Empirijska sociološka istraživanja u SR Makedoniji" (Empirical sociological research in SR Macedonia), *Revija za Sociologiju* (3-4), 78 : 93-99.

125 KORNEEV, M. Ja. "Usilenie apologetičeskoj funkcii sovermennoj francuzskoj buržuaznoj sociologii" (The reinforcement of the contemporary French bourgeois sociology apologetic function), *IN: Sovremennaja buržuaznaja sociologija na službe gosudarstvenno-monopolističeskogo kapitalizma.* Leningrad, 79 : 40-52.

126 KULCSÁR, Kálmán. *Sociological research in Hungary.* New Delhi, Ravindra Pr., 79, 43 p. [published by the Hungarian Information and Cultural Centre.]

127 MUKHERJEE, Ramkrishna. "Trends in Indian sociology", *Contributions to Indian Sociology* 13, jul-dec 79 : 319-332.

128 OSIPOV, G. V. *Teorija i praktika sociologičeskih issledovanij v SSSR* (Theory and practice of sociological research in the USSR). Moskva, Nauka, 79, 343 p.

129 PAPCKE, Sven. "Die deutsche Soziologie zwischen Totalitarismus und Demokratie" (The German sociology between totalitarianism and democracy), *Aus Politik und Zeitgeschichte* 20, 80 : 3-19.

130 PINTO, Diana. "La sociologie dans l'Italie de l'après guerre 1950-1980", *Revue francçaise de Sociologie* 21, apr-jun 80 : 233-250.

131 RADEMAKER, L.; [ed.]. *Sociologie in Nederland* (Sociology in the Netherlands). Deventer, Van Loghum Slaterus, 79, 173 p.

132 ROKKAN, Stein; [ed.]. *A quarter century of international social science: Papers and reports on developments, 1952-1977.* New Delhi, Concept, 79, viii-388 p. [publications of the International Social Science Council.]

133 ŠPAKOV, R. P. "Sociologija FRG v sisteme gosudarstvenno-monopolističeskogo kapitalizma" (The FRG sociology in the State monopolist capitalism system), *IN: Sovremennaja buržuaznaja sociologija na službe gosudarstvenno-monopolističeskogo kapitalizma.* Leningrad, 79 : 20-39.

134 ŠPORER, Željka. "Položaj sociologije na tehničkim fakultetima" (The place and function of sociology at technical faculties), *Revija za Sociologiju* (3-4), 78 : 86-92. [Yugoslavia.]

135 STERN, Paul C. *Evaluating social science research.* New York, Oxford University Press, 79, 240 p. CR: Richard A. ZELLER, *Contemporary Sociology (Albany)* 9(6), nov 80 : 821.

136 UEDA, Mamoru. "Taisho democracy-ki ni okeru Nihon shakaigaku (jo)" (The Japanese sociology at Taisho democracy age), *Shakaigaku tsushin* 10, 80 : 6-21.

137 Bibl.XXIX-89. WONG, Siu-Lun. *Sociology and socialism in contemporary China.* CR: Lung-Chang, YOUNG, *Contemporary Sociology (Albany)* 9(4), jul 80 : 553-554.

10320. **Applied research. Interdisciplinary research**
Recherche appliquée. Recherche interdisciplinaire

[See also / voir aussi: 199, 1047]

138 ABT, Clark C.; [ed.]. *Perspectives on the costs and benefits of applied social research.* Cambridge, MA, Council for Applied Social Research with the assistance of Abt Books, 79, xi-288 p.

139 FERNÁNDEZ VARGAS, Valentina. "Un ejemplo de investigación interdisciplinar: el Instituto de Investigaciones Interétnicas e Interculturales de la Universidad de Niza" (An example of interdisciplinary research: the Interethnic and Intercultural Research Institute of Nice University), *Revista internacional de Sociología* 37(32), oct-dec 79 : 525-545.

140 MIRSKIJ, È. M. *Meždisciplinarnye issledovanija i disciplinarnaja organizacija nauki* (Interdisciplinary research and disciplinary organization of science). Moskva, Nauka, 80, 304 p.

141 ROTHMAN, Jack. *Social R & D; research and development in the human services.* Englewood Cliffs, NJ, Prentice-Hall, 80, xiii-290 p.

142 VAN DE VALL, Mark; BOLAS, Cheryl. "Applied social discipline research or social policy research: the emergence of a professional paradigm in sociological research", *American Sociologist* 15, aug 80 : 128-137.

143 VAN TRIER, W. E. "Actualités bibliographiques: la recherche-action", *Déviance et Société* jun 80 : 179-193.

144   VARGA, Károly; [ed.]. *Szervezeti akciókutatás 1977/78. Vol. 1: Problémafelt á rś és elök észitö akciók; Vol. 2: Elmélet vezérelt vizsgá latok és folyta tó dó akciók* (Action research in organizations. Vol. 1: Defining of problems and preliminary actions; Vol. 2: Theory directed investigations and further actions). Budapest, MTA KESZ, 79, Vol. 1: 189; Vol. 2: 301 p. [published by the Institute of sociology of the Hungarian Academy of Sciences.]

10330.   Research centre
Centre de recherche

[See also / voir aussi: 480, 1047, 3530]

145   IGRICKIJ, Tu. I. "Burzuaznaja sovetologija v sovremennoj bor'be idij" (Bourgeois sovietology in the contemporary ideological culture), *Voprosy Istorii* 53(11), nov 79 : 71-89. [research centres in the Soviet Union.]
146   KOZLOV, D. F. "Razvitie sovetskoj sociologičeskoj nauki v moskovskom Universiteta (1917-1979)" (Development of Soviet sociological sciences at the Moscow University, 1917-1979), *Vestnik Moskovskogo Universiteta. Serija Filosofija* 33, nov-dec 79 : 34-44.

10340.   Organization of research. Research policy
Organisation de la recherche. Politique de la recherche

[See also / voir aussi: 139]

147   "Social science and public policy: funding research", *Society* 17, sep-oct 80 : 6-16. [by the National Science Foundation, USA.]
148   ANDREWS, Frank; [ed.]. *Scientific productivity. The effectiveness of research groups in six countries.* Cambridge, Cambridge University Press, 79, 512 p. CR: Friedhelm NEIDHARDT, *Kölner Zeitschrift für Soziologie und Sozialpsychologie* 32(3), sep 80 : 620-624.
149   ASHRAF, Jaweed. CMEA integration in science and education. New Delhi, Sterling, 79, viii-167 p.
150   BROOKMAN, Frits Henry. *The making of a science policy. A historical study of the institutional and conceptual background to Dutch science policy in a West-European perspective.* Amsterdam, Academische Pers, 79, ix-511 p. CR: Frank R. PFETSCH, *Kölner Zeitschrift für Soziologie und Sozialpsychologie 32(3), sep 80 : 620.*
151   CAVEING, Maurice. "La recherche dans les sciences de l'homme: la montée des périls", *Raison présente* 52, oct-nov-dec 79 : 45-63. [France.]
152   COLE, Jonathan R. *Fair science: women in the scientific community.* New York, Free Press, 79, 336 p. CR: Barbara F. RESKIN, *Contemporary Sociology (Albany)* 9(6), nov 80 : 793-795.
153   GIACOMONI, Silvia. *Miseria e nobiltà della ricerca in Italia: le fondazioni e gli istituti di studi economico-sociali* (Poverty and nobility of research in Italy: foundations and institutions of economic and social studies). Milano, Feltrinelli, 79, 267 p.
154   HIEBER, Lutz. "Die Auswirkungen der Einrichtung von Grossforschungszentren und Sonderforschungsbereichen auf die naturwissenschaftlich-technische Forschung in den Universitäten" (The effects of big science and of the concentration of support on special research areas on scientific and technological research in the universities), *Zeitschrift für Soziologie* 80 : 159-178.
155   JOLLES, H. M. "De Nederlandse sociologie als eenheid van beleid" (Dutch sociology as a unit in science policy), *Sociologische Gids* 27, mai-jun 80 : 225-238.
156   JUZUFOVIČ, G. K. *Nauka pri socializme: politiko-ekonomičeskie problemy* (Science under socialism: political and economic problems). Leningrad, Izdatel'stvo Leningradskogo Universiteta, 80, 120 p.
157   MATSUMOTO, Miwao. "Kagakusha shūdan to seidoka no mondai — shoki Merton no kagaku-shakaigaku saikō" (The scientific community and the problems of institutionalization — A reexamination of the early studies of R. K. Merton), *Shakaigaku hyoron* 31, 80 : 15-30.
158   MIKEŠIN, N. I. "Konkretno-sociologičeskie issledovanija i zadača opredelenija potenciala naučnogo kollektiva" (Concrete sociological research and the objective of determination of a scientific collectivity potential), *IN: Problemy dejatel'nosti ucenogo i naučnyh kolektivov'. VII.* Moskva, 79 : 76-80.
159   MORELL, Jonathan Alan. *Program evaluation in social reseach.* New York, Pergammon Press, 79, xvi-193 p.

160 PHILIPPART, A.; [et al.]. "Politique de la science, langages et information", *Économies et Sociétés. Cahiers de l'ISÉA* 13(11-12), nov-dec 79 : 1525-1777.

161 REUTER, Helga; TRIPIER, Pierre. "Travail et créativité dans un marché interne: le cas du système français de recherche universitaire", *Sociologie du Travail* 22, jul-sep 80 : 241-256.

162 RJABUŠKIN, T. V.; [ed.]. *Territorial'naja vyborka v sociologičeskih issledovanijah* (Territorial choice in sociological research). Moskva, Nauka, 80, 218 p.

163 SHINN, Terry. "Division du savoir et spécificité organisationnelle. Les laboratoires de recherche industrielle en France", *Revue française de Sociologie* 21, jan-mar 80 : 3-34.

164 UNESCO. *La Coopération interrégionale en sciences sociales.* Paris, Unesco, 79, 92 p.

10350. Research equipment
Équipement de la recherche

[See also / voir aussi: 471, 4676]

165 BONNET, André G. "Les microprocesseurs et leurs futures applications", *Social Science Information* 19, 80 : 413-422.

166 France. Mission à l'informatique. *Actes du Colloque international informatique et société: 24-28 septembre 1979, Paris.* Paris, la Documentation française, 80, 5 vols: 284, 305, 329, 247, 253 p.

167 NILSEN, Svein E. "Microelectronics; useful for some, harmful for others", *Social Science Information* 19, 80 : 423-434.

168 RADA, Juan F. "Microelectronics and information technology: a challenge for research in the social sciences", *Social Science Information* 19, 80 : 435-465.

169 SILVER, Gerald A. *The social impact of computers.* New York, Harcourt Brace Jovanovich, 79, x-342 p.

10360. Sociological association
Association de sociologie

170 BOORSTIN, Robert O. *Professional societies in the People's Republic of China.* Washington, DC, National Council for US-China Trade, 79, 501 p.

171 HOLLIER, Denis; [ed.]. *Le Collège de sociologie: 1937-1939: textes de George Bataille, Roger Caillois, René M. Guastalla, Pierre Klossowski, et al.* Paris, Gallimard, 79, 599 p. [Collection Idées; 413.]

10400. CONGRES. MEETING
CONGRÈS. RÉUNION

[See also / voir aussi: 114]

172 "Zum 3. Kongress der marxistisch-leninistischen Soziologie in der DDR" (The Third Congress of Marxist-Leninist sociology in the GDR), *Deutsche Zeitschrift für Philosophie* 28, 80 : 1-128.

173 "Xth Congress of the European Society for Rural Sociology, Córdoba, April 5-10, 1979: Economic growth and regional development", *Sociologia ruralis* 20(1-2), 80 : 7-130. [special issue.]

174 JAAKKOLA, Risto; BRUNN, Kettil. "Observations on the 9th World Congress of Sociology, Uppsala, 1978", *Acta sociologica* 22, 79 : 377-383.

175 MASLOVA, O. M. "Sovetsko-pol'skaja konferencija po metodike sociologičeskih issledovanij" (Soviet-Polish Conference on sociological research methods), *Sociologičeskie Issledovanija* 79 : 209-212.

176 PERHEENTUPA, Olli; [ed.]. I. Finnish-Soviet symposium of sociology, Helsinki 24-25 January 1978. Helsinki, 80, 141 p.

177 SALCEDO, Juan. "Del centro, la periferia y el conflicto: a proposito del X Congreso Europeo de Sociología Rural" (Centre, periphery and conflict: about the Xth European Congress of Rural Sociology), *Revista española de Investigaciones sociológicas* apr-jun 79 : 131-139. [Córdoba, 9-10 apr 1979.]

10500. DOCUMENT. INFORMATION PROCESSING
DOCUMENT. TRAITEMENT DE L'INFORMATION

10510. Documentation
Documentation

[See also / voir aussi: 374, 811, 1984, 2056, 2143]

178 ARNDT, Johan; GRØNHAUG, Kjell; TROYE, Sigurd V. "Information exchange among scientists: a two-step sociometric study", *Sociology* 14, aug 80 : 441-448.
179 BARRON, Iann; CURNOW, Ray. *The future with microelectronics: Forecasting the effects of information technology.* London, Pinter, New York, Nichols, 79, 243 p.
180 BRAJNOVIĆ, Luka. *El ámbito científico de la información* (The scientific framework of information). Pamplona, Ediciones Universidad de Navarra, 79, 178 p.
181 BROADBENT, Kieran P. *Dissemination of scientific information in the People's Republic of China.* Ottawa, International Development Research Centre, 80, 60 p.
182 HERNON, Peter. *Use of government publications by social scientists.* Norwood, NJ, Ablex Pub. Corp., 79, xiii-173 p.
183 Bibl.XXIX-1927. KLAPP, Orrin E. *Opening and closing: strategies of information adaptation in society.* CR: Marvin B. SCOTT, *American Journal of Sociology* 86(2), sep 80 : 431-433. [also CR: R. S. PERINBANAYAGAM, Contemporary Sociology (Albany) 9(3), mai 80 : 414-415.]
184 KRJUČKOVA, L. N. "Ob ispol'zovanii informacii v sociologičeskom issledovanii" (On the information utilization in sociological research), *IN: Social'nye aspekty razvitija ličnosti. Ispol'zovanie informacionnyh sistem dlja ego prognozirovanija.* Moskva, 78 : 132-140.
185 KUŠAKOV, Š. S. "Suščnost' i osnovnye tipy social'noj informacii" (Nature and essential patterns of social information), *Trudy Samarkandskogo Universiteta* 357, 78 : 74-86.
186 KUZNECOV, A. G.; [et. al.]. "Ob ispol'zovanie pokazatelej obraza žizni dlja informacionno-analizirujuščej sistemy v sociologii" (On the utilization of the way of life indexes for the information analysis system in sociology), *IN: Social'nye aspekty razvitija ličnosti. Ispol'zovanie informacionnyh sistem dlja ego prognozirovanija.* Moskva, 78 : 150-159.
187 LE COADIC, Yves F. "La diffusion des articles scientifiques de chimie. Approche mathématique et sociologique", *Revue française de Sociologie* 21, jan-mar 80 : 37-48.
188 MARTIN, Michael W.; SELL, Jane. "The marginal utility of information: its effects upon decision-making", *Sociological Quarterly* 21, 80 : 233-242.
189 RELYEA, Harold C. "Freedom of information, privacy, and official secrecy: the evolution of federal government information policy concepts", *Social Indicators Research* (1-4), jan 80 : 137-156.
190 ŠINKARENKO, V. V. "Problemy ispol'zovanija sociologičeskoj informacii v partijnoj rabote" (Problems of the sociological information utilization in the Party activity), *Sociologičeskie Issledovanija* 80 : 28-33.
191 STANKEVIČ, L. "Ideologičeskaja funkcija francuzskoj sociologii informacii" (Ideological function of the French sociology of information), *IN: Sovremennaja buržuaznaja sociologija na službe gosudarstvenno-monopolističeskogo kapitalizma.* Leningrad, 79 : 121-131.
192 STEINBUCH, Karl. "Informationssysteme und Kommunikation in der heutigen Gesellschaft" (Information systems and communication in contemporary society), *Universitas. Zeitschrift für Wissenschaft, Kunst und Literatur* 35, 80 : 267-273.
193 VAČNADZE, G. N. "Meždunarodnyj obmen informaciej i social'noe razvitie" (International exchange of informations and social development), *IN: Sociologičeskie problemy obrazovanija, kul'tury i nauki.* Moskva, 78 : 113-120.
194 VAN BOL, Jean-Marie. "Les politiques de la communication en Belgique", *Textes et Documents* 324, 79 : 5-129.
195 WAGNER, Jon; [ed.]. *Images of information: still photography in the social sciences.* Beverly Hills, Sage Publications, 79, 311 p.
196 WILSON, T. D. "On information science and the social sciences", *Social Sciences Information Studies* oct 80 : 5-12.

10520. Document analysis. Reference book
Analyse documentaire. Ouvrage de référence

[See also / voir aussi: 77, 232, 550, 2442, 3150, 4857]

197 BUSS, Eugen; SCHÖPS, Martina. *Kompendium für das wissenschaftliche Arbeiten in der Soziologie* (Compendium for scientific work in sociology). Heidelberg, Quelle und Meyer, 79, 181 p. CR: Siegfried TASSEIT, *Kölner Zeitschrift für Soziologie und Sozialpsychologie* 32(1), mar 80: 182-183.

198 RADEMAKER, L.; VAN HOORN, R. J. P. *Kleine sociologische literatuurgids* (Small guide to sociological literature). De Meern, Spectrum, 80, 118 p.

199 RIGNEY, Daniel; BARNES, Donna. "Patterns of interdisciplinary citation in the social sciences", *Social Science Quarterly* 61, jun 80 : 114-127.

10530. Documentation centre
Centre de documentation

[See also / voir aussi: 5378]

200 ERMAKOVA, O. V.; IODKOVSKAJA, L. V. "Opyt sozdanija informacionnogo massiva banka sociologičeskih dannyh (na materialah otečestvennoj literatury po sociologii)" (An essay of a data bank creation on sociological research; from materials of Soviet literature on sociology), *IN: Social'nye aspekty razvitija ličnosti. Ispol'zovanie informacionnyh sistem dlja ego prognozirovanija.* Moskva, 78 : 160-168.

201 OSBURN, Charles B. *Academic research and library resources: changing patterns in America.* Westport, CT, Greenwood Press, 79, xx-187 p.

202 TYLER, William G.; [ed.]. *Data banks and archives for social science research on Latin America.* Gainsville, FL, Consortium of Latin American Studies Programs, 75, iv-124, 103 p.

10540. Documentalist
Documentaliste

203 GARRISON, Dee. *Apostles of culture: the public librarian and American society, 1876-1920.* New York, Macmillan Information, 79, xvi-319 p.

10550. Terminology
Terminologie

[See also / voir aussi: 531, 1857, 2300, 2903]

204 Bibl.XXIX-167. GALLINO, Luciano. *Dizionario di sociologia* (Dictionary of sociology). CR: René KÖNIG, *Kölner Zeitschrift für Soziologie und Sozialpsychologie* 32(1), mar 80 : 157-158.

205 MIALARET, Gaston. *Vocabulaire de l'éducation: éducation et sciences de l'éducation.* Paris, Presses universitaires de France, 79, xxii-457 p.

206 MITCHELL, G. Duncan; [ed.]. *A new dictionary of the social sciences.* The Hague, Paris, New York, Mouton, 79, viii-244 p.

207 TOMOVIĆ, Vladislav A.; [ed.]. *Definitions in sociology: convergence, conflict, and alternative vocabularies: a manual for writers of term papers, research reports, and theses.* St. Catharines, Ont., Diliton Publications, 79, ix-195 p.

208 VIET, Jean. *International thesaurus of cultural development/Thesaurus international du développement culturel.* Paris, UNESCO, 80, xvi-498 p.

10560. Biography
Biographie

[See also / voir aussi: 2954]

209 "Robert S. Lybd", *Journal of the History of Sociology* 79-80 : 10131.
210 "In memoriam Ante Fiamengo", *Revija za Sociologiju* (3-4), 78 : 114-115.
211 "In memoriam Oleg Mandić", *Revija za Sociologiju* (3-4), 78 : 116-117.
212 BECHELLONI, Giovanni. "Camillo Pellizzi", *Rassegna italiana di Sociologia* 20, oct-dec 79 : 545-556.
213 BODEN, Margaret A. *Jean Piaget.* New York, Viking Press, 80, xii-176 p.
214 CALOT, Gérard. "In memoriam Paul Vincent (1912-1979)", *Population* 34, nov-dec 79 : 979-984.
215 COUSER, G. Thomas. *American autobiography: the prophetic mode.* Amherst, University of Massachusetts Press, 79, vi-222 p.

216 HOBART, Charles. "In memoriam Charles Hynam", *Canadian Journal of Sociology* 80 : ix-10.
217 JANIĆIJEVIĆ, Miloslav. "In memoriam Dr. Ante Fiamengo, 1913-1979", *Sociologija* 21, 79 : 213-214.
218 MACKSCHEIDT, Klaus. "Fritz Karl Mann, 10.12.1883 - 14.9.1979", *Kölner Zeitschrift für Soziologie und Sozialpsychologie* 32, 80 : 625-627.
219 MAY, Georges Claude. *L'autobiographie*. Paris, Presses universitaires de France, 79, 229 p.
220 MERTON, Robert K.; [et al.]. "[In memory of] Talcott Parsons, 1902-1979", *American Sociologist* 15, mai 80 : 60-71.
221 RAUSHENBUSH, Winifred. *Robert E. Park: biography of a sociologist*. Durham, NC, Duke University Press, 79, xii-206 p. CR: Robert E. L. FARIS, *Contemporary Sociology (Albany)* 9(2) mar 80: 264-265. [Park, Robert Ezra, 1864-1944.]
222 RICHMOND, Katy; [et al.]. "Jean Martin: a tribute", *Australian and New Zealand Journal of Sociology* 15, nov 79 : 2-5. [1923-1979.]
223 SKINNER, Burrhus Frederic. *The shaping of a behaviorist: part two of an autobiography*. New York, Knopf, 79, 373 p. [distributed by Random House.]
224 TIRYAKIAN, Edward A. "Talcott Parsons, 1902-1979", *Cahiers internationaux de Sociologie* 68, jan-jun 80 : 171-172.
225 VALLEE, Frank F. "In memoriam John Porter 1921-1979", *Canadian Journal of Sociology* 80 : vii-10.
226 WESTPHAL-HELLBUSCH, Sigrid. "Hilde Thurnwald 15.2.1890-7.8.1979", *Sociologus* 30, 80 : 97-101.

10570. Article. Periodical
         Article. Périodique

[See also / voir aussi: 44, 239]

227 BALLÉ, Catherine. "Sociologie du Travail et sociologie du changement", *Sociologie du Travail* 22, jan-mar 80 : 38-54.
228 BERTACCHINI, Renato. *Le riviste del Novecento: introduzione e guida allo studio dei periodici italiani: storia, ideologia e cultura* (The periodicals of the 20th century: introduction and guide to the study of Italian periodicals: history, ideology and culture). Firenze, le Monnier, 79, 248 p.
229 SKIFF, Anthony. "Toward a theory of publishing or perishing", *American Sociologist* 15, aug 80 : 175-183.
230 SPECTOR, Malcolm; FAULKNER, Robert R. "Thoughts on five new journals and some old ones", *Contemporary Sociology* jul 80 : 477-482. [survey essay.]
231 TEEVAN, James J. "Journal prestige and quality of sociological articles", *American Sociologist* 15, mai 80 : 109-112.
232 VILLA, Francesco. "Vent'anni di "Sociologie du Travail" (1959-1978): elementi per una bibliografia ragionata" (Twenty years of Sociologie du Travail 1959-1978: elements for a systematic bibliography), *Studi di Sociologia* 17, apr-jun 80 : 208-234.

10580. Proceedings. Report
         Actes. Rapport

10590. Textbook. Thesis
         Manuel. Thèse

[See also / voir aussi: 699, 980]

233 BABBIE, Earl R. *Sociology, an introduction*. Belmont, Calif., Wadsworth Pub. Co., 80, xiv-611 p. [first edition published in 1977 under title: Society by agreement.]
234 BOURDIEU, Pierre. *Eléments de sociologie*. Paris, Éditions de minuit, 80, 268 p.
235 COHEN, Bruce J.; HARRISON, Madelyn M. *Schaum's outline of theory and problems of introduction to sociology*. New York, McGraw-Hill, 79, 216 p.
236 HERRICK, Robert L. "Nineteen pictures of a discipline: a review of recent introductory sociology textbooks", *Contemporary Sociology* sep 80 : 617-626. [survey essay.]
237 MEIER, Robert F. "Different criminologies: a survey of recent introductory criminology textbooks", *Contemporary Sociology* sep 80 : 626-631. [survey essay.]
238 Bibl.XXIX-202. MENDRAS, Henri; [ed.]. *Éléments de sociologie*. CR: Philippe BESNARD, *Revue française de Sociologie* 21(1), jan-mar 80: 146-147.

239 OROMANER, Mark. "Influentials in sociological textbooks and journals, 1955 and 1970", *American Sociologist* 15, aug 80 : 169-174.
240 REINHARZ, Shulamit. *On becoming a social scientist.* San Francisco, Jossey-Bass Publishers, 79, xviii-422 p. CR: Ted George GOERTZEL, *Contemporary Sociology (Albany)* 9(5), sep 80: 659-662.
241 VILLEMEZ, Wayne J. "Explaining inequality: a survey of perspectives represented in introductory sociology textbooks", *Contemporary Sociology* jan 80 : 35-39. [survey essay.]

11. METHODOLOGY. THEORY
MÉTHODOLOGIE. THÉORIE

11100. EPISTEMOLOGY. RESEARCH METHOD. THEORY
EPISTÉMOLOGIE. MÉTHODE DE RECHERCHE. THÉORIE

11110. Philosophy. Theory
Philosophie. Théorie

[See also / voir aussi: 67, 68, 69, 125, 223, 342, 356, 383, 728, 788, 934, 975, 980, 1062, 1107, 1138, 1247, 1248, 1262, 1324, 1376, 1640, 1647, 1669, 1947, 1959, 1967, 2041, 2241, 2581, 2801, 2803, 2807, 3038, 4692, 5501, 5517, 5615]

242 "Aspects of Weberian scholarship", *British Journal of Sociology* 31, sep 80 : 313-440.
243 "Marxism and structuralism", *Insurgent Sociologist* sum 79 : 4-73.
244 AGULLA, Juan C. *De la sociología del conocimiento a la teoría crítica: Karl Mannheim y Max Horkheimer* (From the Sociology of Knowledge to Critical Theory: Karl Mannheim and Max Horkheimer). Buenos Aires, Editorial del Instituto Torcuanto Di Tella, 79, 58 p.
245 ALEXANDER, Richard D. *Darwinism and human affairs*. Seattle, University of Washington Press, 79, xxiv-317 p.
246 ANDERSSON, Sten. *Positivism kontra hermeneutik* (Positivism against hermeneutics). Göteborg, Korpen, 79, 119 p.
247 ASSMAN, Peter. "Value-relations and general theory: Parsons' critique of Weber", *Zeitschrift für Soziologie* jan 80 : 100-111.
248 BANNISTER, Robert C. *Social Darwinism: science and myth in Anglo-American social thought*. Philadelphia, Temple University Press, 79, 292 p. CR: Donald K. PICKENS, *Social Science Quarterly* 61(2), sep 80: 317-321.
249 BARKER, Martin. "Kant as a problem for Weber", *British Journal of Sociology* 31, jun 80 : 224-245.
250 BAUM, John Alan. *Montesquieu and social theory*. Oxford, New York, Pergamon Press, 80, viii-191 p.
251 Bibl.XXIX-215. BAUMAN, Zygmut. *Hermeneutics and social science*. CR: H. P. RICKMAN, *British Journal of Sociology* 31(1), mar 80: 111-112.
252 BERKSON, William. "Skeptical rationalism", *Inquiry* 22, 79 : 281-320.
253 Bibl.XXIX-218. BIEN, Joseph; [ed.]. *Phenomenology and the social sciences: a dialogue*. CR: Frances Chaput WAKSLER, *Contemporary Sociology (Albany)* 9(2), mar 80 : 304-305.
254 BILBAO, Andrés. "Marx y la crisis del marxismo"(Marx and crisis of marxism), *Sistema. Revista de Ciencias sociales* 37, 80 : 37-49.
255 BOLOGH, Roslyn Wallach. *Dialectical phenomenology: Marx's method*. Boston, Routledge & Kegan Paul, 79, xiii-287 p.
256 BRAUN, Karl-Heinz. *Kritik des Freudo-Marxismus: zur marxist. Aufhebung d. Psychoanalyse* (Criticism of Freudian-Marxism). Köln, Pahl-Rugenstein, 79, 224 p.
257 BUSINO, Giovanni. "Sociological theory and modern society: Pareto and Freud", *Revue européenne des Sciences sociales. Cahiers Vilfredo Pareto* 18(52), 80 : 123-132.
258 CHUA, Beng-Huat. "The structure of the contemporary sociological problematic: a Foucaultian view", *American Sociologist* 15, mai 80 : 82-93.
259 CONNERTON, Paul. *The tragedy of enlightenment: an essay on the Frankfurt School*. Cambridge, New York, Cambridge University Press, 80, xi-162 p.
260 COTESTA, Vittorio. "Forma di relazione sociale e produzione teorica nella 'Ideologia tedesca' di K. Marx e F. Engels" (Form of social relations and theoretical production in K. Marx and F. Engels' "German ideology"), *Critica sociologica* 50, 79 : 139-155.
261 CRISPINI, Franco. *Neokantismo, strutturalismo, scienze umane: Gurvitch e Goldmann* (Neo-Kantism, structuralism, sciences of man — Gurvitch and Goldmann). Cosenza, Lerici, 79, 326 p.
262 DAHRENDORF, Ralf. *Lebenschancen. Anläufe zur sozialen und politischen Theorie* (Life chances: approach to social and political theory). Frankfurt-am-Main, Suhrkamp, 79, 240 p. CR: Roland REICHWEIN; Gerhard BRANDT, *Soziologische Revue* 3(4), 80: 375-388. [also published in English: Chicago, University of Chicago Press, 79: ix-181p.]

263   Bibl.XXIX-229. DANFORD, John W. *Wittgenstein and political philosophy: a reexamination of the foundations of social science.* CR: David D. LAITIN, *American political Science Review* 74(1), mar 80: 159-160.
264   DAVIS, Lawrence Howard. *Theory of action.* Englewood Cliffs. NJ, Prentice-Hall, 79, viii-152 p.
265   DE LUCCA, John. "La philosophie enterrera-t-elle ses fossoyeurs?", *Diogène* 108, oct-dec 79 : 3-21.
266   DERKSEN, A. Th. "Hoe anti-positivistisch was Max Weber in zijn sociaal-empirisch onderzoek?" (How anti-positivist was Max Weber in his social-empirical research?), *Sociologische Gids* 27, sep-oct 80 : 354-375.
267   DISCO, Cornelis. "Critical theory as ideology of the new class. Rereading Jürgen Habermas", *Theory and Society* sep 79 : 159-214.
268   FAUGHT, Jim. "Presuppositions of the Chicago School in the work of Everett C. Hughes", *American Sociologist* 15, mai 80 : 72-82.
269   FLERE, Sergej. "O nekim pojavama u razvoju savremene (buržoaske) sociologije" (On some phenomena in the development of contemporary (bourgeois) sociology), *Sociologija* 22(1-2), 80 : 93-110.
270   FOUGEYROLLAS, Pierre. *Sciences sociales et marxisme.* Paris, Payot, 79, 271 p.
271   FREIBERG, J. W.; [ed.]. *Critical sociology: European international perspectives.* New York, Irvington, 79, xvi-408 p. CR: Rhonda F. LEVINE, *Contemporary Sociology (Albany)* 9(5), sep 80: 718-179. [distributed by Halsted Press.]
272   FRITLINSKIJ, V. S.; MARČENKO, G. I. "Special'nye sociologičeskie teorii v marksistskoj sociologii" (Special sociological theories in the Marxist sociology), *IN: Metodoličeskie problemy sociologičeskogo issledovanija.* Moskva, 79 : 120-145.
273   Bibl.XXIX-243. FRY, John. *Marcuse — dilemma and liberation: a critical analysis.* CR: Barry SMART, *Contemporary Sociology (Albany)* 9(1), jan 80 : 151.
274   FURMANOV, G. L. *Istoričeskij materializm kak obščesociologičeskaja teorija-leninskoe filosofsko-sociologičeskoe nasledie i sovremennost'* (Historical materialism as a general sociological theory: the Leninist philosophical and sociological heritage and the contemporary era). Moskva, Izdatel'stvo Moskovskogo Universiteta, 79, 214 p.
275   Bibl.XXIX-246. GANDY, D. Ross. *Marx and history: from primitive society to the communist future.* CR: Ronald J. HUNT, *American political Science Review* 74(1), mar 80 : 163.
276   Bibl.XXIX-250. GIDDENS, Anthony. *Emile Durkheim.* CR: Roland ROBERTSON, *Contemporary Sociology* 9(4), jul 80: 584.
277   GORIN, Zeev. "Socialism and dependency in Parsons' theory of evolution", *Sociological Quarterly* 21, 80 : 243-258.
278   GOULDNER, Alvin Ward. *The two Marxisms: contradictions and anomalies in the development of theory.* New York, Seabury Press, 80, viii-397 p.
279   HANLY, Charles Mervyn Taylor. *Existentialism and psychoanalysis.* New York, International Universities Press, 79, 298 p.
280   HAUBTMANN, Pierre. *La Philosophie sociale de P.-J. Proudhon.* Grenoble, Presses universitaires de Grenoble, 80, 293 p.
281   HAYES, Adrian C. "A semi-formal explication of Talcott Parsons' theory of action", *Sociological Inquiry* 50, 80 : 39-56.
282   HECHTER, Michael. "Notes on marxism and sociology in the USA", *Theory and Society* nov 79 : 377-386.
283   ISRAEL, Joachim. *The language of dialectics and dialectics of language.* Copenhagen, Munksgaard, Atlantic Highlands, NJ, Humanities Press, 79, xvii-263 p.
284   JAUSS, Hans Robert. "Limites et tâches d'une herméneutique littéraire", *Diogène* 109, jan-mar 80 : 102-133.
285   JORGENSEN, Danny L. "Florian Znaniecki's sociological theorizing", *Journal of the History of Sociology* 80 : 85-107.
286   KÄSLER, Dirk. *Einführung in das Studium Max Webers* (Introduction to the study of Max Weber). München, Beck, 79, 291 p. CR: Hans GRÜNBERGER, *Soziologische Revue* 3(2), 80: 162-163.
287   KJAHRIK, L. O. "K kritike normativnogo determinizma v sovremennoj buržuaznoj sociologii" (Critics of normative determinism in the contemporary bourgeois sociology), *Sociologičeskie Issledovanija* 79 : 170-177.
288   KORENG, Christine. *Norm und Interaktion bei Jürgen Habermas* (Norm and interaction in Jürgen Habermas). Düsseldorf, Patmos Verlag, 79, 136 p.

289	KURZWEIL, Edith. *The age of structuralism: Lévi-Strauss to Foucault.* New York, Colombia University Press, 80, xi-256 p.
290	LANE, James. "The relationship between analysis and theory in Pareto's general sociology", *Revue européenne des Sciences sociales. Cahiers Vilfredo Pareto* 18(52), 80 : 171-188.
291	LLOBERA, Josep R. "Durkheim, the Durkheimians and their collective misrepresentation of Marx", *Social Science Information* 19, 80 : 385-411.
292	LONG, Tom. "Marx and Western marxism in the 1970's", *Berkeley Journal of Sociology* 24-25, 80 : 13-66.
293	LOPREATO, Joseph. "Pareto's sociology in a sociobiological key", *Revue européenne des Sciences sociales. Cahiers Vilfredo Pareto* 18(52), 80 : 133-162.
294	LUHMANN, Niklas. "Talcott Parsons: zur Zukunfts eines Theorieprogramms" (Talcott Parsons: on the future of a theoretical programme), *Zeitschrift für Soziologie* jan 80 : 5-17.
295	MACGREGOR, David. "Evaluating the Marxist tradition", *Contemporary Sociology* jul 80 : 486-488. [survey essay.]
296	MAFFESOLI, Michel. "L'imaginaire dans la tradition sociologique: Vilfredo Pareto", *Revue européenne des Sciences sociales. Cahiers Vilfredo Pareto* 18(52), 80 : 163-170.
297	MARTEL, Martin U.; HAYES, Adrian C. "Some new directions for action theory", *Sociological Inquiry* 49, 79 : 77-82.
298	MAYES, Sharon S. "Sociological thought in Emile Durkheim and George Fitzhugh", *British Journal of Sociology* 31, mar 80 : 78-94.
299	Bibl.XXIX-283. MCCARTHY, Thomas. *The critical theory of Jürgen Habermas.* CR: Gillian ROSE, *British Journal of Sociology* 31(1). mar 80: 110-111.
300	MEYER, Thomas. "Neuere Literatur über die Theorie von Marx" (New literature on marxist theory), *Forum DS* 79 : 171-221.
301	MIRKOVIĆ, Damir. "Dijalektička misao Georga Zimela" (Dialectic thought of Georg Simmel), *Sociologija* 21, 79 : 267-290.
302	MIRKOVIĆ, Damir. "Dijalektička misao Georga Zimela" (Dialectic thought of Georg Simmel), *Sociologija* 21, 79 : 267-290.
303	MITSUHASHI, Toshimitsu. "Mexico ni okeru Auguste Comte jisshoshugi no juyo to tenkai" (Auguste Comte's positivism — Its introduction and development in the Mexican socio-political context), *Jochi daigaku kokusaigaku ronshu* 80 : 67-81.
304	MONTORO ROMERO, Ricardo. "La reconstrucción del materialismo histórico de Jürgen Habermas" (Reconstruction of Jürgen Habermas' historical materialism), *Revista española de Investigaciones sociológicas* 12, oct-dec 80 : 117-139.
305	MÜNCH, Richard. "Über Parsons zu Weber: von der Theorie der Rationalisierung zur Theorie der Interpenetration" (On Parsons to Weber: from the theory of rationalization to the theory of interpenetration), *Zeitschrift für Soziologie* jan 80 : 18-53.
306	MUNTERS, Q. J. "E. W. Hofstee: tussen speculatieve fantasie en empirisch realisme" (E. W. Hofstee: between speculative fancy and empirical realism), *Mens en Maatschappij* 255, sep 80 : 221-244.
307	NATSUKARI, Yasuo. "Durkheim ni okeru shakai-kan rikai eno ichi-shiza" (A standpoint of a comprehension of Durkheim's social view), *Shakaigaku ronso* 78, 80 : 13-27.
308	NEDELMANN, Birgitta. "Strukturprinzipien der soziologischen Denkweise Georg Simmels" (Structural principles of Georg Simmel's sociological thought), *Kölner Zeitschrift für Soziologie und Sozialpsychologie* 32, 80 : 559-572.
309	OBRDLIKOVA, Bruo J. "J. L. Fisher's sociological thought: the first attempt at structural-functional theory of society", *Indian Journal of social Research* 20, dec 79 : 180-190.
310	ØSTERBERG, Dag. "Essays on materialism", *International Journal of Sociology* 79-80 : 3-111.
311	PAGÈS, Max. "Introduction à l'analyse dialectique", *Connexions* 29, 80 : 51-67.
312	PALMER, Jeremy N. J. "The damp stones of positivism: Erich von Däniken and paranormality", *Philosophy of the social Sciences* jun 79 : 129-148.
313	PARKER, James Hill. "A critique of Parsons' pattern variables", *International Journal of contemporary Sociology* 15(3-4), jul-oct 78 : 273-282.
314	PARKIN, Frank. *Marxism and class theory: a bourgeois critique.* London, Tavistock, 79. CR: Garin MACKENZIE, *British Journal of Sociology* 31(4), dec 80: 582-584. [also CR: Guenther ROTH, Contemporary Sociology (Albany), 9(2), mar 80: 306-307.]

315   Bibl.XXIX-298. PARSONS, Talcott. *Action theory and the human conditions.* CR: Michael LESSNOFF, *British Journal of Sociology* 31(2), jun 80, 300-302. [also CR: Jonathan H. TURNER, Contemporary Sociology (Albany), 9(3), mai: 380-383.]
316   PETERSEN, William. *Malthus.* Cambridge, MA, Harvard University Press, 79, vi-302 p. CR: Jacques DUPÂQUIER; Nathan KEYFITZ, *Contemporary Sociology (Albany)* 9(4), jul 80: 462-269. [also CR: Mark PERLMAN, Journal of economic Literature 18(3), sep 80 : 1100-1103.]
317   PETTAZZI, Carlo. Th. Wiesengrund Adorno: linee di origine e di sviluppo del pensiero (1903-1949) (Th. Wiesengrund Adorno: origin and development lines of his thought). Firenze: La nuova Italia, 79, xvi-295 p.
318   PREWO, Rainer. *Max Webers Wissenschaftsprogramm* (Max Weber's scientific programme). Frankfurt am Main, Suhrkamp, 79, 613 p. CR: Dirk Käsler, *Soziologische Revue* 3(4), 80: 418-421.
319   PROTTI, Mauro. "Teoria come prassi e 'politico' in Th. W. Adorno" (Theory as praxis and the political in Th. W. Adorno), *Rassegna italiana di Sociologia* 21, apr-jun 80 : 265-289.
320   RAY, L. J. "Critical theory and positivism: Popper and the Frankfurt School'', *Philosophy of the social Sciences* jun 79 : 149-173.
321   RENZINA, I. M. "Kritičeskij analiz problemy sootnošenija teorij i metoda v sovremennoj buržuaznoj sociologii" (Critical analysis of the theories and method correlation problem in the bourgeois contemporary sociology), *IN: Metodologičeskie problemy sociologičeskogo issledovanija.* Moskva, 79 : 93-119.
322   Bibl.XXIX-310. ROSE, Gillian. *The melancholy science: an introduction to the thought of Theodor W. Adorno.* CR: Elliott EISENBERG, *American Journal of Sociology* 85(5), mar 80 : 1262-1264.
323   RUTKEVIČ, M. N. "Dialektika i sociologija''(Dialectics and sociology), 80.
324   SCHLUCHTER, Wolfgang. *Die Entwicklung des okzidentalen Rationalismus: eine Analyse von Max Webers Gesellschaftsgeschichte* (The development of western rationalism: an analysis of Max Weber's social history). Tübingen, J. C. B. Mohn (Siebeck), 79, ix-280 p. CR: Mary FULBROOK, *British Journal of Sociology* 31(3), sep 80 : 452-453. [also CR: Niklas LUHMANN, Soziologische Revue, 3(3), 80: 243-250.]
325   SENSAT, Julius Jr. *Habermas and Marxism: an appraisal.* Beverly Hills, CA, Sage Publications, 79, 176 p.
326   Bibl.XXIX-316. SKINNER, B. F. *Reflections on behaviorism and society.* CR: George C. HOMANS, *American Journal of Sociology* 86(2), sep 80: 389-393.
327   Bibl.XXIX-320. SNIZEK, William E.; FUHRMANN, Ellsworth R.; MILLER, Michael K.; [eds.]. *Contemporary issues in theory and research: a metasociological perspective.* CR: Leon H. WARSHAY, *Contemporary Sociology (Washington)* 9(4), jul 80 : 585-586.
328   SZTOMPKA, Piotr. *Sociological dilemmas: toward a dialectic paradigm.* New York, Academic Press, 79, xvii-362 p.
329   TILLEY, Nicholas. "Popper, positivism and ethnomethodology'', *British Journal of Sociology* 31, mar 80 : 28-45.
330   TIRYAKIAN, E. A. "L'École durkheimienne à la recherche de la société perdue: la sociologie naissante et son milieu culturel'', *Cahiers internationaux de Sociologie* 66, jan-jun 79 : 97-114.
331   TODISCO, Orlando. *Karl Marx, analisi critica della metodologia sociale* (Karl Marx, critical analysis of the social methodology). Roma, Edizioni paoline, 79, 392 p.
332   TOURAINE, Alain. *La voix et le regard.* Paris, Seuil, 78, 315 p. CR: Guy MINGUET, *Revue française de Sociologie* 21(1), jan-mar 80: 121-133.
333   UMEZAWA, Takashi. "Kinō-shugi shakai ni okeru setsumei" (An explanation in sociological functionalism), *Keio gijuku daigaku daigaku'in shakaigaku kenkyuka kiyo* 20, 80 : 55-63.
334   VALLAS, Steven P. "The lesson of Mannheim's historicism'', *Sociology* 13, nov 79 : 459-474.
335   VAN DER BERG, Axel. "Critical theory: is there still hope?'', *American Journal of Sociology* 86, nov 80 : 449-478.
336   VOS, Henk de. "Interpretatie als identificatie: de keuze van de hermeneutische traditie'' (Interpretation as identification: the choice of the hermeneutic tradition), *Mens en Maatschappij* 55, 80 : 39-58.
337   YASUDA, Saburo. "Weber kōiron no kaishaku to hihan — 'Shakaigaku no konpon mondai'" (A critical commentary on the action theory of Max Weber), *Kwansei gakuin daigaku shakaigakubu kiyo* 40, 80 : 111-130.

338 ŽEMIN, M. V. "Istoričeskij materializm i metodologičeskie problemy analiza čelovečeskogo obščenija" (Historical materialism and methodological problems of human relations analysis), IN: Filosofsko-metodologičeskie problemy obščestvennogo razvitija. Moskva, 79 : 59-66.

11120. Epistemology. Explanation. Understanding
Epistémologie. Explication. Compréhension

[See also / voir aussi: 263, 287, 355, 404, 482, 516, 566, 992, 1351, 1891, 1956, 2315, 2617, 2812, 3263, 3280, 3331, 4318, 4470, 5013, 5276, 5459, 5542, 5655, 6083]

339 ALBERT, Hans; STAPF, Kurt H.; [eds.]. *Theorie und Erfahrung: Beitragen zur Grundlagenproblematik der Sozialwissenschaften* (Theory and practice: Essays on foundation problems of social sciences). Stuttgart, Klett-Cotta, 79, 382 p. CR: Gerald L. EBERLEIN, *Soziologische Revue* 3(4), 80: 442-443.

340 ALBERT, Hans; TOPITSCH, Ernst; [eds.]. *Werturteilsstreit* (Value judgment dispute). Darmstadt, Wissenschaftliche Buchgesellschaft, 79, xi-568 p.

341 ALDRUP, Dieter. "Wertfreiheit und Verantwortlichkeit in den Gesellschaftswissenschaften" (Freedom as regards values and responsibility in the social sciences), *Jahrbuch für Sozialwissenschaft* 31, 80 : 70-101.

342 ALEXANDER, Jeffrey C. "Paradigm revision and 'Parsonianism' ", *Canadian Journal of Sociology* 79 : 343-358.

343 AUDI, Robert. "Wants and intentions in the explanation of action", *Journal for the Theory of social Behaviour* oct 79 : 227-249.

344 Bibl.XXIX-355. BESTUŽEV-LADA, I. V.; [ed.]. *Prognozirovanie v sociologičeskih issledovanijah: metodologičeskie problemy* (Forecasting in sociological research: methodological problems). CR: Jiri KOLAJA, *Contemporary Sociology (Albany)* 9(2), mar 80: 273-274.

345 BIRNBAUM, Michael H.; STEGNER, Steven E. "Source credibility in social judgment: bias, expertise, and the judge's point of view", *Journal of Personality and social Psychology* 37, jan 79 : 75-86.

346 BOLDER, Axel. "Zur Prognose von Bildungs- und Berufswahlentscheidungen im Chancenzuweisungsprozess" (On the prediction of educational and occupational choice decisions in chance attribution process), *Kölner Zeitschrift für Soziologie und Sozialpsychologie* 32, 80 : 262-280.

347 Bibl.XXIX-342. BOURDIEU, Pierre. La distinction. Critique sociale du jugement. CR: Etienne GEHIN; Nicholas HERPIN, *Revue française de Sociologie* 21(3), jul-sep 80 : 439-448. [also CR: Philippe RAYNAUD, Esprit, 3, mar 80 : 82-93.]

348 BUTRICK, Richard. *Deduction and analysis*. Washington, University Press of America, 80, vi-100 p.

349 ČABROVSKIJ, V. A. "Problema nadežnosti prognozov" (Problems of the forecasts security), *Problemy social'nogo Prognozirovanija* 79 : 75-80.

350 CASSELL, Eric J. "Changing ideas of causality in medicine", *Social Research* 46, 79 : 728-743.

351 CHEN, Huey-Tsyh; ROSSI, Peter H. "The multi-goal, theory-driven approach to evaluation: a model linking basic and applied social science", *Social Forces* 59, sep 80 : 106-122.

352 CLARKE, Ignatius Frederick. *The pattern of expectation, 1644-2001*. New York, Basic Books, 79, xi-344 p.

353 COLAPINTO, Jorge. "The relative value of empirical evidence", *Family Process* 18, 79 : 427-441.

354 COOK, Thomas D.; REICHARDT, Charles S.; [eds.]. *Qualitative and quantitative methods in evaluation research*. Beverly Hills, CA, Sage Publications, 79, 160 p.

355 CORTÉS, Fernando H. "Causalidad, pronóstico y regresión" (Causality, forecast and regression), *Revista mexicana de Sociología* 41, jul-sep 79 : 963-1011.

356 DANDEKER, Christopher; SCOTT, John. "The structure of sociological theory and knowledge", *Journal for the Theory of social Behaviour* oct 79 : 303-325.

357 DATTA, Lois-Ellin; PERLOFF, Robert; [eds.]. *Improving evaluations*. Beverly Hills, CA, Sage Publications, 79, 280 p.

358 DETEL, Wolfgang. "Funktionale Erklärungen bei Marx" (Functional explanations in Marx), *Analyse und Kritik* 79 : 147-163.

359   ECKBERG, Douglas Lee; HILL, Lester, Jr. "The paradigm concept and sociology: a critical review", *American sociological Review* 44, dec 79 : 925-937.

360   EDEL, Abraham. *Analyzing concepts in social science.* New Brunswick, NJ, Transaction Books, 79, xiv-351 p.

361   ELISEEV, V. E. "Učenie marksizma o zakonah obščestva i social'noe predvidenie" (The Marxist teaching on the society laws and social forecast), *Problemy social'nogo Prognozirovanija* 79 : 3-8.

362   FAL'KO, V. I. "O konstruktivnom podhode v prognozirovanii" (On the constructive approach in forecasts), *Problemy social'nogo Prognozirovanija* 79 : 58-67.

363   FALCO, Maria J.; [ed.]. *Through the looking glass: epistemology and the conduct of inquiry — an anthology.* Washington, DC, University Press of America, 79, viii-408 p. CR: Eugene F. MILLER, *American political Science Review* 74(3), sep 80: 797-799.

364   FERGUSON, Tamara J.; WELLS, Gary L. "Priming of mediators in causal attribution", *Journal of Personality and social Psychology* 38, mar 80 : 461-470.

365   FRAZIER, Charles E. "Initial cause and societal reaction theory", *International Journal of contemporary Sociology* 15(3-4), jul-oct 78 : 397-413.

366   GENDIN, A. M. "O ponjatii predvidenija"(On the "forecast" concept), *Problemy social'nogo Prognozirovanija* 79 : 32-43.

367   GLAUSER, Daniel. "Problèmes de l'interprétation sociologique des phénomènes de redondance et de stéréotypie dans un système de catégories", *Schweizerische Zeitschrift für Soziologie/Revue suisse de Sociologie* mar 80 : 65-85.

368   GORR, Michael. "Agency and causation", *Journal for the Theory of social Behaviour* mar 79 : 1-14.

369   HALL, Richard H.; CLARK, John P. "An ineffective effectiveness study and some suggestions for future research", *Sociological Quarterly* 21, 80 : 119-134.

370   HARRIS, Christopher Charles. *Fundamental concepts and the sociological enterprise.* London, Croom Helm, 80, 248 p.

371   HEKMAN, Susan J. "Weber's concept of causality and the modern critique", *Sociological Inquiry* 49, 79 : 67-76.

372   IWAWAKI, Saburo; EYSENCK, Sybil B. G.; EYSENCK, Hans J. "The universality of typology: a comparison between English and Japanese schoolchildren", *Journal of social Psychology* 112, oct 80 : 1-9.

373   JÄGER, Michael; [et al.]. *Subjektivität als Methodenproblem* (Subjectivity as a methodological problem). Köln, Pahl-Rugenstein, 79, 244 p.

374   Bibl.XXIX-364. KATZER, Jeffrey; COOK, Kenneth H.; CROUCH, Wane W. *Evaluating information: a guide for users of social science research.* CR: R. J. SCHOENBERG, *Contemporary Sociology (Albany)* 9(1), jan 80: 106-107.

375   KAWASAKI, Ken'ichi. "Shakaigaku to keiken — seidoka to kagakuteki nenshiki no kihon mondai" (Sociology and experience: fundamental problems of institutionalization and scientific cognition), *Sociologos* 80 : 46-57.

376   KUČENKO, V. I.; [ed.]. *Voprosy prognozirovanija obščestvennyh javlenij* (Questions on the social events forecast). Kiev, Naukova Dumka, 78, 194 p.

377   LANE, James. "Freedom, determinism, and sociological explanation", *Revue européenne des Sciences sociales. Cahiers Vilfredo Pareto* 18(52), 80 : 77-121.

378   LEWIS, George H.; LEWIS, Jonathan F. "The dog in the night-time: negative evidence in social research", *British Journal of Sociology* 31, dec 80 : 544-558.

379   LITTLE, Roderick J. A.; PULLUM, Thomas W. "The general linear model and direct standardization. A comparison", *Sociological Methods and Research* mai 79 : 475-501.

380   MAKI, Judith E.; THORNGATE, Warren B.; MCCLINTOCK, Charles G. (Prediction and perception of social motives), *Journal of Personality and social Psychology* 37, feb 79 : 203-220.

381   MANISCALCO, Maria Luisa. "Conoscenza e metodo in Pareto" (Knowledge and methodology in Pareto), *Studi di Sociologia* 18, apr-jun 80 : 139-152.

382   MARČENKO, G. I. "Metodologičeskie osnovy klassifikacii sociologičeskih issledovanij" (Methodological bases of the sociological research classification), *IN: Metodologičeskie problemy sociologičeskogo issledovanija.* Moskva, 79 : 49-92.

383   MCHOUL, Alexander. "The practical methodology of reading in science and everyday life: reading Althusser reading Marx", *Philosophy of the social Sciences* 10, jun 80 : 129-150.

384   MCMILLAN, James H. "Children's causal attribution in achievement situations", *Journal of social Psychology* 112, oct 80 : 31-39.

385 MEYER, John P. "Causal attribution for success and failure: a multivariate investigation of dimensionality, formation, and consequences", *Journal of Personality and social Psychology* 38, mai 80 : 704-718.
386 MILLER, Michael K. "An operational framework for policy modeling in the social sciences", *Social Indicators Research* jul 79 : 373-387.
387 NATSOULAS, Thomas. "Against phenomenal objects", *Journal for the Theory of social Behaviour* 10, jul 80 : 97-114.
388 NERSESSIAN, Nancy J. "The roots of epistemological 'anarchy'", *Inquiry* 22, 79 : 423-440.
389 NIKIFOROB, V. M. "Metodologičeskie osnovy predvidenija buduščego kommunističeskimi partijami razvityh kapitalističeskih stran" (Methodological bases of the future forecast by the communist parties in the developed capitalist countries), *Problemy social'nogo Prognozirovanija* 79 : 15-24.
390 OKUDA, Kazuhiko. "Jisshōteki kenkyu no hōhōron-teki kentō" (A methodological examiniation on verification), *Senshū keieigaku ronshū* 29, 80 : 75-121.
391 RICH, Robert F.; [ed.]. *Translating evaluation into policy.* Beverly Hills, CA, Sage Publications, 79, 160 p.
392 ROSSI, Peter H.; [et al.]. *Evaluation. A systematic Approach.* Beverly Hills, CA, Sage Publications, 79, 256 p.
393 RUSSELL, James. "The status of genetic epistemology", *Journal for the Theory of social Behaviour* mar 79 : 53-70.
394 SABINI, John; SILVER, Maury. "Baseball and hot sauce: a critique of some attributional treatment of evaluation", *Journal for the Theory of social Behaviour* 10, jul 80 : 83-95.
395 SAMČENKO, V. N. "Social'noe predvidenie i svoboda" (Social forecast and freedom), *Problemy social'nogo Prognozirovanija* 79 : 51-57.
396 ŠARYČEV, Ju. M. "Social'noe predvidenie i osnovnye napravlenija razvitija socialističeskogo obščestva" (Social forecast and essential tendencies of the socialist society development), *IN: Metodologija upravlenija obščestvennym, sistemami v uslovijah razvitogo socializma.* 78 : 24-33.
397 SEGRE, Sandro. "Oggettività conoscitiva e teoria della società in Max Weber" (Scientific objectiveness and theory of society in Max Weber), *Rassegna italiana di Sociologia* 20, oct-dec 79 : 665-687.
398 SEPPILLI, Tullio. "Neutralita e oggettivita nelle scienze sociali. Linee per una riflessione critica sul rapporto tra conoscenza e prassi" (Neutrality and objectiveness in social sciences. Indications for a critical reflexion on the relationship between knowledge and practice), *Problemi del Socialismo* 20(15), jul-sep 79 : 77-92.
399 STEINVORTH, Ulrich. "Modellkonstruktion und empirische Überprüfbarkeit in Marx' ''Kapital''" (Model building and empirical verification in Marx' "Capital"), *Analyse und Kritik* 79 : 164-181.
400 SURMIN, Ju. P. "Social'nyj ėksperiment kak metod ėmpiričeskoj obrabotki prognozov" (Social experiment as a method of forecasts empirical treatment), *Problemy social'nogo Prognozirovanija* 79 : 67-75.
401 VAN DER PLIGT, Joop; VAN DIJK, Jos A. "Polarization of judgment and preference for judgmental labels", *European Journal of social Psychology* jul-sep 79 : 233-241.
402 VAN PARIJS, Philippe. "Functional explanation and the linguistic analogy", *Philosophy of the social Sciences* dec 79 : 425-443.

11130. Research method. Sociological analysis
Méthode de recherche. Analyse sociologique

403 ALDERETE, Nuñez. *Métodos de investigación social* (Social research methods). Buenos Aires, Moharra, 79.
404 ALMARAZ, José. "La transición del modelo interactivo al sistémico en Parsons" (The transition from the interactive to the systems analytic model in Parsons), *Revista española de Investigaciones sociológicas* oct-dec 79 : 5-32.
405 ANGLE, John. "Work and earnings: cumulative experience method of analysis of longitudinal surveys", *Sociological Methods and Research* nov 79 : 209-231.
406 BALLESTERO, Enrique. *El encuentro de las ciencias sociales. Un ensayo de metodología* (The meeting of social sciences. A methodological essay). Madrid, Alianza Editorial, 80, 134 p.

407 BLALOCK, H. M. Jr. "Measurement and conceptualization problems: the major obstacle to integrating theory and research", *American sociological Review* 44, dec 79 : 881-894.
408 BOGDANOVIĆ, Marija. "Lazarsfeldovo shvatanje sociologije i njenog metoda" (Lazarsfeld's conception of sociology and its method), *Sociologija* 21(1-2), 79 : 57-76.
409 BOHRNSTEDT, George W.; [ed.]. "Social science methodology: the past twenty-five years", *American behavioral Scientist* 23, jul-aug 80 : 779-928.
410 BOLLEN, Kenneth A.; WARD, Sally. "Ratio variables in aggregate data analysis. Their uses, problems, and alternatives", *Sociological Methods and Research* mai 79 : 431-450.
411 BORGATTA, Edgar F.; JACKSON, David J. "Aggregate data analysis. An overview", *Sociological Methods and Research* mai 79 : 379-383.
412 BORUCH, Robert F.; CECIL, Joe S. *Assuring the confidentiality of social research data*. Philadelphia, University of Pennsylvania Press, 79, viii-312 p.
413 Bibl.XXIX-419. BOTTOMORE, Tom; NISBET, Robert; [eds.]. *A history of sociological analysis*. CR: Randall COLLINS; Anthony M. ORUM, *Contemporary Sociology (Albany)* 9(6), nov 80: 742-754. [also CR: Alvin BOSKOFF, American Journal of Sociology, 86(2), sep 80: 425-427.]
414 BOYD, Lawrence H.; IVERSEN, Gudmund R. *Contextual analysis: concepts and statistical techniques*. Belmont, CA, Wadsworth Pub. Co., 79, xxvi-274 p.
415 BYNNER, John; STRIBLEY, Keith M.; [eds.]. *Social research: principles and procedures*. London, New York, Longman, 79, 354 p.
416 CAVALLO, Roger E. *The role of systems methodology in social science research*. Boston, M. Nijhoff, 79, ix-202 p.
417 CHIESI, Antonio M. "L'analisi dei reticoli sociali: teoria e metodi" (Social network analysis: theory and methods), *Rassegna italiana di Sociologia* 21, apr-jun 80 : 291-310.
418 CHURCHMAN, Charles West. *The systems approach*. New York, NY, Dell Pub. Co., 79, xi-243 p.
419 CHURCHMAN, Charles West. *The systems approach and its enemies*. New York, Basic Books, 79, xii-221 p.
420 DITTERICH, Kuno; SCHNEIDER, Hans. *Systemanalyse und Prozessstrategie* (Systems analysis and process strategy). München, Theimig, 79, xii-207 p.
421 ECKES, Thomas; ROSSBACH, Helmut. *Clusteranalysen* (Cluster analysis). Berlin, Köln, Mainz, Kohlhammer, 80, 124 p.
422 ENEROTH, Bo. *Kvalitativ metod för samhällsvetenskaplig forskning* (Qualitative method for sociological research). Stockholm, Akademilitt, 79, 95 p.
423 EPPLE, Karl. *Theorie und Praxis der Systemanalyse* (Theory and practice of systems analysis). München, Minerva-Publikation, 79, x-268 p.
424 FAVRE, Pierre. "Découvertes, expérimentations et paradigmes dans les travaux sur le sommeil", *Revue française de Sociologie* 21, apr-jun 80 : 259-285. [à propos de LEMAINE, Gérard et al. Stratégies et choix dans la recherche, à propos des travaux sur le sommeil. Paris, Mouton, 77, 218p. Avec une réponse de G. LEMAINE: 287-288.]
425 FELSON, Marcus. "Human chronography", *Sociology and social Research* 65, oct 80 : 1-9.
426 FIKSEL, Joseph. "Dynamic evolution in societal networks", *Journal of mathematical Sociology* 80 : 27-46.
427 FREESE, Lee; [ed.]. *Theoretical methods in sociology: seven essays*. Pittsburgh, University of Pittsburgh Press, 80, xii-377 p.
428 FRIJLING, B. W.; VAN HOESEL, P. H. M.; LEEUW, F. L. "Universitair beleidsgericht onderzoek in de sociale wetenschappen. Een theoretische beschouwing en enkele organisatorische opmerkingen" (University research in social sciences. A theoretical consideration and some organizational remarks), *Mens en Maatschappij* 55, 80 : 117-135.
429 GLETTLER, Monika. "Anwendbarkeit und Grenzen der komparatistischen Methode in der Nationalismus-Forschung" (Use and limitation of the comparative method in the research on nationalism), *Österreichische Osthefte* 21, 79 : 203-214.
430 GOULD, Peter; GATRELL, Anthony. "A structural analysis of a game: the Liverpool v. Manchester United Cup Final of 1977", *Social Networks* jul 80 : 253-273.
431 GRAS, Alain. "Le temps de l'évolution et l'air du temps", *Diogène* 108, oct-dec 79 : 68-94.
432 GREIMAS, A. J.; [et al.]. *Introduction à l'analyse du discours en sciences sociales*. Paris, Hachette, 79, 254 p.

433 HARTWIG, Frederick. *Exploratory data analysis*. London, Beverly Hills, Sage Publications, 80, 84 p.
434 HASTINGS, Donald W.; BERRY, Linda G.; [eds.]. *Cohort analysis: a collection of interdisciplinary readings*. Oxford, OH, Scripps Foundation for Research in Population Problems, 79, 349 p.
435 HOPF, Christel; WEINGARTEN, Elmar; [eds.]. Qualitative Sozialforschung (Qualitative social research). Stuttgart, Klett Cotta, 79, 255 p.
436 JACKMAN, Robert W. "A note on the measurement of growth rates in cross-national research", *American Journal of Sociology* 86, nov 80 : 604-617.
437 KLINGBEIL, Detlev. "Zeit als Prozess und Ressource in der sozialwissenschaftlichen Humangeographie" (Time as process and resource in human geography), *Geographische Zeitschrift* 68, 80 : 1-32.
438 KNOKE, David; ROGERS, David L. "A blockmodel analysis of interorganizational networks", *Sociology and social Research* 64, oct 79 : 28-52.
439 KRIPPENDORFF, Klaus. *Content Analysis. An introduction to its Methodology*. Beverly Hills, CA, Sage Publications, 80, 192 p.
440 KÜCHLER, Manfred. "Qualitätive Sozialforschung. Modetrend oder Neuanfang?" (Qualitative social research. Latest fashion or new beginning?), *Kölner Zeitschrift für Soziologie und Sozialpsychologie* 32, 80 : 373-386.
441 KUMAR, Krishna; [ed.]. *Bonds without bondage: explorations in transcultural interactions*. Honolulu, University Press of Hawaii, 79, vi-302 p. [published for the East-West Center.]
442 LASLETT, Barbara. "Beyond methodology: the place of theory in quantitative historical research", *American sociological Review* 45, apr 80 : 214-228.
443 LEINFELLNER, Werner; KÖHLER, Eckehart; BERGHEL, Hal; [eds.]. *Methodological developments in social science*. Dordrecht-Boston, Reidel, 79, 398 p. CR: Thomas ACHATZ, *Kölner Zeitschrift für Soziologie und Sozialpsychologie* 32(1), mar 80: 178-180.
444 LEMAINE, Gérard. "Science normale et science hypernormale. Les stragégies de différenciation et les stratégies conservatrices dans les sciences", *Revue française de Sociologie* 21, oct-dec 80 : 499-527.
445 LEMING, Michael R. "Research methods: the first class", *Teaching Sociology* jan 79 : 133-137.
446 LEPSIUS, M. Rainer. "Stein Rokkans Beitrag zur vergleichenden Strukturforschung Westeuropas" (Stein Rokkan's contribution to comparative research on the structure of Western Europe), *Zeitschrift für Soziologie* apr 80 : 115-117.
447 LEVINE, Robert V.; WEST, Laurie J.; REIS, Harry T. "Perceptions of time and punctuality in the United States and Brazil", *Journal of Personality and social Psychology* 38, apr 80 : 541-550.
448 LINCOLN, James R.; ZEITZ, Gerald. "Organizational properties from aggregate data: separating individual and structural effects", *American sociological Review* 45, jun 80 : 391-408.
449 LINDEMAN, Richard Harold; MERENDA, Peter F; GOLD, Ruth Z. *Introduction to bivariate and multivariate analysis*. Glenview, IL, Scott, Foresman, 80, 444 p.
450 LOY, Pamela. "Content analysis of journal articles as a technique for historical research", *Journal of the History of Sociology* 79 : 93-101.
451 MARRADI, Alberto. "Strategie per l'elaborazione elettronica dei dati nelle scienze sociali" (Strategy for electronic data processing in social sciences), *Rassegna italiana di Sociologia* 21, jan-mar 80 : 117-132.
452 MATSUMOTO, Kazuyoshi. "Parsons no system-ron to jōhÇo seigyo" (Parsons' system theory and his interpretation of cybernetic control), *Tohoku shakaigaku kenkyukai shakaigaku kenkyu* 39, 80 : 25-50.
453 MERTON, Robert K.; COLEMAN, James S.; ROSSI, Peter H.; [eds.]. *Qualitative and quantitative social research: papers in honor of Paul F. Lazarsfeld*. New York, Free Press, 79, xviii-413 p.
454 Bibl.XXIX-398. MITROFF, Ian I.; KILMANN, Ralph H. *Methodological approaches to social sciences*. CR: Henry TEUNE, *American political Science Review* 74(3), sep 80: 805-806. [also CR: Stephen TURNER, *Contemporary Sociology* (Albany), 9(5), sep 80 : 687-688.]
455 NAGEL, Stuart S.; NEEF, Marian. *Policy analysis in social science research*. Beverly Hills, CA, Sage Publications, 79, 300 p.
456 PATTON, Michael Quinn. *Qualitative research methods*. Beverly Hills, Sage Publications, 80, 381 p.

457 PEÑA-MARIN, Cristina. "Una aproximación interaccional al análisis del discurso" (An interaction approach to the analysis of speech), *Revista española de Investigaciones sociológicas* 12, oct-dec 80 : 141-157.
458 PERRUCHET, Pierre. *L'Analyse différentielle du conditionnement humain.* Paris, Éditions du Centre national de la recherche scientifique, 80, 119 p.
459 RESTIVO, Sal P. "Elements of a general theory in macrosociology", *International Journal of contemporary Sociology* 15(3-4), jul-oct 78 : 249-271.
460 ROGERS, Susan Carol. "Espace masculin, espace féminin. Essai sur la différence", *Études rurales* 74, apr-jun 79 : 87-110.
461 ROSENTHAL, Robert; RUBIN, Donald B. "Comparing within- and between-subjects studies", *Sociological Methods and Research* aug 80 : 127-136.
462 SAGANENKO, G. I. *Sociologičeskaja informacija: statističeskaja ocenka nadežnosti ishodnyh dannyh sociologičeskih issledovanij* (The sociological information: a statistical estimation of security of sociological research data). Leningrad, Nauka, 79, 142 p.
463 Bibl.XXIX-414. SCHWARTZ, Howard; JACOBS, Jerry. *Qualitative sociology: a method to the madness.* CR: R. J. ANDERSON, *British Journal of Sociology* 31(4), dec 80, 586-588. [also CR: Robert R. FAULKNER, Contemporary Sociology (Albany), 9(5), sep 80, 720-721.]
464 SHIMODA, Naoharu. "Hōhōron-teki shukan-shugi to kyakkan-shugi" (Methodological subjectivism vs. objectivism in sociology), *Kagaku tetsugaku* 13, 80 : 7-21.
465 Bibl.XXIX-440. SHYE, Samuel; [ed.]. *Theory construction and data analysis in the behavioral sciences.* CR: Bernard P. COHEN, *Contemporary Sociology (Albany)* 9(4), jul 80: 563-564.
466 TANDON, B. C.; [ed.]. *Research methodology in social sciences.* Allahabad, Chaitanya Pub. House, 79, vi-271 p.
467 TAYLOR, K. Wayne; CHAPPELL, Neena L. "Multivariate analysis of qualitative data", *Canadian Review of Sociology and Anthropology* 17, mai 80 : 93-108.
468 VAN PRAAG, Bernard M. S.; KAPTEYN, Arie; VAN HERWAARDEN, Floor G. "The definition and measurement of social reference spaces", *Netherlands' Journal of Sociology* 15, jul 79 : 13-25.
469 Bibl.XXIX-403. WALIZER, Michael H.; WIENIR, Paul L. *Research methods and analysis: searching for relationships.* CR: J. David LEWIS, *Contemporary Sociology (Albany)* 9(1), jan 80 : 109-110.
470 WEIMER, Walter B. *Notes on the methodology of scientific research.* Hillsdale, NJ., Lawrence Erlbaum Assoc., 79, 257 p. CR: Jerry B. MICHEL, *Contemporary Sociology (Albany)* 9(4), jul 80: 552-553.
471 WOOD, Michael. "Alternatives and options in computer content analysis", *Social Science Research* sep 80 : 273-286.

11200. DATA COLLECTION. EXPERIMENT
RASSEMBLEMENT DES DONNÉES. EXPÉRIENCE

11210. Experimentation. Observation
Expérimentation. Observation

472 "Ethical problems of fieldwork", *Social Problems* 27, feb 80 : 259-378.
473 BRIONES, Guillermo; ESCALANTE, Carlos. *Técnicas de medición en ciencias sociales* (Measurement techniques in social sciences). Bogotá, Ediciones Tercer Mundo, 79, 97 p.
474 CARMINES, Edward G.; ZELLER, Richard A. *Reliability and validity assessment.* Beverly Hills, CA, Sage Publications, 79, 70 p.
475 DOKTOROV, B. Z. *O nadežnosti izmerenija v sociologičeskom issledovanii* (The measurement security in sociological research). Leningrad, Nauka, 79, 128 p.
476 FASSNACHT, Gerhard. *Systematische Verhaltensbeobachtung — Einführung in die Methodologie und Praxis* (Systematic observation of behaviour. Introduction to methodology and practice). München, Basel, E. Reinhardt, 79, 218 p.
477 Bibl.XXIX-449. FIEDLER, Judith. *Field research: a manual for logistics and management of scientific studies in natural settings.*
478 GOLANT, Stephen M.; MCCUTCHEON, Allan L. "Objectivity, quality of life indicators and the external validity of community research findings", *Social Indicators Research* (1-4), jan 80 : 207-235. [Evanston, Ill..]
479 GOTTDIENER, M. "Field research and video tape", *Sociological Inquiry* 49, 79 : 59-66.
480 JAMIN, Jean. "Naissance de l'observation anthropologique: la Société des Observateurs de l'Homme, 1799-1805", *Cahiers internationaux de Sociologie* 67, jul-dec 79 : 313-335.

481 KOCH, James L.; RHODES, Susan R. "Problems with reactive instruments in field research", *Journal of applied behavioral Science* 15, oct-dec 79 : 485-506.
482 LIEBHAFSKY, E. E.; GNUSCHKE, John E.; MCKEE, William L. "Value judgments inherent in criticisms of CPS measurement of unemployment", *Social Science Quarterly* 61, sep 80 : 237-252. [Current Population Survey, USA.]
483 MARTIN, Michael W.; SELL, Jane. "The role of the experiment in the social sciences", *Sociological Quarterly* 20, 79 : 581-590.
484 NAMIHIRA, Isao. "Tagenteki shihyo ni yoru sonraku kaiso-kozo no bunseki -Ikemajima, Gushikami-son Minatogawa, Hateruma-jime no hikaku"(A tentative analysis of village community stratification by multiple indexes), *Okinawa kokusai daigaku bungakubu kiyo* 80 : 19-45.
485 NEUMANN, Yoram. "Measures of association: comparability, symmetry, and level of measurement", *Social Science* 54, 79 : 215-222.
486 POLSBY, Nelson W. "Empirical investigations of mobilization of bias in community power research", *Political Studies* 27, dec 79 : 527-541.
487 ROBERTS, Fred S. *Measurement theory with applications to decision making, utility, and the social sciences*. Reading, MA, Addison-Wesley, 79, xxii-420 p.
488 SEILER, Lauren H.; MURTHA, James. "Federal regulation of social research using 'human subjects': a critical assessment", *American Sociologist* 15, aug 80 : 146-157.
489 SPRADLEY, James P. *Participant observation*. New York, Holt, Rinehart and Winston, 80, xi-195 p.
490 TOTOKI, Toshichika; [et al.]. "Chiiki shakai kenkyu no rironteki sai-kenkto" (Community study — Some theoretical problems), *Keio daigaku hogaku kenkyu* 53, 80 : 25-40.
491 WEISS, Carol H.; BUCUVALAS, Michael J. "Truth tests and utility tests: decision-makers' frames of reference for social science research", *American sociological Review* 45, apr 80 : 302-313.
492 ZELLER, Richard A.; CARMINES, Edward G. *Measurement in the social sciences: the link between theory and data*. Cambridge, New York, Cambridge University Press, 80, x-198 p.
493 ZENTNER, Henry. "The concept of validity in sociology: a phenomenological perspective", *Indian Journal of social Research* 20, aug 79 : 119-126.

11220. Sampling. Survey
Échantillonnage. Enquête

494 BIRCH, Alfred L.; SCHMID, Alfred A. "Public opinion surveys as guides to public policy and spending", *Social Indicators Research* (1-4), jan 80 : 299-311.
495 DAVIS, James A. "Conservative weather in a liberalizing climate: change in selected NORC General Social Survey Items, 1972-78", *Social Forces* 58, jun 80 : 1129-1156.
496 FREEDMAN, Deborah S.; THORNTON, Arland; CAMBURN, Donald. "Maintaining response rates in longitudinal studies", *Sociological Methods and Research* aug 80 : 87-98.
497 HAKIM, C. "Integrated social data systems: the role of household censuses and surveys as sources of social, demographic and manpower data in Britain", *Social Science Information Studies* oct 80 : 13-21.
498 HOMAN, Roger. "The ethics of covert methods", *British Journal of Sociology* 31, mar 80 : 46-59. [Covert research enquiry conducted in a community of primitive sectarians described as "old-time pentecostals". With a comment by Martin BULMER: 59-65.]
499 Bibl.XXIX-465. LECLERC, Gérard. *L'observation de l'homme: une histoire des enquêtes sociales*. CR: Remi CLIGNET, *Contemporary Sociology (Albany)* 9(2), mar 80: 260-261. [also CR: Jacques SALIBA, Revue française de Sociologie, 21(3), jul-sep 80 : 466-468.]
500 MACLEAN, Mavis; GENN, Hazel. *Methodological issues in social surveys*. Atlantic Highlands, NJ, Humanities Press, 79, viii-118 p.
501 MOSS, Louis; GOLDSTEIN, Harvey; [eds.]. *The Recall method in social surveys*. London, University of London Institute of Education, 79, 176 p. [distributed by NFER Pub. Co., Windsor, Eng..]
502 ROOF, Wade Clark. "The ambiguities of 'religious preference' in survey research — a methodological note", *Public Opinion Quarterly* 44, 80 : 403-407.

11230. Interview. Questionnaire
Entretien. Questionnaire

[See also / voir aussi: 906, 2150]

503 BIBLARZ, Arturo; RICHARDSON, Chad; BIBLARZ, Dolores Noonan. "'Please don't take this personal, but...' Differential effects of personal and impersonal approaches to position inquiry letters", *American Sociologist* 15, aug 80 : 163-169.

504 BLAIR, Edward. "Using practice interviews to predict interviewer behaviors", *Public Opinion Quarterly* 44, 80 : 257-260.

505 BRADBURN, Norman M.; [et al.]. *Improving interview method and questionnaire design.* San Francisco: Jossey-Bass, 79, xvi-214 p.

506 DEMAIO, Theresa J. "Refusals: who, where and why", *Public Opinion Quarterly* 44, 80 : 223-233.

507 DIJKSTRA, Wil. "Response bias in the survey interview; an approach from balance theory", *Social Networks* jul 80 : 285-304.

508 EVANS, David R.; [et al.]. *Essential interviewing: a programmed approach to effective communication.* Monterey, CA, Brooks/Cole Pub. Co., 79, ix-271 p.

509 FLUTTERT, P. H. M. "Wat is een response van 80% waard?: een onderzoeksnotitie" (What does a high proportion of returns say? A research note), *Sociologische Gids* 27, mar-apr 80 : 160-165.

510 GILBERT, G. Nigel. "Being interviewed: a role analysis", *Social Science Information* 19, 80 : 227-236.

511 HETEBRIJ, M. "Een model voor een interviewtheorie" (A model for an interview theory), *Mens en Maatshcappij* 55, sep 80 : 280-297.

512 JORDAN, Lawrence; MARCUS, Alfred C.; REEDER, Leo G. "Response styles in telephone and household interviewing: a field experiment", *Public Opinion Quarterly* 44, 80 : 210-222.

513 SCHAEFFER, Nora Cate. "Evaluating race-of-interviewer effects in a national survey", *Sociological Methods and Research* mai 80 : 400-419.

514 SOSDIAN, Carol P.; SHARP, Laure M. "Nonresponse in mail surveys: access failure or respondent resistance", *Public Opinion Quarterly* 44, 80 : 396-402.

515 WEEKS, M. F.; [et al.]. "Optimal times to contact sample households", *Public Opinion Quarterly* 44, 80 : 101-114.

11240. Personality measurement. Test
Mesure de la personnalité. Test

[See also / voir aussi: 2524]

516 ALEKSEEVA, V. G. "Mesto cennostnyh orientacij v postroenii tipologii ličnosti" (Place of value orientations in the personality typology elaboration), *Sociologičeskie Issledovanija* 80 : 34-43.

517 Bibl.XXIX-497. FISKE, Donald W. *Strategies for personality research.* CR: Paul Davidson REYNOLDS, *Contemporary Sociology (Albany)* 9(1), jan 80: 144-145.

11250. Sociodrama
Sociodrame

11300. MATHEMATICAL ANALYSIS. STATISTICAL ANALYSIS
ANALYSE MATHÉMATIQUE. ANALYSE STATISTIQUE

11310. Algebra. Calculus. Logic
Algèbre. Calcul. Logique

[See also / voir aussi: 2001]

518 BRADLEY, Raymond. *Possible worlds: an introduction to logic and its philosophy.* Indianapolis: Hackett Pub. Co., 79, xxi-391 p.

519 ELSTER, Jon. *Logic and society: contradictions and possible worlds,* Chichester-New York-Brisbane-Toronto, John Wiley and Sons 78 : viii-235 p. [See also the symposium devoted to this book in Inquiry 23(2), jun 80 : 139-232.]

520 Bibl.XXIX-506. ELSTER, Jon. *Logic and society: contradictions and possible worlds.* CR: Omar K. MOORE, *Contemporary Sociology (Albany)* 9(1), jan 80 : 82-93.
521 HARARY, Frank; KOMMEL, Helene J. "Matrix measures for transitivity and balance", *Journal of mathematical Sociology* 79 : 199-210.
522 PICK, James B.; HOLLADAY, John C. "An alternative approach to analyzing convergence by Leslie matrices", *Journal of mathematical Sociology* 79 : 283-324.
523 ROBINSON, John Alan. *Logic: form and function: the mechanization of deductive reasoning.* Edinburgh, University Press, 79, vi-312 p.
524 RUSSELL, Kevin. "Controversies: the use of matrix substructuring for an analysis of divergent explanatory perspectives", *Scottish Journal of Sociology* jan 80 : 53-85.
525 SARTORI, Giovanni. *La politica: logica e metodo in scienze sociali* (Politics: logic and method in the social sciences). Milano, SugarCo, 79, 321 p.

11320. Statistical analysis
Analyse statistique

526 AGRESTI, Alan; AGRESTI, Barbara Finlay. *Statistical methods for the social sciences.* San Francisco, Dellen Pub. Co., 79, xvi-554 p.
527 ALLISON, Paul D. "Analyzing collapsed contingency tables without actually collapsing", *American sociological Review* 45, feb 80 : 123-130.
528 ANDERSEN, Erlin B. *Discrete statistical methods with social science applications.* Amsterdam, New York, North-Holland Pub. Co., 80, xiii-383 p. [sole distributors for the U.S.A. and Canada, American Elsevier Pub. Co., New York.]
529 ARNEY, William Ray. "Statistics as language", *Teaching Sociology* jan 79 : 173-177.
530 BATYGIN, G. S. "Logiko-teoretičeskoe obosnovanie pokazatelej v sociologičeskih issledovanijah" (A logical and theoretical elaboration of indexes in sociological research), *Sociologičeskie Issledovanija* 79 : 136-145.
531 BATYGIN, G. S. "Tezaurus social'nyh pokazatelej obraza žizni" (Thesaurus of the way of life indicators), *IN: Trud kak osnova socialističeskogo obraza žizni.* Moskva, 79 : 117-126.
532 BEBBINGTON, A. C.; DAVIES, Bleddyn. "Territorial need indicators: a new approach", *Journal of social Policy* apr 80 : 145-168.
533 BÖHNING, Dankmar; WILKE, Helmut. "Statistische Analysepakete und ihre Einbeziehung in social-wissenschaftliche Studiengänge"(Statistical programming packages and their integration into social-scientific curricula), *Zeitschrift für Soziologie* jul 80 : 290-307.
534 BORGATTA, Edgar F.; [ed.]. *Aggregate data. Analysis and interpretation.* Beverly Hills, CA, Sage Publications, 80, 192 p.
535 BULMER, Martin. "Why don't sociologist make more use of official statistics?", *Sociology* 14, nov 80 : 505-523.
536 BURGAT, Paul; CHARDON, Pierre-André. "Analyse des tableaux de contingence par des modèles loglinéaires. Comparaison avec l'analyse des correspondances", *Revue européenne des Sciences sociales. Cahiers Vilfredo Pareto* 18(51), 80 : 5-20.
537 CRITTENDEN, Kathleen S.; MONTGOMERY, Andrew C. "A system of paired asymmetric measures of association for use with ordinal dependent variables", *Social Forces* 58, jun 80 : 1178-1194.
538 DIEKMANN, Andreas. "A dynamic stochastic version of the Pitcher-Hamblin-Miller model of 'collective violence' ", *Journal of mathematical Sociology* 79 : 277-282.
539 DOREIAN, Patrick. "Linear models with spatially distributed data: spatial disturbances or spatial effects?", *Sociological Methods and Research* aug 80 : 29-60.
540 DOREIAN, Patrick; HUMMON, Norman. "Estimating differential equation models on time series: some simulation evidence", *Sociological Methods and Research* aug 79 : 3-33.
541 DUNCAN, Otis Dudley. "Constrained parameters in a model for categorical data", *Sociological Methods and Research* aug 79 : 57-68.
542 ELGIE, R. A. "Territorial social indicator construction: an alternative perspective and example", *Social Indicators Research* jun 80 : 175-197.
543 EMDE, Reimund. *Sozialindikatoren und Systemvergleich: zur Analyse intersystemarer Beziehungen* (Social indicators and system comparison: on the inter-system relations analysis). Frankfurt/Main, New York, Campus-Verlag, 79, 179 p.
544 FENNESSEY, James; D'AMICO, Ronald. "Collinearity, ridge regression, and investigator judgment", *Sociological Methods and Research* feb 80 : 309-340.
545 FERRISS, Abbott L.; [ed.]. "The US Federal effort in social indicators development", *Social Indicators Research* apr 79 : 129-282.

546 FISHBURN, Peter C. "Evaluative comparisons of distributions of a social variable: ordering methods", *Social Indicators Research* jan 79 : 103-126.
547 FOX, John. "Effect analysis in structural equation models: extensions and simplified methods of computation", *Sociological Methods and Research* aug 80 : 3-28.
548 FÜSTÖS, László; MANCHIN, Győző Róbert; TÓTH, Károly. *SZOCPROG. Társadalomstatisztikai programrendszer* (SOCPROG. A program system of social statistics). Budapest, MTA Szociológiai Kutatóintézet, 78, 86 p. [publ. by the Inst. of Sociology of the Hungarian Academy of Sciences.]
549 GILLESPIE, Michael W.; FOX, John. "Specification error and negatively correlated disturbances in "parallel" simultaneous-equation models", *Sociological Methods and Research* feb 80 : 273-308.
550 GILMARTIN, Kevin J.; [et al.]. *Social indicators: an annotated bibliography of current literature.* New York, Garland Pub., 79, xii-123 p.
551 GIRT, John L. "A measure of quality of opportunity", *Social Indicators Research* jan 79 : 91-102.
552 GULEZIAN, R. C. *Statistics for decision making.* Philadelphia, Saunders, 79, xvii-665 p.
553 GUTTMAN, Louis. "Malos usos en estadística"(Bad uses in statistics), *Revista española de Investigaciones sociológicas* apr-jun 79 : 101-127.
554 HINKLE, Dennis E.; WIERSMA, William; JURS, Stephen G. *Applied statistics for the behavioral sciences.* Chicago, Rand McNally College Pub. Co., 79, xiv-489 p.
555 HODGE, Robert W.; KLORMAN, Ricardo. "Dynamic social indicator models: some problems of analysis and interpretation", *Sociology and social Research* 64, oct 79 : 1-27.
556 HOLT, D. "Log-linear models of contingency table analysis: on the interpretation of parameters", *Sociological Methods and Research* feb 79 : 330-336.
557 HOLTMANN, Dieter. "Interpretationsprobleme und Verwendung der Residuen in der multiplen Regression" (Problems of interpretation and use of the residuals in multiple regression), *Zeitschrift für Soziologie* oct 80 : 384-399.
558 Bibl.XXIX-517. HORTON, Raymond L. *The general linear model: data analysis in the social and behavioural sciences.* CR: William R. KELLY, *Contemporary Sociology (Albany)* 9(1), jan 80 : 105.
559 HUBERT, J. J. "Linguistic indicators", *Social Indicators Research* jun 80 : 223-255.
560 IGRA, Amnon. "Three methods of estimating a model of group effects: a comparison with reference to school effect studies", *Sociological Methods and Research* aug 80 : 61-86.
561 IRVINE, John; MILES, Ian; EVANS, Jeff; [eds.]. *Demystifying social statistics.* London, Pluto Press, 79, 390 p. CR: E. S. LYON, *British Journal of Sociology* 31(3), sep 80 : 453-455.
562 IVERSEN, Gudmund R. "Decomposing chi-square: a forgotten technique", *Sociological Methods and Research* nov 79 : 143-157.
563 JACKSON, David J; [ed.]. *Factor analysis and measurement in sociological research. A multidimensional perspective.* Beverly Hills, CA, Sage Publications, 80, 278 p.
564 JACKSON, David J.; BORGATTA, Edgar F.; GOLDSMITH, Harold F. (Data analysis in factorial ecology), *Sociological Methods and Research* feb 79 : 356-368.
565 JURA, Michel. "Les indicateurs sociaux", *Consommation* 26(3-4), jul-dec 79 : 7-27.
566 KENNY, David A. *Correlation and causality.* New York, Wiley, 79, xiii-277 p. [in social sciences.]
567 KNOX, Paul L. "Measures of accessibility as social indicators: a note", *Social Indicators Research* (1-4), jan 80 : 367-377.
568 KOSAKA, Katsuaki. "Kokyo seisaku to shakai shihyo -shakai keikakuron eno josho" (Public policy and social indicators), *Kokusai shika daigaku ronso* 22, 80 : 79-88.
569 KRITZER, Herbert M. "Comparing partial rank order correlations from contingency table data", *Sociological Methods and Research* mai 80 : 420-433.
570 KUECHLER, Manfred. "The analysis of nonmetric data: the relation of dummy dependent variable regression using and additive-saturated Grizzle-Starmer-Koch model", *Sociological Methods and Research* mai 80 : 369-388.
571 KURIAN, George Thomas. *The book of world rankings.* New York, Facts on File, 79, xiii-430 p.
572 LAND, Kenneth C.; MCMILLAN, Marilyn M. "Demographic data and social indicators", *Sociology and social Research* 64, apr 80 : 348-377.
573 LEACH, Chris. *Introduction to statistics: a nonparametric approach for the social sciences.* Chichester, Eng., New York, Wiley, 79, xv-339 p.
574 LEE, Trevor; MARANS, Robert W. "Objective and subjective indicators: effects of scale discordance on interrelationships", *Social Indicators Research* mar 80 : 47-64.

575 Bibl.XXIX-539. LEIPERT, Christian. *Gesellschaftliche Berichterstattung. Eine Einführung in Theorie und Praxis sozialer Indikatoren* (Social reporting. A research on the theory and practice of social indicators). CR: Eike BALLERSTEDT, *Soziologische Revue* 3(4), 80: 425-426.

576 MACDONALD, K. I. "Interpretation of residual paths and decomposition of variance", *Sociological Methods and Research* feb 79 : 289-329.

577 MACMILLAN, Alexander; DAFT, Richard L. "Relationships among ratio variables with common components: fact or artifact", *Social Forces* 58, jun 80 : 1109-1128.

578 MARCOTORCHINO, J. F.; MICHAUD, Pierre. *Optimisation en analyse ordinale des données.* Paris, New York, Masson, 79, xii-211 p.

579 MCCLEARY, Richard; [et al.]. *Applied time series analysis for the social sciences.* London, Beverly Hills, Sage Publications, 80, 328 p.

580 MCDOWALL, David. *Interrupted time series analysis.* Beverly Hills, CA, Sage Publications, 80, 80 p.

581 MOORMAN, Jeanne E. "Aggregation bias: an empirical demonstration", *Sociological Methods and Research* aug 79 : 69-94.

582 Nations unies. Statistique (Bureau). *L'Amélioration des statistiques sociales dans les pays en développement: cadre conceptuel et méthodes.* New York, Nations Unies, 79, vii-108 p.

583 OSIPOV, G. V.; ANDREENKOV, V. G.; [eds.]. *Issledovanie postroenija pokazatelej social'nogo razvitija i planirovanija* (Research on indexes elaboration on social development and planning). Moskva, Nauka, 79, 229 p.

584 PARKER, Robert Nash. "Correlation in time series regression: the Geary test", *Sociological Methods and Research* aug 80 : 99-114.

585 PENDLETON, Brian F.; WARREN, Richard D.; CHANG, H. C. "Correlated denominators in multiple regression and change analyses", *Sociological Methods and Research* mai 79 : 451-474.

586 REVENSTORF, Dirk. *Faktorenanalyse* (Factor analysis). Stuttgart, Berlin, Köln, Mainz, Kohlhammer, 80, 188 p.

587 SALAU, Ademola T. "Toward a reappraisal of social indicators for housing in developing nations", *Social Indicators Research* jul 79 : 293-299.

588 SMITH, Kent W.; SASAKI, M. S. "Decreasing multicollinearity: a method for models with multiplicative functions", *Sociological Methods and Research* aug 79 : 35-56.

589 STAVIG, Gordon R. "Measuring the magnitude of agreement between paired values for a single case", *Sociology and social Research* 64, apr 80 : 379-388.

590 STIPAK, Brian. "Are there sensible ways to analyze and use subjective indicators of urban service quality?", *Social Indicators Research* oct 79 : 421-438.

591 SWAFFORD, Michael. "Three parametric techniques for contingency table analysis: a nontechnical commentary", *American sociological Review* 45, aug 80 : 664-690.

592 TAYLOR, Charles Lewis; [ed.]. *Indicator systems for political, economic, and social analysis.* Koenigstein, Verlag A. Hain, Cambridge, MA, Oelgeschlager, Gunn & Hain, 80, x-242 p.

593 TUNSTALL, Daniel B. "Developing indicators of environmental quality: the experience of the Council on Environmental Quality", *Social Indicators Research* jul 79 : 301-347.

594 VOLKOV, O. È. "K razrabotke sistemy indikatorov razvitija socialističeskogo proizvodstvennogo kollektiva" (On the indicators system elaboration of the socialist production collectivity development), IN: *Social'naja struktura sovetskogo obščestva i socialističeskij obraz žizni. II.* Moskva, 78 : 41-52.

595 WARREN, Richard D.; FEAR, Frank A.; KLONGLAN, Gerald E. "Social-indicator model building: a multiple-indicator design", *Social Indicators Research* (1-4), jan 80 : 269-297.

596 Bibl.XXIX-530. WILDT, Albert R.; AHTOLA, Olli T. *Analysis of covariance.* CR: Richard A. ZELLER, *Contemporary Sociology (Albany)* 9(2), mar 80: 278-279.

597 ZAPF, Wolfgang. "Applied social reporting: a social indicators system for West German society", *Social Indicators Research* oct 79 : 397-419.

11330. Cybernetics. Information theory
Cybernétique. Théorie de l'information

[See also / voir aussi: 452]

598 BEA, Franz Xaver; BOHNET, Armin; KUMESCH, Herbert; [eds.]. *Systemmodelle: Anwendungsmöglichkeiten d. systemtheoret. Ansatzes* (System models: system theory application

possibilities). München, Wien, Oldenbourg, 79, 270 p. CR: Herbert STACHOWIAK, *Soziologische Revue* 3(1), 80: 31-32.
599 GARCIIA COTARELO, Ramón. *Crítica de la teoría de sistemas* (Criticism of systems theory). Madrid, Centro de Investigaciones Sociológicas, 79, 166 p.
600 GEORGE, Frank Honywill. *Philosophical foundations of cybernetics.* Tunbridge Wells, Abacus Press, 79, ix-157 p.
601 HANNAN, Michael T.; TUMA, Nancy Brandon. "Methods for temporal analysis", *Annual Review of Sociology* 79 : 303-328.
602 PETERSEN, Ib Damgaard. *Kybernetiske systemers udviklingslove* (Development of cybernetic systems). København, Københavns Universitets Institut for Samfundsfag, 79, vi-333 p.
603 PICARD, Claude François; CAMION, Paul. *Théorie de l'information: développements récents et applications.* Paris, Éditions du Centre national de la recherche scientifique, 78, 506 p.

11340. Graph theory
Théorie des graphes

604 BURT, Ronald S. "Autonomy in a social topology", *American Journal of Sociology* 85, jan 80 : 892-925.
605 BURT, Ronald S. "Relational equilibrium in social topology", *Journal of mathematical Sociology* 79 : 211-252.
606 CAPOBIANCO, Michael F.; MOLLUZZO, John C. "The strength of a graph and its application to organizational structure" (Social Networks), *Social Networks* jul 80 : 275-283.
607 EVERETT, Martin; NIEMINEN, Juhani. "Partitions and homomorphisms in directed and undirected graphs", *Journal of mathematical Sociology* 80 : 91-111.
608 FRANK, Ove; HARAY, Frank. "Balance in stochastic signed graphs", *Social Networks* apr 80 : 155-163.
609 HARARY, Frank; [ed.]. *Topics in graph theory.* New York, New York Academy of Sciences, 79, 208 p.

11350. Stochastic processes. Statistical decision. Game theory
Processus stochastiques. Décision statistique. Théorie des jeux

610 ALLISON, Paul D. "Estimation of testing for a Markov model of reinforcement", *Sociological Methods and Research* mai 80 : 434-453.
611 BRUMELLE, Shelby L.; GERCHAK, Yigal. "A stochastic model allowing interaction among individuals and its behavior for large populations", *Journal of mathematical Sociology* 80 : 73-90.
612 CONLISK, John; SOMMERS, Paul. "Eigenvector status proxies in Markov chain mobility models", *Sociological Methods and Research* nov 79 : 159-178.
613 KARMESHU; PATHRIA, R. K. "Stochastic evolution of competing social groups", *Journal of mathematical Sociology* 80 : 59-71.
614 KINDERMANN, Ross P.; SNELL, J. Laurie. "On the relation between Markov random fields and social networks", *Journal of mathematical Sociology* 80 : 1-13.
615 ROSENTHAL, Robert. "New equilibria for noncooperative two-person games", *Journal of mathematical Sociology* 80 : 15-26.
616 SOMMERS, Paul; CONLISK, John. "Eigenvalue immobility measures for Markov chains", *Journal of mathematical Sociology* 79 : 253-276.

11360. Attitude scale
Échelle d'attitude

[See also / voir aussi: 926, 1240]

617 CLOGG, Clifford C. "Characterizing the class organization of labour market opportunity: a modified latent structure approach", *Sociological Methods and Research* feb 80 : 243-272.
618 Bibl. XXIX-525. GOODMAN, Leo A. *Analyzing qualitative/categorical data: log-linear models and latent structure analysis.* CR: Howard ROSENTHAL, *Contemporary Sociology (Albany)* 9(2), mar 80 : 207-212.

619	GREENE, V. L. "Canonical analysis and optimal criterion validity scaling", *Social Science Research* mar 80 : 55-59.
620	JOHNSON, David W.; NOREM-HEBEISEN, Ardyth A. "A measure of cooperative, competitive, and individualistic attitudes", *Journal of social Psychology* 109, dec 79 : 253-261.
621	PIAZZA, Thomas. "The analysis of attitude items", *American Journal of Sociology* 86, nov 80 : 584-603.
622	PRESSER, Stanley; SCHUMAN, Howard. "The measurement of a middle position in attitude surveys", *Public Opinion Quarterly* 44, 80 : 70-85.
623	RAY, J. J. "The comparative validity of Likert projective, and forced-choice indices of achievement motivation", *Journal of social Psychology* 111, jun 80 : 63-72.
624	STRAUSS, David J. "Chance in Guttman scaling", *Social Science Research* mar 80 : 76-82.

12. INDIVIDUAL. GROUP. ORGANIZATION
INDIVIDU. GROUPE. ORGANISATION

12100. PSYCHOLOGY. SOCIAL PSYCHOLOGY. SOCIOMETRY.
PSYCHOLOGIE. PSYCHOLOGIE SOCIALE. SOCIOMÉTRIE

12110. Psychoanalysis. Social psychology
Psychanalyse. Psychologie sociale

[See also / voir aussi: 279, 809, 836, 983, 1562, 1858, 2809, 4005]

625 ALARCÓN, Reynaldo; [ed.]. "La psicología en el Perú" (Psychology in Peru), *Revista latinoamericana de Psicología* 12, 80 : 199-394.
626 ALBRECHT, Stan L.; CHADWICK, Bruce A.; THOMAS, Darwin L. *Social psychology.* Englewood Cliffs, NJ, Prentice-Hall, 80, xi-463 p.
627 ALEXANDER, Theron. *Developmental psychology.* New York, Van Nostrand, 80, xi-477 p.
628 ALLEN, Donald E.; GUY, Rebecca F.; EDGLEY, Charles K. *Social psychology as social process.* Belmont, CA, Wadsworth Pub. Co., 80, xii-477 p.
629 AMADO, Georges. *De l'enfant à l'adulte: la psychanalyse au regard de l'être.* Paris, Presses universitaires de France, 79, 288 p.
630 BÉGUIN, Guy; JOSHI, Purushottam. *Psychologie sociale.* Québec, Presses de l'Université Laval, 79, 479 p.
631 BLANCO ABARCA, Amalio. "La psicología social: desorientación y aplicación a la realidad española" (Social psychology: confusion and application to the Spanish reality), *Revista española de Investigaciones sociológicas* 12, oct-dec 80 : 159-194.
632 BLOOMFIELD, T. M. "Psychoanalysis: a human science?", *Journal for the Theory of social Behaviour* oct 79 : 271-287.
633 BOLTON, Neil; [ed.]. *Philosophical problems in psychology.* London, New York, Methuen, 79, xiii-207 p.
634 BORNEWASSER, Manfred; [et al.]. *Einführung in die Sozialpsychologie.* Heidelberg, Quelle und Meyer, 79, 248 p.
635 BOUTILIER, Robert G.; ROED, J. Christian; SVENDSEN, Ann C. "Crises in the two social psychologies: a critical comparison", *Social Psychology Quarterly* 43, mar 80 : 5-17. [PSP: Psychological social psychology; SSP: Sociological social psychology.]
636 BUSS, Allan R.; [ed.]. *Psychology in social context.* New York, Irvington Publishers, 79, xii-407 p. [distributed by Halsted Press.]
637 CAMPOS SANTELICES, Armando; BRENES, Abelardo; QUEVEDO REYES, Santiago. "Crisis, dependencia, y contradicciones de la psicología en América Latina" (Crisis, dependence and contradictions of psychology in Latin America), *Revista latinoamericana de Psicología* 12, 80 : 11-27.
638 Bibl.XXIX-584. DOISE, Willem; DESCHAMPS, Jean-Claude; MUGNY, Gabriel. *Psychologie sociale expérimentale.* CR: Philippe BESNARD, *Revue française de Sociologie* 21(2), apr-jun 80: 313-314.
639 FAW, Terry. Schaum's outline of theory and problems of child psychology. New York, McGraw-Hill, 80, 296 p.
640 FOSCHI, Martha. "Theory, experimentation and cross-cultural comparison in social psychology", *Canadian Journal of Sociology* 80 : 91-102.
641 GINSBURG, Gerald P.; [ed.]. *Emerging strategies in social psychological research.* Chichester, New York, Wiley, 79, 319 p.
642 GROUPE DESGENETTES. "La sociopsychanalyse institutionnelle", *Connexions* 29, 80 : 69-80.
643 HERMANN, Theo. *Psychologie als Problem: Herausforderungen d. psycholog. Wiss.* (Psychology as a problem: challenge of psychological knowledge). Stuttgart, Klett-Cotta, 79, 196 p.
644 ISRAEL, Joachim. *Om relationistisk socialpsykologi* (On relationist social psychology). Göteborg, Korpen, 79, 128 p.
645 JONES, Russell A.; HENDRICK, Clyde; EPSTEIN, Yakov M. *Introduction to social psychology.* Sunderland, MA, Sinauer Associates, 79, xvii-542 p.

646	KLINE, Paul. *Psychometrics and psychology*. London, New York, Academic Press, 79, ix-381 p.
647	KOTLER, Tamara; CHETWYND, Jane. "Changes in family members during psychotherapy", *Human Relations* 33, 80 : 101-110.
648	LAMBERTH, John. *Social psychology*. New York, Macmillan, 80, ix-609 p.
649	LEVY-LEBOYER, Claude. *Psychologie et environnement*. Paris, Presses universitaires de France, 80, 211 p.
650	LEVY-LEBOYER, Claude. *Psychologie et environnement*. Paris, Presses universitaires de France, 80, 211 p.
651	LEYENS, Jacques Philippe. *Psychologie sociale*. Bruxelles, P. Mardaga, 79, 194 p. CR: Philippe BESNARD, *Revue française de Sociologie* 21(2), apr-jun 80: 313-314.
652	MARIN, Gerardo. "Hacia una psicología social comunitaria" (Towards a community social psychology), *Revista latinoamericana de Psicología* 12, 80 : 171-180.
653	Bibl.XXIX-607. PENNER, Lluis A. *Social psychology: a contemporary approach*. CR: Richard J. BUTSCH, *Contemporary Sociology (Albany)* 9(4), jul 80: 582-583.
654	QURESHI, Mohammed Younus. *Statistics and behavior: an introduction*. Washington, University Press of America, 80, x-322 p.
655	ROUCHY, Jean-Claude. "Vers une psychologie psychanalytique", *Connexions* 29, 80 : 17-37.
656	SPENCER, Martin E. "The social psychology of Max Weber", *Sociological Analysis* 40, 79 : 240-253.
657	ZAVALLONI, Marisa; LOUIS-GUERIN, Christiane. "Social psychology at the crossroads: its encounter with congnitive and ecological psychology and the interactive perspective", *European Journal of social Psychology* jul-sep 79 : 307-321.

12120. Psychological factor
Facteur psychologique

12200. INDIVIDUAL. PERSONALITY
INDIVIDU. PERSONNALITÉ

12210. Ego. Identity
Ego. Identité

[See also / voir aussi: 1616]

658	DE SILVA, Lynn A. *The problem of the self in Buddhism and Christianity*. New York, Barnes & Noble, 79, xv-185 p.
659	ERBRING, Lutz; YOUNG, Alice A. "Individuals and social structure: contextual effects as endogenous feedback", *Sociological Methods and Research* mai 79 : 396-430.
660	HOGAN, Robert; [ed.]. "Personality processes and individual differences", *Journal of Personality and social Psychology* 39, oct 80 : 669-750.
661	KON, I. "Ja' kak kul'tura istoričeskij fenomen" ("I" as a cultural and historical phenomenon), *Obščestvennye Nauki (Moskva)* 79 : 143-158.
662	LANA, Robert E. "Giambattista Vico and the history of social psychology", *Journal for the Theory of social Behaviour* oct 79 : 251-263.
663	OBRADOVIĆ, Josip. "Grana industrije i ponašanje pojedinca u procesu donošenja odluka" (Branch in industry and the individual behaviour in the process of decision making), *Sociologija* 21, 79 : 369-395.
664	REITZES, Donald C.; BURKE, Peter J. "College student identity: measurement and implications", *Pacific sociological Review* 23, jan 80 : 45-66.
665	ROYCE, Joseph R. "Toward a viable theory of individual differences", *Journal of Personality and social Psychology* 37(10), oct 79 : 1927-1931.
666	YOSHIDA, Tadashi. "Shakai no sôi to jiga no sôiteki keisei ni tsuite" (A study of the stages of ego corresponding to three levels of society), *Oitemon gakuin daigaku bungakubu kiyo* 14, 80 : 67-86.

12220. Egocentrism. Self concept
Égocentrisme. Conception de soi

[See also / voir aussi: 717, 846, 887, 908, 1303, 1361, 1865, 1892, 2101, 2475, 3061, 3088, 3097, 3672, 4527, 5063, 5430]

667   BENSMAN, Joseph; LILIENFELD, Robert. *Between public and private: the lost boundaries of the self.* New York, Free Press, 79, xii-196 p.
668   BIGGS, Simon. "The me I see: acting participating, and viewing and their implications for videofeedback", *Human Relations* 33, aug 80 : 575-588.
669   BLAKAR, Rolv Mikkel; PEDERSEN, Tobe Beate. "Control and self-confidence as reflected in sex-bound patterns in communication: an experimental approach", *Acta sociologica* 23, 80 : 33-53.
670   BROCKNER, Joel. (Self-esteem, self-consciousness, and task performance: replications, extensions, and possible explanations), *Journal of Personality and social Psychology* 37, mar 79 : 447-461.
671   BROCKNER, Joel. "The effects of self-esteem, success-failure, and self-consciousness on task performance", *Journal of Personality and social Psychology* 37(10), oct 79 : 1732-1741.
672   BRODY, Baruch A. *Identity and essence.* Princeton, NJ, Princeton University Press, 80, 164 p.
673   BURKE, Peter J. "The self-measurement requirements from an interactionist perspective", *Social Psychology Quarterly* 43, mar 80 : 18-29.
674   BURNS, R. B. *The self concept in theory, measurement, development, and behaviour.* London, New York, Longman, 79, 333 p.
675   BURRIDGE, Kenelm. *Someone, no one: an essay on individuality.* Princeton, NJ, Princeton University Press, 79, xi-270 p.
676   BUSS, Arnold Herbert. *Self-consciousness and social anxiety.* San Francisco, W. H. Freeman, 80, xii-270 p.
677   CARVER, Charles S. "A cybernetic model of self-attention processes", *Journal of Personality and social Psychology* 37, aug 79 : 1251-1281.
678   D'AGOSTINO, F. B. "Individualism and collectivism: the case of language", *Philosophy of the social Sciences* mar 79 : 27-47.
679   DENSCOMBE, Martyn; ROBINS, Lynton. "Self-assessment and essay writing", *Teaching Sociology* oct 80 : 63-78.
680   DESCHAMPS, Jean-Claude; [et al.]. "L'identité sociale et les rapports de domination", *Schweizerische Zeitschrift für Soziologie / Revue suisse de Sociologie* mar 80 : 109-140.
681   DRURY, Darrel W. "Black self-esteem and desegregated schools", *Sociology of Education* 53, apr 80 : 88-103.
682   DRURY, Darrel W.; MCCARTHY, John D. "The social psychology of name change: reflections on a serendipitous discovery", *Social Psychology Quarterly* 43, sep 80 : 310-320.
683   FARLEY, Reynolds; RICHARDS, Toni; WURDOCK, Clarence. "School desegregation and white flight: an investigation of competing models and their discrepant findings", *Sociology of Education* 53, jul 80 : 123-139. [USA.]
684   FILIPP, Sigrun-Heide; [ed.]. *Selbstkonzept-Forschung* (Self-concept research). Stuttgart, Klett-Cotta, 79, 304 p.
685   FODDY, W. H.; FINIGHAN, W. R. "The concept of privacy from a symbolic interaction perspective", *Journal for the Theory of social Behaviour* 10, mar 80 : 11-17.
686   KAHLE, Lynn R.; KULKA, Richard A.; KLINGEL, David M. "Low adolescent self-esteem leads to multiple interpersonal problems: a test of social-adaptation theory", *Journal of Personality and social Psychology* 39, sep 80 : 496-502.
687   KONDRAT'EVA, O. I. "O nekotoryh napravlenijah issledovanija problemy samoutverždenija ličnosti" (On some tendencies of research on the personality self-consolidation problem), IN: *Metodologičeskie problemy nauki.* Novosibirsk, 79 : 142-149.
688   LATORRE, Ronald A. *Sexual identity.* Chicago, Nelson-Hall, 79, x-171 p.
689   Bibl.XXIX-646. MACFARLANE, Alan. *The origins of English individualism: the family, property, and social transition.* CR: Lester R. KURTZ, *American Journal of Sociology* 86(2), sep 80: 403-407. [also CR: George C. HOMANS, *Contemporary Sociology* (Albany), 9(2), mar 80 : 262-263.]
690   MACKINNON, Neil J.; ANISEF, Paul. "Self-assessment in the early educational attainment process", *Canadian Review of Sociology and Anthropology* 16, aug 79 : 305-319.
691   MAHLER, Margaret S. *Separation-individuation.* New York, J. Aronson, 79, vi-263 p.
692   MARKHAM, William T.; BONJEAN, Charles M.; CORDER-BOLZ, Judy. "Self-expression at work: a theory-based questionnaire instrument", *Journal of applied behavioral Science* 16, apr-jun 80 : 167-191.
693   MUGUERZA, Javier. "La crisis de identidad de la filosofía de la identidad" (The crisis of identity of the philosophy of identity), *Sistema. Revista de Ciencias sociales* 36, 80 : 19-36.

694 OGAWA, Hiroshi. "Tokumeisei to shakai no sonritsu — A. Schutz no tokumeisei no gainen o megutte" (Anonymity and genesis of society — An analysis of Alfred Schutz' concept of anonymity), *Shakaigaku hyoron* 31, 80 : 17-30.
695 PETROVA, É. N. "Samosoznanie ličnosti kak social'naja problema" (The personality self-consciousness as a social problem), *IN: Vsestoronnee razvitie ličnosti sovetskogo čeloveka*. Sverdlovsk, 79 : 95-196.
696 PLINER, Patricia; BLANKSTEIN, Kirk R.; SPIGEL, Irwin M.; [eds.]. *Perception of emotion in self and others*. New York, Plenum Press, 79, x-204 p.
697 PORTER, Judith R.; WASHINGTON, Robert. "Black identity and self-esteem: a review of studies of Black self-concept, 1968-1978", *Annual Review of Sociology* 79 : 53-74.
698 POST, Peter W.; RAO, D. C. "Effect of skin color on self-esteem", *Social Biology* 26, 79 : 51-54.
699 REITZES, Donald C. "Beyond the looking glass self: Cooley's social self and its treatment in introductory textbooks", *Contemporary Sociology* sep 80 : 631-640. [survey essay.]
700 Bibl.XXIX-652. ROSENBERG, Morris. *Conceiving the self*. CR: Sheldon STRYKER, *Contemporary Sociology (Albany)* 9(3), mai 80, 383-385.
701 ROTHBARD, Murray N. *Individualism and the philosohpy of the social sciences*. San Francisco, CATO Institute, 79, 67 p.
702 ROUNDTREE, George A. *Self-esteem and social adjustment: an experimental study of the effects of a mathematical educational model on self-esteem of male prison inmates*. Calcutta, Minerva, 79, xviii-131 p.
703 SCHAFER, Robert B.; BRAITO, Rita. "Self-concept and role performance evaluation among marriage partners", *Journal of Marriage and Family* 41, nov 79 : 801-810.
704 SCHEIER, Michael F. "Effects of public and private self-conciousness on the public expression of personal beliefs", *Journal of Personality and social Psychology* 39, sep 80 : 514-521.
705 SCHEIER, Michael F.; CARVER, Charles S. "Private and public self-attention, resistance to change and dissonance reduction", *Journal of Personality and social Psychology* 39, sep 80 : 390-405.
706 SHIINO, Nobuo. "Shakaiteki sekai to identity"(Social world and identity), *Sociologos* 80 : 66-78.
707 STANGVIK, Gunnar. *Self-concept and school segregation*. Göteborg, Acta Universitatis Gothoburgensis, 79, 528 p.
708 TAKAHASHI, Yoshinori. "Jiko teiji to audience"(Some aspects of self-audience relationship — A theoretical study), *Shakaigaku hyoron* 31, 80 : 2-16.
709 TESSER, Abraham. "Self-esteem maintenance in family dynamics", *Journal of Personality and social Psychology* 39, jul 80 : 77-91.
710 VAHIDUDDIN, Syed. "À la rencontre de l'homme avec lui-même", *Diogène* 109, janmar 80 : 59-71.
711 WEGNER, Daniel M.; GIULIANO, Toni. "Arousal-induced attention to self", *Journal of Personality and social Psychology* 38, mai 80 : 719-726.
712 YATABE, Takeo. "Kachi toshiteno kojin-shugi"(Individualism as a value in modern society), *Shakaigaku kenkyu* 39, 80 : 1-24.

12230. Personality
Personnalité

[See also / voir aussi: 660, 666, 812, 852, 910, 1042, 1185, 1224, 1354, 1360, 1390, 1392, 1441, 1456, 1469, 1476, 1525, 1624, 1626, 2237, 2391, 2486, 2861, 4296, 4587, 4695, 4892, 5213, 5351, 5444, 5630, 5641, 5660]

713 ABIMOV, R. "Kollektiv i razvitija trudovoj aktivnosti ličnosti" (Collectivity and the development of the personality labour activity), *Kommunist Tatarii* 79 : 24-29.
714 ABRAMSON, Paul R. *Personality*. New York, Holt, Rinehart and Winston, 80, xv-377 p.
715 ANDRUŠČENKO, V. P. "Trud i socializacija ličnosti v obščestve zrelogo socializma" (Labour and the personality socialization in the mature socialism society), *Voprosy naučnogo Kommunizma* 42, 79 : 60-68.
716 ARHANGEL'SKIJ, L. M.; [ed.]. *Socializm i ličnost'* (Socialism and personality). Moskba, Mysl', 79, 357 p.

717 BAGLEY, Christopher; [et al.]. *Personaltiy, self-esteem, and prejudice.* Farnborough, Saxon House, 79, ix-244 p.

718 BARRON, Frank X. *The shaping of personality: conflict, choice, and growth.* New York, Harper & Row, 79, xxiv-359 p.

719 BERLIZOVA, G. "Vlijanie kul'turnoj revoljucii na social'nuju aktivnost' ličnosti kak harakternuju čertu socialističeskogo obraza žizni" (Influence of the cultural revolution on the personality social activity as a characteristics aspect of the socialist way of life), *IN: Social'naja odnorodnost' i svoboda ličnosti v razvitom socialističeskom obščestve.* Ivanovo, 78 : 116-121.

720 BIAGGIO, Mary K. "Anger arousal and personality characteristics", *Journal of Personality and social Psychology* 39, aug 80 : 352-356.

721 BOBNEVA, M. "Social'noe razvitie ličnosti: psihologičeskaja problema" (The personality social development: a psychological problem), *Obščestvennye Nauki (Moskva)* 80 : 89-101.

722 CATTELL, Raymond Bernard. *The structure of personality in its environment.* New York, Springer Pub. Co., 79, xxiv-421 p.

723 CONSTANTINI, Edmond; CRAIK, Kenneth H. "Personality and politicians: California party leaders, 1960-1976", *Journal of Personality and social Psychology* 38, apr 80 : 641-661.

724 ČUBČENKO, M. T. *Rol' trudovyh kollektivov v formirovanii internacional'nogo soznanija ličnosti* (The labour collectivities role in the formation of the personality international consciousness). 79.

725 CUSINATO, Mario. *Personalità e famiglia*(Personality and family). Padova, Libreria editrice universitaria Pàtron, 79, 227 p.

726 DENISJUK, N. P. *Tradicii i formirovanie ličnosti* (Traditions and formation of personality). Minsk, Izdatel'stvo BGU imeni V. I. Lenina, 79, 136 p.

727 DORMAGEN-KREUTZBECK, Inge. *Soziologie der Persönlichkeit* (Sociology of personality). Köln, Pahl-Rugenstein, 79, 393 p.

728 GAN, Ju. V. "Formirovanie marksistskoj koncepcii vsestoronne razvitoj ličnosti, 1844-1846" (Formation of the Marxist conception of the global personality development, 1844-1846), *IN: Vsestoronnee razvitie ličnosti sovetskogo čeloveka.* Sverdlovsk, 79 : 81-94.

729 GORČENKO, G. V. "Avtoritet ličnosti v sisteme socialističeskogo obraza žizni" (The personality authority in the system of the socialist way of life), *IN: Socialističeskij obraz žizni i ličnost'.* 79 : 112-123.

730 HERGENHAHN B. R. *An introduction to theories of personality.* Englewood Cliffs, NJ, Prentice-Hall, 80, xvi-382 p.

731 HETTEMA, P. J. *Personality and adaptation.* Amsterdam, New York, North-Holland Pub. Co., 79, x-228 p.

732 ISMAILOV, I. A. "Marksistsko-leninskoe ponimanie ličnosti" (The personality marxist-leninist conception), *Naučnye Trudy Azerbajdžanskogo Universiteta. Serija juridičeskij Nauk* 79 : 3-11.

733 IVANČUK, N. V. "Vsestoronne razvitija ličnost' i sistema eè potrebnostej" (The totally developed personality and system of its needs), *IN: Vsestoronnee razvitie ličnosti sovetskogo čeloveka.* Sverdlovsk, 79 : 28-38.

734 JANOVSKIJ, R. "Formirovanie ličnosti i social'naja aktivnost' učenogo" (The personality formation and the scientist's social activity), *Obščestvennye Nauki (Moskva)* 79 : 20-37.

735 JAREMKO, Matt E. *Cognitive-behavioral reflections on some dimensions of personality.* Washington, DC, University Press of America, 80, iv-232 p.

736 KAMYŠEV, Ė. N. "Proizvodstvennaja dejatel'nost' kak osnova ponimanija kommunističeskoj ličnosti" (Production activity as a basis of the communist personality conception), *IN: Social'nye voprosy vospitanija i obrazovanija.* Tomsk, 79 : 44-51.

737 KAVALEROV, A. I. "Socialističeskij byt v formirovanii i razvitie ličnosti" (Socialist customs in the personality formation and development), *Ličnost' i Obščestvo* 79 : 46-56.

738 KIM, Moonja Park; ROSENBERG, Seymour. "Comparison of two structural models of implicit personality theory", *Journal of Personality and social Psychology* 38, mar 80 : 375-389.

739 KISELEVA, L. A. "K voprosy o strukture i soderžanii socialističeskogo tipa ličnosti" (On the structure and content of the socialist type personality), *Sociologičeskie Issledovanija* 80 : 44-51.

740 KISLOV, S. A. "Socializm i razvitie ličnosti rabočego" (Socialism and the worker's personality development), *IN: Problema čeloveka: gumanističeskie i social'nye aspekty.* Petrozavodsk, 79 : 102-116.
741 KLENOVA, N. V. "Socialističeskoe sorevnovanie kak faktor vsestoronnego razvitija ličnosti" (Socialist competition as a factor of the global personality development), *IN: Vsestoronnee razvitie ličnosti sovetskogo čeloveka.* Sverdlovsk, 79 : 71-80.
742 KLJUEV, A. V. "Ličnost' kak sub'ekt političeskoj aktivnosti" (Personality as a subject of political activity), *Političeskaja Organizacija Obščestva i Upravlenija pri Socializme* 79 : 91-103.
743 KOL'GA, T. V. "Istoki formirovanija aktivnoj žiznennoj pozicii ličnosti socialističeskogo tipa" (Sources of the socialist type personality vital position formation), *IN: Problemy socialističeskogo obraza žizni v uslovijah razvitogo socializma.* Moskva, 80 : 68-79.
744 KOROGODIN, I. T. "Sovokupnyj trud kak ėkonomičeskaja osnova razvitija ličnosti" (Collective labour as an economic basis of personality development), *IN: Ėkonomičeskie i duhovnye osnovy razvitija ličnosti.* Voronež, 79 : 6-13.
745 KUDRJAVCEV, V. N.; KAZIMIRCUK, V. L.; [eds.]. *Ličnost' i uvaženie k zakonu: sociologičeskij aspekt* (Personality and the respect to law: the sociological aspect). Moskva, Nauka, 79, 285 p.
746 KURILOVIČ, V. S. "Process truda kak faktor soveršenstvovanija ličnosti" (Labour process as a factor of the personality improvement), *IN: Ėkonomičeskie i duhovnye osnovy razvitija ličnosti.* Voronež, 79 : 13-20.
747 KUZMA, Ja. "Formirovanie socialističeskogo tipa ličnosti" (Formation of the personality socialist type), *Voprosy naučnogo Kommunizma* 42, 79 : 46-50.
748 KVASNIKOVA, S. M. "Vlijanie razvitija sfery obsluživanija na vsestoronnee razvitie ličnosti" (Influence of the sphere services development on the personality global development), *IN: Ėkonomičeskie i duhovnye osnovy razvitija ličnosti.* Voronež, 79 : 37-43.
749 LADYŽINSKIJ, Ja. P. "O formirovanii ličnosti rabočego novogo tipa v socialističeskom obščestve (po materialam sociologičeskih issledovanij)" (On the formation of a new type of worker personality in the socialist society: from materials of sociological research), *IN: Razvitoj socialism: oznovnye čerty.* Saratov, 79 : 49-55.
750 LEŠČINER, B. I. *Struktura ličnosti i nekotorye zakonomernosti formirovanija eё soznanija* (The personality structure and some formation laws of its knowledge). Tomsk, Izdatel'stvo Tomskogo Universiteta, 79, 161 p.
751 LOGANOV, I. I. *Svoboda ličnosti* (The personality freedom). Moskva, Mysl', 80, 158 p.
752 MAKAREVIČ, G. A. "Socialističeskij trud kak osnova vsestoronnego razvitija ličnosti" (Socialist labour as a basis of the personality total development), *IN: XXV s'ezd KPSS i voprosy social'no-političeskogo razvitija sovetskogo obščestva.* Minsk, 79 : 106-119.
753 MANSUROV, N. S.; [ed.]. *Osnovnye faktory formirovanija ličnosti v uslovijah razvitogo socializma* (Essentials factors of personality formation under conditions of developed socialism). Moskva, Institut Sociologičeskih Issledovanij AN SSSR, 79, 77 p.
754 MEHRABIAN, Albert; O'REILLY, Eric. "Analysis of personality measure in terms of basic dimensions of temperament", *Journal of Personality and social Psychology* 38, mar 80 : 492-503.
755 MILLS, Carol J.; BOHANNON, Wayne E. "Character structure and jury behavior: conceptual and applied implications", *Journal of Personality and social Psychology* 38, apr 80 : 662-667.
756 NISHIYAMA, Toshihiko. "Gainen zushiki °jiga kakuritsu' to sono sosaka -kinoteki kosatsu tetteika eno ichi-shian" ('Ego-maturation' and its operationalization — a tentative framework toward functional analysis of personality), *Sapienchia* 14, 80 : 1-25.
757 NOVIKOV, B. V. "Nekotorye aspekty teorii social'noj aktivnosti ličnosti" (Some aspects of the theory of the personality social activity), *Voprosy naučnogo Kommunizma* 42, 79 : 38-45.
758 OREŠNIKOV, I. M.; RODIONOV, B. A. "Vlijanie NTR na razvitie ličnosti" (The scientific and technical revolution influence on personality development), *IN: Razvitie soznanija ličnosti v uslovijah razvitogo socializma.* Iževsk, 78 : 90-101.
759 ORUDŽEV, V. M.; SUŠINSKIJ, V. V. "Kommunizm i vsestoronnee razvitie ličnosti" (Communism and the personality global development), *IN: Filosofsko-metodologičeskie problemy obščestvennogo razvitija.* Moskva, 79 : 77-85.
760 SADOVSKAJA, V. S. "Nekotorye faktory formirovanija social'no aktivnoj ličnosti" (Some factors of a socially active personality formation), *IN: XXV s'ezd KPSS i voprosy social'no-političeskogo razvitija sovetskogo obščestva 'ezd KPSS i problemy kul'tury razvitogo socializma.* Moskva, 79 : 40-51.

761   STANKEVIČ, L.; SVETLAEV, V. D. "Ličnost' v sisteme obščestvennyh otnošenij" (The personality in the social relations system), *Ličnost' i Obščestvo* 79 : 31-38.
762   STAUB, Ervin; [ed.]. *Personality: basic aspects and current research.* Englewood Cliffs, NJ, Prentice-Hall, 80, xiv-386 p.
763   STOLBUN, È. B.; NIKITINA, I. N. "Metodologičeskie osobennosti sociologičeskogo issledovanija problemy ličnosti" (Methodological characteristics of the personality problems sociological research), *IN: Metodologičeskie problemy sociologičeskogo issledovanija.* Moskva, 79 : 146-173.
764   SUPRUN, A. V. "Nauka kak faktor razvitija ličnosti" (Science as a factor of personality development), *IN: Social'naja aktivnost' ličnosti. II.* Volgograd, 78 : 153-162.
765   SYROEŠKINA, M. K. "Formirovanie ličnosti v razvitom socialističeskom obščestve" (The personality formation in the developed socialist society), *Sociologičeskie Issledovanija* 79 : 217-218.
766   ULANOVA, È. A. "Vzaimodejstvie individual'nogo i massovogo soznanija v processe formirovanija novogo čeloveka v socialističeskom obščestve" (Interaction between individual and mass consciousness in the formation process of a new man in the socialist society), *IN: Aktivnost' ličnosti v uslovijah naučno-tehničeskoj revoljucii.* Leningrad, 79 : 62-67.
767   VITRUK, N. V. "Ličnost' i eě političeskaja aktivnost' v obščestve razvitogo socializma" (Personality and its political activity in the developed socialist society), *IN: Politika mira i razvitie političeskih sistem 1978.* Moskva, 79 : 161-169.
768   VODGREEVA, L. V. "Metodologičeskie predposylki issledovanija processa formirovanija socialističeskoj ličnosti" (Methodological conditions of the research on the socialist personality formation process), *Vestnik Moskovskogo Universiteta. Teorija naučnogo Kommunizma* 79 : 51-58.
769   ZAGULJAEV, V. A.; ZAGULJAEVA, L. A. "Kollektivistskoe soznanie ličnosti i problema kompleksnogo podhoda k ěgo formirovaniju" (The personality collectivist consciousness and the complex approach problem to its formation), *IN: Kommunističeskoe vospitanie molodeži.* Moskva, 79 : 113-120.
770   ZINČENKO, Ju. G. "Samovospitanie kak faktor vozrastanija social'noj aktivnosti socialističeskoj ličnosti" (Self-education as an elevation factor of the socialist personality social activity), *IN: Aktivnost' ličnosti v uslovijah naučno-tehničeskoj revoljucii.* Leningrad, 79 : 42-61.

12240.   Cognition. Emotion. Motivation
Cognition. Émotion. Motivation

771   *(La) Peur.* Paris, Desclée De Brouwer, 79, 167 p.
772   "Effet (L') de lecture", *Revue des Sciences humaines* 46(177), 80 : 1-117.
773   ADAMS, Jack A. *Learning and memory, an introduction.* Homewood, IL, Dorsey Press, 80, rev. ed., xi-378 p.
774   AIGINGER, Karl. "Empirische Informationen zur Bildung von Erwartungen" (Empirical informations on the formations of expectations), *IFO-Studien* 25(1/2), 79 : 83-135.
775   ALLEN, Walter R. "Preludes to attainment: race, sex, and student achievement orientations", *Sociological Quarterly* 21, 80 : 65-79.
776   ANDERSSON, Inga. *Tankestilar och hemmiljö* (Cognitive styles and home environment). Göteborg, Acta Universitatis Gothoburgensis, 79, 285 p.
777   ANFALOVA, S. L. "Dialektika potrebnosti v social'noj aktivnosti v členov razvitogo socialističeskogo obščestva" (Dialectics of needs in the social activity of the developed socialist society members), *IN: Dialektika ěstestvenno-naučnogo i social'nogo poznanija.* Moskva, 79 : 50-54.
778   ANSELM, Sigrun. *Angst und Solidarität: eine krit. Studie zur Psychoanalyse d. Angst* (Anxiety and solidarity — a critical study on psychoanalysis of anxiety). München, Kindler, 79, 229 p.
779   AZOUVI, François. "La peste, la mélancolie et le diable, ou l'imaginaire", *Diogène* 108, oct-dec 79 : 124-143.
780   BABIN, B. A. "Obščestvenno-političeskaja aktivnost' v sisteme social'nyh potrebnostej" (Socio-political activity in the social needs system), *IN: Doklady Instituta sociologičeskih issledovanij AN SSSR na XI vsemirnom kongresse meždunarodnoj Associacii političeskih nauk (Moskva, 12-18 aug. 1979 gg.).* Moskva, 79 : 72-83.

781	BABIN, B. A. "O zakone vozvyšenija potrebnostej v ėpohu naučno-tehničeskoj revoljucii" (On the needs elevation law at the scientific and technical revolution era), IN: Naučno-tehničeskaja revoljucija i problemy razvitija obščestva i kollektivov. 79 : 5-13.
782	BABIN, B. A. "Nekotorye voprosy izučenija potrebnostej kak faktora social'nogo razvitija" (Some questions on the needs study as a social development factor), IN: Social'naja struktura sovetskogo obščestva i socialističeskij obraz žizni. II. Moskva, 78 : 151-159.
783	BARNES, Barry. "Il sociologo e il concetto di razionalità" (The sociologist and concept of rationality), Critica sociologica 51-52, 79-80 : 6-10.
784	BHARADWAJ, Lakshmi K.; WILKENING, Eugene A. "Life domain predictors of satisfaction with personal efficacy", Human Relations 33, mar 80 : 165-181.
785	BIERHOFF, Hans Werner. Kognitive Organisation, Wahl und Voraussage (Cognitive organization, choice and forecasting). Göttingen, Toronto, Zürich, Verlag für Psychologie Hogrefe, 79, 224 p.
786	BOLDT, Edward D. "On aligning actions in simple societies", Canadian Review of Sociology and Anthropology 16, aug 79 : 249-259.
787	BOSIO, Albino C.; [ed.]. Sulla creatilltà (On creativity). Milano, Via e pensiero, 79, x-164 p.
788	BOUDON, Raymond. Widersprüche sozialen Handels (Contradictions of social action). Darmstadt, Neuwied, Luchterhand, 79, 196 p. [essays originally published in R. Boudon's La crise de la sociologie and his Effets pervers et ordre social.]
789	BOURDIEU, Pierre. Le Sens pratique. Paris, Éditions de minuit, 80, 475 p.
790	BOXER, Philip J. "Supporting reflective learning: towards a reflexive theory of form", Human Relations 33, 80 : 1-22.
791	BRANSFORD, John D. Human cognition: learning, understanding, and remembering. Belmont, CA, Wadsworth Pub. Co., 79, xii-300 p.
792	BRISKMAN, Larry. "Creative product and creative process in science and art", Inquiry 23, mar 80 : 83-106.
793	BUCK, Ross. "Nonverbal behavior and the theory of emotion: the facial feedback hypothesis", Journal of Personality and social Psychology 38, mai 80 : 811-824.
794	BUGELSKI, Bergen Richard. Principles of learning and memory. New York, Praeger, 79, xvii-419 p.
795	CARRIER, James G. "Misrecognition and knowledge", Inquiry 22, 79 : 321-342.
796	CATANIA, A. Charles. Learning. Englewood Cliffs, NJ, Prentice-Hall, 79, xi-406 p.
797	CHANCE, Paul. Learning and behavior. Belmont, CA, Wadsworth Pub. Co., 79, xiv-247 p.
798	CHERKAOUI, Mohamed. "Les déterminants socioculturels des modes de pensée", Cahiers internationaux de Sociologie 67, jul-dec 79 : 337-347.
799	COULTER, Jeff. The social construction of mind: studies in ethnomethodology and linguistic philosophy. Totowa, NJ, Rowman and Littlefield, 79, ix-190 p. CR: Paul DREW, British Journal of Sociology 31(3), sep 80 : 451-452.
800	CRANDALL, James E. "Adler's concept of social interest: theory, measurement, and implications for adjustment", Journal of Personality and social Psychology 39, sep 80 : 481-495.
801	DAVIS, Fred. Yearning for yesterday: a sociology of nostalgia. New York, Free Press, 79, 146 p. CR: Gary Alan FINE, Contemporary Sociology (Albany) 9(3), mai 80: 410-411.
802	DENZIN, Norman K. "A phenomenology of emotion and deviance", Zeitschrift für Soziologie jul 80 : 251-261.
803	DICKINSON, Anthony; BOAKES, Robert A.; [eds.]. Mechanisms of learning and motivation: a memorial volume to Jerzy Konorski. Hillsdale, NJ, Erlbaum Associates, New York, distributed by Halsted Press Division of Wiley, 79, xiii-468 p.
804	DONAHOE, John W. Learning, language, and memory. New York, Harper & Row, 80, xv-513 p.
805	DUBOST, Jean. "De la sociologie de l'action à l'action sociologique: la pratique d'intervention d'Alain Touraine", Connexions 29, 80 : 143-166.
806	DUVIGNAUD, Françoise. "Pour une sociologie de l'effroi: note sur l'épouvantail", Cahiers internationaux de Sociologie 66, jan-jun 79 : 151-160.
807	DUVIGNAUD, Jean. "Roger Caillois et l'imaginaire", Cahiers internationaux de Sociologie 66, jan-jun 79 : 91-96.
808	EGLIN, Peter. "Resolving reality disjunctures on Telegraph Avenue: a study of practical reasoning", Canadian Journal of Sociology 79 : 359-377.
809	EISER, J. Richard. Cognitive social psychology: a guidebook to theory and research. London, New York, McGraw-Hill Book Co., 80, xv-361 p.
810	EYSENCK, Hans J. The structure and measurement of intelligence. Berlin, New York, Springer-Verlag, 79, 253 p.

811 FADEN, Ruth R.; BEAUCHAMP, Tom L. "Decision-making and informed consent: a study of the impact of disclosed information", *Social Indicators Research* (1-4), jan 80 : 313-336.
812 FAJNBURG, Z. I. "K voprosu ob istoričeskih tipah samorealizacii ličnosti" (On historical patterns of the personality self-realization), *IN: Vsestoronnee razvitie ličnosti sovetskogo čeloveka.* Sverdlovsk, 79 : 18-27.
813 FERRAROTTI, Franco. "Verso una razionalità non razionalistica" (Towards a non-rational rationality), *Critica sociologica* 51-52, 79-80 : 11-17.
814 FINOCCHIARO, Maurice A. "The psychological explanation of reasoning: logical and methodological problems", *Philosophy of the social Sciences* sep 79 : 277-291.
815 FODOR, Eugene M.; FARROW, Dana L. "The power motive as an influence on use of power", *Journal of Personality and social Psychology* 37(11), nov 79 : 2091-2097.
816 GALLACHER, H. P. "Over het interpreteren van handelingen — kernpunten uit het debat tussen Schutz en Parsons" (Interpreting action: central issues in the Schutz-Parsons debate), *Sociologische Gids* 27, sep-oct 80 : 376-392.
817 GAPONOV, A. K. "Potrebnosti čeloveka kak odna iz celej social'nogo upravlenija pri socializme" (Human needs as an objective of social management under socialism), *Naučnyj Kommunizm* 79 : 29-37.
818 GEAN, William D. "Emotion, emotional feeling and passive bodily change", *Journal for the Theory of social Behaviour* mar 79 : 39-51.
819 GHOLSON, Barry. *The cognitive-developmental basis of human learning: studies in hypothesis testing.* New York, Academic Press, 80, xiv-250 p.
820 GLASS, Arnold Lewis; HOLYOAK, Keith James; SANTA, John Lester. *Cognition.* Reading, MA, Addison-Wesley Pub. Co., 79, xix-521 p.
821 GLEICHMANN, Peter Reinhart. "Einige soziale Wandlungen des Schlafens" (Some social changes of sleeping habits), *Zeitschrift für Soziologie* jul 80 : 236-250.
822 GRATTON, Lynda C. "Analysis of Maslow's need hierarchy with three social class groups", *Social Indicators Research* (1-4), jan 80 : 463-476. [lower, working and middle class.]
823 GRUEN, Eckhard. *Angst und Gesellschaft: sozialpsycholog. Aspekte polit. Sozialisation* (Anxiety and society: socio-psychological aspects of political socialization). 79, vi-96 p.
824 HALE, Gordon A.; LEWIS, Michael; [eds.]. *Attention and cognitive development.* New York, Plenum Press, 79, xv-366 p.
825 HERBER, Hans-Jörg. *Motivationstheorie und pädagogische Praxis* (Motivation theory and educational practice). Stuttgart, Berlin, Köln, Mainz, Kohlhammer, 79, 187 p.
826 HOLLING, Heinz; LIEPMANN, Detlev. "Zum Zusammenhang zwischen gesellschaftlicher Struktur und kognitiven Leistungen" (The relationship between social structure and cognitive performance), *Kölner Zeitschrift für Soziologie und Sozialpsychologie* 32, 80 : 484-507.
827 HOWE, Michael J. A. *The psychology of human learning.* New York, Harper & Row, 80, xiv-448 p.
828 JEAN, Georges. *Les Voies de l'imaginaire enfantin.* Paris, Armand Colin, 79, 168 p.
829 JENNESSEN, Heinz. *Leistungsmotiventwicklung und Fernsehen* (Achievement motivation and television). Bochum, Studienverlag Brockmeyer, 80, 310 p.
830 JONES, Frank L. "Obsession plus pseudo-science equals fraud: Sir Cyril Burt, intelligence and social mobility", *Australian and New Zealand Journal of Sociology* 16, mar 80 : 48-56.
831 KEKES, John. "The centrality of problem-solving", *Inquiry* 22, 79 : 405-421.
832 KICKERT, Walter J. M. *Organisation of decision-making: a systems-theoretical approach.* Amsterdam, New York, North-Holland Pub. Co., 80, xiii-277 p. [sole distributors for the U.S.A. and Canada, Elsevier North-Holland, New York.]
833 KLAUSMEIER, Herbert John. *Cognitive learning and development: information-processing and Piagetian perspectives.* Cambridge, MA, Ballinger Pub. Co., 79, xiii-370 p.
834 KLEINBECK, Uwe. "Leistungsmotivation in Arbeit und Betrieb" (Achievement motivation in work and enterprise), *Betriebswirtschaft* 39, 79 : 481-492.
835 KÖHLER, Wolfgang R. "Logischer Empirismus und normative Entscheidungstheorie" (Logical empiricism and normative decision theory), *Analyse und Kritik. Zeitschrift für Sozialwissenschaften* 79 : 192-199.
836 KOLM, Serge-Christophe. "Psychanalyse et théorie des choix", *Social Science Information* 19, 80 : 269-339.
837 KOŠELJUK, L. F. "Razvitie tvorčeskih sposobnostej kak rezerv povyšenija social'noj mobil'nosti" (Development of creative possibilities as a reserve of the social mobility

elevation), *IN: Problemy social'nogo upravlenija na promyšlennom predprijatii. VIII.* 78 : 33-41.
838 KSENOFONTOVA, V. V. "Obščestvennye potrebnosti i žiznennye plany molodogo pokolenija" (Social needs and life plans of the young generation), *IN: Vsestoronnee razvitie ličnosti sovetskogo čeloveka.* Sverdlovsk, 79 : 46-53.
839 KUSHMAN, John; LANE, Sylvia. "A multivariate analysis of factors affecting perceived life satisfaction and psychological well-being among the elderly", *Social Science Quarterly* 61, sep 80 : 264-277.
840 LAUTREY, Jacques. *Classe sociale, milieu familial, intelligence.* Paris, Presses universitaires de France, 80, 283 p.
841 LEPENIES, Wolf. "The critique of learning and science, and the crisis of orientation", *Social Science Information* 19, 80 : 1-37.
842 LEVY, Alan B.; BELL, Roger A.; LIN, Elizabeth. "Life satisfaction — aspirations and alcohol use: a preliminary report", *Social Indicators Research* dec 80 : 441-452.
843 LIEBHART, Ernst H. "Information search and attribution: cognitive processes mediating the effect of false autonomic feedback", *European Journal of social Psychology* jan-mar 79 : 19-37.
844 LUCKHAM, Bryan; KAMARÁS, István. *Olvasmányválasztás Manchesterben és Miskolcon. Szociológiai vizsgálat angol és magyar könyvtárhasználók körében* (Choice of reading in Manchester and in Miskolc. Sociological research among English and Hungarian library users). Budapest, Könyvtártudományi és Módszertani Központ, 80. [published by the Centre for Library Science of the Hungarian National Library.]
845 LUPASCO, Stéphane. *L'Univers psychique: ses dialectiques constitutives et sa connaissance de la connaissance.* Paris, Denoël, Gonthier, 79, 243 p.
846 MACDONALD, Graham F.; [ed.]. *Perception and identity: essays presented to A. J. Ayer with his replies.* Ithaca, NY, Cornell University Press, 79, 358 p.
847 MAHLER, Fred. "Aspirations et créativité sociale", *Revue de l'Institut de Sociologie* (3-4), 79 : 351-383.
848 MICHALOS, Alex C. "Satisfaction and happiness", *Social Indicators Research* dec 80 : 385-422.
849 MIHAJLOV, N. N. "'Potrebnost' v trude-dominantnaja potrebnost' čeloveka" (The labour need is the man's dominant need), *Problemy social'noj Aktivnosti* 78 : 53-67.
850 MIHAJLOV, N. N. "Razumnye potrebnosti pri socializme: kriterij ocenki" (Rational needs under socialism: an elaboration criterion), *Problemy social'noj Aktivnosti* 78 : 96-111.
851 MOČALOV, B. M.; [ed.]. *Potrebnosti i spros v razvitom socialisičeskom obščestve* (Needs and demand in the developed socialist society). Moskva, Moskovskij Institut Narodnogo Hozjajstva imeni G. V. Plehanova, 79, 141 p.
852 MOROZOV, I. K. "Potrebnost' kak faktor formirovanija cennostnogo otnošenija i social'noj aktivnosti ličnosti" (Need as a factor of a valuable orientation formation and of the personality social activity), *Problemy social'noj Aktivnosti* 78 : 67-80.
853 NUTTIN, Joseph. *Théorie de la motivation humaine: du besoin au projet d'action.* Paris, Presses universitaires de France, 80, 304 p.
854 OBRADOVIĆ, Josip. "Grana industrije i ponašanje pojedinca u procesu donošenja odluka" (Industrial branch and individual behaviour in decision making process), *Sociologija* 21, 79 : 369-396.
855 PELLAUMAIL, Marcelle Maugin. *Le masochisme dit féminin.* Montréal, Stanké, 79, 214 p.
856 PLUTCHIK, Robert. *Emotion, a psychoevolutionary synthesis.* New York, Harper & Row, 80, xix-440 p.
857 RADKOWSKI, Georges-Hubert De. *Les jeux du désir: de la technique à l'économie.* Paris, PUF, 80, 262 p.
858 RAHMANIN, V. S. "Socialističeskij obraz žizni i sdvigi v strukture potrebnostej" (The socialist way of life and changes in needs structure), *IN: Socialističeskij obraz žizni i ličnost'.* 79 : 6-26.
859 RAMIREZ, Francis; ROLOT, Christian. "L'intelligibilité du rire est-elle une recherche pertinente?", *Revue de l'Institut de Sociologie* (3-4), 79 : 195-206.
860 RESCHER, Nicholas. *Cognitive systematization: a systems-theoretic approach to a coherentist theory of knowledge.* Totowa, NJ, Rowman and Littlefield, 79, xii-211 p.
861 RIBORDY, Sheila C.; HOLMES, David S.; BUCHSBAUM, Helen K. "Effects of affective and cognitive distractions on anxiety reduction", *Journal of social Psychology* 112, oct 80 : 121-127.
862 SAHKULJAN, R. O. *Potrebnosti i upravlenie ih razvitiem: ėkonomičeskij aspekt* (Needs and management of their development: the economic aspect). Ėrevan, Ajastan, 79, 151 p.

863 SCOTT, William Abbott; [et al.]. *Cognitive structure, theory and measurement of individual differences*. Washington, V.H. Winston, 79, x-252 p. [distributed solely by Halsted Press, New York.]
864 SEARLE, John R. "The intentionality of intention and action", *Inquiry* 22, 79 : 253-280.
865 SETA, John J.; HASSAN, Riad K. "Awareness of prior success or failure: a critical factor in task performance", *Journal of Personality and social Psychology* 39, jul 80 : 70-76.
866 SHIRAKURA, Yukio. "Shugoteki kettei no shakaigakuteki bunseki" (A sociological analysis of collective decisions), *Gendai shakaigaku* 80 : 140-183.
867 SIMPSON, Carl; BAKER, Kathryn; MELLINGER, Glen. "Conventional failures and unconventional dropouts: comparing different types of university withdrawals", *Sociology of Education* 53, oct 80 : 203-214.
868 SIMS, David. "A framework for understanding the definition and formulation of problems in teams", *Human Relations* 32(11), nov 79 : 909-921.
869 SMOL'KOV, V. G.; FEDININ, V. K.; [eds.]. *Razvitoj socializm i tvorčestvo mass: aktual'nye voprosy teorii i praktiki socialističeskogo sorevnovanija* (Developed socialism and mass creation: topical questions on the socialist stimulation theory and practice). Moskva, Politizdat, 79, 240 p.
870 SNIDER, Earle L. "Explaining life satisfaction: it's the elderly's attitudes that count", *Social Science Quarterly* 61, sep 80 : 253-263.
871 SOLSO, Robert L. *Cognitive psychology*. New York, Harcourt, Brace, Jovanovich, 79, xi-499 p.
872 STEELMAN, Lala Carr; MERCY, James A. "Unconfounding the confluence model: a test of sibship size and birth-order effects on intelligence", *American sociological Review* 45, aug 80 : 571-582.
873 STICHWEH, Rudolf. "Rationalität bei Parsons" (Rationality in Parsons), *Zeitschrift für Soziologie* jan 80 : 54-78.
874 TESSER, Abraham. "When individual dispositions and social pressure conflict: a catastrophe", *Human Relations* 33, jun 80 : 393-407.
875 UMINO, Michio. "Kojinteki kettei to shakaiteki kettei (1) ishikettei katei model no kochiku" (Individual decision-making and social decision-making. I. Building a decision-making model), *Kwansei gakuin daigaku shakaigakubu kiyo* 41, 80 : 13-25.
876 VIŠNEVSKIJ, M. I. "Potrebnosti i neobhodimost'" (Needs and necessity), *IN: Filosofija i naučnyj kommunizm. VI.*. Minsk, 79 : 44-52.
877 VYDRIN, D. I. "Kategorija 'potrebnost' v istoričeskom materializme i v koncepcijah 'kačestva žizni' metodologičeskie aspekty problemy" (The "need" category in historical materialism and in the "quality of life" conceptions; methodological aspects of the problem), *IN: Dialektika obščestvennogo razvitija: teoretičeskie i metodologičeskie problemy*. Moskva, 79 : 45-55.
878 WEISBERG, Robert W. *Memory, thought, and behaviour*. New York, Oxford University Press, 80, xx-458 p.
879 WICKELGREN, Wayne A. *Cognitive psychology*. Englewood Cliffs, NJ, Prentice-Hall, 79, xi-436 p.
880 WINCKELMANN, Johannes. "Die Herkunft von Max Webers Entzauberungs-Konzeption" (The origin of Max Weber's concept of disenchantment), *Kölner Zeitschrift für Soziologie und Sozial-Psychologie* 32, mar 80 : 12-53.
881 YASUDA, Takashi. "Yokkyu no shakai riron — A. Heller no shosetsu ni yosete" (The theory of need from a socio-historical point of view — Comment on A. Heller's theory of need), *Shakaigaku nenpo* 80 : 1-20.
882 ŽILINA, L. N.; SOKOLOV, V. M. "Problemy formirovanija razumnyh potrebnostej v material'nyh blagah (sociologiceskij aspect)" (Problems of the rational needs formation in material goods: the sociological aspects), *Sociologičeskie Issledovanija* 80 : 52-59.

12300. INTERPERSONAL RELATIONS
RELATIONS INTERPERSONNELLES

12310. Human relations. Sociability
Relations humaines. Sociabilité

[See also / voir aussi: 611, 1185, 1598]

883 AIDA, Toshihiko. "Nihonjin no taijin kankei no tokushitsu — 'Kotoba' kara no sekkin" (Characteristics of Japanese interpersonal relations), *NHK hoso bunka kenkyu nenpo* 25, 80 : 203-221.

884	CAPELLE, Ronald G. *Changing human systems.* Toronto, International Human Systems Institute, 79, xviii-204 p.
885	CHELUNE, Gordon J.; [et al.]. *Self-disclosure: origins, patterns, and implications of openness in interpersonal relationships.* San Francisco, Jossey-Bass, 79, xviii-396 p.
886	COSER, Lewis A. "The notion of civility in contemporary society", *Archives européennes de Sociologie* 21, 80 : 3-13.
887	DERBER, Charles. *The pursuit of attention: power and individualism in everyday life.* Boston, MA, G. K. Hall, 79, x-110 p.
888	EIDELSON, Roy J. "Interpersonal satisfaction and level of involvement: a curvilinear relationship", *Journal of Personality and social Psychology* 39, sep 80 : 460-470.
889	ESCOVAR, A., Luis. "Efectos de la estructura social y la alienación sobre las actitudes interpersonales de los campesinos" (Effects of social structure and alienation on peasants' interpersonal attitudes), *Revista latinoamericana de Psicología* 12, 80 : 37-49.
890	GOVE, Walter R.; HUGHES, Michael. "Reexamining the ecological fallacy: a study in which aggregate data are critical in investigating the pathological effects of living alone", *Social Forces* 58, jun 80 : 1157-1177.
891	KELLEY, Harold H. *Personal relationships: their structures and processes.* Hillsdale, NJ, L. Erlbaum Associates, 79, xii-183 p. [distributed by Halsted Press, New York.]
892	LESLY, Philip. *How we discommunicate.* New York, AMACOM, 79, xi-227 p.
893	MICHAEL, Robert T.; FUCHS, Victor R.; SCOTT, Sharon R. "Changes in the propensity to live alone: 1950-1976", *Demography* 17, feb 80 : 39-56.
894	OBOZOV, N. N. *Mežličnostnye otnošenija* (Inter-personal relations). Leningrad, Izdatel'stvo Leningradskogo Universitet, 79, 151 p.
895	PARADEISE, Catherine. "Sociabilité et culture de classe", *Revue française de Sociologie* 21, oct-dec 80 : 571-597.
896	REED, John Shelton. "Getting to know you: the contact hypothesis applied to the sectional beliefs and attitudes of white Southerners", *Social Forces* 59, sep 80 : 123-135.
897	Bibl.XXIX-1435. SAYRE, Robert. *Solitude in society: a sociological study in French literature.* CR: Priscilla P. CLARK, *Contemporary Sociology (Albany)* 9(4), jul 80 : 530-531.
898	SELMAN, Robert L. *The growth of interpersonal understanding: developmental and clinical analyses.* London, New York, Academic Press, 80, xvii-343 p.
899	STEINER, Ivan D.; [ed.]. "Interpersonal relations and group processes", *Journal of Personality and social Psychology* 39, oct 80 : 625-668.
900	VINOKUROVA, V. A. "O mežličnostnyh otnošenijah v neformal'nyh gruppah"(On interpersonal relations in non-formal groups), *IN: Sel'skaja molodež' Jakutii.* 79 : 80-94.

12320. Social perception
Perception sociale

[See also / voir aussi: 696, 1209, 1268, 1566, 1602, 2559, 5946]

901	BURT, Ronald S.; [et al.]. "Network power structures from informant perceptions", *Human Organization* 39, 80 : 121-133.
902	FELSON, Richard B.; BOHRNSTEDT, George W. "'Are the good beautiful or the beautiful good?' The relationship between children's perceptions of ability and perceptions of physical attractiveness", *Social Psychology Quarterly* 42, dec 79 : 386-392. [with a comment by Richard T. CAMPBELL: 393-398.]
903	FORGAS, Joseph P.; ARGYLE, Michael; GINSBURG, Gerald P. "Social episodes and person perception: the fluctuating structure of an academic group", *Journal of social Psychology* 109, dec 79 : 207-222.
904	FURTH, Hans G. *The world of grown-ups: children's conceptions of society.* New York, Elsevier North Holland, 80, x-221 p.
905	GOVE, Walter R.; [ed.]. *The Labelling of Deviance. Evaluating a Perspective.* Beverly Hills, CA, Sage Publications, 80, 400 p.
906	JACKSON, Douglas N.; PEACOCK, Andrew C.; SMITH, Joelle P. "Impressions of personality in the employment interview", *Journal of Personality and social Psychology* 39, aug 80 : 294-307.
907	KNUDSON, Roger M.; SOMMERS, Alison A.; GOLDING, Stephen L. "Interpersonal perception and mode of resolution in marital conflict", *Journal of Personality and social Psychology* 38, mai 80 : 751-763.
908	LEWIS, Michael; BROOKS-GUNN, Jeanne. *Social cognition and the acquisition of self.* New York, Plenum Press, 79, xix-296 p.

909 MESSÉ, Lawrence A.; [et al.]. "Interpersonal consequences of person perception processes in two social contexts", *Journal of Personality and social Psychology* 37, mar 79 : 369-379.

910 NEWMAN, Alexander. "First impressions: reliability and implicit personality theory", *Journal of social Psychology* 111, aug 80 : 259-268.

911 RIVERA, Alba Nydia. "Factores que determinan la atribución de altruismo" (The factors that cause observers to label an actor as altruistic), *Revista latinoamericana de Psicología* 12, 80 : 63-77.

912 SRULL, Thomas K.; WYER, Robert S. Jr. "Category accessibility and social perception: some implications for the study of person memory and interpersonal judgments", *Journal of Personality and social Psychology* 38, jun 80 : 841-856.

913 STEWART, Robert A.; POWELL, Graham E.; CHETWYND, S. Jane. *Person perception and stereotyping*. Farnborough, Eng., Saxon House, 79, ix-318 p.

914 TROPE, Yaacov; BURNSTEIN, Eugene. "Inference about others from their reports about themselves", *European Journal of social Psychology* jul-sep 79 : 291-305.

915 ZWEIGENHAFT, Richard L.; HAYES, Karen N.; HAAGEN, C. Hess. "The psychological impact of names", *Journal of social Psychology* 110, apr 80 : 203-210.

12330. Interpersonal attraction
Attraction interpersonnelle

[See also / voir aussi: 902, 911, 997, 1134, 2184, 3057, 3103]

916 BENSON, Peter; [et al.]. "Intrapersonal correlates of nonspontaneous helping behavior", *Journal of social Psychology* 110, feb 80 : 87-95.

917 BIGELOW, Brian John. "Developmental changes in the conceptual friendship expectations associated with children's friendship preferences", *Human Relations* 33, apr 80 : 225-239.

918 BLACK, Charlene R.; WEINSTEIN, Eugene A.; TANUR, Judith M. "Development of expectations of altruism versus self-interest", *Journal of social Psychology* 111, jun 80 : 105-112.

919 CLARK, Margaret S.; MILLS, Judson. "Interpersonal attraction in exchange and communal relationships", *Journal of Personality and social Psychology* 37, jan 79 : 12-24.

920 COOPER, Lucille; [et al.]. "The effects of cooperative, competitive, and individualistic experiences on interpersonal attraction among heterogeneous peers", *Journal of social Psychology* 111, aug 80 : 243-252.

921 DAVIS, Deborah; PERKOWITZ, William T. "Consequences of responsiveness in dyadic interaction: effects of probability of response and proportion of content-related responses on interpersonal attraction", *Journal of Personality and social Psychology* 37, apr 79 : 534-550.

922 FORGAS, Joseph P.; DOBOSZ, Barbara. "Dimensions of romantic involvement: towards a taxonomy of heterosexual relationships", *Social Psychology Quarterly* 43, sep 80 : 290-299.

923 KENRICK, Douglas T.; BAUMANN, Donald J.; CIALDINI, Robert B. "A step in the socialization of altruism as hedonism: effects of negative mood on children's generosity under public and private conditions", *Journal of Personality and social Psychology* 37, mai 79 : 778-789.

924 KENRICK, Douglas T.; JOHNSON, Gregory A. "Interpersonal attraction in aversive environments: a problem for the classical conditioning paradigm?", *Journal of Personality and social Psychology* 37, apr 79 : 572-579.

925 KON, Igor S. *Freundschaft. Geschichte und Sozialpsychologie der Freundschaft als soziale Institution und individuelle Beziehung* (Friendship. History and social psychology of friendship as a social institution and individual relation). Reinbek bei Hamburg, Rowohlt Taschenbuch Verlag GmbH, 79, 204 p. CR: Jean-Claude DARBOIS, *Revue française de Sociologie* 21(3), jul-sep 80: 475-476.

926 LANGEHEINE, Rolf. Strukturanalytische Untersuchungen der Schulklasse: e. Analyse mit Hilfe multidimensionaler Skalierungsmodelle (Structural analysis of the school class: a research using multidimensional scaling models). Frankfurt am Main, Bern, Las Vegas, Lang, 79, 280 p.

927 MUSSEN, Paul H.; EISENBERG-BERG, Nancy. *Helfen, schenken, anteilnehmen. Untersuchungen zur Entwicklung des prosozialen Verhaltens* (Helping, granting, sharing. Research

on the development of pro-social behaviour). Stuttgart, Klett-Cotta, 79, 168 p. CR: Angela SCHUCH, *Soziologische Revue* 3(4), 80: 416-418.

928 NEWCOMB, Theodore M. "A nonconfirmation of a plausible hypothesis: reciprocity of interpretation of attraction", *Social Psychology Quarterly* 42, dec 79 : 299-306.

929 REIS, Harry T.; NEZLEK, John; WHEELER, Ladd. "Physical attractiveness in social interaction", *Journal of Personality and social Psychology* 38, apr 80 : 604-617.

930 REISMAN, John M. *Anatomy of friendship.* New York, Irvington Publishers, 79, vi-260 p.

931 SCHWARTZ, Gary; [et al.]. *Love and commitment.* Beverly Hills, CA, Sage Publications, 80, 272 p.

932 TASHAKKORI, Abbas; INSKO, Chester A. "Interpersonal attraction and the polarity of similar attitudes: a test of three balance models", *Journal of Personality and social Psychology* 37(12), dec 79 : 2262-2277.

933 TITUS, Sandra L. "A function of friendship: social comparisons as a frame of reference for marriage", *Human Relations* 33, jun 80 : 409-431.

934 URICOECHEA, Fernando. "La théorie de la solidarité de Durkheim: une critique", *Cahiers internationaux de Sociologie* 66, jan-jun 79 : 115-123.

12340. Interpersonal influence
Influence interpersonnelle

[See also / voir aussi: 673, 2657, 3452]

935 CHILD, John; PEARCE, Sandra; KING, Lisa. "Class perception and social identification of industrial supervisors", *Sociology* 14, aug 80 : 363-399.

936 GREENE, Les R.; MORRISON, Thomas L.; TISCHLER, Nancy G. "Aspects of identification in the large group", *Journal of social Psychology* 111, jun 80 : 91-97.

937 PEAY, Marilyn Y. "Changes in attitude and beliefs in two-person interaction situations", *European Journal of social Psychology* 10, oct-dec 80 : 367-377.

938 RIM, Y. "Personality and means of influence in marriage", *Human Relations* 32(10), oct 79 : 871-875.

939 ROBERTS, Michael C.; SANTOGROSSI, David A.; THELEN, Mark H. "The effects of being imitated on adult attraction to children", *Journal of social Psychology* 111, aug 80 : 253-258.

940 SCHWARZWALD, Joseph; GOLDENBERG, Judith. "Compliance and assistance to an authority figure in perceived equitable or nonequitable situations", *Human Relations* 32(10), oct 79 : 877-888.

12350. Interpersonal conflict
Conflit interpersonnel

[See also / voir aussi: 970, 1560, 3971, 5111]

941 ANZIEU, Didier. "L'agressivité entre les groupes et à l'intérieur des groupes", *Revue des Travaux de l'Académie des Sciences morales et politiques* 131, 78 : 175-187.

942 BANDURA, Albert. *Aggression. Eine sozial-lerntheoretische Analyse* (Aggression. A social learning theoretical analysis). Stuttgart, Klett-Cotta, 79, 407 p. CR: Hans WERBIK, *Soziologische Revue* 3(3), 80: 334-335.

943 BATTEGAY, Raymond. *Aggression, ein Mittel der Kommunikation?* (Aggression, a means of communication?). Bern, H. Huber, 79, 144 p.

944 DA GLORIA, Jorge; RIDDER, Richard De. "Sex differences in aggression: are current notions misleading?", *European Journal of social Psychology* jan-mar 79 : 49-66.

945 DONNERSTEIN, Edward. "Aggressive erotica and violence against women", *Journal of Personality and social Psychology* 39, aug 80 : 269-277.

946 EDMUNDS, George; KENDRICK, D. C. *The measurement of human aggressiveness.* Chichester, Eng., Horwood, New York, Halsted Press, 80, 223 p.

947 FENIGSTEIN, Allan. "Does aggression cause a preference for viewing media violence?", *Journal of Personality and social Psychology* 37(12), dec 79 : 2307-2317.

948 FESHBACH, Seymour; FRACZEK, Adam; [eds.]. *Aggression and behavior change: biological and social processes.* New York, Praeger, 79, xi-299 p.

949 JAFFE, Yoram; YINON, Yoel. "Retaliatory aggression in individuals and groups", *European Journal of social Psychology* apr-jun 79 : 177-186.

950 MACKAL, Paul K. *Psychological theories of aggression: a social psychologist's reflections about aggression.* Amsterdam, New York, North-Holland Pub. Co., 79, xvi-216 p. [sole distributors for the USA and Canada, Elsevier North-Holland, 79.]
951 MILBURN, Michael A. "Theories of aggression: a critique and possible reformulation", *Human Relations* 33, jun 80 : 353-368.
952 MURNIGHAM, J. Keith; SZWAJKOWSKI, Eugene. "Coalition bargaining in four games that include a veto player", *Journal of Personality and social Psychology* 37(11), nov 79 : 1933-1946.
953 SCHMUTTE, Gregory T.; TAYLOR, Stuart P. "Physical aggression as a function of alcohol and pain feedback", *Journal of social Psychology* 110, apr 80 : 235-244.
954 TEDESCHI, James T; [et al.]. "First impressions, norms, and reactions to threats", *Human Relations* 33, sep 80 : 647-657.
955 WHITE, Leonard A. "Erotics and aggression: the influence of sexual arousal, positive effect, and negative effect on aggresive behavior", *Journal of Personality and social Psychology* 37, apr 79 : 591-601.
956 ZILLMANN, Dolf. *Hostility and aggression.* Hillsdale, NJ, L. Erlbaum Associates, 79, x-422 p. [distributed by the Halsted Press, New York.]
957 ZIPPO, Ida. *L'aggressività: analisi e problematica del fenomeno* (Aggressiveness: analysis and problems of the phenomenon). Roma, Bulzoni, 79, 119 p.

12360. Intergroup relations
Relations intergroupes

[See also / voir aussi: 1203, 2019]

958 "Négociation (La)", *Pouvoirs* 15, 80 : 5-120.
959 BENJAMIN, A. J.; LEVI, A. M. "Process minefields in intergroup conflict resolution: the Sdot Yam workshop", *Journal of applied behavioral Science* 15, oct-dec 79 : 507-519.
960 BLALOCK, Hubert M. Jr.; WILKEN, Paul H. *Intergroup processes: a micro-macro perspective.* New York: Free Press, 79, x-645 p.
961 COMMINS, Barry; LOCKWOOD, John. "The effects of status differences, favoured treatment and equity on intergroup comparisons", *European Journal of social Psychology* jul-sep 79 : 281-289.
962 DI GIAMCOMO, J. P. "Intergroup alliances and rejections within a protest movement (analysis of the social representatins)", *European Journal of social Psychology* 10, oct-dec 80 : 329-344.
963 DOLGODILIN, B. G. "Ob'ektivnaja osnova i sub'ektivnye faktory social'nogo antagonizma" (Objective basis and subjective factors of social antagonism), *IN: Ob'ektivnoe i sub'ektivnoe v obščestvennom razvitii.* Vladivostok, 79 : 56-62.
964 ELDRIDGE, Albert F. *Images of conflict.* New York, St. Martin's Press, 79, ix-229 p. CR: Betty A. NESVOLD, *American political Science Review* 74(4), dec 80: 1054-1055.
965 GOODSTEIN, Leonard D.; LUBIN, Bernard; LUBIN, Alice W.; [eds.]. *Cases in conflict management.* La Jolla, CA, University Associates, 79, iv-236 p.
966 GULLIVER, P. H. *Disputes and negotiations: a cross-cultural perspective.* New York, Academic Press, 79, xxi-293 p.
967 KAHAN, James P.; RAPOPORT, Amnon. "The influence of structural relationships on coalition formation of four-person apex games", *European Journal of social Psychology* oct-dec 79 : 339-361.
968 LEWIS, Arnold. "The peace ritual and Israeli images of social order", *Journal of Conflict Resolution* 23, dec 79 : 685-703.
969 MARKS, Arnaud F. "Intergroup relationships in the Caribbean: a field of long-range sociological research", *Boletín de Estudios latinoamericanos y del Caribe* 26, jun 79 : 39-66.
970 MILLER, Charles E. "A test of four theories of coalition formation: effects of payoffs and resources", *Journal of Personality and social Psychology* 38, jan 80 : 153-164.
971 MILLER, Jon. "Access to interorganizational networks as a professional resource", *American sociological Review* 45, jun 80 : 479-496.
972 Bibl.XXIX-876. MITCHELL, Jack N. *Social exchange, dramaturgy and ethnomethodology.* CR: T. R. YOUNG, *Contemporary Sociology (Albany)* 9(1), jan 80: 148-149.
973 MOLNAR, J. J.; ROGERS, D. L. "A comparative model of interorganizational conflict", *Administrative Science Quarterly* 24, 79 : 405-425.
974 OTT, Sanra. "Blessed bread, 'first neighbours' and asymmetric exchange in the Basque country", *Archives européenes de Sociologie* 21, 80 : 40-58.

975 PROCENKO, A. F. "Voprosy social'nogo konflikta v buržuaznoj 'sociologii konflikta'" (Questions on social conflict in the bourgeois "sociology of conflict"), *IN: Filosofsko-metodologičeskie problemy obščestvennogo razvitija.* Moskva, 79 : 162-167.

976 RACINE, Luc. *Théories de l'échange et circulation des produits sociaux.* Montréal, Les Presses de l'Université de Montréal, 79, 397 p.

977 RAELIN, Joseph A. "A mandated basis of inter-organizational relations: the legal-political network", *Human Relations* 33, jan 80 : 57-68.

978 SARASON, Seymour, B.; LORENTZ, Elizabeth. *The challenge of resource exchange network.* San Francisco, Jossey-Bass, 79, 283 p. CR: Karen S. COOK, *Contemporary Sociology (Albany)* 9(6), nov 80: 842-843.

979 WEHR, Paul. *Conflict regulation.* Boulder, Colo., Westview Press, 79, xx-245 p. CR: Robin M. WILLIAMS Jr.., *Contemporary Sociology (Albany)* 9(6), nov 80: 827-829.

980 WELLS, Alan. "Conflict theory and functionalism: introductory sociology textbooks, 1928-1976", *Teaching Sociology* jul 79 : 429-437.

981 WILDER, David A.; THOMPSON, John E. "Intergroup contact with independent manipulations of in-group and out-group interaction", *Journal of Personality and social Psychology* 38, apr 80 : 589-603.

982 WORCHEL, Stephen; NORVELL, Nancy. "Effect of perceived environmental conditions during cooperation on intergroup attraction", *Journal of Personality and social Psychology* 38, mai 80 : 764-772.

12400. GROUP
GROUPE

12410. Group dynamics
Dynamique de groupe

[See also / voir aussi: 1207, 4674]

983 "Groupe-analyse et groupe Balint. Approche psychanalytique des groupes", *Connexions* 31, 80 : 7-166.

984 AOI, Kazuo. *Sho-shudan no shakaigaku* (Sociology of groups). Tokyo, Tokyo daigaku shuppankai, 80, 355 p.

985 BARRETT-LENNARD, G. T. "A new model of communicational-relational systems in intensive groups", *Human Relations* 32(10), oct 79 : 841-849.

986 BERNARD, H. Russell; KILLWORTH, Peter D.; SAILER, Lee. "Informant accuracy in social network data IV: a comparison of clique-level structure in behavioral and cognitive network data", *Social Networks* jul 80 : 191-218.

987 BOYD, John Paul. "The universal semigroup of relations", *Social Networks* apr 80 : 91-117.

988 COOPER, Lowell; GUSTAFSON, James P. "Toward a general theory of group therapy", *Human Relations* 32(11), nov 79 : 967-981.

989 DOREIAN, Patrick. "On the evolution of group and network structure", *Social Networks* jul 80 : 235-252.

990 FOSTER, Brian L. "Formal network studies and the anthropological perspective", *Social Networks* feb 79 : 241-255.

991 FREEMAN, Linton C. "Centrality in social networks. I. Conceptual clarification. II. Experiental results", *Social Networks* feb 79 : 215-239. [continued in 2(2), apr 80 : 119-141.]

992 HAMMER, Muriel. "Predictability of social connections over time", *Social Networks* apr 80 : 165-180.

993 KAPLAN, Robert E.; OBERT, Steven L.; VAN BUSKIRK, William R. "The etiology of encounter group casualties: 'second facts'", *Human Relations* 33, feb 80 : 131-148.

994 KELLERMAN, Henry. *Group psychotherapy and personality: intersecting structures.* New York, Grune & Stratton, 79, xxi-345 p.

995 PITTS, Forrest R. "The medieval river trade network of Russia revisited", *Social Networks* feb 79 : 285-292.

996 ROBACK, Howard B.; ABRAMOWITZ, Stephen I.; STRASSBERG, Donald S. *Group psychotherapy research: commentaries and selected readings.* Huntington, NY, R. E. Krieger Pub. Co., 79, xiv-239 p.

997 RUNGER, George; WASSERMAN, Stanley. "Longitudinal analysis of friendship networks", *Social Networks* apr 80 : 143-154.

998 TSAI, Yung-Mei; SIGELMAN, Lee. "Stratification and mobility in big-time college football: a vacancy chain analysis", *Sociological Methods and Research* mai 80 : 487-497.
999 VAN POUCKE, Willy. "Network constraints on social action: preliminaries for a network theory", *Social Networks* apr 80 : 181-190.

12420. Primary group. Training group
Groupe primaire. Groupe de formation

[See also / voir aussi: 755, 900, 5378, 5548]

1000 "What's happened to small group research?", *Journal of applied behavioral Science* 15, 79 : 272-423.
1001 ALBERS, Wulf; BAMBERG, Günter; SELTEN, Reinhard; [eds.]. *Entscheidungen in kleinen Gruppen* (Decisions in small groups). Königstein/Ts., Hain, 79, 230 p.
1002 BABINGTON-SMITH, Bernard; FARRELL, Brian Anthony; [eds.]. *Training in small groups: a study of five methods.* Oxford, New York, Pergamon Press, 79, xii-144 p.
1003 BADALATO, Gabriella; DI IULLO, Maria Gabriella. *Gruppi terapeutici e gruppi di formazione* (Theurapeutic groups and training groups). Roma, Bulzoni, 79, 209 p.
1004 COHEN, Roberta G.; LIPKIN, Gladys B. *Therapeutic group work for health professionals.* New York, Springer Pub. Co., 79, xi-276 p.
1005 GOROFF, Norman N.; [ed.]. *Concepts for group processes.* Hebron, Conn., Practitioners' Press, 79, 288 p.
1006 GUSTAFSON, James P.; COOPER, Lowell. "Unconscious planning in small groups", *Human Relations* 32(12), dec 79 : 1039-1064.
1007 IBÁÑEZ, Jesús. *Más allá de la sociología: el grupo de discusión: teoría y crítica* (Beyond sociology: the discussion group: theory and critique). Madrid, Siglo Veintiuno de España, 79, 428 p.
1008 IVANOV, M. A.; KRIČEVSKIJ, R. L. "social'no-psihologičeskie aspekty razvitogo maloj gruppy" (Socio-psychological aspects of a small group development), *IN*: *Psihologo-pedagogičeskie problemy kollektiva i ličnosti.* Moskva, 78 : 8-18.
1009 KOWITZ, Albert C.; KNUTSON, Thomas J. *Decision making in small group: the search for alternatives.* Boston, MA, Allyn and Bacon, 80, xi-226 p.
1010 LENNÉER-AXELSON, Barbro; THYLEFORS, Ingela. *Arbetsgruppens psykologi* (Working group psychology). Stockholm, Natur o. kultur, 79, 158 p.
1011 MABRY, Edward A.; BARNES, Richard E. *The dynamics of small group communication.* Englewood Cliffs, NJ, Prentice-Hall, 80, x-276 p.
1012 MEADOWS, Ian S. G. "Organic structure and innovation in small work groups", *Human Relations* 33, jun 80 : 369-382.
1013 PETKOVIČ, Vlajko. "Uloga sociologa u regulisanju neformalne organizacije" (The sociologist's role in the regulation of informal organizations), *Sociologija* 21(1-2), 79 : 171-186.
1014 SHAW, Marvin E. *Dinámica de grupo. Psicología de la conducta de los pequeños grupos* (Group dynamics. Psychology of small group management). Barcelona, Editorial Herder, 80, 517 p.
1015 SMITH, Peter B. "The T-group trainer-group facilitator or prisoner of circumstance?", *Journal of applied behavioral Science* 16, jan-mar 80 : 63-77.
1016 Bibl.XXIX-891. WILSON, Stephen. Informal groups: an introduction. CR: Barbara F. MEEKER, *Contemporary Sociology (Albany)* 9(5), sep 80: 718.

12430. Group size
Dimension du groupe

[See also / voir aussi: 921, 1231, 1366, 2090, 2108, 2955, 3085, 3764]

1017 DAVIS, Floyd James; [ed.]. *Understanding minority-dominant relations: sociological contributions.* Arlington Heights, IL, AHM Pub. Corp., 79, xv-496 p. CR: Peter KIVISTO, *Contemporary Sociology (Albany)* 9(3), mai 80: 427-428.
1018 ELLYSON, Steve L.; [et al.]. "Visual dominance behavior in female dyads: situational and personality factors", *Social Psychology Quarterly* 43, sep 80 : 328-336.
1019 HALLINAN, Maureen T.; HUTCHINS, Edwin E. "Structural effects on dyadic change", *Social Forces* 59, sep 80 : 225-245.

1020 JOHNSON, Nan E.; NISHIDA, Ryoko. "Minority-group status and fertility: a study of Japanese and Chinese in Hawaii and California", *American Journal of Sociology* 86, nov 80 : 496-511.
1021 MIROWSKY, John II; ROSS, Catherine E. "Minority status, ethnic culture, and distress: a comparison of Blacks, Whites, Mexicans, and Mexican Americans", *American Journal of Sociology* 86, nov 80 : 479-495.
1022 OPP, Karl-Dieter. "Group size, emergence, and composition laws: are there macroscopic theories sui generis?", *Philosophy of the social Sciences* dec 79 : 445-455.
1023 ROPER, Robert T. "Jury size. Impact on verdict's correctness", *American Politics Quarterly* oct 79 : 438-452.
1024 SZÁSZ, János. *A nemzetiségi közművelődés művelődésszociológiai kutatása* (Sociological investigation of minority culture and education in Hungary). Budapest, M. Hirdető, Ny., 80, 104 p. [Published by the Ministry of Culture.]
1025 WHITE, C. J. Mower. "Factors affecting balance, agreement and positivity biases in POQ and POX triads", *European Journal of social Psychology* apr-jun 79 : 129-148.
1026 WOLF, Sharon. "Behavioural style and group cohesiveness as sources of minority influence", *European Journal of social Psychology* oct-dec 79 : 381-395.

12440. Group integration
Intégration du groupe

[See also / voir aussi: 899, 903, 1166, 1191, 1817]

1027 "Aspects of group tensions in cross-cultural perspectives", *International Journal of Group Tensions* (1-2), 78.
1028 CROTT, Helmut. *Soziale Interaktion und Gruppenprozesse* (Social interaction and group process). Stuttgart, Berlin, Köln, Mainz, Kohlhammer, 79, 290 p.
1029 DONCOV, A. I. *Problemy gruppovoj spločennosti* (Problems of group solidarity). Moskva, Izdatel'stvo Moskovskogo Universiteta, 128 p.
1030 GOTTSEGEN, Gloria B. *Group behavior: a guide to information sources.* Detroit, Gale Research Co., 79, x-219 p.
1031 KELL, Carl L. *Fundamentals of effective group communication.* New York, Macmillan, 80, ix-198 p.
1032 LAUGHLIN, Patrick R.; ADAMOPOULOS, John. "Social combination processes and individual learning for six-person cooperative groups on an intellective task", *Journal of Personality and social Psychology* 38, jun 80 : 941-947.
1033 MCCORMICK, Michael B.; LUNDGREN, Earl F.; CECIL, Earl A. "Group search and decision-making processes: a laboratory test of Soelberg's confirmation hypothesis", *Journal of social Psychology* 110, feb 80 : 79-86.
1034 MILLER, Charles E.; ANDERSON, Patricia Doede. "Group decision rules and the rejection of deviates", *Social Psychology Quarterly* 42, dec 79 : 354-363.
1035 MOROCCO, Catherine Cobb. "The development and function of group metaphor", *Journal for the Theory of social Behaviour* mar 79 : 15-27.
1036 THUNE, Elizabeth S.; MANDERSCHEID, Ronald W.; SILBERGFELD, Sam. "Status or sex roles as determinants of interaction patterns in small, mixed-sex groups", *Journal of social Psychology* 112, oct 80 : 51-65.

12450. Group membership
Appartenance au groupe

[See also / voir aussi: 560, 936, 1026, 1131, 1174, 1829]

1037 COCKERHAN, William C.; COHEN, Lawrence E. "Obedience to orders: issues of morality and legality in combat among US army paratroopers", *Social Forces* 58, jun 80 : 1272-1288.
1038 FIREBAUGH, Glenn. "Assessing group effects. A comparison of two methods", *Sociological Methods and Research* mai 79 : 384-395.
1039 GARRETT, William R. "Reference groups and role strains related to spiritual well-being", *Sociological Analysis* 40, 79 : 43-58.
1040 HOWARD, John W.; ROTHBART, Myron. "Social categorization and memory for in-group and outgroup behavior", *Journal of Personality and social Psychology* 38, feb 80 : 301-310.

1041 LINVILLE, Patricia W.; JONES, Edward E. "Polarized appraisals of out-group members", *Journal of Personality and social Psychology* 38, mai 80 : 689-703.

1042 MEADOWS, Ian S. G. "Organic structure, satisfaction, and personality", *Human Relations* 33, jun 80 : 383-392.

1043 MIENER, Ed; [et al.]. "Deindividuation: effects of group size, density, number of observers, and group member similarity on self-consciousness and disinhibited behavior", *Journal of Personality and social Psychology* 39, sep 80 : 449-459.

1044 TURNER, J. C.; BROWN, R. J.; TAJFEL, H. "Social comparison and group interest in ingroup favouritism", *European Journal of social Psychology* apr-jun 79 : 187-204.

1045 WITTE, Erich H. *Das Verhalten in Gruppensituationen* (Behaviour in group situations). Göttingen, Hogrefe, 79, 400 p. CR: Gisela TROMMSDORFF, *Soziologische Revue* 3(4), 80: 414-416.

12460. Group performance
Performance du groupe

[See also / voir aussi: 1012, 1032, 1147]

1046 CLARK, Lawrence P.; ARENSON, Sidney J. "Effects of social and spatial density on group performance of an interactive motor task", *Journal of social Psychology* 111, aug 80 : 205-210.

1047 GILLESPIE, David F.; BIRMBAUM, Philip H. "Status concordance, coordination, and success in inter-disciplinary research teams", *Human Relations* 33, jan 80 : 41-56.

1048 RACINE, Luc. "Échange et circulation d'objets dans des groupes d'enfants en activité libre", *Social Science Information* 19, 80 : 543-580.

1049 SOUTO, Cláudio. "Die sozialen Prozesse, eine theoretische Reduktion" (The social processes, a theoretical reduction), *Archiv für Rechts- und Sozialphilosophie* 66, 80 : 27-52.

12500. BUREAUCRACY. ORGANIZATION
BUREAUCRATIE. ORGANISATION

12510. Sociology of organization
Sociologie des organisations

[See also / voir aussi: 144, 606, 4528, 5939, 6254]

1050 BALDUCCI, Massimo. *Introduzione alla analisi delle organizzazioni* (Introduction to organizational analysis). Milano, F. Angeli, 79, 219 p.

1051 BARKER, Dave. *TA and training: the theory and use of transactional analysis in organisations.* Farnborough, Gower Press, 80, ix-225 p.

1052 BARNHILL, J. Allison. *Approaches to administrative analysis.* Toronto, New York, McGraw-Hill Ryerson, 79, ix-374 p.

1053 BLUEDORN, Allen C. "Cutting the Gordian Knot: a critique of the effectiveness tradition in organizational research", *Sociology and social Research* 64, jul 80 : 477-499.

1054 BROWN, Warren B.; MOBERG, Dennis J. *Organization theory and management: a macro approach.* New York, Wiley, 80, xxv-685 p.

1055 DESSLER, Gary. *Organization theory: integrating structure and behavior.* Englewood Cliffs, NJ, Prentice-Hall, 80, xiv-429 p.

1056 KLAGES, Helmut; [ed.]. *Beiträge der Organisationsforschung zur Analyse industrieller Gesellschaften* (Contributions of organizational studies to the understanding of industrial societies). Berlin, Duncker und Humblot, 79, 151 p. CR: Karl GABRIEL, *Soziologische Revue* 3(4), 80: 428-430.

1057 KOROLAINEN, Sakari. *On the conceptual and logical foundations of the general theory of human organizations. A cybernetic approach.* Helsinki, 80, 154 p.

1058 LAMMERS, Cornelis J.; HICKSON, David J.; [eds.]. *Organizations alike and unlike: international and interinstitutional studies in the sociology of organizations.* London, Boston, Routledge & Kegan Paul, 79, xvi-451 p.

1059 MOWDAY, Richard T.; STEERS, Richard M.; [eds.]. *Research in organizations: issues and controversies.* Santa Monica, Goodyear Pub. Co., 79, xv-350 p.

1060 OSBORN, Richard; HUNT, James G.; JAUCH, Lawrence R. *Organization theory: an integrated approach.* New York, Wiley, 80, xx-611 p.

1061 PETIT, François. *Introduction à la psychosociologie des organisations.* Toulouse, Privat, 79, 352 p.

1062 PINDER, Craig C.; MOORE, Larry F.; [eds.]. *Middle range theory and the study of organizations*. Boston, MA., M. Nijhoff Pub., 80, xiv-413 p.
1063 Bibl.XXIX-925. ROBERTS, Karlene H.; HULIN, Charles L.; ROUSSEAU, Denise M. *Developing an interdisciplinary science of organizations*. CR: Carroll SERON, *Contemporary Sociology (Albany)* 9(1), mar 80, 113-115.
1064 SHIOBARA, Tsutomu. "Shakaigaku ni okeru soshiki kenkyu" (Sociological researches on organization), *Nenpo ningen kagaku* 80 : 9-16.
1065 SHIOBARA, Tsutomu. "Soshiki kenkyu to shakaigaku" (Organizational science and sociology), *Soshiki kagaku* 14, 80 : 10-19.
1066 TICHY, Noel; FOMBRUN, Charles. "Network analysis in organizational settings", *Human Relations* 32(11), nov 79 : 923-965.

12520. Complex organization
Organisation complexe

[See also / voir aussi: 1079, 2542]

1067 ALEMAN, Ulrich Von; HEINZE, Rolf G.; [eds.]. *Verbände und Staat. Vom Pluralismus zum Korporatismus* (Associations and State. From pluralism to corporatism). Opladen, Westdeutscher Verlag, 79, 266 p. CR: Günther TEUBNER, *Soziologische Revue* 3(1), 80: 38-40.
1068 CAROUX, Jacques; CAROUX, Françoise. "Le mouvement associatif, critique du système des partis", *Politique aujourd'hui* 5-6, mai-jun 80 : 73-82.
1069 KRAMER, Ralph M. "Voluntary agencies in the welfare state: an analysis of the vanguard role", *Journal of social Policy* oct 79 : 473-488.
1070 KRAMER, Ralph M. "Governmental-voluntary agency relationships in the Netherlands", *Netherlands' Journal of Sociology* 15, dec 79 : 155-173.
1071 KRAMER, Ralph M. "Public fiscal policy and voluntary agencies in welfare states", *Social Service Review* 53, mar 79 : 1-14.
1072 SALINAS RAMOS, Francisco. "El asociacionismo agrario en España" (Agrarian association in Spain), *Documentación social* 40, 80 : 163-193.

12530. Bureaucracy
Bureaucratie

[See also / voir aussi: 45, 977, 1013, 1140, 1200, 1449, 4544, 4564, 5297, 5456, 5485, 6216]

1073 "Demokratische Gessellschaft und Bürokratie" (Democratic society and bureaucracy), *Neue Gesellschaft* 26(12), 79 : 1076-1125.
1074 ALDRICH, Howard E. *Organizations and environments*. Englewood Cliffs, NJ, Prentice-Hall, 79, 384 p. CR: VAN HOUTEN, Donald R., *Contemporary Sociology (Albany)* 9(4), jul 80: 566-567.
1075 ALEXANDER, E. R. "The design of alternatives in organizational contexts: a pilot study", *Administrative Science Quarterly* 24, 79 : 382-404.
1076 ANTONIO, Robert J. "The contradiction of domination and production in bureaucracy: the contribution of organizational efficiency to the decline of the Roman Empire", *American sociological Review* 44, dec 79 : 895-912.
1077 BENAISSA, Said. "Décentralisation et autogestion en Yougoslavie", *Revue algérienne des Sciences juridiques, économiques et politiques* 16, jun 79 : 335-358.
1078 BERG, Per-Olof. *Emotional structures in organizations: a study of the process of change in a Swedish company*. Lund, Studentlitt. in coop. with the Foundation for economic research, 79, 287 p.
1079 BONAZZI, G. "Pour une sociologie du bouc émissaire dans les organisations complexes", *Sociologie du Travail* 22, jul-sep 80 : 300-323.
1080 BOSETZKY, Horst. "Forms of bureaucratic organization in public and industrial administration — trends in the Federal Republic of Germany", *Social Science Information* 19, 80 : 107-137.
1081 BOUHOUCH, A. "Bureaucracy and its impact on the social integration in the Arab world: a descriptive analysis", *Journal of the social Sciences* jan 80 : 1-13.
1082 BUITENHUIS, Cornelius H. *Organization in innovation, innovation in organization: the matrix as a stimulus to renewal*. Assen, Van Gorcum, 79, xv-158 p.

1083 CALHOUN, C. J. "Democracy, autocracy, and intermediate associations in organizations: flexibility or unrestrained change?", *Sociology* 14, aug 80 : 345-361.
1084 CLEGG, Stewart. *The theory of power and organization.* London, Boston, Routledge & Kegan Paul, 79, x-176 p.
1085 CLEGG, Stewart; DUNKERLEY, David. *Organization, class and control.* International Library of Sociology. London and Boston, Routledge & Kegan Paul, 80, x-614 p.
1086 CONNOR, Patrick E. *Organizations, theory and design.* Chicago, Science Research Associates, 80, xvii-549 p.
1087 CROZIER, Michel; FRIEDBERG, Erhard. *Macht und Organisation* (Power and organization). Königstein/Ts., Athenäum, 79, x-392 p.
1088 EDEN, Colin; JONES, Sue; SIMS, David. *Thinking in organizations.* London, Macmillan, 79, x-182 p.
1089 EIFF, Wilfried von. *Organisationsentwicklung* (Organizational development). Berlin, Duncker & Humblot, 79, 289 p.
1090 FUDETANI, Minoru. "Soshiki dotairon no gendaiteki kadai" (Modern problems on the theory of organizational dynamics), *Bukkyo-daigaku daigakuin kenkyu kiyo* 64, 80 : 41-59.
1091 FUDETANI, Minoru. *Gensho to shiteno soshiki shakai* (Organizational society as phenomena). Kyoto, Sekai shisosha, 198 p.
1092 GANNON, Martin J. *Organizational behavior; a managerial and organizational perspective.* Boston, Little, Brown, 79, xxii-484 p.
1093 GIBSON, Cyrus F. *Managing organizational behavior: achieving results through understanding and action.* Homewood, IL, R. D. Irwin, 80, xvi-668 p.
1094 GOLEMBIEWSKI, Robert T. *Orienting perspectives and micro-level interventions.* New York, M. Dekker, 79, xi-363 p.
1095 HAAS, David F. *Interaction in the Thai bureaucracy: structure, culture, and social exchange.* Boulder, CO, Westview Press, 79, xii-180 p.
1096 HAMILTON, Gary G.; BIGGART, Nicole Woolsey. "Making the dilettante an expert: personal staffs in public bureaucracies", *Journal of applied behavioral Science* 16, apr-jun 80 : 192-210.
1097 HOUGLAND, James G. Jr.; WOOD, James R. "Control in organizations and the commitment of members", *Social Forces* 59, sep 80 : 85-105.
1098 HUSEMAN, Richard C.; CARROLL, Archie B.; [eds.]. *Readings in organizational behavior: dimensions of management actions.* Boston, Allyn and Bacon, 79, xiv-432 p.
1099 INBAR, Michael. *The future of bureaucracy.* Beverly Hills, CA, Sage Publications, 79, 248 p.
1100 KALAŠNIKOV, N. I. "Bjurokratija v razvivajuščiemsja obščestve: na primere Indonezii i Tailanda" (Bureaucracy in the developing society: from Indonesia and Thailand examples), *IN: Issledovanija sociologičeskih problem razvivajuščihsja stran.* 78 : 167-178.
1101 KARMEL, Barbara; [ed.]. *Point & counterpoint in organizational behavior.* Hinsdale, IL, Dryden Press, 80, xiv-154 p.
1102 Bibl.XXIX-958. KARPIK, Lucien; [ed.]. *Organization and environment: theory, issues, and reality.* CR: Michael A. DU BICK, *Contemporary Sociology (Albany)* 9(1), mar 80 : 111-112.
1103 KERR, Steven; [ed.]. *Organizational behavior.* Columbus, Ohio, Grid Pub., 79, x-460 p.
1104 KIRTON, Michael. "Adaptors and innovators in organization", *Human Relations* 33, apr 80 : 213-224.
1105 KOBAYASHI, Koichiro. *Kankyō hendō ni tomonau kodō gijutsu-shudogata kigyō no soshiki bunka no henka katei ni kansuru jisshoteki kenkyu* (Changes in organizational culture of high-technology oriented enterprises in changing environments). Tokyo, Toyo daigaku shakaigaku kenkyushitsu, 153 p.
1106 KOUZES, James M.; MICO, Paul R. "Domain theory: an introduction to organizational behavior in human service organizations", *Journal of applied behavioral Science* 15, oct-dec 79 : 449-469.
1107 LERNER, Bertha. "La teoría marxista clásica y el problema de la burocracia" (The classical marxist theory and the problem of bureaucracy), *Revista mexicana de Sociología* 41, oct-dec 79 : 1317-1334.
1108 LITTRELL, W. Boyd; SJOBERG, Gideon; [eds.]. "Bureaucracy in the eighties", *Journal of applied behavioral Science* 16, jul-aug-sep 80 : 263-447.
1109 Bibl.XXIX-963. LOUIS, Karen Seashore; SIEBER, Sam Dixon. *Bureaucracy and the dispersed organization: the educational extension agent experiment.* CR: Bruce M. HACKETT, *Contemporary Sociology (Albany)* 9(5), sep 80, 694-695.
1110 MAGYARI BECK, István. *Alkotás a szervezetben. Az alkotó munka irányítására vonatkozó felfogások és szervezeti megoldások elméleti és empírikus vizsgálata* (Creativity in organizations.

ing the guidance of creative work). Budapest, Akadémiai K., 80, 169 p.
1111 MANGHAM, I. L. *The politics of organizational change.* Westport, CT, Greenwood Press, 79, xii-221 p.
1112 MARTIN, Patricia Yancey. "Size in residential service organizations", *Sociological Quarterly* 20, 79 : 565-579.
1113 MAZMANIAN, Daniel A.; NIENABER, Jeanne. *Can organizations change? Environmental protection, citizen participation, and the corps of engineers.* Washington, DC, Brookings Institution, 79, x-220 p. CR: Walter A. ROSENBAUM, *American political Science Review* 74(1), mar 80: 210-211. [also CR: E. Jackson BAUR, Contemporary Sociology (Albany), 9(5), sep 80: 695-696.]
1114 MEYER, Marshall W. *Change in public bureaucracies.* Cambridge, New York, Cambridge University Press, 79, ix-216 p.
1115 MILES, Robert H.; RANDOLPH, W. Alan; [eds.]. *The Organization game: a simulation in organizational behavior, design, change, and development.* Santa Monica, CA, Goodyear Pub. Co., 79, x-325 p.
1116 MILLER, George A.; CONATY, Joseph. "Differentiation in organization: replication and cumulation", *Social Forces* 59, sep 80 : 265-174.
1117 MILLER, Jon. "Decision-making and organizational effectiveness: participation and perceptions", *Sociology of Work and Occupations* feb 80 : 55-79.
1118 MINER, John B. *Theories of organizational behavior.* Hinsdale, IL, Dryden Press, 80, x-435 p.
1119 MOORE, Michael. "Public bureaucracy in the post-colonial State: some questions on 'autonomy' and 'dominance' in South Asia", *Development and Change* 11, jan 80 : 137-148.
1120 NADLER, David A.; CAMMANN, Cortlandt; MIRVIS, Philip H. "Developing a feedback system for work units: a field experiment in structural change", *Journal of applied behavioral Science* 16, jan-mar 80 : 41-62.
1121 OSZLAK, Oscar. "Notas críticas para una teoría de la burocracia estatal" (Critical notes for a theory of the State bureaucracy), *Desarrollo económico (Buenos Aires)* 19(74), jul-sep 79 : 211-250.
1122 PAGÈS, Max; [et al.]. *L'Emprise de l'organisation.* Paris, Presses universitaires de France, 79, 261 p.
1123 PITT, Douglas. "Mr. Illich's multiplier: the strange death of the bureaucratic organization", *British Journal of Sociology* 31, jun 80 : 277-291.
1124 PORRAS, Jerry I.; WILKINS, Alan. "Organization development in a large system: an empirical assessment", *Journal of applied behavioral Science* 16, oct-dec 80 : 506-534.
1125 Bibl.XXIX-977. PROTTAS, Jeffrey Manditch. *People-processing: the street-level bureaucrat in public service bureaucracies.* CR: Alfred J. KAHN, *Contemporary Sociology (Albany)* 9(5), sep 80 : 715-716.
1126 REHN, Götz. *Modelle der Organisationsentwicklung* (Models of organizational development). Bern, P. Haupt, 79, 357 p. CR: Peter NIEDER, *Soziologische Revue* 3(1), 80: 47-48.
1127 RIZZI, Bruno. *La burocratización del mundo*(World bureaucratization). Barcelona, Península, 80, 248 p.
1128 ROSS, G. Alexander. "The emergence of organization sets in three ecumenical disaster recovery organizations: an empirical and theoretical exploration", *Human Relations* 33, jan 80 : 23-39.
1129 SCANLAN, Burt K.; KEYS, J. Berward. *Management and organizational behavior.* New York, Wiley, 79, xx-663 p.
1130 ŠPORER, Željka. "Organizacije i znanje"(Organizations and knowledge), *Sociologija* 21, 79 : 255-266.
1131 STYSKAL, Richard A. "Power and commitment in organizations: a test of the participation thesis", *Social Forces* 58, mar 80 : 925-943.
1132 WEED, Frank J. "Bureaucratization as reform: the case of the public welfare movement, 1900-1929", *Social Science Journal* 16, 79 : 79-89.
1133 ZEY-FERRELL, Mary. *Dimensions of organizations: environment, context, structure, process, and performance.* Santa Monica, CA, Goodyear Pub. Co., 79, xix-390 p.

12600. LEADERSHIP. ROLE
COMMANDEMENT. RÔLE

12610. Authority
Autorité

[See also / voir aussi: 680, 1037, 1803, 1826, 3555, 5456]

1134   BAUDRILLARD, Jean. *De la Séduction*. Paris, Galilée, 79, 248 p.
1135   CAMIC, Charles. "Charisma: its varieties, preconditions, and consequences", *Sociological Inquiry* 50, 80 : 5-23.
1136   COLEMAN, James S. "Authority systems", *Public Opinion Quarterly* 44, 80 : 143-163.
1137   Bibl.XXIX-994. GOODE, William J. *The celebration of heroes: prestige as a social control system*. CR: George C. HOMANS; Wilbert E. MOORE ., *Contemporary Sociology* 9(2), mar 80 : 178-182.
1138   LINDSKOUG, Kerstin. *Hänförelse och fmuft: om karisma och rationalitet i Max Webers sociologi* (Enchantment and reason: on charisma and rationality in Max Weber's sociology). Lund, Dialog, 79, 211 p.
1139   SINGH, Ramadhar; BOHRA, Kayyum A. "Fabourableness of leadership situations studies with information integration theory", *European Journal of social Psychology* jul-sep 79 : 253-264.
1140   SPITTLER, Gerd. "Abstraktes Wissen als Herrschaftsbasis. Zur Entstehungsgeschichte bürokratischer Herrschaft im Bauernstaat Preussen" (Abstract knowledge as authority basis. On the history of bureaucratic power in the peasant state of Prussia), *Kölner Zeitschrift für Soziologie und Sozialpsychologie* 32, 80 : 574-604.
1141   THEOBALD, Robin. "The role of charisma in the development of social movements", *Archives de Sciences sociales des Religions* 25, jan-mar 80 : 83-100.
1142   WRONG, Dennis Hume. *Power, its forms, bases, and uses*. New York, Harper and Row Publishers, 79, viii-326 p.

12620. Leadership
Commandement

[See also / voir aussi: 1182, 5168, 5210]

1143   BYRON, R. F. "Skippers and strategies: leadership and innovation in Shetland fishing crews", *Human Organization* 39, 80 : 227-232.
1144   DAY, Phyllis J. "Charismatic leadership in the small organization", *Human Organization* 39, 80 : 50-58.
1145   INSKO, Chester A.; [et al.]. "Social evolution and the emergency of leadership", *Journal of Personality and social Psychology* 39, sep 80 : 431-448.
1146   JOHNSON, Doyle Paul. "Dilemmas of charismatic leadership: the case of the People's Temple", *Sociological Analysis* 40, 79 : 315-323. ;961[Guyana.]
1147   KOCH, James L. "Effects of goal specificity and performance feedback to work groups on peer leadership performance, and attitudes", *Human Relations* 32(10), oct 79 : 819-840.
1148   KUZMITZ, Frank E.; [ed.]. *Leadership in a dynamic society*. Indianapolis, Bobbs-Merrill Educational Pub., 79, xvi-75 p.
1149   LALL, Bernard M.; LALL, Geeta R. *Dynamic leadership*. Mountain View, CA, Pacific Press Pub. Association, 79, 270 p.
1150   RICH, Richard C. "The dynamics of leadership in neighbourhood organizations", *Social Science Quarterly* 60, mar 80 : 570-587.
1151   SHARNI, Shoshana. "From alienation to admiration: developmental stages of group leaders in encounters with culturally deprived mothers", *Human Relations* 32, sep 79 : 737-749.
1152   SHIVERS, Jay Sanford. *Recreational leadership: group dynamics and interpersonal behavior*. Princeton, NJ, Princeton Book Co., 80, ix-268 p.
1153   STEIN, R. Timothy; HELLER, Tamar. "An empirical analysis of the correlations between leadership status and participation rates reported in the literature", *Journal of Personality and social Psychology* 37(11), nov 79 : 1993-2002.
1154   VAN WORMER, Katerine S.; BATES, Frederick L. "A study of leadership roles in an Alabama prison for women", *Human Relations* 32, sep 79 : 793-801.

1155 ZORINA, Z. A. "Avtoritet rukovoditelja v sisteme upravlenija" (The leader's authority in a management system), *IN: Metodologija upravlenija obščestvennymi sistemami v uslovijah razvitogo socializma.* 78 : 146-154.

12630. Role
Rôle

[See also / voir aussi: 703, 1039, 2937, 3202, 5121, 5538, 5648]

1156 BIDDLE, Bruce. *Role theory: expectations, identities, and behaviors.* New York, Academic Press, 79, x-416 p.
1157 BOCHNER, Stephen; LIN, Anli; MCLEOD, Beverly M. "Anticipated role conflict of returning overseas students", *Journal of social Psychology* 110, apr 80 : 265-272.
1158 CARLSTON, Donald E. "A closer examination of subject roles", *Journal of Personality and social Psychology* 38, jun 80 : 857-870.
1159 CONNELL, R. W. "The concept of role and what to do with it", *Australian and New Zealand Journal of Sociology* 15, nov 79 : 7-17.
1160 CROGHAN, Martin J. *Role models and readers: a sociological analysis.* Washington, University Press of America, 80, ix-170 p.
1161 FERLIGOJ, Anuška; MEŽNARIĆ, Silva; ULE, Mirjana. "Raspodela svakodnevnih uloga u porodici izmedu projekcije (društva) i stvarnosti (porodice)" (Division of everyday family roles between that which is desired (society) and the reality (family)), *Sociologija* 21, 79 : 419-439.
1162 GEORGE, Linda K. *Role transitions in later life.* Monterey, CA, Brooks/Cole Pub. Co., 80, xiii-159 p.
1163 HERZOG, Walter. "Antezedenzien der Rolleninternalisierung: eine begriffliche und empirische Analyse" (Antecedents of role interiorization: a conceptual and empirical analysis), *Kölner Zeitschrift für Soziologie und Sozialpsychologie* 32, 80 : 240-261.
1164 KAMIKO, Takeji. "Gendai kazoku no yakuwari kozo" (The role structure of the modern family), *Jido shinri* 34, 80 : 1-12.
1165 KANBARA, Fumiko. "Yukuwari cycle shūsei model" (A revised model of "role cycle"), *Soshioroji* 25, 80 : 55-77.
1166 KEER, Norbert L.; NERENZ, David R.; HERRICK, David. "Role playing and the study of jury behavior", *Sociological Methods and Research* nov 79 : 337-355.
1167 KURIOKA, Mikiei. "Yakuwari riron no ichikeiko" (A trend in role theory), *Soshioroji* 25, 80 : 37-53.
1168 NOLAN, Patrick D. "'Role distance" is suicide: a cumulative development in theory", *Sociology and social Research* 64, oct 79 : 99-104.
1169 OLSON, Joan Toms. "Role conflict between housework and child care", *Sociology of Work and Occupations* nov 79 : 430-456.
1170 POSNER, Barry Z.; RANDOLPH, W. Alan. "Perceived situational moderators of the relationship between role ambiguity, job satisfaction, and effectiveness", *Journal of social Psychology* 109, dec 79 : 237-244.
1171 SKVORETZ, John; FARARO, Thomas J.; AXTEN, Nick. "Role-programme models and the analysis of institutional structure", *Sociology* 14, feb 80 : 49-67.

12700. ATTITUDE. OPINION
ATTITUDE. OPINION

12710. Behaviour
Comportement

[See also / voir aussi: 458, 870, 937, 1237, 1577, 2090, 2997, 3050, 3304, 3415, 5112, 5950, 6178]

1172 BAGOZZI, Richard P.; BURNKRANT, Robert E. "Attitude organization and the attitude-behavior relationship", *Journal of Personality and social Psychology* 37, jun 79 : 913-929.
1173 BISHOP, George D.; HAMILTON, David L.; MCCONAHAY, John B. "Attitudes and nonattitudes in the belief systems of mass publics", *Journal of social Psychology* 110, feb 80 : 53-64.

1174 BRANDSTÄTTER, Hermann; KLEIN-MODDENBORG, Volker. "A modified proportional change model of attitude change by group discussion", *European Journal of social Psychology* oct-dec 79 : 363-380.

1175 BROWN, Richard H. "Ordre et révolution dans les formes normales du discours et de la conduite", *Cahiers internationaux de Sociologie* 68, jul-dec 79 : 69-81.

1176 DAVIDSON, Andrew R.; JACCARD, James J. "Variables that moderate the attitude-behavior relation: results of a longitudinal survey", *Journal of Personality and social Psychology* 37, aug 79 : 1364-1376.

1177 EISER, J. Richard; PANCER, S. Mark. "Attitudinal effects of the use of evaluative biased language", *European Journal of social Psychology* jan-mar 79 : 39-47.

1178 EISER, J. Richard; VAN DER PLIGT, Joop; GOSSOP, Michael R. "Categorization, attitude and memory for the source of attitude statements", *European Journal of social Psychology* jul-sep 79 : 243-251.

1179 FRIDERES, James S.; WARNER, Lyle G. "Attitude-action relationships", *Canadian Review of Sociology and Anthropology* 17, mai 80 : 109-121.

1180 GLOVER, John A.; GARY, Albert L. *Behavior modification: an empirical approach to self-control.* Chicago, Nelson-Hall, 79, 198 p.

1181 GRÖSCHKE, Dieter. *Zur Rekonstruktion der Verhaltensmodifikation: wissenschaftstheoret. u. wissenschaftssoziolog. Aspekte d. Klin. Psychologie* (On reconstruction of behaviour modification). Frankfurt/ Main, Haag und Herchen, 79, ii-293 p.

1182 HUNTER, John E.; HUNTER, Ronda F.; LOPIS, John E. "A causal analysis of attitudes toward leadership training in a classroom setting", *Human Relations* 32(11), nov 79 : 889-907.

1183 JUDD, Charles M.; MILBURN, Michael A. "The structure of attitude systems in the general public: comparisons of a structural equation model", *American sociological Review* 45, aug 80 : 627-643.. [with a rejoinder by Philip E. CONVERSE: 644-646.]

1184 KAHLE, Lynn R.; BERMAN, John J. "Attitudes cause behaviors: a cross-legged panel analysis", *Journal of Personality and social Psychology* 37, mar 79 : 315-321.

1185 KARDOS, Lajos; [ed.]. *Attitudes, interaction and personality.* Budapest, Akadémiai Kiado, 80, 149 p.

1186 KAZDIN, Alan E. *Behavior modification in applied settings.* Homewood, IL, Dorsey Press, Georgetown, Ont., Irwin-Dorsey, 80, xiii-416 p.

1187 LABORIT, Henri. *L'inhibition de l'action: biologie, physiologie, psychologie, sociologie.* Paris, New York, Masson, 79, vi-214 p.

1188 LARSEN, Knut S. "Social categorization and attitude change", *Journal of social Psychology* 111, jun 80 : 113-118.

1189 MANIS, Melvin; ROTHBART, Myron; [eds.]. "Attitudes and social cognition", *Journal of Personality and social Psychology* 39, oct 80 : 532-624.

1190 NEFF, James Alan. "Interactional versus hypothetical others: the use of vignettes in attitude research", *Sociology and social Research* 64, oct 79 : 105-125.

1191 PAICHELER, Geneviève. "Polarization of attitudes in homogeneous and heterogeneous groups", *European Journal of social Psychology* jan-mar 79 : 85-96.

1192 PECKHAM, Morse. *Explanation and power: the control of human behavior.* New York, Seabury Press, 79, xix-290 p.

1193 PLAX, Timothy G.; ROSENFELD, Lawrende B. "Individual differences in the credibility and attitude change relationship", *Journal of social Psychology* 111, jun 80 : 79-89.

1194 RODEWALD, Herbert Keith. *Stimulus control of behavior.* Baltimore, University Park Press, 79, vii-162 p.

1195 ROMER, Daniel. "Distraction, counterarguing and the internationalization of attitude change", *European Journal of social Psychology* jan-mar 79 : 1-17.

1196 SCHUESSLER, Karl; WALLACE, Michael. "Components in comunality of mental attitude items", *Sociological Focus* 12, oct 79 : 247-261.

1197 UNGAR, Sheldon. "Attitude inferences from behavior performed under public and private conditions", *Social Psychology Quarterly* 43, mar 80 : 81-89.

1198 WHITE, Gregory L. "Consensus and justification effects on attitude following counterattitudinal behavior", *Sozial Psychology Quarterly* 43, sep 80 : 321-327.

1199 ZANNA, Mark P.; OLSON, James M.; FAZIO, Russell H. "Attitude-behavior consistency: an individual difference perspective", *Journal of Personality and social Psychology* 38, mar 80 : 432-440.

12720. Cognitive dissonance. Prejudice
Dissonance cognitive. Préjugé

[See also / voir aussi: 507, 717, 943, 4778]

1200   ALVAREZ, Rodolfo; [et al.]. *Discrimination in organizations*. San Francisco, Jossey-Bass, 79, xxvi-425 p.
1201   BECK, E. M. "Discrimination and white economic loss: a time series examination of the radical model", *Social Forces* 59, sep 80 : 148-168.
1202   BRANTHWAITE, Alan; DOYLE, Susan; LIGHTBOWN, Nicholas. "The balance between fairness and discrimination", *European Journal of social Psychology* apr-jun 79 : 149-163. [with a reply by TURNER, John C. ibid. 10(2), apr-jun 80: 131-147.]
1203   CSEPELI, György; [ed.]. *Előítéletek és csoportközi viszonyok. Válogatott tanulmányok* (Prejudice and intergroup relations. Selected studies). Budapest, Közgazdasági és Jogi Kiado, 80, 454 p.
1204   Bibl.XXIX-1050. DWYER, Daisy Hilse. *Images and self-images: male and female in Morocco*. CR: Kay A. SNYDER., *Contemporary Sociology (Albany)* 9(2), mar 80: 292-293.
1205   GLASSNER, Barry. *Essential interactionism: on the intelligibility of prejudice*. Boston, Routledge and Kegan Paul, 80, 185 p. CR: Michael A. OVERINGTON, *Contemporary Sociology (Albany)* 9(6), nov 80: 844-845.
1206   GLOOR, Pierre-André; [et al.]. "Représentations collectives et images de l'autre. Mythes et utopies", *Revue européenne des Sciences sociales. Cahiers Vilfredo Pareto* 18(53), 80 : 7-135.
1207   JACKMAN, Mary R.; SENTER, Mary Scheuer. "Images of social groups: categorical or qualified?", *Public Opinion Quarterly* 44, 80 : 341-361.
1208   LESTER, Richard A. *Reasoning about discrimination: the analysis of professional and executive work in federal antibias programs*. Princeton, NJ, Princeton University Press, 80, xv-384 p. CR: Robert S. FRIEDMAN, *American political Science Review* 74(4), dec 80: 1089-1090.
1209   PETRUNIK, Michael. "The rise and fall of 'labelling theory': the construction and destruction of a sociological strawman", *Canadian Journal of Sociology* 80 : 213-233.
1210   TAYLOR, Howard F.; HORNUNG, Carlton A. "On a general model for social and cognitive consistency", *Sociological Methods and Research* feb 79 : 259-288.

12730. Dogmatism. F scale
Dogmatisme. Échelle F

[See also / voir aussi: 2521, 2542, 2670, 3780, 3801, 5455]

1211   ALTVATER, Elmar; [et al,]. *Tendenze autoritarie del capitalismo sviluppato* (Authoritarian trends of developed capitalism). Milano, F. Angeli, 79, 159 p.
1212   BOOTH, Ken. *Strategy and ethnocentrism*. New York, Holmes and Meier, 79, 191 p. CR: Richard SMOKE, *American political Science Review* 74(2), jun 80: 578-579.
1213   HAYNAL, André; MOLNAR, Miklos; PUYMÈGE, Gérard de. *Le fanatisme : ses racines : un essai historique et psychanalytique*. Paris, Stock, 80, 357 p.
1214   HEAVEN, P. C. L. "Authoritarianism, prejudice, and alienation among Afrikaners", *Journal of social Psychology* 110, feb 80 : 39-42.
1215   RAY, John J. "Authoritarianism in California 30 years later — with some cross-cultural comparisons", *Journal of social Psychology* 111, jun 80 : 9-17.
1216   SMITH, Leslie Whitener; PETERSEN, Karen Kay. "Rural-urban differences in tolerance: Stouffer's 'culture shock' hypothesis revisited", *Rural Sociology* 45, 80 : 256-271.
1217   STEIBER, Steven R. "The influence of the religious factor on civil and sacred tolerance, 1958-71", *Social Forces* 58, mar 80 : 811-832.
1218   SUTHERLAND, S. L.; TANENBAUM, E. J. "Submissive authoritarians", *Canadian Review of Sociology and Anthropology* 17, feb 80 : 1-23.

12740. Opinion
Opinion

[See also / voir aussi: 494, 704, 1173, 1700, 1854, 2175, 2628, 3065, 3099, 3332, 4590, 4612, 4747, 5420, 5989, 6014]

1219   ALEHIN, V. A. "Rol' obščestvennogo mnenija v formirovanii nravstvennoj osnovy socialističeskogo obraza žizni" (Role of public opinion in the formation of the socialist way of life moral basis), *IN: Socialističeskij obraz žizni i ličnost'.* Voronež, 79 : 104-112.

1220   ALEKSEEV, B. K.; [et al.]. "Izučenie obščestvennogo mnenija: opyt i problemy" (Public opinion study: experiment and problems), *Sociologičeskie Issledovanija* 79 : 23-32.

1221   BISHOP, George F.; [et al.]. "Pseudo-opinions on public affairs", *Public Opinion Quarterly* 44, 80 : 198-209.

1222   ČERNYŠEVA, A. V. "Rol' obščestvennogo mnenija v razvitom socialističeskom obščestve" (The public opinion role in the developed socialist society), *IN: Istoričeskij materializm i sovremennoe obščestvennoe razvitie.* Moskva, 79 : 62-69.

1223   DURANDIN, Guy. "La manipulation de l'opinion", *Revue des Travaux de l'Académie des Sciences morales et politiques* 131, 78 : 143-160.

1224   ĔRUNOV, B. A. "Obščestvennoe mnenie i ličnost' v uslovijah sovremennoj kul'tury" (Public opinion and the personality under conditions of contemporary culture), *IN: Rol' duhovnoj kul'tury v razvitii ličnosti.* 79 : 20-25.

1225   FRANK, Tibor; HOPPÁL, Mihály; [eds.]. *Hiedelemrendszer és társadalmi tudat* (Belief-system and social consciousness). Budapest, Mass Communication Research Centre, Tömegkommunikációs Kutatóközpont, 80, vol 1: 340; vol 2: 301 p. [Proceedings of the conference The nature, origin and role of beliefs in social consciousness, Visegrád, 28-30th April 1975.]

1226   GORŠKOV, M. K.; ŠEREGI, F. Ê. "Dinamika obščestvennogo mnenija molodeži" (Dynamics of the youth public opinion), *Sociologičeskie Issledovanija* 79 : 33-40.

1227   HANIN, Ju. L. *Psihologija obščenija v sporte* (The public opinion psychology in sport). Moskva, Fizkul'tura i Sport, 80, 208 p.

1228   HOLSTI, Ole R.; ROSENAU, James N. "Does where you stand depend on when you were born? The impact of generation on post-Vietnam foreign policy beliefs", *Public Opinion Quarterly* 44, 80 : 1-22.

1229   IVANOVA, L. N. "Metodologičeskie principy konkretno-sociologičeskogo issledovanija obščestvennogo mnenija" (Methodological problems of the public opinion concrete sociological research), *IN: Metodologija častnyh nauk.* Irkutsk, 79 : 143-148.

1230   LASSWELL, Harold Dwight; LERNER, Daniel; SPEIER, Hans; [eds.]. *Emergence of public opinion in the West.* Honolulu, University Press of Hawaii, for the East-West Center, xiii-561 p.

1231   LEVINE, John M.; RUBACK, R. Barry. "Reaction to opinion deviance: impact of a Fence-Straddler's rationale on majority evaluation", *Social Psychology Quarterly* 43, mar 80 : 73-81.

1232   MAHMUDOVA, Z. A. "Obščestvennoe mnenie i normy kommunističeskoj morali" (Public opinion and communist morals norms), *Naučnye Trudy Azerbajdžanskogo Universiteta. Serija juridičeskij Nauk* 79 : 18-24.

1233   MENANTEAU-HORTA, Dario. "El rol de la opinión pública en la integración de America latina" (The role of public opinion in the integration of Latin America), *Revista española de Investigaciones sociológicas* apr-jun 79 : 151-164.

1234   MONGARDINI, Carlo. "Le condizioni del consenso"(The conditions of consensus), *Studi di Sociologia* 18, apr-jun 80 : 123-138.

1235   ROGILO, V. V. "Obščestvennoe mnenie i nravstvennye otnošenija v trudovom kollektive" (Public opinion and ethical relations in a labour collectivity), *IN: Kommunističeskaja idejnost' — osnova aktivnoj žiznennoj pozicii.* Moskva, 79 : 210-217.

1236   SAFAROV, R. A. "Političeskij status obščestvennogo mnenija" (Public opinion political status), *Sociologičeskie Issledovanija* 79 : 11-22.

1237   SCHUMAN, Howard; PRESSER, Stanley. "Public opinion and public ignorance: the fine line between attitudes and nonattitudes", *American Journal of Sociology* 85, mar 80 : 1214-1225.

1238   SWANN, William B. Jr.; SNYDER, Mark. "On translating beliefs into action: theories of ability and their application in an instructional setting", *Journal of Personality and social Psychology* 38, jun 80 : 879-888.

1239   TAYLOR, D. Garth. "Procedures for evaluating trends in public opinion", *Public Opinion Quarterly* 44, 80 : 86-100.

1240   TILLINGHAST, Diana Stover. "Direct magnitude estimation scales in public opinion surveys", *Public Opinion Quarterly* 44, 80 : 377-384.

1241   WATTS, William A.; HOLT, Lewis E. "Persistence of opinion change induced under conditions of forewarning and distraction", *Journal of Personality and social Psychology* 37, mai 79 : 778-789.

12750. Ideology
Idéologie

[See also / voir aussi: 13, 1206, 1290, 1347, 1614, 1627, 1863, 1962, 2030, 2066, 2098, 2147, 2284, 2378, 2535, 2977, 3042, 3051, 3056, 3589, 3681, 4433, 4612, 5211, 5422, 5468, 6014]

1242 "Populism and popular ideologies", *Laru Studies* (2-3), jan 80 : 1-168.
1243 BARNETT, Steve; SILVERMAN, Martin G. *Ideology and everyday life: anthropology, neomarxist thought, and the problem of ideology and the social whole.* Ann Arbor, University of Michigan Press, 79, ix-179 p.
1244 Bibl.XXIX-1075. BARRETT, Michele; [et al.]. *Ideology and cultural production.* CR: R. J. TRISTRAM, *British Journal of Sociology* 31(4), dec 80: 589-590.
1245 BERNARDI, Walter. *Morelly e Dom Deschamps: utopia e ideologia nel secolo dei lumi* (Morelly and Dom Deschamps: Utopia and ideology in the 18th century). Firenze, L. S. Olschki, 79, 273 p.
1246 ENGELHARDT, W. W. "Zum Verhältnis von sozialen Utopien und politischen Konzeptionen" (On the relationship between social utopia and political conceptions), *Sozialer Fortschritt* 29, 80 : 1-6; 41-45.
1247 GRAMPA, Giuseppe. *Ideologia e poetica: marxismo e ermeneutica per il linguaggio religioso* (Ideology and poetics: marxism and hermeneutics for the religious language). Milano, Vita e pensiero, 79, xiv-337 p.
1248 GUCCIONE MONROY, Nino. *Critica e ideologia* (Criticism and ideology). Palermo, S. F. Flaccovio, 79, 153 p.
1249 HALL, Stuart. "Über Ideologieforschung in Grossbritannien" (The ideological research in Great Britain), *Argument (Berlin)* 21(118), 79 : 846-856.
1250 HIRST, Paul Q. *On law and ideology.* Atlantic Highlands, NJ, Humanities Press, 79, vii-181 p.
1251 IPOLA, Emilio De. "Populismo e ideología"(Populism and ideology), *Revista mexicana de Sociología* 41, jul-sep 79 : 925-960.
1252 JÓZSA, Péter. *Adalékok az ideológia és a jelentés elméletéhez* (Contributions to the theory of ideology and meaning). Budapest, NPI, 79, 247 p.
1253 KNJAZEVA, M. B. "Social'nye funkcii kommunističeskogo ideala" (Social functions of the communist ideal), *Kommunističeskoe Vospitanie* 79 : 41-50.
1254 LARRAIN, Jorge. "Durkheim's concept of ideology", *Sociological Review* 28, feb 80 : 129-139.
1255 LARRAIN, Jorge. *The concept of ideology.* London, Hutchinson, 79, 256 p. CR: Nicholas ABERCROMBIE, *British Journal of Sociology* 31(4), dec 80: 588-589.
1256 MANUEL, Frank E.; MANUEL, Fritzie P. *Utopian thought in the Western world.* Cambridge, Harvard University Press, 79, vi-896 p. CR: Robert Booth FOWLER, *American political Science Review* 74(2), jun 80: 484-485.
1257 MCCARTHY, Timothy. "Marx and the problem of ideology", *Social Science* 54, 79 : 204-209.
1258 MELIK-KARAMOV, R. É. "Ideologičeskij faktor i vozrastanie ėgo roli v razvitii nacional'nyh otnošenij razvitogo socializma" (Ideological factor and elevation of its role in the development of the developed socialism national relations), *Naučnye Trudy Azerbajdžanskogo Universiteta. Serija juridičeskij Nauk* 79 : 66-75.
1259 MIKAMI, Takeshi. "'Ideology to Utopia' ni okeru Utopia-teki ishiki no ichi" (The position of the Utopian mentality in "Ideology and Utopia"), *Soshioroji* 24, 80 : 1-15.
1260 MOSEJKO, A. N. "Osnovnye social'nye funkcii ideologii v obščestvennoj sisteme razvivajuščihsja stran: po materialam afrikanskogo regiona" (Ideology essential social functions in the developing countries social system: from an African region materials), *IN: Issledovanija sociologičeskih problem razvivajuščihsja stran..* 78 : 201-218.
1261 SALLE, Philippe. *L'Homo anti-atomicus ou Naissance d'un nouvel idéal occidental.* Paris, A. Moreau, 79, 379 p.
1262 SCAGLIA, Antonio. *Illusione capitalistica e utopia marxista: elementi di teoria sociologica e problematiche istituzionali* (Capitalist illusion and marxist utopia: elements of sociological theory and institutional problematics). Milano, F. Angeli, 79, v-278 p.
1263 SUMNER, Colin. *Reading ideologies: an investigation into the Marxist theory of ideology and law.* London, New York, Academic Press, 79, xiii-313 p.
1264 TEUNIS, H. B. "Ideologie en maatschappelijke ontwikkeling. George Duby over 'Les trois ordres ou l'imaginaire du féodalisme'" (Ideology and social development. About

George Duby 'Les trois ordres ou l'imaginaire du féodalisme'), *Mens en Maatschappij* 55, 80 : 136-147.
1265   WUNENBURGER, Jean Jacques. *L'utopie: ou, La crise de l'imaginaire.* Paris, Delarge, 79, 254 p. CR: Étienne GÉHIN, *Revue française de sociologie* 21(2), apr-jun 80: 309-312.
1266   ŽURAVLEV, G. T. *Sociologičeskie issledovanija effektivnosti ideologičeskoj raboty* (Sociological research on the ideological activity efficiency). Moskva, Mysl', 80, 252 p.

12760. Collective behaviour
Comportement collectif

[See also / voir aussi: 538, 1555, 4367, 5281]

1267   ABRAMS, Robert. *Foundations of political analysis: an introduction to the theory of collective choice.* New York, Columbia University Press, 80, xii-357 p.
1268   EDWARDS, David J. A. "Perception of crowding and tolerance for interpersonal proximity and separation in South Africa", *Journal of social Psychology* 110, feb 80 : 9-17.
1269   FROLOVA, M. A. "Klassovyj harakter manipulirovanija massovym soznaniem v buržuaznom obščestve" (Class character of the mass consciousness manipulation in the bourgeois society), *Kommunističeskoe Vospitanie* 79 : 113-121.
1270   GORJUNOV, V. "Aktivnost' mass — istočnik sily socialističeskogo stroja" (The masses activity is the source of the socialist system force), *Kommunist vooruzennyk Sil* 16, 79 : 13-21.
1271   OLIVER, Pamela. "Rewards and punishments as selective incentives for collective action: theoretical investigations", *American Journal of Sociology* 85, mai 80 : 1356-1375.
1272   Bibl.XXIX-1115. PERRY, Joseph B. Jr.; PUGH, M. D. *Collective behavior: response to social stress.* CR: Thomas C. HOOD, *Contemporary Sociology (Albany)* 9(4), jul 80: 583.
1273   RUSSELL, Clifford S.; [ed.]. *Collective decision making: Applications from public choice theory.* Baltimore, London, Johns Hopkins University Press for Resources for the Future, 79, xvi-296 p.
1274   SOLOV'EV, O. M. "Razvitie social'no-političeskoj aktivnosti mass v uslovijah socialističeskoj demokratii" (The mass socio-political activity development under conditions of socialist democracy), *Politiceskaja Organizacija Obscestva i Upravlenija pri Socializme* 79 : 8-18.
1275   Bibl.XXIX-1220. WRIGHT, Sam. *Crowds and riots: a study in social organization.* CR: Clark MCPHAIL, *Contemporary Sociology (Albany)* 9(2), mar 80: 302-303.

13. CULTURE. SOCIALISATION. SOCIAL LIFE
CULTURE. SOCIALISATION. VIE SOCIALE

13100. CULTURE. SOCIAL ENVIRONMENT. VALUE
CULTURE. MILIEU SOCIAL. VALEUR

13110. Social and cultural anthropology
Ethnologie

[See also / voir aussi: 799, 1613]

1276 FABIAN, Johannes. "Rule and process: thoughts on ethnography as communication", *Philosophy of the social Sciences* mar 79 : 1-26.
1277 KUPER, Adam. "The man in the study and the man in the field. Ethnography, theory and comparison in social anthropology", *Archives européenes de Sociologie* 21, 80 : 14-39.
1278 MCHOUL, A. W. "'Cultural creation': unsociological aspects of Goldmann's sociology of culture", *Sociology* 14, nov 80 : 567-580.
1279 WILLENDER, Alfred. *L'Héroine travail: essais de sociologie de la culture.* Genève, Grounauer, 79, 252 p.

13120. Civilization. Culture. Society
Civilisation. Culture. Société

1280 "Enfants (Les) et les cultures", *Cultures* 79 : 7-173.
1281 "Estudios mexicanos" (Mexican studies), *Revista mexicana de Sociología* 41, jul-sep 79 : 621-835.
1282 "Estudios norteamericanos sobre Mexico"(North American studies on Mexico), *Revista mexicana de Sociología* 41, oct-dec 79 : 1123-1296.
1283 ABDULOVA, G. Ja. "Socialističeskij obraz žizni i ravenstvo polov" (The socialist way of life and the equality of sexes), *Naučnye Trudy Azerbajdžanskogo Universiteta. Serija juridičeskij Nauk* 79 : 45-50.
1284 ALEKSEEV, V. N. *Socialističeskij obraz žizni* (The socialist way of life). Kišinev, Kartja Moldovenjaskě, 79, 105 p.
1285 ALTMAN, Irwin; CHEMERS, Martin. *Culture and environment.* Monterey, CA, Brooks/Cole Pub. Co., 80, xiv-337 p.
1286 ANDOR, Csaba. *Jel — kultúra — kommunikáció. Interdiszciplináris szempontok a kultúrakutatásban* (Signs — culture — communication. Interdisciplinary aspects in the research of culture). Budapest, Gondolat, 80, 203 p.
1287 ANDRÁSSY, Mária; VITÁNYI, Iván. *Ifjúság és kultúra. A fiatalok kulturális, művészeti magatartása* (Youth and culture. Cultural and artistic behaviour of young peoples). Budapest, Kossuth Kiadó, 79, 164-4 p.
1288 ARIAN, Asher; [ed.]. *Israel — a developing society.* Assen, The Netherlands, Van Gorcum, 80, 456 p.
1289 ASANTE, Molefi Kete; VANDI, Abdulai S. *Contemporary Black Thought: Alternative Analyses in Social and Behavioral Science.* Beverly Hills, CA, Sage Publications, 80, 304. p.
1290 BAJOIT, G. "Modèle culturel, idéologie et théorie de l'histoire", *Recherches sociologiques* 11, 80 : 3-30.
1291 BESPAMJATNYH, N. N. "Internacionalizacija obraza zizni belorusskogo naroda v razvitom socialističeskom obščestve" (The internationalization of the Belorussian people's way of life in the developed socialist society), *IN: Issledovanija po obščestvennym i gumanitarnym naukam.* Grodno, 78 : 3-10.
1292 BESTUŽEV-LADA, I. V. "K sisteme social'nyh pokazatelej obraza žizni razvitogo socialističeskogo obščestva" (The social indexes system of the developed socialist society way of life), *IN: Teoretičeskie problemy razvitogo socializma. I. Plenarnoe zasedanie.* Moskva, 79 : 128-150.
1293 BESTUŽEV-LADA, I. V.; BATYGIN, G. S.; [eds.]. *Teoretičeskie i metodologičeskie problemy issledovanija obraza žizni* (Theoretical and methodological problems of the way of life research). Moskva, Institut Sociologičeskih Issledovanij AN SSSR, 79, 182 p.

1294 BROMLEJ, Ju. V.; KALTAHČJAN, S. T. "Aktual'nye problemy marksistsko-leninskoj teorii nacii i nacional'nyh otnŏsenij i bor'ba idej" (Topical problems of the Marxist-Leninist theory of nation and international relations and the ideological struggle), *Naučnye Doklady vysšej Školy. Naučnyj Kommunizm* 80 : 58-69.

1295 CAMPA, Arthur Leon. *Hispanic culture in the Southwest*. Norman, University of Oklahoma Press, 79, xii-316 p.

1296 CAMPBELL, Colin. "Accounting for the counter culture", *Scottish Journal of Sociology* jan 80 : 37-51.

1297 ČEMODANOV, M. P. "Sovetskij obraz žizni i obščestvennaja pozicija učenogo" (The Soviet way of life and the scientist's social situation), *IN: Sovetskaja intelligencija i ee rol' v duhovnoj žizni razvitogo socializma*. Moskva, 79 : 47-52.

1298 CERTEAU, Michel de. *L'invention du quotidien. 1. Arts de faire*. Paris, Union générale d'éditions, 80, 377 p.

1299 CIPKO, A. S.; [ed.]. *Socialističeskij obraz žizni: sbornik statej učenyh socialističeskih stran* (The socialist way of life: a handbook of the scientists papers from the socialist states). Moskva, Progress, 79, 213 p.

1300 CLAUSEN, Lars. "Grün ist die Hoffnung. Neue Literatur zu 'alternativen' Lebensformen" (Green is the hope. New literature on 'alternative' life styles), *Soziologische Revue* 80 : 147-155. [review article.]

1301 COSTA, Francisque; [et al.]. *La Civilisation britannique*. Paris, Presses universitaires de France, 80, 441 p.

1302 CRIST, Raymond E.; PAGANINI, Louis A. "The rise and fall of Maya civilization", *American Journal of Economics and Sociology* 39, jan 80 : 23-30.

1303 ČUGUNOV, V. I. "Socialističeskij obraz žizni i individual'nost" (The socialist way of life and individuality), *IN: Problemy socialističeskogo obraza žizni v uslovijah razvitogo socializma*. Moskva, 78 : 16-32.

1304 Culture (La) et la communication. *Cultures* 80 : 7-158.

1305 DABŽANOVA, Ž. B. "Sovetskij obraz žizni i social'naja rol' ženščiny v obščestve (na primere Kazahstana)" (The Soviet way of life and the women's social role in society: from the Kazakhstan example), *IN: Utverždenie sovetskogo obraza žizni v Kazahstane i voprosy vospitanija novogo čeloveka*. Alma-Ata, 79 : 38-46.

1306 DAMBAEVA, V. D. "Socialističeskij obraz žizni i nekotorye aspekty duhovnogo mira sovremennogo molodogo pokolenija" (The socialist way of life and some aspects of the contemporary young generation spiritual world), *IN: Utverždenie sovetskogo obraza žizni v Kazahstane i voprosy vospitanija novogo čeloveka*. Alma-Ata, 79 : 46-53.

1307 DANILOV, V. K. "Socialističeskij obraz žizni i ėgo ėkonomičeskij aspekt" (The socialist way of life and its economic aspect), *IN: Razvitie obščestvennogo truda i potrebnostej v uslovijah razvitogo socializma*. Moskva, 79 : 59-74.

1308 DAVYDOV, Ju. N. "Kontrkul'tura i krizis socializacii molodeži" (Counterculture and crisis of the youth socialization), *IN: Molodež', NTR, kapitalizm*. Moskva, 79 : 245-287.

1309 DENISKO, L. N.; ĖFIMEC, V. D. "Socialističeskij obraz žizni i obščestvennye idealy sovetskogo studenčestva" (The socialist way of life and the Soviet students social ideals), *Problemy Filosofii* 48, 79 : 61-66.

1310 DMITRIEV, A. N.; DMITRIEVA, Ė. Ja. "Kul'tura, mirovozzrenie, tvorčestvo i ličnost" (Culture, world conception, creation and personality), *Naučnye Trudy Kujbyševskogo pedagogičeskogo Instituta* 198, 77 : 55-64.

1311 DOUGLAS, Jack D.; [et al.]. *Introduction to the sociologies of everyday life*. Boston, Allyn and Bacon, 80, xiii-201 p.

1312 DŽABBAROV, I. M. "Sovetskij obraz žizni i preodolenie perežitkov Islama v bytu" (The Soviet way of life and the Islam survival elimination in customs), *IN: Voprosy teorii i praktiki ateističeskogo vospitanija*. Taškent, 79 : 154-170.

1313 ERDEI, Ferenc. *A magyar társadalomról* (On Hungarian society). Budapest, Adadémiai Kiadó, 80, 402 p.

1314 FARUŠKIN, M.; PADERIN, V. "Internacionalizm našego obraza žizni" (Internationalism of our way of life), *Kommunist Tatarii* 79 : 79-84.

1315 FREEDMAN, Maurice. *The study of Chinese society: essays*. Stanford, CA, Stanford University Press, 79, xxiv-491 p. CR: Stephan FEUCHTWANG, *British Journal of Sociology* 31(4), dec 80 : 598-600. [edited by G. W. Skinner.]

1316 FRY, John Allan; [ed.]. *Economy, class and social reality: issues in contemporary Canadian society*. Toronto, Butterworths, 79, viii-459 p.

1317 GEERTZ, Clifford; GEERTZ, Hildred; ROSEN, Lawrence. *Meaning and order in Moroccan society: three essays in cultural analysis.* Cambridge, Cambridge University Press, 79, xii-510 p.
1318 GINER, Salvador. *Sociedad masa: crítica del pensamiento conservador* (Mass society: criticism of the conservative thought). Barcelona, Ediciones Península, 79, 429 p.
1319 GONZALEZ GAVIOLA, Horacio. *Sociología básica, cómo funciona una sociedad?* (Basic sociology, how a society is functioning). Buenos Aires, Paulina, 80, 104 p.
1320 GONZÁLEZ, Mariano. *Análisis dialéctico de la sociedad española: estructura, clases, contradicciones* (Dialectical analysis of Spanish society: structure, social classes, contradictions). Madrid, HOAC, 79, 511 p.
1321 GOTTLIEB, Roger S. "The dialectics of national identity: left-wing antisemitism and the Arab-Israeli conflict", *Socialist Review* sep-oct 79 : 19-52.
1322 HABIBULIN, K. A.; [ed.]. *Cennostnye orientacii socialističeskogo obraza žizni* (Valuable orientations of the socialist way of life). Leningrad, Leningradskij Gosudarstvennyj Pedatogičeskij Institut imeni A. I. Gercena, 79, 166 p.
1323 HAGUE, John A.; [ed.]. *American character and culture in a changing world: some twentieth-century perspectives.* Westport, CT, Greenwood Press, 79, xiv-395 p.
1324 HAJKO, Dalimír. *Filozofia a socialistická kultúra* (Philosophy and socialist culture). Bratislava, Veda, 79, 111 p.
1325 HALLIK, K. S. "Nacional'nye i internacional'noe v socialističeskom obraze žizni" (National and international in the socialist way of life), IN: *Socialističeskij obraz žizni. I.* Tallin, 78 : 19-30.
1326 HAMA, Hideo. "'Nichijo' no shakaigaku — Nichijo seikatsu no sekai to rikai shakaigaku" (Alfred Schutz and the sociology of Alltag: World of everyday life and interpretative sociology), *Osaka daigaku nenpo ningen kagaku* 80 : 113-126.
1327 HANOVA, O. V. "Ponjatie kul'tury i ėgo vzaimosvjaz's ponjatiem obraza žizni" (Culture concept and its interaction with the way of life concept), *Metodologičeskie Voprosy Nauki* 78 : 112-132.
1328 HARE, A. Paul; SAVAGE, Michael. "Sociology of South Africa", *Annual Review of Sociology* 79 : 329-350.
1329 HARE, Alexander Paul; WIENDIECK, Gerd; BROEMBSEN, Max H. von; [eds.]. *South Africa: sociological analyses.* Cape Town, New York, Oxford University Press, 79, 430 p.
1330 HARRIS, Marvin. *Cultural materialism: the struggle for a science of culture.* New York, Random House, 79, xii-381 p. CR: PRYOR, Frederic L., *Journal of economic Literature* 18(1), mar 80: 106-109.
1331 HASHIZUME, Daisaburo. "Shakai wa hitotsuno sochi deatte, shakaiteki genjitsu o umidasu" (Society is an apparatus which produces social realities), *Soshiorogosu* 80 : 102-109.
1332 HEBDIGE, Dick. *Subculture, the meaning of style.* London, Methuen, 79, viii-195 p.
1333 HIMELFARB, Alexander; RICHARDSON, C. James. *People, power, and process: sociology for Canadians.* Toronto, New York, McGraw-Hill Ryerson, 79, 353 p.
1334 HUSZÁR, Tibor. *Contemporary Hungarian society.* Budapest, Corvina, 79, 48 p.
1335 HYDYROV, T. "Internacionalizm socialističeskogo obraza žizni i kritika domyslov antikommunistov o nacional'nyh otnošenijah v SSSR" (Internationalism of the socialist way of life and critics of anticommunist conceptions on national relations in the USSR), *Izvestija Akademii Nauk Turkmenskoj SSR. Serija obščestvennaja Nauk* 79 : 3-9.
1336 IKEDA, Yoshisuke; TOYOSHIMA, Kakujō; TAKAHASHI, Noriaki; [eds.]. *Gendai shakai to shakaigaku* (Modern society and sociology). Kyoto, Horitsu bunkasha, 80, 310 p.
1337 IOANID, Ileana. *Societati şi cultură* (Society and culture). Bucureşti, Editura Politică, 79, 227 p.
1338 IOVČUK, M. T.; KOGAN, L. N. "Duhovnaja kul'tura socializma" (Socialism spiritual culture), IN: *Konstitucija obščenarodnogo gosudarstva. Voprosy teorii.* Moskva, 79 : 162-187.
1339 IVANOV, Ė. I. "K izučeniju socialističeskogo obraza žizni" (On the socialist way of life research), IN: *Metodologičeskie i social'nye problemy razvitija nauki.* Moskva, 79 : 58-65.
1340 IVANOV, Ė. I. "Metodologičeskie problemy izučenija socialističeskogo obraza žizni. Nauka i obraz žizni" (Methodological problems of the socialist way of life study. Science and way of life), IN: *Osnovy obščestvennogo stroja i politiki SSSR.* Moskva, 79 : 89-94.
1341 JAGCHID, Sechin; HYER, Paul. *Mongolia's culture and society.* Boulder, Colo., Westview Press, 79, xvi-461 p.

1342 JAVEAU, Claude. "Sur le concept de vie quotidienne et sa sociologie", *Cahiers internationaux de Sociologie* 68, jan-jun 80 : 31-45.

1343 JENSEN, Stefan; NAUMANN, Jens. "Commitments — Medienkomponente einer ökonomischen Kulturtheorie?" (Commitments. Media components of an economic theory of culture), *Zeitschrift für Soziologie* jan 80 : 79-99.

1344 JOHNSON, Lesley. *The cultural critics: from Matthew Arnold to Raymond Williams*. London, Boston, Routledge & Kegan Paul, 79, viii-235 p.

1345 JOHNSTON, Barry V.; DASILVA, Fabio. "Conceptualizing ideational culture: a critique and phenomenological alternative", *International Journal of contemporary Sociology* 15(3-4), jul-oct 78 : 292-302.

1346 KALBOUSS, George. *Russian culture: an outline*. Columbus, Ohio State University Libraries Publications Committee, 79, iv-203 p.

1347 KALIKA, Ju. A.; [ed.]. *Socialističeskij obraz žizni i ideologičeskaja bor'ba: ukazatel' literatury opublikovannoj v SSR v 1967-1978 gg.* (The socialist way of life and the ideological struggle: a review of the literature published in the USSR in the 1976-1978 years). Moskva, INION AN SSSR, 79, 155 p.

1348 KASPI, André. *La Vie quotidienne aux États-Unis au temps de la prospérité: 1919-1929*. Paris, Hachette, 80, 349 p.

1349 KASPI, André; BERTRAND, Claude-Jean; HEFFER, Jean. *La civilisation américaine*. Paris, Presses universitaires de France, 79, 437 p.

1350 KEJZEROV, N. "Obraz žizni v bor'be idej" (The way of life in the ideological struggle), *Pod Znamenem Leninizma* 79 : 56-61.

1351 KIDA, Akio. "'Shakai' gainen o megutte (ge)"(On the category of "Society"), *Atarashii shakaigaku no tameni* 20, 80 : 22-33.

1352 KISELEV, N. N.; TOŠČENKO, Ž. T. "Soveršenstvovanie socialističeskogo obraza žizni kak problema upravlenija" (The socialist way of life improvement as a management problem), *Problemy naučnogo Kommunizma (Moskva)* 13, 79 : 44-66.

1353 KOBECKIJ, V. D.; SAVEL'EV, S. N. "Stanovlenie sovetskogo obraza žizni i preodolenie religioznogo byta" (The Soviet way of life in the future and the elimination of religious customs), *IN: Social'no filosofskie aspekty kritiki religii*. Leningrad, 79 : 28-39.

1354 KOGAN, L. N. "Socialističeskaja kul'tura i vsestoronnee garmoničeskoe razvitie ličnosti" (Socialist culture and harmonious personality development), *IN: Vsestoronnee razvitie ličnosti sovetskogo čeloveka*. Sverdlovsk, 79 : 5-17.

1355 KONYK, G. "NTR i socialističeskij obraz žizni" (The scientific and technical revolution and the socialist way of life), *Kommunist Tatarii* 12, 79 : 27-34.

1356 KULCSÁR, Kálmán. *A mai magyar társadalom*(The contemporary Hungarian society). Budapest, Kossuth Kiadó, 80, 329 p.

1357 KUZNECOV, A. G.; SIL'DMJAE, T. I. "Voprosy matematiko-statističeskogo modelirovanija obraza žizni" (Questions on the way of life mathematical and statistical models elaboration), *IN: Trud kak osnova socialističeskogo obraza žizni*. Moskva, 79 : 181-201.

1358 LAR'KOV, A. M. *Nacii i nacional'nye otnošenija razvitogo socialističeskogo obščestva* (Nations and national relations in the developed socialist society). Moskva, Izdatel'stvo Moskovskogo Universiteta, 80, 147 p.

1359 LEVAŠOV, V. I.; UDARCEVA, I. F. "Nckotorye problemy soveršenstvovanija socialističeskogo obraza žizni" (Some problems concerning improvement in the socialist way of life), *IN: Osnovy obščestvennogo stroja i politiki SSSR*. Moskva, 79 : 95-103.

1360 LEVIT, S. Ja.; [ed.]. *Socialističeskaja kul'tura, obraz žizni i ličnost'* (The socialist culture, way of life and personality). Moskva, INION AN SSSR, 79, 231 p.

1361 LIRUS, Julie. *Identité antillaise: contribution à la connaissance psychologique et anthropologique des Guadeloupéens et des Martiniquais*. Paris, Éditions caribéennes, 79, 263 p.

1362 LIVŠIC, Ju. M.; PAROL', V. I. "Socialističeskij obraz žizni kak kriterij razvitogo socializma" (The socialist way of life as a developed socialism criticism), *IN: Social'nye processy razvitogo socialističeskogo obščestva i ideologičeskaja bor'ba*. Tallin, 79 : 112-118.

1363 LYONS, Francis Stewart Leland. *Culture and anarchy in Ireland, 1890-1939*. Oxford, Clarendon Press, New York, Oxford University Press, 79, vi-184 p.

1364 MAEYAMA, Takashi. "Brazil no bunka to kachi taikei ni tsuite no shiron" (On culture and value system in Brazil — A preliminary note), *Tsukuba daigaku Latin America tokubetsu project nenji hokokusho* 80 : 51-61.

1365 MAFFESOLI, Michel. *La Conquête du présent: pour une sociologie de la vie quotidienne*. Paris, Presses universitaires de France, 79, 200 p.

1366 MANN, Arthur. *The one and the many: reflections on the American identity*. Chicago, University of Chicago Press, 79, xii-209 p.

1367 MINAMI, Hiroshi. *Nihonjin no shinri to seikatsu* (Psychology and life of the Japanese people). Tokyo, Keiso shobo, 80, 3rd, 420 p.

1368 MORIN, Michel; BERTRAND, Claude. *Le territoire imaginaire de la culture*. Montréal, Hurtubise HMH, 79, 182 p.

1369 MURNIEK, Ē. Ē. "Socialistićeskij obraz žizni: tendencii razvitija na sele: po materialam Latvijskoj SSR" (The socialist way of life: tendencies of its development in a village: from the Letton SSR materials), *Izvestija Akademii Nauk latvijskoj SSR* 79 : 62-73.

1370 NAGY, Katalin S. *Eredmények a lakáskultúra vizsgálatból* (Results of the research about life style and taste in connection with dwelling habits). Budapest, Népművelési Intézet, 79, 53 p.

1371 NAKAMOTO, Hiromichi; HISHIYAMA, Kenji. *Shakai genron* (Principles of society). Tokyo, Aoki shoten, 80, 269 p.

1372 NEKIPELOVA, L. V. "Dialektika nacional'nogo i internacional'nogo v socialistićeskom obraze žizni" (Dialectics of the national and the international in the socialist way of life), *IN: Dialektika social'nogo poznanija*. Moskva, 79 : 73-78.

1373 O'CONNELL, Agnes N. "Correlates of life style: personality, role concept, attitudes, influences and choices", *Human Relations* 33, aug 80 : 589-601.

1374 OGMUNDSON, R. "Toward study of the endangered species known as the anglophone Canadian", *Canadian Journal of Sociology* 80 : 1-12.

1375 OVČINSKIJ, V. S. "Obraz žizni kak ob'ekt kriminologićeskogo izučenija" (Way of life as an object of criminological study), *Trudy Omskogo vysšej Školy Milicii* 28, 78 : 91-102.

1376 PETERMANN, Thomas. *Claude-Henri de Saint-Simon: die Gesellschaft als Werkstatt* (Claude-Henri de Saint-Simon: society as workshop). Berlin, Duncker und Humblot, 79, 241 p. CR: Richard Martinus EMGE, *Kölner Zeitschrift für Soziologie und Sozialpsychologie* 32(3), sep 80: 605-606.

1377 PETERSON, Richard A. "Revitalizing the culture concept", *Annual Review of Sociology* 79 : 137-166.

1378 POLENBERG, Richard. *One nation divisible: class, race, and ethnicity in the United States since 1938*. New York, Viking Press, 80, 363 p.

1379 POPOV, S. I. "Vzaimosvjaz' meždu količestvennymi i kačestvennymi harakteristikami obrazov žizni" (Interaction between quantitative and qualitative characteristics of way of life), *IN: Social'naja struktura sovetskogo obšćestva i socialistićeskij obraz žizni. II.* Moskva, 78 : 5-14.

1380 POPOVA, I. M. "Koncepcija stimulirovanija i problemy social'nogo regulirovanija obraza žizni" (Stimulation conception and problems of the way of life social regulation), *IN: Social'naja struktura sovetskogo obšćestva i socialistićeskij obraz žizni. II.* Moskva, 78 : 83-94.

1381 PURTOV, V. I. "K voprosu o metodologii issledovanija obraza žizni" (On the methodology of the way of life research), *Problemy Filosofii* 48, 79 : 132-135.

1382 RASULOV, R. A. "Nacional'nye interesy v razvitom socialistićeskom obšćestve SSSR" (National interests in the USSR developed socialist society), *Naučyne Trudy Azerbajdžanskogo Universiteta. Serija juridićeskij Nauk* 79 : 59-64.

1383 ROBINSON, David J.; [ed.]. *Social fabric and spatial structure in colonial Latin America*. Ann Arbor, MI, published for the Dept. of Geography, Syracuse University by University Microfilms International, 79, xviii-478 p.

1384 ROGOVIN, V. Z. "Kačestvennaja storono obraza žizni obšćestva kak kriterij social'nogo progressa" (The society way of life qualitative aspect as a criterion of social progress), *IN: Social'naja struktura sovetskogo obšćestva i socialistićeskij obraz žizni. II.* Moskva, 78 : 30-40.

1385 RONCERAY, Hubert de; [ed.]. *Sociologie du fait haïtien*. Québec, Presses de l'Université du Québec, 79, xvi-270 p.

1386 ŠABUROVA, L. A. "Voprosy obraza žizni v teorii naučnogo kommunizma" (Way of life questions in the theory of scientific communism), *IN: Social'nye i poltićeskie otnošenija v razvitom socialistićeskom obšćestve*. 79 : 116-125.

1387 SCHIRAY, Michel; SIGAL, Silvia. "Expérimentations sociales et changement de styles de vie", *Politique aujourd'hui* 7-8, 79 : 91-103.

1388 SELIVERSTOVAJA, T. N.; [ed.]. *Problemy socialistićeskogo obraza žizni v uslovijah razvitogo socializma* (Problems of the socialist way of life under conditions of developed socialism). Moskva, Izdatel'stvo Moskovskogo Universiteta, 80, 123 p.

1389 SINGHAL, D. P. *Modern Indian society and culture.* Meerut, Meenakshi, 80, vi-280 p.
1390 ŠINKARUK, V. I. ; [ed.]. *Socialističeskij obraz žizni i vsestoronnee razvitie ličnosti* (The socialist way of life and the personality global development). Kiev, Naukova Dumka, 79, 343 p.
1391 SMITH, Richard Joseph. *Traditional Chinese culture: an interpretive introduction.* Houston, TX, William Marsh Rice University, 79, iii-74 p.
1392 SOLOŠENKO, V. I. "Socialističeskij obraz žizni i razvitie ličnosti" (The socialist way of life and the personality development), *IN: XXV s'ezd KPSS i voprosy social'no-političeskogo razvitija sovetskogo obščestva.* Minsk, 79 : 140-159.
1393 SOW, Alpha I.; [et al.]. *Introduction to African culture: general aspects.* Paris, UNESCO, 79, 184 p.
1394 SPEARRITT, Peter; WALKER, David Robert; [eds.]. *Australian popular culture.* Sydney, Boston, Allen & Unwin, 79, x-255 p.
1395 SWARTZ, Marc J.; JORDAN DAVID K. *Culture: the anthropological perspective.* New York, Wiley, 80, vi-476 p.
1396 SZÁNTÓ, Miklós; [ed.]. *Tanulmányok az életmódról* (Studies on the way of life). Budapest, Gondolat, 80, 285 p.
1397 SZÁNTÓ, Miklós; [ed.]. *Ways of life. Hungarian sociological studies.* Budapest, Corvina Pr., 77, 404 p.
1398 TAKENAKA, Kazuo; KOMAI, Hiroshi; [eds.]. *Gendai shakairon* (Contemporary society). Tokyo, Nihon hyoronsha, 80, 268 p.
1399 TITMA, M. H. "Sub'ektivnye predposylki socialističeskogo obraze žizni" (Subjective conditions of the socialist way of life), *IN: Socialističeskij obraz žizni. I.* 78 : 69-79.
1400 TRAVIN, I. I. *Material'no-veščnaja sreda i socialističeskij obraz žizni* (Material environment and the socialist way of life). Leningrad, Nauka, 79, 117 p.
1401 TYHEEVA, Ju. C. "Metodologičeskie problemy issledovanija obraza žizni" (Methodological problems of the way of life research), *IN: Dialektika social'nogo poznanija.* Moskva, 79 : 67-73.
1402 VAN STEENBERGEN, Bart; FELLER, Gordon. "Emerging lifestyle movements: alternative to overdevelopment", *Alternatives* nov 79 : 275-305.
1403 VIZITEJ, É. "Socialističeskij obraz žizni i éstetičeskaja kul'tura" (The socialist way of life and aesthetic culture), *Kommunist Moldavii* 79 : 83-85.
1404 Bibl.XXIX-1240. WILLIS, Paul E. *Profane culture.* CR: Will WRIGHT, *American Journal of Sociology* 85(5), mar 80: 1312-1316.
1405 WOLF, Mauro. *Sociologie della vita quotidiana*(Sociology of everyday life). Roma, L'espresso, 79, 217 p.
1406 ZOPF, Paul E. *Cultural accumulation in Latin America.* Washington, DC, University Press of America, 80, viii-385 p.

13130. Cultural dynamics. Cultural relations
Dynamique culturelle. Relations culturelles

1407 AL-CHARIM, Maher. *Le Patrimoine culturel palestinien.* Paris, le Sycomore, 80, 233 p.
1408 ALCOCK, Antony E.; TAYLOR, Brian K.; WELTON, John M.; [eds.]. *The Future of cultural minorities.* New York, St. Martin's Press, 79, viii-221 p.
1409 ANDER, Oscar Fritiof. *The cultural heritage of the Swedish immigrant: selected references.* New York, Arno Press, 79, xix-191 p.
1410 ASANTE, Molefi Kete; [et al.]; [eds.]. *Handbook of intercultural communication.* Beverly Hills, CA, Sage Publications, 79, 482 p.
1411 AVRAMENKO, V. N. "Kul'turnye potrebnosti v sisteme faktorov razvitija socialističeskogo obraza žizni" (Cultural needs in the development factors system of the socialist way of life), *IN: XXV s'ezd KPSS i problemy kul'tury razvitogo socializma.* Moskva, 79 : 52-72.
1412 BASIN, É. Ja. "Prestižnoe prisvoenie kul'tury kak harakternaja čerta buržuaznogo obraza žizni" (Culture distinguished assimilation as a characteristic aspect of the bourgeois way of life), *IN: Sociologičeskie problemy obrazovanija, kul'tury i nauki.* Moskva, 78 : 94-104.
1413 CAMILLERI, C. "Crise socio-culturelle et crise d'identité dans les sociétés du Tiers-Monde: l'exemple des sociétés maghrébines", *Psychologie française* 24(3-4), 79 : 259-268.
1414 CH'ÊN, Jerome. *China and the West: society and culture, 1815-1937.* Bloomington, Indiana University Press, 79, 488 p.

1415 CHU, Godwin C.; HSU, Francis L. K.; [eds.]. *Moving a mountain: cultural change in China.* Honolulu, University Press of Hawaii, 79, ix-446 p. CR: Alan P. L. LIU, *American political Science Review* 74(3), sep 80: 838-839.
1416 DALES, Richard C. *The intellectual life of western Europe in the middle ages.* Washington, University Press of America, 80, 313 p.
1417 EISENSTADT, S. N. "Cultural orientations, institutional entrepreneurs, and social change: comparative analysis of traditional civilizations", *American Journal of Sociology* 85, jan 80 : 840-869.
1418 ELIOU, Marie. "Érosion et permanence de l'identité culturelle", *Cahiers internationaux de Sociologie* 66, jan-jun 79 : 79-90.
1419 GAMŌ, Masao; SHIMODA, Naoharu; YAMAGUCHI, Masao; [eds.]. *Rekishi-teki bunka-zō — Nishimura, Asahitaro hakase koki kinen* (Historical picture of culture: essays in memory of Dr. Asahitaro Nishimura). Tokyo, Shinsensha, 443 p.
1420 GOLOVNEV, A. I.; MEL'NIKOV, A. P. *Sbliženie nacional'nyh kul'tur v processe kommunističeskogo stroitel'stva* (The bringing together of national cultures in the process of communism edification). Minsk, BGU imeni V. I. Lenina, 79, 176 p.
1421 GONČARENKO, N. V. "Preemstvennost' kak faktor razvitija kul'tury" (Heritage as a factor of culture development), IN: *Sociolgičeskie problemy obrazovanija, kul'tury i nauki.* Moskva, 78 : 62-72.
1422 GRANDGUILLAUME, Gilbert. "Langue, identité et culture nationale au Maghreb", *Peuples méditerranéens/Mediterranean Peoples* oct-dec 79 : 3-28.
1423 HARVEY, Edwin R. *Cultural policy in Argentina.* Paris, Unesco, 79, 92 p.
1424 INDOVINA, Emma. "Confronto tra aggregazione culturale e poli di sviluppo nel Messinese" (Confrontation between cultural aggregation and development poles in the Messine era), *Sociologia (Roma)* 13(2-3), mai-dec 79 : 223-238.
1425 KREISEL, Werner. "Assimilation in Hawaii am Beispiel des Vordringens der englischen Sprache" (Assimilation in Hawaii, exemplified by the advance of the English language), *Sociologus* 30, 80 : 29-51.
1426 LEVY, Emanuel. "National and imported culture in Israel", *Sociological Focus* 13, jan 80 : 37-53.
1427 LIEGEOIS, Jean-Pierre. "Le discours de l'ordre, pouvoirs publics et minorités culturelles", *Esprit* mai 80 : 17-44.
1428 MITTERLING, Philip I. *U.S. cultural history: a guide to information sources.* Detroit, Gale Research Co., 80, ix-581 p.
1429 MOODIE, Meredith Aldrich. "The development of national identity in white South African schoolchildren", *Journal of social Psychology* 111, aug 80 : 169-180.
1430 ORIOL, Michel. "Identité produite, identité instituée, identité exprimée: confusions des théories de l'identité nationale et culturelle", *Cahiers internationaux de Sociologie* 66, jan-jun 79 : 19-28.
1431 PIRZIO-BIROLI, Detalmo. *Rivoluzione culturale africana* (African cultural revolution). Roma, Bari, Laterza, 79, 274 p.
1432 POCHE, Bernard. "Mouvement régional et fondements territoriaux de l'identité sociale: le mouvement régionaliste savoyard", *Cahiers internationaux de Sociologie* 66, jan-jun 79 : 63-77.
1433 REMY, Jean; VOYÉ, Liliane. "Le mouvement flamand, dialectique du culturel et de l'économique", *Plural Societies* 10, sum 79 : 3-36.
1434 SÁGI, Mária; VITÁNYI, Iván. *The transmission of culture in the family in the age of the scientific-technical revolution.* Budapest, Institute for Culture, 80, 27 p. ;961[Hungary.]
1435 SCHAFER, D. Paul. *Canada's international cultural relations.* Ottawa, Department of External Affairs, 79, 66 p.
1436 SOLE, Carlota. "La identificación de los immigrantes con la 'cultura catalana'" (Assimilation of the Catalan culture by the immigrants), *Revista española de Investigaciones socioloógicas* jan-mar 80 : 119-137.
1437 SUBRAMANIAM, Venkateswarier. *Cultural integration in India: a socio-historical analysis.* New Delhi, Ashish, 79, 228 p.
1438 SUSATO, Shigeru; [ed.]. *Bunka no hendō -hendō no jidai* (Cultural change in modern Japan). Tokyo, Asakura shoten, 80, 252 p.
1439 TIBI, Bassam. "Akkulturation und interkulturelle Kommunikation: ist jede Verwestlichung kulturimperialistisch?" (Acculturation and intercultural communication. Is always westernization culturally imperialist?), *Gegenwartskunde* 29, 80 : 173-190.
1440 VELTMAN, Calvin J. "Le sort de la francophonie aux États-Unis", *Cahiers québécois de Démographie* apr 80 : 43-58.

1441 VIŠNEVSKIJ, Ju. R. "Ědinstvo socialističeskoj kul'tury i vsestoronnee razvitie ličnosti" (The socialist culture unity and the global development of personality), *Sbornik naučnyh Trudov (Sverdlovskij pedagogičeskij Institut)* 315, 79 : 44-55.

13140. Norm. Social control. Value
Norme. Régulation sociale. Valeur

[See also / voir aussi: 247, 642, 874, 1084, 1171, 1364, 1493, 1505, 1557, 1578, 1579, 1591, 1595, 1789, 2066, 2086, 2362, 2576, 2706, 2766, 2867, 3035, 3540, 3552, 4067, 4599, 4702, 4964, 5084, 5279, 5280, 5337, 5357, 5421, 5434, 5535, 6039, 6235]

1442 "Nouvelles approches des structures artificielles dans les sociétés industrielles. Actes du colloque des 2-3-4 février 1979: autonomisation des artefacts dans les sociétés industrielles", *Connexions* 30, 80 : 7-113.

1443 AKIMOVA, V. V. "Kul'tura proizvodstva v sisteme cennostej socialističeskogo obraza žizni" (Culture production in the systems of the socialist way of life values), *IN: Cennostnye orientacii socialističeskogo obraza žizni.* Leningrad, 79 : 58-66.

1444 BABAJAN, L. V. "Ob internacionalizacii cennostnyh orientacij v meždunacional'nom obščenii" (On the internationalization of value orientations in the international public opinion), *IN: Cennostnye orientacii socialističeskogo obraza žizni.* Leningrad, 79 : 135-140.

1445 BRATT, Nancy. *Samfund, normer og normdannelse* (Society, norms and norm conformity). København, Forum, 79, 214 p.

1446 BREWER, Harold. *The dominant society: power politics of the future.* Ventura, CA, Toy Piper Press, 80, 252 p.

1447 ČALDAROVIČ, Mladen. "Odnos vrednota i pojedinih oblika društvene svijesti" (The relationship of values and individual forms of social consciousness), *Revija za Sociologiju* (1-2), 78 : 16-28.

1448 CHU, Lily. "The sensitivity of Chinese and American children to social influences", *Journal of social Psychology* 109, dec 79 : 175-186.

1449 COMSTOCK, Donald E. "Dimensions of influence in organizations", *Pacific sociological Review* 23, jan 80 : 67-84.

1450 CROZIER, Michel. "La transformation des modes de contrôle social et la crise des régulations traditionnelles", *Tocqueville Review* wint 80 : 40-54.

1451 CURTIS, Bruce; EDGINTON, Barry. "Uneven institutional development and the 'staple' approach: a problem of method", *Canadian Journal of Sociology* 79 : 257-273.

1452 DILLINGHAM, Gerald. "The value stretch: an empirical test", *Sociology and social Research* 64, jan 80 : 249-262.

1453 DIÓSI, Pál. *Csoportviszonyok és értékválasztások a Frankovics Ifjúsági Klubban. Esettanulmány* (Group situation and choice of values at a youth education centre. A case study). Budapest, Népművelési Propaganda Iroda, 79, 100 p.

1454 DOMHOFF, G. William; [ed.]. "Power structure research", *Insurgent Sociologist* (2-3), aut 79-wint 80 : 3-142.

1455 DUX, Günther. "Der Ursprung der Normen. Die Bedeutung der Sprache für ihre Entwicklung" (The origin of norms. The meaning of language for their development), *Archiv für Rechts und Sozialphilosophie* 66, 80 : 53-76.

1456 ĚVTUŠENKO, I. I. "K voprosu o social'nyh cennostjah i aktivnosti ličnosti" (Question on social values and the personality activity), *IN: Istoričeskij materializm i sovremennoe obščestvennoe razvitie.* Moskva, 79 : 102-110.

1457 FOUREZ, Gérard. *Choix éthiques et conditionnement social: introduction à une philosophie morale.* Paris, Le Centurion, 79, 253 p.

1458 GANESH, S. R. "From thin air to firm ground: empirical guidelines for a general processual model of institution building", *Human Relations* 32, sep 79 : 751-779.

1459 Bibl.XXIX-1329. GOLDENBERG, I. Ira. *Oppression and social intervention.* CR: RULE, James B., *Contemporary Sociology (Albany)* 9(4), jul 80: 580.

1460 GOLOTA, V. S. "K probleme vzaimosvjazi social'nyh norm v processe upravlenija" (On the social norms interaction in the management process), *IN: Problemy upravlenija v uslovijah razvitogo socializma.* Moskva, 79 : 28-39.

1461 GOLOTA, V. S. "O ponjatii sistemy social'nyh norm razvitogo socialističeskogo obščestva" (On the social norms system of the developed socialist society), *IN: Social'nye i političeskie otnosenija v razvitom socialističeskom obščestve.* Moskva, 79 : 39-47.

1462 GRABB, Edward G. "Differences in sense of control among French- and English-Canadian adolescents", *Canadian Review of Sociology and Anthropology* 17, mai 80 : 169-175.
1463 HAFERKAMP, Hans. "Normbildung und Gesetzgebung im Theorienvergleich" (Norm formation and legislation in theoretical comparison), *Kölner Zeitschrift für Soziologie und Sozialpsychologie* 32, 80 : 296-311.
1464 HODŽIĆ, Alija. "Vrijednosne orijentacije omladine" (Value orientations of young people), *Revija za Sociologiju* (1-2), 78 : 54-61.
1465 JACOBSEN, Chanoch; VAN DER VOORDT, Theo J. M. "Interpreting modal frequencies to measure social norms", *Sociological Methods and Research* mai 80 : 470-486.
1466 KAPITÁNY, Ágnes; KAPITÁNY, Gábor. *Rendetlen, értékek, értéktelen rendek avagy: Utelágazásnál táblák nélkül* (Disordered values — valueless order: in other words: at a crossroad without road marks). Budapest, Népművelési Intézet, 80, 100 p.
1467 KAZAMA, Daiji; AKIYAMA, Toyoko. "Japanese value orientations: persistence and change", *Studies of Broadcasting* 16, mar 80 : 5-26.
1468 KLAGES, Helmut; KMIECIAK, Peter; [eds.]. *Wertwandel und gesellschaftlicher Wandel* (Value change and social change). Frankfurt/Main, New York, Campus-Verlag, 79, 725 p.
1469 KONOPLEV, V. F. "Vlijanie cennostnoj orientacii učitelja na formirovanie ličnosti škol'nika" (Influence of the teacher's value orientation on the student's personality formation), *IN: Cennostnye orientacii socialističeskogo obraza žizni.* Leningrad, 79 : 108-118.
1470 KUKUŠKIN, V. I. "Ob internacionalizacii cennostnyh orientacij molodeži v uslovijah socialističeskogo obraza žizni" (On the internationalization of the youth value orientations under conditions of the socialist way of life), *IN: Cennostnye orientacii socialističeskogo obraza žizni.* Leningrad, 79 : 125-135.
1471 LAMO DE ESPINOSA, Emilio. "Marx y la teoría del poder social extraño" (Marx and the theory of the foreign social power), *Sistema. Revista de Ciencias sociales* 34, 80 : 3-36.
1472 LEBEDEV, L. K.; KRONEVAL'D, I. I. "Vlijanie kul'turnyh potrebnostej na cennostnye orientacii ličnosti" (The cultural needs influence on the personality value orientations), *IN: Cennostnye orientacii socialističeskogo obraza žizni.* Leningrad, 79 : 86-95.
1473 LISTVIN, V. F.; KLIMOV, V. A. "Kontrol' kak funcii socialističeskogo upravlenija" (Control as a socialist management function), *IN: Aktual'nye voprosy social'no-politiceskogo razvitija obščestva v uslovijah zrelogo socializma.* Saratov, 79 : 96-115.
1474 LIVET, Pierre. "Modèles de sociétés: clôture du pouvoir et consommation de pouvoirs", *Cahiers internationaux de Sociologie* 67, jul-dec 79 : 277-295.
1475 LJAHOVA, L. N. "Social'nye normy kak forma obščestvennogo samoregulirovanija" (Social norms as a form of social self-regulation), *IN: Metodologija upravlenija obščestvennymi sistemami v uslovijah razvitogo socializma.* Izevsk, 78 : 54-62.
1476 MAJOROVA, È. F.; MILOSLAVOVA, I. A. "Vlijanie sem'i na samorealizaciju i formirovanie social'no-političeskoj orientacii podrostka" (The family influence on the self-realization and formation of the adolescent's socio-political orientation), *IN: Cennostnye orientacii socialističeskogo obraza žizni.* Leningrad, 79 : 149-158.
1477 MEYER, Ruth. "Cambio de valores en la población suiza" (Change of values in the Swiss population), *Revista española de Investigaciones sociológicas* jul-sep 79 : 7-34.
1478 MUGNY, Gabriel; DOISE, Willem. "Niveaux d'analyse dans l'étude expérimentale des processus d'influence sociale", *Social Science Information* 18, 79 : 819-876.
1479 OGRYZKOV, V. M. "Sociologičeskie aspekty standartizacii" (Sociological aspects of standardization), *Sociologičeskie Issledovanija* 79 : 95-100.
1480 PAZY, Asya; LOMRANZ, Jacob. "Value conceptions of American and Israeli youth", *Journal of social Psychology* 111, aug 80 : 181-187.
1481 PLAHOV, V. D. "Social'nye normy i cennostyne orientacii" (Social norms and value orientations), *Ličnost' i Obščestvo* 79 : 22-31.
1482 POPA, Cornel. "Sisteme de norme, libertate şi aspiratii in societatea socialista" (Norm systems, freedom and aspirations in socialist society), *Revista de Filozofie* 26, sep-oct 79 : 561-568.
1483 RANKIN, William L.; GRUBE, Joel A. "A comparison of ranking and rating procedures for value system measurement", *European Journal of social Psychology* 10, jul-sep 80 : 233-246.
1484 ROBERTS, Alden E.; GILLESPIE, David F. "Durkheim revisited: a critique of Hirschi's control theory", *Indian Journal of social Research* 20, apr 79 : 45-48.

1485 RUSSELL, J. Curtis; FIRESTONE, Ira J.; BARON, Reuben M. "Seating arrangement and social influence: moderated by reinforcement meaning and internal-external control", *Social Psychology Quarterly* 43, mar 80 : 103-109.

1486 SELWYN, T. "The order of men and the order of things: an examination of food transactions in an Indian Village", *International Journal of the Sociology of Law* aug 80 : 297-317.

1487 SIRIN, A. D. *Specifika zakonov obščestva i ih rol' v regulirovanii obščestvennyh processov* (The society laws specificity and their role in the social processes regulation). Tomsk, Izdatel'stvo Tomskogo Universiteta, 79, 208 p.

1488 SZEBENYI, Péterné. *Társadalmunk normái középiskolások tudatában* (Social norms in the mind of grammar school pupils). Budapest, Tankönyvkiadó, 80, 408 p.

1489 TAYLOR, Steven J.; BOGDAN, Robert. "Defending illusions: the institution's struggle for survival", *Human Organization* 39, 80 : 209-218.

1490 VIŠNEVSKIJ, Ju. R. "Cennostnye orientacii v sisteme ědinoj socialističeskoj kul'tury" (Value orientations in the system of the unique socialist culture), *IN: Cennostnye orientacii socialističeskogo obraza žizni.* Leningrad, 79 : 28-36.

1491 VORONCOV, A. V. "O cennostnyh orientacijah sel'skoj molodeži v sovremennoj kolhoznoj derevne" (On the rural youth value orientations in the contemporary collective farm), *IN: Cennostnye orientacii socialističeskgo obraza žizni.* Leningrad, 79 : 95-107.

1492 WATARI, Akeshi. "M. Foucault no kenryoku bunseki to shakaigaku-teki kadai" (M. Foucault's power-analysis and the sociological problems), *Shakaigaku hyoron* 31, 80 : 60-76.

13150. Alienation. Socialization. Social conformity
Aliénation. Socialisation. Conformité sociale

[See also / voir aussi: 37, 538, 702, 715, 802, 889, 905, 929, 947, 962, 1028, 1081, 1151, 1153, 1189, 1214, 1225, 1234, 1275, 1308, 1447, 1515, 1601, 1635, 1657, 1663, 1740, 2049, 2116, 2117, 2198, 2207, 2232, 2304, 2312, 2418, 2431, 2477, 2694, 2829, 2932, 2993, 3024, 3025, 3031, 3036, 3095, 3373, 3405, 3459, 3484, 3499, 3508, 3695, 3873, 4236, 4578, 4998, 5026, 5093, 5355, 5383, 5384, 5388, 5496, 5598, 5666, 5697, 5703, 5710, 5811, 5938, 5981, 6010, 6191]

1493 ADAMS, Murray C. "The functions of institutional deviance", *Indian Journal of social Research* 20, dec 79 : 151-155.

1494 AGNEW, Robert S. "Success and anomie: a study of the effect of goals on anomie", *Sociological Quarterly* 21, 80 : 53-64.

1495 Bibl.XXIX-1377. ALEXANDER, Yonah; CARLTON, David; WILKINSON, Paul; [eds.]. *Terrorism: theory and practice.* CR: Michael STOHL, *American political Science Review* 74(2), jun 80 : 577-578.

1496 ALTROCCHI, John. *Abnormal behavior.* New York, Harcourt Brace Jovanovich, 80, xxvi-755 p.

1497 AMVROSOV, A. A. "Ukreplenie social'noj odnorodnosti sovetskogo obščestva" (The reinforcement of Soviet society social homogeneity), *IN: Social'naja struktura sovetskogo obščestva i socialističeskij obraz žizni. I.* Moskva, 78 : 5-14.

1498 ARUTJUNJAN, S. G. "Dostiženie polnoj social'noj odnorodnosti socialističeskogo obščestva" (Results of a complete social homogeneity of the socialist society), *Voprosy naučnogo Kommunizma* 79 : 75-90.

1499 BACRY, Daniel; TERNISIEN, Michel. *La Torture: la nouvelle inquisition.* Paris, Fayard, 80, 454 p.

1500 BARBERO AVANZINI, Bianca. "Partezipazione sociale e participazione scolastica" (Social and school participation), *Studi di Sociologia* 17, jan-mar 79 : 18-30. ;961[Italy.]

1501 BARDIS, Panos D. "Social interaction and social processes", *Social Science* 54, 79 : 147-167. [see also International behavioural Scientist, (12), 78: 7-32.]

1502 BAUMGÄRTEL, Frank; [ed.]. *Familiensozialisation* (Family socialization). Braunschweig, Westermann, 79, 370 p.

1503 BAUMRIND, Diana. "New directions in socialization research", *American Psychologist* 35, jul 80 : 639-652.

1504 Bibl.XXIX-1381. BECKER, George. *The mad genius controversy: a study in the sociology of deviance.* CR: Manfred STANLEY, *Contemporary Sociology (Albany)* 9(3), mai 80 : 409-410.

1505 BEL'SKIJ, K. T.; KISELEV, V. P. "O zakonomernostjah formirovanija pravosoznanija v socialističeskom obščestva" (On the legal consciousness formation of laws in the socialist society), *IN: Problema social'noj zakonomernosti.* Gor'kij, 78 : 160-171.

1506 BEUCHELT, Eno. "Sozialisation in Tourismus. Kulturen — Erziehung zur Dienstleistung?" (Socialization in tourism. Cultural education for service?), *Sociologus* 30, 80 : 65-76.

1507 BHARADWAJ, Lakshmi K.; WILKENING, Eugene A. "Life domain satisfactions and personal social integration", *Social Indicators Research* (1-4), jan 80 : 337-351.

1508 BIANCHI, Antonella; GRANATO, Fiore; ZINGARELLI, Delia. *Marginalità e lotte dei marginali*. Milano, F. Angeli, 79, 391 p. [Italy.]

1509 BLAKE, Nancy; [et al.]. *Le discours de la violence dans la culture américaine.* Lille, Publications de l'Université de Lille, 79, 197 p.

1510 BONANATE, Luigi. "Some unanticipated consequences of terrorism", *Journal of Peace Research* 16, 79 : 197-211.

1511 BOURDIEU, Pierre. "Le mort saisit le vif", *Actes de la Recherche en Sciences sociales* 32-33, apr-jun 80 : 3-14. [Introduction au numéro intitulé "Paternalisme et maternage".]

1512 CAIRNS, Robert B.; [ed.]. *The Analysis of social interactions: methods, issues, and illustrations.* Hillsdale, NJ, Lawrence Erlbaum Associates, 79, x-243 p. [distributed by the Hallsted Press, New York.]

1513 CARACUIC, Traian. *Confruntări sociale în capitalismul contemporan* (Social confrontations in contemporary capitalism). București, Editura Politica, 79, 277 p.

1514 CASTILLO, Juan José; [et al.]. *Para acabar con la alienación* (In order to end with alienation). Madrid, Taller de Sociología, 78, 267 p.

1515 CHAUCHAT, Hélène. "Facteurs biographiques de la marginalité et familles 'marginaloïdes'. Étude de processus d'adaptation sociale", *Cahiers internationaux de Sociologie* 68, jan-jun 80 : 95-126.

1516 COLE, Michelle. *Violent sheep: the tyranny of the meek.* New York, Times Books, 80, xi-178 p.

1517 CONRAD, Peter; SCHNEIDER, Joseph W. *Deviance and medicalization, from badness to sickness.* St. Louis, Mosby, 80, xvii-311 p.

1518 DE LEO, Gaetano; SALVINI, Alessandro. *Normalità e devianza: processi scientifici e istituzionali nella costruzione della personalità deviante* (Normality and deviance: scientific and institutional processes in the construction of deviant personality). Milano, G. Mazzotta, 78, 277 p.

1519 DERKSEN, A. Th. "Anomie is niet identiek aan normoloosheid bij Durkheim" (Anomie is not synonym of normlessness in Durkheim), *Mens en Maatschappij* 55, 80 : 186-189.

1520 DOMENACH, Jean-Luc. "Une crise sociale en Chine: la société henanaise de l'été 1956 à l'été 1957", *Annales-Economies-Sociétés-Civilisations* 34, sep-oct 79 : 1069-1093.

1521 ERLANGER, Howard S. "Estrangement, machismo and gang violence", *Social Science Quarterly* 60, sep 79 : 235-248.

1522 ERMOLINA, G. "K ponjatiju social'noj odnorodnosti" (On the concept of social homogeneity), *IN: Social'naja odnorodnost' i svoboda ličnosti v razvitom socialističeskom obščestve.* Ivanovo, 78 : 3-20.

1523 FEDOTOV, S. K. "Obščestvennaja psihologija v strukture obščestvennogo soznanija" (Social psychology in the social consciousness structure), *IN: Razvitie soznanija ličnosti v uslovijah razvitogo socializma.* Iževsk, 78 : 20-28.

1524 FERRAROTTI, Franco. *Alle radici della violenza* (At the roots of violence). Milano, Rizzoli, 79, 186 p.

1525 FETISOV, V. P. "Socializacija i vsestoronne razvitie ličnosti" (Socialization and the personality total development), *IN: Ėkonomiceskie i duhovnye osnovy razvitija licnosti.* Voronež, 79 : 105-109.

1526 FLYNN, Edith Elisabeth; [ed.]. "Violence in American society", *American behavioral Scientist* 23, mai-jun 80 : 637-776.

1527 FORGAS, J. P. *Social episodes: the study of interaction routines.* London, New York, Academic Press, 79, xi-324 p. [published in cooperation with the European Association of Experimental Social Psychology.]

1528 FRYE, Charles A.; [ed.]. *Values in conflict: Blacks and the American ambivalence toward violence.* Washington, DC, University Press of America, 80, iii-169 p.

1529 GERMANI, Gino. *Marginality.* New Brunswick, NJ, Transaction Books, 80, vii-98 p. CR: Wilber A. CHAFFEE, *American political Science Review* 74(4), dec 80: 1113-1114.

1530 GOLDSTONE, Jack A. "The weakness of organization: a new look at Gamson's The strategy of social protest", *American Journal of Sociology* 85, mar 80 : 1017-1060. [with a comment by William A. GAMSON: 1043-1060. (See Bibl.XXV-1391).]

1531 Bibl.XXIX-1401. GOODE, Erich. *Deviant behaviour: an interactionist approach.* CR: Ronald C. KRAMER, *Contemporary Sociology (Albany)* 9(4), jul 80: 533-534.

1532 GRIESE, Hartmut M. *Sozialisation im Erwachsenenalter* (Socialization in adult age). Weinheim, Basel, Beltz, 79, 315 p.
1533 GRIMSHAW, Allen D. "Social interactional and sociolinguistic rules", *Social Forces* 58, mar 80 : 789-810.
1534 HABERMAS, Jürgen. "Psychic Thermidor and the rebirth of rebellious subjectivity", *Berkeley Journal of Sociology* 24-25, 80 : 1-12.
1535 HEISE, David R. *Understanding events: affect and the construction of social action*. Cambridge, New York, Cambridge University Press, 79, x-197 p.
1536 HERCEG, Josip. "Alijenacija i moral — nekoliko napomena o socijalizmu i moralu" (Alienation and morale: some remarks on socialism and morale), *Revija za Sociologiju* (1-2), 78 : 62-66.
1537 HILLERY, George A. Jr.; DUDLEY, Charles J.; THOMPSON, Thomas P. "A theory of integration and freedom", *Sociological Quarterly* 20, 79 : 551-563.
1538 HILLS, Stuart L. *Demystifying social deviance*. New York, McGraw-Hill, 80, xiii-210 p.
1539 IKEDA, Katsunori. "Sogai no chosa ni nokoru mondai" (The problems of alienation in social research), *Shakaigaku ronso* 77, 80 : 62-76.
1540 ISAAC, Larry; MUTRAN, Elizabeth; STRYKER, Sheldon. "Political protest orientations among Black and White adults", *American sociological Review* 45, apr 80 : 191-213.
1541 ITKIN, S. M. "O nekotoryh zakonomernostjah voznikovenija i preodolenii social'noj illjuzii kak fenomena obščestvennogo soznanija" (On some laws of the coming of social illusion and elimination as a social consciousness phenomenon), *IN: Problema social'noj zakonomernosti*. Gor'kij, 78 : 172-180.
1542 JACOB, Jeffrey C. "Urban poverty, children, and the consumption of popular culture: a perspective on marginality theses from a Latin American squatter settlement", *Human Organization* 39, 80 : 233-241. ;961[Guatemala City.]
1543 KAES, René. "Soixante-huit: effet d'après-coup et travail de la négativité. Situation de la chose psychosociale", *Connexions* 29, 80 : 39-49. ;961[France, 1968.]
1544 KARP, David Allen; YOELS, William C. *Symbols, selves, and society: understanding interaction*. New York, Lippincott, 79, xii-212 p.
1545 KELLY, Delos H.; [comp.]. *Deviant behavior: readings in the sociology of deviance*. New York, St. Martin's Press, 79, xiv-769 p.
1546 KLOCKARS, Carl B.; O'CONNOR, Finnbarr W.; [eds.]. *Deviance and decency: the ethics of research with human subjects*. Beverly Hills, Sage Publications, 79, 284 p.
1547 KUMAGAI, Fumie. "Seishonen no shakaika kokusai hikaku -Nichi-In-Bei no baai" (Socialization of youth in Japan, India, and the USA), *Kyoiku shakaigaku kiyo* 35, 80 : 85-98.
1548 KUMAGAI, Fumie. "Katei-nai boryoku no rironteki kosatsu" (Theoretical approaches to family violence), *Shakaigaku hyoron* 31, 80 : 36-44.
1549 KUMAI, Haruo. "Gendai shakai ni okeru chiiki seikatsu no henyō to 'shakai kankei' ni tsuite no ichi-kōsatsu" (Community life and social relations in contemporary society), *Waseda daigaku shakaigaku nenshi* 21, 80 : 153-167.
1550 KUPRJAŠIN, G. L. "Ob"ektivnye osnovy stanovlenija polnoj social'noj odnorodnosti obščestva" (Objective bases of the future of society's total social homogeneity), *IN: Social'nye i polititčeskie otnošenija v razvitom socialističeskom obščestve*. 79 : 70-81.
1551 LAMNEK, Siegfried. *Theorien abweichenden Verhaltens* (Deviant behavior theories). München, Fink, 79, 340 p.
1552 LEMPERT, Wolfgang; HOFF, Ernst; LAPPE, Lothar. *Konzeptionen zur Analyse der Sozialisation durch Arbeit* (Concepts on the analysis of socialization through work). Berlin, Max-Planck-Institut für Bildungsforschung, 79, x-624 p.
1553 LINDQUIST, Neil; HIRABAYASHI, Gordon. "Coping with marginal situations: the case of gay males", *Canadian Journal of Sociology* 79 : 87-104.
1554 MARKOWITZ, Jürgen. *Die soziale Situation: Entwurf e. Modells zur Analyse d. Verhältnisses zwischen personalen Systemen u. ihrer Umwelt* (The social situation: outline of a model for the analysis of relations between personal systems and their environment). Frankfurt am Main, Suhrkamp, 79, 217 p.
1555 MASSELOS, Jim. "Social segregation and crowd cohesion: reflections around some preliminary data from 19th century Bombay city", *Contributions to Indian Sociology* 13, jul-dec 79 : 145-167.
1556 MAURICE, F.; MIAILLE, M. "Violence et violence du droit: débat", *Déviance et Société* jun 80 : 149-177.

1557 MCKIRNAN, David J. "The identification of deviance: a conceptualization and initial test of a model of social norms", *European Journal of social Psychology* 10, jan-mar 80 : 75-93.
1558 MIDLARSKY, Manus I.; [et al.]. "Why violence spreads: the contagion of international terrorism", *International Studies Quarterly* 24, jun 80 : 262-298.
1559 Bibl.XXIX-14250. MILLER, Gale. *Odd jobs: the world of deviant work*. CR: Joseph HARRY, *American Journal of Sociology* 86(1), jul 80: 217-218.
1560 MIRET MAGDALENA, Enrique. "Reflexiones en torno a la violencia y la agresividad" (Reflexions about violence and aggressiveness), *Sistema. Revista de Ciencial sociales* 38-39, 80 : 125-143.
1561 MORDKOVIČ, V. G. "Social'naja aktivnost' i nekotorye voprosy antiobščestvennogo povedenija individa" (Social activity and some questions on a man's antisocial behaviour), *Problemy social'noj Aktivnosti* 78 : 111-126.
1562 MOSCOVICI, S. "Mai 1968 et la psychologie sociale", *Connexions* 29, 80 : 127-141.
1563 NECVIT, L. F. "Social'no-psihologičeskie problemy stimulirovanija obščestvennoj aktivnosti" (Socio-psychological problems of the social activity stimulation), *Problemy Filosofii* 48, 79 : 113-120.
1564 NEWMAN, Graeme R. *Understanding violence*. New York, Harper & Row, 79, x-310 p.
1565 O'DELL, Felicity Ann. *Socialization through children's literature: the Soviet example*. New York, Cambridge University Press, 79, 278 p. CR: Michael SWAFFORD, *Contemporary Sociology (Albany)* 9(5), sep 80 : 716-717.
1566 POSNER, Judith. "Introspecting into deviance: two project reports on labeling theory", *Teaching Sociology* jan 79 : 139-146.
1567 ROSE, Peter I.; [ed.]. *Socialization and the life cycle*. New York, St. Martin's Press, 79, x-412 p.
1568 SACHS, Wladimir M.; MEDITZ, Marybeth L. "A concept of active adaptation", *Human Relations* 32(12), dec 79 : 1081-1093.
1569 SCHUR, Edwin M. *Interpreting deviance: a sociological introduction*. New York, Harper & Row, 79, xiv-539 p.
1570 SCHUR, Edwin M. *The politics of deviance: stigma contests and the uses of power*. Englewood Cliffs, NJ, Prentice-Hall, 80, xi-241 p.
1571 SERRANO, Maria Eugenia C. de. "Violencia y subversión en Colombia" (Violence and subversion in Colombia), *Revista javeriana* 93(464), mai 80 : 309-322.
1572 SGRITTA, Giovanni B.; LESCHIUTTA, Pier Paolo; SAPORITI, Angelo. "Marginalità e riproduzione sociale in un contesto urbano. Modelli interpretativi ed esperienze di intervento politico-sociale" (Marginality and social reproduction in an urban context. Interpretive models and experiences of political and social intervention), *Rassegna italiana di Sociologia* 20, jul-sep 79 : 389-438.
1573 SHUPE, Anson D. "Social participation and voting turnout: the case of Japan", *Comparative political Studies* 12, jul 79 : 229-256.
1574 SIMMEL, Edward C.; [ed.]. *Early experiences and early behavior: implications for social development*. New York, Academic Press, 80, xiii-217 p.
1575 SKOGSTAD, Grace. "Agrarian protest in Alberta", *Canadian Review of Sociology and Anthropology* 17, feb 80 : 55-73.
1576 SMIRNOVA, G. "K voprosu o stiranii social'nyh različij meždu rabočim klassom i intelligenciej" (On the elimination of social differences between the working class and the intelligentsia), *IN: Social'naja odnorodnost' i svoboda ličnosti v razvitom socialističeskom obštestve*. 78 : 59-66.
1577 SMITH, Clagett G.; TEITLER, Robert J.; BOREN, Larry C. "Personality concomitants of varying attitudes towards the use of violence for settlement of disputes at three different levels: interpersonal, intergroup, and international", *Sociological Inquiry* 49, 79 : 45-54.
1578 SOKOLOVIĆ, Džemal. "Teorija otuđenija i radna teorija veijednosti" (The theory of alienation and a working theory of values), *Sociologija* 21, 79 : 231-253. [for the first part see Bibl. XXIX-1438.]
1579 SOKOLOVIĆ, Džemal. "Teorija otuđenja i radna teorija vrijednosti" (The theory of alienation and a working theory of values), *Sociologija* 21(1-2), 79 : 29-56. [continued 21(3), 79: 231-253.]
1580 STARR, Paul D.; ROBERTS, Alden E. "The marginal man theory: an empirical test from Malaysia", *Sociology and social Research* 64, jul 80 : 514-527.
1581 STIPAK, Brian. "Analysis of policy issues concerning social integration", *Policy Sciences* 12, jun 80 : 41-60.

1582   STRAUS, Murray Arnold. *Behind closed doors: violence in the American family.* Garden City, NY, Anchor Press/Doubleday, 80, 1st, viii-301 p.
1583   STRYKER, Sheldon. *Symbolic interactionism: a social structural version.* Menlo Park, CA, Benjamin/Cummings Pub. Co., 80, xiv-161 p.
1584   VAN DER WUSTEN, H. "The United Kingdom and its Irish contenders, 1800-1922", *Netherlands' Journal of Sociology* 16, 80 : 171-184.
1585   VAZQUEZ FIGUEROA, Onel. "Exito y aspiraciones en la socialización formal des estudiante puertorriqueño" (Success and aspirations in formal socialization of the Puerto Rican student), *Revista de Ciências sociales* 20(3-4), dec 79 : 307-346.
1586   VINCENT, G.; [et al.]. *Études sur la socialisation scolaire.* Paris, Editions du CNRS, 79, 136 p. CR: Jean-Claude CHAMBOREDON, *Revue française de Sociologie* 21(2), apr-jun 80: 289-295.
1587   VOLČOK, G. I. "Sojuz raboĉego klassa i krest'janstva: faktor rascvet i sbliženija socialističeskih nacij" (The union of the working class with the peasantry: the factor of development and bringing together of the socialist nations), *IN: Internacionalizacija obščestvennoj žizni ob'ektivnaja zakonomernost' kommunističeskogo stroitel'stva.* 79 : 80-86.
1588   VOLODINA, N. G. "Istoričeskij optimizm-zakonomernost' razvitija obščestvennogo soznanija na stupeni zrelogo socializma" (Historical optimism in the law of social consciousness development under mature socialism), *IN: Problema social'noj zakonomernosti.* Gor'kij, 78 : 144-153.
1589   VREDENBURGH, Donald J.; SHERIDAN, John E. "Individual and occupational determinants of life satisfaction and alienation", *Human Relations* 32(12), dec 79 : 1023-1038.
1590   WINICK, Charles; [ed.]. *Deviance and mass media.* Beverly Hills, CA, Sage, 79, 309 p. CR: Michael R. MEND, *Contemporary Sociology (Albany)* 9(4), jul 80: 534-535.
1591   WOLLMAN, Winnifred K.; BACHNER, Mary Lynn; PETERSON, Christopher. "Specificity of values and the prediction of prosocial behavior", *Journal of social Psychology* 111, jun 80 : 35-40.
1592   YAMAMURA, Yoshiaki. "Shakai-ka no ronri" (The perspective of socialization), *Seinen shinri* 21 & 22, 80 : 154-172; 176-193.
1593   ZAVTUR, A. "Na puti k polnoj social'noj odnorodnosti obščestva" (Towards the society complete social homogeneity), *Kommunist Moldavii* 80 : 71-79.
1594   ZELLER, Richard A.; NEAL, Arthur G.; GROAT, H. Theodore. "On the reliability and stability of alienation measures: a longitudinal analysis", *Social Forces* 58, jun 80 : 1195-1204.

13200.   **CUSTOM. TRADITION**
          COUTUME. TRADITION

[See also / voir aussi: 974, 2791, 2853, 3698]

1595   CHANDLER, Charles R. "Traditionalism in a modern setting: a comparison of Anglo- and Mexican-American value orientations", *Human Organization* 38, 79 : 153-159.
1596   ČIMIĆ, Esad. "Između tradicija i tradicionalizma" (Between tradition and traditionalism), *Revija za Sociologiju* (1-2), 78 : 29-36.
1597   DESCAMPS, Marc Alain. *Psychosociologie de la mode.* Paris, Presses universitaires de France, 79, 212 p. CR: Philippe BESNARD, *Revue française de Sociologie* 21(3), jul-sep 80 : 474-475.
1598   FAVRE, Pierre. "La différenciation sociale des pratiques alimentaires et des pratiques de sociabilité", *Revue française de Sociologie* 21, oct-dec 80 : 629-632.
1599   GRIGNON, Claude; GRIGNON, Christiane. "Styles d'alimentation et goûts populaires", *Revue française de Sociologie* 21, oct-dec 80 : 531-569.
1600   HERPIN, Nicolas. "Comportements alimentaires et contraintes sur les emplois du temps", *Revue française de Sociologie* 21, oct-dec 80 : 599-628.
1601   MANISCALCO, Maria Luisa. "Moda e socializzazione" (Fashion and socialization), *Sociologia (Roma)* 13, jan-apr 79 : 87-101.

13300.   **ETHICS. MORALS**
          ÉTHIQUE. MORALE

[See also / voir aussi: 49, 101, 472, 498, 1219, 1232, 1235, 1457, 1536, 1661, 1677, 1909, 2151, 2806, 3182, 3390, 3672, 4583, 4670, 5213, 5737, 5811]

1602 ARKKELIN, Daniel; OAKLEY, Thomas; MYNATT, Clifford. "Effects of controllable versus uncontrollable factors on responsibility attributions: a single-subject approach", *Journal of Personality and social Psychology* 27, jan 79 : 116-123.
1603 BAHM, Archie J. *Axiology, the science of values; Ethics, the science of oughtness.* Albuquerque, World Books, 80. [2 vol. in 1.]
1604 BAMBROUGH, Renford. *Moral scepticism and moral knowledge.* Atlantic Highlands, NJ, Humanities Press, 79, 166 p.
1605 BASOV, B. P. "Social'naja otvetstvennost' ličnosti v uslovijah razvitogo socializma" (Individual social responsibility under conditions of developed socialism), *IN: Razvitie soznanija ličnosti v uslovijah razvitogo sozializma.* Iževsk, 78 : 38-49.
1606 BEAUCHAMP, Tom L.; [et al.]. *Matters of life and death: new introductory essays in moral philosophy.* New York, Random House, 80, lst, xvi-343 p.
1607 BIERMAN, Arthur Kalmer. *Life and morals: an introduction to ethics.* New York, Harcourt Brace Jovanovich, 80, xii-596 p.
1608 BLJUMKIN, V. A.; MAZAEVA, E. B. "Rol' kommunističeskogo nravstvennogo ideala v formirovanii idejnyh i moral'nyh kačestv sovetskoj molodeži" (Role of the communist ethical ideal in the formation of the Soviet youth ideological and moral qualities), *Problemy Filosofii* 48, 79 : 34-42.
1609 CHAMBADAL, Paul. *Savoir, devoir, pouvoir: la science moderne et les fondements de l'éthique.* Paris, Copernic, 79, 203 p.
1610 CHANDEL, Bhuvan. *Marxian ethics: some preliminary considerations.* New Delhi, Munshiram Manoharlal, 79, 216 p.
1611 COLOMER FERRANDIZ, Fernando. "La ética como filosofía primera en el pensamiento de E. Levinas" (Ethics as first philosophy in E. Levinas' thought), *Cuadernos de Realidades sociales* 16-17, 80 : 79-95.
1612 Bibl.XXIX-1468. DIENER, Edward; CRANDALL, Rick. *Ethics in social and behavioral research.* CR: Ted R. VAUGHAN., *Contemporary Sociology (Albany)* 9(1), jan 80 : 104-105.
1613 DINGWALL, Robert. "Ethics and ethnography", *Sociological Review* 28, nov 80 : 871-891.
1614 FORSYTH, Donelson R. "A taxonomy of ethical ideologies", *Journal of Personality and social Psychology* 39, jul 80 : 175-184.
1615 FRENCH, Peter A. *The scope of morality.* Minneapolis, University of Minnesota Press, 79, xxii-212 p.
1616 GRJADUNOVA, L. I. *Social'naja otvetstvenost' ličnosti v uslovijah razvitogo socializma* (Individual social responsibility under conditions of developed socialism). Kiev, Višča Škola, 79, 134 p.
1617 GUSTAFSON, James M. *Christian ethics and the community.* New York, Pilgrim Press, 79, 224 p.
1618 JUNGHÄNEL, Günter; TACKMANN, Sigrid. *Moral und Arbeiterklasse* (Morals and working class). Berlin, Dietz, 79, 184 p.
1619 KAINZ, Howard P. *Ethica dialectica: a study of ethical oppositions.* The Hague, Nijhoff, 79, x-163 p.
1620 MARGOLIS, Joseph. "The prospects of an objective morality", *Social Research* 46, 79 : 744-765.
1621 MAŠKOVA, L. T. "Moral'naja norma kak faktor stabilizacii sem'i" (Moral norm as a family stabilization factor), *IN: Marksistsko-leninskaja filosofija i problemy razvitija nauki i praktiki.* Leningrad, 79 : 149-154.
1622 PHARO, Patrick. "Éthique et mutation économique. Étude d'un cas: l'élevage des veaux en Corrèze", *Revue française de Sociologie* 21, jul-sep 80 : 355-377.
1623 PICKERING, W. S. F.; [ed.]. *Durkheim: essays on morals and education.* London, Boston, Routledge & Kegan Paul, 79, xiv-214 p.
1624 PLAHOTNYJ, A. F.; LEVČENKO, E. V. "Problema social'noj otvetstvennosti kak kačestva ličnosti" (Social responsibility problem as a personality quality), *Problemy Filosofii* 48, 79 : 3-12.
1625 POLOVEC, V. M. "Nravstvennye problemy žizni malyh sel" (Ethical problems of the small villages life), *IN: Kommunističeskaja idejnost'* — *osnova aktivnoj žiznennoj pozicii.* Moskva, 79 : 222-230.
1626 RUDKOVSKIJ, E. I. *Svoboda i otvetstvennost' ličnosti* (Freedom and the personality responsibility). Minsk, Izdatel'stvo BGU imeni V. I. Lenina, 79, 152 p.
1627 SHALIN, Dmitri N. "Between the ethos of science and the ethos of ideology", *Sociological Focus* 12, oct 79 : 275-293.

1628 SIMON, Robert L.; ZEGURA, Stephen L. (Sociobiology and morality), *Social Research* 46, 79 : 766-786.
1629 SINGER, Peter. *Practical ethics.* Cambridge, New York, Cambridge University Press, 79, viii-237 p.
1630 SOKOLOV, V. M. "Konkretno-sociologičeskie issledovanija effektivnosti nravstvennogo vospitanija" (Concrete sociological research on the ethical education efficiency), *IN: Voprosy partijnogo rukovodstva nravstvennym vospitaniem.* Moskva, 79 : 194-203.
1631 STROH, Guy W. *American ethical thought.* Chicago, Nelson-Hall, 79, xxv-311 p.
1632 SUZUKI, Hiroshi. "Community moral to shakai idō no bunseki zushiki" (Frame of analysis of the community morals and social mobility), *Gendai shakaigaku no chihei to shōten* 80 : 257-263.
1633 VOLKOV, I. N. "Kollektivnaja i individual'naja otvetstvennost'" (Collective and individual responsibility), *IN: Socialističeskij obraz žizni.* I. 78 : 31-43.
1634 WESBROOK, Stephen D. "Morale proficiency and discipline", *Journal of political and military Sociology* 80 : 43-54.
1635 WINDMILLER, Myra; LAMBERT, Nadine; TURIEL, Elliot; [eds.]. *Moral development and socialization.* Boston, MA, Allyn and Bacon, 80, xi-264 p.

13400. LAW. REGULATION
LOI. RÉGLEMENTATION

[See also / voir aussi: 745, 1250, 1263, 1556, 1962, 3473, 4462, 5125, 5519, 5734, 5940]

1636 "Change in the common law: legal and economic perspectives", *Journal of legal Studies* mar 80 : 189-427.
1637 "'Modern' versus 'traditional' law", *Verfassung und Recht in Übersee* 12, 79 : 95-158.
1638 AREMU, L.O. "Criminal responsibility for homicide in Nigeria and supernatural beliefs", *International and comparative Law Quarterly* 29, jan 80 : 112-131.
1639 BENDA-BECKMANN, Franz von. "Modernes Recht und traditionelle Gesellschaften" (Modern law and traditional societies), *Verfassung und Recht in Übersee* 12, 79 : 337-351.
1640 BOBOTOV, S. V. *Buržuaznaja sociologija prava* (Bourgeois sociology of law). Moskva, 78, 220 p.
1641 CAIN, Maureen; HUNT, Alan; [eds.]. *Marx and Engels on law.* New York, Academic Press, 79, 281 p. CR: Austin T. TURK, *Contemporary Sociology (Albany)* 9(4), jul 80 : 556-557.
1642 CAMPBELL, C. M.; WILES, Paul; [eds.]. *Law and society.* New York, Barnes & Noble Books, 79, x-310 p.
1643 ČEFRANOV, V. A. "Otnositel'naja samostojatel'nost' pravovogo soznanija kak metodologičeskaja problema" (Relative independence of legal consciousness as a methodological problem), *Problemy Filosofii* 48, 79 : 12-17.
1644 CHARBONNEAU, Simon; PADIOLEAU, Jean G. "La mise en oeuvre d'une politique publique réglementaire: le défrichement des bois et forêts", *Revue française de Sociologie* 21, jan-mar 80 : 49-75.
1645 COHEN, Fred. *The law of deprivation of liberty: a study in social control: cases and materials.* St. Paul, MN, West Pub. Co., 80, xxxviii-755 p.
1646 DE CASTRO, Celso Antonio Pinheiro. *Sociologia e direito: fundamentos de sociologia geral, sociologia aplicada ao direito* (Sociology and law: foundations of general sociology, sociology applied to law). São Paulo, Editora Atlas, 79, 240 p.
1647 DIAZ, Elías. "Marx y la teoría marxista del Derecho y del Estado" (Marx and the marxist theory of law and state), *Sistema. Revista de Ciencias sociales* 38-39, 80 : 29-66.
1648 DIXON, David. "'Class law': the Street Betting Act of 1906", *International Journal of the Sociology of Law* mai 80 : 101-128.
1649 DWYER, Daisy Hilse. "Law actual and perceived: the sexual politics of law in Morocco", *Law and Society Review* 13, spr 79 : 739-756.
1650 HENRY, Jean-Robert; BALIQUE, François. *La Doctrine coloniale du droit musulman algérien: bibliographie systématique et introduction critique.* Paris, Editions du Centre national de la recherche scientifique, 79, 178 p.
1651 HUNT, Alan. "The radical critique of law: an assessment", *International Journal of the Sociology of Law* feb 80 : 33-46.
1652 Bibl.XXIX-1524. JOHNSON, Harry M.; [ed.]. *Social system and legal process: theory, comparative perspectives, and special studies.* CR: Austin T. TURK, *Contemporary Sociology (Albany)* 9(1), jan 80: 99-100.

1653 Bibl.XXIX-1526. KAMENKA, Eugene; BROWN, Robert; TAY, Alice Erh-Soon; [eds.]. *Law and society: the crisis in legal ideals.* CR: Lloyd Davis RAINES, *Contemporary Sociology (Albany)* 9(4), jul 80: 557.

1654 KAMENKA, Eugene; TAY, Alice Erh-Soon; [eds.]. *Justice: ideas and ideologies.* New York, St. Martin's Press, 80, viii-184 p. CR: John G. GUNNELL, *American political Science Review* 74(4), dec 80: 1056-1057.

1655 KATEB, George. "On the 'legitimation crisis'", *Social Research* 46, 79 : 695-727.

1656 KIM, Chin; LAWSON, Craig M. "The law of the subtle mind: the traditional Japanese conception of law", *International and comparative Law Quarterly* 28, jul 79 : 491-513.

1657 KOZJUBRA, N. I. *Socialistič̆eskoe pravo i obšč̆estvennoe soznanie* (The socialist law and the social consciousness). Kiev, Naukova Dumka, 79, 207 p.

1658 KULCSÁR, Kálmán. "Social changes and the legal structure: a discussion of the socialist experience", *International Journal of the Sociology of Law* feb 80 : 61-81.

1659 KULCSÁR, Kálmán. *Rechtssoziologische Abhandlungen* (Studies on the sociology of law). Budapest, Akadémiai K., 80, 242 p.

1660 MERRYMAN, John Henry; [et al.]. *Law and social change in Mediterranean Europe and Latin America: a handbook of legal and social indicators for comparative study.* Stanford, CA, Stanford Law School, 79, xvi-618 p. [distributed by Oceana Publications, Dobbs Ferry, NY.]

1661 RAZ, Joseph. *The authority of law: essays on law and morality.* Oxford, Clarendon Press, New York, Oxford University Press, 79, ix-292 p.

1662 Bibl.XXIX-1542. REASONS, Charles E.; RICH, Robert L.; [eds.]. *The sociology of law: a conflict perspective.* CR: Jon SNODGRASS, *Contemporary Sociology (Albany)* 9(2), mar 80, 270-271.

1663 RICH, Robert M. *The sociology of criminal law: evolution of deviance in Anglo-American society.* Toronto, Butterworths, 79, 282 p.

1664 RODRÍGUEZ PANIAGUA, José María. *Derecho y sociedad* (Law and society). Madrid, Tecnos, D.L., 79, 151 p.

1665 SAJÓ, András. *Jogkövetés és társadalmi magatartás* (Law observation and social behaviour). Budapest, Akadémiai K., 80, 343 p.

1666 SAJÓ, András; [ed.]. *Jog és szociológia. Válogatott tanulmányok* (Law and sociology. Selected studies). Budapest, Közgazdasági és Jogi K., 79, 442 p.

1667 SALITOT-DION, Michèle. "Coutume et système d'héritage dans l'ancienne Franche-Comté", *Études rurales* 74, apr-jun 79 : 5-22.

1668 SCHOLLER, Heinrich. "Le rôle du judiciaire dans la modernisation du droit dans les pays d'Afrique", *Verfassung und Recht in Übersee* 12, 79 : 364-369.

1669 STEFANI, Manuela Angela. "Marxismo e diritto"(Marxism and law), *Critica sociologica* 50, 79 : 190-208. [continued in 51-52, 1979-1980: 122-166.]

1670 STEIN, Peter. *Legal evolution: the story of an idea.* Cambridge, Eng., New York, Cambridge University Press, 80, xi-131 p.

1671 TAYLOR, Ian. "The law and order issue in the British general election and Canadian federal election of 1979: crime, populism and the state", *Canadian Journal of Sociology* 80 : 285-311.

1672 VAN ROUVEROY VAN NIEUWAAL, E. A. B. "Bases juridiques du droit coutumier au Togo dans l'époque coloniale allemande, 1884-1914", *Verfassung und Recht in Übersee* 13, 80 : 27-34.

13500. MAGIC. MYTHOLOGY. RELIGION
MAGIE. MYTHOLOGIE. RELIGION

13510. Religion. Sociology of religion
Religion. Sociologie religieuse

[See also / voir aussi: 1247, 1858, 4090, 5678]

1673 BERTRAND, Michèle. *Le statut de la religion chez Marx et Engels.* Paris, Éditions sociales, 79, 189 p.

1674 BRELICH, Angelo. *Storia delle religioni, perchè?*(History of religions, why?). Napoli, Liguori, 79, 257 p.

1675 CLAYTON, John Powell. *The concept of correlation. Paul Tillich and the possiblity of a mediating theology.* The Hague, Paris, New York, Mouton, 80, xii-178 p.

1676 DECONCHY, J. P.; [et al.]. "Expérimentation et psychologie de la religion", *Archives de Sciences sociales des Religions* 25, jan-mar 80 : 151-160.

1677   EVANS, Donald D. *Struggle and fulfillment: the inner dynamics of religion and morality.* Cleveland, Collins, 79, 238 p.

1678   GIUDICI, Amilcare. *Processo alla religione: introduzione culturale al problema religioso* (Questioned religion: cultural introduction to the religious problem). Milano, G. Mazzotta, 79, 173 p.

1679   HERBERT, Robert T. *Paradox and identity in theology.* Ithaca, NY, Cornell University Press, 79, 197 p.

1680   LADRIÈRE, Paul. "Une philosophie catholique aux frontières des sciences sociales des religions", *Archives de Sciences sociales des Religions* 48, oct-dec 79 : 213-221.

1681   LOTZ, Johannes Baptist. *Die Religion in ihrer Bedeutung für die technische Kultur: eine Besinnung auf die Einheit des menschlichen Wirkens* (The religion and its meaning for the technical culture). München, G. Olzog, 79, 136 p.

1682   Bibl.XXIX-1567. MARTIN, David. *The dilemmas of contemporary religion.* CR: Rocco CAPORALE, *American Journal of Sociology* 86(3), nov 80: 682-684. [also CR: Marion DEARMAN, Contemporary Sociology (Albany), 9(2), mar 80: 288.]

1683   MILANESI, Giancarlo. "Religione e famiglia nella recente letteratura sociologica" (Religion and family in the recent sociological literature), *Studi di Sociologia* 17, jul-sep 79 : 273-307.

1684   MUYSKENS, James L. *The sufficiency of hope: conceptual foundations of religion.* Philadelphia, Temple University Press, 79, xv-170 p.

1685   NISHIYAMA, Shigeru. "Gendai shukyo no doko to tenbo -shin-shukyo o chushin toshite" (Today's trend and anticipatory transformation of contemporary religion), *Jurisuto zokan sogo tokushu* 21, 80 : 163-169.

1686   Bibl.XXIX-1576. SCHOFFELEERS, Matthew; MEIJERS, Daniel. *Religion, nationalism and economic action: critical questions on Durkheim and Weber.* CR: Robert WUTHNOW, *Contemporary Sociology (Albany)* 9(6), nov 80: 835-836.

1687   SCHUON, Frithjof. *De l'unité transcendante des religions.* Paris, Seuil, 79, 185 p.

1688   TERABAYASHI, Osamu. "Durkheim no shukyoron josetsu" (Durkheim on religion: introductory remarks), *Shukugawa gakuin tanki daigaku kenkyu kiyo* 80 : 16-30.

1689   WIMBERLEY, Ronald C. "Continuity in the measurement of civil religion", *Sociological Analysis* 40, 79 : 59-62.

1690   WUTHNOW, Robert; [ed.]. *The Religious dimension: new directions in quantitative research.* New York, Academic Press, 79, xiv-376 p.

13520.   Magic. Primitive religion
Magie. Religion primitive

1691   ALLAN, Sarah; COHEN, Alvin P.; [eds.]. *Legend, lore and religion in China: essays in honor of Wolfram Eberhard on his seventieth birthday.* San Francisco, Chinese Materials Center, 79, xxiv-269 p.

1692   BEN-YEHUDA, Nachman. "The European witch craze of the 14th to 17th centuries: a sociologist's perspective", *American Journal of Sociology* 86, jul 80 : 1-31.

1693   CARDINI, Franco. *Magia, stregoneria, superstizioni nell'Occidente medievale* (Magic, witchcraft, superstition in the medieval West). Firenze, La nuova Italia, 79, 241 p.

1694   HARRISON, John Fletcher Clews. *The second coming: popular millenarianism, 1780-1850.* New Brunswick, NJ, Rutgers University Press, 79, xvii-277 p.

1695   HARVEY, Youngsook Kim. *Six Korean women: the socialization of shamans.* St. Paul, West Pub. Co., 79, xi-326 p.

1696   LE TENNEUR, René. *Magie, sorcellerie et fantastique en Normandie: des premiers hommes à nos jours.* Coutances, OCEP, 79, 499 p.

1697   LEE, Jung Young. *Korean Shamanistic rituals.* The Hague, Paris, New York, Mouton, 80, xvi-250 p.

1698   LLOYD, Geoffrey Ernest Richard. *Magic, reason and experience.* Cambridge, Eng., New York, Cambridge University Press, 79, xii-335 p.

1699   MAPPEN, Marc; [ed.]. *Witches & historians: interpretations of Salem.* Huntingdon, NY, R. E. Krieger Pub. Co., 80.

1700   SOSIS, Ruth H.; STRICKLAND, Bonnie R.; HALEY, William E. "Perceived locus of control and beliefs about astrology", *Journal of social Psychology* 110, feb 80 : 65-71.

1701   TYSON, G. A. "Occupation and astrology or season of birth: a myth", *Journal of social Psychology* 110, feb 80 : 73-80.

1702   YINGER, J. Milton. "Salvation and witches in a 'secular' age", *Contemporary Sociology* jul 80 : 472-477. [survey essay.]

13530. Buddhism. Christianity
Bouddhisme. Christianisme

[See also / voir aussi: 658, 1312, 1617, 1650, 1680, 1808, 1838, 2059, 2584, 2840, 2975, 3244, 3261, 3473, 3827, 5415, 5416, 5478, 5673, 5807, 5973]

1703 "Recherces sur l'Islam: histoire et anthropologie", *Annales-Economies-Sociétés-Civilisations* 35(3-4), mai-aug 80 : 415-867.
1704 "World (The) of Islam", *Current History* 78(456), apr 80 : 145-186.
1705 "A symposium on the Soviet immigrant", *Journal of Jewish communal Service* 56, sep 79 : 50-76.
1706 AKRAMUZZAMAN. *A sociological profile of Islam.* Dacca, Islamic Foundation, Bangladesh, 79, 125 p.
1707 AMORE, Roy C.; [ed.]. *Developments in Buddhist thought: Canadian contributions to Buddhist studies.* Waterloo, Ontario, 79, 193 p. [published for the Canadian Corporation for Studies in Religion by Wilfrid Laurier University Press.]
1708 BADAWI, 'Abd al-Rahmǎn. *Quelques figures et thèmes de la philosophie islamique.* Paris, G.-P. Maisonneuve et Larose, 79, 253 p.
1709 BEN SAÏD, Laurent; [et al.]. *Juifs (Les) en France.* Paris, Hachette, 79, 309 p.
1710 BENNIGSEN, Alexandre. "Islam in the Soviet Union", *Soviet Jewish Affairs* 79 : 3-14.
1711 BERQUE, Jacques. *L'Islam au défi.* Paris, Gallimard, 80, 311 p.
1712 BHEBE, Ngwabi. *Christianity and traditional religion in western Zimbabwe, 1859-1923.* London, Longman, 79, xiv-190 p.
1713 BLOFELD, John Eaton Calthorpe. *Taoism: the quest for immortality.* London, Boston, Unwin Paperbacks, 79, xii-195 p.
1714 BOISARD, Marcel A. *L'Islam et la morale internationale.* Paris, A. Michel, 79, 436 p.
1715 BOND, George; JOHNSON, Walton; WALKER, Sheila S.; [eds.]. *African Christianity: patterns of religious continuity.* New York, Academic Press, 79, xvi-175 p.
1716 BOROWITZ, Eugene B. *Understanding Judaism.* New York, Union of American Hebrew Congregations, 79, xv-231 p.
1717 BOYCE, Mary. *Zoroastrians, their religious beliefs and practices.* London, Boston, Routledge & Kegan Paul, 79, xxi-252 p.
1718 BRADSHAW, Jane. *Eight major religions in Britain.* London, E. Arnold, 79, 173 p.
1719 CALDAROLA, Carlo. *Christianity, the Japanese way.* Leiden, Brill, 79, viii-234 p.
1720 CAMBIER, Guy; [ed.]. *Christianisme d'hier et d'aujourd'hui: hommages à Jean Préaux.* Bruxelles, Éditions de l'Université de Bruxelles, 79, 160 p.
1721 CLEBSCH, William A. *Christianity in European history.* New York, Oxford University Press, 79, xii-315 p.
1722 Bibl.XXIX-1618. COLEMAN, John A. *The evolution of Dutch Catholicism, 1958-1974.* CR: Roland ROBERTSON, *Contemporary Sociology (Washington)* 9(4), jul 80: 575.
1723 DE SILVA, M. W. Padmasiri. *An introduction to Buddhist psychology.* New York, Barnes & Noble Books, 79, xii-134 p.
1724 DEKMEJIAN, R. Hrair. "The anatomy of islamic revival: legitimacy crisis, ethnic conflict and the search for islamic alternatives", *Middle East Journal* 34, wint 80 : 1-12.
1725 DHUNJIBHOY, Ros-han. "Islamismo y socialismo"(Islam and socialism), *Nueva Sociedad* 47, mar-apr 80 : 59-71.
1726 DĪKSHITA, Jagadīśa Datta. *Brāhmana tathā Bauddha vicāradhārā kā tulanātmaka adhyayana* (A comparative study of Brahmanism and Buddhism). Dillī, Bhāratīya Vidyā Prakāśana, 79, xvi-488 p.
1727 DRIEDGER, Leo. "Jewish identity: the maintenance of urban religious and ethnic boundaries", *Ethnic and racial Studies* jan 80 : 67-88.
1728 EVERY, George. *Understanding eastern Christianity.* Bangalore, Dharmaram Publications, 78, xxiv-136 p. [published for Centre for Indian and Inter-Religious Studies.]
1729 FALATURI, Abdoldjawad. "Der Islam. Eine Religion mit gesellschaftlichem und politischem Engagement" (Islam. A religion with social and political engagement), *Beiträge zur Konfliktforschung* 10, 80 : 49-70.
1730 FREIDENREICH, Harriet Pass. *The Jews of Yugoslavia: a quest for community.* Philadelphia, Jewish Publication Society of America, 79, xiv-323 p.
1731 GARRISSON-ESTÈBE, Janine. *L'homme protestant.* Paris, Hachette, 80, 254 p.
1732 GATES, Alan Frederick. 79.
1733 GOTTWALD, Norman Karol. *The tribes of Yahweh: a sociology of the religion of liberated Israel, 1250-1050 B.C.E..* Maryknoll, NY, Orbis Books, 79, xxv-916 p.

1734   GOWING, Peter G. *Muslim Filipinos: heritage and horizon.* Quezon City, Philippines, New Day Publishers, 79, xiii-286 p.
1735   GREELEY, Andrew M. "Sociology of American Catholics", *Annual Review of Sociology* 79 : 91-111.
1736   GREILSAMMER, Ilan. "The democratization of a community: French Jewry and the Fonds social juif unifié", *Jewish Journal of Sociology* 21, dec 79 : 109-124.
1737   GRIZZARD, Nigel; RAISMAN, Paula. "Inner city Jews in Leeds", *Jewish Journal of Sociology* 12, jun 80 : 21-33.
1738   GUTMANN, Emanuel. "Religion and its role in national integration in Israel", *Middle East Review* 12, aut 79 : 31-36.
1739   HALBERSTAM, Joshua; [ed.]. "Contemporary American judaism", *American behavioral Scientist* 23, mar-apr 80 : 461-632.
1740   HIMMELFARB, Harold S. "Agents of religious socialization among American Jews", *Sociological Quarterly* 20, 79 : 477-494.
1741   HOLLAND, Barron; [comp.]. *Popular Hinduism and Hindu mythology: an annotated bibliography.* Westport, CO, Greenwood Press, 79, xxiv-394 p.
1742   KAHANE, Reuven. "Religious diffusion and modernization: a preliminary reflexion on the spread of Islam in Indonesia and its impact on social change", *Archives européenes de Sociologie* 21, 80 : 116-138.
1743   KALIR, Joseph. *Introduction to Judaism.* Washington, DC, University Press of America, 80, viii-159 p.
1744   KEE, Howard Clark. *Christian origins in sociological perspective: methods and resources.* Philadelphia, Westminster Press, 80, 204 p.
1745   KIMBROUGH, S. T. *Israelite religion in sociological perspective: the work of Antonin Causse.* Wiesbaden, Harrassowitz, 78, xvi-154 p.
1746   KLEIN, Joel. *Psychology encounters Judaism.* New York, Philosophical Library, 79, 128 p.
1747   KRAFT, Charles II. *Christianity in culture: a study in dynamic Biblical Theologizing in cross-cultural perspective.* Maryknoll, NY, Orbis Books, 79, xviii-445 p.
1748   KUPISCH, Karl. *Die Freiheit des geschichtlichen Denkens: Protestantismus u. Geschichte* (The freedom of historical thought: protestantism and history). Stuttgart, Steinkopf, 79, 154 p.
1749   LACHS, Samuel Tobias; WACHS, Saul P. *Judaism.* Niles, IL, Argus Communications, 79, x-101 p.
1750   LACKNER, Wolfram. *Kirche ohne Religion: Ende d. Protestantismus?* (Church without religion: the end of protestantism?). Saterland, Saterland-Verlag, 79, 152 p.
1751   LADRIÈRE, Paul. "L'intransigeance des origines et le devenir du catholicisme actuel", *Cahiers internationaux de Sociologie* 67, jul-dec 79 : 297-311.
1752   LANGE, Maurice de. *Contemporary culture and Christianity.* Chicago, Franciscan Herald Press, 79, 76 p.
1753   LIEBMAN, Arthur. *Jews and the Left.* New York, Wiley, 79, 676 p. CR: Joe R. FEAGIN, *Contemporary Sociology (Albany)* 9(5), sep 80: 702-703.
1754   LIU, Da. *The Tao and Chinese culture.* New York, Schocken Books, 79, vii-168 p.
1755   LOOME, Thomas Michael. *Liberal catholicism, reform catholicism, modernism: a contribution to a new orientation in modernist research.* Mainz, Matthias-Grünewald-Verlag, 79, vii-452 p.
1756   MALEK, Abdel. "El Islam político"(Political Islam), *Revista mexicana de Sociología* 41, jul-sep 79 : 909-923.
1757   METZ, Johann Baptist; [ed.]. *Christianity and the bourgeoisie.* New York, Seabury Press, 79, viii-126 p.
1758   MICHEL, Patrick. "Le catholicisme polonais. Approches sociologiques", *Archives de Sciences sociales des Religions* 25, jan-mar 80 : 161-175.
1759   NADVI. SYED HABIBUL HAQ. *Dimensions of Islam through fourteen centuries.* Cape Town, Board of Extra-Mural Studies , University of Cape Town, 79, vii-157 p.
1760   NEWSOM, Carroll Vincent. *The roots of Christianity.* Englewood Cliffs, NJ, Prentice-Hall, 79, ix-263 p.
1761   NICOLAS, Guy. "Sociétés africaines, monde arabe et culture islamique", *Mois en Afrique* 15(172-173), apr-mai 80 : 47-64.
1762   OLIVER, Ian P. *Buddhism in Britain.* London, Rider, 79, 224 p.
1763   OOSTHUIZEN, Gerhardus Cornelis. *Afro-Christian religions.* Leiden, Brill, 79, 51,48 p.
1764   PARRINDER, Geoffrey. *La sabiduría de los primeros budistas* (The wisdom of the first Buddhists). Buenos Aires, El Ateneo, 80, 99 p.
1765   PARRINDER, Geoffrey. *La sabiduría del bosque, las Upanishad* (The wisdom of the forest, the Upanishad). Buenos Aires, El Ateneo, 80, 111 p.

1766 PERÉZ-REMÓN, Joaquin. *Self and non-self in early Buddhism*. The Hague, Paris, New York, Mouton, 80, 400 p.

1767 PHILIPPE, Béatrice; KRIEGEL, Annie. *Être juif dans la Societé française, du Moyen-Âge à nos jours*. Paris, Éditions Montalba, 79, 315 p.

1768 PREBISH, Charles S. *American Buddhism*. North Scituate, MA, Duxbury Press, 79, xix-220 p.

1769 PRESTON, Ronald H. *Religion and the persistence of capitalism: the Maurice Lectures for 1977 and other studies in Christianity and social change*. London, SCM Press, 79, ix-182 p.

1770 RAPHAEL, Marc Lee. *Jews and Judaism in a midwestern community, Columbus, Ohio, 1840-1975*. Columbus, Ohio Historical Society, 79, x-483 p.

1771 REISMAN, Bernard. *The Jewish experiential book: the quest for Jewish identity*. New York, Ktav Pub. House, 79, xii-449 p.

1772 RUDAVSKY, David. *Modern Jewish religious movements: a history of emancipation and adjustment*. New York, Behrman House, 79, 460 p.

1773 SARDAR, Ziauddin. *The future of Muslim civilisation*. London, Croom Helm, 79, 288 p.

1774 SCHLOEGL, Irmgard. *La sabiduría del Zen* (The Zen's wisdom). Buenos Aires, El Ateneo, 80, 107 p. [Creencias, religión y mística.]

1775 SCHNAPPER, Dominique. *Juifs et israélites*. Paris, Gallimard, 80, 281 p.

1776 SÉGUY, Jean. *Christianisme et société: introduction à la sociologie de Ernst Troeltsch*. Paris, les Éditions du Cerf, 80, 334 p.

1777 SELTZER, Robert M. *Jewish people, Jewish thought: the Jewish experience in history*. New York, Macmillan, 80, xxi-874 p.

1778 SHEPHERD, Michael A. "Cheltenham Jews in the nineteenth century", *Jewish Journal of Sociology* 21, dec 79 : 125-133.

1779 SMART, Ninian. *The phenomenon of Christianity*. London, Collins, 79, 320 p.

1780 SMITH, Wilfred Cantwell. *On understanding Islam*. The Hague, Paris, New York, Mouton, 80, 352 p.

1781 SPERO, Moshe Halevi. *Judaism and psychology: halakhic perspectives*. New York, Ktav Pub. House, Meshiva University Press, 80, xv-275 p.

1782 STEINBERG, Bernard. "Jewish education in the United States: a study in religio-ethnic response", *Jewish Journal of Sociology* 21, jun 79 : 5-35.

1783 TAMNEY, Joseph B. "Established religiosity in modern society: Islam in Indonesia", *Sociological Analysis* 40, 79 : 125-135.

1784 THEISSEN, Gerd. *Studien zur Soziologie des Urchristentums* (Studies on the sociology of early christianity). Tübingen, Mohr, 79, vi-317 p.

1785 TIBI, Bassam. "Islam und sozialer Wandel im moderner Orient" (Islam and social change in modern East), *Archiv für Rechts- und Sozialphilosophie* 65, 79 : 483-502.

1786 WARBURG, Gabriel R. "Islam in Sudanese politics", *Jerusalem Quarterly* 13, aut 79 : 47-61.

1787 WARNER, R. Stephen. "Theoretical barriers to the understanding of Evangelical Christianity", *Sociological Analysis* 40, 79 : 1-9.

1788 WEINFELD, Morton. "The Jews of Quebec: perceived antisemitism, segregation, and emigration", *Jewish Journal of Sociology* 12, jun 80 : 5-20.

1789 WEISBROD, Aviva; SHERMAN, Martin F.; SHERMAN, Nancy C. "Values as a function of religious commitment in Judaism", *Journal of social Psychology* 110, feb 80 : 101-107.

1790 WELCH, Holmes; SEIDEL, Anna; [eds.]. *Facets of Taoism: essays in Chinese religion*. New Haven, Yale University Press, 79, 301 p.

1791 WILLIS, John Ralph; [ed.]. *Studies in West African Islamic history*. London, F. Cass, 79, 308 p.

1792 WILLIS, John Ralph; [ed.]. *The Cultivators of Islam*. London, F. Cass, 79, x-325 p.

1793 WILSON, John Frederick. *Public religion in American culture*. Philadelphia, Temple University Press, 79, ix-198 p.

1794 YAJIMA, Yutaka. *Ōita kirishitan ruizokuchō no kenkyū* (A history of the early christian record in Oita). Tokyo, Musashino shobō, 80, 414 p.

1795 YAROSKY, Michael D. "The Jewish community of Quebec province: bridging the past and the present", *Journal of Jewish communal Service* 56, sep 79 : 19-27.

13540. Church. Religious community. Sect
Église. Communauté religieuse. Secte

1796 *Monachesimo nel Terzo mondo* (Monasticism in the Third World). Roma, Edizioni paoline, 79, 288 p.

1797 ALSTON, Jon P.; AGUIRRE, B. E. "Congregational size and the decline of sectarian commitment: the case of the Jehovah's witnesses in South and North America", *Sociological Analysis* 40, 79 : 63-70.

1798 ARMSTRONG, Orland Kay; ARMSTRONG, Marjorie. *The Baptists in America*. Garden City, NY, Doubleday, 79, xvii-485 p.

1799 BASSETT, William; HUIZING, Peter; [eds.]. *The Finances of the Church*. New York, Seabury Press, 79, x-146 p.

1800 BAUBÉROT, Jean. "L'élaboration du document 'Eglise et pouvoirs'", *Archives de Sciences sociales des Religions* 25, jan-mar 80 : 7-27.

1801 BOLZ, Wolfgang. *Religiöser Gruppenprotest: die ausserkirchlichen religiösen Gruppen als Herausforderung an die Kirchen*. 160 p.

1802 BURNHAM, Kenneth E. *God comes to America: Father Divine and the Peace Mission Movement*. Boston, Lambeth Press, 79, 167 p. CR: Thomas Ford HOULT, *Contemporary Sociology (Albany)* 9(4), jul 80: 574-575.

1803 CHAGNON, Roland. *Les charismatiques au Québec*. Montréal, Québec, Amérique, 79, 211 p.

1804 CHAMIE, Joseph. "Religious groups in Lebanon: a descriptive investigation", *International Journal of Middle East Studies* 11, apr 80 : 175-187.

1805 DE ROSA, Gabriele. "Seminario sulla storia della parrochia in Italia nell'età contemporanea" (Seminar on the history of the parish in Italy in the contemporary era), *Sociologia (Roma)* 13(2-3), mai-dec 79 : 3-38.

1806 DELLA FAVE, L. Richard; HILLERY, George A. Jr. "Status inequality in a religious community: the case of a Trappist Monastery", *Social Forces* 59, sep 80 : 62-84.

1807 DOWNTON, James V. Jr. *Sacred journeys; the conversion of young Americans to Divine Light Mission*. New York, Columbia University Press, 79, ix-241 p. CR: Roy WALLIS, *American Journal of Sociology* 86(3), nov 80: 657-661.

1808 ELAZAR, Daniel J.; MONSON, Rela Geffen. "The synagogue Havurah: an experiment in restoring adult fellowship to the Jewish community", *Jewish Journal of Sociology* 21, jun 79 : 67-81.

1809 FERRER BENIMELI, José Antonio. *Masonería española contemporánea* (Spanish freemasonry today). Madrid, Siglo Veintiuno, 80. [2 vols..]

1810 FRACCHIA, Charles A. *Living together alone: the new American monasticism*. San Francisco, Harper & Row, 79, 186 p.

1811 HALSEY, William M. *The survival of American innocence: Catholicism in an era of disillusionment, 1920-1940*. Notre Dame, IN, University of Notre Dame Press, 80, xv-230 p.

1812 HERMANS, Manfred. *Kirche als soziale Organisation: zwischen Partizipation u. Herrschaft* (Church and social organization: between participation and authority). Düsseldorf, Patmos Verlag, 79, 160 p.

1813 HOUGLAND, James G. Jr.; WOOD, James R. "'Inner circles' in local churches: an application of Thompson's theory", *Sociological Analysis* 40, 79 : 226-239.

1814 KAUFFMAN, J. Howard. "Social correlates of spiritual maturity among North American Mennonites", *Sociological Analysis* 40, 79 : 27-42.

1815 KELLY, George Anthony. *The battle for the American church*. Garden City, NY, Doubleday, 79, xi-513 p. [Catholic Church in the United States.]

1816 KONDZIELA, Joachim. "Sozialer und politischer Wandel in Polen und die gesellschaftliche Position der katholischen Kirche" (Social and political change in Poland and the social position of the Catholic Church), *Jarhbuch für christliche Sozialwissenschaften* 21, 80 : 57-72.

1817 LEE, Raymond L. M.; ACKERMAN, S. E. "Conflict and solidarity in a Pentecostal group in urban Malaysia", *Sociological Review* 28, nov 80 : 809-827.

1818 LEONE, Mark P. *Roots of modern Mormonism*. Cambridge, MA, Harvard University Press, 79, ix-250 p.

1819 LERNOUX, Penny. "The Latin American Church", *Latin American Research Review* 15, 80 : 201-211.

1820 LONG, Theodore E.; HADDEN, Jeffrey K. "Sects, cults and religious movements", *Sociological Analysis* 40, 79 : 279-282.

1821 MALLISON, John. *Building small groups in the Christian community*. West Ryde, N.S.W., Renewal Publications, 79, 238 p.

1822 NISHIYAMA, Shigeru; MORIOKA, Kiyomi. "From structural to a life-cycle theory of religious organization", *Japanese Journal of religious Studies* (2-3), 80 : 167-207.
1823 PANNET, Robert. *La paroisse de l'avenir: l'avenir de la paroisse.* Paris, Fayard, 79, 333 p.
1824 RICHARDSON, James T.; STEWART, Mary White; SIMMONDS, Robert B. *Organized miracles: a study of a contemporary, youth, communal, fundamentalist organization.* New Brunswick, NJ, Transaction Books,, 79, xxviii-368 p. CR: Roy WALLIS, *American Journal of Sociology* 86(3), nov 80: 657-661.
1825 SCHNELLER, Raphael. "Continuity and change in ultra orthodox education", *Jewish Journal of Sociology* 12, jun 80 : 35-45.
1826 SÉGUY, Jean. "La protestation implicite: groupes et communautés charismatiques", *Archives de Sciences sociales des Religions* 48, oct-dec 79 : 187-212.
1827 SHUPE, Anson D. Jr.; BROMLEY, David G. "The Moonies and the anti-cultists: movement and countermovement in conflict", *Sociological Analysis* 40, 79 : 325-334.
1828 STARK, Rodney; BAINBRIDGE, William Sims. "Networks of faith: interpersonal bands and recruitment to cults and sects", *American Journal of Sociology* 85, mai 80 : 1376-1395. [USA.]
1829 SZAFRAN, Robert F. "The effect of executive and professional membership values on the timing and influence of structural innovation in religious organizations", *Sociology of Work and Occupations* mai 80 : 188-209. [US Catholic diocesan organizations.]
1830 TANNER, Jerald. *The changing world of Mormonism.* Chicago, Moody Press, 80, 591 p.

13550. Clergy. Religious authority
Clergé. Autorité religieuse

1831 BROUGHTON, Walter; MILLS, Edgar W. Jr. "Resource inequality and accumulative advantage: stratification in the ministry", *Social Forces* 58, jun 80 : 1288-1301.
1832 FINCH, Janet. "Devising conventional performances: the case of clergy men's wives", *Sociological Review* 28, nov 80 : 851-870.
1833 GANNON, Thomas M. "The effect of segmentation in the religious clergy", *Sociological Analysis* 40, 79 : 183-196.
1834 Bibl.XXIX-1689. JULES-ROSETTE, Bennetta; [ed.]. *The new religions of Africa: priests and priestesses in contemporary cults and churches.* CR: Jack GLAZIER, *Contemporary Sociology (Albany)* 9(6), nov 80: 834-835.
1835 KAWASAKI, Kikuko. "Shukyoteki ken'i no ruikei — J. Wach to M. Weber o megutte" (Types of religious authority — J. Wach and M. Weber), *Shakaigaku ronso* 78, 80 : 53-68.
1836 KOLLER, Norman B.; RETZER, Joseph D. "The sound of silence revisited", *Sociological Analysis* 40, 80 : 155-161. [Attitudes of clergy toward controversial social and political issues.]
1837 NELSEN, Hart M.; MAGUIRE, Mary Ann. "The two worlds of clergy and congregation: dilemma for mainline denominations", *Sociological Analysis* 41, 80 : 74-80.
1838 TOWLER, Robert; COXON, Anthony P. M. *The fate of the Anglican clergy: a sociological study.* London, Macmillan, 79, x-248 p.

13560. Cult. Rite
Culte. Rite

[See also / voir aussi: 1820, 2046, 2063, 2278]

1839 ANTIER, Jean Jacques. *Le pèlerinage retrouvé.* Paris, Le Centurion, 79, 300 p.
1840 BALCH, Robert W. "Looking behind the scenes in a religious cult: implications for the study of conversion", *Sociological Analysis* 41, 80 : 137-143.
1841 BRAINBRIDGE, William Sims; STARK, Rodney. "Cult formation: three compatible models", *Sociological Analysis* 40, 79 : 283-295.
1842 BROMLEY, David G.; SHUPE, Anson D. Jr. "The Tnevnoc cult", *Sociological Analysis* 40, 79 : 361-366.
1843 CASPARIS, Johan. "The bridal shower: an American rite of passage", *Indian Journal of social Research* 20, apr 79 : 11-21.
1844 CHARTIER, Robert. "Discipline et invention. Les fêtes en France, XVe-XVIIe siècle", *Diogène* 110, apr-jun 80 : 51-71.
1845 GAY, Volney Patrick. *Freud on ritual: reconstruction and critique.* Missoula, MT, Scholars Press, 79, ix-212 p.

1846 GUIART, Jean. *Les Hommes et la mort: rituels funéraires à travers le monde.* Paris, Le Sycomore, 79, 331 p. [Objets et mondes, Muséum national d'histoire naturelle.]

1847 JULES-ROSETTE, Bennetta. "Changing aspects of women's initiation in Southern Africa: an exploratory study", *Canadian Journal of African Studies* 13, 80 : 389-405.

1848 LEWIS, Gilbert. *Day of shining red: an essay on understanding ritual.* Cambridge, New York, Cambridge University Press, 80, xvi-233 p.

1849 OFSHE, Richard. "The social development of the Synanon cult: the managerial strategy of organizational transformation", *Sociological Analysis* 41, 80 : 109-127.

1850 QUEREILHAC DE KUSSROW, Alicia. *La fiesta de San Baltazar* (St. Baltasar's feast). Buenos Aires, Editorial Tekné, 79, 79 p.

1851 RAGHAVAN, V. *Festivals, sports, and pastimes of India.* Ahmedabad, B. J. Institute of Learning and Research, 79, x-287 p.

1852 STARK, Rodney; BAINBRIDGE, William Sims; DOYLE, Daniel P. "Cults of America: a reconnaissance in space and time", *Sociological Analysis* 40, 79 : 347-359.

1853 TURNER, Harold W. *From Temple to Meeting House: The Phenomenology and Theology of Places of Worship.* The Hague-Paris-New York, Mouton, 79, 404 p.

1854 TURNER, Stephen. "Translating ritual beliefs", *Philosophy of the social Sciences* dec 79 : 401-423.

13570. Myth. Religious doctrine
Mythe. Doctrine religieuse

[See also / voir aussi: 1776]

1855 "Religion (La) dans les grands courants de la sociologie allemande", *Social Compass* 27, 80 : 5-158.

1856 ASHWORTH, C. E. "Flying saucers, spoon-bending and Atlantis: a structural analysis of new mythologies", *Sociological Review* 28, mai 80 : 353-376.

1857 COTTERELL, Arthur. *A dictionary of world mythology.* New York, Putnam, 80, 1st American edition, 256 p.

1858 DECONCHY, J. P. "Méthodologie expérimentale et psychologie de la religion: note documentaire et thématique", *Social Science Information* 19, 80 : 581-606.

1859 DELANEY, Cornelius F.; [ed.]. *Rationality and religious belief.* Notre Dame, IN, University of Notre Dame Press, 79, viii-168 p.

1860 DONOVAN, Peter. *Interpreting religious experience.* New York, Seabury Press, 79, 120 p.

1861 DUGANDŽIJA, Nikola. "Religije varijacije"(Religious variations), *Revija za Sociologiju* (1-2), 78 : 37-45.

1862 DURAND, Gilbert. *Figures mythiques et visages de l'oeuvre: de la mythocritique à la mythanalyse.* Paris, Berg international, 79, 327 p.

1863 DURIĆ, Mihailo. *Mythos, Wissenschaft, Ideologie*(Myth, science, ideology). Amsterdam, Rodopi, 79, ii-219 p.

1864 EMERTON, J. A.; [ed.]. *Prophecy.* The Hague, Paris, New York, Mouton, 80, 240 p.

1865 FALLDING, Harold. "Made in the likeness of God; or, the religious realization of human identity; or, religion without illusion", *Sociological Analysis* 40, 79 : 147-157.

1866 FERRARO, Guido. *Il linguaggio del mito: valori simbolici e realtà sociale nelle mitologie primitive* (Language of the myth: symbolic value and social reality in primitive mythology). Milano, Feltrinelli, 79, 254 p.

1867 FERRAROTTI, Franco. "The destiny of reason and the paradox of the sacred", *Social Research* 46, 79 : 648-681.

1868 FISCHER, Roland. "Mémoire et prédiction. Pour une psycho-biologie de la divination", *Diogène* 108, oct-dec 79 : 22-46.

1869 HAINING, Peter. *Superstitions.* London, Sidgwick & Jackson, 79, 175 p.

1870 HARGROVE, Barbara W. *The sociology of religion: classical and contemporary approaches.* Arlington Heights, IL, AHM Pub. Corp., 79, viii-342 p.

1871 INGRAM, Larry C. "Teaching the sociology of religion: the student's religious autobiography", *Teaching Sociology* jan 79 : 161-171.

1872 JUNQUERA, Carlos. "Una aproximación al estudio del mito en la actualidad" (An approach to the study of myth in present time), *Cuadernos de Realidades sociales* 16-17, 80 : 291-304.

1873 KIECKHEFER, Richard. *Repression of heresy in medieval Germany.* Philadelphia, University of Pennsylvania Press, 79, xiv-161 p.

1874 LÉVI-STRAUSS, Claude. *Myth and meaning.* New York, Schocken Books, 79, vii-54 p.

1875 MARTIN, David; [et al.]. *Estudios de sociología de la religión* (Studies in the sociology of religion). Zaragoza, Universidad de Zaragoza, Facultad de Empresariales, Dto. de Sociología, 79, 169 p.
1876 MOLNAR, Thomas. *Theist and Atheist. A typology of non-belief.* The Hague, Paris, New York, Mouton, 80, viii-220 p.
1877 MULAGO, Vincent. *Simbolismo religioso africano: estudio comparativo con el sacramentalismo cristiano* (African religious symbolism: a comparison with the Christian sacramentalism). Madrid, [s.n.], 79, xxxi-333 p.
1878 SMITH, Wilfred Cantwell. *Faith and belief.* Princeton, NJ, Princeton University Press, 79, ix-347 p.
1879 SPROUL, Barbara C. *Primal myths: creating the world.* San Francisco, Harper & Row, 79, vii-373 p.
1880 TAPPER, Bruce Elliot. "Windows and goddesses: female roles in deity symbolism in a South Indian village", *Contributions to Indian Sociology* 13, jan-jun 79 : 1-31.
1881 WILSON, Robert R. *Prophecy and society in ancient Israel.* Philadelphia, Fortress Press, 80, vii-322 p.
1882 WOODS, Richard; [ed.]. *Understanding mysticism.* Garden City, NY, Image Books, 80, xi-586 p.

13580. Religious behaviour
Comportement religieux

[See also / voir aussi: 502, 1217, 1783, 3088]

1883 "Religión y brujería" (Religion and witchcraft), *Revista javeriana* 92(459), oct 79 : 303-355. [Colombia.]
1884 "Religions (Les) de la classe ouvrière", *Social Compass* 27(2-3), 80 : 167-305.
1885 ABBOTT, Andrew. "Religion, psychiatry, and problems of everyday life", *Sociological Analysis* 40, 80 : 164-171.
1886 BARRISH, Gerald; WELCH, Michael. "Student religiosity and discriminatory attitudes toward women", *Sociological Analysis* 41, 80 : 66-73.
1887 BEIT-HALLAHMI, Benjamin. "Personal and social components of the Protestant ethics", *Journal of social Psychology* 109, dec 79 : 263-267.
1888 BOLOGNINI, Franco. *Libertà religiosa e diritto matrimoniale italiano: profili sisstematici* (Religious liberty and marriage law in Italy: systematic profiles). Milano, A. Giuffrè, 79, iv-247 p.
1889 CAMPBELL, Keith E.; GRANBERG, Donald. "Religiosity, and attitude toward the Vietnam War: a research note using national samples", *Sociological Analysis* 40, 79 : 254-256.
1890 FAURY, Jean. *Cléricalisme et anticléricalisme dans le Tarn: 1848-1900.* Toulouse, le Mirail, 80, 532 p. [Service des publications de l'université de Toulouse.]
1891 FILSNGER, Erik E.; FAULKNER, Joseph E.; WARLAND, Rex H. "Empirical taxonomy of religious individuals: an investigation among college students", *Sociological Analysis* 40, 79 : 136-146.
1892 GILLESPIE, Virgil Bailey. *Religious conversion and personal identity: how and why people change.* Birmingham, AL, Religious Education Press, 79, xi-246 p.
1893 HAACK, Friedrich-Wilhelm. *Jugendreligionen: Ursachen, Trends, Reaktionen* (Religions of youth: causes, trends, reactions). München, Claudius-Verlag, München, Pfeiffer, 79, 435 p.
1894 KIM, Byong-suh. "Religious deprogramming and subjective reality", *Sociological Analysis* 40, 79 : 197-207.
1895 LORENTZEN, Louise J. "Evangelical life style concerns expressed political action", *Sociological Analysis* 41, 80 : 144-154.
1896 MALONEY, George A. *Following Jesus in the real world: asceticism today.* Albany, Clarity Pub., 79, 30 p.
1897 MUELLER, G. H. "The dimensions of religiosity", *Sociological Analysis* 41, 80 : 1-24.
1898 ORTIZ ECHAMIZ, Silvia. "Origen, desarrollo y características del espiritualismo en México" (Origin, development and characteristics of spiritualism in Mexico), *América indígena* 39, jan-mar 79 : 147-170.
1899 PACE, Enzo. "The debate on popular religion in Italy", *Sociological Analysis* 40, 79 : 71-75.

1900 RUSSO, Carlo. "La religiosità popolare nell' età moderna. Problemi e prospettive" (Popular religiosity in modern times. Problems and prospects), *Prospettive settanta* jul-sep 79 : 345-379.

1901 SIMARD, Jean. *Un patrimoine méprisé: la religion populaire des Québécois*. Cité de LaSalle, Québec, Hurtubise HMH, 79, x-309 p.

1902 SMIDT, Corwin. "Civil religious orientations among elementary school children", *Sociological Analysis* 41, 80 : 25-40.

1903 TAMNEY, Joseph B. "Functional religiosity and modernization in Indonesia", *Sociological Analysis* 41, 80 : 55-65.

1904 ZAÑARTU, Mario. "Elementos sociales de la conciencia cristiana" (Social elements of Christian consciousness), *Revista de Fomento social* 35(140), 80 : 495-508.

1905 ZARET, David. "Ideology and organization in puritanism", *Archives européenes de Sociologie* 21, 80 : 83-115.

13590. Church and State. Religious practice
Église et État. Pratique religieuse

[See also / voir aussi: 1353, 1724, 1801, 1820, 1973, 2533, 3378]

1906 ACERBI, Antonio. *Le Chiesa nel tempo: sguardi sui progetti di relazione tra Chiesa e società civile negli ultimi cento anni* (The Church through the time: an overview of projects on relationships between the Church and civil society in the last hundred years). Milano, Vita e pensiero, 79, vi-315 p.

1907 ALVES, Márcio Moreira. *A Igreja e a política no Brasil* (Church and politics in Brazil). São Paulo, Editora Brasiliense, 79, 268 p.

1908 BIDDULPH, Howard L. "Religious participation of youth in the USSR", *Soviet Studies* 31, jul 79 : 417-433.

1909 BIRD, Frederick. "The pursuit of innocence: new religious movements and moral accountability", *Sociological Analysis* 40, 79 : 335-346.

1910 BOITER, Albert. *Religion in the Soviet Union*. Beverly Hills, CA, Sage Publications, 80, 80 p.

1911 BORI, Pier Cesare; BETTIOLO, Paolo. *Movimenti religiosi in Russia prima della rivoluzione (1900-1917)* (Religious movements in Russia before the revolution, 1900-1917). Brescia, Queriniana, 79?, 318 p.

1912 BRINKERHOFF, Merlin B.; BURKE, Kathryn L. "Disaffiliation: some notes on 'failing from the faith'", *Sociological Analysis* 41-54, 80 : 41.

1913 CAMPICHE, Roland. "La religion, source de conflits ou ciment de l'unité suisse?", *Archives de Sciences sociales des Religions* 25, jan-mar 80 : 43-57.

1914 CAPRARO, Giuseppe. "Religione e società in Italia: alla ricerca di un'ipotesi esplicative e di una tipologia descrittiva" (Religion and society in Italy: towards an interpretative hypothesis and a descriptive study), *Studi di Sociologia* 17, jan-mar 79 : 81-94.

1915 CARMODY, Denise Lardner. *Women & world religions*. Nashville, Abingdon, 79, 172 p.

1916 DANN, Graham M. S. "Religion and cultural identity: the case of Umbanda", *Sociological Analysis* 40, 79 : 208-225.

1917 DIXON, Richard D. "Tourism and church attendance: empirical findings", *Sociological Analysis* 40, 79 : 256-260.

1918 FERRARI, Silvio. "Chiesa e Stato in Inghilterra" (Church and State in England), *Ponte* 35(11-12), 30 nov-31 dec 79 : 1342-1352.

1919 GARELLI, Franco. "Giovani e fenomeno religioso in una società complessa" (Young people and religious phenomenon in a complex society), *Aggiornamenti sociali* 31, jan 80 : 7-20.

1920 GLAZIER, Stephen D. "Religion and contemporary religious movements in the Caribbean: a report", *Sociological Analysis* 40, 80 : 181-183.

1921 GUIZZARDI, Gustavo. *La religione della crisi: per una teoria sociologica dello scambio del prodotto religioso* (Religion of crisis: for a sociological theory of changing religious product). Milano, Edizioni di Comunità, 79, xvi-228 p.

1922 HADDEN, Jeffrey K. "Religion and the construction of social problems", *Sociological Analysis* 41, 80 : 99-108.

1923 Bibl.XXIX-1772. HAMMOND, John L. *The politics of benevolence: revival religion and American voting behaviour*. CR: Paul KLEPPNER, *American political Science Review* 74(2), jun 80 : 502-503. [also CR: Benton JOHNSON, Contemporary Sociology (Albany), 9(6), nov 80: 833-834.]

1924	HOUGLAND, James G. Jr.; WOOD, James R. "Correlates of participation in local churches", *Sociological Focus* 13, oct 80 : 343-358. [Protestant churches, Indianapolis, IA.]
1925	ISAMBERT, François-A. "Religion et politique", *Archives de Sciences sociales des Religions* 25, jan-mar 80 : 77-81.
1926	KAWASAKI, Kikuko. "Iran ni okeru Shiah-ha no kaisei -shukyo-shakaigaku shiron toshite" (The revival of Shiah in Iran — An essay on sociology of religion), *Teikyo tanki daigaku kiyo* 80 : 121-137.
1927	KELLEY, Dean M.; [ed.]. "The uneasy boundary: Church and State", *Annals of the American Academy of political and social Science* 446, nov 79 : 1-161.
1928	LALIVE D'EPINAY, Christian; ALEXANDER, Daniel. "Formative d'un Etat-Nation et minorité ethno-culturelle", *Archives de Sciences sociales des Religions* 25, jan-mar 80 : 101-118.
1929	LOVELACE, Richard F. *Dynamics of spiritual life: an evangelical theology of renewal.* Downers Grove, IL, Inter-Varsity Press, 79, 455 p.
1930	MAÎTRE, Jacques. "Processus politiques et dynamique religieuse", *Archives de Sciences sociales des Religions* 25, jan-mar 80 : 147-149.
1931	Bibl.XXIX-1787. MARTIN, David. *A general theory of secularization.* CR: Robert TOWLER, *British Journal of Sociology* 31(4), dec 80: 608-609.
1932	ROBBINS, Thomas; ANTHONY, Dick. "Sociology of contemporary religious movements", *Annual Review of Sociology* 79 : 75-89.
1933	ROBERTSON, Roland. "Religious movements and modern societies: toward a progressive problem shift", *Sociological Analysis* 40, 79 : 297-314.
1934	ROTHROCK, George A. *The Huguenots: a biography of a minority.* Chicago, Nelson-Hall, 79, xxv-201 p.
1935	ROUSSEAU, André. "Différenciation religieuse et position de classe", *Archives de Sciences sociales des Religions* 25, jan-mar 80 : 29-42. [France.]
1936	SARRIAS, Cristóbal. "Aproximación sociológica a los movimientos matrimoniales en España" (Sociological approach to matrimonial movements in Spain), *Razón y Fé* 200(983), dec 79 : 404-416.
1937	SHIFMAN, Pinhas. "Religious affiliation in Israeli interreligions law", *Israel Law Review* 15, jan 80 : 1-48.
1938	STRAUS, Roger A. "Religious conversion as a personal and collective accomplishment", *Sociological Analysis* 40, 79 : 158-165.
1939	TAVARES, Jean. "La "synthèse" chrétienne, dépassement vers l' "au-delà" ", *Actes de la Recherche en Sciences sociales* 34, sep 80 : 45-65.
1940	TURNER, Harold W. *Religious innovation in Africa: collected essays on new religious movements.* Boston, MA, G. K. Hall, 79, x-354 p.
1941	WILLIAMS, Peter W. *Popular religion in America: symbolic change and the modernization process in historical perspective.* Englewood Cliffs, NJ, Prentice-Hall, 80, xiv-244 p.
1942	WILSON, Bobby M. "Church participation: a social space analysis in a community of Black in-migrants", *Journal of Black Studies* 10, dec 79 : 198-217.
1943	WIMBERLEY, Ronald C.; CHRISTENSON, James A. "Civil religion and Church and State", *Sociological Quarterly* 21, 80 : 35-40.
1944	YIP, Ka-che. *Religion, nationalism, and Chinese students: the anti-Christian movement of 1922-1927.* Bellingham, Center for East Asian Studies, Western Washington University, 80, iii-133 p.

13600. SCIENCE. SOCIOLOGY OF KNOWLEDGE
SCIENCE. SOCIOLOGIE DE LA CONNAISSANCE

[See also / voir aussi: 11, 148, 244, 283, 356, 424, 444, 764, 1130, 1627, 1863]

1945	ANTIPINA, Z. G. "Metodologičeskie osnovy poznanija rituala kak social'nogo fenomena" (Methodological bases of the ritual knowledge considered as a social phenomenon), *IN: Metodologija častnyh nauk.* Irkutsk, 79 : 122-132.
1946	ARDITTI, Rita; BRENNAN, Pat; CAVRAK, Steve; [eds.]. *Science and liberation.* Boston, MA, South End Press, 80, vii-398 p.
1947	ARISUE, Ken. "Hihanteki shakaigaku no chishiki kozo -paradigm gainen o jiku toshite" (The structure of knowledge in critical sociology), *Keio gijuku daigaku daigaku'in shakaigaku kenkyuka kiyo* 20, 80 : 37-45.
1948	BÉKÉS, Ferenc. *Ismeretszintmérés, ismeretstruktúra, ismerettipológia. A felnőtt lakosság körében végzett eddigi ismeretszint-vizsgálatok alapján* (Measuring the level of knowledge, structure

and typology of knowledge, on the base of surveys among the adult population). Mass Communication Research Centre, Budapest, Tömegkomm, Kutatóközpont, 80, 167 p.
1949 BERGER, Gaston. *Recherches sur les conditions de la connaissance: essai d'une théorétique pure.* New York, Garland Pub., 79, 193 p.
1950 BERLIN, Isaiah. *Against the current: essays in the history of ideas.* New York, Viking Press, 80, liii-394 p.
1951 BLANKENAGEL, Alexander. "Wissenschaftsfreiheit aus der Sicht der Wissenschaftssoziologie" (Scientific freedom from the point of view of sociology of knowledge), *Archiv des öffentlichen Rechts* 105, 80 : 35-78.
1952 BÖHME, Gernot; ENGELHARDT, Michael Von; [eds.]. *Entfremdete Wissenschaft* (Alienated science). Frankfurt-am-Main, Suhrkamp Verlag, 79, 308 p. CR: Dirk KÄSLER, *Soziologische Revue* 3(1), 80: 50-52.
1953 BRAINBRIDGE, William Sims; STARK, Rodney. "Scientology: to be perfectly clear", *Sociological Analysis* 41, 80 : 128-136.
1954 BRANNIGAN, Augustine. "Naturalistic and sociological models of the problem of scientific discovery", *British Journal of Sociology* 31, dec 80 : 559-573.
1955 BROWN, B.; COUSINS, M. "The linguistic fault: the case of Foucault's archaeology", *Economy and Society* aug 80 : 251-278.
1956 CARAMELLI, Nicoletta. *Epistemologia genetica e teoria della conoscenza in J. Piaget* (Genetic epistemology and theory of knowledge in J. Piaget). Milano, F. Angeli, 79, 135 p.
1957 CAVELL, Stanley. *The claim of reason: Wittgenstein, skepticism, morality and tragedy.* Oxford, Clarendon Press, New York, Oxford University Press, 79, xii-511 p.
1958 ČEMODANOV, M. P. "Kriziz buržuaznyh koncepcij roli tehniki i nauki" (Crisis of the bourgeois concepts on the role of science and technology), *IN: Metodologičeskie problemy sovremennoj nauki.* Moskva, 79 : 221-236.
1959 DANKENBRING, William F. *The first genesis: the saga of creation vs evolution.* Altadena, CA, Triumph Pub., 79, 417 p.
1960 DUVIGNAUD, Jean. *Sociologie de la connaissance: études.* Paris, Payot, 79, 286 p.
1961 FARKAS, János; [ed.]. *Sociology of science and research.* Budapest, Akadémiai Kiadó, 79, 503 p. [Papers of the International Sociology of Science Conference in Budapest, Sept. 7-9 1977.]
1962 FUHRMAN, Ellsworth R. *The sociology of knowledge in America, 1883-1915.* Charlottesville, University Press of Virginia, 80, xx-268 p.
1963 GOBERNADO, Arribas, Rafael. *Ideología, lenguaje y derecho: aplicación de un modelo de sociología del conocimiento al derecho* (Ideology, language and law: application of a sociology of knowledge model to law). Madrid, Cupsa, 78, 265 p.
1964 GOFF, Tom W. *Marx and Mead: Contributions to a sociology of knowledge.* London-Boston, Henley, Routledge and Kegan Paul, 80, viii-166 p. CR: Walter HERZOG, *Kölner Zeitschrift für Soziologie und Sozialpsychologie* 32(4), dec 80: 790-792.
1965 GONZALEZ BLASCO, Pedro. "Reflexiones sobre el subdesarrollo científico en España" (Reflexions on the scientific underdevelopment in Spain), *Sistema. Revista de Ciencias sociales* 36, 80 : 53-63.
1966 GONZALEZ BLASCO, Pedro; JIMENEZ BLANCO, José; LOPEZ PIÑERO, José. *Historia y sociología de la ciencia en España* (History and sociology of science in Spain). Madrid, Alianza Editorial, 79, 224 p.
1967 HOLZNER, Burkart; MARX, John H. *Knowledge application: the knowledge system in society.* Boston, Allyn and Bacon, 79, xxiii-388 p.
1968 HORUC, L. E. "Sovremennye tendencii v buržuaznoj sociologii poznanija" (Contemporary tendencies in the bourgeois sociology of knowledge), *IN: Social'naja priroda poznanija.* Moskva, 79 : 196-222.
1969 JOHNSON, Oliver A. *Skepticism and cognitivism: a study in the foundations of knowledge.* Berkeley, University of California Press, 79, xiii-293 p.
1970 KENNEDY, Devereaux. "Michel Foucault: the archeology and sociology of knowledge", *Theory and Society* sep 79 : 269-297.
1971 KNORR, Karin D. "Tinkering toward success: prelude to a theory of scientific practice", *Theory and Society* nov 79 : 347-376.
1972 KODAMA, Toshihiko. "Kagaku shakaigaku no keisei to tenkai" (The emergence and the development of 'sociology of science'), *Shakaigaku hyoron* 30, 79 : 81-87.
1973 KUKLICK, Henrika. "Restructuring the past: toward an appreciation of the social context of social science", *Sociological Quarterly* 21, 80 : 5-21.
1974 LEMERT, Charles. "Science, religion and secularization", *Sociological Quarterly* 20, 79 : 445-461.

1975 LUBRANO, Linda L.; SOLOMON, Susan Gross; [eds.]. *The Social context of Soviet science.* Boulder, CO, Westview Press, 80, xv-240 p.

1976 MACHADO NETO, Antônio Luiz. *Formação e temática da sociologia do conhecimento* (Formation and themes of the sociology of knowledge). São Paulo, Editora Convívio, 79, 240 p.

1977 MANSILLA, H. C. F. "La conciencia científica ante las amenazas de nuestro tiempo" (Scientific consciousness facing contemporary threats), *Cuadernos de Realidades sociales* 16-17, 80 : 5-18.

1978 MAUSKOPF, Seymour H.; [ed.]. *The reception of unconventional science.* Boulder, CO, Westview Press, 79, 137 p. CR: George RITZER, *Contemporary Sociology (Albany)* 9(3), mai 80, 416-418.

1979 MAXWELL, Nicholas. "Science, reason, knowledge, and wisdom: a critique of specialism", *Inquiry* 23, mar 80 : 19-81.

1980 MELLOR, D. H.; [ed.]. *Science, belief, and behaviour: essays in honour of R. B. Braithwaite.* Cambridge, Eng., New York, Cambridge University Press, 80, xii-227 p.

1981 MEYER, Michel. *Découverte et justification en science: kantisme, néopositivisme et problématologie.* Paris, Klincksieck, 79, 365 p.

1982 MORAZÉ, Charles; [et al.]. *Science and the factors of inequality: lessons of the past and hopes for the future.* Paris, Unesco, 79, 269 p.

1983 MOREHOUSE, Ward; [ed.]. *Science, technology and the social order.* New Brunswick, NJ, Transaction Books, 79, vi-277-427 p.

1984 MULKAY, Michael Joseph. *Science and the sociology of knowledge.* London, Boston, G. Allen & Unwin, 79, 132 p. CR: John DEBRIZZI, *Contemporary Sociology (Albany)* 9(3), mai 80 : 418-419.

1985 NADEL, Edward. "Formal communication, journal concentration and the rise of a discipline in physics", *Sociology* 14, aug 80 : 401-416.

1986 Bibl.XXIX-1857. NAMER, Gérard. *Machiavel et les origines de la sociologie de la connaissance.* CR: Odile RUDELLE, *Revue française de Science politique* 30(1), feb 80: 153-154.

1987 NEWTON-SMITH, William. "Is science rational?", *Social Science Information* 19, 80 : 469-499.

1988 Bibl.XXIX-5671. NITSCHKE, August. *Revolutionen in Naturwissenschaft und Gesellschaft.* Stuttgart-Bad Cannstatt, Frommann-Holzboog, 79, 207 p. CR: Walter L. BÜHL, *Soziologie und Sozialpsychologie* 32(4), dec 80: 796-798. [nos. 402 and 403 have been telescoped.]

1989 NOWAK, Leszek. *The structure of idealization: towards a systematic interpretation of the Marxian idea of science.* Dordrecht, Boston, D. Reidel, 80, xi-277 p.

1990 NOWOTNY, Helga; ROSE, Hilary; [eds.]. "Countermovements in the sciences. The sociology of the alternatives to big science", 79 : xv-1-289. [in: Sociology of the Sciences. A Yearbook.]

1991 PRENDERGAST, Christopher. "The problem of unity of knowledge in Comte's philosophy of science", *Sociological Inquiry* 49, 79 : 25-35.

1992 PRIGOGINE, Ilya; STENGERS, Isabelle. *La nouvelle alliance: métamorphose de la science.* Paris, Gallimard, 79, 302 p.

1993 ROLL-HANSEN, Nils. "The controversy between biometricians and Mendelians: a test case for the sociology of scientific knowledge", *Social Science Information* 19, 80 : 501-517.

1994 SANTUCCIO, Mario. *Scienza e società* (Science and society). Milano, F. Angeli, 79, 280 p.

1995 SCHÄFER, Wolf. "Finalization in perspective: toward a revolution in the social paradigm of science", *Social Science Information* 18, 79 : 915-943.

1996 SCHEURER, Paul B. *Révolutions de la science et permanence du réel.* Paris, PUF, 79, 366 p.

1997 SEMENOV, N. N. "Nekotorye voprosy sociologii nauk" (Some questions on sociology of science), *IN: Nauka-narodnomu hozjajstvu.* 79 : 239-271.

1998 Bibl.XXIX-1856. SIMONDS, A. P. *Karl Mannheim's sociology of knowledge.* CR: Charles CAMIC, *American Journal of Sociology* 86(2), sep 80: 422-425. [also CR: Arthur Lennart KALLEBERG, American political Science Review, 74(1), mar 80: 265-266.]

1999 SOKOLOV, S. V. "Obščestvennoe i individual'noe soznanie" (Social and individual knowledge), *Izvestija Akademii Nauk latvijskoj SSR* 79 : 15-27.

2000 SPÖRER, Željka. "Organizacija i znanije"(Organisation and knowledge), *Sociologija* 21, 79 : 255-266.

2001 STEBBINS, Robert A. "Avocational science: the amateur routine in archaeology and astronomy", *International Journal of comparative Sociology (Leiden)* 21(1-2), mar-jun 80 : 34-48.

2002 STRATUP, Richard. "The sociology of mathematics", *Sociology and social Research* 64, jan 80 : 151-167.
2003 SUHOTIN, A. K.; [ed.]. *Sovremennaja nauka i naučnoe poznanie* (Contemporary science and scientific knowledge). Tomsk, Izdatel'stvo Tomskogo Universiteta, 79, 189 p.
2004 WISMAN, Jon D. "The sociology of knowledge as a tool for research into the history of economic thought", *American Journal of Economics and Sociology* 39, jan 80 : 83-94.
2005 WISMAN, Jon D. "Values and modes of rationality in economic science", *International Journal of social Economics* 80 : 137-148.
2006 WUTHNOW, Robert. "The emergence of modern science and world system theory", *Theory and Society* sep 79 : 215-243.

13700. COMMUNICATION. LANGUAGE
COMMUNICATION. LANGAGE

13710 Linguistics. Semiotics
Linguistique. Sémiotique

[See also / voir aussi: 402, 559, 799, 1533, 2085, 2157]

2007 AARONSON, Doris; RIEBER, Robert W.; [eds.]. *Psycholinguistic research: implications and applications.* Hillsdale, NJ, L. Erlbaum Associates, New York, 79, x-534 p. [distributed by the Halsted Press division of Wiley.]
2008 ADDA, R.; [et al.]. *Néologie et lexicologie; hommage à Louis Guilbert.* Paris, Larousse, 79, 223 p.
2009 AUROUX, Sylvain. *La Sémiotique des encyclopédistes: essai d'épistémologie historique des sciences du langage.* Paris, Payot, 79, 333 p.
2010 BLANCHARD, Marc Eli. *Description: Sign, Self, Desire. Critical theory in the wake of semiotics.* The Hague, Paris, New York, Mouton, 80, viii-300 p.
2011 BOTHA, Rudolph I. *The Conduct of Linguistic Inquiry.* The Hague, Paris, New York, Mouton, 80, 448 p.
2012 BÜLOW, Edeltraud; SCHMITTER, Peter; [eds.]. *Integrale Linguistik* (Integral linguistics). Amsterdam, John Benjamins, 79, xiii-817 p.
2013 CALVERT, Donald R. *Description phonetics.* New York, Brian C. Decker Div. Thieme-Stratton, 80, xiv-247 p.
2014 CANART, Paul. *Studies in comparative semantics.* New York, St. Martin's Press, 79, xvii-166 p.
2015 DELEDALLE, Gérard. *Théorie et pratique du signe: introduction à la sémiotique de Charles S. Peirce.* Paris, Payot, 79, 215 p.
2016 DESHPANDE, Madhav M. *Sociolinguistic attitudes in India: an historical reconstruction.* Ann Arbor, Karoma Publishers, 79, xvi-162 p.
2017 ECO, Umberto. *The role of the reader: explorations in the semiotics of texts.* Bloomington, Indiana University Press, 79, viii-273 p.
2018 FILLMORE, Charles J.; KEMPLER, Daniel; WANG, William S.-Y.; [eds.]. *Individual differences in language ability and language behavior.* New York, Academic Press, 79, xv-346 p.
2019 Bibl.XXIX-1886. GILES, Howard; [ed.]. *Language, ethnicity and intergroup relations.* CR: David E. LOPEZ, *Contemporary Sociology (Albany)* 9(6), nov 80: 811-812.
2020 GREIMAS, Algirdas Julien; COURTÉS, Joseph. *Sémiotique: dictionnaire raisonné de la théorie du langage.* Paris, Hachette, 79, vi-422 p.
2021 HANCOCK, Ian F.; [ed.]. "Romani sociolinguistics", *International Journal of the Sociology of Language* 19, 79 : 5-144.
2022 HELBO, André; [ed.]; [et al.]. *Le Champ sémiologique: perspectives internationales.* Bruxelles, Éditions Complexe, 79.
2023 HÉNAULT, Anne. *Les enjeux de la sémiotique: introduction à la sémiotique générale.* Paris, Presses universitaires de France, 79, 191 p.
2024 HERVEY, S. G. J. *Axiomatic semantics: a theory of linguistics semantics.* Edinburgh, Scottish Academic Press, 79, xxvii-313 p.
2025 HUDSON, R. A. *Sociolinguistics.* Cambridge, Eng., New York, Cambridge University Press, 80, xii-250 p.
2026 KAUFER, David S. "The competence/performance distinction in linguistic theory", *Philosophy of the social Sciences* sep 79 : 257-275.
2027 MULDER, Jan W. F.; HERVEY, S. G. J. *The strategy of linguistics: papers on the theory and methodology of axiomatic functionalism.* Edinburgh, Scottish Academic Press, 80, v-236 p.

2028 NARULA, Shamsher Singh. *Social roots of Indian linguistics.* New Delhi, Oriental Publishers & Distributors, 79, 212 p.
2029 PELC, Jerzy; [ed.]. *Semiotics in Poland, 1894-1969.* Dordrecht, Holland, Boston, D. Reidel Pub. Co., 79, xxvi-504 p.
2030 ROSSI-LANDI, Ferruccio. *Semiotica e ideologia* (Semiotics and ideology). Milano, Bompiani, 79, 331 p.
2031 SAARINEN, Esa; [ed.]. *Game-theoretical semantics: essays on semantics.* Dordrecht, Holland, Boston, D. Reidel Pub. Co., 79, xiv-292 p.
2032 SABOURIN, Conrad; BLAIS, Denise Daoust. *Linguistique et sociolinguistique: recherches en cours au Québec.* Montréal, Service des publications, Direction des communications, Office de la langue française, 79, 54 p.
2033 WINNER, Irene Portis; UMIKER-SEBEOK, Jean; [eds.]. *Semiotics of Culture.* The Hague, Paris, New York, Mouton, 79, vi-290 p.

13720. Communication. Sign
Communication. Signe

[See also / voir aussi: 183, 669, 685, 892, 1276, 1286, 1304, 1544, 1583, 2015, 2083, 2088, 2150, 2176, 2280, 3084, 3487, 3498, 5047]

2034 BALDI, Paolo. "La notion de signification dans la théorie des actes de langage", *Studi italiani di Linguistica teorica ed applicata* (1-2-3), 79 : 31-43.
2035 BATES, Elizabeth. *The emergence of symbols: cognition and communication in infancy.* New York, Academic Press, 79, xvi-387 p.
2036 BERNIER, Charles L.; YERKEY, A. Neil. *Cogent communication: overcoming reading overload.* Westport, CT, Greenwood Press, 79, xii-280 p.
2037 BULLOWA, Margaret; [ed.]. *Before speech: the beginning of interpersonal communication.* Cambridge, New York, Cambridge University Press, 79, viii-400 p.
2038 CARR, Jacquelyn B. *Communicating and relating.* Menlo Park, CA, Benjamin/Cummings Pub. Co., 79, xv-413 p.
2039 CIPRIANI, Roberto. "Simbolismo, politica e religione"(Symbolism, politics and religion), *Sociologia (Roma)* 13, jan-apr 79 : 25-50.
2040 COOMBS, Gary. "Opportunities, information networks and the migration-distance relationship", *Social Networks* feb 79 : 257-276. [Example of the Chumash Indians to Santa Barbara, CA, 18th century.]
2041 FISCHER-LICHTE, Erika. *Bedeutung: Probleme e. semiot. Hermeneutik u. Ästhetik* (Meaning: problem in semiotic hermeneutics and aesthetics). München, Beck, 79, 233 p.
2042 GRABBE, Holger. *Kommunikationseinrichtungen als urbanitätsstiftende Strukturen* (Communication facilities as fundamental structures of urbanity). Bielefeld, Pfeffer, 79, 145 p.
2043 HARDT, Hanno; [ed.]. *Communication and capitalism. Early German and American perspectives.* Beverly Hills, CA, Sage Publications, 79, 248 p.
2044 HARPER, Nancy L. *Human communication theory: the history of a paradigm.* Rochelle Park, NJ, Hayden Book Co., 79, 321 p.
2045 HARRIS, Howard; LIPMAN, Alan. "Social symbolism and space usage in daily life", *Sociological Review* 28, mai 80 : 415-428.
2046 HENRICKS, Thomas S. "Ascending and descending meaning: a theoretical inquiry into play and ritual", *Sociologial Inquiry* 50, 80 : 25-37.
2047 ISAMBERT, François-A. *Rite et efficacité symbolique: essai d'anthropologie sociologique.* Paris, Éditions du Cerf, 79, 224 p.
2048 JEDLICKA, Davor. "Opportunities, information networks and international migration streams", *Social Networks* feb 79 : 277-284. [From Japan to Hawaiian Islands.]
2049 KOWALEWSKI, David. "The protest uses of symbolic politics: the mobilization functions of protester symbolic resources", *Social Science Quarterly* 61, jun 80 : 95-113.
2050 LASSWELL, Harold Dwight; LERNER, Daniel; SPEIER, Hans; [eds.]. *The Symbolic instrument in early times.* Honolulu, University Press of Hawaii, 79, xiv-631 p. [published for the East-West Center.]
2051 MALETZKE, Gerhard. *Kommunikationsforschung als empirische Sozialwissenschaft* (Communication research as an empirical social science). Berlin, Spiess, 80, 93 p.
2052 MARTIN, Bernice. "The sacralization of disorder: symbolism in rock music", *Sociological Analysis* 40, 79 : 87-124.
2053 MAZUR, Allan; [et al.]. "Physiological aspects of communication via mutual gaze", *American Journal of Sociology* 86, jul 80 : 50-74.

2054   NOCE, Augusto del. *Agonía de la sociedad opulenta* (The end of affluent society). Pamplona, EUNSA, 79, 227 p.
2055   POČEPKO, V. V. "K voprosu o roli kommunikacii eê sredstv v duhovnoj kul'ture obščestva" (On the communication role and its means in the societal spiritual culture), *IN: Problemy čeloveka i obščestva v filosofii i naučnom kommunizme.* Leningrad, 79 : 62-70.
2056   RICHARDSON, R. J.; ERICKSON, Bonnie H.; NOSANCHUK, T. A. "Community size, network structure and the flow of information", *Canadian Journal of Sociology* 79 : 379-392.
2057   RODIONOV, B. A. "Social'nye kommunikacii v socialističeskom trudovom kollektive" (Social communications in the socialist labour collectivity), *IN: Metodologija upravlenija obščestvennymi sistemami v uslovijah razvitogo socializma.* 78 : 109-115.
2058   ROIZ, Miguel. "La contaminación informativa e incomunicación social" (Informative contamination and social incommunication), *Documentación social* 38, 80 : 135-156.
2059   SHOLEM, Gershom. "La symbolique des couleurs dans la tradition et la mystique juives", *Diogène* 108, oct-dec 79 : 95-123.
2060   SKYVINGTON, William. "Les systèmes de communication, la science de la communication", *Revue internationale des Sciences sociales* 32, 80 : 222-238.
2061   STEVENS, John D. *Communication History: reconceptualizing the past.* Beverly Hills, CA, Sage Publications, 80, 160 p.
2062   STROPPA, Claudio; [ed.]. *I Processi di comunicazione nell'ambito urbano* (Communication processes in the urban environment). Bologna, Pàtron, 79, 372 p.
2063   SUPEK-ZUPAN, Olga. "Simboličko ponašanje u suvremenoj kulturi: smisao poklada" (Symbolic behaviour in contemporary culture: the meaning of carnival), *Sociologija* 21, 79 : 291-303.
2064   TAMIR, Lois M. *Communication and the aging process: interaction throughout the life cycle.* New York, Pergamon Press, 79, xix-195 p.
2065   TEHRANIAN, Majid. "La malédiction de la modernité: dialectique de la modernisation et de la communication", *Revue internationale des Sciences sociales* 32, 80 : 263-280.
2066   TOTARO, Francesco. *Produzione del senso: forme del valore e dell'ideologia* (Meaning production: forms of values and ideology). Milano, Vita e pensiero, 79, viii-221 p.
2067   VAN HATTUM, Rolland James. *Communication disorders: an introduction.* New York, Macmillan, 80, xiii-578 p.
2068   WARTELLA, Ellen; [ed.]. *Children Communicating. Media and Development of Thought, Speech, Understanding.* Beverly Hills, CA, Sage Publications, 79, 288 p.
2069   WIREDU, Kwasi. "Le concept de communication humaine: une perspective philosophique", *Revue internationale des Sciences sociales* 32, 80 : 214-221.

13730.   Language
            Langage

[See also / voir aussi: 457, 529, 678, 804, 1177, 1247, 1422, 1455, 1963, 2020, 2034, 2259, 2284, 2381, 2601, 3394, 3487, 3699, 5627]

2070   "Actes (Les) de discours"(Communications (Paris)), *Communications (Paris)* 32, 80 : 7-284.
2071   "Apprentissage et connaissance d'une langue étrangère", *Langages* 14(57), mar 80 : 5-126.
2072   "Langages et sociétés", *Pensée* 209, jan 80 : 3-129.
2073   ADENIRAN, Adekunle. "Personalities and policies in the establishment of English in Northern Nigeria, 1900-1943", *International Journal of the Sociology of Language* 22, 79 : 57-77.
2074   ALDER, Max K. *Non-vocal language and language substitutes: a sociolinguistic study.* Hamburg, Buske, 79, 206 p.
2075   AMMON, Ulrich; [ed.]. "Dialect and standard in highly industrialized societies", *International Journal of the Sociology of Language* 21, 79 : 155.
2076   BERK-SELIGSON, Susan. "Sociolinguistic view of the Mexican-American speech community", *Latin American Research Review* 15, 80 : 65-110.
2077   BERRUTO, Gaetano. "Problemi e metodi nell' 'analisi del discorso' " (Problems and methods of speech analysis), *Studi italiani di Linguistica teorica ed applicata* (1-2-3), 79 : 45-71.
2078   BRAGA, Giorgio. "International languages: concept and problems", *International Journal of the Sociology of Language* 22, 79 : 27-49.
2079   CALVET, Louis Jean. *Linguistique et colonialisme: petit traité de glottophagie.* Paris, Payot, 79, 236 p.

2080 CAMPBELL, Lyle; MITHUN, Marianne; [eds.]. *The Languages of Native America: historical and comparative assessment.* Austin, University of Texas Press, 79, 1034 p.
2081 CASSEN, Bernard. "L'espagnol et l'anglais à Porto-Rico. Historique d'une tentative d'ethnocide linguistique", *Amérique latine* jul-sep 80 : 12-20.
2082 CRUTTENDEN, Alan. *Language in infancy and childhood: a linguistic introduction to language acquisition.* New York, St. Martin's Press, 79, xiv-193 p.
2083 DENKEL, Arda. "The speaker's communicative intent", *Journal for the Theory of social Behaviour* 10, mar 80 : 19-38.
2084 DUIPMANS, D. "Fries of Nederlands? Een onderzoek naar het taalgedrag van tweetaligen" (Frisian of Dutch? The behaviour towards language of bilinguals), *Sociologische Gids* 27, sep-oct 80 : 409-425.
2085 EDWARDS, Walter F. "The sociolinguistic significance of some Guyanese speech acts", *International Journal of the Sociology of Language* 22, 79 : 79-101.
2086 FOWLER, Roger; [et al.]. *Language and control.* London, Boston, Routledge & K. Paul, 79, 224 p.
2087 FRENCH, Peter A.; UEHLING, Theodore Edward; WETTSTEIN, Howard K.; [eds.]. *Contemporary perspectives in the philosophy of language.* Minneapolis, University of Minnesota Press, 79, viii-417 p.
2088 FRIEDRICH, Paul. *Language, context, and the imagination: essays.* Stanford, CA, Stanford University Press, 79, xiv-523 p. [selected and introduced by Anwar S. DIL.]
2089 HALL, Judith A. "Voice tone and persuasion", *Journal of Personality and social Psychology* 38, jun 80 : 924-934.
2090 HJELMQUIST, Erland; BRENNER, Sten-Olaf. "The mediation of attitudes by speech in dyadic conversations", *Human Relations* 32(12), dec 79 : 983-997.
2091 IBRAGIMOV, H. A. "Opyt sociologičeskogo issledovanija sootnošenija jazykov i nacional'nogo (ètničeskogo) samozosnanija (na primere gorodskogo naselenija Dagestana)" (An essay of sociological research on the correlation between languages and national (ethnic) consciousness (with the example of Daghestan urban population)), *IN: Social'no-ètničeskoe kul'turnoe razvitie gorodskogo naselenija Dagestana.* Mahačkala, 79 : 51-66.
2092 JARDEL, Jean-Pierre. "Langues et pouvoir en pays créolophones", *Pluriel* 21, 80 : 59-68.
2093 JOHNSON, C. L. "Perceptual sociology: using the semantic differential technique in the classroom", *Teaching Sociology* oct 80 : 87-94.
2094 KARAM, Francis X. "Processes of increasing mutual intelligibility between language varieties", *International Journal of the Sociology of Language* 22, 79 : 115-137.
2095 KASSAPU, S. N. "Pour deux langues africaines de communication", *Peuples noirs — Peuples africains* (12), nov-dec 79 : 60-84.
2096 KHLEIF, Bud B. *Language, Ethnicity, and Education in Wales.* The Hague, Paris, New York, Mouton, 80, xiv-316 p.
2097 KNAPP, Mark L. *Essentials of nonverbal communication.* New York, Holt, Rinehart and Winston, 80, viii-264 p.
2098 KRESS, Gunther R.; HODGE, Robert. *Language as ideology.* London, Boston, Routledge & Kegan Paul, 79, x-163 p.
2099 KURZAWA, Lothar. *Zeichen, Körper, Schrift: zur Interpretation d. Sprache in Hegels Psychologie* (Signs, body, writing: on the interprepation of language in Hegel's psychology). Marburg/Lahn, Guttandin und Hoppe, 79, 214 p.
2100 LAMB, David. *Language and perception in Hegal and Wittgenstein.* Amersham, Eng., Avebury, 79, xiii-135 p.
2101 LAMY, Paul; [ed.]. "Language planning and identity planning", *International Journal of the Sociology of Language* 20, 79 : 5-107.
2102 LINDBLOM, B.; ÖHMAN, S.; [eds.]. *Frontiers of speech communication research.* London, New York, Academic Press, 79, xxv-393 p.
2103 MALMBERG, Bertil. *Le langage: signe de l'humain.* Paris, Picard, 79, 289 p.
2104 MANESSY, Gabriel; WALD, Paul. *Plurilinguisme: normes, situations, stratégies: études sociolinguistiques.* Paris, Éditions L'Harmattan, 79, 283 p. [publ. par le Centre d'étude des plurilinguismes, Université de Nice.]
2105 MAYER, Kurt B. "Language groups in Switzerland", *Plural Societies* 10(3-4), aut-wint 79 : 53-70.
2106 MCCORMACK, William C.; WURM, Stephen A.; [eds.]. *Language and society: anthropological issues.* The Hague, Mouton, 79, xv-771 p.

2107 MOLES, Abraham A. "A French point of view on the predominance of English", *International Journal of the Sociology of Language* 22, 79 : 51-56.
2108 NATALE, Michael; ENTIN, Elliot; JAFFE, Joseph. "Vocal interruptions in dyadic communication as a function of speech and social anxiety", *Journal of Personality and social Psychology* 37, jun 79 : 865-878.
2109 OKOH, Nduka. "Bilingualism and divergent thinking among Nigerian and Welsh school children", *Journal of social Psychology* 110, apr 80 : 163-170.
2110 PSATHAS, George; [ed.]. *Everyday language: studies in ethnomethodology*. New York, Irvington Publishers, 79, 299 p. [distributed by Halsted Press.]
2111 RADDEN, Günter. *Ein Profil soziolinguistischer Variation in einer amerikanischen Kleinstadt* (Profile of sociolinguistic variation in a small American town). Frankfurt a.M., Bern, Cirencester, Lang, 79, vii-437 p.
2112 RICH, Marvian C. "Verbal reports and mental processes: issues of accuracy and awareness", *Journal for the Theory of social Behaviour* mar 79 : 29-37.
2113 ROMMETVEIT, Ragnar; BLAKAR, Rolv Mikkel; [eds.]. *Studies of language, thought, and verbal communication*. London, New York, Academic Press, 79, xxi-466 p.
2114 ROSENTHAL, Robert; [ed.]. *Skill in nonverbal communication: individual differences*. Cambridge, MA, Oelgeschlager, Gunn & Hain, 79, xviii-270 p.
2115 SAGER, J. C.; [ed.]. "Standardization of nomenclature", *International Journal of Sociology of Language* 23, 80 : 5-104.
2116 Bibl.XXIX-1981. SCHENKEIN, Jim; [ed.]. *Studies in the organization of conversational interaction*. CR: Hugh MEHAN; J. Lee MEIHLS, *American Journal of Sociology* 86(2), sep 80: 435-436.
2117 SCHERER, Klaus R.; GILES, Howard; [eds.]. *Social markers in speech*. Cambridge, Eng., New York, Cambridge University Press; Paris, Éditions de la Maison des sciences de l'homme, 79, xiii-395 p.
2118 SCHWITZGEBEL, R. Kirkland; TAYLOR, Robert W. "Impression formation under conditions of spontaneous and shadowed speech", *Journal of social Psychology* 110, apr 80 : 253-263.
2119 SHOPEN, Timothy; [ed.]. *Languages and their status*. Cambridge, MA, Winthrop Publishers, 79, xii-335 p.
2120 SREEDHAR, M. V. "The functions of bilingualism in Nagaland", *International Journal of the Sociology of Language* 22, 79 : 103-113. [Assam.]
2121 STEVENS, Paul. "Modernism and authenticity as reflected in language attitudes: the case of Tunisia", *Civilisations* 30(1-2), jun 80 : 37-59.
2122 WOLFLE, Lee M. "The enduring effects of education on verbal skill", *Sociology of Education* 53, apr 80 : 104-114.

13740. Audience
Audience

[See also / voir aussi: 708, 1160, 1183, 2017, 2149]

13750. Advertising. Propaganda
Publicité. Propagande

[See also / voir aussi: 1223, 1269, 2089, 5463]

2123 BERGLER, Reinhold. *Zigarettenwerbung und Zigarettenkonsum: eine psychologische Studie* (Cigarette advertising and cigarette consumption: a psychological study). Bern, H. Huber, 79, 191 p.
2124 CHEBAT, Jean-Claude. "Analyse du débat sur le contexte économique de la publicité", *Revue de l'Institut de Sociologie* (3-4), 79 : 207-221.
2125 GOVAERTS, France. "Modèle de croissance publicitaire et idéologie de la consommation", *Revue de l'Institut de Sociologie* (3-4), 79 : 223-237.
2126 LEVKOV, Ju. Ja.; PROTOPOPOVA, A. A. *Psihologopedagogičeskie aspekty propagandy* (Psychological and pedagogical aspects of propaganda). Syktyvkar, Komi Knižnoe Izdatel'stvo, 79, 63 p.
2127 PATEMAN, Trevor. "How to do things with images. An essay on the pragmatics of advertising", *Theory and Society* jul 80 : 603-622.
2128 POGUDIN, V. I. "Vzaimodejstvie i svjazi propagandy i agitacii" (Interaction and ties between propaganda and discussion), *Voprosy Teorii i Metodov ideologičeskoj Raboty* (11), 79 : 23-39.

2129	ROLOFF, Michael E.; MILLER, Gerald R.; [eds.]. *Persuasion. New directions in theory and research*. Beverly Hills, CA, Sage Publications, 80, 312 p.
2130	ROŠIN, S. K. "Reklama i 'psihologija potrebitelja'" (Advertising and the consumer's psychology), *IN: Psihologičeskie mehanizmy reguljacii social'nogo povedenija*. Moskva, 79 : 305-320.
2131	SPROULE, J. Michael. *Argument: language and its influence*. New York, McGraw-Hill, 80, xiii-464 p.

13760. Mass communication
Communication de masse

[See also / voir aussi: 829, 947, 1343, 1590, 2503, 3034, 3590, 3963, 4324, 5343, 5355, 5989]

2132	"Children and television", *Journal of Broadcasting* 24, spr 80 : 117-265.
2133	"Satellites for rural development", *Journal of Communications* 29, aut 79 : 89-114.
2134	"Growing older: perceptions and representations", *Journal of Communications* 30, wint 80 : 37-88.
2135	"Medios de comunicación social en España ante la década de los años ochenta" (Mass communication media in Spain facing the 1980's), *Razón y Fé* 202(990), jul-aug 80 : 1-24.
2136	ACQUAVIVA, Sabino S.; [ed.]. *Mass media, famiglia e transformazioni sociali* (Mass media, family and social transformations). Firenze, Sansoni, 80, 256 p.
2137	ADLER, Laure. *Les premiers journalistes, 1830-1850*. Paris, Payot, 79, 239 p. CR: François GRESLE, *Revue française de Sociologie* 21(2), apr-jun 80: 312.
2138	AIDA, Toshihiko. "Masukomi juyo kodo no henka"(Changes in the Mass Communication responses of the Japanese audience), *Nenpo shakai shinrigaku* 21, 80 : 109-132.
2139	ALLEN, Richard L.; BIELBY, William T. "Blacks' relationship with the print media", *Journalism Quarterly* 56, aut 79 : 488-496.
2140	ALLEN, Richard L.; CLARKE, David E. "Ethnicity and mass media behaviour: a study of Blacks and Latinos", *Journal of Broadcasting* 24, wint 80 : 23-34.
2141	ANDERSON, Digby C.; SHARROCK, W. W. "Biasing the news: technical issues in 'media studies'", *Sociology* 13, nov 79 : 367-385.
2142	ANDRÁSSY, Mária. *A kulturális ipar — a tömegkommunikáció — hatása a magyar nők szocio-kulturális viselkedésére* (Effects of the cultural industry — i.e. of mass media — on the sociocultural behaviour of Hungarian women). Institute for Research of Culture, Budapest, Művelődéskutató Intézet, 80, 83 p.
2143	BECKER, Jörg. "Die internationale Medienpolitik der Bundesrepublik zwischen Prinzipien und Interessen" (The international media policy of the Federal Republic between principles and interests), *Rundfunk und Fernsehen* 28, 80 : 224-234.
2144	BELTRÁN S., Luis Ramiro. "Massenmedien in Lateinamerika" (Mass media in Latin America), *Rundfunk und Fernsehen* 28, 80 : 21-39.
2145	BERGER, Arthur Asa. *Television as an instrument of terror: essays on media, popular culture, and everyday life*. New Brunswick, NJ, Transaction Books, 80, xii-214 p.
2146	BERGLER, Reinhold; SIX, Ulrike. *Psychologie des Fernsehens* (Psychology of television). Bern, H. Huber, 79, 302 p. CR: Michael HACHENBERG, *Kölner Zeitschrift für Soziologie und Sozialpsychologie* 32(2), jun 80: 407-408.
2147	BERTINI, Antonio. *Cinema e ideologia nella Germania di Weimar* (Cinema and ideology in Weimar Germany). Cosenza, Pellegrini, 79, 172 p.
2148	BINET, Jacques. "Apport et influence du cinéma négro-africain", *Diogène* 110, apr-jun 80 : 72-89.
2149	BORTZ, Jürgen; BRAUNE, Paul. "The effects of daily newspapers on their readers. Exemplary presentation of a study and its results", *European Journal of social Psychology* 10, apr-jun 80 : 165-193.
2150	BOSSHART, Louis. *Dynamik der Fernseh-Unterhaltung. Eine kommunikationswissenschaftliche Analyse und Synthese* (Dynamics of the televised interview. An analysis and synthesis in communication sciences). Freiburg, Universitätsverlag, 79, 248 p. CR: Alphons SILBERMANN, *Kölner Zeitschrift für Soziologie und Sozialpsychologie* 32(2), jun 80 : 404-405.
2151	BRINKGREVE, C.; KORZEC, M. "Feelings, behaviour, morals in the Netherlands: 1938-1978. Analysis and interpretation of an advice column", *Netherlands' Journal of Sociology* 15, dec 79 : 123-140.

2152   BRODERSOHN, Victor. "Mass media use, issue knowledge and political involvement" (Economic structure and social development in El Salvador), *Public Opinion Quarterly* 44, 80 : 241-248.
2153   CÂMPEANU, Pavel. *Oamenii şi televiziunea: privirc sociologicĂ asupra telespectatorului* (Television audiences: sociological research on televiewers). Bucureşti "Meridiane", 79, 241 p.
2154   CANTOR, Muriel G. *Prime-time television. Content and control.* Beverly Hills, CA, Sage Publications, 80, 152 p.
2155   CARRERA VILLAR, Francisco. "Ethos-Pathos-Logos: Formulación original aristotélica, distorsiones interpretativas y vigencia en comunicación persuasiva de masas" (Ethos-pathos-logos: original Aristotelian formulation, interpretative distorsions and enforcement in persuasive mass communication), *Cuadernos de Realidades sociales* 16-17, 80 : 19-56.
2156   CARROLL, John M. *Toward a Structural Psychology of Cinema.* The Hague, Paris, New York, Mouton, 80, 224 p.
2157   CHATEAU, Dominique; JOST, François. *Nouveau cinéma, nouvelle sémiologie: essai d'analyse des films d'Alain Robbe-Grillet.* Paris, Union générale d'édition, 79, 314 p.
2158   COMSTOCK, George. *Televison in America.* Beverly Hills, CA, Sage Publications, 80, 160 p.
2159   COPPA, Frank J.; [ed.]. *Screen and society: the impact of television upon aspects of contemporary civilization.* Chicago, Nelson-Hall, 79, xxvii-217 p.
2160   CVETAEVA, N. N. "Televidenie kak faktor potreblenija kul'tury" (Television as a factor of cultural consumption), *IN: Sociologičeskie problemy obščestvennogo mnenija i dejatel'nosti sredstv massovoj informacii.* Moskva, 79 : 67-74.
2161   DILLNER, Gisela. *Massenkommunikation in Ecuador*(Mass communication in Ecuador). Frankfurt/Main, Vervuert, 79, 312 p.
2162   DOELKER, Christian. *"Wirklichkeit" in den Medien* ("Reality" in the media). Zug, Klett & Balmer, 79, 191 p.
2163   DOOB, Anthony N; MACDONALD, Glenn E. "Television viewing and fear of victimization: is the relationship causal?", *Journal of Personality and social Psychology* 37, feb 79 : 170-179.
2164   DRIDZE, T. M. *Organizacija i metody lingvo-psihologičeskogo issledovanija massovoj kommunikacii* (Organization and methods of the linguistic and psychosociological research on mass communication). Moskva, Izdatel'stvo Moskovskogo Universiteta, 79, 281 p.
2165   EURICH, Claus. *Kommunikative Partizipation und partizipative Kommunikationsforschung* (Communicative participation and participative communication research). Frankfurt, R. G. Fischer, 80, 412 p.
2166   FAULSTICH, Werner; [ed.]. *Kritische Stichwörter zur Medienwissenschaft* (Critical comments on media science). München, W. Fink, 79, 437 p.
2167   FLICHY, Patrice. *Les Industries de l'imaginaire: pour une analyse économique des media.* Grenoble, Presses universitaires de Grenoble, Paris, INA, 80, 277 p. [publ. par l'Institut national de l'audiovisuel.]
2168   Bibl.XXIX-2011. FRIEDMANN, Georges. *Ces merveilleux instruments. Essai sur les communications de masse.* CR: Jean-René TRÉANTON, *Revue française de Sociologie* 21(3), jul-sep 80 : 474.
2169   GARCIA JIMENEZ, Jcsús. *Radiotelevisión y política cultural en el franquismo* (Radiotelevision and cultural policy during the Franco regime). Madrid, Instituto "Balmes" Consejo Superior de Investigaciones Científicas, 80, 692 p.
2170   GILBOA, Eylan. "Studying mass media roles: the use of simulation in national and international politics", *Teaching political Science* oct 79 : 73-88.
2171   GOFFREDO, Donato; [et al.]. *Comunicazione e partecipazione* (Communication and participation). Roma, Edizioni paoline, 79, 299 p. [Italy.]
2172   GRUHN, Werner. *Wissenschaft und Technik in deutschen Massenmedien: ein Vergleich zwischen der Bundesrepublik Deutschland und der DDR* (Science and technique in German mass media: a comparison between the Federal Republic of Germany and the GDR). Deutsche Gesellschaft für Zeitgeschichtliche Fragen, Vertrieb, Institut für Gesellschaft und Wissenschaft an der Universität Erlangen-Nürnberg, 79, xvii-430 p.
2173   GRUSŠIN, B. A.; ONIKOV, L. A.; [eds.]. *Massovaja informacija v sovetskom promyšlennom gorode: opyt kompleksnogo sociologičeskogo issledovanija* (Mass information in a Soviet industrial town: an essay of complex sociological research). Moskva, Politizdat, 80, 446 p.
2174   GUREVIČ, P. S. "Massovaja informacija kak faktor kul'turnyh izmenenij" (Mass information as a factor of cultural change), *IN: Sociologičeskie problemy obrazovanija, kul'tury i nauki.* Moskva, 78 : 105-112.

2175	HANÁK, Katalin; SZILÁGYI, Erzsébet. *Egy különös jelenség. "A halottlátó" a tömegkommunikációs eszközök tükrében és a közvéleményben* (A strange phenomenon. "The necromancer" as reflected by mass media and in public opinion). Budapest. Tömegkommunikációs Kutatóközpont, 79, 86 p.
2176	HARDT, Hanno. *Social theories of the press: early German and America perspectives.* Beverly Hills, Sage Publications, 79, 240 p.
2177	HOLZ, Josephine R.; WRIGHT, Charles R. "Sociology of mass communications", *Annual Review of Sociology* 79 : 193-217.
2178	HOROWITZ, Irving Louis. "Marketing social science", *Society* 17, nov-dec 79 : 12-53. [social science publishing in the USA.]
2179	HUERTA Y PALACIOS, Felipe. "Prensa infantil y juvenil: problemática ética" (Child and youth press: ethical problems), *Cuadernos de Realidades sociales* 16-17, 80 : 307-326.
2180	HUGHES, Michael. "The fruits of cultivation analysis: a reexamination of some effects of television watching", *Public Opinion Quarterly* 44, 80 : 287-302.
2181	JEANCOLAS, Jean Pierre. *Le cinéma des Français: la Ve République, 1958-1978.* Paris, Stock, 79, 477 p.
2182	JOWETT, Garth; LINTON, James M. *Movies as a mass communication.* Beverly Hills, CA, Sage Publications, 80, 149 p.
2183	KOROBEINIKOV, Valery S. "Conflits de médias dans la société industrielle moderne", *Revue international des Sciences sociales* 32, 80 : 254-262.
2184	KOROBEJNIKOV, V. S. "Vazimodejstvie sredstv massovoj informacii i ličnosti pri socializme" (Interaction between mass media and personality under socialism), *IN: Sociologičeskie problemy obščestvennogo mnenija i dejatel'nosti sredstv massovoj informacii.* Moskva, 79 : 7-16.
2185	KUNCZIK, Michael. *Massenkommunikation: eine Einführung* (Mass communication: an introduction). Köln, Wien, Böhlau, 79, vi-246 p.
2186	LIGBOAJAH, Frank Okwu. "Developing indigenous communication in Nigeria", *Journal of Communications* 29, aug 79 : 40-45.
2187	LITTUNEN, Yrjö. "Les problèmes culturels liés à la radiodiffusion directe par satellites", *Revue internationale des Sciences sociales* 32, 80 : 302-324.
2188	LUSCHER, Kurt. "Gesellschaftspolitische Aspekte des Kabelfernsehens. Thesen aus sozialökologischer Sicht" (Socio-political aspects of cable television. Theses from a socio-ecological viewpoint), *Publizistik* 24, jul-sep 79 : 344-352. [Germany FR.]
2189	MALASSINET, Alain. *Société et cinéma: les années 1960 en Grande Bretagne, essai d'interprétation sociologique.* Paris, Minard, 79, 223 p.
2190	MANAEV, O. T. "O povyšenii ëffektivnosti sredstv massovoj informacii promyšlennogo predprijatija" (On the elevation of the mass media efficiency in an industrial enterprise), *IN: Sociologičeskie problemy obščestvennogo mnenija i dejatel'nosti sredstv massovoj informacii.* Moskva, 79 : 39-48.
2191	MATTELART, Armand; MATTELART, Michèle. *De l'Usage des médias en temps de crise: les nouveaux profils des industries de la culture.* Paris, A. Moreau, 79, 447 p.
2192	MCCOMBS, Maxwell E.; BECKER, Lee B. *Using mass communication theory.* Englewood Cliffs, NJ, Prentice-Hall, 79, x-148 p.
2193	MEADOWS, Paul. "The press and the communication media: a technological perspective", *International Journal of comparative Sociology (Leiden)* 21(1-2), mar-jun 80 : 65-73.
2194	MEYN, Hermann. *Massenmedien in der Bundesrepublik Deutschland* (Mass media in the Federal Republic of Germany). Berlin, Colloquium Verlag, 79, 173 p.
2195	MONNIER-RABALL, Jacques. *Simuler/dissimuler: essai sur les simulacres de masse.* Paris, Payot, 79, 211 p.
2196	MOSCO, Vincent. *Broadcasting in the United States: innovative challenge and organization control.* Norwood, NJ, Ablex Publishing Corporation, 79, 153 p. CR: Mark R. LEVY, *Contemporary Sociology (Albany)* 9(6), nov 80: 812-813.
2197	PÉREZ ESPINO, Efraín. "El monopolio de la televisión comercial en México" (Commercial television monopoly in Mexico), *Revista mexicana de Sociología* 41, oct-dec 79 : 1435-1468.
2198	PHILLIPS, David P. "Airplane accidents, murder, and the mass media: towards a theory of imitation and suggestion", *Social Forces* 58, jun 80 : 1001-1024.
2199	PISANO, Laura. "Lecteurs de la presse quotidienne et monopole de l'information en Sardaigne (1967-1975)", *Peuples méditerranéens/Mediterranean Peoples* oct-dec 79 : 101-123.
2200	PRIMEAU, Ronald. *The rhetoric of television.* New York, Longman, 79, xii-275 p.

2201 SABAT, Khabil. "Les mass media en Egypte", *Revue de l'Occident musulman et de la Méditerranée* 27, 79 : 135-156.
2202 SHINDLER, Colin. *Hollywood goes to war: films and American Society, 1939-1952.* London, Boston, Routledge & K. Paul, 79, xv-152 p.
2203 SILBERMANN, Alphons. "La sociologie des mass media et de la communication de masse", *Revue internationale des Sciences sociales* 32, 80 : 239-253.
2204 SPLICHAL, Slavko; [et al.]. "Understanding criteria of news selection in mass communication: a clustering approach", *Quality and Quantity* 14, oct 80 : 605-618.
2205 SPRAFKIN, Joyce N.; SILVERMAN, L. Theresa; RUBINSTEIN, Eli A. "Reactions to sex on television: an exploratory study", *Public Opinion Quarterly* 44, 80 : 303-315.
2206 STEIN, Jay Wobith. *Mass media, education, and a better society.* Chicago, Nelson-Hall, 79, xi-164 p.
2207 SURBECK, Elaine; ENDSLEY, Richard C. "Children's emotional reactions to TV violence: effects of film character, reassurance, age, and sex", *Journal of social Psychology* 109, dec 79 : 269-281.
2208 TAKANE, Masaaki; [ed.]. *Jōhō shakai to mass media* (Information society and mass media). Tokyo, Shibundo, 80, 248 p.
2209 TAN, Alexis S. "Mass media use, issue knowledge and political involvement", *Public Opinion Quarterly* 44, 80 : 241-248.
2210 THIHER, Allen. *The cinematic muse: critical studies in the history of French cinema.* Columbia, University of Missouri Press, 79, vi-216 p.
2211 UGBOAJAH, Frank Okwu. "Strukturprobleme der Medien in Afrika. Das Beispiel Nigeria" (Structure problems of the media in Africa. The example of Nigeria), *Rundfunk und Fernsehen* 28, 80 : 40-55.
2212 VIGNOLLE, Jean-Pierre. "Mélange des genres, alchimie sociale: la production des disques de variétés", *Sociologie du Travail* 22, apr-jun 80 : 129-151.
2213 WEBSTER, Frank; ROBINS, Kevin. "Mass communications and information technology", *Socialist Register* 79 : 285-316.
2214 WEBSTER, James, G.; COSCARELLI, William C. "The relative appeal to children of adult versus children's television programming", *Journal of Broadcasting* 23, aut 79 : 437-451.

13800. ART
ART

13810. Aesthetics. Artist. Museum
Esthétique. Artiste. Musée

[See also / voir aussi: 1862, 2254, 4585]

2215 AMABILE, Teresa L. "Effects of external evaluation on artistic creativity", *Journal of Personality and social Psychology* 37, feb 79 : 221-233.
2216 BARRAZA, Eduardo. "Bertolt Brecht y el desarrollo de las fuerzas productivas artísticas" (Berthold Brecht and the development of artistic productive forces), *Revista mexicana de Sociología* 41, jul-sep 79 : 879-908
2217 BURGBACHER-KRUPKA, Ingrid. *Strukturen zeitgenossischer Kunst. Eine empirische Untersuchung zur Rezeption der Werke von Beuys, Darboven, Flavin, Long, Walther* (Structures of the contemporary art. An empirical research on the works of Beuys, Darboven, Flavin, Long, Walther). Stuttgart, Ferdinand Enke Verlag, 79, viii-208 p. CR: Rainer WICK, *Kölner Zeitschrift für Soziologie und Sozialpsychologie* 32(4), dec 80: 819-820.
2218 FRANCÈS, Robert. *Psychologie de l'art et de l'esthétique.* Paris, Presses universitaires de France, 79, 313 p.
2219 GALEAZZI, Umberto. *L'estetica di Adorno: arte, linguaggio, società repressiva* (Adorno's aesthetics: art, language, repressive society). Roma, Città nuova, 79, 275 p.
2220 GARCÍA CANCLINI, Néstor. *La producción simbólica: teoría y método en sociología del arte* (Symbolic production: theory and method in sociology of art). México, Siglo Veintiuno Editores, 79, 162 p.
2221 GIZATOV, K. "Estetičeskie potrebnosti sovetskogo obščestva" (Aesthetic needs of the Soviet society), *Kommunist Tatarii* 79 : 34-40.
2222 GOLDVARB, Jeffrey C. "The repressive context of art work", *Theory and Society* jul 80 : 623-632.
2223 HENDON, William Scott. *Analyzing an art museum.* New York, Praeger, 79, xvi-263 p.

2224 HOLT, Elizabeth Gilmore; [ed.]. *The triumph of art for the public: the emerging role of exhibitions and critics.* Garden City, NY, Anchor Press, Doubleday, 79, 530 p. CR: Remi CLIGNET, *Contemporary Sociology (Albany)* 9(4), jul 80: 529-530.

2225 JENKINS, Hugh. *The culture gap: an experience of government and the arts.* London, Boston, Marion Bovars, 79, x-271 p.

2226 KORNIENKO, V. S. "Rol' iskusstva v utverždenii socialističeskogo obraza žizni" (Role of art in the socialist way of life strengthening), *Problemy Filosofii* 48, 79 : 48-54.

2227 KRIS, Ernst; KURZ, Otto. *Legend, myth and magic in the image of the artist: an historical experiment.* New Haven, Yale University Press, 79, xvi-159 p.

2228 KRJUČKOVA, V. A. *Sociologija iskusstva i modernizm* (Sociology of art and modernism). Moskva, Izobrazitel'noe Iskusstvo, 79, 215 p.

2229 KUDRJAVCEVA, S. P.; [et al.]. "Problemy upravlenija hudožestvennoj dejatel'nost'ju v uslovijah razvitogo socialističeskogo obščestva" (Problems of the artistic activity management under conditions of the developed socialist society), *IN: Problemy naučnogo upravlenija socialističekim obščestvom.* Riga, 78 : 70-79.

2230 MEYER, Karl E. *The art museum: power, money, ethics.* New York, William Morrow and Co., 79, 352 p. CR: Douglas M. FOX, *American political Science Review* 74(2), jun 80 : 509-510.

2231 MINAMI, Hiroshi. *Nihonjin no geijutsu to bunka* (Art and culture of the Japanese people). Tokyo, Keiso shobo, 80, 2nd, 348 p.

2232 PLOTNIKOV, S. N. "Dialektika razvitija hudožestvennoj kul'tury (k metodologii social'nogo poznanija)" (Dialectics of the artistic culture development; methodology of social consciousness), *IN: Sociolgičeskie problemy obrazovanija, kul'tury i nauki.* Moskva, 78 : 51-61.

2233 POMMEREHNE, Werner W.; FREY, Bruno S. "Les musées dans une perspective économique", *Revue internationale des Sciences sociales* 32, 80 : 345-362.

2234 RAMIREZ, Juan Antonio. "Corrientes metodológicas en la historia del arte. Un balance provisional" (Methodological trends in the history of art: a draft balance-sheet), *Cuadernos de Realidades sociales* 16-17, 80 : 205-222.

2235 SÂRBU, Viorel. *Arta și acțiunea socială* (Art and social action). Timișoara, "Facla", 79, 291 p.

2236 SCHOEFER, Christine. "The power of creation — Lukács and Clark on politics and art in France after 1848", *Berkeley Journal of Sociology* 24-25, 80 : 159-183.

2237 SWIDERSKI, Edward M. *The philosophical foundations of Soviet aesthetics: theories and controversies in the post-war years.* Dordrecht, Holland, Boston, D. Reidel Pub. Co., 79, xviii-225 p.

2238 VETOSKINA, T. A. "Tvorčestvo kak faktor razvitija ličnosti" (Creation as a factor of personality development), *IN: Vsestoronnee razvitie ličnosti sovetskogo čeloveka.* Sverdlovsk, 79 : 54-61.

2239 VIZITEJ, É. B. "Rol' èstetičeskogo vospitanija v soversenstvovanii socialističeskogo obraza žizni" (The aesthetic education role in the improvement of the socialist way of life), *IN: Kommunističeskoe vospitanie trudjaščihsja sostavnaja čast' stroitel'stva kommunizma.* Kišinev, 80 : 126-134.

13820. Literature
Littérature

[See also / voir aussi: 284, 772, 897, 1565, 2979, 3680]

2240 "Archives orales: une autre histoire?", *Annales-Economies-Sociétés-Civilisations* 35, jan-feb 80 : 124-199.

2241 BENNETT, Tony. *Formalism and Marxism.* London, Methuen, 79, xii-200 p.

2242 CIORANESCU, Alexandre. "Troisième articulation: la littérature", *Diogène* 109, jan-mar 80 : 3-24.

2243 CONTENTI, Alessandra. "Come si fabbrica uno scrittore popolare" (How to write a popular novel), *Critica sociologica* 50, 79 : 52-71.

2244 CORSINI, Gianfranco. "La sociologia della letteratura: dieci anni dopo. Dalla infruttuosa ricerca di paternità alla difficile ricerca di una identità" (The sociology of literature ten years later. From the unfruitful action for affiliation to the difficult research of an identity), *Critica sociologica* 50, 79 : 12-24.

2245 CUSSLER, Margaret. "Il sistema economico letterario" (The economic system of literature), *Critica sociologica* 50, 79 : 25-40.

2246 EAGLETON, Mary. *Attitudes to class in the English novel from Walter Scott to David Storey.* London, Thames and Hudson, 79, 159 p.

2247 ESAER, Eric. "Langage de l'art. Réflexions sur un prétexte rimbaldien", *Revue de l'Institut de Sociologie* (3-4), 79 : 299-349.

2248 FEHÉR, Ferenc. "Sul rapporto fra G. Lukács e L. Goldmann" (About the relationship between G. Lukács and L. Goldmann), *Critica sociologica* 50, 79 : 72-75.

2249 FERNÁNDEZ FONT, Jorge. "Apuntes para una lectura social de la obra literaria" (Indications for a social reading of literary works), *Revista mexicana de Sociología* 41, jul-sep 79 : 863-878.

2250 FERRAROTTI, Franco. "Mercato delle lettere, cultura populare e sociologia della letteratura" (Literary market, popular culture and sociology of literature), *Critica sociologica* 50, 79 : 6-11.

2251 HALL, John A. *The sociology of literature.* London, New York, Longman, 79, 162 p.

2252 HEGAZY, Samir. *Littérature et société en Egypte. (De la guerre de 1967 à celle de 1973).* Paris, L'Harmattan, 79, 162 p.

2253 JOTWANI, Motilal Wadhumal; [ed.]. *Contemporary Indian literature and society.* New Delhi, Heritage, 79, xi-251 p.

2254 KOGAN, L. N.; MATJUŠIN, B. G. "Neprofessional'noe literaturnoe tvorčestvo: opyt sociologičeskogo issledovanija" (The non-professional literary creation: an essay of sociological research), IN: *Vsestoronnee razvitie ličnosti sovetskogo čeloveka.* Sverdlovsk, 79 : 62-70.

2255 LUNGHI, Marco. *Oralità e trasmissione in Africa Nera: saggio etnologico* (Oral tradition in Black Africa: ethnological essay). Milano, Vita e pensiero, 79, ix-216 p.

2256 NYIOÖ, L.; [ed.]. *Literature and its interpretation.* The Hague, Paris, New York, Mouton, 80, 302 p.

2257 OEMARJATI, Boen S. "Social issues in recent Indonesian literature", *Southeast Asian Affairs* 79 : 134-141.

2258 SCHWENGER, Johannes. *Literaturproduktion. Zwischen Selbstverwirklichung und Vergesellschaftung* (Literary production. Between self-achievement and socialization). Stuttgart, Metzler, 79, 130 p. CR: Richart ALBRECHT, *Kölner Zeitschrift für Soziologie und Sozialpsychologie* 34(4), dec 80, 821-825.

2259 SIMPSON, Ekundayo. "Bilinguisme et création littéraire en Afrique", *Présence africaine* 111, 79 : 44-60.

2260 STUSSI, Alfredo; [ed.]. *Letteratura italiana e culture regionali* (Italian literature and regional cultures). Bologna, Zanichelli, 79, 239 p.

2261 THIESSE?, Anne-Marie. "L'éducation sociale d'un romancier. Le cas d'Eugène Sue", *Actes de la Recherche en Sciences sociales* 32-33, apr-jun 80 : 51-63.

2262 VITTA, Maurizio. "Letteratura e società nel 'Marito di Elena' di G. Verga" (Literature and society in G. Verga's "Ellen's husband"), *Critica sociologica* 51-52, 79-80 : 18-50.

2263 WILSON, Robert Neal. *The writer as social seer.* Chapel Hill, NC, University of North Carolina Press, 79, xiv-172 p.

13830. Fine arts
Beaux-arts

[See also / voir aussi: 195, 3469, 5365]

2264 CHOAY, Françoise. *La Règle et le modèle: sur la théorie de l'architecture et de l'urbanisme.* Paris, Editions du Seuil, 80, 374 p.

2265 MUKERJI, Chandra. "Mass culture and the modern world-system. The rise of the graphic arts", *Theory and Society* sep 79 : 245-268.

13840. Music
Musique

[See also / voir aussi: 2052]

2266 HERNDON, Marcia; MCLEOD, Norma. *Music as culture.* Norwood, PA, Norwood Editions, 79, v-196 p.

2267 KEALY, Edward R. "From craft to art: the case of sound mixers and popular music", *Sociology of Work and Occupations* feb 79 : 3-29.

2268 LÉVY, Ernst. *Des rapports entre la musique et la société; suivi de Réflexions.* Neuchâtel, Éditions de la Baconnière, 79, 66 p.
2269 LOSONCZI, Ágnes. *Bedarf, Funktion, Wertwechsel in der Musik. Musiksoziologische Untersuchung des Musiklebens in Ungarn nach 1945* (Needs, functions, change of values in music. Sociological research of the musical life in Hungary after 1945). Budapest, Akadémiai K., 80, 184 p.
2270 RADOCY, Rudolf E.; BOYLE, J. David. *Psychological foundations of musical behavior.* Springfield, IL, C. C. Thomas, 79, vii-349 p.
2271 VIGNOLLE, Jean-Pierre. "Mixing genres and reaching the public: the production of popular music", *Social Science Information* 19, 80 : 79-105.
2272 ZOLBERG, Vera L. "Displayed art and performed music: selective innovation and the structure of artistic media", *Sociological Quarterly* 21, 80 : 219-231.

13850. Dramatic art
Art dramatique

[See also / voir aussi: 2272, 5366]

2273 DMITRIEVSKIJ, V. N. *Voprosy sociologičeskogo izučenija teatra* (Questions on the theatre sociological study). Leningrad, Leningradskij Gosudarstvennyj Institut Teatra, Muzyji i Kinematografii, 79, 179 p.
2274 DMITRIEVSKIJ, V. N.; DOKTOROV, B. Z.; [eds.]. *Teatr i molodež': opyt sociologičeskogo issledovanija* (Theatre and youth: an essay of sociological research). Moskva, Vserossijskoe Teatral'noe Obščestvo, 79, 291 p.
2275 GOLDFARB, Jeffrey C. *The persistence of freedom: the sociological implications of Polish student theater.* Boulder, Westview Press, 80, xii-159 p.
2276 GUTIÉRREZ, Sonia; [ed.]. *Teatro popular y cambio social en América Latina* (Popular theatre and social change in Latin America). Costa Rica, Editorial Universitaria Centro Americana, 79, 487 p.

13860. Folk art
Art populaire

[See also / voir aussi: 4077]

2277 CHANEY, David C. *Fictions and ceremonies: representations of popular experience.* New York, St. Martin's Press, 79, 156 p.
2278 COLLOMB, Gérard. "'Parler folklore': les fêtes au village en Savoie", *Cahiers internationaux de Sociologie* 68, jan-jun 80 : 83-93.
2279 FERNANDES, Florestan. *Folclore e mudança social na cidade de São Paulo* (Folklore and social change in the City of São Paulo). Petrópolis, Brasil, Vozes, 79, 410 p.
2280 SUPEK-ZUPAN, Olga. "Simboličko ponašanje u suvremenoj kulturi: smisao poklada" (Symbolic behaviour in contemporary culture: the meaning of Carnival), *Sociologija* 21, 79 : 291-303.
2281 THOMPSON, Kenneth. "Folklore and sociology", *Sociological Review* 28, mai 80 : 249-275.

13900. EDUCATION
ÉDUCATION

13910. Educational sociology
Sociologie de l'éducation

[See also / voir aussi: 205, 825, 1024, 1623, 2544, 2776, 2980, 3354]

2282 ALONSO HINOJAL, Isidoro. "Bernstein en la encrucijada de la sociología de la educación" (Bernstein at the crossroads of the sociology of education), *Revista española de Investigaciones sociológicas* 11, jul-sep 80 : 55-74.
2283 ARDOINO, Jacques; [et al.]. *Education et relations: introduction à une analyse plurielle des situations éducatives.* Paris, Gauthier-Villars, Unesco, 80, 183 p.
2284 BISSERET, Noëlle. *Education, class language and ideology.* London, Boston, Routledge & K. Paul, 79, vii-145 p.

2285 BRINKMANN, Wilhelm; [ed.]. *Erziehung, Schule, Gesellschaft* (Education, school, society). Bad Heilbrunn/Obb., Klinkhardt, 80, 208 p.
2286 BURGESS, Robert G. "Project teaching in the sociology of education: a case study", *Teaching Sociology* jan 79 : 179-194.
2287 Bibl.XXIX-2176. COLLINS, Randall. *The credential society: an historical sociology of education and stratification.* CR: Christopher J. HURN, *Contemporary Sociology (Albany)* 9(4), jul 80 : 501-505.
2288 COLONNA, Salvatore. *Società educante e umanizzazione sociale* (Educational society and social humanization). Lecce, Milella, 79, 252 p.
2289 COOK, Martha A.; ALEXANDER, Karl L. "Design and substance in educational research: adolescent attainments, a case in point", *Sociology of Education* 53, oct 80 : 187-202.
2290 CORNATON, Michel. *La Trans-formation permanente: pouvoir, autorité, puissance dans l'éducation et la formation.* Lyon, Presses universitaires de Lyon, 79, 278 p.
2291 DAMIANO, Elio; SCURATI, Cesare. *La ricerca pedagogica: problemi e orientamenti* (Educational research: problems and orientations). 79, 157 p.
2292 DUBEY, Darrell L.; EDEM, D. A.; THAKUR, A. S. *An introduction to the sociology of Nigerian education.* London, Macmillan, 79, viii-100 p.
2293 EGGERS, Philipp; STEINBACHER, Franz. *Pädagogische Soziologie* (Sociology of education). Bad Heilbrunn/Obb., Klinkhardt, 79, 184 p.
2294 FÜHR, Christoph. Das Bildungswesen in der Bundesrepublik Deutschland: e. Überblick (Education in the Federal Republic of Germany: an overview). Weinheim, Basel, Beltz, 79, 202 p.
2295 GOLDSCHMIDT, Dietrich; SCHÖFTHALER, Traugott. "The establishment of educational sociology in the Federal Republic of Germany 1945-1979", *Education (Tübingen)* 20, 79 : 7-25.
2296 GOODMAN, Jerry D. "The economic returns of education: an assessment of alternative models", *Social Science Quarterly* 60, sep 79 : 269-283. [USA.]
2297 GUROVA, R. G.; KIRILLOVA, M. A.; [eds.]. *Sociologopedagogičeskie issledovanija v kapitalističeskih stranah: kritičeskij analiz* (Educational sociology research in the capitalist countries; a critical analysis). Moskva, 78, 139 p.
2298 ISAMBERT-JAMATI, Viviane. "Travail, rapports sociaux, éducation en Europe. Esquisse historique de la chute de l'Empire à l'entre-deux-guerres", *Sociologie et Sociétés* 12, apr 80 : 9-21.
2299 LABINOWICZ, Ed. *The Piaget primer: thinking, learning, teaching.* Menlo Park, CA, Addison-Wesley, 80, ix-310 p.
2300 LANDSHEERE, G. *Dictionnaire de l'évaluation et de la recherche en éducation; avec lexique anglais-français.* Paris, Presses universitaires de France, 79, viii-338 p.
2301 LEON, Antoine. *Introduction à l'histoire des faits éducatifs.* Paris, Presses universitaires de France, 80, 245 p.
2302 LOCH, Werber. *Lebenslauf und Erziehung* (Life cycle and education). Essen, Neue Deutsche Schule, Verlagsges., 79, 187 p.
2303 LYNCH, James. *Education for community: a cross-cultural study in education.* Basingstoke, Eng., Macmillan Education, 79, xii-212 p.
2304 MANZ, Wolfgang. *Erziehung und Gesellschaft: pädag., psycholog. u. soziolog. Aspekte schul. Sozialisation* (Education and society: pedagogical, psychological and sociological aspects of school socialization). München, Kösel, 80, 136 p.
2305 MARBURGER, Helga. *Entwicklung und Konzepte der Sozialpädagogik* (Development and concept of social pedagogy). München, Juventa-Verlag, 79, 188 p.
2306 MCKENZIE, Richard B. *The political economy of the educational process.* Boston, M. Nijhoff Pub., 79, xi-199 p.
2307 MILLER, Steven I. "Sociology of education as social science: a brief analysis of some analytical and empirical issue", *Indian Journal of social Research* 20, apr 79 : 22-27.
2308 NAKAJIMA, Akinori. *Shakaigaku-teki kyoiku shiso no keisei* (Formation of sociological thought on education). Tokyo, Kazama shobo, 80, 289 p.
2309 NISHINE, Kazuo. "M. Weber no kyoiku shakai-gaku" (Max Weber's sociology of education), *Hiroshima daigaku gakuko kyoikugakubu kiyo* 80 : 1-9.
2310 RIBOLZI, Luisa. "Sviluppi e prospettive di sociologia dell'educazione" (Developments and prospects in sociology of education), *Studi di Sociologia* 17, oct-dec 79 : 347-367.
2311 SÁGI, Mária. *Művelődés és személyiség* (Culture and personality). Budapest, Népművelési Propaganda Iroda, 80, 138 p. [Research methods in psychology of education.]

2312	SGROI, Emanuele; [ed.]. *Educazione e socializzazione* (Education and socialization). Milano, A. Giuffrè, 79, xi-386 p.
2313	VAN SCOTTER, Richard D.; KRAFT, Richard J.; HAAS, John D. *Foundations of education: social perspectives*. Englewood Cliffs, NJ, Prentice-Hall, 79, xi-416 p.
2314	WILLIAMSON, Bill. *Education, social structure, and development: a comparative analysis.* New York, Holmes & Meier Publishers, 79, xii-238 p. CR: Mike HICKOX, *British Journal of Sociology* 31(3), sep 80: 446.
2315	WOLF, Richard M. *Evaluation in education: foundations of competency assessment and program review*. New York, Praeger Publishers, 79, xii-217 p.

13920. Educational system. Educational policy
Système d'enseignement. Politique de l'enseignement

[See also / voir aussi: 681, 707, 2096, 2265, 2298, 2986, 3059, 3236, 3613, 3624, 3755, 3760, 5077, 5078]

2316	"Symposium on education reform in Greece", *Comparative Education Review* 22, feb 78 : 1-98.
2317	"Evaluating educational reform", *Comparative Education Review* 22, oct 78 : 367-479.
2318	"Women and education", *Harvard educational Review* 49, nov 79 : 413-526.
2319	"Bildungspolitik" (Educational policy), *Neue Gesellschaft* 27, mar 80 : 215-231. [Germany FR.]
2320	"Problemas cruciales de la enseñanza en España" (Crucial problems of the educational system in Spain), *Revista de Fomento social* 35(138), apr-jun 80 : 125-283.
2321	AMODIO, Emanuele. *Oppressione e cultura: sulla produzione culturale subalterna* (Oppression and culture: on subordinate cultural production). Ragusa, Sicilia Punto L.-Coop, Zuleima, 80, 56 p. [Italy.]
2322	ARCHER, Margaret S. *Social origins of educational systems*. Beverly Hills, CA, Sage Publications, 79, 824 p.
2323	ARLIČENKOVA, EN. "Vospitanie ličnosti i obras žizni" (Individual education and the way of life), *IN: Problemy kompleksnogo podhoda k kommunističeskomu vospitaniju molodeži v svete rešenij XXV s'ezda KPSS*. Tomsk, 79 : 36-41.
2324	AXT, Friedrich. *Leopold Sedar Senghor und die Erziehungspolitik in der Republik Senegal* (Leopold Sedar Senghor and educational policy in the Republic of Senegal). Frankfurt a.M., Bern, Cirencester, U.K., Lang, 79, 108 p.
2325	BAKER, Eva L.; QUELLMALZ, Edys S.; [eds.]. *Educational testing and evaluation*. Beverly Hills, CA, Sage Publications, 80, 244 p.
2326	BALLION, Robert. "L'enseignement privé, une école sur mesure?", *Revue française de Sociologie* 21, apr-jun 80 : 203-231.
2327	BEDALL, Fritz K. "Elternrecht und Gleichheit der Bildungschancen" (Parental rights and educational opportunities), *Zeitschrift für Bevölkerungswissenschaft* 79 : 3-11.
2328	BEEBY, Clarence Edward. *Assessment of Indonesian education: a guide in planning*. Wellington, New Zealand Council for Educational Research, 79, xiv-349 p.
2329	BELANGER, Paul. "Une pratique de contre-école: l'expérience éducative du mouvement de libération nationale dans les zones libérées de la Guinée-Bissau", *Sociologie et Sociétés* 12, apr 80 : 155-168.
2330	BEREND, Ivan T. "Les réformes de l'éducation dans les pays orientaux d'Europe centrale: l'exemple hongrois", *Perspectives (Unesco)* 10, 80 : 182-187.
2331	BOLGOV, V. I. "K postroeniju sistemy pokazatelej kul'turnogo urovnja trudjaščihsja" (On the elaboration of the workers' cultural level indexes), *IN: Sociologičeskie problemy obrazovanija, kul'tury i nauki*. Moskva, 78 : 73-83.
2332	BOUDON, Raymond; LAGNEAU, Janina. "L'inégalité des chances devant l'enseignement en Europe occidentale", *Perspectives (Unesco)* 19, 80 : 196-204.
2333	BRIDGE, R. Gary; JUDD, Charles M.; MOOCK, Peter R. *The determinants of educational outcomes: The impact of families, peers, teachers, and schools*. Cambridge, MA, Harper & Row, Ballinger, 79, xxii-357 p.
2334	BÜTTEMEYER, Wilhelm; MÖLLER, Bernhard; [eds.]. *Der Positivismusstreit in der deutschen Erziehungswissenschaft* (The positivism dispute in German education). München, Fink Verlag, 79, 269 p. CR: Heiner DRERUP, *Soziologische Revue* 3(3), 80: 306-308.
2335	CARNOY, Martin; [et al.]. *Can educational policy equalise income distribution in Latin America?*. Westmead, Eng., Saxon House, 79, ix-110 p. [published on behalf of the International Labour Office.]

2336   Bibl.XXIX-2295. CATALDO, Everett F.; GILES, Michael W.; GATLIN, Douglas S. *School desegragation policy.* CR: Barbara M. GIBBS, *Contemporary Sociology (Albany)* 9(2), mar 80 : 251.

2337   CHEE, Tham Seong. "Issues in Malaysian education: past, present and future", *Journal of Southeast Asian Studies* 10, sep 79 : 321-350.

2338   CLEMENT, Werner. *Bildungsexpansion und Arbeitsmarkt* (Educational development and labour market). Wien, Signum-Verlag, 80, 439 p.

2339   COLEMAN, James S. *Equality of educational opportunity.* New York, Arno Press, 79, 2 vols. p.

2340   EZEAKU, L. C. "Education in Nigeria: its functional and dysfunctional roles", *Developing Economies* 17, jun 79 : 162-172.

2341   FAKSH, Mahmud A. "The consequences of the introduction and spread of modern education: education and national integration in Egypt", *Middle Eastern Studies* 16, mai 80 : 42-55.

2342   FILOGRASSO, Nando. *Gli obiettivi dell'educazione: fondamenti epistemologici* (Aims of education: epistemological foundations). Venezia, Marsilio, 79, 1st, 249 p.

2343   FITZPATRICK, Sheila. *Education and social mobility in the Soviet Union, 1921-1934.* Cambridge, Eng., New York, Cambridge University Press, 79, x-355 p.

2344   GREEN, Thomas F. *Predicting the behavior of the educational system.* Syracuse, NY, Syracuse University Press, 80, xviii-200 p.

2345   GRUNDMAN, Adolph H. "School desegregation and social science: the Virginia experience", *Research in Law and Sociology* 78 : 229-250.

2346   HAAG, Daniel; MUNARI, Silvio. *Educational administration.* Paris, Unesco, Geneva, IBE, 79, 67 p. [sold by Unipub, New York.]

2347   HALSEY, A. H.; HEATH, A. F.; RIDGE, J. M. *Origins and destination: family, class, and education in modern Britain.* Oxford, Clarendon Press, New York, Oxford University Press, 80, ix-240 p.

2348   HANSON, E. Mark. *Educational administration and organizational behavior.* Boston, MA, Allyn and Bacon, 79, x-395 p.

2349   HAWKINS, John N. "National-minority education in the People's Republic of China", *Comparative Education Review* 22, feb 78 : 147-162.

2350   HAZARD, William R.; ROSENBLUM, Victor G; [eds.]. "Education: progress and prospects", *American behavioral Scientist* 23, nov-dec 79 : 139-296.

2351   HENEVELD, Ward. "Indonesian education in the seventies: problems of rapid growth", *Southeast Asian Affairs* 79 : 142-154.

2352   HOHL, Janine. "Les politiques scolaires à l'égard des milieux défavorisés et l'émergence d'un nouveau mode de production pédagogique", *Sociologie et Sociétés* 12, apr 80 : 133-154.

2353   HOLMES, Brian. *International guide to education systems.* Paris, Unesco, 79, 288 p.

2354   IMMEGART, Glenn L.; BOYD, William L.; [eds.]. *Problem-finding in educational administration: trends in research and theory.* Lexington, MA, Lexington Books, 79, xix-297 p.

2355   INGRAM, Cregg F. *Fundamentals of educational assessment.* New York, Van Nostrand, 80, xii-404 p.

2356   JACQUEMIN, Alix. "Prolongation de la scolarité obligatoire et inégalités sociales", *Orientation scolaire et professionnelle* apr-mai-jun 80 : 141-160.

2357   JAKOPOVIČ, Ivan. "Teorijski pristup i rezultati istraživanja 'kulturni standard radničke klase u Zagrebu'" (Theoretical approach and research results on 'Cultural standard of the working class in Zagreb'), *Sociologija* 22(1-2), 80 : 71-84.

2358   JAKOPOVIČ, Ivan. "Teorijski pristup i rezultati istraživanja 'Kulturni standard radničke klase u Zagrebu'" (Theoretical approach and research results on "Cultural standard of the working class in Zagreb"), *Sociologija* 22(1-2), 80 : 71-84.

2359   KIRSCH, Hans Christian. *Bildung im Wandel: Schule gestern, heute u. morgen* (Education in change: schools yesterday, today and tomorrow). Düsseldorf, Wien, Econ, 79, 448 p.

2360   KOGAN, L. N.; BARSUK, V. L.; [eds.]. *Issledovanie kul'turnoj dejatel'nosti i kul'turnogo urovnja naselenija gorodov Urala* (Research on the Ural towns population cultural activity and cultural level). Sverdlovsk, Ural'nyj Naučnyj Centr AN SSSR, 79, 156 p.

2361   KRAUTKRÄMER, Ursula. *Staat und Erziehung: Bergründung öffentlicher Erziehung bei Humboldt, Kant, Fichte, Hegel und Schleiermacher* (State and education: background of public education in Humboldt, Kant, Fichte, Hegel and Schleiermacher). München, J. Berchmans, 79, 314 p.

2362   KUMBULA, Tendayi J. *Education and social control in Southern Rhodesia.* Palo Alto, CA, R & E Research Associates, 79, vi-168 p.

2363	KWONG, Julia. *Chinese education in transition: prelude to the Cultural Revolution*. Montreal, McGill-Queen's University Press, 79, x-207 p.
2364	LAMBERT, Richard D.; [ed.]. "New directions in international education", *Annals of the American Academy of political and social Science* 449, mai 80 : 1-164.
2365	LATCHEM, C. R. *An educational development system for Northern Ireland: a study of expressed needs, opinions, research studies, and recommendations*. London, Council for Educational Technology, 79, 165 p.
2366	LEWAN, Kenneth. "Bildungspolitik in Ägypten"(Educational policy in Egypt), *Dritte Welt* 79 : 257-263.
2367	LITT, Edgar; PARKINSON, Michael. *US and UK educational policy: a decade of reform*. New York, Praeger, 79, x-161 p. CR: Edward P. MORGAN, *American political Science Review* 74(4), dec 80: 1119-1120.
2368	LITT, Jean-Louis; [ed.]. "L'école? Pour quoi faire?", *Recherches sociologiques* 11, 80 : 107-236.
2369	LUNDMAN, Lars. *Socioeconomisk differentiering i grundskolan = Socio-economic differentiation in comprehensive schools*. Lund, Liber Läromedel / Gleerup, 79, 356 p.
2370	MARE, Robert D. "Social background and school continuation decisions", *Journal of the American statistical Association* 75(370), jun 80 : 295-305.
2371	MCGINN, Noel F.; [et al.]. *Education and development in Korea*. Cambridge, MA, Council on East Asian Studies, Harvard University, 80, xxvi-285 p. [distributed by Harvard University Press.]
2372	MINGAT, Alain. "Essai sur la demande d'éducation", 79.
2373	MINOT, Jacques. *L'éducation nationale*. Paris, Berger-Levrault, 79, 276 p.
2374	MOISSET, Jean J. "Les politiques d'intégration des systèmes économiques et scholaires dans les pays africains: le cas du Mali", *Canadian Journal of African Studies* 13, 80 : 461-469.
2375	MUSHKATEL, Alvin; MUSHKATEL, Linda G. "The effect of school desegregation on housing prices", *Social Science Journal* 17, jan 80 : 67-78.
2376	NEAL, Walter Douglas; [ed.]. *Education in Western Australia*. Nedlands, W. A., University of Western Australia for the Education Committee of the 150th Anniversary Celebrations, 79, xvii-306 p. [for the Education Committee of the 150th Anniversary Celebrations.]
2377	Organization for Economic Cooperation and Development. *Austria, school policy*. Paris, OECD, 79, 106 p.
2378	PUELLES BENITES, Manuel de. *Educación e ideología en la España contemporánea* (Education and ideology in contemporary Spain). Barcelona, Labor, 80, 522 p.
2379	PUGLIESE, Enrico. "I giovani tra scuola e lavoro nel Mezzogiorno: risultati di un'inchiesta su Napoli" (Young people between school and working life in Southern Italy: results from a research in Naples), *Critica sociologica* 50, 79 : 228-243.
2380	RAJAONAH, Voahangy. "Réflexion sur l'éducation en Afrique", *Présence africaine* 111, 79 : 19-30.
2381	RAM, Bali; VERMA, Ravi. "Anglophone-francophone differences in returns to schooling in Canada", *International Journal of comparative Sociology (Leiden)* 21(1-2), mar-jun 80 : 49-64.
2382	RAULS, Martina. *Schulische Bildung und Unterentwicklung in Paraguay* (School education and underdevelopment in Paraguay). Saarbrücken, Fort Lauderdale, Breitenbach, 79, ix-185 p.
2383	RIST, Ray C. "On the education of guest-worker children in Germany: public policies and equal educational opportunity", *Comparative Education Review* 23, oct 79 : 355-369.
2384	RIVERO HERRERA, José. *La educación no-formal en la reforma peruana* (Non-formal education in Peruvian reforms). Buenos Aires, UNESCO-CEPAL, Proyecto Desarrolo y Educación en América Latina y el Caribe, 79, 93 p.
2385	ROSOLI, Gianfausto. "La scolarizzazione dei figli degli emigrati: analisi e indicazioni" (Educational provision to migrant workers' children: analysis and indications), *Studi Emigrazione* 17(57), mar 80 : 3-152.
2386	ROSS, Alec M. "Education and national development", *India international Centre Quarterly* oct 79 : 307-315. [India.]
2387	SÁ, Nicanor Palhares. *Política educacional e populismo no Brasil* (Educational policy and populism in Brazil). São Paulo, Cortez & Moraes, 79, 107 p.
2388	SAMOFF, Joel. "Education in Tanzania: class formation and reproduction", *Journal of modern African Studies* 17, mar 79 : 47-69.

2389 SAXENA, Sateshwari. *Educational planning in India: a study in approach and methodology.* New Delhi, Sterling, 79, viii-202 p.
2390 Bibl.XXIX-2314. SELAKOVICH, Daniel. *Ethnicity and the schools: educating minorities for mainstream America.* CR: Janet E. POPPENDIECK, *Contemporary Sociology (Albany)* 9(1), jan 80, 86-87.
2391 SEMENOV, V. A. "Buržuaznaja 'massovaja kul'tura' i eě vlijanie na ličnost" (Bourgeois mass culture and its influence on the personality), *IN: Rol' duhovnoj kul'tury v razvitii ličnosti.* 79 : 97-103.
2392 SINE, Babacar. *Non-formal education and education policy in Ghana and Senegal.* Paris, Unesco, 79, 35 p.
2393 SINGHHI, Narendra Kumar. *Education and social change.* Jaipur, Rawat Publications, 79, xiii- 309 p. [India.]
2394 TAKANE, Masaaki. *Chiteki kyōsō shakai no susume* (Essays on educational system in Japan). Tokyo, Toyo keizai shinposha, 80, 213 p.
2395 THRUSH, John C.; SMITH, Philip R. *Japan's economic growth and educational change, 1950-1970.* Lincoln, NE, EBHA Press, 80, 90 p.
2396 TURČENKO, V. N. "Sistema obrazovanija kak faktor social'nogo progressa sibirskoj derevni" (Education system as a factor of the Siberian village social progress), *IN: Social'naja struktura sovetskogo obščestva i socialističeskij obraz žizni. I.* Moskva, 78 : 178-184.
2397 United Nations Educational, Scientific and Cultural Organization. *Educational reforms: experiences and prospects.* Paris, UNESCO, 79, 232 p.
2398 VANAS, Norbert. "Die österreichische Schule nach zehn Jahren Schulreform" (The Austrian school after ten years of school reform), *Österreichische Monatshefte* 35(11-12), nov-dec 79 : 23-31.
2399 WAGAW, Teshome G. *Education in Ethiopia: prospect and retrospect.* Ann Arbor, University of Michigan Press, 79, xv-256 p.
2400 WEIS, Lois. "Education and reproduction of inequality: the case of Ghana", *Comparative Education Review* 23, feb 79 : 41-51.
2401 WINKLER, Donald R. "The distribution of educational resources in Paraguay: implications for equality of opportunity", *Comparative Education Review* 24, feb 80 : 73-86.
2402 WURDOCK, Clarence. "Public school resegregation after desegregation: some preliminary findings", *Sociological Focus* 12, oct 79 : 263-274. [USA.]

13930. Primary education. Secondary education
Enseignement primaire. Enseignement secondaire

[See also / voir aussi: 1902, 2543, 5647]

2403 ALLEN, K. Eileen. *Mainstreaming in early childhood education.* Albany, NY, Delmar Publishers, 80, vi-261 p.
2404 AXT, Friedrich. *Sekundarschulwesen in der Republik Senegal* (Secondary education in the Republic of Senegal). Frankfurt a M., Bern, Cirencester, U.K., Lang, 79, 322 p.
2405 BASSIRI-MOVASSAGH, Schahin. *Grundschule in Iran*(Elementary education in Iran). Frankfurt am Main, Bern, Las Vegas, Lang, 79, x-298 p.
2406 BEINKE, Lothar; STUBER, Fritz. *Fachhochschule und Weiterstudium: e. empir. Unters. zur Sozialstruktur d. Fachhochschulstudenten* (Technical schools and further education: an empirical research on the social structure of technical school students). Bad Honnef, Bock und Herchen, 79, 198 p. [Germany FR.]
2407 BELPERRON, Roland. *On a sauvé l'école du village.* Paris, Éditions Syros, 79, 140 p.
2408 CHABAUTY, Marie Luce. *Les enfants de la maternelle.* Paris, Centurion, 79, 237 p.
2409 FILIPPOV, F. R. "Vseobščee srednee obrazovanie v SSSR i social'noe razvitie sovetskogo obščestva" (The USSR secondary school and the Soviet society social development), *IN: Sociologičeskie problemy obrazovanija, kul'tury i nauki.* Moskva, 78 : 121-136.
2410 Fundación del Niño. *Programa hogares de cuidado diario en Venezuela. Estudio de evaluación* (Day care homes program in Venezuela. Evaluation study). Caracas, Fundación del Niño, 78-79. [10 vols. various pagings.]
2411 GOLDSCHMIDT, Dietrich; ROEDER, Peter M.; [eds.]. *Alternative Schulen? Gestalt und Funktion der nichtstaatlichen Schulen im Rahmen öffentlicher Bildungssysteme* (Alternative schools? Form and function of private schools within the framework of the public system of education). Stuttgart, Klett-Cotta Verlag, 79, 623 p. CR: Walther Von DIETRICH, *Soziologische Revue* 3(3), 80: 305-306.

2412 JOHANNINGMEIER, Erwin V. *Americans and their schools.* Chicago, Rand McNally College Pub. Co., 80, xiii-328 p.
2413 KOČERGIN, A. N.; LISS, L. F. "Vysšaja škola kak ob'ekt sistemno-sociologičeskogo issledovanija" (High school as an object of systemic and sociological research), *IN: Sociologičeskie problemy obrazovanija, kul'tury i nauki.* Moskva, 78 : 150-159.
2414 KUSHMAN, John E. "A public choice model of day care center services", *Social Science Quarterly* 60, sep 79 : 295-308. ;961[USA.]
2415 MARTIN, Christopher. *A short history of English schools, 1750-1965.* Hove, Wayland, 79, ix-118 p.
2416 MASSOT, Alain. "Destins scolaires des étudiants de secondaire: Une analyse comparative des secteurs français et anglais", *Recherches sociographiques* 20, sep-dec 79 : 383-401. [Canada.]
2417 MCCARTHY, Melodie A.; HOUSTON, John P. *Fundamentals of early childhood education.* Cambridge, MA, Winthrop Publishers, 80, xi-366 p.
2418 MEIJNEN, G. W. "Schooltypen in het lager onderwijs en milieuspecifieke leerprestaties" (Types of schools in elementary education and milieu-specific teaching), *Mens en Maatschappij* 55, dec 80 : 385-410.
2419 SIEBER, R. Timothy. "Schoolrooms pupils, and rules: the role of informality in bureaucratic socialization", *Human Organization* 38, aut 79 : 273-282.

**13940. School environment
Milieu scolaire**

[See also / voir aussi: 1500, 1586]

2420 COHEN, Elizabeth G.; MILLER, Russell H. "Coordination and control of instruction in schools", *Pacific sociological Review* 23, oct 80 : 446-473.
2421 Bibl.XXIX-2359. DAFT, Richard L.; BECKER, Selwyn W. *The innovative organization: innovation adoption in school organizations.* CR: Arnold D. KALUZNY., *American Journal of Sociology* 85(5), mar 80: 1272-1273.
2422 DÉHAN, Nadia; PERCHERON, Annick; BERTHÉLÉMY-THOMAS, Martine. "La démocratie à l'école", *Revue française de Sociologie* 21, jul-sep 80 : 379-407.

**13950. Higher education
Enseignement supérieur**

[See also / voir aussi: 89, 116, 161, 372, 664, 775, 867, 1157, 1309, 1469, 1488, 1585, 1886, 1891, 1944, 2406, 2416, 2422, 2559, 2771, 2950, 2986, 3375, 3769, 3781, 3855, 4769, 5067, 5109, 5357, 5633, 5952, 6241]

2423 "Issues in contemporary higher education", *Comparative Education Review* 22, jun 78 : 185-351.
2424 "Student activism", *Higher Education* nov 79 : 603-699.
2425 "Higher education, psychology and the Black American" (Journal of Black Studies), *Journal of Black Studies* 10, mar 80 : 269-364.
2426 "Universität und Gesellschaft"(University and society), *Österreichische Zeitschrift für Politikwissenschaft* 80 : 261-353. [Austria.]
2427 "Administration (L') des universités", *Revue française d'Administration publique* 14, apr-jun 80 : 1-130.
2428 ALBORNOZ, Orlando. *Teoría praxis de la educación superior venezolana* (Theory and praxis of higher education in Venezuela). Caracas, Facultad de Humanidades y Educación, Escuela de Educación, UCV., 79, 172 p.
2429 ALTBACH, Philip G. *Comparative higher education: research trends and bibliography.* London, Mansell, 79, xi-206 p.
2430 ARIMOTO, Akira. "Kōtō-Kyōiku no hatten ruikei to kaikaku" (The development patterns of higher education and reform), *Ōsaka kyōiku daigaku kyōikugaku ronshū* 80 : 37-47.
2431 BARDIS, Panos D. "Attitudes toward violence among university students in India", *International Review of modern Sociology* jan-jun 79 : 61-75.
2432 BEREDAY, George Z. F. *Democratization of higher education.* Paris, Unesco, Geneva, IBE, available from Unipub, New York, 79, 78 p. [prepared for the International Bureau of Education.]
2433 BOURRICAUD, François. "L'avenir de l'institution universitaire en France", *Commentaire* (11), aut 80 : 492-499.

2434 BOUSSARD, Isabel. "Les étudiants et la participation. Les élections aux Conseils d'UER et d'Universités", *Revue française de Sociologie* 21, jan-mar 80 : 77-96.
2435 BUSH, Peter; DIGHT, Susan. *Undergraduate income and expenditure.* London, H. M. Stationery Office, 79, ix-69 p. [United Kingdom.]
2436 CARTER, Charles Frederick. *Higher education for the future.* Oxford, Blackwell, 80, ix-149 p.
2437 COBO SUERO, J. M. *La enseñanza superior en el mundo* (Higher education in the world). Madrid, Narcea de Ediciones, 79, 358 p.
2438 CUMMINGS, William K.; AMANO, Ikuo; KITAMURA, Yazuyuki; [eds.]. *Changes in the Japanese university: a comparative perspective.* New York, Praeger, 79, xxi-261 p.
2439 DANDURAND, Pierre; FOURNIER, Marcel; BERNIER, Léon. "Développement de l'enseignement supérieur, classes sociales et luttes nationales au Québec", *Sociologie et Sociétés* 12, apr 80 : 101-131.
2440 DÉRI, Miklósné; [ed.]. *Pályakezdő diplomások négy szocialista országban* (Graduates in four socialist countries). Budapest, Felsőoktatási Pedagógiai Kutatóközpont, 79, 348 p. [Czechoslovakia, German DR, Hungary, Poland.][published by the Institute for Higher Education.]
2441 FARAGÓ, Magdolna S. *Az egyetemi, főiskolai hallgatók beilleszkedése a felsőoktatásba* (Adaptation of undergraduates to higher education). Budapest, Felsőoktatási Pedagógiai Kutatközpont, 79, 239 p. [published by the Research Centre for Higher Education, Budapest.]
2442 FOMERAND, Jacques. *Higher education in Western Europe and North America: a selected and annotated bibliography.* NYC (i.e. New York), 79, 229 p. [available from Council for European Studies.]
2443 GEIGER, Roger L. "The changing demand for higher education in the seventies: adaptations within the three national systems", *Higher Education* mai 80 : 255-276.
2444 GERBOD, Paul. "Note sur la condition matérielle et morale de l'étudiant français", *Revue française de Sociologie* 21, apr-jun 80 : 251-258.
2445 GRANT, Gerald; RIESMAN, David. *The perpetual dream: reform and experiment in the American college.* Chicago, University of Chicago Press, 79, 474 p. CR: Joseph BEN-DAVID, *Contemporary Sociology (Albany)* 9(4), jul 80: 505-508.
2446 GRANT, Gerald; [et al.]. *On competence: a critical analysis of competence-based reforms in higher education.* San Francisco, Jossey-Bass Publishers, 79, xxii-592 p.
2447 GRIGOR'EV, S. I. "Studenčeskij kollektiv v političeskoj sisteme obščestva razvitogo socializma" (The students collectivity in the political system of the developed socialist society), *IN: Konstitucija SSSR i aktual'nye problemy teorii naucnogo kommunizma.* Moskva, 79 : 81-87.
2448 HAMMERICH, Kurt. "Die soziale Herkunft von Schülern als Thema schulpolitischer Argumentation" (The social origin of students as a theme of school political argumentation), *Kölner Zeitschrift für Soziologie und Sozialpsychologie* 32, 80 : 457-483.
2449 HEARN, James C. "Major choice and the well-being of college men and women: an examination from developmental, organizational, and structural perspectives", *Sociology of Education* 53, jul 80 : 164-178.
2450 HOFFMAN, Phillip P.; KAMERLING, David S. "Comparative geography of higher education in the United States and the USSR: an initial investigation", *Soviet Geography* 20, sep 79 : 412-439.
2451 INGRAM, Larry C. "Broken frame and emergent meaning: the case of student evaluation of teaching", *Human Relations* 32, sep 79 : 803-818.
2452 JACQUES, Jeffrey M. "The split labor market and ethnic antagonism: a case study in higher education", *Sociology of Education* 53, oct 80 : 225-235.
2453 JENSEN, Jens-Jorgen. *Universitet, forskning og samfund i DDR* (University, research and society in the GDR). Esbjerg, Sydjyak Universitetsforlag, 79, 451 p.
2454 KALINKIN, E. "Usilenie roli vyssej skoly v ekonomiceskomi social'nom razvitii SSSR" (Increasing the role of higher education in the economic and social development of the USSR), *Ekonomičeskie Nauki* 22(10), oct 80 : 14-20.
2455 KAMALAVIJAYAN, D. *Problems of higher education in India: an annotated bibliography of source material.* Gurgaon, Indian Documentation Service, 79, xxii-116 p.
2456 KLUCZYNSKI, Jan. "L'enseignement supérieur dans les pays socialistes d'Europe", *Perspectives (Unesco)* 10, 80 : 212-218.
2457 KONDRAŠOV, V. P. "O determinacii i urovnjah social'noj aktivnosti studenčeskoj molodeži" (On the determination and levels of the student youth social activity), *IN: Filosofija i naučnyj kommunizm. VI..* Minsk, 79 : 114-119.

2458 LABRADOR, Carmen; COBO, Juan M. "Problemas de la regionalización de la enseñanza superior en el Estado español" (Regionalization problems of higher education in the Spanish state), *Cuadernos de Realidades sociales* 16-17, 80 : 143-154.
2459 LEWIS, Darrell R.; BECKER, William E. Jr.; [eds.]. *Academic rewards in higher education*. Cambridge, MA, Harper & Row, Ballinger, 79, xx-339 p. CR: Margaret S. GORDON, *Journal of economic Literature* 18(3), sep 80: 1142-1143.
2460 LICHTER, Robert S. "Young rebels: a psychopolitical study of West German male radical students", *Comparative Politics* 12, oct 79 : 27-48.
2461 LISOVSKIJ, V. T. "Ličnost' studenta kak ob'ekt sociologičeskogo issledovanija: tipologičeskie osobennosti ličnosti sovremennogo sovetskogo studenta" (The students personality as an object of sociological research: typological characteristics of the contemporary Soviet student's personality), *IN: Social'nye aspekty razvitija ličnosti. Ispol'zovanie informacionnyh sistem dlja ego prognozirovanija*. Moskva, 78 : 97-109.
2462 LOWY, Michael. "Students and class struggle in Brazil", *Latin American Perspectives* aut 79 : 101-107.
2463 MARTÍN MORENO, Jaime. *Universidad, fábrica de parados: informe sociológico sobre las necesidades de graduados universitarios en España y sus perspectivas de empleo* (University and production of unemployed: sociological report on the needs for graduates in Spain and their employment prospects). Barcelona, Ediciones Vicens-Vives, 79, vii-193 p.
2464 MARTINDALE, Don. "Patrons and clients: the sociology of academic advising", *International Journal of contemporary Sociology* 16(3-4), jul-oct 79 : 2-187.
2465 MONCADA, Alberto. "El consumo de educación superior en Madrid" (Consumption of higher education in Madrid), *Revista española de Investigaciones sociológicas* apr-jun 79 : 141-150.
2466 OKADA, Makoto. "Bonchi toshi ni ritsuchi suru daigaku" (The re-location of higher education, its functions for the local communities and the society as a whole), *Nihon toshigakukai nenpo* 14, 80 : 55-64. [Japan.]
2467 PEISERT, Hansgert; FRAMHEIM, Gerhild. *Das Hochschulsystem in der Bundesrepublik Deutschland* (The higher education system in the Federal Republic of Germany). Stuttgart, Klett-Cotta, 79, 194 p.
2468 Bibl.XXIX-2411. PEMPEL, T. J. *Patterns of Japanese policymaking: experiences from higher education*. CR: Haruhiro FUKUI, *American political Science Review* 74(1), mar 80, 265-266.
2469 PHILLIPS, Donald E. *Student protest, 1960-1969: an analysis of the issues and speeches*. Washington, University Press of America, 80, xi-176 p.
2470 PREMFORS, Rune. *The politics of higher education in a comparative perspective: France, Sweden, United Kingdom*. Stockholm, Group for the Study of Higher Education and Research Policy of the University of Stockholm, 80, v-260 p.
2471 PSACHAROPOULOS, George; KAZAMIAS, Andreas M. "Student activism in Greece: a historical and empirical analysis", *Higher Education* mar 80 : 127-138.
2472 RANGEL GUERRA, Alfonso. *La educacion superior en México* (Higher education in Mexico). México, El Colegio de México, 79, vii-146 p.
2473 RAO, V. Nandini; RAO, Prakasa V. V.; BENJAMIN, Rommel. "Sex, parental background, and drinking bahavior of Black collegians", *International Journal of the Sociology of the Family* jan-jun 79 : 47-66.
2474 REDDY, N. Y. *Values and attitudes of Indian youth: a psychological study of rural and urban students*. New Delhi, Light and Life, 80, vi-244 p.
2475 REITZES, Donald T. "College student identities and behaviors", *Sociological Focus* 13, apr 80 : 113-124.
2476 RIBOLZI, Giancarlo. "Gli studenti nella scuola secondaria superiore: alla ricerca di un nuovo modello di participazione" (High school students: towards new participation patterns), *Studi di Sociologia* 17, jan-mar 79 : 31-40. [Italy.]
2477 ROOTES, Christopher A. "Student radicalism: politics of moral protest and legitimation problems of the modern capitalist state", *Theory and Society* mai 80 : 473-502.
2478 SABATHIL, Gerhard. "Objectif de gestion et objectifs comptables pour les universités publiques. Le cas allemand", *Annales de l'Économie publique, sociale et coopérative* 67, oct-dec 79 : 27-42.
2479 SUIMENKO, È. I. "Social'no-akseleratornaja funkcija vysšego obrazovanija v socialističeskom obščestva" (Socio-accelerating function of higher formation in socialist society), *IN: Social'naja struktura sovetskogo obščestva i socialističeskij obraz žizni. I.*. Moskva, 78 : 155-165.

2480   TOURAINE, Alain. *Lutte étudiante.* Paris, Seuil, 78, 382 p. CR: Guy MINGUET, *Revue française de Sociologie* 21(1), jan-mar 80: 121-133.
2481   TOURAINE, Alain. "Déclin ou transformation des universités", *Perspectives (Unesco)* 10, 80 : 205-211.
2482   Bibl.XXIX-2427. VAN DE GRAAF, John H.; [et al.]. *Academic power: patterns of authority in seven national systems of higher education.* CR: Robert L. HALL, *Contemporary Sociology (Albany)* 9(2), mar 80: 280.
2483   VLAŠKALIĆ, Tihomir. "La nouvelle position de l'enseignement supérieur dans la société", *Questions actuelles du Socialisme* 30, apr 80 : 30-40.
2484   WEBLER, Wolf-Dietrich. "The sixties and the seventies: aspects of student activism in West Germany", *Higher Education* mar 80 : 155-168.
2485   ZELEPUKIN, A. V. "Studenčestvo v social'noj strukture sovetskogo obščestva" (Students in the Soviet society social structure), *IN: Razvitoj socializm: osnovnye čerty i osobennosti.* Saratov, 79 : 72-85.
2486   ŽIHAREVA, Z. A.; KARAUŠ, A. A. "Struktura social'noj aktivnosti ličnosti studenta i nekotorye puti eě formirovanija v uslovijah zaočnago obrazovanija" (Structure of the student personality social activity and some means of its formation under conditions of oral teaching), *Naučnye Trudy. Moskovskij zaočnyj pedagogičeskij Institut* 58, 79 : 157-184.
2487   ŽIVKOVIČ, Miroslav. "Kako je rasporeten jugoslovenski intelektualni kapital" (Distribution of the intellectual capital in Yugoslavia), *Sociologija* 21, 79 : 341-367.

**13960.   Adult education
            Éducation des adultes**

2488   "Literacy and the future of print", *Journal of Communications* 30, wint 80 : 89-204.
2489   ALEKSEEVA, L. K.; [et al.]. "Upravlenie processami razvitija duhovnoj kul'tury trudjaščihsja v uslovijah razvitogo socializma" (Management of the workers' intellectual culture development process under conditions of developed socialism), *IN: Metodologija upravlenija obščestvennymi sistemami v uslovijah razvitogo socializma.* Iževsk, 78 : 126-138.
2490   ANDERSON, Richard E. *Participation and persistence in American adult education: implications for public policy and future research from a multivariate analysis of a national data base.* New York, College Entrance Examination Board, 79, x-43 p.
2491   APPS, Jerold W. *Problems in continuing education.* New York, McGraw-Hill, 79, vii-204 p.
2492   BERNARD, Lucien. *Mythe de l'alphabétisation et des moyens de communication collective en Amérique Latine: une mise au point sur la technologie éducative.* Port-au-Prince, Haiti, Ateliers Fardin, 79, 141 p.
2493   BHOLA, H. S. *Evaluating functional literacy.* Amersham, Hulton, for the International Institute for Adult Literacy Methods, 79, xvi-164 p. [Iran.]
2494   BOWN, Lalage J.; TOMORI, Sunday Hezekiah Olu; [eds.]. *A Handbook of adult eduction for West Africa.* London, Hutchinson, 79, 296 p.
2495   BRÖDEL, Rainer. *Bildungserfahrungen von Industriearbeitern* (Continuing education of industrial workers). Frankfurt/Main, New York, Campus Verlag, 79, 419 p. CR: SESINK, Werner, *Soziologische Revue* 3(3), 80: 303-305.
2496   CANTOR, Leonard Martin. *Further education today: a critical review.* London, Boston, Routledge & K. Paul, 79, viii-255 p.
2497   CLEMENT, Werner; EDDING, Friedrich; [eds.]. *Recurrent education und berufliche Flexibilitätsforschung* (Recurrent education and occupational flexibility research). Berlin, Duncker und Humblot, 79, 188 p.
2498   COLELLA, Brizio. *L'educazione permanente nella realtà sociale* (Life-long education in social reality). Lecce, Milella, 79, 139 p. [Italy.]
2499   COUVERT, Roger. *The evaluation of literacy programmes: a practical guide.* Paris, Unesco, 79, 168 p.
2500   CROPLEY, A. J.; [ed.]. *Lifelong education, a stocktaking.* Hamburg, Unesco Institute for Education, 79, xi-115 p.
2501   DELALIĆ, Eşref. *Workers' universities in Yugoslavia: an adult education modality.* Vancouver, Centre for Continuing Education, University of British Columbia, 79, xiii-170 p.
2502   FERRY, Gilles. "Problèmatiques et pratiques de l'éducation des adultes", *Revue française de Pédagogie* 50, jan-feb-mar 80 : 42-53.
2503   FLORES JARAMILLO, Renán. *El uso de la prensa en la alfabetización de adultos* (The use of press for literacy). Madrid, Magisterio Español, 79, 1st, 182 p. [Spain.]
2504   GADOTTI, Moacir. *L'Éducation contre l'éducation: l'oubli de l'éducation au travers de l'éducation permanente.* Lausanne, Editions l'Age d'homme, 79, 149 p.

2505 GELPI, Ettore. *A future for lifelong education.* Manchester, Department of Adult and Higher Education, University of Manchester, 79. [2 vols..]
2506 GISLER, Dany. "Corps, langage, politique; une expérience d'alphabétisation en Guadeloupe", *Actes de la Recherche en Sciences sociales* 32-33, apr-jun 80 : 105-110.
2507 GRAFF, Harvey J. *The literacy myth: literacy and social structure in the nineteenth-century city.* New York, Academic Press, 79, xxii-352 p.
2508 HINZEN, Heribert. *Erwachsenenbildung und Entwicklung in Tanzania* (Adult education and development in Tanzania). Hamburg, Institut für Afrika-Kunde im Verbund der Stiftung Deutsches Übersee-Institut, 79, xiv-439 p.
2509 KOZÁK, Gyula. *Család — iskola — továbbtanulás. A különböző társadalmi rétegekbe tartozó fiatalok továbbtanulását, pályaválasztását meghatározó szociokulturális tényezők — különös tekintettel a családra és az iskolára* (Family — school — higher education. Factors determining the further education of students of different social background; the role of family, school and social environment). Budapest, Felsooktatási Pedagógiai Kutatóközpont, 80, 222 p.
2510 KOZOL, Jonathan. *Prisoners of silence: breaking the bonds of adult illiteracy in the United States.* New York, Continuum, 80, xiii-113 p.
2511 KRISHAN, Gopal; SHYAM, Madhav. "Regional aspects of urban-rural differential in literacy in India: 1971", *Journal of developing Areas* 13, oct 78 : 11-21.
2512 LENZ, Werner. *Grundlagen der Erwachsenenbildung*(Fundamentals of adult education). Stuttgart, Berlin, Köln, Mainz, Kohlhammer, 79, 170 p.
2513 LIMAGE, Leslie J. "L'analphabétisme dans les pays industrialisés: un commentaire sociologique", *Perspectives (Unesco)* 10, 80 : 151-167.
2514 PADUA, Jorge. *El analfabetismo en América Latina: un estudio empírico con especial referencia a los casos de Perú, México y Argentina* (Illiteracy in Latin America: an empirical study, with reference to Peru, Mexico and Argentina). México, El Colegio de México, 79, vi-192 p.
2515 PELTONEN, Matti. "Aikuiskasvatus ja sen tehtävät" (Adult education and its tasks), *Kasvatus* 11, 80 : 5-8.
2516 SATO, Mamoru. "Shogai kyoiku to hattatsu katei"(The lifelong education and the developmental process), *Kyoiku shakaigaku kenkyu* 35, 80 : 15-24.
2517 SATO, Mamoru. "Akita-ken ni okeru shogai kyoiku no tenkai" (The developing process of the life-long education system in Akita prefecture), *Nihon shogai kyoiku gakukai nenpo* 80 : 21-44.
2518 STUBBS, Michael. *Language and literacy: the sociolinguistics of reading and writing.* London. Boston, Routledge & Kegan Paul, 80, xii-188 p.
2519 VIŠNEVSKIJ, I. B.; GOLOVAČEV, S. B. "Ekonomičeskoe obrazovanie i social'naja aktivnost' trudjaščihsja" (Economic education and the workers' social activity), *Politiceskaja Organizacija Obščestva i Upravlenija pri Socializme* 79 : 57-69.
2520 ZLOTNIKOV, R. A. "Ob osnovnyh tendencijah formirovanija i razvitija duhovnyh potrebnostej sovetskogo raboçego" (On essential tendencies of the formation and development of the Soviet worker's intellectual needs), *IN: Social'nye aspekty razvitija ličnosti. Ispol'zovanie informacionnyh sistem dlja ego prognozirovanija.* Moskva, 78 : 47-55.

13970. Civic education. Technical education
Instruction civique. Enseignement technique

2521 CORBETT, Michael. "Education and contextual tolerance: group-relatedness and consistency reconsidered", *American Politics Quarterly* jul 80 : 345-359.
2522 GEARHEART, B. R. *Special education for the '80s.* St. Louis, C. V. Mosby Co., 80, xviii-498 p.
2523 GLEESON, Denis. "'Streaming' at work and college: on the social differentiation of craft and technician apprentices in technical education", *Sociological Review* 28, nov 80 : 745-761.
2524 JACOBSEN, Walter. "Politische Erziehung und Motivationsforschung" (Political education and motivation research), *Aus Politik und Zeitgeschichte* 16, 80 : 45-53.
2525 LYSON, Thomas A. "Going to college: an emerging rung on the agricultural ladder", *Rural Sociology* 44, wint 79 : 773-790.
2526 MUEL-DREYFUS, Francine. "L'initiative privée; le "terrain" de l'éducation spécialisée", *Actes de la Recherche en Sciences sociales* 32-33, jun 80 : 15-50.
2527 NELSON, Hart M. "Religious transmission versus religious formation: preadolescent-parent interaction", *Sociological Quarterly* 21, 80 : 207-218.

2528 SCHRAMM, Karin. "Une formation commerciale pour l'avenir", *Revue internationale du Travail* 119, jan-feb 80 : 123-136.

**13980. Academic achievement. School failure
Réussite des études. Échec scolaire**

2529 BURSTEIN, Leigh; FISCHER, Kathleen B.; MILLER, M. David. "The multilevel effects of background on science achievement: a cross-national comparison", *Sociology of Education* 53, oct 80 : 215-225.

2530 CHERKAOUI, Mohamed. *Les paradoxes de la réussite scolaire, Sociologie comparée des systèmes d'enseignement.* Paris, Presses universitaires de France, 79, 223 p. CR: Claude DUBAR, *Revue française de sociologie* 21(3), jul-sep 80: 472-473.

2531 GREENSPAN, Stanley I. *Intelligence and adaptation: an integration of psychoanalytic and Piagetian developmental psychology.* New York, International Universities Press, 79, 408 p.

2532 KAIL, Robert. *The development of memory in children.* San Francisco, W. H. Freeman, 79, ix-168 p.

2533 MUELLER, Charles W. "Evidence on the relationship between religion and educational attainment", *Sociology of Education* 53, jul 80 : 140-152. [USA.]

**13990. Pedagogy. Teaching. Teacher
Pédagogie. Enseignement. Enseignant**

[See also / voir aussi: 533, 1469, 2451, 2486, 4501, 5010, 6049]

2534 ALTBACH, Philip G.; SLAUGHTER, Sheila; [eds.]. "The academic profession", *Annals of the American Academy of political and social Science* 448, mar 80 : 1-150.

2535 APPLE, Michael W. *Ideology and curriculum.* London, Boston, Routledge & K. Paul, 79, viii-203 p.

2536 BALLÓN, Eduardo; [et al.]. *La condición del maestro en el Perú* (Teacher's status in Peru). Lima, Desco, 79, 173 p.

2537 BARROW, Robin. *The Canadian curriculum: a personal view.* London, Ont., Faculty of Education, University of Western Ontario, 79, 118 p.

2538 BATUDAEV, I. A.; OSINSKIJ, I. I. "Rol' učitel'skoj intelligencii v social'nom razvitii derevni" (Role of educational intelligentsia in the village social development), *IN: Problemy social'nogo razvitija obščestva zrelogo socializma.* 78 : 13-27. [USSR.]

2539 BELL, Gordon H. *Developing teacher education in the European community: a case study in innovation.* Middlesbrough, Eng., Centre for Teacher Education, Teeside Polytechnic, 79, 82 p.

2540 BRONSEMA, Gerhard. *Lehrerausbildung in Wandel* (Teacher training in evolution). Baltmannsweiler, Burgbücherei Schneider, 79, x-287 p. [Germany FR.]

2541 COBALTI, Antonio; DEI, Marcello. *Insegnanti, innovazione e adattamento: una ricerca sociologica sugli insegnanti della secondaria superiore* (Teachers, innovation and adaptation: a sociological research on high school teachers). Firenze, La nuova Italia, 79, vi-327 p. [Italy.]

2542 COX, Harold. "Professional orientation, associational membership, and teacher militancy", *Sociological Inquiry* 50, 80 : 57-64.

2543 DWORKIN, Anthony Gary. "The changing demography of public school teachers: some implications for faculty turnover in urban areas", *Sociology of Education* 53, apr 80 : 65-73.

2544 GARDINER, W. Lambert. *The psychology of teaching.* Monterey, CA, Brooks/Cole Pub. Co., 80, xiii-384 p.

2545 GOLDINGER, Barbro. *Familjegrupper i skolan* (Family group and school). Stockholm, Wahlström & Widstrand, 79, 116 p.

2546 HAES, Julian. "The problem of cultural relativism: Habermas and the curriculum", *Sociological Review* 28, nov 80 : 717-743.

2547 HARP, John; BETCHERMAN, Gordon. "Contradictory class locations and class action: the case of school teachers' organizations in Ontario and Quebec", *Canadian Journal of Sociology* 80 : 145-162.

2548 KING, Ronald. "The search for the 'invisible' pedagogy", *Sociology* 13, nov 79 : 445-458.

2549 KOLBE, Manfred. *Reformkonzeptionen der Lehrerbildung in Schweden* (Teacher training reform concepts in Sweden). Weinheim, Basel, Beltz, 79, x-198 p.

2550 KULSHRESTHA, S. P. *Emerging value-pattern of teachers and new trends of education in India.* New Delhi, Light & Life Publishers, 79, xxii-336 p.

2551 LYSON, Thomas A. "Factors associated with the choice of a typical or atypical curriculum among college women", *Sociology and social Research* 64, jul 80 : 559-571.

2552 MOOIJ, Ton. "Multi-level onderzoek van samenwerking in het part-time onderwijs" (Multi-level research of cooperation in part-time teaching), *Mens en Maatschappij* 55, 80 : 148-169.

2553 NOBLE, Trevor. "Recruitment to teaching in the years of expansion", *British Journal of Sociology* 31, mar 80 : 95-109.

2554 Organisation de coopération et de développement économiques. *La Profession enseignante: nouvelles orientations.* Paris, O.C.D.E., 79, 169 p.

2555 Organization for Economic Cooperation and Development. *Teacher policies in a new context.* Paris, OECD, 79, 163 p.

2556 VANKOVA, Libuse. "Informace o vysledcich vyzkumu verejneho mineni k problematice vychovy k manzelstvi a rodicovstvi" (An opinion survey on the problems of marriage and parents' education), *Populacni Zpravy* 1-2, 78 : 32-37.

2557 WILKE, Arthur S. *The hidden professoriate: credentialism, professionalism, and the tenure crisis.* Westport, CT, Greenwood Press, 79, 290 p. CR: Lionel S. LEWIS, *Contemporary Sociology (Albany)* 9(4), jul 80 : 508-512.

2558 WILSON, Logan. *American academics: then and now.* New York, Oxford University Press, 79, 309 p. CR: Lionel S. LEWIS, *Contemporary Sociology (Albany)* 9(2), mar 80 : 317-319.

2559 WONG, Morrison G. "Model students? Teachers' perceptions and expectations of their Asian and white students", *Sociology of Education* 53, oct 80 : 236-246.

14. SOCIAL STRUCTURE
STRUCTURE SOCIALE

14100. SOCIAL SYSTEM
SYSTÈME SOCIAL

[See also / voir aussi: 446, 468, 659, 826, 889, 968, 1260, 1320, 1652, 1983, 2314, 2894, 3940, 4420, 4620, 6088]

2560 AITOV, N. A. "Harakternye čerty social'noj struktury razvitogo socialističeskogo obščestva" (Characteristics of the developed socialist society social structure), *IN: Razvitoj socializm: oznovnye čerty*. Saratov, 79 : 37-49.

2561 Bibl.XXIX-2558. BARTH, Fredrik; [ed.]. *Scale and social organization*. CR: Richard E. BLANTON, *Contemporary Sociology (Albany)* 9(2), mar 80: 221.

2562 BELOVA, L. V. "K voprosu o mehanizme dejstvija social'nyh zakonov v socialističeskom obščestve" (On the mechanism of the social laws action in the socialist society), *IN: Ob'ektivnoe i sub'ektivnoe v obščestvennom razvitii*. Vladivostok, 79 : 62-67.

2563 BOLTE, Karl Martin. *Leistung und Leistungsprinzip. Zur Konzeption, Wirklichkeit und Möglichkeit eines gesellschaftlichen Gestaltungsprinzips. Ein Beitrag zur Sozialkunde der Bundesrepublik Deutschland* (Achievement and achievement principle. On the concept, reality and possibility of a social formation principle. An essay on the social information of the Federal Republic of Germany). Opladen, Leske und Budrich Verlag, 79, 107 p. CR: Elisabeth FLITNER, *Soziologische Revue* 3(1), 80 : 36-38.

2564 BOULDING, Kenneth Ewart; BOULDING, Elise; BURGESS, Guy M. *The social system of the planet earth*. Reading, MA, Addison-Wesley, 80, xvii-233 p.

2565 CHASE, Richard. "Structural-functional dynamics in the analysis of socio-economic systems: adaptation of structural change processes to biological systems of human interaction", *American Journal of Economics and Sociology* 39, jan 80 : 49-64.

2566 DOLGIH, N. S. "Dinamika social'no-klassovej struktury obscestva v SFRJu" (Dynamics of the class social structure in Yugoslavia), *Rabočij Klass i sovremennyj Mir* mar-apr 80 : 106-118.

2567 DŽUNUSOV, M. S. *Tendencii izmenenija social'no-klassovoj struktury sovetskih nacij i narodnostej* (Tendencies of change of Soviet nations and peoples class structure). Moskva, Institut Sociologičeskih Issledovanij AN SSSR, 78, 198 p.

2568 FLORIAN, Radu. *Introducere în teoria marxistă a determinismului social* (Introduction to the marxist theory of social determinism). București, Editura Științifică și Enciclopedica, 79, 373 p.

2569 GEL'BRAS, V. G. "Social'naja struktura kitajskogo obščestva" (Social structure of Chinese society), *Rabočij Klass i sovremennyj Mir* mai-jun 80 : 69-76.

2570 GESER, Hans. "Kleine sozialsysteme: Strukturmerkmale und Leistungskapazitäten. Versuch einer theoretischen Integration" (Small social system: structural characteristics and achievement capacity. Towards a theoretical integration), *Kölner Zeitschrift für Soziologie und Sozialpsychologie* 32, 80 : 205-239.

2571 GINER DE SAN JULIAN, Salvador. "La estructura social de la libertad" (The social structure of freedom), *Revista española de Investigaciones sociológicas* 11, jul-sep 80 : 7-27.

2572 HAYASHI, Yatomi. "Kokyo sentaku riron to shin-shakai chitsujo keisei no kokoromi" (The theory of public choice and the general theory of social system), *Zaiseigaku kenkyu* 80 : 45-53.

2573 JOSSELIN DE JONG, P. E. de. *Minangkabau and Negri Sembilan: socio-political structure in Indonesia*. New York, AMS Press, 80, viii-208 p.

2574 KRICKIJ, V. I. "Metodologičeskie problemy izučenija social'noj struktury razvitogo socialističeskogo obščestva" (Methodological problems of the study of the developed socialist society social structure), *IN: Istoričeskij materializm i sovremennoe obščestvennoe razvitie*. Moskva, 79 : 10-16.

2575 KUPRIJAN, A. P. "Social'nyj determinizm kak metodologičeskaja problema sovremennogo obščestvennogo razvitija" (Social determinism as a methodological problem of the contemporary social development), *IN: Social'nye processy razvitogo socialističeskogo obščestva i ideologičeskaja bor'ba*. Tallin, 79 : 24-30.

2576 LOMBARD, Jacques. "Systèmes sociaux et modes de répression", *Cahiers internationaux de Sociologie* 67, jul-dec 79 : 349-364.
2577 MACURA, Milos; [ed.]. *Effect of current demographic change in Europe on social structure.* Beograd, Ekonomski Institut, 79, viii-215 p.
2578 MANICAS, Peter. "The concept of social structure", *Journal for the Theory of social Behaviour* 10, jul 80 : 65-82.
2579 MESIHOVIĆ, Nijaz. "Veberov pristup istraživanju društvene strukture" (Weber's approach to the study of the social structure), *Sociologija* 21(1-2), 79 : 77-88.
2580 MIHAJLOV, S. V. "Izmenenija v social'noj strukture kapitalističeskogo obščestva" (Social structure change of the capitalist society), *Rabočij Klass i sovremennyj Mir* jan-feb 80 : 45-53.
2581 NAMER, Gérard. *Le système social de Rousseau: de l'inégalité économique à l'inégalitié politique.* Paris, Éditions Anthropos, 79, 212 p.
2582 NEDOREZOV, A. I. "Preobrazovanie social'no — klassovoj struktury v socialističeskih stranah Europy" (Transformation of social and class structures in European socialist countries), *Voprosy Istorii* 54, apr 80 : 49-69.
2583 PINNARO, Gabriella; POGLIESE, Enrico. "Changes in the social structure of Southern Italy", *International Journal of urban and regional Research* dec 79 : 492-515.
2584 QURESHI, Anwar Iqbal. *The economic and social system of Islam.* Lahore, Islamic Book Service, 79, viii-135 p.
2585 RUTKEVIČ, M. N. "Social'naja struktura sovetskogo obščestva i eě razvitie" (The Soviet society social structure and its development), IN: *Konstitucija obščenarodnogo gosudarstva. Voprosy teorii.* Moskva, 79 : 143-161.
2586 SCHÄFERS, Bernhard. *Sozialstruktur und Wandel der Bundesrepublik Deutschland* (Social structure and change of the Federal Republic of Germany). Stuttgart, Enke, 79, xv-335 p.
2587 TANI, Katsuhide. *Gendai shakai no kozo to hendo* (The social structure and social change of modern society in Japan). Tokyo, Nansosha, 80, 174 p.
2588 TEGTMEYER, Heinrich; [ed.]. *Soziale Strukturen und individuelle Mobilität: Beitr. zur soziodemograph. Analyse d. Bundesrepublik Deutschland* (Social structures and individual mobility: Essays on the socio-demographic analysis of the Federal Republic of Germany). Boppard am Rhein, Boldt, 79, 336 p.
2589 WATANABE, Motoki. "Blau no shakaiteki kōkan riron ni tsuite" (On Blau's social exchange theory), *Risshō daigaku shakaigaku-shakaifukushigakukai ronsō* 15, 80 : 1-12.
2590 WEINSTEIN, Michael; WEINSTEIN, Deena. "Freud et le problème de l'ordre social ou le retour à Hobbes", *Diogène* 108, oct-dec 79 : 47-67.
2591 YAMAOKA, Eiichi. "Shakai kankei to shakai ishiki" (Social organization and social relationships), *Bukkyō daigaku shakaigaku kenkyūjo kiyō* 80 : 43-53.

14200. SOCIAL STRATIFICATION
STRATIFICATION SOCIALE

14210. Social differentiation
Différenciation sociale

[See also / voir aussi: 1598, 1806, 2332, 2339, 2356, 2400, 2672, 2692, 2919, 3157, 3199, 3666, 3686, 3691, 4418, 4489, 4515, 4766, 5071, 5196, 5744, 5763, 5793, 5848, 6095, 6206, 6244]

2592 Bibl.XXIX-2595. ADAM, Barry D. *The survival of domination: inferiorization and everyday life.* CR: Murray WEBSTER JR., *American Journal of Sociology* 58(6), mai 80 : 1478-1480.
2593 Bibl.XXIX-2596. AGGER, Robert E. *A little white lie: institutional division of labor and life.* CR: Sidney M. WILLHELM., *Contemporary Sociology (Albany)* 9(1), jan 80 : 90-91.
2594 BELL, Wendell; ROBINSON, Robert V. "Cognitive maps of class and racial inequalities in England and the United States", *American Journal of Sociology* 86, sep 80 : 320-349.
2595 Bibl.XXIX-2601. BENOKRAITIS, Nijole V.; FEAGIN, Joe R. *Affirmative action and equal opportunity: action, inaction, reaction.* CR: Allan P. SINDLER, *American political Science Review* 74(1), mar 80 : 186-187.
2596 BERG-SCHLOSSER, Dirk. "Soziale Differenzierung und Klassenbildung in Kenia, Entwicklungen und Perspektiven" (Social differentiation and class formation in Kenya: developments and prospects), *Politische Vierteljahresschrift* 20, 79 : 313-329.
2597 BILKES, C. G. C.; TILLEKENS, G. "'L'histoire se répète!' Een kritische reflectie op de geschiedschrijving van het stratificatie-onderzoek" ("'L'histoire se répète!" A

critical reflection on the history of stratification research), *Mens en Maatschappij* 54, nov 79 : 451-461.
2598 Bibl.XXIX-2603. BLUMBERG, Rae Lesser. *Stratification: socioeconomic and sexual inequality.* CR: Patricia A. TAYLOR, *Contemporary Sociology (Albany)* 9(3), mai 80: 438-439.
2599 COVELLO, Vincent T.; ASHBY, Jacqueline. "Inequality in a divided society: an analysis of data from Northern Ireland", *Sociological Focus* 13, apr 80 : 87-98.
2600 DAHLSTRÖM, Edmund. "Division of labour, class stratification, and cognitive development", *Acta sociologica* 23(2-3), 80 : 133-155.
2601 DEN OUDEN, J. H. B. "Social stratification expressed through language: a case study of a South Indian village", *Contributions to Indian Sociology* 13, jan-jun 79 : 33-59.
2602 FOLEY, John W. "Toward macro-social accounting: measures and scales of racial, sexual, and spatial equality in 243 US SMSA's", *Social Indicators Research* oct 79 : 445-461.
2603 FONER, Anne. "Ascribed and achieved bases of stratification", *Annual Review of Sociology* 79 : 219-242.
2604 GALLINO, Luciano. "Effetti dissociativi dei processi associativi in una società altamente differenziata" (Dissociative effects of associative processes in a society highly differenciated), *Quaderni di Sociologia* 28, mar 79 : 1-23. [Italy.]
2605 HAMMOUDI, A. "Segmentarity, social stratification, political power and sainthood: reflections on Gellner's theses", *Economy and Society* aug 80 : 279-303.
2606 HWA-BAO CHANG, Henry. "Social stratification in Hong Kong: a critical analysis", *International Journal of contemporary Sociology* 15(3-4), jul-oct 78 : 338.353.
2607 ITSKHOKIN, ALEKSANDR. "The dual system", *American Journal of Sociology* 85, mai 80 : 1317-1336. [with a comment by Randall COLLINS: 1337-1339.]
2608 JACOBS, David. "Inequality and police strength — the conflict theory and coercive control in metropolitan areas", *Amercian sociological Review* 44, dec 79 : 913-925.
2609 JEFFRIES, Vincent; RANSFORD, H. Edward; [comp.]. *Social stratification: a multiple hierarchy approach.* Wellesley, MA, Allyn and Bacon, 80, xii-596 p.
2610 KALLEBERG, Arne L.; GRIFFIN, Larry J. "Class, occupation, and inequality in job rewards", *American Journal of Sociology* 85, jan 80 : 731-768. [USA.]
2611 LAMBERT, Ronald D.; HUNTER, Alfred A. "Social stratification, voting behaviour, and the images of Canadian federal political parties", *Canadian Review of Sociology and Anthropolgy* 16, aug 79 : 287-304. [Canada.]
2612 MITRA, Asok; MUKHERJI, Shekhar. *Population food and land inequality in India: a geography of hunger and insecurity.* Bombay, Allied, 80, xvii-112 p.
2613 Bibl.XXIX-2624. MOORE, Barrington Jr. *Injustice: the social bases of obedience and revolt.* CR: John WAHLKE, *American political Science Review* 74(2), jun 80: 485-486.
2614 OSMANI, S. R. "On the normative measurement of inequality", *Bangladesh Development Studies* 78 : 417-442.
2615 PEARCE, I. O.; ODEBIYI, I. A. "The impact of socio-economic inequalities on health", *Africa Development* oct-dec 79 : 64-83. [Nigeria.]
2616 PERRY, Charles S.; BAUDER, Ward W. "Equality, economic resources, and structural differentiation: dimensions of development in the Northeast United States", *Social Indicators Research* sep 80 : 327-340.
2617 PILIPENKO, D. A. "K metodologii razrabotki ponjatija 'social'nyj sloj'" (Methodology of the "social stratum" concept elaboration), IN: *Metodologičeskie problemy nauki.* Novosibirsk, 79 : 137-142.
2618 SABERWAL, Satish. "Inequality in colonial India", *Contributions to Indian Sociology* 13, jul-dec 79 : 241-264.
2619 SAWER, Marian. "Socialism and the legitimation of inequality", *Australian and New Zealand Journal of Sociology* 16, mar 80 : 56-62.
2620 SCHAEFER, David Lewis; [ed.]. *The new egalitarianism: questions and challenges.* Port Washington, NY, Kennikat Press, 79, 248 p. CR: Harry C. BREDEMEIER, *Contemporary Sociology (Albany)* 9(3), mai 80: 425-426.
2621 ŠKARATAN, O. I.; [et al.]. "Harakter vneproizvodstvennoj dejatel'nosti i social'naja differenciacja gorožan" (Character of the non-productive activity and the citizens social differentiation), *Sociologičeskie Issledovanija* 79 : 104-110.
2622 SMITH, Arthur B. Jr. "The law and equal employment opportunity: what's past should not be prologue", *Industrial and Labor Relations Review* 33, jul 80 : 493-505.
2623 STRASSER, Hermann. "Stratum and class formation: principles of a theory of social inequality", *Canadian Journal of Sociology* 80 : 103-120.

2624	STUMPF, Stephen A.; GELLER, Martin M.; FREEDMAN, Richard D. "Equal employment opportunity regulation and change in compensation practices", *Journal of applied behavioral Science* 16, jan-mar 80 : 29-40.
2625	TERPSTRA, J. "Preventie en sociale ongelijkheid: een interpretatie van onderzoeksresultaten" (Prevention and social inequality: an interpretation of research-findings), *Sociologische Gids* 27, mar-apr 80 : 146-159.
2626	ULTEE, W. C. "Over sociale ongelijkheid. Vooruitgang in het naoorlogse socialistische denken?" (About social inequality. Is there any progress in postwar socialist thought?), *Mens en Maatschappij* 54, nov 79 : 420-445.
2627	Bibl.XXIX-2638. VANFOSSEN, Beth E. *The structure of social inequality.* CR: Larry LYON, *Contemporary Sociology (Albany)* 9(3), mai 80: 450-452.
2628	VERCAUTEREN, P. "La croyance égalitaire", *Recherches sociologiques* 11, 80 : 31-57.
2629	VILLETI, Roberto. "Trabajo dividido y trabajo forzado" (Divided labour and forced labour), *Sistema. Revista de Ciencias sociales* 34, 80 : 37-70.
2630	WEDDERBURN, Dorothy. "Some reflections on inequality and class structure", *Stamp Memorial Lecture* 79 : 1-20.

14220. Caste. Slavery
Caste. Esclavage

[See also / voir aussi: 3550]

2631	BLASSINGAME, John W. *The slave community: plantation life in the antebellum South.* New York, Oxford University Press, 79, xviii-414 p.
2632	CUNLIFFE, Marcus. *Chattel slavery and wage slavery: the Anglo-American context, 1830-1860.* Athens, University of Georgia Press, 79, xix-128 p.
2633	DESINGU SETTY, E. "Caste hierarchy: the crumbling edifice", *Social Welfare* 25, dec 78 : 1-3. [India.]
2634	ESCOTT, Paul D. *Slavery remembered: a record of twentieth-century slave narratives.* Chapel Hill, University of North Carolina Press, 79, xv-221 p.
2635	GASH, Norman. *Aristocracy and people: Britain, 1815-1865.* Cambridge, MA, Harvard University Press, 79, 375 p.
2636	GERBET, Marie Claude. *La noblesse dans le royaume de Castille: étude sur ses structures sociales en Estrémadure (1454-1516).* Paris, Publications de la Sorbonne, 79, 540 p.
2637	JOSHI, Barbara R. "'Ex-untouchable': problems, progress and policies in Indian social change", *Pacific Affairs* 53, sum 80 : 193-222.
2638	KAMBLE, B. R. *Caste and philosophy in pre Buddhist India.* Aurangbad, Parimal, 79, 288 p.
2639	KHAN, Mumtaz Ali. *Scheduled castes and their status in India.* New Delhi, Uppal, 80, xiv-276 p.
2640	MATTOSO, Katia M. de Queirós. *Être esclave au Brésil: XVIe-XIXe.* Paris, Hachette, 79, 317 p.
2641	PANDE, S. U. "The politicisation of the special constitutional provisions and the perpetuation of casteism", *Indian political Science Review* 14, jan 80 : 80-90.
2642	PARISH, Peter J. *Slavery: the many faces of a Southern institution.* Durham, British Association for American Studies, 79, 48 p.
2643	RAMAMURTY, M. V. "Caste and class", *Radical Humanist* 43(12), dec 79 : 5-10.
2644	SARADAMONI, K. *Emergence of a slave caste: Pulays of Kerala.* New Delhi, Peoples Publishing House, 80, xiii-259 p.
2645	SENGUPTA, Syamalkanti. *Caste, status, group, aggregate and class: an inquiry into the social stratification in rural West Bengal.* Calcutta, Firma KLM, 79, xi-182 p.
2646	STERN, Henri. "Power in modern India: caste or class? An approach and case study", *Contributions to Indian Sociology* 13, jan-jun 79 : 61-84.
2647	WATSON, James L.; [ed.]. *Asian and African systems of slavery.* Berkeley, University of California Press, 80, 348 p.

14230. Social class
Classe sociale

[See also / voir aussi: 314, 822, 840, 935, 1085, 1378, 1576, 1618, 1757, 1884, 1935, 2246, 2284, 2347, 2357, 2358, 2439, 2462, 2566, 2582, 2600, 2623, 2630, 2645, 2646, 2723, 2742, 2780, 2890, 3387, 3416, 3456, 3529, 3536, 3563, 3586, 3594, 3700, 3721, 3744, 3750, 4014, 4067, 4098, 4124, 4300, 4379, 4431, 4454, 4457, 4697, 4698, 4949, 5084, 5090, 5281, 5450, 5479, 5668, 5674, 5719, 5728, 5764, 5861, 6090, 6230]

2648 "Conflits de classes et conflits de nations", *Mondes en Développement* 26, 79 : 171-355.
2649 "Work and the working class", *Theory and Society* jan 80 : 1-214. [special issue.]
2650 ŌKAJI, Toshio. "Rōdōsha kaikyū no gainen to seisanteki rōdō" (The concept of the working class and productive labour), *Sōka daigaku daigakuin kiyo* 80 : 209-226.
2651 AMIN, Samir. "The class structure of the contemporary imperialist system", *Monthly Review* 31, jan 80 : 9-26.
2652 ANDERSEN, Jørgen Goul. *Mellemlagene i Danmark* (Middle classes in Denmark). Århus, Politica, 79, 305 p.
2653 BATATU, Hanna. *The old social classes and the revolutionary movements in Iraq: a study of Iraq's old landed and commercial classes and of its communists, Ba'thists, and free officers.* Princeton, NJ, Princeton University Press, 79, xxiv-1283 p. CR: James A. BILL, *American political Science Review* 74(2), jun 80: 529-530.
2654 BOVENKERK, F. "Rehabilitatie van het rapalje — hoe en waarom Marx en Engels het lompenproletariaat ten onrechteh hebben afgeschilderd als een reactionaire kracht" (Rehabilitation of the rabble: how and why Marx and Engels have pictured the 'lumpenproletariat' unjustly as a force of political reaction), *Sociologische Gids* 27, mai-jun 80 : 191-224.
2655 Bibl.XXIX-2695. BRUCE-BRIGGS, B.; [ed.]. *The new class?*. CR: Steven BRINT, *Contemporary Sociology (Albany)* 9(5), sep 80: 651-653.
2656 BUCK, Trevor W. "Regional class differences: an international study of capitalism", *International Journal of urban and regional Research* dec 79 : 516-526.
2657 CANNON, Lynn Weber. "On the absolute or relative basis of perception: the case for middle class identification", *Social Indicators Research* sep 80 : 347-363.
2658 Bibl.XXIX-2701. COLEMAN, Richard P,; RAINWATER, Lee; MCCLELLAND, Kent A. *Social standing in America: new dimensions of class*. CR: Erik Olin WRIGHT, *American Journal of Sociology* 85(6), mai 80: 1433-1439. [also CR: Peter H. ROSSI, Contemporary Sociology (Albany), 9(1), jan 80: 40-44; Karl-Wilhelm GRÜMER, Kölner Zeitschrift für Soziologie und Sozialpsychologie, 32(1), mar 80: 167-170.]
2659 CONNELL, R. W. "A critique of the Althusserian approach to class", *Theory and Society* nov 79 : 303-345.
2660 COTGROVE, Stephen; DUFF, Andrew. "Environmentalism, middle-class radicalism and politics", *Sociological Review* 28, mai 80 : 333-351.
2661 DAVIES, Robert H. *Capital, state and white labour in South Africa, 1900-1960: An historical materialist analysis of class formation and class relations.* Atlantic Highlands, NJ, Humanities Press, 79, viii-414 p.
2662 DOMHOFF, G. William; [ed.]. *Power structure research.* Beverly Hills, CA, Sage Publications, 80, 270 p.
2663 DUCLOS, Denis. "Classe ouvrière et environnement", *Sociologie du Travail* 22, jul-sep 80 : 324-345.
2664 EREMENKO, A. M. "Nekotorye voprosy formirovanija raboĉego klassa v stranah socialistiĉeskoj orientacii (Tropiĉeskaja Afrika)" (Some questions on the working class formation in the socialism-oriented countries: Tropical Africa), *IN: Dialektika social'nogo poznanija*. Moskva, 79 : 98-104.
2665 FOSSAERT, Robert. *La Socieété. Les classes.* Paris, Seuil, 80, 487 p. [Tombe 4.]
2666 FOX, William S.; PHILLIBER, William W. "Class convergence: an empirical test", *Sociology and social Research* 64, jan 80 : 236-248.
2667 GANDÁSEGUI, Marco A. *La lucha de clases y la Zona del Canal* (Class struggle and the Canal Zone). Panamá, Asociación Panameña de Sociología, 73-79, 24 p.
2668 GILMORE, David D. *The people of the plain: class and community in lower Andalusia.* New York, Columbia University Press, 80, xi-247 p.
2669 GORDON, L. A.; KLOPOV, E. V. "Obŝĉie ĉerty social'nogo razvitija raboĉego klassa v stranah socialistiĉeskogo sodružestva" (Common characteristics of the social development of working class in the socialist community countries), *Raboĉij Klass i sovremennyj Mir* nov-dec 79 : 80-91.
2670 GRABB, Edward G. "Marxist categories and theories of class: the case of working-class authoritarianism", *Pacific sociological Review* 23, oct 80 : 359-376.
2671 GRAND'MAISON, Jacques. *La nouvelle classe et l'avenir du Québec.* Montréal, Stanké, 79, 272 p.
2672 GURIN, Patricia; MILLER, Arthur H.; GURIN, Gerald. "Stratum identification and consciousness", *Social Psychology Quarterly* 43, mar 80 : 30-47.
2673 HARVEY, Fernand; HOULE, Gilles. *Les classes sociales au Canada et au Québec: bibliographie annotée.* Québec, Institut supérieur des sciences humaines, Université Laval, 79, 288 p.

2674 HAYASHI, Yatomi. "Senshin shakai to shokaikyu"(The advanced societies and social classes), *Atarashii shakaigaku no tameni* 21, 80 : 11-17.

2675 IMANOV, G. R.; RAGIMOV, A. A. "Rabocij klass i razvitie social'noj struktury sovetskogo obščestva" (Working class and development of the social structure of Soviet society), *Voprosy Filosofii* 33, mai 80 : 90-100.

2676 JAHANGIR, Burhanuddin Khan. *Differentiation, polarisation, and confrontation in rural Bangladesh.* Dacca, Centre for Social Studies, 79, 324 p.

2677 JOHNSON, Robert Eugene. *Peasant and proletarian: the working class of Moscow at the end of the nineteenth century.* New Brunswick, NJ, Rutgers University Press, 79, xii-225 p.

2678 JULLIARD, Jacques; [et al.]. *Crise et avenir de la classe ouvrière.* Paris, Éditions du Seuil, 79, 121 p.

2679 JUNG, Harold. "Class struggle in El Salvador", *New Left Review* 122, jul-aug 80 : 3-25.

2680 KEDDIE, Vincent. "Class identification and party preference among manual workers: the influence of community, union membership and kinship", *Canadian Review of Sociology and Anthropology* 17, feb 80 : 24-36.

2681 KESSLER, Ronald C.; CLEARY, Paul D. "Social class and psychological distress", *American sociological Review* 45, jun 80 : 463-478.

2682 KOJTLA, H. "Rabočij klass i kul'turnyj progress socializma" (The working class and the socialism cultural progress), IN: *Social'nye processy razvitogo socialističeskogo obščestva i ideologičeskaja bor'ba.* Tallin, 79.

2683 KOLBANOVSKIJ, V. V.; DENISOVSKIJ, G. M. "Social'noe razvitie rabočego klassa i avtomatizacija" (Social development of the working class and automation), IN: *Social'naja struktura sovetskogo obščestva i socialističeskij obraz žizni. I.*. Moskva, 78 : 40-51.

2684 KOVAC, F. "Ravočij klass v social'nej strukture sovremennoj Vengrii" (The working class in the social structure of contemporary Hungary), *Rabočij Klass i sovremennyj Mir* nov-dec 79 : 92-98.

2685 KREML, William P. *The middle class burden.* Durham, NC, Carolina Academic Press, 79, xiv-153 p.

2686 LEVITT, Ian; SMOUT, Christopher. *The state of the Scottish working class in 1843: a statistical and spatial enquiry based on the data from the Poor Law Commission Report of 1844.* Edinburgh, Scottish Academic Press, 79, x-284 p.

2687 LOMNITZ-ADLER, Claudio. "Clase y etnicidad en Morelos: una nueva interpretación" (Class and ethnicity in Morelos: a new interpretation), *América indígena* 39, jul-sep 79 : 439-475.

2688 LOPES, José Sérgio Leite; [et al.]. *Mudança social no Nordeste: a reprodução da subordinação: estudos sobre trabalhadores urbanos*(Social change in the Northeast; reproduction of dependence: studies on urban workers). Rio de Janeiro, Paz e Terra, 79, 226 p.

2689 LUBECK, Paul; WALTON, John. "Urban class conflict in Africa and Latin America", *International Journal of urban and regional Research* mar 79 : 3-28.

2690 MARESCA, Sylvain. "Grandeur et permanence des grandes familles paysannes", *Actes de la Recherche en Sciences sociales* 31, jan 80 : 35-61.

2691 MARKITAN, S. "Veduščaja rol' rabočego klassa v upravlenii gosudarstvom razvitogo socializma" (The working class leading role in the management of the developed socialism state), *Kommunist Moldavii* 79 : 60-67.

2692 MARKOV, N. V. "Puti preodolenija social'nyh različij vnutri rabočego klassa" (Means of eliminating social differences inside the working class), *Problemy naučnogo kommunizma (Moskva)* 13, 79 : 194-210.

2693 MARTINELLI, Franco. *Struttura di classe e comunicazione culturale* (Class structure and cultural communication). Napoli, Liguori, 79, 201 p. : 961[Italy.]

2694 MERRIMAN, John M.; [ed.]. *Consciousness and class experience in nineteenth-century Europe.* New York, Holmes & Meier Publishers, 79, vii-261 p.

2695 MITSUHASHI, Toshimitsu. "Gendai Mexico chukan kaikyu no keizai-teki ichi to genjo no sho-sokumen -hoho-ron-jo no tenbo ni mukete" (The economic position of the Mexican middle classes and their actual situation in society. Towards a methodological perspective), *Iberoamericana* 80 : 22-35.

2696 MONTOYA, Rodrigo. "Changes in rural class structure under the Peruvian agrarian reform", *Latin American Perspectives* aut 78 : 113-126.

2697 MOYANA, Tafire nyika. "Creating an African middle class: the political economy of education and exploitation in Zimbabwe", *Journal of Southern African Affairs* jul 79 : 325-346.

2698 MUTTI, Antonio. "Elementi per un'analisi della borghesia di stato" (Elements for an analysis of the state bourgeoisie), *Quaderni di Sociologia* 28, mar 79 : 24-70.

2699 PALMER, Bryan D. "Working-class Canada: recent historical writing", *Queen's Quarterly* 86, wint 79-80 : 594-616.
2700 PEREZ PICAZO, María Teresa. *Oligarquía urbana y campesinado en Murcia, 1875-1902* (Urban oligarchy and peasantry in Murcia, 1875-1902). Murcia, Academia Alfonso X El Sabio, 79, xxiii-302 p.
2701 PERRING, Charles. "A moment in the 'proleterianization' of the new middle class: race, value and division of labour in the copperbelt, 1946-1966", *Journal of Southern African Studies* apr 80 : 183-213.
2702 Bibl.XXIX-2763. PETRAS, James. *Critical perspectives on imperialism and social class in the Third World.* CR: Eldon KENWORTHY, *American political Science Review* 74(3), sep 80 : 885-886.
2703 PIVA, Michael J. *The condition of the working class in Toronto, 1900-1921.* Ottawa, University of Ottawa Press, 79, xviii-190 p.
2704 PRZEWORSKI, Adam; RUBIN, Barnett R.; UNDERHILL, Ernest. "The evolution of the class structure of France, 1901-1968", *Economic Development and cultural Change* 28, jul 80 : 725-752.
2705 ROŽKO, A. M. "Rabočij klass i social'nogo priroda KPSS" (The working class and the CPSU social nature), *IN: Aktual'nye voprosy social'no-političeskogo razvitija obščestva v uslovijah zrelogo socializma.* Saratov, 79 : 3-14.
2706 ROŽKOVA, A. P. "Orientacija na upravlenčeskuju dejatel'nost' v strukture cennostej rabočego klassa" (Orientation towards a management activity in the working class values structure), *IN: Socialističeskij obraz žizni i ličnost'.* 79 : 78-90.
2707 SAINT MARTIN, Monique De. "Une grande famille", *Actes de la Recherche en Sciences sociales* 31, jan 80 : 4-21.
2708 SALES, Arnaud. *La bourgeoisie industrielle au Québec.* Montréal, Presses de l'Université de Montréal, 79, 322 p.
2709 SCHREIBER, E. M. "Class awareness and class voting in Canada: a reconsideration of the Ogmudson thesis", *Canadian Review of Sociology and Anthropology* 17, feb 80 : 37-44. [with a response by R. OGMUNDSON: 45-54.]
2710 SKLAR, Richard. "The nature of class domination in Africa", *Journal of modern African Studies* 17, dec 79 : 531-552.
2711 TEZANOS, José F. "La sociología del recelo; o como trivializar el debate sobre las clases sociales" (The sociology of distrust, or how is the debate on social classes to be vulgarized?), *Sistema. Revista de Ciencias sociales* 34, 80 : 117-138.
2712 USENIN, V. I.; KREVNEVIČ, V. V.; [eds.]. *Rabočij klass v uslovijah naučno-tehničeskoj revoljucii* (The working class under conditions of the scientific and technical revolution). Moskva, Nauka, 79, 310 p.
2713 VANNEMAN, Reeve D. "US and British perceptions of class", *American Journal of Sociology* 85, jan 80 : 769-790.
2714 VDOVIN, A. I. "O prirode rabočego klassa pri socializme" (On the working class nature under socialism), *IN: Metodologičeskie i metodičeskie problemy izučenija rabočego klassa socialističeskogo obščestva.* 79 : 4-29.
2715 VELTMEYER, Henry C. "The working class in Halifax", *Scottish Journal of Sociology* apr 79 : 225-261.
2716 VINOGRADOV, Vladimir. "Politique anticrise et lutte de classe", *Nouvelle Revue internationale* 23, feb 80 : 135-148.
2717 VOLČOK, G. I.; GERASTEVIČ, È. A. "Social'noklassovaja struktura obščestva razvitogo socializma i tendencii eě razvitija" (Socio-class structure of the developed socialist society and tendencies of its development), *IN: XXV s'ezd KPSS i voprosy social'no-političeskogo razvitija sovetskogo obščestva.* Minsk, 79 : 28-38.
2718 WESOLOWSKI, Wlodzimierz. *Classes, strata and power.* Boston, Routledge and Kegan Paul, 79, 159 p. CR: Frank PARKIN, *Contemporary Sociology (Albany)* 9(6), nov 80 : 802-804.
2719 WINSON, Anthony. "Class structure and agrarian transition in Central America", *Latin American Perspectives* aut 78 : 27-48.
2720 ZAGLADIN, V. V. *Istoričeskaja missija rabočego klassa i sovremennoe rabočee dviženie* (The working class historical mission and the contemporary labour movement). Moskva, Znanie, 79, 63 p.
2721 ZAJMIST, F. L. "Povyšenie veduščej roli rabočego klassa-osnova soveršenstvovanija političeskoj sistemy sovetskcgo obščestva" (The elevation of the working class leading role is the basis of the Soviet society political system improvement), *IN: Konstitucija SSSR i aktual'nye problemy teorii naučnogo kommunizma.* Moskva, 79 : 8-14.

2722 ZINOV'EVA, R. A. "Urbanizacija i migracija kak uslovija razvitija raboČego klassa Latinskoj Ameriki" (Urbanization and migration as conditions of development of the Latin American working class), *IN: Problemy sovremennogo raboČego dviŽenija Latinskoj Ameriki.* Moskva, 80 : 139-156.

14240. Status
Status

[See also / voir aussi: 1036, 2370, 2448, 3206, 3250, 3712, 3753, 4381, 4391, 6201]

2723 BOURDIEU, Pierre. "Le capital social", *Actes de la Recherche en Sciences sociales* 31, jan 80 : 2-3.
2724 CAMPBELL, Richard T.; HENRETTA, John C. "Status claims and status attainment: the determinants of financial well-being", *American Journal of Sociology* 86, nov 80 : 618-629.
2725 CROSBIE, Paul V. "The effect of sex and size on status ranking", *Social Psychology Quarterly* 42, dec 79 : 340-353.
2726 GRÜMER, Karl-Wilhelm; HELD, Gerhard; ROHLINGER, Harald. "Situationskontexte als Einflussfaktoren der Statuswahrnehmung" (Situation contexts as determinants in the process of status perception), *Zeitschrift für Soziologie* jul 80 : 275-284.
2727 O'CONNELL, Agnes N. "Effects of manipulated status on performance, goal setting, achievement motivation, anxiety, and fear of success", *Journal of social Psychology* 112, oct 80 : 75-89.
2728 TERADA, Ryoichi. "Chii fuseigoron no setsumei wakugumi to sono kon'nichiteki igi -sotaiteki hakudatsuron tono taihi ni oite" (Frameworks of status inconsistency theory and their contemporary significance — in comparison with theory of relative deprivation), *Tokyo toritsu daigaku shakaigaku ronko* 80 : 84-106.
2729 ZELDITCH, Morris Jr.; LAUDERDALE, Pat; STUBLAREC, Stephen. "How are inconsistencies between status and ability resolved?", *Social Forces* 58, jun 80 : 1025-1043.
2730 ZIMMERMANN, Ekkart. "Statusinkonsistenz in der Bundesrepublik Deutschland. Ein Stiefkind sozialstruktureller Analyse?" (Status inconsistency in the Federal Republic of Germany. A bastard of the socio-structural analysis?), *Kölner Zeitschrift für Soziologie und Sozialpsychologie* 32, 80 : 325-338.

14250. Elite. Intellectual
Élite. Intellectuel

[See also / voir aussi: 267, 1576, 1939, 3685, 3991, 4102, 4116, 5237, 5467, 6015]

2731 AITOV, N. A. "O nekotoryh diskussionnyh voprosah izuČenija sovetskoj intelligencii" (On some questions under discussion concerning the Soviet intelligentsia study), *SociologiČeskie Issledovanija* 79 : 29-34.
2732 AJELLO, Nello. *Intellettuali e PCI 1944-1958* (Intellectuals and ICP, 1944-1958). Bari, Laterza, 79, 567 p.
2733 B'CHIR, Badra. "Réflexions sur le concept d'élite chez le sociologue arabe", *Revue tunisienne de Sciences sociales* 15(53), 78 : 41-58.
2734 BERKOWITZ, S. D. "Structural and non-structural models of elites: a critique", *Canadian Journal of Sociology* 80 : 13-30.
2735 BOKAREV, N. N. "Rol' social'noj aktivnosti intelligencii SSSR" (Role of the USSR intelligentsia social activity), *IN: Social'naja struktura sovetskogo obŠČestva i socialistiČeskij obraz Žizni. I..* Moskva, 78 : 64-75.
2736 BRATHWAITE, Farley. "Race, social class and the origins of occupational elites in Trinidad and Tobago", *Boletín de Estudios latinoamericanos y del Caribe* 28, jun 80 : 13-30.
2737 CANFORO, Luciano. *Intellettuali in Germania: tra reazione e rivoluzione* (Intellectuals in Germany: between reaction and revolution). Bari, De Donato, 79, 171 p. [1888-1918.]
2738 COHEN, Lenard J. "Partisans, professionals and proletarians: elite change in Yugoslavia", *Canadian Slavonic Papers* 21, dec 79 : 446-478.
2739 FERNER, Anthony. "The dominant class and industrial development in Peru", *Journal of Development Studies* 15, jul 79 : 268-288.
2740 GIOVAGNOLI, Agostino. "Sulla formazione della classe dirigente democristiana" (On the formation of the democristian ruling class), *Mulino* 29(267), jan-feb 80 : 102-129. [Italy.]

2741 GLAZOVA, E. P.; [et al.]. "Nekotory social'nye harakteristiki pravjaščej élity v kapitalističeskih stranah" (Some social characteristics of the leading elite in the capitalist countries), *IN: Rabočij klass v mirovom revoljucionnom processe: Ežegodnik 1979*. Moskva, 79 : 138-149.

2742 GOULDNER, Alvin Ward. *The future of intellectuals and the rise of the new class: a frame of reference, theses, conjectures, arguments, and an historical perspective on the role of intellectuals and the intelligentsia in the international class contest of the modern era.* New York, Seabury Press, 79, 121 p.

2743 GRAYSON, J. Paul; GRAYSON, L. M. "Canadian literary and other elites: the historical and institutional bases of shared realities", *Canadian Review of Sociology and Anthropology* 17, nov 80 : 338-356.

2744 HIGLEY, John; DEACON, Desley; SMART, Don. *Elites in Australia*. London, Boston, Routledge & K. Paul, 79, xiv-317 p. CR: Andrew HOPKINS, *Australian and New Zealand Journal of Sociology* 16(1), mar 80: 73-78.

2745 HLOPHE, Stephen S. "Ruling families and power struggles in Liberia", *Journal of African Studies* sum 79 : 75-82.

2746 HUSSAIN, Asaf. *Elite politics in an ideological state: the case of Pakistan*. Folkestone, Eng., Dawson, 79, 212 p.

2747 Bibl.XXIX-2825. INGHAM, John N. *The iron barons: a social analysis of an American urban elite, 1874-1965.* CR: John C. LEGGETT, *American Journal of Sociology* 85(4), jan 80 : 976-978.

2748 IVAŠKEVIČ, I. M.; ŠLJAHTUN, P. A. "Ob uglublenii social'noj neodnorodnosti umstvennogo truda v sovremennom kapitalističeskom obsčestve" (On the deepening of the intellectual labour social heterogeneity in the contemporary capitalist society), *Voprosy naučnogo Kommunizma* 43, 79 : 110-118.

2749 JAFAR, Mohammad. "The Arab ruling classes in the 1970s", *Khamsin* 80 : 73-85.

2750 JANOVER, Louis. *Les intellectuels face à l'histoire: essai*. Paris, Éditions Galilée, 80, 296 p.

2751 KUGEL', S. A.; ŠČELIŠČ, P. E. "Naučnaja intelligencija SSSR: faktory i tendencii razvitija professional'noj struktury" (The USSR scientific intelligentsia: factors and tendencies of the professional structure development), *IN: Sociologičeskie problemy obrazovanija, kul'tury i nauki.* Moskva, 78 : 160-172.

2752 LIMA DOS SANTOS, Maria de Lourdes. "Sobre os intelectuais portugueses no século xix" (On Portuguese intellecutals in the xixth century), *Análise social* 15, 79 : 69-115.

2753 MAKSIMENKO, V. I. "'Političeskaja subkul'tura' intelligencii v razvivajuščihsja stranah" (Intelligentsia "political subculture" in the developing countries), *IN: Issledovanija sociologičeskih problem razvivajuščihsja stran.* Moskva, 78 : 136-150.

2754 MALIK, Yogendra K. *North Indian intellectuals: an attitudinal profile.* Leiden, Brill, 79, xii-187 p.

2755 MARCUS, Judith. "Ideas and intellectuals in the age of the masses", *Contemporary Sociology* jul 80 : 482-486. [survey essay.]

2756 MAYHEW, Bruce H.; SCHOLLAERT, Paul T. "Social morphology of Pareto's economic elite", *Social Forces* 59, sep 80 : 25-43.

2757 MOORE, Gwen; [et al.]. "National elite networks in Australia and the United States", *Australian and New Zealand Journal of Sociology* 16, mar 80 : 14-23.

2758 NIKONOV, K. M.; EVDOKIMOV, P. G. "O vozzrastanii roli intelligencii v processe internacionalizacii duhovnoj žizni sovetskogo naroda" (On the elevation of the intelligentsia role in the internationalization process of Soviet people's cultural life), *IN: Rol' socialističeskoj intellitencii v internacional'nom vospitanii trudjaščihsja.* 79 : 1-9.

2759 OSINSKIJ, I. I. "Marksizm-leninizm ob istoričeskoj neobhodimosti formirovanija socialističeskoj intelligencii, eé meste v novom obščestve" (Marxism-Leninism on the historical necessity of the formation of a socialist intelligentsia, its place in the new society), *IN: Problemy social'nogo razvitija obščestva zrelogo socializma.* Irkutsk, 78 : 28-56.

2760 REKUNOV, F. N. "Sovetskaja intelligencija i socialističeskij obraz žizni" (Soviet intelligentsia and the socialist way of life), *IN: Sovetskaja intelligencija i eé rol' v duhovnoj žizni razvitogo socializma.* Moskva, 79 : 45-47.

2761 RENDÓN CORONA, Armando. "Enfoques sobre la élite del poder" (Focus on power elite), *Revista mexicana de Sociología* 41, oct-dec 79 : 1335-1367.

2762 ROZENBERG, C. R. *Naučno-tehničeskaja revoljucija i intelligencija* (The scientific and technical revolution and the intelligentsia). Alma-Ata, Kazahstan, 79, 147 p.

2763 SEGRE, Dan V. "Colonialization and decolonization: the case of Zionist and African elites", *Comparative Studies in Society and History* 22, jan 80 : 23-41.

2764	SEMENOV, V. S. "Mesto i rol'intelligencii v social'noj strukture razvitogo socialističeskogo obščestva" (Intelligentsia place and role in the social structure of the developed socialist society), IN: Nekotorye teoretičeskie problemy formirovanija i razvitija sovetskoj intelligencii na puti k kommunizmu. 79 : 31-54.
2765	SIEWERT, Hans-Jörg. Lokale Elitesysteme (Local elite system). Königstein/Ts., Hain, 79, 231 p. CR: Herbert GRYMER, Soziologische Revue 3(3), 80: 310-312.
2766	SINGH, R. A. P. "Rural elites and decision-making value-norms", Indian Journal of social Research 20, dec 79 : 161-167. [India.]
2767	STEPANJAN, C. A. "Zakonomernosti formirovanija sovetskoj intelligencii i osnovnye ètapy eè razvitija na puti k kommunizmu" (Laws of the Soviet intelligentsia formation and essential stages of its development in the way of communism), IN: Nekotorye teoretičeskie problemy formirovanija i razvitija sovetskoj intelligencii na puti k kommunizmu. 79 : 3-30.
2768	STUDLAR, Donley. "Elite responsiveness or elite autonomy: British immigration policy reconsidered", Ethnic and racial Studies apr 80 : 207-223.
2769	Bibl.XXIX-2847. SULEIMAN, Ezra N. Elites in French society: the politics of survival. CR: Bernard E. BROWN, American political Science Review 74(1), mar 80: 276-277.
2770	TÓTH, Pál Péter. A magyar értelmiség két világháború közötti történetéhez. Interjúk(Contributions to the history of the Hungarian intelligentsia of the interwar period. Interviews). Budapest, Oktatási Min., 80, vol.1. 314 p. [Published by the Ministry of Education.]
2771	TRILLING, Leon. "Technological elites in France and the United States", Minerva 17, sum 79 : 225-243.
2772	WEINBAUM, M. G. "Dimensions of elite change in the Middle East", Comparative political Studies 12, jul 79 : 123-150.
2773	WURFEL, David. "Elites of wealth and elites of power, the changing dynamic: a Philippine case study", Southeast Asian Affairs 79 : 233-245.
2774	ŽIVKOVIČ, Miroslav. "Kako je raspoređen jugoslovenski intelektualni kapital" (Distribution of the intellectual capital in Yugoslavia), Sociologija 21, 79 : 341-367.

14260. Social mobility
Mobilité sociale

[See also / voir aussi: 830, 837, 1632, 2343, 2588, 2864, 3282, 3429, 3559, 3666, 3876, 4949, 5081, 5484]

2775	ALLERBECK, Klaus; STORK, Hans Rainer. "Soziale Mobilität in Deutschland 1833-1970. Eine Reanalyse" (Social mobility in Germany, 1833-1970. A new analysis), Kölner Zeitschrift für Soziologie und Socialpsychologie 32, mar 80 : 93-110.
2776	ALLMAN, James. Social mobility, education and development in Tunisia. Leiden, Brill, 79, x-172 p.
2777	ANDORKA, Rudolf; ZAGÓRSKI, Krzysztof. A társadalmi mobilitás Magyarországon és Lengyelországban. Az 1972. és 1973. évi adatfelvétel összehasonlító elemzése (Social mobility in Hungary and Poland. A comparative analysis of 1972 and 1973 data). Budapest, Statisztikai Kiadó, 79, 75 p.
2778	BIBBY, John. "Measures of social mobility based on income inequality measures", Quality and Quantity 14, oct 80 : 619-633.
2779	COLEMAN, D. A. "A study of marriage and mobility in Reading, England", Journal of biosocial Science 11, oct 79 : 369-389.
2780	GOLDTHROPE, John H.; LLEWELLYN, Catriona; PAYNE, Colive. Social mobility and class structure in modern Britain. Oxford, Clarendon Press, New York, Oxford University Press, 80, viii-310 p.
2781	GOODMAN, Neal R. "A note on measures of female mobility", Sociological Inquiry 49, 79 : 55-57.
2782	HARROP, Martin. "Popular conceptions of mobility", Sociology 14, feb 80 : 89-98.
2783	KARASAWA, Kazuyoshi. "Chiiki shakai no tokusei to shakai ido" (The factor of social mobility in Japan), Shakaigaku ronso 79, 80 : 28-43.
2784	OLESNEVIČ, L. A. "Rol' i zadači planirovanija social'noj mobil'nosti na promyšlennom predprijatii" (Role and objectives of the social mobility planning in an industrial enterprise), IN: Problemy social'nogo upravlenija na promyšlennom predprijatii. VIII. Kiev, 78 : 3-6.
2785	SCARDIGLI, Victor; MERCIER, Pierre-Alain. "Ascension sociale et pauvreté", Orientation scolaire et professionnelle apr-mai-jun 80 : 99-109.

2786 SOARES, Gláucio Ari Dillon. "Mobilidade e política" (Mobility and politics), *Revista brasileira de Estudos políticos* 50, jan 80 : 103-119. ;961[Brazil.]

2787 VOVKANYČ, S. I. "Suščnost' social'noj mobil'nosti proizvodstvennogo kollektiva v uslovijah naučno-tehničeskoj revoljucii" (Nature of a production collectivity social mobility under conditions of the scientific and technical revolution), *IN: Problemy social'nogo upravlenija na promyšlennom predprijatii. VIII.*. 78 : 7-17.

14300. SOCIAL CHANGE
CHANGEMENT SOCIAL

14310. History
Histoire

[See also / voir aussi: 118, 275, 324, 1290, 1748, 1844, 2686, 2700, 2737, 2829, 2832, 2841, 3012, 3127, 3368, 3519, 3552, 3660, 3721, 4132, 4754, 4813, 5061, 5181, 5218, 5229, 5241, 5251, 5714, 5838]

2788 "Social history", *Theory and Society* sep 80 : 667-777. [special issue.]

2789 BLESSING, Werner K. "Umwelt und Mentalität im ländlichen Bayern. Eine Skizze zum Alltagswandel im 19. Jahrhundert" (Environment and mentality in rural Bavaria. A sketch of daily change in the 19th century), *Archiv für Sozialgeschichte* 19, 79 : 1-42.

2790 CALVI, Giulia. *Società industriale e cultura operaia negli Stati Uniti (1890-1917)* (Industrial society and culture of the working class in the United States: 1890-1917). Roma, Bulzoni, 79, 299 p.

2791 CARACCIOLO, Alberto. "Between tradition and innovation: Italian studies in modern social history", *Social Research* 47, 80 : 404-425.

2792 CRUDEN, Robert. *Many and one: a social history of the United States.* Englewood Cliffs, NJ, Prentice-Hall, 80, x-441 p.

2793 DAY, John. "Fernand Braudel and the rise of capitalism", *Social Research* 47, 80 : 507-518.

2794 DE SPIRITO, Angelomichele. "Per un approccio antropologico di storia locale" (For an anthropological approach to local history), *Sociologia (Roma)* 13(2-3), mai-dec 79 : 69-98.

2795 GEURTS, Pieter Antoon Marie; MESSING, F. A. M.; [eds.]. *Theoretische en methodologische aspecten van de economische en sociale geschiedenis* (Theoretical and methodological aspects of the economic and social history). Den Haag, Nijhoff, 79. [2 vols..]

2796 HANDLIN, Oscar. *Truth in history.* Cambridge, MA, Belknap Press, 79, xi-437 p.

2797 HAUPT, Georges. *L'historien et le mouvement social.* Paris, F. Maspéro, 80, 341 p.

2798 JONES, R. Ben. *Economic and social history of England, 1770-1977.* London, Longman, 79, viii-320 p.

2799 KOCKA, Jürgen. "Theory and social history: recent developments in West Germany", *Social Research* 47, 80 : 426-457.

2800 MATHIAS, Peter. *The transformation of England: essays in the economic and social history of England in the eighteenth century.* London, Methuen, 79, x-324 p.

2801 MCCARTHY, Timothy. "Politics, ideology, and class: some methodological problems in the Marxian interpretation of history", *Social Science* 55, 80 : 94-98.

2802 NARASIMHAIAH, B. *Neolithic and megalithic cultures in Tamil Nadu.* Delhi, Sundeep, 80, xi-257 p.

2803 NIELD, Keith. "A symptomatic dispute? Notes on the relation between Marxian theory and historical practice in Britain", *Social Research* 47, 80 : 479-506.

2804 PILIPENKO, N. V. "Vzaimo svjaz' neobhodimosti i slučajnosti v social'no-istoričeskih processah" (Interaction between necessity and hazard in socio-historical processes), *Sociologičeskie Issledovanija* 79 : 45-52.

2805 REIS, Jaime; MÓNICA, Maria Filomena; LIMA DOS SANTOS, Maria de Lourdes; [eds.]. "O século XIX em Portugal", *Análise social* 16(1-2), 80 : 2-445.

2806 ROTH, Guenther. *Max Weber's vision of history: ethics and methods.* Berkeley, University of California Press, 79, xi-211 p. CR: Robert J. ANTONIO, *American Journal of Sociology* 86(3), nov 80: 666-668. [also CR: Martin RIESEBRODT, *Kölner Zeitschrift für Soziologie und Sozialpsychologie,* 32(4), dec 80: 787-788.]

2807 TOPOLSKI, Jerzy. "Methodological problems of applications of the Marxist theory to historical research", *Social Research* 47, 80 : 458-478.

2808	WALTERS, Ronald G. "Signs of the times: Clifford Geertz and historians", *Social Research* 47, 80 : 537-556.
2809	WEHLER, Hans-Ulrich. "Psychoanalysis and history", *Social Research* 47, 80 : 519-536.
2810	ZARET, David. "From Weber to Parsons and Schutz: the eclipse of history in modern social theory", *American Journal of Sociology* 85, mar 80 : 1180-1201.

14320. Future
Futur

[See also / voir aussi: 2990]

2811	HANNIGAN, John A. "Fragmentation in science: the case of futurology", *Sociological Review* 28, mai 80 : 317-332.
2812	POLUĔKTOV, A. M. "Kategorija stanovlenija i prognozirovanie" ("Future" category and forecast), *Problemy Filosofii* 47, 79 : 132-137.
2813	RUYER, Raymond. "Le statut de l'avenir et le monde invisible", *Diogène* 109, jan-mar 80 : 41-58.
2814	SIEBERT, Horst. "Soziologie der Weiterbildung"(Sociology of the future), *Soziologische Revue* 80 : 389-401. [review article.]

14330. Social change
Changement social

[See also / voir aussi: 18, 193, 227, 782, 1264, 1384, 1417, 1468, 1658, 1660, 1742, 1785, 1903, 2065, 2136, 2279, 2393, 2409, 2567, 2575, 2586, 2587, 2637, 2675, 2688, 2789, 2797, 3044, 3050, 3180, 3240, 3253, 3273, 3483, 3597, 3622, 3698, 3903, 3974, 4091, 4191, 4324, 4410, 4575, 4603, 4605, 4614, 4619, 5395, 5437, 5549, 5668, 5706, 5771, 5859, 6045]

2815	ABBOTT, Susan; VAN WILLIGEN, John; [eds.]. *Predicting sociocultural change.* Athens, University of Georgia Press, 80, 147 p.
2816	ABEDISEID, Mohammad. "Probleme des sozio-ökonomischen und politischen Wandels in der Arabischen Welt" (Problems of socio-economic and political change in the Arab World), *Dritte Welt* 79 : 234-256.
2817	AYA, Rod. "Theories of revolution reconsidered: contrasting models of collective violence", *Theory and Society* jul 79 : 39-99.
2818	BOGOMOLOV, A. P. *Problemy mirnogo razvitija revoljucii* (Problems of the peaceful development of revolution). Misnk, Izdatel'stvo BGV imeni V. I. Lenina, 79, 224 p.
2819	BOGOMOLOV, T. B. "Osobennosti obščestvennogo progressa v uslovijah rasvitogo socializma" (Social progress characteristics under conditions of developed socialism), *IN: Problemy social'nogo razvitija obščestva zrelogo socializma.* Irkutsk, 78 : 123-134.
2820	BREYTENBACH, Willie J. "Changes in South-African society", *South Africa International* 10, jan 80 : 153-164.
2821	CAPRIO, Giovanni. *Haiti, wirtschaftliche Entwicklung und periphere Gesellschaftsformation* (Haiti, economic development and peripheric society formation). Frankfurt/Main, Haag und Herchen, 79, 338 p.
2822	CHEMS, Albert. "Organizations as instruments of social change in post-industrial societies", *Organization Studies* 80 : 109-122.
2823	COCHIN, Augustin. *L'esprit du jacobinisme. Une interprétation sociologique de la Révolution française.* Paris, Presses universitaires de France, 79, 198 p.
2824	CROOK, John Hurrell. "Social change in Indian Tibet", *Social Science Information* 19, 80 : 139-166.
2825	DEMENČONOK, Ė. V.; SEMENOU, Ju-N. "Kritika sovremennyh buržuaznyh koncepcij obščestvennogo progressa" (Criticism of the present bourgeois concepts of social progress), *Voprosy Filosofii* 32(12), dec 79 : 101-113.
2826	DIAZ ARAUJO, Enrique. "¿Cuánto cuesta una revolución?" (How much does a revolution cost?), *Boletín de Ciencias políticas y sociales* 25(12), 79 : 81-111.
2827	DZJABKO, N. N. "O suščnosti i dlitel'nosti social'nogo progressa" (On the maturity and continuance of the social progress), *IN: Problema čeloveka v dialektičeskom materializma.* Perm', 79 : 149-155.
2828	EISENSTADT, S. N. "El marco social y las condiciones de la revolución" (The social framework and the conditions of revolution), *Revista de Estudios políticos* 12, nov-dec 79 : 63-83.

2829 FAJARDO, Dario. *Violencia y desarrollo: transformaciones sociales en tres regiones cafetaleras del Tolima, 1936-70* (Violence and development: social transformations in three coffee producing regions of the Tolima, 1936-1970). Bogotà, Fondo Editorial Suramérica, 79, 217 p.

2830 FATHALY, Omar I.; PALMER, Monte. "Opposition to change in rural Libya", *"International Journal of Middle East Studies* 11, apr 80 : 247-261.

2831 FEDOSEEV, P. N. "Nauka ob obščestve i obščestvennyj progress" (Science on society and social progress), *IN: Politika mira i razvitie političeskih sistem 1978*. Moskva, 79 : 7-25.

2832 FEDOTOVA, O. D. "Ponjatie 'obščestvenno-èkonomičeskaja formacija' i konkrentno-istoričeskoe obščestvo" (The "socio-economic formation" concept and the concrete historical society), *IN: Dialektika social'nogo poznanija*. Moskva, 79 : 46-53.

2833 FEHR, Helmut. *Soziale Kontinuität und sozialer Wandel* (Social continuity and socialchange). Frankfurt/Main, New York, Campus-Verlag, 79, ii-230 p.

2834 BARCIA-PETIT, Jorge; SCHÄFERS, Bernhard. "Sozialer Wandel in Spanien.Über einige Prozesse der Modernisierung und sozialer Mobilisierung" (Social change in Spain. On some modernization processes and social mobilization), *Schweizerische Zeitschrift für Soziologie/Revue suisse de Sociologie* mar 80 : 87-108.

2835 GAVRILOV, A. P. "Toždestvo i različie celej i rezul'tatov v obščestvennom razvitii" (Identity and difference of objectives and results in the social development), *Kategorii Dialektiki* 79 : 142-148.

2836 GAVRILOV, A. P. "Problema nesovpavlenija čelej i rezul'tatov v obščestvennom razvitii" (Problems of the objectives and no-coincidence results in social development), *IN: Problema social'noj zakonomernosti*. Gor'kij, 78 : 74-81.

2837 GOROVSKIJ, F. Ja.; [ed.]. *Edinstvo internacional'nogo i nacional'nogo v mirovom revoljucionnom processe* (Unity of the international and national in the world revolutionary process). Kiev, Višča Škola, 79, 295 p.

2838 GUSOV, A. Z. "Social'nye otnošenija kak ob'ekt planirovanija social'nogo raz vitija" (Social relations as an object of social developing planning), *IN: Osnovy obščestvennogo stroja i politiki SSSR*. Moskva, 79 : 76-82.

2839 HALLIDAY, Fred. "The genesis of the Iranian Revolution", *Third World Quarterly* oct 79 : 1-16.

2840 ISMAEL, J. S.; ISMAEL, T. Y. "Social change in Islamic society: the political thought of Ayatollah Khomeini", *Social Problems* 27, jun 80 : 601-619.

2841 KALBERG, Stephen. "Max Weber's types of rationality: cornerstones for the analysis of rationalization processes in history", *American Journal of Sociology* 85, mar 80 : 1145-1179.

2842 KAWAMURA, Nozomu. "Nihon ni okeru 'kindai-ka' to 'toshika' " ("Modernization" and "Urbanization" in Japan), *Tokyo toritsu daigaku jinbungaku-ho* 143, 80 : 63-68.

2843 KELLY, William R.; CUTRIGHT, Phillips. "Modernization and the demographic transition: cross-sectional and longitudinal analysis of a revised model", *Sociological Focus* 13, oct 80 : 315-329.

2844 KLINGMAN, David. "Temporal and spatial diffusion in the comparative analysis of social change", *American Political Science Review* 74, mar 80 : 123-137.

2845 KODICA, N. "Razrabotka K. Marksom metodologičeskih osnov obščestvennogo progressa" (The elaboration of the social progress methodological bases by K. Marx), *Kommunist Moldavii* 79 : 18-25.

2846 KOYANO, Shōgo; WATANUKI, Jōji; KOMAI, Hiroshi; [eds.]. *Asian per spectives on social development: Proceedings of the second conference of Asian sociologists held in Uppsala, August 1978*. Tokyo, Japan Sociological Society, 116 p.

2847 KRAUS, Willy. *Wirtschaftliche Entwicklung und sozialer Wandel in der Volksrepublik China* (Economic development and social change in the People's Republic of China). Berlin, Heidelberg, New York, Springer, 79, xxi-738 p.

2848 KUZIN, V. "Leninism i sovremennyj revoljucionnyj process" (Leninism and the contemporary revolutionary process), *Kommunist Tatarii* 79 : 10-17.

2849 MARSDEN, Lorna R.; HARVEY, Edward B. *Fragile federation: social change in Canada*. Toronto, New York, McGraw-Hill Ryerson, 79, xiii-242 p.

2850 MCDONALD, Angus W. Jr. *The urban origins of rural revolution: elites and the masses in Hunan Province, China, 1911-1927*. Berkeley, University of California Press, 79, xi-369 p. CR: John R. HANDELMAN. *American political Science Review* 74(2), jun 80 : 555-556.

2851 MEŽEVIC, M. N. *Social'noe razvitie i gorod: filosofskie i sociologičeskie aspekty* (Social development and town: philosphical and sociological aspects). Leningrad, Nauka, 79, 175 p.

2852	MORDKOVIČ, V. G. "Puti obščestvennogo razvitija social'naja aktivnost' čeloveka" (The social development ways and the man's social activity), *IN: Social'nye aspekty razvitija ličnosti. Ispol'zovanie informacionnyh sistem dlja ego prognozirovanija.* Moskva, 78 : 31-46.
2853	MUSHAKOJI, Kinhide. "Tradition and change in developing countries", *Science and public Policy* feb 80 : 20-29.
2854	NISBET, Robert. *History of the idea of progress.* New York, Basic Books, 80, xi-370 p.
2855	NOYES, Richard. "The time horizon of planned social change: I. Why utopian movements always promise amelioration in the future. II. How the advocates of social reform may expedite their purpose through temporal calibration", *American Journal of Economics and Sociology* 39, jan 80 : 65-77. [continued in 39 (3), jul 80 : 261-272.]
2856	PRESTON, Richard A.; [ed.]. *Perspectives on revolution and evolution.* Durham, NC, Duke University Press, 79, xiv-300 p. CR: J. Paul GRAYSON, *American political Science Review* 74(2), jun 80: 566-567.
2857	RANKOVIĆ, Miodrag. "Teorija modernizacija kao varijanta neoevolucionizma u savremenoj sociologiji" (The theory of modernisation as an alternative of neo-evolutionism in contemporary sociology), *Sociologija* 21(1-2), 79 : 5-27.
2858	ROHRER, Wayne C. "Social change and quality of life in the USA", *Social Indicators Research* dec 80 : 481-493.
2859	RUMJANCEVA, T. M. "Dialektika prošlogo nastojaščego-buduščego v uslovijah razvitogo socialisticeskogo obščestva" (Dialectics of the past, the present and the future under conditons of the developed socialist society), *Problemy social'nogo Prognozirovanija* 79 : 24-32.
2860	SANO, Katsutaka. "Shakai-shugika to kindaika" (The theory of socialism and modernization), *Nagoya daigaku shakaigaku ronshu* 80 : 9-20.
2861	SHAFFER, David R. *Social and personality development.* Monterey, CA, Brooks/Cole Pub. Co., 79, xiii-624 p.
2862	SHANNEIK, Ghazi. "Ölreichtum und sozialer Wandel:das Beispiel Kuwaits" (Oil resources and social change: the example of Kuwait), *Orient (Opladen)* 20, sep 79 : 25-48.
2863	STRASSER, Hermann; RANDALL, Susan C. *Einführung in die Theorien des sozialen Wandels* (Introduction to social change theories). Darmstadt, Neuwied, Luchterhand, 79, 390 p.
2864	TEGTMEYER, Heinrich. "Sozialer Wandel als Folge struktureller oder individueller Mobilität. Beziehungen zwischen theoretischer Konzeption und empirischem Befund" (Social change as a consequence of structural or individual mobility. Relations between theoretical conception and empirical findings), *Zeitschrift für Bevölkerungswissenschaft* 78 : 351-364.
2865	Bibl.XXIX-2927. TILLY, Charles. From mobilization to revolution. CR: Edward N. MULLER, *American political Science Review* 74(4), dec 80: 1071-1073. [also J. Craig JENKINS, Contemporary Sociology (Albany) 9(1), jan 80: 133-135; Erich WEEDE, Kölner Zeitschrift für Soziologie und Sozialpsychologie 32(4), dec 80: 798-801; François CHAZEL, Revue française de Sociologie 21(4), oct-dec 80: 653-658.]
2866	TRAVIN, I. I. "Rol' material'no-veščnoj sredy v processah social'nogo razvitija" (Role of the material environment in the social development processes), *IN: Naučno-tehničeskaja revoljucija i problemy razvitija obščestva i kollektivov.* Moskva, 79 : 49-60.
2867	TRISTRAM, R. J. "Values, analysis and the study of revolution", *Sociology* 14, feb 80 : 69-87. [continued in 14(2), mai 80: 247-259.]
2868	VAGO, Steven. *Social change.* New York, Holt, Rinehart and Winston, 80, xiii-434 p.
2869	VAN CAUWENBERGH, A.; COOL, K. "Verandering, logica, macht en symbolen. Een nieuwe analyse voor het management van de verandering" (Change, logics, power and symbols. A new analysis of the management of change), *Economisch en sociaal Tijdschrift* 33, 79 : 677-697.
2870	VAN NIEUWENHUIJZE, Christoffel Anthonie Oliver. *Social development: supplement or corrective to economic development?.* The Hague, Institute of Social Studies, 79, 44 p.
2871	WEBER, Kenneth R. "Ecology, economy and demography: some parameters of social change in Hispanic New Mexico", *Social Science Journal* 17, jan 80 : 53-64.
2872	ZENTNER, Henry. "Prolegomena to a theory of socio-cultural change and development; Toynbee's challenge-response hypothesis revisited", *Indian Journal of social Research* 20, apr 79 : 28-35.

14340. Changing society
Société en transformation

[See also / voir aussi: 1056, 1417, 1442, 1667, 1738, 2341, 2382, 2513, 2822, 3617, 4152, 4425, 4577, 5426, 5688, 5708, 5740, 5772]

2873 "Dominación, hegemonía y desarrollo"(Domination, hegemony and development), *Revista mexicana de Sociología* 41, apr-jun 79 : 377-595.

2874 "Thomas Hobbes: de la société civile, de sa matière, de sa forme et de son pouvoir", *Revue européenne des Sciences sociales. Cahiers Vilfredo Pareto* 18(49), 80 : 7-254.

2875 ANDORKA, Rudolf. "Long-term development of Hungary, measured by social indicators", *Social Indicators Research* mar 80 : 1-13.

2876 ARPAL, Jesús. *La sociedad tradicional en el País Vasco* (Traditional society in the Basque country). San Sebastian, L. Haranburu, 79, 356 p.

2877 ČESNOKOV, G. D. "Evoljucija teorij industrial'nogo obščestva v buržuaznoj sociologii" (Evolution of the industrial society theories in the bourgeois society), *IN: Sovremennaja buržuaznaja sociologija na službe gosudarstvenno-monopolističeskogo kapitalizma.* Leningrad, 79 : 53-68.

2878 CLAESSENS, Dieter; CLAESSENS, Karin. *Kapitalismus und Kultur — Entstehung und Grundlagen der bürgerlichen Gesellschaft* (Capitalism and culture. Origin and bases of the civil society). Frankfurt-am-Main, Suhrkamp, 79, 220 p. CR: Leo KOFLER, *Soziologische Revue* 3(2), 80: 157-158.

2879 DEIANA, Giuseppe. "La Puglia socio-economica: un'ipotesi interpretativa del sottosviluppo" (An interpretative hypothesis about underdevelopment in Puglia), *Studi di Sociologia* 17, oct-dec 79 : 395-412.

2880 EMBID, Alfredo. "Civilización industrial y sus efectos en el individuo" (Industrial civilization and its effects on the individual), *Documentación social* 38, 80 : 58-70.

2881 GRIMM, Klaus. *Theorien der Unterentwicklung und Entwicklungsstrategien. Eine Einführung* (Theories of underdevelopment and development strategies. An introduction). Opladen, Westdeutcher Verlag, 79, 242 p. CR: Erich WEEDE, *Kölner Zeitschrift für Soziologie und Sozialpsychologie* 32(2), jun 80 : 401-404.

2882 Bibl.XXIX-2960. HALSEY, A. H. *Change in British society: based on the Reith lectures.* CR: Roland ROBERTSON, *Contemporary Sociology (Albany)* 9(1), jan 80: 153-154.

2883 Bibl.XXIX-2966. JANOWITZ, Morris. *The last half-century: societal change and politics in America.* CR: Ralph H. TURNER; Everett Carll LADD; James D. WRIGHT, *Contemporary Sociology (Albany)* 9(5), sep 80: 607-616.

2884 KWEE, Swan-liat; [et al.]. *Nederland op weg naar een post-industriële samenleving?* (The Netherlands on the way to a post-industrial society?). Assen, Gorcum, 79, 273 p.

2885 LI, V. F.; [ed.]. *Issledovanie sociologičeskih problem razvivajuščihsja stran: teorija socialističeskoj struktury* (Research on the developing countries sociological problems: theory on the socialist structure). Moskva, Nauka, 78, 237 p.

2886 Bibl.XXIX-2976. MCVEY, Ruth T.; [ed.]. *Southeast Asian transitions: approaches through social history.* CR: Donald E. WEATHERBEE, *American political Science Review* 74(2), jun 80, 556-557.

2887 MEYER, John W.; HANNAN, Michael T.; [eds.]. *National development and the world system: Educational, economic, and political change, 1950-1970.* Chicago and London, University of Chicago Press, 79, x-334 p.

2888 OGURA, Mitsuo. "Kaihatsu shakaigaku to kohatsuteki hatten no mondai" (Sociology of development and the problems of late development), *Kokusai seiji* 64, 80 : 114-136.

2889 SHAUKAT ALI, Dr. *Nation building development and administration: a Third World perspective.* Lahore, Aziz Publishers, 79, 464 p.

2890 SIROTA, N. M. "Kritika marksistami SŠA teori 'postindustrial'nogo obščestva' po voprosu o meste i roli rabočego klassa pri kapitalizme" (The "post-industrial society" theory critics by US marxists and the question of the working class place and role under capitalism), *Naučnyj Kommunizm* 79 : 95-104.

2891 TAYLOR, John G. *From modernization to modes of production: A critique of the sociologies of development and underdevelopment.* Atlantic Highlands, NJ, Humanities Press, 79, xii-335 p.

2892 TIBI, Bassam. *Internationale Politik und Entwicklungsländer-Forschung: Materialien zu einer ideologiekritischen Entwicklungssoziologie* (International politics and developing country research: materials for an ideological criticism of development sociology). Frankfurt am Main, Suhrkamp, 79, 223 p. CR: Gerhard GROHS, *Kölner Zeitschrift für Soziologie und Sozialpsychologie* 32(11), dec 80; 816. [also Horst BÜSCHER, Soziologische Revue 3(2), 80: 196-198.]

2893 Bibl.XXIX-2992. VU, Thy Quyen. *Die vietnamesische Gesellschaft im Wandel. Kolonialismus und gesellschaftliche Entwicklung in Vietnam* (The Vietnamese society in change. Colonialism and social development in Vietnam). CR: Klaus-Georg RIEGEL, *Soziologische Revue* 3(1), 80: 84-86.

15. POPULATION. FAMILY. ETHNIC GROUP
POPULATION. FAMILLE. GROUPE ETHNIQUE

15100. DEMOGRAPHY. GENETICS
DÉMOGRAPHIE. GÉNÉTIQUE

15110. Population research
Recherche démographique

[See also / voir aussi: 2940]

2894 ALEKSANDROVA, L. M.; KOROSTELEV, G. M. "Zakony narodonaselenija i ih mesto v sisteme obščestvennyh zakonov" (Population laws and their place in the social laws system), *IN: Problema social'noj zakonomernosti.* Gor'kij, 78 : 36-42.

2895 BOGUE, Donald Joseph. *Techniques for making functional population projections.* Chicago, Community and Family Study Center, the University of Chicago, 79, v-125 p.

2896 Canada. Statistics Canada. *La population du Canada: perspectives démographiques.* Ottawa, Statistics Canada, 79, 32 p.

2897 Canada. Statistics Canada. *Population projections for Canada and the provinces, 1976-2001 = Projections démogrqphiques pour le Canada et les provinces, 1976-2001.* Ottawa, Statistics Canada, 79, 472 p.

2898 FOOT, David K. *Public policy and future population in Ontario.* Toronto, Ontario Economic Council, 79, 57 p.

2899 FREDETTE, Jean-Marc. "Collecte et traitement des données sur les naissances, les mariages, les divorces et les décès au Québec: rêves et réalité", *Cahiers québécois de Démographie* apr 80 : 117-138.

2900 GREGORY, Joel W. "La démographie africaniste ou la recherche d'une technicité qui devient biais idéologique", *Canadian Journal of African Studies* 13(1-2), 79 : 195-208.

2901 KEYFITZ, Nathan. "Population appearances and demographic reality", *Population and Development Review* mar 80 : 47-64.

2902 LALONDE, Carole. "La démographie au Québec", *Cahiers québécois de Démographie* apr 80 : 7-26.

2903 LEGUINA, Joaquín. "Algunas precisiones en torno a la terminología demográfica" (Some precisions about demographical terminology), *Revista internacional de Sociología* 37(32), oct-dec 79 : 493-506.

2904 MOISEENKO, V. M.; [ed.]. *Teorija i praktika issledovanija narodonaselenija* (Theory and practice of demographic research). Moskva, Izdatel'stvo Moskovskogo Universiteta, 79, 185 p.

2905 NAM, Charles B. "The progress of demography as a scientific discipline", *Demography* 16, nov 79 : 485-492.

2906 PÉRON, Yves. "L'analyse démographique et la famille: prémisses d'une autocritique", *Cahiers québécois de Démographie* dec 79 : 99-112.

2907 PETRENKO, É. S.; JAROŠENKO, T. M. *Social'no-demografičeskie pokazateli v sociologičeskih issledovanijah* (Socio-demographical indexes in sociological research). Moskva, Statistika, 79, 166 p.

2908 SALAS, Rafael M. *International population assistance: the first decade: a look at the concepts and policies which have guided the UNFPA in its first ten years.* Oxford, New York, Pergamon Press, 79, xxvii-456 p. [United Nations Fund for Population Activities.]

2909 SALCEDO, Juan; [ed.]. "Trabajos sobre sociología de la población en España" (Works on sociology of population in Spain), *Revista española de Investigaciones sociológicas* 10, apr-jun 80 : 9-248.

2910 Bibl.XXIX-3016. TAEUBER, Karl E.; BUMPASS, Larry; SWEET, James A.; [eds.]. *Social demography.* CR: Nathan KEYFITZ, *American Journal of Sociology* 85(6), mai 80 : 1456-1457. [also CR: Georges SABAGH, Contemporary Sociology (Albany), 9(1), jan 80 : 78-79.]

2911 URLANIS, B. C. "Demografičeskaja nauka i demografičeskaja politika" (Demography and population policy), *Vestnik Akademii Nauk SSSR* 49, jan 80 : 41-49. [USSR.]

2912 VJATKIN, A. R. *Naselenie Birmy: istoriko-demografičeskij očerk* (The Burma population: an historical and demographical study). Moskva, Nauka, 79, 168 p.

2913   ZITO, George V. *Population and its problems.* New York, Human Sciences Press, 79, 283 p.

15120.   Household. Man. Woman
Ménage. Homme. Femme

[See also / voir aussi: 95, 152, 460, 669, 688, 775, 855, 944, 1036, 1283, 1305, 1521, 1847, 1880, 1886, 2205, 2318, 2598, 2725, 2781, 3050, 3055, 3076, 3097, 3166, 3211, 3395, 3505, 3519, 3523, 3583, 3592, 3636, 3738, 4463, 4501, 4716, 4912, 4922, 5022, 5025, 5049, 5067, 5070, 5562, 5623, 5796, 5827, 5845, 5850, 5923, 5962, 5963, 5981, 5983, 6226]

2914   "Animal rights....", *Inquiry* 22(1-2), 79 : 1-247.
2915   "Women and the city", *International Journal of urban and regional Research* oct 78 : 390-566.
2916   "Women in Latin America", *Signs* aut 79 : 204p.
2917   "Women and the American city", *Signs* spr 80 : 274p.
2918   "Women. Sex and sexuality", *Signs* sum 80 : 569-800.
2919   ACKER, Joan R. "Women and stratification: a review of recent literature", *Contemporary Sociology* jan 80 : 25-35. [survey essay.]
2920   ALLEMANN-TSCHOPP, Annemarie. *Geschlechtsrollen. Versuch einer interdisziplinären Synthese* (Sex roles. Attempt at an interdisciplinary synthesis). Bern, Stuttgart, Wien, Verlag Hans Huber, 79, 218 p. CR: Kajo PIEPER, *Soziologische Revue* 3(2), 80: 184-185.
2921   AMNEUS, Daniel. *Back to patriarchy.* New Rochelle, NY, Arlington House, 79, 221 p.
2922   ANDIAPPAN, P. "Remedies for sex discrimination in employment in India and the United States", *Revue internationale des Sciences administratives* 45, 79 : 268-274.
2923   ANTOS, Joseph R.; CHANDLER, Mark; MELLOW, Wesley. "Sex differences in union membership", *Industrial and Labor Relations Review* 33, jan 80 : 162-169.
2924   BACA ZINN, Maxime. "Employment and education of Mexican-American women: the interplay of modernity and ethnicity in eight families", *Harvard educational Review* 50, feb 80 : 47-62.
2925   BERNARD, Larry Craig. "Multivariate analysis of new sex role formulations and personality", *Journal of Personality and social Psychology* 38, feb 80 : 323-336.
2926   BLEKHER, Feiga. *The Soviet woman in the family and in society: (a sociological study).* New York, Wiley, 80, ix-234 p.
2927   BOKEMEIER, Janet L.; TAIT, John. "Women as power actors: a comparative study of rural communities", *Rural Sociology* 45, sum 80 : 238-255.
2928   BOURGUIGNON, Erika; [et al.]. *A world of women: anthropological studies of women in the societies of the world.* New York, NY, Praeger, 80, xv-364 p.
2929   BROWN, Randall S.; MOON, Marilyn; ZOLOTH, Barbara S. "Occupational attainment and segregation by sex", *Industrial and Labor Relations Review* 33, jul 80 : 506-517.
2930   BURR, Jeanne; [ed.]. *Sex roles: rights & values in conflict.* New York, Facts on File, 79, vii-216 p.
2931   CARVAJAL, Manuel J.; GEITHMAN, David T. "Sex differences in earnings in a low-income country: the case of Costa Rica", *International Journal of the Sociology of the Family* jul-dec 79 : 143-160.
2932   CENSI, Antonietta. "Elementi per un'analisi della socializzazione al ruolo femminile" (Elements for an analysis of the female role socialization), *Critica sociologica* 51-52, 79-80 : 107-121.
2933   CLARK, Lorenne M. G.; LANGE, Lynda; [eds.]. *The Sexism of social and political theory: women and reproduction from Plato to Nietzsche.* Toronto, Buffalo, University of Toronto Press, 79, xvii-141 p.
2934   CURTI, Merle. *Human nature in American thought: a history..* Madison, University of Wisconsin Press, 80, xvii-453 p. CR: Alan P. GRIMES, *American political Science Review* 74(4), dec 80 : 1054.
2935   DE KORTE, M.; VERNOOIJ-PIETERSE, E. W. M. J. Th. "De richtlijnen inzake gelijke behandeling van mannen en vrouwen in de sociale zekerheid" (The guidelines for deleting sex discrimination in social legislation), *Sociaal Maandblad Arbeid* 34, jun 79 : 364-371. ;961[Netherlands.]
2936   DUBBERT, Joe L. *A man's place: masculinity in transition.* Englewood Cliffs, NJ, Prentice-Hall, 79, xi-323 p.
2937   Bibl.XXIX-3024. DUNCAN, Beverly; DUNCAN, Otis Dudley. *Sex typing and social roles: a research report.* CR: Cynthia Fuchs EPSTEIN, *Contemporary Sociology (Albany)* 9(4), jul 80 : 515-517.

2938 ECKERT, Roland; [ed.]. *Geschlechtsrollen und Arbeitsteilung: Mann u. Frau in soziolog. Sicht* (Sex roles and working conditions: men and women from a sociological point of view). München, Beck, 79, 308 p.

2939 EYSENCK, Hans J.; WILSON, Glenn. *The psychology of sex*. London, J. M. Dent, 79, 208 p.

2940 FEIJOO, María del Carmen. *La mujer, el desarrollo y las tendencias de población, en América Latina* (Woman, development and population trends in Latin America). Buenos Aires, Centro de Estudios de Estado y Sociedad, 80, 62 p.

2941 FELDBERG, Roslyn L.; GLENN, Evelyn Nakaro. "Male and female: job versus gender models in the sociology of work", *Social Problems* 26, jun 79 : 524-538.

2942 FISHER, Elizabeth. *Woman's creation: sexual evolution and the shaping of society*. Garden City, NY, Anchor Press, 79, 1st, xvii-484 p.

2943 GARCIA, Brígida; OLIVEIRA, Orlandina de. "Una caracterización sociodemográfia de las unidades domésticas en la ciudad de México" (A socio-demographic characterization of households in Mexico City), *Demografía y Economía* 13, 79 : 1-18.

2944 Bibl.XXIX-3029. GIELE, Janet Zollinger. *Women and the future: changing sex roles in modern America*. CR: Teresa Donati MARCIANO, *Contemporary Sociology (Albany)* 9(5), sep 80 : 704-706.

2945 GOMBERG, Edith S.; FRANKS, Violet; [eds.]. *Gender and disordered behavior: sex differences in psychopathology*. New York, Brunner/Mazel, 79, xv-538 p.

2946 Bibl.XXIX-3076. GREGORY, Michael S.; SILVERS, Anita; SUTCH, Diane; [eds.]. *Sociology and human nature*. CR: Eugene ROSA, *Contemporary Sociology (Albany)* 9(2), mar 80 : 308-309.

2947 GUYER, Jane I. "Food, cocoa and the division of labor by sex in two West African societies", *Comparative Studies in Society and History* 22, jul 80 : 355-373.

2948 HAKIM, Catherine. *Occupational segregation: A comparative study of the degree and pattern of the differentiation between men and women's work in Britain, the United States, and other countries*. London, Department of Employment, 79, 65 p. [Research Paper No. 9.]

2949 HARBI, Mohamed; DUFRANCATEL, Christiane. "Les femmes dans la révolution algérienne", *Révoltes logiques* 11, wint 79-80 : 77-102.

2950 HATTORI, Noriko. "Joshi gakusei no seibetsu yakuwari taido to sono kazokuteki yo'in" (Sex-role attitudes of female students and their family factors), *Soshioroji* 25, 80 : 79-100.

2951 HINDELANG, Michael J. "Sex differences in criminal activity", *Social Problems* 27, dec 79 : 143-156.

2952 HIRANO, Takako; [et al.]. "Josei no shokugyō seikatsu to sei-yakuwari" (Women's occupational life and sex role), *Shakaigaku hyoron* 30, 79 : 17-37.

2953 HOYENGA, Katharine; HOYENGA, Kermit T. *The question of sex differences: psychological, cultural, and biological issues*. Boston, Little, Brown and Co., 79, 474 p. CR: Shelley COVERMAN, *Contemporary Sociology (Albany)* 9(3), mai 80: 435-437.

2954 HUNT, Janet G. "Sex stratification and male biography: from deprivation to ascendance", *Sociologial Quarterly* 21, 80 : 143-156.

2955 ICKES, William; SCHERMER, Brian; STEENO, Jeff. "Sex and sex-role influences in same-sex dyads", *Social Psychology Quarterly* 42, dec 79 : 373-385.

2956 JONES, Linda M.; MCBRIDE, Joanne L. "Sex-role stereotyping in children as a function of maternal employment", *Journal of social Psychology* 111, aug 80 : 219-223.

2957 KAMIKO, Takeji. "Sei-sabetsu to sei-yakuwa-ri" (Sex discrimination and sex roles), *Jinbun kenkyu* 32, 80 : 5-24.

2958 KANBARA, Fumiko. "Seikatsu kōzō kara mita shufu yakuwari model -toshi kazoku ni okeru hitotsu no kenshō" (The housewife role model from the view point of the living-structure — An examination about today's urban family), *Shakaigaku hyoron* 31, 80 : 31-59.

2959 KRAMPEN, Günter. "Sozialisationsbezogene Antezedenzbedingungen von normativen Geschlechtsrollen-Orientierungen. Weitere Befunde zur GRO-Skala" (Antecedents of normative sex-role orientations. Further results concerning the sex-role orientations scale), *Zeitschrift für Soziologie* oct 80 : 378-383.

2960 LAWS, Judith Long. *The second X: sex role and social role*. New York, Elsevier-New York, 79, x-405 p.

2961 Bibl.XXIX-3041. LEIBOWITZ, Lila. *Females, males, families: a biosocial approach*. CR: Elizabeth W. MOEN, *Contemporary Sociology (Albany)* 9(5), sep 80: 708-709.

2962 LEMENNICIER, Bertrand. "La spécialisation des rôles conjugaux. Les gains du mariage et la perspective du divorce", *Consommation* 27, jan-mar 80 : 27-71.

2963 LUEPTOW, Lloyd. "Consensus, change and stability in sex role orientation, 1974-77", *Sociological Focus* 13, apr 80 : 125-141.

2964 MARTIN, Patricia Yancey; [et al.]. "The significance of gender as a social and demographic correlate of sex-role attitudes", *Sociological Focus* 13, oct 89 : 383-396.

2965 MAY, Robert. *Sex and fantasy: patterns of male and female development.* New York, Norton, 80, xi-226 p.

2966 MCCONAGHY, Maureen J. "Sex-role contravention and sex education directed toward young children in Sweden", *Journal of Marriage and Family* 41, nov 79 : 893-904.

2967 MEGURO, Yoriko. *Shufu blues — On'na yakuwari towa nanika* (The housewife blues — what is the female role?). Tokyo, Chikuma shobo, 200 p.

2968 MITANI, Tetsuo. "Setai to kazoku ni kansuru ichi-shiron" (A preliminary note on the household and the family), *Hokkaido daigaku bungakubu kiyo* 28, 80 : 173-191.

2969 NEMEROWICZ, Gloria Morris. *Children's perceptions of gender and work roles.* New York, Praeger, 79, xiv-201 p.

2970 Bibl.XXIX-3050. NIELSEN, Joyce McCarl. *Sex in society, perspectives on stratification.* CR: Elizabeth M. ALMQUIST, *Contemporary Sociology (Albany)* 9(5), sep 80: 709.

2971 O'KELLY, Charlotte G. *Women and men in society.* New York, D. Van Nostrand Co., 80, vi-345 p.

2972 OSEI, Gabriel Kingsley. *Caribbean women: their history and habits.* London, African Publication Society, 79, 191 p. [available from International Publications Service, Collings, New York.]

2973 OSTERMAN, Paul. "Sex discrimination in professional employment: a case study", *Industrial and Labor Relations Review* 32, jul 79 : 451-464.

2974 PARSONS, Jacquelynne E.; [ed.]. *The Psychology of sex differences and sex roles.* Washington, Hemisphere Pub. Corp., 80, xv-319 p.

2975 PEEK, Charles W.; BORWN, Sharon. "Sex prejudice among white protestants: like or unlike ethnic prejudice?", *Social Forces* 59, sep 80 : 169-185.

2976 PERRY, David G.; BUSSEY, Kay. "The social learning theory of sex differences: imitation is alive and well", *Journal of Personality and social Psychology* 37(10), oct 79 : 1699-1712.

2977 PETRYSZAK, Nicholas G. L. "Human nature, ideology and social theory", *Archiv für Rechts- und Sozialphilosophie* 66, 80 : 1-25.

2978 PLECK, Elizabeth H.; PLECK, Joseph H. *The American man.* Englewood Cliffs, NJ, Prentice-Hall, 80, xii-433 p.

2979 PRINGLE, Mary Beth; STERICKER, Anne; [eds]. *Sex roles in literature.* New York, Longman, 80, xvii-286 p.

2980 RINDFUSS, Ronald R.; BUMPASS, Larry; ST. JOHN, Craig. "Education and fertility: implications for the roles women occupy", *American sociological Review* 45, jun 80 : 431-447.

2981 SACKS, Karen. *Sisters and wives: the past and future of sexual equality.* Westport, CT, Greenwood Press, 79, 274 p.

2982 SCANZONI, John; SZINOVACZ, Maximiliane. *Family decision-making. A developmental sex role model.* Beverly Hills, CA, Sage Publications, 80, 320 p.

2983 SCHAFFER, Kay F. *Sex-role issues in mental health.* Reading, MA, Addison-Wesley Pub. Co., 80, xii-227 p.

2984 SENARCLENS, Marina de. "Le rôle de la femme dans la vie économique et sociale", *Revue économique et sociale* 37, dec 79 : 200-209.

2985 SHIRAMIZU, Shigehiko. "Chiiki shakai no henka to shufu no katsudō" (The social activities of the women's groups in the changing villages), *Takachiho ronsō* 80, 80 : 185-226.

2986 STOCKTON, Nancy; [et al.]. "Sex role and innovative major choice among college students", *Journal of vocational Behavior* 16, jun 80 : 360-367.

2987 STORMS, Michael D. "Sex role identity and sex role stereotypes", *Journal of Personality and social Psychology* 37(10), oct 79 : 1779-1789.

2988 TANNAHILL, Reay. *Sex in history.* New York, Stein and Day, 80, 480 p.

2989 THOMPSON, Mary K.; BROWN, Julia S. "Feminine roles and variations in women's illness behaviors", *Pacific sociological Review* 23, oct 80 : 405-422.

2990 TROMMSDORFF, Gisela; BURGER, Christine; FÜCHSLE, Traudl. "Geschlechtsdifferenzen in der Zukunftsorientierung" (Sex differentiation and orientation to the future), *Zeitschrift für Soziologie* oct 80 : 366-377.

2991 UNGER, Rhoda Kesler. *Female and male: psychological perspectives.* New York, Harper & Row, 79, x-564 p.

2992 WATT, Ian. "Linkages between industrial radicalism and the domestic role among working women", *Sociological Review* 28, feb 80 : 55-74.
2993 WEITZMAN, Lenore J. *Sex role socialization: a focus on women*. Palo Alto, CA, Mayfield Pub. Co., 79, 105 p. CR: Kay Richards BROSCHART, *Contemporary Sociology (Albany)* 9(6), nov 80: 838-839.
2994 WILLIAMS, Juanita H.; [ed.]. *Psychology of women: selected readings*. New York, Norton, 79, 506 p. CR: Mary Glenn WILEY, *Contemporary Sociology (Washington)* 9(3), mai 80 : 444-445.

15130. Eugenism. Heredity
Eugénisme. Hérédité

[See also / voir aussi: 3726]

2995 BALDWIN, John D.; BALDWIN, Janice I. "Sociobiology or balanced biosocial theory?", *Pacific sociological Review* 23, jan 80 : 3-27.
2996 BLANK, Robert H. "Human genetic technology: some political implications", *Social Science Journal* 16, oct 79 : 1-19.
2997 CHAGNON, Napoleon A.; IRONS, William; [eds.]. *Evolutionary biology and human social behavior: an anthropological perspective*. North Scituate, MA, Duxbury Press, 79, xvi-623 p.
2998 FREEDMAN, Daniel G. *Human sociobiology: a holistic approach*. New York, Free Press, 79, ix-242 p.
2999 ISAMBERT, François-A. "Ethique et génétique. De l'utopie eugénique au contrôle des malformations congénitales", *Revue française de Sociologie* 21, jul-sep 80 : 331-354.
3000 JENCKS, Christopher. "Heredity, environment, and public policy reconsidered", *American sociological Review* 45, oct 80 : 273-736.
3001 LEVY, Charles Kingsley. *Biology, human perspectives*. Santa Monica, CA, Goodyear Pub. Co., 79, xiii-562 p.
3002 MURPHY, Edmond A. "Quantitative genetics: a critique", *Social Biology* 26, 79 : 126-141.
3003 RUSE, Michael. "Genetics and the quality of life", *Social Indicators Research* (1-4), jan 80 : 419-441.

15200. AGE GROUP
GROUPE D'ÂGE

15210. Age. Cohort. Generation
Âge. Cohorte. Génération

[See also / voir aussi: 3137, 3213, 5850, 5962]

3004 FONER, Anne. "The sociology of age stratification: a review of some recent publications", *Contemporary Sociology* nov 80 : 771-779. [survey essay.]
3005 HERSHEY, Daniel; WANG, Hsuan-Hsien. *A new age-scale for humans*. Lexington, MA, Lexington Books, 80, xiii-156 p.
3006 WITT, David D.; [et al.]. "The changing association between age and happiness: emerging trend or methodological artifact/'', *Social Forces* 58, jun 80 : 1302-1307.

15220. Childhood
Enfance

[See also / voir aussi: 384, 691, 827, 828, 902, 904, 1280, 1448, 1574, 2035, 2109, 2132, 2207, 2214, 3540, 5338, 5927, 6230]

3007 BERTRAND, Arthur; CEBULA, Joseph P. *Tests, measurement, and evaluation: developmental approach*. Reading, MA, Addison-Wesley Pub. Co., 80, xiii-321 p.
3008 BOULDING, Elise. *Children's rights and the wheel of life*. New Brunswick, NJ, Transaction Books, 79, xv-179 p.
3009 BRYAN, James H.; BRYAN, Tanis H. *Exceptional children*. Sherman Oaks, CA, Alfred Pub. Co., 79, xiii-424 p.
3010 COLLETTA, Nancy Donohue. "Child-rearing and maternal satisfaction in one- and two-parent families", *International Journal of the Sociology of the Family* jan-jun 79 : 27-33.
3011 CRAIG, Grace J. *Child development*. Englewood Cliffs, NJ, Prentice-Hall, 79, xiii-524 p.

3012 CRUBELLIER, Maurice. *L'enfance et la jeunesse dans la société française 1800-1950*. Paris, A. Colin, 79, 389 p. CR: Françoise MAYEUR, *Revue française de Sociologie* 21(4), oct-dec 80 : 662-666.
3013 DONATI, Pierpaolo. "Infanzia e territorio sociale: dopo la crisi del Puerocentrismo" (Childhood and social field: after the crisis of child-centrism), *Sociologia (Roma)* 13(2-3), mai-dec 79 : 171-209.
3014 ERESUND, Pia; TESHA, Nancy. *The situation of children in Tanzania*. Stockholm, Swedish International Development Authority, 79, 95 p.
3015 FASSHEBER, Marianne. *Auswirkungen familiärer und schulischer Einflüsse auf die Entwicklung von Kindern* (Family impact and school influence on child development). Göttingen, Toronto, Zürich, Verlag für Psychologie Hogrefe, 80, 216 p.
3016 FILIPPOV, F. R. "Deti v strane razvitogo socializma" (Children in the developed socialist country), *Sociologičeskie Issledovanija* 79 : 51-62.
3017 HO, Teresa J. "Time costs of child rearing in the rural Philippines", *Population and Development Review* dec 79 : 643-662.
3018 ISHWARAN, K.; [ed.]. *Childhood and adolescence in Canada*. Toronto, New York, McGraw-Hill Ryerson, 79, 386 p.
3019 KHAN, Mumtaz Ali. *Sociological aspects of child development: a study of rural Karnataka*. New Delhi, Concept, 80, 212 p.
3020 LEVITIN, Teresa E; [eds.]. "Children of divorce", *Journal of social Issues* 35, 79 : 1-186.
3021 LIEGLE, Ludwig. "Kindheit und Familie im interkulturellen Vergleich" (Childhood and family in cross-cultural comparison), *Hauswirtschaft und Wissenschaft* 28, 80 : 151-157.
3022 MUSSEN, Paul H.; [et al.]. *Essentials of child development and personality*. New York, Harper & Row, 80, x-451 p.
3023 NADIEN, Margot B. *The child's psychosocial development: from birth to early adolescence*. Wayne, NJ, Avery Pub. Group, 80, xi-164 p.
3024 NISI, Cesare. *Sviluppo infantile e realtà sociale* (Child development and social reality). Bologna, Pàtron, 79, 268 p.
3025 PINZAS R., Juana. "El desarrollo de conceptos sociales en niños peruanos" (Social concept development in Peruvian children), *Revista latinoamericana de Psicología* 12, 80 : 29-35.
3026 RYBACK, David; [et al.]. "Child-rearing practices reported by students in six cultures", *Journal of social Psychology* 110, apr 80 : 153-162. [Ethiopia, Republic of China, Thailand, Israel, India, USA.]
3027 SARAFINO, Edward P.; ARMSTRONG, James W. *Child and adolescent development*. Glenview, IL, Scott, Foresman, 80, 605 p.
3028 TASHIRO, Fujio; KANDA, Osamu; [eds.]. *Jido kensho -Nihon no kodomo no kenri sengen* (Children's charter -declaration of Japanese children's rights). Tokyo, Hokuju shuppan, 80, 249 p.
3029 ZERN, David S. "Child-rearing practices and social complexity: effect of disequilibrium on cognitive development", *Journal of social Psychology* 110, apr 80 : 171-175.

15230. Youth
Jeunesse

[See also / voir aussi: 686, 838, 1220, 1287, 1306, 1308, 1453, 1462, 1464, 1470, 1480, 1491, 1547, 1608, 1893, 1908, 1919, 2179, 2274, 2289, 2474, 3012, 3018, 3365, 3716, 5801, 5803, 5813, 5896]

3030 "Jugend" (Youth), *Gewerkschaftliche Monatshefte* 31, 80 : 357-420.
3031 "Youth protest in the sixties", *Sociological Focus* 13, aug 80 : 173-313. [special issue. USA and Sri Lanka.]
3032 ARDILA ESPINEL, Noe. "La adolescencia: factores críticos" (Adolescence: critical factors), *Revista latinoamericanos de Psicología* 12, 80 : 441-454.
3033 BAMBER, J. H. *The fears of adolescents*. London, New York, Academic Press, 79, viii-228 p.
3034 BERMAN, David R.; STOOKEY, John A. "Adolescents, television, and support for government", *Public Opinion Quarterly* 44, 80 : 330-340.
3035 BIDDLE, Bruce J.; BANK, Barbara J.; MARLIN, Marjorie M. "Parental and peer influence on adolescents", *Social Forces* 58, jun 80 : 1057-1079.
3036 BOROVIK, V. S. "Formirovanie social'noj otvetstvennosti molodoži v uslovijah razvitogo socializma" (The formation of youth social responsibility under conditions of

developed socialism), *IN: Problemy formirovanija dostojnoj smeny rabočego klassa v uslovijah razvitogo socializma.* Moskva, 79 : 108-128.

3037 BOVKUN, V. V. "Obraz žizni molodeži i ego razvitie socialističeskom obscestve" (The youth way of life and its development in the socialist society), *IN: Social'naja struktura sovetskogo obščestva i socialističeskij obraz žizni. II.* Moskva, 78 : 63-71.

3038 BRITVIN, V. G.; MANSUROV, V. A. "Nekotory mirovozzrenčeskie predstavlenija molodeži" (Some youth world conception representations), *IN: Social'nye aspekty razvitija ličnosti. Ispol'zovanie informacionnyh sistem dlja ego prognozirovanija.* Moskva, 78 : 76-87.

3039 DACEY, John Stewart. *Adolescents today.* Santa Monica, CA, Goodyear Pub. Co., 79, 442 p.

3040 DUTTER, Lee E.; SELIKTAR, Ofira. "Attitudes of Israeli youth toward the Middle East conflict", *Journal of Peach Research* 16, 79 : 135-153.

3041 FAVRÈ, Chantal. *Les Motards: le phénomène moto, les jeunes et leur vie communautaire.* Toulouse, Privat, 80, 160 p.

3042 FEDOROV, G. T. *Molodež' i sovremennaja ideologičeskaja bor'ba* (Youth and the contemporary ideological struggle). Kiev, Višča Škola, 79, 183 p.

3043 GIULIANO, Luca. "Orientamenti per una sociologia della gioventù" (Orientations for a sociology of youth), *Revue internationale de sociologie / International Review of Sociology* 15(1-2-3), apr-aug-dec 79 : 25-48.

3044 GUROVA, R. G. "Gotovnost' molodezi k vypolneniju osnovnyh social'nyh funkcij kak faktor obščestvennogo razvitija" (The youth preparation for the essential social functions execution as a factor of social development), *IN: Social'nye aspekty razvitija ličnosti. Ispol'zovanie informacionnyh sistem dlja ego prognozirovanija.* Moskva, 78 : 69-75.

3045 KRIVORUČENKO, V. K. "Komsomol v političeskoj sisteme socialističeskogo obščestva" (Komsomol in the socialist society political system), *Vestnik Moskovskogo Universiteta. Teorija naučnogo Kommunizma* 79 : 19-28.

3046 LARKIN, Ralph W. *Suburban youth in cultural crisis.* New York, Oxford University Press, 79, xi-259 p.

3047 LARMIN, O. V.; LIPICKIJ, V. S.; [eds.]. *Molodež', NTR, kapitalizm* (Youth, scientific and technical revolution, capitalism). Moskva, Izdatel'stvo Moskovskogo Universiteta, 79, 288 p.

3048 LERNER, Richard M.; SPANIER, Graham B. *Adolescent development: a life-span perspective.* New York, McGraw-Hill, 80, xx-537 p.

3049 LIPSITZ, Joan. *Growing up forgotten: a review of research and programs concerning early adolescence.* New Brunswick, NJ, Transaction Books, 80, xvi-267 p.

3050 LUEPTOW, Lloyd B. "Social change and sex-role change in adolescent orientations toward life, work and achievement: 1964-1975", *Social Psychology Quarterly* 43, mar 80 : 48-58.

3051 MJALKIN, A. V.; [ed.]. *Molodež' v sovremennoj ideologičeskoj bor'be* (Youth in the contemporary ideological struggle). Moskva, VKS pri CK VLKSM, 79, 138 p.

3052 MOŠNJAGA, V. P. "O meste i roli meždunarodnogo demokratičeskogo molodežnogo dviženija v mirovom revoljucionnom processe" (On the place and role of the democratic youth movement in the world revolutionary process), *IN: Meždunarodnoe molodežnoe dviženie.* Moskva, 79 : 3-22.

3053 MURRAY, Christopher; [ed.]. *Youth in contemporary society.* Windsor, Eng., Humanities Press, 79, 306 p. CR: Jere M. COHEN, *Contemporary Sociology (Albany)* 9(4), jul 80 : 546.

3054 NAUMENKO, G. F. *Molodež' socialističeskogo goroda: byt, tradicii, obyčai* (The socialist town youth: customs, traditions, uses). Kiev, Naukova Dumka, 79, 155 p.

3055 PENDERGAST, Shirley; PROUT, Alan. "What will I do...? Teenage girls and the construction of motherhood", *Sociological Review* 28, aug 80 : 517-535.

3056 PETROV, I. I. "Idejnaja bor'ba vokrug molodežnyh problem v FRG" (The ideological struggle about youth problems in the FRG), *IN: Molodež' v sovremennoj ideologičeskij bor'be.* Moskva, 79 : 56-70.

3057 POPOV, B. N. "Otnošenie molodeži k voprosam ljubvi, braka i sem'i" (Youth relations to love, marriage and family questions), *IN: Sel'skaja molodež' Jakutii.* Jakutsk, 79 : 60-79.

3058 ROSENMAYR, Leopold; ALLERBECK, Klaus; [eds.]. "Youth and society", *Sociologie contemporaine/Current Sociology* 27(2-3), 79 : 362.

3059 ROSSI, Robert J.; GILMARTIN, Kevin J. "Social indicators of youth development and educational performance: a programmatic statement", *Social Indicators Research* (1-4), jan 80 : 157-191.

3060 SIEGERT, Michael T. *Adoleszenzkrise und Familienumwelt* (Adolescence crisis and family environment). Frankfurt/Main, New York, Campus-Verlag, 79, 280 p.
3061 SIMMONS, Roberta G.; [et. al.]. "Entry into early adolescence — the impact of school structure, puberty, and early dating on self-esteem", *American sociological Review* 44, dec 79 : 948-967.
3062 SUBKIN, V. N. *Nacalo puti: problemy molodezi v zerkale sociologii i literatury* (The beginning of the road: youth problems in sociology and literature). Moskva, Molodaja Gvardija, 79, 224 p.
3063 TOMASKEVIC, V. E.; PLAKSIJ, S. I. "Nekotorye pokazateli obščestvennoj aktivnosti gorodskoj i sel'skoj molodeži" (Some indexes of the urban and rural youth social activity), *Sociologiceskie Issledovanija* 79 : 121-122.
3064 ZARUBIN, A. G. "Molodež' Zapada i sovremennyj pravnyj radikalizm" (Western youth and contemporary right radicalism), *IN: Aktual'nye problemy ideologičeskoj bor'by. II.* Moskva, 79 : 86-93.
3065 ZLOBINA, E. G. "Obščenie molodeži v sisteme buržuaznogo i socialističeskogo obraza žizni" (Youth public opinion in the bourgeois and socialist ways of life), *IN: Aktual'nye problemy ideologičeskoj bor'by. I.* Moskva, 79 : 162-167.

15240. Adult
Adulte

[See also / voir aussi: 1532]

3066 HOGAN, Dennis P. "The transition to adulthood as a career contingency", *American sociological Review* 45, apr 80 : 261-276.
3067 ROGERS, Dorothy. *The adult years: an introduction to aging.* Englewood Cliffs, NJ, Prentice-Hall, 79, xiv-482 p.

15250. Old age
Vieillesse

[See also / voir aussi: 839, 870, 1162, 2064, 2134, 3532, 3560, 3675, 5816, 5922, 5930, 5960]

3068 "Vieillesse et mort", *Gérontologie et Société* 12, mar 80 : 176.
3069 "Vieillissement, retraite, loisir", *Loisir et Société* nov 79 : 277-447.
3070 ABALLEA, François; [et al.]. "Habitat des personnes âgées et avenir du patrimoine immobilier rural", *Recherche sociale (Paris)* 74, apr-jun 80 : 72 p.
3071 BAUM, Martha; BAUM, Rainer, C. *Growing old: a societal perspective.* Englewood Cliffs, NJ, Prentice-Hall, 80, x-306 p.
3072 Bibl.XXIX-3168. BERGHORN, Forrest J.; [et al.]. *The urban elderly: a study of life satisfaction.* CR: Elmer SPREITZER; Carla JORDAN, *Contemporary Sociology (Albany)* 9(5), sep 80: 673-674.
3073 BERSEE, A. P. M. "De economische positie van de bejaarden in de Verenigde Staten" (The economic conditions of aged in the United States), *Bevolking en Gezin* dec 79 : 295-310.
3074 BORGATTA, Edgar F.; MCCLUSKEY, Neil G.; [eds.]. *Aging and society. Current research perspectives.* Beverly Hills, CA, Sage Publications, 80, 224 p.
3075 CASALS, Ignacio. "Hacia una sociología de la ancianidad en España" (Toward a sociology of old age in Spain), *Revista española de Investigaciones sociológicas* 11, jul-sep 80 : 91-111.
3076 CHAPPELL, Neena L.; HAVENS, Betty. "Old and female: testing the double jeopardy hypothesis", *Sociological Quarterly* 21, 80 : 157-171.
3077 CHUDACOFF, Howard P.; HAREVEN, Tamara K. "From the empty nest to family dissolution: life course transitions into old age", *Journal of Family History* 79 : 69-83.
3078 DECKER, David L. "Sociological theory and the social position of the aged", *International Journal of contemporary Sociology* 15(3-4), jul-oct 78 : 303-317. ;961[USA.]
3079 DMITRIEV, A. V. *Social'nye problemy ljudej požilogo vozrasta* (Social problems of aged people). Leningrad, Nauka, 80, 103 p.
3080 DOWD, James J. *Stratification among the aged.* Monterey, CA, Brooks/ Cole Pub. Co., 80, xii-153 p.

3081   GOLANT, Stephen M.; [comp.]. *Location and environment of elderly population*. Washington, V. H. Winston, New York, Halsted Press, 79, viii-214 p.
3082   GREEN, Brent; [et al.]; [eds.]. "Old age: environmental complexity and policy interventions", *Journal of social Issues* 36, 80 : 1-164.
3083   GUILLEMARD, Anne-Marie. *La Vieillesse et l'État*. Paris, PUF, 80, 238 p.
3084   HAZAN, Haim. "Continuity and change in a tea-cup: on the symbolic nature of tea-related behaviour among the aged", *Sociological Review* 28, aug 80 : 497-516.
3085   JACKSON, Jacquelyne Johnson. *Minorities and aging*. Belmont, CA, Wadsworth Pub. Co., 80, xiv-256 p.
3086   JOHNSON, Elizabeth S.; WILLIAMSON, John B. *Growing old: the social problems of aging*. New York, Holt, Rinehart and Winston, 80, viii-196 p.
3087   KANE, L.; ANDERSEN, N. A. *Health Status and needs of the urban aged: a survey of the aged population of the inner city and near eastern suburbs of Sydney, 1975*. Kensington, School of Health Administration, University of New South Wales, 79, 111 p.
3088   KEARL, Michael. "Time, identity, and the spiritual needs of the elderly", *Sociological Analysis* 40, 80 : 172-180.
3089   KOHUT, Sylvester; KOHUT, Jeraldine Joanne; FLEISHMAN, Joseph J. *Reality orientation for the elderly*. Oradell, NJ, Medical Economics Co., Book Division, 79, xii-108 p.
3090   LA GORY, Mark. "The age segregation process: explanation for American cities", *Urban Affairs Quarterly* 16, sep 80 : 59-80.
3091   LAWTON, Mortimer Powell. *Environment and aging*. Monterey, CA, Brooks/Cole Pub. Co., 80, xii-186 p.
3092   LINDGREN, Jarl. "Aging: a demographic and an economic problem", *Yearbook of Population Research in Finland* 17, 79 : 84-90.
3093   MADDOX, George L. "Sociology of later life", *Annual Review of Sociology* 79 : 113-135.
3094   MALINCHAK, Alan A. *Crime and gerontology*. Englewood Cliffs, NJ, Prentice-Hall, 80, xvi-207 p.
3095   MANCINI, Jay A.; [et al.]. "Social network interaction among older adults: implications for life satisfaction", *Human Relations* 33, aug 80 : 541-554.
3096   MARSHALL, Victor W. *Last chapters, a sociology of aging and dying*. Monterey, CA, Brooks/Cole Pub. Co., 80, xii-227 p.
3097   MATTHEWS, Sarah H. *The social world of old women. Management of self identity*. Beverly Hills, CA, Sage Publications, 79, 200 p.
3098   PERKINSON, Margaret A. "Alternate roles for the elderly: an example from a Midwestern retirement community", *Human Organization* 39, 80 : 219-226.
3099   PETTY, David L. *An analysis of attitudes and behaviors of young adults toward the aged*. Palo Alto, CA, R & E Research Associates, 79, vii-119 p.
3100   RADEBOLD, Hartmut; GRUBER, Franz. *Psychosoziale Gerontologie* (Psychosocial gerontology). Freiburg im Breisgau, Lambertus-Verlag, 79, 341 p.
3101   RILEY, Matilda White; [ed.]. *Aging from birth to death: interdisciplinary perspectives*. Boulder, CO, Westview Press, 79, 196 p. CR: Russell A. WARD, *Contemporary Sociology (Albany)* 9(5), sep 80: 674.
3102   RODRIGUEZ, Ibañez, Jose Enrique. "Perspectiva sociológica de la vejez" (Sociological perspective of old age), *Revista española de Investigaciones sociológicas* jul-sep 79 : 77-97.
3103   ROSENFELD, Jeffrey P. "Old age beneficiaries: kinship, friendship and (dis)inheritance", *Sociology and social Research* 64, oct 79 : 86-98. [USA.]
3104   SAUVY, Alfred. "Les conséquences sociales et morales du vieillissement de la population", *Canadian Studies in Population* 79 : 107.
3105   SCHULZ, Heike. *Soziale Beziehungen im Alter: Integration durch 'Insulation'* (Social relations in old age: integration through 'insulation'). Frankfurt/ Main, New York, Campus Verlag, 79, 183 p.
3106   SCHWARTZ, Arthur N.; PETERSON, James A. *Introduction to gerontology*. New York, Holt, Rinehart and Winston, 79, 300 p. CR: Frank J. WHITTINGTON, *Contemporary Sociology (Albany)* 9(4), jul 80, 524-525.
3107   SHANAS, Ethel. "Older people and their families: the new pioneers", *Journal of Marriage and Family* 42, feb 80 : 9-15.
3108   SHIMIZU, Hiroaki. "Nōson rōjin no kyojū keitai -Miyagi-ken Shibahime-chō to Kagohima-ken ūra-cho no higaku kenkyū" (Living arrangement of aged people in rural areas: A comparison of rural areas in northeastern and southwestern districts), *Jinko mondai kenkyu* 156, 80 : 39-53.
3109   STAHURA, John. "Ecological determinants of the aging of suburban populations", *Sociological Quarterly* 21, 80 : 107-118.

3110	WALKER, Alan. "The social creation of poverty and dependency in old age", *Journal of social Policy* jan 80 : 49-76.
3111	WILLIAMSON, John B.; [et al.]. *Aging and society*. New York, Holt, Rinehart and Winston, 80, viii-450 p.
3112	YUZAWA, Yasuhiko; [ed.]. *Sekai no rōjin no ikikata* (Life style of aged in different countries). Tokyo, Yūhikaku, 80, 235 p.

15300. POPULATION EVULUTION. POPULATION POLICY
ÉVOLUTION DE LA POPULATION. POLITIQUEDÉMOGRAPHIQUE

15310. Population growth
Accroissement de la population

[See also / voir aussi: 572, 2360, 2577, 2843, 3054, 3155, 3295, 3396, 3617, 4295, 4319, 4387, 6188]

3113	ANDERSON, Robert Moffat; TURNER, B. D.; TAYLOR, Lionel Ray; [eds.]. *Population dynamics: the 20th symposium of the British Ecological Society, London, 1978*. Oxford, Blackwell Scientific Publications, 79, viii-434 p. [distributor, USA and Canada, Halsted Press.]
3114	BALLESTER ROS, Ignacio. "El movimiento natural de la población en España" (The natural movement of population in Spain), *Revista de Estudios de la Vida local* 39(205), jan-mar 80 : 127-142.
3115	BHARARA, L. P.; MALHOTRA, S. P. "Some socio-economic characteristics of human resource structure in an arid village of Rajasthan", *Indian Journal of social Research* 20, dec 79 : 191-202.
3116	BLAYO, Yves. "Les populations des régions en développement", *Population* 34, nov-dec 79 : 1116-1127.
3117	BOND, Andrew R.; LYDOLPH, Paul E. "Soviet population change and city growth, 1970-79: a preliminary report", *Soviet Geography* 20, oct 79 : 461-488.
3118	BREZNIK, Sušan. "Age composition and ageing of the population", *Yugoslav Survey* 20, nov 79 : 47-56.
3119	BROWN, David L. "Metropolitan reclassification: some effects on the characteristics of the population in metropolitan and nonmetropolitan counties", *Rural Sociology* 44, wint 79 : 791-801. [USA.]
3120	CASSI, Laura. "Osservazioni sulle variazioni di popolazione dei centri urbani italiani dal 1951" (Observations on population variations of Italian urban centres from 1951 to 1971), *Rivista geografica italiana* 86, sep 79 : 321-337.
3121	CELM, Ralph S. "Regional patterns of population change", *Geographical Review* 70, apr 80 : 137-156.
3122	CORNELIUS, Ivar; LENGSFELD, Wolfgang. "Die demographische Situation in der Bundesrepublik Deutschland im Jahre 1976" (The demographic situation in the Federal Republic of Germany in 1976), *Zeitschrift für Bevölkerungswissenschaft* 79 : 65-111.
3123	Bibl.XXIX-3193. Council of Europe. *Population decline in Europe: implications of a declining stationary population*. CR: Nathan KEYFITZ, 9(3), mai 80: 402-403.
3124	DI MAIO, Alfred J. Jr. "The Soviet Union and population", *Comparative political Studies* 13, apr 80 : 97-136.
3125	DIOP, L. M. "Approche géographique de l'optimum de population. Place réelle et importance relative du problème de l'accroissement demographique dans le monde actuel, notamment en zone intertropicale", *Bulletin de l'Institut fondamental d'Afrique noire* 40, jan 78 : 179-207.
3126	DUNSTAN, John. "The effect of crowding on behaviour: empirical measures for testing theoretical models", *Urban Studies* 16, oct 79 : 299-307.
3127	DUPÂQUIER, Jacques. *La Population rurale du Bassin parisien à l'époque de Louis XIV*. Paris, Editions de l'Ecole des hautes études en sciences sociales, 79, 440 p.
3128	Bibl.XXIX-3198. DYER, Colin. *Population and society in twentieth century France*. CR: Leslie Page MOCH, *Contemporary Sociology (Albany)* 9(1), jan 80: 76-77.
3129	EL-SAYED EL-BUSHRA. "Some demographic indicators for Khartoum conurbation, Sudan", *Middle Eastern Studies* 15, oct 79 : 259-309.
3130	FABRI, Marcel Y. "*Relations entre les facteurs démographiques et socio-économiques dans le contexte du développement*", *Bulletin démographique des Nations Unies* 10, 77 : 1-13.

3131   FILANGIERI, Angerio. *Territorio e popolazione nell'Italia meridionale: evoluzione storica* (Territory and population in southern Italy: historical evolution). Milano, F. Angeli, 80, 389 p.
3132   FINKLE, Jason L.; MCINTOSH, Alison. "Political perceptions of population stabilization and decline", *Policy Studies Review Annual* 78 : 575-586.
3133   FRANQUEVILLE, André. "Croissance démographique et immigration à Yaoundé", *Cahiers d'Outre-Mer* 32(128), oct-dec 79 : 231-254.
3134   Bibl.XXIX-3202. FRIEDLANDER, Dov; GOLDSCHEIDER, Calvin. *The population of Israel.* CR: Ronald FREEDMAN, *Contemporary Sociology* 9(3), mai 80: 403-404.
3135   GANIAGE, Jean. "La population du Beauvaisis. Transformations économiques et mutations démographiques (1790-1975)", *Annales de Géographie* 54(491), jan-feb 80 : 1-36.
3136   GAZZETTI, Fernando. *Economia del declino demografico: premessa alla politica demografica* (Economics of population decrease: a premise of population policy). Roma, Casa editrice Mediterranea, 79, 78 p. [Italy.]
3137   HAJDA, Lubomyz. "Nationality and age in Soviet population change", *Soviet Studies* 32, oct 80 : 475-499.
3138   HERRERA, Ligia. "Estructura agraria y distribución de la población en México" (Agrarian structure and population distribution in Mexico), *Demografía y Economía* 12, 78 : 203-255.
3139   HIRSCHMAN, Charles. "Demographic trends in peninsular Malaysia, 1947-75", *Population and Development Review* mar 80 : 103-125.
3140   International Union for the Scientific Study of Population. *Economic and demographic change: Issues for the 1980's: Proceedings of the conference, Helsinki, 1978.* Liege, Belgium, Author, 79, 3 vols.: 464 p., 449 p., 350 p.
3141   JOHNSON, Kenneth M.; PURDY, Ross L. "Recent non-metropolitan population change in fifty-year perspective", *Demography* 17, feb 80 : 57-70. ;961[USA.]
3142   KELLY, Phyllis B. "A model of population increase in the Mazahua region, Mexico", *América indígena* 39, apr-jun 79 : 371-380.
3143   LAND, Ney; ALMEIDA, Arilza Nazareth de. "População e depopulação em grupos indígenas" (Population and population decline in indigenous groups), *América indígena* 39, apr-jun 79 : 339-369. [Brazil.]
3144   LANGANEY, André. "Diversité et histoire humaine", *Population* 34, nov-dec 79 : 985-1006.
3145   LATTES, Alfredo E. *La dinámica de la población rural en la Argentina entre 1870 y 1970* (The dynamics of rural population in Argentina between 1870 and 1970). Buenos Aires, Centro de Estudios de Población (CENEP), 79, 42 p.
3146   LEWIS, Robert A.; ROWLAND, Richard H. *Population redistribution in the USSR: its impact on society, 1897-1917.* New York, Praeger, 79, xx-485 p.
3147   LEWIS, Robert A.; ROWLAND, Richard H. *Population redistribution in the USSR: its impact on society, 1897-1917.* New York, Praeger, 79, xx-485 p.
3148   LIEBERMAN, Samuel S. *Prospects for development and population growth in Iran.* New York, Population Council, 79, 39 p.
3149   LIEBERMAN, Samuel S. "A community approach to aggregate demographic patterns in rural Turkey", *Research in economic Anthropology* 80 : 349-383.
3150   LINARES, Emma. *Bibliografía argentina de población 1970-1978* (Argentine bibliography of population 1970-1978). Buenos Aires, Fundación para el Desarrollo de América Latina, 79, 111 p.
3151   LOVE, Douglas; PASHUTE, Lincoln. "The effects of population size growth, and concentration upon scientific productivity", *Research in Population Economics* 78 : 127-142.
3152   MAZET, Claude. "Croissance démographique et concentration urbaine au Pérou. L'accentuation des déséquilibres à la fin du 20. siècle", *Jahrbuch für Geschichte von Staat, Wirtschaft und Gesellschaft Lateinamerikas* 16, 79 : 379-406.
3153   MOYA PONS, Frank. "Datos para el estudio de la demografía aborigen en Santo Domingo" (Data for the study of aboriginous demography in Santo Domingo), *Jahrbuch für Geschichte von Staat, Wirtschaft und Gesellschaft Lateinamerikas* 16, 79 : 1-11.
3154   MURRAY, Bertram G. *Population dynamics: alternative models.* New York, Academic Press, 79, ix-212 p.
3155   MURRAY, Martin. "Étude démographique de St-Jean-de-Cherbourg, une paroisse gaspésienne du XXème siècle", *Cahiers québécois de Démographie* dec 79 : 59-76.
3156   MYNTII, Cynthia. "Population processes in rural Yemen: temporary emigration, breastfeeding, and contraception", *Studies in Family Planning* 10(10), oct 79 : 282-289.

3157 NAMIHIRA, Isao. *Chiho toshi no kaiso-kozo-Okinawa toshi no bunseki* (Social stratification in local cities — a case of Okinawa cities). Okinawa, Okinawa jiji shuppan, 80, 258 p.
3158 Organisation de coopération et de développement économiques. *L'Évolution démographique de 1950 à 1990*. Paris, O.C.D.E., 79, 150 p.
3159 Organization for Economic Cooperation and Development. Centre for Educational Research and Innovation. *Child and family: demographic development in the OECD countries*. Paris, OECD, 79, 218 p.
3160 PANKRATOVA, M. G. "Évoljucija količestvennyh harakteristik sel'skoj sem'i v SSSR" (Evolution of the rural family quantitative characteristics in the USSR), *IN: Social'naja struktura sovetskogo obščestva i socialističeskij obraz žizni. II*. Moskva, 78 : 170-179.
3161 RALLU, Jean-Louis. "Situation démographique de la Polynésie française", *Population* 35, apr 80 : 385-415.
3162 RJABUŠKIN, T. V.; GALECKAJA, R. A. *Dinamika i struktura naselenija v socialističeskom obščestve* (The population dynamics and structure in the socialist society). Moskva, Statistika, 79, 223 p.
3163 RODRIGUEZ ALCAIDE, José J. "Estructura de la población agraria mundial" (Structure of the world agricultural population), *Revista de Estudios agro-sociales* 29(112), 80 : 9-20.
3164 ROSE, Harold M. "The diminishing urban promise: economic retrenchment, social policy and race", *Urban Affairs annual Review* 17, 79 : 183-210.
3165 ROWLAND, Richard H. "Declining and stagnant towns of the USSR", *Soviet Geography* 21, apr 80 : 195-218.
3166 SEKI, Kiyohide; ŌYAMA, Nobuyoshi. *Hyakuman toshi no fujin -Sapporo-shi ni okeru fujin no seikatsu kōzō to seikatsu shiko ni kansuru hōkokusho* (Women of a million population city; social life and intention for living of women in Sapporo). Sapporo, Sapporo-shi, 80, 188 p.
3167 SIDHU, Manjit S. "Population distribution in peninsular Malaysia: historical trends and contemporary issues", *Asian Profile* oct 79 : 459-480.
3168 SINHA, V. C. *Dynamics of India's population growth*. New Delhi, National, 79, xv-506 p.
3169 SLY, David, F.; TAYMAN, Jeffrey. "Metropolitan morphology and population mobility: the theory of ecological expansion reexamined", *American Journal of Sociology* 86, jul 80 : 119-138.
3170 SOLNICKOVA, Lenka. "La développement démographique en Tchécoslovaquie en 1978", *Demosta* 12, 79 : 69-73.
3171 SOSKIN, S. N. "Obrazovanie kak faktor progressa social'noj struktury sel'skogo naselenija Kazahstana" (Formation as a factor of progress of the Kazahstan rural population social structure), *IN: Social'naja struktura sovetskogo obščestva i socialističeskij obraz žizni. I*. Moskva, 78 : 110-121.
3172 STAROVEROV, V. I. "Razvitie social'noj struktury sel'skogo naselenija SSSR v uslovijah zrelogo socializma" (Development of the USSR rural population social structure under conditions of mature socialism), *IN: Social'naja struktura sovetskogo obščestva i socialističeskij obraz žizni. I*. Moskva, 78 : 76-90.
3173 STOCKWELL, Edward G.; LAIDLAW, Karen A. "A note on the association between population growth and economic development in low-income countries", *Rural Sociology* 45, 80 : 132-138.
3174 Bibl.XXIX-3248. TAPINOS, G.; PIOTROW, Phyllis T. *Six billion people: demographic dilemmas and world politics*. CR: Jeffrey S. PASSEL, *Contemporary Sociology (Albany)* 9(5), sep 80 : 699-700.
3175 TEACHMAN, Jay D. "Analysis of population diversity: measures of qualitative variation", *Sociological Methods and Research* feb 80 : 341-362.
3176 THUMERELLE, P. J. "Crise économique et décroissance démographique. L'exemple de la région Nord-Pas-de-Calais", *Annales de Géographie* 89(492), mar-apr 80 : 144-156.
3177 VALENTEJ, D. I.; BODROVA, V. V. "Demografičeskie processy v stranah-članah SĖV" (Demographic processes in the CMEA countries), *IN: Naselenie i trudovye resursy v socialističeskih stranah*. Moskva, 79 : 3-21.
3178 VARZAR'. P. M.; RUSANDU, I. K. "Soderžanie truda i nekotory voprosy obščestvennoj aktivnosti sel'skih truženikov" (Labour content and some questions on the rural workers' social activity), *Izvestija Akademii Nauk moldavskoj SSR. Serija obščestvennyh Nauk* 79 : 42-49. ;961[USSR].
3179 YINON, Oded. "Egypt's population explosion", *Jerusalem Quarterly* 15, spr 80 : 106-120.

15320. Morbidity
Morbidité

[See also / voir aussi: 2989, 5874, 6184, 6197, 6201]

3180 AGAPITIDIS, Sotiris; NICOLAIDOU, Silia. "Certains groupes de personnes sous-privilégiées en rapport avec le développement social en Grèce", *Revue internationale de sociologie / International Review of Sociology* 15(1-2-3), apr-dec 79 : 3-24.

3181 ALEMI, Ali A.; MOHSENI, Manouchehr. "A causal concept of disease in an Iranian community", *Journal of biosocial Science* 10, oct 78 : 347-351.

3182 ARRINGTON, Robert L. "Pra ctical reason, responsibility and the psychopath", *Journal for the Theory of social behaviour* mar 79 : 71-89.

3183 BATES, Erica M.; WILSON, Paul R. *Mental disorder or madness?: alternative theories.* St. Lucia, Australia, University of Queensland Press, 79, vi-257 p.

3184 BERKOWITZ, Edward D. "The politics of mental retardation during the Kennedy administration", *Social Science Quarterly* 61, jun 80 : 128-143.

3185 BOLDERSON, Helen. "The origins of the disabled persons employment quota and its symbolic significance", *Journal of social Policy* apr 80 : 169-186.

3186 BROOKS, Nancy A. "The social consequences of disability: an experiential approach", *Teaching Sociology* jul 80 : 425-438.

3187 Bibl.XXIX-3272. BROWN, George W.; HARRIS, Tirril. *Social origins of depression: a study of psychiatric disorder in women.* CR: Phoebe Kazdin SCHNITZER, *Contemporary Sociology (Albany)* 9(1), jan 80: 123-124.

3188 CASSILETH, Barrie R.; [ed.]. *The Cancer patient: social and medical aspects of care.* Philadelphia, Lea & Febiger, 79, xii-332 p.

3189 CHARLES, Edgar D.; KRONENFELD, Jennie J.; [eds.]. *Social and economic impact of coronary artery disease.* Lexington, MA, Toronto, Heath, Lexington Books, 80, xii-141 p.

3190 CLELAND, Charles Carr. *The profoundly mentally retarded.* Englewood Cliffs, NJ, Prentice-Hall, 79, xii-211 p.

3191 GALLAGHER, Bernard J. *The sociology of mental illness.* Englewood Cliffs, NJ, Prentice-Hall, 80, x-357 p.

3192 GLIEDMAN, John; ROTH, William. *The unexpected minority: handicapped children in America.* New York, Harcourt Brace Jovanovich, 80, xvi-525 p.

3193 GONZALEZ RODRÍGUEZ, Benjamin. "Las bases sociales de la enfermedad mental" (Social bases of mental illness), *Revista española de Investigaciones sociológicas* apr-jun 79 : 85-99.

3194 GREENWALD, Howard P. *Social problems in cancer control.* Cambridge, MA, Ballinger Pub. Co., 80, xv-291 p.

3195 GROSSARTH-MATICEK, Ronald. *Krankheit als Biographie. Ein medizinsoziologisches Modell der Krebsentstehung und -therapie* (Disease as biography. A medical sociology model of cancer origin and therapy). Köln, Kiepenheuer und Witsch, 79, 362 p. CR: Arnold LANGENMAYR, *Soziologische Revue* 3(3), 80: 318-322.

3196 GROSSARTH-MATICEK, Ronald. *Soziales Verhalten und die Krebserkrankung* (Social behaviour and the beginning of cancer). Weinheim-Basel, Beltz, 79, 393 p. CR: Arnold LANGENMAYR, *Soziologische Revue* 3(3), 80: 318-322.

3197 GRUNEWALD, Karl. *Psykiskt utvecklingsstörda och deras livsvillkor i siffror — Facts and figures on the mentally retarded and their living conditions in Sweden — Die geistig Behinderten in Schweden und ihre Lebensbedingungen in Zahlen.* Stockholm, Socialstyre, Liber distribution, 79, 89 p.

3198 KOSHAL, Rajindar K.; KOSHAL, Manjulika. "Externalities of air pollution: estimates of heart diseases", *Social Indicators Research* mar 80 : 65-79. [USA.]

3199 RUNDE, Peter; HEINZE, Rolf G.; [eds.]. *Chancengleichheit für Behinderte. Sozialwissenschaftliche Analysen für die Praxis* (Equal opportunity for handicapped. Social science analysis for practice). Neuwied-Darnstadt, Luchterhand, 79, 272 p. CR: Karlheinz WÖHLER, *Soziologische Revue* 3(1); 80: 65-68.

3200 SCULL, A. T. *Museums of madness: the social organization of insanity in 19th century England.* London, Allen Lane, 79, 275 p. CR: Shulamit RAMON, *British Journal of Sociology* 31(4), dec 80: 606-607.

3201 TAYLOR, Frederick Kräupl. *The concepts of illness, disease, and morbus.* Cambridge, Eng., New York, Cambridge University Press, 79, ix-131 p.

3202 TWADDLE, Andrew C. *Sickness behavior and the sick role.* Boston, MA, G. K. Hall, 79, 239 p.

3203 WELLINGTON, Dorothy Gaites; MACDONALD, Eleanor J.; WOLF, Patricia F. *Cancer mortality: environmental and ethnic factors.* New York, Academic Press, 79, xii-258 p.

3204   ZAZZO, René; [ed.]. *Les Débilités mentales*. Paris, A. Colin, 79, 473 p.

15330. Mortality
Mortalité

[See also / voir aussi: 1846, 3068, 3096, 3356, 3415, 6219]

3205   *Mort (La) dans la vie africaine*. Paris, Présence africaine, 79, 335 p.
3206   ADAMCHUK, Donald J. "Emerging trends in the relationship between infant mortality and socio-economic status", *Social Biology* 26, 79 : 16-29.
3207   ANKER, Richard; KNOWLES, James C. "An empirical analysis of mortality differentials in Kenya at the macro and micro levels", *Economic Development and cultural Change* 29, oct 80 : 165-185.
3208   BOURGEOIS-PICHAT, Jean. "Les perspectives de baisse future de la mortalité dans le monde", *Bulletin démographique des Nations Unies* 11, 78 : 12-41.
3209   CARSE, James P. *Death and existence: a conceptual history of human mortality*. New York, Wiley, 80, xiv-473 p.
3210   CHARMAZ, Kathy. *The social reality of death: death in contemporary America*. Reading, MA, Addison-Wesley, 80, xi-335 p.
3211   D'SOUZA, Stan; CHEN, Lincoln C. "Sex differentials in mortality in rural Bangladesh", *Population and Development Review* jun 80 : 257-270.
3212   DUFOUR, Desmond; PÉRON, Yves. *Vingt ans de mortalité au Québec: les causes de décès, 1951-1971*. Montréal, Presses de l'Université de Montréal, 79, 204 p.
3213   FOX, A. John; BULUSU, Lak; KINLEN, Leo. "Mortality and age differences in marriage", *Journal of biosocial Science* 11, apr 79 : 117-131.
3214   FOX, Renée C.; [ed.]. "The social meaning of death", *Annals of the American Academy of political and social Science* 447, jan 80 : 1-146.
3215   GOLDMAN, Noreen. "Far Eastern patterns of mortality", *Population Studies* 34, mar 80 : 5-19.
3216   LAND, Kenneth C.; MCMILLAN, Marilyn M. "A macrodynamic analysis of changes in mortality indexes in the United States, 1946-1975: some preliminary results", *Social Indicators Research* (1-4), jan 80 : 1-46.
3217   LANE, Roger. *Violent death in the city: suicide, accident, and murder in nineteenth-century Philadelphia*. Cambridge, MA, Harvard University Press, 79, xiii-193 p. CR: Tom W. SMITH, *American Journal of Sociology* 86(2), sep 80 : 441-443.
3218   LIPFERT, Frederick W. "Differential mortality and the environment: the challenge of multicollinearity in cross-sectional studies", *Energy Systems and Policy* 80 : 367-400.
3219   NAM, Charles B.; WEATHERBY, Norman L.; OCKAY, Kathleen A. "Causes of death which contribute to the mortality crossover effect", *Social Biology* 25, 78 : 306-314.
3220   NORMANDEAU, Louise; LÉGARÉ, Jacques. "La mortalité infantile des Inuits du Nouveau-Québec", *Canadian Review of Sociology and Anthropology* 16, aug 79 : 260-274.
3221   PEBLEY, Anne R.; DELGADO, Hernan; BRINEMANN, Elena. "Fertility desires and child mortality experience among Guatemalan women", *Studies in Family Planning* 10, apr 79 : 129-136.
3222   PETRIOLI, Luciano; BERTI, Mario. *Modelli de mortalità* (Life tables). Milano, F. Angeli, 79, 365 p.
3223   SCHOEN, Robert; WOODROW, Karen. "Life tables for the United States", *Demography* 17, aug 80 : 297-322.
3224   SMUCKER, Céleste, M.; [et al.]. "Neo-natal mortality in South Asia: the special role of tetanus", *Population Studies* 34, jul 80 : 321-335.
3225   STOETZEL, Jean. "Les Français et leurs morts", *Population* 35, jun 80 : 529-542.
3226   TCHIVELA, Tchichellé. "La mortalité des enfants en République populaire du Congo", *Peuples noirs — Peuples africains* mai-jun 80 : 10-22.
3227   VERON, Jacques. "La mortalité en Asia méridionale et orientale", *Population* 35, feb 80 : 136-166.
3228   VEYS, D. "De ontwikkeling van de levensverwachting in België" (The evolution of life expectancy in Belgium), *Bevolking en Gezin* dec 79 : 283-294.
3229   WILSON, M. G. A. "Infant death in metropolitan Australia, 1970-1973", *Canadian Studies in Population* 79 : 127-142.

15340. Fertility. Natality
Fécondité. Natalité

[See also / voir aussi: 872, 1020, 2980, 3285, 3291, 3343, 3344, 3414, 3447, 3495, 3528, 3536, 3797, 4110, 4811, 4812, 4845]

3230 AGHAJANIAN, Akbar. "The relationship of income and consumption of modern goods to fertility: a study of working class families in Iran", *Journal of biosocial Science* 11, apr 79 : 219-226.
3231 AROWOLO, Oladele O. "Fertility of urban Yoruba working women: a case study of Ibadan city", *Nigerian Journal of economic and social Studies* 19, mar 77 : 37-66.
3232 BALAKRISHNAN, T. R.; EBANKS, G. E.; GRINDSTAFF, C. F. *La fécondité au Canada, 1971.* Ottawa, Statistique Canada, 79, 290 p. [issued also in English under title: Patterns of fertility in Canada, 1971.]
3233 BEHM, Hugo; GUZMAN, José Miguel. "El descenso de la fecundidad en Costa Rica y sus diferencias socio-economicas, 1960-1970" (Socio-economic differentials and fertility decline in Costa Rica from 1960 to 1970), *Notas de Población* (21), dec 79.
3234 BONGAARTS, John. *The fertility impact of traditional and changing childspacing practices in tropical Africa.* New York, Population Council, 79, 27 p.
3235 BUTZ, William P.; WARD, Michael. "Will US fertility remain low? A new economic interpretation", *Population and Development Review* dec 79 : 663-688.
3236 CALDWELL, John C. "Mass education as a determinant of the timing of fertility decline", *Population and Development Review* jun 80 : 225-255.
3237 CALOT, Gérard. "Données comparées sur l'évolution de la fécondité selon le rang de naissance en Allemagne fédérale et en France, 1950-1977", *Population* 34, numéro spécial 79 : 1291-1348.
3238 CALOT, Gérard. "Niveau de vie et nombre d'enfants: un bilan de la législation familiale et fiscale française de 1978", *Population* 35, feb 80 : 9-56.
3239 CALOT, Gérard. "Natalité française et politique démographique", *Revue des Travaux de l'Académie des Sciences morales et politiques* 130, 77 : 171-198.
3240 CHANG, H. C.; WARREN, Richard D.; PENDLETON, Brian F. "Testing and clarifying a macro model of socio-economic change and fertility", *Social Biology* 26, 79 : 30-50.
3241 COALE, Ansley J. *Human fertility in Russia since the nineteenth century.* Princeton, NJ, Princeton University Press, 79, xxiii-285 p. CR: David M. HEER, *Contemporary Sociology (Albany)* 9(5), sep 80: 653-657.
3242 Bibl.XXIX-3339. COCHRANE, Susan Hill. *Fertility and education: what do we really know?.* CR: Frances E. KOBRIN, *Contemporary Sociology (Albany)* 9(6), nov 80: 807-808.
3243 COWARD, J. "Recent characteristics of Roman Catholic fertility in Northern and Southern Ireland", *Population Studies* 34, mar 80 : 31-44.
3244 DELLA PERGOLA, Sergio. "Patterns of American Jewish fertility", *Demography* 17, aug 80 : 261-274.
3245 FERNANDEZ, Juan A.; GAUVREAU, Danielle. "Souhaits individuels et comportement du couple en matière de fécondité", *Cahiers québécois de Démographie* dec 79 : 77-98.
3246 FERNANDO, Dallas F. S. "The continuing fertility decline in Sri Lanka", *Journal of biosocial Science* 12, jan 80 : 51-60.
3247 FESTY, Patrick. *La Fécondité des pays occidentaux de 1870 à 1970.* Paris, Presses universitaires de France, 79, 392 p. [préf. de Jean BOURGEOIS-PICHAT.]
3248 FREJKA, Tomas. "Fertility trends and policies: Czechoslovakia in the 1970s", *Population and Development Review* mar 80 : 65-93.
3249 GARCIA Y GAMA, Irma Olaya. "Diferenciales de fecundidad en México, 1970" (Fertility differentials in Mexico, 1970), *Demografía y Economía* 13, 79 : 49-81.
3250 GOOD, Mary-Jo DelVecchio; FARR, G. M.; GOOD, B. J. "Social status and fertility: a study of a town and three villages in Northwestern Iran", *Population Studies* 34, jul 80 : 311-320.
3251 HAINES, Michael R. *Fertility and occupation: population patterns in industrialization.* New York, Academic Press, 79, xiii-9275 p. CR: Ramon E. DAUBON, *Journal of economic Literature* 18(3), sep 80, 1134-1136.
3252 HASHIMOTO, Masanori. "Demand for children in Japan during modernization", *Research in Population Economics* 80 : 295-320.

3253 HOPKINS VALENTINE, Carol; REVSON, Joanne E. "Cultural traditions, social change, and fertility in sub-Saharan Africa", *Journal of modern African Studies* 17, sep 79 : 453-472.

3254 JULEMONT, Ghislaine. "Une enquête nationale sur la fécondité: attentes et souhaits (1966, 1970, 1975). Quelques aspects du changement", *Population et Famille* (47), 79 : 1-43. [France.]

3255 KASHIWAZAKI, Hiroshi. "Fertility differentials of Japanese agricultural settlers in Eastern Bolivia", *Journal of biosocial Science* 11, jan 79 : 27-37.

3256 KETKAR, Suhas L. "Female education and fertility: some evidence from Sierra Leone", *Journal of developing Areas* 13, oct 78 : 23-33.

3257 KIM, Yoon Shin. "Fertility of the Korean population in Japan influenced by a folk superstition in 1966", *Journal of biosocial Science* 11, oct 79 : 457-464.

3258 KNODEL, John. "From natural fertility to family limitation: the onset of fertility transition in a sample of German villages", *Demography* 16, nov 79 : 493-521.

3259 KOCHER, James E. *Rural development and fertility change in tropical Africa: evidence from Tanzania.* East Lansing, Dept. of Agricultural Economics, Michigan State University, 79, viii-95 p.

3260 Bibl.XXIX-3367. KOHLI, Martin; [ed.]. *Soziologie des Lebenslaufs* (Life cycle sociology). CR: Reinhard MANN, *Kölner Zeitschrift für Soziologie und Sozialpsychologie* 32(4), dec 80 : 825-826.

3261 KYRIAZIS, Natalie. "Sequential fertility decision making: Catholics and Protestant in Canada", *Canadian Review of Sociology and Anthropology* 16, aug 79 : 275-286.

3262 LAPIERRE-ADAMCYK, Évelyne. *Socio-economic correlates of fertility in Canadian metropolitan areas, 1961 and 1971.* Ottawa, Statistics Canada, 79, 101 p.

3263 LEE, Ronald D. " Vue d'ensemble des nouvelles méthodes pour prévoir la fécondité", *Bulletin démographique des Nations Unies* 11, 78 : 6-11.

3264 MAHADEVAN K. *Sociology of fertility: determinants of fertility differentials in South India.* New Delhi, Sterling, 79, xxviii-158 p.

3265 MANUEL, Ron C.; DODDER, Richard A. "Birth order effects continued inconsistencies", *International Review of modern Sociology* jan-jun 79 : 93-102.

3266 MARIS, Bernard. "Famille, fécondité et choix économiques. Une critiique des modèles micro-économiques de fécondité", *Consommation* 26(3-4), jul-dec 79 : 107-129.

3267 MOSK, Carl. "Rural-urban fertility differences and the fertility transition", *Population Studies* 34, mar 80 : 77-90.

3268 OKORE, A. O. "Rural-urban fertility differentials in Southern Nigeria: an assessment of some available evidence", *Population Studies* 34, mar 80 : 171-179.

3269 PILARSKI, Adam M. "The impact of fertility on hours of work: a cross-country comparison", *Research in Population Economics* 78 : 69-91.

3270 POTTS, Malcolm; SELMAN, Peter. *Society and fertility.* Plymouth, Macdonald and Evans, 79, x-374 p.

3271 REPETTO, Robert C. *Economic equality and fertility in developing countries.* Baltimore, published for Resources for the Future by John Hopkins University Press, 79, xv-186 p. CR: David E. HORLACHER, *Journal of economic Literature* 18(4), dec 80: 1626-1627.

3272 RETEL-LAURENTIN, Anne. *Causes de l'infécondité dans la Volta noire.* Paris, Presses universitaires de France, 79, 100 p.

3273 ROMANIUC, A. "Increase in natural fertility during the early stages of modernization: evidence from an African case study", *Population Studies* 34, jul 80 : 293-310.

3274 RYFFEL-GERICKE, Christiane. "Die Geburt des ersten Kindes. Erste Ergebnisse aus Tiefinterviews mit Zürcher Ehefrauen" (The birth of the first child. First results from in-depth interviews of wives in Zurich), *Schweizerische Zeitschrift für Soziologie/Revue suisse de Sociologie* mar 80 : 43-63.

3275 SAEZ, Armand. "La fécondité en Espagne depuis le début du siècle", *Population* 34, nov-dec 79 : 1007-1022.

3276 TAAMALLAH, Khamaïs. "Essai d'application de la méthode de William Brass en vue d'estimer le niveau de fécondité des femmes tunisiennes", *Revue tunisienne de Sciences sociales* 15(53), 78 : 209-215.

3277 TABAH, Léon. "Fertility trends in the developed world", *Populi* 79 : 47-54.

3278 TACKE, Walter. "Glück, Zufriedenheit und generative Verhaltensvorstellungen. Ergebnisse einer globalen Umfrage" (Happiness, contentment and conceptions of reproductive behavior. Results of a worldwide enquiry), *Zeitschrift für Bevölkerungswissenschaft* 78 : 395-423.

3279 VOGELSANG, Harald; FEICHTINGER, Gustav. "Exponentielle Niveau- und Musteränderung der Fertilität. Eine Analyse mittels stabiler Vergleichsbevölkerungen" (Exponentials changes in the level and pattern of fertility. An analysis performed on the basis of corresponding stable populations), *Zeitschrift für Bevölkerungswissenschaft* 79 : 31-63.

3280 WESTOFF, Charles F. "La prédiction des tendances de la fécondité dans les pays développés", *Bulletin démographique des Nations Unies* 11, 78 : 1-5.

3281 YEAUKEY, D.; DOWNING, Douglas C. "The effects of marital dissolution and remarriage on fertility in urban Latin America", *Population Studies* 33, nov 79 : 537-547.

3282 ZIMMER, Basil George. *Urban family building patterns: the social mobility-fertility hypothesis reexamined.* Washington, U.S. Govt. Print. Off., 79, xv-193 p. [available from National Technical Information Service, Springfield, VA.]

15350. Family planning
Planification de la famille

[See also / voir aussi: 2911, 3136, 3156, 3234, 3239, 3258, 3521, 3544, 4157, 4852]

3283 "Population theory in China", *International Journal of Politics* aut 79 : 3-128.

3284 ATKINSON, Gary; MORACZEWSKI, Albert. *A moral evaluation of contraception and sterilization: a dialogical study.* St. Louis, MO, Pope John XXIII Medical-Moral Research and Education Center, 79, viii-115 p.

3285 BAVADRA, T. U.; KIERSKI, J. "Fertility and family planning in Fiji", *Studies in Family Planning* 11, jan 80 : 17-23.

3286 BERELSON, Bernard; HAVEMAN, R. H. *On allocating resources for fertility reduction in developing countries.* New York, Population Council, 79, 85 p.

3287 BERELSON, Bernard; HAVEMAN, R. H. "On allocating resources for fertility reduction in developing countries", *Population Studies* 34, jul 80 : 227-238.

3288 BERELSON, Bernard; LIEBERSON, Jonathan. "Government efforts to influence fertility: the ethical issues", *Population and Development Review* dec 79 : 581-613.

3289 BERELSON, Bernard; MAULDIN, Wayman Parker; SEGAL, Sheldon Jerome. *Population, current status, and policy options.* New York, Population Council, 79, 71 p.

3290 BERTRAND, Jane T.; PINEDA, Maria Antonieta; SANTISO G., Roberto. "Ethnic differences in family planning acceptance in rural Guatemala", *Studies in Family Planning* 10(8-9), aug-sep 79 : 238-245.

3291 BRACKETT, James W.; CHAO, John C.; RAVENHOLT, R. T. "The role of family planning in recent rapid fertility declines in developing countries", *Studies in Family Planning* (12), dec 78 : 314-323.

3292 BROWNE, Elspeth. *The empty cradle: fertility control in Australia.* Kensington, N.S.W., N.S.W. University Press, 79, 146 p.

3293 BRUIJN, Jan de. *Geschiedenis van de abortus in Nederland* (History of abortion in the Netherlands). Amsterdam, Van Gennep, 79, 330 p.

3294 CARAEL, Michel. "Espacement des naissances, nutrition et écologie au Kivu (Zaïre)", *Population et Famille* (47), 79 : 81-99.

3295 CHAKRABORTY, B. "Problems and prospects of population-education in India's rural setting", *Indian Journal of social Research* 20, dec 79 : 175-179.

3296 CHAMBERLAIN, Ann. "The estimation of costs and effectiveness of community-based family planning services", *International Journal of social Economics* 80 : 260-272.

3297 CHAUNU, Pierre; LEGRAND, Jean. *Un Futur sans avenir: histoire et population.* Paris, Calmann-Lévy, 79, 315 p.

3298 CHEN, Peter S. J.; FAWCETT, James T.; [eds.]. *Public policy and population change in Singapore.* New York, Population Council, 79, vii-275 p.

3299 CHIBA, Motoko; FRANZ, Margaret-Mary. "Abortion, contraception and motherhood in post-war Japan and the United States", *International Journal of Women's Studies* 80 : 66-75.

3300 COLLOMB, Philippe. "La diffusion des méthodes contraceptives modernes en France de 1971 à 1978", *Population* 34, nov-dec 79 : 1045-1066.

3301 DE SANDRE, Paolo. "Commentaire sur les idéologies et les politiques déomgraphiques", *Genus* 34(1-2), 78 : 131-144.

3302 DJERASSI, Carl. *The politics of contraception.* Stanford, CA, Stanford Alumni Association, 79, 2 vols., xxv-267 p.

3303 DUTTA, Ranajit. "Abortion in India, with particular reference to West Bengal", *Journal of biosocial Science* 12, apr 80 : 191-200.

3304 EVERS, Mark; MCGEE, Jeanne. "The trend and pattern in attitudes toward abortion in the United States, 1965-1977", *Social Indicators Research* (1-4), jan 80 : 251-267.

3305 FISEK, Nusret H.; SOMBULOGU, K. "The effects of husband and wife education on family planning in rural Turkey", *Studies in Family Planning* (10-11), oct-nov 78 : 280-285.

3306 FORREST, Jacqueline Darroch; SULLIVAN, Ellen. "Abortion in the United States", *Family Planning Perspectives* 11, nov-dec 79 : 329-341.

3307 FRANCOME, Caroline; FRANCOME, Colin. "Towards an understanding of the American abortion rate", *Journal of biosocial Science* 11, jul 79 : 303-313.

3308 FREZEL-LOZEY, Michel. "L'avortement: incidence de la contraception et motivations. Une enqête à Bordeaux", *Population* 35, jun 80 : 545-564.

3309 GALLEN, Moira. "Abortion choices in the Philippines", *Journal of biosocial Science* 11, jul 79 : 281-288.

3310 HAWKINS, Denis Frank; ELDER, Murdoch George. *Human fertility control: theory and practice*. London, Boston, Butterworths, 79, x-483 p.

3311 HULKKO, Jouko. "Population development and population policy in Finland", *Yearbook of Population Research in Finland* 17, 79 : 15-31.

3312 JOHNSON, J. Timothy. "Influences of family planning acceptance: an analysis of background and program factors in Malaysia", *Studies in Family Planning* 10, jan 79 : 15-24.

3313 KALAJDŽIEV, V.; NAUMOV, N. "Demografičeskaja situacija i politika narodonaselenija v Narodnoj Respublike Bolgarii" (The demographical situation and the population policy in the People's Republic of Bulgaria), IN: *Naselenie i trudovye resursy v socialističeskih stranah*. Moskva, 79 : 22-38.

3314 KANTROW, Louise. "Philadelphia gentry: fertility and family limitation among an American aristocracy", *Population Studies* 34, mar 80 : 21-30.

3315 KAR, Snehendu B.; TALBOT, John M. "Attitudinal and nonattitudinal determinants of contraception: a cross-cultural study", *Studies in Family Planning* 11, feb 80 : 51-64.

3316 KELLER, Alan. "Contraceptive acceptability research: utility and limitations", *Studies in Family Planning* 10(8-9), aug-sep 79 : 230-237.

3317 KOCHER, James E. "Population policy in India: recent development and current prospects", *Population and Development Review* jun 80 : 299-310.

3318 LAMY, Marie-Laurence; JOURDAIN, Alain; LEVAILLANT, Jean-Marc. "Aspects sociaux et médicaux de l'avortement. Deux enquêtes en Bretagne et à Créteil", *Population* 35, jun 80 : 565-579.

3319 LATIF MIA, M. A.; [et al.]. "Basic information on family formation and family planning in rural Bangladesh", *Rural Demography* (1-2), 78 : 39-59.

3320 LEÑERO OTERO, Luis. *Valores ideológicos y las políticas de población en México* (Ideological values and population policy in Mexico). México, Editorial Edicol, 79, 236 p.

3321 LERIDON, Henri; [et al.]. "La contraception en France en 1978. Une enquête INED-INSEE", *Population* 34, numéro spécial 79 : 1349-1390.

3322 MONTGOMERY, John D.; LASSWELL, Harold Dwight; MIGDAL, Joel S.; [eds.]. *Patterns of policy: comparative and longitudinal studies of population events*. New Brunswick, NJ, Transaction Books, 79, vi-345 p.

3323 MORRIS, Leo; [et al.]. "Contraceptive prevalence in Paraguay", *Studies in Family Planning* (10-11), oct-nov 78 : 272-279.

3324 MOSKOFF, William. "Pronatalist policies in Romania", *Economic Development and cultural change* 28, apr 80 : 597-614.

3325 MUHUA, Chen. "Birth planning in China", *Family Planning Perspectives* 11, nov-dec 79 : 348-354.

3326 MUKHERJEE, Bishwa Nath. *Prediction of family planning and family size from modernity value orientations of Indian women*. Honolulu, East-West Center, 79, v-50 p.

3327 NARKAVONNAKIT, Tongplaew. "Abortion in rural Thailand: a survey of practitioners", *Studies in Family Planning* 10(8-9), aug-sep 79 : 223-229.

3328 NOR LAILY AZIZ, Datin; TAN, Boon Ann; KUAN, Lin Chee. *The Malaysia national family planning programme: some facts and figures*. Kuala Lumpur, Lembaga Perancang Keluarga Negara, 79, vii-84 p.

3329 OSWALD, Christian. *Familienplanung als volkswirtschaftliches Investitionsproblem aufgezeigt am Beispiel der kolumbianischen Bevölkerungspolitik* (Family planning as a national economic

investment problem from the example of population policy in Colombia). Diessenhofen, Rüegger, 79, 242 p.
3330 PATHAK, Shankar. *Social welfare, health, and family planning in India.* New Delhi, Marwah Publications, 79, 296 p.
3331 PICK DE WEISS, Susan. "Hacia un modelo predictivo de la planificación familiar" (Towards a forecasting model of family planning), *Revista latinoamericana de Psicología* 12, 80 : 119-125.
3332 PONGRÁCZ, Tiborné; MOLNÁR, Edit S. *A gyermekvállalásról és a népesedéspolitikáról alkotott vélemények több gyermeket gondozó anyák körében* (Opinions about the population policy and about having more children. A poll among mothers caring already for two or more children). Budapest, Statisztikai Kiadó, 80, 152 p.
3333 POTTS, Malcolm; BHIWANDIWALA, Pouru; [eds.]. *Birth control, an international assessment.* Baltimore, University Park Press, 79, xi-305 p.
3334 RICE, Charles E. *Beyond abortion: the theory and practice of the secular state.* Chicago, Franciscan Herald Press, 79, vii-159 p.
3335 RIDKER, Ronald G. "The no-birth bonus scheme: the use of savings accounts for family planning in South India", *Population and Development Review* mar 80 : 31-46.
3336 ROBERTS, Alasdair. "Illegitimacy in Catholic Upper Banffshire", *Scottish Journal of Sociology* apr 79 : 213-224. [18-19th centuries. Scotland.]
3337 ROWLEY, John. "Family planning in India: living with frustration", *Populi* 78 : 7-10.
3338 SABATELLO, Eilan F. "Patterns of illegitimacy in Israël", *Jewish Journal of Sociology* 21, jun 79 : 53-65.
3339 SEGUÍ GONZÁLEZ, Luis. *Política de población*(Population policy). Montevideo, Ediciones Jurídicas A. M. Fernández, 79, 167 p. [Uruguay.]
3340 SERVERIN, E. "De l'avortement à l'interruption volontaire de grossesse: l'histoire d'une requalification sociale", *Déviance et Société* mar 80 : 1-17.
3341 SINCLAIR, Daniel B. "The legal basis for the prohibition on abortion in Jewish law", *Israel Law Review* 15, jan 80 : 109-130.
3342 SINGH, Jyoti Shankar; [ed.]. *World population policies.* New York, Praeger Special Studies, 79, xiv-228 p.
3343 SOMPHONG SHEVASUNT; [et al.]. *Fertility and family planning in rural northern Thailand.* Chicago, Community and Family Study Center, University of Chicago, 79, xii-210 p.
3344 SRINIVASAN, K.; REDDY, P. H.; RAJU, K. N. M. "From one generation to the next: changes in fertility, family size preferences, and family planning in an Indian state between 1851 and 1975", *Studies in Family Planning* (10-11), oct-nov 78 : 258-271.
3345 STUBBS, Michael. "Population policy in the Arab countries", *Populi* 79 : 48-53.
3346 SZABADY, Egon. "Problemy naselenija Vengrii na sovremennom ètape" (The Hungarian population problem in the contemporary era), *IN: Naselenie i trudovye resursy v socialističeskih stranah.* Moskva, 79 : 39-53.
3347 THORNTON, Arland; KIM, Joochul. "Perceived impact of financial considerations on childbearing in the United States", *Research in Population Economics* 80 : 351-363.
3348 VAN PRAAG, Philip. *Het bevolkingsvraagstuk in België* (The population problem in Belgium). Antwerpen, Sikkel, Nederlandsche Boekhandel, 79, 149 p.
3349 VAN PRAAG, Philip. "Belgium. Population policies and demographic evolution in retrospect", *Zeitschrift für Bevölkerungswissenschaft* 78 : 365-381.
3350 WEAVER, Jerry L. "The politics of Latin American family-planning policy", *Journal of developing Areas* 12, jul 78 : 415-437.
3351 WHITE, Lynn K. "The correlates of urban illegitimacy in the United States, 1960-1970", *Journal of Marriage and Family* 41, nov 79 : 715-726.

15400. MARRIAGE. FAMILY
MARIAGE. FAMILLE

15410. Sexual behaviour
Comportement sexuel

[See also / voir aussi: 945, 955, 2918, 3721, 6151]

3352 "Changing patterns of sexual behavior", *Proceedings of the annual Symposium of the Eugenic Society* 80 : 214p.
3353 BARRY, Kathleen. *Female sexual slavery.* Englewood Cliffs, NJ, Prentice-Hall, 79, viii-274 p.

3354 BILL, Helga. *Sexualität und Narzissmus: psychoanalyt. Grundlagen d. Erziehung* (Sexuality and narcissism: psychoanalytical bases of education). Frankfurt am Main, Fachbuchhandlung für Psychologie, 79, 218 p.

3355 BORNEMAN, E.; [ed.]. *Sexualität: Materialien zur Sexualforschung.* Weinheim, Basel, Beltz, 79, 247 p.

3356 BRAIN, James Lewton. *The last taboo: sex and the fear of death.* Garden City, NY, Anchor Press, 79, 256 p.

3357 BULLOUGH, Vern L. *Homosexuality, a history.* New York, New American Library, 79, ix-196 p.

3358 BULLOUGH, Vern L.; [ed.]. *The Frontiers of sex research.* Buffalo, NY, Prometheus Books, 79, vi-190 p.

3359 DE LORA, Joann S.; [et al.]. *Understanding human sexuality.* Boston, Houghton Mifflin, 80, xiv-366 p.

3360 DECKER, John F. *Prostitution: regulation and control.* Littleton, CO, F. B. Rothman, 79, xxvi-572 p.

3361 Bibl.XXIX-3456. DELPH, Edward William. *The silent community: public homosexual encounters.* CR: Frederick L. WHITAM, *Contemporary Sociology (Albany)* 9(2), mar 80: 228-229.

3362 FORWARD, Susan. *Betrayal of innocence: incest and its devastation.* Harmondsworth, Eng., New York, Penguin Books, 79, 198 p.

3363 HAGEN, Richard. *The bio-sexual factor.* Garden City, NY, Doubleday, 79, 279 p. CR: Penelope J. GREENE, *Contemporary Sociology (Albany)* 9(6), nov 80: 786-789.

3364 HARRY, Joseph; [ed.]. "Homosexuality", *International Review of modern Sociology* jul-dec 79 : 133-295.

3365 HASS, Aaron. *Teenage sexuality: a survey of teenage sexual behavior.* New York, Macmillan, 79, 203 p.

3366 HYDE, Janet Shibley. *Understanding human sexuality.* New York, McGraw-Hill, 79, 565 p. CR: Joyce McCarl NIELSEN, *Contemporary Sociology (Albany)* 9(6), nov 80: 836-838.

3367 ISHIKAWA, Yoshiyuki. "Incest Taboo-ko" (Some consideration of incest taboo), *Tokushima daigaku gakugei kiyo shakai-kagaku* 29, 80 : 1-18.

3368 JEAY, Madeleine. "Sexuality and family in fifteenth century France: are literacy sources a mask or a mirror?", *Journal of Family History* 79 : 328-345.

3369 JUSTICE, Blair; JUSTICE, Rita. *The broken taboo: sex in the family.* New York, Human Sciences Press, 79, 304 p.

3370 KARASU, Toksoz B.; SOCARIDES, Charles W.; [eds.]. *On sexuality: psychoanalytic observations.* New York, International Universities Press, 79, xv-412 p.

3371 Bibl.XXIX-3463. KATCHADOURIAN, Herant A.; LUNDE, Donald T.; TROTTER, Robert. *Human sexuality: brief edition.* CR: Joyce McCarl NIELSEN, *Contemporary Sociology (Albany)* 9(6), nov 80: 836-838.

3372 KELLY, Gary F. *Sexuality: the human perspective.* Woodbury, NY, Barron's, 80, viii-312 p.

3373 KHAN, M. Masud R. *Alienation in perversions.* New York, International Universities Press, 79, 245 p.

3374 KRAFT, William F. *Sexual dimensions of the celibate life.* Kansas City, KS, Andrews and McMeel, 79, x-221 p.

3375 KURIAN, George. "A comparative perspective in premarital heterosexual attitudes of students", *Social Science* 55, 80 : 29-34. [in traditional and modern societies, led by Scandinavian countries.]

3376 LANTERI-LAURA, Georges. *Lecture des perversions: histoire de leur appropriation médicale.* Paris, New York, Barcelone, Masson, 79, 160 p.

3377 LEVINE, Martin P.; [ed.]. *Gay men: the sociology of male homosexuality.* New York, Harper & Row, 79, vi-346 p. CR: Barry M. DANK, *Contemporary Sociology (Albany)* 9(3), mai 80 : 441-442.

3378 LOPEZ, Enrique Hank. *Eros and ethos: a comparative study of Catholic, Jewish, and Protestant sex behavior.* Englewood Cliffs, NJ, Prentice-Hall, 79, xvi-180 p.

3379 MASTERS, William H.; JOHNSON, Virginia E. *Homosexuality in perspective.* Boston, MA, Little, Brown, 79, xiv-450 p.

3380 MORANDI, Franco. *Crisi e futuro della sessualità* (Crisis and future of sexuality). Assisi, Cittadella editrice, 79, 108 p.

3381 PRUS, Robert C.; IRINI, Styllianoss. *Hookers, rounders, and desk clerks: the social organization of the hotel community.* Toronto, Gage Pub., 80, vi-279 p.

3382 SCHICKEDANZ, Hans-Joachim. *Homosexuelle Prostitution* (Homosexual prostitution). Frankfurt/Main, New York, Campus-Verlag, 79, vi-252 p. [Germany FR.]

3383	SCHULZ, David A. *Human sexuality*. Englewood Cliffs, NJ, Prentice-Hall, 79, 511 p. CR: Joyce McCarl NIELSEN, *Contemporary Sociology (Albany)* 9(6), nov 80: 836-838.
3384	STORMS, Michael D. "Theories of sexual orientation", *Journal of Personality and social Psychology* 38, mai 80 : 783-792.
3385	SYMONS, Donald. *The evolution of human sexuality*. New York, Oxford University Press, 79, vii-358 p. CR: Miriam M. JOHNSON, *Contemporary Sociology (Albany)* 9(6), nov 80 : 791-793.
3386	VICTOR, Jeffrey S. *Human sexuality: a social psychological approach*. Englewood Cliffs, NJ, Prentice-Hall, 80, xv-396 p.
3387	WEINBERG, Martin S.; WILLIAMS, Conlin J. "Sexual embourgeoisment? Social class and sexual activity: 1938-1970", *American sociological Review* 45, feb 80 : 33-48.
3388	WOLF, Deborah Goleman. *The Lesbian community*. Berkeley, University of California Press, 79, 196 p. CR: Meredith GOULD, *Contemporary Sociology (Albany)* 9(3), mai 80 : 445-446.

15420. Marriage. Nuptiality
Mariage. Nuptialité

[See also / voir aussi: 703, 907, 933, 938, 1832, 1936, 2556, 2779, 3020, 3057, 3213, 3281, 3374, 3391, 3395, 3483, 3486, 3516, 3568, 3793, 5110, 5472]

3389	ARROM, Silvia M. "Marriage patterns in Mexico City, 1811", *Journal of Family History* 78 : 376-391.
3390	BAHR, Howard M.; HARVET, Carol D. "Correlates of morale among the newly widowed", *Journal of social Psychology* 110, apr 80 : 219-233.
3391	BIDEAU, Alain. "A demographic and social analysis of widowhood and remarriage: the example of the castellany of Thoissey-en-Dombes, 1670-1840", *Journal of Family History* 80 : 28-43.
3392	BRUNBORG, Helge. *Cohabitation without marriage in Norway = Samliv uten vigsel i Norge*. Oslo, Central Bureau of Statistics, 79, 30 p.
3393	CARLSON, E. D. "Divorce rate fluctuation as a cohort phenomenon", *Population Studies* 33, nov 79 : 523-536.
3394	CASTONGUAY, Charles. "L'exogamie précoce et la prévision des taux de transfert linguistique", *Recherches sociographiques* 20, sep-dec 79 : 403-408.
3395	CAVALLARO, Renato. "Ruolo della donna e beni dotali in un comune del Molise (sec. XVIII-XIX-XX)" (Role of the wife and dowry in a commune of Molise, 18th-19th-20th centuries), *Sociologia (Roma)* 13, jan-apr 79 : 51-86.
3396	CHOJNACKA, Helena. "Polygyny and the rate of population growth", *Population Studies* 34, mar 80 : 91-108.
3397	CORWIN, Patty Arneson. "An exploratory study of stress in marital relationships and life style of missile launch officers", *Journal of social Psychology* 111, aug 80 : 237-242.
3398	CSIZMADIA, Andor; [et al.]. *Études sur l'histoire du droit de mariage de Hongrie*. Pécs, Kiadja a Pécsi Tudomanyegyetem allam-es Jogtudomanyi kara, 79, 48 p.
3399	DEBENHAM, Jerry; SMITH, Gerald. "MATESIM: simulating decision making in marriage formation", *Teaching Sociology* jan 79 : 147-160.
3400	FRINKING, B.; [et al.]. *Een sociaal-demografische analyse van de huwelijkssluiting in Nederland* (A socio-demographic analysis of marriage in the Netherlands). 's-Gravenhage, Staatsuitgeverij, 79, 206 p.
3401	FRISBIE, W. Parker; BEAN, Frank D.; EBERTSTEIN, Isaac W. "Recent changes in marital instability among Mexican Americans: convergence with Black and Anglo trends?", *Social Forces* 58, jun 80 : 1205-1220.
3402	GALLER, Heinz P. "Schulische Bildung und Heiratsverhalten" (School education and marriage behaviour), *Zeitschrift für Bevölkerungswissenschaft* 79 : 199-213.
3403	GIBSON, Colin. "Childlessness and marital instability: a re-examination of the evidence", *Journal of biosocial Science* 12, apr 80 : 121-132.
3404	GLICK, Paul C.; SPANIER, Graham B. "Married and unmarried cohabitation in the USA", *Journal of Marriage and Family* 42, feb 80 : 19-30.
3405	GOTTMAN, John Mordechai. *Marital interaction: experimental investigations*. New York, Academic Press, 79, xvi-315 p.
3406	HALEM, Lynne Carol. *Divorce reform: changing legal and social perspectives*. New York, Free Press, London, Collier Macmillan, 80, xii-340 p.

3407 HENSLIN, James M.; [ed.]. *Marriage and family in a changing society*. New York, Free Press, 80, xv-550 p. [USA.]
3408 HINESTROSA, Fernando. "Comentarios sobre el divorcio en América latina" (Comments on divorce in Latin America), *Revista de la Universidad Externado de Colombia* 20(2-3), dec 79 : 177-185.
3409 HOEKSTRA, C. "Partnerkeuze en geografische afstand een explorerend artikel over huwelijksvelden" (Mate selection and geographical distance between the husband and wife), *Bevolking en Gezin* jul 79 : 167-181.
3410 HUBER, Joan; SPITZE, Glenna. "Considering divorce: an expansion of Becker's theory of marital instability", *American Journal of Sociology* 86, jul 80 : 75-89.
3411 HUGHES, Diane Owen. "From brideprice to dowry", *Journal of Family History* 78 : 262-296.
3412 HUNT, Morton y Bernice. *La experiencia del divorcio* (The experience of divorce). Buenos Aires, Sudamericana, 79, 412 p.
3413 HUTCHISON, Ira W.; HUTCHISON, Katherine R. "The impact of divorce upon clergy career mobility", *Journal of Marriage and Family* 41, nov 79 : 847-855.
3414 KARIM, Mehtab S. *Socioeconomic and cultural aspects of marriage and fertility in urban Pakistan*. Honolulu, Hawaii, East-West Center, 79, v-26 p.
3415 KEITH, Pat M.; GOUDY, Willis J.; POWERS, Edward. "Marital status, family activity, and attitudes toward life and death", *International Journal of the Sociology of the Family* jan-jun 79 : 95-109.
3416 KINGSLEY, Su; MCEWAN, John. "Social classes for women of differing marital status", *Journal of biosocial Science* 10, oct 78 : 353-359.
3417 KIPPER, James K. Jr.; EDWARDS, John N. "Marital decision making: or not to be a doctor's wife", *Social Science* 55, 80 : 35-41.
3418 KIRWEN, Michael C. *African widows: an empirical study of the problems of adapting Western Christian teachings on marriage to the leviratic custom for the care of widows in four rural African societies*. Maryknoll, NY, Orbis Books, 79, viii-253 p.
3419 KOJIMA, Hiroshi. "Kekkon no shakai keizaigaku" (Socio-economic theories of marriage), *Waseda daigaku keizaigaku kenkyu nenpō* 19, 80 : 184-187.
3420 KURIAN, George; [ed.]. *Cross-cultural perspectives of mate-selection and marriage*. Westport, CO, Greenwood Press, 79, xiii-462 p.
3421 LAKATOS, Mária. *A fiatal gyermekes özvegy nők helyzete* (Social condition of young widows with children). Budapest, Statisztikai K., Demographic Research Institute, Central Statistical Office, 79, 55 p.
3422 LEE, Gary R. "Marital structure and economic systems", *Journal of Marriage and Family* 41, nov 79 : 701-713.
3423 LEMAIRE, Jean G. *Le Couple, sa vie, sa mort: la structuration du couple humain*. Paris, Payot, 79, 357 p.
3424 LEVINGER, George Klaus; MOLES, Oliver C.; [eds.]. *Divorce and separation: context, causes, and consequences*. New York, Basic Books, 79, xx-363 p.
3425 LINDGREN, Jarl. "A new phenomenon: cohabitation outside marriage", *Yearbook of Population Research in Finland* 17, 79 : 53-57.
3426 LOBBAN, Richard. "Class, endogamy, and urbanization in the "three towns" of the Sudan", *African Studies Review* 22, dec 79 : 99-114.
3427 MAZEAUD, Henri. "Nouveaux divorces à la française", *Revue des Travaux de l'Académie des Sciences morales et politiques* 131, 78 : 281-293.
3428 MIRA, Joan F. "Organisation sociale et stratégie matrimoniale dans la région de Valence (Espagne)", *Études rurales* 75, jul-sep 79 : 77-96.
3429 MUELLER, Charles W.; POPE, Hallowell. "Divorce and female remarriage mobility: data on marriage matches after divorce for white women", *Social Forces* 58, mar 80 : 726-738.
3430 PAHL, Jan. "Patterns of money management within marriage", *Journal of social Policy* jul 80 : 313-335.
3431 PEACH, Ceri. "Which triple meltingpot? A re-examination of ethnic intermarriage in New Haven", *Ethnic and racial Studies* jan 80 : 1-16.
3432 PROKOPEC, Jiri; [et al.]. "Předpoklady k manželstvi" (Dispositions to marriage), *Demografie* 22, 80 : 31-38.
3433 QUILODRAN, Julieta. "La nupcialidad en las areas rurales de México" (Nuptiality in rural areas of Mexico), *Demografía y Economía* 13, 79 : 263-316.
3434 RADIVOJEVIC, Biljana. "Sklapanje i razvod braka" (Marriage and divorce), *Jugoslovenski Pregled* 23(11-12), nov-dec 79 : 393-398. [Yugoslavia.]

3435   RADIVOJEVIC, Biljana. "Marriage and divorce", *Yugoslav Survey* 21, feb 80 : 61-70.
3436   RAMU, G. N.; [ed.]. *Courtship, marriage and the family in Canada*. Toronto, Macmillan of Canada, 79, 219 p.
3437   RECCHINI DE LATTES, Zulma; WAINERMAN, Catalina H. "Marital status and women's work in Argentina: a cohort analysis", *Genus* 34(3-4), 78 : 40-50.
3438   ROBINSON, Vaughan. "Patterns of South Asian ethnic exogamy and endogamy in Britain", *Ethnic and racial Studies* oct 80 : 427-443.
3439   RÜCKERT, Gerd-Rüdiger; LENGSFELD, Wolfgang; HENKE, Winfried. *Partnerwahl* (Mate selection). Boppard am Rhein, Boldt, 79, 149 p.
3440   SANMARTIN ARCE, Ricardo. "Simulación por computador de un modelo para el análisis de la estrategía matrimonial y hereditaria en una comunidad mediterránea" (Computer simulation of a model for the analysis of marriage and inheritance strategy in a Mediterranean community), *Revista española de Investigaciones sociológicas* 12, oct-dec 80 : 87-116.
3441   SAROUKHANI, Bagher. "Dower (Mahriyeh): a tradition in mate selection in Iran", *International Journal of the Family* jan-jun 79 : 17-25.
3442   SAWADA, Tetsuro. "Gendai no rikon" (On contemporary divorce), *Aichi kyoiku daigaku shakai-kagaku ronshu* 19, 80 : 27-52.
3443   SCHAEFFER, Richard. "Racial endogamy in Great Britain: a cross-national perspective", *Ethnic and racial Studies* apr 80 : 224-235.
3444   SCHECHTMAN GROSSBARD, Amyra. "The economics of polygamy", *Research in Population Economics* 80 : 321-350.
3445   SCHOEN, Robert; COHEN, Lawrence E. "Ethnic endogamy among Mexican American grooms: a reanalysis of generational and occupational effects", *American Journal of Sociology* 86, sep 80 : 359-366.
3446   SCHULTZ, Sandra L. "Marriage preferences and ethnic boundaries: the Greek-American case", *International Journal of the Sociology of the Family* jul-dec 79 : 197-208.
3447   SCHULTZ, T. Paul. "The influence of fertility on labor supply of married women: simultaneous equation estimates", *Research in Labor Economics* 78 : 273-351.
3448   SMITH, Peter, C. "Asian marriage patterns in transition", *Journal of Family History* 80 : 58-97.
3449   SNYDER, Douglas K. "Multidimensional assessment of marital satisfaction", *Journal of Marriage and Family* 41, nov 79 : 813-823.
3450   SPANIER, Graham B.; GLICK, Paul C. "Mate selection differentials between Whites and Blacks in the United States", *Social Forces* 58, mar 80 : 707-725.
3451   SPANIER, Graham B.; LACHMAN, Margie E. "Factors associated with adjustment to marital separation", *Sociological Focus* 13, oct 80 : 369-381.
3452   SZINOVACZ, Maximiliane. "Marital adjustment and satisfaction with marital decisonmaking", *International Journal of the Sociology of the Family* jan-jun 79 : 67-94.
3453   VITEK, Karel. "Vysledky pruzkumu pricin rozvodovosti v CSSR a smery jejiho reseni" (Causes of divorce in Czechoslovakia and means to reduce them), *Populacni Zpravy* 1-2, 78 : 12-18.
3454   YASIN, Bu Ali. "Marriage crisis in Syria", *Jerusalem Quarterly* 15, spr 80 : 121-132.

**15430.   Family
           Famille**

[See also / voir aussi: 104, 647, 709, 725, 840, 872, 1161, 1164, 1434, 1476, 1502, 1515, 1548, 1582, 1621, 1683, 2136, 2473, 2906, 2956, 2961, 2968, 2982, 3010, 3021, 3035, 3057, 3060, 3077, 3103, 3282, 3344, 3368, 3407, 3436, 3465, 3467, 3549, 3568, 3602, 3626, 3793, 3840, 3914, 4080, 4086, 4140, 4427, 4594, 4610, 4753, 4809, 4816, 4833, 4845, 4870, 5048, 5062, 5777, 6157, 6230]

3455   "Familles et pouvoirs", *Informations sociales* 34(4-5), 80 : 3-112.
3456   "Familles en classe ouvrière", *Masses ouvrières* 35(356), nov-dec 79 : 3-100. [France.]
3457   "Changement (Le) des structures familiales et la Sécurité sociale: la situation en Australie", *Revue internationale de la Sécurité sociale* 32, 79 : 3-22.
3458   "Incidence (L') du changement des structures familiales sur la Sécurité sociale: le cas de la République de Corée", *Revue internationale de la Sécurité sociale* 32, 79 : 23-34.
3459   ACOCK, Alan C.; BENGTSON, Vern L. "Socialization and attribution processes: actual versus perceived similarity among parents and youth", *Journal of Marriage and Family* 42, aug 80 : 501-515.

3460   AGRESTI, Barbara Finlay. "Household composition, the family cycle, and economic hardship in a postbellum southern country: Walton County, Florida, 1870-1885", *International Journal of the Sociology of the Family* jul-dec 79 : 245-258.
3461   ALSTEIN, Howard; SIMON, Rita J. "Adoption in America: an examination of traditional and innovative schemes", *Research in social Problems and public Policy* 79 : 93-111.
3462   AOI, Kazuo; SHOJI, Kokichi; [eds.]. *Kazoku to chiiki no shakaigaku* (Sociology of family and community). Tokyo, Tokyo daigaku shuppankai, 80, 251 p.
3463   AZIZ, K. M. A. *Kinship in Bangladesh.* Dacca, International Centre for Diarrhoeal Disease Research, 79, xviii-228 p.
3464   BAHR, Howard M. "Changes in family life in Middletown, 1924-77", *Public Opinion Quarterly* 44, 80 : 35-52.
3465   BAKER, Hugh D. R. *Chinese family and kinship.* New York, Columbia University Press, 79, xii-243 p.
3466   BARBERO AVANZINI, Bianca. "Famiglie a Milano. Una ricerca sociologica sui modelli familiari emergenti" (Family in Milan: a sociological study of emerging family patterns), *Studi di Sociologia* 18, apr-jun 80 : 95-111.
3467   BELSKY, Jay. "The interrelation of parental and spousal behavior during infancy in traditional nuclear families: an exploratory analysis", *Journal of Marriage and Family* 41, nov 79 : 749-755.
3468   BLOCK, James E. "Beyond parenthood: toward a guardianship model for parenting", *Social Policy* 10, mar-apr 80 : 41-46.
3469   BOERDAM, Jaap; MARTINIUS, Warna Oosterbaan. "Family photographs — a sociological approach", *Netherlands' Journal of Sociology* 16, oct 80 : 95-119.
3470   BOWEN, Barbara. "One-parent families", *Ditchley Journal* spr 80 : 15-18.
3471   BURR, Wesley R.; [et al.]. *Contemporary theories about the family.* New York, Free Press, 79. CR: Jerold HEISS, *Contemporary Sociology (Albany)* 9(2), mai 80: 201-204. [2 vols..]
3472   CALISE, Mauro. "Struttura familiari e mobilità del lavoro: alle origini della industrializzazione in Italia" (Family structure and labour mobility: at the origins of industrialization in Italy), *Rassegna italiana di Sociologia* 20, jul-sep 79 : 439-460.
3473   CARROLL, Lucy. "The Muslim family laws, ordianance, 1961: provisions and procedures — a reference paper for current research", *Contributions to Indian Sociology* 13, jan-jun 79 : 117-143.
3474   CHERLIN, Andrew; HORIUCHI, Shiro. "Retrospective reports of family structure: a methodological assessment", *Sociological Methods and Research* mai 80 : 454-469.
3475   COOMBS, Lolagene C. "Underlying family-size preferences and reproductive behavior", *Studies in Family Planning* 10, jan 79 : 25-36.
3476   COWARD, John. "Regional variations in family size in the Republic of Ireland", *Journal of biosocial Science* 12, jan 80 : 1-14.
3477   DAILEY, Timothy B. "Parental power breeds violence against children", *Sociological Focus* 12, oct 79 : 311-322. [in American society.]
3478   DAS, Man Singh; BARDIS, Panos D. *The family in Asia.* London-Boston-Sydney, Allen and Unwin, 79, 431 p. CR: Gisela TROMMSDORFF, *Kölner Zeitschrift für Soziologie und Sozialpsychologie* 32(4), dec 80: 816-818.
3479   DAVIDS, Leo. "Family changes in Canada 1971-1976", *Journal of Marriage and Family* 42, feb 80 : 177-183.
3480   Bibl.XXIX-3642. DAY, Dawn. *The adoption of Black children: counteracting institutional discrimination.* CR: Noel CAZENAVE, *Contemporary Sociology (Albany)* 9(2), mar 80 : 286-287.
3481   DEERE, Carmen Diana. "The differentiation of the peasantry and family structure: a Peruvian case study", *Journal of Family History* 78 : 422-438.
3482   DEL CAMPO, Salustiano. "El ciclo vital de la familia occidental contemporánea" (The life cycle of the contemporary Western family), *Sistema. Revista de Ciencias sociales* 37, 80 : 73-95.
3483   DUBEY, S. M.; [et al.]. *Family, marriage and social change on the Indian fringe.* New Delhi, Cosmo, 80, xi-283 p.
3484   EL SAFTY, Madiha. "Parental attitudes toward the socialization of children in the Egyptian Muslim middle class families", *International Journal of the Sociology of the Family* jul-dec 79 : 177-195.
3485   FINE, Marvin J. *Parents vs. children: making the relationship work.* Englewood Cliffs, NJ, Prentice-Hall, 79, xi-174 p.
3486   FONSECA, Mabel. *Family and marriage in India.* Jaipur, Sachin, 80, xii-291 p.

3487　　FRANKENBERG, Hartwig. *Familienkonflikte und ihre sprachliche Bewältigung* (Family dispute and its verbal settlement). Frankfurt/Main, Haag und Herchen, 79, iii-275 p.
3488　　FURGIUELE, Giovanni. *Libertà e famiglia* (Freedom and family). Milano, A. Giuffrè, 79, viii-321 p. [Italy.]
3489　　GALLAS, Howard B; [ed.]. "Teenage parenting: social determinants and consequences", *Journal of social Issues* 36, 80 : 1-160.
3490　　GEISMAR, Ludwig L.; GEISMAR, Shirley. *Families in an urban mold: policy implications of an Australian-U.S. comparison.* New York, Pergamon Press, 79, xvii-221 p.
3491　　GIAMPAGLIA, Giuseppe; YOUNG, Frank W. "The structural context of family welfare in the regions of Italy", *Social Indicators Research* (1-4), jan 80 : 443-462.
3492　　GOUGH, Kathleen. "Dravidian kinship and modes of production", *Contributions to Indian Sociology* 13, jul-dec 79 : 265-291.
3493　　GREELEY, Andrew; [ed.]. *The Family in crisis or in transition: a sociological and theological perspective.* New York, Seabury Press, 79, viii-112 p.
3494　　HAAVIO-MANNILA, Elina; JALLINOJA, Riitta. *Changes in the life patterns of families in Finland.* Helsinki, 80, 125 p.
3495　　HALE, Nathan Cabot. *Birth of a family: the new role of the father in childbirth.* Garden City, NY, Anchor Press, 79, 195 p.
3496　　HARČEV, A. G. "Aktual'nye problemy dal'nejšego razvitija sovetskoj sim'i" (Topical problems of the Soviet family future development), *IN: Sem'ja v sisteme nravstvennogo vospitanija. Aktual'nye problemy vospitanija podrostkov.* Moskva, 79 : 11-24.
3497　　HEDLUND, Dalva E.; BERKOWITZ, Alan. "The incidence of social-psychological stress in farm families", *International Journal of the Sociology of the Family* jul-dec 79 : 233-243.
3498　　HENKEL, Christoph. *Die Privatisierung der Familie als soziales Problem für die familiale Kommunikation* (Family privatization as a social problem for family communication). Frankfurt am Main, Bern, Las Vegas, Lang, 79, 372 p.
3499　　HESSELER, Michael. "Die Institution der Adoption und die Diskussion einer Sozialisationsperspektive" (Institution of the adoption and discussion of a socialization perspective), *Soziale Welt* 31, 80 : 230-256.
3500　　JANKOVA, Z. A.; [ed.]. *Stabil'nost' sem'i kak social'naja problema* (Family stability as a social problem). Moskva, Institut Sociologičeskie Issledovanij AN SSSR, 78, 193 p.
3501　　JAROSZ, Maria. *Problemy dezorganizacji rodziny* (Problems of family disorganization). Warszawa, Państwowe Wydawn. Naukowe, 79, 223 p.
3502　　KAMIKO, Takeji. "Gendai shakai ni okeru kazoku no kyoikuteki kino" (The educational function of the family in the modern society), *Jido shinri* 35, 80 : 1-15.
3503　　KEEFE, Susan E.; PADILLA, Amado M.; CARLOS, Manuel L. "The Mexican-American extended family as an emotional support system", *Human Organization* 38, 79 : 144-152.
3504　　KENNEDY, Theodore R. *You gotta deal with it: Black family relations in a Southern community.* New York, Oxford University Press, 80, vi-215 p.
3505　　KIM, Kwang Chung; KIM, Hei Chu; HURH, Won Moo. "Division of household tasks in Korean immigrant families in the United States", *International Journal of the Sociology of the Family* jul-dec 79 : 161-175.
3506　　KOYAMA, Takashi; MORIOKA, Kiyomi; KUMAGAI, Fumie; [eds.]. *Family and household in changing Japan.* Tokyo, The Japan Society for the promotion of Sciences, 201 p.
3507　　KRELL, Robert; RABKIN, Leslie. "The effects of sibling death on the surviving child: a family perspective", *Family Process* 18, 79 : 471-477.
3508　　KUMAGAI, Fumie. "Katei-nai boryoku -kazoku no nakano ningen kankei" (Violence in the family: family dynamics), *Shinri to sozo* 16, 80 : 109-121.
3509　　LAAJUS, Sävy. "Perheen kehitykselliset häiriöt" (The developmental disturbances in the family), *Psykologia* 80 : 211-219.
3510　　LEETE, Richard. *Changing patterns of family formation and dissolution in England and Wales 1964-76.* London, Her Majesty's Stationery Office, 79, xiv-130 p.
3511　　LENCLUD, Gérard. "Des feux introuvables. L'organisation familiale dans un village de la Corse traditionnelle", *Études rurales* 76, oct-dec 79 : 7-50.
3512　　Bibl.XXIX-3656. LERNER, Richard M.; SPANIER, Graham B.; [eds.]. *Child influences on marital and family interaction: a life-span perspective.* CR: Laurence D. STEINBERG, *Contemporary Sociology (Albany)* 9(4), jul 80: 545-546.
3513　　LICHTMAN, Allan J.; CHALLINOR, Joan R.; [eds.]. *Kin and communities: families in America.* Washington, Smithsonian Institution Press, 79, 335 p.

3514 LOMNITZ, Larissa; LIZAUR, Marisol Perez. "The history of a Mexican urban family", *Journal of Family History; 30278 : 392-409.*

3515 LUEPTOW, Lloyd B.; MCCLENDON, McKee J.; MCKEON, John W. "Father's occupation and son's personality: findings and questions for the emerging linkage hypothesis", *Sociological Quarterly* 20, 79 : 463-475.

3516 MANCINI, Jay A. "Social indicators of family life satisfaction: a comparison of husbands and wives", *International Journal of the Sociology of the Family* jul-dec 79 : 221-231.

3517 MARSCHAK, Marianne. *Parent-child interaction and youth rebellion.* New York, Gardner Press, 80, xi-293 p. [distributed by Halsted Press.]

3518 MCDONALD, Gerald W. "Determinants of adolescent perceptions of maternal and paternal power in the family", *Journal of Marriage and Family* 41, nov 79 : 757-770.

3519 MEDJUCK, Sheva. "Family and household composition in the nineteenth century: the case of Moncton, New Brunswick 1851 to 1871", *Canadian Journal of Sociology* 79 : 275-286.

3520 MÉTRAL, Marie Odile. *La famille: les illusions de l'unité.* Paris, Éditions ouvrières, 79, 119 p.

3521 MITTERAUER, Michael. "Familienformen und Illegitimität in ländlichen Gebieten Österreichs" (Family forms and illegitimacy in rural areas of Austria), *Archiv für Sozialgeschichte* 19, 79 : 123-188.

3522 MOSSIGE, Svein; PETTERSEN, Rita Bast; BLAKAR, Rolv Mikkel. "Egocentrism and inefficiency in the communication of families containing schizophrenic members", *Family Process* 18, 79 : 404-425.

3523 MULLINS, Elizabeth I. "Perceived parental role satisfaction and daughter's sex-role attitudes and aspirations", *Sociological Focus* 13, oct 80 : 397-412.

3524 NASU, Soichi; KAMIKO, Takeji; [eds.]. *Kazoku byori no shakaigaku* (The sociology of family pathology). Tokyo, Baifukan, 80, 222 p.

3525 NISHIMURA, Hiroko. "Tanshin kazoku no seikatsu jittai chosa" (Research on the one-parent family in Kōchi-city), *Soka daigaku sociologica* 80 : 1-21.

3526 NISHIMURA, Hiroko. "Igirisu no tanshin kazoku mondai to sono taio — Finer Report igo" (One-parent family: problems and counter plans after Finer Report), *Soka daigaku soritsu 10-shunen kinen ronbunshu* 80 : 630-639.

3527 O'NEILL, Onora; RUDDICK, William; [eds.]. *Having children: philosophical and legal reflections on parenthood.* New York, Oxford University Press, 79, 362 p. CR: Lloyd Davis RAINES, *Contemporary Sociology (Albany)* 9(4), jul 80 : 546-547.

3528 PAYNE, Judy. "Talking about children: an examination of accounts about reproduction and family life", *Journal of biosocial Science* 10, oct 78 : 367-374.

3529 PIOTRKOWSKI, Chaya S. *Work and the family system: a naturalistic study of working-class and lower-middle-class families.* New York, Free Press, 79, xiii-337 p.

3530 PIRA DEGIARDE, Elvina. "La concezione dinamica della realtá familiare nei contributi dell'Istituto di Sociologia dell'Università di Louvain la Neuve" (The dynamic conception of the family in contributions of the Sociology Institute of Louvain-la-Neuve University), *Studi di Sociologia* 17, oct-dec 79 : 388-394.

3531 PITROU, Agnès. *Vie familiale et vie professionnelle: relations et interactions: état des recherches sociologiques en France.* Montrouge, ANACT, 79, 32 p.

3532 RAGAN, Pauline K.; [ed.]. *Aging parents.* Los Angeles, Ethel Percy Andrus Gerontology Center, University of Southern California, 79, v-295 p.

3533 RAINWATER, Lee; REIN, Martin. "Tracking family experience in the seventies", *Contemporary Sociology* nov 80 : 779-785. [survey essay.]

3534 RAMOS, Donald. "City and country: the family in Minas Gerais, 1804-1838", *Journal of Family History* 78 : 361-375.

3535 RHONHEIMER, Martin. *Familie und Selbstverwirklichung* (Family and self-actualization). Köln, Verlag Wissenschaft u. Politik, 79, 159 p.

3536 RIBEAUD, Marie Catherine. *La maternité en milieu sous-prolétaire.* Paris, Stock, 79, 275 p.

3537 ROHNER, Ronald. "Worldwide tests of parental acceptance-rejection theory", *Behaviour Science Research* 15, 80 : 88.

3538 ROSSI, Fiorenzo. "Introduzione alla studio della famiglia: Stato e prospettive delle fonti disponibili" (Introduction to the study of family: situation and prospects of available sources), *Genus* 34(3-4), 78 : 122-131.

3539 ROUSSEL, Louis. "La crise de la famille", *Recherche* 111, mai 80 : 544-553.

3540 RUIZ, Sonia G. de; RUBIANO, Aida G. "Influencia de la autoridad familiar sobre la estructuración de los valores de los hijos" (Influence of family authority on the structuration of children's values), *Revista latinoamericana de Psicología* 12, 80 : 513-520.

3541　ŠALAGINOVA, L. I. "Stanovlenie socialističeskih semejnyh otnošenij" (The future of socialist family relations), *IN: Social'nye i političeskie otnošenija v razvitom socialističeskom obščestve.* 79.

3542　ŠALAGINOVA, L. I. "Stanovlenie socialističeskih semejnyh otnošenij" (The future of socialist family relations), *IN: Social'nye i političeskie otnošenija v razvitom socialističeskom obščestve.* 79 : 109-115.

3543　SCHLESINGER, Benjamin. "One-parent families: knowns and unknowns", *Social Science* 55, 80 : 25-28.

3544　SCHWARZ, Karl. "Einkommen und Kinderzahl"(Income and number of children), *Zeitschrift für Bevölkerungswissenschaft* 79 : 299-315.

3545　SEKI, Takatoshi. "Toshi kazoku no shinzoku kankei ni kansuru ichi-kōsatsu" (A study of kinship in urban families), *Gendai shakaigaku* 80 : 3-37.

3546　ŠEŠČUKOVA, G. V. "Socialističeskaja sem'ja kak sistema otnošenij" (Socialist family as a relations system), *IN: Voprosy naučnogo kommunizma.* 79 : 82-91.

3547　ŠEŠUKOVA, G. V. "Social'naja rol' semejnogo vospitanija" (Social role of the family education), *Kommunističeskoe Vospitanie* 79 : 98-104.

3548　SHIMIZU, Yoshifumi. "Nihon no shinzoku soshiki hendo ni kansuru ichi-kōsatsu -Nagano-ken Saku-shi Tokiwa no baai" (A study on the change of kinship organization in Japanese rural society), *Baika tanki daigaku kenkyū kiyō* 29, 80 : 113-154.

3549　Bibl.XXIX-3588. SHIMKIN, Demitri B.; SHIMKIN, Edith M.; FRATE, Dennis A.; [eds.]. *The extended family in black societies.* CR: Aubrey Wendell BONNETT, *Contemporary Sociology (Albany)* 9(2), mar 80: 254.

3550　SINGH, Hira. "Kin, caste and Kisan movements in Marwar: some questions to the conventional sociology of kin and caste", *Journal of Peasant Studies* oct 79 : 101-118.

3551　SLUZKI, Carlos E. "Migration and family conflict", *Family Process* 18, dec 79 : 379-390.

3552　SMITH, Daniel Scott. "Life course, norms and the family system of older Americans in 1900", *Journal of Family History* 79 : 285-298.

3553　SMITH, James P.; WARD, Michael. "Asset accumulation and family size", *Demography* 17, aug 80 : 243-260.

3554　SMITH, Raymond T. "The family and the modern world system: some observations from the Caribbean", *Journal of Family History* 78 : 337-360.

3555　SMITH, Thomas Ewin. "Parental social power. Race and sex differences and similarities", *Youth and Society* 11, dec 79 : 215-236.

3556　SODEI, Takako; FUJISAKI, Hiroko. "Gendai no kazoku mondai" (Contemporary family problems), *Kikan rōdōho bessatsu* 80 : 58-65.

3557　SPANIER, Graham B. "The life cycle of American families: an expanded analysis", *Journal of Family History* 80 : 98-112.

3558　STACEY, Judith. "Toward a theory of family and revolution: reflections on the Chinese case", *Social Problems* 26, jun 79 : 499-508.

3559　STEVENS, Gillian; BOYD, Monica. "The importance of mother: labor force participation and intergenerational mobility of women", *Social Forces* 59, sep 80 : 186-199.

3560　TAKAHASHI, Hiroko. "Rōjin fuyō to kazoku"(Family and elderly support), *Shinri to sozo* 16, 80 : 144-159.

3561　TAMURA, Kenji. *Kodomo kara mita oya no joken*(Parents' conditions as children see them). Tokyo, Takahashi shoten, 80, 253 p.

3562　TILLY, Louise A. "Individual lives and family strategies in the French proletariat", *Journal of Family History* 79 : 137-152.

3563　TORRADO, Susana. "Clases sociales, familia y comportamiento demográfico: orientaciones metodológicas" (Social classes, family and demographic behaviour: methodoligical orientations), *Demografía y Economía* 12, 78 : 343-376.

3564　TUFTE, Virginia; MYERHOFF, Barbara; [eds.]. *Changing images of the family.* New Haven, Yale University Press, 79, ix-403 p.

3565　TYRELL, Hartmann. "Altes und neues von der Familie" (Old and new considerations about family), *Soziologische Revue* 80 : 11-21.

3566　VALENTEJ, D. I.; [ed.]. *Sem'ja segodnja* (Family today). Moskva, Statistika, 79, 119 p. [USSR.]

3567　VAN DEN BERGHE, Pierre L. *Human family systems: an evolutionary view.* New York, Elsevier, 79, viii-254 p.

3568　VERDON, Michel. "From the social to the symbolic equation: the progress of idealism in contemporary anthropological representations of kinship, marriage, and the family", *Canadian Review of Sociology and Anthropology* 17, nov 80 : 315-329.

3569 VERNIER, Bernard. "La circulation des biens, de la main d'oeuvre et des prénoms à Karpathos: du bon usage des parents et de la parenté", *Actes de la Recherche en Sciences sociales* 31, jan 80 : 63-87.

3570 WAINERMAN, Catalina H. "Family relations in Argentina: diachrony and synchrony", *Journal of Family History* 78 : 410-421.

3571 WEISS, Robert Stuart. *Going it alone: the family life and social situation of the single parent.* New York, Basic Books, 79, xvi-303 p.

3572 WILSON-DAVIS, K. "Ideal family size in the Irish Republic", *Journal of biosocial Science* 12, jan 80 : 15-20.

3573 YUZAWA, Yasuhiko. "Nihon no katei wa hontou ni yande irunoka" (Analyzing trends in Japanese family pathology), *Asahi Journal* 22(21), 80 : 106-112.

15440. Woman's status
Condition de la femme

[See also / voir aussi: 1204, 1305, 2142, 2598, 3256, 3416, 3711, 4791, 4799, 4810, 4820, 4841, 5225]

3574 "Ce que pensent des femmes spécialistes dans de petits pays", *Impact. Science et Société* 30, jan-mar 80 : 3-74.

3575 "Frau und Gesellschaft" (Women and society), *Neue Gesellschaft* 27, feb 80 : 100-140. [Germany FR.]

3576 ACOSTA-BELÉN, Edna; CHRISTENSEN, Elia Hidalgo; [eds.]. *The Puerto Rican woman.* New York, Praeger, 79, xi-169 p.

3577 AHMAD, Zubeida. "Comment améliorer le sort des femmes de la campagne?", *Revue internationale du Travail* 119, jul-aug 80 : 455-469.

3578 AMEKRANE, Malika. *Die Stellung der Frau im zeitgenössischen Islam: dargest. am Beispiel Marokkos* (Woman's status in contemporary Islam, from the example of Morocco). Frankfurt a. M., Bern, Cirencester, UK, Lang, 79, 247 p.

3579 ANDERSEN, Margaret L. "Affluence, contentment and resistance to feminism: the case of the corporate gypsies", *Research in social Problems and public Policy* 79 : 139-160.

3580 Bibl.XXIX-3681. ARDENER, Shirley; [ed.]. *Defining females: the nature of women in society.* CR: Jane E. ROSSER, *British Journal of Sociology* 31(3), sep 80: 445-446. [also CR: Shelley COVERMAN, Contemporary Sociology (Albany) 9(3), mai 80: 435-437.]

3581 BAILLEAU LAJOINIE, Simone. *Conditions de femmes en Afghanistan.* Paris, Editions sociales, 80, 222 p.

3582 BAKER, Mary Anne; [et al.]. *Women today: A multidisciplinary approach to women's studies.* Monterey, CA, Wadsworth, Brooks/Cole, 80, xi-307 p.

3583 BALOG, Miklósné. "A nö helyzetének és szerepének alakulása a családban" (Reinforcement of the woman's status and role in the family), *Demográfia* 22(2-3), 79 : 212-226.

3584 BANSAL, Usha Rani. "Women welfare in independent India", *Indian Journal of social Research* 20, dec 79 : 168-174.

3585 BARDWICK, Judith M. *In transition: how feminism, sexual liberation, and the search for self-fulfillment have altered America.* New York, Holt, Rinehart and Winston, 79, 203 p. CR: Myra Marx FERREE, *Contemporary Sociology (Washington)* 9(3), mai 80: 437-438.

3586 BARRIG, Maruja. *Cinturón de castidad: la mujer de clase media en el Perú* (Chastity belt: the middle class woman in Peru). Lime, Mosca Azul, 79, 210 p.

3587 BELLENZIER, Maria T. "Il neofemminismo italiano: situazione e prospettive" (Italian neo-feminism: situation and prospects), *Aggiornamenti sociali* 31, mar 80 : 181-194.

3588 BOSLOOPER, Thomas David. *The image of woman.* New York, distributed by the Rose of Sharon Press, 80, 1st, 228 p.

3589 BOUCHIER, David. "The deradicalisation of feminism: ideology and utopia in action", *Sociology* 13, nov 79 : 387-402.

3590 BUTLER, Flora Cornelia. "Changes in women's status in women's magazine fiction: differences by social class", *Social Problems* 26, jun 79 : 558-569.

3591 CABANA, Alfredo; JARAMILLO, Luz; SILVA, Renán. *Guía bibliográfica de estudios sobre la mujer y la educación* (Bibliographical directory of studies on women and education). Bogotá, Universidad Pedagógica Nacional, Centro de Investigaciones, 79, 68 p.

3592 EICHLER, Margrit. "Sex equality and political participation of women in Canada. Some survey results", *Revue internationale de sociologie / International Review of Sociology* 15(1-2-3), apr-aug-dec 79 : 49-75.

3593   Bibl.XXIX-3708. EVANS, Sara. *Personal politics*. CR: T. Allen CAINE, *Contemporary Sociology (Albany)* 9(5), sep 80: 710-712.
3594   FERREE, Myra Marx. "Working class feminism: a consideration of the consequences of employment", *Sociological Quarterly* 21, 80 : 173-184.
3595   GAIOTTI DE BIASE, Paola. *Questione femminile e femminismo nella storia della Republica* (Women's problem and feminism in the history of the Republic). Brescia, Morcelliana, 79, 256 p.
3596   GALEY, Margaret E. "Promoting nondiscrimination against women: the UN Commission on the status of women", *International Studies Quarterly* 23, jun 79 : 273-302.
3597   GANAPATHY, T. N. "Women and the changing society", *Indian Journal of social Research* 20, dec 79 : 156-160.
3598   GERNER-ADAMS, Debbie J. "The changing status of Islamic women in the Arab world", *Arab Studies Quarterly* apr 79 : 324-353.
3599   Bibl.XXIX-3711. GLENNON, Lynda M. *Women and dualism*. CR: Athena THEODORE, *Contemporary Sociology (Albany)* 9(1), jan 80: 135-136.
3600   GOLDSTEIN, Leslie Friedman. *The constitutional rights of women: cases in law and social change*. New York: Longman, 79, xiii-414 p.
3601   GONZALEZ, Anabel. *El feminismo en España hoy* (Feminism in Spain today). Bilbao, Zero, Madrid, distribuidor exclusivo, ZYX, 79, 312 p.
3602   Bibl.XXIX-3714. HAMILTON, Roberta. *The liberalism of women: a study of patriarchy and capitalism*. CR: Roslyn L. FELDBERG, *American Journal of Sociology* 85(5), mar 80 : 1250-1252. [also CR: Meredith GOULD, Contemporary Sociology (Albany), 9(1), jan 80 : 126-127.]
3603   HAMMAN, Mona. "Women and industrial work in Egypt: the Chubra El-Kheima case", *Arab Studies Quarterly* wint 80 : 50-69.
3604   HECKERMAN, Carol Landau; [ed.]. *The evolving female: women in psychosocial context*. New York, Human Sciences Press, 80, 368 p.
3605   HEITLINGER, Alena. *Women and state socialism: sex inequality in the Soviet Union and Czechoslovakia*. London, Macmillan, 79, xi-241 p.
3606   HERNE, Florence. "Frauen in den EG-Länder — ein Situationsvergleich" (Women in the EEC countries — a comparison of status), *Blätter für deutsche und internationale Politik* 24(12), dec 79 :ʻ1498-1507.
3607   HERNES, Helga; VOJE, Kirsten. "Women in the corporate channel in Norway: a process of natural exclusion?", *Scandinavian political Studies* 80 : 163-185.
3608   HOKSBERGEN, R. A. C.; MAASSEN, G. H. "Hoever gaat de onderwijsemancipatie van de vrouw?" (How far does the educational emancipation of women go?), *Mens en Maatschappij* 55, 80 : 5-38.
3609   INOUE, Teruko. *Joseigaku to sono shuhen* (Toward a better understanding of women's issues). Tokyo, Keiso shobo, 239 p.
3610   JACOBS, Eva; [et al.]; [eds.]. *Woman and society in eighteenth-century France*. London, Athlone Press, NJ, 79, xviii-285 p. [distributed by Humanities Press, Atlantic Highlands, NJ.]
3611   JAIN, Devaki; [et al.]. "Role of rural women in community life: a case study from India", *Economic Bulletin for Asia and Pacific* 29, dec 78 : 84-126.
3612   JAKSIC, Slobodan. "Socijalni razvoj i položaj žene u svetu" (Social development and women's status in the world), *Socijalizam* 23, 80 : 133-146.
3613   KANDA, Michiko. "Fujin mondai to kyoiku kikai" (Women and educational opportunities), *Kyoikugaku kenkyu* 47, 80 : 1-10.
3614   KAPLAN, Marion A. *The Jewish feminist movement in Germany: the campaigns of the Jüdischer Frauenbund, 1904-1938*. Westport, CO, Greenwood Press, 79, viii-229 p.
3615   KAUR, Amrit. "Women education in Punjab", *Indian Journal of social Research* 20, apr 79 : 36-44.
3616   KHONDE, Ptiukuta. "Le rôle de la femme zaïroise dans le développement rural", *Zaïre-Afrique* 20(142), feb 80 : 73-79.
3617   LAIDLAW, Karen A.; PUGH, M. D.; STOCKWELL, Edward G. "A note on the status of women as a factor in population growth in less developed countries", *Sociological Focus* 13, jan 80 : 67-74.
3618   LEACOCK, E.; [et al.]. *Women in Latin America: an anthology from Latin American perspectives*. Riverside, CA, Latin American Perspectives, 79, 164 p.
3619   LOPEZ GARRIGA, María M. "Estrategías de auto-afirmación en mujeres puertorriqueñas" (Self-affirmation strategies of Puerto Rican women), *Revista de Ciências sociales* 20(3-4), dec 78 : 259-286.

3620	MACCURTAIN, Margaret; Ó CORRÁIN, Donncha; [eds.]. *Women in Irish society: the historical dimension*. Westport, CT, Greenwood Press, 79, 125 p.
3621	MAKHLOUF, Carla. *Changing veils: women and modernization in North Yemen*. London, Croom Helm, 79, 103 p.
3622	MANDLE, Joan D. *Women & social change in America*. Princeton, Princeton Book Co., 79, 228 p.
3623	MARTORELLI, Horacio. *Mujer y sociedad: estudio sobre las diversas situaciones sociales de las mujeres en el medio rural uruguayo* (Woman and society: study on the various social conditions of women in the Uruguayan rural environment). Montevideo, CIEDUR-F.C.U., 79, 84 p.
3624	Bibl.XXIX-3731. MAYEUR, Françoise. *L'éducation des filles en France au XIXe siyecle*. CR: François GRESLE, *Revue française de Sociologie* 21(2), apr-jun 80: 296-298.
3625	MEGURO, Yoriko. *On'na yakuwari — sei-shihai no bunseki* (A feminist analysis of the relations between women and men). Tokyo, Kakiuchi shuppansha, 216 p. [Japan.]
3626	MIES, Maria. *Indian women and patriarchy: conflicts and dilemmas of students and working women*. New Delhi, Concept, 80, 311 p.
3627	MOLYNEUX, Maxime D. "State policy and the position of women in South Yemen", *Peuples méditerranéens/Mediterranean Peoples* 12, jul-sep 80: 33-49.
3628	MOSSUZ-LAVAU, Janine; SINEAU, Mariette. *Les Femmes françaises en 1978, insertion sociale, insertion politique*. Paris, CNRS-CDSH, 80, xxvii-362 p.
3629	MUELLER, Charles W.; PARCEL, Toby L.; PAMPEL, Fred C. "The effect of marital-dyad status inconsistency on women's support for equal rights", *Journal of Marriage and Family* 41, nov 79: 779-791.
3630	Nihon. Rōdōshō. Fujin Shōnenkyoku. *The status of women in Japan*. Tokyo, Women's and Young Workers' Bureau of Labor, 79, 41 p.
3631	PATEL, Rashida. *Women and law in Pakistan*. Karachi, Faiza Publishers, 79, xxxii-194 p.
3632	RICHMOND-ABBOTT, Marie. *The American woman: her past, her present, her future*. New York, Holt, Rinehart and Winston, 79, 276 p. CR: Teresa Donati MARCIANO, *Contemporary Sociology (Albany)* 9(5), sep 80: 704-706.
3633	RIVERA, Annamaria. "Donna e mondo contadino: il caso della Puglia" (Women and rural society: the case of the Apulia), *Critica sociologica* 51-52, 79-80: 89-106.
3634	SABROSKY, Judith A. *From rationality to liberation: the evolution of feminist ideology*. Westport, CT, Greenwood Press, 79, viii-175 p.
3635	SAS, Judit H. *Normák és sztereotípiák a nőkről* (Norms and stereotypes about women). Budapest, Tömegkommunikációs Kutatóközpont, 80, 24 p. [published by the Mass Communication Research Centre.]
3636	SCANZONI, John. "Sex-role influences on married women's status attainments", *Journal of Marriage and Family* 41, nov 79: 793-800.
3637	SCHAPS, David, M. *Economic rights of women in ancient Greece*. Edinburgh, Edinburgh University Press, 79, vi-165 p. CR: S. Todd LOWRY, *Journal of economic Literature* 18(4) dec 80: 1574-1575.
3638	SCHRAMM, Sarah Slavin. *Plow women rather than reapers: an intellectual history of feminism in the United States*. Metuchen, NJ, Scarecrow Press, 79, ix-441 p. CR: Nannerl O. KEOHANE, *American political Science Review* 74(1), mar 80: 177-178.
3639	SEGALEN, Martine. *Mari et femme dans la société paysanne*. Paris, Flammarion, 80, 211 p.
3640	SIGEL, Roberta S.; REYNOLDS, John V. "Generational differences and the women's movement", *Political Science Quarterly* 94, wint 79-80: 635-648. [USA.]
3641	SOFFAN, Linda U. "Le rôle de la femme dans l'économie des Emirats arabes noirs", *Travail et Société* jan 80: 3-19.
3642	SOLNICKOVA, Lenka. "Situation de la femme en République tchécoslovaque", *Demosta* 12, 79: 74-78.
3643	SOTO, Shirlene Ann. *The Mexican woman: a study of her participation in the Revolution, 1910-1940*. Palo Alto, CA, R & E Research Associates, 79, iv-118 p.
3644	TAPPER, Nancy. "Matrons and mistresses: women and boundaries in two Middle Eastern tribal countries", *Archives européenes de Sociologie* 21, 80: 59-79.
3645	WEEKES-VAGLIANI, Winifred; GROSSAT, Bernard. *Women in development at the right time for the right reasons*. Paris, Development Centre of the Organisation for Economic Co-operation and Development, Washington, D.C., 80, 330 p.
3646	WEX, Helga; KOLLENBERG, Udo. *Frau und Industriegesellschaft* (Woman and industrial society). Köln, Deutscher Insituts-Verlag, 79, 254 p.
3647	WOLCHIK, Sharon L. "The status of women in a socialist order: Czechoslovakia, 1948-1978", *Slavic Review* 38, dec 79: 583-602.

15500. ETHNIC GROUP
GROUPE ETHNIQUE

15510. Ethnicity. Tribe
Ethnicité. Tribu

[See also / voir aussi: 681, 683, 697, 697, 775, 1021, 1289, 1335, 1378, 1771, 1782, 1942, 2019, 2096, 2139, 2140, 2349, 2390, 2473, 2687, 2924, 3446, 3450, 3673, 3734, 3737, 3753, 3871, 3983, 4306, 4397, 4498, 5462, 5562, 5638, 5651, 5931]

3648 "Research on and by Chicanos: three perspectives", *Social Problems* 27, dec 79 : 186-219.

3649 ALLARDT, Erik. "Prerequisites and consequences of ethnic mobilization in modern society", *Scandinavian political Studies* 80 : 1-20.

3650 ATA, Abe. "The Lebanese in Melbourne: ethnicity, inter-ethnic activities and attitudes to Australia", *Australian Quarterly* 51, sep 79 : 37-54.

3651 Bibl.XXIX-3761. AZARYA, Victor. *Aristocrats facing change: the Fulbe in Guinea, Nigeria, and Cameroon.* CR: Bernard MAGUBANE, *Contemporary Sociology (Albany)* 9(5), sep 80 : 680-681.

3652 Bibl.XXIX-3764. BASH, Harry H. *Sociology, race and ethnicity: a critique of American ideological intrusions upon sociological theory.* CR: Willaim M. NEWMAN, *Contemporary Sociology* 9(6), nov 80: 829-30.

3653 Bibl.XXIX-3766. BEAN, Frank D.; FIRSBIE, W. Parker; [eds.]. *The demography of racial and ethnic groups.* CR: Robert SCHOEN, *Contemporary Sociology (Albany)* 9(4), jul 80 : 536-537.

3654 BEN RAFAEL, Eliezer. "Réalité ethnique et conflit social: le cas israélien", *Cahiers internationaux de Sociologie* 68, jan-jun 80 : 127-148.

3655 BIDDISS, Michael Denis; [ed.]. *Images of race.* New York, Holmes & Meier, 79, 259 p.

3656 BOULDING, Elise. "Ethnic separatism and world development", *Research in social Movements, Conflicts and Changes* 79 : 259-281.

3657 BROMLEJ, Ju. V. "Issledovanija nacional'nyh otnošenij v SSSR" (Research on national relations in the USSR), *Obscestvennye Nauki (Moskva)* 79 : 202-212.

3658 BRUIJNE, G. A. de. "The Lebanese in Surinam", *Boletín de Estudios latinoamericanos y del Caribe* 26, jun 79 : 15-38.

3659 CAMARILLO, Albert. *Chicanos in a changing society: from Mexican pueblos to American barrios in Santa Barbara and southern California, 1848-1930.* Cambridge, MA, Harvard University Press, 79, xiii-326 p.

3660 CARMACK, Robert M. *Historia social de los quichés* (A social history of the Quichés). Guatemala, C. A., Editorial "José de Pineda Ibarra", 79, 455 p.

3661 CARTER, Thomas P.; SEGURA, Roberto D. *Mexican Americans in school: a decade of change.* New York, College Entrance Examination Board, 79, 436 p. CR: Victor RIOS, *Contemporary Sociology (Albany)* 49(4), jul 80: 538-539.

3662 CEAUȘESCU, Nicolae. *Soluţionarea problemei naţionale în România* (To solve the nationalities' problem in Romania). București, Editura Politică, 79, 141 p.

3663 CHANG, Pav-Min. "Continuity and change: the growth and distribution patterns of Chinese in the United States", *Asian Profile* oct 79 : 419-429.

3664 CHIRIF, Alberto; [comp.]. *Etnicidad y ecología* (Ethnicity and ecology). Lima, Centro de Investigación y Promoción Amazónica, 79, 186 p.

3665 COLBURN, David R.; POZZETTA, George E.; [eds.]. *America and the new ethnicity.* Port Washington, NY, Kennikat Press, 79, 243 p.

3666 DARROCH, A. Gordon. "Another look at ethnicity, stratification and social mobility in Canada", *Canadian Journal of Sociology* 79 : 1-25.

3667 DEVERRE, Christian; REISSNER, Raul. "Les figures de l'Indien-problème. L'évolution de l'indigénisme mexicain", *Cahiers internationaux de Sociologie* 68, jan-jun 80 : 149-169.

3668 DÍAZ-POLANCO, Héctor; [et al.]. *Indigenismo, modernización y marginalidad: una revisión crítica.* México, Centro de Investigación para la Integración Social, J. Pablos, 79, 222 p.

3669 DRYSDALE, Alisdair. "Ethnicity in the Syrian officer corps: a conceptualization", *Civilisations* 29(3-4), dec 79 : 359-374.

3670 ELLEMERS, J. E. "Minorities and policy-making in the Netherlands: South Moluccans and other aliens in comparative perspective", *Netherlands' Journal of Sociology* 15, dec 79 : 97-122.

3671 ELLIOTT, Jean Leonard; [ed.]. *Two nations, many cultures: ethnic groups in Canada.* Scarborough, Ont., Prentice-Hall of Canada, 78, xiii-395 p.

3672	Bibl.XXIX-3787. EPSTEIN, A. L. *Ethos and identity: three studies in ethnicity.* CR: Joane NAGEL, *9(5), sep 80 : 700-701*.
3673	EVANS, Art. "The importance of race among Black sociologists", *Sociological Quarterly* 21, 80 : 23-34.
3674	FARAGO, Uri. "Changes in the ethnic identity of Russian immigrant students in Israël (1973-75)", *Jewish Journal of Sociology* 22, jun 79 : 37-52.
3675	GELFAND, Donald E.; KUTZIK, Alfred J.; [eds.]. *Ethnicity and aging: theory, research and policy.* New York, Springer Pub. Co., 79, xii-372 p.
3676	GOGLIO, S.; GUBERT, R.; PAOLI, A. *Etnie fra declino e risveglio: un'indagine sociologica sulla coscienza etnica nell'area dolomitica del Trentino-Alto Adige* (Ethnicity between decline and revival: a sociological survey on ethnic consciousness in the Dolomitic area of Trentino-Alto Adige). Milano, F. Angeli, 79, 237 p.
3677	GOLDSTEIN, Jay E.; BIENVENUE, Rita M.; [eds.]. *Ethnicity and ethnic relations in Canada: a book of readings.* Toronto, Butterworths, 80, 336 p.
3678	HALL, Raymond L.; [ed.]. *Ethnic autonomy: comparative dynamics, the Americas, Europe, and the developing world.* New York, Pergamon Press, 79, xxxii-458 p.
3679	HARVEY, Denis E. *The gypsies: waggon-time and after.* London, Batsford, 79, 144 p.
3680	HEALY, John Joseph. *Literature and the aborigine in Australia, 1770-1975.* New York, St. Martin's Press, 79, x-305 p.
3681	HELLY, Denise. *Idéologie et ethnicié: les Chinois Macao à Cuba, 1847-1886.* Montréal, Presses de l'Université de Montréal, 79, 345 p.
3682	HRABA, Joseph. *American ethnicity.* Itasca, IL, F. E. Peacock, 79, ix-386 p.
3683	HURH, Won Moo. "Towards a Korean-American ethnicity: some theoretical models", *Ethnic and racial Studies* oct 80 : 444-464.
3684	Instituto de Sociologia Aplicada de Madrid. "El Libro Blanco: Los Gitanos españoles" (The White Book: The Spanish gypsies), *Cuadernos de Ralidades sociales* 16-17, 80 : 329-358.
3685	JAMARD, Jean-Luc. "Les Blancs créoles de la Martinique: minorité ethnique privilégiée et classe dominante?", *Social Science Information* 19, 80 : 167-197.
3686	JUDD, Carol M. "Native labour and social stratification in the Hudson Bay Company's Northern Department 1770-1870", *Canadian Review of Sociology and Anthropology* 17, nov 80 : 305-314. [Indians and mixed bloods.]
3687	KATZENSTEIN, Mary Fainsod. *Ethnicity and equality: the Shiv Sena Party and preferential policies in Bombay.* Ithaca, NY, Cornell University Press, 79, 237 p. CR: Daniel R. GRAVES, *American political Science Review* 74(3), sep 80: 843-844.
3688	KOZLOV, Victor. "The classification of ethnic communities: the present position in the Soviet debate", *Ethnic and racial Studies* apr 80 : 123-139.
3689	LEON-PORTILLA, Miguel. "Etnias indígenas y cultura nacional mestiza" (Indigenous ethnic groups and national mestiza culture), *América indígena* 39, jul-sep 79 : 601-621. [Mexico.]
3690	LEPERVANCHE, Marie De. "From race to ethnicity", *Australian and New Zealand Journal of Sociology* 16, mar 80 : 24-37.
3691	LI, Peter S. "A historical approach to ethnic stratification: the case of the Chinese in Canada, 1858-1930", *Canadian Review of Sociology and Anthropology* 16, aug 79 : 320-332.
3692	LVERSON, Hoyt. "The scars of bondage: Black Americans as subjects in behavioral science research", *Journal of social Psychology* 109, dec 79 : 187-200.
3693	MAYER, Enrique; MASFERRER, Elio. "La población indígena de América en 1978" (The indigenous population of America in 1978), *América indígena* 39, apr-jun 79 : 217-337.
3694	MERRY, Sally Engle. "Racial integration in an urban neighborhood: the social organization of strangers", *Human Organization* 39, spr 80 : 59-69.
3695	MIRANDE, Alfredo. "Deviance and oppression: the application of labeling to racial and ethnic minorities", *International Journal of contemporary Sociology* 15(3-4), jul-oct 78 : 375-396.
3696	MONTERO, Darrel. *Vietnamese Americans: patterns of resettlement and socio-economic adaptation in the United States.* Boulder, CO, Westview Press, 79, xvii-218 p.
3697	MORISSET, Jean. "The demand for ethnic autonomy in the Canadian North West", *Journal of social and political Studies* wint 79 : 345-357.
3698	NACHMIAS, Chava; SADAN, Ezra. "Ethnic environment and modernity: reexamining the role of tradition in development", *Research in social Movements, Conflicts and Changes* 79 : 219-231. [Israel.]

3699 NIELSEN, François. "The Flemish movement in Belgium after World War II: a dynamic analysis", *American sociological Review* 45, feb 80 : 76-94.
3700 OTITE, Onigu. "Ethnicity and class in a plural society: Nigeria", *Research in Race and ethnic Relations* 79 : 87-107.
3701 PERRY, Huey L. "The socioeconomic impact of Black political empowerment in a rural Southern locality", *Rural Sociology* 45, 80 : 207-221. [Greene County, Alabama.]
3702 PHADNIS, Urmila. "Ethnicity and nation-building in South Asia: a case study of Sri Lanka", *India Quarterly* 35, jul-sep 79 : 329-350.
3703 POHORECKY, Zenon. *Guide to Saskatchewan ethnic organizations, 1978-1979.* Saskatoon, Sask., Saskatchewan Culture and Youth, 79, 208 p.
3704 PRICE, John A. *Indians of Canada: cultural dynamics.* Scarborough, Ont., Prentice-Hall of Canada, 79, x-261 p.
3705 RAITZ, Karl B. "Themes in the cultural geography of European ethnic groups in the United States", *Geographical Review* 69, jan 79 : 79-94.
3706 REMY, Jean; VOYÉ, Liliane. "Le mouvement flamand. Dialectique du culturel et de l'économique", *Cahiers internationaux de Sociologie* 66, jan-jun 79 : 29-61.
3707 ROCARD, Marcienne. *Les Fils du soleil: la minorité mexicaine à travers la littérature des États-Unis.* Paris, G.-P. Maisonneuve et Larose, 80, 493 p.
3708 Bibl.XXIX-3833. SCHAEFER, Richard T. *Racial and etchnic groups.* CR: Nijole BENOKRAITIS, *Contemporary Sociology (Albany)* 9(3), mai 80: 432-433.
3709 Bibl.XXIX-3834. SCHERMERHORN, R. A. *Ethnic plurality in India.* CR: Man Singh DAS, *Contemporary Sociology (Albany)* 9(1), jan 80: 120-121.
3710 SCHOONENBOOM, Jan. "Ethnic minorities", *Planning and Development in the Netherlands* XI, 79 : 36-57.
3711 SHODEID, Moshe. "Ethnic identity and the position of women among Arabs in an Israeli town", *Ethnic and racial Studies* apr 80 : 188-206.
3712 SZAFRAN, Robert F.; PETERSON, Robert W.; SCHOENHERR, Richard A. "Ethnicity and status attainment: the case of the Roman Catholic Church", *Sociological Quarterly* 21, 80 : 41-51.
3713 THOMSON, Dale C. "Canadian ethnic pluralism in context", *Plural Societies* 11, spr 80 : 55-75.
3714 TREJO, Arnulfo D.; [ed.]. *The Chicanos: as we see ourselves.* Tucson, University of Arizona Press, 79, 221 p. CR: Edward MURGUÍA, *Contemporary Sociology (Albany)* 9(6), nov 80 : 832.
3715 VYAS, N. N.; MANN, R. S.; [eds.]. *Indian tribes in transition.* Jaipur, Rawat, 80, ix-187 p.
3716 YOUNG, Frank J. "Ethnicity as a determinant of political culture among Taiwan youth", *Asian Profile* dec 79 : 517-526.

15520. **Interethnic relations. Racism**
Relations interethniques. Racisme

[See also / voir aussi: 1214, 1378, 1788, 2452, 2975, 3480, 3677, 3695, 3728, 3761, 3801, 3839, 4226, 5070, 5172, 5911]

3717 ADAM, Heribert; GILIOMEE, Hermann. *Ethnic power mobilized: can South Africa change?.* New Haven, Yale University Press, 79, xii-308 p.
3718 ALDERFER, Clayton P.; [et al.]. "Diagnosing race relations in management", *Journal of applied behavioral Science* 16, apr-jun 80 : 135-166.
3719 ALTON SMITH, D. "Government employment and Black-White relative wages", *Journal of human Resources* 25, wint 80 : 77-86.
3720 BAGNI, Bruce N. "Discrimination in the name of the Lord: a critical evaluation of discrimination by religious organizations", *Columbia Law Review* 79, dec 79 : 1515-1549.
3721 BALLHATCHET, Kenneth. *Race, sex, and class under the Raj: imperial attitudes and policies and their critics, 1793-1905.* New York, St. Martin's Press, 80, viii-199 p.
3722 BARGER, W. K. "Eskimos on trial: adaptation, inter-ethnic relations, and social control in the Canadian North", *Human Organizations* 39, 80 : 242-249.
3723 BARRERA, Mario. *Race and class in the Southwest: a theory of racial inequality.* Notre Dame, University of Notre Dame Press, 79, x-261 p.
3724 BECKER, Henry Jay. "Racial segregation among places of employment", *Social Forces* 58, mar 80 : 761-776.

3725	BELTH, Nathan C. *A promise to keep: a narrative of the American encounter with anti-Semitism.* New York, Times Books, 79, xiv-305 p.
3726	BIERVLIET, H.; [et al.]. "Biologism, racism and eugenics in the anthropology and sociology of the 1933s", *Netherlands' Journal of Sociology* 16, apr 80 : 69-92.
3727	BLALOCK, Hubert M. Jr. *Black-white relations in the 1980s: toward a long-term policy.* New York: Praeger, 79, viii-208 p. [USA.]
3728	BLASI, Anthony J. *Segregationist violence and civil rights movements in Tuscaloosa.* Washington, University Press of America, 80, vi-168 p.
3729	BRERETON, Bridget. *Race relations in colonial Trinidad, 1870-1900.* Cambridge, New York, Cambridge University Press, 79, x-251 p.
3730	CAPLAN, Gerald. *Arab and Jew in Jerusalem: explorations in community mental health.* Cambridge, MA, Harvard University Press, 80, viii-300 p.
3731	CAZIER, Pierre; [et al.]. *De l'antijudaïsme antique à l'antisémitisme contemporain.* Lille, Presses universitaires de Lille, 79, 290 p.
3732	CHASE, Allan. *The legacy of Malthus: the social costs of the new scientific racism.* Urbana, University of Illinois Press, 80, xxix-686 p.
3733	CLARE, John. "Racial discrimination", *Ditchley Journal* spr 80 : 39-44. [UK and USA.]
3734	CUMMINGS, Scott. "White ethnics, racial prejudice, and labor market segmentation", *American Journal of Sociology* 85, jan 80 : 938-950.
3735	DOBKOWSKI, Michael N. *The tarnished dream: the basis of American anti-Semitism.* Westport, CT, Greenwood Press, 79, x-291 p.
3736	DORN, Edwin. *Rules and racial equality.* New Haven-London, Yale University Press, 79, xii-158 p. CR: Robert H. STERN, *American political Science Review* 74(4), dec 80 : 1078-1079.
3737	FARLEY, Reynolds; HATCHETT, Shirley; SCHUMAN, Howard. "A note on changes in Black racial attitudes in Detroit, 1968-1976", *Social Indicators Research* oct 79 : 439-443.
3738	FINKELSTEIN, Michael. "The judicial reception of multiple regression studies in race and sex discrimination cases", *Columbia Law Review* 80, mai 80 : 737-754.
3739	FONTAINE, Pierre-Michel. "Research in the political economy of Afro-Latin América", *Latin American Research Review* 15, 80 : 111-141.
3740	FRANKEL, Philip. "The politics of passes: control and change in South Africa", *Journal of modern African Studies* 17, jun 79 : 199-217.
3741	GALVÃO, Eduardo Enéas. *Encontro de sociedades: indios e brancos no Brasil* (Encounter of societies: Indios and Whites in Brazil). Rio de Janeiro, Paz e Terra, 79, 300 p.
3742	GARRISON, Howard H. "Ethnic rela ions in urban Zambia: the case of intergroup friendship choice", *Sociology and social Research* 64, oct 79 : 70-85.
3743	GOODWIN, Carole. *The Oak Park strategy: community control of racial change.* Chicago, University of Chicago Press, 79, xiii-240 p.
3744	GRABB, Edward G. "Social class, authoritarism and social contact: recent trends", *Sociology and social Research* 64, jan 80 : 208-220. [racial attitudes in the USA.]
3745	GREENE, Penelope J. "The doll technique and racial attitudes", *Pacific sociological Review* 23, oct 80 : 474-490.
3746	HANSON, Richard A.; REYNOLDS, Rebecca. *Child development: concepts, issues, and readings.* St. Paul, West Pub. Co., 80, xii-544 p.
3747	HELLMANN, Ellen; LEVER, Henry; [eds.]. *Conflict and progress: fifty years of race relations in South Africa.* Johannesburg, Macmillan South Africa, 79, x-278 p.
3748	HEUMAN, Gad J. *Between Black and White: race, politics, and the free coloreds in Jamaica, 1792-1865.* Westport, CO, Greenwood Press, 80.
3749	HOLMES, Colin. *Anti-Semitism in British society, 1876-1939.* New York, Holmes & Meier Publishers, 79, viii-328 p.
3750	HUI, Lim Mah. "Ethnic and class relations in Malaysia", *Journal of contemporary Asia* 10(12), 80 : 130-154.
3751	HURH, Won Moo. "Universalistische Ethik und partikularistische Praxis in den Rassenbeziehungen der USA: eine humanistische perspektive" (The universalistic ethic and particularistic practice in US-American race relations: a humanistic perspective), *Sociologus* 30, 80 : 149-168.
3752	JACKMAN, Mary R.; JACKMAN, Robert W. "Racial inequalities in home ownerships", *Social Forces* 58, jun 80 : 1221-1234.
3753	KELLY, William R.; SNYDER, David. "Racial violence and socioeconomic changes among Blacks in the United States", *Social Forces* 58, mar 80 : 739-760.

3754 KILLIAN, Lewis M. "The race relations industry as a sensitizing concept", *Research in social Problems and public Policy* 79 : 113-137.
3755 KIRP, David L. *Doing good by doing little: race and schooling in Britain.* Berkeley, University of California Press, 79, xi-164 p. CR: Elizabeth H. CRIGHTON, *American political Science Review* 74(3), sep 79 : 843-844.
3756 KLOSS, Heinz. "Power sharing versus partition in South Africa", *South Africa International* 10, oct 79 : 49-56.
3757 LAGORY, Mark; MAGNANI, Robert J. "Structural correlates of Black-White occupational differenciation: will US regional differences remain?", *Social Problems* 27, dec 79 : 157-169.
3758 LAURENCE, John. *Race, propaganda and South Africa.* London, Gollancz, 79, 215 p.
3759 LEIGH, Duane E. "Unions and nonwage racial discrimination", *Industrial and Labor Relations Review* 32, jul 79 : 439-450.
3760 LEVER, Henry. "Education and ethnic attitudes in South Africa", *Sociology and social Research* 64, oct 79 : 53-69.
3761 LEVINE, Stephen; SPOONLEY, Paul. "New Zealand attitudes on apartheid", *Australian and New Zealand Journal of Sociology* 15, nov 79 : 67-68.
3762 LONGSHORE, Douglas. "Color connotations and racial attitudes", *Journal of Black Studies* 10, dec 79 : 183-197.
3763 LOW, Alfred D. *Jews in the eyes of the Germans: from the Enlightenment to Imperial Germany.* Philadelphia, Institute for the study of Human Issues, 79, x-509 p.
3764 LUHMAN, Reid; GILMAN, Stuart. *Race and ethnic relations: the social and political experience of minority groups.* Belmont, CA, Wadsworth Pub. Co., 80, xi-337 p.
3765 MAGUBANE, Bernard. *The political economy of race and class in South Africa.* New York, Monthly Review Press, 79, xiii-364 p. CR: Joe R. FEAGIN, *Contemporary Sociology (Albany)* 9(6), nov 80: 823-825.
3766 MCLEMORE, S. Dale. *Racial and ethnic relations in America.* Boston, Allyn and Bacon, 80, xv-379 p.
3767 MENCKE, John G. *Mulattoes and race mixture: American attitudes and images, 1865-1918.* Ann Arbor, MI, UMI Research Press, 79, xiii-267 p.
3768 MUNSHI, Surendra. "Tribal absorption and sanskritisation in Hindu society", *Contributions to Indian Sociology* 13, jul-dec 79 : 293-317.
3769 MYNHARDT, Johan C. "Prejudice among Afrikaans- and English-speaking students", *Journal of social Psychology* 110, feb 80 : 9-18.
3770 NAMIHIRA, Isao. "Tori-nokosareta shudan -konketsuji no identity o kangaeru" (The forgotten people — Identity problems of mixed-blood children), *Aoi umi* 93, 80 : 21-30.
3771 NARAYAN, Rudy. *Black vs. White: discrimination against immigrants.* Delhi, Kunj, 80, 110 p.
3772 PALLEY, Marian Lef; PRESTON, Michael B.; [eds.]. *Race, sex, and policy problems.* Lexington, MA, Lexington Books, 79, xvi-271 p.
3773 PARRILLO, Vincent N. *Strangers to these shores: race and ethnic relations in the United States.* Boston, Houghton Mifflin, 80, xii-496 p.
3774 PAVALKO, Ronald M. "Racism and the new immigration: a reinterpretation of the assimilation of white ethnics in American society", *Sociology and social Research* 65, oct 80 : 56-77.
3775 PETTIGREW, Thomas F.; [ed.]. *The sociology of race relations: reflection and reform.* New York, Free Press, 80, xxxiii-445 p.
3776 POTGIETER, Pieter Jacobus Johannes Stephanus; [comp.]. *Index to literature on race relations in South Africa, 1910-1975.* Boston, MA, G. K. Hall, 79, viii-555 p.
3777 QUANN, Dorothy. *Racial discrimination in housing: a discussion paper on the type of prejudices and the recent incidence of racial discrimination in rental and ownership housing across Canada.* Ottawa, Canadian Council on Social Development, 79, v-62 p.
3778 QUINLEY, Harold E.; GLOCK, Charles Y. *Anti-semitism in America.* New York, Free Press, 79, xviii-237 p.
3779 RADEN, David. "Prejudice and hostile behavior: a laboratory study of an attitude-behavior relationship", *Sociological Focus* 13, apr 80 : 143-153.
3780 RAY, J. J. "Racism and authoritarianism among white South Africans", *Journal of social Psychology* 110, feb 80 : 29-37.
3781 REGENS, James L.; BULLOCK, Charles S. "Congruity of racial attitudes among Black and White students", *Social Science Quarterly* 60, dec 79 : 511-522. [USA].
3782 RUSHING, William A. "Race as a contingency in mental hospitalisation", *Sociology and social Research* 64, jan 80 : 168-182.

3783 SCHLEMMER, Lawrance. "Political and economic pressures, corporate group structures and ethnic ideologies in the modernization of race relations in South Africa", *Plural Societies* sum 77 : 77-97.
3784 SHAFFER, Linda J.; WILSON, R. Mark. "Racial discrimination in occupational choice", *Industrial Relations* 19, 80 : 199-205.
3785 STASIULIS, Daiva K. "Pluralist and Marxist perspectives on racial discrimination in South Africa", *British Journal of Sociology* 31, dec 80 : 463-490.
3786 TAIT, John. "Interner Kolonialismus und ethnisch-soziale Segregation im Sudan. Nigerianisch-Westafrikanische Arbeitsmigranten und das Arbeitsmarktsystem in der Gezira" (Internal colonialism and ethnic and social segragation in Sudan. Nigerian and West African migrant workers and the labour market sytem in Gezira), *Afrika Spectrum* 14, 79 : 361-382.
3787 TAMARIN, George R. "Jewish-Arab relations in Israël following the 1973 war", *Plural Societies* wint 76 : 27-45.
3788 TAMARIN, George R. "Three decades of ethnic coexistence in Israel", *Plural Societies* 11, spr 80 : 3-46.
3789 TAYLOR, Marylee C. "Fraternal deprivation and competitive racism: a second look", *Sociology and social Research* 65, oct 80 : 37-55.
3790 UNNEVER, James D.; FRAZIER, Charles E.; HENRETTA, John C. "Race differences in criminal sentencing", *Sociological Quarterly* 21, 80 : 197-206.
3791 VAN DER BERGHE, Pierre L. "Tourism as ethnic relations: a case study of Cuzco, Peru", *Ethnic and racial Studies* oct 80 : 375-392.
3792 WASSERMAN, Ira M. "A reanalysis of the Wallace movement", *Journal of political and military Sociology* 79 : 243-256.
3793 YORKE, Michael. "Kinship, marriage and ideology among the Raj Gonds: a tribal system in the context of South India", *Contributions to Indian Sociology* 13, jan-jun 79 : 85-116.

15600. MIGRATION
MIGRATION

15610. Migrant. Migration policy
Migrant. Politique migratoire

[See also / voir aussi: 2722, 3551, 3786, 4717, 4828]

3794 "Mouvements de population", *Revue juridique et politique — Indépendance et Coopération* 34, jan-mar 80 : 9-150.
3795 AMSELLE, Jean-Loup. "Migration et société néotraditionnelle: le cas des Bambara du Jitumu (Mali)", *Cahiers d'Études africaines* 18, 78 : 487-502.
3796 BERROCAL, Luciano. "Développement économique et processus migratoire en Espagne", *Studi Emigrazione* 17(58), jun 80 : 233-255.
3797 GOLDSTEIN, Sidney. "Migration and fertility in Thailand, 1960-1970", *Canadian Studies in Population* 78 : 167-180.
3798 HAMMAR, Tomas. "Immigration research in Sweden", *International Migration Review* 14, spr 80 : 93-115.
3799 HERRAN, Carlos A. "Migraciones temporarias y articulación social: el valle de Santa Maria, Catamarca" (Seasonal migrations and social articulation: the Santa Maria Valley, Catamarca), *Desarrollo económico (Buenos Aires)* 19(74), jul-sep 79 : 161-187. [Buenos Aires.]
3800 HOMRA, A. V. *Migracija naselenija: voprosy, teorii, metodiki issledovanija* (Migration of population: questions, theory, methods of research). Kiev, Naukova Dumka, 79, 146 p.
3801 KALIN, Rudolf; BERRY, J. W. "Geographic mobility and ethnic tolerance", *Journal of social Psychology* 112, oct 80 : 129-134.
3802 KUBAT, Daniel; MERHLÄNDER, Ursula; GEHMACHER, Ernst; [eds.]. *The politics of migration policies: the first world in the 1970s*. New York, Center for Migration Studies, 79, xxx-294 p.
3803 LYMAN, Stanford M. "Stewart Culin and the debate over trans-Pacific migration", *Journal for the Theory of social Behaviour* mar 79 : 91-115.
3804 Bibl.XXIX-3915. MCNEILL, William H.; ADAMS, Ruth S.; [eds.]. *Human migration: patterns and policies*. CR: Rosemarie ROGERS, *American political Science Review* 74(3), sep 80 : 881-882. [also CR: Helen I. SAFA, Contemporary Sociology (Albany), 9(2), mar 80 : 236-237.]

3805 MCVEY, Wayne W. Jr. "Migration and the smaller communities", *Canadian Studies in Population* 78 : 13-23.
3806 OGILVY, A. A. "Migration. The influence of economic change", *Futures* 11, oct 79 : 383-394.
3807 Organisation de coopération et de développement économiques. Centre de développement. *Les Migrations en Afrique de l'Ouest: compte-rendu du Séminaire tenu à Ouagadougou, Haute-Volta, du 16 au 19 janvier 1979*. Paris, Centre de développement de l'O.C.D.E., 79, ii-86 p.
3808 PICHE, Victor. "La sociologie des migrations au Québec", *Canadian Studies in Population* 78 : 37-53.
3809 REBORATTI, Carlos E. "Migraciones y frontera agraria: Argentina y Brasil en la cuenca de Alto Paraná-Uruguay" (Migrations and agricultural border — Argentina and Brazil in the basin of the upper Parana-Uruguay), *Desarrollo enconómico (Buenos Aires)* 19(74), jul-sep 79 : 189-209. [Buenos Aires.]
3810 RUSSELL, Lillian M.; RIVES, Norfleet, W. Jr. "Household migration plans: a multivariate probit model", *Sociological Methods and Research* aug 79 : 95-109.
3811 STEARMAN, Allyn MacLean. "Migrantes andinos en el Oriente boliviano: el caso de Santa Cruz" (Andean migrants in the Bolivian East: the case of Santa Cruz), *América indígena* 39, apr-jun 79 : 381-400.

15620. External migration
Migration externe

[See also / voir aussi: 1157, 1436, 1942, 2048, 2768, 3156, 3674, 3683, 3696, 3774, 3814, 3835, 3852, 3871, 4195, 4731, 4798, 5695]

3812 "Une expérience de développement: comment pallier l'exode des compétences", *Développement et Progrès socio-économique* jan-mar 80 : 53-66.
3813 "Immigration: la métamorphose", *Informations sociales* 33(9-10), 79 : 2-138. [[France].]
3814 "Caribbean migration to New York", *International Migration Review* 13, 79 : 204-332.
3815 "International migration in Latin America", *International Migration Review* 13, 79 : 407-526.
3816 "Brain drain", *Issue. A quarterly Journal of Opinion* wint 79 : 3-59.
3817 "Quatrième séminaire sur l'adaptation et l'intégration des immigrants permanents", *Migrations internationales* 17(1-2), 79 : 1-259.
3818 "Demain, les immigrés", *Revue nouvelle* 36, sep 80 : 135-262. [Belgique.]
3819 ALOUNE, Youssef. *L'Emigration maghrébine en France*. Tunis, Cérès Productions, 79, 182 p.
3820 ALPALHAO, Joao Antonio; PEREIRA DA ROSA, Victor M. "L'émigration portugaise: réflexion sur ses causes et conséquences", *Migrations internationales* 17(3-4), 79 : 290-296.
3821 ANWAR, Muhammad. *The myth of return: Pakistanis in Britain*. London, Heinemann, 79, x-278 p.
3822 AVERY, Donald. *"Dangerous foreigners": European immigrant workers and labour radicalism in Canada, 1896-1932*. Toronto, McClelland and Stewart, 79, 204 p.
3823 BAROU, Jacques. "Immigration familialc et division de l'espace urbain: le cas des communautés turques et maghrébines dans une petite ville industrielle du Sud-Est de la France", *Civilisations* 30(1-2), jun 80 : 83-95.
3824 BASRAN, G. S. "Canadian immigration policy: the case of non-white immigrants", *Indian Journal of social Research* 20, aug 79 : 127-139.
3825 BERMAN, Gerald S. "Why North Americans migrate to Israel", *Jewish Journal of Sociology* 21, dec 79 : 135-144.
3826 BERNSTEIN, Deborah. "Immigrants and society — a critical view of the dominant school of Israeli sociology", *British Journal of Sociology* 31, jun 80 : 246-264.
3827 BIRMAN, Igor. "Jewish emigration from the USSR: some observations", *Soviet Jewish Affairs* 79 : 46-63.
3828 BLEJER, Mario I.; GOLDBERG, Itshak. "Return migration-expectations versus reality: a case study of Western immigrants to Israël", *Research in Population Economics* 80 : 433-449.
3829 CAZORLA PEREZ, José. "Mentalidad 'modernizante' trabajo y cambio en les retornados andaluces" ('Modernizing' mentality, work and change of return immigrants in Andalucia), *Revista española de Investigaciones sociológicas* 11, jul-sep 80 : 29-53.

3830 CHAZALETTE, Andrée. *Le retour au pays des familles de travailleurs immigrés: désirs, départs et conditions de réussite.* Lyon, Groupe de sociologie urbaine, 79, 163 p.

3831 CHISWICK, Barry R. "Immigrants and immigration policy", *Contemporary economic Problems* 78 : 285-325.

3832 CORNELISEN, Ann. *Strangers and pilgrims: the last Italian migration.* New York, Holt, Rinehart, and Winston, 80, 1st, xi-304 p.

3833 Bibl.XXIX-3963. CORWIN, Arthur F.; [ed.]. *Immigrants — and immigrants: perspectives on Mexican labor migration to the United States.* CR: Merle WEINER, *Contemporary Sociology (Albany)* 9(5), sep 80: 722-723.

3834 DUPONT-GONIN, Pierre. "Migrations et développement: des réfugiés Humong en Guyane", *Revue des Études coopératives* 198, 79 : 23-49.

3835 FAKHFAKH, Françoise. "L'émigration à partir de Tunis-Sus et le retour des émigrés dans la région", *Revue tunisienne de Sciences sociales* 15(53), 78 : 101-139.

3836 FISHER, Maxine P. *Indians of New York city: a study of immigrants from India.* New Delhi, Heritage, 80, 165 p.

3837 FOGEL, Walter. "United States immigration policy and unsanctioned migrants", *Industrial and Labor Relations Review* 33, apr 80 : 295-311. [with a comment by Michael J. PIORE: 312-314.]

3838 FRANZINA, Emilio. *Merica! Merica!: emigrazione e colonizzazione nelle lettere dei contadini veneti in America Latina, 1876-1902* (Merica! Merica!: emigration and colonization through the Venetian people's letters in Latin America, 1876-1902). Milano, Feltrinelli economica, 79, ITA p.

3839 Bibl.XXIX-3968. FREEMAN, Gary P. *Immigrant labor and racial conflict in industrial societies: the French and British exprience, 1945-1975.* CR: Donley T. STUDLAR, *American political Science Review* 74(1), mar 80 : 235-236.

3840 GAVAKI, Efie. "The Greek family in Canada: continuity and change and the process of adjustment", *International Journal of the Sociology of the Family* jan-jun 79 : 1-16.

3841 GERKING, Shelby D.; MUTTI, John H. "Costs and benefits of illegal immigration: key issues for government policy", *Social Science Quarterly* 61, jun 80 : 71-85.

3842 GHOSH, B. N. "Some economic aspects of India's brain drain into the USA", *Migrations internationales* 17(3-4), 79 : 280-289.

3843 GITELMAN, Zvi. "Baltic and non Baltic immigrants in Israel: political and social attitudes and behavior", *Studies in comparative Communism* 12, spr 79 : 74-90.

3844 HANDLIN, Oscar. *Boston's immigrants: a study in acculturation.* Cambridge, MA, Belknap Press of Harvard University Press, 79, xvii-382 p.

3845 HEMSAY, Nicolas. "L'immigration dans la péninsule arabique", *Maghreb-Machrek* 85, jul-aug-sep 79 : 55-60.

3846 HOUTART, François; LEMERCINIER, Geneviève. "Réfugiés au Vietnam et minorités chinoises", *Civilisations* 29(3-4), dec 79 : 268-292.

3847 Instituto español de emigración. *Informe sobre la emigración española. Junio 1979* (Report on the Spanish emigration, June 1979). Madrid, Ministerio de Trabajo, 79, 52 p.

3848 KEELY, Charles B. *U.S. immigration: a policy analysis.* New York, Population Council, 79, x-87 p.

3849 KHELLIL, Mohand. *L'Exil kabyle: essai d'analyse du vécu des migrants.* Paris, Editions l'Harmattan, 80, 207 p.

3850 KING, Haitung; LOCKE, Frances B. "Chinese in the United States: a century of occupational transition", *International Migration Review* 14, 80 : 15-42.

3851 KING, Russell; STRACHAN, Alan. "The effects of return migration on a Gozitan village", *Human Organization* 39, 80 : 175-179. [Malta.]

3852 KLINAR, Peter. "Procesi socializacije in etnične identifikacije (druge generacije migrantov)" (Socialization process and ethnic identification: the second generation of migrants), *Teorija in Praksa* 17, mai 80 : 540-557.

3853 KRANE, Ronald E.; [ed.]. *International labor migration in Europe.* New York, Praeger Publishers, 79, xi-250 p. CR: Philip L. MARTIN, *Contemporary Sociology (Albany)* 9(3), mai 80: 404-406.

3854 KÜNNE, Wilfried. *Die Aussenwanderung jugoslawischer Arbeitskräfte* (Labour force emigration in Yugoslavia). Königstein/Ts., Hanstein, 79, xii-269 p.

3855 LAKSHMANA RAO, G. *Brain-drain and foreign students: a study of the attitudes and intentions of foreign students in Australia, the U.S.A., Canada, and France.* New York, St. Martin's Press, 79, xiv-235 p.

3856 LEE, Gloria; WRENCH, John. "'Accident-prone immigrants': an assumption challenged", *Sociology* 14, nov 80 : 551-566. [UK.]

3857   LEZAMA, Pedro de. "Problemas actuales de los emigrantes en Europa" (Present problems of emigrants in Europe), *Razón y Fé* 202(991), aug-sep 80 : 141-159.
3858   MAJAVA, Altti. *Migration from and to Finland 1979*. Helsinki, Ministry of labour, 80, 48 p.
3859   MONTERO, Darrel. "Vietnamese refugees in America: toward a theory of spontaneous international migration", *International Migration Review* 13, 79 : 624-648.
3860   MORELLI, Anne. "L'immigration et les prêtres italiens de Belgique", *Revue de l'Institut de Sociologie* (3-4), 79 : 239-249.
3861   MZABI, Hassouma. "Quelques aspects de l'émigration dans le Sud tunisien: exemple du gouvernorat de Médenine", *Revue tunisienne de Géographie* 79 : 141-152.
3862   Nations Unies. Affaires économiques et sociales (Département). *Tendances et caractéristiques des migrations internationales depuis 1950*. New York, Nations Unies, 80, vii-176 p.
3863   PASSARIS, Constantine E. "Absorptive capacity and Canada's post-war immigration policy", *Migrations internationales* 17(3-4), 79 : 297-303.
3864   PORTES, Alejandro; PARKER, Robert Nash; COBAS, José A. "Assimilation or consciousness: perceptions of US society among recent Latin immigrants to the United States", *Social Forces* 59, sep 80 : 200-224.
3865   REICHERT, Josh; MASSEY, Douglas S. "Patterns of US migration from a Mexican sending community: a comparison of legal and illegal migrants", *International Migration Review* 13, 79 : 599-623.
3866   Bibl.XXIX-3976. REX, John; TOMLINSON, Sally. *Colonial immigrants in a British city: a class analysis*. CR: Pierre L. VAN DEN BERGHE, *Contemporary Sociology (Albany)* 9(5), sep 80, 662-665.
3867   RICHMOND, Anthony H.; KALBACH, Warren E.; VERMA, Ravi. *Factors in the adjustment of immigrants and their descendants*. Ottawa, Statistics Canada, 80, 481 p.
3868   SAYAD, Abdelmalek. "Immigration et conventions internationales", *Peuples méditerranéens/Mediterranean Peoples* oct-dec 79 : 29-49.
3869   SBATELLO, Eitan. "Patterns of occupational mobility among new immigrants to Israel", *Migrations internationales* 17(3-4), 79 : 267-279.
3870   SCOTT, Franklin Daniel. *Trans-Atlantica: essays on Scandinavian migration and culture*. New York, Arno Press, 79, 208 p.
3871   SCOURBY, Alice. "Three generations of Greek Americans: a study in ethnicity", *International Migration Review* 14, 80 : 43-52.
3872   SHOKEID, Moshe. "Reconciling with bureaucracy: Middle Eastern immigrants' moshav in transition", *Economic Development and cultural Change* 29, oct 80 : 187-205.
3873   SMITH, M. Estelle. "The Portuguese female immigrant: the 'marginal man'", *International Migration Review* 14, 80 : 77-92.
3874   STOKVIS, P. R. D. "Het Nederlandse emigratiepatroon van de jaren 1840 in Europees perspectief" (The Dutch emigration pattern around 1840 in European perspective), *Sociologische Gids* 27, jan-feb 80 : 9-33.
3875   TERMOTE, Marc. "Une mesure de l'impact économique de l'immigration internationale: le cas du Québec, 1951-1974", *Canadian Studies in Population* 78 : 55-68.
3876   TOEPFER, Helmuth; SUIÇMEZ, Vural. "Sektorale und regionale Mobilität von Rückwanderern in die Türkei. Ein Beispiel aus der Provinz Trabzon" (Sectoral and regional mobility of return migrants in Turkey. The example of Trebizonde province), *Orient (Opladen)* 20, dec 79 : 92-107.
3877   VALLAT, Colette. "Immigration et sous-prolétariat en Italie", *Méditerranée* 38, 80 : 67-75.
3878   WACHTER, Michael L. "The labour market and illegal immigration: the outlook for the 1980s", *Industrial and Labor Relations Review* 33, apr 80 : 342-354.
3879   WARREN, Robert; PECK, Jennifer Marks. "Foreign-born emigration from the United States: 1960 to 1970", *Demography* 17, feb 80 : 71-84.
3880   WILSON, Kenneth L.; PORTES, Alejandro. "Immigrant enclaves: an analysis of the labor market experiences of Cubans in Miami", *American Journal of Sociology* 86, sep 80 : 295-319.
3881   WOODRUM, Eric; RHODES, Colbert; FEAGIN, Joe R. "Japanese American economic behavior: its types, determinants and consequences", *Social Forces* 58, jun 80 : 1235-1254.
3882   ZUBRZYCKI, Jerzy. "Polish emigration to British Commonwealth countries: a demographic survey", *International Migration Review* 13, 79 : 649-672.

15630. Internal migration
Migration interne

[See also / voir aussi: 2040, 3133, 4113, 4264, 4402, 4828]

3883 "Job location and the journey to work", *Socio-economic planning Sciences* 14, 80 : 57-77.
3884 ABASIEKONG, Edet M. "Migrant urban workers and rural property ownership — a case study of migrants in Calabar, Nigeria", *International Review of modern Sociology* jan-jun 79 : 49-59.
3885 BOCK, P. G.; ROTHENBERG, Irene Fraser. *Internal migration policy and new towns: the Mexican experience.* Urbana, University of Illinois Press, 79, 156 p.
3886 BONNAR, Desmond M. "Migration in the South East of England: an analysis of the interrelationship of housing, socio-economic status and labour demand", *Regional Studies* 13, 79 : 345-359.
3887 CEBULA, Richard J. *The determinants of human migration.* Lexington, MA, Lexington Books, 79, vi-147 p.
3888 COUSINEAU, Jean-Michel. *La mobilité interprovinciale de la main-d'oeuvre au Canada: le cas de l'Ontario, de la Nouvelle-Écosse et du Nouveau-Brunswick.* Montréal, Département de science économique, Université de Montréal, 79, 22 p.
3889 CURTAIN, Richard. "The structure of internal migration in Papua-New Guinea", *Pacific Viewpoint* 21, mai 80 : 42-61.
3890 DONGMO, Jean-Louis. "L'attraction migratoire nationale des deux capitales camerounaises: Douala et Yaoundé", *Cahiers d'Outre-Mer* 33(129), jan-mar 80 : 49-64.
3891 DONNEA, François-Xavier de; [et al.]. "Modèles du choix du mode de transport domicile-travail à Bruxelles, Liège et Namur", *Annales de Sciences économiques appliquées* 35, 79 : 49-77.
3892 ELKAN, Walter. "Labor migration from Botswana, Lesotho, and Swaziland", *Economic Development and cultural change* 28, apr 80 : 583-596.
3893 Équipe écologie et anthropologie des sociétés pastorales. *Pastoral production and society = Production pastorale et société: proceedings of the international meeting on nomadic pastoralism, Paris 1-3 Dec. 1976.* Cambridge, Eng., New York, Cambridge University Press, 79, vii-493 p.
3894 ESCALLIER, R. "Espace urbain et flux migratoires: le cas de la métropole économique marocaine: Casablanca", *Méditerranée* 38, 80 : 3-14.
3895 ESSER, Hartmut; [et al.]. *Arbeitsmigration und Integration. Sozialwissenschaftliche Grundlagen* (Labour migration and integration. Social science foundations). Königstein/Ts., Hanstein Verlag, 79, 360 p. CR: Peter MEYER, *Kölner Zeitschrift für Soziologie und Sozialpsychologie* 32(4), dec 80: 828-829.
3896 EZEANYAGU, E. "L'exode rural et le développement régional: cas du Nigeria", *Africa Development* oct-dec 79 : 15-55.
3897 FARGUES, Philippe. *Les Champs migratoires internes en Syrie.* Beyrouth, Centre d'études et de recherches sur le Moyen-Orient contemporain, 79, 74 p.
3898 FRANKE, Michael. "Perzeption von Wanderarbeit bei bäuerlichen Tallensi" (Perception of labour migration among Tellensi peasants), *Sociologus* 30, 80 : 132-148.
3899 FUTTON, Philip N. *The journey to work in the United States, 1975.* Washington, U.S. Dept. of Commerce, Bureau of the Census, 79, iii-29 p. [for sale by the Supt. of Docs., U.S. Govt. Print. Off..]
3900 GECK, Hinrich-Matthias. *Die griechische Arbeitsmigration* (Greek labour migration). Königstein/Ts., Hanstein, 79, xiv-284 p.
3901 GILL, Flora. *Economics and the Black exodus: an analysis of Negro emigration from the Southern United States, 1910-70.* New York, Garland Pub., 79, iii-186 p.
3902 HAY, Michael J. "A structural equations model of migration in Tunisia", *Economic Development and cultural Change* 28, jan 80 : 345-358.
3903 ISAJIW, Wsevolod. "Urban migration and social change in contemporary Soviet Ukraine", *Canadian Slavonic Papers* 22, mar 80 : 58-66.
3904 KAYASTHA, S. L.; MUKHERJI, Shekhar. "Spatial disorganisation and internal migration in India: some strategies for restructuring the space economy and development", *Canadian Studies in Population* 79 : 45-61.
3905 KEELY, Charles B. *Asian worker migration to the Middle East.* New York, Population Council, 80, ix-57 p.
3906 KRISHNAN, P.; ROWE, G. "Internal migration in Bangladesh", *Rural Demography* (1-2), 78 : 1-24.

3907 LAMB, Richard F. "Intra-regional migration patterns in rural United States, 1950-1975", *Canadian Studies in Population* 78 : 131-139.
3908 LEE-YING, Soon. "Migrant-native socioeconomic differences in a major metropolitan area of peninsular Malaysia: its implications on migration policy in a multi-ethnic society", *Journal of developing Areas* 13, oct 78 : 35-48.
3909 LICHTER, Daniel T. "Household migration and the labor market position of married women", *Social Science Research* mar 80 : 83-97. [USA.]
3910 LICHTER, Daniel T.; HEATON, Tim; FUGUITT, Glenn V. "Trends in the selectivity of migration between metropolitan and nonmetropolitan areas: 1955-1975", *Rural Sociology* 44, wint 79 : 645-666. [USA.]
3911 MACRAE, Duncan Jr.; CARLSON, John R. "Collective references as predictors of interstate migration", *Social Indicators Research* mar 80 : 15-32. [USA.]
3912 MAJUMDAR, Prasanta S.; MAJUMBAR, Ila. *Rural migrants in an urban setting; a study of two shanty colonies in the capital city of India*. India, Hindustan Pub. Corp., 78, xvi-176 p.
3913 MARR, W. L.; MCCREADY, D. J.; MILLERD, F. W. "Canadian interprovincial migration and education, 1966-1971", *Canadian Studies in Population* 78 : 1-11.
3914 MURRAY, Colin. "Migrant labour and changing family structure in the rural periphery of Southern Africa", *Journal of Southern African Studies* apr 80 : 139-156.
3915 MWANZA, Jacob M. "Rural-urban migration and urban employment in Zambia", *Developing Economies* 17, jun 79 : 172-181.
3916 NAROFF, Joël L.; OSTRO, Bard David. "The impact of decentralization on the journey to work and pollution", *Economic Geography* 56, jan 80 : 63-72.
3917 O'CONNOR, Kervin; MAHER, C. A. "Change in the spatial structure of a metropolitan region: work-residence relationships in Melbourne, 1961-1971", *Regional Studies* 13, 79 : 361-380.
3918 PACCOU, Yves. *Le recensement des nomades mauritaniens*. Paris, Groupe de démographie africaine, 79, 71 p.
3919 PEEK, Peter; STANDING, Guy. "L'exode rural et les politiques gouvernementales dans les pays à faible revenu", *Revue international du Travail* 118, nov-dec 79 : 793-810.
3920 PITIÉ, Jean. *L'exode rural*. Paris, Presses universitaires de France, 79, 128 p. CR: François GRESLE, *Revue française de Sociologie* 21(2), apr-jun 80: 316-317.
3921 PLAUT, Thomas R. *Net migration into Texas and its regions: Trends and patterns*. Austin, Bureau of Business Research, University of Texas, 79, 54 p.
3922 PREMI, Mahendra K. *Urban outmigration*. New Delhi, Sterlin, 80, xvi-184 p.
3923 PRYOR, Robin J.; [ed.]. *Migration and development in South-East Asia: a demographic perspective*. Kuala Lumpur, New York, Oxford University Press, 79, xxi-354 p.
3924 ROWLAND, D. T. "Evaluating the functions of internal migration in settlement systems", *Canadian Studies in Population* 78 : 99-111.
3925 SHAW, R. Paul. "Migrations et construction de logements. Une stratégie pour réorienter les mouvements vers les villes", *Revue internationale du Travail* 119, jul-aug 80 : 501-516.
3926 SHULMAN, Norman; DRASS, Robert E. "Motives and modes of internal migration: relocation in a Canadian City", *Canadian Review of Sociology and Anthropology* 16, aug 79 : 333-342.
3927 STARK, Oded. *Technological change and rural-to-urban migration of labour: A micro-economic causal relationship in the context of less developed economies*. Liege, Belgium, International Union for the Scientific Study of Population, 79, xii-85 p. [IUSSP Papers, No. 11.]
3928 SUAREZ, Maria Matilde; TORREALBA, Ricardo. "Las migraciones internas en Venezuela, 1926-1971" (Internal migrations in Venezuela, 1926-1971), *Boletín de Estudios latinoamericanos y del Caribe* 28, jun 80 : 31-57.
3929 SWANSON, Louis E.; LULOFF, A. E.; WARLAND, Rex H. "Factors influencing willingness to move: an examination of nonmetropolitan residents", *Rural Sociology* 44, wint 79 : 719-735.
3930 TÓTH, Árpád. *Bejáró munkások az Ózdi Kohászati Üzemekben* (Commuting workers of the Metallurgical Plants in the town of Ózd). Budapest, SZEKI, 80, 86 p. [publ. by the Research Institute of Hungarian Trade Unions.]
3931 URIBE CASTANEDA, Manuel; CASO RAPHAEL, Agustín. "Procesos migratorios interestatales: el caso de México" (Inter-state migratory processes: the Mexico case), *Demografía y Economía* 13, 79 : 224-233.
3932 VAN GESTEL, P. W. C. "De binnenlandse migratie in demografisch perspektief" (Internal migration from a demographic point of view), *Bevolking en Gezin* jul 79 : 121-144.

3933 VEDRIS, Mladen. "Modern migration movement from Yugoslavia to West European countries", *Yugoslav Survey* 20, mai 79 : 87-102.
3934 WANG, Charlotte Shiang; SEWELL, William H. "Residence, migration, and earnings", *Rural Sociology* 45, 80 : 185-206.
3935 WARD, John O.; SANDERS, John H. "Nutritional determinants and migration in the Brazilian Northeast: a case study of rural and urban Ceara", *Economic Development and cultural Change* 29, oct 80 : 141-163.
3936 WARDWELL, John M.; GILCHRIST, C. Jack. "Employment deconcentration in the nonmetropolitan migration turnaround", *Demography* 17, mai 80 : 145-158.
3937 WHITE, James W.; [et al.]; [eds.]. *The Urban impact of internal migration.* Chapel Hill, Institute for Research in Social Science, University of North Carolina at Chapel Hill, 79, xi-173 p.

16. ENVIRONMENT. COMMUNITY. RURAL. URBAN
ENVIRONNEMENT. COMMUNAUTÉ. RURAL. URBAIN

16100. ECOLOGY. GEOGRAPHY. POPULATION SETTLEMENT
ÉCOLOGIE. GÉOGRAPHIE. HABITAT

16110. Human geography
Géographie humaine

[See also / voir aussi: 437, 564, 593, 649, 650, 1285, 3000, 3109, 3664, 4479]

3938 "Design and environmental analysis", *Cornell Journal of social Relations* 13, wint 78 : 103-192.
3939 BARNEA, Metei; CALCIU, Alexandru. *Ecologie umană sănătatea populației umane în interdependență cu mediul* (Human ecology: health of human population in relation to its environment). București, Editura Medicală, 79, 799 p.
3940 BERNSTEIN, Irwin S.; SMITH EUCLID O.; [eds.]. *Primate ecology and human origins: ecological influences on social organization*. New York, Garland STPM Press, 79, xvii-362 p.
3941 BURNHAM, P. C.; ELLEN, R. F.; [eds.]. *Social and ecological systems*. London, New York, Academic Press, 79, viii-314 p.
3942 CALDO, Costantino. *Geografia umana* (Human geography). Palermo, Palumbo, 79, 354 p.
3943 CHARTER, S. P. R. *Man on earth: a preliminary evaluation of the ecology of man*. Los Angeles, Guild of Tutors Press, 79, xxxii-264 p.
3944 DUNLAP, Riley A.; CATTON, William R. Jr. "Environmental sociology", *Annual Review of Sociology* 79 : 243-273.
3945 ERICKSON, Paul A. *Ecological impact assessment: principles and applications*. New York, Academic Press, 79, xviii-395 p.
3946 ĖSINA, T. A.; KOVALEV, A. M. "Mesto ėkologičeskoj problematiki v teorii naučnogo kommunizma" (Place of ecological problems in the theory of scientific communism), *Vestnik Moskovskogo Universiteta. Teorija naučnogo Kommunizma* 79 : 44-51.
3947 ESPINET, Blai; VILLAR, Rafael. *El medi ambient*. Barcelona, Dopesa, 79, 108 p.
3948 ESTER, P. "Milieubesef in Nederland" (Environmental concern in the Netherlands), *Sociologische Gids* 27, mar-apr 80 : 120-145.
3949 GLAGOW, Manfred. "Umwelt und Gesellschaft — eine Einführung in die politische Ökologie" (Environment and society: an introduction to political ecology), *Soziologische Revue* 80 : 279-288. [review article.]
3950 GOPAL, Brij; BHARDWAJ, N. *Elements of ecology*. New Delhi, Vikas, 79, vi-200 p.
3951 HALFON, Efraim; [ed.]. *Theoretical systems ecology: advances and case studies*. New York, Academic Press, 79, xvi-516 p.
3952 KAMINSKI, Gerhard. *Psicología ambiental* (Environmental psychology). Buenos Aires, Troquel, 79, 352 p.
3953 KISELEV, N. N. *Ob'ekt ėkologii i ego ėvoljucija: filosofsko-metodologičeskij aspekt* (Ecology object and its evolution: the philosophical and methodological aspects). Kiev, Naukova Dumka, 79, 135 p.
3954 KUČERENKO, N. F. "Ėkologičeskie aspekty obraza žizni trudjaščihsja: obzor sovetskih i francuzskih istočnikov" (Ecological aspects of the workers' way of life: a review of Soviet and French sources), *IN: Social'no-ėkologičeskie problemy kapitalističeskogo goroda*. Moskva, 79 : 182-209.
3955 MALMBERG, Torsten. *Human Territoriality*. The Hague, Paris, New York, Mouton, 80, 320 p.
3956 MARCUZZI, Giorgio. *European ecosystems*. The Hague, Boston, W. Junk, 79, x-779 p.
3957 MARKOVIĆ, Mihailo. "Pogled u svetu na odnos čoveka i životne okoline" (Man and natural environment), *Sociologija* 22(1-2), 80 : 27-43.
3958 MARKOVIĆ, Mihailo. "Pogled u svetu na odnos čoveka i životne okoline" (Man and natural environment), *Sociologija* 22(1-2), 80 : 27-43.
3959 MILETI, Dennis S. "Human adjustment to the risk of environmental extremes", *Sociology and social Research* 64, apr 80 : 327-347.
3960 MLINAR, Zdravko. "Ekološke koncepcije, prostornodruštvene promjene i razvoj" (Ecological conceptions, spatio-social changes and development), *Revija za Sociologiju* (1-2), 78 : 75-88.

3961 SACHS, Ignacy. *Stratégies de l'écodéveloppement.* Paris, Editions Economie et humanisme: les Editions ouvrières, 80, 140 p.
3962 SAUTTER, Gilles. "Some thoughts about human ecology", *Social Science Information* 18, 79 : 991-998.
3963 SCHOENFELD, A. Clay; [et al.]. "Constructing a social problem: the press and the environment", *Social Problems* 27, oct 79 : 38-61.
3964 SYRBU, I. F. "Naučnoe poznanie problem vzaimodejstvija obščestva i prirody na sovremennom ètape" (A scientific knowledge of the society and nature interaction problems at the contemporary era), *Izvestija Akademii Nauk moldavskoj SSR. Serija obščestvennyh Nauk* 79 : 36-42.
3965 VAN LIERE, Kent D.; DUNLAP, Riley E. "The social bases of environmental concern: a review of hypotheses, explanations and empirical evidence", *Public Opinion Quarterly* 44, 80 : 181-197.

16120. Nature. Soil. Water
Nature. Sol. Eau

[See also / voir aussi: 2663, 3198, 3218, 5612]

3966 BOWONDER, B. "Environmental management and the Third World", *Science and public Policy* jun 80 : 185-198.
3967 DEL VAL, Alfonso. "El movimiento ecologista y la política ambiental en España" (The ecologist movement and environmental policy in Spain), *Documentación social* 38, 80 : 157-172.
3968 GROH, Dieter; SIEFERLE, Rolf-Peter. "Experience of nature in bourgeois society and economic theory; outlines of an interdisciplinary research project", *Social Research* 47, 80 : 557-581.
3969 LOWE, George D.; PINHEY, Thomas K.; GRIMES, Michael D. "Public support for environmental protection: new evidence from national surveys", *Pacific sociological Review* 23, oct 80 : 423-445.
3970 LOWE, Julian; LEWIS, David. "Comprehensive versus piecemeal approaches to environmental control", *International Journal of social Economics* 80 : 274-285.
3971 SHERROD, Drury R.; MOORE, Bert S.; UNDERWOOD, Bill. "Environmental noise, perceived control and aggression", *Journal of social Psychology* 109, dec 79 : 245-252.

16130. Citizen. Inhabitant
Citoyen. Habitant

[See also / voir aussi: 2985, 3924]

3972 BHOOSHAN, B. S.; [ed.]. *Towards alternative settlement strategies.* New Delhi, Heritage, 80, 404 p.
3973 BOYDEN, Stephen Vickers. *An integrative ecological approach to the study of human settlements.* Paris, Unesco, 79, 87 p.
3974 CHOMBART DE LAUWE, Paul-Henry. "Appropriation de l'espace et changement social", *Cahiers internationaux de Sociologie* 66, jan-jun 79 : 141-150.
3975 CUENYA, Beatriz. *Políticas de asentamientos humanos* (Human settlements policies). Buenos Aires, Sociedad Interamericana de Planificación, 79, 188 p.
3976 DONELSON, Stuart. *Financiamiento para los asentamientos humanos en América Latina* (Financing for human settlements in Latin America). Buenos Aires, Centro de Estudios Urbanos y Regionales, 79, 167 p.
3977 ENYEDI, György; MÉSZÁROS, Júlia; [eds.]. *Development of settlement systems.* Budapest, Akadémiai Kiadó, 80, 264 p.
3978 GOLANY, Gideon. *Arid zone settlement planning: the Israeli experience.* New York, Pergamon Press, 79, xvii-567 p.
3979 JANOWITZ, Morris. "Observations on the sociology of citizenship: obligations and rights", *Social Forces* 59, sep 80 : 1-24.
3980 MACANDREWS, C. "The role and potential use of land settlements in development policies", *Sociologia ruralis* 19(2-3), 79 : 116-134.
3981 MENGHO, Maurice. "L'habitat rural au Congo: reflet du milieu naturel, expression culturelle", *Cahiers d'Outre-Mer* 33(129), jan-mar 80 : 65-86.

3982 MUSEUR, Michel. "La composition et la structure socio-économique des unités résidentielles — amezzagh — des Touareg de l'Ahaggar", *Revue de l'Institut de Sociologie* (3-4), 79 : 251-297.
3983 NEICE, David C. *Ethnicity and Canadian citizenship: a metropolitan study.* Ottawa, Secretary of State, 79, xv-188 p.

16200. COMMUNITY
COMMUNAUTÉ

[See also / voir aussi: 2668, 3805, 4187, 4603, 5360]

3984 AOKI, Shinji. "Community-ron sai-kentō eno ichi-shikaku" (A perspective on reexamination of community theories), *Shakaigaku nenpo* 80 : 63-82.
3985 BILMES, Jack M. "The evolution of decisions in a Thai village: a quasi-experimental study", *Human Organization* 38, 79 : 169-178.
3986 BLAKELY, Edward J.; [ed.]. *Community development research: concepts, issues, and strategies.* New York, Human Sciences Press, 79, 224 p. [USA].
3987 BUTTEL, Frederick H.; MARTINSON, Oscar B.; WILKENING, A. E. "Size of place and community attachment: a reconsideration", *Social Indicators Research* oct 79 : 475-485.
3988 CLINTON, Charles Anthony. *Local success and Federal failure: a study of community development and educational change in the rural South.* Cambridge, MA, Abt Books, 79, xxvii-183 p.
3989 CUNNINGHAM, J. Barton. "Community program assessment: a functional approach", *Social Indicators Research* (1-4), jan 80 : 71-89.
3990 DEWALT, Billie R. "Alternative adaptative strategies in a Mexican ejido: a new perspective on modernization and development", *Human Organization* 38, 79 : 134-143.
3991 DIGGINS, William; WRIGHT, James D.; ROSSI, Peter H. "Local elites and city hall: the case of natural disaster risk mitigation policy", *Social Science Quarterly* 60, sep 79 : 203-217. [USA].
3992 ERICKSEN, Eugene P.; ERICKSEN, Julia A.; HOSTETLER, John A. "The cultivation of the soil as a moral directive: population growth, family ties, and the maintenance of community among the Old Order Amish", *Rural Sociology* 45, spr 80 : 49-68.
3993 GITTEL, Marilyn; [et al.]. *Limits to Citizen Participation: The Decline of Community Organizations.* Beverly Hills, CA, Sage publications, 80, 280 p.
3994 GUTERBOCK, Thomas M. "Community attachment and machine politics: voting patterns in Chicago's wards", *Social Science Quarterly* 60, sep 79 : 185-202.
3995 HOPE, Kempe R. "Social change and rural regional community development in the United States", *Community Development Journal* 15, apr 80 : 110-116.
3996 HUMBLET, Jean E. "Émergence des communautés et des régions en Belgique", *Plural Societies* 10, sum 79 : 37-48.
3997 ISLAMI, Hivzi. "Problemi društvenog razvitka kosovskog sela" (Some social developing problems in the village of SAP of Kosova), *Sociologija* 21, 79 : 397-418.
3998 ISLAMI, Hivzi. "Problemi društvenog razvitka kosovskog sela" (Some social developing problems in the village of SAP of Kosovo), *Sociologija* 21, 79 : 397-418.
3999 KETTL, Donald F. "Can the cities be trusted? The community development experience", *Political Science Quarterly* 94, aut 79 : 437-451. [USA.]
4000 KIKUCHI, Masao; HAYAMI, Yujiro. "Inducements to institutional innovations in an agrarian community", *Economic Development and cultural Change* 29, oct 80 : 21-36.
4001 LADEWIG, Howard; MCCANN, Glenn C. "Community satisfaction: theory and measurement", *Rural Sociology* 45, spr 80 : 110-131.
4002 LIMOUZIN, Pierre. "Les facteurs de dynamisme des communes rurales françaises. Méthode d'analyse et résultats", *Annales de Géographie* 89(495), sep-oct 80 : 549-587.
4003 LOGAN, John R.; SEMYONOV, Moshe. "Growth and succession in suburban communities", *Sociological Quarterly* 21, 80 : 93-105.
4004 MLINAR, Zdravko. "Socialistički razvoj sela: materijalna izgradnja i mijenjanje svijesti" (The socialist development of the village: material development and changes in consciousness), *Sociologija sela* 17(65-66), 79 : 16-32.
4005 MONTERO, Maritza. "La psicología social y el desarrollo de comunidades en América" (Social psychology and community development in America), *Revista latinoamericana de Psicología* 12, 80 : 159-170.

4006 MOXLEY, Robert L. "Marginality-centrality, household differentiation, and generational differences in a communal social network in Peru", *International Journal of contemporary Sociology* 15(3-4), jul-oct 78 : 440-457.
4007 MUÑOZ, Ricardo F.; [et al.]; [eds.]. *Social and psychological research in community settings.* San Francisco, Jossey-Bass, 79, xx-394 p.
4008 OKPALA, Donatus C. I. "Towards a better conceptualization of rural community development: Empirical findings from Nigeria", *Human Organization* 39, 80 : 161-169.
4009 PREMUS, Robert. "Community selection and equilibrium spatial structure of communities", *Growth and Change* 10, jul 79 : 25-36.
4010 SHIRLEY, Ian F. *Planning for community: the mythology of community development and social planning.* Palmerston North, N. Z., Dunmore Press, 79, 173 p.
4011 SUZUKI, Hiroshi; MIURA, Noriko. "Kogyoka chiiki no seikatsu kozo" (Community change and industrialization — A case study of Kanda town), *Tetsugaku nenpo* 39, 80 : 137-158.
4012 ZATEEV, V. I. "K voprosu o ponjatii 'social'naja obščnost'" (On the concept of "social community"), *IN: Problemy social'nogo razvitija obščestva zrelogo socializma.* 78 : 3-12.

16300. RURAL. URBAN
RURAL. URBAIN

16310. Rural sociology
Sociologie rurale

[See also / voir aussi: 173, 177, 484, 889, 1216, 1486, 1575, 1625, 1880, 2133, 2396, 2538, 2538, 2601, 2690, 2696, 2766, 2789, 2850, 2927, 3108, 3138, 3259, 3267, 3268, 3295, 3433, 3481, 3497, 3511, 3548, 3616, 3623, 3633, 3639, 3698, 3898, 3981, 3985, 3998, 4004, 4017, 4027, 4033, 4050, 4096, 4166, 4171, 4239, 4292, 4331, 4370, 4428, 4493, 4615, 4615, 4616, 4619, 5074, 5083, 5472, 5624, 5657, 6190, 6195, 6248]

4013 "Rural development in India", *Administrative Change* (1-2), jul 78-jun 79 : 1-235.
4014 "Peasants, capitalism, and the class struggle in rural Latin America", *Latin American Perspectives* aut 78 : 2-126.
4015 AKAT'EV, Ju. V. "O nekotoryh osobennostjah razvitija social'nyh processov na sele v uslovijah razvitogo socializma (po materialam sociologičeskih issledovanij kolhozov i sovhozov Baškirskoj ASSR)" (On some characteristics of the social processes development in the villages under conditions of developed socialism: from materials of sociological research concerning the Bachkiry ASSR state and collective farms), *IN: Razvitoj socializm: osnovnye čerty i osobennosti.* Saratov, 79 : 61-72.
4016 ALBEGOVA, I. F. "Rol' inženerno-techničeskoj intelligencii sovhozov v social'nom preobrazovanija sela" (Role of the State farms engineers and technical intelligentsia in the village socialist transformation), *IN: Social'nye problemy sovremennogo sela. II..* Jaroslavl', 78 : 110-119.
4017 ANDO, Keiichiro; [ed.]. *Tokai, mura no seikatsushi* (Village life in Tokai district). Nagoya, Chunichi shinbun honsha, 80, 240 p.
4018 ANSARI, A. Wahid. *Changing village in India.* New Delhi, Chetana, 80, xii-351 p.
4019 BAHARUDDIN, Shamsul Amri. "The development of the underdevelopment of the Malaysian peasantry", *Journal of contemporary Asia* 79 : 434-454.
4020 BAN, Sung Hwan; [et al.]. *Rural development.* Cambridge, MA, Council on East Asian Studies, Harvard University, 80, xxv-468 p. [distributed by Harvard University Press.]
4021 BARROS, Afonso de. "Portuguese agrarian reform and economic and social development", *Sociologia ruralis* 20(1-2), 80 : 82-96.
4022 BARROS, Afonso De. "La reforma agraria en Portugal. De las ocupaciones de tierras a la formación de las neuvas unidades de producción" (The agrarian reform in Portugal. From land occupations to the formation of the new production units), *Agricultura y Sociedad* 14, 80 : 49-78.
4023 BEALS, Alan R. *Gopalpur, a south Indian village.* New York, Holt, Rinehart and Winston, 80, x-125 p.
4024 BELL, Rudolph M. *Fate and honor, family and village: demographic and cultural change in rural Italy since 1800.* Chicago, University of Chicago Press, 79, xiii-269 p.
4025 BELLONCLE, Guy. *Le chemin des villages: formation des hommes et développement rural en Afrique.* Paris, l'Harmattan, Agence de coopération culturelle et technique, 79, 286 p.
4026 BERNAL, Antonio-Miguel. *La lucha por la tierra en la crisis del antiguo régimen* (The struggle for land in the crisis of the ancient regime). Madrid, Taurus, 79, 489 p. [Spain.]

4027 BERNIER, Bernard. "The Japanese peasantry and economic growth since the land reform 1946-47", *Bulletin of concerned Asian Scholars* 12, jan-mar 80 : 40-52.
4028 BLANC, Michel; ALLAIRE, Gilles. "Types d'exploitations et couches sociales dans l'agriculture", *Revue géographique des Pyrénées et du Sud-Ouest* 50, apr 79 : 343-369. [France.]
4029 BONDARENKO, A. A. "Kul'turnoe sbliženie goroda i derevni — važnyj faktor povyšenija social'noj aktivnosti sel'skih tružženikov" (Intellectual bringing together of towns and villages is an essential factor of the rural workers' social activity elevation), *Političeskaja Organizacija Obščestva i Upravlenija pri Socializme* 79 : 129-135.
4030 BONNAIN, Rolande. "King Log: might and power in a rural community in the Pyrenees", *Peasant Studies* sum 78 : 155-171. [France.]
4031 BOUET, Guy. *L'Evolution récente de la vie rurale en Limousin.* Paris, H. Champion, 79, 669 p. [France.]
4032 BOUSCHARAIN, Gérard. "L'expérience de développement rural en Tanzanie: les villages ujamaa", *Annuaire des Pays de l'Océan indien* 78 : 159-182.
4033 BOX, Louk. "Urban bias, rural sociology and development strategy", *Sociologia ruralis* 20(1-2), 80 : 116-130.
4034 BRADSHAW, Ted K.; BLAKELY, Edward J. *Rural communities in advanced industrial society: development and developers.* New York, Praeger, 79, xi-188 p.
4035 BRISCOE, John. "Energy use and social structure in a Bangladesh village", *Population and Development Review* dec 79 : 615-641.
4036 BUNDY, Colin. *The rise and fall of the South African peasantry.* Berkeley, University of California Press, 79, 276 p.
4037 BURGAT, François. "Villages socialistes algériens à l'épreuve des réalités", *Maghreb-Machrek* 86, oct-nov-dec 79 : 56-62.
4038 BURKE, Robert V. "Green Revolution technologies and farm class in Mexico", *Economic Development and cultural Change* 28, oct 79 : 135-154.
4039 BUTORINA, E. V. "Social'naja struktura rabotnikov kolhoznogo proizvodstva i osnovnye napravlenija eè razvitija" (Social structure of the collective farmers and essential tendencies of its development), IN: *Social'nye problemy sovremennogo sela. II.* Jaroslavl', 78 : 68-96.
4040 BUTTEL, Frederick H. "Agricultural structure and rural ecology: toward a political economy of rural development", *Sociologia ruralis* 20(1-2), 80 : 44-62.
4041 CANEVET, Corentin. "De la polyculture paysanne à l'intégration: les couches sociales dans l'agriculture", *Norois* 26(104), oct-dec 79 : 507-522.
4042 CASTILLO, Gelia T. *Beyond Manila: Philippine rural problems in perspective.* Ottawa, International Development Research Centre, 79, 420 p.
4043 CEHELSKY, Marta. *Land reform in Brazil: the management of social change.* Boulder, CO, Westview Press, 79, xv-261 p.
4044 CELA CONDE, Camilo José. *Capitalismo y campesinado en la Isla de Mallorca* (Capitalism and peasantry in the island of Majorca). Madrid, Siglo XXI de España Editores, 79, 239 p.
4045 CHAMBOREDON, Jean-Claude. "Les usages urbains de l'espace rural: du moyen de production au lieu de récréation", *Revue française de Sociologie* 21, jan-mar 80 : 97-119. [à propos de MARIE, Michel; VIARD, Jean. La campagne inventée. Paris, 1977, 238p.]
4046 CHAUDHRY, Mahinder D.; [ed.]. *Rural development.* Leiden, E. J. Brill, 79, x-198 p.
4047 CIFRIĆ, Ivan. "Seljaštvo kao socijalna i politička snaga u društvenom razvoju Jugoslavije" (The peasantry — a social and political force in the social development of Yugoslavia), *Sociologija sela* 17(65-66), 79 : 47-60.
4048 CLARK, Gardner. "Modernization without urbanization. On Switzerland as a model of job development outside large urban areas", *Schweizerische Zeitschrift für Soziologie/Revue suisse de Sociologie* mar 80 : 1-42.
4049 CLARK, Samuel. *Social origins of the Irish land war.* Princeton, NJ, Princeton University Press, 79, x-418 p.
4050 CROSS, Malcolm; MARKS, Arnaud; [eds.]. *Peasants, plantations and rural communities in the Caribbean.* Guildford, Eng., Dept. of Sociology of the University of Surrey, 79, xvi-304 p.
4051 CVJETIĆANIN, Vlado; PULJIZ, Vlado. "Faktori promjena u individualnoj poljoprivredi i udruživanje poljoprivrednika" (Factors of change in privately owned agriculture and the association of farmers), *Sociologija sela* 17(65-66), 79 : 73-87.

4052 DAS, Harish Chandra. *Resources and responses in two Orissan villages: the influence of the new state capital, 1950-1970.* Calcutta, Punthi Pustak, 79, xxii-327 p.

4053 DELBOS, Geneviève. "À l'ombre des usines, comme si de rien n'était... industrialisation et maintien d'une communauté paysanne en Lorraine", *Études rurales* 76, oct-dec 79 : 83-96.

4054 Bibl.XXIX-4193. DIXON, Ruth B. *Rural women at work: strategies for development in South Asia.* CR: Linda J. WAITE, *Contemporary Sociology (Albany)* 9(5), sep 80: 681-682.

4055 DOLZER, Hermann. *Die bäuerliche Gesellschaft, zwischen Traditionalität und Modernität?* (Peasant society, between tradition and modernity?). Frankfurt am Main, Bern, Cirencester, U.K., Lang, 79, 246 p. [Peru.]

4056 DORE Y CABRAL, Carlos. "Reforma agraria y luchas sociales en la Republica dominicana, 1966-1978" (Agrarian reform and social struggle in the Dominican Republic, 1966-1978), *Estudios sociales centroamericanos* (25; 26), jan-apr 80; mai-aug 80 : 91-123; 9-36.

4057 DOWLAT, Manijeh; [et al.]. "Les paysans et la révolution iranienne", *Peuples méditerranées/Mediterranean Peoples* 10, jan-mar 80 : 19-42.

4058 DRAIN, Michel. "La réforme agraire portugaise", *Méditerranée* 37, 79 : 41-54.

4059 ELWERT, Georg. "Überleben in Krisen, kapitalistische Entwicklung und traditionelle Solidarität. Zur Ökonomie und Sozialstruktur eines westafrikanischen Bauerndorfes" (Survival in crises, capitalist development, and traditional solidarity. Economy and social structure of a West African peasant village.), *Zeitschrift für Soziologie* oct 80 : 343-365.

4060 FABRE, Annie. "Socialisme et aménagements ruraux en RPS d'Albanie", *Revue de Géographie de Lyon* 55, 80 : 53-68.

4061 FOSTER, George McClelland. *Tzintzuntzan: Mexican peasants in a changing world.* New York, Elsevier-New York, 79, 392 p.

4062 FRANDA, Marcus. *India's rural development: an assessment of alternatives.* Bloomington, Indiana University Press, 80, xi-306 p. CR: Manindra Kumar MOHAPATRA, *American political Science Review* 74(4), dec 80 : 1111-1112.

4063 FRELASTRE, Georges. "Les nouvelles orientations du développement rural de la Côte d'Ivoire", *Mois en Afrique* 15(176-177), aug-sep 80 : 37-80.

4064 FRENCH, J. Lawrence. "Rural community modernization, inequality and local political involvements", *Social Science Quarterly* 60, dec 79 : 401-417.

4065 FREYHOLD, Michaela von. *Ujamaa villages in Tanzania: analysis of a social experiment.* New York, Monthly Review Press, 79, xviii-201 p. CR: Gerhard GROHS, *Kölner Zeitschrift für Soziologie und Sozialpsychologie* 32(4), dec 80: 814-815.

4066 FUHR, Harald. *Agrarreform und Bauernbewegung in Peru* (Agrarian reform and peasant movement in Peru). Frankfurt/Main, New York, Campus-Verlag, 79, xv-190 p.

4067 GALLI, Rosemary. "Rural development as social control: international agencies and class struggle in the Colombian countryside", *Latin American Perspectives* aut 78 : 71-89.

4068 GAVRIKOV, V. P. "Stanovlenie socialističeskogo obraza žizni sovetskogo krest'janstva" (The future of the Soviet peasantry socialist way of life), *IN: Social'no-ėkonomičeskie problemy razvitogo socialističeskogo obščestva.* Kalinin, 79 : 23-32.

4069 GINER, Salvador; SEVILLA-GUZMÁN, Eduardo. "The demise of the peasant: some reflections on ideological inroads into social theory", *Sociologia ruralis* 20(1-2), 80 : 13-27.

4070 GOODALL, John S. *The story of an English village.* New York, Atheneum, 79, 61 p.

4071 GREMLIZA, Dorothee. *Die Agrarreform in Peru von 1969* (The agrarian reform in Peru, 1969). Meisenheim am Glan, Hain, 79, 301 p.

4072 HALLOWELL, Christopher. *People of the bayou: Cajun life in lost America.* New York, Dutton, 79, 141 p.

4073 HANISCH, Rolf; TETZLAFF, Rainer; [eds.]. *Die Überwindung der ländlichen Armut in der Dritten Welt: Probleme u. Perspektiven kleinbäuerl. Entwicklungsstrategien* (The victory of rural poverty in the Third World: problems and prospects of small rural development strategies). Frankfurt am Main, Metzner, 79, vi-339 p.

4074 HANNAN, Damian. *Displacement and development: class, kinship, and social change in Irish rural communities.* Dublin, Economic and Social Research Institute, 79, 231 p.

4075 HANSEN, David O.; SCHNEIDER, Ivo A.; PAULA VITOR, Vicente de. "Rural sociology in Brazil — institutional growth, 1965-1977", *International Review of modern Sociology* jan-jun 79 : 31-48.

4076 HARGOPAL, G. *Administrative leadership in rural development in India.* New Delhi, Light and Life, 80, xi-231 p.

4077   HARTLEY, Dorothy. *Lost country life.* New York, Pantheon Books, 79, ix-374 p.
4078   HARVEY, Charles; [et al.]. *Rural employment and administration in the Third World: development methods and alternative strategies.* Farnborough, Eng., Saxon House, 79, xi-111 p.
4079   HAUBERT, Maxime. "Dynamismes paysans, structures sociales et développement rural", *Communautés* 51, jan-mar 80 : 51-66.
4080   HEREDIA, Beatriz Maria Alásia de. *A morada da vida: trabalho familiar de pequenos produtories do Nordeste do Brasil* (The home: family work of small producers in the Northeast of Brazil). Rio de Janeiro, Paz e Terra, 79, 164 p.
4081   HOBBS, Daryl J. "Rural development: intentions and consequences", *Rural Sociology* 45, spr 80 : 7-25.
4082   JANVRY, Alain de; GROUND, Lynn. "Types and consequences of land reform in Latin America", *Latin American Perspectives* aut 78 : 90-112.
4083   JHA, B. N. *Problems of land utilization: a case study of Kosi region.* New Delhi, Classical, 80, vi-251 p.
4084   KAMBLE, N. D. *Poverty within poverty: a study of the weaker sections in a Deccan village.* New Delhi, Sterling, 70, 134 p.
4085   KARDELJ, Edvard. "Povezivanje samostalnog ličnog rada zemljoradnika u sistem samoupravnog udruženog rada" (Establishing links between the independent personal labour farmers and the system of self-managed associated labour), *Sociologija sela* 17(65-66), 79 : 3-15. [Yugoslavia.]
4086   KARNOOUH, Claude. "Penser 'maison', penser 'famille'. Résidence domestique et parenté dans les sociétés rurales de l'est de la France", *Études rurales* 75, jul-sep 79 : 35-75.
4087   KASSAB, Ahmed. *L'évolution de la vie rurale dans les régions de la Moyenne Medjerda et de Béja-Mateur.* Tunis, Université de Tunis, 79, 675 p.
4088   KAWAMOTO, Akira. "Soma chiikikaihatsu to noson -Mura shigotoron kara mite-" (The developing of the Sōma district and its effects upon the village structure), *Meijigakuin ronsō* 301(55), 80 : 29-67.
4089   KAWAMOTO, Akira. "Okayama-ken nōson no shakai kōzō to sono henyō" (The social structure and its change of rural society in Okayama Prefecture), *Meijigakuin ronsō* 307(56), 80 : 1-41.
4090   KAWASAKI, Esho; FUNAHASHI, Kazuo. "Shiga ni okeru shukyo to sonraku kozo -Kotosan-son Ojigahata no jirei" (Religion and social structure in the village: A case study of Ojigahata, Shiga), *Bukkyo bunka kenkyujo kiyo* 19, 80 : 57-81.
4091   KAYSER, Bernard. "Le changement social dans les campagnes françaises", *Economie rurale* 135, jan-feb 80 : 5-11.
4092   KAYSER, Bernard. *Petites villes et pays dans l'aménagement rural.* Paris, Éditions du C.N.R.S., 79, 149 p.
4093   KAYSER, Bernard; SCHEKTMAN-LABRY, Geneviève. "Formation d'une nouvelle paysannerie moyenne; enquêtes en Haut-Armagnac", *Revue géographique des Pyrénées et du Sud-Ouest* 50, apr 79 : 293-314. [France.]
4094   KEIM, Willard D. *The Korean peasant at the crossroads: a study of attitudes.* Bellingham, Western Washington University, 79, vii-172 p.
4095   KERVINIO, Monique; CAVESTRO, William. "Le développement socialiste et les transformations sociales dans le village en Hongrie", *Recherches internationales à la Lumière du Marxisme* 20(90), 77 : 70-91.
4096   KHADER, B. "Paysannerie et réforme agraire", *Recherches sociologiques* 11, 80 : 59-84.
4097   KLEIN, Martin A.; [ed.]. *Peasants in Africa: Historical and Comparative Perspectives.* London, Beverly Hills, Sage Publications, 80, 320 p.
4098   KOHNERT, Dirk. "Rural class differentiation in Nigeria — Theory and practice. A quantitative approach in the case of Nupeland", *Afrika Spectrum* 14, 79 : 295-315.
4099   KOLANKIEWICZ, George. "The new 'awkward class': the peasant worker in Poland", *Sociologia ruralis* 20(1-2), 80 : 28-43.
4100   KOTOV, G. G.; MEL'NIKOV, V. F. *Ėkonomičeskie i social'nye problemy sela na sovremennom ėtape* (Villages economic and social problems in the contemporary era). Moskva, Kolos, 79, 225 p. [USSR.]
4101   KRISHNA SWAMY, S. Y. *Ruralism: a new socio-economic philosophy.* Bangalore, IBH, 80, viii-131 p.
4102   KRUZMETRA, M. R. "Sel'skohozjajtvennaja inteligencija i obščestvenno-političeskaja žizn' sela: [na materialah Latvijskoj SSR]" (Rural intelligentsia and the village sociopolitical life. From the SSR of Lettonia materials), *IN: Nekotorye problemy razvitija sovetskoj intelligencii i vozrastanie eë roli v stroitel'stve kommunizma.* Moskva, 79 : 22-27.

4103 KUITENBROUWER, Joost B. W. *Rural transformation in China.* The Hague, Institute of Social Studies, 79, 54 p.

4104 KVOČKIN, M. P. *A tiskah antagonizmov: obostrenie protivopoložnosti mezdu gorodomi derevnej v uslovijah sovremennogo kapitalizma* (On the antagonisms gearing: accentuation of the oppositions between towns and villages under conditions of contemporary capitalism). Minsk, Izdatel'stvo BGU imeni V. I. Lenina, 80, 160 p.

4105 KWAŚNIEWICZ, Krystyna. *Doroczne i rodzinne zwyczaje na tle współczesnych przeoborazen wsi pod-krakowskiej: studium wsi Niegoszowice w woj. Krakowskim*(The evolution of a village in the Krakow area: impact on its annual rites and family customs). Wrocław: Zakład narodowy im Ossolińskich wyd Polskiej akademii nauk, 79, 148 p.

4106 LATZ, Arinna. *Il était une fois un village....: étude psychosociologique des conséquences de la transfor- mation d'un environnement: étude réalisée sur le village de Salles-en-Provence.* Bruxelles, Ed. de l'Université de Bruxelles, 79, 127 p.

4107 LEE, Eddy. "L'évolution des idées en matière de développement rural", *Revue internationale du Travail* 119, jan-feb 80 : 103-121.

4108 LEE, Linda. "Factors affecting land use change at the urban-rural fringe", *Growth and Change* 10, oct 79 : 25-31.

4109 LEVEEN, E. Phillip. "Enforcing the Reclamation Act and rural development in California", *Rural Sociology* 44, wint 79 : 667-690.

4110 LIEBERMAN, Samuel S. *Rural development and fertility transition in South Asia: the case for a broad-based strategy.* New York, NY, Population Council, 80, 52 p.

4111 LUNDAHL, Mats. *Peasants and poverty: a study of Haiti.* London, Croom Helm, 79, 699 p.

4112 MABRY, Bevars D. "Peasant economic behaviour in Thailand", *Journal of Southeast Asian Studies* 10, sep 79 : 400-419.

4113 MAGNARELLA, Paul J. *The peasant venture: tradition, migration, and change among Georgian peasants in Turkey.* Cambridge, MA, Schenkman Pub. Co., 79, ix-175 p.

4114 MANIG, Winfried. "The spatial dimensions of rural development — factors determining the size of operational areas of farmers' associations on Taiwan", *Asia Quarterly* 79 : 229-254.

4115 MARDUEL, Marie-Laure; ROBERT, Michel. *Les Sociétés rurales françaises: éléments de bibliographie.* Paris, Ed. du CNRS, 80, 262 p. [Ecrits et travaux du Groupe de sociologie rurale du CNRS, 3.]

4116 MARESCA, Sylvain. "Ébauche d'une analyse sociologique des élites paysannes. Cinq biographies de dirigeants paysans", *Études rurales* 76, oct-dec 79 : 51-81. [France.]

4117 MARKOVIĆ, Petar. "Edvard Kardelj — mislilac i teoretičar agrarnog razvitka" (Edvard Kardelj — thinker and theoretician of agrarian development), *Sociologija sela* 17(65-66), 79 : 33-43. [with a bibliography of his works: 44-46.]

4118 MARTORELLI, Horacio. *Espacio y poder: notas sobre las relaciones entre el sistema de poder y la organización del espacio en el ámbito rural* (Space and power: notes on the relations between the power system and space organization in rural environment). Montevideo, Fundación de Cultura Universitaria, 79, 27 p.

4119 MATSJUK, A. K. "O dialektike social'noj professional'noj struktur sela v uslovijah razvitogo socializma" (Dialectics of the village social and professional structure under conditions of developed socialism), *IN: Aktual'nye problemy razvitogo socializma.* Karanganda, 78 : 119-128.

4120 MAUREL, Marie-Claude. "L'organisation de l'espace rural soviétique: cadres de vie et trames spatiales", *Annales de Géographie* 88(489), sep-oct 79 : 549-580.

4121 MAUREL, Marie-Claude. *La campagne collectivisée: société et espace rural en Russie.* Paris, Ed. Anthropos, 80, x-300 p.

4122 MAŽURAN, Rudolf. "Osobni rad i udruživanje individualnih poljoprivrednika u SR Hrvatskoj" (Personal labour and the association of private farmers in Croatia), *Sociologija sela* 17(65-66), 79 : 88-99.

4123 Bibl.XXIX-4261. MCHENRY, Dean E. Jr. *Tanzania's ujamaa villages: the implementation of a rural development strategy.* CR: Joel SAMOFF, *American political Science Review* 74(4), dec 80, 1120-1121.

4124 MEDLER, Jerry; MUSHKATEL, Alvin. "Urban -rural class conflict in Oregon land use planning", *Western political Quarterly* 32, sep 79 : 338-349.

4125 MEGRJAN, G. B. "XXV s'ezd KPSS o preodolenii suščestvennyh različij meždu gorodom i derevnej" (The CPSU XXVth Congress and the elimination of existing differences between towns and villages), *Voprosy naučnogo Kommunizma* 79 : 91-107.

4126 MENDRAS, Henri. *Le voyage au pays de l'utopie rustique.* Le Paradou, Éditions Actes/Sud, 79, 167 p. CR: Bernard PICON, *Revue française de Sociologie* 21(4), oct-dec 80: 659-660.

4127 MERTENS, Walter; ALATAS, Secha. "Rural-urban definition and urban agriculture in Indonesia", *Majalah Demografi Indonesia* (10), dec 78 : 40-70.

4128 METTELIN, Pierre. "Évolution de la politique de développement rural en Tanzanie depuis l'indépendance", *Mois en Afrique* 15(170-171), feb-mar 80 : 75-103.

4129 MICHAÏLOF, Serge. "La préparation des projets de développement rural", *Annales économiques* 11, 77 : 147-168.

4130 MISHRA, R. P.; SUNDARAM, K. V. *Multi-level planning and integrated rural development in India.* New Delhi, Tata-McGraw Hill, 80, xv-560 p.

4131 MOGENSEN, Gunnar Viby; MØRKENBERG, Henrik; SUNDBO, Jon. *Småbyer i landdistrikter = Villages in rural areas: population development and living conditions.* København, Socialforskningsinstituttet, 79, 424 p.

4132 MOOSER, Josef. "Gleichheit und Ungleichheit in der ländlichen Gemeinde. Sozialstruktur und Kommunalverfassung im östlichen Westfalen vom späten 18. bis in die Mitte des 19. Jahrhunderts" (Equality and inequality in rural communities. Social structure and communal administration in Eastern Westfalia from the end of the 18th Century to the mid-19th century), *Archiv für Sozialgeschichte* 19, 79 : 231-262.

4133 NEWBY, Howard. *Green and pleasant land?.* London, Hutchinson, 79, 287 p. CR: Keith TRIBE, *British Journal of Sociology* 31(4), dec 80: 591-592. [English rural structure, 1960-1970.]

4134 NEWBY, Howard. "Rural sociology", *Sociologie contemporaine/Current Sociology* 28, spr 80 : 141.

4135 NINOMIYA, Tetsuo. "Rural sociology in Japan: Milestones in development", *Rural sociology in an international context* 80 : 30-46.

4136 NOLAN, Peter; WHITE, Gordon. "Socialist development and rural inequality: the Chinese countryside in the 1970's", *Journal of Peasant Studies* oct 79 : 3-48.

4137 NWAKA, Geoffrey I. "Land administration and urban development: a Nigerian case study", *Civilisations* 30(1-2), jun 80 : 73-82.

4138 OBERAI, A. S.; SINGH, Manmohan H. K. "Les migrations, les envois de fonds et le développement rural. Conclusions d'une étude faite dans le Pendjab indien", *Revue internationale du Travail* 119, mar-apr 80 : 245-258.

4139 PANČENKO, P. P. *Naučnye osnovy razvitija obščestvenno-političeskoj žizni sela:* [na materialah USSR, 1959-1978] (Scientific bases of the village socio-political life; from USSR materials, 1959-1978). Kiev, Višča Škola, 79, 279 p.

4140 Bibl.XXIX-4167. PARISH, William L.; WHYTE, Martin King. *Village and family life in contemporary China.* CR: Ezra F. VOGEL, *American Journal of Sociology* 86(2), sep 80 : 399-401.

4141 PAUSEWANG, Siegfried. "A new international economic order for the peasant in the Third World?", *Sociologia ruralis* 20(1-2), 80 : 97-115.

4142 PEREZ LEDESMA, Manuel. "En torno a los movimientos campesinos chinos" (About the Chinese peasant movements), *Agricultura y Sociedad* 14, 80 : 197-209.

4143 PIATIER, André; [et al.]. *Radioscopie des communes de France: ruralité et relations villes-campagnes: une recherche pour l'action.* Paris, Economica, 79, 549 p.

4144 PICARD, Louis. "Rural development in Botswana: administrative structures and public policy", *Journal of developing Areas* 13, apr 79 : 283-300.

4145 PLANCK, Ulrich; ZICHE, Joachim. *Land- und Agrarsoziologie* (Land and agrarian sociology). Stuttgart, Ulmer, 79, 520 p. CR: Gerd SPITTLER, *Kölner Zeitschrift für Soziologie und Sozialpsychologie* 32(3), sep 80: 606-612.

4146 POFFENBERGER, Mark; ZURBUCHEN, Mary S. "The economics of village Bali: three perspectives", *Economic Development and cultural Change* 29, oct 80 : 91-133.

4147 POPKIN, Samuel L. *The rational peasant: the political economy of rural society in Vietnam.* Berkeley, University of California Press, 79, xxi-306 p. CR: Ronald H. HERRING, *American political Science Review* 74(2), jun 80: 565-566.

4148 POPKIN, Samuel L. "The rational peasant: political economy of peasant society", *Theory and Society* mai 80 : 411-471.

4149 RAGHAVA RAO, D. V. *Panchayats and rural development.* New Delhi, Ashish, 80, xi-96 p.

4150 REINING, Priscilla Copeland; LENKERD, Barbara; [eds.]. *Village viability in contemporary society.* Boulder, CO, published by Westview Press for the American Association for the Advancement of Science, 80, xxv-355 p.

4151 ROCHEGUDE, A. "Quelques idées sur la méthodologie d'une réforme agro-foncière: l'exemple du Mali", *African Perspectives* 79 : 83-96.

4152	SACOUMAN, R. J. "Semi-proletarianization and rural underdevelopment in the Maritimes", *Canadian Review of Sociology and Anthropology* 17, aug 80 : 232-245. [Canada.]
4153	SANCHEZ JIMENEZ, José. "Marginación y conflicto en la sociedad rural española" (Maginalization and conflict in Spanish rural society), *Documentación social* 38, 80 : 90-120.
4154	SCHRYER, Frans J. *The rancheros of Pisaflores: the history of a peasant bourgeoisie in twentieth-century Mexico*. Toronto, Buffalo, University of Toronto Press, 80, xii-210 p.
4155	SCHWARTZ, Alf. "Le déclassement du villageois zaïrois: une approche psycho-sociologique de développement inégal", *Canadian Journal of African Studies* 14, 80 : 113-133.
4156	SCHWIMMER, Brian. "The organization of migrant farmer communities in Southern Ghana", *Canadian Journal of African Studies* 14, 80 : 221-238.
4157	SELIGSON, Mitchell A. "Public policies in conflict: land reform and family planning in Costa Rica", *Comparative Politics* 12, oct 79 : 49-62.
4158	SEVILLA GUZMÁN, Eduardo. *La evolución del campesinado en España: elementos para una sociología política del campesinado* (The evolution of peasantry in Spain: elements for a political sociology of peasantry). Barcelona, Ediciones Península, 79, 332 p.
4159	SHARMA, Sudesh K.; BHATTA CHARYA, Mohit. "Changing strategies of rural development in India", *Journal of Administration Overseas* 19, jan 80 : 4-9.
4160	SHARMA, Sudesh Kumar. "Rural development in India: programmes, strategies and perspectives", *Community Development Journal* 15, jan 80 : 2-9.
4161	SISODIA, G. S. "Panchayat leader's level of the procedural provisions and rules of Panchayats — a study in rural institution", *Indian Journal of social Research* 20, aug 79 : 79-87.
4162	STANFORD, Richard A.; [ed.]. *Rural development in Pakistan*. Durham, NC, Carolina Academic Press, 80, xv-164 p.
4163	STAROVEROV, V. I.; [et al.]. *Derevnja v uslovijah integracii: social'nye problemy* (The village under conditions of integration: social problems). Moskva, Mysl', 79, 272 p. [USSR.]
4164	TAGUCHI, Masami. "Sengo no nihon nōson shakaigaku no tenkai -Fukutake nōson shakaigaku no hihan to keishō" (Development of rural sociology in post-war Japan), *Risshô daigaku tanki daigakubu kiyo* 10, 80 : 5-20.
4165	TAKSANOV, A. K. *Kompleksnyj podhod k social'nomu preobrazovaniju derevni* (A complex approach to the village social transformation). Taškent, Uzbekistan, 79, 147 p.
4166	TIMUŠ, A. I. "Agrarno-promyšlennaja integracija social'noe razvitie derevni" (Agro-industrial integration and the village social development), IN: *Social'naja struktura sovetskogo obščestva i socialističeskij obraz žizni. I.*. Moskva, 78 : 91-109.
4167	UMAPATHY, N. "Tribunals for land reforms in Andhra Pradesh", *Journal of Administration Overseas* 19, jan 80 : 37-46.
4168	United States. Library of Congress. Congressional Research Service. *Rural development: an overview*. Washington, U.S. Govt. Print. Off., 79, ix-257 p.
4169	Universite de Nice. *Communautés rurales et pouvoirs dans les pays méditerranéens XVIe-XXe siècles*. Nice, Centre de la méditerranée moderne et contemporaine, 80, 267 p.
4170	University of Ottawa. Institute for International Co-operation. *Le développement rural en Afrique: priorités, problèmes et perspectives = Rural development in Africa: priorities, problems and prospects*. Ottawa, Éditions de l'Université d'Ottawa, 79, 203 p.
4171	USMANOV, N. "O roli socialističeskogo goroda v preobrazovanii sel'skogo byta" (On the socialist town role in the transformation of rural customs), *Obščestvennye Nauki v Uzbekistane* 79 : 18-23.
4172	UYANGA, Joseph T. *A geography of rural development in Nigeria*. Washington, DC, University Press of America, 80, x-173 p.
4173	VALDERRAMA, Mariano; LUDMANN, Patricia. *La oligarquía terrateniente, ayer y hoy* (Land owners oligarchy, yesterday and today). Lima, Departamento de Ciencias Sociales, P Universidad Católica del Perú, 79, ii-411 p. [Peru.]
4174	VERHAGEN, Koenraad. "Changes in Tanzanian rural development policy 1975-1978", *Development and Change* 11, apr 80 : 285-295.
4175	VERRIPS, Jojada. "The polder and the heavens above: an anthropological study of a Dutch village 1850-1971", *Netherlands' Journal of Sociology* 16, apr 80 : 49-67.
4176	VIBY MOGENSEN, Gunnar; MØRKEBERG, Henrik; SUNDBO, Jon. *Småbyer i landdistrikter* (Villages in rural areas, population development and living conditions). København, Teknisk forlag, 79, 424 p.

4177 VILAIN, Michel. "L'expérimentation administrative en aménagement rural. Expériences-pilotes ou politique de variété", *Revue française de Science politique* 30, oct 80 : 959-984.

4178 VÖLGYES, Ivan; LONSDALE, Richard E.; AVERY, William P.; [eds.]. *The Process of rural transformation: Eastern Europe, Latin America, and Australia.* New York, Pergamon Press, 80, ix-347 p.

4179 WICKBERG, Edgar. "Land reform in mainland China and Taiwan", *Peasant Studies* aut 78 : 250-262.

4180 YAMAGUCHI, Soko. "Hokuriku no ichi kaso sanson ni okeru chiiki kaihatsu to jūmin no seikatsu -Toyama-ken Higashitonami-gun Toga-mura Momosegawa no baai" (Regional development and life of the inhabitants of depopulated mountain village in Hokuriku district), *Fudai keizai ronshū* 24, 78 : 68-95. [see also: ibid: 26(2) 80: 62-92.]

4181 YAMAGUCHI, Soko. "Hokuriku ni okeru -sanson shakai no hendō to jūmin no seikatsu -Toyama-ken Nei-gun Yatsuo-machi Ōhase no baai" (Social change and life of the inhabitants of a depopulated mountain village in Hokuriku district), *Toyamadaigaku Nihonkai kenkyujo kenkyu nenpo* 80 : 65-120.

4182 YAMAOKA, Eiichi. "Tanba, Tango to Ōmi nōson tono hikaku -hitotsu no shiron" (A comparative study of agricultural villages in Ōmi and Tanba, Tango), *Bukkyo daigaku shakaigakubu ronso* 14, 80 : 43-66.

4183 YODEN, Hiromichi. "Mura to 'Mura'" (The administrative village and the village community), *Kwansei gakuin daigaku shakaigakubu kiyo* 40, 80 : 85-92.

4184 ZANDSTRA, Hubert; [et al.]. Caqueza: living rural development. Ottawa, International Development Research Centre, 79, 321 p.

4185 ZASLAVSKAJA, T. I. "Sel'skij sektor kak ob'ekt dolgosročnogo social'nogo prognozirovanija" (Rural sector as an object of long-term social forecast), *IN: Metodologičeskie problemy sovremennoj nauki.* Moskva, 79 : 32-55.

4186 ZASLAVSKAJA, T. I. "Metodologija izučenija i prognozirovanija razvitija derevni" (Methodology of the village development study and forecast), *Obščestvennye Nauki (Moskva)* 79 : 90-106.

4187 ZASLAVSKAJA, T. I.; [et al.]. "Ob opyte kollektivnogo prognozirovanija social'no-ėkonomičeskogo razvitija derevni" (On an essay of a collective forecast of a village's socio-economic development), *IN: Nauka, organizacija i upravlenie.* 79 : 122-150.

4188 ZAVALA, Hector Luis Morales. "Développement rural, science et pouvoir politique: Divergences ou convergences?", *Impact. Science et Société* 30, jul-sep : 181-191.

4189 ZEMCOV, L. G.; [ed.]. *Problemy kul'tury i obrazovanija sovremennogo sela* (Culture and education problems in a contemporary village). Ul'janovsk, Uljanovskij Gosudarstvennyj Pedagogičesij Institut imeni I.N. Ul'Janova, 78, 137 p.

4190 ZIERER, Otto. *Aus Knechtschaft zur Freiheit: die Geschichte des Bauerntums* (From serfdom to freedom: the history of peasantry). Salzburg, Verl. Das Bergland-Buch, 79, 352 p.

4191 ŽUPANČIĆ, Milan. "Podruštvovljavanje poljoprivrede u marksističkoj teoriji društvenog razvoja" (The socialization of agriculture in the Marxist theory of social development), *Sociologija sela* 17(65-66), 79 : 61-72.

16320. Urban sociology
Sociologie urbaine

[See also / voir aussi: 587, 590, 1150, 1370, 1542, 1572, 2062, 2111, 2173, 2264, 2279, 2375, 2608, 2689, 2722, 2842, 2851, 2915, 2917, 3046, 3070, 3072, 3090, 3109, 3117, 3152, 3165, 3217, 3351, 3426, 3777, 3823, 3866, 3925, 4003, 4011, 4086, 4092, 4137, 4204, 4270, 4274, 4276, 4297, 4302, 4311, 4312, 4341, 4355, 4597, 4786, 5775, 6038]

4192 "Ensayos sobre desarrollo urbano y regional en América latina"(Essays on urban and regional development in Latin America), *Boletín de Estudios latinoamericanos y del Caribe* 27, dec 79 : 3-95.

4193 "Revalorisation des espaces anciens", *Espaces et Sociétés* 30-31, jul-dec 79 : 3-156.

4194 "Urbanisme et utopie", *Espaces et Sociétés* 32-33, jan-jun 80 : 3-176.

4195 "Logement des immigrés (Le)", *Hommes et Migrations* 991, mai 80 : 1-28. [France.]

4196 "Symposium on housing policy", *Policy Studies Journal* 79 : 203-399. [USA.]

4197 "Bordeaux, mutations d'un espace urbain", *Revue géographique des Pyrénées et du Sud-Ouest* 51, jan 80 : 9-84.

4198 "Structure (The) of neighbourhood services", *Social Service Delivery Systems* 78 : 7-270.

4199 "Fiscal retrenchment and urban policy", *Urban Affairs annual Review* 17, 79 : 305 p.

4200 "Urban revitalization", *Urban Affairs annual Review* 18, 80 : 7-308.
4201 AHLBRANDT, Roger S.; CUNNINGHAM, James V. *A new public policy for neighborhood preservation*. New York, Praeger, 79, xxv-276 p.
4202 AGRESTI, Barbara Finlay. "Measuring residential segregation in nineteenth-century American cities", *Sociological Methods and Research* mai 80 : 389-399.
4203 AGUIRRE, B. E.; [et al.]. "The residential patterning of Latin American and other ethnic populations in metropolitan Miami", *Latin American Research Review* 15, 80 : 35-63.
4204 AITOV, N. A. *Social'noe razvitie gorodov: suščnost'i prespektivy* (Towns social development: nature and prospects). Moskva, Znanie, 79, 64 p.
4205 AKIMOTO, Ritsuo; OHTA, Hideaki. *Toshi to saigai*(Urban society and disaster). Tokyo, Gakubunsha, 80, 182 p.
4206 AKSOY, Sevim. "The housing problems of Istanbul and the Gecekondu phenomenon", *Planning and Administration* spr 80 : 39-48.
4207 ALDRIDGE, Meryl. *The British new towns: a programme without a policy*. London, Boston, Routledge & Kegan Paul, 79, xiv-219 p.
4208 ALLINSON, Gary D. *Suburban Tokyo: a comparative study in politics and social change*. Berkeley, University of California Press, 79, xv-258 p.
4209 ALLON, Natalie. *Urban life styles*. Dubuque, IA, W. C. Brown Co. Publishers, 79, xvi-215 p. [USA.]
4210 AMATO, Matthew F. *Jersey City, a city in socio-economic and political change*. Hickville, NY, Exposition Press, 80, ix-60 p.
4211 ANDRUSZ, Greg. "Some key issues in Soviet urban development", *International Journal of urban and regional Research* jun 79 : 157-179.
4212 APPLEYARD, Donald; [ed.]. *The Conservation of European cities*. Cambridge, MA, MIT Press, 79, ix-308 p.
4213 ARANOVICH, Carmen; MAGUITAM, Olga Quitarra de. *Concentración urbana y macrocefalismo argentino* (Urban concentration and Argentine macrocephalism). Buenos Aires, Centro Editor, 80.
4214 Bibl.XXIX-4461. ASCHENBRENNER, Joyce; COLLINS, Lloyd R.; [eds.]. *The process of urbanism: a multidisciplinary approach*. CR: Lawrence G. FELICE, *Contemporary Sociology (Albany)* 9(6), nov 80: 808-809.
4215 AYENI, Bola. *Concepts and techniques in urban analysis*. New York, St. Martin's Press, 78, 372 p.
4216 BAKER, Terence J.; O'BRIEN, L. M. *The Irish housing system: a critical overview*. Dublin, Economic and Social Research Institute, 79, xi-272 p.
4217 BALCHIN, Paul N. *Housing improvement and social inequality: case study of an inner city*. Farnborough, Eng., Saxon House, 79, xv-259 p. [United Kingdom.]
4218 Bibl.XXIX-1105. BALDASSARE, Mark. *Residential crowding in urban America*. CR: Candace Hinson WISWELL, *Contemporary Sociology (Albany)* 9(4), jul 80: 535-536.
4219 BARAT, Josef. *Introdução aos problemas urbanos brasileiros: teoria, análise e formulação de política* (Introduction to Brazilean urban problems: theory, analysis and policy-making). Rio de Janeiro, Editora Campus, 79, 249 p.
4220 BARDO, J. W.; HUGHEY, J. B. "A second-order factor analysis of community satisfaction in a Midwestern city", *Journal of social Psychology* 109, dec 79 : 231-235.
4221 BASTIE, Jean; DÉSERT, Bernard. *L'Espace urbain*. Paris, New York, Barcelona, [etc.], Masson, 80, 381 p.
4222 BELLETTINI, Athos. "La croissance urbaine en Italie et ses tendances récentes. Le cas de Bologne", *Genus* 34(3-4), 78 : 20-39.
4223 BENTHAM, Eraham; MOSELEY, Malcolm J. "Socio-economic change and disparities within the Paris agglomeration: does Paris have an" inner city problem"?", *Regional Studies* 14, 80 : 55-71.
4224 BÉRES, Csaba. *Lakótelep — kertes házak helyén. Az életforma-váltás szociológiai problémái egy szanálási övezetben* (New settlement instead of small houses with a garden. Sociological problems of the change of life style in a reconstruction area in the city of Debrecen). Debrecen, Megyei, Könyvtár, 79, 318 p.
4225 Bibl.XXIX-4355. BERNDT, Heide. *Die Natur der Stadt* (Nature of the city). CR: Thomas KRÄMER-BADONI, *Soziologische Revue* 3(2), 80: 186-187.
4226 BERRY, Brian Joe Lobley. *The open housing question: race and housing in Chicago, 1966-1976*. Cambridge, MA, Ballinger Pub. Co., 79, xxii-517 p.
4227 BERTRAND, William E.; LEVINE, Arnold. "A rapid survey technique for 'appropriate technology' in developing urban areas", *Social Indicators Research* (1-4), jan 80 : 237-249. [Cali, Colombia.]

4228 BORGHORST, Hermann. *Die wechselseitige Abhängigkeit von Bund und Kommunen in der Stadtsanierungspolitik der Vereinigten Staaten von Amerika*(The interdependence of state and local government in urban renewal policy in the USA). Berlin, Duncker und Humblot, 79, 321 p.

4229 BORTOLI, Michele. *Urbanistica in Gran Bretagna: da New Lanark a Milton Keynes* (Town planning in Great Britain: from New Lanark to Milton Keynes). Lucca, M. Pacini Fazzi, 79, 142 p.

4230 BORUKHOV, Eli; [et al.]. "The social ecology of Tel Aviv: a study in factor analysis", *Urban Affairs Quarterly* 15, dec 79 : 183-205.

4231 BRAUJEU-GARNIER, Jacqueline. *Géographie urbaine*. Paris, A. Colin, 80, 360 p.

4232 BRAZZODURO, Marco. "L'abusivismo come modalità di crescita urbana: il caso di Roma" (Misues of authority as a means of urban growth: the case of Rome), *Revue internationale de sociologie / International Review of Sociology* 16, apr 80 : 53-92.

4233 BRUNEAU, Jean Claude. *Ziguinchor en Casamance: la croissance urbaine dans les pays tropicaux*. Talence, Centre d'études de géographie tropicale, 79, 163 p.

4234 BRYCE, Herrington J.; [ed.]. *Revitalizing cities*. Lexington, MA, Lexington Books, 79, xvii-298 p.

4235 BUNKŚE, Edmunds V. "The role of a humane environment in Soviet urban planning", *Geographical Review* 69, oct 79 : 379-394.

4236 ČALDAROVIĆ, Ognjen. "Planiranje grada i procesi socijalne integracije" (City planning and the processes of social integration), *Revija za Sociologiju* (1-2), 78 : 96-102.

4237 ČALDAROVIĆ, Ognjen; [et al.]. "Vrednote i komplementarnost stambenih prostora" (Values and the complementarity of housing spaces), *Revija za Sociologiju* (1-2), 78 : 67-74.

4238 CEPPE, Jean Louis. *La pratique de la ville dans l'aménagement du territoire*. Les Sables d'Olonne, France, Cercle d'or, Paris, Chaix, 79, 217 p.

4239 ČERKASOV, G. N.; MEŽEVIČ, M. N. "Aktual'nye problemy razvitija gorodov i pereustrojstva sela: social'naja suščnost' upravlenija" (Topical problems of the towns development and village reorganization: the management social nature), *IN: Social'naja struktura sovetskogo obščestva i socialističeskij obraz žizni. II*. Moskva, 78 : 160-169.

4240 CHALINE, Claude. *La Dynamique urbaine*. Paris, Presses universitaires de France, 80, 206 p.

4241 CHANG, Parris H. "Control of urbanisation — the Chinese approach", *Asia Quarterly* 79 : 215-229.

4242 CHARRIE, Jean-Pierre. "Agen, quelques aspects de la croissance urbaine", *Revue géographique des Pyrénées et du Sud-Ouest* 50, oct 79 : 541-560.

4243 CHERKI, Eddy; MEHL, Dominique. *Les Nouveaux embarras de Paris: de la révolte des usagers des transports aux mouvements de défense de l'environnement*. Paris, F. Maspero, 79, 218 p.

4244 CHERNOFF, Michael L.; REITZES, Donald C. "A revised view of distance-density relationships", *Sociology and social Research* 64, apr 80 : 389-404.

4245 CHEVALLIER, Maurice. *Le phénomène pavillonnaire dans la région urbaine de Lyon et autour de Bourg en Bresse: anciens et nouveaux pavillonnaires (enquête auprès de 120 ménages: rapport d'étude)*. Lyon, Groupe de sociologie urbaine, 79, 168 p.

4246 CHI, Peter S. K.; GRIFFIN, Maryann D. "Social indicators for measuring residential satisfaction in marginal settlements in Costa Rica", *Social Indicators Research* dec 80 : 453-465.

4247 CHOLDIN, Harvey, M. "Crowding and slums: a statistical exploration", *Research in social Problems and public Policy* 79 : 179-194. [USA, Los Angeles.]

4248 CIBRIAN, Ramior. "Procesos de urbanización y problemas energéticos" (Urbanization processes and energy problems), *Revista española de Investigaciones sociológicas* 11, jul-sep 80 : 115-126. [Spain.]

4249 CLARK, W. A. V.; MOORE, Eric G.; [eds.]. *Residential mobility and public policy*. Beverly Hills, CA, Sage Publications, 80, 312 p.

4250 CLAY, Phillip L. *Neighborhood renewal: middle-class resettlement and incumbent upgrading in American neighborhoods*. Lexington, MA, Lexington Books, 79, xi-114 p.

4251 Bibl.XXIX-4389. COUSINS, Albert N.; NAGPAUL, Hans. *Urban life: the sociology of cities and urban society*. CR: Richard DEWEY, *Contemporary Sociology (Albany)* 9(4), jul 80 : 537-538.

4252 CRESPO, Angel. "El proceso de desarrollo urbano en América latina y el Ecuador" (The urban development process in Latin America and Ecuador), *Desarrollo indoamericano* 15(57), apr 80 : 43-58.

4253 CRIBIER, Françoise. "Les Français et leurs résidences secondaires", *Revue des Travaux de l'Académie des Sciences morales et politiques* 131, 78 : 341-353.

4254 CURVIN, Robert; PORTER, Bruce. *Blackout looting! New York City, July 13, 1977.* New York, Gardner Press, 79, 240 p. CR: Ralph H. TURNER, *Contemporary Sociology (Albany)* 9(4), jul 80 : 532-533.

4255 DESHPANDE, C. D.; ARUNACHALAM, B.; BHAT, L. S. *Impact of a metropolitan city on the surrounding region: a study of South Kolaga, Maharashtra.* New Delhi, Concept, 80, xv-142 p.

4256 DMITRIEV, A. V.; MEŽEVIČ, M. N. "Obščie i osovennye čerty urbanizacii v uslovijah socializma i kapitalizma" (Urbanization general and particular characteristics under conditions of socialism and capitalism), *IN: Naučno-tehničeskaja revoljucija i problemy razvitija obščestva i kollektivov.* Moskva, 79 : 26-37.

4257 DONNISON, David. *The good city: A study of urban development and policy in Britain.* London, Heineman Educational Books, 80, 221 p. [with Paul Soto. Centre for Environmental Studies series.]

4258 DORAN, Michael F.; LANDIS, Renée A. "Origin and persistence of an innercity slum in Nassau", *Geographical Review* 70, apr 80 : 182-193.

4259 DUC NHUAN, Nguyen. "Desurbanisation et développement régional au Vietnam (1955-77)", *International Journal of urban and regional Research* jun 78 : 330-350.

4260 ELLIOTT, Brian. "Manuel Castells and the new urban sociology", *British Journal of Sociology* 31, mar 80 : 151-158.

4261 ELLIOTT, Brian; MCCRONE, David. "Urban development in Edinburgh: in contribution to the political economy of place", *Scottish Journal of Sociology* jan 80 : 1-26.

4262 FLY, Jerry W.; REINHART, George R. "Racial separation during the 1970s: the case of Birmingham", *Social Forces* 58, jun 80 : 1255-1262.

4263 FRENCH, Richard Anthony; HAMILTON, F. E. Ian; [eds.]. *The Socialist city: spatial structure and urban policy.* Chichester, New York, Wiley, 79, xviii-541 p.

4264 FREY, William H. "Black in-migration, white flight and the changing economic base of the central city", *American Journal of Sociology; 30285, mai 80 : 1396-1497.* [USA.]

4265 FRIEDEN, Bernard J. "Housing allowances: an experiment that worked", *Public Interest* 59, spr 80 : 15-35.

4266 FRIEDRICHS, Christopher R,. *Urban society in an age of war: Nördlingen, 1580-1720.* Princeton, NJ, Princeton University Press, 79, xvii-350 p.

4267 FUJITA, Hiro'o. "Nihon toshi no shakaigaku-teki tokushitsu -shuken-sei to chonaikai" (On social character of Japanese city), *Shakaigaku hyoron* 30, 79 : 2-16.

4268 GAUBE, Heinz. *Iranian cities.* New York, New York University Press, 79, xviii-132 p.

4269 GLUCK, Peter R.; MEISTER, Richard J. *Cities in transition: social changes and institutional responses in urban development.* New York, New Viewpoints, 79, xiii-237 p. [USA.]

4270 GOETZE, Rolf. *Understanding neighborhood change: the role of expectations in urban revitalization.* Cambridge, MA, Ballinger Pub. Co., 79, xx-162 p.

4271 Bibl.XXIX-4313. GOLANY, Gideon; [ed.]. *International urban growth policies: new town contributions.* CR: Cynthia L. TOBIAS, *Contemporary Sociology (Albany)* 9(3), mai 80: 404.

4272 GONZÁLEZ SALAZAR, Gloria. "Medio ambiente, urbanismo y planeación" (Environment, urbanism and planning), *Problemas del Desarrollo* 10(40), nov 79-jan 80 : 81-105. [Mexico.]

4273 GOODMAN, John L., Jr. *Regional housing assistance allocations and regional housing needs.* Washington, DC, Urban Institute, 79, 50 p. [an Urban Institute Paper on Housing.]

4274 GRAFMEYER, Yves; JOSEPH, Isaac; [eds.]. *L'École de Chicago. Naissance de l'écologie urbaine.* Paris, Éditions du Champ Urbain, 79, 335 p. CR: J.-R. TRÉANTON, *Revue française de Sociologie* 21(1), jan-mar 80: 148.

4275 GRIBET, Marie-France. "De la multinationale à l'usine éclatée. Des villes désarticulées dans la France profonde", *Hérodote* 17, jan-mar 80 : 61-88.

4276 GUEST, Avery M. "Suburbanization of ethnic groups", *Sociology and social Research* 64, jul 80 : 498-513. [USA.]

4277 GUEST, Avery M.; BROOKS, Anna M. "Stone's hypothesis of 'personalizing' shopping as compensation for urban depersonalization: a reconsideration", *Sociological Inquiry* 50, 80 : 83-88.

4278 HAMER, Andrew Marshall; [ed.]. *Urban Atlanta: Redefining the role of the city.* Atlanta, Georgia State University, College of Business Administration, Business Publishing Division, 80, iv-256 p.

4279 HAMM, Bernd; [ed.]. *Lebensraum, Stadt: Beitr. zur Sozialökologie dt. Städte* (Life space town: essay on the social ecology of German towns). Frankfurt/Main, New York, Campus Verlag, 79, 223 p. CR: Heide BERNDT, *Soziologische Revue* 3(3), 80, 322-323.

4280   HANDELMAN, Howard. *High-rises and shantytowns: housing the poor in Bogotá and Caracas.* Hanover, NH, American Universities Field Staff, 79, 21 p.
4281   HANNERZ, Ulf. *Exploring the city: inquiries toward an urban anthropology.* New York, Columbia University Press, 80, x-378 p.
4282   HARTSHORN, Truman A. *Interpreting the city: an urban geography.* New York, Wiley, 80, x-498 p.
4283   HATCH, Elvin. *Biography of a small town.* New York, Columbia University Press, 79, 293 p.
4284   HEATON, Tim; [et al.]. "Residential preferences. Community satisfaction, and the intention to move", *Demography* 16, nov 79 : 565-573.
4285   HEEGER, H. P. "The Dutch solution to the problem of a residential environment", *Planning and Development in the Netherlands* XI, 79 : 3-16.
4286   HERLYN, Ulfert. "Einführung in die Soziologie der Stadt und des Städtebaus" (Introduction to urban sociology), *Soziologische Revue* 80 : 139-146. [review article.]
4287   HINZ, Heide; HINZ, Michael. "Zur französischen Debatte um die Stadtsoziologie — Castells' Versuch der Neuformulierung der 'Stadtfrage'" (The French debate on urban sociology. Castells' attempt at a new formulation of the urban problem), *Leviathan* 79 : 441-449.
4288   HOLLINGSWORTH, J. Rogers; HOLLINGSWORTH, Ellen Jane. *Dimensions in urban history: historical and social science perspectives on middle-sized American cities.* Madison, University of Wisconsin Press, 79, viii-184 p. CR: Harvey BOULAY, *American political Science Review* 79(3), sep 80: 824-825.
4289   HOWARD, William A.; WYMAN, Sherman; [eds.]. "Urban studies in an era of societal discontinuity: a symposium", *Social Science Journal* 17, jan 80 : 1-87.
4290   HUGO, Graeme. "Some demographic factors influencing recent and future demand for housing in Australia", *Australian Quarterly* 51, dec 79 : 4-25.
4291   ISOMURA, Eiichi. *Chihō no jidai: Sōzō to sentaku no shihyō* (Toward the age of urban and local communities). Tokyo, Tokaidaigaku shuppankai, 80, 209 p.
4292   JAKUŠOV, A. I. *Preodolenie suščestvennyh različij meždu gorodom i derevnej v uslovijah razvitogo socializma* (The elimination of existing differences between towns and villages under conditions of developed socialism). Moskva, Vysšaja Škola, 79, 263 p.
4293   JANSSEN, Roel. "Some ideological aspects of urban planning in Latin America: a critique of the Turner model of self-help housing with special reference to Bogota", *Boletín de Estudios latinoamericanos y del Caribe* 27, dec 79 : 69-76.
4294   JEDIDI, Mohamed. "La croissance urbaine dans le Sahel tunisien", *Revue tunisienne de Géographie* 79 : 41-58.
4295   JOLY, Jacques. "Évolution démographique et sociale de Grenoble (1976-1979)", *Revue de Géographie alpine* 68, 80 : 5-20.
4296   JUNUSOV, Ju. Ju. "Gorodskaja sreda i eë vlijanie na formirovanie ličnosti: po materialam Dagestanskoj ASSR" (Urban environment and its influence on the personality formation from the ASSR Daghestan materials), *IN: Social'no-ėtničeskoe i kul'turnoe razvitie gorodskogo naselenija Dagestana.* Mahačkala, 79 : 37-50.
4297   KENDIG, Hal. *New life for old suburbs: post-war land use and housing in the Australian inner city.* Sydney, Boston, Allen & Unwin, 79, 192 p.
4298   KILLEN, James. "Urban transportation problems and issues in Dublin", *Administration (Dublin)* 27, sum 79 : 151-166.
4299   KISTRIEV, Ė. F. "Urbanizacija kak tendencija internacionalizacii obščestvennoj zizni i eë ėtničeskie posledstvija" (Urbanization as a tendency of the social life internationalization and its ethnic consequences), *IN: Social'no-ėtničeskoe i kul'turnoe razvitie gorodskogo naselenija Dagestana.* Mahačkala, 79 : 5-19.
4300   KOYANO, Shōgo. *Toshi kyojū ni okeru tekio gijutsu no tenkai — Saiminso no dōkō o chushin ni* (The development of technology adapted to urban life — Focusing on the lower socioeconomic class). Tokyo, Kokusai rengō daigaku, 31 p.
4301   KRAUSSE, Gerald H. "Problems and prospects of low-income settlements in Southeast Asian cities", *Asian Profile* aug 79 : 359-377.
4302   KUKLICK, Henrika. "Chicago sociology and urban planning policy: sociological theory as occupational ideology", *Theory and Society* nov 80 : 821-845.
4303   KUNDU, Amitabh. *Measurement of urban processes: a study in regionalisation.* Bombay, Popular, 80, vx-246 p. [India.]
4304   LABORIE, Jean-Paul. *Les Petites villes.* Paris, Editions du CNRS, 79, 363 p.
4305   LACAZE, Jean Paul. *Introduction à la planification urbaine: imprécis d'urbanisme à la française.* Paris, Moniteur, 79, xiv-302 p.

4306 LAKE, Robert W.; CARIS CUTTER, Susan. "A typology of black suburbanization in New Jersey since 1970", *Geographical Review* 70, apr 80 : 167-181.
4307 LANSLEY, Stewart. *Housing and public policy*. London, Croom Helm, 79, 246 p.
4308 LEAL MALDONADO JESÚS. "Vivienda y sociedad"(Housing and society), *Revista española de Investigaciones sociológicas* oct-dec 79 : 89-102. [Spain.]
4309 LITOVKA, O. P. "Urbanization in the USSR: problems of spatial differentiation", *Soviet Geography* 21, jan 80 : 30-36.
4310 LOJKINE, Jean. "Politique urbaine et pouvoir local", *Revue française de Sociologie* 21, oct-dec 80 : 633-651.
4311 MARSHALL, Harvey. "White movement to the suburbs: a comparison of explanations", *American sociological Review* 44, dec 79 : 975-994.
4312 MARSHALL, Harvey; STAHURA, John. "The impact of racial composition and racial transition on the status of American suburbs", *Sociological Inquiry* 50, 80 : 75-82.
4313 MASSEY, Douglas S. "Effects of socioeconomic factors on the residential segregation of Blacks and Spanish Americans in US urbanized areas", *American sociological Review* 44, dec 79 : 1015-1022.
4314 MASSEY, Douglas S. "Residential segregation of Spanish Americans in United States urbanized areas", *Demography* 16, nov 79 : 553-563.
4315 MATEJU, Petr; [et al.]. "Social structure, spatial structure and problems of urban research: the example of Prague", *International Journal of urban and regional Research* jun 79 : 181-202.
4316 MATSUMOTO, Kazuyoshi. "Tōhoku 64-shi no kōzō to katei -inshi bunsekiho o chūshin toshita shakaigaku bunseki" (Structure and process of 64 cities in Tohoku district), *Tōhoku kōgyō daigaku kiyō bunkakei-hen* 25, 80 : 1-21.
4317 MCKAY, David H.; COX, Andrew W. *The politics of urban change*. London, Croom Helm, 79, 297 p.
4318 MCKEOWN, Kieran. "The epistemological foundation of the urban sociology of Manuel Castells: a critique", *Scottish Journal of Sociology* jan 80 : 27-36.
4319 MEFVEDKOVA, A. L. "Components in the evolution of urban systems: theory and empirical testing", *Soviet Geography* 21, jan 80 : 15-30.
4320 MELLING, Joseph; [ed.]. *Housing, social policy and the state*. London, Croom Helm, 80, 233 p.
4321 MERRETT, Stephen. *State housing in Britain*. London, Boston, Routledge & Kegan Paul, 79, xviii-376 p.
4322 MEYNAUD, Hélène Y. *Urbanisme et aménagement du territoire en Ouzbekistan: 1917-1978*. Paris, Institut d'Etudes politiques, 79, xviii-355 p.
4323 MILLER, Roberta Balstad. *City and hinterland: a case study of urban growth and regional development*. Westport, CT, Greenwood Press, 79, xiv-179 p. [USA.]
4324 MISHRA, V. M. "Communication and urbanization — modernization processes in South Asia", *Indian Journal of social Research* 20, apr 79 : 64-73.
4325 MLINAR, Zdravko. "Jedinstvo suprotnosti u urbanističkom i prostornom planiranju" (The unity of opposites in town-planning), *Sociologija* 21(1-2), 79 : 89-106.
4326 MORGAN, B. S. "Occupational segregation in metropolitan areas in the United States 1970", *Urban Studies* 17, feb 80 : 63-70.
4327 MORTON, Henry W. "Housing problems and policies of Eastern Europe and the Soviet Union", *Studies in comparative Communism* 12, wint 79 : 300-321.
4328 MURIE, Alan; FORREST, Ray. "Wealth, inheritance and housing policy", *Policy and Politics* jan 80 : 1-19.
4329 MUSIL, Jiří. "Urbanization in socialist countries", *International Journal of Sociology* 10(2-3), 80 : vii-xi-3-185.
4330 NAGPAUL, Hans. "Approaches and strategies for the improvement of slums and squatter settlements in metropolitan India: a bibliographical essay", *Indian Journal of social Research* 20, aug 79 : 105-118.
4331 NEWBY, Howard. "Urbanización y estructura de clases rurales: reflexiones en torno al estudio de un caso" (Urbanization and structure of rural classes: considerations about a case study), *Agricultura y Sociedad* 14, 80 : 9-48.
4332 NIVEN, Douglas. *The development of housing in Scotland*. London, Croom Helm, 79, 136 p.
4333 NORTON, R. D. *City life-cycles and American urban policy*. New York, Academic Press, 79, xv-182 p.
4334 OBUDHO, R. A.; EL-SHAKHS, Salah; [eds.]. *Development of urban systems in Africa*. New York, Praeger, 79, xxv-406 p.

4335 ŌMI, Tetsuo. "Dai-toshi shuhen chiiki no kyoju kankyo ni taisuru jumin no ishiki" (People's consciousness to the residential environment in the urban fringe of metropolitan area), *Waseda daigaku shakai-kagaku tokyu* 25, 80 : 33-59.

4336 OMRAN, Abdel R. "Urbanization and the explosive growth of Arab cities", *Populi* 79 : 13-17.

4337 Organization for Economic Cooperation and Development. *Managing transport: managing of transport systems to improve the urban environment.* Paris, OECD, 79, 299 p.

4338 PARIS, Chris; BLACKABY, Bob. *Not much improvement: house improvement policy in Birmingham.* London, Heinemann, 79, 208 p. CR: Elizabeth LEBAS, *British Journal of Sociology* 31(3), sep 80: 460-461.

4339 PEACE, Adrian. "Prestige, power and legitimacy in a modern Nigerian town", *Canadian Journal of African Studies* 13(1-2), 79 : 25-51.

4340 PHILLIPS, W. S. K. "Social structure and mobility in an urban setting", *Social Action* 30, apr-jun 80 : 138-161.

4341 PIEPER, Richard. *Soziologie im Städtebau* (Sociology in urban planning). Stuttgart, Enke, 79, v-170 p.

4342 PINCHEMEL, Philippe; VIGARIÉ, A.; [eds.]. *Villes et ports: développement portuaire, croissance spatiale des villes, environnement littoral.* Paris, Éditions du CNRS, 79, 595 p. [Second Colloque franco-japonais de géographie, Paris, Marseille, Fos..., 25 septembre-8 octobre, 78.]

4343 PIOLLE, Xavier. *Les citadins et leur ville: approche de phénomènes urbains et recherche méthodologique.* Toulouse, Privat, 79, 432 p.

4344 PONS, Valdo. "Urban problems in developing countries: review article", *Third World Quarterly* jul 80 : 522-535.

4345 POULOSE, K. Thomas. *Experiences and experiments in town and country planning.* Trivandrum, C. Mathews, 79, xxvii-192 p. [India.]

4346 PRADO VALLADARES, Liciado. "Working the system: squatter response to resettlement in Rio de Janeiro", *International Journal of urban and regional Research* mar 78 : 12-25.

4347 PRENANT, André. "La mutation en cours des modes de croissance urbaine en Algérie. Un hommage à Jean Dresch", *Hérodote* 17, jan-mar 80 : 119-159.

4348 RANNIKKO, Pertti. "Urbanismin tila ja tulevaisuus" (The present state and future of urbanism), *Sosiologia* 80 : 195-204.

4349 REES, Philip H. *Residential patterns in American cities.* Chicago, University of Chicago, Dept. of Geography, 79, xvi-405 p.

4350 REICHERT, Henri; REMOND, Jean Daniel. *Analyse sociale de la ville.* Paris, New York, Barcelone, Masson, 80, 226 p.

4351 REPS, John William. *Cities of the American West: a history of frontier urban planning.* Princeton, NJ, Princeton University Press, 79, xii-827 p.

4352 RIDDELL, J. Barry. "Is continuing urbanization possible in West Africa?", *African Studies Review* 23, apr 80 : 69-79.

4353 RIDLER, Neil B. "Development through urbanization: a partial evaluation of the Colombian experiment", *International Journal of urban and regional Research* mar 79 : 49-59.

4354 RIVLIN, Helen Anne B.; HELMER, Katherine; [eds.]. *The Changing Middle Eastern city.* Binghamton, Center for Social Analysis, 80, xiii-262 p. [Program in Southwest Asian and North African Studies, State University of New York at Binghamton.]

4355 RO, Kwang H.; CHANG, Tai O. "Urbanization and housing policy in South Korea", *Asian Profile* dec 79 : 531-546.

4356 ROBERTS, M. Hugh P. *An urban profile of the Middle East.* New York, St. Martin's Press, 79, 239 p.

4357 ROGOVIN, V. Z. "Nekotorye voprosy social'noj politiki v sfere žil'ja" (Some questions on social policy in the dwelling sphere), *IN: Social'nye garantii i problemy soveršenstvovanija raspredelitel'nyh otnošenij.* Moskva, 79 : 86-129.

4358 ROOF, Wade Clark. "Southern birth and racial residential segregation: the case of northern cities", *American Journal of Sociology* 86, sep 80 : 350-358. [USA.]

4359 ROSENTHAL, Donald B. *Urban revitalization.* London, Beverly Hills, Sage Publications, 80, 320 p.

4360 ROTHERNUND, Dietmar; [et al.]; [eds.]. *Urban growth and rural stagnation: studies in the economy of an Indian coalfield and its rural hinterland.* New Delhi, Manohar, 80, xxvi-493 p.

4361 SALAU, Ademola T. "Nigeria's housing policies and programmes: a preliminary assessment", *Planning and Administration* spr 80 : 49-54.

4362 SAULA, Ademola T. "Housing in Africa: toward a reassessment of problems, policies and planning strategies", *Civilisations* 29(3-4), dec 79 : 322-339.

4363	SAYAD, Abdelmalek. "Le foyer des sans-famille", *Actes de la Recherche en Sciences sociales* 32-33, apr-jun 80 : 89-104.
4364	SCHULTHEISS, Flory Jones; [ed.]. *The Small town.* New York, Scribner, 79, vi-296 p.
4365	SCHUTZ, Howard G.; BLAKELY, Edward J. "Social indicators in policy planning: applying the public marketing model in Yuba City, California", *Social Indicators Research* (1-4), jan 80 : 193-206.
4366	SCHWARTZ, Barry. "The suburban landscape: new variations on an old theme", *Contemporary Sociology* jul 80 : 640-650. [survey essay.]
4367	SEVERY, Lawrence J. "Residential migration and crowding", *Journal of Population* 79 : 358-370.
4368	SIEMINSKI, Waldemar. "The social goals of residential communities in Poland", *International Journal of urban and regional Research* jun 79 : 220-227.
4369	SINGH, Andrea Meneffe; DE SOUZA, Alfred. *The urban poor slum and pavement dwellers in the major cities of India.* New Delhi, Manohar, 80, 144 p.
4370	SINHA, M. M. P. *Impact of urbanization on the land use in the rural-urban fringe: a case study of Patna.* New Delhi, Concept, 80, 258 p.
4371	SLATER, David. "Towards a political economy of urbanization in peripheral capitalist societies: problems of theory and method with illustrations from Latin America", *International Journal of urban and regional Research* mar 78 : 26-52.
4372	SMITH, Barry N.; THORNS, David C. "Housing markets and sub markets: an analysis of the role of financial institutions in the allocation of housing", *Australian and New Zealand Journal of Sociology* 16, mar 80 : 4-13.
4373	SMITH, Michael P. *The city and social theory.* New York, St. Martin's Press, 79, xiii-315 p. CR: Elinor R. BOWEN, *American political Science Review* 74(4), dec 80: 1066-1067.
4374	SMITH, Wallace F. *Desarrollo urbano* (Urban development). Buenos Aires, Troquel, 79, 449 p.
4375	SMITH, Woodruff, D. "The emergence of German urban sociology 1900-1910", *Journal of the History of Sociology* 79 : 1-16.
4376	SNIDER, Earle L. "Some social indicators for multiple family housing", *Social Indicators Research* jun 80 : 157-173. [USA.]
4377	SNOW, David A.; LEAHY, Peter J. "The making of a Black slum-ghetto: a case study of neighborhood transition", *Journal of applied behavioral Science* 16, oct-dec 80 : 459-481.
4378	SOEN, Dan; [ed.]. *New trends in urban planning: studies in housing, urban design, and planning.* Oxford, New York, Pergamon Press, 79, ix-357 p.
4379	ŠOMINA, E. S. "Tendencii urbanizacii i rabocij klass SSA" (Urbanization' trends and working class in the USA), *Rabočij Klass i sovremennyj Mir* sep-oct 79 : 85-92.
4380	SOUZA, Washington Peluso Albino de. "O direito econômico e o fenômeno urbano actual" (Economic law and the present urban phenomenon), *Revista brasileira de Estudos políticos* 50, jan 80 : 121-156. [Brazil.]
4381	STAHURA, John. "Suburban status evolution persistence: a structural model", *American sociological Review* 44, dec 79 : 937-947.
4382	STAMBOULI, Fredj. "L'urbanisation du Tiers Monde", *Revue tunisienne de Sciences sociales* 15(53), 78 : 205-208.
4383	STARK, Oded. "On slowing metropolitan city growth", *Population and Development Review* mar 80 : 95-102.
4384	STEEVES, Allan D. "The dissociation of occupation and residence", *Canadian Review of Sociology and Anthropology* 17, mai 80 : 154-168.
4385	STERNLIEB, George; [et al.]. *America's housing: Prospects and problems.* New Brunswick, NJ, Rutgers University, Center for Urban Policy Research, 80, xiv-562 p.
4386	STILWELL, Frank J.B. "Australian urban and regional development in the late 1970's: an overview", *International Journal of urban and regional Research* dec 79 : 527-541.
4387	STOJANOVIČ, Branislav. "Gradovi i gradsko stanovništvo" (Towns and urban population), *Jugoslovenski Pregled* 23(10), oct 79 : 349-356. [Yugoslavia.]
4388	STONE, Michael E. "The housing problem in the United States: origins and prospects", *Socialist Review* 10, jul-aug 80 : 65-119.
4389	TANADA, Hirofumi. "Dai-toshi kogai no kokyo jutaku danchi kyojusha no sumikae to chiikikan ido" (Residence shift and mobility in the suburban housing development), *Waseda daigaku shakaigaku nenshi* 21, 80 : 133-152. [Japan.]
4390	TAUBMANN, Wolfgang. "Bremen, Entwicklung und Struktur der Stadtregion" (Bremen, development and structure of the urban area), *Geographische Rundschau* 32, 80 : 206-218.

4391	TERADA, Ryoichi. "Dai-toshi ni okeru shakai seikatsujo no kyojusei -chii fuseigo to sanka kodo" (Social fitness in the dwelling area of metropolis: status inconsistency and participation), *Tokyo toritsu daigaku sogo toshi kenkyu* 80 : 22-36.
4392	TOBIN, Gary A.; [ed.]. *The changing structure of the city: what happened to the urban crisis.* Beverly Hills, CA, Sage Publications, 79, 320 p. CR: Benjamin BAKER, *American political Science Review* 74(2), jun 80 : 519-520.
4393	TRIVEDI, Harshad R. *Housing and community in old Delhi: the Katra form of urban settlements.* Delhi, Atmaram, 80, xvii-121 p.
4394	TUROWSKI, Jan. *Środowisko mieszkalne w świadomości ludności miejskiej* (Community centers and urban population consciousness). Wrocław, Zakład Narodowy im. Ossolińskich, 79, 268 p.
4395	URANO, Masaki. "Dai-toshi no kyojū kankyō to chiiki seikatsu"(Residential environment in the metropolitan area and social life), *Nihon toshigakukai nenpo* 14, 80 : 137-154.
4396	URANO, Masaki. "Dai-toshi no han'i to sono hatten keitai ni tsuite" (The metropolitan area and its development process), *Sociologos* 80 : 32-43.
4397	VARADY, David P. *Ethnic minorities in urban areas: a case study of racially changing communities.* Boston, M. Nijhoff, 79, xiv-187 p. CR: Douglas LONGSHORE, *Contemporary Sociology (Albany)* 9(6), nov 80: 809-810. [sole distributors for North America, Kluwer Boston, Hingham, MA..]
4398	VIDOR, Ferenc; [ed.]. *Urbanisztika. Válogattot tanulmányok* (Urban problems. Selected studies). Budapest, Gondolat, 79, 562 p.
4399	VOROTILOV, V. A.; ČERKASOV, G. N.; [eds.]. *Metodologija social'no-ėkonomičeskogo planirovanija goroda* (Methodology of a town socio-economic planning). Leningrad, Nauka, 80, 193 p.
4400	VUJOVIĆ, Sreten. "Stambena kriza i ljudske potrebe" (Housing crises and human needs), *Sociologija* 21, 79 : 441-465.
4401	VUJOVIĆ, Sreten. "Stambena kriza i ljudske potrebe" (Housing crises and human needs), *Sociologija;30221, 79 : 441-456.*
4402	WAGNER, F. E.; WARD, John O. "Urbanization and migration in Brazil", *American Journal of Economics and Sociology* 39, aug 80 : 249-259.
4403	WARD, Sally K. "National linkages and city planning: a note on the correlates of planning expenditures", *Social Science Quarterly* 61, sep 80 : 308-317.
4404	WATANUKI, Jōji. "International dimensions of Japanese cities", *Kokusaigaku kenkyu* 80 : 31-48.
4405	WILLEMS, Emilio. "Die Barackensiedlungen Lateinamerikas als städtische "Frontier"" (The slums of Latin America as urban frontier), *Kölner Zeitschrift für Soziologie und Sozialpsychologie* 32, 80 : 281-295.
4406	Bibl.XXIX-4290. WILSON, Robert A.; SCHULZ, David A. *Urban sociology.* CR: George E. ARQUITT Jr., *Contemporary Sociology (Albany)* 9(3), mai 80: 408-409.
4407	YAZAKI, Takeo. *"Hatten-tojokoku no toshi mondai; Hongkong teishotokuso no jutaku mondai o jirei toshite"* (Housing conditions and quality of living of the low income groups in Hong Kong), *Keiō daigaku hogaku kenkyu* 53, 80 : 217-262.
4408	ZAGORODNAJA, Ė. M. *Urbanizacija Moldavskoj SSR: regional'nye osobennosti, ėkonomičeskie problemy* (The Moldavian SSR urbanization: regional characteristics, economic problems). Kišinev, Štiinca, 80, 132 p.
4409	ZUKIN, Sharon. "A decade of the new urban sociology", *Theory and Society* jul 80 : 575-601.

17. ECONOMICS
SCIENCE ÉCONOMIQUE

17100. ECONOMIC SOCIOLOGY
SOCIOLOGIE ÉCONOMIQUE

[See also / voir aussi: 3968, 4537]

4410 BECATTINI, Giacomo. *Scienza economica e trasformazioni sociali* (Economics and social transformations). Firenze, La nuova Italia, 79, xiii-285 p.
4411 HAYASE, Toshio. *Keizai shakaigaku no mondai*(Problems of economic sociology). Tokyo, Yachiyo shuppan, 249 p.
4412 MAYER, Thomas; [ed.]. "Economics: progress and prospects", *American behavioral Scientist* 23, jan-feb 80 : 299-456.
4413 MELOTTI, Umberto. *Sociologia, storia e marxismo: saggi di sociologia economica* (Sociology, history and marxism: essays of economic sociology). Milano, Unicopli, 79, 213 p.
4414 VOJNIC, Dragomier. "Samoupravljange i ekonomske nauke" (Self-management and economic sciences), *Politička Misao* 17(1-2), 80 : 63-85. [Yugoslavia.]

17200. ECONOMIC SYSTEM
SYSTÈME ÉCONOMIQUE

17210. Economic doctrine
Doctrine économique

[See also / voir aussi: 3422, 3884]

4415 BERKOWITZ, S. D. "Forms of state economy and the development of Western Canada", *Canadian Journal of Sociology* 79 : 287-312.
4416 LOPEZ ROA, Angel Luis. "La propiedad como hecho económico" (Property as an economic fact), *Documentación social* 40, 80 : 25-46.
4417 MUKAI, Toshimasa. "Keizai taikeiron ni tsuite no ichi-kosatsu" (A consideration of the theory of economic system), *Kokumin keizai zasshi* 141, 80 : 33-53.
4418 NAVARRO, José. "Propiedad y poder en una sociedad desigual" (Property and power in an unequal society), *Documentación social* 40, 80 : 7-24.
4419 PAREL, Anthony; FLANAGAN, Thomas; [eds.]. *Theories of property: Aristotle to the present: essays*. Waterloo, Ont., Wilfred Laurier University Press, 79, viii-395 p. [published for the Calgary Institute for the Humanities.]
4420 SANCHEZ JIMENEZ, José. "Las luchas por la propiedad privada y su influencia en la organización de la sociedad" (Struggles for private property and their impact on social organization), *Documentación social* 40, 80 : 47-84.

17220. Capitalism. Collectivism
Capitalisme. Collectivisme

[See also / voir aussi: 90, 133, 396, 678, 719, 729, 739, 753, 765, 766, 767, 777, 851, 858, 869, 1211, 1222, 1258, 1262, 1264, 1269, 1274, 1283, 1292, 1322, 1325, 1339, 1340, 1347, 1352, 1358, 1359, 1372, 1382, 1390, 1400, 1412, 1441, 1443, 1461, 1470, 1473, 1482, 1498, 1505, 1513, 1587, 1616, 1657, 1769, 2043, 2079, 2226, 2229, 2447, 2479, 2560, 2562, 2574, 2580, 2651, 2664, 2691, 2717, 2741, 2759, 2764, 2793, 2859, 2877, 2878, 2893, 3016, 3047, 3054, 3162, 3541, 3542, 3546, 3968, 4044, 4119, 4507, 4539, 4540, 4578, 4629, 4699, 4703, 4905, 5075, 5086, 5105, 5317, 5347, 5356, 5424, 5463, 5470, 5471, 5475, 5477, 5483, 5510, 5512, 5583, 5591, 5630, 5733, 6015, 6019, 6069, 6081]

4421 "Mouvement (Le) coopératif au Royaume-Uni", *Revue de la Coopération internationale* 72, 79 : 136-156.
4422 AITOV, N. A. "Nekotorye voprosy upravlenija social'nymi processami v razvitom socialističeskom obščestve" (Some questions on the social processes management in the developed socialist society), *Naučnyj Kommunizm* 79 : 21-29.

4423   ANŽIGANOV, V. S. "O zakonomernostjah pererastanija ranee otstalyh narodov SSSR v socialističeskie nacii" (On the laws of the underdeveloped peoples transformation into socialist nations), *Naučnyj Kommunizm* 79 : 55-63.
4424   BENETTI, Carlo; CARTELIER, Jean. *Marchands, salariat et capitalistes.* Paris, Maspero, 80, 207 p.
4425   BERBEROGLU, Berch. "Toward a theory of state capitalist development in the Third World", *International Review of modern Sociology* jan-jun 79 : 17-29.
4426   BROWN, Lawrence A.; [et al.]. "Innovation diffusion and development in a Third World setting: the cooperative movement in Sierra Leone", *Social Science Quarterly* 60, sep 79 : 249-268.
4427   CANCIAN, Francesca M.; GOODMAN, Louis Wold; SMITH, Peter H. "Capitalism, industrialisation, and kinship in Latin America: major issues", *Journal of Family History* 78 : 314-336.
4428   CHAPMAN ORBEGOSO, Luis Alberto. *Introducción al estudio histórico del feudalismo en el Perú* (Introduction to the historical study of feudalism in Peru). Lima, Perú, Universidad Nacional Mayor de San Marcos, Departamento Académico de Ciencias Histórico-Sociales, 79, 55 p.
4429   COHEN, Jere. "Rational capitalism in Renaissance Italy", *American Journal of Sociology* 85, mai 80 : 1340-1355.
4430   CORELLI, Emilio. *Il movimento cooperativo in Italia ieri e oggi* (The cooperative movement in Italy yesterday and today). Torino, Stampatori Università, 79, 122 p.
4431   COURNANEL, Alain; [ed.]. *Capitalisme et lutte des classes en Afrique australe.* Paris, Presses universitaires de France, 79, 223 p.
4432   Bibl.XXIX-4531. DUBY, Georges. *Les trois ordres ou l'imaginaire du féodalisme.* CR: James K. LINDSEY, *Revue française de Sociologie* 21(3), jul-sep 80: 468-472.
4433   GORJAČEVA, A. I.; [ed.]. *Social'nye processy razvitija socialističeskogo obščestva i ideologičeskaja bor'ba* (Social processes of the developed socialist society and the ideological struggle). Tallin, AN ESSR, 79, 173 p.
4434   HOWARTH, F. "The co-operative movement in Jordan", *Yearbook of agricultural Cooperation* 79 : 105-124.
4435   KULIČENKO, M. "Dialektika nacional'nogo i internacional'nogo v uslovijah razvitogo socializma" (Dialectics of the national and international under conditions of developed socialism), *Kommunist Moldavii* (11), 79 : 38-44.
4436   LA PEÑA, Sergio De. "Acumulacíon capitalista y población" (Capitalist accumulation and population), *Revista mexicana de Sociología* 41, oct-dec 79 : 1369-1383.
4437   LACROIX, Jean. "Le choix coopératif", *Revue des Études coopératives* 198, 79 : 3-22.
4438   LOUIS, Raymond. "Diagnostic du mouvement coopératif colombien", *Revue des Études coopératives* 198, 79 : 67-80.
4439   MANDLE, Jay R. "Marxist analyses and capitalist development in the Third World", *Theory and Society* nov 80 : 865-876.
4440   MAROUTIAN, Mélanie. "Les coopératives de production au Portugal", *Revue des Études coopératives* 198, 79 : 82-105.
4441   MARSHALL, Gordon. "The Weber thesis and the development of capitalism in Scotland", *Scottish Journal of Sociology* apr 79 : 173-211.
4442   MAYORGA, Rcné Antonio. "Problemas metodológicos de la dialéctica y del análisis marxista del Estado capitalista" (Methodological problems of dialectics and marxist analysis of the capitalist state), *Revista mexicana de Sociología* 41, oct-dec 79 : 1385-1419.
4443   MEYER, Gerd. *Sozialistische Systeme: Theorie- u. Strukturanalyse.* Opladen, Leske und Budrich, 79, 310 p. [Eastern Europe.]
4444   MUTCH, Robert E. "Colonial America and the debate about transition to capitalism", *Theory and Society* nov 80 : 847-863.
4445   NIKOL'NIKOV, G. L.; [ed.]. *Razvitoe socialističeskoe obščestvo i mirovoj revoljucionnyj process* (The developed socialist society and the world revolutionary process). Kiev, Višča Škola, 79, 339 p.
4446   OUTTERS-JAEGER, Ingelies. *The development impact of barter in developing countries: synthesis report.* Paris, Development Centre of the Organisation for Economic Cooperation and Development, 79, 130 p.
4447   PINHO, Benevides D. "Anatomie du mouvement coopératif brésilien", *Communautés* 50, oct-dec 79 : 42-56.
4448   PIPITONE, Ugo. "Crisis, estancamiento y restructuración de la economía capitalista" (Crisis, stagnation and restructuration of the capitalist economy), *Revista mexicana de Sociología* 41, oct-dec 79 : 1469-1500.

4449 POPOV, A. N.; ČEREDNJAK, P. G. "Formirovanie social'noj odnorodnosti obščestva zrelogo socializma" (Formation of the mature socialism society social homogeneity), *Naučnyj Kommunizm* 79 : 3-12.
4450 QUINNEY, Richard; [ed.]. *Capitalist society: readings for a critical sociology*. Homewood, IL, Dorsey Press, 79, x-440 p.
4451 ŠABALIN, V. A. "Pravo razvitogo socialističeskogo obščestva" (The developed socialist society law), *Nekotorye filosofskie Problemy Gosudarstva i Prava* 79 : 34-49.
4452 SACOUMAN, R. J. "The differing origin, organization, and impact of Maritime and Prairie cooperative movements to 1940", *Canadian Journal of Sociology* 79 : 199-221.
4453 SCHNEIDER, João Elmo. "Développement capitaliste et sous-développements coopératifs au Brésil", *Communautés* 51, jan-mar 80 : 67-79.
4454 SCOTT, John. *Corporations, classes, and capitalism*. London, Hutchinson, 79, 219 p. CR: Frank LONGSTRETH, *British Journal of Sociology* 31(4), dec 80: 590-591.
4455 SEGRE, Sandro. "Apologia indiretta del capitalismo la razionalità formale come ideologia in Max Weber" (Indirect apology of capitalism: the formal rationality as an ideology in Max Weber), *Rassegna italiana di Sociologia* 21, apr-jun 80 : 209-238.
4456 ŠMEL'KOV, M. I. "Dve stadii razvitija socialističeskogo obščestva i osnovnoj kriterij razvitogo socializma" (Two stages of the socialist society development and the essential criterion of developed socialism), *Naučnyj Kommunizm* 79 : 3-12.
4457 SOLOV'EV, O. M. "Klassovyj harakter socialističeskoj demokratii" (Class character of the socialist democracy), *Politiěeskaja Organizacija Obščestva i Upravlenie pri Socializme* 79 : 84-96.
4458 TABBONI, Simonetta. "Sviluppi del dibattito sull'origine del capitalismo" (Developments of the discussion on the origins of capitalism), *Rassegna italiana di Sociologia* 20, jul-sep 79 : 495-505.
4459 VAN DEN HAAG, Ernest; [ed.]. *Capitalism, sources of hostility*. New Rochelle, NY, published by Epoch Books for the Heritage Foundation, 79, 206 p.
4460 VASIL'ČUK, Ju. A.; RYDVANOV, N. F.; [eds.]. *Ėkonomičeskij krizis i položenie trudjaščihsja v 70-e gody: problemy sovremennyh bezraboticy i inflacii v razvityh kapitalističeskih stranah* (The economic crisis and the workers: situation in the seventies: problems of contemporary unemployment and inflation in the developed capitalist countries).
4461 VETROV, V. A. "Ponjatie tradicij socialističeskoj demokratii" (The concept of the socialist democracy traditions), *IN: Problemy upravlenija v uslovijah razvitogo socializma*. Moskva, 79 : 39-52.
4462 WEITZER, Ronald. "Law and legal ideology: contributions to the genesis and reproduction of capitalism", *Berkeley Journal of Sociology* 24-25, 80 : 137-157.
4463 WINTER, Michael F.; ROBERT, Ellen R. "Male dominance, late capitalism, and the growth of instrumental reason", *Berkeley Journal of Sociology* 24-25, 80 : 249-280.

**17300. ECONOMIC SITUATION. STANDARD OF LIVING
SITUATION ÉCONOMIQUE. NIVEAU DE VIE**

Situation économique. Niveau de vie

**17310. Economy. Economic development
Économie. Développement économique**

[See also / voir aussi: 1622, 3645, 3796, 4876, 5058, 5516]

4464 HARDY, Melissa A. "Economic growth, distributional inequality and political conflict in industrial societies", *Journal of political and military Sociology* aut 79 : 209-227.
4465 JAEGER, Carlo. *Ein Modell der Wirtschaftsgesellschaft* (A model of the economic society). Frankfurt am Main, Bern, Cirencester/U.K., Lang, 79, 127 p.
4466 JOHNSON, Harry G. *Economía y sociedad* (Economics and society). Buenos Aires, El Ateneo, 79, 315 p.
4467 SHIN, Doh C. "Does rapid economic growth improve the human lot? Some empirical evidence", *Social Indicators Research* jun 80 : 199-221.
4468 TOLBERT, Charles; HORAN, Patrick M.; BECK, E. M. "The structure of economic segmentation: a dual economy approach", *American Journal of Sociology* 85, mar 80 : 1095-1116.

**17320. Income. Living conditions
Revenu. Conditions de vie**

[See also / voir aussi: 478, 877, 1507, 2335, 2724, 2778, 2858, 3003, 3103, 3238, 3491, 3544, 4407, 4464, 4701, 4806, 5172, 5202, 5212, 5773]

4469 ABRAHAMSON, Mark. "Sudden wealth, gratification and attainment: Durkheim's anomie of affluence reconsidered", *American sociological Review* 45, feb 80 : 49-57.

4470 AITOV, N. A. "Ponjatie uslovij žizni" (The "standard of living" concept), *IN: Social'naja struktura sovetskogo obščestva i socialističeskij obraz žizni. II.* Moskva, 78 : 72-82.

4471 ANDREWS, Frank; INGLEHART, Ronald F. "The structure of subjective well-being in nine Western societies", *Social Indicators Research* jan 79 : 73-90.

4472 ANDREWS, Frank; MCKENNELL, Aubrey C. "Measures of self-reported well-being: their affective, cognitive, and other components", *Social Indicators Research* jun 80 : 127-155.

4473 ANGELUSZ, Róbert; NAGY, Lajos Géza; TARDOS, Róbert. Munkásvélemények az életszínvonalról, a személyes anyagi és az gazdasági helyzetről (Blue-collar opinions about living standards and about the financial situation of the country and of the individuals). Budapest, Tömegkommunikációs, 79, 69 p.

4474 BAUDOIN, P. "'Petits héritiers, petits héritages...', ou de l'héritage, des droits de succession et de l'inégalité de la richesse en Belgique(1952 à 1961 et 1968 à 1974)", *Recherches sociologiques* 11, 80 : 85-102.

4475 BAUMGARTNER, Tom; BURNS, Tom R. "Inflation: the outcome of institutionalized social struggle over income distribution", *Acta sociologica* 23(2-3), 80 : 177-186.

4476 BELLEN, H.; VAN HERBRUGGEN, C. "Evaluating the quality of life in Belgium", *Social Indicators Research* sep 80 : 311-326.

4477 BIANCHI, Suzanne M. "Racial differences in per capita income, 1960-76: the importance of household size, headship, and labor force participation", *Demography* 17, mai 80 : 129-144.

4478 BLUHM, Lhis H. "The curvilinear level-of-living hypothesis: a new look at cultural lag", *Rural Sociology* 44, wint 79 : 691-704.

4479 BUBOLZ, Margaret M.; [et al.]. "A human ecological approach to quality of life: conceptual framework and results of a preliminary study", *Social Indicators Research* (1-4), jan 80 : 103-136.

4480 BURT, Ronald S.; FISCHER, Michael G.; CHRISTMAN, Kenneth P. "Structures of well-being: sufficient conditions for identification as restricted co-variance models", *Sociological Methods and Research* aug 79 : 111-120.

4481 COELLEN, Stephen P. "Regression analysis of regional quality of life", *Social Indicators Research* dec 80 : 467-479. [Pennsylvania, USA.]

4482 FERNANDEZ, Roberto. *Sistema de la calidad de vida* (Quality of life system). Buenos Aires, Troquel, 79, 134 p.

4483 GILLINGHAM, Robert; REECE, William S. "Analytical problems in the measurement of the quality of life", *Social Indicators Research* (1-4), jan 80 : 91-101.

4484 GRAZIOSI, Mariolina. "Problemi nella misurazione del benessere sociale: indicatori oggettivi e soggettivi" (Problems of social welfare measurement: objective and subjective indicators), *Quaderni di Sociologia* 28, mar 79 : 71-101.

4485 HANKISS, Elemér; MANCHIN, Róbert; FÜSTÖS, László. *Országos élet minöség vizsgálat* (National survey of the quality of life). Budapest, Magyar Tudományos Akadémia Népmüvelési Intézete, 79, 2-121 p. [Hungary.]

4486 HENDERSON, D. W.; ROWLEY, J. C. R. "Decomposition of an aggregate measure of income distribution", *Social Indicators Research* (1-4), jan 80 : 353-366.

4487 JAGODZINSKI, Wolfgang; WEEDE, Erich. "Weltpolitische und ökonomische Determinanten einer ungleichen Einkommensverteilung. Eine international vergleichende Studie" (World political and economic determinants of unequal distribution of income — an internationally comparative study), *Zeitschrift für Soziologie* 80 : 132-148.

4488 KAHN, Lawrence M. "Wage growth and endogenous experience", *Industrial Relations* 19, 80 : 50-63.

4489 KOO, Hagen; HONG, Doo-Seung. "Class and income inequality in Korea", *American sociological Review* 45, aug 80 : 610-626.

4490 LINDEN, Eugene. *Affluence and discontent: the anatomy of consumer societies.* New York, Viking Press, 79, xiv-178 p.

4491 MACAROV, David. "A note on some socio-economic perspectives on the quality of working life", *International Journal of social Economics* 80 : 149-150.

4492 MAYHEW, Bruce H.; SCHOLLAERT, Paul T. "The concentration of wealth: a sociological model", *Sociological Focus* 13, jan 80 : 1-35.

4493 MCGRANAHAN, David A. "The spatial structure of income distribution in rural regions", *American sociological Review* 45, apr 80 : 313-324. [USA.]

4494 MCKENNELL, Aubrey C.; ANDREWS, Frank. "Models of cognition and affect in perceptions of well-being", *Social Indicators Research* sep 80 : 257-298.

4495 MOBERG, David O. "The development of social indicators for quality of life research", *Sociological Analysis* 40, 79 : 11-26.

4496 MOLM, Linda D. "The development of social exchange under incompatible social contingencies", *Social Psychology Quarterly* 42, dec 79 : 324-339.

4497 MUKHERJEE, M.; RAY, A. K.; RAJYALAKSHMI, C. "Physical quality of life index: some international and Indian applications", *Social Indicators Research* jul 79 : 283-292.

4498 NANDI, Proshanta K. *The quality of life of Asian Americans: an exploratory study in a middle size community.* Chicago, IL, Pacific/Asian American Mental Health Research Center, 80, xvi-204 p.

4499 NEWTON, Keith; LECKIE, Norman; PETTMAN, Barrie O. "The quality of working life", *International Journal of social Economics* 79 : 199-234.

4500 PEN, Jan. "A clear case of leveling: income equalization in the Netherlands", *Social Research* 46, 79 : 682-694.

4501 PEZZULLO, Thomas R.; BRITTINGHAM, Barbara E.; [eds.]. *Salary equity: Detecting sex bias in salaries among college and university professors.* Lexington, MA, Toronto, Heath, Lexington Books, 79, 162 p. CR: Marianne FERBER, *Journal of economic literature* 18(1), mar 80: 170-172.

4502 PINKER, Robert. *The idea of welfare.* London, Heinemann Educational, 79, x-276 p. CR: Ray JONES, *British Journal of Sociology* 31(4), dec 80: 598.

4503 RICHMOND, Anthony H.; VERMA, Ravi P. "Income inequality in Canada: ethnic and generational aspects", *Canadian Studies in Population* 78 : 25-36.

4504 ROSENBAUM, James E. "Hierarchical and individual effects on earnings", *Industrial Relations* 19, 80 : 1-14.

4505 RUSS-EFT, Darlene. "Indentifying components comprising neighborhood quality of life", *Social Indicators Research* jul 79 : 349-372.

4506 SIMON, Rita J.; RAU, William; FELLOWS, Mary Louise. "Public versus statutory choice of heirs: a study of public attitudes about property distribution at death", *Social Forces* 58, jun 80 : 1263-1271.

4507 ŠIRALIEV, A. I.; RASULOVA, S. K. "Nekotorye napravlenija povyšenija urovnja žizni naslenija v razvitom socialističeskom obščestve" (Some tendencies of the population standard of living elevation in the developed socialist society), *Naučnye Trudy Azerbajdžanskogo Universiteta. Serija juridičeskij Nauk* 79 : 9-17.

4508 STOETZEL, Jean. "Le cours de la vie selon la condition sociale. Une étude des revenus selon l'âge dans les diverses professions", *Revue française de Sociologie* 21, apr-jun 80 : 155-170.

4509 SZALAI, Alexander; ANDREWS, Frank. *The quality of life.* Beverly Hills, CA, Sage Publications, 80, 272 p.

4510 URBINA, Fernando. "Desarrollo y calidad de vida" (Development and quality of life), *Documentación social* 38, 80 : 7-47.

4511 UTTLEY, Stephen. "The welfare exchange reconsidered", *Journal of social Policy* apr 80 : 187-205.

4512 VISARIA, Pravin. "Poverty and living standards in Asia", *Population and Development Review* jun 80 : 189-223.

4513 VUIJSJE, Flip. "Crisis, welvaart en verdelingsstrijd" (Crisis, welfare and distributional conflicts), *Sociologische Gids* 27, sep-oct 80 : 393-408.

4514 WASSERMAN, Ira M.; CHUA, Lily Aurora. "Objective and subjective social indicators of the quality of life in American SMSA'S: a reanalysis", *Social Indicators Research* sep 80 : 365-381. [Standard Metropolitan Statistical Areas.]

4515 WEEDE, Erich. "Beyond misspecification in sociological analyses of income inequality", *American sociological Review* 45, jun 80 : 497-501.

4516 WELCH, Stephen W. "Union-nonunion construction wage differentials", *Industrial Relations* 19, 80 : 152-162.

4517 YOUNG, Ruth C. "The quality of life in the Caribbean: a political interpretation", *Social Indicators Research* sep 80 : 299-310.

4518 YOUNG, Ruth C.; MACCANNELL, Dean. "Predicting the quality of life in the United States", *Social Indicators Research* jan 79 : 23-40.

17400. ENTERPRISE. PRODUCTION
ENTREPRISE. PRODUCTION

17410. Business economics. Management
Économie de l'entreprise. Gestion

[See also / voir aussi: 1077, 2706, 2869, 4414, 4454, 4981, 5107, 5113, 5271, 5404, 5412, 6099]

4519 ALLEN, Thomas Harrell. *The bottom line: communicating in the organization.* Chicago, Nelson Hall, 79, viii-168 p.
4520 ALONSO SOTO, Francisco. "La empresa autogestionada como alternativa socio-económica" (The self-managed enterprise as a socioeconomic alternative), *Documentación social* 40, 80 : 195-211.
4521 ANDRE-BRUNET, Adolphe. "L'entreprise et les hommes", *Revue des Travaux de l'Académie des Sciences morales et politiques* 131, 78 : 225-245.
4522 BANNER, David K. *Business and society: Canadian issues.* Toronto, New York, McGraw-Hill Ryerson, 79, xi-388 p.
4523 BARON, James N.; BIELBY, William T. "Bringing the firms back in: stratification, segmentation, and the organization of work", *American sociological Review* 45, oct 80 : 737-765.
4524 BAUER, Michel; COHEN, Élie. "Le gouvernement de la grande entreprise: pouvoir de la propriété ou appropriation du pouvoir?", *Sociologie du Travail* 22, apr-jun 80 : 193-212.
4525 BAUER, Michel; COHEN, Élie. "Les limites du pouvoir des cadres: l'organisation de la négociation comme moyen d'exercice de la domination", *Sociologie du Travail* 22, jul-sep 80 : 276-299.
4526 BRUSA, Luigi. *Strutture organizzative d'impresa* (Organizational structure of the enterprise). Milano, Giuffrè, 79, xi-223 p.
4527 BRUSATTI, Alois. "Der Individualismus als geistige Grundlage des europäischen Unternehmers" (Individualism as the mental foundation of European entrepreneurs), *Zeitschrift für Unternehmensgeschichte* 24, 79 : 3-11.
4528 BURRELL, Gibson; MORGAN, Gareth. *Sociological paradigms and organisational analysis: elements of the sociology of corporate life.* London, Heinemann, 79, xiv-432 p.
4529 BURT, Ronald S.; CHRISTMAN, Kenneth P.; KILBURN, Harold C. Jr. "Testing a structural theory of corporate cooptation: interorganizational directorate ties as a strategy for avoiding market constraints on profits", *American sociological Review* 45, oct 80 : 821-841.
4530 ČERNENKO, M. S.; [ed.]. *Naučno-tehničeskij progress i problemy social'nogo razvitija socialističeskogo predprijatija* (The scientific and technical progress and problems of the socialist enterprise social development). Kiev, Izdatel'stvo pri Kievskom Gosudarstvennom Universitet, 79, 157 p. [USSR.]
4531 CROUZET, Alain. *Structure et pouvoir dans l'entreprise: l'organique des entreprises nationales et multinationales.* Neuilly-sur-Seine, Editions du Pont d'Arc, 79, 351 p.
4532 EELLS, Richard. *The political crisis of the enterprise system.* New York, Macmillan, London, Collier Macmillan, 80, xxii-101 p. [Studies of the Modern Corporation series, Graduate School of Business, Columbia University.]
4533 GRIGAS, R. *Social'naja organizacija predprijatija i eë funkcii* (The enterprise social organization and its functions). Vil'njus, Mintis, 80, 317 p.
4534 GRIGAS, R. S. "Razvitie social'nyh funkcij socialisticeskogo predprijatija v uslovijah naučno-tehničeskoj revoljucii" (The development of the socialist enterprise social functions under conditions of the scientific and technical revolution), *IN: Sociologičeskie problemy obrazovanija, kul'tury i nauki.* Moskva, 78 : 16-28.
4535 GUILLERM, Alain. *L'autogestion généralisée.* Paris, C. Bourgois, 79, 215 p. CR: Trinh Van THAO, *Revue française de Sociologie* 21(1), jan-mai 80: 135-138.
4536 HÄBERLE, Eckehard J. *Strukturwandel der Unternehmung: Unters. zur Produktionsform d. bürgerl. Gesellschaft in Deutschland von 1870-1914* (Structure change of the enterprise: research on the production form of the bourgeois society in Germany from 1870 to 1914). Frankfurt/Main, Haag und Herchen, 79, x-456 p.
4537 HONDRICH, Karl-Otto. "Betriebswirtschaftslehre als Sozialwissenschaft — zum Verhältnis von Soziologie und Ökonomie" (Business economics as social science: on the relation between sociology and economics), *Soziologische Revue* 80 : 269-277. [review article.]

4538 HUSSEY, David E.; LANGHAM, M. J. *Corporate planning: the human factor.* Oxford, New York, Pergamon Press, 79, xv-298 p.
4539 KLEER, Jerzy. "Einige theoretische Probleme des sozialistischen Genossenschaftswesens" (Some theoretical problems of socialist cooperatives), *Zeitschrift für das gesamte Genossenschaftswesen* 29, 79 : 312-325.
4540 KOCKA, Jürgen. "Familie, Unternehmer und Kapitalismus. An Beispielen aus der frühen deutschen Industrialisierung" (Family, entrepreneur and capitalism. An example from the early German industrialization), *Zeitschrift für Unternehmensgeschichte* 23, 79 : 99-135.
4541 KREITNER, Robert. *Management, a problem-solving process.* Boston, Houghton Mifflin, 80, xix-554 p.
4542 KUZMANOVIĆ, Bora. "Naučno savetovanje o istrazivanju samoupravljanja" (Scientific symposium on the study of self-management), *Gledista* 21(3-4), mar-apr 80 : 97-105.
4543 LAMBERT, Jacques. *L'information ascendante dans les entreprises.* Paris, Entreprise moderne d'édition, 79, 166 p.
4544 LARÇON, Jean Paul; REITTER. ROLAND. *Structures de pouvoir et identité de l'entreprise.* Paris, F. Nathan, 79, 174 p.
4545 LIEBAU, Eberhard. *Organisation und Entscheidung: krit. Analyse d. Theorie d. Unternehmungsorganisation* (Organization and decision: a critical analysis of the theory of enterprise organization). Frankfurt/Main, New York, Campus-Verlag, 79, 322 p.
4546 LOUIS, Dieter. "Zur Stabilität von kooperativen Organisationen" (On the stability of cooperative organizations), *Zeitschrift für das gesamte Genossenschaftswesen* 29, 79 : 295-311.
4547 MCINTYRE, J.; SHULL, F. "Managerial perceptions of role discretion as related to selected organizational and personal variables. An international study", *Management international Review* 19, 79 : 69-79.
4548 MERKULOV, A. N. "Suščnost' socialističeskogo samoupravlenija" (Nature of the socialist self-management), IN: *Filosofskaja mysl' i aktual'nye problemy poznanija mira.* Leningrad, 79 : 211-215.
4549 MERKULOV, A. N. "Stanovlenie i razvitie socialističeskogo samouprovlenija" (The future and development of the socialist self-management), IN: *Marksistskoleninskaja filosofija i problemy razvitija nauki i praktiki.* Leningrad, 79 : 230-235.
4550 MILANOVIĆ, Vladimir. "Protivrečnosti i sukobi u udruženom radu" (Contradictions and conflicts in the associated labour), *Sociologija* 21, 79 : 481-488.
4551 MILLER, J. A. "Participation structure and two-way communication", *Management international Review* 19, 79 : 89-101.
4552 MLINAR, Zdravko. "Samoupravljanje i sociologija" (Self-management and sociology), *Sociologija* 22(1-2), 80 : 45-70.
4553 MLINAR, Zdravko. "Samoupravljanje i sociologija" (Self-management and sociology), *Sociologija* 22(1-2), 80 : 45-70.
4554 O'CONNELL, Sandra E. *The manager as communicator.* San Francisco, Harper & Row, 79, xii-192 p.
4555 PEPE, Cosetta. *Le imprese in Cina: analisi dei modelli gestionali e delle strutture organizzative* (Enterprises in China: analysis of management models and organizational structures). Milano, F. Angeli, 79, 175 p.
4556 PERROUX, François; [et al.]. "Science de gestion", *Économies et Sociétés. Cahiers de l'ISÉA* 13(4-5-6), apr-jun 79 : 453-1043.
4557 POST, James E. "The corporation in the public policy process — a view toward the 1980s", *Sloan Management Review* 21, aut 79 : 45-52.
4558 ROVATI, Giancarlo. "Dall'imprenditore dirigente al dirigente imprenditore: chiarimenti teorici per una ricerca empirica" (Manager-entrepreneur and entrepreneur-manager: some theoretical guidelines for an empirical research), *Studi di Sociologia* 17, jan-mar 79 : 40-58.
4559 SCOTT, John; HUGHES, Michael. "Capital and communication in Scottish business", *Sociology* 14, feb 80 : 29-47.
4560 SHILS, Edward B.; ZUCKER, William. "Developing a model for internal corporate entrepreneurship", *Social Science* 54, aut 79 : 195-203.
4561 STAROVEROV, V. I. "Social'nye rezul'taty i posledstvija mezhozjajstvennoj kooperacii i agropromyšlennoj integracii" (Social results and consequences of the interenterprise cooperation and the agroindustrial integration), *Sociologičeskie Issledovanija* 79 : 63-76.

4562 TACCHI, Enrico Maria. "La 'funzione organizzazione' nel quadro dello sviluppo strutturale dell'impresa italiana" (The Organization Department in the framework of the structural development of the Italian firms), *Studi di Sociologia* 17, apr-jun 80 : 193-207.
4563 TOŠ, Peter. "Socio-economic position of workers in associated labour", *Socialism in Yugoslav Theory and Practice* (12), 79 : 75-99.
4564 UMEZAWA, Tadashi. *Gendai no management to soshiki kaihatsu* (Management and organization development). Tokyo, Tsushin jigyo kyoiku shinkokai, 79, 210 p.
4565 VINOGRADOV, V. D.; SMIRNOV, B. V. "Upravlenčeskie otnošenija v sisteme proizvodstva: priroda i soderzanie" (Management relations in the production system: nature and content), *Političeskaja Organizacija Obščestva i Upravlenie pri Socializme* 79 : 96-107.
4566 VLOEBERGHS, D. "Manager (De) als communicator"(The manager as communicator), *Economisch en sociaal Tijdschrift* 33, 79 : 645-662.
4567 WIDERKEHR, Doris E. "Autonomy overshadowed: a Bolivian cooperative within the nationalized mining industry", *Human Organization* 39, 80 : 153-160.
4568 WILKEN, Paul H. *Entrepreneurship: a comparative and historical study.* Norwood, NJ, Ablex Publ. Corp., 79, xiv-306 p.

17420. Productivity. Technology
Productivité. Technologie

[See also / voir aussi: 83, 148, 758, 781, 1012, 1104, 1355, 1958, 1965, 2421, 2683, 2762, 2791, 3047, 3151, 3492, 3927, 4227, 4424, 4534, 4565, 4694, 4756, 4992, 5087, 5096]

4569 ABDIL'DIN, Z. M.; [ed.]. *Naučno-tehničeskaja revoljucija i duhovnoj mir čeloveka: filosofsko-sociologičeskie problemy* (The scientific and technical revolution and man's spiritual world: philosophical and sociological problems). Alma-Ata, Nauka, 79, 358 p.
4570 AGUESSY, Honorat. "Les rapports entre échanges technologiques et l'identité culturelle: adaptation des transferts et mutations sociales", *Revue de l'AUPELF* 17, mai 80 : 120-136.
4571 AMKSABEDIAN, Jorge. "El proceso social en la inovación y en la transferencia tecnológica" (Social process in innovation and technology transfer), *Revista latinoamericana de Psicología* 12, 80 : 109-117.
4572 ANDRIANOVA, G. M. "Vlijanie NTR na socialističeskij obraz zizni" (Influence of the scientific and technical revolution on the socialist way of life), *IN: Marksistsko-leninskaja filosofija i problemy razvitija nauki i praktiki: sbornik aspirantskih rabot.* Leningrad, 78 : 155-160.
4573 ARONOV, A. B.; TEREHOV, A. M. "Vlijanie naučno-tehničeskoj revoljucii na izmenenie haraktera i soderžanija truda" (The scientific and technical revolution influence on the labour character and content change), *IN: Puti sbliženija klassov i social'nyh sloev v uslovijah socializma.* Kemerovo, 78 : 55-65.
4574 ARTANOVSKIJ, S. N. "Naučno-tehničeskaja revoljucija i sovremennaja kul'tura" (The scientific and technical revolution and contemporary culture), *IN: Ėkonomika i kul'tura.* Leningrad, 78 : 3-17.
4575 BARON, C. "La politique énergétique et le progrés social dans les pays en développement", *Revue internationale du Travail* 119, sep-oct 80 : 575-594.
4576 BAUM, Richard; [ed.]. *China's four modernizations: The new technological revolution.* Westview Special Studies on China and East Asia, Boulder, CO, Westview Press, 80, xx-307 p.
4577 BEAU, Jean-Louis. *Socialisme et mode de production: pour reciviliser les sociétés industrielles.* Paris, Presses universitaires de France, 80, xii-192 p.
4578 BORUHSOV, G. "NTR i stanovlenie social'noj odnorodnosti socialističeskogo obščestva" (The scientific and technical revolution and the future of the socialist society social homogeneity), *IN: Social'naja odnorodnost' i svoboda ličnosti v razvitom socialističeskom obščestve.* Ivanovo, 78 : 67-76.
4579 BOWONDER, B. "Appropriate technology for developing countries: some issues", *Technological Forecasting and Social Change* 15, sep 79 : 55-67.
4580 BOYD, John Paul. "Three orthogonal models of the adoption of agricultural innovation", *Rural Sociology* 45, 80 : 309-324.
4581 CARRIEU, Marie-Josèphe; [et al.]. *Nucléopolis: matériaux pour l'analyse d'une société nucléaire.* Grenoble, Presses universitaires de Grenoble, 79, 517 p.
4582 CASTELLANO, Vittorio. "Au delà du mythe du progrès techno-scientifique", *Revue internationale de sociologie / International Review of Sociology* 16, apr 80 : 3-18.
4583 DOU, Alberto; [et al.]. *Aspectos éticos del desarrollo tecnológico* (Ethical aspects of technological development). Bilbao, Mensajero, 80, 296 p.

4584 DURAND, Claude. "Les ouvriers et le progrès technique: Mont-Saint-Martin vingt ans après", *Sociologie du Travail* 22, jan-mar 80 : 4-21.
4585 ELLUL, Jacques. "Remarks on technology and art", *Social Research* 46, 79 : 805-833.
4586 GAL'PERIN, Ja. S. "Naučno-tehničeskaja revoljucija aktual'nye problemy poznanija ličnosti: k voprosu postreonie ědinoj sistemy čelovekopoznanija" (The scientific and technical revolution and topical problems of the personality knowledge), *IN: Filosofskie problemy poznanija. III.*. 79 : 150-159.
4587 GAL'PERIN, Ja. S. "Naučno-tehničeskaja revoljucija aktual'nye problemy poznanija ličnosti: k voprosu postreonie ědinoj sistemy čelovekopoznanija" (The scientific and technical revolution and topical problems of personality knowledge), *IN: Filosofskie problemy poznanija. III.* Čeljabinsk, 78 : 150-159.
4588 GAUDIN, Thierry. *L'Écoute des silences: les institutions contre l'innovation?*. Paris, Union générale d'éditions, 79, 283 p.
4589 GOSS, Kevin F. "Consequences of diffusion of innovations", *Rural Sociology* 44, wint 79 : 754-772.
4590 GRUZDEV, A. I. "Naučno-tehničeskij progress i obščestvennoe mnenie" (Scientific and technical progress and the public opinion), *IN: Aktivnost' ličnosti v uslovijah naučnotehničeskoj revoljucii.* Leningrad, 79 : 34-41.
4591 HECHTER, Michael; BRUSTEIN, William. "Regional modes of production and patterns of state formation in Western Europe", *American Journal of Sociology* 85, mar 80 : 1061-1094.
4592 JACOBSSON, Staffan. "Technical change: employment and distribution in LDCs", *Science and public Policy* apr 80 : 124-135.
4593 JUIRŽIS, R. V. "NTR i revoljucija v proizvoditel'nyh silah" (The scientific and technical revolution in productive forces), *IN: Dialektika social'nogo poznanija.* Moskva, 79 : 53-60.
4594 KĚLAM, A. I.; RANNIK, Ě. Ě. "O vlijanii naučno-tehničeskoj revoljucii na sem'ju" (On the scientific and technical revolution influence on the family), *IN: Naučno-tehničeskaja revoljucija i problemy razvitija obščestva i kollektivov.* Moskva, 79 : 137-143.
4595 KOZLOV, M. P. *Dialektika tehničeskogo i kul'turnogo progressa i sociologičeskij aspekt vzaimosvjazeji vzaimodejstvija* (Dialectics of the technical and cultural progress: the sociological aspects of the interrelation and interaction). Saratov, Izdatel'stvo Saratovskogo Universiteta, 79, 260 p.
4596 KRUGLOV, V. V.; TE, Ju. G. "Social'nye aspekty naučno-tehničeskogo progressa" (Social aspects of the scientific and technical progress), *Sociologičeskie Issledovanija* 79 : 104-112.
4597 LAMBRIGHT, W. Henry. *Technology transfer to cities: process of choice at the local level.* Boulder, CO, Westview Press, 79, xv-188 p. CR: Michael L. VASU, *American political Science Review* 74(2), jun 80: 505.
4598 LIGA, M. B. "Naučno-tehničeskaja revoljucija i nekotorye osobennosti ěmpiričeskogo bazisa social'nogo poznanija" (The scientific and technical revolution and some characteristics of the social consciousness empirical basis), *IN: Aktivnost' ličnosti v uslovijah naučno-tehničeskoj revoljucii.* Leningrad, 79 : 107-117.
4599 LONG, Franklin A.; OLESON, Alexandra; [eds.]. *Appropriate technology and social values — A critical appraisal.* Cambridge, MA, Harper & Row, Ballinger, 80, viii-215 p. [in association with the American Academy of Arts and Sciences.]
4600 MARSH, Robert M.; MANNARI, Hiroshi. "Technological implication theory: A Japanese test", *Organizational studies* 80 : 161-183.
4601 MAURICE, Marc. "Le déterminisme technologique dans la sociologie du travail (1955-1980)", *Sociologie du Travail* 22, jan-mar 80 : 22-36.
4602 PARYGIN, B. D. "Naučno-tehničeskij progress i social'no-psichologičeskij klimat kollektiva" (The scientific and technical progress and the collectivity socio-psychological climate), *IN: Naučno-tehničeskaja revoljucija i problemy razvitija obščestva i kollektivov.* Moskva, 79 : 99-107.
4603 PRATTIS, J. I. "Modernization and modes of production in the North Atlantic: a critique of policy formation for the development of marginal maritime communities", *American Journal of Economics and Sociology* 39, oct 80 : 305-319.
4604 ROBINSON, Austin; [ed.]. *Appropriate technologies for Third World development: proceedings of a conference held by the International Economic Association at Teheran, Iran.* New York, St. Martin's Press, 79, xix-417 p.
4605 RYAN, Charles. "The choices in the next energy and social revolution", *Technological Forecasting and social Change* 16, mar 80 : 191-208.

4606 SHEPARD, Jon M.; KIM, Dong I.; HOUGLAND, James G. Jr. "Effects of technology in industrialized and industrializing societies", *Sociology of Work and Occupations* nov 79 : 457-481.
4607 SINGELMANN, Joachim; BROWNING, Harley L. "Industrial transformation and occupational change in the US, 1960-70", *Social Forces* 59, sep 80 : 246-264.
4608 SMIRNOV, B. M. "Naučno-tehničeskij progress i protivorečija truda" (The scientific and technical progress and the labour contradictions), *IN: Aktual'nye problemy razvitija truda v uslovijah naučno-tehničeskogo progressa.* Moskva, 79 : 13-30.
4609 Bibl.XXIX-4683. STANLEY, Manfred. *The technological conscience: survival and dignity in an age of expertise.* CR: John H. KUNKEL, *Contemporary Sociology (Albany)* 9(3), mai 80, 419-420.
4610 TAKEYASU, Hideko. "Gijutsu kakushin to kazoku-nōson kanai kogyō no mura o jirei ni" (Technological change and family), *Oitemon gakuin daigaku bungakubu kiyo* 13, 80 : 63-84.
4611 THORNTON, Peter; [ed.]. "Technology and society", *International Journal of social Economics* 80 : 3-54.
4612 TOURAINE, Alain; [et al.]. *La prophétie antinucléaire.* Paris, Seuil, 80, 374 p. CR: Michel AMIOT, *Sociologie du Travail* 22(4), oct-dec 80: 415-424.
4613 URENA, Enrique M. "Sociedad tecnológica, sociología crítica y conciencia marxista" (Technological society, critical sociology and marxist consciousness), *Razón y Fe* 200(982), nov 79 : 272-281.
4614 VILENSKIJ, M. A. "Vzaimosvjaz' naučno-tehničeskogo i social'nogo progressa kak neobhodimoe uslovie rešenija ekologičeskoj problemy" (Interaction of the scientific and technical progress and the social progress as a necessary condition of the ecological problem solution), *IN: Naučno-tehničeskaja revoljucija i rešenie ekologičeskih problem.* Moskva, 78 : 16-27.

17430. Agriculture. Commerce. Industry
Agriculture. Commerce. Industrie

[See also / voir aussi: 1491, 2190, 2739, 3251, 3472, 4011, 4016, 4039, 4053, 4427, 4540, 4606, 4762, 4894, 5085, 5386]

4615 ALBEGOVA, I. F. "Rol' inženerno-tehničeskoj intelligencii sovhozov v social'nom preobrazovanii sela" (Role of engineering and technical intelligentsia in state farms in the village social transformation), *IN: Social'nye problemy sovremennogo sela. II.* Jaroslavl', 78 : 110-119.
4616 ALCÁNTARA FERRER, Sergio. *Industrias colectivas del pueblo: un estudio de caso sobre industrialización rural en el sur de Jalisco* (Collective cottage industries: a case study on rural industrialization in the north of Jalisco). México, D. F., Centro de Estudios Sociológicos, El Colegio de México, 79, 50 p.
4617 BASAR, Hasmet. "Problems of agricultural co-operation in Turkey", *Yearbook of agricultural Cooperation* 79 : 125-128.
4618 BEAUCHAMP, Claude. "Les débuts de la coopération et du syndicalisme agricoles, 1900-1930: quelques éléments de la pratique", *Recherches sociographiques* 20, sep-dec 79 : 337-381.
4619 BERGER, Michael. *The devil wagon in God's country: the automobile and social change in rural America, 1893-1929.* Hamden, CT, Archon Books, 79, 269 p.
4620 BLAU, Peter. "Implications of growth in services for social structure", *Social Science Quarterly* 61, jun 80 : 3-22.
4621 BUSCH, Lawrence. "Structure and negotiation in the agricultural sciences", *Rural Sociology* 45, spr 80 : 26-48.
4622 DEFILIPPIS, Josip. "Tendencije ekonomske reprodukcije seoskih gospodarstava" (Tendencies of economic reproduction on peasant farms), *Sociologija sela* 17(65-66), 79 : 126-137.
4623 DELOUYA, Brrik. "Le kibboutz, un socialisme à visage humain", *Revue des Études coopératives* 198, 79 : 125-134.
4624 FLEURET, Patrick; FLEURET, Anne. "Nutrition, consumption, and agricultural change", *Human Organization* 39, 80 : 250-260.
4625 FRANCIS, Arthur. "Families, firms, and finance capital: the development of UK industrial firms with particular reference to their ownership and control", *Sociology* 14, feb 80 : 1-27.

4626 FUDETANI, Minoru. "Sangyo soshikiron no kon'nichiteki kadai" (Current topics on the theories of industrial organization), *Bukkyo daigaku shakaigakubu ronso* 14, 80 : 23-35.

4627 GELJUHA, A. M.; KEFELI, V. B. "Issledovanie processov sbliženija raboćego klassa i tehničeskoj intelligencii na promyšlennyh predprijatijah SSSR" (Research on the working class and technical intelligentsia bringing together processes in the USSR industrial enterprises), IN: *Social'naja struktura sovetskogo obšćestva i socialističeskij obraz žizni*. I. Moskva, 78 : 145-154.

4628 HOPKINS, Raymond F.; PUCHALA, Donald J.; TALBOT, Ross B. *Food, politics, and agricultural development: case studies in the public policy of rural modernization*. Boulder, CO, Westview Press, 79, xv-311 p.

4629 JAMIESON, Ian. "Capitalism and culture: a comparative analysis of British and American manufacturing organizations", *Sociology* 14, mai 80 : 217-245.

4630 JUDET, Pierre. "Conséquences sociales de l'industrialisation dans les pays en voie de développement", *Revue de l'AUPELF* 17, mai 80 : 99-110.

4631 KHAN, Azizur Rahman; GHAI, Dharam. *Collective agriculture and rural development in Soviet central Asia*. New York, St. Martins Press, 80, xi-120 p.

4632 KONOPNICKI, Maurice; RAFAEL, Eliezer Ben; RAMBAUD, Placide. *Le Nouveau kibboutz*. Bruxelles, L. Musin, 79, 206 p.

4633 KONOVALJUK, O. I. "Kritika buržuaznyh fal'sifikacij mesta i roli kolhoznogo krest'janstva v SSSR" (Critics of the bourgeois falsifiers on the USSR collective farmers place and role), *Naučnyj Kommunizm* 79 : 104-111.

4634 LINDE, Hans. "Proto-Industrialisierung. Zur Justierung eines neuen Leitbegriffs der sozialgeschichtlichen Forschung" (Proto-industrialization. The justification of a new concept of socio-historical research), *Geschichte und Gesellschaft* 80 : 103-124.

4635 LIVET, Roger. *Les Nouveaux visages de l'agriculture française*. Paris, Éditions Économie et humanisme, Éditions ouvrières, 80, 210 p.

4636 MAURICE, Marc; [et al.]. "Societal differences in organizing manufacturing units: a comparison of France, West Germany and Great Britain", *Organization Studies* 80 : 59-86.

4637 MONJARDET, Dominique. "Organisation, technologie et marché de l'entreprise industrielle", *Sociologie du Travail* 22, jan-mar 80 : 76-96.

4638 NELSON, Franklyn L. "The process of Western industrialization: density, organization and technology", *International Journal of contemporary Sociology* 15(3-4), jul-oct 78 : 318-337.

4639 OGURA, Mitsuo. "Tanzania no kogyoka to 'shakai-shugi'" (Industrialization and 'socialism' in Tanzania), *Kyosan-shugi to kokusai seiji* 80 : 84-105.

4640 OMMINS, P. "Imbalances in agricultural modernisation — with illustrations from Ireland", *Sociologia ruralis* 20(1-2), 80 : 63-81.

4641 PERRY, Charles S. "Industrialization, income and inequality: further considerations", *Rural Sociology* 45, 80 : 139-146. [USA, Kentucky, 1960-70.]

4642 PODOŠEVKO, V. D. "Kolhoznaja demokratija v uslovijah razvitogo socializma" (Collective farms democracy under conditions of developed socialism), IN: *XXV s'ezd KPSS i voprosy social'no-političeskogo razvitija sovetskogo obšćestva*. Minsk, 79 : 60-74.

4643 RAMSAY, Charles E.; RICKSON, Roy E. "Industrial change and classical theory", *International Journal of comparative Sociology (Leiden)* 21(1-2), mar-jun 80 : 74-87.

4644 SADAN, Ezra; WEINTRAUB, Dov. "Ethnicity, nativity and economic performance of cooperatives smallholding farms in Israel", *Economic Development and cultural Change* 28, apr 80 : 487-507.

4645 SCHREMMER, Eckart. "Industrialisierung vor der Industrialisierung. Anmerkungen zu einem Konzept der Proto-Industrialisierung" (Industrialization before industrialization. Remarks on a concept of proto-industrialization), *Geschichte und Gesellschaft* 80 : 420-448.

4646 SIMÓ, Tibor. *Társadalmi tagozódás a mezőgazdasági termelőszövetkezetekben. Műhelytanulmány* (Social strata on agricultural co-operative farms. A work-shop study). Budapest, Kossuth K., 80, 249 p. [published by the Inst. of Social Sciences the Hungarian Workers' Party.]

4647 STEINBERG RATNER, Ronnie. "The social meaning of industrialization in the United States: determinants of the scope of coverage under wage and hour standards legislation 1900-1970", *Social Problems* 27, apr 80 : 448-466.

4648 ŠTERN, Vilko; KOVAČIĆ, Matija; GUZELJ, Jože. "Iskustva na uključivanju seljačkih gospodarstva u sistem udruženog rada na području SR Slovenije" (Experiences in

establishing links between peasant farms and the system of association labour in Slovenia), *Sociologija sela* 17(65-66), 79 : 100-114.
4649 WELLS, R. G. J. "Better ways of living through co-operatives", *Yearbook of agricultural Cooperation* 79 : 1-16.
4650 WILS, Frits C. M. *Industrialization, industrialists, and the nation-state in Peru: a comparative/sociological analysis.* Berkeley, Institute of International Studies, University of California, 79, xii-273 p.

17500. CONSUMPTION. MARKET. PRICE
CONSOMMATION. MARCHÉ. PRIX

17510. Consumer behaviour
Comportement du consommateur

[See also / voir aussi: 58, 774, 2130]

4651 BERK, Richard A.; [et al.]. "Reducing consumption in periods of acute scarcity: the case of water", *Social Science Research* jun 80 : 99-120.
4652 BINET, Jacques. "Nouvelles habitudes de consommation", *Projet* 139, nov 79 : 1061-1068.
4653 FREY, Bruno S. "Ökonomie als Verhaltenswissenschaft" (Economics as a behavioural science), *Jahrbuch für Sozialwissenschaft* 31, 80 : 21-35.
4654 GERŐ, Zsuzsa; HRUBOS, Ildikó; [eds.]. *Fogyasztásszociológia. Szöveggyűjtemény* (Sociology of consumption. A textbook). Budapest, Tankönyvkiadó, Karl Mark University of Economics, 79, 191 p.
4655 HÉNAULT, Georges Maurice. *Le consommateur.* Montréal, Presses de l'Université du Québec, 79, x-212 p.
4656 HOUG, Tora. "Households and markets: theories and new research consumption activities", *Acta sociologica* 23, 80 : 21-31. [Norway.]
4657 JENCKS, Christopher; [et al.]. *Who gets ahead? The determinants of economic success in America.* New York, Basic Books, 79, 397 p. CR: William T. BIELBY; McKee J. McCLENDON, *Contemporary Sociology (Albany)* 9(6), nov 80: 754-762.
4658 SCHNABL, Hermann. *Verhaltenstheorie und Konsumerentscheidung* (Behavioural theory and consumer decision). Tübingen, Mohr, 79, viii-332 p. CR: Günther SCHANZ, *Soziologische Revue* 3(4), 80: 413-414.
4659 SCHNABL, Hermann. *Verhaltenswissenschaftliche Konsumtheorie* (Behavioural economic theory of consumption). Stuttgart, Berlin, Köln, Mainz, Kohlhammer, 79, 150 p.
4660 SHIOTA, Shizuo. "Shōhisha life style to kobai kodo" (Lifestyle of consumer and buying behaviour), *Chukyo shogaku ronso* 27, 80 : 131-170.
4661 ZALTMAN, Gerald; WALLENDORF, Melanie. *Consumer behavior: basic findings and managerial implications.* New York, Wiley, 79, xiv-567 p.

17520. Demand. Supply
Demande. Offre

[See also / voir aussi: 741]

4662 ALEXANDROVA, A. A. "Social'no-političeskaja rol'socialističeskogo sorevnovanija i soveršenstvovanii socialističeskogo obraza žizni"(The socialist competition socio-political role in the socialist way of life improvement), *IN: Problemy socialističeskogo obraza žizni v uslovijah razvitogo socializma.* Moskva, 80 : 93-103.
4663 BRAUN, Hans-Gert. "Märkte in traditionalen Gesellschaften" (Markets in traditional societies), *IFO-Studien* 25(1-2), 79 : 65-82.
4664 HORAN, Patrick M.; BECK, E. M.; TOLBERT, Charles M. II. "The market homogeneity assumption: on the theoretical foundations of empirical knowledge", *Social Science Quarterly* 61, sep 80 : 278-292.
4665 PAVLJUK, N. Ja. "Upravlenie obščestvom i organizacija socialističeskogo sorevnovanija" (The society management and the socialist competition organization), *IN: Problemy upravlenija v uslovijah razvitogo socializma.* Moskva, 79 : 78-92.

17600. CREDIT. FINANCING. MONEY
CRÉDIT. FINANCEMENT. MONNAIE

[See also / voir aussi: 3430, 5276]

4666 BEIGIE, Carl E. *Inflation is a social malady.* London, Washington, DC, British-North American Committee, 79, x-81 p.

4667 BERTILSSON, Margareta; EYERMAN, Ron. "Interest as a problematic concept in Marxist social science", *Acta sociologica* 22, 79 : 361-375.

4668 RATCLIFF, Richard E. "Banks and corporate lending: an analysis of the impact of the internal structure of the capitalist class on the lending behavior of banks", *American sociological Review* 45, aug 80 : 553-570.

4669 SMELT, Simon. "Money's place in society", *British Journal of Sociology* 31, jun 80 : 204-223.

4670 ZELIZER, Viviana A. Rotman. *Morals and markets: the development of life insurance in the United States.* New York, Columbia University Press, 79, xiv-208 p. CR: Carol A. HEIMER, *American Journal of Sociology* 86(1), jul 80: 220-223.

17700. ECONOMIC POLICY. PLANNING
POLITIQUE ÉCONOMIIQUE. PLANIFICATION

[See also / voir aussi: 2881, 3980, 4259, 4322, 5270, 5534]

4671 ABPLANALP, Peter A.; HETTLAGE, Robert. "Wirtschaftspolitik und kommunikative Umwelt in der 'neuen politischer Ökonomie': einige soziologische Bedenken" (Economic policy and communicative environment in the "new economic policy": some sociological remarks), *Jahrbuch für Sozialwissenschaft* 30, 79 : 293-311.

4672 BURKITT, Brian. "The sources of economic power", *International Journal of social Economics* 80 : 122-131.

4673 GVISHIANI, Dzhermen M. "La science et la technique face aux problèmes du développement", *Revue internationale des Sciences sociales* 32, 80 : 165-171.

4674 KATUNARIČ, Vjeran. "Vrijednosni aspekti planiranja — prihvačanje novih grupa" (The value aspects of planning — the problem of accepting the new social groups), *Revija za Sociologiju* (1-2), 78 : 46-53.

4675 VAN DEN DOEL, J. "Een theorie van de Chinese economische politiek" (A theory of Chinese economic policy), *Sociologische Gids* 27, mar-apr 80 : 98-119.

18. LABOUR
TRAVAIL

**18100. INDUSTRIAL SOCIOLOGY. SOCIOLOGY OF WORK
SOCIOLOGIE INDUSTRIELLE. SOCIOLOGIE DU TRAVAIL**

[See also / voir aussi: 75, 232, 2941, 4601, 4990]

4676 ANDERSON, Ronald E.; MORTIMER, Jeylan T.; [eds.]. "Sociology of computer work", *Sociology of Work and Occupations* mai 79 : 131-250.
4677 DÜLL, Klaus; [et al.]. "Regards étrangers sur la sociologie du travail française: débat", *Sociologie du Travail* 22, jan-mar 80 : 55-75.
4678 FORM, William. "Comparative industrial sociology and the convergence hypothesis", *Annual Review of Sociology* 79 : 1-25.
4679 HERKOMMER, Sebastian; BIERBAUM, Heinz. *Industriesoziologie; Bestandsaufnahme, Kritik, Weiterentwicklung* (Industrial sociology: state-of-the-art, critique, further development). Stuttgart, Enke, 79, vi-221 p. CR: Gert SCHMIDT, *Kölner Zeitschrift für Soziologie und Sozialpsychologie* 32(4), dec 80: 803-805.
4680 JUBBER, Ken; [ed.]. *South Africa industrial relations and industrial sociology*. Cape Town, Juta, 79, xix-260 p.
4681 LA ROSA, Michele. *La sociologia del lavoro in Italia e in Francia* (The sociology of work in Italy and France). Milano, F. Angeli, 79, 149 p.
4682 LANDY, Frank J.; TRUMBO, Don A. *Psychology of work behavior*. Homewood, IL, Dorsey Press, 80, xiv-626 p.
4683 PAMPEL, Fred C. "Changes in labor force participation and income of the aged in the United States, 1947-76", *Social Problems* 27, dec 79 : 125-142.
4684 RIBEAUX, Peter; POPPLETON, Stephen E. *Psychology and work: an introduction*. London, Macmillan, 79, xvi-362 p.
4685 Bibl.XXIX-4779. ROSE, Michael. *Servants in post-industrial power?: sociologie du travail in modern France*. CR: Scott M. LASH, *British Journal of Sociology* 31(3), sep 80: 456-458. [also CR: Arne L. KALLEBERG, Contemporary Sociology (Albany), 9(5), sep 80 : 724.]
4686 SAUERMANN, Peter. *Betriebspsychologie*(Industrial psychology). Stuttgart, Enke, 79, viii-202 p.
4687 SCHMIDT, Gert. "Max Webers Beitrag zur empirischen Industrieforschung" (Max Weber's essay on empirical industrial research), *Kölner Zeitschrift für Soziologie und Sozialpsychologie* 32, 80 : 76-92.
4688 SCHMIDT, Gert. "Zur Geschichte der Industriesoziologie in Deutschland" (On the history of industrial sociology in Germany), *Soziale Welt* 31, 80 : 257-278.
4689 WATSON, Tony J. "Industrial sociology: theory, research and teaching: some problems and proposals", *Journal of Management Studies* 16, mai 79 : 117-138.
4690 YAGI, Tadashi. "Rōdō shakaigaku kenkyū no seika to kadai" (Results and tasks of 1980's sociology of work in Japan), *Gekkan rōdō mondai* 282, 80 : 56-61.
4691 ZÜNDORF, Lutz; [ed.]. *Industrie- und Betriebssoziologie* (Industrial and business sociology). Darmstadt, Wissenschaftliche Buchgesellschaft, 79, vi-431 p. CR: Gert, SCHMIDT, *Soziologische Revue* 3(2), 80: 172-174.
4692 ŽUPANOV, Josip. "Sociologija, marksizma i industrijska sociologija" (Sociology, marxism and industrial sociology), *Sociologija* 22(1-2), 80 : 15-25.

**18200. EMPLOYMENT. LABOUR MARKET
EMPLOI. MARCHÉ DU TRAVAIL**

**18210. Labour. Manpower
Travail. Main-d'oeuvre**

[See also / voir aussi: 111, 715, 744, 746, 849, 2338, 2452, 3447, 3472, 3734, 3786, 3878, 3880, 4772, 4776, 4824, 4975, 5166, 5318]

4693 "Work", *Philosophical Forum* 10(2-4), wint 78-sum 79 : 147-384.
4694 ABDURAHMANOV, I. I. "Nekotorye principy dialektiki izmenenija soderžanija i haraktera truda v uslovijah naučno-tehničeskoj revoljucii" (Some dialectics principles

of the labour content and character change under conditions of the scientific and technical revolution), *IN: Dialektika i naučnoe poznanie*. Taškent, 79 : 217-221.

4695 ADLER, Frank. "Travail et développement de la personnalité en République démocratique allemande", *Revue internationale des Sciences sociales* 32, 80 : 473-495.

4696 ANTHONY, Peter David. "Le travail et la perte du sens", *Revue internationale des Sciences sociales* 32, 80 : 444-455.

4697 BAUDELOT, Christian; ESTABLET, Roger; TOISER, Jacques. *Qui travaille pour qui?*. Paris, F. Maspero, 79, 247 p.

4698 BLACKBURN, Robert Martin; MANN, Michael. *The working class in the labour market*. London, Macmillan, 79, x-369 p. [United Kingdom.]CR: David BODDY, *British Journal of Sociology* 31(4), dec 80 : 593-594.

4699 BLINOV, N. M. *Trudovaja dejatel'nost' kak osnova socialističeskogo obraza žizni* (Labour activity as the basis of the socialist way of life). Moskva, Nauka, 79, 143 p.

4700 BLUMENBERG, Hans. *Arbeit am Mythos* (Labour and myth). Frankfurt am Main, Suhrkamp, 79, 699 p.

4701 CHAPPELL, Neena L. "Paid labor: confirming a conceptual distinction between commitment and identification", *Sociology of Work and Occupations* feb 80 : 81-116.

4702 CHERNS, Albert. "Travail et valeurs: changements dans les sociétés industrielles", *Revue internationale des Sciences sociales* 32, 80 : 456-471.

4703 DIERCKXSENS, Wim. *Capitalismo y población: la reproducción de la fuerza de trabajo bajo el capital* (Capitalism and population: manpower reproduction under capital). Ciudad Universitaria Rodrigo Facio, Costa Rica, Editorial Universitaria Centroamericana, 79, 293 p.

4704 ESPENSHADE, Thomas J.; HANUMANTHA RAYAPPA, P. "The behavior of laborforce participation rates in low-income countries", *Majalah Demografi Indonesia* (10), dec 78 : 1-24.

4705 GAUDEMAR, Jean-Paul de. *La mobilisation générale*. Paris, Éditions du Champ urbain, 79, 285 p. [France.]

4706 GLUHOV, P. I. "O stanovlenii truda kak pervoj žiznennoj potrebnosti čeloveka v uslovijah socializma" (On the labour future as the first human need under conditions of socialism), *Naučnyj Kommunizm* 79 : 21-28.

4707 HANAŠ, S. A. "Formirovanie kommunističeskogo otnošenija k trudu kak social'nopolitičeskaja problema razvitogo socializma" (Formation of a communist relation to labour as a socio-political problem of developed socialism), *Naučnye Trudy Kujbyševskogo pedagogičeskogo Instituta* 198, 77 : 12-22.

4708 HENRIKSEN, Ingrid; [et al.]. *Arbejdsløshedsundersøgelserne. 1. Efterspørgsel og udbud på arbejdsmarkedet* (Unemployment surveys. 1. Demand and supply of the labour market). København, Teknisk forlag, 79, 368 p. [Denmark.]

4709 HOROWITZ, Stanley A.; SHERMAN, Allan. "A direct measure of relationship between human capital and productivity", *Journal of human Resources* 25, wint 80 : 67-76.

4710 KALLEBERG, Arne L.; SØRENSEN, Aage B. "Sociology of labor markets", *Annual Review of Sociology* 79 : 351-379.

4711 KAWAKITA, Takashi. "Shokuba eno teichaku to ido" (Workers' mobility), *Julist zokan* 18, 80 : 122-126.

4712 KAZTMAN, Rubén; REYNA, José Luis; [comp.]. *Fuerza de trabajo y movimientos laborales en América Latina* (Labour force and labour movements in Latin America). México, Colegio de México, 79, viii-337 p.

4713 KONDA, Suresh L.; STEWMAN, Shelby. "An opportunity labor demand model and Markovian labor supply models: comparative tests in an organization", *American sociological Review* 45, apr 80 : 276-301.

4714 KONDRATIEV, Vladimir. "Les ressources humaines et la politique de la main-d'oeuvre dans la RSS de Biélorussie", *Revue international du Travail* 118, nov-dec 79 : 775-791.

4715 KRADER, Lawrence. *A treatise of social labor*. Assen, Van Gorcum, 79, ix-513 p.

4716 LAND, Kenneth C.; PAMPEL, Fred C. "Aggregate male and female labor force participation functions: an analysis of structural differences, 1947-1977", *Social Science Research* mar 80 : 37-54. [USA.]

4717 LINKE, Wilfried. "Voraussichtliche Entwicklung der Erwerbsbevölkerung in Europa bis 1990 und Konsequenzen der Wanderungsbewegungen" (Presumable development of the economically active population in Europe up to 1990 and consequences of the migratory movement), *Zeitschrift für Bevölkerungswissenschaft* 78 : 383-393.

4718 LIPSKY, David B. *The labor market experience of workers displaced and relocated by plant shutdowns: the General Foods case*. New York, Garland Pub., 79, 417 p.

4719   LUTZ, M. A. "Vers une théorie plus générale du travail", *Revue internationale des Sciences sociales* 32, 80 : 543-556.
4720   LYON, Larry; ABELL, Troy. "Male entry into the labor force: estimates of occupational rewards and labor market discrimination", *Sociological Quarterly* 21, 80 : 81-92.
4721   MANEVIČ, Ě. L. *Voprosy truda v SSSR* (Labour questions in the USSR). Moskva, Nauka, 80, 216 p.
4722   ROSENBERG, Sam. "Male occupational standing and the dual labor market", *Industrial Relations* 19, 80 : 34-49.
4723   ROTT, Renate. *Industrialisierung und Arbeitsmarkt: Aspekte d. soziöökonom. Entwicklung d. Arbeits- u. Gewerkschaftspolitik in Kolumbien u. Mexiko* (Industrialization and labour market: aspects of the socio-economic development of labour and trade union policy in Colombia and Mexico). Königstein/Ts., Hain, 79, xii-592 p.
4724   SALIM AHMED, Ahmed. "La situation de la main-d'oeuvre au Soudan", *Travail et Société* jul 80 : 315-333.
4725   SCHWIMMER, Erik. "Les limites de l'idéologie économique: essai d'anthropologie comparée sur les concepts du travail", *Revue internationale des Sciences sociales* 32, 80 : 557-573.
4726   SIT, Victor F. S.; NG, S. H. "La main-d'oeuvre mobile de Hong-Kong", *Revue internationale du Travail* 119, jul-aug 80 : 545-555.
4727   VALKENBURG, F. C.; VISSERS, A. M. C. "Segmentation of the labour market: the theory of the dual labour market", *Netherlands' Journal of Sociology* 16, 80 : 155-170.
4728   VISCUSI, W. Kip. *Employment hazards: an investigation of market performance.* Cambridge, Harvard University Press, 79, viii-311 p.
4729   VOROB'EV, N. Ě. "Trud kak potrebnost" (Labour as a need), IN: *Ěkonomičeskie i duhovnye osnovy razvitija ličnosti.* Voronež, 79 : 68-75.
4730   VOUTYRAS, Stavros. "Le travail: conception classique et conception romantique", *Revue internationale des Sciences sociales* 32, 80 : 433-443.

18220.   Employment. Unemployment
Emploi. Chômage

[See also / voir aussi: 482, 3185, 3594, 4827, 5656]

4731   "Chômeurs et immigrés. Chômage et immigration", *Hommes et Migrations* 992, jun 80 : 1-22. [France.]
4732   ADLER-KARLSSON, Gunnar. "Gedanken zur Vollbeschäftigung" (Reflexions on full employment), *Mitteilungen aus der Arbeitsmarkt- und Berufsforschung* 12, 79 : 481-505.
4733   ANTOS, Joseph R.; MELLOW, Wesley. *The youth labor market: a dynamic overview.* Washington, U.S. Dept. of Labor, Bureau of Labor Statistics, 79, x-189 p.
4734   BAX, E. H. "Oriëntaties van lager geschoolde werkloze en werkende mannelijke jongeren. Eeen vergelijkend onderzoek" (Orientations of lower skilled unemployed and working male youth. A comparative research), *Mens en Matschappij* 54, nov 79 : 361-386.
4735   BECCARIA, Luis; ORSATTI, Alvaro. "Sobre el tamaño del desempleo oculto en el mercado de tranbajo urbano de la Argentina" (On the problem of disguised unemployment in the urban labour market in Argentina), *Desarrollo económico (Buenos Aires)* 19(74), jul-sep 79 : 251-267. [Buenos Aires.][with a rejoinder by Carlos F. Sanchez: 269-274.]
4736   BERNARD, C. "Les approches du chômage déguisé dans l'agriculture des pays sous-développés: bilan critique", *Économies et Sociétés. Cahiers de l'ISÉA* 14, jan 80 : 21-110.
4737   BODERMAN, Eli. "The perils of job-hunting", *American Sociologist* 15, aug 80 : 157-162.
4738   BOSANQUET, Nick. "'Structuralism' and structural unemployment'", *British Journal of Industrial Relations* 17, nov 79 : 299-313.
4739   BOULD, S. "Unemployment as a factor in early retirement decisions", *American Journal of Economics and Sociology* 39, apr 80 : 123-136.
4740   CARR, Timothy James. *A comparative study of the duration of unemployment of young and middle-aged men.* Columbus, OH, Ohio State University, College of Administrative Science Center for Human Resource Research, 79, v-126 p.
4741   CASSON, Mark. *Youth unemployment.* London, Macmillan Press, New York, Holmes & Meier, 79, xii-141 p. CR: Paul OSTERMAN, *Journal of economic Literature* 18(3), sep 80 : 1128-1129.
4742   CLOGG, Clifford C. *Measuring underemployment: demographic indicators for the United States* New York, Academic Press, 79, xiii-279 p.

4743	DERBER, Charles. "Underemployment and the American dream", *Sociological Inquiry* 49, 79 : 37-44.
4744	DESPIERRE, Jean; SOREL, Nicole. "Approche de la représentation du chômage chez les jeunes", *Orientation scolaire et professionnelle* oct-nov-dec 79 : 347-364.
4745	FÜRTH, Thomas. *De arbetslösa och 1930-talskrisen: en kollektivbiografi över hjälpsökande arbetslösa i Stockholm 1928-1936* (The unemployed and the crisis of the nineteen thirties: a collective biography of applicants for unemployment relief in Stockholm 1928-1936). Stockholm, Stockholms kommunalförvaltning, 79, 301 p.
4746	GOEDE, M. P. M. de.; MAASSEN, G. H. "Meningen over werklozen en arbeidsongeschikten" (Opinions about unemployment and unemployables), *Mens en Maatschappij* 55, sep 80 : 245-279.
4747	GOEDE, Martijn P. M. de; MAASSEN, Gerard H. *De publieke opinie over niet-werken* (The public opinion about unemployed). Lisse, Swets & Zeitlinger, 79, ix-126 p. [Netherlands.]
4748	GORDON, Margaret S. *Youth education and unemployment problems: an international perspective.* Berkeley, CA, Carnegie Council on Policy Studies in Higher Education, 79, xvii-170 p.
4749	HÖRTE, Sven Åke. *Ungdomsarbetslöshet: ett sociologiskt perspektiv* (Youth unemployment: a sociological perspective). Stockholm, Rabén & Sjögren, 79, 205 p. [Sweden.]
4750	JANNE, Henri. *Education and youth employment in Belgium.* Berkeley, CA, Carnegie Council on Policy Studies in Higher Education, 79, viii-112 p. [Education and Youth Employment in Contemporary Societies Series.]
4751	LAVAL, Bernard. "Les théories récentes de l'emploi et du chômage", *Revue française des Affaires sociales* 34, apr-jun 80 : 57-104.
4752	Bibl.XXIX-4828. MANGUM, Garth L.; SENINGER, Stephen F. *Coming of age in the ghetto: a dilemma of youth unemployment.* CR: William P. KUVLESKY, *Contemporary Sociology (Albany)* 9(1), jan 80 : 157.
4753	MOEN, Phyllis. "Measuring unemployment: family considerations", *Human Relations* 33, mar 80 : 183-192.
4754	NIESS, Frank. *Geschichte der Arbeitslosigkeit*(History of unemployment). Köln, Pahl-Rugenstein, 79, 250 p.
4755	PANG, Eng Fong. "Emploi, développement et besoins essentiels á Singapour", *Revue internationale du Travail* 119, jul-aug 80 : 533-543.
4756	ROTHWELL, Roy; ZEGVELD, Walter. *Technical change and employment.* New York, St. Martin's Press, 79, ix-178 p.
4757	SANDELL, Steven H. "Job search by unemployed women; determinants of the asking wage", *Industrial and Labor Relations Review* 33, apr 80 : 368-378.
4758	SCHNAPPER, Dominique. *Le Vécu du chômage: essai d'interprétation sociologique.* Paris, Ministère du travail et de la participation, 79, 61 p.
4759	SMITH, Ralph E.; [et al.]. "Youth and employment", *Youth and Society* 11, sep 79 : 3-136.
4760	THOMAS, Gail E.; SCOTT, Will B. "Black youth and the labor market. The unemployment dilemma", *Youth and Society* 11, dec 79 : 163-189.
4761	TIPPELT, Rudolf. "Soziale Haltungen und politische Einstellungen arbeitsloser Jugendlicher — Ergebnisse und Tendenzen einer empirischen Untersuchung" (Social attitudes and political opinions of young unemployed. Results and trends of an empirical study), *Neue Praxis* 79 : 273-282. [Germany FR.]
4762	VAN DER HOEVEN, Rolph. "L'emploi, les besoins essentiels et l'industrialisation: réflexions sur l'objectif de Lima", *Revue internationale du Travail* 119, jul-aug 80 : 471-486.
4763	VOHLAND, Ulrich. "Jugendarbeitslosigkeit" (Youth unemployment), *Recht der Jugend und des Bildungswesens* 27, 79 : 395-401.

18230. Employment service. Job evaluation
Service d'emploi. Évaluation d'emploi

[See also / voir aussi: 2622, 2624, 2922, 2929, 2948, 2973, 3724, 4943]

4764	BALDUS, David C.; COLE, James W. L. *Statistical proof of discrimination.* Colorado Springs, CO, Shepard's inc. of Colorado Springs, 80, xx-386 p.
4765	BHAGAT, Rabi S.; CHASSIE, Marilyn B. "Effects of changes in job characteristics on some theory-specific attitudinal outcomes: results from a naturally occurring quasi-experiment", *Human Relations* 33, mai 80 : 297-313.

4766 BURSTEIN, Paul; MACLEOD, Margo W. "Prohibiting employment discrimination: ideas and politics in the Congressional debate over equal employment opportunity legislation", *American Journal of Sociology* 86, nov 80 : 512-533.
4767 COSTA, E.; PHAN-THUY, N. "Promouvoir l'emploi par une utilisation plus poussée de la capacité industrielle", *Revue internationale du Travail* 119, mai-jun 80 : 309-323.
4768 CURRAN, James; STANWORTH, John. "Self-selection and the small firm worker — a critique and an alternative view", *Sociology* 13, nov 79 : 427-444.
4769 FREEMAN, Richard B. "Employment opportunities in the doctorate manpower market", *Industrial and Labor Relations Review* 33, jan 80 : 185-197.
4770 GAPPERT, Gary. "Employment policy in postaffluent America", *Urban Affairs annual Review* 17, 79 : 159-181.
4771 GENNARD, John. *Job security and industrial relations.* Paris, Organisation for Economic Co-operation and Development, 79, 78 p.
4772 GREENWALD, Bruce C. N. *Adverse selection in the labor market.* New York, Garland Pub., 79, 290 p.
4773 JANSEN, Abraham. *Ethiek en praktijk van personeelsselectie* (Ethics and practice of personnel selection). Assen, Gorcum, 79, xii-275 p.
4774 KIGGUNDU, Moses N. "An empirical test of the theory of job design using multiple job ratings", *Human Relations* 33, mai 80 : 339-351.
4775 KORNEGAY, Francis A. *Equal employment: mandate and challenge.* New York, Vantage Press, 79, xviii-308 p.
4776 KRECKEL, Reinhard. "Unequal opportunity structure and labour market segmentation", *Sociology* 14, nov 80 : 525-550.
4777 LAGRANGE, François. "La politique de l'emploi en France", *Travail et Société* apr 80 : 131-145.
4778 LARKIN, Judith Candib; PINES, Harvey A. "No fat persons need apply: experimental studies of the overweight stereotype and hiring preference", *Sociology of Work and Occupations* aug 79 : 312-327.
4779 LERNER, Barbara. "Employment discrimination: adverse impact, validity, and equality", *Supreme Court Review* 79 : 17-49.
4780 MCCORMICK, Ernest James. *Job analysis: methods and applications.* New York, Amacom, 79, vii-371 p.
4781 PETTMAN, Barrie O.; [ed.]. "Discrimination in the labour market", *International Journal of social Economics* 80 : 167-237. [U.K. racial, religious in Northern Ireland.]
4782 REIDY, Elizabeth. "Welfarists and the market: a study of the self-employment assistance programme in the Philippines", *Development and Change* 11, apr 80 : 297-312.
4783 SLOCUM, John W. Jr.; SIMS, Henry P. Jr. "A typology for integrating technology, organization, and job design", *Human Relations* 33, mar 80 : 193-212.
4784 TREIMAN, Donald J. *Job evaluation: an analytic review: interim report to the Equal Employment Opportunity Commission: staff paper prepared for the Committee on Occupational Classification and Analysis, Assembly of Behavioral and Social Sciences, National Research Council.* Washington, National Academy of Sciences, 79, xii-170 p.

18240. Woman worker. Young worker
Travailleur féminin. Jeune travailleur

[See also / voir aussi: 2383, 2385, 2956, 2992, 3437, 3559, 3822, 3830, 3909, 4054, 4363, 4752, 4937, 4938, 4951, 5025, 5030, 5089]

4785 "Problemi attuali dell'emigrazione e degli stranieri" (Present problems of emigration and of foreigners), *Affari sociali internazionali* (1-2), 80 : 137-180.
4786 "Habitat et cadre de vie des travailleurs émigrés", *Recherche sociale (Paris)* 73, jan-mar 80 : 3-106.
4787 "Working women and families", *Sage Yearbooks in Women's Policy Studies* 79 : 9-291.
4788 "Women and work", *Sociology of Work and Occupations* Aug 80 : 259-384. [USA.]
4789 ADAMS, Carolyn Teich; WINSTON, Kathryn Teich. *Mothers at work: public policies in the United States, Sweden, and China.* New York, Longman, 80, 312 p.
4790 AGASSI, Judith B. *Women on the job: the attitudes of women to their work.* Lexington, MA, Lexington Books, 79, vii-263 p.
4791 AGGARWAL, R. C. "Role of women in achieving social goals of economic development", *Indian Journal of social Research* 20, aug 79 : 88-104.
4792 ANDIAPPAN, P. *Women and work.* Bombay, Somaiya, 80, x-155 p. [India.]

4793 ANDREEV, N. N. "Razvitie obščestvenno-političeskoj aktivnosti molodyh inženerno-tehničeskih rabotnikov v sovremennyh uslovijah" (The development of the young engineering and technical workers socio-political activity under contemporary conditions), *IN: Sovetskaja intelligencija i eë rol' v duhovnoj žizni razvitogo socializma*. Moskva, 79 : 145-150.

4794 BANERJEE, Sumanta. *Child labour in India: a general review, with case studies of the brickmaking and zari embroidery industries.* London, Anti-slavery Society, 79, 46 p. [available from Third World Publications, Birmingham, England.]

4795 BECKMAN, Linda J.; HOUSER, Betsy Bosak. "Perceived satisfactions and costs of motherhood and employment among married women", *Journal of Population* 79 : 306-327.

4796 BENATIA, Farouk. "Quelques hypothèses sur le travail féminin en Algérie", *Revue internationale des Sciences sociales* 32, 80 : 496-512.

4797 BENNETT, Sheila K.; ELDER, Glen H. Jr. "Women's work in the family economy: a study of depression hardship in women's lives", *Journal of Family History* 79 : 153-176.

4798 BINDER, Johann; SIMOES, Mario. "Psychische Beschwerden bei ausländischen Arbeitern: eine Untersuchung bei portugiesischen Arbeitsemigranten" (Psychiatric complaints among foreign workers. A field study among Portuguese immigrants), *Zeitschrift für Soziologie* jul 80 : 262-274.

4799 BIRYOUKOVA, A. P. "La législation protectrice spéciale et l'égalité de chances pour les travailleuses en URSS", *Revue internationale du Travail* 119, jan-feb 80 : 53-68.

4800 BLANC, Olivier. "La population active féminine à travers les statistiques", *Revue économique et sociale* 37, dec 79 : 231-242.

4801 BORISKIN, A. N. "Adaptacija molodyh rabočih k obrazu žizni socialističeskogo proizvodstvennogo kollektiva" (The young workers' adaptation to the production collectivity way of life), *IN: Socialističeskij obraz žizni i ličnost'*. Voronež, 79 : 61-78. [USSR.]

4802 BOUILLAGUET-BERNARD, Patricia; GAUVIN, Annie. "Le travail féminin. Famille et système productif", *Consommation* 26, apr-jun 79 : 53-98.

4803 BRIDGES, William P. "Industry marginality and female employment: a new appraisal", *American sociological Review* 45, feb 80 : 58-75.

4804 BUŠUEV, A. M.; [ed.]. *Trudovaja aktivnost' molodeži: sostojanie, puti povyšenija* (The youth labour activity: content and means of its elevation). Moskva, VKS pri CK VLKSM, 79, 140 p. [USSR.]

4805 CAPELLIN, Paola. "Estructura productiva capitalista y trabajo femenino: las condiciones de existencia de la fuerza de trabajo femenino en Brasil" (Capitalist production structure and women's work: living conditions of female manpower in Brazil), *Demografía y Economía* 12, 78 : 37-45.

4806 CARLIER, A. "Arbeidsaanbod van de vrouw: relatieve inkomensbenadering" (Female manpower: the relative income assumption), *Bevolking en Gezin* jul 79 : 183-200.

4807 CASTROS-ALMEIDA, Carlos. "Réflexions sur la situation des migrants de la deuxième génération en Europe occidentale", *Revue internationale du Travail* 118, nov-dec 79 : 811-823.

4808 CHENOWETH, Lillian; MARET, Elizabeth. "The career patterns of mature American women", *Sociology of Work and Occupations* mai 80 : 222-251.

4809 CHINCHILLA, Norma S. "Familia, economía y trabajo de la mujer en Guatemala" (Family, economy and female labour in Guatemala), *Demografía y Economía* 12, 78 : 99-112.

4810 CONNELL, H. B. "La législation protectrice et l'égalité des chances des femmes devant l'emploi en Australie", *Revue internationale du Travail* 119, mar-apr 80 : 213-232.

4811 CRAMER, James C. "Fertility and female employment: problems of causal direction", *American sociological Review* 45, apr 80 : 167-190.

4812 DE FRONZO, James. "Female labor force participation and fertility in 48 States: cross sectional and change analyses for the 1960-70 decade", *Sociology and social Research* 64, jan 80 : 263-278.

4813 DUBLIN, Thomas. *Women at work: the transformation of work and community in Lowell, Massachusetts, 1826-1860.* New York, Columbia University Press, 79, xiii-312 p.

4814 ECKART, Christel; [et al.]. *Frauenarbeit in Familie und Fabrik* (Women's work in family and factory). Frankfurt-am-Main, Campus, 79, 630 p. CR: Ilona OSTNER, *Soziologische Revue* 3(3), 80: 297-299.

4815 EHRLICH, Avishai. "Zionism, demography and women's work", *Khamsin* 80 : 87-105.

4816 EWER, Phyllis A.; CRIMMINS, Eileen; OLIVER, Richard. "An analysis of the relationship between husband's income, family size and wife's employment in the early stages of marriage", *Journal of Marriage and Family* 41, nov 79 : 727-738.

4817   FEINSTEIN, Karen Wolk; [ed.]. *Working women and families.* Beverly Hills, CA, Sage Publications, 79, 295 p.
4818   FEULNER, Patricia N. *Women in the profession: a social-psychological study.* Palo Alto, CA, R & E Research Associates, 79, viii-86 p. [USA.]
4819   GODSCHALK, J. J. "Foreign labour and dirty work", *Netherlands' Journal of Sociology* 15, jul 79 : 1-11.
4820   GÖMÖRI, Edith. "La législation protectrice et l'égalité des femmes devant l'emploi en Hongrie", *Revue internationale du Travail* 119, jan-feb 80 : 69-79.
4821   HARPER, Jan; RICHARDS, Lyn. *Mothers and working mothers.* Ringwood, Vic., Penguin Books Australia, 79, 304 p. [Australia.]
4822   Bibl.XXIX-4856. HARRIS, Barbara J. *Beyond her sphere: women and the professions in American history.* CR: Gaye TUCHMAN, *American Journal of Sociology* 86(2), sep 80 : 437-438.
4823   HUMMER, Patricia M. *The decade of elusive promise: professional women in the United States, 1920-1930.* Ann Arbor, UMI Research Press, 79, vi-182 p.
4824   JOHNSON, George E. "The labor market effects from Western Europe", *Industrial and Labor Relations Review* 33, apr 80 : 331-341.
4825   KAWAKITA, Takashi. "Sho-kibo kigyo konenrei rodosha no shokureki to kaisosei" (Older workers in small business, their career and stratification), *Gendai nihon keizai shakai kenkyu* 80 : 56-67.
4826   KAWAKITA, Takashi. "Sho-kibo kigyo no konenrei koyosha" (Older workers in small business), *Ibaragi daigaku jinbun-gakubu kiyo shakai-kagaku* 13, 80 : 33-74.
4827   KEIFER, Ellen. "Frauenerwerbslosigkeit"(Women's unemployment), *Aus Politik und Zeitgeschichte* 24, 80 : 27-37.
4828   KNEŽEVIĆ, Radoslav. "Položaj i socijalna zaštita jugoslovenskih radnika u zapadnoevropskim zemljama u svetlu promenjenih migracionih politika tih zemalja" (The position and social welfare of Yugoslav workers in Western European countries in the light of the changed migration policies of these countries), *Sociologija* 21(1-2), 79 : 107-133.
4829   KUTSCH, Marlies. *Die Frau im Berufsleben* (Women in occupational life). Freiburg im Breisgau, Basel, Wien, Herder, 79, 141 p. [Germany FR.]
4830   LANSBURY, Russell. "Les travailleurs âgés; l'expérience australienne", *Travail et Société* jan 80 : 77-94.
4831   LEY, Katharina. *Frauen in der Emigration : eine soziologische Untersuchung der Lebens- und Arbeitssituation italienischer Frauen in der Schweiz* (Women in emigration: a socological research on life and occupational situation of Italian women in Switzerland). Frauenfeld [etc.], Huber, 79, 171 p.
4832   LIPPE, Angelika. *Die Situation der erwerbstätigen Frau in Frankreich und ihre Rolle in den französischen Gewerkschaften seit 1965* (The situation of the salaried woman in France and her role in French trade unions since 1965). Berlin, A. Lippe, 79, ii-90 p.
4833   LUSTIG, Nora; RENDÓN, Teresa. "Condición de actividad y posición occupational de la mujer, y características socioeconómicas de la familia en México" (Female employment, occupational status and socioeconomic characteristics of family in Mexico), *Demografía y Economía* 12, 78 : 75-98.
4834   MANDERSON, Lenore. "Women and work", *Kabar Seberang* 5-6, 79 : 94-111.
4835   MARET, Elizabeth; CHENOWETH, Lillian. "The labor force patterns of mature rural women", *Rural Sociology* 44, wint 79 : 736-753.
4836   MARTIN, Philip L.; MILLER, Mark J. "Guestworkers: lessons from Western Europe", *Industrial and Labor Relations Review* 33, apr 80 : 315-330.
4837   MENDELIEVICH, Elias; [ed.]. *Children at work.* Geneva, International Labour Office, 79, ix-176 p.
4838   METZKER, Maria. "La discrimination ouverte ou déguisée contre les femmes dans les conventions collectives. Conclusions d'une enquête autrichienne", *Revue internationale du Travail* 119, mar-apr 80 : 259-270.
4839   MILKMAN, Ruth. "Organizing the sexual division of labor: historical perspectives on 'women's work' and the American labor movement", *Socialist Review* 10, jan-feb 80 : 95-150.
4840   MOSSUZ-LAVAU, Janine; SINEAU, Mariette. "L'ouvrière française et la politique", *Sociologie du Travail* 22, apr-jun 80 : 213-231.
4841   NIELSEN, Ruth. "La législation protectrice des femmes et les pays nordiques", *Revue internationale du Travail* 119, jan-feb 80 : 41-52.
4842   NORTHCOTT, Herbert C. "Women, work and health", *Pacific sociological Review* 23, oct 80 : 393-404.

4843	OPPENHEIMER, Valerie K. "Structural sources of economic pressures for wives to work: an analytical framework", *Journal of Family History* 79 : 177-197.
4844	PEIL, Margaret. "Urban women in the labor force", *Sociology of Work and Occupations* nov 79 : 482-501.
4845	PRESSER, Harriet B.; BALDWIN, Wendy. "Child care as a constraint on employment: prevalence, correlates, and bearing on the work and fertility nexus", *American Journal of Sociology* 85, mar 80 : 1202-1213.
4846	RAINWATER, Lee. "Mothers' contribution to the family money economy in Europe and the United States", *Journal of Family History* 79 : 198-210.
4847	RAVNIC, Anton. "Status stranog radnika u privredi" (Foreign workers' status in the economy), *Zbornik pravnog Fakulteta u Zagrebu* 29(3-4), 79 : 271-312.
4848	RECCHINI DE LATTES, Zulma. "Las mujeres en la actividad económica en Argentina, Bolivia y Paraguay" (Women in economic activity in Argentina, Bolivia and Paraguay), *Demografía y Economía* 13, 79 : 19-48.
4849	RIGER, Stephanie; GALLIGAN, Pat. "Women in management: an exploration of competing paradigms", *American Psychologist* 35(10), oct 80 : 902-910.
4850	RIMBAUD, Christiane. "Le travail des enfants", *Revue française des Affaires sociales* 33, oct-dec 79 : 115-130.
4851	Bibl.XXIX-4870. RIST, Ray C. *Guestworkers in Germany: the protest for pluralism.* CR: Barbara E. SCHMITTER, *American Journal of Sociology* 86(3), nov 80: 669-701. [also CR: Donald F. ROY, Contemporary Sociology (Albany), 9(3), mai 80: 406-407.]
4852	SCANZONI, John. "Work and fertility control sequences among younger married women", *Journal of Marriage and Family* 41, nov 79 : 739-745.
4853	SCHILDKROUT, Enid. "Le travail des enfants: une nouvelle approche", *Revue internationale des Sciences sociales* 32, 80 : 513-524.
4854	Bibl.XXIX-4872. SEIDMAN, Ann; [ed.]. *Working women: a study of women in paid jobs.* CR: Julia A. ERICKSEN, *Contemporary Sociology (Albany)* 9(3), mai 80: 439-440.
4855	SEKI, Hideo. "Emploi et vieillissement démographique. Le cas du Japon", *Revue internationale du Travail* 119, mai-jun 80 : 355-369.
4856	SEMYONOV, Moshe. "The social context of women's labor force participation: a comparative analysis", *American Journal of Sociology* 86, nov 80 : 534-550.
4857	SINGER-KEREL, Jeanne. *Les travailleurs étrangers. Migrations Internationales de main-d'oeuvre, 1974, 1978.* Paris, Centre national de la recherche scientifique, Centre de documentation sciences humaines, 79, 158 p.
4858	SINGH, K. P. "Economic development and female labour force participation: the case of the Punjab", *Social Action* 30, apr-jun 80 : 128-137.
4859	SPITZE, Glenna D.; WAITE, Linda J. "Labor force and work attitudes: young women's early experiences", *Sociology of Work and Occupations* feb 80 : 3-32.
4860	SUTTON, John R. "Some determinants of women's trade union membership", *Pacific sociological Review* 23, oct 80 : 377-391.
4861	TESAROVA, Dyna. "L'emploi des femmes en République socialiste tchécoslovaque", *Demosta* 12, 79 : 79-83.
4862	THOMSON, Elizabeth. "The value of employment to mothers of young children", *Journal of Marriage and Family* 42, aug 80 : 551-566.
4863	VAČKO, G. V. "Formirovanie potrebnostej v obščestvenno-političeskoj dejatel'nosti u molodyh rabočih" (The needs formation in the young worker's socio-political activity), IN: *Problemy socialističeskogo obraza žizni v uslovijah razvitogo socializma.* Moskva, 80 : 42-54.
4864	VAN DEN BERG, Lotty. "Moroccan families in the Netherlands", *Netherlands' Journal of Sociology* 15, jul 79 : 73-82.
4865	VILLEY, Olivier. "La main d'oeuvre étrangère et la crise en France", *Travail et Emploi* apr 80 : 83-92.
4866	VITA, László. *16-29 éves fiatalok különböző gazdasági aktivitású csoportjainak helyzetét jellemző adatok* (Data about the situation of young people of the age 16-29 from different occupational strata). Budapest, Statisztikai K., 80, 199 p. [Hungary].[pub. by the Demographic Research Institute, Central Statistical Office.]
4867	VLASSOF, Michael. "Labour demand and economic utility of children: a case study in rural India", *Population Studies* 33, nov 79 : 415-428.
4868	VRAIN, Phillippe; GONTIER, Geneviève. *Les ouvriers vieillissants de la région parisienne: activité professionnelle et conditions de travail.* Paris, Presses universitaires de France, 79, 514 p.

4869 WAINERMAN, Catalina H.; NAVARRO, Marysa. *El trabajo de la mujer en la Argentina; un análisis preliminar de las ideas dominantes en las primeras décadas del siglo XX* (Women's labor in Argentina: A preliminary analysis of ideas prevalent in the first decades of the 20th century). Buenos Aires, Centro de Estudios de Población (CENEP), 79, 49 p. [Cuaderno del CENEP No. 7.]

4870 WAITE, Linda J. "Working wives and the family life cycle", *American Journal of Sociology* 86, sep 80 : 272-294. [USA. Data from the National Longitudinal Survey of the Education and Labor Market Experiences of Young Women.]

4871 YOHALEM, Alice M. *The careers of professional women: commitment and conflict*. Montclair, NJ, Allanheld Osmun, 79, 225 p. CR: Glenna D. SPITZE, *Contemporary Sociology (Washington)* 9(6), nov 80: 839-840.

18300. PERSONNEL MANAGEMENT. WORKING CONDITIONS
ADMINISTRATION DU PERSONNEL. CONDITIONS DE TRAVAIL

18310. Labour standard. Work study
Norme de travail. Étude du travail

[See also / voir aussi: 2629, 4709, 4955, 4976, 5111, 5128, 5175, 5184]

4872 "La gestion sociale dans l'entreprise", *Annales de Sciences économiques appliquées* 35, 79 : 11-144.

4873 BERTHEL, Jürgen. *Personal-Management*(Personnel management). Stuttgart, Poeschel, 79, xiii-356 p.

4874 BUTERA, Federico. "La questione dell'organizzazione del lavoro in Italia" (The problem of work organization in Italy), *Rassegna sindacale Quaderni* 18(83), mar-apr 80 : 154-171.

4875 ČESNOKOV, B. A. "Socialističeskoe sorevnovanie i ègo rol' v povyšenii social'noj aktivnosti trudjaščihsa v proizvodstvennom kollektive" (Socialist stimulation and its role in elevating the workers' social activity in production collectivity), *IN: Puti sbliženija klassov i social'nyh sloev v uslovijah socializma*. Kemerovo, 78 : 66-75.

4876 CHRISTENSEN, Allan. *Arbejdsorganisation og konjunkturudvikling* (Work organization and business cycle). Aalborg; Aalborg universitetscenter, 79, 112 p. [distribueret af Aalborg Universitets-forlag.]

4877 CZAK, Kazimierz. "Theoretical principles of ergology as a science of the complex organization of work", *Management international Review* 19, 79 : 109-114.

4878 DESATNICK, Robert L. *The expanding role of the human resources manager*. New York, AMACOM, 79, vii-230 p.

4879 DONALDSON, Les. *Behavioral supervision: practical ways to change unsatisfactory behavior and increase productivity*. Reading, MA, Addison-Wesley Pub. Co., 80, xiii-178 p.

4880 ELLIOTT, John. "Management by consent", *Ditchley Journal* spr 80 : 27-38.

4881 GORŠKOV, A. A. "Ukreplenie socialističeskoj discipliny truda v proizvodstvennom kollektive kak upravljaemyj process" (The socialist discipline of labour reinforcement in a production collectivity as a managed process), *IN: Problemy upravlenija v uslovijah razvitogo socializma*. Moskva, 79 : 66-78.

4882 GUILLON, Roland. *Enseignement et organisation du travail du XIXe siècle à nos jours*. Paris, la Documentation française, 80, 127 p.

4883 GULOMOV, O. *Stimuly trudovoj dejatel'nosti: sociologičeskij aspekt* (Incentives of labour activity: the sociological aspect). Dušanbe, Doniš, 79, 169 p.

4884 GUR'JANOV, S. T.; GORBUNOVA, L. N. *Social'noe regulirovanie trudovoj dejatel'nosti na socialističeskom promyšlennom predprijatii* (Social regulation of the labour activity in a socialist industrial enterprise). Moskva, Izdatel'stvo Moskovskogo Universiteta, 79, 179 p.

4885 GUR'JANOV, S. T.; ZVORYKIN, A. A. *Social'noe upravlenie rabočim kollektivom* (Social management of a labour collectivity). Moskva, Izdatel'stvo Moskovskogo Universiteta, 79, 155 p.

4886 HACKMAN, J. Richard; OLDHAM, Greg R. *Work redesign*. Reading, MA, Addison-Wesley, 80, xvii-330 p.

4887 HENEMAN, Herbert G. III; [et al.]. *Personnel/human resource management*. Homewood, IL, R. D. Irwin, 80, xiv-585 p.

4888 HOOGENDOORN, J. *Inleiding personeelplanning*(Introduction to personnel management). Alphen aan den Rijn, Samsom, 79, 172 p.

4889 International Labor Office. *New forms of work organisation. I: Denmark, Norway, and Sweden, France, Federal Republic of Germany, United Kingdom, United States*. Geneva, International Labour Office, 79.

4890 KLINGNER, Donald E. *Public personnel management: contexts and strategies.* Englewood Clifs, NJ, Prentice-Hall, 80, xii-480 p.

4891 KOLÁŘ, Jaroslav; ŠPAŇHEL, Josef. "Sociální vztáhy a výkonnost pracovních kolektivů" (Social relations and output of working groups), *Sociologický Časopis* 14, 78 : 476-488.

4892 KORNEV, V. V. "Povyšenie proizvoditel'nosti truda i razvitie ličnosti" (The labour productivity elevation and the personality development), *IN: Ėkonomičeskie i duhovnye osnovy razvitija ličnosti.* Voronež, 79 : 20-29.

4893 KUDCHEDKAR, L. S. *Aspects of personnel management and industrial relations.* New Delhi, Tata McGraw-Hill, 79, xi-154 p. [India.]

4894 LAMBERT, G. E.; CAVALIÉ, J. L.; PASCAL, R.; [eds.]. *Ergonomie et améliorations des conditions de travail en agriculture.* Toulouse, IRACT, 79, 322 p. [Colloque organisé par l'Institut de recherche pour l'amélioration des conditions de travail.]

4895 LOBOS, Júlio A. *Administração de recursos humanos* (Human resource management). São Paulo, Atlas, 79, 407 p.

4896 MCKINNON, Malcolm H. "Work instrumentalism reconsidered: a replication of Goldthorpe's Luton project", *British Journal of Sociology* 31, mar 80 : 1-27.

4897 MILLER, Edwin; BURACK, Elmer H.; ALBRECHT, Maryann H.; [eds.]. *Management of human resources.* Englewood Cliffs, NJ, Prentice-Hall, 80, viii-455 p.

4898 MODOUX, Gérard; CONWAY, Madeleine. *La Gestion et l'administration du personnel dans les petites et moyennes entreprises.* Berne, Éditions Cosmos, 79, 136 p.

4899 NOVIT, Mitchell S. *Essentials of personnel management.* Englewood Cliffs, NJ, 79, xii-244 p.

4900 RÉGNIER, Jacques. *Pour une évaluation ergonomique: l'évaluation ergonomique des nouvelles formes d'organisation du travail dans les entreprises industrielles.* Montrouge, ANACT, 79, 38 p. [France.] [étude réalisée pour l'amélioration des conditions de travail.]

4901 RICE, Craig S. *Power secrets of managing people.* Englewood Cliffs, NJ, Prentice-Hall, 80, 249 p.

4902 ROWLAND, Kendrith M.; [et al.]; [eds.]. *Current issues in personnel management.* Boston, MA, Allyn and Bacon, 80, 452 p.

4903 SÖDERBERG, Sven. *Psykologioch arbetsorganisation* (Psychology and work organization). Malmö, LiberLäromedel, 79, 269 p.

4904 TROY, Norbert. "Zur Bedeutung der Stresskontrolle. Experimentelle Untersuchungen über Arbeit unter Zeitdruck" (On the meaning of stress control. Experimental researches on work under time pressure), *Zeitschrift für Arbeitswissenschaft* 80 : 103-108.

4905 VLADYČENKO, I. M.; [ed.]. *Sistema upravlenija trudom v razvitom socialističeskom obščestve* (The system of personnel management in the developed socialist society). Moskva, Ėkonomika, 80, 543 p.

4906 YOUNG, W. McEwan. "Le travail par équipes et les horaires variables sont-ils compatibles?", *Revue internationale du Travail* 119, jan-feb 80 : 1-19.

18320. Working conditions
Conditions de travail

[See also / voir aussi: 692, 724, 1169, 1170, 1552, 1600, 3269, 4491, 4499, 4573, 4608, 4693, 4790, 4859, 4894, 4906, 4928, 4945, 4960, 5023, 5089, 5097, 5110, 5320, 5543]

4907 "Partage (Le) du travail", *Droit social* jan 80 : 66-147.

4908 "Contrats (Les) de travail à durée déterminée", *Droit social* 9-10, oct 80 : 3-91.

4909 "Scandinavian and Swedish work research", *Economic and industrial Democracy* mai 80 : 147-287.

4910 "Humanisierung der Arbeit" (Humanization of work), *Gewerkschaftliche Monatshefte* 31, 80 : 213-291.

4911 "'"homo faber" (L') de demain: interaction entre l'homme et ses outils", *Impact. Science et Société* 30, apr-jun 80 : 89-169.

4912 "Women and household labor", *Sage Yearbooks in Women's Policy Studies* 80 : 291 p.

4913 "Enquête sur les conditions de travail, octobre 1978. Premiers résultats", *Statistiques du Travail. Supplément au Bulletin mensuel* 71, 79 : 147 p. [France.]

4914 "Temps (Le) de travail", *Travail et Emploi* jan 80 : 5-90.

4915 ADAMCZUK, Lucian; ZAGÓRSKI, Krzysztof. "The time budget in sociodemographic statistics", *Social Indicators Research* dec 80 : 423-439. [Polish time budget of 1976.]

4916 Agence nationale pour l'amélioration des conditions de travail. *Les Composantes mentales du travail ouvrier*. Montrouge, ANACT, 80, 64 p. [Étude réalisée par le Centre de recherches sociologiques de Toulouse.]

4917 ALONSO OLEA, Manuel. "La extinción del contrato de trabajo por decisión del trabajador" (The termination of labour contract by worker's decision), *Revista de Política social* 126, apr-jun 80 : 137-149.

4918 ANDORKA, Rudolf; FALUSSY, Béla. *Időmérleg. A 15-69 éves népesség napi időfelhasználása 1976/77. évben* (Time budget. Use of time among the population aged 15-69 in 1976-1977). Budapest, Statisztikai Kiado, 80, 270 p. [Hungary.]

4919 Bibl.XXIX-4932. ANDRISANI, Paul J.; [et al.]. *Work attitudes and labor market experience: evidence from the national longitudinal surveys*. CR: Arne L. KALLEBERG, *American Journal of Sociology* 86(3), nov 80: 662-664.

4920 BENDIXEN, Peter. "Humanisierung der Arbeit als gegenwärtiges betriebswirtschaftliches Thema" (Humanization of work as a business economics theme today), *Universitas. Zeitschrift für Wissenschaft, Kunst und Literatur* 35, 80 : 689-695.

4921 BERAUD, Jean-Marc. "L'influence de la suspension du contrat de travail sur les relations institutionnelles dans l'entreprise", *Droit social* feb 80 : 151-164.

4922 BERK, Sarah Fenstermaker; [ed.]. *Women and household labor*. Beverly Hills, Sage Publications, 80, 295 p.

4923 BIELENSKI, Harald. "Barrieren gegen eine flexiblere Arbeitszeitgestaltung" (Barriers against a flexible formation of working time), *Mitteilungen aus der Arbeitsmarkt- und Berufsforschung* 12, 79 : 300-312.

4924 BÖCKLE, Ferdinand. *Flexible Arbeitszeit im Produktionsbereich* (Flexible working time in production management). Frankfurt am Main, Bern, Las Vegas, Lang, 79, 221 p.

4925 BOVONE, Laura. "Etica del lavoro e motivazioni al lavoro nell'Italia contemporanea" (Work ethics and motivations to work in contemporary Italy), *Studi di Sociologia* 17, apr-jun 79 : 130-146.

4926 BRAGG, Emma W. *A profile of work motivation attitudes of apparel workers*. Ann Arbor, MI, published for Tennessee State University by University Microfilms International, 79, xix-265 p.

4927 BRIDGES, William P. "White collar work orientations: social and occupational components", *Sociology and social Research* 64, jul 80 : 542-558.

4928 BUTLER, Suellen; SKIPPER, James K. Jr. "Waitressing, vulnerability, and job autonomy: the case of the risky tip", *Sociology of Work and Occupations* nov 80 : 487-502.

4929 DEBOUZY, Marianne. "Aspects du temps industriel aux États-Unis au début du XIXe siècle", *Cahiers internationaux de Sociologie* 67, jul-dec 79 : 197-220.

4930 DEMONIO, Lucien. "La quadrature du cycle: logiques et contraintes en milieu rural", *Cahiers internationaux de Sociologie* 67, jul-dec 79 : 221-236.

4931 DEUTSCHMANN, Christoph; DYBOWSKI-JOHANNSON, Karin. "Wirtschaftliche und soziale Determinanten der Arbeitszeitpolitik" (Economic and social determinants of the working time policy), *Mitteilungen aus der Arbeitsmarkt- und Berufsforschung* 12, 79 : 313-327.

4932 DEWAR, R.; WERBEL, J. "Universalistic and contingency predictions of employee satisfaction and conflict", *Administrative Science Quarterly* 24, 79 : 426-449.

4933 DULL, Klaus. "Gesellschaftliche Interventionen in Arbeitsbedingungen" (Social interventions in working conditions), *Soziale Welt* 31, 80 : 333-353. [Germany FR.]

4934 EDWARDS, P. K. "Attachment to work and absence behavior", *Human Relations* 32(12), 79 : 1065-1080.

4935 Bibl.XXIX-4946. EDWARDS, Richard. *Contested terrain: the transformation of the workplace in the twentieth century*. CR: Paul GOLDMAN, *Contemporary Sociology (Albany)* 9(4), jul 80 : 570-571.

4936 FITZPATRICK, John S. "Adapting to danger: a participant observation study of an underground mine", *Sociology of Work and Occupations* mai 80 : 131-158.

4937 GILMOUR, Peter. "Career and jobs: women's attitudes at work", *Journal of general management* aut 79 : 80-87.

4938 GRANDJEAN, Burke D.; TAYLOR, Patricia A. "Job satisfaction among female clerical workers: 'status panic' of the opportunity structure of office work?", *Sociology of Work and Occupations* feb 80 : 33-53.

4939 GRUENBERG, Barry. "The happy worker: an analysis of educational and occupational differences in determinants of job satisfaction", *American Journal of Sociology* 86, sep 80 : 247-271.

4940 GRUNEBERG, Michael M. *Understanding job satisfaction*. Wiley, 79, xi-170 p.

4941 GUSTAVSEN, Bjørn. "Le choix d'une stratégie pour améliorer le milieu de travail", *Revue internationale du Travail* 119, mai-jun 80 : 291-308.

4942 HALABY, Charles N. "Dynamic models and attainment in the workplace", *Social Science Research* mar 80 : 1-36.

4943 HEINZE, Rolf G.; [et al.]. "Arbeitszeitflexibilisierung als beschäftigungspolitisches Instrument" (Working time flexibility as an employment policy instrument), *Mitteilungen aus der Arbeitsmarkt- und Berufsforschüng* 12, 79 : 276-288.

4944 HUSZÁR, Tibor. *Adalékok a munkaerkölcs történetéhez és szociológiájához* (Contributions to the history and sociology of attitudes towards work). Budapest, Oktatási Minisztérium, 80, 155 p.

4945 JAKOBS, Ludwig. *Humanisierungstendenzen am Arbeitsplatz* (Humanization trends in the working place). Bochum, Studienverlag Brockmeyer, 79, 278 p.

4946 JARRY, Elisabeth. "Les temps sociaux dans le Chablisien", *Cahiers internationaux de Sociologie* 67, jul-dec 79 : 237-262.

4947 KAFRY, Kitsa; PINES, Ayala. "The experience of tedium in life and work", *Human Relations* 33, jul 80 : 477-503.

4948 KAZUTOSHI, Koshiro. "Perceptions of work and living attitudes of the Japanese", *Japan Quarterly* 27, jan-mar 80 : 46-55.

4949 KNIGHT, Graham. "Work orientation and mobility ideology in the working-class", *Canadian Journal of Sociology* 79 : 27-41.

4950 KÖPPL, Bernd. *Intensivierung kontra Humanisierung: d. Arbeitssituation unqualifizierter Industriearbeiter* (Intensification versus humanization: unskilled industrial worker's working conditions). Frankfurt/Main, New York, Campus-Verlag, 79, 183 p.

4951 KRAVČENKO, V. M. "Cennost' truda v obraze žizni molodyh rabočih" (The labour value in the young workers' way of life), *IN: Socialističeskij obraz žizni i ličnost'.* Voronež, 79 : 38-50.

4952 KUBICEK, Herbert. "Dimensionen der Humanisierung des Arbeitslebens" (Dimensions of the humanization of working life), *Betriebswirtschaft* 39, 79 : 663-679.

4953 LENOIR, Remi. "La notion d'accident du travail: un enjeu de luttes", *Actes de la Recherche en Sciences sociales* 32-33, apr-jun 80 : 77-88.

4954 MAGUIRE, Tom; ROMANIUK, Eugene W.; MACRURY, Katherine A. *Development of scales on attitudes towards the world of work.* Edmonton, Can., Minister's Advisory Committee on Student Achievement, 79. [2 vols.]

4955 MAKO, Csaba. "Une expérience d'enrichissement du travail dans l'industrie hongroise", *Sociologie du Travail* 22, oct-dec 80 : 390-407.

4956 MANNARI, Hiroshi. "The Japanese factory reconsidered", *Rice University* 66, 80 : 189-200.

4957 MANNARI, Hiroshi; MARSH, Robert M. "Nihon no kojo no shoshiki kozo: Gijutsu kettei riron no kensho" (Organizational structure of Japanese factories: A test of technological implications theory), *Soshiki kagaku* 14, 80 : 61-75.

4958 MCLENNAN, Roy; LIEW, Tuck. "Work group behaviour in a New Zealand factory", *Australian and New Zealand Journal of Sociology* 16, mar 80 : 84-85.

4959 MERCURE, Daniel. "L'étude des temporalités sociales. Quelques orientations", *Cahiers internationaux de Sociologie* 67, jul-dec 79 : 263-276.

4960 MINC, L. È. *Social'no-èkonomičeskie i sociologičeskie problemy balansa truda i bjudžeta vremeni* (Socio-economic and sociological problems of the labour and time budget balance). Moskva, Nauka, 79, 213 p.

4961 MORTIMER, Jeylan T. *Changing attitudes toward work.* Scarsdale, NY, Work in America Institute, 79, 55 p.

4962 NELSON, Linda. "Household time: a cross-cultural example", *Sage Yearbooks in Women's Policy Studies* 80 : 169-190.

4963 NIEUWENBURG, C. K. F. "Enige macro-economische aspecten van arbeidstijdverkorting" (Some macroeconomic aspects of hours of work reduction), *Sociaal Maandblad Arbeid* 34, jan 79 : 36-47.

4964 OLDHAM, Jack. "Social control of voluntary work activity: the gift horse syndrome", *Sociology of Work and Occupations* nov 79 : 379-403.

4965 OLK, Thomas; [et al.]. "Lohnarbeit und Arbeitszeit" (Salaried work and working time), *Leviathan* 79 : 151-173. [continued in vol. 7(3), 1979: 376-407.]

4966 OVČINNIKOV, V. F.; DOBRYNIN, I. A. "Orientacija na tvorčeskij trud kak social'naja cennost'" (Orientation to creative labour as a social value), *Ličnost' i Obščestvo* 79 : 39-46.

4967 OWEN, John D. *Working hours: An economic analysis.* Lexington, MA, Toronto, Heath, Lexington Books, 79, xiv-206 p. CR: Harold L. SHEPPARD, *Journal of economic Literature* 18(3), sep 80: 1132-1133.

4968 PANETRAT, P. "Les budgets-temps soviétiques", *Économies et Sociétés. Cahiers de l'ISÉA* 13(7-8-9-10). jul-aug-sep-oct 79 : 1221-1389.

4969 PASCALE, Richard Tanner; MAGUIRE, Mary Ann. "Comparison of selected work factors in Japan and the United States", *Human Relations* 33, jul 80 : 433-455.

4970 PATRUŠEV, V. D. "Metodika izučenija bjudžeta vremeni trudjaščihsja" (Methods of the worker's time-budget study), *Sociologičeskie Issledovanija* 80 : 129-139.

4971 PATRUŠEV, V. D.; [ed.]. *Tendencii izmenenija bjudžeta vremeni trudjaščihsja* (Change tendencies of the workers' time budget). Moskva, Institut Sociologiceskih Issledovanij AN SSSR, 79, 176 p. [USSR.]

4972 PERABO, Christa. *Humanisierung der Arbeit* (Humanization of work). Giessen, Focus-Verlag, 79, 221 p. [Germany FR.]

4973 PFEFFER, Jeffrey. "A partial test of the social information processing model of job attitudes", *Human Relations* 33, jul 80 : 457-476.

4974 RATNER, Ronnie Steinberg. "La paradoxe de la protection: la législation sur la durée maximale du travail aux États-Unis", *Revue internationale du Travail* 119, mar-apr 80 : 195-211.

4975 REYHER, Lutz; [et al.]. "Arbeitszeit und Arbeitsmarkt" (Working time and labour market), *Mitteilungen aus der Arbeitsmarkt- und Berufsforschung* 12, 79 : 381-402.

4976 ROHMERT, Walter. "Humanisierung der Arbeit durch Ergonomie?" (Humanization of work through ergonomics), *Zeitschrift für Arbeitswissenschaft* 80 : 65-69.

4977 RONEN, Simcha; KRAUT, Allen I. "An experimental examination of work motivation taxonomies", *Human Relations* 33, jul 80 : 505-516.

4978 RUCH, Richard S. "A path analytic study of the structure of employee job satisfaction: the critical role of top management", *Journal of vocational Behavior* 15, dec 79 : 277-293.

4979 RUTGAJZER, V. M.; SMAROV, A. I. "Bjudzer vremeni naselenija i metodologiceskie voprosy ego prognozviovanija" (Population time-budget and methodological problems of forecasting it), *Ekonomika i matematičeskie Metody* 16, mai-jun 80 : 435-448.

4980 SAINT-JOURS, Yves. "Existe-t-il un contrat de travail de droit public?", *Droit social* feb 80 : 187-195.

4981 SAVALL, Henri. *Reconstruire l'entreprise: analyse socio-économique des conditions de travail.* Paris, Dunod, 80, xix-275 p.

4982 SCHÄUBLE, Gerhard. *Die Humanisierung der Industriearbeit* (The humanization of industrial work). Frankfurt/Main, New York, Campus-Verlag, 79, 303 p.

4983 STAUDT, Erich. "Die Bedeutung der mikroökonomischen Analyse zur Beurteilung und Durchsetzung neuer Arbeitszeitstrukturen" (The meaning of the microeconomic analysis for the criticism and success of new working time structures), *Mitteilungen aus der Arbeitsmarkt- und Berufsforschung* 13, 79 : 328-339.

4984 TATUR, Melanie. "Sozialplanung und Humanisierung der Arbeit in der Sowjetunion" (Social planning and humanization of work in the Soviet Union), *Leviathan* 79 : 415-440.

4985 TERIET, Bernhard. "Vom Work-Sharing zum Job-Sharing" (From work-sharing to job-sharing), *Zeitschrift für Arbeitswissenschaft* 80 : 84-88.

4986 THIEME, Hans. "Zur Rolle des Arbeitsvertrages als betriebliches Leitungsinstrument" (The role of the labour contract as an instrument of business management), *Staat und Recht* 28(11), 79 : 977-986. [German DR.]

4987 TITMA, Mikk. "Formation of young people's orientation towards work", *Acta sociologica* 22, 79 : 345-359. [USSR.]

4988 VALTICOS, Nicolas. "L'avenir des normes internationales du travail", *Revue internationale du Travail* 118, nov-dec 79 : 721-740.

4989 VAUGHT, Charles; SMITH, David L. "Incorporation and mechanical solidarity in an underground coal mine", *Sociology of Work and Occupations* mai 80 : 159-187.

4990 WACHTLER, Günther. *Humanisierung der Arbeit und Industriesoziologie* (Humanization of work and industrial sociology). Stuttgart, Berlin, Köln, Mainz, Kohlhammer, 79, 180 p.

4991 WRIGHT, James D.; HAMILTON, Richard F. "Education and job attitudes among blue-collar workers", *Sociology of Work and Occupations* feb 79 : 59-83.

4992 ŽARIKOV, F. S. "Umstvennyj trud v uslovijah sovremennoj naučno-tehničeskoj revoljucii" (Intellectual work under conditions of the contemporary scientific and technical revolution), *IN: Problemy intensifikacii obučenija.* Moskva, 79 : 7-15.

18330. Labour turnover
Renouvellement de la main-d'oeuvre

[See also / voir aussi: 3069, 4739, 4934, 5696]

4993 BARBIER, Jean Marie. "Situation de travail, poursuite d'un projet de formation et procès de transformation personnelle", *Revue française de Sociologie* 21, jul-sep 80 : 409-437.
4994 BEGNOCHE SMITH, Catherine. "Influence of internal opportunity structure and sex of worker on turnover patterns", *Administrative Science Quarterly* 24, sep 79 : 362-381.
4995 BEVERIDGE, W. E. "Retirement and life significance: a study of the adjustment to retirement of a sample of men at management level", *Human Relations* 33, jan 80 : 69-78.
4996 BRADFORD, Leland Powers; BRADFORD, Martha I. *Retirement: coping with emotional upheavals.* Chicago: Nelson-Hall, 79, xii-202 p.
4997 BRYANT, Christopher G. A. "Worker advancement and political order in a state socialist society: a case study of Poland", *Sociological Review* 28, feb 80 : 105-128.
4998 CASCIOLI, Alfio. *Assenteismo e alienazione* (Absenteeism and alienation). Milano, F. Angeli, 79, 130 p.
4999 EHRENBERG, Ronald G. "Retirement system characteristics and compensating wage differentials in the public sector", *Industrial and Labor Relations Review* 33, jul 80 : 470-483.
5000 HALL, Arden; JOHNSON, Terry R. "The determinants of planned retirement age", *Industrial and Labor Relations Review* 33, jan 80 : 241-254.
5001 HALL, Robert Ernest; LILIEN, David M. *The measurement and significance of labor turnover.* Washington, National Commission on Employment and Unemployment Statistics, 79, v-49 p. [for sale by the Supt. of Docs., U.S. Govt. Print. Off..]
5002 JARDILLIER, Pierre; BAUDUIN, Henri. *L'absentéisme: mythes et réalités.* Paris, Entreprise moderne d'édition, 79, xiv-171 p.
5003 KEMP, Fred; BUTTLE, Bernard. *Focus on retirement.* London, Kogan Page, 79, 198 p.
5004 KLEILER, Frank M. *Can we afford early retirement?.* Baltimore, Johns Hopkins University Press, 79, ix-163 p. CR: N. A. BARR, *Economica (London)* 47(188), nov 80 : 488-489.
5005 MIKALACHKI, A.; GANDZ, Jeffrey. "Measuring absenteeism", *Relations industrielles* 34, 79 : 516-545.
5006 MONNIER, Alain. "Les limites de la vie active et la retraite. II. Les condition du passage à la retraite: réalités et projets", *Population* 35, feb 80 : 109-136.
5007 TRACY, Martin. *Retirement age practices in ten industrial societies, 1960-1976.* Geneva, International Social Security Association, 79, ix-170 p.
5008 WAGNER, Jon. "Strategies of dismissal: ways and means of avoiding personal abuse", *Human Relations* 33, sep 80 : 603-622.
5009 WEISS, Dimitri. "L'absentéisme", *Revue française des Affaires sociales* 33, oct-dec 79 : 49-95.
5010 WINKLER, Donald R. "The effects of sick-leave policy on teacher absenteeism", *Industrial and Labor Relations Review* 33, jan 80 : 232-240.
5011 WOOD, Stephen. "Managerial reactions to job redundancy through early retirements", *Sociological Review* 28, nov 80 : 783-807.

18400. OCCUPATION. VOCATIONAL TRAINING
PROFESSION. FORMATION PROFESSIONNELLE

18410. Occupational sociology
Sociologie de la profession

[See also / voir aussi: 105, 3757, 4607, 5029, 5034, 6235, 6242]

5012 "Professionalisierung in historischer Perspektive" (Professionalization in historical perspective), *Geschichte und Gesellschaft* 80 : 311-402.
5013 BERGFELD, Hans-Joachim Edmund. *Empirische Untersuchung einer berufsfeldbezogenen Arbeitstypologie* (Empirical research of a labour typology based on occupational fields). Berlin, Köln, Beuth, 79, v-329 p.
5014 BLAIR, Roger D.; RUBIN, Stephen; [eds.]. *Regulating the professions: A public-policy symposium.* Lexington, MA, Toronto, Heath, Lexington Books, 80, viii-327 p.
5015 COLASANTO, Michele. "La "nuova" professionalità: temi e problemi per una ipotesi di lavoro" (The "new" professionality: topics and problems for a hypothesis), *Studi di Sociologia* 17, apr-jun 79 : 183-192.

5016 Bibl.XXIX-4959. COXON, Anthony P. M.; JONES, Charles L. *Class and hierarchy: the social meanings of occupations.* CR: Trevor W. JONES, *British Journal of Sociology* 31(4), dec 80 : 584-586.

5017 COXON, Anthony P. M.; JONES, Charles L. *Measurement and meanings: techniques and methods of studying occupational cognition.* London, Macmillan, 79, 305 p. CR: Trevor W. JONES, *British Journal of Sociology* 31(4), dec 80: 584-586.

5018 CULLEN, John B. *The structure of professionalism: A quantitative examination.* New York, PBI-Petrocelli Books, 78, xiii-290 p. [distributed by McGraw-Hill.]

5019 FIELDING, A. G.; PORTWOOD, D. "Professions and the State — towards a typology of bureaucratic professions", *Sociological Review* 28, feb 80 : 23-53.

5020 HERAUD, Brian J. *Sociology in the professions.* London, Open Books, 79, viii-219 p.

5021 HOGAN, Daniel B. *The regulation of psychotherapists. I. A study in the philosophy and practice of professional regulation.* Cambridge, MA, Ballinger, 79, 412 p. CR: Kurt W. BACK, *Contemporary Sociology (Albany)* 9(6), nov 80, 846-847.

5022 IZRAELI, Dafna N. "Sex structure of occupations: the Israeli experience", *Sociology of Work and Occupations* nov 79 : 404-429.

5023 MARKOVIĆ, Danilo Z. "Prilo određivanju predmeta sociologije zaštite na radu" (A contribution to the specification of the subject matter of the sociology of occupational safety), *Revija za Sociologiju* (1-2), 78 : 89-95.

5024 ODENYO, Amos O. "Professionalization amidst change: the case of the emerging legal profession in Kenya", *African Studies Review* 22, dec 79 : 33-44.

5025 ROSENFELD, Rachel A. "Women's occupational careers: individual and structural explanations", *Sociology of Work and Occupations* aug 79 : 283-311.

5026 STERN, Robert N.; MURPHY, Kevin R. "Professional socialization and attitudes toward collective bargaining: an exploration among law students", *Sociology of Work and Occupations* nov 80 : 431-456.

5027 UGLJEŠIĆ, Dubravka. "Mjesto i uloga sociologa na području zapošljavanja" (The sociologist's place and role in the employment field), *Revija za Sociologiju* (3-4), jul-dec 79 : 80-85.

18420. Occupational life. Vocational guidance
Vie professionnelle. Orientation professionnelle

[See also / voir aussi: 1829, 2542, 2736, 2952, 3066, 3413, 3531, 3784, 3869, 4748, 4833, 4938, 4987, 4993, 5116, 5513, 6241, 6243]

5028 ACERO, Liliana. "Workers' skills in Latin America: an approach towards self-reliant development", *Development and Change* 11, jul 80 : 367-389.

5029 ALBRECHT, Gary L. "Defusing technological change in juvenile courts: the probation officer's struggle for professional autonomy", *Sociology of Work and Occupations* aug 79 : 259-282.

5030 AMANO, Masako; [et al.]. *Josei jinzairon* (Development of occupational ability of women). Tokyo, Yuhikaku, 80, 200 p.

5031 ANGLE, John; STEIBER, Steven R.; WISSMANN, David A. "Educational indicators and occupational achievement", *Social Science Research* mar 80 : 60-75.

5032 BALKWELL, James W.; BATES, Frederick L.; GARBIN, Albeno P. "On the intersubjectivity of occupational status evaluations: a test of a key assumption underlying the "Wisconsin Model" of status attainment", *Social Forces* 58, mar 80 : 865-903.

5033 BARON, James N. "Indianapolis and beyond: a structural model of occupational mobility across generations", *American Journal of Sociology* 85, jan 80 : 815-839.

5034 BECK, Ulrich; BRATER, Michael; WEGENER, Bernd. *Berufswahl und Berufszuweisung. Zur sozialen Verwandtschaft von Ausbildungsberufen* (Occupational choice and occupational assignment. On the social relationship of training occupations). Frankfurt-am-Main, New York, Campus Verlag, 79, 195 p. CR: Gerhard HELD, *Kölner Zeitschrift für Soziologie und Sozialpsychologie* 32(1), mar 80 : 175-177.

5035 BELLAMY, G. Thomas; O'CONNOR, Gail; KARAN, Orv C.; [eds.]. *Vocational rehabilitation of severely handicapped persons: contemporary service strategies.* Baltimore, University Park Press, 79, 276 p.

5036 BERTAUX, D. "La détermination sociale des destinées individuelles", *Economie et Humanisme* 250, nov-dec 79 : 7-27.

5037 BISHOP, James M. "Institutional and operational knowledge in work: a sensitizing framework", *Sociology of Work and Occupations* aug 79 : 328-352.

5038 BLAU, Judith R. "Expertise and power in professional organization", *Sociology of Work and Occupations* feb 79 : 103-123.

5039 BOURRICAUD, François. "La crise de l'autorité professionnelle: avocats, magistrats, médicins et professeurs", *Commentaire* aut 79 : 382-389.
5040 BOVONE, Laura. "Per una ricognizione teorica dell'ipotesi dell'alternanza scuola-lavoro" (For a theoretical recognition of the possibility of education/work hypothesis), *Studi di Sociologia* 18, apr-jun 80 : 113-122.
5041 BUCHMANN, Michael A. *Berufsstrukturen in Entwicklungsländern* (Occupational structure in developing countries). Tübingen, Basel, Erdmann, 79, 439 p.
5042 ČERNOVOLENKO, V. F.; [et al.]. *Prestiž professij i problemy social'no-professional'noj orientacii molodeži: opyt sociologičeskogo issledovanija* (Occupational prestige and problems of the youth socio-occupational orientation: an essay of sociological research). Kiev, Naukova Dumka, 79, 214 p. [USSR.]
5043 CORTELAZZI, Silvia; PICCOLI, Italo. "I quadri regionali della formazione professionale: ruolo, professionalità e atteggiamenti sindacali" (Professional development: regional middle-management role, professionality and unionistic attitudes), *Studi di Sociologia* 17, apr-jun 79 : 147-182. [Italy.]
5044 DOMBOS, Paul. "Some recent changes in the Swedish occupational structure", *Acta sociologica* 22, 79 : 321-343.
5045 ERLANGER, Howard S. "The allocation of status within occupations: the case of the legal profes sion", *Social Forces* 58, mar 80 : 882-903.
5046 FERGE, Zsuzsa; [ed.]. *Pedagógusok és tanulók a szakmunkásképzésben* (Teachers and pupils in vocational training schools). Budapest, MTA KESZ, vol. 1, 76; vol. 2, 79, 175; 290 p. [Hungary.]
5047 FISCHER, Heinz-Dietrich; [ed.]. *Spektrum der Kommunikationsberufe* (Structure of communication occupations). Köln, Deutscher Ärzte-Verlag, 79, 299 p. [Germany FR.]CR: Alphons SILBERMANN, *Kölner Zeitschrift für Soziologie und Sozialpsychologie* 32(2), jun 80: 405-407.
5048 GECAS, Viktor. "Family and social structural influences on the career orientations of rural MexicanAmerican youth", *Rural Sociology* 45, sum 80 : 272-289.
5049 GRANDJEAN, Burke D.; BERNAL, Helen Hazuda. "Sex and centralization in a semiprofession", *Sociology of Work and Occupations* feb 79 : 84-102.
5050 HARANNE, Markku. "Dialectics between occupational and party structures: Finland since World War II", *Acta sociologica* 23(2-3), 80 : 83-95.
5051 HERZ, Thomas Aage; WIEKEN-MAYSER, Maria. *Berufliche Mobilität in der Bundesrepublik* (Occupational mobility in the Federal Republic). Frankfurt am Main, New York, Campus Verlag, 79, 127 p. CR: Klaus ALLERBECK, *Soziologische Revue* 3(4), 80: 434-435.
5052 KOURVETARIS, George A. "Structure and process: the waiter's role in a middle class restaurant", *International Journal of contemporary Sociology* 15(3-4), jul-oct 78 : 414-439.
5053 LITVAK, Isaiah A.; MAULE, Christopher J. "Politiques et pratiques en matière de congé de formation dans certaines entreprises du Canada", *Travail et Société* apr 80 : 209-224.
5054 MARTIN, Michel L. "Note sur l'hérédité professionelle chez les officiers de l'armée de terre française", *Annales de l'Université des Sciences sociales de Toulouse* 27, 79 : 321-335.
5055 MATHIESEN, Anders. "Polarization of the qualification structure of the Danish labour force: the role of the educational system in post-war Denmark", *Acta sociologica* 23(2-3), 80 : 157-172.
5056 MAUPEOU-ABBOUD, Nicole de. "Les politiques patronales de formation et leurs finalités", *Sociologie du Travail* 22, apr-jun 80 : 171-192.
5057 MAYER, Karl Ulrich. "Strukturwandel im Beschäftigungssystem und berufliche Mobilität zwischen Generationen" (Structural change in the occupational system and occupational mobility between generations), *Zeitschrift für Bevölkerungswissenschaft* 79 : 267-296.
5058 MCCLENDON, McKee J. "Occupational mobility and economic development: a cross-national analysis", *Sociological Focus* 13, oct 80 : 331-342.
5059 MEJÍA, Alfonso; PIZURKI, Helena; ROYSTON, Erica. *Physician and nurse migration: analysis and policy implications: report of a WHO study*. Geneva, World Health Organization, 79, xiv-476 p.
5060 MESSNER, Steven F. "Blau's theory of occupational differentiation: problems in empirical examination", *Sociology of Work and Occupations* nov 80 : 395-424. [with a comment by Peter M. Blau, ibid.: 425-430.]
5061 MÓNICA, Maria Filomena. "Uma aristocracia operária: os chapeleiros, 1870-1914" (A working aristocracy: the hat-makers, 1870-1914), *Analise social* 15, 79 : 859-945. [Portugal.]
5062 MONTLIBERT, Christian De. "L'éducation morale des familles; l'extension du métier de puéricultrice", *Actes de la Recherche en Sciences sociales* 32-33, apr-jun 80 : 65-76.

5063 MORTIMER, Jeylan T.; LORENCE, Jon. "Occupational experience and the self-concept: a longitudinal study", *Social Psychology Quarterly* 42, dec 79 : 307-323.

5064 MYKLEBOST, Hallstein. *Norges tettsteder: folketall og naeringsstruktur = Norway's urban settlements: population and occupational structure.* Bergen, Universitetsforl., 79, 118 p.

5065 OHRIMENKO, V. A. "Sociologopedagogičeskie problemy v sisteme 'obrazovanie-proizvodstvo'" (Sociological and pedagogical problems in the "formation-production" system), *IN: Social'naja struktura sovetskogo obščestva i socialističeskij obraz žizni. I.* Moskva, 78 : 185-198.

5066 ONO, Yoshibumi. "Byōin ishi no shokugyōseikatsu ishiki -shigoto manzokudo ni tsuite" (Professional life -consciousness of hospital physicians), *Byōin* 39, 80 : 1093-1095.

5067 PERRUCCI, Carolyn Cummings. "Gender and achievement: the early careers of college graduates", *Sociological Focus* 13, apr 80 : 99-111.

5068 READ, Jane. "An analysis of occupational ranking by careers officers", *Sociological Review* 28, aug 80 : 537-548.

5069 RENAUD, Jean; BERNARD, Paul; BERTHIAUME, Monique. "Éducation, qualification professionnelle et carrière au Québec", *Sociologie et Sociétés* 12, apr 80 : 23-52.

5070 ROSENFELD, Rachel A. "Race and sex differences in career dynamics", *American sociological Review* 45, aug 80 : 583-609.

5071 ROTHMAN, Robert A. "Occupational roles: power and negotiation in the division of labor", *Sociological Quarterly* 20, 79 : 495-515.

5072 SCHREIBER, Carol Tropp. *Changing places: men and women in transitional occupations.* Cambridge, MA, MIT Press, 79, xiv-244 p. [USA.]

5073 SEWELL, William H.; HAUSER, Robert M.; WOLF, Wendy C. "Sex, schooling, and occupational status", *American Journal of Sociology* 86, nov 80 : 551-583.

5074 SHARDA, Bam Dev. "Occupational prestige in rural India", *Rural Sociology* 44, wint 79 : 705-718.

5075 ŠKARATAN, O. I. "Social'nyj sloj i professija v klassovoj strukture socialističeskogo obščestva" (Social strata and occupations in the socialist society class structure), *IN: Social'naja struktura sovetskogo obščestva i socialističeskij obraz žizni. I..* Moskva, 78 : 15-27.

5076 SPENNER, Kenneth I. "Temporal changes in work content", *American sociological Review* 44, dec 79 : 968-975. [USA.]

5077 TANGUY, Lucie. "Appropriation et privation des savoirs dans et par l'école", *Sociologie et Sociétés* 12, apr 80 : 53-66.

5078 TINTO, Vincent. "College origins and patterns of status attainment: schooling among professional and business-managerial occupations", *Sociology of Work and Occupations* nov 80 : 457-486.

5079 VICTOR, Jean. "L'évolution de la structure des qualifications des ouvriers en courte période (1965-1970)", *Issues* (3-4), 79 : 83-113.

5080 VOHLAND, Ulrich. *Berufswahlunterricht: Theorie, Didaktik, Methodik u. Modelle* (Vocational education: theory, didactics, method and model). Bad Heilbrunn, Obb., Klinkhardt, 80, 294 p.

18500. EMPLOYEE. TECHNICIAN. WORKER
EMPLOYÉ. TECHNICIEN. TRAVAILLEUR

18510. Worker
Travailleur

[See also / voir aussi: 740, 749, 1143, 2331, 2523, 2680, 3178, 3954, 4584, 4950, 4970, 4991, 5198, 5348, 5412, 6029]

5081 BAKLICKAJA, O. P. "Social'no-psihologičeskaja adaptacija rabotnikov v sisteme social'noj mobil'nosti kollektiva" (The workers' sociopsychological adaptation in the system of the collectivity social mobility), *IN: Problemy social'nogo upravlenija na promyšlennom predprijatii. VIII.* Kiev, 78 : 42-49. [USSR.]

5082 BAREŽEV, V. A.; ZAJDFUDIM, P. H. "Puti dal'nejšego povyšenija social'noj aktivnosti sovetskih trudjaščihsja v svete novoj Konstitucii SSSR" (Progress in the development of the Soviet workers social activity as seen in the light of the USSR Constitution), *Političeskaja Organizacija Obščestva i Upravlenija pri Socializme* 79 : 44-57.

5083 BARZILOV, S. I. "Social'naja priroda agrarnogo otrjada rabočego klassa" (Social nature of the working class agrarian branch), *IN: Aktual'nye voprosy social'no-političeskogo razvitija obščestva v uslovijah zrelogo socializma.* Saratov, 79 : 39-57.

5084 CANNON, Lynn Weber. "Normative embourgeoisement among manual workers: a reexamination using longitudinal data", *Sociological Quarterly* 21, 80 : 185-195.
5085 CONZE, Werner; ENGELHARDT, Ulrich; [eds.]. *Arbeiter im Industrialisierungsprozess* (Workers in the industrialization process). Stuttgart, Klett-Cotta, 79, 513 p.
5086 DRONOV, V. T.; LAZUKA, S. A. "Rol' socialističeskoj organizacii obščestva v vozrastanii social'noj aktivnosti trudjaščihsja" (Role of the society socialist organization in the elevation of the workers' social activity), *Političeskaja Organizacija Obščestva i Upravlenija pri Socializme* 79 : 34-43.
5087 GAUDEMAR, Jean-Paul de; [ed.]. *Usines et ouvriers: figures du nouvel ordre productif*. Paris, F. Maspéro, 80, 164 p.
5088 GLASERIVA, Jaroslava. "K soucasnemu stavu v pratovnich silach v CS. zemedelstvi z uzemniho pohledu" (Present situation of agricultuaral manpower in Czechoslavakia), *Demografie* 21, 79 : 289-301.
5089 HACK, Lothar; [et al.]. *Leistung und Herrschaft: soziale Strukturzusammenhänge subjektiver Relevanz bei jüngeren Industriearbeitern* (Performance and authority: subjective relevance of social structure cohesion among young industrial workers). Frankfurt/Main, New York, Campus-Verlag, 79, v-647 p.
5090 Bibl.XXIX-5013. HIRSCH, Susan E. *Roots of the American working class: the industrialization of crafts in Newark, 1800-1860*. CR: Stephen BRIER, *Contemporary Sociology (Albany)* 9(1), jan 80: 96-97.
5091 KAHAN, Arcadius; RUBLE, Blair A.; [eds.]. *Industrial labor in the U.S.S.R.*. New York, Pergamon Press, 79, xv-421 p.
5092 KAHN, Michèle; MINK, Georges. "Les ouvriers en URSS: statut économique et social", *Courrier des Pays de l'Est* 234, nov 79 : 3-98.
5093 KUDERA, Werner; [et al.]. *Gesellschaftliches und politisches Bewusstsein von Arbeitern: e. empir. Unters.* (Workers' social and political consciousness: an empirical research). Köln, Frankfurt am Main, Europäische Verlagsanstalt, 79, 377 p. [Germany FR.]
5094 LJUČVAJTIS, S. Ju. "Trudovaja i obščestvennaja aktivnost' sovetskih rabočih" (The Soviet workers' labour and social activity), *IN: Sociologičeskie problemy obrazovanija, kul'tury i nauki*. Moskva, 78 : 5-15.
5095 PAWULA, Harry. *Die Industriearbeiter, Kern der sozialistischen Arbeiterklasse: e. Beitr. zur Struktur d. Arbeiterklasse im Sozialismus* (The industrial worker, the corner stone of the socialist working class). Berlin, Deutscher Verlag der Wissenschaften, 79, 119 p.
5096 SEVKO, V. B. "Formirovanie rabočego novogo tipa v uslovijah naučno-tehničeskoj revoljucii" (Formation of a new type of worker under the conditions of scientific and technical revolution), *Vestnik Moskovskogo Universiteta. Teorija naučnogo Kommunizma* 79 : 12-19.
5097 SIZOVA, T. P. "Rost obrazovanija i otnošenie rabočih k trudu" (Formation growth and the workers' relation to labour), *IN: Aktual'nye voprosy social'no-političeskogo razvitija obščestva v uslovijah zrelogo socializma*. Saratov, 79 : 57-69.
5098 TARASOV, Ju. N. "Puti i formy soveršenstvovanija obraza zizni sel'skih truženikov" (Means and forms of the rural workers' way of life improvement), *IN: Trud kak osnova socialističeskogo obraza žizni*. Moskva, 79 : 127-143.
5099 TÓTH, Árpád. *Nagyüzemi munkások művelődése és műveltsége Ózdon* (Culture and education of industrial workers in the town Ózd). Budapest, NPI, 79, 83 p. [publ. by the Research Institute of Hungarian Trade Unions.]
5100 VERRET, Michel. *L'espace ouvrier*. Paris, A. Colin, 79, 231 p.
5101 Bibl.XXIX-5031. VERRET, Michel; CREUSEN, Joseph. *L'ouvrier français*. CR: René MOURIAUX, *Revue française de Science politique* 30(1), feb 80: 155-156.

18520. Employee
Employé

[See also / voir aussi: 4473, 4927, 4938, 5187, 5198]

5102 FRAISSE, Geneviève. *Femmes toutes mains: essai sur le service domestique*. Paris, Seuil, 79, 245 p.
5103 MARTIN-FUGIER, Anne. *La Place des bonnes: la domesticité féminine à Paris en 1900*. Paris, B. Grasset, 79, 382 p.
5104 MCNALLY, Fiona. *Women for hire: a study of the female office worker*. London, Macmillan, 79, 210 p. CR: Pauline HUNT, *British Journal of Sociology* 31(4), dec 80: 592-593.
5105 RUSSKIH, B. G. "Služaščie — nespecialisty v social'noj strukture razvitogo socialističeskogo obščestva" (Non-specialists — employees in the developed socialist

society social structure), *IN: Razvitoj socializm: osnovnye čerty i osobennosti.* Saratov, 79 : 102-109.

5106   TOIVONEN, Timo. "Toimihenkilöiden taloudellisen aseman muutoksesta 1900-luvulla" (Changes in the economic position of white-collar workers during this century), *Sosiologia* 80 : 205-215.

18530. Manager. Technician
Cadre. Technicien

[See also / voir aussi: 1113, 4016, 4524, 4525, 4558, 4978, 5175]

5107   BOERGER, Martin. "Annotations on the dilemma of management-development. Leadership training, aspiration and realization", *Management international Review* 19, 79 : 89-93.

5108   BOLTANSKI, Luc. "L'université, les entreprises et la multiplication des salariés bourgeois, 1960-1975", *Actes de la Recherche en Sciences sociales* 34, sep 80 : 17-44.

5109   BOLTANSKI, Luc. "Croissance universitaire et montée des cadres en France (1960-1975)", *Sociologie et Sociétés* 12, apr 80 : 67-100.

5110   BURKE, Ronald J.; WEIR, Tamara; DUWORS, Richard E. Jr. "Work demands on administrators and spouse well-being", *Human Relations* 33, apr 80 : 253-278.

5111   CHOW, Esther Ngan-Ling; GRUSKY, Oscar. "Productivity, aggressiveness, and supervisory style", *Sociology and social Research* 65, oct 80 : 23-36.

5112   DAVIS, Charles E.; WEST, Jonathan P. "Attitudinal differences among supervisors in the public sector", *Industrial and Labor Relations Review* 32, jul : 496-505.

5113   FLEET, D van S. Al-Tuhaih. "A cross-cultural analysis of perceived leader behaviors"), *IN: Management International Review.* 79 : 81-87.

5114   GOLDING, David. "Establishing blissful clarity in organizational life: managers", *Sociological Review* 28, nov 80 : 763-782.

5115   Bibl.XXIX-5042. GRUNBERG, Gérard; MOURIAUX, René. *L'univers politique et syndical des cadres.* [France.]CR: Gérard VINCENT, *Revue française de Science politique* 30(3), jun 80 : 609-612.

5116   LAATZ, Wilfried. *Ingenieure in der Bundesrepublik Deutschland. Gesellschaftliche Lage und politisches Bewusstsein* (Engineers in the Federal Republic of Germany. Social status and political consciousness). Frankfurt-am-Main, New York, Campus, 79, 380 p. CR: Alfred OPPOLZER, *Soziologische Revue* 3(4), 80: 435-437.

5117   LAWRENCE, Peter A. *Managers and management in West Germany.* New York, St. Martin's Press, 80, 202 p.

5118   LEGGATT, Timothy. "Managers in industry: their interorganizational mobility", *Human Relations* 32(10), oct 79 : 851-869. [United Kingdom.]

5119   MARGOLIS, Diane Rothbard. *The managers: corporate life in America.* New York, Morrow, 79, 313 p.

5120   REDDING, S. G. *The working class manager: beliefs and behaviour.* Farnborough, Eng., Saxon House, 79, vii-154 p.

5121   RIBAS, Armando P. *El rol del empresario en la sociedad* (The manager's social role). Buenos Aires, El Ateneo, 80, 124 p.

5122   STENING, Bruce W.; EVERETT, James E. "Japanese managerial attitudes at home and abroad", *Journal of social Psychology* 111, jun 80 : 19-25.

5123   STEPHENS, D. B.; [et al.]. "A comparative study of the managerial need structure in the US and Peruvian textile industries", *Management industrial Review* 20, 80 : 103-109.

5124   TALAMO, Magda. *I Dirigenti industriali in Italia: autorità, comando e responsabilità sociali* (Industrial managers in Italy: authority, leadership and social responsibility). Torin, G. Einaudi, 79, vi-201 p.

18540. Liberal profession
Profession libérale

5125   "Legal (The) profession", *International Journal of the Sociology of Law* nov 79 : 331-432.

18600. LABOUR MANAGEMENT RELATIONS
RELATIONS DU TRAVAIL

[See also / voir aussi: 4680, 4771, 4893, 5161, 5176, 5199, 5250, 6082]

5126   "Industrial relations in Ireland", *Administration (Dublin)* 27, aut 79 : 282-329.

5127	"Arbeitsbeziehungen" (Labour relations), *Politische Vierteljahresschrift* 20, 79 : 241-281. [Germany FR.]
5128	BACHY, Jean-Paul. *Administration du travail et conflits collectifs*. Sceaux, Centre de recherches en sciences sociales du travail, Université Paris-Sud, 79, 164 p.
5129	BAYART, Philippe. *Les relations sociales dans l'enterprise*. Paris, Chotard, 79, 342 p. [France.]
5130	BEDARIDA, François; GIUILY, Eric; RAMEIX, Gérard. *Syndicats et patrons en Grande-Bretagne*. Paris, les Éditions ouvrières, 80, 188 p.
5131	BRIEF, Arthur P.; ALDAG, Ramon J.; RUSSELL, Craig J. "An analysis of power in a work setting", *Journal of social Psychology* 109, dec 79 : 289-295.
5132	BURAWOY, Michael. *Manufacturing consent: changes in the labor process under monopoly capitalism*. Chicago, University of Chicago Press, 79, xvii-267 p.
5133	CLEGG, Hugh Armstrong. *The changing system of industrial relations in Great Britain*. Oxford, B. Blackwell, 79, xi-479 p.
5134	CORDOVA, Efien. "Les relations collectives de travail en Amérique latine: essai de réexamen", *Travail et Société* jul 80 : 247-263.
5135	CUTHBERT, Norman H.; DOBBINS, Richard. "Industrial democracy, economic democracy and the ownership of British industry: scenarios for the 1980s", *International Journal of social Economics* 80 : 286-295.
5136	DAMACHI, Ukandi Godwin; SEIBEL, Hans Dieter; TRACHTMAN, Lester; [eds.]. *Industrial relations in Africa*. New York, St. Martin's Press, 79, xiii-373 p.
5137	DMITERKO, D. Ja. "Trudovoj kollektiv v sisteme obščestvennyh otnošenij" (Labour collectivity in the social relations system), *Vestnik Moskovskogo Universiteta. Teorija naučnogo Kommunizma* 79 : 29-37.
5138	HANAMI, Tadashi. *Labor relations in Japan today*. Tokyo, Kodansha International, 79, 253 p. [distributed in the United States through Harper & Row, New York.]
5139	HANAMI, Tadashi A. *Labour law and industrial relations in Japan*. Deventer, Kluwer, 79, 157 p.
5140	HOLLEY, William H.; JENNINGS, Kenneth M. *The labor relations process*. Hinsdale, IL, Dryden Press, 80, 656 p. [USA.]
5141	HUMPHREY, John. "Auto workers and the working class in Brazil", *Latin American Perspectives* aut 79 : 71-89.
5142	KAHN-FREUND, Otto. *Labour relations: heritage and adjustment*. Oxford, Eng., New York, Oxford University Press for the British Academy, 79, 102 p.
5143	KELLER, Berndt; GROSER, Manfre. "'Industrial and Labor Relations' als interdisziplinärer Ansatz. Zum gegenwärtigen Stand von Theorie und Methode" (Industrial and Labor Relations: an interdisciplinary approach. Current discussion on theory and method), *Zeitschrift für Soziologie* oct 80 : 396-415.
5144	KEN'ICHI, Furuya. "Labor-management relations in postwar Japan", *Japan Quarterly* 27, jan-mar 80 : 29-38.
5145	LEVINE, Solomon B. "Changing strategies of unions and management: evaluation of four industrialised countries", *British Journal of industrial Relations* 18, mar 80 : 70-81.
5146	MARTIN, Benjamin; KASSALOW, Everett M.; [eds.]. *Labor relations in advanced industrial societies: issues & problems*. Washington, DC, Carnegie Endowment for International Peace, 80, xiii-206 p.
5147	MAURICE, Marc; SELLIER, François. "A societal analysis of industrial relations: a comparison between France and West Germany", *British Journal of industrial Relations* 17, nov 79 : 322-336.
5148	MEYERS, Frederic. *Mexican industrial relations from the perspective of the Labor Court*. Los Angeles, Institute of Industrial Relations, University of California, 79, 103 p.
5149	MITCHELL, Richard. "Australian industrial relations and labour law policy: a postwar review", *Australian Quarterly* 52, aut 80 : 40-59.
5150	MÜLLER-JENTSCH, Walther. "Nouvelles formes de conflit et stabilité institutionnelle. Évolution récente des relations professionnelles en RFA", *Sociologie du Travail* 22, apr-jun 80 : 152-170.
5151	PARK, Young-Ki. "Labor and business environment in Korea", *Asian Economies* 31, dec 79 : 5-44.
5152	PENNACCHI, Laura. "Il sistema di interconnessioni fra ciclo di lavorazione e forza-lavoro nell'industria petrolchimica" (The system of interconnections between labour cycle and labour force in the petrochemical industry), *Rassegna italiana di Sociologia* 20, oct-dec 79 : 593-628.
5153	QUALE, Thoralf Ulrik. "Industrial democracy in Norway", *Journal of general Management* aut 79 : 37-45.

5154 REYNAUD, Jean-Daniel. "Industrial relations and political systems: some reflections on the crisis in industrial relations in Western Europe", *British Journal of Industrial Relations* 18, mar 80 : 1-13.
5155 SCHAIN, Martin A. "The dynamics of labor policy in France: industrial relations and the French trade union movement", *Tocqueville Review* wint 80 : 77-109.
5156 SMITH, Robin. "Industrial relations policies and political change: the EEC code for South African subsidiaries", *British Journal of Industrial Relations* 18, mar 80 : 99-114.
5157 TROCSANYI, Laszlo. "Questions fondamentales en matière de rapports de travail dans les pays socialistes européens", *Annuaire de l'URSS et des Pays socialistes européens* 78 : 315-330.
5158 WILKINSON, Robert E. "America's labor relations system: the law and the practice", *Annales de la Faculté de Droit d'Istanbul* 25(42), 79 : 3-58.

18610. Labour law
Droit du travail

[See also / voir aussi: 5230]

5159 "Décisions judiciaires en matière de droit du travail", *Revue internationale du Travail* 119, jan-feb 80 : 81-101.
5160 ABRAHAMSSON, Bengt; BROSTRÖM, Anders. *The rights of labor.* Beverly Hills, CA, Sage Publications, 80, 367 p.
5161 NATTRASS, Jill. "Labour reforms, private enterprise, economic growth and equity in South Africa", *South Africa International* 10, jan 80 : 101-112.
5162 SATYENDRA, N. "The role of labour laws in a developing economy", *Sri Lanka Labour Gazette* 30, jan 79 : 11-17.
5163 SUPIOT, Alain. "Le juge et le droit du travail. Compte rendu d'une recherche", *Droit social* mai 80 : 59-72.
5164 VOISSET, Michèle. "Droit du travail et crise", *Droit social* jun 80 : 287-298.

18620. Employers' organization
Organisation patronale

[See also / voir aussi: 5056]

5165 ALIPRANTIS, Nikitas. "Les organisations patronales en France: éléments de leur attitude et idéologie judiciaire", *Droit social* mai 80 : 73-83.

18630. Trade union
Syndicat

[See also / voir aussi: 594, 1067, 2720, 2923, 3759, 4618, 4712, 4832, 4860, 4881, 5155, 5297, 5493, 5540]

5166 "Sindacato e mobilità del lavoro"(Trade union and labour mobility), *Rassegna sindacale Quaderni* 17(78-79), mai-aug 79 : 3-74. [Italy.]
5167 "Sindacato, repressione e sviluppo 1955-1963" (Trade union, repression and development, 1955-1963), *Rassegna sindacale Quaderni* 17(80), sep-oct 79 : 3-179. [Italy.]
5168 ACHARJI, Nilima. *Trade union leadership profile.* New Delhi, Ambika, 80, xvi-110 p.
5169 ANDERSON, John C. "Local union democracy. In search of criteria", *Relations industrielles* 34, 79 : 431-449.
5170 ARONOWITZ, Stanley. "The labor movement and the left in the United States", *Socialist Review* mar-apr 79 : 9-62.
5171 AYBERK, Ural; REY, Jean-Noël. "Le mouvement syndical dans une société industrielle; l'exemple de la Suisse", *Revue européenne des Sciences sociales. Cahiers Vilfredo Pareto* 18(52), 80 : 193-224.
5172 BECK, E. M. "Labor unionism and racial income inequality: a time-series analysis of the post-world war II period", *American Journal of Sociology* 85, jan 80 : 791-814. [USA.]
5173 BELLARDI, Lauralba; NARDINOCCHI, Giorgio; PISANI, Elena. *Sindacati e contrattazione collettiva in Italia nel 1976-77* (Trade unions and collective agreements in Italy in 1976-1977). Milano, F. Angeli, 79, 331 p.
5174 BERGMANN, Joachim; [ed.]. *Beiträge zur Soziologie der Gewerkschaften* (Essay on the sociology of trade unions). Frankfurt am Main, Suhrkamp, 79, 439 p. CR: Christoph LAU, *Soziologische Revue* 3(1), 80: 43-44.

5175 BEYER, Janice M.; TRICE, Harrison M.; HUNT, Richard E. "The impact of federal sector unions on supervisors' use of personnel policies", *Industrial and Labor Relations Review* 33, jan 80 : 212-231.

5176 BIENEFELD, M. A. "Trade unions, the labour process, and the Tanzanian State", *Journal of modern African Studies* 17, dec 79 : 553-593.

5177 BLÜM, Norbert. *Gewerkschaften zwischen Allmacht und Ohnmacht, Ihre Rolle in der pluralistischen Gesellschaft* (Trade unions between all-power and non-power. Their role in a pluralist society). Stuttgart, Bonn Aktuell, 79, 208 p.

5178 BRETT, Jeanne M. "Behavioral research on unions and union management systems", *Research in organizational Behavior* 80 : 177-213.

5179 BROCKHAUS, Christian. *Lohnarbeit als Existenzgrund von Gewerkschaften* (Salaried work as the reason for the existence of trade unions). Frankfurt/Main; New York: Campus-Verlag, 79, x-288 p.

5180 BUTLER, Stuart. "The political power of British trade unions", *Journal of social and political Studies* wint 79 : 321-344.

5181 CARONE, Edgard. *Movimento operário no Brasil, 1877-1944* (Labour movement in Brazil, 1877-1944). São Paulo, DIFEL, 79, 578 p.

5182 CHAISON, Gary N. "Union mergers and international unionism in Canada", *Relations industrielles* 34, 79 : 768-777.

5183 CHITAYAT, Gideon. *Trade union mergers and labor conglomerates.* New York, NY, Praeger, 79, xiii-225 p.

5184 CLARK, Kim B. "The impact of unionization on productivity: a case study", *Industrial and Labor Relations Review* 33, jul 80 : 451-469.

5185 CÓRDOVA, E.; OZAKI, M. "Les clauses de sécurité syndicale. Étude internationale", *Revue internationale du Travail* 119, jan-feb 80 : 21-40.

5186 Bibl.XXIX-5109. COUFFIGNAL, Georges. *Les syndicats italiens et la politique. Méthode de lutte, structures, stratégie de 1945 à nos jours.* CR: Daniel CLEMENT, *Revue française de Sociologie* 21(4), oct-dec 80 : 666-670.

5187 CROMPTON, Rosemary. "Trade unionism and the insurance clerk", *Sociology* 13, nov 79 : 403-426.

5188 DE SOUZA MARTINS, Heloisa Helena Teixera. *O estado e a burocratização do sindicato no Brasil* (State and trade unions bureaucratization in Brazil). São Paulo, Editora Hucitec, 79, xi-190 p.

5189 DEPPE, Frank. *Autonomie und Integration: Materialien zur Gewerkschaftsanalyse* (Self-government and integration: materials on trade union analysis). Marburg, Verlag Arbeiterbewegung u. Gesellschaftswiss., 79, 243 p. [Germany FR.]CR: Joachim BERGMANN, *Soziologische Revue* 3(2), 80: 165-167.

5190 DUBOIS, Pierre. "Niveaux de main-d'oeuvre et organisation du travail ouvrier. Étude de cas français et anglais", *Sociologie du Travail* 22, jul-sep 80 : 257-275.

5191 EDELSTEIN, J. David. "Trade unions in British producers' cooperatives", *Industrial Relations* 18, 79 : 358-363.

5192 EDELSTEIN, J. David; WARNER, Malcolm. *Comparative union democracy: organisation and opposition in British and American unions.* New Brunswick, NJ, Transaction Books, 79, xii-388 p.

5193 ENGELHARDT, Ulrich. "Zur Entwicklung der Streikbewegungen in der ersten Industrialisierungsphase und zur Funktion von Streiks bei der Konstituierung der Gewerkschaftsbewegung in Deutschland" (The development of strike movements in the first phase of industrialization and the function of strike in the constitution of the trade union movement in Germany), *Internationale wissenschaftliche Korrespondenz zur Geschichte der deutschen Arbeiterbewegung* 15, 79 : 547-569.

5194 ENGLAND, Joe. "Les facteurs clés du syndicalisme et des conflits du travail à Hong Kong", *Travail et Société* jul 80 : 289-314.

5195 FINCHAM, Robin; ZULU, Grace. "Les conseils d'entreprise en Zambie. La mise en oeuvre de la démocratie active industrielle", *Travail et Société* apr 80 : 187-208.

5196 GALLIE, Duncan. "Trade union ideology and worker's conceptions of class inequality in France", *West European Politics* jan 80 : 10-32.

5197 GALVIN, Miles E. *The organized labor movement in Puerto Rico.* London, Cranbury, NJ, Associated University Presses, 79, 241 p.

5198 GASPARINI, Giovanni. "Orientamenti sindacali dei lavoratori e organizzazione sindacale: considerazioni in margine ad una ricerca sugli impiegati" (Workers' trade union orientations and trade union organizations: considerations in connection with research on the employees), *Studi di Sociologia* 17, apr-jun 79 : 111-129.

5199   GHOSH, S. C. "The British trade unions and the Labour Law. The case of the Industrial Relations Act, 1971", *Relations industrielles* 35, 80 : 251-278.

5200   GREBING, Helga. "Gewerkschaften in der Gesellschaft" (Trade unions in society), *Gewerkschaftliche Monatshefte* 31, 80 : 149-157.

5201   GUSOV, A. Z. "Social'nye otnošenija proizvodstvennogo kollektiva" (Social relations of the production collectivity), *IN: Socialističeskij proizvodstvennyj kollektiv.* Moskva, 79 : 82-97.

5202   HALFPENNY, Peter; ABELL, Peter. "National wage rate claims and settlements: an exploratory study of trade union bargaining power", *Sociology* 14, mai 80 : 183-215. [UK.]

5203   HANDELMAN, Howard. *Organized labor in Mexico: oligarchy and dissent.* Hanover, NH, AUFS, 79, 13 p.

5204   HENDRIE, Delia; KOOY, Alide. *Trade unions in South Africa: some statistics.* Cape Town, Division of Research, School of Economics, University of Cape Town, 79, 86 p.

5205   HIRSCH, Barry T. "The determinants of unionization: an analysis of interarea differences", *Industrial and Labor Relations Review* 33, jan 80 : 147-161.

5206   HYCLAK, Thomas. "The effect of unions on earnings inequality in local labor markets", *Industrial and Labor Relations Review* 33, oct 79 : 77-84.

5207   IBARROLA, Jésus. "Le syndicalisme européen de 1945 à nos jours: jalons pour une recherche", *Pensée* 208, dec 79 : 109-131.

5208   ICHNIOWSKI, Casey. "Economic effects of the fire-fighters' union", *Industrial and Labor Relations Review* 33, jan 80 : 198-211.

5209   IVANOV, V. N.; TIHONOV, N. M. "Social'noe upravlenie v proizvodstvennom kollektive" (Social management in the production collectivity), *IN: Buduščee nauki. XII.* Moskva, 79 : 246-258.

5210   JASPAL SINGH. *India's trade union leaders.* New Delhi, National, 80, xiv-260 p.

5211   Bibl.XXIX-5127. JEFFRIES, Richard. *Class, power and ideology in Ghana: the railwaymen of Sekondi.* CR: Paul S. GRAY, *Contemporary Sociology (Albany)* 9(6), nov 80: 847-848.

5212   KAHN, Lawrence M. "Unionism and relative wages: direct and indirect effects", *Industrial and Labor Relations Review* 32, jul 79 : 520-532.

5213   KARMAZINOV, L. S. "Rol' proizvodstvennogo kollektiva v nravstvennom vospitanii ličnosti" (The production collectivity role in the personality moral education), *IN: XXV s'ezd KPSS i voprosy social'no-političeskogo razvitija sovetskogo obščestva.* Minsk, 79 : 120-139.

5214   KAWANISHI, Hirosuke. "Rōdō kumi'ai no kasseika o meguru jisshoteki kenkyū" (Field work on the development of labor unions), *Kikan rōdōho bessatsu* 80 : 81-89.

5215   KELLER, Berndt. "Zur Interessenpolitik von Beamtenverbänden" (On the interest politics of civil service unions), *Zeitschrift für Soziologie* apr 80 : 194-212.

5216   KIDNER, Richard. *Trade union law.* London, Stevens, 79, xxxiv-343 p. [United Kingdom.]

5217   KLJUČNIKOV, A. I. "Cel' i osnovnye zadači social'nogo planirovanija proizvodstvennyh kollektivov" (Objective and essential tasks of the production collectivities social planning), *IN: Aktual'nye voprosy social'no-političeskogo razvitija obščestva v uslovijah zrelogo socializma.* Saratov, 79 : 116-130.

5218   KLONNE, Arno. *Die deutsche Arbeiterbewegung* (The German labour movement). Düsseldorf, E. Diederichs, 80, 382 p.

5219   KORSNES, Olav. "Duality in the role of unions and unionists: the case of Norway", *British Journal of industrial Relations* 17, nov 79 : 362-375.

5220   KÜHNE, Robert J. *Co-determination in business: workers' representatives in the boardroom.* New York, Praeger, 80, xi-126 p.

5221   LALIBERTÉ, G.-Raymond. "Dix-huit ans de corporatisme militant. L'École sociale populaire de Montréal, 1933-1950", *Recherches sociographiques* 21(1-2), jan-aug 80 : 55-96.

5222   LIAUZU, Claude. *Militants, grévistes et syndicats: études du mouvement ouvrier maghrébin.* Nice, Centre de la Méditerranée moderne et contemporaine, 79, 230 p.

5223   LICHTENSTEIN, Nelson. "The communist experience in American trade unions", *Industrial Relations* 19, 80 : 119-130. [with a reply by Robert H. Zeiger: 131-135 and by Roger Keeran: 136-139.]

5224   MARENGO, Franco Damaso. *The code of British trade union behavior.* Farnborough, Eng., Saxon House, 79, x-200 p.

5225   MARUANI, Margaret. *Les syndicats à l'épreuve du féminisme.* Paris, Syros, 79, 274 p. CR: Pierre DUBOIS, *Revue française de Sociologie* 21(4); oct-dec 80: 670-672.

5226 MOISES, José Alvaro. "Current issues in the labor movement in Brazil", *Latin American Perspectives* aut 79 : 51-70.

5227 MONTGOMERY, David. *Workers' control in America: studies in the history of work, technology and labor struggles.* Cambridge, Eng., New York, Cambridge University Press, 79, x-189 p.

5228 MÜLLER, Dirk H. "Probleme gewerkschaftlicher Organisation und Perspektiven im Rahmen eines arbeitsteiligen Organisationskonzeptes" (Problem of trade union organization and perspectives within the framework of a labour organization concept), *Internationale wissenschaftliche Korrespondenz zur Geschichte der deutschen Arbeiterbewegung* 15, 79 : 569-580.

5229 NAVAS, Luis. *El movimiento obrero en Panamá, 1880-1914* (Labour movement in Panama, 1880-1914). Ciudad Universitaria Rodrigo Facio, Costa Rica, Editorial Universitaria Centroamericana, 79, 176 p.

5230 NAVRÁTIL, Oldřich; PUDÍK, Vladimír. *Czechoslovak trade unions and labour law.* Prague, Práce, 79, 83 p.

5231 NICHOLSON, Nigel; URSELL, Gill; BLYTON, Paul. "Social background attitudes and behaviour of white-collar shop stewards", *British Journal of industrial Relations* 18, jul 80 : 231-239.

5232 PANITCH, Leo. "Recent theorizations of corporatism: reflections on a growth industry", *British Journal of Sociology* 31, jun 80 : 159-187.

5233 PEREZ DIAZ, Victor M. "Elecciones sindicales, afiliación y vida sindical local de los obreros españoles de hoy" (Trade-union elections, affiliation and local trade-union life of the Spanish workers today), *Revista española de Investigaciones sociológicas* apr-jun 79 : 11-52.

5234 PLOWMAN, David. "Some aspects of trade union development in Papua New Guinea", *Australian Outlook* 33, dec 79 : 326-338.

5235 REGINI, Marino. "Labour unions, industrial action and politics", *West European Politics* oct 79 : 49-66. [Italy.]

5236 REGINI, Marino; ESPING-ANDERSON, Gösta. "Trade Union strategies and social policy in Italy and Sweden", *West European Politics* jan 80 : 107-123.

5237 REYNOLDS, Morgan O. "The intellectual muddle over labor unions", *Journal of social and political Studies* aut 79 : 269-281.

5238 RICHARDSON, Ray; CATLIN, Steve. "Trade union density and collective agreement patterns in Britain", *British Journal of industrial Relations* 17, nov 79 : 376-385.

5239 RODRIGUES, Leôncio Martins. "Tendências futuras do sindicalismo brasileiro" (Future trends of Brazilian trade unionism), *Revista de Administração de Emprêsas* 19, oct-dec 79 : 45-54.

5240 ROUILLARD, Jacques. *Les syndicats nationaux au Québec de 1900 à 1930.* Québec, Presses de l'Université Laval, 79, 342 p.

5241 SAGNES, Jean. *Le Mouvement ouvrier du Languedoc: syndicalistes et socialistes de l'Hérault, de la fondation des Bourses du travail à la naissance du Parti communiste.* Toulouse, Privat, 80, 320 p.

5242 SARTIN, P. "Rôle et action des comités d'entreprise", *Travail et Méthodes* 374-375, jun-jul 80 : 35-41.

5243 SAYERS BAIN, George; ELSHEIKH, Farouk. "Unionisation in Britain: an inter-establishment analysis based on survey data", *British Journal of industrial Relations* 18, jul 80 : 169-178.

5244 SERVAIS, Jean-Michel. "La liberté syndicale, l'inviolabilité des locaux syndicaux, le secret de la correspondance et des conversations syndicales", *Revue internationale du Travail* 119, mar-apr 80 : 233-244.

5245 SMITH, Russell L.; HOPKINS, Anne H. "Public employee attitudes toward unions", *Industrial and Labor Relations Review* 32, jul 79 : 484-495.

5246 STEINBERG, Hans-Josef. *Die deutsche sozialistische Arbeiterbewegung bis 1914* (The German socialist labour movement up to 1914). Frankfurt/Main, New York, Campus, 79, xi-379 p.

5247 STREECK, Wolfgang. "Vergleichende Gewerkschaftsforschung und 'Gewerkschaftstheorien'" (Comparative labour movement research and labour movement theories), *Soziologische Revue* 80 : 289-294. [review article.]

5248 THOMSON, A. W. J. "Trade unions and the Corporate State in Britain", *Industrial and Labor Relations Review* 33, oct 79 : 36-54.

5249 TIBI, Bassam. "Trade unions as an organizational form of political opposition in Afro-Arab States — The case of Tunisia", *Orient (Opladen)* 20, dec 79 : 75-91.

5250   WEISS, Dimitri. *Politique, partis et syndicats dans l'entreprise.* Paris, Éditions d'organisation, 79, 127 p.
5251   WENDT, Bernd-Jürgen. "Historische Aspekte der englischen Arbeiterbewegung. Ein Literaturbericht" (Historical aspect of the British labour movement. A literature survey), *Archiv für Sozialgeschichte* 19, 79 : 527-564.
5252   ZUBANOV, A. G. "Sposob proizvodstva kak glavnaja, determinanta migracii naselenija" (Means of production as an essential factor of the population migration), IN: *Trud kak osnova socialističeskogo obraza žizni.* Moskva, 79 : 144-155.

18640. Labour conflict
Conflit du travail

[See also / voir aussi: 5128, 5194, 5227, 5295]

5253   "Review of industrial disputes in India during 1977", *Indian Labour Journal* 20, mai 79 : 777-955.
5254   BLANKENBURG, Erhard; SCHÖNHOLZ, Siegfried. *Zur Soziologie des Arbeitsgerichtsverfahrens* (On the sociology of labour court procedures). Neuwied, Darmstadt, Luchterhand, 79, 202 p. [Germany FR.]
5255   BLEITRACH, Danielle; CHENU, Alain. *L'usine et la vie: luttes régionales: Marseille et Fos.* Paris, F. Maspero, 79, 217 p.
5256   BLONDIAU, Heribert. *Streiks und Streikverhalten im Metall- und Baubereich der BRD* (Strikes and strike behaviour in metal and construction industry of the FRG). Frankfurt/Main, R. G. Fischer, 79, 328 p. [Germany FR.]
5257   BOULLE-BARBIEUX, C. "Méthodologie statistique dans l'étude des conflits du travail", *Économies et Sociétés. Cahiers de l'ISÉA* 14, jan 80 : 133-143.
5258   BRETT, Jeanne M.; GOLDBERG, Stephen B. "Wildcat strikes in bituminous coal mining", *Industrial and Labor Relations Review* 32, jul 79 : 465-483.
5259   BRUNETTA, Giuseppe. "Conflitti di lavoro in Italia (1950-1979)" (Labour conflicts in Italy, 1950-1979), *Aggiornamenti sociali* 31, jun 80 : 465-476.
5260   CAMARDA, Alessandro; PELI, Santo. *La conflittualità operaia in Italia, 1900-1926* (Labour conflicts in Italy, 1900-1926). Messina, Firenze, G. D'Anna, 79, 192 p.
5261   CHERMESH, Ran. "Strikes: the issue of social responsibility", *British Journal of industrial Relations* 17, nov 79 : 337-346.
5262   CLARKE, R. O. "Labour-management disputes: a perspective", *British Journal of industrial Relations* 18, mar 80 : 15-25.
5263   CREIGH, S. S. "Research note: stoppage of work incidence in the United Kingdom, 1913-1977", *International Journal of social Economics* 80 : 296-300.
5264   CRONIN, James E. *Industrial conflict in modern Britain.* London, Croom Helm, Totowa, NJ, Rowman and Littlefield, 79, 242 p.
5265   DUBOIS, Pierre. "Recherche statistiques et monographiques sur les grèves", *Revue française des Affaires sociales* 34, apr-jun 80 : 29-55.
5266   ERSOV, S. A.; MAKARENKO, N. A. "Zabrastovočnoe dviženie rabočego klassa v stranah kapitala v 70-X godah" (Working class' strike movements in capitalist countries in the 70s), *Novaja i novejšaja Istorija* 23, mai-jun 80 : 21-38.
5267   GROTH, Margit Velsing. *Strejker i Danmark 1969-1972: en empirisk analyse.* København, Nyt fra Samfundsvidenskaberne, 79, 178 p.
5268   HANAMI, Tadashi A. "Le règlement des conflits du travail dans le monde", *Revue internationale des Sciences sociales* 32, 80 : 525-541.
5269   HEPPLE, B. A. "Lock-outs in Great Britain", *Recht der Arbeit* 33, 80 : 25-32.
5270   JACKSON, Dudley. "The disappearance of strikes in Tanzania: incomes policy and industrial democracy", *Journal of modern African Studies* 17, jun 79 : 219-251.
5271   JOVANOV, Neca. "La grève et le projet autogestionnaire en Yougoslavie", *Sociologie du Travail* 22, oct-dec 80 : 408-414.
5272   KALBITZ, Rainer. *Aussperrungen in der Bundesrepublik* (Lockouts in the Federal Republic). Köln, Frankfurt am Main, Europäische Verlagsanstalt, 79, 176 p.
5273   KIRSCH, Martin. "Le lock-out en droit français", *Recht der Arbeit* 33, 80 : 32-39.
5274   LACROIX, Robert; DUSSAULT, François. *La grève: ses facteurs déterminants et son effet sur les hausses de salaire: une synthèse critique.* Montréal, Université de Montréal, 79, 41 p.
5275   LYONS, Dan. "Are Luddites confused?", *Inquiry* 22, 79 : 381-404.
5276   NEUMANN, George R. "The predictability of strikes: evidence from the stock market", *Industrial and Labor Relations Review* 33, jul 80 : 525-535.

5277 OECHSLER, Walter A. *Konfliktmanagement: Theorie u. Praxis industrieller Arbeitskonflikte* (Conflict management: theory and practice of industrial labour disputes). Wiesbaden, Gabler, 79, 132 p.

5278 Organization for Economic Cooperation and Development. *Labour disputes: a perspective.* Paris, OECD, 79, 52 p.

5279 PERA, Guiseppe. "Die Aussperrung im italienischen Recht" (The lockout in Italian Law), *Recht der Arbeit* 33, 80 : 39-43.

5280 REYNAUD, Jean-Daniel. "Conflict and social regulation", *British Journal of industrial Relations* 17, nov 79 : 314-321.

5281 REYNAUD, Jean-Daniel. "Conflits du travail, classes sociales et contrôle social", *Sociologie du Travail* 22, jan-mar 80 : 97-115.

5282 SEGRESTIN, Denis. "Les communautés pertinentes de l'action collective. Canevas pour l'étude des fondements sociaux des conflits du travail en France", *Revue française de Sociologie* 21, apr-jun 80 : 171-202.

5283 SISAYE, Seleshi. "Industrial conflict and labor politics in Ethiopia: a study of the March 1974 general strike", *Plural Societies* sum 77 : 49-76.

5284 SMITH, Michael R. "Characterizations of Canadian strikes. Some critical comments", *Relations industrielles* 34, 79 : 592-605.

5285 TUNCOMAG, Kenan. "Die Beilegung der Arbeitsstreitigkeiten in der Türkei", *Annales de la Faculté de Droit d'Istanbul* 25(42), 79 : 285-316.

5286 VETTER, Jan. "Lockouts under United States law", *Recht der Arbeit* 33, 80 : 43-48.

18650. Arbitration. Mediation
Arbitrage. Médiation

[See also / voir aussi: 5026, 5071, 5202]

5287 BARBASH, Jack. "Collective bargaining and the theory of conflict", *Relations industrielles* 34, 79 : 646-659.

5288 BRIGGS, Steven Stambaugh; ANDERSON, John C. "An empirical investigation of arbitrator acceptability", *Industrial Relations* 19, 80 : 163-174.

5289 DEATON, D. R.; BEAUMONT, P. B. "The determination of bargaining structure: some large scale survey evidence for Britain", *British Journal of industrial Relations* 18, jul 80 : 202-216.

5290 DERBER, Milton. "Collective bargaining, mutuality and workers participation in management: an international analysis", *Relations industrielles* 35, 80 : 187-201.

5291 FARBER, Henry S.; KATZ, Harry C. "Interest arbitration, outcomes, and the incentive to bargain", *Industrial and Labor Relations Review* 33, oct 79 : 55-63.

5292 FEUILLE, Peter. "Selected benefits and costs of compulsory arbitration", *Industrial and Labor Relations Review* 33, oct 79 : 64-76.

5293 GRAY, Paul S. "Collective bargaining in Ghana", *Industrial Relations* 19, 80 : 175-191.

5294 HARTMAN, Paul T.; FRANKE, Walter M. "The changing bargaining structure in construction: wide-area and multicraft bargaining", *Industrial and Labor Relations Review* 33, jan 80 : 170-184.

5295 HUXLEY, Christopher. "The state, collective bargaining and the shape of strikes in Canada", *Canadian Journal of Sociology* 79 : 223-239.

5296 KÄLLSTRÖM, Kent. *Lokala kollektivavtal = Collective bargaining on the plant level.* Stockholm, LiberFörlag, 79, 281 p.

5297 KOCHAN, Thomas A. "Collective bargaining and organizational behavior research", *Research in organizational Behavior* 80 : 129-176.

5298 LEWIN, David; HORTON, Raymond D.; KUHN, James W. *Collective bargaining and manpower utilization in big city governments.* Montclair, NJ, Allanheld, Osmun, New York, Universe Books, 79, vxi-155 p.

5299 LEWIN, David; HORTON, Raymond D.; KUHN, James W. *Collective bargaining and manpower utilization in big city governments.* Montclair, NJ, Allanheld, Osmun, New York, Universe Books, 79, xvi-155 p.

5300 Organization for Economic Cooperation and Development. *Collective bargaining and government policies: conference held at Washington, DC, 10-13 July 1978.* Paris, OECD, 79, 338 p.

5301 PONAK, Allen; HARIDAS, T. P. "Collective bargaining attitudes of registered nurses in the United States and Canada. A Wisconsin-Ontario comparison", *Relations industrielles* 34, 79 : 576-590.

5302   Bibl.XXIX-5192. REYNAUD, Jean-Daniel. *Les syndicats, les patrons et l'État. Tendances de la négociation collective en France.* CR: Jean-Marie DUPREZ, *Revue française de Sociologie* 21(1), jan-mar 80, 138-140.

5303   ROBERTS, Benjamin Charles; OKAMOTO, Hideaki; LODGE, George C. *Collective bargaining and employee participation in Western Europe, North America and Japan: report of the Trilateral Task Force on Industrial Relations to the Trilateral Commission.* New York, The Commission, 79, xvii-90 p.

5304   SOMERS, Gerald G.; [ed.]. *Collective bargaining: Contemporary American experience.* Madison, WI, Industrial Relations Research Association, 80, vi-588 p. [Industrial Relations Research Association Series.]

5305   TEPLE, Edwin R.; MOBERLY, Robert B. *Arbitration and conflict resolution.* Washington, Bureau of National Affairs, 79, xvii-595 p.

5306   WETZEL, Kurt; GALLAGHER, Daniel G. "The Saskatchewan government's internal arrangements to accommodate collective bargaining", *Relations industrielles* 34, 79 : 452-469.

**18660.   Collective agreement. Joint management
Convention collective. Cogestion**

[See also / voir aussi: 4838, 5173, 5238, 5290]

5307   "Special issue on economic democracy and collective ownership", *Economic and industrial Democracy* aug 80 : 313-415.

5308   "Workers' participation in management: an international comparison", *Industrial Relations* 18, aut 79 : 247-385.

5309   BELL, D. Wallace. *Industrial participation.* London, Pitman, 79, viii-239 p.

5310   BELOUSOV, R. A. *Učastie trudjaščihsja v upravlenii socialističeskim proizvodstvom* (The workers' participation in the socialist production management). Minsk, 80, 30 p. [USSR.]

5311   BERENBACH, Shari. "Peru's social property: limits to participation", *Industrial Relations* 18, 79 : 370-375.

5312   BERTSCH, Gary K.; OBRADOVIĆ, Josip. "Participation and influence in Yugoslav self-management", *Industrial Relations* 18, 79 : 322-329.

5313   BLINOV, Nikolaj Michajlovič. "Ke kritice současných buržoazních koncepcí účasti pracujících na řízení socialistické a kapitalistické výroby" (Criticism of contemporary bourgeois theories of workers' participation to socialist and capitalist production), *Sociologický Časopis* 14, 78 : 456-464.

5314   BOKAREV, N. N. *Rasširenie učastija trudjaščihsja v upravlenii proizvodstvom* (The enlargement of the workers' participation to the production management). Moskva, Nauka, 79, 223 p.

5315   BRAUMANN, Freddy. *Partizipation und Beitriebsorganisation in China* (Participation and enterprise organization in China). Bochum, Studienverlag Brockmeyer, 79, vii-286 p.

5316   COMISSO, Ellen Turkish. *Workers' control under plan and market: implications of Yugoslav self-management.* New Haven, CT, Yale University Press, 79, x-285 p. CR: Fedor I. CICAK, *American political Science Review* 74(4), dec 80: 1109-1110.

5317   DIDORČUK, L. S.; JAKUBA, E. A. "Vozrastanie roli trudovogo kollektiva kak sub'ekta obščestvennyh otnošenij v razvitom socialističeskom obščestve" (The elevation of the labour collectivity role as a subject of social relations in the developed socialist society), *Problemy Filosofii* 48, 79 : 102-113.

5318   FRY, John A.; [ed.]. *Industrial democracy and labour market policy in Sweden.* Oxford, New York, Pergamon Press, 79, xii-1563 p.

5319   GOLDBERG, Walter. "Verhandelte oder kodifizierte Mitbestimmung. Ein Vergleich der Mitbestimmungsregelungen in der Bundesrepublik Deutschland und in Schweden" (Discussed or codified joint management. A comparison of joint management rules in the Federal Republic of Germany and Sweden), *Betriebswirtschaft* 40, 80 : 205-227.

5320   GREENBERG, Edward S. "Participation in industrial decision making and work satisfaction: the case of producer cooperatives", *Social Science Quarterly* 60, mar 80 : 551-569.

5321   HÁGELMAYER, Istvánné. *A kollektív szerződzęs ataøkzęrdzęsęi* (Collective labour agreements). Budapest, Akadémiai Kiadó, 79, 342 p. [Hungary.]

5322   HÉTHY, Lajos. *As üzemi demokrácia és a munkások* (Workers and shop-floor democracy). Budapest, Kossuth Kiado, 80, 264 p.

5323 JECCMINIS, Chris A. "Employee's participation in management: international experiences and the prospects for Canada", *Relations industrielles* 34, 79 : 490-512.

5324 KNIGHT, Ian B. *Company organisation and worker participation: a survey commissioned by the Department of Employment of attitudes and practices in industrial democracy with special emphasis on the prospects for employee directors.* London, H.M. Stationery Off., 79, x-158 p.

5325 KOZIARA, Edward C. (Workers' participation in Malta), *Industrial Relations* 18, 79 : 381-384.

5326 LAPPE, Marlies. "Die Mitbestimmung in sozialen Angelegenheiten" (Joint management in social matters), *Arbeitsrecht der Gegenwart* 16, 79 : 55-90.

5327 LUND, Reinhard. "Indirect participation, influence and power: some Danish experiences", *Organization Studies* 80 : 147-160.

5328 MARCHINGTON, Mick. *Responses to participation at work: a study of the attitudes and behavior of employees, shop stewards and managers in a manufacturing company.* Farnborough, Eng., Gower Pub. Co., 80, xii-213 p.

5329 MARTIN, Dominique; GOETSCHY, Janine. *Participation et pouvoir dans l'entreprise: la démocratie industrielle en Europe: étude française sur la distribution du pouvoir dans l'entreprise.* Sceaux, CRESST, 80, ix-554-13 p.

5330 ROSENBERG, Richard D.; ROSENSTEIN, Eliezer. "Participation and productivity; an empirical study", *Industrial and Labor Relations Review* 33, apr 80 : 355-367.

5331 SEIWERT, Lothar. *Mitbestimmung und Zielsystem der Unternehmung* (Joint management and objectives of the enterprise). Göttingen, Vandenhoeck und Ruprecht, 79, 472 p.

5332 STAEHELIN, Rudolf M. *Mitbestimmung in Europa*(Joint management in Europe). Zürich, Schulthess, 79, 562 p.

5333 VAN ZWAM, H. J. "Nieuwe vormen van medezeggenschap" (New forms of participation), *Sociaal Maandblad Arbeid* 34(10), oct 79 : 621-634. [workers' participation in the Netherlands.]

5334 WESTENHOLZ, Ann. "Workers' participation in Denmark", *Industrial Relations* 18, 79 : 376-380.

5335 WITTE, Eberhard. "Das Einflusspotential der Arbeitnehmer als Grundlage der Mitbestimmung. Eine empirische Untersuchung." (Worker's influence potential as the foundation of joint management. An empirical research.), *Betriebswirtschaft* 40, 80 : 3-26.

5336 ZWERDLING, Daniel. *Workplace democracy: A guide to workplace ownership, participation, and self-management experiments in the United States and Europe.* New York, Harper & Row, Harper Colopron Books, 80, xii-195 p.

18700. LEISURE
LOISIR

[See also / voir aussi: 3069]

5337 "Loisir et changements de valeur", *Loisir et Société* apr 80 : 7-110.

5338 GRACIA SANZ, Jesús. "El ocio de los niños"(Leisure of children), *Documentación social* 39, 80 : 77-91.

5339 HANKE, Helmut. *Freizeit in der DDR* (Leisure in the GDR). Berlin, Dietz Verlag, 79, 182 p.

5340 LEVASSEUR, Roger. "Contributions à une sociologie de l'action culturelle", *Loisir et Société* apr 80 : 113-132.

5341 RIBOUREL, Jacques. *Le temps du plaisir: les loisirs et le travail.* Paris, Presses de la Cité, Solar, 79, 184 p. [France.]

5342 ROIZ, Miguel. "Sociología del tiempo libre y ocio de los trabajadores españoles" (Sociology of leisure time and leisure of the Spanish workers), *Documentación social* 39, 80 : 7-35.

5343 ROMANO, Vicente. "Ocio y comunicación de masas" (Leisure and mass communication), *Documentación social* 39, 80 : 65-76.

5344 WICKERMAN, R. W. "The new leisure society. An economic analysis", *Futures* 12, jun 80 : 191-200.

5345 ZUZANEK, Jiri. "The work leisure relationship in Soviet sociological discussion", *Canadian Slavonic Papers* 22, mar 80 : 122-128.

18710. Leisure time
Temps de loisir

5346 ALEJABEITIA, Carmen. "Crítica del significado del ocio" (Critique of the meaning of leisure), *Documentación social* 39, 80 : 37-50.

5347   CYRKUN, A. F.; [ed.]. *Svobodnoe vremja pri socializme referativnyj sbornik* (Leisure time under socialism: a handbook). Moskva, INION AN SSSR, 79, 268 p.
5348   DUBSON, B. I. *Social'no-ekonomičeskie problemy svobodnogo vremeni trudjaščihsja v uslovijah sovremennogo kapitalizma* (Socio-economic problems of the workers' leisure time under conditions of contemporary capitalism). Moskva, Nauka, 80, 200 p.
5349   DUFOUR, Roland. *Mythologie du week-end.* Paris, Ed. du Cerf, 80, 365 p.
5350   EICHLER, Gert. *Spiel und Arbeit. Zur Theorie der Freizeit* (Play and work. On the theory of leisure time). Stuttgart, Bad Cannstatt, Frommann, 79, 223 p.
5351   GNYRJA, É. S. "Svobodnoe vremja o garmoničeskoe razvitie ličnosti" (Leisure time and harmonious personality development), *IN:* Problemy kompleksnogo podhoda k kommunističeskomu vospitaniju molodeži v svete rešenij XXV s'ezda KPSS. Tomsk, 79 : 18-26.
5352   KOLLENBERG, Udo. *Freizeit und Wirtschaft* (Leisure time and economy). Köln, Deutscher Instituts-Verlag, 79, 179 p.
5353   NAVARRO, José. "Ocio y tiempo libre en la juventud española" (Leisure and leisure time of the Spanish youth), *Documentación social* 39, 80 : 93-108.
5354   ORLOV, G. P.; BUKREEV, V. I. "Sociologičeskie problemy aktivnogo otdyha" (Sociological problems of active rest), *IN: Social'naja struktura sovetskogo obščestva socialističeskij obraz žizni. II.* Moskva, 78 : 107-115.
5355   ORTIZ, Lourdes. "Alienación, industria de la cultura y tiempo del ocio" (Alienation, cultural industry and leisure time), *Documentación social* 39, 80 : 51-63.
5356   ŠMAKOV, V. I. "Svobodnyj trud — rešajuščij faktor utverždenija social'noj odnorodnosti socialističeskogo obščestva"(Leisure time is a decisive factor of the socialist society social homogeneity strengthening), *IN: Konstitucija SSSR i aktual'nye problemy teorii naučnogo kommunizma.* Moskva, 79 : 48-54.
5357   TREGUBOV, B. A. "Cennostnye orientacii studenčeskoj molodeži v svobodnoe vremja" (Value orientations of the student youth in leisure time), *Ličnost' i Obščestvo* 79 : 89-98.

18720.   Leisure utilization
Utilisation des loisirs

[See also / voir aussi: 430, 998, 1152, 1227, 1506, 1851, 1917, 2046, 3791, 5495]

5358   "Sociologie du sport (La): perspectives et analyses", *Recherches sociologiques* 10, 79 : 341-452.
5359   "Sport (Le) et la société", *Sciences sociales. Académie des Sciences de l'URSS* 80 : 13-65. [USSR.]
5360   ASCANIO, Alfredo. "Turismo y desarrollo de la comunidad: una experiencia venezolana" (Tourism and community development: a Venezuelan experience), *Revista de Estudios agro-sociales* 28(109), oct-dec 79 : 53-69.
5361   BOTE GOMEZ, Venancio. "El turismo rural en España: una estrategía artesanal para un turismo masivo" (Rural tourism in Spain: a primary strategy for mass tourism), *Revista de Estudios agro-sociales* 28(109), oct-dec 79 : 29-51.
5362   COTTA, Alain. *La société ludique: la vie envahie par le jeu.* Paris, B. Grasset, 80, 286 p.
5363   DE KADT, Emanuel; [et al.]. *Tourism: Passport to development? Perspectives on the social and cultural effects of tourism in developing countries.* New York, Oxford, Toronto, Tokyo, Oxford University Press for the World Bank and UNESCO, 79, xviii-360 p.
5364   DUVIGNAUD, Jean. *Le Jeu du jeu.* Paris, Balland, 80, 158 p.
5365   ENGLAND, Richard. "Architecture pour touristes", *Revue internationale des Sciences sociales* 32, 80 : 46-58.
5366   FISCHER, Heinz-Dietrich; MELNIK, Stefan Reinhard; [eds.]. *Entertainment, a cross-cultural examination.* New York, Hastings House, 79, xxi-330 p.
5367   GARCIA FERRANDO, Manuel. "Problemas sociales del trabajo deportivo: el caso de los atletas españoles de élite" (Social problems of the sport work: the case of the Spanish elite athletes), *Revista española de Investigaciones sociológicas* oct-dec 79 : 33-87.
5368   GRABURN, Nelson H. H. "Enseignement de l'anthropologie du tourisme", *Revue internationale des Sciences sociales* 32, 80 : 59-73.
5369   Bibl.XXIX-5247. GUTTMAN, Allan. *From ritual to record: the nature of modern sports.* CR: Thomas S. HENRICKS, *American Journal of Sociology* 85(5), mar 80: 1294-1296.
5370   HÄGELE, Werner. *Spiel und Sport: e. soziolog. Begriffsanalyse* (Play and sport: a sociological concept analysis). Ahrensburg bei Hamburg, Czwalina, 79, 96 p.
5371   HANKS, Michael. "Race, sexual status and athletics in the process of educational achievement", *Social Science Quarterly* 60, dec 79 482-496 : 482-496.

5372 HØIVIK, Tord; HEIBERG, Turid. "Tourisme entre le centre et la périphérie et autodépendance", *Revue internationale des Sciences sociales* 32, 80 : 74-108.
5373 HOPF, Wilhelm. *Kritik der Sportsoziologie*(Critique of sport sociology). Lollar/Lahn, Achenbach, 79, 152 p.
5374 KALLICK-KAUFMANN, Maureen; REUTER, Peter; [eds.]. "Gambling in the US: public finance or public problem?", *Journal of social Issues* 35, 79 : 1-185.
5375 KRAUS, Richard G. *Social recreation: a group dynamics approach.* St. Louis, Mosby, 79, vii-194 p.
5376 LANFANT, Marie-Françoise. "Le tourisme international, fait et acte social; une problématique", *Loisir et Société* apr 80 : 135-157.
5377 LANFANT, Marie-Françoise. "Le tourisme dans le processus d'internationalisation", *Revue internationale des Sciences sociales* 32, 80 : 14-45.
5378 LEBEDINSKIJ, N. F.; PERSIANOV, R. M. "Rol' klubov i bibliotek v ispol'zovanii svobodnogo vremeni i trudjaščihsja" (The clubs and libraries role in the workers' leisure time utilization), *IN: Ėkonomika i kul'tura.* Leningrad, 78 : 56-75.
5379 LEE, Barrett, A.; ZEISS, Carol A. "Behavioral commitment to the role of sport consumer: an exploratory analysis", *Sociology and social Research* 64, apr 80 : 405-419.
5380 MARJANOVIĆ, Radovan. "Socijalne funkcije sporta" (The social functions of sport), *Sociologija* 21(1-2), 79 : 135-158.
5381 MIHOVILOVIĆ, Miro A. "Le s loisirs et le tourisme en Europe", *Revue internationale des Sciences sociales* 32, 80 : 109-124.
5382 OLWIG, Karen Fog. "National parks, tourism and local development: a West Indian case", *Human Organization* 39, 80 : 22-31.
5383 PATRIKSSON, Göran. *Socialisation och involvering i idrott* (Socialization and involvement in sport). Göteborg, Acta Universitatis Gothoburgensis, 79, vii-234 p.
5384 ROADBURG, Alan. "Factors precipitating fan violence: a comparison of professional soccer in Britain and North America", *British Journal of Sociology* 31, jun 80 : 265-276.
5385 ROGALEWSKI, Olaf. "Le tourism polanais dans le monde", *Revue internationale des Sciences sociales* 32, 80 : 125-140.
5386 ROSNER, Menahem. "Changes in leisure culture in the kibbutz", *Loisir et Société* nov 79 : 451-481.
5387 SIGELMAN, Lee; CARTER, Robert. "Win one for the giver? Alumni giving and bigtime college sports", *Social Science Quarterly* 60, sep 79 : 284-294. [USA.]
5388 SMITH, Michael D. "Towards an explanation of hockey violence: a reference other approach", *Canadian Journal of Sociology* 79 : 105-124.
5389 Bibl.XXIX-5258. SNYDER, Eldon E.; SPREITZER, Elmer. *Social aspects of sport.* CR: Wilbert M. LEONARD II, *Contemporary Sociology (Albany)* 9(6), nov 80: 813-814.
5390 STOLJAROV, V. I. "Social'nye problemy sporta" (Social problems of sport), *Filosofskie Nauki* 22, jul-aug 80 : 3-13.
5391 STOLJAROV, V. I.; KRAVČIK, Z.; [eds.]. *Sport i obraz žizni* (Sport and the way of life). Moskva, Fizkul'tura i Sport, 79, 278 p.
5392 TOKUHISA, Tamao. "Le tourisme à l'intérieur en provenance et à destination du Japon", *Revue internationale des Sciences sociales* 32, 80 : 141-163.
5393 VALENTINOVA, N. G.; MIL'ŠTEJN, O. A. "Sport, optimizm, ličnost': problemy i tendencii" (Sport, optimism, personality: problems and tendencies), *IN: Social'nye aspekty razvitija ličnosti. Ispol'zovanie informacionnyh sistem dlja ėgo prognozirovanija.* Moskva, 78 : 122-131.
5394 VIZITEJ, N.; TREST'JAN, A. "Sport kak social'noe javlenie" (Sport as a social phenomenon), *Kommunist Moldavii* (11), 79 : 71-75.
5395 WOOD, Robert E. "International tourism and cultural change in Southeast Asia", *Economic Development and cultural Change* 28, apr 80 : 561-581.

19. POLITICS. STATE. INTERNATIONAL RELATIONS
POLITIQUE. ÉTAT. RELATIONS INTERNATIONALES

19100. POLITICAL SCIENCE. POLITICAL SOCIOLOGY
SCIENCE POLITIQUE. SOCIOLOGIE POLITIQUE

5396 AKIMOTO, Ritsuo; MORI, Hiroshi; SORANAKA, Seiji; [eds.]. *Seiji shakaigaku nyumon* (An introduction to political sociology). Tokyo, Yuhikaku, 80, 295 p.

5397 BADIE, Bertrand; GERSTLÉ, Jacques. *Sociologie politique.* Paris, PUF, 79, 127 p.

5398 BOTTOMORE, Tom. *Political sociology.* London, Hutchinson, 79, 176 p.

5399 FEDOSEEV, A. A. "Političeskaja sociologija sovremennogo amerikanskogo imperializma" (Political sociology of the contemporary American imperialism), *IN: Sovremennaja buržuaznaja sociologija službe gosudarstvenno monopolističeskogo kapitalizma.* Leningrad, 79 : 3-19.

5400 GARCIA FERRANDO, Manuel. "Problemas metodológicos y técnicos de investigación en la Sociología política" (Methodological and technical problems of research in political sociology), *Revista española de Investigaciones sociológicas* jul-sep 79 : 35-61.

5401 KHOSHKISH, A. *The socio-political complex: an interdisciplinary approach to political life.* Oxford, New York, Pergamon Press, 79, 1st, x-396 p.

5402 KOURVETARIS, George A.; DOBRATZ, Betty; [eds.]. *Political sociology: readings in research and theory.* New Brunswick, NJ, Transaction Books, 80, ix-443 p.

5403 MAYER, Jacob Peter. *Max Weber and German politics.* New York, Arno Press, 79, 160 p.

5404 PASIC, Najdan. "Samoupravljanje i političke nauke" (Self-management and political sciences), *Politička Misao* 17(1-2), 80 : 49-62. [Yugoslavia.]

5405 RÖHRICH, Wilfried. *Sozialgeschichte politischer Ideen: d. bürgerl. Gesellschaft* (Social history of political ideas: the civil society). Reinbek bei Hamburg, Rowohlt, 79, 233 p.

5406 SMITH, David Hordon. "Political psychology and the proliferation of interdisciplinary fields in the social behavioral sciences", *Political Psychology* aut 79 : 106-112. [continued in 2(1), spr 80: 85-92.]

19200. POLITICAL DOCTRINE. POLITICAL THOUGHT
DOCTRINE POLITIQUE. PENSÉE POLITIQUE

19210. Political philosophy
Philosophie politique

[See also / voir aussi: 263, 1246, 6000]

5407 "Political ideology: its impact on contemporary political transformations", *International political Science Review* 80 : 301-424.

5408 "(La) Philosophie politique de G. W. F. Hegel", *Revue européenne des Sciences sociales. Cahiers Vilfredo Pareto* 18(52), 80 : 7-217.

5409 BLOM, H. W. "Political science in the golden age. Criticism, history and theory in Dutch seventeeth century political thought", *Netherlands' Journal of Sociology* 15, jul 79 : 47-71.

5410 BOBBIO, Norberto; [et al.]. "La filosofia politica di Luigi Sturzo" (Luigi Sturzo's political philosophy), *Sociologia (Roma)* 14(1-2), jan-aug 80 : 5-301.

5411 Bibl.XXIX-5272. BOUCHIER, David. *Idealism and revolution: new ideologies of liberation in Britain and the United States.* CR: Larry D. SPENCE ., *American political Science Review* 74(1), mar 80: 151.

5412 CURRAN, James. "The political world of the small firm worker", *Sociological Review* 28, feb 80 : 75-103.

5413 FRANK, Lawrence P. "Ideological competition in Nigeria: urban populism versus elite nationalism", *Journal of modern African Studies* 17, sep 79 : 433-452.

5414 LAŠINA, M. V.; LAŠIN, A. G. "Politika i ideologija (k metodologii issledovanija)" (Politics and ideology: the research methodology), *IN: Politika mira i razvitie političeskih sistem 1978.* Moskva, 79 : 41-47.

5415 NAJJAR, F. M. "Democracy in Islamic political philosophy", *Studia islamica* 51, 80 : 107-122.

5416 NAJJAR, F. M. "Democracy in Islamic political philosophy", *Studia islamica* 51, 80 : 107-122.
5417 PUGAČEV, V. P. "Aktivnaja rol' političeskoj ideologii v kommunističeskom stroitel'stve" (The political ideology active role in the communist edification), *Vestnik Moskovskogo Universiteta. Teorija naučnogo Kommunizma* 79 : 20-29.

19220. Power
Pouvoir

[See also / voir aussi: 2605, 5180, 5689]

5418 MINSON, Jeff. "Strategies for socialists? Foucault's conception of power", *Economy and Society* feb 80 : 1-43.
5419 Bibl.XXIX-5290. PARENTI, Michael. *Power and the powerless.* CR: Christopher HUXLEY, *Contemporary Sociology (Albany)* 9(6), mar 80: 117-118.
5420 TURKEL, Gerald. "Legitimation, authority, and consensus formation", *International Journal of the Sociology of Law* feb 80 : 19-32.
5421 WALLIMANN, Isidor; [et al.]. "Misreading Weber: the concept of 'Macht' ", *Sociology* 14, mai 80 : 261-275.

19230. Communism. Nationalism
Communisme. Nationalisme

[See also / voir aussi: 137, 429, 716, 736, 759, 1253, 1318, 1362, 1536, 1686, 1944, 2101, 2619, 2626, 4577]

5422 "Faschismus und Ideologie" (Fascism and ideology), *Argument (Berlin)* 21(117), 79 : 645-677.
5423 "Razvitoj socializm i problemy teorii i praktiki"(Developed socialism: theoretical and practical problems), *Pod Znamenem Leninizma* 12, 79 : 29-49.
5424 "Actual socialisms", *Theory and Society* mar 80 : 233-407.
5425 "Meždunarodnoe značenie real'nogo socializma" (International meaning of real socialism), *Vestnik Moskovskogo Uniersiteta. Teorija naučnogo Kommunizma* 79 : 3-11.
5426 AJUBDŽANOV, Ja. Ja. "Nekotorye osobennosti nemarksistskih koncepcij socializma v razvivajuščihsja stranah Azii i Afriki" (Some characteristics of the socialist non-marxist conceptions in the Asian and African developing countries), *Sbornik naučnyh Trudov Taškentskogo Universiteta* 584, 78 : 121-129.
5427 ARUSTAMJAN, M. A. "O sootnošenii zakonomernosti socialističeskogo stroitel'stva i razvitija socializma kak mirovoj sistemy" (On the correlation between the socialist edification laws and the development of socialism as a world system), *Voprosy naučnogo Kommunizma* 79 : 60-74.
5428 AYÇOBERRY, Pierre. *La question nazie: essai sur les interprétations du national-socialisme, 1922-1975.* Paris, Éditions du Seuil, 79, 314 p.
5429 BALLER, È. A. *Kommunizm, kul'tura, čelovek* (Communism, culture, man). Moskva, Sovetskaja Rossija, 79, 256 p.
5430 BECKWITH, Burnham P. *Socialist essays, from individualism to socialism.* Palo Alto, CA, 80, vi-258 p.
5431 BLASCHKE, Jochen; [ed.]. *Handbuch der westeuropäischen Regionalbewegung* (Handbook of Western European regional movement). Frankfurt-am-Main, Syndikat Autoren- und Verlagsgesellschaft, 80, 335 p. CR: René KÖNIG, *Kölner Zeitschrift für Soziologie und Sozialpsychologie* 32(4), dec 80: 831-834.
5432 CATALANO, Franco. *Fascismo e piccola borghesia: crisi economica, cultura e dittatura in Italia (1923-1925)* (Fascism and small bourgeoisie: economic crisis, culture and dictatorship in Italy, (1923-1925)). Milano, Feltrinelli economica, 79, 401 p.
5433 DERJAPA, M. R. "Osobennosti projavlenija ob'ektivnyh zakonov socializma" (Characteristics of the socialism objective laws manifestation), *Naučnyj Kommunizm* 79 : 13-20.
5434 FEATHER, N. T. "Value correlates of conservatism", *Journal of Personality and social Psychology* 37, sep 79 : 1617-1630.
5435 FEDOSEEV, P. N.; [et al.]. *Čto takoe "demokratičeskij socializm"* (What is "democratic socialism"). Moskva, Politizdat, 79, 2nd, 248 p.
5436 FERRAS, Robert. "La dualité catalane entre l'idéologie régionaliste et les stratégies économiques", *Hérodote* 16(4th trim), 79 : 113-135.

5437 FILATOV, A. "Socializm i obščestvennyj progress" (Socialism and social progress), *Kommunist Tatarii* 79 : 87-91.
5438 FISHER, Donald. "American philanthropy and the social sciences in Britain, 1919-1939; the reproduction of a conservative ideology", *Sociological Review* 28, mai 80 : 277-315.
5439 FRIŠ, A. S.; [ed.]. *Razvitoj socializm i aktual'nye problemy naučnogo kommunizma* (Developed socialism and topical problems of scientific communism). Moskva, Nauka, 79, 334 p.
5440 GLUMIN, V. I. *Kommunističeskaja ubeždennost' sovetskogo čeloveka* (Communist conviction of the Soviet man). Alma-Ata, Kazahstan, 80, 184 p.
5441 GREIFFEN HAGEN, Martin. "The dilemma of conservatism in Germany", *Journal of contemporary History* 14, oct 79 : 611-625.
5442 JANKOWSKI, James P. "Nationalism in twentieth century Egypt", *Middle East Review* 12, aut 79 : 37-47.
5443 KVOČKIN, M. P. "O vseobščej značimosti osnovnyh zakonov razvitija socializma" (On the general meaning of the socialism development essential laws), *IN: Filosofija i naučnyj kommunism. VI.* Minsk, 79 : 60-70.
5444 LEBEDEV, B. "Ličnoe i obščestvennoe v uvlovijah zrelogo socializma" (Personal and social under conditions of mature socialism), *Kommunist Tatarii* 79 : 11-17.
5445 LUARD, David Evan Trant. *Socialism without the state.* New York, St. Martin's Press, 79, 184 p.
5446 MASCOTTO, Jacques; SOUCY, Pierre-Yves. *Sociologie politique de la question nationale.* Montréal, Éditions coopératives Albert St-Martin, 79, 180 p.
5447 MONNEROT, Jules. *Sociologie du communisme: échec d'une tentative religieuse au XXe siècle.* Paris, Éditions libres, 79, xxiv-570 p.
5448 OSIPOV, V. I. "K voprosu o periodizacii razvitogo socializma" (On the periodization of developed socialism), *IN: Razvitoj socializm: osnovnye čerty i osobennosti.* Saratov, 79 : 16-29.
5449 PACHTER, Henry; [ed.]. "State (The) of socialism", *Social Research* 47, 80 : 3-198.
5450 PONTUSSON, Jonas. "Gramsci and Eurocommunism: a comparative analysis of conceptions of class rule and socialist transition", *Berkeley Journal of Sociology* 24-25, 80 : 185-248.
5451 REID, Philippe. "L'émergence du nationalisme canadien-français: l'idéologie du Canadien (1806-1842)", *Recherches sociographiques* 21(1-2), jan-aug 80 : 11-53.
5452 ROGAČEV, P. M.; SVERDLIN, M. A. *Patriotizm, klassy, revoljucija* (Patriotism, classes, revolution). Moskva, Politizdat, 79, 208 p.
5453 SADYKOV, F. B. "Suščnost' i kriterii razvitogo socializma" (Developed socialism nature and criteria), *IN: Razvitoj socializm: osnovnye čerty i osobennosti.* Saratov, 79 : 5-16.
5454 ŠAHNAZAROV, G. "Socializm: dostiženija, problemy, gorizonty" (Socialism: results, problems, horizons), *Obščestvennye Nauki (Moskva)* 79 : 5-24.
5455 SCHENK, Josef. "Gemeinsamkeiten und Unterschiede von Konservatismus und Autoritarismus" (Similarities and differences of conservatism and authoritarianism), *Zeitschrift für Soziologie* oct 80 : 390-395.
5456 SCHMIEDERER, Ursula. "Zum Problem von Bürokratie und Herrschaft im realen Sozialismus" (On the problem of bureaucracy and authority in real socialism), *Soziologische Revue* 80 : 403-411. [review article.]
5457 SIEDENTOPF, Heinrich. "Regionalismus in Italien" (Regionalism in Italy), *Archiv für Kommunalwissenschaften* 18, 79 : 224-240.
5458 SMITH, Anthony D. S. *Nationalism in the twentieth century.* New York, New York University Press, 79, x-257 p.
5459 STEPANIANTS, Marietta. "Development of the concept of nationalism", *Muslim World* 49, jan 79 : 28-41.
5460 SUMBATJAN, Ju. G. "Real'nyj socializm i ėgo buržuaznaje fal'sifikatory" (Real socialism and its bourgeois falsifiers), *Vestnik Moskovskogo Universiteta. Teorija naučnogo Kommunizma* 79 : 63-71.
5461 TOURAINE, Alain. *L'Après socialisme.* Paris, B. Grasset, 80, 283 p.
5462 VANDYCKE, Robert. "La question nationale: où en est la pensée marxiste?", *Recherches sociographiques* 21(1-2), jan-aug 80 : 97-129.

19240. Democracy. Dictatorship
Démocratie. Dictature

[See also / voir aussi: 76, 2723, 3314]

5463 BESSONOV, B. "Problemy demokratii i buržuaznaja propaganda" (Democracy problems and bourgeois propaganda), *Meždunarodnaja Žizn'* 79 : 50-60.

5464 BOLLEN, Kenneth A. "Issues in the comparative measurement of political democracy", *American sociological Review* 45, jun 80 : 370-390.
5465 CHUA, Beng-Huat. "Democracy as textual accomplishment", *Sociological Quarterly* 20, 79 : 541-549.
5466 EHRLICH, Howard J.; [et al.]; [eds.]. *Reinventing anarchy: what are anarchists thinking these days?*. Boston, Routledge and Kegan Paul, 79, 371 p. CR: George FISCHER, *Contemporary Sociology (Albany)* 9(5), sep 80: 709-710.
5467 FEYERABEND, Paul. "Democracy, elitism, and scientific method", *Inquiry* 23, mar 80 : 3-18.
5468 GREHNEV, V. S. *Problema demokratii v sovremennoj ideologičeskoj bor'be* (The democracy problem in the contemporary ideological struggle). Moskva, Molodež v sovremennoj ideologičeskoj bor'be, 79, 24-41 p.
5469 GROSRICHARD, Alain. *Structure du sérail: la fiction du despotisme asiatique dans l'Occident classique*. Paris, Seuil, 79, 234 p.
5470 LEONIDOV, E. "V. I. Lenin o buržuaznoj demokratii i sovremennost" (V. I. Lenin on the bourgeois democracy and the contemporary era), *Meždunarodnaja Žizn'* 12, 79 : 71-81.
5471 MAKAREVIČ, V. A.; TOLKAČEVA, S. S. "Novaja stupen'razvitija socialističeskoj demokratii" (The new degree of the socialist democracy development), *IN: XXV s'ezd KPSS i voprosy social'no-političeskogo razvitija sovetskogo obščestva*. Minsk, 79 : 39-59.
5472 MERLLIÉ, Dominique; COUSQUER, Jean-Yves. "Mariage et relations familiales dans l'aristocratie rurale: deux entretiens", *Actes de la Recherche en Sciences sociales* 31, jan 80 : 22-34.
5473 PREBISCH, Raúl; [et al.]. *Las condiciones sociales de la democracia* (Social conditions of democracy). Buenos Aires, El Cid, 79, 248 p.
5474 SEJERSTED, Francis. "Democracy and 'the rule of law'. Some historical experiences of contradictions in the striving for good government", *Social Science Information* 18, 79 : 945-966.
5475 TOLKAČEVA, S. S. "Narodnyj kontrol' kak odna iz form razvitija socialističeskoj demokratii" (People's control as a form of the socialist democracy development), *IN: XXV s'ezd KPSS i voprosy social'no-političeskogo razvitija sovetskogo obščestva*. Minsk, 79 : 75-91.

19300. CONSTITUTION. STATE
CONSTITUTION. ÉTAT

19310. Political system
Système politique

[See also / voir aussi: 1067, 1647, 2432, 2447, 4591, 4997, 5019, 5521, 5581, 5583, 5721, 5728]

5476 "State (The)", *Daedalus* aut 79 : 1-74.
5477 "State and social formation in the capitalist periphery", *Insurgent Sociologist* spr 80 : 3-67.
5478 "Régimes (Les) islamiques", *Pouvoirs* 12, 80 : 5-154.
5479 ANDERSEN, Heine. "Organizations, classes and the growth of state interventionism in Denmark", *Acta sociologica* 23(2-3), 80 : 113-131.
5480 ANTALFFY, György. *Állam, politikai rendszer, társadalom. Az állam — és jogelmélet és a politológia határkér-déseiről* (State, political system, society. Fundamentals of the theory of state and law). Budapest, Közgazdasági és Jogi K., 79, 342 p.
5481 BADIE, Bertrand; BIRNBAUM, Pierre. *Sociologie de l'État*. Paris, B. Grasset, 79, 250 p.
5482 BELOV, G. A. "O zakonah funkcionirovanija i razvitija političeskih otnošenij socialističeskogo obščestva" (On the laws of the political relations functioning and development in the socialist society), *Vestnik Moskovskogo Universiteta. Teorija naučnogo Kommunizma* 79 : 12-20.
5483 BELYH, A. K. "Političeskaja organizacija socialističeskogo obščestva kak sistema" (Political organization of the socialist society as a system), *Političeskaja Organizacija Obščestva Upravlenie pri Socializme* 79 : 9-24.
5484 BOY, Daniel. "Système politique et mobilité sociale", *Revue française de Science politique* 30, oct 80 : 925-958.
5485 BURNS, Tom. "Sovereignty, interests and bureaucracy in the modern state", *British Journal of Sociology* 31, dec 80 : 491-506.

5486 ČIRKIN, V. E. "'Političeskaja 'modernizacija' razvivajuščihsja stran: teorija i real'nost" (The developing countries political "modernization": theory and reality), *IN: Politika mira i razvitie političeskih sistem 1978.* Moskva, 79 : 208-221.

5487 Bibl.XXIX-5332. COHEN, Ronald; SERVICE, Elman R.; [eds.]. *Origins of the State: the anthropology of political evolution.* CR: Richard P. SCHAEDEL, *Contemporary Sociology (Albany)* 9(5), sep 80: 696-697.

5488 GARCIA COTARELLO, Ramón. "Sobre la extinción del Estado" (On the withering of the state), *Sistema. Revista de Ciencias sociales* 38-39, 80 : 65-95.

5489 GORDIEVSKIJ, A. A. "Rol' Konstitucii SSSR v soveršenstvovanii socialističeskogo obraza žizni" (The USSR Constitution role in the socialist way of life improvement), *IN: Konstitucija SSSR i aktual'nye problemy teorii naučnogo kommunizma.* Moskva, 79 : 114-118.

5490 HATTORI, Tōru. "Feuerbach no kokka, kyōdōtai ni tsuite" (On Feuerbach's theory of state and community), *Ritsumeikan sangyō-shakai ronshū* 24, 80 : 1-23.

5491 HATTORI, Tōru. "Shoki Marx no kokka-ron ni ni tsuite" (On early Marx's state theory), *Ritsumeikan sangyō-shakai ronshū* 26, 80 : 115-138.

5492 Bibl.XXIX-5336. HAYWARD, J. E. S.; BERKI, R. N.; [eds.]. *State and society in contemporary Europe.* CR: Valerie BUNCE, *American political Science Review* 74(4), dec 80 : 1117-1118.

5493 HOLTON, R. J. "Syndicalist theories of the State", *Sociological Review* 28, feb 80 : 5-21.

5494 KOCH, Koen. "The new marxist theory of the State or the rediscovery of the limitation of a structural functionalist paradigm", *Netherlands' Journal of Sociology* 16, apr 80 : 1-19.

5495 KUSHMAN, John E.; GROTH, Alexander; CHILDS, Robin. "Political systems and international travel", *Social Science Quarterly* 60, mar 80 : 604-616.

5496 LAPORTA, Francisco J. "Estado y violencia: Sugerencias para una toma de posición" (State and violence: suggestions for adopting a definite position), *Sistema. Revista de Ciencias sociales* 38-39, 80 : 111-123.

5497 Bibl.XXIX-5285. LITTLEJOHN, Gary; [et al.]; [eds.]. *Power and the State.* CR: William G. ROY, *Contemporary Sociology (Albany)* 9(2), mar 80: 282-283.

5498 ODUEV, S. F. "Svoboda neobhodimost' i otvetstvennost' v socialističeskom obščestve i ih realizacija v Konstitucii SSSR" (Freedom, necessity and responsibility in the socialist society and its realization in the USSR constitution), *IN: Real'nyj socializm.* Moskva, 79 : 144-166.

5499 ODUEV, S. F. "Konstitucija razvitogo socializma: svoboda, neobhodimost' i otvetstvennost" (The Constitution of developed socialism: freedom, necessity and responsibility), *IN: Teoretičeskie problemy razvitogo socializma. I. Plenarnoe zasedanie.* Moskva, 79 : 197-216.

5500 PECES-BARBA, Gregorio. "Consideraciones sobre el significado y el valor de Estado" (Considerations about the meaning and value of state), *Sistema. Revista de Ciencias sociales* 38-39, 80 : 3-27.

5501 PLEŠAKOV, A. I. "Političeskij režim — kategorija istoričeskogo materializma" (Political system as a category of historical materialism), *IN: Istoričeskij materializm i sovremennoe obščestvennoe razvitie.* Moskva, 79 : 36-42.

5502 Bibl.XXIX-5343. POGGI, Gianfranco. *The development of the modern state: a sociological introduction.* CR: Charles TILLY, *American political Science Review* 74(1), mar 80: 266-267.

5503 PÖLS, Werner; [ed.]. *Staat und Gesellschaft im politischen Wandel: Beitr. zur Geschichte d. modernen Welt* (State and society in political change: essays on the history of modern world). Stuttgart, Klett-Cotta, 79, x-554 p.

5504 ROCCA, James V. "Reflections on twenty years of the Fifth French Republic. An evaluation and a prognosis", *Social Science* 55, 80 : 3-12.

5505 ROZANOV, A. A. "K voprosu o dialektike obščego i osobennogo v stanovlenii i razvitii političeskoj sistemy real'nogo socializma" (Dialectics of the general and particular in the future and development of the real socialism political system), *IN: Real'nyj socializm.* Moskva, 79 : 66-88.

5506 SALAZAR, Diego Renato. *Teoría del estado*(Theory of State). Bogotá, Librería Jurídicas Wilches, 79, vi-241 p.

5507 SCHMIDT, Samuel. "El Estado y su autonomia"(The state and its autonomy), *Problemas del Desarrollo* 10(40), nov 79-jan 80 : 53-80.

5508 SELIN, V. N. "Konstitucija SSSR i kriterij razvitogo socialističeskogo obščestva" (The USSR Constitution and the developed socialist society criteria), *IN: Konstitucija SSSR i aktual'nye problemy teorii naučnogo kommunizma.* Moskva, 79 : 54-59.

5509 TAMAKI, Matsuo. "Hatten tojō shakai no kokka keisei" (State formation in developing societies), *Gendai no esupuri bessatsu hendo suru shakai to ningen* 80 : 99-112.
5510 TIHOMIROV, Ju. A. "Razvitie naučnyh znanij o socialističeskom gosudarstve" (The development of scientific knowledge on the socialist state), *IN: Politika mira i razvitie političeskih sistem 1978*. Moskva, 79 : 34-40.
5511 TIRYAKIAN, Edward A. "Quebec, Wales, and Scotland: three nations in search of a State", *International Journal of comparative Sociology (Leiden)* 21(1-2), mar-jun 80 : 1-13.
5512 TOPORNIN, B. N. "Dinamika političeskoj sistemy razvitogo socialističeskogo obščestva" (Dynamics of the developed socialist society political system), *IN: Politika mira i razvitie političeskih sistem*. Moskva, 79 : 144-152.
5513 ULTEE, Wout C. "Is education a positional good? An empirical examination of alternative hypotheses on the connection between education and occupational level", *Netherlands' Journal of Sociology* 16, oct 80 : 135-153.
5514 ZEMELMAN, Hugo. "Acerca del estudio del Estado: notas metodológicas" (About the study of state: methodological notes), *Revista mexicana de Sociología* 41, jul-sep 79 : 1041-1048.
5515 ŽURAVLEV, M. M. "Konstitucija i sovetskij obraz žizni" (Constitution and the Soviet way of life), *IN: Konstitucionnoe razvitie socialističeskogo obščestva*. Moskva, 79 : 121-126.
5516 ZYLENBERBERG, Jacques. "Modèles d'État, modèles de croissance: le cas latino-américain", *Civilisations* 30(1-2), jun 80 : 60-72.

19320. Human rights
Droits de l'homme

[See also / voir aussi: 377, 1537, 1626, 2571]

5517 "Fundamental human rights and marxism", *Social Praxis* (1-2), 79 : 93-126.
5518 BARMENKO, A. I. *Svoboda sovetsti v SSSR* (Liberty of conscience in the USSR). Moskva, Mysl', 79, 223 p.
5519 BUCHHOLZ, Erich; DAHN, Ulrich. "Rechte und Freiheiten der Bürger und sozialistisches Strafrecht" (Civil rights and liberties, and socialist penal law), *Staat und Recht* 28(12), 79 : 1079-1089. [German DR.]
5520 BURSTEIN, Paul. "Attitudinal, demographic and electoral components of legislative change: Senate voting on civil rights", *Sociology and social Research* 64, jan 80 : 221-235.
5521 ČHIKVADZE, V. M. "Ideologičeskoe protivoborstvo dvuh social'no-političeskih sistem i prava čeloveka" (Ideological opposition of the two socio-political systems and the human rights), *IN: Socializm i ličnost'*. Moskva, 79 : 145-162.
5522 DI GIOVANNI, Alberto. "Il contributo teoretico di Luigi Sturzo al problema dei diritti dell'uomo" (The theoretical contribution by Luigi Sturzo to the problem of human rights), *Sociologia (Roma)* 13(2-3), mai-dec 79 : 53-67.
5523 KUVAČIČ, Ivan. "O pojmovima čast, dostojanstvo, građanska prava u svijetlu suodnošenja ljudskog i institucionalnog" (On the concepts of honor, dignity, human rights in light of the co-relationship of the human and the institutional), *Revija za Sociologiju* (1-2), 78 : 8-15.
5524 MIALARET, Gaston; [ed.]. *The Child's right to education*. Paris, Unesco, 79, 258 p.
5525 SHIBATA, Shingo. "Fundamental human rights and Marxism", *Social praxis* (1-2), 80 : 117-126.
5526 WOODS, L. B. *A decade of censorship in America: the threat to classrooms and libraries, 1966-1975*. Metuchen, N.J., Scarecrow Press, 79, xii-183 p.

19330. Political representation
Représentation politique

5527 SHORTRIDGE, Ray M. "Democracy's golden age? Voter turnout in the Midwest, 1840-1872", *Social Science Quarterly* 60, mar 80 : 617-629.

19340. Government
Gouvernement

[See also / voir aussi: 2608, 5924, 5931, 5985]

5528 BRIGHAM, John; BROWN, Don W.; [eds.]. *Policy Implementation: Choosing between penalties and incentives*. Beverly Hills, CA, Sage Publications, 80, 272 p.

5529 ENDRUWEIT, Günter. *Struktur und Wandel der Polizei. Organisations- und berufssoziologische Untersuchungen über die Polizei in der Bundesrepublik Deutschland und in den USA* (Structure and change of the police. Research in organizational and occupational sociology on police in the Federal Republic of Germany and the USA). Berlin, Duncker und Humblot, 79, 222 p. CR: Roland GIRTLER, *Soziologische Revue* 3(3), 80: 299-301.

5530 FIJNAUT, C. "Les origines de l'appareil policier moderne en Europe de l'Ouest continentale", *Déviance et Société* mar 80 : 19-41.

5531 KNEMEYER, Franz-Ludwig. "Polizei" (Police), *Economy and Society* mai 80 : 172-196. [with an introduction by Keith TRIBE: 168-171.]

5532 KNIESNER, Thomas J.; MCINTOSH, John V. "Predicting presidentiel performance: a human capital approach", *Social Science Research* jun 80 : 178-192.

5533 KNUTSSON, Jahannes; [et al.]; [eds.]. *Police and the social order: contemporary research perspectives.* Stockholm, National Swedish council for crime prevention, 79, 383 p.

5534 LEHNER, Franz. *Grenzen des Regierens. Eine Studie zur Regierungsproblematik hochindustrialisierter Demokratien* (Limits of government. A study on government problems of highly industrialized democracies). Königstein/Ts., Athenäum, 79, x-232 p.

5535 LIEBERMAN, Carl. "The use of mediating institutions in implementing public policy", *Social Science* 55, 80 : 13-18. [family, church and neighborhood.]

5536 LUNDMAN, Richard J.; [ed.]. *Police behavior: a sociological perspective.* New York, Oxford University Press, 80, xv-332 p.

5537 POOLE, Eric D.; REGOLI, Robert M. "An examination of the effects of professionalism on cynicism among police", *Social Science Journal* 16, oct 79 : 59-66.

5538 REGOLI, Robert M.; POOLE, Eric D. "Police professionalism and role conflict: a comparison of rural and urban departments", *Human Relations* 33, apr 80 : 241-252.

5539 REINER, Robert. "Fuzzy thoughts: the police and law-and-order politics", *Sociological Review* 28, mai 80 : 377-413.

5540 Bibl.XXIX-5372. REINER, Robert. *The blue-coated worker: a sociological study of police unionism.* CR: William J. GRIMSHAW, *American Journal of Sociology* 86(3), nov 80 : 705-707. [also CR: V. L. ALLEN, British Journal of Sociology 31(4), dec 80 : 594-596.]

5541 SAMORA, Julian; BERNAL, Joe; PEÑA, Albert. *Gunpowder justice: a reassessment of the Texas Rangers.* Notre Dame, IN, University of Notre Dame Press, 79, 179 p. CR: Robert M. REGOLI, *Contemporary Sociology (Albany)* 9(3), mai 80: 399-400.

5542 STEINBERGER, Peter J. "Typologies of public policy: meaning construction and the policy process", *Social Science Quarterly* 61, sep 80 : 185-197. [followed by a discussion by Elinor OSTROM: 198-202, Ira SHARKANSKY: 203-206, and the author: 206-207.]

5543 VAN MAANEN, John; KATZ, Ralph. "Police perceptions of their work environment: an exploratory study into organization space and time", *Sociology of Work and Occupations* feb 79 : 31-58.

19350. Parliament
Parlement

19360. Judiciary power
Pouvoir judiciaire

[See also / voir aussi: 5866]

5544 BAKER, Ralph; MEYER, Fred A. *The criminal justice game: politics and players.* North Scituate, MA, Duxbury Press, 80, 257 p.

5545 GIBSON, James L. "Environmental constraints on the behavior of judges: a representational model of a judicial decision making", *Law and Society Review* 14, wint 80 : 343-370.

5546 HEYDEVRAND, Wolf. "The technocratic administration of justice", *Research in Law and Sociology* 79 : 29-64.

5547 MOTIWAL, O. P. *Changing aspects of law and justice in India.* Allahabad, Chugh, 79, xiii-616 p.

5548 ROWLAND, C. K. "The relationship between grand jury composition and performance", *Social Science Quarterly* 60, sep 79 : 323-327.

19400. PUBLIC ADMINISTRATION
ADMINISTRATION PUBLIQUE

19410. Civil service. Technocracy
Fonction publique. Technocratie

[See also / voir aussi: 62, 1114, 5215, 6085]

5549 "Reforma administrativa y cambio social" (Administrative reform and social change), *Revista mexicana de Ciencias políticas y sociales* 24(92), apr-jun 78 : 5-199. [Mexico.]
5550 AL-TERAIFI, Al-Agab A. "Recent administrative reforms in the Sudan", *Revue internationale des Sciences administratives* 45, 79 : 136-146.
5551 BIHARI, Mihály; [ed.]. *Közigazgatás és politika. Tanulmányok a közigazgatás köréből* (Public administration and politics. Studies in public administration). Budapest, Kossuth Kiado, 80, 233 p.
5552 CHAPMAN, Richard A. "L'élitisme dans le recrutement des haut-fonctionnaires en Grande-Bretagne", *Revue française d'Administration publique* 12, oct-dec 79 : 19-33.
5553 CÓRDOVA, Efrén. "Les relations professionnelles dans la fonction publique en Amérique latine", *Revue internationale du Travail* 119, sep-oct 80 : 625-640.
5554 FONYÓ, Gyula; [ed.]. *A közigazgatás személyi állománya. Tanulmányok az összetétel, az anyagi és erkölcsi megbecsülés köréből* (Studies on the staff of public administration. Social composition of the stratum, its financial and moral estimation). Budapest, Közgazdasági és Jogi Kiadó, 80, 479 p. [Hungary.]
5555 GREMION, Catherine. *Profession, décideurs; pouvoir des hauts fonctionnaires et réform de l'État.* Paris, Gauthier-Villars, 79, xiv-454 p.
5556 GUSTAVSEN, Bjørn. "Legal-administrative reforms and the role of social research", *Acta sociologica* 23, 80 : 3-19.
5557 LEE, Robert D. *Public personnel systems.* Baltimore, University Park Press, 79, xv-434 p.
5558 PAPP, Ignác. *Közigazgatás, társadalom, hatékonyság* (Public administration, society, efficacy). Szeged, Acta Univ. Szegediensis de Attila József nom., 79, 54 p. [Acta juridica et politica, Tom. 26. Fasc. 5.]
5559 RINGELING, A. B. "Administrative discretion: a study of policy administration by officials as illustrated by the so-called 'spijtoptantenbeleid'", *Netherlands' Journal of Sociology* 16, oct 80 : 121-134.

19420. Central government. Local government
Administration centrale. Administration locale

[See also / voir aussi: 2765, 3701, 3991, 4030, 4149, 4161, 4310, 5298, 5299]

5560 "Urban policy making", *Sage Yearbooks in Politics and public Policy* 79 : 7-283.
5561 DRESSAYRE, Philippe. "Suburbanisation et pouvoir local", *Revue française de Science politique* 30, jun 80 : 533-559.
5562 KARNIC, Albert K.; WELCH, Susan. "Sex and ethnic differences in municipal representation", *Social Science Quarterly* 60, dec 79 : 465-481. [USA.]
5563 KOBAYASHI, Kōichirō; TANAKA, Toyoji. "Chiho jichitai ni okeru gyōsei kadai no hendō to gyōsei-shoshiki no henkaku — Niigata-ken Nishikanbara-gun Yahiko-mura yakuba ni okeru action research (jo)" (Organizational changes in changing administrative tasks of a local government), *Tokyo daigaku shakaigaku kenkyujo nenpo* 11, 80 : 1-53.
5564 MILLER, Tom. "The emergence and impact of participatory ideas on Swedish planning and local government", *Scandinavian political Studies* 79 : 333-349.
5565 ROSSETTI, Carlo Guiseppe. "Spazio e tempo in Nuerland e la sociologia del dominio coloniale" (Space and time in Nuerland and the sociology of colonial power), *Quaderni di Sociologia* 28, mar 79 : 103-133.
5566 SAUNDERS, Peter R. *Urban politics: a sociological interpretation.* London, Hutchison, 79, 383 p. [United Kingdom.]
5567 SAVITCH, H. V. *Urban policy and the exterior city: Federal, State, and corporate impacts upon major cities.* New York, Pergamon Press, 79, xv-359 p. [USA.]
5568 UESUGI, Takamichi. "Dai-toshi ni okeru chiiki shisaku to shakai-kyoiku gyōsei" (Community policy and administration in a big city), *Nihon shakai-kyōiku gakukai kiyō* 16, 80 : 19-26.

5569 "Prospects for the American Left in the 1980's", *Berkeley Journal of Sociology* 24-25, 80 : 281-314.
5570 "Parti unique et multipartisme", *Mois en Afrique* 15(174-175), jun-jul 80 : 18-129. [Afrique.]
5571 BADA, José; BAYONA, Bernardo; BETÉS, Luis. *La izquierda, de origen christiano? estudio sociológico de la izquierda aragonesa* (The Left, from Christian origin? Sociological study of the Aragonese Left). Zaragoza, Cometa, 79, 168 p.
5572 BESPALOV, N. E. "V. I. Lenin o klassovom haraktere kommunističeskoj partii" (V. I. Lenin on the Communist Party class character), *Naučnye Trudy po Istorii KPSS* 101, 79 : 3-10.
5573 BOUDOUIN, Jean. "Les phénomènes de contestation au sein du Parti communiste française (avril 1978-mai 1979)", *Revue française de Science politique* 30, feb 80 : 78-111.
5574 BURLES, Jean. *Le Parti communiste dans la société française*. Paris, Éditions sociales, 79, 176 p.
5575 CHAI, Trong R. "The communist party of China: the process of institutionalization", *Asian Affairs (London)* 11, feb 80 : 43-54.
5576 COTTER, Cornelius P.; BIBBY, John. "Institutional development of parties and the thesis of party decline", *Political Science Quarterly* 95, spr 80 : 1-27. [USA.]
5577 DJATLOVA, M. M.; FINOGENOV, V. F. "Politika KPSS — važnejšij faktor izmenenija social'no-klassovoj struktury obščestva razvitogo socializma" (The CPSU policy is an essential factor of change of the developed socialism society socio-class structure), *IN: Razvitie socialističeskoe obščestvo-prodolženie dela Velikogo Oktjabrja*. Leningrad, 79 : 21-36.
5578 EPSTEIN, Léon D. "What happened to the British party model?", *American political Science Review* 74, mar 80 : 9-22.
5579 GAJFULLIN, U.; MUHAMEDOV, S. "Osnovnye zakonomernosti razvitija KPSS" (Essential laws of the CPSU development), *Kommunitst Tatarii* 79 : 11-18.
5580 IRVINE, William P.; GOLD, H. "Do frozen cleavages ever go stale? the bases of the Canadian and Australian party systems", *British Journal of political Science* 10, apr 80 : 187-218.
5581 JAKUPOV, N. M. "KPSS — rukovodjaščee jadro političeskoj sistemy sovetskogo obščestva" (The CPSU is the leading cell of the Soviet society political system), *Naučnye Trudy po Istorii KPSS (Kiev)* 104, 80 : 3-9.
5582 KAS'JENENKO, V. I. *Rol' KPSS v formirovanii socialističeskogo obraza žizni* (The CPSU role in the socialist way of life formation). Moskva, Politizdat, 79, 279 p.
5583 KSENOFONTOV, S. V. "Rukovodjaščaja rol' KPSS v političeskoj sisteme razvitogo socializma" (The CPSU leading role in the developed socialism political system), *Političeskaja Organizacija Obščestva i Upravlenie pri Socializme* 79 : 34-45.
5584 LARIONOV, A. G. "Sociologičeskie issledovanija i effektivnost' partijnoj raboty" (Sociological research and the Party activity efficiency), *Sociologičeskie Issledovanija* 80 : 215-218.
5585 MADISON, Dan L.; [et al.]. "Organizational politics: an exploration of managers' perceptions", *Human Relations* 33, feb 80 : 79-100.
5586 MOREHINA, G. G. "Kommunističeskaja partija v uslovijah razvitogo socializma" (The Communist Party under conditions of developed socialism), *IN: Vozrastanie roli obščestvennyh nauk v kommunističeskom stroitel'stve*. Moskva, 79 : 11-21.
5587 PANEBIANCO, Angelo. "Imperativi organizzativi, conflitti interni e ideologia nei partiti comunisti" (Organizational prescriptions, internal conflicts and ideology in communist parties), *Rivista italiana di Scienza politica* dec 79 : 511-536.
5588 REID MARTZ, Mary Jeanne. "Studying Latin American political parties: dimensions, past and present", *Journal of Latin American Studies* 12, mai 80 : 139-167.
5589 REITER, Howard L. "Party factionalism: national conventions in the new era", *American Politics Quarterly* jul 80 : 303-318.
5590 RIGHI, Roberto. "La teoria del partito politico in Max Weber" (The theory of political party in Max Weber), *Rassegna italiana di Sociologia* 21, apr-jun 80 : 239-264.
5591 ROŽKOV, V. P. "Marksistko-leninskaja partija i demokratičeskij harakter upravlenija socialističeskim obščestvom" (The marxist-leninist party and the democratic character of the socialist society management), *IN: Social'no-političeskogo razvitija obščestva v uslovijah zrelogo socializma*. Saratov, 79 : 14-30.
5592 SCHONFELD, William R. "La stabilité des dirigeants des partis politiques: le personnel des directions nationales du Parti socialiste et du mouvement gaulliste", *Revue française de Science politique* 30, jun 80 : 477-505.
5593 SPATARO, Giuseppe. "Dal Partito Popolare alla Democrazia Cristiana" (From the People's Party to Christian Democracy), *Sociologia (Roma)* 13(2-3), mai-dec 79 : 39-52. [Italy.]

5594 STEININGER, Rudolf. "Max Webers Parteienkonzept und die Parteienforschung" (Max Weber's concept of party and the party research), *Kölner Zeitschrift für Soziologie und Sozialpsychologie* 32, 80 : 54-75.

5595 ŽIDANOV, A. I. "Nekotorye voprosy dejatel'nosti neproletarskih demokratičeskih partij v uslovijah stroitel'stva socializma" (Some questions on the non-proletarian democratic parties activity under the conditions of socialism edification), *Vestnik Moskovskogo Universiteta. Teorija naučnogo Kommunizma* 79 : 26-34.

19520. Pressure group. Protest movement
Groupe de pression. Mouvement contestataire

[See also / voir aussi: 332, 1132, 1141, 1432, 1571, 2653, 3656, 3967]

5596 ALBERONI, Francesco. "Movimenti sociali e società italiana" (Social movements and Italian society), *Rassegna italiana di Sociologia* 20, jul-sep 79 : 359-388.

5597 ALLUM, Percy. "Les groupes de pression en Italie", *Revue française de Science politique* 30, oct 80 : 1048-1072.

5598 BARKAN, Steven E. "Strategic, tactical and organizational dilemmas of the protest movement against nuclear power", *Social Problems* 27, oct 79 : 19-37.

5599 BECKMANN, Michael. *Theorie der sozialen Bewegung* (Theory of social movements). München, Minerva-Publikation, 79, 370 p. CR: Clausjohann LINDNER, *Kölner Zeitschrift für Soziologie und Sozialpsychologie* 32(2), jun 80: 413. [also CR: Helmut FEHR, Soziologische Revue, 3(2), 80: 163-165.]

5600 CASTELLS, Manuel. "Urban social movements and the struggle for democracy: the citizens' movement in Madrid", *International Journal of urban and regional Research* mar 78 : 133-146.

5601 CERI, Paolo. "Il movimento operaio e i nuovi movimenti nella sociologia di Alain Touraine" (The labour movement and the new movements in Alain Touraine's sociology), *Quaderni di Sociologia* 28, mar 79 : 134-139.

5602 CORDERO, Christina; JENNETT, Christine. "Social scientists and social movements", *Australian and New Zealand Journal of Sociology* 16, mar 80 : 38-47.

5603 DOFFNY, Jacques; AKIWOWO, Akinsola; [eds.]. *National and ethnic movements.* Beverly Hills, CA, Sage Publications, 80, 300 p. [Africa; Asia.]

5604 DUMONT, Fernand. "Mouvements nationaux et régionaux d'aujourd'hui", *Cahiers internationaux de Sociologie* 66, jan-jun 79 : 5-17.

5605 FISICHELLA, Domenico. "Gruppi di interesse e gruppi di pressione nella democrazia moderna; uno schema di interpretazione" (Interest groups and pressure groups in modern democracy: an explanatory scheme), *Rivista italiana di Scienza politica* 10, apr 80 : 53-72.

5606 INDO, Kazuo. "Pressure groups in the Diet elections of postwar Japan — the role of trade unions and business groups", *Kobe University Law Review* 13, 79 : 1-24.

5607 KAU, James B.; RUBIN, Paul H. "Public interest lobbies: membership and influence", *Public Choice* 34, 79 : 45-54.

5608 KIM, G. F. "Mirovoj socializm i nacional'no-osvoboditel'noe dviženie" (World socialism and the national liberation movement), *IN: Politika mira i sotrudničestva.* Moskva, 79 : 172-187.

5609 MEDLIN, Virgil D. "Russia, 1917: reluctant revolutionaries succumbed to the paradox of revolution", *Social Science Journal* 16, oct 79 : 21-29.

5610 MELUCCI, Alberto. "The new social movements: a theoretical approach", *Social Science Information* 19, 80 : 199-226.

5611 POPOV, V. V. "Vlijanie sub'ektivnogo faktora na vozniknovenie revoljucionnoj situacii" (The subjective factor influence on the revolutionary situation rise), *Vestnik Moskovskogo Universiteta. Teorija naučnogo Kommunizma* 80 : 30-38.

5612 SIMCOCK, Bradford L. "Developmental aspects of antipollution protest in Japan", *Research in social Movements, Conflicts and Changes* 79 : 83-103.

5613 SNOW, David A.; ZURCHER, Louis A. Jr.; EKLAND-OLSON, Sheldon. "Social networks and social movements: a microstructural approach to differential recruitment", *American sociological Review* 45, oct 80 : 787-801.

5614 ZALD, Mayer N.; MCCARTHY, John D.; [eds.]. *The dynamics of social movements: resource mobilization, social control, and tactics.* Cambridge, MA, Winthrop Publishers, 79, viii-274 p.

19530. Political majority. Political opposition
ajorité politique. Opposition politique

[See also / voir aussi: 5249, 5677]

19600. POLITICAL BEHAVIOUR. ELECTIONS. POLITICS
COMPORTEMENT POLITIQUE. ÉLECTIONS. POLITIQUE

19610. Political leader. Political society
Leader politique. Société politique

[See also / voir aussi: 723, 5503]

5615 BIRJUKOV, N. I. "Krizis buržuaznoj sociologii političeskogo liderstva" (Crisis of the bourgeois sociology on political leadership), IN: Vlijanie uspehov mirovogo socializma na razvitie social'no-političeskih processov v zarubežnom mire. 79 : 40-47.

5616 GAXIE, Daniel. "Les logiques du recrutement politique", *Revue française de Science politique* 30, fev 80 : 5-45.

5617 GREGORY, Ann. "Dimensions of elite integration: the Javanization of the Indonesian political elite", *Kabar Seberang* 5-6, 79 : 171-180.

5618 TEZANOS, José F. "Radiografía de dos Congresos. Una aportación al estudio sociológico de los cuadros políticos del socialismo español" (Radiography of two congresses. A contribution to the sociological study of political leadership in Spanish socialism), *Sistema. Revista de Ciencias sociales* 35, 80 : 79-99.

19620. Political attitude. Political participation
Attitude politique. Participation politique

[See also / voir aussi: 767, 823, 1540, 1895, 1925, 1930, 2152, 2209, 2680, 2786, 3034, 3064, 3592, 3716, 4064, 4840, 5050, 5750]

5619 ACOCK, Alan C.; SCOTT, Wilbur J. "A model for predicting behavior: the effect of attitude and social class on high and low visibility political participation", *Social Psychology Quarterly* 43, mar 80 : 59-72.

5620 Bibl.XXIX-5495. BALOYRA, Enrique A.; MARTZ, John D. *Political attitudes in Venezuela: societal cleavages and political opinion.* CR: David Eugene BLANK, *American political Science Review* 74(2), jun 80 : 528-529.

5621 Bibl.XXIX-5498. BENSON, George C. S. *Political corruption in America.* CR: Pat LAUDERDALE, *Contemporary Sociology (Albany)* 9(4), jul 80 : 531-532.

5622 BILLIG, Michael; COCHRANE, Raymond. "Values of British political extremists and potential extremists: a discriminant analysis", *European Journal of social Psychology* apr-jun 79 : 205-222.

5623 BLACK, Jerome H.; MCGLEN, Nancy E. "Male-female political involvement differentials in Canada, 1965-1974", *Canadian Journal of political Science* 12, sep 79 : 471-497.

5624 BOOTH, John A.; SELIGSON, Mitchell A. "Peasants as activists: a reevaluation of political participation in the countryside", *Comparative political Studies* 12, apr 79 : 29-59.

5625 BRAUN, Karl-Heinz. "Subjektive Bedingungen politischen Handelns in der Bundesrepublik" (Subjective conditions of political behaviour in the Federal Republic of Germany), *Blätter für deutsche und internationale Politik* 25, apr 80 : 448-463.

5626 BREDOW, Wilfried von. "Extremismus und politische Tabus" (Radicalism and political taboos), *Liberal (Bonn)* 21(12), dec 79 : 907-919. [Germany FR.]

5627 CORCORAN, Paul E. *Political language and rhetoric.* St. Lucia, Australia, University of Queensland Press, 79, xvii-216 p. [distributed by Prentice-Hall International, Hemel Hempstead, Eng..]

5628 COTTA, Maurizio. "Il concetto di partecipazione politica: linea di un inquadramento teorico" (The concept of political participation lines for a theoretical framework), *Rivista italiana di Scienza politica* aug 79 : 193-228.

5629 DALTON, Russell J. "Reassessing parental socialization: indicator unreliability versus generational transfer", *American political Science Review* 74, jun 80 : 421-631.

5630 DIDUR, I. A. "Rol' političeskogo soznanija v formirovanii social'no aktivnoj ličnosti razvitogo socializma" (The political consciousness role in the formation of the personality social activity under developed socialism), *Problemy Filosofii* 48, 79 : 42-48.

5631	DIETZ, Henry; MOORE, Richard J. *Political participation in a non-electoral setting: the urban poor in Lima, Peru.* Athens, Ohio University, Center for International Studies, 79, vii-102 p.
5632	EPSTEIN, Laurily Keir. "Individual and contextual effects on partisanship", *Social Science Quarterly* 60, sep 79 : 314-322.
5633	GAUTAM, Moham; GANDHI, Raj. "Some aspects of the political socialization of the graduate students of Calgary", *Indian Journal of social Research* 20, apr 79 : 1-10.
5634	GRABB, Edward G. "Relative centrality and political isolation: Canadian dimensions", *Canadian Review of Sociology and Anthropology* 16, aug 79 : 343-355.
5635	GREIFFENHAGEN, Martin; GREIFFENHAGEN, Sylvia. *Ein schwieriges Vaterland. Zur politischen Kultur Deutschlands* (A difficult fatherland. On the political culture of Germany). München, List Verlag, 79, 484 p. CR: Dirk KÄSLER, *Kölner Zeitschrift für Soziologie und Sozialpsychologie* 32(2), jun 80: 391-393.
5636	HOWELL, Susan E. "The behavioral component of changing partisanship", *American Politics Quarterly* jul 80 : 279-302.
5637	IVANOV, V. N. "Nekotorye aspekty issledovanija dejstvennosti političeskoj kommunikacii" (Some aspects of efficiency research on political communication), *IN: Doklady Instituta sociologičeskih issledovanij AN SSR na XI vsemirnom kongress meždunarodnoj Associacii politiceskih nauk (Moskva, 12-18 aug. 1979 gg.).* Moskva, 79 : 87-94.
5638	IYENGAR, Shanto. "Political knowledge among Indian children and adolescents: an examination of the 'mass ignorance' thesis", *Social Science Quarterly* 60, sep 79 : 328-335.
5639	KATONA, Imre. *Mi a különbség? Közéleti vicceinkről* (What's the difference? Sociology of political jokes in Hungary). Budapest, Magvető, 80, 181 p.
5640	KISSLER, Leo. *Politische Sozialisation* (Political socialization). Baden-Baden, Nomos-Verlagsgesellschaft, 79, 158 p.
5641	KLJUEV, A. V. *Političeskaja aktivnost' ličnosti pri socializme: suščnost' i faktory ee povyšenija* (The personality political activity under socialism: nature and factors of its elevation). Leningrad, Izdatel'stvo Leningradskogo Universiteta, 80, 136 p.
5642	KNOKE, David; MACKE, Anne; FELSON, Marcus. "Using social indicators to forecast partisan alignments in congressional election years", *Social Indicators Research* (1-4), jan 80 : 47-61.
5643	KOGAN, L. N. "Političeskaja kul'tura socializma" (Political culture of socialism), *Naučnyj Kommunizm* 79 : 56-63.
5644	KRAUSS, Ellis S.; FRENDRICH, James M. "Political socialization of US and Japanese adults: the impact of adult roles on college leftism", *Comparative political Studies* 13, apr 80 : 3-32.
5645	LEVY, Shlomit. "The cylindrical structure of political involvement", *Social Indicators Research* oct 79 : 463-473.
5646	LISTHAUG, Ola; KINDSETH, Ola. "Sex, resources, and political participation: direct and indirect effects", *Scandinavian political Studies* 79 : 373-383.
5647	MALIK, Yogendra K. "Party identifications and political attitudes among the secondary school children of North India", *Asia Quarterly* 79 : 259-275.
5648	MCGLEN, Nancy E. "The impact of parenthood on political participation", *Western political Quarterly* 33, sep 80 : 297-313.
5649	MILLER, W. L. "What was the profit in following the crowd? The effectiveness of party strategies on immigration and devolution", *British Journal of political Science* 10, jan 80 : 15-38.
5650	MOMMEN, André. *De stratgie van het politiserend vormingswerk: een marxistische analyse* (The strategy of political socialization: a marxist analysis). Alphen aan den Rijn, Samsom, 79, 127 p.
5651	NELSON, Dale C. "Ethnicity and socio-economic status as sources of participation: the case for ethnic political culture", *American political Science Review* 73, dec 79 : 1024-1038.
5652	NIELSEN, Hans Jorgen; SAUERBERG, Steen. "Upstairs and downstairs in Danish politics: an analysis of political apathy and social structure", *Scandinavian political Studies* 80 : 59-78.
5653	ORNSTEIN, Michael D.; [et al.]. "Region, class and political culture in Canada", *Canadian Journal of political Science* 13, jun 80 : 227-271.
5654	RAMIREZ, Manuel. "La socialización política en España: una empresa para la democracia" (Political socialization in Spain: an enterprise for democracy), *Sistema. Revista de Ciencias sociales* 34, 80 : 91-115.
5655	SAMUELS, Warren J. "Two concepts of 'politicization'", *Social Science* 55, 80 : 67-70.

5656 SCOTT, Wilbur J.; ROPERS, Richard H. "Unemployment and political partisanship: support for the null hypothesis", *Sociological Focus* 13, oct 80 : 359-368.

5657 SELIGSON, Mitchell A. "Trust, efficacy and modes of political participation: a study of Costa Rican peasants", *British Journal of political Science* 10, jan 80 : 75-99.

5658 SELIGSON, Mitchell A. "A problem-solving approach to measuring political efficacy", *Social Science Quarterly* 60, mar 80 : 630-642.

5659 SIDANUIS, Jim; EKEHAMMAR, Bo. "Political socialization: a multivariate analysis of Swedish political attitude and preference data", *European Journal of social Psychology* jul-sep 79 : 265-279.

5660 SMORGUNOVA, V. Ju. "Funkcionirovanie političeskoj kul'tury ličnosti v uslovijah NTR" (The personality political culture functioning under conditions of the scientific and technical revolution), *IN: Aktivnost' ličnosti v uslovijah naučno-tehničeskoj revoljucii*. 79 : 2-11.

5661 STERN, Mark; MARTIN, Jeanne. "Socialization and participation in politics and the women's movement: a study of fathers, mothers, and daughters", *GPSA Journal* aut 79 : 117-140.

5662 TEDIN, Kent L. "Assessing peer and parent influence on adolescent political attitudes", *American Journal of political Science* 24, feb 80 : 136-154.

5663 TEMPLETON, Kenneth S. Jr.; [ed.]. *The politicization of society.* Indianapolis, Liberty Press, 79, 541 p.

5664 TERADA, Atsuhiro. "Seijiteki shakai-ka no sai-kentō" (Reconsideration on political socialization), *Shakaigaku ronso* 78, 80 : 28-37.

5665 TESSLER, Mark A.; HAWKINS, Linda L. "The political culture of Jews in Tunisia and Morocco", *International Journal of Middle East Studies* 11, 80 : 59-86.

5666 TIERNEY, John. "Political deviance: a critical commentary on a case study", *Sociological Review* 28, nov 80 : 829-850.

5667 TORRES ADRIÁN, Mario Julio. "Radicalismo o izquierdismo en el Perú: un análisis de opiniones políticas" (Radicalism or leftism in Peru: an analysis of political opinions), *Revista mexicana de Sociología* 41, oct-dec 79 : 1501-1534.

5668 TRAUGOTT, Mark. "Determinants of political orientation: class and organization in the Parisian insurrection of June 1848", *American Journal of Sociology* 86, jul 80 : 32-49.

5669 VERCHOMIN-HARASYMIW, Elaïne. "Civic education in the Soviet Union: a model for political socialization", *Canadian Slavonic Papers* 22, mar 80 : 43-57.

19630. Elections
           Élections

[See also / voir aussi: 1573, 1671, 1923, 2611, 2709, 3994]

5670 CHAFFEE, Steven H.; CHOE, Sun Yuel. "Time of decision and media use during the Ford-Carter campaign", *Public Opinion Quarterly* 44, 80 : 53-69.

5671 FAURE, Yves-André. "L'évolution politique: élections et partis en Afrique noire", *Année africaine* 78 : 214-250.

5672 GOOT, Murray. "Age differences in party preferences and policy positions", *Australian Quarterly* 52, aut 80 : 60-74.

5673 GREISLAMMER, Alain. "Sociologie électorale du protestantisme français", *Archives de Sciences sociales des Religions* 25, jan-mar 80 : 119-145.

5674 GUTERBOCK, Thomas M. "Social class and voting choices in Middletown", *Social Forces* 58, jun 80 : 1044-1056.

5675 KITAJIMA, Shigeru. "Asahikawa shicho senkyo ni okeru tohyo kodo ni kansuru ichi-kosatsu -kakushin shisei kara hoshu shisei eno sentaku no sho-yoin" (Review of the voting behaviour in Asahikawa mayoral election 1978), *Asahakawa daigaku kiyo* 10, 80 : 41-58.

5676 KRÖLL, Friedhelm. "Die Mythologisierung der Wahlkabine: zur Kritik der herrschenden Wahlforschung" (The mythologization of the polling-booth: on the criticism of the dominant electoral sociology), *Blätter für deutsche und internationale Politik* 25, apr 80 : 464-475.

5677 MADDOX, William W. "Changing electoral coalitions from 1952-1976", *Social Science Quarterly* 60, sep 79 : 309-313. [USA.]

5678 MORGAN, David R.; MEIER, Kenneth J. "Politics and morality: the effect of religion on referenda voting", *Social Science Quarterly* 61, jun 80 : 144-148.

5679 PAGE, Benjamin I.; JONES, Calvin C. "Reciprocal effects of policy preferences, party loyalties and the vote", *American political Science Review* 73, dec 79 : 1071-1089.

5680 PARISI, Arturo; PASQUINO, Gianfranco. "Changes in Italian electoral behaviour: the relationships between parties and voters", *West European Politics* oct 79 : 6-30.

5681 POWELL, Lynda Watts. "A Bayesian approach to a sequential three-decision problem: voting and the uses of information in electoral choice", *Journal of mathematical Sociology* 79 : 177-198.

5682 ROMERO VILLAFRANCA, Rafael; ZUNICA RAMAJO, Luisa. "Geografía electoral española. Una aplicación del análisis factorial de correspondencias de los resultados de las elecciones del 10 de marzo de 1979" (Spanish electoral geography. An application of correspondence factor analysis to the electoral results of the 10th March 1979), *Revista española de Investigaciones sociológicas* jan-mar 80 : 139-167.

5683 ROSE, Richard; [ed.]. *Electoral participation: a comparative analysis.* Beverly Hills, CA, Sage Publications, 80, 360 p.

5684 ROSENTHAL, U. "De verborgen invloed van verkiezingen: symboliek, ritueel, regelmaat en anticiperende effecten" (The latent influence of elections: symbolics, ritual, regularity and anticipated effects), *Mens en Maatschappij* 55, 80 : 59-76.

5685 WIMBERLEY, Ronald C. "Civil religion and the choice for president: Nixon in '72", *Social Forces* 59, sep 80 : 44-61.

19640. Politics
Politique

[See also / voir aussi: 1925, 1930, 2039, 2236, 2660, 4464, 5539, 5738]

5686 BARKAN, Steven E. "Political trials and resource mobilization: towards an understanding of social movement litigation", *Social Forces* 58, mar 80 : 944-961.

5687 BEN RAFAEL, Eliezer; LISSAK, Moshe. *Social aspects of guerilla and anti-guerilla warfare.* Jerusalem, Magnes Press, Hebrew University, 79, 96 p.

5688 BENJAMIN, Roger. *The limits of politics: Collective goods and political change in postindustrial societies.* Chicago, London, University of Chicago Press, 80, xiii-148 p.

5689 BRAZZODURO, Marco. "Politica e potere nella crisi italiana" (Politics and power in the Italian crisis), *Revue internationale de sociologie / International Review of Sociology* 15(1-2-3), apr-aug-dec 79 : 131-148.

5690 DIRKS, Nicholas B. "The structure and meaning of political relations in a South Indian little kingdom", *Contributions to Indian Sociology* 13, jul-dec 79 : 169-206.

5691 HANSEN, Joseph. *The Leninist strategy of party building: the debate on guerrilla warfare in Latin America.* New York, Pathfinder Press, 79, 608 p.

5692 ROACH, Janet, K.; ROACH, Jack L. "Turmoil in command of politics: organizing the poor", *Sociological Quarterly* 21, 79 : 259-270.

5693 THOMPSON, William R.; CHRISTOPHERSON, Jon A. "A multivariate analysis of the correlates of regime vulnerability and proneness of the military coup", *Journal of political and military Sociology* aut 79 : 283-289.

5694 Bibl.XXIX-5595. WEINSTEIN, Michael. *Meaning and appreciation: time and modern political life.* CR: Burkart HOLZNER, *Contemporary Sociology (Albany)* 9(4), jul 80 : 573-574.

19700. ARMY. MILITARY SOCIOLOGY
ARMÉE. SOCIOLOGIE MILITAIRE

[See also / voir aussi: 1037, 1634, 3669, 5054, 5068]

5695 AZARYA, Victor; KIMMERLING, Baruch. "New immigrants in the Israeli armed forces", *Armed Forces and Society* spr 80 : 455-482.

5696 BLUEDORN, Allen C. "Structure, environment, and satisfaction: toward a causal model of turnover from military organizations", *Journal of political and military Sociology* aut 79 : 181-207.

5697 BRYANT, Clifton D. *Khaki-collar crime: deviant behavior in the military context.* New York, Free Press, 79, xii-388 p.

5698 CHISHOLM, Rupert F.; GAUNTNER, Donald E.; MUNZENRIDER, Robert F. "Pre-enlistment expectations/perceptions of army life, satisfaction, and re-enlistment of volunteers", *Journal of political and military Sociology* 80 : 31-42.

5699 COCKERHAM, William C.; COHEN, Lawrence E. "Attitudes of US army paratroopers towards participation in the quelling of civil disturbances", *Journal of political and military Sociology* 79 : 257-269.

5700 ECCLES, Henry Effingham. *Military power in a free society*. Newport, RI, Naval War College Press, 79, xv-275 p. [for sale by Supt. of Docs., U. S. Govt. Print. Off., Washington, DC.]

5701 EHREN, A. M. A.; TEITLER, G. "On the relationship between the Dutch and their armed forces", *Netherlands' Journal of Sociology* 15, jul 79 : 27-45.

5702 EVANS, M. D.; FELSON, Marcus; LAND, Kenneth C. "Developing social indicators research on the military in American society", *Social Indicators Research* mar 80 : 81-102.

5703 GABRIEL, Richard A. "Legitimate avenues of military protest in a democratic society", *Social Science* 54, aut 79 : 223-230.

5704 HALTINER, Karl; MEYER, Ruth. "Aspects of the relationship between military and society in Switzerland", *Armed Forces and Society* aut 79 : 49-81.

5705 HONG, Dvo-Scung. "Retired US military elites: post-military employment and its sociopolitical implications", *Armed Forces and Society* spr 79 : 451-466.

5706 KEPPLINGER, Hans Mathias; HACHENBERG, Michael. "Die fordernde Minderheit. Eine Studie zum sozialen Wande durch abweichendes Verhalten am Beispiel der Kriegsdienstverweigerung" (The claimed minority. A study of social change through different behaviours by the example of non-compliance with military service), *Kölner Zeitschrift für Soziologie und Sozialpsychologie* 32, 80 : 508-534.

5707 KLEIN, Paul; LIPPERT, Ekkehard. *Militär und Gesellschaft: Bibliographie zur Militärsoziologie* (Military and society: bibliography on military sociology). München, Bernard & Graefe, 79, vii-139 p.

5708 LAIDLAW, Karen A. "The military and the Third World — a case for the convergence hypothesis?", *International Review of modern Sociology* jan-jun 79 : 1-15.

5709 LEJEUNE, Bernard. *Les Casernements de l'armée de terre et de la gendarmerie mobile: contribution à une étude sociologique sur l'insertion du militaire dans la vie de la nation*. Paris, Foundation nationale des sciences politiques, Centre de sociologie de la défense nationale, 79, 2 vols, 225, 149 p.

5710 LILIENSIEK, Peter. *Bedingungen und Dimensionen militärischer Sozialisation: e. Beitr. zur Bundeswehrsoziologie* (Conditions and dimensions of military sozialization: an essay on the sociology of the Bundeswehr). Frankfurt am Main, Bern, Cirencester, U.K., Lang, 79, ix-285 p.

5711 MARGIOTTA, Franklin D.; [ed.]. *The changing world of the American military*. Boulder, CO, Westview Press, 79, xxii-488 p. CR: Lawrence, J. KORB, *American political Science Review* 74(1), mar 80: 209-210.

5712 MARTIN, Michel L. "Le soldat prétorien, la politicque et le changement social en Afrique noire: des causes militaires d'un échec", *Année africaine* 78 : 119-150.

5713 POZZI, Enrico. *Introduzione alla sociologia militare* (Introduction to military sociology). Napoli, Liguori, 79, 298 p.

5714 SERMAN, William. *Les origines des officiers français. 1848-1870*. Paris, Publications de la Sorbonne, 79, 406 p.

5715 Bibl.XXIX-5620. SHIBUTANI, Tamotsu. *The derelicts of company K: a sociological study of demoralization*. CR: Kurt LANG, *American Journal of Sociology* 86(1), jul 80 : 200-202.

5716 SNYDER, William; NYBERG, Kenneth L. "Gays and the military: an emerging policy issue", *Journal of political and military Sociology* 80 : 71-84.

5717 STEMPLOWSKI, Ryszard. *Wojsko i społeczeństwo w Trzecim Świecie* (Army and society in the Third World). Warszawa, Czytelnik, 79, 557 p.

5718 Bibl.XXIX-5622. TRIMBERGER, Ellen Kay. *Revolution from above: military bureaucrats and development in Japan, Turkey, Egypt, and Peru*. CR: Barbara Hockey KAPLAN, *American Journal of Sociology* 85(5), mar 80 : 1305-1306. [also CR: James PETRAS, *Contemporary Sociology* (Albany), 9(5), sep 80 : 712-713.]

5719 USEEM, Michael. "Educational and military experience of young men during the Vietnam era: non-linear effects of parental social class", *Journal of political and military Sociology* 80 : 15-29.

5720 ZELINKA, Fritz F. *Präferenzen sozialwissenschaftlicher Militärforschung in der Bundesrepublik Deutschland* (Preferences of social science military research in the Federal Republic of Germany). Frankfurt am Main, Bern, Cirencester/U.K., Lang, 79, v-171 p.

19800. **INTERNATIONAL RELATIONS**
RELATIONS INTERNATIONALES

19810. International law. International organization
Droit international. Organisation internationale

[See also / voir aussi: 1212, 1714]

5721 BENCHIKH, Madjid. "De quelques aspects théoriques et pratiques de la notion de démocratisation des relations internationales", *Revue algérienne des Sciences juridiques, économiques et politiques* 15, dec 78 : 9-20.

5722 BUTENKO, A. "Internacionalizm kak ključevaja kategorija marksizma" (Internationalism as an essential category of marxism), *Obščestvennye Nauki (Moskva)* 80 : 48-61.

5723 EISENSTADT, S. N. "Some reflections on the dynamics of international systems", *Sociological Inquiry* 49, 7913 : 5-12.

5724 EVANS, Peter. "Beyond center and periphery: a comment on the contribution of the world system approach to the study of development", *Sociological Inquiry* 49, 79 : 15-20.

5725 JONES, Thomas E. "Wallerstein's neglect of Nelson's 'rationales'", *Sociological Inquiry* 49, 79 : 21-24. [about WALLERSTEIN, Immanuel. The modern world system: capitalist agriculture and the origins of the European world economy in the 16th century. New York, Academic Press, 1974; and NELSON, Benjamin. The idea of usury. Chicago, University of Chicago Press, 1949.]

5726 KABAČENKO, A. P. *Razvitie proletarskogo internacionalizma* (Development of proletarian internationalism). Moskva, Izdatel'stvo Moskovskogo Universiteta, 79, 247 p.

5727 NIKULIN, A. I. "Nekotorye voprosy psihologii v propagande teorii i politiki proletarskogo internacionalizma" (Some psychological questions in the propaganda of the proletarian internationalism theory and politics), *IN: Social'no-ėkonomičeskie problemy razvitogo socialističeskogo obščestva.* Kalinin, 79 : 76-84.

5728 PETTMAN, Ralph. *State and class: a sociology of international affairs.* New York, St. Martin's Press, 79, 270 p.

5729 POPOV, B. S. "O kriterijah proletarskogo internacionalizma v sovremennyh uslovijah" (On the proletarian internationalism criteria under contemporary conditions), *IN: Proletarskij internacionalizm: voprosy ideologii i kul'tury.* Moskva, 79 : 5-14.

5730 TENJANKO, Ju. P. "Kritika buržuaznyh fal'sifikacij principa socialističeskogo internacionalizma" (Criticism of the bourgeois falsifications of the socialist internationalism principle), *Voprosy obščestvennyh Nauk* 43, 80 : 66-71.

19820. Foreign policy. Sovereignty
Politique étrangère. Souveraineté

[See also / voir aussi: 2702, 5399]

5731 BAUTISTA MALPICA, Matilde. "Un análisis de la idea de imperialismo en Rudolf Hilferding" (Analysis of Rudolf Hilferding's concept of imperialism), *Cuadernos de Realidades sociales* 16-17, 80 : 57-78.

5732 CERNY, Philip G. "Foreign policy leadership and national integration", *British Journal of international Studies* 79 : 59-85.

5733 SABALIN, V. A. "Suščnost'" i sistema socialističeskogo narodovlastija" (Nature and system of the socialist people's sovereignty), *Političeskaja Organizacija Obščestva i Upravlenie pri Socializme* 79 : 45-60.

5734 TAMAI, Minoru. "T. Hobbes no shizengo ni yoru kokka shukenron no ichi-kosatsu" (A study on the sovereignty through the natural law in T. Hobbes), *Tokyo kogei daigaku kogakubu kiyo* 80 : 74-83.

5735 ZAHAROV, F. I. "Nauka o revoljucii i ideologičeskie aspekty strategii imperializma" (Science on revolution and ideological aspects of the imperialism strategy), *IN: Problemy kommunističeskogo dviženija.* 79 : 234-248.

19830. International cooperation. War
Coopération internationale. Guerre

[See also / voir aussi: 1889, 2648]

5736 Bibl.XXIX-5645. LOCKHART, Charles. *Bargaining in international conflicts.* CR: Charles S. GOCHMAN, *American political Science Review* 74(1), mar 80 : 299-300.

5737 PASKINS, Barrie; DOCKRILL, Michael. *The ethics of war.* Minneapolis, University of Minnesota Press, 79, xii-332 p.
5738 SANDERS, Jerry. "Shaping the cold war consensus: the Soviet threat, interelite conflict, and mass politics in the Korean War era", *Berkeley Journal of Sociology* 24-25, 80 : 67-136.
5739 SOBOLEV, A. I.; [ed.]. *Mirnoe sosuščestvovanie i bor'ba za social'nyj progress* (Peaceful coexistence and the struggle for social progress). Moskva, Politizdat, 79, 319 p.
5740 VERSTRYNGE ROJAS, Jorge. *Una sociedad para la guerra: (los efectos de la guerra en la sociedad industrial)* (A society for the war: effects of war on the industrial society). Madrid, Centro de Investigaciones Sociológicas, 79, 403 p.
5741 VIDICH, Arthur. "Prospects for peace in a nuclear world", *Journal of political and military Sociology* 80 : 85-97.

19840. Disarmament. Weapon
Désarmement. Arme

[See also / voir aussi: 5741]

20. SOCIAL PROBLEM. SOCIAL SERVICE. SOCIAL WORK
PROBLÈME SOCIAL. SERVICE SOCIAL. TRAVAIL SOCIAL

20100. SOCIAL PROBLEM
PROBLÈME SOCIAL

20110. Applied sociology
Sociologie appliquée

[See also / voir aussi: 142, 159, 332, 378, 440, 1539, 5556]

5742 BAILEY, Joe. *Ideas and intervention: social theory for practice.* London, Boston, Routledge & Kegan Paul, 80, vii-156 p.
5743 BROCH, Tom; [et al.]. *Kvalitative metoder i dansk samfundsforskning* (Qualitative methods and Danish social research). København, Nyt fra Samfundsvidenskaberne, 79, 379 p.
5744 BUCHHOFER, Bernd; LÜDTKE, Hartmut. "Arbeitsteilung und Statusunterschiede in der empirischen Sozialforschung: eine Untersuchung der Interview-Projektforschung 1968-1972" (Division of labor and social differentiation in social research: a survey of interview projects 1968-1972), *Zeitschrift für Soziologie* apr 80 : 179-193.
5745 DAVIDJUK, G. P. *Prikladnaja sociologija* (Applied sociology). Minsk, Vyšejšaja Škola, 79, 220 p.
5746 DEMARTINI, Joseph R. "Constraints to the development of curricula in applied sociology", *American Sociologist* 15, aug 80 : 138-145.
5747 DEMARTINI, Joseph R. "Applied sociology: an attempt at clarification and assessment", *Teaching Sociology* jul 79 : 331-354.
5748 EATON, Joseph W. "The mushrooming of applied sociology", *Contemporary Sociology* nov 80 : 768-771. [survey essay.]
5749 HOFFMANN-RIEM, Christa. "Die Sozialforschung einer interpretativen Soziologie. Der Datengewinn" (Social research in interpretative sociology. The data acquisition), *Kölner Zeitschrift für Soziologie und Sozialpsychologie* 32, 80 : 339-372.
5750 HUIZER, Gerrit. "Ciencia social aplicada y acción política: notas sobre nuevos enfoques" (Applied social science and political action: notes on new research fields), *Revista mexicana de Sociología* 41, jul-sep 79 : 1013-1040.
5751 MAYER, Robert R.; GREENWOOD, Ernest. *The design of social policy research.* Englewood Cliffs, NJ, Prentice-Hall, 80, xi-290 p.
5752 Bibl.XXIX-5673. RULE, James. *Insight and social betterment: a preface to applied social science.* CR: Derba KALMUSS, *Contemporary Sociology (Albany)* 9(2), mar 80: 300-301.
5753 SCOTT, Robert A.; SHORE, Arnold R. *Why sociology does not apply: a study of the use of sociology in public policy.* New York, Elsevier, 79, xviii-265 p.

20120. Social pathology
Pathologie sociale

5754 EITZEN, D. Stanley. *Social problems.* Boston, Allyn and Bacon, 80, 534 p.
5755 KUMAR, Krishan. "Thoughts on the present discontents in Britain", *Theory and Society* jul 80 : 539-574.
5756 LEONARDI, Franco. "Un'analisi concettuale dei processi di disgregazione sociale" (A conceptual analysis of the social disintegration processes), *Politico* 45, mar 80 : 43-64.
5757 ROBINSON, T. Russell; SISMONDO, Sergio. "Analysis of social pathologies in a policy context: a paradigm for action", *Social Indicators Research* jan 79 : 41-72.

20130. Disaster
Catastrophe

[See also / voir aussi: 3856, 4205]

20140. Poverty
Pauvreté

[See also / voir aussi: 2785, 3110, 4111, 4755, 4762, 5841, 6053]

5758 "Nourriture (La): pour une anthropologie bio-culturelle de l'alimentation", *Communications (Paris)* 31, 79 : 1-210.

5759 AUSTIN, James E. *Confronting urban malnutrition: the design of nutrition programs*. Baltimore, Johns Hopkins University Press, 80, xi-119 p. [published for the World Bank.]

5760 AZIZ, Sartaj. "Abolishing hunger: the complex reality of food", *Third World Quarterly* oct 79 : 17-27.

5761 Bibl.XXIX-5693. BALLA, Bálint. *Soziologie der Knappheit. Zum Verständnis individueller und gesellschaftlicher Mangelzustände* (Sociology of scarcity. On individual intelligence and social deficiency conditions). CR: Alfred BELLEBAUM, *Kölner Zeitschrift für Soziologie und Sozialpsychologie* 32(1), mar 80 : 158-159.

5762 BEQUELE, Assefa; VAN DER HOEVEN, Rolph. "Pauvreté et inégalité en Afrique tropicale", *Revue internationale du Travail* 119, mai-jun 80 : 387-399.

5763 BERGHMAN, J. "Pauvreté et inégalités en Belgique — un aperçu", *Revue belge de Sécurité sociale* 21, sept 79 : 549-586.

5764 CARBONARO, Antonio. *Povertà e classi sociali: per la critica sociologica delle ideologie sui processi di pauperizzazione* (Poverty and social classes: for the sociological critique of ideologies on impoverishment). Milano, F. Angeli, 79, 184 p.

5765 CHALFANT, H. Paul. *Sociological aspects of poverty: a bibliography*. Monticello, IL, Vance Bibliographies, 80, 77 p.

5766 COHN, Steven; WOOD, Robert. "Basic human needs programming: an analysis of Peace Corps data", *Development and Change* 11, apr 80 : 313-332.

5767 Bibl.XXIX-5698. DAVIS, Karen; SCHOEN, Cathy. *Health and the war on poverty: a ten-year appraisal*. CR: Lloyd Davis RAINES, *Contemporary Sociology (Albany)* 9(5), sep 80 : 689-690.

5768 DREWNOWSKI, Jan. "Poverty: its measuring and measurement", *Policy Studies Review Annual* 78 : 280-305.

5769 FRANKE, Richard W.; CHASIN, Barbara H. *Seeds of famine: ecological destruction and the development dilemma in the west African Sahel*. Montclair, NJ; Allanheld, Osmun, 80, xi-266 p.

5770 GHAI, Dharam. "Les besoins essentiels: des paroles aux actes. Quelques exemples pris au Kenya", *Revue internationale du Travail* 119, mai-jun 80 : 371-385.

5771 Bibl.XXIX-5702. GRØNDBJERG, Kirsten; STREET, David; SUTTLES, Gerald D. *Poverty and social change*. CR: Edgar LITT, *American political Science Review* 74(1), mar 80 : 198-199.

5772 GUTIERREZ LEYTON, Mario. *Lactancia y desarrollo socioeconomico* (Lactation and socio-economic development). Buenos Aires, Facultad Latinoamericana de Ciencias Sociales, 80, 18 p.

5773 HAVEMAN, R. H. "Poverty, income distribution and social policy: the last decade and the next", *Policy Studies Review Annual* 78 : 306-327. [USA.]

5774 HEJDA, Stanislav. "L'alimentation et l'état de nutrition de la population en République socialiste tchécoslovaque", *Demosta* 12, 79 : 118-123.

5775 LAWLESS, Paul. *Urban deprivation and government initiative*. London, Boston, Faber, 79, 251 p.

5776 LISK, Franklyn; VAN DER HOEVEN, Rolph. "Mesure et interprétation de la pauvreté en Sierra Leone", *Revue internationale du Travail* 118, nov-dec 79 : 755-773.

5777 MUSGROVE, Philip. "Household size and composition, employment and poverty in urban Latin America", *Economic Development and cultural Change* 28, jan 80 : 249-266.

5778 NELSON, Jack A. *Hunger for justice: the politics of food and faith*. Maryknoll, NY, Orbis Books, 80, viii-230 p.

5779 OSMOND, Marie Withers; SCHRADER, David F. (Paths to poverty in the United States), *International Review of modern Sociology* jan-jun 79 : 77-91.

5780 PAGLIN, Morton. *Poverty and transfers in-kind: A re-evaluation of poverty in the United States*. Stanford, CA, Hoover Institution Press, 80, 98 p.

5781 RELEMBERG, N. S.; [et al.]. *Los pobres de Venezuela* (Poormen in Venezuela). Buenos Aires, El Cid, 79, 173 p.

5782 SHEEHAN, Glen; HOPKINS, Mike. *Basic needs performance: an analysis of some international data*. Geneva, International Labour Off., 79, 138 p.

5783 SINGH, R. R.; [ed.]. *Social work perspectives on poverty*. New Delhi, Concept, 80, 304 p.

5784 STAMBOULI, Fredj. "Populations néo-citadines et besoins humains fondamentaux, le cas de Djebel Lahmar en Tunisie", *Dritte Welt* 79 : 302-324.

5785 TÉVOÉDJRÈ, Albert. *Poverty: wealth of mankind*. New York, London, Pergamon Press, 79, iv-182 p. CR: David J. GOULD, *American political Science Review* 74(2), jun 80 : 602-603.

5786 THOME, Joseph R. "Legal and social structures and the access of the Latin American rural poor to the State allocation of goods and services", *Research in Law and Sociology* 79 : 251-274.

5787 TOWNSEND, Peter. *Poverty in the United Kingdom: a survey of household resources and standards of living.* Berkeley, University of California Press, 79, 1216 p.
5788 TREBLE, James H. *Urban poverty in Britain, 1830-1914.* New York, St. Martin's Press, 79, 216 p.
5789 VAN GINNEKEN, W.; JOIN-LAMBERT, L.; LECAILLON, J. "La pauvreté persistante dans les pays industriels à économie de marché", *Revue internationale du Travail* 118, nov-dec 79 : 741-753.
5790 VELJKOVIČ, Vera. "Struktura ishrane i njena zavisnost od uticaja vanekonomskih činilaca" (The structure of nutrition and its dependence on the influence of extra-economic factors), *Sociologija* 21(1-2), 79 : 159-169.
5791 VERBER, Christian Von. "Ernährungsgewohnheiten: zur Soziologie der Ernährung" (Nutrition habits: towards a sociology of nutrition), *Zeitschrift für Soziologie* jul 80 : 221-235.
5792 YORNET, Mario. *Elementos para una sociología de la escasez* (Elements for a sociology of scarcity). Buenos Aires, Fundación para la Investigación de los Problemas Económicos y Sociales, 80. [2 vols..]
5793 YOUNG, Ruth C. "Poverty and inequality in the United States: a non-Marxist explanation", *Social Indicators Research* mar 80 : 103-113.

20150. Alcoholism. Drug
Alcoolisme. Stupéfiants

[See also / voir aussi: 842, 2123, 2473]

5794 *(El) Problema actual de la coca en la sociedad peruana: diferentes enfoques* (Present problems of cocaine in Peruvian society: different viewpoints). Lima, Centro de Investigaciones Socio-Económicas, Taller de Coyuntura Agraria, Universidad Nacional Agraria, 79, 110 p.
5795 "Colloque international (25è) sur la prévention et le traitement de l'alcoolisme", *Toxicomanies* 12(3-4), jul-dec 79 : 141-424.
5796 ASHBROOK, Debra L. *Women and heroin abuse: a survey of sexism in drug abuse administration.* Palo Alto, CA, R. & E. Research Associates, 79, ix-115 p.
5797 BABAIAN, E. A. "Contrôle des stupéfiants et prévention de la toxicomanie en URSS", *Bulletin des Stupéfiants* 31, jan-mar 79 : 13-21.
5798 BARLING, Julian; FINCHAM, Frank. "Alcohol, psychological conservatism, and sexual interest in male social drinkers", *Journal of social Psychology* 112, oct 80 : 135-144.
5799 BAUMAN, Karl E. *Predicting adolescent drug use: utility structure and marijuana.* New York, Praeger, 80, x-181 p.
5800 BERGERET, Jean; [ed.]. *Le Toxicomane et ses environnements.* Paris, Presses universitaires de France, INSERM, 79, 229 p.
5801 BESCHNER, George M.; FRIEDMAN, Alfred S.; [eds.]. *Youth drug abuse: problems, issues, and treatment.* Lexington, MA, Lexington Books, 79, xxxi-681 p.
5802 Bibl.XXIX-5726. BEYER, Janice M.; TRICE, Harrison M. *Implementing change: alcoholism policies in work organizations.* CR: Paul T. SCHOLLAERT, *Contemporary Sociology (Albany)* 9(4), jul 80: 567-568.
5803 BLANE, Howard T.; CHAFETZ, Morris E. [eds.]. *Youth, Alcohol, and Social Policy Conference, Arlington, VA, 1978.* New York, Plenum Press, 79, xxvi-424 p. [USA.]
5804 BLOCKER, Jack S. Jr.; [ed.]. *Alcohol, reform, and society: the liquor issue in social context.* Westport, CT, Greenwood Press, 79, x-289 p.
5805 BRUNSWICK, Ann F.; BOYLE, John M. "Patterns of drug involvement. Developmental and secular influences on age at initiation", *Youth and Society* 11, dec 79 : 139-162.
5806 CASTRO, Maria Elena; [et al.]. "Les drogues et l'alcool dans la population scolaire au Mexique et au Canada: usage, problèmes et disponibilités", *Bulletin des Stupéfiants* 31, jan-mar 79 : 41-48.
5807 GLASSNER, Barry; BERG, Bruce. "How Jews avoid alcohol problems", *American sociological Review* 45, aug 80 : 647-664.
5808 GOLDMAN, Albert Harry. *Grass roots: marijuana in America today.* New York, Harper & Row, 79, 262 p.
5809 GONZÁLEZ DURO, Enrique. *Consumo de drogas en España* (Drug addiction in Spain). Madrid, Villalar, 79, 323 p.
5810 LIA, Domenico. "Rilevi sociologici e culturali connessi al fenomeno di utilizzazione di droghe nella città di Amsterdam" (Sociological and cultural remarks in connection

with the drug addiction phenomenon in Amsterdam), *Studi di Sociologia* 17, jul-sep 79 : 308-328.
5811   LIDZ, Charles W.; WALKER, Andrew L.; GOULD, Leroy C. *Heroin, deviance and morality*. Beverly Hills, CA, Sage Publications, 80, 240 p.
5812   MANNING, Peter K. *The narc's game: organizational and informational limits on drug law enforcement*. Cambridge, MA, MIT Press, 80, xiv-316 p.
5813   MAYER, John E.; FILSTEAD, William J.; [eds.]. *Adolescence and alcohol*. Cambridge, MA, Ballinger Pub. Co., 80, xvi-288 p.
5814   MENDLEWICZ, J.; VAN PRAAG, Herman Meïr; [eds.]. *Alcoholism: a multidisciplinary approach*. Basel, New York, S. Karger, 79, 138 p.
5815   MEUDT, Volker. *Drogen und Öffentlichkeit* (Drugs and publicity). München, Minerva-Publikation, 79, vii-354 p. CR: Aldo LEGNARO, *Kölner Zeitschrift für Soziologie und Sozialpsychologie* 32(4), dec 80: 826-827.
5816   MISHARA, Brian L.; KASTENBAUM, Robert. *Alcohol and old age*. New York, Grune & Stratton, 80, ix-220 p.
5817   NOVAK, William. *High culture: marijuana in the lives of Americans*. New York, Knopf, 80, xxv-289 p. [distributed by Random House.]
5818   PASCALE, Robert; HURD, Mava; PRIMAVERA, Louis H. "The effects of chronic marijuana use", *Journal of social Psychology* 110, apr 80 : 273-283.
5819   PLANT, Martin. *Drinking careers: occupations, drinking habits, and drinking problems*. London, Tavistock Publications, 79, xiv-167 p. [UK.]
5820   POMMEREHNE, Werner W.; HARTMANN, Hans C. "Ein ökonomischer Ansatz zur Rauschgiftkontrolle" (An economic essay on drug control), *Jahrbuch für Sozialwissenschaft* 31, 80 : 102-143.
5821   ROBERTS, James S. "Der Alkoholkonsum deutscher Arbeiter im 19. Jahrhundert" (The alcohol consumption of the German worker in the 19th century), *Geschichte und Gesellschaft* 80 : 220-242.
5822   SANDMAIER, Marian. *The invisible alcoholics: women and alcohol and alcohol abuse in America*. New York, McGraw-Hill, 80, xviii-298 p.
5823   STRACK, Jay. *Drugs and drinking: the all American cop-out*. Nashville, Sceptre Books, Nelson, 79, 195 p.
5824   VAN DER BURGH, Chris; HEAVEN, P. C. L. *The aetiology of drug use: a social-psychological examination*. Pretoria, South African Human Sciences Research Council, Institute for Sociological Demographic and Criminological Research, 79, v-40 p.
5825   WHITE, Gregory L.; ZIMBARDO, Philip G. "The effects of threat of surveillance and actual surveillance on expressed opinions toward marijuana", *Journal of social Psychology* 111, jun 80 : 49-61.
5826   WÜTHRICH, Peter. *Alkohol in der Schweiz* (Alcohol in Switzerland). Frauenfeld, Stuttgart, Huber, 79, 188 p.

20160.   Crime. Delinquency
Délit. Délinquance

[See also / voir aussi: 237, 702, 1154, 1168, 1375, 1521, 2951, 3094, 3790, 5029, 5846, 5868, 5911, 5926, 5977, 5984, 5992]

5827   "Femme délinquante", *Annales de l'Université des Sciences sociales de Toulouse* 27, 79 : 229-305.
5828   "Crime policy and the criminal justice system", *Policy Studies* 79 : 743-799. [[USA].]
5829   ALBRECHT, Peter-Alexis; LAMNEK, Siegfried. *Jugendkriminalität im Zerrbild der Statistik: ein Analyse von Daten und Entwicklungen* (Juvenile delinquency in the deceptive mirror of statistics: an analysis of data and developments). München, Juventa-Verlag, 79, 184 p.
5830   ALLEN, Nancy H. *Homicide, perspectives on prevention*. New York, Human Sciences Press, 80, 191 p.
5831   ALPERT, Geoffrey P.; [ed.]. *Legal Rights of Prisoners*. Beverly Hills, CA, Sage Publications, 80, 280 p.
5832   ARLACCHI, Pino. "Mafia e tipi di società" (Mafia and types of society), *Rassegna italiana di Sociologia* 21, jan-mar 80 : 3-49.
5833   ATHENS, Lonnie H. *Violent criminal acts and actors: a symbolic interactionist study*. Boston, Routledge & Kegan Paul, 80, xiii-104 p.
5834   BAILEY, William C. "Deterrence and the celerity of the death penalty: a neglected question in deterrence research", *Social Forces* 58, jun 80 : 1308-1333.

5835 BAILEY, William C. "A multivariate cross sectional analysis of the deterrent effect of the death penalty", *Sociology and social Research* 64, jan 80 : 183-207.

5836 BALKAN, Sheila; BERGER, Ronald J.; SCHMIDT, Janet. *Crime and deviance in America: a critical approach.* Belmont, CA, Wadsworth Pub. Co., 80, 408 p.

5837 BALLONI, Augusto. *Devianza e giustizia minorile: teorie e ricerche* (Deviance and juvenile corrections: theory and research). Milano, F. Angeli, 79, 302 p. [Italy.]

5838 BANERJI, Sures Chandra. *Crime and sex in ancient India.* Calcutta, Naya Prokash, 80, xvi-184 p.

5839 BANKSTON, William B.; ALLEN, David H. "Rural social areas and patterns of homicide: an analysis of lethal violence in Louisiana", *Rural Sociology* 45, sum 80 : 223-237.

5840 BARTOL, Curt R. *Criminal behaviour: a psychosocial approach.* Englewood Cliffs, NJ, Prentice-Hall, 80, xiii-434 p.

5841 BERK, Richard A.; LENIHAN, Kenneth L.; ROSSI, Peter H. "Crime and poverty: some experimental evidence from ex-offenders", *American sociological Review* 45, oct 80 : 766-786. [USA.]

5842 BERK, Richard A.; [et al.]. "Bringing the cops back in: a study of efforts to make the criminal justice system more responsive to incidents of family violence", *Social Science Research* sep 80 : 193-215. [USA.]

5843 BERKMAN, Ronald. *Opening the gates: the rise of the prisoners' movement.* Lexington, MA, Lexington Books, 79, xii-200 p.

5844 BERNS, Walter. *For capital punishment: crime and the morality of the death penalty.* New York, Basic Books, 79, x-214 p. CR: Ernest VAN DEN HAAG, *American political science Review* 74(2), jun 80: 470-471.

5845 BERTRAND, Marie-Andrée. *La Femme et le crime.* Montréal, l'Aurore, 79, 224 p.

5846 BLOOM, Howard S. "Evaluating human service and correctional programs by modeling the timing of recidivism", *Sociological Methods and Research* nov 79 : 179-208.

5847 BOTTOMLEY, A. Keith. *Criminology in focus: past trends and future prospects.* New York, Barnes & Noble Books, 79, ix-181 p.

5848 BRAITHWAITE, John. *Inequality, crime, and public policy.* London, Boston, Routledge and K. Paul, 79, xiii-332 p.

5849 BRAITHWAITE, John; BILES, David. "Crime victimisation rates in Australian cities", *Australian and New Zealand Journal of Sociology* 16, mar 80 : 79-83.

5850 BRAUNGART, Margaret; BRAUNGART, Richard G.; HOYER, William J. "Age, sex, and social factors in fear of crime", *Sociological Focus* 13, jan 80 : 55-66.

5851 BROWN, Don W.; MCDOUGAL, Stephen L. "Non-compliance with law: a utility analysis of city crime rates", *Policy Studies Review Annual* 78 : 554-573.

5852 BURSIK, Robert J. Jr. "The dynamics of specialization in juvenile offenses", *Social Forces* 58, mar 80 : 851-864.

5853 BURT, Martha R. "Cultural myths and supports for rape", *Journal of Personality and social Psychology* 38, feb 80 : 217-230.

5854 BUTELER, Patricio. "Panorama actual de la criminología" (Present situation of criminology), *Boletín de Ciencias políticas y sociales* 24, 79 : 189-209.

5855 CANTOR, David; COHEN, Lawrence E. "Comparing measures of homicide trends: methodological and substantive differences in the vital statistics and uniform crime report time series, 1933-1975", *Social Science Research* jun 80 : 121-145. [USA.]

5856 CARR-HILL, R. A.; STERN, N. H. *Crime, the police and criminal statistics: An analysis of official statistics for England and Wales using econometric methods.* London, New York, San Francisco, Harcourt Brace Jovanovich, Academic Press, 79, xiv-356 p.

5857 CHANG, Dae H.; [ed.]. *Introduction to criminal justice: theory and application.* Dubuque, IA, Kendall/Hunt Pub. Co., 79, ix-395 p.

5858 COHEN, Lawrence E.; FELSON, Marcus; LAND, Kenneth C. "Property crime rates in the United States: a macrodynamic analysis, 1947-1977; with ex ante forecasts for the mid-1980s", *American Journal of Sociology* 86, jul 80 : 90-118.

5859 Conseil de l'Europe. *Transformation sociale et délinquance juvénile.* Conseil de l'Europe, Affaires juridiques, Comité européen pour les problèmes criminels. Strasbourg, Conseil de l'Europe, 79, 158 p.

5860 DODGE, Calvert R. *A world without prisons: alternatives to incarceration throughout the world.* Lexington, MA, Lexington Books, 79, xxi-273 p.

5861 DUVALL, Donna; BOOTH, Alan. "Social class, stress and physical punishment", *International Review of modern Sociology* jan-jun 79 : 103-117.

5862 EISENBERG, Ulrich. *Kriminologie* (Criminology). Köln, Berlin, Bonn, München, Heymann, 79, xix-692 p.
5863 ELLIOTT, Delbert S.; AGETON, Suzanne S. "Reconciling race and class differences in self-reported and official estimates of delinquency", *American sociological Review* 45, feb 80 : 95-110.
5864 ELLIS, Desmond. "The prison guard as carceral Luddite: a critical review of the MacGuigan Report on the penitentiary system in Canada", *Canadian Journal of Sociology* 79 : 43-64.
5865 Bibl.XXIX-5780. EMPEY, Lamar T. *American delinquency: its meaning and construction.* CR: Travis HIRSHI, *Contemporary Sociology (Albany)* 9(3), mai 80 : 372-373.
5866 EMPEY, Lamar T.; [ed.]. *The Future of childhood and juvenile justice.* Charlottesville, University Press of Virginia, 80, vi-422 p.
5867 ERICSON, Richard; [ed.]. "Special issue on criminology", *Canadian Journal of Sociology* 80 : 209-311.
5868 ERISTAIN, Tonio. "Treatment of young delinquents in Spain and the Basque country from 1936 to 1978", *International Journal of the Sociology of Law* aug 80 : 277-296.
5869 FALKIN, Gregory P. *Reducing delinquency: a strategic planning approach.* Lexington, MA, Lexington Books, 79, xix-212 p.
5870 FARBEROW, Norman L.; [ed.]. *The many faces of suicide: indirect self-destructive behavior.* New York, McGraw-Hill, 80, xvi-446 p.
5871 FARLEY, Reynolds. "Homicide trends in the United States", *Demography* 17, mai 80 : 177-188.
5872 FEELEY, Malcolm M. *The process is the punishment: handling cases in a lower criminal court.* New York, Russell Sage Foundation, 79, xxii-323 p. CR: Burton M. ATKINS, *American political Science Review* 74(3), sep 80: 820-822.
5873 FEIN, Helen. *Accounting for genocide: national response and Jewish victimization during the Holocaust.* New York, Free Press, 79, 468 p. CR: Irving Louis HOROWITZ, *Contemporary Sociology (Albany)* 9(4), jul 80: 489-492.
5874 FINGARETTE, Herbert; HASS, Ann Fingarette. *Mental disabilities and criminal responsibility.* Berkeley, University of California Press, 79, xi-321 p. [USA.]
5875 FOUST, Cleon H.; WEBSTER, D. Robert; [eds.]. *An Anatomy of criminal justice: a system overview.* Lexington, MA, Lexington Books, 80, xiv-325 p.
5876 FRIEDENBERG, Edgar Z. "The punishment industry in Canada", *Canadian Journal of Sociology* 80 : 273-283.
5877 GEIS, Gilbert; STOTLAND, Ezra; [eds.]. *White-collar crime: theory and research.* Beverly Hills, CA, Sage Publications, 80, 320 p.
5878 GIANNITI, Francesco. *L'importanza della psicologia e della sociologia nel processo penale* (The importance of psychology and sociology in criminal procedure). Bologna, Pàtron, 79, 29 p.
5879 GIBBSON, Don C. *The criminological enterprise: theories and perspectives.* Englewood Cliffs, NJ, Prentice-Hall, 79, 226 p. CR: Robert F. MEIER, *Contemporary Sociology (Albany)* 9(3), mai 80 : 374-376.
5880 GILCHRIST, Bruce W. "Disproportionality in sentences of imprisonment", *Columbia Law Review* 79, oct 79 : 1119-1167.
5881 GOETHALS, J. "Actualités bibliographiques: les effets psycho-sociaux des longues peines d'emprisonnement", *Déviance et Société* mar 80 : 81-101.
5882 GRABOSKY, P. N. *Social Indicators Research* (1-4), jan 80 : 63-70.
5883 GREENBERG, David F. "Crime deterrence research and social policy", *Policy Studies* 77 : 461-475.
5884 GREENBERG, Martin S.; [et al.]. "Social and emotional determinants of victim crime reporting", *Social Psychology Quarterly* 42, dec 79 : 364-372.
5885 GROTH, A. Nicholas. *Men who rape: the psychology of the offender.* New York, Plenum Press, 79, xviii-227 p.
5886 GUIBOURDENCHE DE CABEZAS, Marta. "El suicidio en Mendoza" (Suicide in Mendoza), *Boletín de Ciencias políticas y sociales* 22, 78 : 135-158.
5887 Bibl.XXIX-5786. HACKLER, James C. *Prevention of youthful crime: the great stumble forward.* CR: Robert B. COATES., *Contemporary Sociology (Albany)* 9(2), mar 80: 230-231.
5888 HAGAN, John. "Symbolic justice: the status politics of the American probation movement", *Sociological Focus* 12, oct 79 : 295-309. [Marxian and Weberian perspectives on crime and law.]
5889 HAGAN, John; LEON, Jeffrey. "The rehabilitation of law: a social-historical comparison of probation in Canada", *Canadian Journal of Sociology* 80 : 235-251.

5890	HAGAN, John; NAGEL-BERNSTEIN, Ilene H.; ALBONETTI, Celesta. "The differential sentence of white-collar offenders in ten federal district courts", *American sociological Review* 45, oct 80 : 802-820. [USA.]
5891	HALLEN, G. C. "Suicide and Karma", *Indian Journal of social Research* 20, apr 79 : 49-63. [India.]
5892	HAMILTON, V. Lee; RYTINA, Steve. "Social consensus on norms of justice: should the punishment fit the crime?", *American Journal of Sociology* 85, mar 80 : 1117-1144.
5893	HANDIN, Kenneth H.; MANCUSO, James C. "Perceptions of the functions of reprimand", *Journal of social Psychology* 110, feb 80 : 43-52.
5894	HARRELL, W. Andrew; GOLTZ, J. Walter. "Effect of victim's need and previous accusation of theft upon bystander's reaction to theft", *Journal of social Psychology* 112, oct 80 : 41-49.
5895	HARTNAGE, Timothy F.; GILLIAN, Mary Ellen. "Female prisoners and the inmate code", *Pacific sociological Review* 23, jan 80 : 85-104.
5896	HEUER, Gerhild. *Selbstmord bei Kindern und Jugendlichen*. Stuttgart, Klett-Cotta, 79, 152 p.
5897	HINDELANG, Michael J.; HIRSCHI, Travis; WEIS, Joseph G. "Correlates of delinquency: the illusion of discrepancy between self-report and official measures", *American sociological Review* 44, dec 79 : 995-1014.
5898	HIRSCHI, Travis; GOTTFREDSON, Michael. *Criminal behavior. Current theory and research*. Beverly Hills, CA, Sage Publications, 80, 160 p.
5899	HOENACK, Stephen A.; WEILER, William C. "A structural model of murder behavior and the criminal justice system", *American economic Review* 70, jun 80 : 327-341.
5900	INCIARDI, James A.; FAUPEL, Charles E. *History and Crime: Implications for criminal justice policy*. Beverly Hills, CA, Sage Publications, 80, 296 p.
5901	INDRA, Jeet Singh. *Indian prison: a sociological enquiry*. Delhi, Concept, 79, x-179 p.
5902	JACKALL, Robert. "Crime in the suites", *Contemporary Sociology* mai 80 : 354-358. [survey essay.]
5903	JACOB, Herbert. *Crime and justice in urban America*. Englewood Cliffs, NJ, Prentice-Hall, 80, ix-198 p.
5904	JANKOVIČ, Ivan. "Rushe-Kirchheimerova sociologija kazne" (Rusche-Kirchheimer's sociology of punishment), *Sociologija* 22(1-2), 80 : 111-125.
5905	JANKOVIČ, Ivan. "Rushe-Kirchheimerova sociologija kazne" (Rusche-Kirchheimer's sociology of punishment), *Sociologija* 22(1-2), 80 : 111-125.
5906	JENSEN, Gary F.; ROJEK, Dean G. *Delinquency, a sociological view*. Lexington, MA, D. C. Heath, 80, viii-408 p.
5907	KELLOUGH, D. G.; BRICKEY, S. L.; GREENAWAY, W. K. "The politics of incarceration: Manitoba, 1918-1939", *Canadian Journal of Sociology* 80 : 253-271.
5908	Bibl.XXIX-5795. KELLY, Delos H.; [ed.]. *Delinquent behavior: interactional and motivational aspects*. CR: Patrick G. DONNELLY, *Contemporary Sociology (Albany)* 9(3), mai 80: 393.
5909	Bibl.XXIX-5797. KORNHAUSER, Ruth Rosner. *Social sources of delinquency: an appraisal of analytic models*. CR: Robert F. MEIER, *American Journal of Sociology* 86(3), nov 80 : 678-680.
5910	LABADIE, J. M. "Limites et chances d'une réflexion psychanalytique en criminologie", *Déviance et Société* déc 79 : 301-322.
5911	LAFREE, Gary D. "The effect of sexual stratification by race on official reactions to rape", *American sociological Review* 45, oct 80 : 842-854. [USA.]
5912	LAFREE, Gary D. "Variables affecting guilty pleas and convictions in rape cases: toward a social theory of rape processing", *Social Forces* 58, mar 80 : 833-850.
5913	LEBLANC, Marc; [et al.]. "La délinquance juvénile: son développement psychosocial durant l'adolescence", *Annales de Vaucresson* 78 : 11-54.
5914	LÉVY, Thierry. *Le désir de punir: essai sur le privilège pénal*. Paris, Fayard, 79, 259 p.
5915	LEYTON, Elliott. *The myth of delinquency: an anatomy of juvenile nihilism*. Toronto, McClelland and Stewart, 79, 220 p.
5916	LITTRELL, W. Boyd. *Bureaucratic justice: police, prosecutors, and plea bargaining*. Beverly Hills, CA, Sage Publications, 79, 284 p.
5917	LÓPEZ, Ernesto. "El poder disciplinario de Foucault" (The disciplinary power in Foucault's works), *Revista mexicana de Sociología* 41, oct-dec 79 : 1421-1432.
5918	LOURDJANE, Ahmed. "La réforme pénitentiaire en Algérie", *Revue algérienne des Sciences juridiques, économiques et politiques* 15, mar 78 : 75-93.
5919	MALAMUTH, Neil M.; HEIM, Maggie; FESHBACH, Seymour. (Sexual responsiveness of college students to rape depictions: inhibitory and disinhibitory effects), *Journal*

of Personality and social Psychology 38, mar 80 : 399-408. [with a comment by Carolyn Wood SHERIF: 409-415.]

5920 MATHIAS, William J.; RESCORLA, Richard C.; STEPHENS, Eugene. *Foundations of criminal justice.* Englewood Cliffs, NJ, Prentice-Hall, 80, x-575 p.

5921 MATHIESEN, Thomas. "The future of control systems, the case of Norway", *International Journal of the Sociology of Law* mai 80 : 149-164.

5922 MATSUMOTO, Toshiaki. "Jisatsu no shinri, shakaiteki yoin ni kansuru kenkyu -jisatsu rojin no life history no bunseki o chushin toshite" (Research on the psychology of suicide and its primary social causes — Life history analysis of elderly people who have committed suicide), *Otsuma joshidaigaku kaseigakubu kiyo* 16, 80 : 135-152.

5923 MAWBY, Rob. "Sex and crime: the results of a self-report study", *British Journal of Sociology* 31, dec 80 : 525-543. [Sample: Sheffield.]

5924 MAXFIELD, Michael G.; LEWIS, Dan A.; SZOC, Ron. "Producing official crimes: verified crime reports as measure of police output", *Social Science Quarterly* 61, sep 80 : 221-236. [USA, Chicago.]

5925 MCCAGHY, Charles H. *Crime in American society.* New York, Macmillan, 80, xiii-368 p.

5926 Bibl.XXIX-5800. MCCALL, George J. *Observing the law: field methods in the study of crime and the criminal justice system.* CR: Judson R. LANDIS, *Contemporary Sociology (Albany)* 9(2), mar 80 : 233-234.

5927 MCCORD, Joan. "Some child-rearing antecedents of criminal behavior in adult men", *Journal of Personality and social Psychology* 37, sep 79 : 1477-1486.

5928 MCDONALD, William F.; [ed.]. *The Prosecutor.* Beverly Hills, CA, Sage Publications, 79, 288 p.

5929 MCMULLAN, John L. "'Maudits voleurs': racketeering and the collection of private debts in Montreal", *Canadian Journal of Sociology* 80 : 121-145.

5930 MILLER, Marv. *Suicide after sixty: the final alternative.* New York, Springer Pub. Co., 79, 118 p.

5931 MIRANDE, Alfredo. "Fear of crime and fear of the police in a Chicano community", *Sociology and social Research* 64, jul 80 : 528-541.

5932 MOLNÁR, József. "Juvenile delinquency in large cities", *Acta juridica (Budapest)* 21(1-2), jan-jun 79 : 63-83.

5933 MOLNÁR, József. "Die Deviation und Jugendkriminalität antisozialen Gruppen" (Deviance and juvenile delinquency of antisocial groups), *Annales Universitatis Scientiarum budapestinensis de Rolando Eötvös nominatae. Sectio iuridica* 20, 78 : 127-138.

5934 MYERS, Martha A. "Personal and situational contingencies in the processing of convicted felons", *Sociological Inquiry* 50, 80 : 65-74.

5935 MYERS, Martha A. "Offended parties and official reactions: victims and the sentencing of criminal defendants", *Sociological Quarterly* 20, 79 : 529-540.

5936 MYERS, Samuel L. "Why are crimes underreported? What is the crime rate? Does it really matter?", *Social Science Quarterly* 61, jun 80 : 23-43. [USA.]

5937 NAAFS, J.; SARIS, W. E. "Diefstal door middel van brak. Diachronische analyse van een delict in Amsterdam" (Theft with house-breaking. Diachronic analysis of a crime in Amsterdam), *Mens en Maatschappij* 54, nov 79 : 387-419.

5938 NAGEL, W. H. "A social-legal view on the suppression of terrorists", *International Journal of the Sociology of Law* aug 80 : 213-226.

5939 NEEDLEMAN, Martin L.; NEEDLEMAN, Carolyn. "Organizational crime: two models of criminogenesis", *Sociological Quarterly* 20, 79 : 517-528.

5940 NETTLER, Gwynn. "Criminal justice", *Annual Review of Sociology* 79 : 27-52.

5941 NIETZEL, Michael T. *Crime and its modification: a social learning perspective.* Elmsford, NY, Pergamon Press, 79, viii-301 p.

5942 O'BRIEN, John T.; MARCUS, Marvin; [eds.]. *Crime and justice in America: critical issues for the future.* New York, Pergamon Press, 79, xx-361 p.

5943 OATMAN, Eric; [ed.]. *Crime and society.* New York, H. W. Wilson Co., 79, 216 p.

5944 OFFER, Daniel; MAROHN, Richard C.; OSTROV, Eric. *The psychological world of the juvenile delinquent.* New York, Basic Books, 79, xi-224 p.

5945 OLIVER, M. J. "Epilepsy, crime and delinquency: a sociological account", *Sociology* 14, aug 80 : 417-440.

5946 ŌMURA, Eishō. *Hikō no shakaigaku*(Social reality in delinquency; the labelling process in Japan). Kyoto, Sekai shiso-sha, 80, 208 p.

5947 OPP, Karl-Dieter; [ed.]. *Strafvollzug und Resozialisierung* (Punishment completion and resocialization). München, Wilhelm Fink Verlag, 79, 394 p. CR: Ekkehard KLAUSA, *Kölner Zeitschrift für Soziologie und Sozialpsychologie* 32(2), jun 80 : 400-401.

5948	OSBORNE, Harold W. "Juvenile delinquency: a survey review of recent texts (1977-1979)", *Contemporary Sociology* mai 80 : 358-367. [survey essay.]
5949	OSCHLIES, Wolf. Jugendkriminalität in Osteuropa(Juvenile delinquency in Eastern Europe). Köln, Wien, Böhlau, 79, xiii-217 p.
5950	OSTHEIMER, John M. "The polls: changing attitudes toward euthanasia", *Public Opinion Quarterly* 44, 80 : 123-128.
5951	PECK, Dennis L. *Fatalistic suicide.* Palo Alto, CA, R & E Research Associates, 79, v-126 p.
5952	PECK, Dennis L.; BHARADWAJ, Lakshmi K. "Personal stress and fatalism as factors in college suicide", *Social Science* 55, 80 : 19-24.
5953	PELFREY, William V. *The evolution of criminology.* Cincinnati, Anderson Pub. Co., 80, v-117 p.
5954	PEPINSKY, Harold E. *Crime control strategies: an introduction to the study of crime.* New York, Oxford University Press, 80, xvii-352 p.
5955	Bibl.XXIX-5808. PEREZ, Joseph F. *The family roots of adolescent delinquency.* CR: Karl SCHONBORN, *Contemporary Sociology (Albany)* 9(3), mai 80 : 392-393.
5956	PERROT, Michelle. *L'Impossible prison: recherches sur le système pénitentiaire au XIXe siècle.* Paris, Éditions du Seuil, 80, 317 p.
5957	PFEIFFER, Dietmar K.; SCHEERER, Sebastian. *Kriminalsoziologie: e. Einf. in Theorien u. Themen* (Criminal sociology: an introduction to theories and topics). Stuttgart, Berlin, Köln, Mainz, Kohlhammer, 79, 168 p.
5958	PHILLIPS, David P. "The deterrent effect of capital punishment: new evidence on an old controversy", *American Journal of Sociology* 86, jul 80 : 139-148.
5959	PINATEL, Jean. *La Criminologie.* Paris, Éditions ouvrières, 79, 224 p.
5960	POLLACK, Lance M.; PATTERSON, Arthur H. "Territoriality and fear of crime in elderly and non-elderly home owners", *Journal of social Psychology* 111, jun 80 : 119-129.
5961	RAFFEL PRICE, Barbara. *Criminal justice research: new models and findings.* Beverly Hills, CA, Sage Publications, 80, 160 p.
5962	RANKIN, Joseph H. "School factors and delinquency: interactions by age and sex", *Sociology and social Research* 64, apr 80 : 420-434.
5963	RASKÓ, Gabriella. "Significance and features of female criminality", *Acta juridica (Budapest)* 21(1-2), jan-jun 79 : 105-120.
5964	REICHEL, Philip L. "Teaching about crime in Communist societies", *Teaching Sociology* jan 80 : 141-162.
5965	REUBAND, Karl-Heinz. "Sanktionsverlagen im Wandel. Die Einstellung zur Todesstrafe in der Bundesrepublik Deutschland seit 1950" (Change in punishment. The situation of capital punishment in the Federal Republic of Germany since 1950), *Kölner Zeitschrift für Soziologie und Sozialpsychologie* 32, 80 : 535-558.
5966	ROBIN, Gerald D. *Introduction to the criminal justice system: principles, procedures, practice.* New York, Harper & Row, 80, xvii-558 p.
5967	SAGARIN, Edward; [ed.]. *Criminology: new concerns.* Beverly Hills, CA, Sage Publications, 79, 191 p.
5968	SAGARIN, Edward; [ed.]. *Taboos in criminology.* Beverly Hills, CA, Sage Publications, 80, 152 p.
5969	SANDER, Günther. *Abweichendes Verhalten in der DDR: Kriminalitätstheorien in e. sozialist. Gesellschaft* (Deviant behaviour in the GDR: criminality theories in a socialist society). Frankfurt/Main, New York, Campus-Verlag, 79, 134 p.
5970	SCHWARZ, Louis; [et al.]. "Role of commitments in the decision to stop a theft", *Journal of social Psychology* 110, apr 80 : 183-192.
5971	SELLIN, Johan Thorsten. *The penalty of death.* Beverly Hills, CA, Sage Publications, 80, 190 p.
5972	SEYLER, M. "La banalisation péitentiaire ou le voeu d'une réforme impossible", *Déviance et Société* jun 80 : 131-147.
5973	SHARMA, Arvind. "Emile Durkheim on suttee as suicide", *International Journal of contemporary Sociology* 15(3-4), jul-oct 78 : 283-291.
5974	SHELLEY, Louise. "The geography of Soviet criminality", *American sociological Review* 45, feb 80 : 111-122.
5975	SHICHOR, David; KELLY, Delos H.; [eds]. *Critical issues in juvenile delinquency.* Lexington, MA, Lexington Books, 80, vii-347 p.
5976	SHUR, Irene G.; LITTELL, Franklin H.; WOLFGANG, Marvin E.; [eds.]. "Reflections on the holocaust: historical, philosophical and educational dimensions", *Annals of the American Academy of political and social Science* 450, jul 80 : 1-256.

5977 Bibl.XXIX-5816. SILBERMAN, Charles E. *Criminal violence, criminal justice.* CR: Donald R. CRESSEY; Clarence SHRAG; James F. SHORT Jr., *Contemporary Sociology (Albany)* 9(3), mai 80: 341-353.

5978 SINDEN, Peter G. "Perceptions of crime in capitalist America: the question of consciousness manipulation", *Sociological Focus* 13, jan 80 : 75-85.

5979 SINGER, L. R. "Supporting surveillance: probation as discipline theorizing care and control: a reintroduction", *International Journal of the Sociology of Law* aug 80 : 251-275.

5980 SINGH, B. K. "Correlates of attitudes toward euthanasia", *Social Biology* 26, 79 : 247-254.

5981 SMITH, Douglas A.; VISHER, Christy A. "Sex and involvement in deviance/crime: a quantitative review of the empirical literature", *American sociological Review* 45, aug 80 : 691-701.

5982 SMITH, M. Dwayne; PARKER, Robert Nash. "Type of homicide and variation in regional rates", *Social Forces* 59, sep 80 : 136-147.

5983 STEFFENSMEIER, Darrell J. "Sex differences in patterns of adult crimes 1965-77: a review and assessment", *Social Forces* 58, jun 80 : 1080-1108.

5984 Bibl.XXIX-5866. STREIB, Victor L. *Juvenile justice in America.* CR: Theodore N. FERDINAND, *Contemporary Sociology (Albany)* 9(1), jan 80: 100-101.

5985 TOBIAS, John Jacob. *Crime and police in England, 1700-1900.* New York, St Martin's Press, 79, 194 p.

5986 TOBY, Jackson. "Crime in American public schools", *Public Interest* 58, wint 80 : 18-42.

5987 TYLER, Tom R. "Impact of directly and indirectly experienced events: the origin of crime-related judgments and behaviors", *Journal of Personality and social Psychology* 39, jul 80 : 13-28.

5988 UHLMAN, Thomas M.; WALKER, N. Darlene. "A plea is no bargain: the impact of case disposition on sentencing", *Social Science Quarterly* 60, sep 79 : 218-234.

5989 VAN DIJK, J. J. M. "L'influence des medias sur l'opinion publique relative à la criminalité: un phénomène exceptionnel?", *Déviance et Société* jun 80 : 107-129.

5990 VAN OUTRIVE, Lode. "Le système pénitentiaire en Belgique: un système bloqué", *Revue interdisciplinaire d'Études juridiques* 79 : 1-35.

5991 WARD, David A. "The theft of criminology from sociology", *Contemporary Sociology* mai 80 : 368-371. [survey essay.]

5992 WEISSER, Michael R. *Crime and punishment in early modern Europe.* Atlantic Highlands, NJ, Humanities Press, 79, xi-193 p.

5993 WICKMAN, Peter M.; WHITTEN, Phillip; LEVEY, Robert. *Criminology, perspectives on crime and criminality.* Lexington, MA, D. C. Heath, 80, 628 p.

5994 WILLIAMS, Kirk R.; GIBBS, Jack P.; ERICKSON, Ma ynard L. "Public knowledge of statutory penalties: the extent and basis of accurate perception", *Pacific sociological Review* 23, jan 80 : 105-127.

20200. SOCIAL POLICY
POLITIQUE SOCIALE

20210. Social action. Social planning
Action sociale. Planification sociale

[See also / voir aussi: 757, 852, 999, 1069, 1352, 1460, 1561, 1922, 2235, 2935, 3963, 4410, 4665, 5217, 5773, 5775, 6122]

5995 ABEL-SMITH, Brian. "The welfare State: breaking the post-war consensus", *Political Quarterly* 51, jan-mar 80 : 17-34. [UK.]

5996 AGAFONOV, O. V. "Social'noe planirovanie — važnejšee sredstvo soveršenstvovanija upravlenija razvitym socialističeskim obščestvom" (Social planning is an essential way for improving the developed socialist society management), *IN: Problemy naučnogo upravlenija socialističeskom obščestvom.* Riga, 78 : 59-69.

5997 ALBER, Jens. "Der Wohlfahrtstaat in der Krise? Eine Bilanz nach drei Jahrzehnten Sozialpolitik in der Bundesrepublik" (A crisis of the Welfare State? An evaluation of 30 years of social policy in the FRG), *Zeitschrift für Soziologie* oct 80 : 313-342.

5998 AMELINE, Claude. "Des bénévoles par millions: l'action sociale volonatire en Grande Bretagne", *Revue française des Affaires sociales* 33, oct-dec 79 : 37-47.

5999 AOI, Kazuo; NAOI, Atsushi; [eds.]. *Fukushi to keikaku no shakaigaku* (Sociology of social welfare and social planning). Tokyo, Tokyo daigaku shuppankai, 80, 270 p.

6000 ARTS, W. "Politieke filosofie en sociologie: het probleem van de verdelende rechtvaardigheid" (Political philosophy and sociology: the problem of distributive justice), *Mens en Maatschappij* 55, dec 80 : 343-384.

6001 BELONOVSKIJ, V. N. "K voprosu stanovlenija sistemy upravlenija socialističeskogo tipa" (On the future of the socialist type management system), *IN: Problemy upravlenija v uslovijah razvitogo socializma.* Moskva, 79 : 18-27.

6002 BERKOWITZ, Edward D. *Creating the welfare state: the political economy of twentieth-century reform.* New York, Praeger, 80, xv-185 p.

6003 BERKOWITZ, Edward D.; MCQUAID, Kim. "Bureaucrats as 'social engineers': federal welfare programs in Herbert Hoover's America", *American Journal of Economics and Sociology* 39, oct 80 : 321-335. [(1920; 1933-1938).]

6004 BERKOWITZ, Edward D.; MCQUAID, Kim. "Welfare reform in the 1950s", *Social Service Review* 54, mar 80 : 45-58.

6005 BOIS, Philippe. "Spécificités de la politique sociale en Suisse", *Revue française des Affaires sociales* 34, jul-sep 80 : 189-209.

6006 BORJAKOV, V. I. "Povyšenie urovnja naučnogo upravlenija social'nymi processami v uslovijah razvitogo socializma" (The elevation of the social processes scientific management level under conditions of developed socialism), *IN: Social'nye i političeskie otnošenija v razvitom socialističeskom obščestve.* Moskva, 79 : 10-20.

6007 BROOKE, Rosalind. *Law, justice, and social policy.* London, Croom Helm, 79, 136 p. [United Kingdom.]

6008 BROWNING, Rufus P.; [et al.]. "Implementation and political change: sources of local variations in federal social programs", *Policy Studies Journal* 80 : 616-632. [USA.]

6009 BURLAJ, E. V.; MEL'NIČENKO, A. I. "O nauke social'nogo upravlenija i eě predmete" (On the science of social management and its object), *Problemy Pravovedenija* 39, 79 : 35-41.

6010 BURTON, John Wear. *Deviance, terrorism & war: the process of solving unsolved social and political problems.* New York, St. Martin's Press, 79, xv-240 p.

6011 CESAREO, Vincenzo. "Consenso e legittimazione nello Stato assistenziale" (Consensus and legitimation in the welfare state), *Studi di Sociologia* 17, jul-sep 79 : 249-256.

6012 CHEVALLIER, Jacques. "La fin de l'Etat providence", *Projet* 143, mar 80 : 262-273.

6013 COLEMAN, James William; CRESSEY, Donald R. *Social problems.* New York, Harper & Row, 80, xvii-584 p.

6014 COUGHLIN, Richard M. *Ideology, public opinion, & welfare policy: attitudes toward taxes and spending in industrialized societies.* Berkeley, Institute of International Studies, University of California, 80, xvi-195 p.

6015 DEGTJAREVA, A. I. "Nekotorye voprosy upravlenija duhovnoj zizn'ju socialističeskogo obščestva" (Some questions on the management of the socialist society intellectual life), *Političeskaja Organizacija Obščestva i Upravlenija pri Socializme* 79 : 113-126.

6016 ESPINOSA, Justiniano. "Una política social para el pueblo colombiano" (A social policy for the Colombian people), *Revista javeriana* 92(459), oct 79 : 363-366.

6017 FELFE, Edeltraut. *Das Dilemma der Theorie vom "Wohlfahrsstaat": e. Analyse d. "schwed. Modells"* (The dilemma of welfare state theory: an analysis of the Swedish model). Berlin, Deutscher Verlag der Wissenschaften, 79, 170 p.

6018 FERGE, Zsuzsa. *Társadalompolitikai tanulmányok* (Studies on societal policy). Budapest, Gondolat, 80, 425 p.

6019 FILIN, Ju. N. "Social'naja obuslovlennost' vozrastanija roli politiki v obščestve razvitogo socializma" (Social determination of the elevation of social policy in the developed socialism society), *Političeskaja Organizacija Obščestva i Upravlenija pri Socializme* 79 : 103-113.

6020 FOURNIER, Jacques; QUESTIAUX, Nicole. *Le pouvoir du social.* Paris, Presses universitaires de France, 79, 288 p.

6021 FOX PIVEN, Francis; CLOWARD, Richard A. "Sozialpolitik und politische Bewusstseinsbildung" (Social policy and political consciousness education), *Leviathan* 79 : 283-307.

6022 FRIEDMANN, John. *The Good Society: a personal account of its struggle with the world of social planning and dialectical inquiry into the roots of radical practice.* Cambridge, MA, MIT Press, 79, xvii-199 p.

6023 FRIEZE, Irene Hanson; BAR-TAL, Daniel; CARROLL, John S.; [eds.]. *New approaches to social problems.* San Francisco, Jossey-Bass, 79, xxii-472 p.

6024 FRITLINSKIJ, V. S. "Metodologičeskie problemy social'nogo planirovanija" (Methodological problems of social planning), *IN: Metodologičeskie problemy sociologičeskogo issledovanija.* Moskva, 79 : 174-223.

6025 GIDDENS, Anthony. *Central problems in social theory: action, structure and contradiction in social analysis*. Berkeley, University of California Press, 79, x-294 p. CR: James MILLER, *American political Science Review* 74(4), dec 80 : 1055-1056.

6026 GINSBURG, Norman. *Class, capital and social policy*. London, Macmillan, 79, xv-192 p. CR: R. V. SEIFERT, *British Journal of Sociology* 31(4), dec 80: 596-598.

6027 GLICK, Leonard; HEBDING, Daniel E. *Introduction to social problems*. Reading, MA, Addison-Wesley Pub. Co., 80, xiii-523 p.

6028 GORBUNOVA, L. N. "Aktual'nye problemy teorii i praktiki social'nogo planirovanija" (Topical problems of the social planning theory and practice), *IN: Socialističeskij proizvodstvennyj kollektiv*. Moskva, 79 : 29-42.

6029 GORDON, L.; KLOPOV, Ė. "Ulučšenie byta trudjaščihsja-ogromnaja oblast' social'noj politiki KPSS i Sovetskogo gosudarstva" (The workers life amelioration is an essential part of the CPSU and Soviet state social policy), *IN: Vo imja čeloveka truda: social'naja politika v sovetskom sojuze i PNR*. Moskva, 79 : 145-166.

6030 GOUGH, Ian. *The political economy of the welfare state*. London, Macmillan, 79, xii-196 p. [United Kingdom.]CR: Robert V. SEIFERT, *British Journal of Sociology* 31(4), dec 80 : 596-598.

6031 GRAYCAR, Adam. "Backlash overload and the welfare State", *Australian Quarterly* 51, sep 79 : 16-28.

6032 GRIGOROV, V. M. "O kompleksom podhode k upravleniju social'nymi processami" (On the complex approach to the social processes management), *Problemy naučnogo Kommunizma (Moskva)* 13, 79 : 67-83.

6033 GRIGOROV, V. M. "O kompleksnom podhode k upravleniju social'nymi processami" (On the complex approach to social processes management), *IN: Problemy naučnogo kommunizma. XIII*. Moskva, 79 : 67-83.

6034 GUR'JANOV, S. T.; ARESTOVA, A. S. *Social'nye problemy trudovogo kollektiva* (Social problems of a labour collectivity). Moskva, Izdatel'stvo Moskovskogo Universiteta, 79, 138 p.

6035 HAM, Chris. "Approaches to the study of social policy making", *Policy and Politics* jan 80 : 55-71.

6036 HASTINGS, William M. *How to think about social problems: a primer for citizens*. New York, Oxford University Press, 79, 251 p. CR: Michael BROOKS, *Contemporary Sociology (Albany)* 9(4), jul 80: 549-550.

6037 HEFFERNAN, W. Joseph. *Introduction to social welfare policy: power, scarcity, and common human needs*. Itasca, IL, F. E. Peacock Publishers, 79, viii-323 p.

6038 HERBERT, David T.; SMITH, David M.; [eds.]. *Social problems and the city: geographical perspectives*. Oxford, New York, Oxford University Press, 79, xi-271 p. [United Kingdom.]

6039 HIGGINS, Joan. "Social control theories of social policy", *Journal of social Policy* jan 80 : 1-23.

6040 HILL, Michael J.; LAING, Peter. *Social work and money*. London, Boston, G. Allen and Unwin, 79, 120 p.

6041 HOROWITZ, Irving Louis. *Constructing policy: dialogues with social scientists in the national political arena*. New York, Praeger Publishers, 79, ix-244 p.

6042 HOROWITZ, Irving Louis. "Methods and strategies in evaluating equity research", *Social Indicators Research* jan 79 : 1-22.

6043 IATRIDIS, Demetrius S. *Social Planning and policy alternatives in Greece*. Athènes, 80, 320 p.

6044 ILIEVA, L. G. "K voprosu o ponjatii "social'naja aktivnost"" (On the concept of "social activity"), *IN: Social'nye problemy sovremennogo sela. II*. Jaroslavl', 78 : 120-138.

6045 ISMAEL, Jacqueline S. "Social policy and social change: the case of Iraq", *Arab Studies Quarterly* sum 80 : 235-248.

6046 ITO, Susumu. *Shihon-shugi taisei no kaikaku to henkaku* (Essays on social policy and democratic socialism). Tokyo, Shin hyoron, 80, 241 p.

6047 JANKOVIČ, Nevenka. "Socijalna politika i njeno ostvarivanje" (Social policy and its implementation), *Jugoslovenski Pregled* 24, mar 80 : 89-100. [Yugoslavia.]

6048 JASSO, Guillermina. "A new theory of distributive justice", *American sociological Review* 45, feb 80 : 3-32.

6049 JONES, Catherine. "Teaching social policy: some European perspectives", *Journal of social Policy* oct 79 : 509-526.

6050 Bibl. XXIX-5892. JONES, Kathleen; BROWN, John; BRADSHAW, Jonathan. *Issues in social policy*. CR: N. J. DEMERATH III, *Contemporary Sociology (Albany)* 9(2), mar 80 : 289-299.

6051 KAL'NOJ, I. I. "Sub'ektivnyj faktor i upravlenie social'nymi processami" (Subjective factor and the social processes management), *Politiĉeskaja Organizacija Obŝĉestva i Upravlenie pri Socializme* 79 : 108-112.

6052 KAWAKITA, Takashi. "Shakai keikaku to shakaigaku" (Social planning and sociology), *Kikan rodoho bessatsu gendai shakaigaku* 80 : 30-40.

6053 KERSTEIN, Robert; JUDD, Dennis R. "Achieving less influence with more democracy: the permanent legacy of the war on poverty", *Social Science Quarterly* 61, sep 80 : 208-220.

6054 KESSELMAN, Steven. *The modernization of American reform: structures and perceptions.* New York, Garland Pub., 79, 645 p.

6055 KRÜGER, Jürgen. "Anmerkungen zur sozialwissenschaftlichen Wiederentdeckung der Sozialpolitik" (Remarks on the social science coverage of social policy), *Archiv für Wissenschaft und Praxis der Sozialen Arbeit* 10, 79 : 241-255.

6056 KUĈENKO, V. I.; [ed.]. *Social'noe poznanie i social'noe upravlenie* (Social knowledge and social management). Kiev, Naukova Dumka, 79, 371 p.

6057 KUHNLE, Stein. "National equality and local-decision making: values in conflict in the development of the Norwegian welfare state", *Acta sociologica* 23(2-3), 80 : 97-111.

6058 KULIKOV, V. S. *Finansy i dal'nejŝij pod'em blagosostojanija sovetskogo naroda* (Finance and future growth of the Soviet people's welfare). Moskva, Finansy, 79, 160 p. [USSR.]

6059 KULKARNI, P. D. *Social policy and social development in India.* Madras, Association of Schools of Social Work in India, 79, 137 p.

6060 LEMAN, Christopher. *The collapse of welfare reform: political institutions, policy, and the poor in Canada and the United States.* Cambridge, MA, MIT Press, 80, xvii-292 p.

6061 LOPATA, P. P. "Suŝĉnost' osnovnye osobennosti social'noj politiki KPSS v uslovijah socializma" (Nature and essential characteristics of the CPSU social policy under conditions of socialism), *Problemy nauĉnogo Kommunizma (Moskva)* 13, 79 : 5-24.

6062 LOPATA, P. P. "Suŝĉnost' i osnovnye osobennosti social'noj politiki KPSS v uslovijah socializma" (Nature and essential characteristics of the CPSU social policy under conditions of socialism), IN: *Problemy nauĉnogo kommunizma. XIII.* Moskva, 79 : 5-24.

6063 MACDONALD, John Stuart. *Planning implementation and social policy: an evaluation of Ciudad Guayana, 1965 and 1975.* Oxford, Eng., New York, Pergamon Press, 79, 211 p.

6064 MARSH, David C.; [ed.]. *Introducing social policy.* London, Boston, Routledge & Kegan Paul, 79, ix-286 p.

6065 MATEJKO, Alexander J. "Work and the Welfare State: experiences from Sweden", *Revue internationale de sociologie / International Review of Sociology* 16, apr 80 : 19-52.

6066 MCBRIDE, William Leon. *Social theory at a crossroads.* Pittsburgh, Duquesne University Press, 80, ix-171 p.

6067 MĈEDLOV, M. P.; [et al.]. *Social'naja politika KPSS v uzlovijah razvitogo socializma* (The CPSU social policy under conditions of developed socialism). Moskva, Politizdat, 79, 432 p.

6068 MEENAGHAN, Thomas M.; WASHINGTON, Robert. *Social policy and social welfare: structure and applications.* New York, Free Press, 80, x-261 p.

6069 MITIN, M. B. "Social'noe upravlenie v socialistiĉeskom obŝĉestve" (Social management in the socialist society), IN: *Konstitucija obŝĉenarodnogo gosudarstva. Voprosy teorii.* Moskva, 79 : 264-289.

6070 NEBESKY, Milos. "Sur quelques aspects de la politique sociale en Tchécoslovaquie", *Aperçus sur l'Économie tchécoslovaque* mai 80 : 23-41.

6071 OLESNEVIĈ, L. A.; [et al.]. *Socia'noe upravlenie: bibliografiĉeskij ukazatel' literatury* [1966-1975] (Social planning: a bibliographical review, 1966-1975). L'vov, L'vovskaja Nauĉnaja Biblioteka imeni V. Stefanina AN USSR, 78, 374 p.

6072 PHILLIPS, Derek L. *Equality, justice, and rectification: an exploration in normative sociology.* London, New York, Academic Press, 79, viii-325 p.

6073 PODMARKOV, V. G. "Metodologiĉeskie problemy social'nogo planirovanija" (Methodological problems of social planning), IN: *Socialistiĉeskij proizvodstvennyj kollektiv.* Moskva, 79 : 98-114.

6074 PODMARKOV, V. G. "Social'noe planirovanie: opty i specifika" (Social planning: essay and specificity), *Sociologiĉeskie Issledovanija* 79 : 20-28.

6075 POMYKALOV, V. V. "Social'naja aktivnost' kak kategorija istotiĉeskogo materializma" (Social activity as a category of historical materialism), *Problemy social'noj Aktivnosti* 78 : 3-28.

6076 PUTIMSKIJ, È. B. "Ponjatie 'ispolnenie' i ègo rol' v social'nom upravlenii" (The "execution" conception and its role in social planning), IN: *Social'no-èkonomiĉeskie problemy razvitogo socialistiĉeskogo obŝĉestva.* Kalinin, 79 : 19-23.

6077 REIN, Martin. "Méthodes pour l'étude de l'interaction entre les sciences sociales et la politique sociale", *Revue internationale des Sciences sociales* 32, 80 : 385-394.

6078 RODRÍGUEZ Y RODRÍGUEZ, Federico. *Introducción en la política social: I, La política social como objeto de conocimiento: II, Los problemas metódicos de la política social* (Introduction to social policy: I, Social policy as an object of knowledge: II, Methodological problems of social policy). Madrid, Fundación Universidad-Empresa, 79, 462 p.

6079 ROGOVIN, V. Z. "Nekotorye voprosy social'nogo upravlenija v uslovijah naučno-tehničeskoj revoljucii" (Some social management questions under the conditions of scientific and technical revolution), *IN: Naučno-tehničeskaja revoljucija i problemy razvitija obščestva i kollektivov*. Moskva, 79 : 14-25.

6080 ROOM, Graham. *The sociology of welfare: social policy, stratification, and political order*. New York, St. Martin's Press, 79, xi-276 p.

6081 ROSENKO, M. N.; [et al.]. "Upravlenie v socialističeskom obščestve i perspektivy ego soveršentsvovanija: (obzor rabot sovetskih avtorov po aktual'nym problemom upravlenija)" (Management in the socialist society and forecasts of its improvement; a review of Soviet authors' works on management topical problems), *Političeskaja Organizacija Obščestva i Upravlenija pri Socializme* 79 : 124-133.

6082 ŠEPEL', V. M. "O ponjatii "social'noe upravlenie": na primere trudovogo kollektiva" (On the "social management" concept: from the labour collectivity example), *Problemy naučnogo Kommunizma (Moskva)* 13, 79 : 25-43.

6083 ŠEPEL', V. M. "O ponjatii 'social'noe upravlenie' (na primere trudovogo kollektiva)" (On the "social management" concept: from the team work example), *IN: Problemy naučnogo kommunizma. XIII*. Moskva, 79 : 25-43.

6084 SMITH, Gilbert. *Social need, policy, practice, and research*. London, Boston, Routledge & Kegan Paul, 80, x-216 p.

6085 SMITH, John H. "The human factor in social administration", *Journal of social Policy* oct 79 : 433-448.

6086 STANDFEST, Erich. *Sozialpolitik als Reformpolitik: Aspekte d. sozialpolit. Entwicklung in d. Bundesr.:publik Deutschland* (Social policy as reform policy: aspects of social policy development in the Federal Republic of Germany). Köln, Bund-Verlag, 79, 139 p.

6087 SULLIVAN, Thomas J.; [et al.]. *Social problems: divergent perspectives*. New York, Wiley, 80, xix-728 p.

6088 SUZUKI, Hiroshi; [ed.]. *Shakai riron to shakai taisei* (Social theory and social system). Kyoto, Akademia shuppankai, 80, 300 p.

6089 TASSEIT, Siegfried. "Zu den Bedingungen sozialer Planung — Konzeption und Praxis eines "Mitbestimmungs-Trainings" für die von sozialer Planung Betroffenen" (The conditions of social planning. Concept and practice of a "joint-management training" for persons concerned with social planning), *Neue Praxis* 79 : 299-312. [Germany FR.]

6090 TIMOFEEV, T. "Social'naja politika KPSS i razvitie rabočego klassa" (The CPSU social policy and the working class development), *IN: Vo imja celoveka truda: social'naja politika v sovetskom sojuze i PNR*. Moskva, 79 : 51-65.

6091 TOKUNAGA, Makoto; [ed.]. *Shakai-shiso-shi*(History of social thoughts). Tokyo, Kobundo, 80, 247 p.

6092 UPADHYAY, Jai Jai Ram. *Licensing power in India: a government action for social welfare*. New Delhi, S. Chand, 80, xii-469 p.

6093 VAN DRIEL, G. J.; HARTOG, J. A.; VAN RAVENZWAAIJ, C. *Limits to the welfare state: an inquiry into the realizability of socioeconomic and political desiderata in a highly industrialized society*. Boston, M. Nijhoff, 80, viii-180 p.

6094 VAN VUGHT, Frans. *Sociale Planning: oorsprong en ontwikkeling van het amerikaanse planningsdenken* (Social planning: origin and development of the American planning concept). Assen, Gorcum, 79, xviii-289 p.

6095 VERMEER, Edward B. "Social welfare provisions and the limits of inequality in contemporary China", *Asian Survey* 19, sep 79 : 856-880.

6096 VINGRÉ, Michel. *Le Social c'est fini: la nouvelle politique sociale: austérité, discipline, retour au marché*. Paris, "Autrement", 80, 228 p.

6097 VINOGRADOV, V. G.; GONČARUK, S. I. "Rol' prognostičeskih funkcij zakonov obščestva v sisteme upravlenija" (Role of society laws forecast functions in the management system), *IN: Problema social'noj zakonomernosti*. Gor'kij, 78 : 43-52.

6098 VOPLENKO, N. N. "Social'naja spravedlivost' i formy eě vyraženija v prave" (Social justice and its expression forms in law), *Sovetskoe Gosudarstvo i Pravo* 52(10), oct 79 : 39-46.

6099 VYLEGŽANIN, D. A.; ARTEMOV, G. P. "Social'noe samoupravlenie kak obščesociologičeskaja kategorija" (Social-self-management as a sociological category), *Političeskaja Organizacija Obščestva i Upravlenie pri Socializme* 79 : 113-119.
6100 WILSON, Dorothy. *The welfare state in Sweden: a study in comparative social administration*. London, Heinemann, 79, ix-171 p.
6101 WISEMAN, Jacqueline P. "Toward a theory of policy intervention in social problems", *Social Problems* 27, oct 79 : 3-18.
6102 YASUDA, Saburo; [et al.]; [eds.]. *Kiso shakaigaku dai l-kan: Shakaiteki kōi* (Fundamental sociology. I. Social action). Tokyo, Toyo keizai shinpōsha, 80, 241 p.
6103 ZDRAVOMYSLOV, A. "Teoretičeskie osnovy social'noj politiki KPSS v oblasti povyšenija blagosostojanija naroda" (Theoretical bases of the CPSU social policy in the people's welfare elevation sector), *IN: Vo imja čeloveka truda: social'naja politika v sovetskom sojuze i PNR*. Moskva, 79 : 102-119.
6104 ŽURAVLEV, G. T. "Problemy optimizacii upravlenija v ideologičeskoj sfere" (Problems of the management optimization in the ideological sphere), *Problemy naučnogo kommunizma (Moskva)* 13, 79 : 84-97.
6105 ZVORYKIN, A. A. "Nekotorye teoretičeskie i metodičeskie voprosy social'nogo upravlenija i planirovanija v proizvodstvennom i naučnom kollektive" (Some theoretical and methodological questions on social management and planning in the production and scientific collectivity), *IN: Socialističeskij proizvodstvennyj kollektiv*. Moskva, 79 : 43-62.

20220. Social security
Sécurité sociale

[See also / voir aussi: 1169, 3457, 3458, 3468, 5786, 6155]

6106 "Reaching the aged. Social services in forty four countries", *Social Service Delivery Systems* 79 : 7-256.
6107 ABERNATHY, Thomas J. Jr. "Selected aspects of Canadian family policy: their formulation, implementation and effects", *International Journal of the Sociology of the Family* jul-dec 79 : 209-219.
6108 BELANGER, Michel. "Les actions d'appui en faveur des personnes âgées", *Revue trimestrielle de Droit sanitaire et social* 15(60), oct-dec 79 : 449-463. [France.]
6109 Bureau International du Travail. Direction. "La sécurité sociale à la croisée des chemins", *Revue internationale du Travail* 119, mar-apr 80 : 147-160.
6110 BURKHAUSER, Richard V. "The early acceptance of social security: an asset maximization approach", *Industrial and Labor Relations Review* 33, jul 80 : 484-492.
6111 CHOWDHRY, D. Paul. *Child welfare development*. Delhi, Atma Ram, 80, xv-443 p.
6112 COOLEN, J. A. I. "Samenhang van voorzieningen voor bejaarden" (Patterns of supply in the health and welfare services for the aged), *Sociologische Gids* 27, jan-feb 80 : 47-66.
6113 DELLAPORTAS, G. "The effectiveness of public assistance payments in reducing poverty", *American Journal of Economics and Sociology* 39, apr 80 : 113-121.
6114 DODOUNEKOVA, Penka. "La Sécurité sociale dans la République populaire de Bulgarie", *Revue internationale de la Sécurité sociale* 31, 78 : 17-30.
6115 ETZIONI, Amitai. "Old people and public policy", *Policy Studies Review Annual* 78 : 608-615.
6116 FENN, Paul. "Sources of disqualification for unemployment benefit, 1960-1976", *British Journal of industrial Relations* 18, jul 80 : 240-253.
6117 FRANK, Werner. "Standort und Perspektiven der Sozialhilfe im System sozialer Sicherung" (Situation and prospects of social assistance in the system of social security), *Archiv für Wissenschaft und Praxis der Sozialen Arbeit* 11, 80 : 13-45.
6118 GERSTER, Florian. "Familienpolitsche Ideologien" (Family policy ideologies), *Theorie und Praxis der sozialen Arbeit* 31, 80 : 93-101.
6119 GIELE, Janet Zollinger. "Social policy and the family", *Annual Review of Sociology* 79 : 275-302.
6120 GÖCKENJAN, Gerd. "Politik und Verwaltung präventiver Gesundheitssicherung" (Preventive health insurance policy and administration), *Sozial Welt* 31, 80 : 156-175.
6121 GOODWIN, Leonard; MOEN, Phyllis. "The evolution and implementation of family welfare policy", *Policy Studies Journal* 80 : 632-651. [USA.]
6122 HATANAKA, Munekazu. *Shakai fukushi, jido fukushi shinko* (An introduction to social welfare and child welfare). Tokyo, Meigen shobo, 159 p.

6123 KHALAKDINA, Margaret. *Early child care in India*. London, New York, Gordon and Breach, 79, iv-212 p.
6124 LAROQUE, Pierre. "La protection sociale des plus de 75 ans: quels sont les problèmes?", *Revue internationale de la Sécurité sociale* 31, 78 : 295-315.
6125 LOUIS, Etienne; MARCILLAC, Louis de. "Les aides financières à la famille: un édifice à reconstruire", *Projet* 144, apr 80 : 468-487.
6126 Bibl.XXIX-5940. MESA-LAGO, Carmelo. *Social security in Latin America: pressure groups, stratification, and inequality*. CR: Henry DIETZ, *American political Science Review* 74(1), mar 80 : 256-257.
6127 MOOTZ, M.; TIMMERMANS, J. M. "Policy for the elderly in the Netherlands", *Planning and Development in the Netherlands* XI, 79 : 58-82.
6128 NICHOLS, Abigail C. "Why welfare mothers work: implications for employment and training services", *Social Service Review* 53, sep 79 : 378-391.
6129 Organization of American States. Social Development Program. *La seguridad social en los países del Grupo Andino* (Social security in Andean Group countries). Washington, Secretaría General, La Organización, 79, 350 p.
6130 PEJOVICH, Svetozar. *Social security in Yugoslavia*. Washington, American Enterprise Institute for Public Policy Research, 79, 46 p.
6131 ŠALAGINOVA, L. I. "Politika kommunističeskoj partii i sovetskogo gosudarstva v oblasti semejnyh otnošenij" (The Communist Party and the Soviet state policy in the family relations sphere), *IN: Problemy socialističeskogo obraza žizni v uslovijah razvitogo socializma*. Moskva, 80 : 55-67.
6132 SCHRAM, Sanford F. "Elderly policy particularism and the new social services", *Social Service Review* 53, mar 79 : 75-91.
6133 SINHA, P. K. *Social security measures in India*. New Delhi, Classical, 80, viii-248 p.
6134 SLESINGER, Doris P. "Racial and residential differences in preventive medical care for infants in low-income populations", *Rural Sociology* 45, spr 80 : 69-90.
6135 VON FRANK, April A. *Family policy in the USSR since 1944*. Palo Alto, CA, R & E Research Associates, 79, v-133 p.
6136 WEI DJAO, A. "Social welfare in Canada: ideology and reality", *Social Praxis* (1-2), 79 : 35-53.
6137 WINTERSTEIN, Helmut. *Das System der sozialen Sicherung in der Bundesrepublik Deutschland* (The social security system in the Federal Republic of Germany). München, Vahlen, 80, 168 p.

20300. SOCIAL WORK
TRAVAIL SOCIAL

[See also / voir aussi: 5783]

6138 ALISSI, Albert S.; [ed.]. *Perspectives on social group work practice: a book of readings*. New York, Free Press, 80, x-405 p.
6139 BAUR, Roland. *Sozialarbeit im Industriebetrieb* (Social work in industrial enterprise). Weinheim, Basel, Beltz, 80, 311 p. [Germany FR.]
6140 BEAUCHARD, Jacques; [ed.]. *Identités collectives et travail social*. Toulouse, Privat, 79, 215 p.
6141 BEAUREGARD, Robert A.; INDIK, Bernard P. *A human service labor market: developmental disabilities*. New Brunswick, Center for Urban Policy Research, Rutgers — The State University of New Jersey, 79, ix-354 p.
6142 CHAUVIÉRE, M. "L'inscription historique du travail social, l'exemple du secteur de l'enfance inadaptée", *Déviance et Société* dec 79 : 323-336.
6143 COMPTON, Beulah Roberts; GALAWAY, Burt. *Social work processes*. Homewood, IL, Dorsey Press, 79, xix-565 p.
6144 COULTON, Claudia J. *Social work quality assurance programs: a comparative analysis*. Washington, National Association of Social Workers, 79, x-102 p.
6145 CURNOCK, Kathleen; HARDIKER, Pauline. *Towards practice theory: skills and methods in social assessments*. London, Boston, Routledge & K. Paul, 79, xii-193 p.
6146 DUTRÉNIT, Jean-Marc; [ed.]. *Sociologie et compréhension du travail social*. Toulouse, Privat, 80, 296 p.
6147 EPSTEIN, Laura. *Helping people: the task-centered approach*. St. Louis, Mosby, 80, xiii-265 p.
6148 FANSHEL, David; [ed.]. *Future of social work research: selected papers*. Washington, DC, National Association of Social Workers, 80, x-198 p. [National Conference on the Future of Social Work Research, October 15-18, 1978, San Antonio, Texas.]

6149	GALPER, Jeffry H. *Social work practice: a radical perspective.* Englewood Cliffs, NJ, Prentice-Hall, 80, ix-261 p.
6150	GERMAIN, Carel B.; GITTERMAN, Alex. *The life model of social work practice.* New York, Columbia University Press, 80, xiii-376 p.
6151	HART, John. *Social work and sexual conduct.* London, Boston, Routledge & K. Paul, 79, ix-206 p.
6152	HO, Man Keung. *Social work methods, techniques, and skills.* Washington, DC, University Press of America, 80, ix-549 p.
6153	IRVINE, Elizabeth E. *Social work and human problems: casework, consultations, and other topics.* Oxford, New York, Pergamon Press, 79, xiii-260 p.
6154	JACKSON, Michael Peart; VALENCIA, B. Michael. *Financial aid through social work.* London, Boston, Routledge & Kegan Paul, 79, 135 p.
6155	LIEBERMAN, Florence. *Social work with children.* New York, Human Sciences Press, 79, 344 p.
6156	MILLO, Efraim. "Sozialarbeit in Israel" (Social work in Israel), *Theorie und Praxis der sozialen Arbeit* 31, 80 : 44-58.
6157	MUNSON, Carlton E.; [ed.]. *Social work with families: theory and practice.* New York, Free Press, 80, xviii-456 p.
6158	NELSEN, Judith C. *Communication theory and social work practice.* Chicago, University of Chicago Press, 80, x-214 p.
6159	ROONEY, James F. "Organizational success through program failure: skid row rescue missions", *Social Forces* 58, mar 80 : 904-924.

20400. SOCIAL SERVICE
SERVICE SOCIAL

20410. Medical sociology. Medicine
Sociologie médicale. Médecine

[See also / voir aussi: 350, 1885, 3195, 6194]

6160	ALBRECHT, Gary L.; HIGGINS, Paul C.; [eds.]. *Health, illness and medicine: a reader in medical sociology.* Chicago, Rand McNally College Pub. Co., 79, xiii-504 p.
6161	BAKAL, Donald A. *Psychology and medicine: psychobiological dimensions of health and illness.* New York, Springer Pub. Co., 79, viii-280 p.
6162	BOUDREAU, Françoise. "The Quebec psychiatric system in transition: a case study in psychopolitics", *Canadian Review of Sociology and Anthropology* 17, mai 80 : 123-137.
6163	BRENNER, M. Harvey; MOONEY, Anne; NAGY, Thomas J.; [eds.]. *Assessing the contributions of the social sciences to health.* Boulder, CO, Westview press for the American Association for the Advancement of Science, 80, xvi-216 p.
6164	Bibl.XXIX-5992. CASTEL, Françoise; CASTEL, Robert; LOVELL, Anne. *La société psychiatrique avancée. Le modèle américain.* CR: Pierre, LANTZ, *Revue française de Sociiologie* 21(1), jan-mar 80: 144-146.
6165	DANIELSON, Ross. *Cuban medicine.* New Brunswick, NJ, Transaction Books, 79, 247 p. CR: Harvey WILLIAMS, *Contemporary Sociology (Albany)* 9(6), nov 80: 815.
6166	Bibl.XXIX-5999. EHRENREICH, John; [eds.]. *The cultural crisis of modern medicine.* CR: Noel PARRY, *British Journal of Sociology* 31(1), mar 80 : 144-145.
6167	ELINSON, Jack; SIEGMANN, Athilia E.; [eds.]. *Sociomedical health indicators.* Farmingdale, NY, Baywood Pub. Co., 79, vi-216 p.
6168	FOX, Renée C. *Essays in medical sociology: journeys into the field.* New York, Wiley, 79, viii-548 p.
6169	Bibl.XXIX-6004. GLASSNER, Barry; FREEDMAN, Jonathan A. *Clinical sociology.* CR: J. Allen WHITT, *Contemporary Sociology (Albany)* 9(1), jan 80: 159-160.
6170	JEROTIĆ, Vladeta; MILANOVIĆ, Vladimir; DESPOTOVIĆ, Aleksandar. "Antipsihijatrija i društvo"(Anti-psychiatry and society), *Sociologija* 22(1-2), 80 : 127-143.
6171	JEROTIĆ, Vladeta; MILANOVIĆ, Vladimir; DESPOTOVIĆ, Aleksandar. "Antipsihijatrija i društvo"(Antipsychiatry and society), *Sociologija* 22(1-2), 80 : 127-143.
6172	KLEIN, Norman; [ed.]. *Culture, curers, and contagion: readings for medical social science.* San Francisco, Chandler & Sharp, 79, viii-246 p.
6173	MECHANIC, David; [ed.]. *Readings in medical sociology.* New York, Free Press, 80, xi-513 p.
6174	ROBITSCHER, Jonas B. *The powers of psychiatry.* Boston, Houghton Mifflin, 80, xviii-557 p.
6175	ROSENGREN, William R. *Sociology of medicine: adversity, conflict and change.* New York Harper & Row, 80, xiii-446 p.

6176   STROMAN, Duane F. *The quick knife: unnecessary surgery USA*. Washington, NY, Kennikat Press, 79, v-178 p. CR: Dale J. JAFFE, *American Journal of Sociology* 86(3), nov 80 : 695-697. [also CR: Elianne RISKA, Contemporary Sociology (Albany) 9(5), sep 80 : 692-693.]

6177   Bibl.XXIX-6012. TUCKETT, David; KAUFERT, Joseph. *Basic readings in medical sociology*. CR: Margaret STACEY, *British Journal of Sociology* 31(1), mar 80: 142-144.

6178   VEENMAN, Justus; JANSMA, Lammert G. "The 1978 Dutch polio epidemic; a sociological study of the motives for accepting or refusing vaccination", *Netherlands' Journal of Sociology* 16, apr 80 : 21-48.

20420. Public health
Santé publique

[See also / voir aussi: 2615, 2983, 4842, 5035, 5767]

6179   "Reforma (La) sanitaria" (Public health reform), *Revista de Fomento social* 35(137), jan-mar 80 : 3-70. [Spain.]

6180   ADAY, Lu Ann; ANDERSEN, Ronald; FLEMING, Gretchen V. *Health care in the U.S.: Equitable for whom?*. Beverly Hills, CA, London, Sage, 80, 415 p.

6181   AHEARN, Mary C. *Health care in rural America*. Washington, United States Dept. of Agriculture, Economics, Statistics, and Cooperatives Service, 79, iii-36 p.

6182   AHMED, Paul I.; COELHO, George V.; KOLKER, Aliza; [eds.]. *Toward a new definition of health: psychosocial dimensions*. New York, Plenum Press, 79, xxxiii-470 p.

6183   ALLEN, Richard C.; [ed.]. *Mental health in America: the years of crisis*. Chicago, Marquis Academic Media, 79, xviii-380 p.

6184   BATES, Erica M. "Decision making in critical illness", *Australian and New Zealand Journal of Sociology* 15, nov 79 : 45-54.

6185   BENSON, Paul R. "Labeling theory and community care of the mentally ill in California: the relationship of social theory and ideology to public policy", *Human Organization* 39, 80 : 134-141.

6186   BOCHEL, Dorothy; MACLARAN, Morag. "Representing the interests of the public?: the case of the Local Health Council in Scotland", *Journal of social Policy* oct 79 : 449-472.

6187   BOLTON, Brian; JAQUES, Marceline Elaine; [eds.]. *The Rehabilitation client*. Baltimore, University Park Press, 79, xiii-237 p.

6188   BORGATTA, Edgar F.; BORGATTA, Marid L. "On determining critical health problem areas: New York City", *Sociological Methods and Research* feb 79 : 369-376.

6189   BOWE, Frank. *Rehabilitating America: toward independence for disabled and elderly people*. New York, Harper & Row, 80, xvii-203 p.

6190   Centro de estudios de asistencia sanitaria. *La asistencia sanitaria en las zonas rurales* (Medical care in rural areas). Madrid, 79, 280 p. [Spain.]

6191   COCKERHAM, William C. "Medical practice and social protest", *Contemporary Sociology* mar 80 : 195-197. [survey essay.]

6192   COSER, Rose Laub. *Training in ambiguity: learning through doing in a mental hospital*. New York, Free Press, 79, 220 p. CR: Donald LIGHT Jr., *Contemporary Sociology (Albany)* 9(4), jul 80 : 568-569.

6193   DUDEK, R. A.; MARCY, N. M. "Public policy and social responsibility with regard to rehabilitation and maintenance of disabled persons", *Technological Forecasting and social Change* 17, mai 80 : 61-72.

6194   FEIERMAN, Steven. *Health and society in Africa: a working bibliography*. Waltham, MA, Crossroads Press, 79, 210 p.

6195   FLAX, James W.; [et al.]. *Mental health and rural America: an overview and annotated bibliography*. Rockville, MD, National Institute of Mental Health, Division of Mental Health Service Programs, 79, viii-216 p. [for sale by the Supt. of Docs., U.S. Govt. Print. Off., Washington.]

6196   FOSTER, Peggy. "The informal rationing of primary medical care", *Journal of social Policy* oct 79 : 489-508.

6197   FRANK, Arthur W. III; GOLDSTEIN, Michael S. "Sociology of mental health and illness", *Annual Review of Sociology* 79 : 167-191; 381-409.

6198   GLASNER, A. Hale. "Professional power and State intervention in medical practice", *Australian and New Zealand Journal of Sociology* 15, nov 79 : 20-29.

6199   LEE, Sidney S. *Quebec's health system: a decade of change, 1967-77*. Toronto, Institute of Public Administration of Canada, 79, 54 p.

6200 LIPPMAN, Lenora. "Community mental health ideology in Victoria", *Australian and New Zealand Journal of Sociology* 15, nov 79 : 39-44.
6201 NAJMAN, J. M.; [et al.]. "Patterns of morbidity, health care utilisation and socio-economic status in Brisbane", *Australian and New Zealand Journal of Sociology* 15, nov 79 : 55-63.
6202 Bibl.XXIX-6040. NAVARRO, V. *Class struggle, the State and medicine: an historical and contemporary analysis of the medical sector in Great Britain.* CR: Nicky HART, *British Journal of Sociology* 31(4), dec 80: 604-605. [also CR: Paul ADAMS, *Contemporary Sociology* (Albany) 9(5), sep 80 : 691-692.]
6203 SECONDULFO, Domenico. "Medico e paziente: elementi per un'analisi sociologica" (Doctor and patient: elements for a sociological analysis), *Studi di Sociologia* 17, oct-dec 79 : 368-387.
6204 THACKERAY, Milton G.; SKIDMORE, Rex A.; FARLEY, O. William. *Introduction to mental health, field and practice.* Englewood Cliffs, NJ, Prentice-Hall, 79, viii-296 p.
6205 WARD, Colleen. "Spirit possession and mental health: a psycho-anthropological perspective", *Human Relations* 33, mar 80 : 149-163.
6206 WILLIS, Evan. "Sister Elizabeth Kenny and the evolution of the occupational division of labour in health care", *Australian and New Zealand Journal of Sociology* 15, nov 79 : 30-38.
6207 WOLINSKY, Fredric D. *The sociology of health: principles, professions, and issues.* Boston, Little, Brown, 80, xiv-449 p.

20430. Hospital
Hôpital

[See also / voir aussi: 3782, 5882, 6192, 6257]

6208 "Health and society", *Milbank Memorial Fund Quarterly* 58, wint 80 : 1-172. [continued in 58(2), spr 80: 173-347.]
6209 "Regulating health care: the struggle for control", *Proceedings of the Academy of political Science* 33, 80 : 1-244. [USA.]
6210 ATKINSON, Paul; DINGWALL, Robert; MURCOTT, Anne; [eds.]. *Prospects for the national health.* London, Croom Helm, 79, 218 p.
6211 BARRETT, S. D. "Social and Economic Aspects of the Health Services", *Irish Banking Review* mar 79 : 11-16.
6212 BARTH, Richard T.; VERTINSKY, Patricia; YANG, Chung-fang. "Some socio-behavioral and other determinants of compliance: a voluntary health service campaign", *Human Relations* 32, sep 79 : 781-792.
6213 BROWN, Ronald Gordon Sclater. *Reorganising the National Health Service: a case study in administrative change.* Oxford, Blackwell, Martin Robertson, 79, xiii-232 p.
6214 DE MIGUEL, Jesús M. "Siete tesis erróneas sobre la política sanitaria española, y una alternativa sociológica critica" (Seven erroneous theses on the Spanish health policy, and a critical sociological alternative), *Revista española de Investigaciones sociológicas* jan-mar 80 : 53-80.
6215 ELLING, Ray H. *Cross-national study of health systems: concepts, methods, and data sources: A guide to information sources.* Detroit: Gale Research, 80, xvii-293 p.
6216 EVAN, William M.; KLEMM, R. Christopher. "Inter-organizational relations among hospitals: a strategy, structure, and performance model", *Human Relations* 33, mai 80 : 315-337.
6217 HAYNES, Robin M.; BENTHAM, C. G. *Community hospitals and rural accessibility.* Farnborough, Eng., Saxon House, 79, vii-200 p.
6218 KORFF, Michael Von. "A statistical model of the duration of mental hospitalization: the mixed exponential distribution", *Journal of mathematical Sociology* 79 : 169-175.
6219 KRICHEWSKY, Maurice. "Mourir à l'hôpital: les soins palliatifs dans les pays anglo-saxons et en France", *Revue française des Affaires sociales* 33, oct-dec 79 : 3-36.
6220 LABASSE, Jean. *L'Hôpital et la ville: géographie hospitalière.* Paris, Hermann, 80, 241 p.
6221 LEICHTER, Howard M. *A comparative approach to policy analysis: health care policy in four nations.* Cambridge, New York, Cambridge University Press, 79, x-326 p.
6222 Bibl.XXIX-6071. MECHANIC, David. *Future issues in health care: social policy and the rationing of medical services.* CR: Harry W. MARTIN, *Contemporary Sociology (Albany)* 9(6), nov 80 : 817-818.
6223 NYMAN, Kauko. "Terveyspalvelusten käyttöön vaikuttaneet tekijät Suomessa vuosina 1964, 1968 ja 1976" (Factors affecting the use of health services in Finland in 1964, 1968 and 1976), *Sosiaalivakuutus* 5-6, 80 : 152-163.

6224 PARSTON, Gregory. *Planners, politics and health services*. London, Croom Helm, 80, 196 p.
6225 RAFFEL, Marshall W. *The U.S. health system: origins and functions*. New York, Wiley, 80, ix-639 p.
6226 RODENSTEIN, Marianne. "Fraueninteressen in Gesundheitspolitik und -forschung" (Women's interests in health policy and medical research), *Soziale Welt* 31, 80 : 176-190.
6227 ROTHMAN, David J. *Conscience and convenience: the asylum and its alternatives in progressive America*. Boston, Little, Brown, 80, xii-464 p.
6228 STOMMES, Eileen; SISAYE, Seleshi. "The development and distribution of health care services in Ethiopia: a preliminary review", *Canadian Journal of African Studies* 13, 80 : 487-495.
6229 STRONG, P. M. *The ceremonial order of the clinic: parents, doctors, and medical bureaucracies*. London, Boston, Routledge & Kegan Paul, 79, xiii-267 p.
6230 UGAZI, Valeria; DI BLASIO, Paola. "Famiglia, classe sociale e ospedalizzazione infantile: uno studio pilota" (Family, social class and children's hospitalization: a pilot study), *Studi di Sociologia* 17, jan-mar 79 : 59-80.
6231 VAN DER ZWAAN, A. H. "Organisatie Nederlandse gezondheidszorg: overzichtsliteratuur" (Organization of Dutch health services: a literature survey), *Mens en Maatschappij* 55, jun 80 : 190-196.
6232 WILLIAMS, Stephen J.; [ed.]. *Issues in health services*. New York, Wiley, 80, xi-371 p.
6233 ZERUBAVEL, Eviatar. *Patterns of time in hospital life: a sociological perspective*. Chicago, University of Chicago Press, 79, xxiv-157 p.

20440. Social worker
Travailleur social

[See also / voir aussi: 5021, 5059, 5066, 5301, 5998, 6198]

6234 "Activité professionnelle des médicins en 1977", *Cahiers de Sociologie et de Démographie médicales* 20, jan-mar 80 : 5-58. [France.]
6235 ANISEF, Paul; BASSON, Priscilla. "The institutionalization of a profession: a comparison of British and American midwifery", *Sociology of Work and Occupations* aug 79 : 353-372.
6236 Bibl.XXIX-6077. AUSTIN, Michael J. *Professionals and paraprofessionals*. CR: Edgar W. MILLS Jr., *Contemporary Sociology (Albany)* 9(5), sep 80: 721-722.
6237 BLAKE, Robert R.; [et al.]. *The Social worker grid*. Springfield, IL, Thomas, 79, vii-192 p.
6238 BRIEF, Arthur P.; ALDAG, Ramon J. "Antecedents of organizational commitment among hospital nurses", *Sociology of Work and Occupations* mai 80 : 210-221.
6239 Canadian Council on Social Development. *Directory of Canadian welfare services, 1979 = Répertoire des services sociaux canadiens, 1979*. Ottawa, The Canadian Council on Social Development, 79, 208 p.
6240 CHARLES, Geneviève. *L'infirmière en France d'hier à aujourd'hui*. Paris, Le Centurion, 79, 246p.
6241 COLDITZ, Graham A.; BATCH, Jennifer. "Student expectations of the medical profession", *Australian and New Zealand Journal of Sociology* 15, nov 79 : 65-66.
6242 DOMINGUEZ-ALCON, Carmen. "Para una sociología de la profesión de enfermería en España" (For a sociology of nursing in Spain), *Revista española de Investigaciones sociológicas* oct-dec 79 : 103-129.
6243 FOSTER, L. E.; WILLIAMS, A. J. "An institutionalised art: therapy as ideological carrier in the 1970's", *Australian and New Zealand Journal of Sociology* 16, mar 80 : 63-72.
6244 GRUBER, Murray L. "Inequality in the social services", *Social Service Review* 54, mar 80 : 59-75.
6245 HILLGAARD, Lis; KEISER, Lis. *Social(be)handling: teori og metode i socialt arbejde* (Social service: theory and method in social work). København, Munksgaard, 79, 268 p.
6246 KANG-WANG, Janet F. "The midwife in Taiwan: an alternative model for maternity care", *Human Organization* 39, 80 : 70-79.
6247 LA ROSA, Michele; ZURLA, Paolo. "I servizi sociali fra esigenza di razionalizzazione e potenzialità innovative: un approccio sociologico" (Social services between requirements of rationalization and innovatory potentialities: a sociological approach), *Studi di Sociologia* 17, jan-mar 79 : 3-17. [Italy.]
6248 LEVY, Danièle; BUI DANG HA DOAN. "L'exercice médical en milieu rural", *Cahiers de Sociologie et de Démographie médicales* 20, apr-jun 80 : 65-142.

6249	MAGILL, Robert S. *Community decision making for social welfare: federalism, city government, and the poor.* New York, Human Sciences Press, 79, 219 p.
6250	MAWBY, R. I.; [et al.]. "Press coverage of social work", *Policy and Politics* oct 79 : 357-376.
6251	MEHR, Joseph. *Human services: concepts and intervention strategies.* Boston, Allyn and Bacon, 80, xv-286 p.
6252	MENDELSOHN, Ronald. *The condition of the people: social welfare in Australia, 1900-1975.* Sydney, Boston, G. Allen & Unwin, 79, 408 p.
6253	PAYNE, Malcolm. *Power, authority, and responsibility in social services: social work in area teams.* London, Macmillan, 79, 253 p.
6254	REIN, Mildred. "Fact and function in human service organizations", *Sociology and social Research* 65, oct 80 : 78-94.
6255	ROSSI, Giovanna. "Ruolo dell'assistente sociale e sistema dei servizi sociali" (The role of social worker and the system of social services), *Studi di Sociologia* 17, jul-sep 79 : 257-272.
6256	SIMPKIN, Michael. *Trapped within welfare: surviving social work.* London, Macmillan, 79, vii-168 p.
6257	SLOAN, Frank A.; ELNICKI, Richard A. "Nurse staffing in hospitals: a microeconomic analysis", *Industrial Relations* 19, 80 : 15-33.
6258	THURSZ, Daniel; VIGILANTE, Joseph; [eds.]. *Reaching People: The structure of Neighborhood Services.* Beverly Hills, CA, Sage Publications, 79, 288 p.
6259	WILLIAMS, Stephen J.; TORRENS, Paul R.; [eds.]. *Introduction to health services.* New York, Wiley, 80, xviii-397 p.

AUTHOR INDEX
INDEX DES AUTEURS

Aaronson, Doris, 2007
Aballea, François, 3070
Abasiekong, Edet M., 3884
Abbott, Andrew, 1885
Abbott, Susan, 2815
Abdil'din, Z. M., 4569
Abdulova, G. Ja., 1283
Abdurahmanov, I. I., 4694
Abediseid, Mohammad, 2816
Abel-Smith, Brian, 5995
Abell, Peter, 5202
Abell, Troy, 4720
Abercrombie, Nicholas, 1255
Abernathy, Thomas J. Jr., 6107
Abimov, R., 713
Abplanalp, Peter A., 4671
Abrahamson, Mark, 4469
Abrahamsson, Bengt, 5160
Abramowitz, Stephen I., 996
Abrams, Robert, 1267
Abramson, Paul R., 714
Abt, Clark C., 138
Acerbi, Antonio, 1906
Acero, Liliana, 5028
Acharji, Nilima, 5168
Achatz, Thomas, 443
Acker, Joan R., 2919
Ackerman, S. E., 1817
Acock, Alan C., 3459, 5619
Acosta-Belén, Edna, 3576
Acquaviva, Sabino S., 2136
Adam, Barry D., 2592
Adam, Heribert, 3717
Adamchuk, Donald J., 3206
Adamczuk, Lucian, 4915
Adamopoulos, John, 1032
Adams, Carolyn Teich, 4789
Adams, Jack A., 773
Adams, Murray C., 1493
Adams, Paul, 6202
Adams, Ruth S., 3804
Aday, Lu Ann, 6180
Adda, R., 2008
Adeniran, Adekunle, 2073
Adler, Frank, 4695
Adler, Laure, 2137
Adler-Karlsson, Gunnar, 4732
Agafonov, O. V., 5996
Agapitidis, Sotiris, 3180
Agassi, Judith B., 4790
Ageton, Suzanne S., 5863
Aggarwal, R. C., 4791
Agger, Robert E., 2593
Aghajanian, Akbar, 3230

Agnew, Robert S., 1494
Agresti, Alan, 526
Agresti, Barbara Finlay, 526, 3460, 4202
Aguessy, Honorat, 4570
Aguirre, B. E., 1797, 4203
Agulla, Juan C., 244
Ahearn, Mary C., 6181
Ahlbrandt, Roger S., 4201
Ahmad, Zubeida, 3577
Ahmed, Paul I., 6182
Ahtola, Olli T., 596
Aida, Akira, 5
Aida, Toshihiko, 883, 2138
Aiginger, Karl, 774
Aitov, N. A., 2560, 2731, 4204, 4422, 4470
Ajello, Nello, 2732
Ajubdžanov, Ja. Ja., 5426
Akat'ev, Ju. V., 4015
Akimoto, Ritsuo, 4205, 5396
Akimova, V. V., 1443
Akiwowo, Akinsola, 5603
Akiyama, Toyoko, 1467
Akramuzzaman, 1706
Aksoy, Sevim, 4206
Al-Charim, Maher, 1407
Al-Teraifi, Al-Agab A., 5550
Alarcón, Reynaldo, 625
Alatas, Secha, 4127
Albegova, I. F., 4016, 4615
Alber, Jens, 5997
Alberoni, Francesco, 5596
Albers, Wulf, 1001
Albert, Hans, 339, 340
Albonetti, Celesta, 5890
Albornoz, Orlando, 2428
Albrecht, Gary L., 5029, 6160
Albrecht, Maryann H., 4897
Albrecht, Peter-Alexis, 5829
Albrecht, Richart, 2258
Albrecht, Stan L., 626
Alcántara Ferrer, Sergio, 4616
Alcock, Antony E., 1408
Aldag, Ramon J., 5131, 6238
Alder, Max K., 2074
Alderete, Nuñez, 403
Alderfer, Clayton P., 3718
Aldrich, Howard E., 1074
Aldridge, Meryl, 4207
Aldrup, Dieter, 341
Alehin, V. A., 1219
Alejabeitia, Carmen, 5346
Aleksandrova, L. M., 2894
Alekseev, B. K., 1220
Alekseev, V. N., 1284

Alekseeva, L. K., 2489
Alekseeva, V. G., 516
Aleman, Ulrich Von, 1067
Alemi, Ali A., 3181
Alexander, Daniel, 1928
Alexander, E. R., 1075
Alexander, Jeffrey C., 342
Alexander, Karl L., 2289
Alexander, Richard D., 245
Alexander, Theron, 627
Alexander, Yonah, 1495
Alexandrova, A. A., 4662
Aliprantis, Nikitas, 5165
Alissi, Albert S., 6138
Allaire, Gilles, 4028
Allan, Sarah, 1691
Allardt, Erik, 3649
Allemann-Tschopp, Annemarie, 2920
Allen, David H., 5839
Allen, Donald E., 628
Allen, K. Eileen, 2403
Allen, Nancy H., 5830
Allen, Richard C., 6183
Allen, Richard L., 2139, 2140
Allen, Thomas Harrell, 4519
Allen, V. L., 5540
Allen, Walter R., 775
Allerbeck, Klaus, 2775, 3058, 5051
Allinson, Gary D., 4208
Allison, Paul D., 527, 610
Allman, James, 2776
Allon, Natalie, 4209
Allum, Percy, 5597
Almaraz, José, 404
Almeida, Arilza Nazareth de, 3143
Almquist, Elizabeth M., 2970
Alonso Hinojal, Isidoro, 2282
Alonso Olea, Manuel, 4917
Alonso Soto, Francisco, 4520
Aloune, Youssef, 3819
Alpalhao, Joao Antonio, 3820
Alpert, Geoffrey P., 5831
Alstein, Howard, 3461
Alston, Jon P., 1797
Altbach, Philip G., 2429, 2534
Altman, Irwin, 1285
Alton Smith, D., 3719
Altrocchi, John, 1496
Altvater, Elmar, 1211
Alvarez, Rodolfo, 1200
Alves, Márcio Moreira, 1907
Amabile, Teresa L., 2215
Amado, Georges, 629
Amano, Ikuo, 2438
Amano, Masako, 5030
Amato, Matthew F., 4210
Amekrane, Malika, 3578
Ameline, Claude, 5998
Amin, Samir, 2651
Amiot, Michel, 4612
Amksabedian, Jorge, 4571
Ammon, Ulrich, 2075

Amneus, Daniel, 2921
Amodio, Emanuele, 2321
Amore, Roy C., 1707
Amselle, Jean-Loup, 3795
Amvrosov, A. A., 1497
Ander, Oscar Fritiof, 1409
Andersen, Erlin B., 528
Andersen, Heine, 5479
Andersen, Jørgen Goul, 2652
Andersen, Margaret L., 3579
Andersen, N. A., 3087
Andersen, Ronald, 6180
Anderson, Digby C., 2141
Anderson, John C., 5169, 5288
Anderson, Patricia Doede, 1034 4211
Anfalova, S. L., 777
Angelusz, Róbert, 4473
Angle, John, 405, 5031
Anisef, Paul, 690, 6235
Anker, Richard, 3207
Ansari, A. Wahid, 4018
Anselm, Sigrun, 778
Antalffy, György, 5480
Anthony, Dick, 1932
Anthony, Peter David, 4696
Antier, Jean Jacques, 1839
Antipina, Z. G., 1945
Antonio, Robert J., 1076, 2806
Antos, Joseph R., 2923, 4733
Anwar, Muhammad, 3821
Anzieu, Didier, 941
Anžiganov, V. S., 4423
Aoi, Kazuo, 984, 3462, 5999
Aoki, Shinji, 3984
Apple, Michael W., 2535
Appleyard, Donald, 4212
Apps, Jerold W., 2491
Aranovich, Carmen, 4213
Archer, Margaret S., 2322
Ardener, Shirley, 3580
Ardila Espinel, Noe, 3032
Arditti, Rita, 1946
Ardoino, Jacques, 2283
Aremu, L. O., 1638
Arenson, Sidney J., 1046
Arestova, A. S., 6034
Argyle, Michael, 903
Arhangel'skij, L. M., 716
Arian, Asher, 1288
Arimoto, Akira, 2430
Arisue, Ken, 1947
Arkkelin, Daniel, 1602
Arlacchi, Pino, 5832
Arličenkova, È. N., 2323
Armstrong, James W., 3027
Armstrong, Marjorie, 1798
Armstrong, Orland Kay, 1798
Arndt, Johan, 178
Arney, William Ray, 529
Aronov, A. B., 4573
Aronowitz, Stanley, 5170
Arowolo, Oladele O., 3231

Arpal, Jesús, 2876
Arquitt, George E. Jr., 4406
Arrington, Robert L., 3182
Arrom, Silvia M., 3389
Artanovskij, S. N., 4574
Artemov, G. P., 6099
Arts, W., 6000
Arunachalam, B., 4255
Arustamjan, M. A., 5427
Arutjunjan, S. G., 1498
Asante, Molefi Kete, 1289, 1410
Ascanio, Alfredo, 5360
Aschenbrenner, Joyce, 4214
Ashbrook, Debra L., 5796
Ashby, Jacqueline, 2599
Ashraf, Jaweed, 149
Ashworth, C. E., 1856
Assman, Peter, 247
Ata, Abe, 3650
Athens, Lonnie H., 5833
Atkins, Burton M., 5872
Atkinson, Gary, 3284
Atkinson, Paul, 6210
Audi, Robert, 343
Auroux, Sylvain, 2009
Austin, James E., 5759
Austin, Michael J., 6236
Avery, Donald, 3822
Avery, William P., 4178
Avramenko, V. N., 1411
Axt, Friedrich, 2324, 2404
Axten, Nick, 1171
Aya, Rod, 2817
Ayberk, Ural, 5171
Ayçoberry, Pierre, 5428
Ayeni, Bola, 4215
Azarya, Victor, 3651, 5695
Aziz, K. M. A., 3463
Aziz, Sartaj, 5760
Azouvi, François, 779

B'Chir, Badra, 2733
Babaian, E. A., 5797
Babajan, L. V., 1444
Babbie, Earl R., 233
Babin, B. A., 780, 781, 782
Babington-Smith, Bernard, 1002
Baca Zinn, Maxime, 2924
Bachner, Mary Lynn, 1591
Bachy, Jean-Paul, 5128
Back, Kurt W., 5021
Bacry, Daniel, 1499
Bada, José, 5571
Badalato, Gabriella, 1003
Badawi, 'Abd al-Rahmǎn, 1708
Badie, Bertrand, 5397, 5481
Bagley, Christopher, 717
Bagni, Bruce N., 3720
Bagozzi, Richard P., 1172
Baharuddin, Shamsul Amri, 4019
Bahm, Archie J., 1603
Bahr, Howard M., 3390, 3464

Bailey, Joe, 5742
Bailey, William C., 5834, 5835
Bailleau Lajoinie, Simone, 3581
Bainbridge, William Sims, 1828, 1852
Bajoit, G., 1290
Bakal, Donald A., 6161
Baker, Benjamin, 4392
Baker, Eva L., 2325
Baker, Hugh D. R., 3465
Baker, Kathryn, 867
Baker, Mary Anne, 3582
Baker, Ralph, 5544
Baker, Terence J., 4216
Baklickaja, O. P., 5081
Balakrishnan, T. R., 3232
Balch, Robert W., 1840
Balchin, Paul N., 4217
Baldassare, Mark, 4218
Baldi, Paolo, 2034
Balducci, Massimo, 1050
Baldus, David C., 4764
Baldwin, Janice I., 2995
Baldwin, John D., 2995
Baldwin, Wendy, 4845
Balique, François, 1650
Balkan, Sheila, 5836
Balkwell, James W., 5032
Balla, Bálint, 5761
Ballé, Catherine, 227
Baller, E. A., 5429
Ballerstedt, Eike, 575
Ballester Ros, Ignacio, 3114
Ballestero, Enrique, 406
Ballhatchet, Kenneth, 3721
Ballion, Robert, 2326
Ballón, Eduardo, 2536
Balloni, Augusto, 5837
Balog, Miklósné, 3583
Baloyra, Enrique A., 5620
Bamber, J. H., 3033
Bamberg, Günter, 1001
Bambrough, Renford, 1604
Ban, Sung Hwan, 4020
Bandura, Albert, 942
Banerjee, Sumanta, 4794
Banerji, Sures Chandra, 5838
Bank, Barbara J., 3035
Bankston, William B., 5839
Banner, David K., 4522
Bannister, Robert C., 248
Bansal, Usha Rani, 3584
Bar-Tal, Daniel, 6023
Barat, Josef, 4219
Barbash, Jack, 5287
Barber, Bernard, 101
Barbero Avanzini, Bianca, 1500, 3466
Barbier, Jean Marie, 4993
Bardis, Panos D., 1501, 2431, 3478
Bardo, J. W., 4220
Bardwick, Judith M., 3585
Barežev, V. A., 5082
Barger, W. K., 3722

Barkan, Steven E., 5598, 5686
Barker, Dave, 1051
Barker, Martin, 249
Barling, Julian, 5798
Barmenko, A. I., 5518
Barnea, Metei, 3939
Barnes, Barry, 783
Barnes, Donna, 199
Barnes, Richard E. 1011
Barnett, Steve, 1243
Barnhill, J. Allison, 1052
Baron, C., 4575
Baron, James N., 4523, 5033
Baron, Reuben M., 1485
Barou, Jacques, 3823
Barr, N. A., 5004
Barraza, Eduardo, 2216
Barrera, Mario, 3723
Barrett, Michele, 1244
Barrett, S. D., 6211
Barrett-Lennard, G. T., 985
Barrig, Maruja, 3586
Barrish, Gerald, 1886
Barron, Frank X, 718
Barron, Iann, 179
Barros, Afonso de, 4021, 4022
Barrow, Robin, 2537
Barry, Brian, 76
Barry, Kathleen, 3353
Barsuk, V. L., 2360
Barth, Fredrik, 2561
Barth, Richard T., 6212
Bartol, Curt R., 5840
Barzilov, S. I., 5083
Basar, Hasmet, 4617
Bash, Harry H., 3652
Basin, E. Ja., 1412
Basov, B. P., 1605
Basran, G. S., 3824
Bassett, William, 1799
Bassiri-Movassagh, Schahin, 2405
Basson, Priscilla, 6235
Bastie, Jean, 4221
Batatu, Hanna, 2653
Batch, Jennifer, 6241
Bates, Elizabeth, 2035
Bates, Erica M., 3183, 6184
Bates, Frederick L., 1154, 5032
Battegay, Raymond, 943
Batudaev, I. A., 2538
Batygin, G. S., 530, 531, 1293
Baubérot, Jean, 1800
Baudelot, Christian, 4697
Bauder, Ward W., 2616
Baudoin, P., 4474
Baudrillard, Jean, 1134
Bauduin, Henri, 5002
Bauer, Michel, 4524, 4525
Baum, John Alan, 250
Baum, Martha, 3071
Baum, Rainer C., 3071
Baum, Richard, 4576

Bauman, Karl E., 5799
Bauman, Zygmut, 251
Baumann, Donald J., 923
Baumgärtel, Frank, 1502
Baumgartner, Tom, 4475
Baumrind, Diana, 1503
Baur, E. Jackson, 1113
Baur, Roland, 6139
Bautista Malpica, Matilde, 5731
Bavadra, T. U., 3285
Bax, E. H., 4734
Bayart, Philippe, 5129
Bayona, Bernardo, 5571
Bea, Franz Xaver, 598
Beals, Alan R., 4023
Bean, Frank D., 3401, 3653
Beau, Jean-Louis, 4577
Beauchamp, Claude, 4618
Beauchamp, Tom L., 811, 1606
Beauchard, Jacques, 6140
Beaumont, P. B., 5289
Beauregard, Robert A., 6141
Bebbington, A. C., 532
Becattini, Giacomo, 4410
Beccaria, Luis, 4735
Bechelloni, Giovanni, 212
Beck, E. M., 1201, 4468, 4664, 5172
Beck, Ulrich, 5034
Becker, George, 1504
Becker, Henry Jay, 3724
Becker, Jörg, 2143
Becker, Lee B., 2192
Becker, Selwyn W., 2421
Becker, William E. Jr., 2459
Beckman, Linda J., 4795
Beckmann, Michael, 5599
Beckwith, Burnham P., 5430
Bedall, Fritz K., 2327
Bedarida, François, 5130
Beeby, Clarence Edward, 2328
Begnoche Smith, Catherine, 4994
Béguin, Guy, 630
Behm, Hugo, 3233
Beigie, Carl E., 4666
Beinke, Lothar, 2406
Beit-Hallahmi, Benjamin, 1887
Békés, Ferenc, 1948
Bel'skij, K. T., 1505
Belanger, Michel, 6108
Belanger, Paul, 2329
Bell, D. Wallace, 5309
Bell, Gordon H., 2539
Bell, Roger A., 842
Bell, Rudolph M., 4024
Bell, Wendell, 2594
Bellamy, G. Thomas, 5035
Bellardi, Lauralba, 5173
Bellebaum, Alfred, 5761
Bellen, H., 4476
Bellenzier, Maria T., 3587
Bellettini, Athos, 4222
Belloncle, Guy, 4025

Index des auteurs

Belonovskij, V. N., 6001
Belousov, R. A., 5310
Belov, G. A., 5482
Belova, L. V., 2562
Belperron, Roland, 2407
Belsky, Jay, 3467
Belth, Nathan C., 3725
Beltrán S., Luis Ramiro, 2144
Belyh, A. K., 5483
Ben Rafael, Eliezer, 3654, 5687
Ben Saïd, Laurent, 1709
Ben-David, Joseph, 2445
Ben-Yehuda, Nachman, 1692
Benaissa, Said, 1077
Benatia, Farouk, 4796
Benchikh, Madjid, 5721
Benda-Beckmann, Franz von, 1639
Bendix, Reinhard, 113
Bendixen, Peter, 4920
Benetti, Carlo, 4424
Bengtson, Vern L., 3459
Benjamin, A. J., 959
Benjamin, Roger, 5688
Benjamin, Rommel, 2473
Bennett, Sheila K., 4797
Bennett, Tony, 2241
Bennigsen, Alexandre, 1710
Benokraitis, Nijole V., 2595, 3708
Bensman, Joseph, 667
Benson, George C. S., 5621
Benson, Paul R., 6185
Benson, Peter, 916
Bentham, C. G., 6217
Bentham, Eraham, 4223
Benton, Ted, 53
Bequele, Assefa, 5762
Beraud, Jean-Marc, 4921
Berberoglu, Berch, 4425
Bereday, George Z. F., 2432
Berelson, Bernard, 3286, 3287, 3288, 3289
Berenbach, Shari, 5311
Berend, Ivan T., 2330
Béres, Csaba, 4224
Berg, Bruce, 5807
Berg, Per-Olof, 1078
Berg-Schlosser, Dirk, 2596
Berger, Arthur Asa, 2145
Berger, Gaston, 1949
Berger, Michael, 4619
Berger, Ronald J., 5836
Bergeret, Jean, 5800
Bergfeld, Hans-Joachim Edmund, 5013
Berghel, Hal, 443
Berghman, J., 5763
Berghorn, Forrest J., 3072
Bergler, Reinhold, 2123, 2146
Bergmann, Joachim, 5174, 5189
Berk, Richard A., 4651, 5841, 5842
Berk, Sarah Fenstermaker, 4922
Berk-Seligson, Susan, 2076
Berki, R. N., 5492
Berkman, Ronald, 5843

Berkowitz, Alan, 3497
Berkowitz, Edward D., 3184, 6002, 6003, 6004
Berkowitz, S. D., 2734, 4415
Berkson, William, 252
Berlin, Isaiah, 1950
Berlizova, G., 719
Berman, David R., 3034
Berman, Gerald S., 3825
Berman, John J., 1184
Bernal, Antonio-Miguel, 4026
Bernal, Helen Hazuda, 5049
Bernal, Joe, 5541
Bernard, C., 4736
Bernard, H. Russell, 986
Bernard, Larry Craig, 2925
Bernard, Lucien, 2492
Bernard, Paul, 5069
Bernardi, Walter, 1245
Berndt, Heide, 4225, 4279
Bernier, Bernard, 4027
Bernier, Charles L., 2036
Bernier, Léon, 2439
Berns, Walter, 5844
Bernsdorf, Wilhelm, 77
Bernstein, Deborah, 3826
Bernstein, Irwin S., 3940
Berque, Jacques, 1711
Berrocal, Luciano, 3796
Berruto, Gaetano, 2077
Berry, Brian Joe Lobley, 4226
Berry, J. W., 3801
Berry, Linda G., 434
Bersee, A. P. M., 3073
Bertacchini, Renato, 228
Berthel, Jürgen, 4873
Berthélémy-Thomas, Martine, 2422
Berthiaume, Monique, 5069
Berti, Mario, 3222
Bertilsson, Margareta, 4667
Bertini, Antonio, 2147
Bertrand, Arthur, 3007
Bertrand, Claude, 1368
Bertrand, Claude-Jean, 1349
Bertrand, Jane T., 3290
Bertrand, Marie-Andrée, 5845
Bertrand, Michèle, 1673
Bertrand, William E., 4227
Bertsch, Gary K., 5312
Beschner, George M., 5801
Besnard, Philippe, 238, 638, 651, 1597
Bespalov, N. E., 5572
Bespamjatnyh, N. N., 1291
Bessonov, B., 5463
Bestužev-Lada, I. V., 344, 1292, 1293
Betcherman, Gordon, 2547
Betés, Luis, 5571
Bettiolo, Paolo, 1911
Beuchelt, Eno, 1506
Beveridge, W. E., 4995
Beyer, Janice M., 5175, 5802
Bhagat, Rabi S., 4765

Bharadwaj, Lakshmi K., 784, 1507, 5952
Bharara, L. P., 3115
Bhardwaj, N., 3950
Bhat, L. S., 4255
Bhatta Charya, Mohit, 4159
Bhebe, Ngwabi, 1712
Bhiwandiwala, Pouru, 3333
Bhola, H. S., 2493
Bhooshan, B. S., 3972
Biaggio, Mary K., 720
Bianchi, Antonella, 1508
Bianchi, Suzanne M., 4477
Bibby, John, 2778, 5576
Biblarz, Arturo, 503
Biblarz, Dolores Noonan, 503
Biddiss, Michael Denis, 3655
Biddle, Bruce, 1156
Biddle, Bruce J., 3035
Biddulph, Howard L., 1908
Bideau, Alain, 3391
Bielby, William T., 2139, 4523, 4657
Bielenski, Harald, 4923
Bien, Joseph, 253
Bienefeld, M. A., 5176
Bienvenue, Rita M., 3677
Bierbaum, Heinz, 4679
Bierhoff, Hans Werner, 785
Bierman, Arthur Kalmer, 1607
Biervliet, H., 3726
Bigelow, Brian John, 917
Biggart, Nicole Woolsey, 1096
Biggs, Simon, 668
Bihari, Mihály, 5551
Bilbao, Andrés, 254
Biles, David, 5849
Bilkes, C. G. C., 2597
Bill, Helga, 3354
Bill, James A., 2653
Billig, Michael, 5622
Bilmes, Jack M., 3985
Binder, Johann, 4798
Binet, Jacques, 2148, 4652
Birch, Alfred L., 494
Bird, Frederick, 1909
Birjukov, N. I., 5615
Birman, Igor, 3827
Birmbaum, Philip H., 1047
Birnbaum, Michael H., 345
Birnbaum, Pierre, 5481
Biryoukova, A. P., 4799
Bishop, George D., 1173
Bishop, George F., 1221
Bishop, James M., 110, 5037
Bisogno, Paolo, 78
Bisseret, Noëlle, 2284
Black, Charlene R., 918
Black, Jerome H., 5623
Blackaby, Bob, 4338
Blackburn, Robert Martin, 4698
Blair, Edward, 504
Blair, Roger D., 5014
Blais, Denise Daoust, 2032

Blakar, Rolv Mikkel, 669, 2113, 3522
Blake, Nancy, 1509
Blake, Robert R., 6237
Blakely, Edward J., 3986, 4034, 4365
Blalock, Hubert M. Jr., 407, 960, 3727
Blanc, Michel, 4028
Blanc, Olivier, 4800
Blanchard, Marc Eli, 2010
Blanco Abarca, Amalio, 631
Blane, Howard T., 5803
Blank, David Eugene, 5620
Blank, Robert H., 2996
Blankenagel, Alexander, 1951
Blankenburg, Erhard, 5254
Blankstein, Kirk R., 696
Blanton, Richard E., 2561
Blaschke, Jochen, 5431
Blasi, Anthony J., 3728
Blassingame, John W., 2631
Blau, Judith R., 5038
Blau, Peter, 4620, 5060
Blayo, Yves, 3116
Bleitrach, Danielle, 5255
Blejer, Mario I., 3828
Blekher, Feiga, 2926
Blessing, Werner K., 2789
Blinov, N. M., 4699, 5313
Bljumkin, V. A., 1608
Block, James E., 3468
Blocker, Jack S. Jr., 5804
Blofeld, John Eaton Calthorpe, 1713
Blom, H. W., 5409
Blondiau, Heribert, 5256
Bloom, Howard S., 5846
Bloomfield, T. M., 632
Bluedorn, Allen C., 1053, 5696
Bluhm, Lhis H., 4478
Blüm, Norbert, 5177
Blumberg, Rae Lesser, 2598
Blumenberg, Hans, 4700
Blyton, Paul, 5231
Boakes, Robert A., 803
Bobbio, Norberto, 5410
Bobneva, M., 721
Bobotov, S. V., 1640
Bochel, Dorothy, 6186
Bochner, Stephen, 1157
Bock, P. G., 3885
Böckle, Ferdinand, 4924
Boddy, David, 4698
Boden, Margaret A., 213
Boderman, Eli, 4737
Bodrova, V. V., 3177
Boerdam, Jaap, 3469
Boerger, Martin, 5107
Bogdan, Robert, 1489
Bogdanović, Marija, 408
Bogdány, Franz Josef, 6
Bogomolov, A. P., 2818
Bogomolov, T. B., 2819
Bogue, Donald Joseph, 2895
Bohannon, Wayne E., 755

Index des auteurs

Bohlke, Robert H., 209
Böhme, Gernot, 1952
Bohnet, Armin, 598
Böhning, Dankmar, 533
Bohra, Kayyum A., 1139
Bohrnstedt, George W., 409, 902
Boils Morales, Guillermo, 119
Bois, Philippe, 6005
Boisard, Marcel A., 1714
Boiter, Albert, 1910
Bokarev, N. N., 2735, 5314
Bokemeier, Janet L., 2927
Bolas, Cheryl, 142
Bolder, Axel, 346
Bolderson, Helen, 3185
Boldt, Edward D., 786
Bolgov, V. I., 2331
Bollen, Kenneth A., 410, 5464
Bologh, Roslyn Wallach, 255
Bolognini, Franco, 1888
Boltanski, Luc, 5108, 5109
Bolte, Karl Martin, 2563
Bolton, Brian, 6187
Bolton, Neil, 633
Bolz, Wolfgang, 1801
Bonanate, Luigi, 1510
Bonazzi, G., 1079
Bond Andrew R., 3117
Bond, George, 1715
Bondarenko, A. A., 4029
Bongaarts, John, 3234
Bonjean, Charles M., 692
Bonnain, Rolande, 4030
Bonnar, Desmond M., 3886
Bonnet, André G., 165
Bonnett, Aubrey Wendell, 3549
Boorstin, Robert O., 170
Booth, Alan, 5861
Booth, John A., 5624
Booth, Ken, 1212
Boren, Larry C., 1577
Borenstein, Audrey, 7
Borgatta, Edgar F., 411, 534, 564, 3074, 6188
Borgatta, Marid L., 6188
Borghorst, Hermann, 4228
Bori, Pier Cesare, 1911
Boriskin, A. N., 4801
Borjakov, V. I., 6006
Borneman, E., 3355
Bornewasser, Manfred, 634
Borovik, V. S., 3036
Borowitz, Eugene B., 1716
Bortoli, Michele, 4229
Bortz, Jürgen, 2149
Boruch, Robert F., 412
Boruhsov, G., 4578
Borukhov, Eli, 4230
Borwn, Sharon, 2975
Bosanquet, Nick, 4738
Bosetzky, Horst, 1080
Bosio, Albino C., 787

Boskoff, Alvin, 413
Boslooper, Thomas David, 3588
Bosshart, Louis, 2150
Bote Gomez, Venancio, 5361
Botha, Rudolph I., 2011
Bottomley, A. Keith, 5847
Bottomore, Tom, 413, 5398
Bouchier, David, 3589, 5411
Boudon, Raymond, 788, 2332
Boudouin, Jean, 5573
Boudreau, Françoise, 6162
Bouet, Guy, 4031
Bouhouch, A., 1081
Bouillaguet-Bernard, Patricia, 4802
Boulay, Harvey, 4288
Bould, S., 4739
Boulding, Elise, 2564, 3008, 3656
Boulding, Kenneth Ewart, 2564
Boulle-Barbieux, C., 5257
Bourdieu, Pierre, 234, 347, 789, 1511, 2723
Bourgeois-Pichat, Jean, 3208
Bourguignon, Erika, 2928
Bourricaud, François, 2433, 5039
Bouscharain, Gérard, 4032
Boussard, Isabel, 2434
Boutilier, Robert G., 635
Bovenkerk, F., 2654
Bovkun, V. V., 3037
Bovone, Laura, 4925, 5040
Bowe, Frank, 6189
Bowen, Barbara, 3470
Bowen, Elinor R., 4373
Bown, Lalage J., 2494
Bowonder, B., 3966, 4579
Box, Louk, 4033
Boxer, Philip J., 790
Boy, Daniel, 5484
Boyce, Mary, 1717
Boyd, John Paul, 987, 4580
Boyd, Lawrence H., 414
Boyd, Monica, 3559
Boyd, William L., 2354
Boyden, Stephen Vickers, 3973
Boyle, J. David, 2270
Boyle, John M., 5805
Brackett, James W., 3291
Bradburn, Norman M., 505
Bradford, Leland Powers, 4996
Bradford, Martha I., 4996
Bradley, Raymond, 518
Bradshaw, Jane, 1718
Bradshaw, Jonathan, 6050
Bradshaw, Ted K., 4034
Bradshaw, Ted R., 79
Braga, Giorgio, 2078
Bragg, Emma W., 4926
Brain, James Lewton, 3356
Brainbridge, William Sims, 1841, 1953
Braithwaite, John, 5848, 5849
Braito, Rita, 703
Brajnović, Luka, 180
Brandstätter, Hermann, 1174

Brandt, Gerhard, 262
Brannigan, Augustine, 1954
Bransford, John D., 791
Branthwaite, Alan, 1202
Brater, Michael, 5034
Brathwaite, Farley, 2736
Bratt, Nancy, 1445
Braujeu-Garnier, Jacqueline, 4231
Braumann, Freddy, 5315
Braun, Hans-Gert, 4663
Braun, Karl-Heinz, 256, 5625
Braune, Paul, 2149
Braungart, Margaret, 5850
Braungart, Richard G., 5850
Brazzoduro, Marco, 4232, 5689
Bredemeier, Harry C., 2620
Bredow, Wilfried von, 5626
Brelich, Angelo, 1674
Brenes, Abelardo, 637
Brennan, Pat, 1946
Brenner, M. Harvey, 6163
Brenner, Sten-Olaf, 2090
Brereton, Bridget, 3729
Brett, Jeanne M., 5178, 5258
Brewer, Harold, 1446
Breytenbach, Willie J., 2820
Breznik, Sušan, 3118
Brickey, S. L., 5907
Bridge, R. Gary, 2333
Bridges, William P., 4803, 4927
Brief, Arthur P., 5131, 6238
Brier, Stephen, 5090
Briggs, Steven Stambaugh, 5288
Brigham, John, 5528
Brinemann, Elena, 3221
Brinkerhoff, Merlin B., 1912
Brinkgreve, C., 2151
Brinkmann, Wilhelm, 2285
Brint, Steven, 2655
Briones, Guillermo, 473
Briscoe, John, 4035
Briskman, Larry, 792
Brittingham, Barbara E., 4501
Britvin, V. G., 3038
Broadbent, Kieran P., 181
Broch, Tom, 5743
Brockhaus, Christian, 5179
Brockner, Joel, 670, 671
Brödel, Rainer, 2495
Brodersohn, Victor, 2152
Brody, Baruch A., 672
Broembsen, Max H. von, 1329
Bromlej, Ju. V., 1294, 3657
Bromley, David G., 1827, 1842
Bronsema, Gerhard, 2540
Brooke, Rosalind, 6007
Brookman, Frits Henry, 150
Brooks, Anna M., 4277
Brooks, Michael, 6036
Brooks, Nancy A., 3186
Brooks-Gunn, Jeanne, 908
Broschart, Kay Richards, 2993

Broström, Anders, 5160
Broughton, Walter, 1831
Brown, B., 1955
Brown, Bernard E., 2769
Brown, David L., 3119
Brown, Don W., 5528, 5851
Brown, George W., 3187
Brown, John, 6050
Brown, Julia S., 2989
Brown, Lawrence A., 4426
Brown, R. J., 1044
Brown, Randall S., 2929
Brown, Richard H., 1175
Brown, Robert, 1653
Brown, Ronald Gordon Sclater, 6213
Brown, Warren B., 1054
Bowne, Elspeth, 3292
Browning, Harley L., 4607
Browning, Rufus P., 6008
Bruce-Briggs, B., 2655
Bruijn, Jan de., 3293
Bruijne, G. A. de, 3658
Brumelle, Shelby L., 611
Brunborg, Helge, 3392
Bruneau, Jean Claude, 4233
Brunetta, Giuseppe, 5259
Brunn, Kettil, 174
Brunswick, Ann F., 5805
Brusa, Luigi, 4526
Brusatti, Alois, 4527
Brustein, William, 4591
Bryan, James H., 3009
Bryan, Tanis H., 3009
Bryant, Christopher G. A., 4997
Bryant, Clifton D., 5697
Bryce, Herrington J., 4234
Bubolz, Margaret M., 4479
Buchhofer, Bernd, 5744
Buchholz, Erich, 5519
Buchmann, Michael A., 5041
Buchsbaum, Helen K., 861
Buck, Ross, 793
Buck, Trevor W., 2656
Bucuvalas, Michael J., 491
Bugelski, Bergen Richard, 794
Bühl, Walter L., 1988
Bui Dang Ha Doan, 6248
Buitenhuis, Cornelius H., 1082
Bukreev, V. I., 5354
Bullock, Charles S., 3781
Bullough, Vern L., 3357, 3358
Bullowa, Margaret, 2037
Bulmer, Martin, 498, 535
Bülow, Edeltraud, 2012
Bulusu, Lak, 3213
Bumpass, Larry, 2910, 2980
Bunce, Valerie, 5492
Bundy, Colin, 4036
Bunkśe, Edmunds V., 4235
Burack, Elmer H., 4897
Burawoy, Michael, 5132
Burgat, François, 4037

Index des auteurs

Burgat, Paul, 536
Burgbacher-Krupka, Ingrid, 2217
Burger, Christine, 2990
Burgess, Guy M., 2564
Burgess, Robert G., 2286
Burke, Kathryn L., 1912
Burke, Peter J., 664, 673
Burke, Robert V., 4038
Burke, Ronald J., 5110
Burkhauser, Richard V., 6110
Burkitt, Brian, 4672
Burlaj, E. V., 6009
Burles, Jean, 5574
Burnham, Kenneth E., 1802
Burnham, P. C., 3941
Burnkrant, Robert E., 1172
Burns, R. B., 674
Burns, Tom, 5485
Burns, Tom R., 4475
Burnstein, Eugene, 914
Burr, Jeanne, 2930
Burr, Wesley R., 3471
Burrell, Gibson, 4528
Burridge, Kenelm, 675
Bursik, Robert J. Jr., 5852
Burstein, Leigh, 2529
Burstein, Paul, 4766, 5520
Burt, Martha R., 5853
Burt, Ronald S., 604, 605, 901, 4480, 4529
Burton, John Wear, 6010
Busch, Lawrence, 4621
Büscher, Horst, 2892
Bush, Peter, 2435
Busino, Giovanni, 257
Buss, Allan R., 636
Buss, Arnold Herbert, 676
Buss, Eugen, 197
Bussey, Kay, 2976
Bušuev, A. M., 4804
Buteler, Patricio, 5854
Butenko, A., 5722
Butera, Federico, 4874
Butler, Flora Cornelia, 3590
Butler, Stuart, 5180
Butler, Suellen, 4928
Butorina, E. V., 4039
Butrick, Richard, 348
Butsch, Richard J., 653
Buttel, Frederick H., 3987, 4040
Büttemeyer, Wilhelm, 2334
Buttle, Bernard, 5003
Butz, William P., 3235
Bynner, John, 415
Byron, R. F., 1143

Cabana, Alfredo, 3591
Čabrovskij, V. A., 349
Cain, Maureen, 1641
Caine, T. Allen, 3593
Cairns, Robert B., 1512
Calciu, Alexandru, 3939
Čaldarola, Carlo, 1719

Čaldarovič, Mladen, 1447
Caldarović, Ognjen, 4236, 4237
Caldo, Costantino, 3942
Caldwell, John C., 3236
Calhoun, C. J., 1083
Calise, Mauro, 3472
Calot, Gérard, 214, 3237, 3238, 3239
Calvert, Donald R., 2013
Calvet, Louis Jean, 2079
Calvi, Giulia, 2790
Camacho, Daniel, 114
Camarda, Alessandro, 5260
Camarillo, Albert, 3659
Cambier, Guy, 1720
Camburn, Donald, 496
Camic, Charles, 1135, 1998
Camilleri, C., 1413
Camion, Paul, 603
Cammann, Cortlandt, 1120
Campa, Arthur Leon, 1295
Campbell, C. M., 1642
Campbell, Colin, 1296
Campbell, Keith E., 1889
Campbell, Lyle, 2080
Campbell, Richard T., 902, 2724
Câmpeanu, Pavel, 2153
Campiche, Roland, 1913
Campos Santelices, Armando, 637
Canart, Paul, 2014
Cancian, Francesca M., 4427
Canevet, Corentin, 4041
Canforo, Luciano, 2737
Cannon, Lynn Weber, 2657, 5084
Cantor, David, 5855
Cantor, Leonard Martin, 2496
Cantor, Muriel G., 2154
Capelle, Ronald G., 884
Capellin, Paola, 4805
Caplan, Gerald, 3730
Capobianco, Michael F., 606
Caporale, Rocco, 1682
Capraro, Giuseppe, 1914
Caprio, Giovanni, 2821
Caracciolo, Alberto, 2791
Caracuic, Traian, 1513
Carael, Michel, 3294
Caramelli, Nicoletta, 1956
Carbonaro, Antonio, 5764
Cardini, Franco, 1693
Caris Cutter, Susan, 4306
Carlier, A., 4806
Carlos, Manuel L., 3503
Carlson, E. D., 3393
Carlson, John R., 3911
Carlston, Donald E., 1158
Carlton, David, 1495
Carmack, Robert M., 3660
Carmines, Edward G., 474, 492
Carmody, Denise Lardner, 1915
Carnoy, Martin, 2335
Carone, Edgard, 5181
Caroux, Françoise, 1068

Caroux, Jacques, 1068
Carr, Jacquelyn B., 2038
Carr, Timothy James, 4740
Carr-Hill, R. A., 5856
Carre Villar, Francisco, 2155
Carrier, James G., 795
Carrieu, Marie-Josèphe, 4581
Carroll, Archie B., 1098
Carroll, John M., 2156
Carroll, John S., 6023
Carroll, Lucy, 3473
Carse, James P., 3209
Cartelier, Jean, 4424
Carter, Charles Frederick, 2436
Carter, Robert, 5387
Carter, Thomas P., 3661
Carvajal, Manuel J., 2931
Carver, Charles S., 677, 705
Casals, Ignacio, 3075
Cascioli, Alfio, 4998
Caso Raphael, Agustín, 3931
Casparis, Johan, 1843
Cassell, Eric J., 350
Cassen, Bernard, 2081
Cassi, Laura, 3120
Cassileth, Barrie R., 3188
Casson, Mark, 4741
Castel, Françoise, 6164
Castel, Robert, 6164
Castellano, Vittorio, 4582
Castells, Manuel, 5600
Castillo, Gelia T., 4042
Castillo, Juan José, 1514
Castonguay, Charles, 3394
Castro, Maria Elena, 5806
Castros-Almeida, Carlos, 4807
Catalano, Franco, 5432
Cataldo, Everett F., 2336
Catania, A. Charles, 796
Catlin, Steve, 5238
Cattell, Raymond Bernard, 722
Catton, William R. Jr., 3944
Cavalié, J. L., 4894
Cavallaro, Renato, 3395
Cavallo, Roger E., 416
Caveing, Maurice, 151
Cavell, Stanley, 1957
Cavestro, William, 4095
Cavrak, Steve, 1946
Cazenave, Noel, 3480
Cazier, Pierre, 3731
Cazorla Perez, José, 3829
Ceauşescu, Nicolae, 3662
Cebula, Joseph P., 3007
Cebula, Richard J., 3887
Cecil, Earl A., 1033
Cecil, Joe S., 412
Čefranov, V. A., 1643
Cehelsky, Marta, 4043
Cela Conde, Camilo José, 4044
Celm, Ralph S., 3121
Čemodanov, M. P., 1297, 1958

Censi, Antonietta, 2932
Ceppe, Jean Louis, 4238
Čerednjak, P. G., 4449
Ceri, Paolo, 5601
Čerkasov, G. N., 4239, 4399
Černenko, M. S., 4530
Černovolenko, V. F., 5042
Cerny, Philip G., 5732
Černyševa, A. V., 1222
Certeau, Michel de, 1298
Cesareo, Vincenzo, 6011
Česnokov, B. A., 4875
Česnokov, G. D., 2877
Ch'ên, Jerome, 1414
Chabauty, Marie Luce, 2408
Chadwick, Bruce A., 626
Chafetz, Morris E., 5803
Chaffee, Steven H., 5670
Chaffee, Wilber A., 1529
Chagnon, Napoleon A., 2997
Chagnon, Roland, 1803
Chai, Trong R., 5575
Chaison, Gary N., 5182
Chakraborty, B., 3295
Chalfant, H. Paul, 5765
Chaline, Claude, 4240
Challinor, Joan R., 3513
Chambadal, Paul, 1609
Chamberlain, Ann, 3296
Chamboredon, Jean-Claude, 1586, 4045
Chamie, Joseph, 1804
Chance, Paul, 797
Chandel, Bhuvan, 1610
Chandler, Charles R., 1595
Chandler, Mark, 2923
Chaney, David C., 2277
Chang, Dae H., 5857
Chang, H. C., 585, 3240
Chang, Parris H., 4241
Chang, Pav-Min, 3663
Chang, Tai O., 4355
Chao, John C., 3291
Chapman, Richard A., 5552
Chapman Orbegoso, Luis Alberto, 4428
Chappell, Neena L., 467, 3076, 4701
Charbonneau, Simon, 1644
Chardon, Pierre-André, 536
Charles, Edgar D., 3189
Charles, Geneviève, 6240
Charmaz, Kathy, 3210
Charon, Joel M., 8
Charrie, Jean-Pierre, 4242
Charter, S. P. R., 3943
Chartier, Robert, 1844
Chase, Allan, 3732
Chase, Richard, 2565
Chasin, Barbara H., 5769
Chassie, Marilyn B., 4765
Chateau, Dominique, 2157
Chauchat, Hélène, 1515
Chaudhry, Mahinder D., 4046
Chaunu, Pierre, 3297

Chauviére, M., 6142
Chazalette, Andrée, 3830
Chazel, François, 2865
Chebat, Jean-Claude, 2124
Chee, Tham Seong, 2337
Chelune, Gordon J., 885
Chemers, Martin, 1285
Chems, Albert, 2822
Chen, Huey-Tsyh, 351
Chen, Lincoln C., 3211
Chen, Peter S. J., 3298
Cheng-Fang, Yang, 115
Chenoweth, Lillian, 4808, 4835
Chenu, Alain, 5255
Cherkaoui, Mohamed, 798, 2530
Cherki, Eddy, 4243
Cherlin, Andrew, 3474
Chermesh, Ran., 5261
Chernoff, Michael L., 4244
Cherns, Albert, 4702
Chetwynd, Jane, 647
Chetwynd, S. Jane, 913
Chevallier, Jacques, 6012
Chevallier, Maurice, 4245
Chi, Peter S. K., 4246
Chiba, Motoko, 3299
Chiesi, Antonio M., 417
Čhikvadze, V. M., 5521
Child, John, 935
Childs, Robin, 5495
Chinchilla, Norma S., 4809
Chirif, Alberto, 3664
Chisholm, Rupert F., 5698
Chiswick, Barry R., 3831
Chitayat, Gideon, 5183
Choay, Françoise, 2264
Choe, Sun Yuel, 5670
Chojnacka, Helena, 3396
Choldin, Harvey M., 4247
Chombart de Lauwe, Paul-Henry, 3974
Chow, Esther Ngan-Ling, 5111
Chowdhry, D. Paul, 6111
Christensen, Allan, 4876
Christensen, Elia Hidalgo, 3576
Christenson, James A., 1943
Christman, Kenneth P., 4480, 4529
Christopherson, Jon A., 5693
Chu, Godwin C., 1415
Chu, Lily, 1448
Chua, Beng-Huat, 258, 5465
Chua, Lily Aurora, 4514
Chudacoff, Howard P., 3077
Churchman, Charles West, 418, 419
Cialdini, Robert B., 923
Cibrian, Ramior, 4248
Cicak, Fedor I., 5316
Cifrić, Ivan, 4047
Čimič, Esad, 9, 1596
Cioranescu, Alexandre, 2242
Cipko, A. S., 1299
Cipriani, Roberto, 2039
Čirkin, V. É., 5486

Claessens, Dieter, 2878
Claessens, Karin, 2878
Clare, John, 3733
Clark, Gardner, 4048
Clark, John P., 369
Clark, Kim B., 5184
Clark, Lawrence P., 1046
Clark, Lorenne M. G., 2933
Clark, Margaret S., 919
Clark, Priscilla P., 897
Clark, S. D., 10
Clark, Samuel, 4049
Clark, W. A. V., 4249
Clarke, David E., 2140
Clarke, Ignatius Frederick, 352
Clarke, R. O., 5262
Clausen, Lars, 1300
Claval, Paul, 11
Clay, Phillip L., 4250
Clayton, John Powell, 1675
Cleary, Paul D., 2681
Clebsch, William A., 1721
Clegg, Hugh Armstrong, 5133
Clegg, Stewart, 1084, 1085
Cleland, Charles Carr, 3190
Clement, Daniel, 5186
Clement, Werner, 2338, 2497
Clignet, Remi, 499, 2224
Clinton, Charles Anthony, 3988
Clogg, Clifford C., 617, 4742
Cloward, Richard A., 6021
Coale, Ansley J., 3241
Coan, Richard W., 80
Coates, Robert B., 5887
Cobalti, Antonio, 2541
Cobas, José A., 3864
Cobo, Juan M., 2458
Cobo Suero, J. M., 2437
Cochin, Augustin, 2823
Cochrane, Raymond, 5622
Cochrane, Susan Hill, 3242
Cockerham, William C., 1037, 5699, 6191
Coelho, George V., 6182
Coellen, Stephen P., 4481
Cohen, Alvin P., 1691
Cohen, Bernard P., 12, 465
Cohen, Bruce J., 235
Cohen, Élie, 4524, 4525
Cohen, Elizabeth G., 2420
Cohen, Fred, 1645
Cohen, Jere, 3053, 4429
Cohen, Lawrence E., 1037, 3445, 5699, 5855, 5858
Cohen, Lenard J., 2738
Cohen, Roberta G., 1004
Cohen, Ronald, 5487
Cohn, Steven, 5766
Colapinto, Jorge, 353
Colasanto, Michele, 5015
Colburn, David R., 3665
Colditz, Graham A., 6241
Cole, James W. L., 4764

Cole, Jonathan R., 152
Cole, Michelle, 1516
Colella, Brizio, 2498
Coleman, D. A., 2779
Coleman, James S., 453, 1136, 2339
Coleman, James William, 6013
Coleman, John A., 1722
Coleman, Richard P,, 2658
Colletta, Nancy Donohue, 3010
Collins, Lloyd R., 4214
Collins, Randall, 413, 2287, 2607
Collomb, Gérard, 2278
Collomb, Philippe, 3300
Colomer Ferrandiz, Fernando, 1611
Colonna, Salvatore, 2288
Comisso, Ellen Turkish, 5316
Commins, Barry, 961
Compton, Beulah Roberts, 6143
Comstock, Donald E., 1449
Comstock, George, 2158
Conaty, Joseph, 1116
Conlisk, John, 612, 616
Connell, H. B., 4810
Connell, R. W., 1159, 2659
Connerton, Paul, 259
Connor, Patrick E., 1086
Conrad, Peter, 1517
Constantini, Edmond, 723
Contenti, Alessandra, 2243
Converse, Philip E., 1183
Conway, Madeleine, 4898
Conze, Werner, 5085
Cook, Karen S., 978
Cook, Kenneth H., 374
Cook, Martha A., 2289
Cook, Thomas D., 354
Cool, K., 2869
Coolen, J. A. I., 6112
Coombs, Gary, 2040
Coombs, Lolagene C., 3475
Cooper, Lowell, 988, 1006
Cooper, Lucille, 920
Coppa, Frank J., 2159
Corbett, Michael, 2521
Corcoran, Paul E., 5627
Corder-Bolz, Judy, 692
Cordero, Christina, 5602
Córdova, E., 5134, 5185, 5553
Corelli, Emilio, 4430
Cornaton, Michel, 2290
Cornelisen, Ann, 3832
Cornelius, Ivar, 3122
Corradi, Juan E., 1998
Corsini, Gianfranco, 2244
Cortelazzi, Silvia, 5043
Cortés, Fernando H., 355
Corwin, Arthur F., 3833
Corwin, Patty Arneson, 3397
Coscarelli, William C., 2214
Coser, Lewis A., 886
Coser, Rose Laub, 6192
Costa, E., 4767

Costa, Francisque, 1301
Cotesta, Vittorio, 260
Cotgrove, Stephen, 2660
Cotta, Alain, 5362
Cotta, Maurizio, 5628
Cotter, Cornelius P., 5576
Cotterell, Arthur, 1857
Couffignal, Georges, 5186
Coughlin, Richard M., 6014
Coulter, Jeff, 799
Coulton, Claudia J., 6144
Cournanel, Alain, 4431
Court, David, 116
Courtés, Joseph, 2020
Couser, G. Thomas, 215
Cousineau, Jean-Michel, 3888
Cousins, Albert N., 4251
Cousins, M., 1955
Cousquer, Jean-Yves, 5472
Couvert, Roger, 2499
Covello, Vincent T., 2599
Coverman, Shelley, 2953, 3580
Coward, J., 3243
Coward, John, 3476
Cox, Andrew W., 4317
Cox, Harold, 2542
Coxon, Anthony P. M., 1838, 5016, 5017
Craig, Grace J., 3011
Craik, Kenneth H., 723
Cramer, James C., 4811
Crandall, James E., 800
Crandall, Rick, 1612
Creigh, S. S., 5263
Crespo, Angel, 4252
Cressey, Donald R., 5977, 6013
Creusen, Joseph, 5101
Cribier, Françoise, 4253
Crighton, Elizabeth H., 3755
Crimmins, Eileen, 4816
Crispini, Franco, 261
Crist, Raymond E., 1302
Crittenden, Kathleen S., 537
Croghan, Martin J., 1160
Crompton, Rosemary, 5187
Cronin, James E., 5264
Crook, John Hurrell, 2824
Cropley, A. J., 2500
Crosbie, Paul V., 2725
Cross, Malcolm, 4050
Crott, Helmut, 1028
Crouch, Wane W., 374
Crouzet, Alain, 4531
Crozier, Michel, 1087, 1450
Crubellier, Maurice, 3012
Cruden, Robert, 2792
Cruttenden, Alan, 2082
Csepeli, György, 1203
Csizmadia, Andor, 3398
Čubčenko, M. T., 724
Cuenya, Beatriz, 3975
Čugunov, V. I., 1303
Cullen, John B., 5018

Index des auteurs

Cummings, Scott, 3734
Cummings, William K., 2438
Cunliffe, Marcus, 2632
Cunningham, J. Barton, 3989
Cunningham, James V., 4201
Curnock, Kathleen, 6145
Curnow, Ray, 179
Curran, James, 4768, 5412
Curtain, Richard, 3889
Curti, Merle, 2934
Curtis, Bruce, 1451
Curvin, Robert, 4254
Cusinato, Mario, 725
Cussler, Margaret, 2245
Cuthbert, Norman H., 5135
Cutright, Phillips, 2843
Cvetaeva, N. N., 2160
Cvjetićanin, Vlado, 4051
Cvjetičantin, Veljko, 117
Cyrkun, A. F., 5347
Czak, Kazimierz, 4877

D'Agostino, F. B., 678
D'Amico, Ronald, 544
D'Souza, Stan, 3211
Da Gloria, Jorge, 944
Dabžanova, Ž. B., 1305
Dacey, John Stewart, 3039
Daft, Richard L., 577, 2421
Dahn, Ulrich, 5519
Dahrendorf, Ralf, 262
Dailey, Timothy B., 3477
Dales, Richard C., 1416
Dalhlström, Edmund, 2600
Dalton, Russell J., 5629
Damachi, Ukandi Godwin, 5136
Dambaeva, V. D., 1306
Damiano, Elio, 2291
Dandeker, Christopher, 356
Dandurand, Pierre, 2439
Danford, John W., 263
Danielson, Ross, 6165
Danilov, V. K., 1307
Dank, Barry M., 3377
Dankenbring, William F., 195
Dann, Graham M. S., 1916
Darbois, Jean-Claude, 925
Darroch, A. Gordon, 3666
Das, Harish Chandra, 4052
Das, Man Singh, 3478, 3709
Dasilva, Fabio, 1345
Datta, Lois-Ellin, 357
Daubon, Ramon E., 3251
Davidjuk, G. P., 5745
Davids, Leo, 3479
Davidson, Andrew R., 1176
Davies, Bleddyn, 532
Davies, Robert H., 2661
Davis, Charles E., 5112
Davis, Deborah, 921
Davis, Floyd James, 1017
Davis, Fred, 801

Davis, James A., 495
Davis, Karen, 5767
Davis, Lawrence Howard, 264
Davydov, Ju. N., 1308
Day, Dawn, 3480
Day, John, 2793
Day, Phyllis J., 1144
De Castro, Celso Antonio Pinheiro, 1646
De Fronzo, James, 4812
De Kadt, Emanuel, 5363
De Korte, M., 2935
De Leo, Gaetano, 1518
De Lora, Joann S., 3359
De Lucca, John, 265
De Miguel, Jesús M., 6214
De Rosa, Gabriele, 1805
De Sandre, Paolo, 3301
De Silva, Lynn A., 658
De Silva, M. W. Padmasiri, 1723
De Souza, Alfred, 4369
De Souza Martins, Heloisa Helena Teixera, 5188
De Spirito, Angelomichele, 2794
Deacon, Desley, 2744
Deaton, D. R., 5289
Debenham, Jerry, 3399
Debouzy, Marianne, 4929
Debrizzi, John, 13, 1984
Decker, David L., 3078
Decker, John F., 3360
Deconchy, J. P., 1676, 1858
Deegan, Mary Jo, 14
Deere, Carmen Diana, 3481
Defilippis, Josip, 4622
Degtjareva, A. I., 6015
Déhan, Nadia, 2422
Dei, Marcello, 2541
Deiana, Giuseppe, 2879
Dekmejian, R. Hrair, 1724
Del Campo, Salustiano, 3482
Del Val, Alfonso, 3967
Delalić, Ešref, 2501
Delaney, Cornelius F., 1859
Delbos, Geneviève, 4053
Deledalle, Gérard, 2015
Delgado, Hernan, 3221
Della Fave, L. Richard, 1806
Della Pergola, Sergio, 3244
Dellaportas, G., 6113
Delouya, Brrik, 4623
Delph, Edward William, 3361
DeMaio, Theresa J., 506
DeMartini, Joseph R., 5746, 5747
Demenčonok, È. V., 2825
Demerath, N. J. III, 6050
Demonio, Lucien, 4930
Den Ouden, J. H. B., 2601
Denisjuk, N. P., 726
Denisko, L. N., 1309
Denisovskij, G. M., 2683
Denkel, Arda, 2083
Denscombe, Martyn, 679

Denzin, Norman K., 802
Deppe, Frank, 5189
Derber, Charles, 887, 4743
Derber, Milton, 5290
Déri, Miklósné, 2440
Derjapa, M. R., 5433
Derksen, A. Th., 266, 1519
Desatnick, Robert L., 4878
Descamps, Marc Alain, 1597
Deschamps, Jean-Claude, 638, 680
Désert, Bernard, 4221
Deshpande, C. D., 4255
Deshpande, Madhav M., 2016
Desingu Setty, E., 2633
Despierre, Jean, 4744
Despotović, Aleksandar, 6170, 6171
Dessler, Gary, 1055
Detel, Wolfgang, 358
Deutschmann, Christoph, 4931
Deverre, Christian, 3667
DeWalt, Billie R., 3990
Dewar, R., 4932
Dewey, Richard, 4251
Dhunjibhoy, Ros-han, 1725
Di Blasio, Paola, 6230
Di Giamcomo, J. P., 962
Di Giovanni, Alberto, 5522
Di Iullo, Maria Gabriella, 1003
Di Maio, Alfred J. Jr., 3124
Diaz, Elías, 1647
Diaz Araujo, Enrique, 2826
Díaz-Polanco, Héctor, 3668
Dickinson, Anthony, 803
Didorčuk, L. S., 5317
Didur, I. A., 5630
Diekmann, Andreas, 538
Diener, Edward, 1612
Dierckxsens, Wim, 4703
Dietrich, Walther Von, 2411
Dietz, Henry, 5631, 6126
Diggins, William, 3991
Dight, Susan, 2435
Dijkstra, Wil, 507
Dīkshita, Jagadīśa Datta, 1726
Dillingham, Gerald, 1452
Dillner, Gisela, 2161
Dingwall, Robert, 1613, 6210
Diop, L. M., 3125
Diósi, Pál, 1453
Dirks, Nicholas B., 5690
Disco, Cornelis, 267
Ditterich, Kuno, 420
Dixon, David, 1648
Dixon, Richard D., 1917
Dixon, Ruth B., 4054
Djatlova, M. M., 5577
Djerassi, Carl, 3302
Dmiterko, D. Ja., 5137
Dmitriev, A. N., 1310
Dmitriev, A. V., 3079, 4256
Dmitrieva, É. Ja., 1310
Dmitrievskij, V. N., 2273, 2274

Dobbins, Richard, 5135
Dobkowski, Michael N., 3735
Dobosz, Barbara, 922
Dobratz, Betty, 5402
Dobrynin, I. A., 4966
Dockrill, Michael, 5737
Dodder, Richard A., 3265
Dodge, Calvert R., 5860
Dodounekova, Penka, 6114
Doelker, Christian, 2162
Doffny, Jacques, 5603
Doise, Willem, 638, 1478
Doktorov, B. Z., 475, 2274
Dolgih, N. S., 2566
Dolgodilin, B. G., 963
Dolzer, Hermann, 4055
Dombos, Paul, 5044
Domenach, Jean-Luc, 1520
Domhoff, G. William, 1454, 2662
Dominguez-Alcon, Carmen, 6242
Donahoe, John W., 804
Donaldson, Les, 4879
Donati, Pierpaolo, 3013
Doncov, A. I., 1029
Donelson, Stuart, 3976
Dongmo, Jean-Louis, 3890
Donnea, François-Xavier de, 3891
Donnelly, Patrick G., 5908
Donnerstein, Edward, 945
Donnison, David, 4257
Donovan, Peter, 1860
Doob, Anthony N, 2163
Doran, Michael F., 4258
Dore y Cabral, Carlos, 4056
Doreian, Patrick, 539, 540, 989
Dormagen-Kreutzbeck, Inge, 727
Dorn, Edwin, 3736
Dou, Alberto, 4583
Douglas, Jack D., 1311
Dowd, James J., 3080
Dowlat, Manijeh, 4057
Downing, Douglas C., 3281
Downton, James V. Jr., 1807
Doyle, Daniel P., 1852
Doyle, Susan, 1202
Drain, Michel, 4058
Drass, Robert E., 3926
Drerup, Heiner, 2334
Dressayre, Philippe, 5561
Drew, Paul, 799
Drewnowski, Jan, 5768
Dridze, T. M., 2164
Driedger, Leo, 1727
Dronov, V. T., 5086
Drury, Darrel W., 681, 682
Drysdale, Alisdair, 3669
Du Bick, Michael A., 1102
Dubar, Claude, 2530
Dubbert, Joe L., 2936
Duberman, Lucile, 15
DuBey, Darrell L., 2292
Dubey, S. M., 3483

Dublin, Thomas, 4813
Dubois, Pierre, 5190, 5225, 5265
Dubost, Jean, 805
Dubson, B. I., 5348
Duby, Georges, 4432
Duc Nhuan, Nguyen, 4259
Duclos, Denis, 2663
Dudek, R. A., 6193
Dudley, Charles J., 1537
Duff, Andrew, 2660
Dufour, Desmond, 3212
Dufour, Roland, 5349
Dufrancatel, Christiane, 2949
Dugandžija, Nikola, 1861
Duipmans, D., 2084
Düll, Klaus, 4677
Dull, Klaus, 4933
Dumont, Fernand, 5604
Duncan, Beverly, 2937
Duncan, Otis Dudley, 541, 2937
Dunkerley, David, 1085
Dunlap, Riley A., 3944
Dunlap, Riley E., 3965
Dunstan, John, 3126
Dupâquier, Jacques, 316, 3127
Dupont-Gonin, Pierre, 3834
Duprez, Jean-Marie, 5302
Durand, Claude, 4584
Durand, Gilbert, 1862
Durandin, Guy, 1223
Durić, Mihailo, 1863
Dussault, François, 5274
Dutrénit, Jean-Marc, 6146
Dutta, Ranajit, 3303
Dutter, Lee E., 3040
Duvall, Donna, 5861
Duvignaud, Françoise, 806
Duvignaud, Jean, 807, 1960, 5364
DuWors, Richard E. Jr., 5110
Dux, Günther, 1455
Dworkin, Anthony Gary, 2543
Dwyer, Daisy Hilse, 1204, 1649
Dybowski-Johannson, Karin, 4931
Dyer, Colin, 3128
Džabbarov, I. M., 1312
Dzjabko, N. N., 2827
Džunusov, M. S., 2567

Eagleton, Mary, 2246
Eaton, Joseph W., 5748
Ebanks, G. E., 3232
Eberlein, Gerald L., 339
Ebertstein, Isaac W., 3401
Eccles, Henry Effingham, 5700
Eckart, Christel, 4814
Eckberg, Douglas Lee, 359
Eckert, Roland, 2938
Eckes, Thomas, 421
Eco, Umberto, 2017
Edding, Friedrich, 2497
Edel, Abraham, 360
Edelstein, J. David, 5191, 5192

Edem, D. A., 2292
Eden, Colin, 1088
Edginton, Barry, 1451
Edgley, Charles K., 628
Edmunds, George, 946
Edwards, David J. A., 1268
Edwards, John N., 3417
Edwards, P. K., 4934
Edwards, Richard, 4935
Edwards, Walter F., 2085
Eells, Richard, 4532
Efimec, V. D., 1309
Eggers, Philipp, 2293
Eglin, Peter, 808
Ehara, Yumiko, 16
Ehren, A. M. A., 5701
Ehrenberg, Ronald G., 4999
Ehrenreich, John, 6166
Ehrlich, Avishai, 4815
Ehrlich, Howard J., 5466
Eichler, Gert, 5350
Eichler, Margrit, 3592
Eidelson, Roy J., 888
Eiff, Wilfried von, 1089
Eisenberg, Elliott, 322
Eisenberg, Ulrich, 5862
Eisenberg-Berg, Nancy, 927
Eisenstadt, S. N., 1417, 2828, 5723
Eiser, J. Richard, 809, 1177, 1178
Eitzen, D. Stanley, 5754
Ekehammar, Bo, 5659
Ekland-Olson, Sheldon, 5613
El Safty, Madiha, 3484
El-Sayed El-Bushra, 3129
El-Shakhs, Salah, 4334
Elazar, Daniel J., 1808
Elder, Glen H. Jr., 4797
Elder, Murdoch George, 3310
Eldridge, Albert F., 964
Elgie, R. A., 542
Elinson, Jack, 6167
Eliou, Marie, 1418
Eliseev, V. E., 361
Elkan, Walter, 3892
Ellemers, J. E., 3670
Ellen, R. F., 3941
Elling, Ray H., 6215
Elliott, Brian, 4260, 4261
Elliott, Delbert S., 5863
Elliott, Jean Leonard, 3671
Elliott, John, 4880
Ellis, Desmond, 5864
Ellul, Jacques, 4585
Ellyson, Steve L., 1018
Elnicki, Richard A., 6257
Elsheikh, Farouk, 5243
Elster, Jon, 519, 520
Elwert, Georg, 4059
Embid, Alfredo, 2880
Emde, Reimund, 543
Emerton, J. A., 1864
Emge, Richard Martinus, 1376

Empey, Lamar T., 5865, 5866
Endruweit, Günter, 81, 5529
Endsley, Richard C., 2207
Eneroth, Bo, 422
Engelhardt, Michael Von, 1952
Engelhardt, Ulrich, 5085, 5193
Engelhardt, W. W., 1246
England, Joe, 5194
England, Richard, 5365
Entin, Elliot, 2108
Enyedi, György, 3977
Epple, Karl, 423
Epstein, A. L., 3672
Epstein, Cynthia Fuchs, 2937
Epstein, Laura, 6147
Epstein, Laurily Keir, 5632
Epstein, Léon D., 5578
Epstein, Yakov M., 645
Erbe, Michel, 118
Erbring, Lutz, 659
Erdei, Ferenc, 1313
Eremenko, A. M., 2664
Eresund, Pia, 3014
Ericksen, Eugene P., 3992
Ericksen, Julia A., 3992, 4854
Erickson, Bonnie H., 2056
Erickson, Maynard L., 5994
Erickson, Paul A., 3945
Ericson, Richard, 5867
Eristain, Tonio, 5868
Erlanger, Howard S., 1521, 5045
Ermakova, O. V., 200
Ermolina, G., 1522
Ersov, S. A., 5266
Erunov, B. A., 1224
Esaer, Eric, 2247
Escalante, Carlos, 473
Escallier, R., 3894
Escott, Paul D., 2634
Escovar, A., Luis, 889
Esina, T. A., 3946
Espenshade, Thomas J., 4704
Espinet, Blai, 3947
Esping-Anderson, Gösta, 5236
Espinosa, Justiniano, 6016
Esser, Hartmut, 3895
Establet, Roger, 4697
Ester, P., 3948
Etzioni, Amitai, 6115
Eurich, Claus, 2165
Evan, William M., 6216
Evans, Art, 3673
Evans, David R., 508
Evans, Donald D., 1677
Evans, Jeff, 561
Evans, M. D., 5702
Evans, Peter, 5724
Evans, Sara, 3593
Evdokimov, P. G., 2758
Everett, James E., 5122
Everett, Martin, 607
Evers, Mark, 3304

Every, George, 1728
Evtušenko, I. I., 1456
Ewer, Phyllis A., 4816
Eyerman, Ron, 4667
Eysenck, Hans J., 372, 810, 2939
Eysenck, Sybil B. G., 372
Ezeaku, L. C., 2340
Ezeanyagu, E., 3896

Fabian, Johannes, 1276
Fabiano, Mauro Antonio, 17
Fabre, Annie, 4060
Fabri, Marcel Y., 3130
Faden, Ruth R., 811
Fajardo, Dario, 2829
Fajnburg, Z. I., 812
Fakhfakh, Françoise, 3835
Faksh, Mahmud A., 2341
Fal'ko, V. I., 362
Falaturi, Abdoldjawad, 1729
Falco, Maria J., 363
Falkin, Gregory P., 5869
Fallding, Harold, 1865
Falussy, Béla, 4918
Fanshel, David, 6148
Faragó, Magdolna S., 2441
Farago, Uri, 3674
Fararo, Thomas J., 1171
Farber, Henry S., 5291
Farberow, Norman L., 5870
Fargues, Philippe, 3897
Faris, Robert E. L., 221
Farkas, János, 1961
Farley, O. William, 6204
Farley, Reynolds, 683, 3737, 5871
Farr, G. M., 3250
Farrell, Brian Anthony, 1002
Farrow, Dana L., 815
Faruškin, M., 1314
Fassheber, Marianne, 3015
Fassnacht, Gerhard, 476
Fathaly, Omar I., 2830
Faught, Jim, 268
Faulkner, Joseph E., 1891
Faulkner, Robert R., 230, 463
Faulstich, Werner, 2166
Faupel, Charles E., 5900
Faure, Yves-André, 5671
Faury, Jean, 1890
Favrè, Chantal, 3041
Favre, Pierre, 424, 1598
Faw, Terry, 639
Fawcett, James T., 3298
Fazio, Russell H., 1199
Feagin, Joe R., 1753, 2595, 3765, 3881
Fear, Frank A., 595
Feather, N. T., 5434
Fedinin, V. K., 869
Fedorov, G. T., 3042
Fedoseev, A. A., 5399
Fedoseev, P. N., 18, 2831, 5435
Fedotov, S. K., 1523

Index des auteurs

Fedotova, O. D., 2832
Feeley, Malcolm M., 5872
Fehér, Ferenc, 2248
Fehr, Helmut, 2833, 5599
Feichtinger, Gustav, 3279
Feierman, Steven, 6194
Feijoo, María del Carmen, 2940
Fein, Helen, 5873
Feinstein, Karen Wolk, 4817
Feldberg, Roslyn L., 2941, 3602
Felfe, Edeltraut, 6017
Felice, Lawrence G., 4214
Feller, Gordon, 1402
Fellows, Mary Louise, 4506
Felson, Marcus, 425, 5642, 5702, 5858
Felson, Richard B., 902
Fenigstein, Allan, 947
Fenn, Paul, 6116
Fennessey, James, 544
Ferber, Marianne, 4501
Ferdinand, Theodore N., 5984
Ferge, Zsuzsa, 5046, 6018
Ferguson, Tamara J., 364
Ferligoj, Anuška, 1161
Fernandes, Florestan, 2279
Fernandez, Juan A., 3245
Fernandez, Roberto, 4482
Fernández Font, Jorge, 2249
Fernández Vargas, Valentina, 139
Fernando, Dallas F. S., 3246
Ferner, Anthony, 2739
Ferrari, Silvio, 1918
Ferraro, Guido, 1866
Ferrarotti, Franco, 813, 1524, 1867, 2250
Ferras, Robert, 5436
Ferree, Myra Marx, 3585, 3594
Ferrer Benimeli, José Antonio, 1809
Ferriss, Abbott L., 545
Ferry, Gilles, 2502
Feshbach, Seymour, 948, 5919
Festy, Patrick, 3247
Fetisov, V. P., 1525
Feuchtwang, Stephan, 1315
Feuille, Peter, 5292
Feulner, Patricia N., 4818
Feyerabend, Paul, 5467
Fiedler, Judith, 477
Fielding, A. G., 5019
Fijnaut, C., 5530
Fiksel, Joseph, 426
Filangieri, Angerio, 3131
Filatov, A., 5437
Filin, Ju. N., 6019
Filipp, Sigrun-Heide, 684
Filippov, F. R., 2409, 3016
Fillmore, Charles J., 2018
Filograsso, Nando, 2342
Filsnger, Erik E., 1891
Filstead, William J., 5813
Finch, Janet, 1832
Fincham, Frank, 5798
Fincham, Robin, 5195

Fine, Gary Alan, 801
Fine, Marvin J., 3485
Fingarette, Herbert, 5874
Finighan, W. R., 685
Finkelstein, Michael, 3738
Finkle, Jason L., 3132
Finocchiaro, Maurice A., 814
Finogenov, V. F., 5577
Firebaugh, Glenn, 1038
Firestone, Ira J., 1485
Firsbie, W. Parker, 3653
Fischer, George, 5466
Fischer, Heinz-Dietrich, 5047, 5366
Fischer, Kathleen B., 2529
Fischer, Michael G., 4480
Fischer, Roland, 1868
Fischer-Lichte, Erika, 2041
Fisek, Nusret H., 3305
Fishburn, Peter C., 546
Fisher, Donald, 5438
Fisher, Elizabeth, 2942
Fisher, Maxine P., 3836
Fisichella, Domenico, 5605
Fiske, Donald W., 517
Fitzpatrick, John S., 4936
Fitzpatrick, Sheila, 2343
Flanagan, Thomas, 4419
Flax, James W., 6195
Fleet, D van S. Al-Tuhaih, 5113
Fleishman, Joseph J., 3089
Fleming, Gretchen V., 6180
Flere, Sergej, 19, 269
Fleuret, Anne, 4624
Fleuret, Patrick, 4624
Flichy, Patrice, 2167
Flitner, Elisabeth, 2563
Flores Jaramillo, Renán, 2503
Florian, Radu, 2568
Fluttert, P. H. M., 509
Fly, Jerry W., 4262
Flynn, Edith Elisabeth, 1526
Foddy, W. H., 685
Fodor, Eugene M., 815
Fogel, Walter, 3837
Foley, John W., 2602
Fombrun, Charles, 1066
Fomerand, Jacques, 2442
Foner, Anne, 2603, 3004
Fonseca, Mabel, 3486
Fontaine, Pierre-Michel, 3739
Fonyó, Gyula, 5554
Foot, David K., 2898
Forgas, J. P., 1527
Forgas, Joseph P., 903, 922
Form, William, 4678
Forrest, Jacqueline Darroch, 3306
Forrest, Ray, 4328
Forsyth, Donelson R., 1614
Forward, Susan, 3362
Foschi, Martha, 640
Fossaert, Robert, 2665
Foster, Brian L., 990

Foster, George McClelland, 4061
Foster, L. E., 6243
Foster, Peggy, 6196
Fougeyrollas, Pierre, 270
Fourez, Gérard, 1457
Fournier, Jacques, 6020
Fournier, Marcel, 2439
Foust, Cleon H., 5875
Fowler, Robert Booth, 1256
Fowler, Roger, 2086
Fox, A. John, 3213
Fox, Douglas M., 2230
Fox, John, 547, 549
Fox, Renée C., 3214, 6168
Fox, William S., 2666
Fox Piven, Francis, 6021
Fracchia, Charles A., 1810
Fraczek, Adam, 948
Fraisse, Geneviève, 5102
Framheim, Gerhild, 2467
Francès, Robert, 2218
Francis, Arthur, 4625
Francome, Caroline, 3307
Francome, Colin, 3307
Franda, Marcus, 4062
Frank, Arthur W. III, 6197
Frank, Lawrence P., 5413
Frank, Ove, 608
Frank, Tibor, 1225
Frank, Werner, 6117
Franke, Michael, 3898
Franke, Richard W., 5769
Franke, Walter M., 5294
Frankel, Philip, 3740
Frankenberg, Hartwig, 3487
Franks, Violet, 2945
Franqueville, André, 3133
Franz, Margaret-Mary, 3299
Franzina, Emilio, 3838
Frassinetti, Antonio Murga, 119
Frate, Dennis A., 3549
Frazier, Charles E., 365, 3790
Frederic L. Pryor, 1330
Fredette, Jean-Marc, 2899
Freedman, Daniel G., 2998
Freedman, Deborah S., 496
Freedman, Jonathan A., 6169
Freedman, Maurice, 1315
Freedman, Richard D., 2624
Freedman, Ronald, 3134
Freeman, Gary P., 3839
Freeman, Linton C., 991
Freeman, Richard B., 4769
Freese, Lee, 427
Freiberg, J. W., 271
Freidenreich, Harriet Pass, 1730
Frejka, Tomas, 3248
Frelastre, Georges, 4063
French, J. Lawrence, 4064
French, Peter A., 1615, 2087
French, Richard Anthony, 4263
Frendrich, James M., 5644

Frey, Bruno S., 2233, 4653
Frey, William H., 4264
Freyhold, Michaela von, 4065
Frezel-Lozey, Michel, 3308
Frideres, James S., 1179
Friedberg, Erhard, 1087
Frieden, Bernard J., 4265
Friedenberg, Edgar Z., 5876
Friedlander, Dov, 3134
Friedman, Alfred S., 5801
Friedman, Robert S., 1208
Friedmann, Georges, 2168
Friedmann, John, 6022
Friedrich, Paul, 2088
Friedrichs, Christopher R., 4266
Frieze, Irene Hanson, 6023
Frijling, B. W., 428
Frinking, B., 3400
Friš, A. S., 5439
Frisbie, W. Parker, 3401
Fritlinskij, V. S., 272, 6024
Frolova, M. A., 1269
Fry, John, 273
Fry, John A., 5318
Fry, John Allan, 1316
Frye, Charles A., 1528
Fuchs, Victor R., 893
Füchsle, Traudl, 2990
Fudetani, Minoru, 1090, 1091, 4626
Fuguitt, Glenn V., 3910
Führ, Christoph, 2294
Fuhr, Harald, 4066
Fuhrman, Ellsworth R., 45, 63, 64, 327, 1962
Fujisaki, Hiroko, 3556
Fujita, Hiro'o, 4267
Fukui, Haruhiro, 2468
Fulbrook, Mary, 324
Funahashi, Kazuo, 4090
Furgiuele, Giovanni, 3488
Furmanov, G. L., 274
Furth, Hans G., 904
Fürth, Thomas, 4745
Füstös, László, 548, 4485
Futton, Philip N., 3899

Gabriel, Karl, 1056
Gabriel, Richard A., 5703
Gadotti, Moacir, 2504
Gaiotti de Biase, Paola, 3595
Gajfullin, U., 5579
Gal'perin, Ja. S., 4586, 4587
Galaway, Burt, 6143
Galeazzi, Umberto, 2219
Galeckaja, R. A., 3162
Galey, Margaret E., 3596
Gallacher, H. P., 816
Gallagher, Bernard J., 3191
Gallagher, Daniel G., 5306
Gallas, Howard B, 3489
Gallen, Moira, 3309
Galler, Heinz P., 3402

Galli, Rosemary, 4067
Gallie, Duncan, 5196
Galligan, Pat, 4849
Gallino, Luciano, 204, 2604
Galper, Jeffry H., 6149
Galvão, Eduardo Enéas, 3741
Galvin, Miles E., 5197
Gamō, Masao, 1419
Gamson, William A., 1530
Gan, Ju. V., 728
Ganapathy, T. N., 3597
Gandásegui, Marco A., 2667
Gandhi, Raj, 5633
Gandy, D. Ross, 275
Gandz, Jeffrey, 5005
Ganesh, S. R., 1458
Ganiage, Jean, 3135
Gannon, Martin J., 1092
Gannon, Thomas M., 1833
Gaponov, A. K., 817
Gappert, Gary, 4770
Garbin, Albeno P., 5032
Garcia, Brígida, 2943
García Canclini, Néstor, 2220
Garcia Cotarello, Ramón, 5488
Garcia Ferrando, Manuel, 5367, 5400
Garcia Jimenez, Jesús, 2169
Garcia y Gama, Irma Olaya, 3249
Garcia-Petit, Jorge, 2834
Garciía Cotarelo, Ramón, 599
Gardiner, W. Lambert, 2544
Garelli, Franco, 1919
Garmendia, Jose Antonio, 20
Garrett, William R., 1039
Garrison, Dee, 203
Garrison, Howard H., 3742
Garrisson-Estèbe, Janine, 1731
Gary, Albert L., 1180
Gash, Norman, 2635
Gasparini, Giovanni, 5198
Gates, Alan Frederick, 1732
Gatlin, Douglas S., 2336
Gatrell, Anthony, 430
Gaube, Heinz, 4268
Gaudemar, Jean-Paul de, 4705, 5087
Gaudin, Thierry, 4588
Gauntner, Donald E., 5698
Gautam, Moham, 5633
Gauvin, Annie, 4802
Gauvreau, Danielle, 3245
Gavaki, Efie, 3840
Gavrikov, V. P., 4068
Gavrilov, A. P., 2835, 2836
Gaxie, Daniel, 5616
Gay, Volney Patrick, 1845
Gazzetti, Fernando, 3136
Gean, William D., 818
Gearheart, B. R., 2522
Gecas, Viktor, 5048
Geck, Hinrich-Matthias, 3900
Geertz, Clifford, 1317
Geertz, Hildred, 1317

Géhin, Étienne, 347, 1265
Gehmacher, Ernst, 3802
Geiger, Roger L., 2443
Geis, Gilbert, 5877
Geismar, Ludwig L., 3490
Geismar, Shirley, 3490
Geithman, David T., 2931
Gel'bras, V. G., 2569
Gelfand, Donald E., 3675
Geljuha, A. M., 4627
Geller, Martin M., 2624
Gelpi, Ettore, 2505
Gendin, A. M., 366
Genn, Hazel, 500
Gennard, John, 4771
George, Frank Honywill, 600
George, Linda K., 1162
Georgievski, Petre, 120
Gerastevič, E. A., 2717
Gerbet, Marie Claude, 2636
Gerbod, Paul, 2444
Gerchak, Yigal, 611
Gerking, Shelby D., 3841
Germain, Carel B., 6150
Germani, Gino, 1529
Gerner-Adams, Debbie J., 3598
Gerő, Zsuzsa, 4654
Gerster, Florian, 6118
Gerstlé, Jacques, 5397
Geser, Hans, 2570
Geurts, Pieter Antoon Marie, 2795
Ghai, Dharam, 4631, 5770
Gholson, Barry, 819
Ghosh, B. N., 3842
Ghosh, S. C., 5199
Giacomoni, Silvia, 153
Giampaglia, Giuseppe, 3491
Gianniti, Francesco, 5878
Gibbs, Barbara M., 2336
Gibbs, Jack P., 5994
Gibbson, Don C., 5879
Gibson, Colin, 3403
Gibson, Cyrus F., 1093
Gibson, James L., 5545
Giddens, Anthony, 276, 6025
Giele, Janet Zollinger, 2944, 6119
Gilbert, G. Nigel, 510
Gilboa, Eylan, 2170
Gilchrist, Bruce W., 5880
Gilchrist, C. Jack, 3936
Giles, Howard, 2019, 2117
Giles, Michael W., 2336
Giliomee, Hermann, 3717
Gill, Flora, 3901
Gillespie, David F., 1047, 1484
Gillespie, Michael W., 549
Gillespie, Virgil Bailey, 1892
Gillian, Mary Ellen, 5895
Gillingham, Robert, 4483
Gilman, Stuart, 3764
Gilmartin, Kevin J., 550, 3059
Gilmore, David D., 2668

Gilmour, Peter, 4937
Giner, Salvador, 1318, 4069
Giner de San Julian, Salvador, 2571
Ginsburg, Gerald P., 641, 903
Ginsburg, Norman, 6026
Giovagnoli, Agostino, 2740
Girt, John L., 551
Girtler, Roland, 5529
Gisler, Dany, 2506
Gitelman, Zvi, 3843
Gittel, Marilyn, 3993
Gitterman, Alex, 6150
Giudici, Amilcare, 1678
Giuily, Eric, 5130
Giuliano, Luca, 3043
Giuliano, Toni, 711
Gizatov, K., 2221
Glagow, Manfred, 3949
Glaser, Edward M., 21
Glaseriva, Jaroslava, 5088
Glasner, A. Hale, 6198
Glass, Arnold Lewis, 820
Glassner, Barry, 1205, 5807, 6169
Glauser, Daniel, 367
Glazier, Jack, 1834
Glazier, Stephen D., 1920
Glazova, E. P., 2741
Gleeson, Denis, 2523
Gleichmann, Peter Reinhart, 821
Glenn, Evelyn Nakaro, 2941
Glennon, Lynda M., 3599
Glettler, Monika, 429
Glick, Leonard, 6027
Glick, Paul C., 3404, 3450
Gliedman, John, 3192
Glock, Charles Y., 3778
Gloor, Pierre-André, 1206
Glover, John A., 1180
Gluck, Peter R., 4269
Gluhov, P. I., 4706
Glumin, V. I., 5440
Gnuschke, John E., 482
Gnyrja, E. S., 5351
Gobernado, Arribas, Rafael, 1963
Gochman, Charles S., 5736
Göckenjan, Gerd, 6120
Godschalk, J. J., 4819
Goede, M. P. M. de, 4747
Goede, M. P. M. de., 4746
Goertzel, Ted George, 70, 240
Goethals, J., 5881
Goetschy, Janine, 5329
Goetze, Rolf, 4270
Goff, Tom W., 1964
Goffredo, Donato, 2171
Goglio, S., 3676
Golant, Stephen M., 478, 3081
Golany, Gideon, 3978, 4271
Gold, H., 5580
Gold, Ruth Z., 449
Goldberg, Itshak, 3828
Goldberg, Stephen B., 5258

Goldberg, Walter, 5319
Goldenberg, I. Ira, 1459
Goldenberg, Judith, 940
Goldfarb, Jeffrey C., 2275
Golding, David, 5114
Golding, Stephen L., 907
Goldinger, Barbro, 2545
Goldman, Albert Harry, 5808
Goldman, Noreen, 3215
Goldman, Paul, 4935
Goldscheider, Calvin, 3134
Goldschmidt, Dietrich, 2295, 2411
Goldsmid, Charles A., 82
Goldsmid, Paula L., 82
Goldsmith, Harold F., 564
Goldstein, Harvey, 501
Goldstein, Jay E., 3677
Goldstein, Leslie Friedman, 3600
Goldstein, Michael S., 6197
Goldstein, Sidney, 3797
Goldstone, Jack A., 1530
Goldthrope, John H., 2780
Goldvarb, Jeffrey C., 2222
Golembiewski, Robert T., 1094
Golota, V. S., 1460, 1461
Golovačev, S. B., 2519
Golovnev, A. I., 1420
Goltz, J. Walter, 5894
Gomberg, Edith S., 2945
Gömöri, Edith, 4820
Gončarenko, N. V., 1421
Gončaruk, S. I., 6097
Gontier, Geneviève, 4868
González, Anabel, 3601
González, Mariano, 1320
Gonzalez Blasco, Pedro, 83, 1965, 1966
González Duro, Enrique, 5809
Gonzalez Gaviola, Horacio, 1319
Gonzalez Rodríguez, Benjamin, 3193
González Salazar, Gloria, 4272
Good, B. J., 3250
Good, Mary-Jo DelVecchio, 3250
Goodall, John S., 4070
Goode, Erich, 1531
Goode, William J., 1137
Goodman, Jerry D., 2296
Goodman, John L., Jr., 4273
Goodman, Leo A., 618
Goodman, Louis Wold, 4427
Goodman, Neal R., 2781
Goodstein, Leonard D., 965
Goodwin, Carole, 3743
Goodwin, Leonard, 6121
Goot, Murray, 5672
Gopal, Brij, 3950
Gorbunova, L. N., 4884, 6028
Gorčenko, G. V., 729
Gordievskij, A. A., 5489
Gordon, Howard Scott, 22
Gordon, L., 6029
Gordon, L. A., 2669
Gordon, Margaret S., 2459, 4748

Gorin, Zeev, 277
Gorjačeva, A. I., 4433
Gorjunov, V., 1270
Goroff, Norman N., 1005
Gorovskij, F. Ja., 2837
Gorr, Michael, 368
Gorškov, A. A., 4881
Gorškov, M. K., 1226
Goss, Kevin F., 4589
Gossop, Michael R., 1178
Gottdiener, M., 479
Gottfredson, Michael, 5898
Gottlieb, Roger S., 1321
Gottman, John Mordechai, 3405
Gottsegen, Gloria B., 1030
Gottwald, Norman Karol, 1733
Goudy, Willis J., 3415
Gough, Ian, 6030
Gough, Kathleen, 3492
Gould, David J., 5785
Gould, Leroy C., 5811
Gould, Meredith, 3388, 3602
Gould, Peter, 430
Gouldner, Alvin Ward, 278, 2742
Govaerts, France, 2125
Gove, Walter R., 890, 905
Gowing, Peter G., 1734
Grabb, Edward G., 1462, 2670, 3744, 5634
Grabbe, Holger, 2042
Grabosky, P. N., 5882
Graburn, Nelson H. H., 5368
Gracia Sanz, Jesús, 5338
Graff, Harvey J., 2507
Grafmeyer, Yves, 4274
Grampa, Giuseppe, 1247
Granato, Fiore, 1508
Granberg, Donald, 1889
Grand'Maison, Jacques, 2671
Grandguillaume, Gilbert, 1422
Grandjean, Burke D., 4938, 5049
Grant, Gerald, 2445, 2446
Gras, Alain, 431
Gratton, Lynda C., 822
Graves, Daniel R., 3687
Gray, Paul S., 5211, 5293
Graycar, Adam, 6031
Grayson, J. Paul, 2743, 2856
Grayson, L. M., 2743
Graziosi, Mariolina, 4484
Grebing, Helga, 5200
Greeley, Andrew, 3493
Greeley, Andrew M., 1735
Green, Brent, 3082
Green, Charles S. III, 84
Green, Thomas F., 2344
Greenaway, W. K., 5907
Greenberg, David F., 5883
Greenberg, Edward S., 5320
Greenberg, Martin S., 5884
Greene, Les R., 936
Greene, Penelope J., 3363, 3745
Greene, V. L., 619

Greenspan, Stanley I., 2531
Greenwald, Bruce C. N., 4772
Greenwald, Howard P., 3194
Greenwood, Ernest, 5751
Gregory, Ann, 5617
Gregory, Joel W., 2900
Gregory, Michael S., 2946
Grehnev, V. S., 5468
Greiffen Hagen, Martin, 5441
Greiffenhagen, Martin, 5635
Greiffenhagen, Sylvia, 5635
Greilsammer, Ilan, 1736
Greimas, A. J., 432
Greimas, Algirdas Julien, 2020
Greislammer, Alain, 5673
Gremion, Catherine, 5555
Gremliza, Dorothee, 4071
Gresle, François, 2137, 3624, 3920
Gribet, Marie-France, 4275
Griese, Hartmut M., 1532
Griffin, Larry J., 2610
Griffin, Maryann D., 4246
Grigas, R., 4533
Grigas, R. S., 4534
Grignon, Christiane, 1599
Grignon, Claude, 1599
Grigor'ev, S. I., 2447
Grigorov, V. M., 6032, 6033
Grimes, Alan P., 2934
Grimes, Michael D., 3969
Grimm, Klaus, 2881
Grimshaw, Allen D., 1533
Grimshaw, William J., 5540
Grindstaff, C. F., 3232
Grizzard, Nigel, 1737
Grjadunova, L. I., 1616
Groat, H. Theodore, 1594
Groh, Dieter, 3968
Grohs, Gerhard, 2892, 4065
Grøndbjerg, Kirsten, 5771
Grønhaug, Kjell, 178
Gröschke, Dieter, 1181
Groser, Manfre, 5143
Grosrichard, Alain, 5469
Grossarth-Maticek, Ronald, 3195, 3196
Grossat, Bernard, 3645
Groth, A. Nicholas, 5885
Groth, Alexander, 5495
Groth, Margit Velsing, 5267
Ground, Lynn, 4082
Groupe Desgenettes, 642
Grube, Joel A., 1483
Gruber, Franz, 3100
Gruber, Murray L., 6244
Gruen, Eckhard, 823
Gruenberg, Barry, 4939
Gruhn, Werner, 2172
Grümer, Karl-Wilhelm, 2726
Grunberg, Gérard, 5115
Grünberger, Hans, 286
Grundman, Adolph H., 2345
Gruneberg, Michael M., 4940

Grunewald, Karl, 3197
Grusky, Oscar, 5111
Grussin, B. A., 2173
Gruzdev, A. I., 4590
Grymer, Herbert, 2765
Gubert, R., 3676
Guccione Monroy, Nino, 1248
Guest, Avery M., 4276, 4277
Guiart, Jean, 1846
Guibourdenche de Cabezas, Marta, 5886
Guillemard, Anne-Marie, 3083
Guillerm, Alain, 4535
Guillon, Roland, 4882
Guizzardi, Gustavo, 1921
Gulezian, R. C., 552
Gulliver, P. H., 966
Gulomov, O., 4883
Gunnell, John G., 1654
Gur'janov, S. T., 4884, 4885, 6034
Gurevič, P. S., 2174
Gurin, Gerald, 2672
Gurin, Patricia, 2672
Gurova, R. G., 2297, 3044
Gusov, A. Z., 2838, 5201
Gustafson, James M., 1617
Gustafson, James P., 988, 1006
Gustavsen, Bjørn, 4941, 5556
Guterbock, Thomas M., 3994, 5674
Gutiérrez, Sonia, 2276
Gutierrez Leyton, Mario, 5772
Gutmann, Emanuel, 1738
Gutmann, Gail, 96
Guttman, Allan, 5369
Guttman, Louis, 553
Guy, Rebecca F., 628
Guyer, Jane I., 2947
Guzelj, Jože, 4648
Guzman, José Miguel, 3233
Gvishiani, Dzhermen M., 4673

Haack, Friedrich-Wilhelm, 1893
Haag, Daniel, 2346
Haagen, C. Hess, 915
Haas, David F., 1095
Haas, John D., 2313
Haavio-Mannila, Elina, 3494
Häberle, Eckehard J., 4536
Habermas, Jürgen, 1534
Habibulin, K. A., 1322
Hachenberg, Michael, 2146, 5706
Hack, Lothar, 5089
Hackett, Bruce M., 1109
Hackler, James C., 5887
Hackman, J. Richard, 4886
Hadden, Jeffrey K., 1820, 1922
Haes, Julian, 2546
Haferkamp, Hans, 1463
Hagan, John, 5888, 5889, 5890
Hägele, Werner, 5370
Hägelmayer, Istvánné, 5321
Hagen, Richard, 3363
Hague, John A., 1323

Haines, Michael R., 3251
Haining, Peter, 1869
Hajda, Lubomyz, 3137
Hajko, Dalimír, 1324
Hakim, C., 497
Hakim, Catherine, 2948
Halaby, Charles N., 4942
Halberstam, Joshua, 1739
Hale, Gordon A., 824
Hale, Nathan Cabot, 3495
Halem, Lynne Carol, 3406
Haley, William E., 1700
Halfon, Efraim, 3951
Halfpenny, Peter, 5202
Hall, Arden, 5000
Hall, John A., 2251
Hall, Judith A., 2089
Hall, Raymond L., 3678
Hall, Richard H., 45, 369
Hall, Robert Ernest, 5001
Hall, Robert L., 2482
Hall, Stuart, 1249
Hallen, G. C., 5891
Halliday, Fred, 2839
Hallik, K. S., 1325
Hallinan, Maureen T., 1019
Hallowell, Christopher, 4072
Halsey, A. H., 2347, 2882
Halsey, William M., 1811
Haltiner, Karl, 5704
Ham, Chris, 6035
Hama, Hideo, 1326
Hamer, Andrew Marshall, 4278
Hamilton, David L., 1173
Hamilton, F. E. Ian, 4263
Hamilton, Gary G., 1096
Hamilton, Richard F., 4991
Hamilton, Roberta, 3602
Hamilton, V. Lee, 5892
Hamm, Bernd, 4279
Hamman, Mona, 3603
Hammar, Tomas, 3798
Hammer, Muriel, 992
Hammerich, Kurt, 2448
Hammond, John L., 1923
Hammoudi, A., 2605
Hanák, Katalin, 2175
Hanami, Tadashi, 5138
Hanami, Tadashi A., 5139, 5268
Hanaš, S. A., 4707
Hancock, Ian F., 2021
Handelman, Howard, 4280, 5203
Handelman, John R., 2850
Handin, Kenneth H., 5893
Handlin, Oscar, 2796, 3844
Hanin, Ju. L., 1227
Hanisch, Rolf, 4073
Hanke, Helmut, 5339
Hankiss, Elemér, 4485
Hanks, Michael, 5371
Hanly, Charles Mervyn Taylor, 279
Hannan, Damian, 4074

Hannan, Michael T., 601, 2887
Hannerz, Ulf, 4281
Hannigan, John A., 2811
Hanova, O. V., 1327
Hansen, David O., 4075
Hansen, Joseph, 5691
Hanson, E. Mark, 2348
Hanson, Richard A., 3746
Hanumantha Rayappa, P., 4704
Haranne, Markku, 5050
Harary, Frank, 521, 609
Haray, Frank, 608
Harbi, Mohamed, 2949
Harčev, A. G., 3496
Hardiker, Pauline, 6145
Hardt, Hanno, 2043, 2176
Hardy, Melissa A., 4464
Hare, A. Paul, 1328, 1329
Hareven, Tamara K., 3077
Hargopal, G., 4076
Hargrove, Barbara W., 1870
Haridas, T. P., 5301
Harp, John, 2547
Harper, Jan, 4821
Harper, Nancy L., 2044
Harrell, W. Andrew, 5894
Harris, Barbara J., 4822
Harris, Christopher Charles, 370
Harris, Howard, 2045
Harris, Marvin, 1330
Harris, Tirril, 3187
Harrison, John Fletcher Clews, 1694
Harrison, Madelyn M., 235
Harrop, Martin, 2782
Harry, Joseph, 1559, 3364
Hart, John, 6151
Hart, Nicky, 6202
Hartjen, Clayton A., 15
Hartley, Dorothy, 4077
Hartman, Paul T., 5294
Hartmann, Hans C., 5820
Hartnage, Timothy F., 5895
Hartog, J. A., 6093
Hartshorn, Truman A., 4282
Hartwig, Frederick, 433
Harvet, Carol D., 3390
Harvey, Charles, 4078
Harvey, Denis E., 3679
Harvey, Edward B., 2849
Harvey, Edwin R., 1423
Harvey, Fernand, 2673
Harvey, Youngsook Kim, 1695
Hashimoto, Masanori, 3252
Hashizume, Daisaburo, 1331
Hass, Aaron, 3365
Hass, Ann Fingarette, 5874
Hassan, Riad K., 865
Hastings, Donald W., 434
Hastings, William M., 6036
Hatanaka, Munekazu, 6122
Hatch, Elvin, 4283
Hatchett, Shirley, 3737

Hattori, Noriko, 2950
Hattori, Tōru, 5490, 5491
Haubert, Maxime, 4079
Haubtmann, Pierre, 280
Haupt, Georges, 2797
Hauser, Robert M., 5073
Haveman, R. H., 3286, 3287, 5773
Havens, Betty, 3076
Hawkins, Denis Frank, 3310
Hawkins, John N., 2349
Hawkins, Linda L., 5665
Hay, Michael J., 3902
Hayami, Yujiro, 4000
Hayase, Toshio, 4411
Hayashi, Yatomi, 2572, 2674
Hayes, Adrian C., 281, 297
Hayes, Karen N., 915
Haynal, André, 1213
Haynes, Robin M., 6217
Hayward, J. E. S., 5492
Hazan, Haim, 3084
Hazard, William R., 2350
Healy, John Joseph, 3680
Hearn, James C., 2449
Heath, A. F., 2347
Heaton, Tim, 3910, 4284
Heaven, P. C. L., 1214, 5824
Hebdige, Dick, 1332
Hebding, Daniel E., 6027
Hechter, Michael, 282, 4591
Heckerman, Carol Landau, 3604
Hedlund, Dalva E., 3497
Heeger, H. P., 4285
Heer, David M., 3241
Heffer, Jean, 1349
Heffernan, W. Joseph, 6037
Hegazy, Samir, 2252
Heiberg, Turid, 5372
Heilman, Samuel C., 85
Heim, Maggie, 5919
Heimer, Carol A., 4670
Heinze, Rolf G., 1067, 3199, 4943
Heise, David R., 1535
Heiss, Jerold, 3471
Heitlinger, Alena, 3605
Hejda, Stanislav, 5774
Hekman, Susan J., 371
Helbo, André, 2022
Held, Gerhard, 2726, 5034
Heller, Tamar, 1153
Hellmann, Ellen, 3747
Helly, Denise, 3681
Helmer, Katherine, 4354
Hemsay, Nicolas, 3845
Hénault, Anne, 2023
Hénault, Georges Maurice, 4655
Henderson, D. W., 4486
Hendon, William Scott, 2223
Hendrick, Clyde, 645
Hendrie, Delia, 5204
Heneman, Herbert G. III, 4887
Heneveld, Ward, 2351

Author index

Henke, Winfried, 3439
Henkel, Christoph, 3498
Henretta, John C., 2724, 3790
Henricks, Thomas S., 2046, 5369
Henriksen, Ingrid, 4708
Henry, Jean-Robert, 1650
Henslin, James M., 3407
Hepple, B. A., 5269
Heraud, Brian J., 5020
Herber, Hans-Jörg, 825
Herbert, David T., 6038
Herbert, Robert T., 1679
Herceg, Josip, 1536
Heredia, Beatriz Maria Alásia de, 4080
Hergenhahn B. R., 730
Herkommer, Sebastian, 4679
Herlyn, Ulfert, 4286
Hermann, Theo, 643
Hermans, Manfred, 1812
Herndon, Marcia, 2266
Herne, Florence, 3606
Hernes, Helga, 3607
Hernon, Peter, 182
Herpin, Nicolas, 347, 1600
Herran, Carlos A., 3799
Herrera, Ligia, 3138
Herrick, David, 1166
Herrick, Robert L., 236
Herring, Ronald J., 4147
Hershey, Daniel, 3005
Hertzler, J. O., 23
Hervey, S. G. J., 2024, 2027
Herz, Thomas Aage, 5051
Herzog, Walter, 1163, 1964
Hesseler, Michael, 3499
Hetebrij, M., 511
Héthy, Lajos, 5322
Hettema, P. J., 731
Hettlage, Robert, 4671
Heuer, Gerhild, 5896
Heuman, Gad J., 3748
Heydevrand, Wolf, 5546
Hickox, Mike, 2314
Hickson, David J., 1058
Hieber, Lutz, 154
Higgins, Joan, 6039
Higgins, Paul C., 6160
Higley, John, 2744
Hill, Lester, Jr., 359
Hill, Michael J., 6040
Hiller, Harry H., 121
Hillery, George A. Jr., 1537, 1806
Hillgaard, Lis, 6245
Hills, Stuart L., 1538
Himelfarb, Alexander, 1333
Himmelfarb, Harold S., 1740
Hindelang, Michael J., 2951, 5897
Hinestrosa, Fernando, 3408
Hinkle, Dennis E., 554
Hinkle, Roscoe C., 24
Hinz, Heide, 4287
Hinz, Michael, 4287

Hinzen, Heribert, 2508
Hirabayashi, Gordon, 1553
Hirano, Takako, 2952
Hirsch, Barry T., 5205
Hirsch, Susan E., 5090
Hirschi, Travis, 5897, 5898
Hirschman, Charles, 3139
Hirshi, Travis, 5865
Hirst, Paul Q., 1250
Hishiyama, Kenji, 1371
Hjelmquist, Erland, 2090
Hlophe, Stephen S., 2745
Ho, Man Keung, 6152
Ho, Teresa J., 3017
Hobart, Charles, 216
Hobbs, Daryl J., 4081
Hodge, Robert, 2098
Hodge, Robert W., 555
Hodžić, Alija, 1464
Hoekstra, C., 3409
Hoenack, Stephen A., 5899
Hoff, Ernst, 1552
Hoffman, Phillip P., 2450
Hoffmann-Riem, Christa, 5749
Hogan, Daniel B., 5021
Hogan, Dennis P., 3066
Hogan, Robert, 660
Hohl, Janine, 2352
Høivik, Tord, 5372
Hoksbergen, R. A. C., 3608
Holladay, John C., 522
Holland, Barron, 1741
Holley, William H., 5140
Hollier, Denis, 171
Holling, Heinz, 826
Hollingsworth, Ellen Jane, 4288
Hollingsworth, J. Rogers, 4288
Holmes, Brian, 2353
Holmes, Colin, 3749
Holmes, David S., 861
Holsti, Ole R., 1228
Holt, D., 556
Holt, Elizabeth Gilmore, 2224
Holt, Lewis E., 1241
Holtmann, Dieter, 557
Holton, R. J., 5493
Holyoak, Keith James, 820
Holz, Josephine R., 2177
Holzner, Burkart, 1967, 5694
Homan, Roger, 498
Homans, George C., 326, 1137
Homra, A. V., 3800
Hondrich, Karl-Otto, 4537
Hong, Doo-Seung, 4489
Hong, Dvo-Scung, 5705
Hood, Thomas C., 1272
Hoogendoorn, J., 4888
Hoogstraten, Johan, 86
Hope, Kempe R., 3995
Hopf, Christel, 435
Hopf, Wilhelm, 5373
Hopkins, Andrew, 2744

Index des auteurs

Hopkins, Anne H., 5245
Hopkins, Mike, 5782
Hopkins, Raymond F., 4628
Hopkins Valentine, Carol, 3253
Hoppál, Mihály, 1225
Horan, Patrick M., 4468, 4664
Horiuchi, Shiro, 3474
Horlacher, David E., 3271
Hornung, Carlton A., 1210
Horowitz, Irving Louis, 2178, 5873, 6041, 6042
Horowitz, Ruth, 477
Horowitz, Stanley A., 4709
Hörte, Sven Åke, 4749
Horton, Raymond D., 5298, 5299
Horton, Raymond L., 558
Horuc, L. É., 1968
Hoshi, Akira, 87
Hostetler, John A., 3992
Houg, Tora, 4656
Houghton, John, 51
Hougland, James G. Jr., 1097, 1813, 1924, 4606
Houle, Gilles, 2673
Hoult, Thomas Ford, 1802
Houser, Betsy Bosak, 4795
Houston, John P., 2417
Houtart, François, 3846
Howard, John W., 1040
Howard, William A., 4289
Howarth, F., 4434
Howe, Michael J. A., 827
Howell, Susan E., 5636
Hoyenga, Katharine, 2953
Hoyenga, Kermit T., 2953
Hoyer, William J., 5850
Hraba, Joseph, 3682
Hrubos, Ildikó, 4654
Hsu, Francis L. K., 1415
Huber, Joan, 3410
Hubert, J. J., 559
Hudson, R. A., 2025
Huerta Y Palacios, Felipe, 2179
Hughes, Diane Owen, 3411
Hughes, Michael, 890, 2180, 4559
Hughey, J. B., 4220
Hugo, Graeme, 4290
Hui, Lim Mah, 3750
Huizer, Gerrit, 5750
Huizing, Peter, 1799
Hulin, Charles L., 1063
Hulkko, Jouko, 3311
Humblet, Jean E., 3996
Hummer, Patricia M., 4823
Hummon, Norman, 540
Humphrey, John, 5141
Hunt, Alan, 1641, 1651
Hunt, Bernice, 3412
Hunt, James G., 1060
Hunt, Janet G., 2954
Hunt, Morton, 3412
Hunt, Pauline, 5104

Hunt, Richard E., 5175
Hunt, Ronald J., 275
Hunter, Alfred A., 2611
Hunter, John E., 1182
Hunter, Ronda F., 1182
Hurd, Mava, 5818
Hurh, Won Moo, 3505, 3683, 3751
Hurn, Christopher J., 2287
Huseman, Richard C., 1098
Hussain, Asaf, 2746
Hussey, David E., 4538
Huszár, Tibor, 25, 1334, 4944
Hutchins, Edwin E., 1019
Hutchison, Ira W., 3413
Hutchison, Katherine R., 3413
Huxley, Christopher, 5295, 5419
Hwa-Bao Chang, Henry, 2606
Hyclak, Thomas, 5206
Hyde, Janet Shibley, 3366
Hydyrov, T., 1335
Hyer, Paul, 1341

Iatridis, Demetrius S., 6043
Ibáñez, Jesús, 1007
Ibarrola, Jésus, 5207
Ibragimov, H. A., 2091
Ichniowski, Casey, 5208
Ickes, William, 2955
Igra, Amnon, 560
Igrickij, Tu. I., 145
Iguíñiz, Javier, 122
Ikeda, Katsunori, 1539
Ikeda, Yoshisuke, 1336
Ilieva, L. G., 6044
Imanov, G. R., 2675
Immegart, Glenn L., 2354
Inbar, Michael, 1099
Inciardi, James A., 5900
Indik, Bernard P., 6141
Indo, Kazuio, 5606
Indovina, Emma, 1424
Indra, Jeet Singh, 5901
Ingham, John N., 2747
Inglehart, Ronald F., 4471
Ingram, Cregg F., 2355
Ingram, Larry C., 1871, 2451
Inoue, Teruko, 3609
Insko, Chester A., 932, 1145
Ioanid, Ileana, 1337
Iodkovskaja, L. V., 200
Iovčuk, M. T., 1338
Ipola, Emilio De, 1251
Irini, Styllianoss, 3381
Irons, William, 2997
Irvine, Elizabeth E., 6153
Irvine, John, 561
Irvine, William P., 5580
Isaac, Larry, 1540
Isajiw, Wsevolod, 3903
Isambert, François-A., 1925, 2047, 2999
Isambert-Jamati, Viviane, 2298
Ishikawa, Yoshiyuki, 3367

Ishwaran, K., 3018
Islami, Hivzi, 3997, 3998
Ismael, J. S., 2840
Ismael, Jacqueline S., 6045
Ismael, T. Y., 2840
Ismailov, I. A., 732
Isomura, Eiichi, 26, 4291
Israel, Joachim, 283, 644
Itkin, S. M., 1541
Ito, Susumu, 6046
Itskhokin, Aleksandr, 2607
Ivančuk, N. V., 733
Ivanov, E. I., 1339, 1340
Ivanov, M. A., 1008
Ivanov, V. N., 5209, 5637
Ivanova, L. N., 1229
Ivaškevič, I. M., 2748
Iversen, Gudmund R., 414, 562
Iwawaki, Saburo, 372
Iyengar, Shanto, 5638
Izraeli, Dafna N., 5022

Jaakkola, Risto, 174
Jaccard, James J., 1176
Jackall, Robert, 5902
Jackman, Mary R., 1207, 3752
Jackman, Robert W., 436, 3752
Jackson, David J., 411, 563, 564
Jackson, Douglas N., 906
Jackson, Dudley, 5270
Jackson, Jacquelyne Johnson, 3085
Jackson, Michael Peart, 6154
Jacob, Herbert, 5903
Jacob, Jeffrey C., 1542
Jacobs, David, 2608
Jacobs, Eva, 3610
Jacobs, Jerry, 463
Jacobsen, Chanoch, 1465
Jacobsen, Walter, 2524
Jacobsson, Staffan, 4592
Jacquemin, Alix, 2356
Jacques, Jeffrey M., 2452
Jaeger, Carlo, 4465
Jafar, Mohammad, 2749
Jaffe, Dale J., 6176
Jaffe, Joseph, 2108
Jaffe, Yoram, 949
Jagchid, Sechin, 1341
Jäger, Michael, 373
Jagodzinski, Wolfgang, 4487
Jahangir, Burhanuddin Khan, 2676
Jain, Devaki, 3611
Jakobs, Ludwig, 4945
Jakopovič, Ivan, 2357, 2358
Jaksic, Slobodan, 3612
Jakuba, E. A., 5317
Jakupov, N. M., 5581
Jakušov, A. I., 4292
Jallinoja, Riitta, 3494
Jamard, Jean-Luc, 3685
James, Dilmus D., 123
James B. Rule, 1459

Jamieson, Ian, 4629
Jamin, Jean, 88, 480
Janićijević, Miloslav, 217
Jankova, Z. A., 3500
Janković, Ivan, 5904, 5905
Janković, Nevenka, 6047
Jankowski, James P., 5442
Janne, Henri, 4750
Janover, Louis, 2750
Janovskij, R., 734
Janowitz, Morris, 2883, 3979
Jansen, Abraham, 4773
Jansma, Lammert G., 6178
Janssen, Roel, 4293
Janvry, Alain de, 4082
Jaques, Marceline Elaine, 6187
Jaramillo, Luz, 3591
Jardel, Jean-Pierre, 2092
Jardillier, Pierre, 5002
Jaremko, Matt E., 735
Jarošenko, T. M., 2907
Jarosz, Maria, 3501
Jarry, Elisabeth, 4946
Jaspal Singh, 5210
Jasso, Guillermina, 6048
Jauch, Lawrence R., 1060
Jauss, Hans Robert, 284
Javeau, Claude, 1342
Jean, Georges, 828
Jeancolas, Jean Pierre, 2181
Jeay, Madeleine, 3368
Jeccminis, Chris A., 5323
Jedidi, Mohamed, 4294
Jedlicka, Allen D., 123
Jedlicka, Davor, 2048
Jeffries, Richard, 5211
Jeffries, Vincent, 2609
Jencks, Christopher, 3000, 4657
Jenkins, Hugh, 2225
Jenkins, J. Craig, 2865
Jennessen, Heinz, 829
Jennett, Christine, 5602
Jennings, Kenneth M., 5140
Jensen, Gary F., 5906
Jensen, Jens-Jorgen, 2453
Jensen, Stefan, 1343
Jerez Mir, Rafael, 27
Jerotić, Vladeta, 6170, 6171
Jha, B. N., 4083
Jimenez Blanco, José, 1966
Johanningmeier, Erwin V., 2412
Johnson, Benton, 1923
Johnson, C. L., 2093
Johnson, David W., 620
Johnson, Doyle Paul, 1146
Johnson, Elizabeth S., 3086
Johnson, George E., 4824
Johnson, Gregory A., 924
Johnson, Harry G., 4466
Johnson, Harry M., 1652
Johnson, J. Timothy, 3312
Johnson, Kenneth M., 3141

Index des auteurs

Johnson, Lesley, 1344
Johnson, Miriam M., 3385
Johnson, Nan E., 1020
Johnson, Oliver A., 1969
Johnson, Robert Eugene, 2677
Johnson, Terry R., 5000
Johnson, Virginia E., 3379
Johnson, Walton, 1715
Johnston, Barry V., 1345
Join-Lambert, L., 5789
Jolles, H. M., 155
Joly, Jacques, 4295
Jones, Calvin C., 5679
Jones, Catherine, 6049
Jones, Charles L., 5016, 5017
Jones, Edward E., 1041
Jones, Frank L., 830
Jones, Kathleen, 6050
Jones, Linda M., 2956
Jones, R. Ben, 2798
Jones, Ray, 4502
Jones, Russell A., 645
Jones, Sue, 1088
Jones, Thomas E., 5725
Jones, Trevor W., 5016, 5017
Jordan, Carla, 3072
Jordan, David K., 1395
Jordan, Lawrence, 512
Jorgensen, Danny L., 285
Joseph, Isaac, 4274
Joshi, Barbara R., 2637
Joshi, Purushottam, 630
Josifovski, Ilija, 124
Josselin de Jong, P. E. de, 2573
Jost, François, 2157
Jotwani, Motilal Wadhumal, 2253
Jourdain, Alain, 3318
Jovanov, Neca, 5271
Jowett, Garth, 2182
Józsa, Péter, 1252
Jubber, Ken, 4680
Judd, Carol M., 3686
Judd, Charles M., 1183, 2333
Judd, Dennis R., 6053
Judet, Pierre, 4630
Juiržis, R. V., 4593
Julemont, Ghislaine, 3254
Jules-Rosette, Bennetta, 1834, 1847
Julliard, Jacques, 2678
Jung, Harold, 2679
Junghänel, Günter, 1618
Junho Pena, Maria Valéria, 28
Junquera, Carlos, 1872
Junusov, Ju. Ju., 4296
Jura, Michel, 565
Jurs Stephen G., 554
Justice, Blair, 3369
Justice, Rita, 3369
Juzufovič, G. K., 156

Kabačenko, A. P., 5726
Kaes, René, 1543

Kafry, Kitsa, 4947
Kahan, Arcadius, 5091
Kahan, James P., 967
Kahane, Reuven, 1742
Kahle, Lynn R., 686, 1184
Kahn, Alfred J., 1125
Kahn, Lawrence M., 4488, 5212
Kahn, Michèle, 5092
Kahn-Freund, Otto, 5142
Kail, Robert, 2532
Kainz, Howard P., 1619
Kal'noj, I. I., 6051
Kalajdžiev, V., 3313
Kalašnikov, N. I., 1100
Kalbach, Warren E., 3867
Kalberg, Stephen, 2841
Kalbitz, Rainer, 5272
Kalbouss, George, 1346
Kalika, Ju. A., 1347
Kalin, Rudolf, 3801
Kalinkin, E., 2454
Kalir, Joseph, 1743
Kalleberg, Arne L., 2610, 4685, 4710, 4919
Kalleberg, Arthur Lennart, 1998
Kallick-Kaufmann, Maureen, 5374
Källström, Kent, 5296
Kalmuss, Derba, 5752
Kaltahčjan, S. T., 1294
Kaluzny, Arnold D., 2421
Kamalavijayan, D., 2455
Kamarás, István, 844
Kamble, B. R., 2638
Kamble, N. D., 4084
Kamenka, Eugene, 1653, 1654
Kamerling, David S., 2450
Kamiko, Takeji, 1164, 2957, 3502, 3524
Kaminski, Gerhard, 3952
Kamyšev, E. N., 736
Kanbara, Fumiko, 1165, 2958
Kanda, Michiko, 3613
Kanda, Osamu, 3028
Kane, L., 3087
Kang-Wang, Janet F., 6246
Kantrow, Louise, 3314
Kapitány, Ágnes, 1466
Kapitány, Gábor, 1466
Kaplan, Barbara Hockey, 5718
Kaplan, Marion A., 3614
Kaplan, Robert E., 993
Kapteyn, Arie, 468
Kar, Snehendu B., 3315
Karam, Francis X., 2094
Karan, Orv C., 5035
Karasawa, Kazuyoshi, 2783
Karasu, Toksoz B., 3370
Karauš, A. A., 2486
Kardelj, Edvard, 4085
Kardos, Lajos, 1185
Karim, Mehtab S., 3414
Karmazinov, L. S., 5213
Karmel, Barbara, 1101
Karmeshu, 613

297

Karnic, Albert K., 5562
Karnoouh, Claude, 4086
Karp, David Allen, 1544
Karpik, Lucien, 1102
Kas'jenenko, V. I., 5582
Kashiwazaki, Hiroshi, 3255
Käsler, Dirk, 286, 318, 1952, 5635
Kaspi, André, 1348, 1349
Kassab, Ahmed, 4087
Kassalow, Everett M., 5146
Kassapu, S. N., 2095
Kastenbaum, Robert, 5816
Katchadourian, Herant A., 3371
Kateb, George, 1655
Katona, Imre, 5639
Katunarič, Vjeran, 4674
Katz, Harry C., 5291
Katz, Ralph, 5543
Katzenstein, Mary Fainsod, 3687
Katzer, Jeffrey, 374
Kau, James B., 5607
Kaufer, David S., 2026
Kaufert, Joseph, 6177
Kauffman, J. Howard, 1814
Kaur, Amrit, 3615
Kavalerov, A. I., 737
Kawakita, Takashi, 4711, 4825, 4826, 6052
Kawamoto, Akira, 4088, 4089
Kawamura, Nozomu, 2842
Kawanishi, Hirosuke, 5214
Kawasaki, Esho, 4090
Kawasaki, Ken'ichi, 375
Kawasaki, Kikuko, 1835, 1926
Kayastha, S. L., 3904
Kaye, Howard L., 7
Kayser, Bernard, 4091, 4092, 4093
Kazama, Daiji, 1467
Kazamias, Andreas M., 2471
Kazdin, Alan E., 1186
Kazimirčuk, V. L., 745
Kaztman, Rubén, 4712
Kazutoshi, Koshiro, 4948
Kealy, Edward R., 2267
Kearl, Michael, 3088
Keddie, Vincent, 2600
Kee, Howard Clark, 1744
Keefe, Susan E., 3503
Keely, Charles B., 3848, 3905
Keer, Norbert L., 1166
Kefeli, V. B., 4627
Keifer, Ellen, 4827
Keim, Willard D., 4094
Keiser, Lis, 6245
Keith, Pat M., 3415
Kejzerov, N., 1350
Kekes, John, 831
Kělam, A. I., 4594
Kell, Carl L., 1031
Keller, Alan, 3316
Keller, Berndt, 5143, 5215
Kellerman, Henry, 994
Kelley, Dean M., 1927

Kelley, Harold H., 891
Kellough, D. G., 5907
Kelly, Delos H., 1545, 5908, 5975
Kelly, Gary F., 3372
Kelly, George Anthony, 1815
Kelly, Phyllis B., 3142
Kelly, William R., 558, 2843, 3753
Kemp, Fred, 5003
Kempler, Daniel, 2018
Ken'ichi, Furuya, 5144
Kendig, Hal, 4297
Kendrick, D. C., 946
Kennedy, Devereaux, 1970
Kennedy, Theodore R., 3504
Kenny, David A., 566
Kenrick, Douglas T., 923, 924
Kenworthy, Eldon, 2702
Keohane, Nannerl O., 3638
Kepevska, Jovanka, 124
Kepplinger, Hans Mathias, 5706
Kerr, Steven, 1103
Kerstein, Robert, 6053
Kervinio, Monique, 4095
Kesselman, Steven, 6054
Kessler, Ronald C., 2681
Ketkar, Suhas L., 3256
Kettl, Donald F., 3999
Keyfitz, Nathan, 316, 2901, 2910, 3123
Keys, J. Berward, 1129
Khader, B., 4096
Khalakdina, Margaret, 6123
Khan, Azizur Rahman, 4631
Khan, M. Masud R., 3373
Khan, Mumtaz Ali, 2639, 3019
Khellil, Mohand, 3849
Khleif, Bud B., 2096
Khonde, Ptiukuta, 3616
Khoshkish, A., 5401
Kick, Edward L., 109
Kickert, Walter J. M., 832
Kida, Akio, 1351
Kidner, Richard, 5216
Kieckhefer, Richard, 1873
Kierski, J., 3285
Kigundu, Moses N., 4774
Kikuchi, Masao, 4000
Kilburn, Harold C. Jr., 4529
Killen, James, 4298
Killian, Lewis M., 3754
Killworth, Peter D., 986
Kilmann, Ralph H., 454
Kim, Byong-suh, 1894
Kim, Chin, 1656
Kim, Dong I., 4606
Kim, G. F., 5608
Kim, Hei Chu, 3505
Kim, Joochul, 3347
Kim, Kwang Chung, 3505
Kim, Moonja Park, 738
Kim, Yoon Shin, 3257
Kimbrough, S. T., 1745
Kimmerling, Baruch, 5695

Index des auteurs

Kindermann, Ross P., 614
Kindseth, Ola, 5646
King, Haitung, 3850
King, Kathleen Piker, 89
King, Lisa, 935
King, Ronald, 2548
King, Russell, 3851
Kingsley, Su, 3416
Kinlen, Leo, 3213
Kipper, James K. Jr., 3417
Kirillova, M. A., 2297
Kirp, David L., 3755
Kirsch, Hans Christian, 2359
Kirsch, Martin, 5273
Kirton, Michael, 1104
Kirwen, Michael C., 3418
Kiselev, N. N., 1352, 3953
Kiselev, V. P., 1505
Kiseleva, L. A., 739
Kislov, S. A., 740
Kissler, Leo, 5640
Kistriev, E. F., 4299
Kitajima, Shigeru, 5675
Kitamura, Yazuyuki, 2438
Kivisto, Peter, 1017
Kjahrik, L. O., 287
Klages, Helmut, 1056, 1468
Klapp, Orrin E., 183
Klausa, Ekkehard, 5947
Klausmeier, Herbert John, 833
Kleer, Jerzy, 4539
Kleiler, Frank M., 5004
Klein, Joel, 1746
Klein, Martin A., 4097
Klein, Norman, 6172
Klein, Paul, 5707
Klein-Moddenborg, Volker, 1174
Kleinbeck, Uwe, 834
Klemm, R. Christopher, 6216
Klenova, N. V., 741
Kleppner, Paul, 1923
Klimov, V. A., 1473
Klinar, Peter, 3852
Kline, Paul, 646
Klingbeil, Detlev, 437
Klingel, David M., 686
Klingman, David, 2844
Klingner, Donald E., 4890
Ključnikov, A. I., 5217
Kljuev, A. V., 742, 5641
Klockars, Carl B., 1546
Klonglan, Gerald E., 595
Klonne, Arno, 5218
Klopov, E., 6029
Klopov, E. V., 2669
Klorman, Ricardo, 555
Kloss, Heinz, 3756
Kluczynski, Jan, 2456
Kmieciak, Peter, 1468
Knapp, Mark L., 2097
Knemeyer, Franz-Ludwig, 5531
Knežević, Radoslav, 4828

Kniesner, Thomas J., 5532
Knight, Graham, 4949
Knight, Ian B., 5324
Knjazeva, M. B., 1253
Knodel, John, 3258
Knoke, David, 438, 5642
Knorr, Karin D., 1971
Knospe, Horst, 77
Knowles, James C., 3207
Knox, Paul L., 567
Knudson, Roger M., 907
Knutson, Thomas J., 1009
Knutsson, Jahannes, 5533
Kobayashi, Kōichirō, 5563
Kobayashi, Koichiro, 1105
Kobeckij, V. D., 1353
Kobrin, Frances E., 3242
Kočergin, A. N., 2413
Koch, James L., 481, 1147
Koch, Koen, 5494
Kochan, Thomas A., 5297
Kocher, James E., 3259, 3317
Kocka, Jürgen, 2799, 4540
Kodama, Toshihiko, 1972
Kodica, N., 2845
Kofler, Leo, 2878
Kogan, L. N., 1338, 1354, 2254, 2360, 5643
Köhler, Eckehart, 443
Köhler, Wolfgang R., 835
Kohli, Martin, 3260
Kohnert, Dirk, 4098
Kohut, Jeraldine Joanne, 3089
Kohut, Sylvester, 3089
Kojima, Hiroshi, 3419
Kojtla, H., 2682
Kol'ga, T. V., 743
Kolaja, Jiri, 344
Kolankiewicz, George, 4099
Kolář, Jaroslav, 4891
Kolbanovskij, V. V., 2683
Kolbe, Manfred, 2549
Kolker, Aliza, 6182
Kollenberg, Udo, 3646, 5352
Koller, Norman B., 1836
Kolm, Serge-Christophe, 836
Komai, Hiroshi, 1398, 2846
Kommel, Helene J., 521
Kon, I., 661
Kon, Igor S., 925
Konda, Suresh L., 4713
Kondrašov, V. P., 2457
Kondrat'eva, O. I., 687
Kondratiev, Vladimir, 4714
Kondziela, Joachim, 1816
König, René, 204, 5431
Konoplev, V. F., 1469
Konopnicki, Maurice, 4632
Konovaljuk, O. I., 4633
Konyk, G., 1355
Koo, Hagen, 4489
Kooy, Alide, 5204
Köppl, Bernd, 4950

299

Korb, Lawrence J., 5711
Koreng, Christine, 288
Korff, Michael Von, 6218
Korneev, M. Ja., 125
Kornegay, Francis A., 4775
Kornev, V. V., 4892
Kornhauser, Ruth Rosner, 5909
Kornienko, V. S., 2226
Korobeinikov, V. S., 2183
Korobejnikov, V. S., 2184
Korogodin, I. T., 744
Korolainen, Sakari, 1057
Korostelev, G. M., 2894
Korsnes, Olav, 5219
Korzec, M., 2151
Kosaka, Katsuaki, 568
Košeljuk, L. F., 837
Koshal, Manjulika, 3198
Koshal, Rajindar K., 3198
Kotler, Tamara, 647
Kotov, G. G., 4100
Kourvetaris, George A., 5052, 5402
Kouzes, James M., 1106
Kovac, F., 2684
Kovačić, Ivan, 29
Kovačić, Matija, 4648
Kovalev, A. M., 3946
Kowalewski, David, 2049
Kowitz, Albert C., 1009
Koyama, Takashi, 3506
Koyano, Shōgo, 2846, 4300
Kozák, Gyula, 2509
Koziara, Edward C., 5325
Kozjubra, N. I., 1657
Kozlov, D. F., 146
Kozlov, M. P., 4595
Kozlov, Victor, 3688
Kozol, Jonathan, 2510
Krader, Lawrence, 4715
Kraft, Charles II, 1747
Kraft, Richard J., 2313
Kraft, William F., 3374
Kramer, Ralph M., 1069, 1070, 1071
Kramer, Ronald C., 1531
Krämer-Badoni, Thomas, 4225
Krampen, Günter, 2959
Krane, Ronald E., 3853
Kraus, Richard G., 5375
Kraus, Willy, 2847
Krause, Elliott A., 30
Krauss, Ellis S., 5644
Krausse, Gerald H., 4301
Kraut, Allen I., 4977
Krautkrämer, Ursula, 2361
Kravčenko, V. M., 4951
Kravčik, Z., 5391
Kreckel, Reinhard, 4776
Kreisel, Werner, 1425
Kreitner, Robert, 4541
Krell, Robert, 3507
Kreml, William P., 2685
Kress, Gunther R., 2098

Krevnevič, V. V., 2712
Kričevskij, R. L., 1008
Krichewsky, Maurice, 6219
Krickij, V. I., 2574
Kriegel, Annie, 1767
Krippendorff, Klaus, 439
Kris, Ernst, 2227
Krishan, Gopal, 2511
Krishna Swamy, S. Y., 4101
Krishnan, P., 3906
Kritzer, Herbert M., 569
Krivoručenko, V. K., 3045
Krjučkova, L. N., 184
Krjučkova, V. A., 2228
Kröll, Friedhelm, 5676
Kronenfeld, Jennie J., 3189
Kroneval'd, I. I., 1472
Krüger, Jürgen, 6055
Kruglov, V. V., 4596
Kruzmetra, M. R., 4102
Ksenofontov, S. V., 5583
Ksenofontova, V. V., 838
Kuan, Lin Chee, 3328
Kubat, Daniel, 3802
Kubicek, Herbert, 4952
Kučenko, V. I., 376, 6056
Kučerenko, N. F., 3954
Küchler, Manfred, 440
Kudchedkar, L. S., 4893
Kudera, Werner, 5093
Kudrjavcev, V. N., 745
Kudrjavceva, S. P., 2229
Kuechler, Manfred, 570
Kugel', S. A., 90, 2751
Kuhn, James W., 5298, 5299
Kühne, Robert J., 5220
Kuhnle, Stein, 6057
Kuitenbrouwer, Joost B. W., 4103
Kuklick, Henrika, 1973, 4302
Kukuškin, V. I., 1470
Kulcsár, Kálmán, 126, 1356, 1658, 1659
Kuličenko, M., 4435
Kulikov, V. S., 6058
Kulka, Richard A., 686
Kulkarni, P. D., 6059
Kulshrestha, S. P., 2550
Kumagai, Fumie, 1547, 1548, 3506, 3508
Kumai, Haruo, 1549
Kumar, Krishan, 5755
Kumar, Krishna, 441
Kumbula, Tendayi J., 2362
Kumesch, Herbert, 598
Kunczik, Michael, 2185
Kundu, Amitabh, 4303
Kunkel, John H., 4609
Künne, Wilfried, 3854
Kuper, Adam, 1277
Kupisch, Karl, 1748
Kuprijan, A. P., 2575
Kuprjašin, G. L., 1550
Kurian, George, 3375, 3420
Kurian, George Thomas, 571

Index des auteurs

Kurilovič, V. S., 746
Kurioka, Mikiei, 1167
Kurtz, Lester R., 689
Kurz, Otto, 2227
Kurzawa, Lothar, 2099
Kurzweil, Edith, 289
Kušakov, Š. S., 185
Kushman, John, 839
Kushman, John E., 2414, 5495
Kutsch, Marlies, 4829
Kutzik, Alfred J., 3675
Kuvačič, Ivan, 31, 32, 5523
Kuvlesky, William P., 4752
Kuzin, V., 2848
Kuzma, Ja., 747
Kuzmanović, Bora, 4542
Kuzmitz, Frank E., 1148
Kuznecov, A. G., 186, 1357
Kvasnikova, S. M., 748
Kvočkin, M. P., 4104, 5443
Kwaśniewicz, Krystyna, 4105
Kwee, Swan-liat, 2884
Kwong, Julia, 2363
Kyriazis, Natalie, 3261

La Gory, Mark, 3090
La Peña, Sergio De, 4436
La Rosa, Michele, 4681, 6247
Laajus, Sävy, 3509
Laatz, Wilfried, 5116
Labadie, J. M., 5910
Labasse, Jean, 6220
Labinowicz, Ed., 2299
Laborie, Jean-Paul, 4304
Laborit, Henri, 1187
Labrador, Carmen, 2458
Lacaze, Jean Paul, 4305
Lachman, Margie E., 3451
Lachs, Samuel Tobias, 1749
Lackner, Wolfram, 1750
Lacroix, Jean, 4437
Lacroix, Robert, 5274
Ladd, Everett Carll Jr., 2883
Ladewig, Howard, 4001
Ladrière, Paul, 1680, 1751
Ladyžinskij, Ja. P., 749
LaFree, Gary D., 5911, 5912
Lagneau, Janina, 2332
Lagory, Mark, 3757
Lagrange, François, 4777
Laidlaw, Karen A., 3173, 3617, 5708
Laing, Peter, 6040
Laitin, David D., 263
Lakatos, Mária, 3421
Lake, Robert W., 4306
Lakshmana Rao, G., 3855
Laliberté, G.-Raymond, 5221
Lalive d'Epinay, Christian, 1928
Lall, Bernard M., 1149
Lall, Geeta R., 1149
Lalonde, Carole, 2902
Lamb, David, 2100

Lamb, Richard F., 3907
Lambert, G. E., 4894
Lambert, Jacques, 4543
Lambert, Nadine, 1635
Lambert, Richard D., 2364
Lambert, Ronald D., 2611
Lamberth, John, 648
Lambright, W. Henry, 4597
Lammers, Cornelis J., 1058
Lamnek, Siegfried, 1551, 5829
Lamo De Espinosa, Emilio, 1471
Lamy, Marie-Laurence, 3318
Lamy, Paul, 2101
Lana, Robert E., 662
Land, Kenneth C., 572, 3216, 4716, 5702, 5858
Land, Ney, 3143
Landis, Judson R., 5926
Landis, Renée A., 4258
Landsheere, G., 2300
Landy, Frank J., 4682
Lane, James, 290, 377
Lane, Roger, 3217
Lane, Sylvia, 839
Lanfant, Marie-Françoise, 5376, 5377
Lang, Kurt, 5715
Langaney, André, 3144
Lange, Lynda, 2933
Lange, Maurice de, 1752
Langeheine, Rolf, 926
Langenmayr, Arnold, 3195, 3196
Langham, M. J., 4538
Lansbury, Russell, 4830
Lansley, Stewart, 4307
Lanteri-Laura, Georges, 3376
Lantz, Pierre, 6164
Lapassade, Georges, 91
Lapierre-Adamcyk, Évelyne, 3262
Laporta, Francisco J., 5496
Lappe, Lothar, 1552
Lappe, Marlies, 5326
Lar'kov, A. M., 1358
Larçon, Jean Paul, 4544
Larionov, A. G., 5584
Larkin, Judith Candib, 4778
Larkin, Ralph W., 3046
Larmin, O. V., 3047
Laroque, Pierre, 6124
Larrain, Jorge, 1254, 1255
Larsen, Knut S., 1188
Lash, Scott M., 4685
Lašin, A. G., 5414
Lašina, M. V., 5414
Laslett, Barbara, 442
Lasswell, Harold Dwight, 1230, 2050, 3322
Latchem, C. R., 2365
Latif Mia, M. A., 3319
LaTorre, Ronald A., 688
Lattes, Alfredo E., 3145
Latz, Arinna, 4106
Lau, Christoph, 5174
Lauderdale, Pat, 2729, 5621

301

Laughlin, Patrick R., 1032
Laurence, John, 3758
Lautrey, Jacques, 840
Laval, Bernard, 4751
Lawless, Paul, 5775
Lawrence, Peter A., 5117
Laws, Judith Long, 2960
Lawson, Craig M., 1656
Lawton, Mortimer Powell, 3091
Lazuka, S. A., 5086
Le Coadic, Yves F., 187
Le Tenneur, René, 1696
Leach, Chris., 573
Leacock, E., 3618
Leahy, Peter J., 4377
Leal Maldonado Jesús, 4308
Lebas, Elizabeth, 4338
Lebedev, B., 5444
Lebedev, L. K., 1472
Lebedinskij, N. F., 5378
LeBlanc, Marc, 5913
Lecaillon, J., 5789
Leckie, Norman, 4499
Leclerc, Gérard, 499
Lee, Barrett, A., 5379
Lee, Eddy, 4107
Lee, Gary R., 3422
Lee, Gloria, 3856
Lee, Jung Young, 1697
Lee, Linda, 4108
Lee, Raymond L. M., 1817
Lee, Robert D., 5557
Lee, Ronald D., 3263
Lee, Sidney S., 6199
Lee, Trevor, 574
Lee-Ying, Soon, 3908
Leete, Richard, 3510
Leeuw, F. L., 428
Légaré, Jacques, 3220
Leggatt, Timothy, 5118
Leggett, John C., 2747
Legnaro, Aldo, 5815
Legrand, Jean, 3297
Leguina, Joaquín, 2903
Lehner, Franz, 5534
Leibowitz, Lila, 2961
Leichter, Howard M., 6221
Leigh, Duane E., 3759
Leinfellner, Werner, 443
Leipert, Christian, 575
Lejeune, Bernard, 5709
Lemaine, Gérard, 424, 444
Lemaire, Jean G., 3423
Leman, Christopher, 6060
Lemennicier, Bertrand, 2962
Lemercinier, Geneviève, 3846
Lemert, Charles, 33, 1974
Leming, Michael R., 445
Lempert, Wolfgang, 1552
Lena, Hugh F., 92
Lenclud, Gérard, 3511
Leñero Otero, Luis, 3320

Lengsfeld, Wolfgang, 3122, 3439
Lenihan, Kenneth L., 5841
Lenkerd, Barbara, 4150
Lennéer-Axelson, Barbro, 1010
Lenoir, Remi, 4953
Lenz, Werner, 2512
Leon, Antoine, 2301
Leon, Jeffrey, 5889
Leon-Portilla, Miguel, 3689
Leonard, Wilbert M. II, 5389
Leonardi, Franco, 5756
Leone, Mark P., 1818
Leonidov, Ě., 5470
Lepenies, Wolf, 841
Lepervanche, Marie De, 3690
Lepsius, M. Rainer, 446
Leridon, Henri, 3321
Lerner, Barbara, 4779
Lerner, Bertha, 1107
Lerner, Daniel, 1230, 2050
Lerner, Richard M., 3048, 3512
Lernoux, Penny, 1819
Leschiutta, Pier Paolo, 1572
Leščiner, B. I., 750
Lesly, Philip, 892
Lessnoff, Michael, 315
Lester, Richard A., 1208
Levaillant, Jean-Marc, 3318
Levašov, V. I., 1359
Levasseur, Roger, 5340
Levčenko, E. V., 1624
Leveen, E. Phillip, 4109
Lever, Henry, 3747, 3760
Levey, Robert, 5993
Levi, A. M., 959
Lévi-Strauss, Claude, 1874
Levine, Arnold, 4227
Levine, John M., 1231
Levine, Martin P., 3377
Levine, Rhonda F., 271
Levine, Robert V., 447
Levine, Solomon B., 5145
Levine, Stephen, 3761
Levinger, George Klaus, 3424
Levit, S. Ja., 1360
Levitin, Teresa E, 3020
Levitt, Ian, 2686
Levkov, Ju. Ja., 2126
Levy, Alan B., 842
Levy, Charles Kingsley, 3001
Levy, Danièle, 6248
Levy, Emanuel, 1426
Lévy, Ernst, 2268
Levy, Mark R., 2196
Levy, Shlomit, 5645
Lévy, Thierry, 5914
Levy-Leboyer, Claude, 649, 650
Lewan, Kenneth, 2366
Lewin, David, 5298, 5299
Lewis, Arnold, 968
Lewis, Dan A., 5924
Lewis, Darrell R., 2459

Index des auteurs

Lewis, David, 3970
Lewis, George H., 378
Lewis, Gilbert, 1848
Lewis, J. David, 469
Lewis, Jonathan F., 378
Lewis, Lionel S., 2557, 2558
Lewis, Michael, 824, 908
Lewis, Robert A., 3146, 3147
Lewis, Stephen, 108
Ley, Katharina, 4831
Leyens, Jacques Philippe, 651
Leyton, Elliott, 5915
Lezama, Pedro de, 3857
Li, Peter S., 3691
Li, V. F., 2885
Lia Domenico, 5810
Liauzu, Claude, 5222
Lichtenstein, Nelson, 5223
Lichter, Daniel T., 3909, 3910
Lichter, Robert S., 2460
Lichtman, Allan J., 3513
Lidz, Charles W., 5811
Liebau, Eberhard, 4545
Lieberman, Carl, 5535
Lieberman, Florence, 6155
Lieberman, Samuel S., 3148, 3149, 4110
Lieberson, Jonathan, 3288
Liebhafsky, E. E., 482
Liebhart, Ernst H., 843
Liebman, Arthur, 1753
Liegeois, Jean-Pierre, 1427
Liegle, Ludwig, 3021
Liepmann, Detlev, 826
Liew, Tuck, 4958
Liga, M. B., 4598
Ligboajah, Frank Okwu, 2186
Light, Donald Jr., 6192
Lightbown, Nicholas, 1202
Lilien, David M., 5001
Lilienfeld, Robert, 667
Liliensiek, Peter, 5710
Lima Dos Santos, Maria de Lourdes, 2752, 2805
Limage, Leslie J., 2513
Limouzin, Pierre, 4002
Lin, Anli, 1157
Lin, Elizabeth, 842
Linares, Emma, 3150
Lincoln, James R., 448
Lindblom, B., 2102
Linde, Hans, 4634
Lindeman, Richard Harold, 449
Linden, Eugene, 4490
Lindgren, Jarl, 3092, 3425
Lindner, Clausjohann, 5599
Lindquist, Neil, 1553
Lindsey, James K., 4432
Lindskoug, Kerstin, 1138
Linke, Wilfried, 4717
Linton, James M., 2182
Linville, Patricia W., 1041
Lipfert, Frederick W., 3218

Lipickij, V. S., 3047
Lipkin, Gladys B., 1004
Lipman, Alan, 2045
Lippe, Angelika, 4832
Lippert, Ekkehard, 5707
Lippman, Lenora, 6200
Lipsitz, Joan, 3049
Lipsky, David B., 4718
Lirus, Julie, 1361
Lisk, Franklyn, 5776
Lisovskij, V. T., 2461
Liss, L. F., 2413
Lissak, Moshe, 5687
Listhaug, Ola, 5646
Listvin, V. F., 1473
Litovka, O. P., 4309
Litt, Edgar, 2367, 5771
Litt, Jean-Louis, 2368
Littell, Franklin H., 5976
Little, Roderick J. A., 379
Littlejohn, Gary, 5497
Littrell, W. Boyd, 1108, 5916
Littunen, Yrjö, 2187
Litvak, Isaiah A., 5053
Liu, Alan P. L., 1415
Liu, Da, 1754
Livet, Pierre, 1474
Livet, Roger, 4635
Livšic, Ju. M., 1362
Lizaur, Marisol Perez, 3514
Ljahova, L. N., 1475
Ljučvajtis, S. Ju., 5094
Llewellyn, Catriona, 2780
Llobera, Josep R., 291
Lloyd, Geoffrey Ernest Richard, 1698
Lobban, Richard, 3426
Lobos, Júlio A., 4895
Loch, Werber, 2302
Locke, Frances B., 3850
Lockhart, Charles, 5736
Lockwood, John, 961
Lodge, George C., 5303
Logan, John R., 4003
Loganov, I. I., 751
Lojkine, Jean, 34, 4310
Lombard, Jacques, 2576
Lomnitz, Larissa, 3514
Lomnitz-Adler, Claudio, 2687
Lomranz, Jacob, 1480
London, Bruce, 92
Long, Franklin A., 4599
Long, Theodore E., 1820
Long, Tom, 292
Longshore, Douglas, 3762, 4397
Longstreth, Frank, 4454
Lonsdale, Richard E., 4178
Loome, Thomas Michael, 1755
Lopata, P. P., 6061, 6062
Lopes, José Sérgio Leite, 2688
Lopez, David E., 2019
Lopez, Enrique Hank, 3378
López, Ernesto, 5917

303

Lopez Garriga, María M., 3619
Lopez Piñero, José, 1966
Lopez Roa, Angel Luis, 4416
Lopis, John E., 1182
Lopreato, Joseph, 293
Lorence, Jon, 5063
Lorentz, Elizabeth, 978
Lorentzen, Louise J., 1895
Łoś, Maria, 50
Losonczi, Ágnes, 2269
Lotz, Johannes Baptist, 1681
Louis, Dieter, 4546
Louis, Etienne, 6125
Louis, Karen Seashore, 1109
Louis, Raymond, 4438
Louis-Guerin, Christiane, 657
Lourdjane, Ahmed, 5918
Love, Douglas, 3151
Lovelace, Richard F., 1929
Lovell, Anne, 6164
Low, Alfred D., 3763
Lowe, George D., 3969
Lowe, Julian, 3970
Lowry, S. Todd, 3637
Lowy, Michael, 2462
Loy, Pamela, 450
Luard, David Evan Trant, 5445
Lubeck, Paul, 2689
Lubin, Alice W., 965
Lubin, Bernard, 965
Lubrano, Linda L., 1975
Lucas, Marín, Antonio, 35
Lucchini, Riccardo, 36
Luckham, Bryan, 844
Ludmann, Patricia, 4173
Lüdtke, Hartmut, 5744
Lueptow, Lloyd, 2963
Lueptow, Lloyd B., 3050, 3515
Luhman, Reid, 3764
Luhmann, Niklas, 294, 324
Luloff, A. E., 3929
Lund, Reinhard, 5327
Lundahl, Mats, 4111
Lunde, Donald T., 3371
Lundgren, Earl F., 1033
Lundman, Lars, 2369
Lundman, Richard J., 5536
Lunghi, Marco, 2255
Lupasco, Stéphane, 845
Luscher, Kurt, 2188
Lustig, Nora, 4833
Lutz, Gene M., 93
Lutz, M. A., 4719
Lverson, Hoyt, 3692
Lydolph, Paul E., 3117
Lyman, Stanford M., 3803
Lynch, James, 2303
Lyon, E. S., 561
Lyon, Larry, 2627, 4720
Lyons, Dan, 5275
Lyons, Francis Stewart Leland, 1363
Lyson, Thomas A., 2525, 2551

Maassen, G. H., 3608, 4746
Maassen, Gerard H., 4747
Mabry, Bevars D., 4112
Mabry, Edward A., 1011
MacAndrews, C., 3980
Macarov, David, 4491
MacCannell, Dean, 4518
MacCurtain, Margaret, 3620
MacDonald, Eleanor J., 3203
Macdonald, Glenn E., 2163
Macdonald, Graham F., 846
Macdonald, John Stuart, 6063
Macdonald, K. I., 576
Macfarlane, Alan, 689
MacGregor, David, 295
Machado Neto, Antônio Luiz, 1976
Mackal, Paul K., 950
Macke, Anne, 5642
Mackenzie, Garin, 314
MacKinnon, Neil J., 690
Mackscheidt, Klaus, 218
Maclaran, Morag, 6186
Maclean, Mavis, 500
MacLeod, Margo W., 4766
MacMillan, Alexander, 577
MacRae, Duncan Jr., 3911
MacRury, Katherine A., 4954
Macura, Milos, 2577
Madan, Gurmukh Ram, 37
Maddox, George L., 3093
Maddox, William W., 5677
Madison, Dan L., 5585
Maeyama, Takashi, 1364
Maffesoli, Michel, 296, 1365
Magill, Robert S., 6249
Magnani, Robert J., 3757
Magnarella, Paul J., 4113
Magubane, Bernard, 3651, 3765
Maguire, Mary Ann, 1837, 4969
Maguire, Tom, 4954
Maguitam, Olga Quitarra de, 4213
Magyari Beck, István, 1110
Mahadevan K., 3264
Maher, C. A., 3917
Mahler, Fred, 847
Mahler, Margaret S., 691
Mahmudova, Z. A., 1232
Maître, Jacques, 1930
Majava, Altti, 3858
Majorova, E. F., 1476
Majumbar, Ila, 3912
Majumdar, Prasanta S., 3912
Makarenko, N. A., 5266
Makarevič, G. A., 752
Makarevič, V. A., 5471
Makhlouf, Carla, 3621
Maki, Judith E., 380
Mako, Csaba, 4955
Maksimenko, V. I., 2753
Malamuth, Neil M., 5919
Malassinet, Alain, 2189
Malek, Abdel, 1756

Index des auteurs

Maletzke, Gerhard, 2051
Malhotra, S. P., 3115
Malik, Yogendra K., 2754, 5647
Malinchak, Alan A., 3094
Mallison, John, 1821
Malmberg, Bertil, 2103
Malmberg, Torsten, 3955
Maloney, George A., 1896
Manaev, O. T., 2190
Manchin, Győző Róbert, 548
Manchin, Róbert, 4485
Mancini, Jay A., 3095, 3516
Mancuso, James C., 5893
Manderscheid, Ronald W., 1036
Manderson, Lenore, 4834
Mandle, Jay R., 4439
Mandle, Joan D., 3622
Manessy, Gabriel, 2104
Manevič, E. L., 4721
Mangham, I. L., 1111
Mangum, Garth L., 4752
Manicas, Peter, 2578
Manig, Winfried, 4114
Manis, Melvin, 1189
Maniscalco, Maria Luisa, 381, 1601
Mann, Arthur, 1366
Mann, Michael, 4698
Mann, R. S., 3715
Mann, Reinhard, 3260
Mannari, Hiroshi, 4600, 4956, 4957
Manning, Peter K., 5812
Mansilla, H. C. F., 1977
Mansurov, N. S., 753
Mansurov, V. A., 3038
Manuel, Frank E., 1256
Manuel, Fritzie P., 1256
Manuel, Ron C., 3265
Manz, Wolfgang, 2304
Mappen, Marc, 1699
Marans, Robert W., 574
Marburger, Helga, 2305
Marčenko, G. I., 272, 382
Marchington, Mick, 5328
Marciano, Teresa Donati, 2944, 3632
Marcillac, Louis de, 6125
Marcotorchino, J. F., 578
Marcus, Alfred C., 512
Marcus, Judith, 2755
Marcus, Marvin, 5942
Marcuzzi, Giorgio, 3956
Marcy, N. M., 6193
Marduel, Marie-Laure, 4115
Mare, Robert D., 2370
Marengo, Franco Damaso, 5224
Maresca, Sylvain, 2690, 4116
Maret, Elizabeth, 4808, 4835
Margiotta, Franklin D., 5711
Margolis, Diane Rothbard, 5119
Margolis, Joseph, 1620
Marin, Gerardo, 652
Maris, Bernard, 3266
Marjanovič, Radovan, 5380

Markham, William T., 692
Markitan, S, 2691
Markov, N. V., 2692
Marković, Danilo Ž., 5023
Marković, Mihailo, 3957, 3958
Marković, Petar, 4117
Markowitz, Jürgen, 1554
Marks, Arnaud, 4050
Marks, Arnaud F., 969
Marlin, Marjorie M., 3035
Marohn, Richard C., 5944
Maroutian, Mélanie, 4440
Marr, W. L., 3913
Marradi, Alberto, 451
Marschak, Marianne, 3517
Marsden, Lorna R., 2849
Marsh, C. Paul, 107
Marsh, David C., 6064
Marsh, Robert M., 4600, 4957
Marshall, Gordon, 4441
Marshall, Harvey, 4311, 4312
Marshall, Victor W., 3096
Martel, Martin U., 297
Martin, Benjamin, 5146
Martin, Bernice, 2052
Martin, Christopher, 2415
Martin, David, 1682, 1875, 1931
Martin, Dominique, 5329
Martin, Harry W., 6222
Martin, Jeanne, 5661
Martin, Michael W., 188, 483
Martin, Michel L., 5054, 5712
Martin, Patricia Yancey, 1112, 2964
Martin, Philip L., 3853, 4836
Martín Moreno, Jaime, 2463
Martin-Fugier, Anne, 5103
Martindale, Don, 33, 38, 2464
Martinelli, Franco, 2693
Martinius, Warna Oosterbaan, 3469
Martinson, Oscar B., 3987
Martorelli, Horacio, 3623, 4118
Martz, John D., 5620
Maruani, Margaret, 5225
Marx, John H., 1967
Mascotto, Jacques, 5446
Masferrer, Elio, 3693
Maškova, L. T., 1621
Maslova, O. M., 175
Masselos, Jim, 1555
Massey, Douglas S., 3865, 4313, 4314
Massot, Alain, 2416
Masters, William H., 3379
Matejko, Alexander J., 6065
Mateju, Petr, 4315
Mathias, Peter, 2800
Mathias, William J., 5920
Mathiesen, Anders, 5055
Mathiesen, Thomas, 5921
Matjušin, B. G., 2254
Matsjuk, A. K., 4119
Matsumoto, Kazuyoshi, 452, 4316
Matsumoto, Miwao, 157

Matsumoto, Toshiaki, 5922
Mattelart, Armand, 2191
Mattelart, Michèle, 2191
Matthews, Sarah H., 3097
Mattoso, Katia M. de Queirós, 2640
Mauldin, Wayman Parker, 3289
Maule, Christopher J., 5053
Maupeou-Abboud, Nicole de, 5056
Maurel, Marie-Claude, 4120, 4121
Maurice, F., 1556
Maurice, Marc, 4601, 4636, 5147
Mauskopf, Seymour H., 1978
Mawby, R. I., 6250
Mawby, Rob, 5923
Maxfield, Michael G., 5924
Maxwell, Nicholas, 1979
May, Georges Claude, 219
May, Robert, 2965
Mayer, Enrique, 3693
Mayer, Jacob Peter, 5403
Mayer, John E., 5813
Mayer, Karl Ulrich, 5057
Mayer, Kurt B., 2105
Mayer, Robert R., 5751
Mayer, Thomas, 4412
Mayes, Sharon S., 298
Mayeur, Françoise, 3012, 3624
Mayhew, Bruce H., 2756, 4492
Mayorga, René Antonio, 4442
Mazaeva, E. B., 1608
Mazeaud, Henri, 3427
Mazet, Claude, 3152
Mazmanian, Daniel A., 1113
Mazur, Allan, 2053
Mažuran, Rudolf, 4122
McBride, Joanne L., 2956
McBride, William Leon, 6066
McCaghy, Charles H., 5925
McCall, George J., 107, 5926
McCann, Glenn C., 4001
McCarthy, John D., 682, 5614
McCarthy, Melodie A., 2417
McCarthy, Thomas, 299
McCarthy, Timothy, 1257, 2801
McCleary, Richard, 579
McClelland, Kent A., 2658
McClendon, McKee J., 3515, 4657, 5058
McClintock, Charles G., 380
McCluskey, Neil G., 3074
McCombs, Maxwell E., 2192
McConaghy, Maureen J., 2966
McConahay, John B., 1173
McCord, Joan, 5927
McCormack, William C., 2106
McCormick, Ernest James, 4780
McCormick, Michael B., 1033
McCready, D. J., 3913
McCrone, David, 4261
McCutcheon, Allan L., 478
McDonald, Angus W. Jr, 2850
McDonald, Gerald W., 3518
McDonald, William F., 5928

McDougal, Stephen L., 5851
McDowall, David, 580
Mčedlov, M. P., 6067
McEwan, John, 3416
McGee, Jeanne, 3304
McGinn, Noel F., 2371
McGlen, Nancy E., 5623, 5648
McGranahan, David A., 4493
McHenry, Dean E. Jr., 4123
McHoul, A. W., 1278
McHoul, Alexander, 383
McIntosh, Alison, 3132
McIntosh, John V., 5532
McIntyre, J., 4547
McKay, David H., 4317
McKee, William L., 482
McKennell, Aubrey C., 4472, 4494
McKenzie, Richard B., 2306
McKeon, John W., 3515
McKeown, Kieran, 4318
McKinnon, Malcolm H., 4896
McKirnan, David J., 1557
McLemore, S. Dale, 3766
McLennan, Roy, 4958
McLeod, Beverly M., 1157
McLeod, Norma, 2266
McMillan, James H., 384
McMillan, Marilyn M., 572, 3216
McMullan, John L., 5929
McNally, Fiona, 5104
McNeill, William H., 3804
McPhail, Clark, 1275
McPherron, Sharon M., 79
McQuaid, Kim, 6003, 6004
McVey, Ruth T., 2886
McVey, Wayne W. Jr., 3805
Meadows, Ian S. G., 1012, 1042
Meadows, Paul, 2193
Mechanic, David, 6173, 6222
Meditz, Marybeth L., 1568
Medjuck, Sheva, 3519
Medler, Jerry, 4124
Medlin, Virgil D., 5609
Meeker, Barbara F., 1016
Meenaghan, Thomas M., 6068
Mefvedkova, A. L., 4319
Megrjan, G. B., 4125
Meguro, Yoriko, 2967, 3625
Mehan, Hugh, 2116
Mehl, Dominique, 4243
Mehr, Joseph, 6251
Mehrabian, Albert, 754
Meier, Kenneth J., 5678
Meier, Robert F., 237, 5879, 5909
Meignant, Alain, 94
Meihls, J. Lee, 2116
Meijers, Daniel, 1686
Meijnen, G. W., 2418
Meister, Richard J., 4269
Mejía, Alfonso, 5059
Mel'ničenko, A. I., 6009
Mel'nikov, A. P., 1420

Index des auteurs

Mel'Nikov, V. F., 4100
Melik-Karamov, R. É., 1258
Melling, Joseph, 4320
Mellinger, Glen, 867
Mellor, D. H., 1980
Mellow, Wesley, 2923, 4733
Melnik, Stefan Reinhard, 5366
Melotti, Umberto, 4413
Melucci, Alberto, 5610
Menanteau-Horta, Dario, 1233
Mencke, John G., 3767
Mend, Michael R., 1590
Mendelievich, Elias, 4837
Mendelsohn, Ronald, 6252
Mendlewicz, J., 5814
Mendras, Henri, 238, 4126
Mengho, Maurice, 3981
Mercier, Pierre-Alain, 2785
Mercure, Daniel, 4959
Mercy, James A., 872
Merenda, Peter F, 449
Merhländer, Ursula, 3802
Merkulov, A. N., 4548, 4549
Merllié, Dominique, 5472
Merrett, Stephen, 4321
Merriman, John M., 2694
Merry, Sally Engle, 3694
Merryman, John Henry, 1660
Mertens, Walter, 4127
Merton, Robert K., 220, 453
Mesa-Lago, Carmelo, 6126
Mesihović, Nijaz, 2579
Messé, Lawrence A., 909
Messing, F. A. M., 2795
Messner, Steven F., 5060
Mészáros, Júlia, 3977
Métral, Marie Odile, 3520
Mettelin, Pierre, 4128
Metz, Johann Baptist, 1757
Metzker, Maria, 4838
Meudt, Volker, 5815
Meyer, Fred A., 5544
Meyer, Gerd, 4443
Meyer, John P., 385
Meyer, John W., 2887
Meyer, Karl E., 2230
Meyer, Marshall W., 1114
Meyer, Michel, 1981
Meyer, Peter, 3895
Meyer, Ruth, 1477, 5704
Meyer, Thomas, 300
Meyers, Frederic, 5148
Meyn, Hermann, 2194
Meynaud, Hélène Y., 4322
Mežević, M. N., 2851, 4239, 4256
Mežnarić, Silva, 1161
Miaille, M., 1556
Mialaret, Gaston, 205, 5524
Michael, Robert T., 893
Michaïlof, Serge, 4129
Michalos, Alex C., 848
Michaud, Pierre, 578

Michel, Jerry B., 470
Michel, Patrick, 1758
Mico, Paul R., 1106
Midlarsky, Manus I., 1558
Miener, Ed, 1043
Mies, Maria, 3626
Migdal, Joel S., 3322
Mihajlov, N. N., 849, 850
Mihajlov, S. V., 2580
Mihovilović, Miro A., 5381
Mikalachki, A., 5005
Mikami, Takeshi, 1259
Mikešin, N. I., 158
Mil'štejn, O. A., 5393
Milanesi, Giancarlo, 1683
Milanović, Vladimir, 4550, 6170, 6171
Milburn, Michael A., 951, 1183
Miles, Ian, 561
Miles, Robert H., 1115
Mileti, Dennis S., 3959
Milkman, Ruth, 4839
Miller, Arthur H., 2672
Miller, Charles E., 970, 1034
Miller, Edwin, 4897
Miller, Eugene F., 363
Miller, Gale, 1559
Miller, George A., 1116
Miller, Gerald R., 2129
Miller, J. A., 4551
Miller, James, 6025
Miller, Jon, 971, 1117
Miller, M. David, 2529
Miller, Mark J., 4836
Miller, Marv, 5930
Miller, Michael K., 327, 386
Miller, Roberta Balstad, 4323
Miller, Russell H., 2420
Miller, Steven I., 2307
Miller, Tom, 5564
Miller, W. L., 5649
Millerd, F. W., 3913
Millo, Efraim, 6156
Mills, Carol J., 755
Mills, Edgar W. Jr., 1831, 6236
Mills, Judson, 919
Miloslavova, I. A., 1476
Minami, Hiroshi, 39, 1367, 2231
Minc, L. É., 4960
Miner, John B., 1118
Mingat, Alain, 2372
Minguet, Guy, 332, 2480
Mink, Georges, 5092
Minot, Jacques, 2373
Minson, Jeff, 5418
Mira, Joan F., 3428
Mirande, Alfredo, 3695, 5931
Miret Magdalena, Enrique, 1560
Mirković, Damir, 301, 302
Mirowsky, John II, 1021
Mirskij, E. M., 140
Mirvis, Philip H., 1120
Mishara, Brian L., 5816

Mishra, R. P., 4130
Mishra, V. M., 4324
Mitani, Tetsuo, 2968
Mitchell, G. Duncan, 206
Mitchell, Jack N., 972
Mitchell, Richard, 5149
Mithun, Marianne, 2080
Mitin, M. B., 6069
Mitra, Asok, 2612
Mitroff, Ian I., 454
Mitsuhashi, Toshimitsu, 303, 2695
Mitterauer, Michael, 3521
Mitterling, Philip I., 1428
Miura, Noriko, 4011
Mjalkin, A. V., 3051
Mlinar, Zdravko, 3960, 4004, 4325, 4552, 4553
Moberg, David O., 4495
Moberg, Dennis J., 1054
Moberly, Robert B., 5305
Močalov, B. M., 851
Moch, Leslie Page, 3128
Modoux, G*erard, 4898
Moen, Elizabeth W., 2961
Moen, Phyllis, 4753, 6121
Mogensen, Gunnar Viby, 4131
Mohapatra, Manindra Kumar, 4062
Mohseni, Manouchehr, 3181
Moiseenko, V. M., 2904
Moises, Jos*e Alvaro, 5226
Moisset, Jean J., 2374
Moles, Abraham A., 2107
Moles, Oliver C., 3424
Möller, Bernahrd, 2334
Molluzzo, John C., 606
Molm, Linda D., 4496
Molnár, Edit S., 3332
Molnar, J. J., 973
Molnár, József, 5932, 5933
Molnar, Miklos, 1213
Molnar, Thomas, 1876
Molyneux, Maxime D., 3627
Mommen, André, 5650
Moncada, Alberto, 2465
Mongardini, Carlo, 1234
Mónica, Maria Filomena, 2805, 5061
Monjardet, Dominique, 4637
Monnerot, Jules, 5447
Monnier, Alain, 5006
Monnier-Raball, Jacques, 2195
Monson, Rela Geffen, 1808
Montero, Darrel, 3696, 3859
Montero, Maritza, 4005
Montgomery, Andrew C., 537
Montgomery, David, 5227
Montgomery, John D., 3322
Montlibert, Christian De, 5062
Montoro Romero, Ricardo, 304
Montoya, Rodrigo, 2696
Moock, Peter R., 2333
Moodie, Meredith Aldrich, 1429
Mooij, Ton, 2552

Moon, Marilyn, 2929
Mooney, Anne, 6163
Moore, Barrington Jr., 2613
Moore, Bert S., 3971
Moore, Eric G., 4249
Moore, Gwen, 2757
Moore, Larry F., 1062
Moore, Michael, 1119
Moore, Omar K., 520
Moore, Richard J., 5631
Moore, Wilbert E., 1137
Moorman, Jeanne E., 581
Mooser, Josef, 4132
Mootz, M., 6127
Moraczewski, Albert, 3284
Morandi, Franco, 3380
Morazé, Charles, 1982
Mordkovič, V. G., 1561, 2852
Morehina, G. G., 5586
Morehouse, Ward, 1983
Morell, Jonathan Alan, 159
Morelli, Anne, 3860
Morgan, B. S., 4326
Morgan, David R., 5678
Morgan, Edward P., 2367
Morgan, Gareth, 4528
Morgan, J. Graham, 95
Mori, Hiroshi, 5396
Morin, Michel, 1368
Morioka, Kiyomi, 1822, 3506
Morisset, Jean, 3697
Mørkeberg, Henrik, 4131, 4176
Morocco, Catherine Cobb, 1035
Morozov, I. K., 852
Morris, Leo, 3323
Morrison, Thomas L., 936
Mortimer, Jeylan T., 4676, 4961, 5063
Morton, Henry W., 4327
Mosco, Vincent, 2196
Moscovici, S., 1562
Mosejko, A. N., 1260
Moseley, Malcolm J., 4223
Mosk, Carl, 3267
Moskoff, William, 3324
Mošnjaga, V. P., 3052
Moss, Louis, 501
Mossige, Svein, 3522
Mossuz-Lavau, Janine, 3628, 4840
Motiwal, O. P., 5547
Mouriaux, René, 5101, 5115
Mowday, Richard T., 1059
Moxley, Robert L., 4006
Moya Pons, Frank, 3153
Moyana, Tafire nyika, 2697
Mucchielli, Roger, 40
Muel-Dreyfus, Francine, 2526
Mueller, Charles W., 2533, 3429, 3629
Mueller, G. H., 1897
Mugny, Gabriel, 638, 1478
Muguerza, Javier, 693
Muhamedov, S., 5579
Muhua, Chen, 3325

Mukai, Toshimasa, 4417
Mukerji, Chandra, 2265
Mukherjee, Bishwa Nath, 3326
Mukherjee, M., 4497
Mukherjee, Ramkrishna, 127
Mukherji, Shekhar, 2612, 3904
Mulago, Vincent, 1877
Mulder, Jan W. F., 2027
Mulkay, Michael Joseph, 1984
Müller, Dirk H., 5228
Muller, Edward N., 2865
Müller, Ursula, 41
Müller-Jentsch, Walther, 5150
Mullins, Elizabeth I., 3523
Munari, Silvio, 2346
Münch, Richard, 305
Muñoz, Ricardo F., 4007
Munshi, Surendra, 3768
Munson, Carlton E., 6157
Munters, Q. J., 306
Munzenrider, Robert F., 5698
Murcott, Anne, 6210
Murguía, Edward, 3714
Murie, Alan, 4328
Murniek, E. E., 1369
Murnigham, J. Keith, 952
Murphy, Edmond A., 3002
Murphy, Kevin R., 5026
Murray, Bertram G., 3154
Murray, Christopher, 3053
Murray, Colin, 3914
Murray, Martin, 3155
Murray, Stephen, 42
Murtha, James, 488
Museur, Michel, 3982
Musgrove, Philip, 5777
Mushakoji, Kinhide, 2853
Mushkatel, Alvin, 2375, 4124
Mushkatel, Linda G., 2375
Musil, Jiří, 4329
Mussen, Paul H., 927, 3022
Mutch, Robert E., 4444
Mutran, Elizabeth, 1540
Mutti, Antonio, 2698
Mutti, John H., 3841
Muyskens, James L., 1684
Mwanza, Jacob M., 3915
Myerhoff, Barbara, 3564
Myers, Martha A., 5934, 5935
Myers, Samuel L., 5936
Myklebost, Hallstein, 5064
Mynatt, Clifford, 1602
Mynhardt, Johan C., 3769
Myntii, Cynthia, 3156
Mzabi, Hassouma, 3861

Naafs, J., 5937
Nachmias, Chava, 3698
Nadel, Edward, 1985
Nadien, Margot B., 3023
Nadler, David A., 1120
Nadvi, Syed Habibul Haq, 1759

Nagel, Joane, 3672
Nagel, Stuart S., 455
Nagel, W. H., 5938
Nagel-Bernstein, Ilene H., 5890
Nagpaul, Hans, 4251, 4330
Nagy, Katalin S., 1370
Nagy, Lajos Géza, 4473
Nagy, Thomas J., 6163
Naitō, Kanji, 43
Najjar, F. M., 5415, 5416
Najman, J. M., 6201
Nakajima, Akinori, 44, 2308
Nakamoto, Hiromichi, 1371
Nam, Charles B., 2905, 3219
Namer, Gérard, 1986, 2581
Namihira, Isao, 484, 3157, 3770
Nandi, Proshanta K., 4498
Naoi, Atsushi, 5999
Narasimhaiah, B., 2802
Narayan, Rudy, 3771
Nardinocchi, Giorgio, 5173
Narkavonnakit, Tongplaew, 3327
Naroff, Joël L., 3916
Narula, Shamsher Singh, 2028
Nasu, Soichi, 3524
Natale, Michael, 2108
Natsoulas, Thomas, 387
Natsukari, Yasuo, 307
Nattrass, Jill, 5161
Naumann, Jens, 1343
Naumenko, G. F., 3054
Naumov, N., 3313
Navarro, José, 4418, 5353
Navarro, Marysa, 4869
Navarro, V., 6202
Navas, Luis, 5229
Navrátil, Oldřich, 5230
Nawton, Rae R., 96
Neal, Arthur G., 1594
Neal, Walter Douglas, 2376
Nebesky, Milos, 6070
Necvit, L. F., 1563
Nedelmann, Birgitta, 308
Nedorezov, A. I., 2582
Needleman, Carolyn, 5939
Needleman, Martin L., 5939
Neef, Marian, 455
Neff, James Alan, 1190
Neice, David C., 3983
Neidhardt, Friedhelm, 148
Nekipelova, L. V., 1372
Nelsen, Hart M., 1837
Nelsen, Judith C., 6158
Nelson, Dale C., 5651
Nelson, Franklyn L., 4638
Nelson, Hart M., 2527
Nelson, Jack A., 5778
Nelson, Linda, 4962
Nemerowicz, Gloria Morris, 2969
Nerenz, David R., 1166
Nersessian, Nancy J., 388
Nesvold, Betty A., 964

Nettler, Gwynn, 97, 5940
Neumann, George R., 5276
Neumann, Yoram, 485
Newby, Howard, 4133, 4134, 4331
Newcomb, Theodore M., 928
Newman, Alexander, 910
Newman, Graeme R., 1564
Newman, William M., 3652
Newra, Raal, 3620
Newsom, Carroll Vincent, 1760
Newton, Keith, 4499
Newton-Smith, William, 1987
Nezlek, John, 929
Ng, S. H., 4726
Nichols, Abigail C., 6128
Nicholson, Nigel, 5231
Nicolaidou, Silia, 3180
Nicolas, Guy, 1761
Nieder, Peter, 1126
Nield, Keith, 2803
Nielsen, François, 3699
Nielsen, Hans Jorgen, 5652
Nielsen, Joyce McCarl, 2970, 3366, 3371, 3383
Nielsen, Ruth, 4841
Nieminen, Juhani, 607
Nienaber, Jeanne, 1113
Niess, Frank, 4754
Nietzel, Michael T., 5941
Nieuwenburg, C. K. F., 4963
Nikiforob, V. M., 389
Nikitina, I. N., 763
Nikol'nikov, G. L., 4445
Nikonov, K. M., 2758
Nikulin, A. I., 5727
Nilsen, Svein E., 167
Ninomiya, Tetsuo, 4135
Nisbet, Robert, 413, 2854
Nishida, Ryoko, 1020
Nishimura, Hiroko, 3525, 3526
Nishine, Kazuo, 2309
Nishiyama, Shigeru, 1685, 1822
Nishiyama, Toshihiko, 756
Nisi, Cesare, 3024
Nitschke, August, 1988
Niven, Douglas, 4332
Nizek, William E., 45
Noble, Trevor, 2553
Noce, Augusto del, 2054
Nolan, Patrick D., 1168
Nolan, Peter, 4136
Nor Laily Aziz, Datin, 3328
Norem-Hebeisen, Ardyth A., 620
Normandeau, Louise, 3220
Northcott, Herbert C., 4842
Norton, R. D., 4333
Norvell, Nancy, 982
Nosanchuk, T. A., 2056
Novak, William, 5817
Novikov, B. V., 757
Novit, Mitchell S., 4899
Nowak, Leszek, 1989

Nowotny, Helga, 1990
Noyes, Richard, 2855
Nuttin, Joseph, 853
Nwaka, Geoffrey I., 4137
Nyberg, Kenneth L., 5716
Nyioö, L., 2256
Nyman, Kauko, 6223

O'Brien, John T., 5942
O'Brien, L. M., 4216
O'Connell, Agnes N., 1373, 2727
O'Connell, Sandra E., 4554
O'Connor, Finnbarr W., 1546
O'Connor, Gail, 5035
O'Connor, Kervin, 3917
O'Dell, Felicity Ann, 1565
O'Kelly, Charlotte G., 2971
O'Neill, Onora, 3527
O'Reilly, Eric, 754
Oakley, Thomas, 1602
Oatman, Eric, 5943
Oberai, A. S., 4138
Obert, Steven L., 993
Obozov, N. N., 894
Obradović, Josip, 663, 854, 5312
Obrdlikova, Bruo J., 309
Obudho, R. A., 4334
Ockay, Kathleen A., 3219
Odebiyi, I. A., 2615
Odenyo, Amos O., 5024
Oduev, S. F., 5498, 5499
Oechsler, Walter A., 5277
Oemarjati, Boen S., 2257
Offer, Daniel, 5944
Ofshe, Richard, 1849
Ogawa, Hiroshi, 694
Ogilvy, A. A., 3806
Ogmundson, R., 1374, 2709
Ogryzkov, V. M., 1479
Ogura, Mitsuo, 2888, 4639
Öhman, S., 2102
Ohrimenko, V. A., 5065
Ohta, Hideaki, 4205
Okada, Makoto, 2466
Ōkaji, Toshio, 2650
Okamoto, Hideaki, 5303
Okoh, Nduka, 2109
Okore, A. O., 3268
Okpala, Donatus C. I., 4008
Okuda, Kazuhiko, 390
Oldham, Greg R., 4886
Oldham, Jack, 4964
Olesnevič, L. A., 2784, 6071
Oleson, Alexandra, 4599
Oliveira, Orlandina de, 2943
Oliver, Ian P., 1762
Oliver, M. J., 5945
Oliver, Pamela, 1271
Oliver, Richard, 4816
Olk, Thomas, 4965
Olson, James M., 1199
Olson, Joan Toms, 1169

Index des auteurs

Olwig, Karen Fog, 5382
Ōmi, Tetsuo, 4335
Ommins, P., 4640
Omran, Abdel R., 4336
Ōmura, Eisho, 5946
Onikov, L. A., 2173
Ono, Yoshibumi, 5066
Oosthuizen, Gerhardus Cornelis, 1763
Opp, Karl-Dieter, 46, 1022, 5947
Oppenheimer, Valerie K., 4843
Oppolzer, Alfred, 5116
Orešnikov, I. M., 758
Oriol, Michel, 1430
Orlov, G. P., 5354
Ornstein, Michael D., 5653
Oromaner, Mark, 98, 239
Orsatti, Alvaro, 4735
Ortiz, Lourdes, 5355
Ortiz Echamiz, Silvia, 1898
Orudžev, V. M., 759
Orum, Anthony M., 413
Osborn, Richard, 1060
Osborne, Harold W., 5948
Osburn, Charles B., 201
Oschlies, Wolf, 5949
Osei, Gabriel Kingsley, 2972
Osinskij, I. I., 2538, 2759
Osipov, G. V., 128, 583
Osipov, V. I., 5448
Osmani, S. R., 2614
Osmond, Marie Withers, 5779
Østerberg, Dag, 310
Osterman, Paul, 2973, 4741
Ostheimer, John M., 5950
Ostner, Ilona, 4814
Ostro, Bard David, 3916
Ostrom, Elinor, 5542
Ostrov, Eric, 5944
Oswald, Christian, 3329
Oszlak, Oscar, 1121
Otite, Onigu, 3700
Ott, Sanra, 974
Outters-Jaeger, Ingelies, 4446
Ovčinnikov, V. F., 4966
Ovčinskij, V. S., 1375
Overington, Michael A., 1205
Owen, John D., 4967
Ōyama, Nobuyoshi, 3166
Ozaki, M., 5185

Paccou, Yves, 3918
Pace, Enzo, 1899
Pachter, Henry, 5449
Paderin, V., 1314
Padilla, Amado M., 3503
Padioleau, Jean G., 1644
Padua, Jorge, 2514
Paganini, Louis A., 1302
Page, Benjamin I., 5679
Pagès, Max, 311, 1122
Paglin, Morton, 5780
Pahl, Jan, 3430

Paicheler, Geneviève, 1191
Pairault, Claude, 99
Palley, Marian Lef, 3772
Palmer, Bryan D., 2699
Palmer, Jeremy N. J., 312
Palmer, Monte, 2830
Pampel, Fred C., 3629, 4683, 4716
Pančenko, P. P., 4139
Pancer, S. Mark, 1177
Pande, S. U., 2641
Panebianco, Angelo, 5587
Panetrat, P., 4968
Pang, Eng Fong, 4755
Panitch, Leo, 5232
Pankratova, M. G., 3160
Pannet, Robert, 1823
Paoli, A., 3676
Papcke, Sven, 129
Papp, Ignác, 5558
Papp, Zsolt, 48
Paradeise, Catherine, 895
Parcel, Toby L., 3629
Parel, Anthony, 4419
Parenti, Michael, 5419
Paris, Chris, 4338
Parish, Peter J., 2642
Parish, William L., 4140
Parisi, Arturo, 5680
Park, Young-Ki, 5151
Parker, James Hill, 313
Parker, Robert Nash, 584, 3864, 5982
Parkin, Frank, 314, 2718
Parkinson, Michael, 2367
Parol', V. I., 1362
Parrillo, Vincent N., 3773
Parrinder, Geoffrey, 1764, 1765
Parry, Noel, 6166
Parsons, Jacquelynne E., 2974
Parsons, Talcott, 315
Parston, Gregory, 6224
Parygin, B. D., 4602
Pascal, R., 4894
Pascale, Richard Tanner, 4969
Pascale, Robert, 5818
Pashute, Lincoln, 3151
Pasic, Najdan, 5404
Paskins, Barrie, 5737
Pasquino, Gianfranco, 5680
Passaris, Constantine E., 3863
Passel, Jeffrey S., 3174
Patel, Rashida, 3631
Pateman, Trevor, 2127
Pathak, Shankar, 3330
Pathria, R. K., 613
Patriksson, Göran, 5383
Patrušev, V. D., 4970, 4971
Patterson, Arthur H., 5960
Patton, Michael Quinn, 456
Paula Vitor, Vicente de, 4075
Pausewang, Siegfried, 4141
Pavalko, Ronald M., 3774
Pavljuk, N. Ja., 4665

Pawula, Harry, 5095
Payne, Colive, 2780
Payne, Judy, 3528
Payne, Malcolm, 6253
Pazy, Asya, 1480
Peace, Adrian, 4339
Peach, Ceri, 3431
Peacock, Andrew C., 906
Pearce, I. O., 2615
Pearce, Sandra, 935
Peay, Marilyn Y., 937
Pebley, Anne R., 3221
Peces-Barba, Gregorio, 5500
Peck, Dennis L., 5951, 5952
Peck, Jennifer Marks, 3879
Peckham, Morse, 1192
Pedersen, Tobe Beate, 669
Peek, Charles W., 2975
Peek, Peter, 3919
Peil, Margaret, 4844
Peisert, Hansgert, 2467
Pejovich, Svetozar, 6130
Pelc, Jerzy, 2029
Pelfrey, William V., 5953
Peli, Santo, 5260
Pellaumail, Marcelle Maugin, 855
Pellizzi, Camillo, 49
Peltonen, Matti, 2515
Pempel, T. J., 2468
Pen, Jan, 4500
Peña, Albert, 5541
Peña-Marin, Cristina, 457
Pendergast, Shirley, 3055
Pendleton, Brian F., 585, 3240
Pennacchi, Laura, 5152
Penner, Lluis A., 653
Pepe, Cosetta, 4555
Pepinsky, Harold E., 5954
Pera, Guiseppe, 5279
Perabo, Christa, 4972
Percheron, Annick, 2422
Pereira Da Rosa, Victor M., 3820
Perez, Joseph F., 5955
Perez Diaz, Victor M., 5233
Pérez Espino, Efraín, 2197
Perez Ledesma, Manuel, 4142
Perez Picazo, María Teresa, 2700
Peréz-Remón, Joaquin, 1766
Perheentupa, Olli, 176
Perinbanaygam, R. S., 183
Perkinson, Margaret A., 3098
Perkowitz, William T., 921
Perlman, Mark, 316
Perloff, Robert, 357
Péron, Yves, 2906, 3212
Perring, Charles, 2701
Perrot, Michelle, 5956
Perroux, François, 4556
Perrucci, Carolyn Cummings, 5067
Perrucci, Robert, 100
Perruchet, Pierre, 458
Perry, Charles S., 2616, 4641

Perry, David G., 2976
Perry, Huey L., 3701
Perry, Joseph B. Jr., 1272
Persianov, R. M., 5378
Petermann, Thomas, 1376
Petersen, Ib Damgaard, 602
Petersen, Karen Kay, 1216
Petersen, William, 316
Peterson, Christopher, 1591
Peterson, James A., 3106
Peterson, Richard A., 1377
Peterson, Robert W., 3712
Petit, François, 1061
Petkovič, Vlajko, 1013
Petras, James, 2702, 5718
Petrenko, E. S., 2907
Petrioli, Luciano, 3222
Petrov, I. I., 3056
Petrova, E. N., 695
Petrunik, Michael, 1209
Petryszak, Nicholas G. L., 2977
Pettazzi, Carlo, 317
Pettersen, Rita Bast, 3522
Pettigrew, Thomas F., 3775
Pettman, Barrie O., 4499, 4781
Pettman, Ralph, 5728
Petty, David L., 3099
Pezzullo, Thomas R., 4501
Pfeffer, Jeffrey, 4973
Pfeiffer, Dietmar K., 5957
Pfetsch, Frank R., 150
Phadnis, Urmila, 3702
Phan-Thuy, N., 4767
Pharo, Patrick, 1622
Philippart, A., 160
Philippe, Béatrice, 1767
Philliber, William W., 2666
Phillips, David P., 2198, 5958
Phillips, Derek L., 6072
Phillips, Donald E., 2469
Phillips, W. S. K., 4340
Piatier, André, 4143
Piazza, Thomas, 621
Picard, Claude François, 603
Picard, Louis, 4144
Piccoli, Italo, 5043
Piche, Victor, 3808
Pick, James B., 522
Pick de Weiss, Susan, 3331
Pickens, Donald K., 248
Pickering, W. S. F., 1623
Picon, Bernard, 4126
Pieper, Kajo, 2920
Pieper, Richard, 4341
Pilarski, Adam M., 3269
Pilipenko, D. A., 2617
Pilipenko, N. V., 2804
Pinatel, Jean, 5959
Pinchemel, Philippe, 4342
Pinder, Craig C., 1062
Pineda, Maria Antonieta, 3290
Pines, Ayala, 4947

Index des auteurs

Pines, Harvey A., 4778
Pinhey, Thomas K., 3969
Pinho, Benevides D., 4447
Pinker, Robert, 4502
Pinnaro, Gabriella, 2583
Pinto, Diana, 130
Pinzas R., Juana, 3025
Piolle, Xavier, 4343
Piotrkowski, Chaya S., 3529
Piotrow, Phyllis T., 3174
Pipitone, Ugo, 4448
Pira Degiarde, Elvina, 3530
Pirzio-Biroli, Detalmo, 1431
Pisani, Elena, 5173
Pisano, Laura, 2199
Pitié, Jean, 3920
Pitrou, Agnès, 3531
Pitt, Douglas, 1123
Pitts, Forrest R., 995
Piva, Michael J., 2703
Pizurki, Helena, 5059
Plahotnyj, A. F., 1624
Plahov, V. D., 1481
Plaksij, S. I., 3063
Planck, Ulrich, 4145
Plant, Martin, 5819
Plaut, Thomas R., 3921
Plax, Timothy G., 1193
Pleck, Elizabeth H., 2978
Pleck, Joseph H., 2978
Plešakov, A. I., 5501
Pliner, Patricia, 696
Plotnikov, S. N., 2232
Plowman, David, 5234
Plutchik, Robert, 856
Počepko, V. V., 2055
Poche, Bernard, 1432
Podgórecki, Adam, 50
Podmarkov, V. G., 6073, 6074
Podoševko, V. D., 4642
Poffenberger, Mark, 4146
Poggi, Gianfranco, 5502
Pogliese, Enrico, 2583
Pogudin, V. I., 2128
Pohorecky, Zenon, 3703
Polenberg, Richard, 1378
Pollack, Lance M., 5960
Poloma, Margaret M., 51
Polovec, V. M., 1625
Pöls, Werner, 5503
Polsby, Nelson W., 486
Poluěktov, A. M., 2812
Pomfret, Alan, 52
Pommerehne, Werner W., 2233, 5820
Pomykalov, V. V., 6075
Ponak, Allen, 5301
Pongrácz, Tiborné, 3332
Pons, Valdo, 4344
Pontusson, Jonas, 5450
Poole, Eric D., 5537, 5538
Popa, Cornel, 1482
Pope, Hallowell, 3429

Popkin, Samuel L., 4147, 4148
Popov, A. N., 4449
Popov, B. N., 3057
Popov, B. S., 5729
Popov, S. I., 1379
Popov, V. V., 5611
Popova, I. M., 1380
Poppendieck, Janet E., 2390
Poppleton, Stephen E., 4684
Porras, Jerry I., 1124
Porter, Bruce, 4254
Porter, Judith R., 697
Portes, Alejandro, 3864, 3880
Portwood, D., 5019
Posner, Barry Z., 1170
Posner, Judith, 1566
Post, James E., 4557
Post, Peter W., 698
Potgieter, Pieter Jacobus Johannes Stephanus, 3776
Potts, Malcolm, 3270, 3333
Poulose, K. Thomas, 4345
Powell, Graham E., 913
Powell, Lynda Watts, 5681
Powers, Edward, 3415
Pozzetta, George E., 3665
Pozzi, Enrico, 5713
Prado Valladares, Liciado, 4346
Pratt, Vernon, 53
Prattis, J. I., 4603
Prebisch, Raúl, 5473
Prebish, Charles S., 1768
Premfors, Rune, 2470
Premi, Mahendra K., 3922
Premus, Robert, 4009
Prenant, André, 4347
Prendergast, Christopher, 1991
Presser, Harriet B., 4845
Presser, Stanley, 622, 1237
Preston, Michael B., 3772
Preston, Richard A., 2856
Preston, Ronald H., 1769
Prewo, Rainer, 318
Price, John A., 3704
Prigogine, Ilya, 1992
Primavera, Louis H., 5818
Primeau, Ronald, 2200
Pringle, Mary Beth, 2979
Procenko, A. F., 975
Prokopec, Jiri, 3432
Protopopova, A. A., 2126
Prottas, Jeffrey Manditch, 1125
Protti, Mauro, 319
Prout, Alan, 3055
Prus, Robert C., 3381
Pryor, Robin J., 3923
Przeworski, Adam, 2704
Psacharopoulos, George, 2471
Psathas, George, 2110
Puchala, Donald J., 4628
Pudík, Vladimír, 5230
Puelles Benites, Manuel de, 2378

Pugačev, V. P., 5417
Pugh, M. D., 1272, 3617
Pugliese, Enrico, 2379
Puljiz, Vlado, 4051
Pullum, Thomas W., 379
Purdy, Ross L., 3141
Purtov, V. I., 1381
Putimskij, È. B., 6076
Puymège, Gérard de, 1213

Quale, Thoralf Ulrik, 5153
Quann, Dorothy, 3777
Quellmalz, Edys S., 2325
Quereilhac de Kussrow, Alicia, 1850
Quereshi, Mohammed Younus, 654
Questiaux, Nicole, 6020
Quevedo Reyes, Santiago, 637
Quilodran, Julieta, 3433
Quinley, Harold E., 3778
Quinney, Richard, 4450
Qureshi, Anwar Iqbal, 2584

Rabinow, Paul, 54
Rabkin, Leslie, 3507
Rabow, Jerome, 55
Racine, Luc, 976, 1048
Rada, Juan F., 168
Radden, Günter, 2111
Radebold, Hartmut, 3100
Rademaker, L., 131, 198
Raden, David, 3779
Radivojevic, Biljana, 3434, 3435
Radkowski, Georges-Hubert De, 857
Radocy, Rudolf E., 2270
Raelin, Joseph A., 977
Rafael, Eliezer Ben, 4632
Raffel, Marshall W., 6225
Raffel Price, Barbara, 5961
Ragan, Pauline K., 3532
Raghava Rao, D. V., 4149
Rashavan, V., 1851
Ragimov, A. A., 2675
Rahmanin, V. S., 858
Raines, Lloyd Davis, 1653, 3527, 5767
Rainwater, Lee, 2658, 3533, 4846
Raisman, Paula, 1737
Raison, Timothy, 56
Raitz, Karl B., 3705
Rajaonah, Voahangy, 2380
Raju, K. N. M., 3344
Rajyalakshmi, C., 4497
Rallu, Jean-Louis, 3161
Ram, Bali, 2381
Ramamurty, M. V., 2643
Rambaud, Placide, 4632
Rameix, Gérard, 5130
Ramirez, Francis, 859
Ramirez, Juan Antonio, 2234
Ramirez, Manuel, 5654
Ramon, Shulamit, 3200
Ramos, Donald, 3534
Ramsay, Charles E., 4643

Ramu, G. N., 3436
Randall, Susan C., 2863
Randolph, W. Alan, 1115, 1170
Rangel Guerra, Alfonso, 2472
Rankin, Joseph H., 5962
Rankin, William L., 1483
Ranković, Miodrag, 2857
Rannik, È. È., 4594
Rannikko, Pertti, 4348
Ransford, H. Edward, 2609
Rao, D. C., 698
Rao, Prakasa V. V., 2473
Rao, V. Nandini, 2473
Raphael, Marc Lee, 1770
Rapoport, Amnon, 967
Raskó, Gabriella, 5963
Rasulov, R. A., 1382
Rasulova, S. K., 4507
Ratcliff, Richard E., 4668
Ratner, Ronnie Steinberg, 4974
Rau, William, 4506
Rauls, Martina, 2382
Raushenbush, Winifred, 221
Ravenholt, R. T., 3291
Ravnic, Anton, 4847
Ray, A. K., 4497
Ray, J. J., 623, 3780
Ray, John J., 1215
Ray, L. J., 320
Raynaud, Philippe, 347
Raz, Joseph, 1661
Read, Jane, 5068
Reasons, Charles E., 1662
Reboratti, Carlos E., 3809
Recchini de Lattes, Zulma, 3437, 4848
Redding, S. G., 5120
Reddy, N. Y., 2474
Reddy, P. H., 3344
Reece, William S., 4483
Reed, John Shelton, 896
Reeder, Leo G., 512
Rees, Philip H., 4349
Regens, James L., 3781
Regini, Marino, 5235, 5236
Régnier, Jacques, 4900
Regoli, Robert M., 5537, 5538, 5541
Rehn, Götz, 1126
Reichardt, Charles S., 354
Reichel, Philip L., 5964
Reichert, Henri, 4350
Reichert, Josh, 3865
Reichwein, Roland, 262
Reid, Philippe, 5451
Reid Martz, Mary Jeanne, 5588
Reidy, Elizabeth, 4782
Rein, Martin, 3533, 6077
Rein, Mildred, 6254
Reiner, Robert, 5539, 5540
Reinhart, George R., 4262
Reinharz, Shulamit, 240
Reining, Priscilla Copeland, 4150
Reis, Harry T., 447, 929

Index des auteurs

Reis, Jaime, 2805
Reisman, Bernard, 1771
Reisman, John M., 930
Reissner, Raul, 3667
Reiter, Howard L., 5589
Reitter. Roland, 4544
Reitzes, Donald C., 664, 699, 4244
Reitzes, Donald T., 2475
Rekunov, F. N., 2760
Relemberg, N. S., 5781
Relyea, Harold C., 189
Remond, Jean Daniel, 4350
Remy, Jean, 1433, 3706
Renaud, Jean, 5069
Rendón, Teresa, 4833
Rendón Corona, Armando, 2761
Renzina, I. M., 321
Repetto, Robert C., 3271
Reps, John William, 4351
Rescher, Nicholas, 860
Rescorla, Richard C., 5920
Reskin, Barbara F., 152
Restivo, Sal P., 459
Retel-Laurentin, Anne, 3272
Retzer, Joseph D., 1836
Reuband, Karl-Heinz, 5965
Reuter, Helga, 161
Reuter, Peter, 5374
Revenstorf, Dirk, 586
Revson, Joanne E., 3253
Rex, John, 3866
Rey, Jean-Noël, 5171
Reyher, Lutz, 4975
Reyna, José Luis, 4712
Reynaud, Jean-Daniel, 5154, 5280, 5281, 5302
Reynolds, John V., 3640
Reynolds, Morgan O., 5237
Reynolds, Paul D., 101, 517
Reynolds, Rebecca, 3746
Rhoades, Lawrence J., 102
Rhodes, Colbert, 3881
Rhodes, Susan R., 481
Rhonheimer, Martin, 3535
Ribas, Armando P., 5121
Ribeaud, Marie Catherine, 3536
Ribeaux, Peter, 4684
Ribolzi, Giancarlo, 2476
Ribolzi, Luisa, 2310
Ribordy, Sheila C., 861
Ribourel, Jacques, 5341
Rice, Charles E., 3334
Rice, Craig S., 4901
Rich, Marvian C., 2112
Rich, Richard C., 1150
Rich, Robert F., 391
Rich, Robert L., 1662
Rich, Robert M., 1663
Richards, Lyn, 4821
Richards, Toni, 683
Richardson, C. James, 1333
Richardson, Chad, 503

Richardson, James T., 1824
Richardson, R. J., 2056
Richardson, Ray, 5238
Richmond, Anthony H., 3867, 4503
Richmond, Katy, 222
Richmond-Abbott, Marie, 3632
Rickman, H. P., 251
Rickson, Roy E., 4643
Riddell, J. Barry, 4352
Ridder, Richard De, 944
Ridge, J. M., 2347
Ridker, Ronald G., 3335
Ridler, Neil B., 4353
Ridoré, Charles, 36
Rieber, Robert W., 2007
Riegel, Klaus-Georg, 2893
Riesebrodt, Martin, 2806
Riesman, David, 2445
Riger, Stephanie, 4849
Righi, Roberto, 5590
Rigney, Daniel, 199
Riley, Matilda White, 3101
Rim, Y., 938
Rimbaud, Christiane, 4850
Rindfuss, Ronald R., 2980
Ringeling, A. B., 5559
Rios, Victor, 3661
Riska, Elianne, 6176
Rist, Ray C., 2383, 4851
Ritzer, George, 1978
Rivera, Alba Nydia, 911
Rivera, Annamaria, 3633
Rivero Herrera, José, 2384
Rives, Norfleet, W. Jr., 3810
Rivlin, Helen Anne B., 4354
Rizzi, Bruno, 1127
Rjabuškin, T. V., 162, 3162
Ro, Kwang H., 4355
Roach, Jack L., 5692
Roach, Janet, K., 5692
Roadburg, Alan, 5384
Roback, Howard B., 996
Robbins, Thomas, 1932
Robert, Ellen R., 4463
Robert, Michel, 4115
Roberts, Alasdair, 3336
Roberts, Alden E., 1484, 1580
Roberts, Benjamin Charles, 5303
Roberts, Fred S., 487
Roberts, James S., 5821
Roberts, Karlene H., 1063
Roberts, M. Hugh P., 4356
Roberts, Michael C., 939
Robertson, Roland, 276, 1722, 1933, 2882
Robin, Gerald D., 5966
Robins, Kevin, 2213
Robins, Lynton, 679
Robinson, Austin, 4604
Robinson, David J., 1383
Robinson, John Alan, 523
Robinson, Robert V., 2594
Robinson, T. Russell, 5757

Robinson, Vaughan, 3438
Robitscher, Jonas B., 6174
Rocard, Marcienne, 3707
Rocca, James V., 5504
Rochegude, A., 4151
Rodenstein, Marianne, 6226
Rodewald, Herbert Keith, 1194
Rodionov, B. A., 758, 2057
Rodrigues, Leôncio Martins, 5239
Rodriguez, Ibañez, Jose Enrique, 3102
Rodriguez Alcaide, José J., 3163
Rodríguez Paniagua, José María, 1664
Rodríguez y Rodríguez, Federico, 6078
Roed, J. Christian, 635
Roeder, Peter M., 2411
Rogačev, P. M., 5452
Rogalewski, Olaf, 5385
Rogers, D. L., 973
Rogers, David L., 438
Rogers, Dorothy, 3067
Rogers, Rosemarie, 3804
Rogers, Sharon J., 103
Rogers, Susan Carol, 460
Rogilo, V. V., 1235
Rogovin, V. Z., 1384, 4357, 6079
Rohlinger, Harald, 2726
Rohmert, Walter, 4976
Rohner, Ronald, 3537
Rohrer, Wayne C., 2858
Röhrich, Wilfried, 5405
Roiz, Miguel, 2058, 5342
Rojek, Dean G., 5906
Rokkan, Stein, 132
Roll-Hansen, Nils, 1993
Roloff, Michael E., 2129
Rolot, Christian, 859
Romaniuc, A., 3273
Romaniuk, Eugene W., 4954
Romano, Vicente, 5343
Romer, Daniel, 1195
Romero Villafranca, Rafael, 5682
Rommetveit, Ragnar, 2113
Ronceray, Hubert de, 1385
Ronen, Simcha, 4977
Roof, Wade Clark, 502, 4358
Room, Graham, 6080
Rooney, James F., 6159
Rootes, Christopher A., 2477
Roper, Robert T., 1023
Ropers, Richard H., 5656
Rosa, Eugene, 2946
Rose, Gillian, 299, 322
Rose, Harold M., 3164
Rose, Hilary, 1990
Rose, Michael, 4685
Rose, Peter I., 1567
Rose, Richard, 5683
Rosen, Lawrence, 1317
Rosenau, James N., 1228
Rosenbaum, James E., 4504
Rosenbaum, Walter A., 1113
Rosenberg, Morris, 700

Rosenberg, Richard D., 5330
Rosenberg, Sam, 4722
Rosenberg, Seymour, 738
Rosenblum, Victor G, 2350
Rosenfeld, Jeffrey P., 3103
Rosenfeld, Lawrende B., 1193
Rosenfeld, Rachel A., 5025, 5070
Rosengren, William R., 6175
Rosenko, M. N., 6081
Rosenmayr, Leopold, 3058
Rosenstein, Eliezer, 5330
Rosenthal, Donald B., 4359
Rosenthal, Howard, 618
Rosenthal, Robert, 461, 615, 2114
Rosenthal, U., 5684
Rošin, S. K., 2130
Rosner, Menahem, 5386
Rosoli, Gianfausto, 2385
Ross, Alec M., 2386
Ross, Catherine E., 1021
Ross, G. Alexander, 1128
Rossbach, Helmut, 421
Rosser, Jane E., 3580
Rossetti, Carlo Guiseppe, 5565
Rossi, Fiorenzo, 3538
Rossi, Giovanna, 6255
Rossi, Peter H., 351, 392, 453, 3991, 5841
Rossi, Robert J., 3059
Rossi-Landi, Ferruccio, 2030
Roth, Guenther, 314, 2806
Roth, William, 3192
Rothbard, Murray N., 701
Rothbart, Myron, 1040, 1189
Rothenberg, Irene Fraser, 3885
Rothernund, Dietmar, 4360
Rothman, David J., 6227
Rothman, Jack, 141
Rothman, Robert A., 5071
Rothrock, George A., 1934
Rothwell, Roy, 4756
Rott, Renate, 4723
Rouchy, Jean-Claude, 655
Rouillard, Jacques, 5240
Roundtree, George A., 702
Rousseau, André, 1935
Rousseau, Denise M., 1063
Roussel, Louis, 3539
Rovati, Giancarlo, 4558
Rowe, G., 3906
Rowland, C. K., 5548
Rowland, D. T., 3924
Rowland, Kendrith M., 4902
Rowland, Richard H., 3146, 3147, 3165
Rowley, J. C. R., 4486
Rowley, John, 3337
Roy, Donald F., 4851
Roy, William G., 5497
Royce, Joseph R., 665
Royston, Erica, 5059
Rozanov, A. A., 5505
Rozenberg, C. R., 2762
Rožko, A. M., 2705

Index des auteurs

Rožkov, V. P., 5591
Rožkova, A. P., 2706
Ruback, R. Barry, 1231
Rubiano, Aida G. de, 3540
Rubin, Barnett R., 2704
Rubin, Donald B., 461
Rubin, Paul H., 5607
Rubin, Stephen, 5014
Rubinstein, Eli A., 2205
Ruble, Blair A., 5091
Ruch, Richard S., 4978
Rückert, Gerd-Rüdiger, 3439
Rudavsky, David, 1772
Ruddick, William, 3527
Rudelle, Odile, 1986
Rudkovskij, E. I., 1626
Ruiz, Sonia G. de, 3540
Rule, James, 5752
Rumjanceva, T. M., 2859
Runde, Peter, 3199
Runger, George, 997
Rusandu, I. K., 3178
Ruse, Michael, 3003
Rushing, William A., 3782
Russ-Eft, Darlene, 4505
Russell, Clifford S., 1273
Russell, Craig J., 5131
Russell, J. Curtis, 1485
Russell, James, 393
Russell, Kevin, 524
Russell, Lillian M., 3810
Russkih, B. G., 5105
Russo, Carlo, 1900
Rutgajzer, V. M., 4979
Rutkevič, M. N., 323, 2585
Ruyer, Raymond, 2813
Ryan, Charles, 4605
Ryback, David, 3026
Rydvanov, N. F., 4460
Ryffel-Gericke, Christiane, 3274
Rytina, Steve, 5892

Sá, Nicanor Palhares, 2387
Saarinen, Esa, 2031
Sabagh, George, 2910
Šabalin, V. A., 4451, 5733
Sabat, Khalil, 2201
Sabatello, Eilan F., 3338
Sabathil, Gerhard, 2478
Saberwal, Satish, 2618
Sabini, John, 394
Sabourin, Conrad, 2032
Sabrosky, Judith A., 3634
Šaburova, L. A., 1386
Sachs, Ignacy, 3961
Sachs, Wladimir M., 1568
Sacks, Karen, 2981
Sacouman, R. J., 4152, 4452
Sadan, Ezra, 3698, 4644
Sadovskaja, V. S., 760
Sadykov, F. B., 5453
Saez, Armand, 3275

Safarov, R. A., 1236
Saganenko, G. I., 462
Sagarin, Edward, 5967, 5968
Sager, J. C., 2115
Sági, Mária, 1434, 2311
Sagnes, Jean, 5241
Šahkuljan, R. O., 862
Šahnazarov, G., 5454
Sailer, Lee, 986
Saint Martin, Monique De, 2707
Saint-Jours, Yves, 4980
Sajó, András, 1665, 1666
Šalaginova, L. I., 3541, 3542, 6131
Salas, Rafael M., 2908
Salau, Ademola T., 587, 4361
Salazar, Diego Renato, 5506
Salcedo, Juan, 177, 2909
Sales, Arnaud, 2708
Saliba, Jacques, 499
Salim Ahmed, Ahmed, 4724
Salinas Ramos, Francisco, 1072
Salitot-Dion, Michèle, 1667
Salle, Philippe, 1261
Salvini, Alessandro, 1518
Samčenko, V. N., 395
Samoff, Joel, 2388, 4123
Samora, Julian, 5541
Samuels, Warren J., 5655
Sanchez Jimenez, José, 4153, 4420
Sandell, Steven H., 4757
Sander, Günther, 5969
Sanders, Jerry, 5738
Sanders, John H., 3935
Sandmaier, Marian, 5822
Sanmartin Arce, Ricardo, 3440
Sano, Katsutaka, 2860
Santa, John Lester, 820
Santiso G., Roberto, 3290
Santogrossi, David A., 939
Santuccio, Mario, 1994
Saporiti, Angelo, 1572
Saradamoni, K., 2644
Sarafino, Edward P., 3027
Sarason, Seymour, B., 978
Sârbu, Viorel, 2235
Sardar, Ziauddin, 1773
Saris, W. E., 5937
Saroukhani, Bagher, 3441
Sarrias, Cristóbal, 1936
Sartin, P., 5242
Sartori, Giovanni, 525
Šaryčev, Ju. M., 396
Sas, Judit H., 3635
Sasaki, M. S., 588
Satariano, William A., 103
Sato, Mamoru, 2516, 2517
Satyendra, N., 5162
Sauerberg, Steen, 5652
Sauermann, Peter, 4686
Saula, Ademola T., 4362
Saunders, Peter R., 5566
Sautter, Gilles, 3962

Sauvy, Alfred, 3104
Savage, Michael, 1328
Savall, Henri, 4981
Savel'ev, S. N., 1353
Savitch, H. V., 5567
Sawada, Tetsuro, 3442
Sawer, Marian, 2619
Saxena, Sateshwari, 2389
Sayad, Abdelmalek, 3868, 4363
Sayers Bain, George, 5243
Sayre, Robert, 897
Sbatello, Eitan, 3869
Scaglia, Antonio, 1262
Scanlan, Burt K., 1129
Scanzoni, John, 2982, 3636, 4852
Scardigli, Victor, 2785
Sčelišč, P. E., 2751
Schaedel, Richard P., 5487
Schaefer, David Lewis, 2620
Schaefer, Richard T., 3708
Schaeffer, Nora Cate, 513
Schaeffer, Richard, 3443
Schafer, D. Paul, 1435
Schafer, Robert B., 703
Schäfer, Wolf, 1995
Schäfers, Bernhard, 2586, 2834
Schaffer, Kay F., 2983
Schain, Martin A., 5155
Schanz, Günther, 4658
Schaps, David, M., 3637
Schäuble, Gerhard, 4982
Schechtman Grossbard, Amyra, 3444
Scheerer, Sebastian, 5957
Scheier, Michael F., 704, 705
Schektman-Labry, Geneviève, 4093
Schelsky, Helmut, 57
Schenk, Josef, 5455
Schenkein, Jim, 2116
Scherer, Klaus R., 2117
Schermer, Brian, 2955
Schermerhorn, R. A., 3709
Scheurer, Paul B., 1996
Schickedanz, Hans-Joachim, 3382
Schildkrout, Enid, 4853
Schiray, Michel, 1387
Schlemmer, Lawrance, 3783
Schlesinger, Benjamin, 3543
Schloegl, Irmgard, 1774
Schluchter, Wolfgang, 324
Schmid, Alfred A., 494
Schmidt, Gert, 4679, 4687, 4688, 4691
Schmidt, Janet, 5836
Schmidt, Samuel, 5507
Schmiederer, Ursula, 5456
Schmitter, Barbara E., 4851
Schmitter, Peter, 2012
Schmutte, Gregory T., 953
Schnabl, Hermann, 4658, 4659
Schnapper, Dominique, 1775, 4758
Schneider, Hans, 420
Schneider, Ivo A., 4075
Schneider, João Elmo, 4453

Schneider, Joseph W., 1517
Schneller, Raphael, 1825
Schnitzer, Phoebe Kazdin, 3187
Schoefer, Christine, 2236
Schoen, Cathy, 5767
Schoen, Robert, 3223, 3445, 3653
Schoenberg, R. J., 374
Schoenfeld, A. Clay, 3963
Schoenherr, Richard A., 3712
Schoffeleers, Matthew, 1686
Schöfthaler, Traugott, 2295
Schollaert, Paul T., 2756, 4492, 5802
Scholler, Heinrich, 1668
Schonborn, Karl, 5955
Schonfeld, William R., 5592
Schönholz, Siegfried, 5254
Schoonenboom, Jan, 3710
Schöps, Martina, 197
Schrader, David F., 5779
Schram, Sanford F., 6132
Schramm, Karin, 2528
Schramm, Sarah Slavin, 3638
Schreiber, Carol Tropp, 5072
Schreiber, E. M., 2709
Schremmer, Eckart, 4645
Schryer, Frans J., 4154
Schuch, Angela, 927
Schuessler, Karl, 1196
Schulter, David B., 58
Schultheiss, Flory Jones, 4364
Schultz, Clarence C., 104
Schultz, Sandra L., 3446
Schultz, T. Paul, 3447
Schulz, David A., 3383, 4406
Schulz, Heike, 3105
Schuman, Howard, 622, 1237, 3737
Schuon, Frithjof, 1687
Schur, Edwin M., 1569, 1570
Schutz, Howard G., 4365
Schwartz, Alf, 4155
Schwartz, Arthur N., 3106
Schwartz, Barry, 4366
Schwartz, Gary, 931
Schwartz, Howard, 463
Schwarz, Karl, 3544
Schwarz, Louis, 5970
Schwarzwald, Joseph, 940
Schwenger, Johannes, 2258
Schwimmer, Brian, 4156
Schwimmer, Erik, 4725
Schwitzgebel, R. Kirkland, 2118
Scott, Franklin Daniel, 3870
Scott, John, 356, 4454, 4559
Scott, Marvin B., 183
Scott, Robert A., 5753
Scott, Sharon R., 893
Scott, Wilbur J., 5619, 5656
Scott, Will B., 4760
Scott, William Abbott, 863
Scourby, Alice, 3871
Scull, A. T., 3200
Scurati, Cesare, 2291

Index des auteurs

Searle, John R., 864
Secondulfo, Domenico, 6203
Segal, Sheldon Jerome, 3289
Segalen, Martine, 3639
Segre, Dan V., 2763
Segre, Sandro, 397, 4455
Segrestin, Denis, 5282
Seguí González, Luis, 3339
Segura, Roberto D., 3661
Séguy, Jean, 1776, 1826
Seibel, Hans Dieter, 5136
Seidel, Anna, 1790
Seidman, Ann, 4854
Seifert, R. V., 6026, 6030
Seiler, Lauren H., 488
Seiwert, Lothar, 5331
Sejersted, Francis, 5474
Seki, Hideo, 4855
Seki, Kiyohide, 3166
Seki, Takatoshi, 3545
Selakovich, Daniel, 2390
Seligson, Mitchell A., 4157, 5624, 5657, 5658
Seliktar, Ofira, 3040
Selin, V. N., 5508
Seliverstovaja, T. N., 1388
Sell, Jane, 188, 483
Sellier, François, 5147
Sellin, Johan Thorsten, 5971
Selman, Peter, 3270
Selman, Robert L., 898
Selten, Reinhard, 1001
Seltzer, Robert M., 1777
Selwyn, T., 1486
Semenou, Ju-N., 2825
Semenov, N. N., 1997
Semenov, V. A., 2391
Semenov, V. S., 2764
Semyonov, Moshe, 4003, 4856
Senarclens, Marina de, 2984
Sengupta, Syamalkanti, 2645
Seninger, Stephen F., 4752
Sensat, Julius Jr., 325
Senter, Mary Scheuer, 1207
Šepel', V. M., 6082, 6083
Seppilli, Tullio, 398
Šeregi, F. É., 1226
Serman, William, 5714
Seron, Carroll, 1063
Serrano, Maria Eugenia C. de, 1571
Servais, Jean-Michel, 5244
Serverin, E., 3340
Service, Elman R., 5487
Šeščukova, G. V., 3546
Sesink, Werner, 2495
Šešukova, G. V., 3547
Seta, John J., 865
Severy, Lawrence J., 4367
Sevilla-Guzmán, Eduardo, 4069, 4158
Sevko, V. B., 5096
Sewell, William H., 3934, 5073
Seyler, M., 5972

Sgritta, Giovanni B., 1572
Sgroi, Emanuele, 2312
Shaffer, David R., 2861
Shaffer, Linda J., 3784
Shalin, Dmitri N., 1627
Shanas, Ethel, 3107
Shanneik, Ghazi, 2862
Sharda, Bam Dev, 5074
Sharkansky, Ira, 5542
Sharma, Arvind, 5973
Sharma, Sudesh K., 4159
Sharma, Sudesh Kumar, 4160
Sharni, Shoshana, 1151
Sharp, Laure M., 514
Sharrock, W. W., 2141
Shaukat Ali, Dr., 2889
Shaw, Marvin E., 1014
Shaw, R. Paul, 3925
Sheehan, Glen, 5782
Shelley, Louise, 5974
Shepard, Jon M., 4606
Shepherd, Michael A., 1778
Sheppard, Harold L., 4967
Sheridan, John E., 1589
Sherif, Carolyn Wood, 5919
Sherman, Allan, 4709
Sherman, Howard, 59
Sherman, Martin F., 1789
Sherman, Nancy C., 1789
Sherrod, Drury R., 3971
Shibata, Shingo, 5525
Shibutani, Tamotsu, 5715
Shichor, David, 5975
Shifman, Pinhas, 1937
Shiino, Nobuo, 706
Shils, Edward B., 4560
Shimizu, Hiroaki, 3108
Shimizu, Yoshifumi, 3548
Shimkin, Demitri B., 3549
Shimkin, Edith M., 3549
Shimoda, Naoharu, 464, 1419
Shin, Doh C., 4467
Shindler, Colin, 2202
Shinn, Terry, 163
Shiobara, Tsutomu, 1064, 1065
Shiota, Shizuo, 4660
Shirakura, Yukio, 866
Shiramizu, Shigehiko, 2985
Shirley, Ian F., 4010
Shivers, Jay Sanford, 1152
Shliapentokh, Vladimir E., 60
Shodeid, Moshe, 3711
Shoji, Kokichi, 3462
Shokeid, Moshe, 3872
Sholem, Gershom, 2059
Shopen, Timothy, 2119
Shore, Arnold R., 5753
Short, James F. Jr., 5977
Shortridge, Ray M., 5527
Shrag, Clarence, 5977
Shull, F., 4547
Shulman, Norman, 3926

Shupe, Anson D., 1573
Shupe, Anson D. Jr., 1827, 1842
Shur, Irene G., 5976
Shyam, Madhav, 2511
Shye, Samuel, 465
Sica, Alan M., 61
Sidanuis, Jim, 5659
Sidhu, Manjit S., 3167
Sieber, R. Timothy, 2419
Sieber, Sam Dixon, 1109
Siebert, Horst, 2814
Siedentopf, Heinrich, 5457
Sieferle, Rolf-Peter, 3968
Siegert, Michael T., 3060
Siegmann, Athilia E., 6167
Sieminski, Waldemar, 4368
Siewert, Hans-Jörg, 2765
Sigal, Silvia, 1387
Sigel, Roberta S., 3640
Sigelman, Lee, 998, 5387
Signorelli, Adriana, 62
Sil'dmjaè, T. I., 1357
Silbergfeld, Sam, 1036
Silberman, Charles E., 5977
Silbermann, Alphons, 2150, 2203, 5047
Silva, Edwart T., 105
Silva, Renán, 3591
Silver, Gerald A., 169
Silver, Maury, 394
Silverman, L. Theresa, 2205
Silverman, Martin G., 1243
Silvers, Anita, 2946
Simard, Jean, 1901
Simcock, Bradford L., 5612
Simmel, Edward C., 1574
Simmonds, Robert B., 1824
Simmons, Roberta G., 3061
Simó, Tibor, 4646
Simoes, Mario, 4798
Simon, Rita J., 3461, 4506
Simon, Robert L., 1628
Simonds, A. P., 1998
Simpkin, Michael, 6256
Simpson, Carl, 867
Simpson, Ekundayo, 2259
Sims, David, 868, 1088
Sims, Henry P. Jr., 4783
Sinclair, Daniel B., 3341
Sinden, Peter G., 5978
Sindler, Allan P., 2595
Sine, Babacar, 2392
Sineau, Mariette, 3628, 4840
Singelmann, Joachim, 4607
Singer, L. R., 5979
Singer, Peter, 1629
Singer-Kerel, Jeanne, 4857
Singh, Andrea Meneffe, 4369
Singh, B. K., 5980
Singh, Hira, 3550
Singh, Jyoti Shankar, 3342
Singh, K. P., 4858
Singh, Manmohan H. K., 4138

Singh, R. A. P., 2766
Singh, R. R., 5783
Singh, Ramadhar, 1139
Singhal, D. P., 1389
Singhhi, Narendra Kumar, 2393
Sinha, M. M. P., 4370
Sinha, P. K., 6133
Sinha, V. C., 3168
Šinkarenko, V. V., 190
Šinkaruk, V. I., 1390
Širaliev, A. I., 4507
Sirin, A. D., 1487
Sirota, N. M., 2890
Sisaye, Seleshi, 5283, 6228
Sismondo, Sergio, 5757
Sisodia, G. S., 4161
Sit, Victor F. S., 4726
Six, Ulrike, 2146
Sizova, T. P., 5097
Sjoberg, Gideon, 1108
Škaratan, O. I., 2621, 5075
Skidmore, Rex A., 6204
Skiff, Anthony, 229
Skinner, B. F., 223, 326
Skinner, G. W., 1315
Skipper, James K. Jr., 4928
Sklar, Richard, 2710
Skogstad, Grace, 1575
Skvoretz, John, 1171
Skyvington, William, 2060
Slater, David, 4371
Slaughter, Sheila, 105, 2534
Slesinger, Doris P., 6134
Šljahtun, P. A., 2748
Sloan, Frank A., 6257
Slocum, John W. Jr., 4783
Sluzki, Carlos E., 3551
Sly, David, F., 3169
Šmakov, V. I., 5356
Smarov, A. I., 4979
Smart, Barry, 273
Smart, Don, 2744
Smart, Ninian, 1779
Šmel'kov, M. I., 4456
Smelt, Simon, 4669
Smidt, Corwin, 1902
Smirnov, B. M., 4608
Smirnov, B. V., 4565
Smirnova, G., 1576
Smith, Anthony D. S., 5458
Smith, Arthur B. Jr., 2622
Smith, Barry N., 4372
Smith, Clagett G., 1577
Smith, Daniel Scott, 3552
Smith, David Hordon, 5406
Smith, David L., 4989
Smith, David M., 6038
Smith, Douglas A., 5981
Smith, Gerald, 3399
Smith, Gilbert, 6084
Smith, James P., 3553
Smith, Joelle P., 906

Smith, John H., 6085
Smith, Kent W., 588
Smith, Leslie Whitener, 1216
Smith, M. Dwayne, 5982
Smith, M. Estelle, 3873
Smith, Michael D., 5388
Smith, Michael P., 4373
Smith, Michael R., 5284
Smith, Peter B., 1015
Smith, Peter H., 4427
Smith, Peter, C., 3448
Smith, Philip R., 2395
Smith, Ralph E., 4759
Smith, Raymond T., 3554
Smith, Richard Joseph, 1391
Smith, Robin, 5156
Smith, Russell L., 5245
Smith, Thomas Ewin, 3555
Smith, Tom W., 3217
Smith, Wallace F., 4374
Smith, Wilfred Cantwell, 1780, 1878
Smith, Woodruff, D., 4375
Smith Euclid O., 3940
Smith-Lovin, Lynn, 74
Smoke, Richard, 1212
Smol'kov, V. G., 869
Smorgunova, V. Ju., 5660
Smout, Christopher, 2686
Smucker, Céleste, M., 3224
Snell, J. Laurie, 614
Snider, Earle L., 870, 4376
Snizek, William E., 63, 64, 327
Snodgrass, Jon, 1662
Snow, David A., 4377, 5613
Snyder, David, 3753
Snyder, Douglas K., 3449
Snyder, Eldon E., 5389
Snyder, Kay A., 1204
Snyder, Mark, 1238
Snyder, William, 5716
Soares, Gláucio Ari Dillon, 2786
Sobolev, A. I., 5739
Socarides, Charles W., 3370
Sodei, Takako, 3556
Söderberg, Sven, 4903
Soen, Dan, 4378
Soffan, Linda U., 3641
Sokolov, S. V., 1999
Sokolov, V. M., 882, 1630
Sokolović, Džemal, 1578, 1579
Sole, Carlota, 1436
Solnickova, Lenka, 3170, 3642
Solomon, Susan Gross, 1975
Sološenko, V. I., 1392
Solov'ev, O. M., 1274, 4457
Solso, Robert L., 871
Sombulogu, K., 3305
Somers, Gerald G., 5304
Šomina, E. S., 4379
Sommers, Alison A., 907
Sommers, Paul, 612, 616
Somphong Shevasunt, 3343

Soranaka, Seiji, 5396
Sorel, Nicole, 4744
Sørensen, Aage B., 4710
Sosdian, Carol P., 514
Sosis, Ruth H., 1700
Soskin, S. N., 3171
Soto, Shirlene Ann, 3643
Soucy, Pierre-Yves, 5446
Souto, Cláudio, 1049
Souza, Washington Peluso Albino de, 4380
Sow, Alpha I., 1393
Špakov, R. P., 133
Špaňhel, Josef, 4891
Spanier, Graham B., 3048, 3404, 3450, 3451, 3512, 3557
Spataro, Giuseppe, 5593
Spearritt, Peter, 1394
Spector, Malcolm, 230
Speier, Hans, 1230, 2050
Spence, Larry D., 5411
Spencer, Martin E., 656
Spenner, Kenneth I., 5076
Spero, Moshe Halevi, 1781
Spigel, Irwin M., 696
Spittler, Gerd, 1140, 4145
Spitze, Glenna, 3410
Spitze, Glenna D., 4859, 4871
Splichal, Slavko, 2204
Spoonley, Paul, 3761
Šporer, Željka, 134, 1130, 2000
Spradley, James P., 489
Sprafkin, Joyce N., 2205
Spreitzer, Elmer, 3072, 5389
Sproul, Barbara C., 1879
Sproule, J. Michael, 2131
Sreedhar, M. V., 2120
Srinivasan, K., 3344
Srull, Thomas K., 912
St. John, Craig, 2980
Stacey, Judith, 3558
Stacey, Margaret, 6177
Stachowiak, Herbert, 598
Staehelin, Rudolf M., 5332
Stahura, John, 3109, 4312, 4381
Stambouli, Fredj, 4382, 5784
Standfest, Erich, 6086
Standing, Guy, 3919
Stanford, Richard A., 4162
Stangvik, Gunnar, 707
Stankevič, L., 191, 761
Stanley, Manfred, 1504, 4609
Stanworth, John, 4768
Stapf, Kurt H., 339
Stark, Oded, 3927, 4383
Stark, Rodney, 1828, 1841, 1852, 1953
Staroverov, V. I., 3172, 4163, 4561
Starr, Paul D., 1580
Stasiulis, Daiva K., 3785
Staub, Ervin, 762
Staudt, Erich, 4983
Stavig, Gordon R., 589
Stavrov, Boris Dimov, 65

Stearman, Allyn MacLean, 3811
Stebbins, Robert A., 2001
Steelman, Lala Carr, 872
Steeno, Jeff, 2955
Steers, Richard M., 1059
Steeves, Allan D., 4384
Stefani, Manuela Angela, 1669
Steffensmeier, Darrell J., 5983
Stegner, Steven E., 345
Steiber, Steven R., 1217, 5031
Stein, Jay Wobith, 2206
Stein, Peter, 1670
Stein, R. Timothy, 1153
Steinbacher, Franz, 2293
Steinberg, Bernard, 1782
Steinberg, Hans-Josef, 5246
Steinberg, Laurence D., 3512
Steinberg Ratner, Ronnie, 4647
Steinberger, Peter J., 5542
Steinbuch, Karl, 192
Steiner, Ivan D., 899
Steininger, Rudolf, 5594
Steinvorth, Ulrich, 399
Stemplowski, Ryszard, 5717
Stengers, Isabelle, 1992
Stening, Bruce W., 5122
Stepaniants, Marietta, 5459
Stepanjan, C. A., 2767
Stephens, D. B., 5123
Stephens, Eugene, 5920
Stericker, Anne, 2979
Stern, Henri, 2646
Stern, Mark, 5661
Stern, N. H., 5856
Stern, Paul C., 135
Stern, Robert H., 3736
Stern, Robert N., 5026
Štern, Vilko, 4648
Sternlieb, George, 4385
Stevens, Gillian, 3559
Stevens, John D., 2061
Stevens, Paul, 2121
Stewart, Mary White, 1824
Stewart, Robert A., 913
Stewman, Shelby, 4713
Stichweh, Rudolf, 873
Stilwell, Frank J.B., 4386
Stipak, Brian, 590, 1581
Stockton, Nancy, 2986
Stockwell, Edward G., 3173, 3617
Stoetzel, Jean, 3225, 4508
Stohl, Michael, 1495
Stojanovič, Branislav, 4387
Stokvis, P. R. D., 3874
Stolbun, Ė. B., 763
Stoljarov, V. I., 5390, 5391
Stommes, Eileen, 6228
Stone, Michael E., 4388
Stookey, John A., 3034
Stork, Hans Rainer, 2775
Storms, Michael D., 2987, 3384
Stotland, Ezra, 5877

Strachan, Alan, 3851
Strack, Jay, 5823
Strassberg, Donald S., 996
Strasser, Hermann, 2623, 2863
Stratup, Richard, 2002
Straus, Murray Arnold, 1582
Straus, Roger A., 1938
Strauss, David J., 624
Streeck, Wolfgang, 5247
Street, David, 5771
Street, James H., 123
Streib, Victor L., 5984
Stribley, Keith M., 415
Strickland, Bonnie R., 1700
Stroh, Guy W., 1631
Stroman, Duane F., 6176
Strong, P. M., 6229
Stroppa, Claudio, 2062
Stryker, Sheldon, 700, 1540, 1583
Stubbs, Michael, 2518, 3345
Stuber, Fritz, 2406
Stublarec, Stephen, 2729
Studlar, Donley, 2768
Studlar, Donley T., 3839
Stumpf, Stephen A., 2624
Stussi, Alfredo, 2260
Styskal, Richard A., 1131
Suarez, Maria Matilde, 3928
Šubkin, V. N., 3062
Subramaniam, Venkateswarier, 1437
Suhotin, A. K., 2003
Suiçmez, Vural, 3876
Suimenko, Ė. I., 2479
Suleiman, Ezra N., 2769
Sullivan, Ellen, 3306
Sullivan, Thomas J., 6087
Sullivan, William M., 54
Sumbatjan, Ju. G., 5460
Sumner, Colin, 1263
Sundaram, K. V., 4130
Sundbo, Jon, 4131, 4176
Supek, Rudi, 66, 67, 68
Supek-Zupan, Olga, 2063, 2280
Supiot, Alain, 5163
Suprun, A. V., 764
Surbeck, Elaine, 2207
Surmin, Ju. P., 400
Susato, Shigeru, 1438
Sušinskij, V. V., 759
Sutch, Diane, 2946
Sutherland, S. L., 1218
Suttles, Gerald D., 5771
Sutton, John R., 4860
Suzuki, Hiroshi, 1632, 4011, 6088
Svendsen, Ann C., 635
Sverdlin, M. A., 5452
Svetlaev, V. D., 761
Swafford, Michael, 591, 1565
Swann, William B. Jr., 1238
Swanson, Louis E., 3929
Swartz, Marc J., 1395
Sweet, James A., 2910

Swiderski, Edward M., 2237
Swingewood, Alan, 7
Symons, Donald, 3385
Syrbu, I. F., 3964
Syroeškina, M. K., 765
Szabady, Egon, 3346
Szacki, Jerzy, 69
Szafran, Robert F., 1829, 3712
Szalai, Alexander, 4509
Szántó, Miklós, 1396, 1397
Szász, János, 1024
Szebenyi, Péterné, 1488
Szilágyi, Erzsébet, 2175
Szinovacz, Maximiliane, 2982, 3452
Szoc, Ron, 5924
Sztompka, Piotr, 328
Szwajkowski, Eugene, 952
Szymanski, Albert, 70

Taamallah, Khamaïs, 3276
Tabah, Léon, 3277
Tabboni, Simonetta, 4458
Tacchi, Enrico Maria, 4562
Tacke, Walter, 3278
Tackmann, Sigrid, 1618
Taeuber, Karl E., 2910
Taguchi, Masami, 4164
Tait, John, 2927, 3786
Tajfel, H., 1044
Takahashi, Hiroko, 3560
Takahashi, Noriaki, 1336
Takahashi, Yoshinori, 708
Takane, Masaaki, 2208, 2394
Takashima, Shōji, 5
Takenaka, Kazuo, 1398
Takeyasu, Hideko, 4610
Taksanov, A. K., 4165
Talamo, Magda, 5124
Talbot, John M., 3315
Talbot, Ross B., 4628
Tamai, Minoru, 5734
Tamaki, Matsuo, 5509
Tamarin, George R., 3787, 3788
Tamir, Lois M., 2064
Tamney, Joseph B., 1783, 1903
Tamura, Kenji, 3561
Tan, Alexis S., 2209
Tan, Boon Ann, 3328
Tanada, Hirofumi, 4389
Tanaka, Toyoji, 5563
Tandon, B. C., 466
Tanenbaum, E. J., 1218
Tanguy, Lucie, 5077
Tani, Katsuhide, 2587
Tannahill, Reay, 2988
Tanner, Jerald, 1830
Tanur, Judith M., 918
Tapinos, G., 3174
Tapper, Bruce Elliot, 1880
Tapper, Nancy, 3644
Tarasov, Ju. N., 5098
Tardos, Róbert, 4473

Tashakkori, Abbas, 932
Tashiro, Fujio, 3028
Tasseit, Siegfried, 197, 6089
Tatur, Melanie, 4984
Taubmann, Wolfgang, 4390
Tavares, Jean, 1939
Tay, Alice Erh-Soon, 1653, 1654
Taylor, Brian K., 1408
Taylor, Charles Lewis, 592
Taylor, D. Garth, 1239
Taylor, Frederick Kräupl, 3201
Taylor, Howard F., 1210
Taylor, Ian, 1671
Taylor, John G., 2891
Taylor, K. Wayne, 467
Taylor, Lionel Ray, 3113
Taylor, Marylee C., 3789
Taylor, Patricia A., 2598, 4938
Taylor, Robert W., 2118
Taylor, Steven J., 1489
Taylor, Stuart P., 953
Tayman, Jeffrey, 3169
Tchivela, Tchichellé, 3226
Te, Ju. G., 4596
Teachman, Jay D., 3175
Tedeschi, James T, 954
Tedin, Kent L., 5662
Teevan, James J., 231
Tegtmeyer, Heinrich, 2588, 2864
Tehranian, Majid, 2065
Teitler, G., 5701
Teitler, Robert J., 1577
Templeton, Kenneth S. Jr., 5663
Tenjanko, Ju. P., 5730
Teple, Edwin R., 5305
Terabayashi, Osamu, 1688
Terada, Atsuhiro, 5664
Terada, Ryoichi, 2728, 4391
Terehov, A. M., 4573
Teriet, Bernhard, 4985
Termote, Marc, 3875
Ternisien, Michel, 1499
Terpstra, J., 2625
Tesarova, Dyna, 4861
Tesha, Nancy, 3014
Tesser, Abraham, 709, 874
Tessler, Mark A., 5665
Tetzlaff, Rainer, 4073
Teubner, Günther, 1067
Teune, Henry, 454
Teunis, H. B., 1264
Tévoédjrè, Albert, 5785
Tezanos, José F., 2711, 5618
Thackeray, Milton G., 6204
Thakur, A. S., 2292
Thao, Trinh Van, 4535
Theissen, Gerd, 1784
Thelen, Mark H., 939
Theobald, Robin, 1141
Theodore, Athena, 3599
Thieme, Hans, 4986
Thiesse, Anne-Marie, 2261

Thiher, Allen, 2210
Thomas, Darwin L., 626
Thomas, David, 71
Thomas, Gail E., 4760
Thome, Joseph R., 5786
Thompson, John E., 981
Thompson, Kenneth, 2281
Thompson, Mary K., 2989
Thompson, Thomas P., 1537
Thompson, William R., 5693
Thomson, A. W. J., 5248
Thomson, Dale C., 3713
Thomson, Elizabeth, 4862
Thorngate, Warren B., 380
Thorns, David C., 4372
Thornton, Arland, 496, 3347
Thornton, Peter, 4611
Thrush, John C., 2395
Thumerelle, P. J., 3176
Thune, Elizabeth S., 1036
Thursz, Daniel, 6258
Thylefors, Ingela, 1010
Tibi, Bassam, 1439, 1785, 2892, 5249
Tichy, Noel, 1066
Tierney, John, 5666
Tihomirov, Ju. A., 5510
Tihonov, N. M., 5209
Tillekens, G., 2597
Tilley, Nicholas, 329
Tillinghast, Diana Stover, 1240
Tilly, Charles, 2865, 5502
Tilly, Louise A., 3562
Timmermans, J. M., 6127
Timofeev, T., 6090
Timuš, A. I., 4166
Tinto, Vincent, 5078
Tippelt, Rudolf, 4761
Tiryakian, E. A., 330
Tiryakian, Edward A., 224, 5511
Tischler, Nancy G., 936
Titma, M. H., 1399
Titma, Mikk, 4987
Titus, Sandra L., 933
Tobias, Cynthia L., 4271
Tobias, John Jacob, 5985
Tobin, Gary A., 4392
Toby, Jackson, 5986
Todisco, Orlando, 331
Toepfer, Helmuth, 3876
Toiser, Jacques, 4697
Toivonen, Timo, 5106
Tokuhisa, Tamao, 5392
Tokunaga, Makoto, 6091
Tolbert, Charles, 4468
Tolbert, Charles M. II., 4664
Tolkačeva, S. S., 5471, 5475
Tomaškevič, V. E., 3063
Tomlinson, Sally, 3866
Tomori, Sunday Hezekiah Olu, 2494
Tomović, Vladislav A., 207
Topitsch, Ernst, 340
Topolski, Jerzy, 2807

Topornin, B. N., 5512
Torrado, Susana, 3563
Torrealba, Ricardo, 3928
Torrens, Paul R., 6259
Torres Adrián, Mario Julio, 5667
Toš, Peter, 4563
Toščenko, Ž. T., 1352
Totaro, Francesco, 2066
Tóth, Árpád, 3930, 5099
Tóth, Károly, 548
Tóth, Pál Péter, 2770
Totoki, Toshichika, 490
Touraine, Alain, 332, 2480, 2481, 4612, 5461
Towler, Robert, 1838, 1931
Townsend, Peter, 5787
Toyoshima, Kakujō, 1336
Trachtman, Lester, 5136
Tracy, Martin, 5007
Traugott, Mark, 5668
Travin, I. I., 1400, 2866
Tréanton, J.-R., 2168, 4274
Treble, James II, 5788
Tregubov, B. A., 5357
Treiman, Donald J., 4784
Trejo, Arnulfo D., 3714
Trest'jan, A., 5394
Tribe, Keith, 4133, 5531
Trice, Harrison M., 5175, 5802
Trilling, Leon, 2771
Trimberger, Ellen Kay, 5718
Tripier, Pierre, 161
Tristram, R. J., 1244, 2867
Trivedi, Harshad R., 4393
Trocsanyi, Laszlo, 5157
Trommsdorff, Gisela, 1045, 2990, 3478
Trope, Yaacov, 914
Trotter, Robert, 3371
Troy, Norbert, 4904
Troye, Sigurd V., 178
Trumbo, Don A., 4682
Tsai, Yung-Mei, 998
Tuchman, Gaye, 4822
Tuckett, David, 6177
Tufte, Virginia, 3564
Tuma, Nancy Brandon, 601
Tuncomag, Kenan, 5285
Tunstall, Daniel B., 593
Turčenko, V. N., 2396
Turiel, Elliot, 1635
Turk, Austin T., 1641, 1652
Turkel, Gerald, 5420
Turner, B. D., 3113
Turner, Harold W., 1853, 1940
Turner, J. C., 1044, 1202
Turner, Jonathan H., 315
Turner, Ralph H., 2883, 4254
Turner, Stephen, 454, 1854
Turowski, Jan, 4394
Twaddle, Andrew C., 3202
Tyheeva, Ju. C., 1401
Tyler, Tom R., 5987

Index des auteurs

Tyler, William G., 202
Tyrell, Hartmann, 3565
Tyson, G. A., 1701

Udarceva, I. F., 1359
Ueda, Mamoru, 136
Uehling, Theodore Edward, 2087
Uesugi, Takamichi, 5568
Ugazi, Valeria, 6230
Ugboajah, Frank Okwu, 2211
Uglješić, Dubravka, 5027
Uhlman, Thomas M., 5988
Ulanova, É. A., 766
Ule, Mirjana, 1161
Ultee, W. C., 2626, 5513
Umapathy, N., 4167
Umezawa, Tadashi, 4564
Umezawa, Takashi, 333
Umiker-Sebeok, Jean, 2033
Umino, Michio, 875
Underhill, Ernest, 2704
Underwood, Bill, 3971
Ungar, Sheldon, 1197
Unger, Rhoda Kesler, 2991
Unnever, James D., 3790
Upadhyay, Jai Jai Ram, 6092
Urano, Masaki, 4395, 4396
Urbina, Fernando, 4510
Urena, Enrique M., 4613
Uribe Castaneda, Manuel, 3931
Uricoechea, Fernando, 934
Urlanis, B. C., 2911
Ursell, Gill, 5231
Useem, Michael, 5719
Usenin, V. I., 2712
Usmanov, N., 4171
Uttley, Stephen, 4511
Uyanga, Joseph T., 4172

Vačko, G. V., 4863
Vačnadze, G. N., 193
Vago, Steven, 2868
Vahiduddin, Syed, 710
Valderrama, Mariano, 4173
Valencia, B. Michael, 6154
Valentej, D. I., 3177, 3566
Valentinova, N. G., 5393
Valkenburg, F. C., 4727
Vallas, Steven P., 334
Vallat, Colette, 3877
Vallee, Frank F., 225
Valticos, Nicolas, 4988
Van Bol, Jean-Marie, 194
Van Buskirk, William R., 993
Van Cauwenbergh, A., 2869
Van de Graaf, John H., 2482
Van De Vall, Mark, 142
Van Den Berg, Lotty, 4864
Van den Berghe, Pierre L., 3567, 3866
Van Den Doel, J., 4675
Van Den Haag, Ernest, 4459, 5844
Van Der Berg, Axel, 335

Van der Berghe, Pierre L., 3791
Van Der Burgh, Chris, 5824
Van der Hoeven, Rolph, 4762, 5762, 5776
Van Der Pligt, Joop, 401, 1178
Van der Voordt, Theo J. M., 1465
Van Der Wusten, H., 1584
Van Der Zwaan, A. H., 6231
Van Dijk, J. J. M., 5989
Van Dijk, Jos A., 401
Van Driel, G. J., 6093
Van Gestel, P. W. C., 3932
Van Ginneken, W., 5789
Van Hattum, Rolland James, 2067
Van Herbruggen, C., 4476
Van Herwaarden, Floor G., 468
Van Hoesel, P. H. M., 428
Van Hoorn, R. J. P., 198
Van Houten, Donald R., 1074
Van Liere, Kent D., 3965
Van Maanen, John, 5543
Van Nieuwenhuijze, Christoffel Anthonie Oliver, 2870
Van Outrive, Lode, 5990
Van Parijs, Philippe, 402
Van Poucke, Willy, 999
Van Praag, Bernard M. S., 468
Van Praag, Herman Meïr, 5814
Van Praag, Philip, 3348, 3349
Van Ravenzwaaij, C., 6093
Van Rouveroy van Nieuwaal, E. A. B., 1672
Van Scotter, Richard D., 2313
Van Steenbergen, Bart, 1402
Van Trier, W. E., 143
Van Vught, Frans, 6094
Van Willigen, John, 2815
Van Wormer, Katerine S., 1154
Van Zwam, H. J., 5333
Vanas, Norbert, 2398
Vanderpool, Christopher K., 76
Vandi, Abdulai S., 1289
Vandycke, Robert, 5462
Vanfossen, Beth E., 2627
Vankova, Libuse, 2556
Vanneman, Reeve D., 2713
Varady, David P., 4397
Varga, Károly, 144
Varzar'. P. M., 3178
Vasil'čuk, Ju. A., 4460
Vasu, Michael L., 4597
Vaughan, Charlotte A., 106
Vaughan, Ted R., 1612
Vaught, Charles, 4989
Vazquez Figueroa, Onel, 1585
Vdovin, A. I., 2714
Vedris, Mladen, 3933
Veenman, Justus, 6178
Veljkovič, Vera, 5790
Veltman, Calvin J., 1440
Veltmeyer, Henry C., 2715
Verber, Christian Von, 5791
Vercauteren, P., 2628

Verchomin-Harasymiw, Elaïne, 5669
Verdon, Michel, 3568
Verhagen, Koenraad, 4174
Verma, Ravi, 2381, 3867
Verma, Ravi P., 4503
Vermeer, Edward B., 6095
Vernier, Bernard, 3569
Vernooij-Pieterse, E. W. M. J. Th., 2935
Veron, Jacques, 3227
Verret, Michel, 5100, 5101
Verrips, Jojada, 4175
Verstrynge Rojas, Jorge, 5740
Vertinsky, Patricia, 6212
Vetoškina, T. A., 2238
Vetrov, V. A., 4461
Vetter, Jan, 5286
Veys, D., 3228
Viby Mogensen, Gunnar, 4176
Victor, Jean, 5079
Victor, Jeffrey S., 3386
Vidich, Arthur, 5741
Vidor, Ferenc, 4398
Viet, Jean, 208
Vigarié, A., 4342
Vigilante, Joseph, 6258
Vignolle, Jean-Pierre, 2212, 2271
Vilain, Michel, 4177
Vilenskij, M. A., 4614
Villa, Francesco, 232
Villar, Rafael, 3947
Villemez, Wayne J., 241
Villeti, Roberto, 2629
Villey, Olivier, 4865
Vincent, G., 1586, 5115
Vingré, Michel, 6096
Vinogradov, V. D., 4565
Vinogradov, V. G., 6097
Vinogradov, Vladimir, 2716
Vinokurova, V. A., 900
Visaria, Pravin, 4512
Viscusi, W. Kip, 4728
Visher, Christy A., 5981
Višnevskij, I. B., 2519
Višnevskij, Ju. R., 1441, 1490
Višnevskij, M. I., 876
Vissers, A. M. C., 4727
Vita, László, 4866
Vitányi, Iván, 1287, 1434
Vitek, Karel, 3453
Vitruk, N. V., 767
Vitta, Maurizio, 2262
Vizitej, É., 1403
Vizitej, É. B., 2239
Vizitej, N., 5394
Vjatkin, A. R., 2912
Vladyčenko, I. M., 4905
Vlaškalić, Tihomir, 2483
Vlassof, Michael, 4867
Vloeberghs, D., 4566
Vodgreeva, L. V., 768
Vogel, Ezra F., 4140
Vogelsang, Harald, 3279

Vohland, Ulrich, 4763, 5080
Voisset, Michèle, 5164
Voje, Kirsten, 3607
Vojnic, Dragomier, 4414
Volčok, G. I., 1587, 2717
Völgyes, Ivan, 4178
Volkov, I. N., 1633
Volkov, O. E., 594
Volodina, N. G., 1588
Von Frank, April A., 6135
Voplenko, N. N., 6098
Vorob'ev, N. E., 4729
Voroncov, A. V., 1491
Vorotilov, V. A., 4399
Vos, Henk de, 336
Voutyras, Stavros, 4730
Vovkanyč, S. I., 2787
Voyé, Liliane, 1433, 3706
Vrain, Phillippe, 4868
Vredenburgh, Donald J., 1589
Vu, Thy Quyen, 2893
Vuijsje, Flip, 4513
Vujović, Sreten, 4400, 4401
Vyas, N. N., 3715
Vydrin, D. I., 877
Vylegžanin, D. A., 6099

Wachs, Saul P., 1749
Wachter, Michael L., 3878
Wachtler, Günther, 4990
Wagaw, Teshome G., 2399
Wagner, F. E., 4402
Wagner, Jon, 195, 5008
Wahlke, John, 2613
Wainerman, Catalina H., 3437, 3570, 4869
Waite, Linda J., 4054, 4859, 4870
Waksler, Frances Chaput, 253
Wald, Paul, 2104
Walizer, Michael H., 469
Walker, Alan, 3110
Walker, Andrew L., 5811
Walker, David Robert, 1394
Walker, N. Darlene, 5988
Walker, Sheila S., 1715
Wallace, Michael, 1196
Wallendorf, Melanie, 4661
Wallimann, Isidor, 5421
Wallis, Roy, 1807, 1824
Walters, Ronald G., 2808
Walton, John, 2689
Wang, Charlotte Shiang, 3934
Wang, Hsuan-Hsien, 3005
Wang, William S.-Y., 2018
Warburg, Gabriel R., 1786
Ward, Colleen, 6205
Ward, David A., 5991
Ward, John O., 3935, 4402
Ward, Michael, 3235, 3553
Ward, Russell A., 3101
Ward, Sally, 410
Ward, Sally K., 4403
Wardwell, John M., 3936

Index des auteurs

Warland, Rex H., 1891, 3929
Warner, Lyle G., 1179
Warner, Malcolm, 5192
Warner, R. Stephen, 1787
Warren, Richard D., 585, 595, 3240
Warren, Robert, 3879
Warshay, Leon H., 33, 327
Wartella, Ellen, 2068
Washington, Robert, 697, 6068
Wasserman, Ira M., 3792, 4514
Wasserman, Stanley, 997
Watanabe, Motoki, 2589
Watanuki, Jōji, 2846, 4404
Watari, Akeshi, 1492
Watson, James L., 2647
Watson, Tony J., 4689
Watt, Ian, 2992
Watts, William A., 1241
Weatherbee, Donald E., 2886
Weatherby, Norman L., 3219
Weaver, Jerry L., 3350
Weber, George H., 107
Weber, Kenneth R., 2871
Webler, Wolf-Dietrich, 2484
Webster, D. Robert, 5875
Webster, Frank, 2213
Webster, James, G., 2214
Webster, Murray Jr., 2592
Wedderburn, Dorothy, 2630
Weed, Frank J., 1132
Weede, Erich, 2865, 2881, 4487, 4515
Weekes-Vagliani, Winifred, 3645
Weeks, M. F., 515
Wegener, Bernd, 5034
Wegner, Daniel M., 711
Wehler, Hans-Ulrich, 2809
Wehr, Paul, 979
Wei Djao, A., 6136
Weiler, William C., 5899
Weimer, Walter B., 470
Weinbaum, M. G., 2772
Weinberg, Martin S., 3387
Weiner, Merle, 3833
Weinfeld, Morton, 1788
Weingarten, Elmar, 435
Weinstein, Deena, 2590
Weinstein, Eugene A., 918
Weinstein, Michael, 2590, 5694
Weintraub, Dov, 4644
Weir, Tamara, 5110
Weis, Joseph G., 5897
Weis, Lois, 2400
Weisberg, Robert W., 878
Weisbrod, Aviva, 1789
Weiss, Carol H., 491
Weiss, Dimitri, 5009, 5250
Weiss, Robert Stuart, 3571
Weisser, Michael R., 5992
Weitzer, Ronald, 4462
Weitzman, Lenore J., 2993
Welch, Holmes, 1790
Welch, Michael, 108, 1886

Welch, Stephen W., 4516
Welch, Susan, 5562
Wellington, Dorothy Gaites, 3203
Wells, Alan, 980
Wells, Gary L., 364
Wells, R. G. J., 4649
Welton, John M., 1408
Wendt, Bernd-Jürgen, 5251
Wendt, Bruno, 72
Werbel, J., 4932
Werbik, Hans, 942
Wesbrook, Stephen D., 1634
Wesolowski, Wlodzimierz, 2718
West, Jonathan P., 5112
West, Laurie J., 447
Westenholz, Ann, 5334
Westie, Frank R., 109
Westoff, Charles F., 3280
Westphal-Hellbusch, Sigrid, 226
Wettstein, Howard K., 2087
Wetzel, Kurt, 5306
Wex, Helga, 3646
Wheeler, Ladd, 929
Whitam, Frederick L., 3361
White, C. J. Mower, 1025
White, Gordon, 4136
White, Gregory L., 1198, 5825
White, James W., 3937
White, Leonard A., 955
White, Lynn K., 3351
Whitt, J. Allen, 6169
Whitten, Phillip, 5993
Whittington, Frank J., 3106
Whyte, Martin King, 4140
Wick, Rainer, 2217
Wickberg, Edgar, 4179
Wickelgren, Wayne A., 879
Wickerman, R. W., 5344
Wickman, Peter M., 5993
Widerkehr, Doris E., 4567
Wieken-Mayser, Maria, 5051
Wiendieck, Gerd, 1329
Wienir, Paul L., 469
Wiersma, William, 554
Wilder, David A., 981
Wildt, Albert R., 596
Wiles, Paul, 1642
Wiley, Mary Glenn, 2994
Wilke, Arthur S., 2557
Wilke, Helmut, 533
Wilken, Paul H., 960, 4568
Wilkening, A. E., 3987
Wilkening, Eugene A., 784, 1507
Wilkins, Alan, 1124
Wilkinson, Paul, 1495
Wilkinson, Robert E., 5158
Willems, Emilio, 4405
Willender, Alfred, 1279
Willhelm, Sidney M., 2593
Williams, A. J., 6243
Williams, Conlin J., 3387
Williams, Harvey, 6165

327

Williams, Juanita H., 2994
Williams, Kirk R., 5994
Williams, Peter W., 1941
Williams, Robin M. Jr., 979
Williams, Stephen J., 6232, 6259
Williamson, Bill, 2314
Williamson, John B., 3086, 3111
Willis, Evan, 6206
Willis, John Ralph, 1791, 1792
Willis, Paul E., 1404
Wils, Frits C. M., 4650
Wilson, Bobby M., 1942
Wilson, Dorothy, 6100
Wilson, Glenn, 2939
Wilson, John Frederick, 1793
Wilson, Kenneth L., 73, 74, 3880
Wilson, Logan, 2558
Wilson, M. G. A., 3229
Wilson, Paul R., 3183
Wilson, R. Mark, 3784
Wilson, Robert A., 4406
Wilson, Robert Neal, 2263
Wilson, Robert R., 1881
Wilson, Stephen, 1016
Wilson, T. D., 196
Wilson-Davis, K., 3572
Wimberley, Ronald C., 1689, 1943, 5685
Winckelmann, Johannes, 880
Windmiller, Myra, 1635
Winick, Charles, 1590
Winkler, Donald R., 2401, 5010
Winner, Irene Portis, 2033
Winson, Anthony, 2719
Winston, Kathryn Teich, 4789
Winter, Michael F., 4463
Winterstein, Helmut, 6137
Wiredu, Kwasi, 2069
Wiseman, Jacqueline P., 6101
Wisman, Jon D., 2004, 2005
Wissmann, David A., 5031
Wiswell, Candace Hinson, 4218
Witt, David D., 3006
Witte, Eberhard, 5335
Witte, Erich H., 1045
Wöhler, Karlheinz, 3199
Wolchik, Sharon L., 3647
Wolf, Deborah Goleman, 3388
Wolf, Mauro, 1405
Wolf, Patricia F., 3203
Wolf, Richard M., 2315
Wolf, Sharon, 1026
Wolf, Wendy C., 5073
Wolfgang, Marvin E., 5976
Wolfle, Lee M., 2122
Wolinsky, Fredric D., 6207
Wollman, Winnifred K., 1591
Wong, Morrison G., 2559
Wong, Siu-Lun, 137
Wood, James L., 59
Wood, James R., 1097, 1813, 1924
Wood, Michael, 471
Wood, Robert, 5766

Wood, Robert E., 5395
Wood, Stephen, 5011
Woodrow, Karen, 3223
Woodrum, Eric, 3881
Woods, L. B., 5526
Woods, Richard, 1882
Woolf, William J. Jr., 110
Worchel, Stephen, 982
Wrench, John, 3856
Wright, Charles R., 2177
Wright, Erik Olin, 2658
Wright, James D., 2883, 3991, 4991
Wright, Sam, 1275
Wright, Will, 1404
Wrong, Dennis Hume, 1142
Wunenburger, Jean Jacques, 1265
Wurdock, Clarence, 683, 2402
Wurfel, David, 2773
Wurm, Stephen A., 2106
Wuthnow, Robert, 1686, 1690, 2006
Wüthrich, Peter, 5826
Wyer, Robert S. Jr., 912
Wyman, Sherman, 4289

Yagi, Tadashi, 4690
Yajima, Yutaka, 1794
Yamaguchi, Masao, 1419
Yamaguchi, Soko, 4180, 4181
Yamamura, Yoshiaki, 1592
Yamaoka, Eiichi, 2591, 4182
Yang, Chung-fang, 6212
Yarosky, Michael D., 1795
Yasin, Bu Ali, 3454
Yasuda, Saburo, 337, 6102
Yasuda, Takashi, 881
Yatabe, Takeo, 712
Yazaki, Takeo, 4407
Yeaukey, D., 3281
Yerkey, A. Neil, 2036
Yinger, J. Milton, 1702
Yinon, Oded, 3179
Yinon, Yoel, 949
Yip, Ka-che, 1944
Yoden, Hiromichi, 4183
Yoels, William C., 1544
Yohalem, Alice M., 4871
Yorke, Michael, 3793
Yornet, Mario, 5792
Yoshida, Tadashi, 666
Young, Alice A., 659
Young, Frank J., 3716
Young, Frank W., 3491
Young, Lung-Chang, 137
Young, Ruth C., 4517, 4518, 5793
Young, T. R., 972
Young, W. McEwan, 4906
Yuzawa, Yasuhiko, 3112, 3573
Yzerman, Thomas J., 111

Zagladin, V. V., 2720
Zagorodnaja, É. M., 4408
Zagórski, Krzysztof, 2777, 4915

Index des auteurs

Zaguljaev, V. A., 769
Zaguljaeva, L. A., 769
Zaharov, F. I., 5735
Zajdfudim, P. H., 5082
Zajmist, F. L., 2721
Zald, Mayer N., 5614
Zaltman, Gerald, 4661
Zañartu, Mario, 1904
Zandstra, Hubert, 4184
Zanna, Mark P., 1199
Zapf, Wolfgang, 597
Zaret, David, 1905, 2810
Žarikov, F. S., 4992
Zarubin, A. G., 3064
Zaslavskaja, T. I., 4185, 4186, 4187
Zateev, V. I., 4012
Zavala, Hector Luis Morales, 4188
Zavalloni, Marisa, 657
Zavtur, A., 1593
Zazzo, René, 3204
Zdravomyslov, A., 6103
Zegura, Stephen L., 1628
Zegveld, Walter, 4756
Zeiss, Carol A., 5379
Zeitz, Gerald, 448
Zelditch, Morris Jr., 2729
Zelepukin, A. V., 2485
Zelinka, Fritz F., 5720
Zelizer, Viviana A. Rotman, 4670
Zeller, Richard A., 135, 474, 492, 596, 1594
Zemcov, L. G., 4189
Zemelman, Hugo, 5514
Žemin, M. V., 338
Zentner, Henry, 493, 2872
Zern, David S., 3029
Zerubavel, Eviatar, 6233
Zey-Ferrell, Mary, 1133
Ziche, Joachim, 4145
Židanov, A. I., 5595

Zierer, Otto, 4190
Žihareva, Z. A., 2486
Žilina, L. N., 882
Zillmann, Dolf, 956
Zimbardo, Philip G., 5825
Zimmer, Basil George, 3282
Zimmermann, Ekkart, 2730
Zinčenko, Ju. G., 770
Zingarelli, Delia, 1508
Zinov'eva, R. A., 2722
Zippo, Ida, 957
Zito, George V., 2913
Živkovič, Miroslav, 2487, 2774
Zlobina, E. G., 3065
Zlotnikov, R. A., 2520
Zolberg, Vera L., 2272
Zoloth, Barbara S., 2929
Zopf, Paul E., 1406
Zorina, Z. A., 1155
Zubanov, A. G., 5252
Zubrzycki, Jerzy, 3882
Zucker, Lynne G., 55
Zucker, William, 4560
Zukin, Sharon, 4409
Zulu, Grace, 5195
Zündorf, Lutz, 4691
Zunica Ramajo, Luisa, 5682
Župančić, Milan, 4191
Županov, Josip, 75, 4692
Žuravlev, G. T., 1266, 6104
Žuravlev, M. M., 5515
Zurbuchen, Mary S., 4146
Zurcher, Louis A. Jr., 5613
Zurla, Paolo, 6247
Zuzanek, Jiri, 5345
Zvorykin, A. A., 4885, 6105
Zweigenhaft, Richard L., 915
Zwerdling, Daniel, 5336

SUBJECT INDEX

Abnormal, 1496
Abortion, 3340
    France, 3308, 3318
    India, 3303
    Israel, 3341
    Japan, 3299
    Netherlands, 3293
    Philippines, 3309
    Thailand, 3327
    USA, 3299, 3304, 3306-3307, 3334
Absenteeism, 4934, 4998, 5005, 5009-5010
    France, 5002
Academic profession, USA, 2534
Academic success, 2529-2530
    USA, 2533
Access to eduction, Western Europe, 2332
Accidents, 3217, 3856
Acculturation, 1439
    Hawaii, 1425
    Spain, 1436
Achievement, 384, 812, 2289
Achievement motivations, 623, 775, 829, 834, 838, 874, 2727
Action, 281, 297, 343, 786, 788-789, 805, 816, 853, 864, 1179, 1187, 1238, 1271, 2595
Action research, 143-144
Action theory, 264, 315, 332, 337
Actionalism, 281, 297
Adams, Henry Carter, 13
Administration of justice, 5544, 5866
    India, 5547
    USA, 5546
Administrative reforms, 5556
    Mexico, 5549
    Sudan, 5550
Adolescence, 3032, 3048-3049, 3060-3061
    Canada, 3018
Adolescents, 686, 2289, 3033-3035, 3039, 3050
    Canada, 1462
    USA, 3365
Adorno, Theodor W., 317, 319, 322, 2219
Adult age, 1532, 3066-3067
Adult education, 2512, 2515
    France, 2502
    Tanzania, 2508
    USA, 2490
    West Africa, 2494
    Yugoslavia, 2501
Advertising, 2123-2125, 2127, 2130
Aesthetics, 2218-2219, 2239
    USSR, 2221, 2237
Affluent society, 2054, 4490

Age, 3005-3006
Age difference, 3213
Age distribution, 3004, 5850, 5962
    USSR, 3137
Aged, 839, 870, 1162, 3076, 3079-3080, 3084, 3088-3090, 3092, 3095, 3097, 3108-3109, 3111-3112, 3532, 3560, 5816, 5922, 5930, 5960
    Australia, 3087
    France, 3070
    USA, 2134, 3073, 3078, 3081, 3085-3086, 3091, 3094, 3098-3099, 3107, 3675
Ageing, 2064, 3069, 3093, 3096, 3101, 3104
Aggression, 942-945, 947, 949-951, 953, 955, 3971
Aggressiveness, 941, 946, 948, 954, 956-957, 1560, 5111
Agrarian reforms, 4096, 4191
    Dominican Republic, 4056
    Mali, 4151
    Peru, 2696, 4066, 4071
    Portugal, 4021-4022, 4058
Agricultural cooperatives, 4649
    Canada, 4618
    Hungary, 4646
    Israel, 4644
    Sierra Leone, 4426
    Turkey, 4617
Agricultural development, 4624, 4628
    Ireland, 4640
Agricultural education, USA, 2525
Agricultural policy, 4628
Agricultural population, 3163
Agricultural workers, 5083, 5098
    Czechoslovakia, 5088
    USSR, 3178
Agriculture, 4621, 4894
    France, 4635
Alcoholism, 842, 5795, 5802, 5804, 5807, 5814, 5816
    Germany, 5821
    Switzerland, 5826
    United Kingdom, 5819
    USA, 5803, 5813, 5822
Alienation, 889, 1151, 1514, 1536, 1539, 1578-1579, 1589, 1594, 3373, 4998, 5355
    South Africa, 1214
Althusser, Louis, 383, 2659
Altruism, 911, 916, 918, 923, 927
Anarchy, 5466
Animals, 2914
Animism, Taiwan, 1732
Anomie, 1494, 1519, 4469

331

Anonymity, 694
Anthropologists, 99
Anti-semitism, 3731
    Germany, 3763
    United Kingdom, 3749
    USA, 3725, 3735, 3778
Antisocial behaviour, 1561
Anxiety, 676, 778, 823, 861, 2681
Apartheid, 3761
    South Africa, 3740
Applied research, 138, 142
Applied sociology, 142, 332, 5742, 5745-5748, 5750, 5752
    USA, 5753
Apprentices, 2523
Apprenticeship, 5056
Appropriate technology, 4227, 4579, 4599, 4604
Arbitration, 5288
    USA, 5305
Architecture, 2264, 5365
Aristocracy, 2723
    France, 5472
    USA, 3314
Army, 1037, 1634, 5717
    Netherlands, 5701
    USA, 5696, 5698-5699
Arrangement of working time, 4907
Art, 1862, 2217-2218, 2224, 2226, 2232, 2234-2235, 4585
    France, 2236
    Japan, 2231
Articles, 229, 231
Artistic creation, 2215-2216, 2222, 2229, 2238, 2254
Artists, 2227
Arts, United Kingdom, 2225
Asceticism, 1896
Aspirations, 842, 847
Associations, 1067, 2542
    France, 1068
    Spain, 1072
Astrology, 1700-1701
Asylums, USA, 6227
Atheism, 1876
Attention, 824
Attitude change, 937, 1174, 1177, 1188, 1193, 1195, 1198, 3050, 5950
Attitude scales, 620-622
Attitude to work, 4790, 4859, 4919, 4926-4927, 4934, 4937, 4944, 4947, 4949, 4951, 4954, 4966, 4973, 4977, 4991, 5097
    Japan, 4948, 4969
    New Zealand, 4958
    USA, 4961, 4969
    USSR, 4987
Attitudes, 870, 1172-1173, 1176, 1178-1179, 1182-1185, 1189-1191, 1196-1197, 1199, 1237, 1577, 2090, 3415, 5112
    Israel, 3040
    Japan, 5122

    Netherlands, 6178
    USA, 3304
Audience, 708, 1183
Authoritarianism, 1211, 1218, 2670, 5455
    South Africa, 1214, 3780
    USA, 1215
Authority, 680, 940, 1037, 1136, 1140, 3555, 5456
Automation, 2683
Automobiles, USA, 4619
Balance theory, 507
Banks, 4668
Bargaining, 958, 966
Bargaining power, 5071, 5202
Barter, developing countries, 4446
Basic needs, 4762, 5766, 5782
    Kenya, 5770
    Singapore, 4755
    Tunisia, 5784
Behaviour, 458, 1175, 1180-1181, 1186-1187, 1192, 1194, 1199, 2997, 3196
Behavioural sciences, 21, 39, 45, 63-64, 73-74, 465, 4653, 5406
    USA, 3692
Behaviourism, 223, 326
Belief, 704, 1173, 1225, 1238, 1700, 1854, 2628
Bernstein, 2282
Bibliographies, 2442, 4857
    Argentina, 3150
Bibliography, 198, 232
Bilingualism, 2084, 2109
    Africa, 2259
    Belgium, 3699
    Canada, 2381
    India, 2120
    Tunisia, 2121
Biographies, 219, 221, 223, 2954
    USA, 215
Birth, 3495
Birth control, 3284, 3333, 4852
    Africa, 3234
    China, 3325
    developing countries, 3286
    USA, 3314, 3347
Birth order, 872, 3265
    Switzerland, 3274
Birth rate, France, 3239
    Japan, 3252
Birth spacing, Zaire, 3294
Blacks, 697, 1289, 2473, 3549, 3673, 4377
    USA, 681, 1942, 2139, 2425, 3450, 3504, 3692, 3701, 3737, 3753, 3781, 4306, 5371
Blau, Peter M., 2589, 5060
Bourdieu, Pierre, 2
Bourgeois society, 1269, 1412, 2877, 3968, 5463, 5470
Bourgeois sociology, 269, 287, 321, 975, 1640, 1968, 5615
    France, 125
Bourgeoisie, 1757, 2698, 2723, 5084

Canada, 2708
France, 2690, 2707
Brahmanism, 1726, 1765
Brain drain, 3812, 3816, 3855
  India, 3842
Brass, William, 3276
Braudel, Fernand, 2793
Broadcasting, 2187
  Nigeria, 2186
  USA, 2196
Brother, 3507
Buddhism, 658, 1707, 1723, 1726, 1764, 1766, 1774
  United Kingdom, 1762
  USA, 1768
Bureaucracy, 1076, 1091, 1096, 1099, 1107-1109, 1114, 1121, 1123, 1125, 1140, 5019, 5456, 5485
  Arab countries, 1081
  Germany FR, 1073, 1080
  Indonesia, 1100
  South Asia, 1119
  Thailand, 1095, 1100
Bureaucratic control, 1013, 1079, 1083-1085, 1087, 1097
Bureaucratization, 1127, 1132
Burt, Cyril, 830
Business communication, 4519, 4543, 4551, 4554, 4559, 4566
Business communities, Canada, 4522
Business cycles, 4876
Business economics, 4537
Business management, 4524-4525, 4538, 4547, 5107, 5113
  China, 4555
Business organization, 4523, 4529
  China, 5315
Caillois, Roger, 807
Cancer, 3188, 3194-3196, 3203
Capital accumulation, 4436
Capital punishment, 5844, 5958, 5971
  Germany FR, 5965
  USA, 5834-5835
Capitalism, 1211, 1262, 1513, 1769, 1905, 2043, 2793, 2878, 3047, 4425, 4429, 4448, 4454-4455, 4458-4459, 4462-4463, 4629, 4703
  developing countries, 4439
  Latin America, 4427
  Southern Africa, 4431
  Spain, 4044
  United Kingdom, 4441
Capitalist countries, 2651, 2741, 4460, 5477
Capitalist society, 2580, 4424, 4436, 4442, 4450
Care of the aged, 6106, 6112, 6115, 6124
  France, 6108
  Netherlands, 6127
  USA, 6132
Carnival, 2280
Casework, 6145, 6147, 6150

Castells, Manuel, 4260, 4287, 4318
Castes, India, 2633, 2637-2639, 2641, 2643-2646, 3550
Catholic Church, 1800, 3712
  Brazil, 1907
  Canada, 1803
  France, 1799
  Latin America, 1819
  Poland, 1816
  USA, 1811, 1815
Catholicism, 1680, 1751, 1755
  Netherlands, 1722
  Poland, 1758
Catholics, Canada, 3261
  Ireland, 3243
  USA, 1735
Causal analysis, 74
Causal explanation, 343, 355, 377
Causal inference, 364, 380, 384-385
Causality, 350, 365, 368, 371, 566
Causes of death, 3217, 3219
  Canada, 3212
Celibacy, 3374
Censorship, USA, 5526
Censuses, Mauritania, 3918
  USA, 482
Character, 755
Charisma, 1135, 1138, 1141, 1803, 1826
Charismatic leaders, 1144
  Guyana, 1146
Chicago School, 268
Child adoption, 3480, 3499
  USA, 3461
Child care, 1169, 3468, 6111, 6122, 6155
  India, 6123
  USA, 6134
Child development, 691, 827-828, 1574, 3007, 3011, 3015, 3022-3024, 3027, 3746
  India, 3019
  Peru, 3025
Child labour, 4837, 4850, 4853
  India, 4794, 4867
Child psychology, 639
Child rearing, 3010, 3026, 3029, 5927
  Philippines, 3017
Childhood, 3013, 3021
  Canada, 3018
Children, 384, 902, 904, 1280, 1448, 2068, 2109, 2207, 3009, 3016, 3020, 3540, 5338, 6230
  France, 3012
  Tanzania, 3014
  USA, 2132, 2214
  USSR, 1565
Children's rights, 3008, 3028
Choice, 836
Christianity, 658, 1617, 1720, 1728, 1744, 1747, 1752, 1757, 1760, 1769, 1776, 1779, 1784, 1787
  Africa, 1715, 1763
  Europe, 1721

Subject index

Japan, 1719, 1794
Taiwan, 1732
USA, 1793
Zimbabwe, 1712
Church and State, 1812, 1906, 1925, 1927, 1943
　Brazil, 1907
　United Kingdom, 1918
Cinema, 2156-2157
　Africa, 2148
　France, 2181, 2210
　Germany, 2147
　United Kingdom, 2189
Citations, 199
Citizenship, 3979
　Canada, 3983
Civiization, Maya, 1302
Civil law, USA, 1636
Civil rights, German DR, 5519
　USA, 5520
Civil servants, Germany FR, 5215
　United Kingdom, 5552
Civil service, France, 5555
　Latin America, 5553
　USA, 3719, 5557
Civil society, 2874, 2878
Civilization, UK, 1301
　USA, 1323, 1349
Class conflicts, 2648, 2689
　Malaysia, 3750
　South Africa, 2661
　USA, 4124
Class consciousness, 2672
　Canada, 2680, 2709
Class culture, 895
Class differentiation, 2656
　Nigeria, 4098
Class domination, Africa, 2710
Class structure, 2600, 2623, 2651, 2717
　Central America, 2719
　Eastern Europe, 2582
　France, 2704
　Italy, 2693
　Peru, 2696
　South Africa, 2661
　United Kingdom, 2630, 2780
Class struggle, 314, 2716
　Brazil, 2462
　Colombia, 4067
　El Salvador, 2679
　Latin America, 4014
　Panama, 2667
　Southern Africa, 4431
Classification, 367, 382
Clergy, 1833, 1836-1837, 3413
　United Kingdom, 1838
Clergymen, 1832
　USA, 1831
Clericalism, France, 1890
Clubs, 5378
Cluster analysis, 421
Coalitions, 967, 970

Cognition, 785, 791, 795, 809, 820, 826, 843, 860, 863, 871, 879, 1956, 2600, 3029
Cognitive development, 776, 824, 833, 2035
Cohort analysis, 434, 3437
Collective agreements, Austria, 4838
　Hungary, 5321
　Italy, 5173
　United Kingdom, 5238
Collective attitudes, 538
Collective bargaining, 5026, 5287, 5290-5291, 5300, 5303
　Canada, 5295, 5301, 5306
　France, 5302
　Ghana, 5293
　Sweden, 5296
　United Kingdom, 5289
　USA, 5294, 5297-5299, 5301, 5304
Collective behaviour, 1271-1272
　France, 5282
Collective choice, 1267, 1273
Collective consciousness, 1269
Collective farming, USSR, 4633
　Yugoslavia, 4648
Collective farms, 1491, 4642
　USSR, 4039, 4631
Collectivism, 678
Colonial government, 5565
Colonialism, 2079
Commercial education, 2528
Communication, 183, 669, 892, 943, 1276, 1286, 1304, 1410, 2036, 2042-2044, 2050, 2053, 2055, 2057-2058, 2061-2062, 2065, 2067-2069, 2083, 4496
　Germany FR, 5047
　Italy, 2171
Communication network, 2040, 2048, 2056, 2060
Communication research, 2051, 2060
　Germany, 2043, 2176
　USA, 2043, 2176
Communication sciences, 2150
Communism, 736, 759, 1253, 5429, 5439, 5447
　USSR, 5440
Community, 3984, 4003, 4007, 4012
　Spain, 2668
Community development, 3986, 3989, 4005, 4010, 4603
　Belgium, 3996
　Canada, 3805
　France, 4002
　Japan, 4011
　Mexico, 3990
　Nigeria, 4008
　Philippines, 4000
　Thailand, 3985
　USA, 3988, 3992, 3995, 3999, 4001, 4009
　USSR, 4187
　Venezuela, 5360
　Yugoslavia, 3997-3998, 4004
Community integration, Peru, 4006
Community participation, 3987, 3993

334

USA, 3991, 3994
Community study, 478, 484, 490, 2794
  USA, 486
Commuting, 3916
  Australia, 3917
  Belgium, 3891
  Canada, 3883
  Hungary, 3930
  USA, 3899
Comparative analysis, 429, 446, 461, 1448, 2844
Competition, 741, 4662, 4665
Complex organizations, 1079
Compulsory arbitration, 5292
Compulsory education, France, 2356
Computer science, 166
Computers, 165, 167-169, 471, 4676
Comsumer behaviour, 4658
Comte, Auguste, 303, 1991
Concepts, 360, 366, 370-371, 1351, 2617, 2733, 4470, 5421, 5459, 5628, 5655, 6075, 6082-6083
Conceptualization, 1345
Conferences, 175
Conflicts, 963-964, 975, 980, 5280
Congregations, 1837
Congresses, 172-174, 177
  Finland, 176
  Latin America, 114
  USSR, 176
Congruity models, 1210
Consensual union, 3425
  Norway, 3392
  USA, 3404
Consensus, 1234, 5420
Conservatism, 1318, 5434, 5438, 5455
  Germany FR, 5441
Constitution, 5499
  USSR, 5489, 5498, 5508, 5515
Consumer behaviour, 2130, 4652, 4655, 4659-4661
  Norway, 4656
  USA, 4651
Consumption, 58, 2125, 4654, 4656, 4659
Content analysis, 432, 439, 450, 457, 471, 2077, 2151
Contextual analysis, 414
Contraception, 3302, 3310, 3315-3316
  France, 3321
  Japan, 3299
  Paraguay, 3323
  USA, 3299
  Yemen, 3156
Contraceptive methods, France, 3300
Cooperative system, 4437
  Brazil, 4447, 4453
  Canada, 4452
  Colombia, 4438
  Italy, 4430
  Jordan, 4434
  Portugal, 4440
  Sierra Leone, 4426

United Kingdom, 4421
Cooperatives, Bolivia, 4567
  Germany FR, 4546
Corporatism, 5232
  Canada, 5221
Correlation, 566, 569, 584
Counter culture, 1296, 1308
Coup d'état, 5693
Covariance, 589, 596
Creativity, 787, 792, 837, 847, 869, 2215
Crimes, 5833, 5848, 5856, 5884, 5902, 5931, 5939, 5943, 5945, 5954, 5960, 5977, 5987
  Europe, 5992
  India, 5838
  United Kingdom, 5985
  USA, 5836, 5850, 5877, 5925, 5978, 5983
Criminal justice, 5878, 5899-5900, 5916, 5926, 5961, 5977
  USA, 5857, 5875, 5903, 5920, 5928, 5942, 5966, 5984
Criminal sentencing, 3790, 5935, 5988
  USA, 5880, 5890, 5911
Criminology, 237, 1375, 5847, 5854, 5862, 5879, 5910, 5953, 5957, 5959, 5964, 5967-5968, 5991, 5993
  Canada, 5867
Critical theory, 244, 267, 271, 299, 1248, 1947
Cross-cultural analysis, 441, 640
Cross-national analysis, 436, 2529, 5058
Crowd, 1268, 1275, 4367
  India, 1555
Culin, Stewart, 3803
Cults, 1820, 1840-1842, 1849, 1853
  USA, 1852
Cultural areas, Mexico, 1302
  USA, 1295
Cultural assimilation, 1412
Cultural change, 1419, 2174, 4595
  Africa, 1431
  China, 1415
  Italy, 4024
  Japan, 1438
  South East Asia, 5395
Cultural consumption, 2160
Cultural development, 208, 1411, 1421, 2682, 5340
  Italy, 2693
Cultural dissemination, Hungary, 1434
Cultural dynamics, Italy, 1424
Cultural environment, 330
Cultural goods, 2212
Cultural heritage, 1421
  Palestine, 1407
  Sweden, 1409
Cultural history, USA, 1428
  Western Europe, 1416
Cultural identity, 1418, 1430, 1432, 3706, 4570
  Belgium, 1433
  Brazil, 1916

Subject index

North Africa, 1413, 1422
South Africa, 1429
Cultural industry, 2167, 2191, 2212, 5355
  Hungary, 2142
Cultural integration, 1420, 1441
  India, 1437
  Israel, 1426
Cultural level, 2331, 2357
  Italy, 2321
  USSR, 2360
  Yugoslavia, 2358
Cultural minorities, 1408
  France, 1427
Cultural patterns, 1290
Cultural pluralism, Canada, 1374
Cultural policy, Argentina, 1423
  Spain, 2169
Cultural relations, 1410
  Canada, 1435
  China, 1414
  USA, 1440
  USSR, 2758
Cultural values, 1417
Culture, 1244, 1280, 1285-1287, 1289, 1304, 1327, 1330, 1337, 1343-1345, 1368, 1377, 1395, 1403-1404, 1443, 1747, 1752, 2033, 2878, 4574, 4629, 5429
  Africa, 1393
  Australia, 1394
  Brazil, 1364
  China, 1391
  Hungary, 1024
  India, 1389
  Ireland, 1363
  Italy, 2260
  Japan, 2231
  Latin America, 1406
  Mexico, 3689
  Mongolia, 1341
  USA, 1323
  USSR, 1346
Culture and personality, 1310
  Guadeloupe, 1361
  Martinique, 1361
Current research, 132, 327
Curriculum, 79, 84, 100, 102, 110, 533, 2535, 2546, 2551, 5746
  Canada, 2537
Customary law, France, 1667
  Togo, 1672
Cybernetics, 452, 600, 602
Däniken, Erich von, 312
Darwin, Charles, 245, 248
Data analysis, 410-411, 433, 448, 465, 558
Data banks, Latin America, 202
  United Kingdom, 497
  USSR, 200
Data processing, 451
Data protection, 412, 462
Day care centres, USA, 2414
  Venezuela, 2410
De-schooling, Guinea-Bissau, 2329

Death, 1846, 3068, 3096, 3209, 3214, 3356, 3415, 6219
  Africa, 3205
  France, 3225
  USA, 3210
Decentralization, Yugoslavia, 1077
Decision, 835, 1034
Decision making, 188, 346, 552, 663, 811, 832, 854, 866, 875, 1001, 1009, 1033, 1117, 3417, 3452, 3985, 6184
  India, 2766
Deduction, 348
Delinquency, 1671, 2951, 5827, 5840, 5851, 5863, 5897-5898, 5906, 5908-5909, 5927, 5941, 5945, 5963, 5981, 5989
  Australia, 5849
  German DR, 5969
  Japan, 5946
  United Kingdom, 5923
  USA, 3094, 5841, 5865, 5924, 5936
  USSR, 5974
Delinquent rehabilitation, 5947
Delinquents, 5845
  USA, 5874
Democracy, 76, 129, 5463-5465, 5467-5468, 5470-5471, 5473-5475
Democratization, 2432, 5721
Demographic research, 2904, 2906-2907
  Africa, 2900
Demographic transition, 2843
Demography, 2901, 2903, 2905, 2910
  Canada, 2899, 2902
  Spain, 2909
  USSR, 2911
Deontology, 1612
  USA, 472
Despotism, 5469
Determinism, 287, 377
Developed countries, 3280
Developing countries, 123, 582, 1260, 2885, 2889, 3173, 3271, 3291, 3617, 3927, 4425, 5708, 5717
Development policy, 3980, 4673
  Italy, 1424
Development strategy, 2881
  South Asia, 4054
Deviance, 802, 905, 1493, 1504, 1517-1518, 1531, 1538, 1545-1546, 1551, 1557, 1559, 1566, 1569-1570, 1590, 1663, 3695, 5666, 5697, 5811, 5981, 6010
Diachronic analysis, 601
Dialectics, 68, 255, 283, 301-302, 311, 323, 328
Dialects, 2075
Dictionaries, 204-207, 1857, 2300
Differential analysis, 458
Directory, 77
Disability, 3186
Disasters, 4205
Discrimination, 1201-1202
  USA, 1200, 1208
Discussion groups, 1007

Diseases, 2989, 3201, 6184
  Iran, 3181
Disguised unemployment, Argentina, 4735
  developing countries, 4736
Dismissal, 5008
Dispute settlement, 959, 965-966, 968, 979, 1577
  Turkey, 5285
Divination, 1868
Division of labour, 2593, 2600, 2629, 5071, 5744, 6206
Divorce, 3020, 3410, 3412-3413, 3442
  Czechoslovakia, 3453
  France, 3427
  Latin America, 3408
  USA, 3393, 3401, 3406, 3424, 3429
  Yugoslavia, 3434-3435
Domestic workers, 5104
  France, 5102-5103
Dowry, 3395, 3411
Drinkers, 2473, 5798
Drug addiction, 5796, 5801, 5805, 5818, 5820, 5824-5825
  Canada, 5806
  France, 5800
  Germany FR, 5815
  Mexico, 5806
  Netherlands, 5810
  Spain, 5809
  USA, 5799, 5808, 5823
  USSR, 5797
Dual society, 2607
Duby, Georges, 1264
Durkheim, Émile, 44, 276, 291, 298, 307, 934, 1168, 1254, 1484, 1519, 1623, 1686, 1688, 4469, 4939, 5973
Durkheimian School, 330
Dyad, 921, 1018-1019, 2090, 2108, 2955
Early childhood, 2035
Ecodevelopment, 3940, 3961
Ecology, 564, 3941, 3943, 3946, 3949-3951, 3953-3955, 3960
  Europe, 3956
  Peru, 3664
Economic and social development, 5772
  Hungary, 2875
Economic behaviour, 774, 4653
  USA, 4657
Economic change, France, 1622
Economic concentration, 4524
  USSR, 4561
Economic development, 3130, 3173, 3645, 4465, 5058
  Canada, 4415
  China, 2847
  Haiti, 2821
  Iran, 3148
  Spain, 3796
Economic growth, 4464, 4467
  Japan, 2395
  Latin America, 5516
Economic history, Canada, 4415

Portugal, 2805
United Kingdom, 2798, 2800
Economic life, 4466
Economic policy, 2716, 4671, 5534
  China, 4675
Economic power, 4672
Economic sociology, 4411, 4413
Economic structure, 4468
Economic systems, 2584, 3422, 4417
  Canada, 4415
Economic thought, 2004, 3968
Economics, 72, 2005, 4410, 4412, 4537, 4653
  Yugoslavia, 4414
Economics of education, 2306, 2454
  USA, 2296
Economists, 76, 99
Education, 205, 1623, 2283-2285, 2290, 2300-2304, 2312, 2314-2315, 2980, 5513
  Canada, 3913
  Germany FR, 2294, 2334
  Hungary, 1024
  Tunisia, 2776
Educational administration, 2346, 2348, 2354
Educational development, Austria, 2338
  Egypt, 2341
Educational guidance, USA, 2370, 2986
Educational leave, Canada, 5053
Educational level, 2323
  South Africa, 3760
Educational needs, 2372
Educational objectives, 2342, 2368
Educational opportunities, 2327, 2369, 2385, 3613
  Germany FR, 2383
  Paraguay, 2401
  USA, 2318, 2339, 2390
Educational output, 2325, 2333, 3059
Educational planning, India, 2389
  Indonesia, 2328
Educational policy, 2361
  Brazil, 2387
  China, 2349
  Egypt, 2366
  Germany FR, 2319
  Ghana, 2392
  Latin America, 2335
  Senegal, 2324, 2392
  United Kingdom, 2367
  USA, 2367
Educational reforms, 2317, 2397
  Austria, 2398
  Canada, 2352
  Greece, 2316
  Hungary, 2330
  Mali, 2374
Educational research, 2289, 2291
Educational systems, 2298, 2322, 2353, 5077
  Africa, 2380
  Australia, 2376
  Austria, 2377
  China, 2363

337

Subject index

Denmark, 5055
Ethiopia, 2399
France, 2373, 3624
Germany FR, 2359
Ghana, 2400
India, 2386, 2393
Indonesia, 2351
Japan, 2394-2395
Korea R, 2371
Malaysia, 2337
Nigeria, 2340
Paraguay, 2382
Peru, 2384
Spain, 2320, 2378
Tanzania, 2388
United Kingdom, 2096, 2347, 2365
USA, 2344, 2350, 2364
USSR, 2343, 2396
Zimbabwe, 2362
Effect, 369
Egalitarianism, 2620
Ego, 658, 661, 666
Elections, 5684
    Black Africa, 5671
    Canada, 1671
    United Kingdom, 1671
Electoral campaigning, USA, 5670, 5677
Electoral sociology, 5676
    Spain, 5682
Electoral systems, USA, 5527
Elite, 2733-2734, 2741, 2744, 2756, 2765, 5467
    Africa, 2763
    Australia, 2757
    Canada, 2743
    France, 2769, 2771, 4116
    India, 2766
    Israel, 2763
    Middle East, 2772
    Pakistan, 2746
    Philippines, 2773
    Trinidad and Tobago, 2736
    United Kingdom, 2768
    USA, 2747, 2757, 2771, 3991
    Yugoslavia, 2738
Emigrants, Algeria, 3849
    Caribbean, 3814
    Europe, 3857
    India, 3836
    Italy, 3838, 3860
    Japan, 3255, 3881
    Korea, 3257
    Mexico, 3833, 3865
    Morocco, 4864
    Portugal, 3873
    Yugoslavia, 3852
Emigration, China, 3850
    Greece, 3871
    Italy, 3832, 4831
    Japan, 2048
    Netherlands, 3874
    North Africa, 3819

Poland, 3882
Portugal, 3820
Scandinavia, 3870
Spain, 3847
Sweden, 1409
Tunisia, 3835, 3861
USA, 3879
USSR, 3827
Yemen, 3156
Yugoslavia, 3854
Emotion, 696, 793, 802, 818, 856
Empirical research, France, 17
Employees, 4927, 5105, 5187, 5198
    Finland, 5106
    Hungary, 4473
Employers, 5056
Employers' organizations, France, 5165
Employment, 3594, 4751, 4759, 4762
    Latin America, 5777
    Singapore, 4755
    United Kingdom, 3185
Employment discrimination, 4772
    USA, 4764, 4775, 4779
Employment opportunities, 2624, 2929, 4776, 4781
    India, 2922
    USA, 2622, 2922, 2973, 3724, 4766, 4769
Employment policy, 4767, 4943
    France, 4777
    Philippines, 4782
    USA, 4770
Employment security, 4771
Endogamy, 3445
    Sudan, 3426
    United Kingdom, 3438, 3443
Energy, 4605
Energy policy, developing countries, 4575
Engels, Friedrich, 260, 1641, 1673
Engineers, 1113
    Germany FR, 5116
Enterprises, 4454, 4523, 4526, 4528, 4531-4534, 4544-4545, 4557, 4981, 5412
    China, 4555
    France, 4521, 5108
    Germany, 4536
    Italy, 4562
    United Kingdom, 4559
    USSR, 4530
Entertainment, 5366
Entrepreneurs, Europe, 4527
    Germany, 4540
Entrepreneurship, 4558, 4568
    USA, 4560
Environment, 593, 649-650, 3000, 3109, 3938, 3941, 3944, 3949, 3952, 3959, 3963, 3965
    Netherlands, 3948
    Spain, 3947
    USA, 3945
Environmental protection, 2663, 3966, 3969-3970

Subject index

Spain, 3967
Epistemology, 263, 339, 353, 356, 363, 375, 381, 383, 388, 393, 1956, 1987, 4318
Equal opportunity, 2595, 2624, 3199
 USA, 2339, 2622, 4766
 Western Europe, 2332
Ergonomics, 4877, 4894, 4896, 4904, 4976
 Scandinavia, 4909
Ethics, 49, 101, 498, 1235, 1457, 1603-1604, 1606-1607, 1609-1615, 1617, 1619, 1622, 1625, 1629-1630, 1661, 1677, 2806, 4583, 5737
 USA, 1631
Ethnic groups, 3446, 3653, 3656, 3708
 Belgium, 3699
 Canada, 3671, 3691, 3703, 3713
 Cuba, 3681
 India, 3709
 Israel, 3698
 United Kingdom, 3679
 USA, 3659, 3705, 4203, 4276, 5562
 USSR, 3688
 West Africa, 3651
Ethnic minorities, 3649, 3695
 Australia, 3650
 Canada, 1727, 3697, 3704
 China, 2349
 Israel, 3654
 Martinique, 3685
 Netherlands, 3670, 3710
 Romania, 3662
 Spain, 3684
 Surinam, 3658
 USA, 2076, 2390, 3648, 3661, 3663, 3665, 3694, 3707, 3714, 4397, 4477, 4498, 5638, 5931
Ethnicity, 697, 1021, 1771, 1782, 2019, 2924, 3652, 3672, 3674, 3678, 3681, 3683, 3690, 3712, 3871, 5651
 Canada, 3666, 3677, 3983
 India, 3687
 Israel, 3711, 4644
 Italy, 3676
 Mexico, 2687
 Nigeria, 3700
 Peru, 3664
 Sri Lanka, 3702
 Syria, 3669
 Taiwan, 3716
 United Kingdom, 2096
 USA, 1378, 2140, 3665, 3675, 3682
Ethnocentrism, 1212
Ethnography, 1276-1277, 1613
Ethnopsychology, 799
Ethos, 1627, 3672
Eugenism, 2999, 3726
Euthanasia, 5950, 5980
Evaluation, 135, 351, 354, 357, 374, 391-392, 394, 2315
Everyday life, 1243, 1298, 1311, 1326, 1342, 1365, 1405, 1885, 2045, 2592
 USA, 1348

Evolutionism, 245, 248, 277, 1959
Examinations, USA, 2355
Exchange, 972, 974, 976, 978
Existentialism, 279
Exogamy, 3394
 United Kingdom, 3438
Expectations, 352, 774
Experimental psychology, 424
Experimentation, 483, 488, 640, 1676
Explanation, 358, 402
Factor analysis, 536, 563-564, 577, 586
Failure, 867
Faith, 1859, 1876, 1878, 1912
Family, 104, 709, 725, 1161, 1164, 1502, 1683, 2136, 2906, 2961, 2968, 3021, 3057, 3282, 3455, 3462, 3469, 3471, 3473, 3482, 3502, 3520, 3524, 3530, 3538, 3564-3565, 3567-3568, 4594, 4610, 4753, 6119, 6157, 6230
 Asia, 3478
 Australia, 3490
 Austria, 3521
 Brazil, 3534
 Canada, 3436, 3479, 3519, 6107
 Caribbean, 3554
 China, 3465, 3558
 Egypt, 3484
 France, 3368, 3456, 3562
 Guatemala, 4809
 India, 3483, 3486
 Italy, 3466, 3491
 Japan, 3506
 Mexico, 3514, 4833
 Peru, 3481
 USA, 1582, 3407, 3490, 3513, 3529, 3552, 3557
 USSR, 1621, 3496, 3566
Family allowances, 6119
 Canada, 6107
 France, 6125
 USA, 6121, 6128
Family disintegration, 3077, 3470, 3493, 3509, 3539, 3551
 Japan, 3573
 Poland, 3501
Family education, 3540, 3547
 Hungary, 1434
Family environment, 840, 872, 1476, 1515, 2473, 3060, 3535
 France, 5062
 USA, 5048
Family group, 647, 2982, 3472, 3474, 3505, 3511, 3522, 3541-3542, 3546, 3560
 Southern Africa, 3914
 USA, 3460
Family integration, 3500, 3840
 Italy, 3488
Family life, 1548, 3464, 3487, 3497-3498, 3508, 3512, 3516, 3528, 3531, 3533, 3541-3542, 3556, 4870
 Argentina, 3570
 Brazil, 4080

339

Subject index

China, 4140
Finland, 3494
United Kingdom, 3510
USA, 3504
Family planning, 3291, 3296, 3329, 3331, 3544, 6118
  Bangladesh, 3319
  Costa Rica, 4157
  developing countries, 3287
  Fiji, 3285
  Germany FR, 3258
  Guatemala, 3290
  India, 3326, 3330, 3335, 3337, 3344
  Latin America, 3350
  Malaysia, 3312, 3328
  Thailand, 3343
  Turkey, 3305
Family policy, USSR, 6131, 6135
Family reconstitution, USA, 3460
Family size, 3475, 3544, 3553, 3563, 4816
  Australia, 3457
  France, 3536
  India, 3344
  Ireland, 3476, 3572
  Korea R, 3458
  Latin America, 5777
Famine, Sahel, 5769
Fanaticism, 1213
Farmers, Canada, 1575
  USSR, 4039
  Yugoslavia, 4051, 4085, 4122
Farming, Mexico, 4038
Farms, Yugoslavia, 4622, 4648
Fascism, 5422
  Italy, 5432
Fashion, 1597, 1601
Father, 3495
Fear, 771, 806, 2163, 3033, 5850, 5931, 5960
Feasts, Argentina, 1850
  India, 1851
Feeding, 5758
  Czechoslovakia, 5774
Female manpower, 2956, 2992, 3447, 3559, 4790, 4795, 4797, 4802, 4806, 4811, 4814, 4816-4817, 4842-4843, 4845, 4849, 4852, 4854, 4856, 4860, 4870-4871,4937, 5025, 5030, 5104
  Algeria, 4796
  Argentina, 3437, 4848, 4869
  Australia, 4810, 4821
  Austria, 4838
  Bolivia, 4848
  Brazil, 4805
  China, 4789
  Czechoslovakia, 4861
  Egypt, 3603
  Europe, 4846
  France, 4832, 4840
  Germany FR, 4827, 4829
  Guatemala, 4809
  Hungary, 4820
  India, 3626, 4791-4792, 4858

Israel, 4815
Mexico, 4833
Nigeria, 3231
Paraguay, 4848
Scandinavia, 4841
South Asia, 4054
South East Asia, 4834
Sweden, 4789
Switzerland, 4800
USA, 3909, 4787-4789, 4803, 4808, 4812-4813, 4818, 4822-4823, 4835, 4839, 4846, 4859, 4862, 4938
USSR, 4799
West Africa, 4844
Feminism, 3589, 3594, 3634
  France, 5225
  Germany, 3614
  Italy, 3587, 3595
  Japan, 3625
  Spain, 3601
  USA, 3579, 3585, 3638
Fertility, 1020, 2980, 3240, 3242, 3245, 3251, 3263, 3266-3267, 3269-3271, 3278-3280, 3282, 3447, 3528, 4110, 4811, 4845
  Africa, 3234, 3273
  Africa South of Sahara, 3253
  Bolivia, 3255
  Canada, 3232, 3261-3262
  Czechoslovakia, 3248
  developed countries, 3277
  Fiji, 3285
  France, 3237-3238, 3254
  Germany FR, 3237, 3258
  India, 3264, 3344
  Iran, 3230, 3250
  Ireland, 3243
  Japan, 3257
  Latin America, 3281
  Mexico, 3249
  Nigeria, 3231, 3268
  Pakistan, 3414
  Sierra Leone, 3256
  Spain, 3275
  Tanzania, 3259
  Thailand, 3343, 3797
  Tunisia, 3276
  USA, 3235, 3244, 4812
  Western countries, 3247
Fertility decline, 3236, 3291
  Costa Rica, 3233
  Sri Lanka, 3246
Fertility rate, USSR, 3241
Festivals, 2063
  France, 1844, 2278
Feudalism, 1264, 4432
  Peru, 4428
Feuerbach, Ludwig, 5490
Fiamengo, Ante, 210, 217
Field work, 477, 479, 481, 1277
  USA, 472
Films, USA, 2182, 2202

Financial market, 5276
Fisher, J. L., 309
Fishermen, United Kingdom, 1143
Fitzhugh, George, 298
Folk art, 2277
Folk culture, United Kingdom, 4077
Folklore, 2278, 2281
    Brazil, 2279
Food habits, 1598-1600
Food requirements, 5778
    India, 2612
Forced labour, 2629
Forecasting, 352
Forecasting techniques, 344, 349, 362, 389, 400, 992, 3263, 3280, 3331, 5276
Forecasts, 346, 355, 361, 366, 376, 395-396, 2812
Foreign policy, 5732
Foreign students, 3855
Foreign workers, 2385, 4798, 4847, 4857
    Canada, 3822
    EEC countries, 4785
    France, 3830, 3839, 4363, 4786, 4865
    Germany FR, 2383, 4851
    Netherlands, 4819, 4864
    Switzerland, 4831
    United Kingdom, 3839
    Western Europe, 4807, 4824, 4828, 4836
Foucault, Michel, 258, 289, 1492, 1955, 1970, 5418, 5917
Frankfurt School, 259, 320
Freedom, 377, 1537, 2571
    USSR, 5518
Freemasonry, Spain, 1809
Freud, Sigmund, 257, 1845, 2590
Friendship, 917, 925, 930, 933, 997, 3103
Frustration, 880
Full employment, 4732
Functional analysis, 358
Functional literacy, Iran, 2493
Functionalism, 309, 333, 980
Further education, Hungary, 2509
    United Kingdom, 2496
Future, 2812-2814, 2990
Futurology, 2811
Gambling, USA, 5374
Game theory, 2031
Games, 430
Gangs, 1521
Geertz, Clifford, 2808
Gellner, Ernest, 2605
General systems theory, 598-599
General theory, 342
Genetics, 2996, 2999, 3002-3003
Genocide, 5873, 5976
Geographic mobility, 3801
Gerontology, 3100, 3106, 3111
Girls, 3055
Goffman, Erving, 1168
Goldmann, Lucien, 261, 1278, 2248
Government policy, 5528, 5534-5535, 5542
Graduates, 5067

socialist countries, 2440
Spain, 2463
USA, 2464, 4769
Yugoslavia, 2487
Gramsci, Antonio, 5450
Graph theory, 606-609
Graphic arts, 2265
Group analysis, 983, 998
Group behaviour, 1030, 1033, 1035, 1166, 1191
Group cohesiveness, 903
Group conformity, 1037
Group dynamics, 985, 993
Group effects, 560, 1038, 1045
Group functioning, 1048-1049
Group influence, 1026, 1043, 1174
Group integration, 1034
Group interaction, 899, 1027-1028, 1031-1032, 1036
Group membership, 936, 1042, 1829
Group participation, 1131
Group performance, 1012, 1023, 1046-1047, 1147
Group psychotherapy, 988, 994, 996
Group size, 1022-1023
Group solidarity, 1029, 1817
Group task, 1032
Group values, 1044
Groups, 984, 989, 1207, 4674
Guerrilla, 5687
    Latin America, 5691
Gurvitch, Georges, 261
Guttman scale, 624
Habermas, Jürgen, 267, 288, 299, 304, 325, 335, 2546
Habitat, Algeria, 3982
    Congo, 3981
Handicapped, 3199
    Greece, 3180
    United Kingdom, 3185
Handicapped children, USA, 3192
Handicapped rehabilitation, 6187, 6192
    USA, 5035, 6189, 6193
Happiness, 848, 3006
Health, 4842, 5767, 6182, 6207
    Nigeria, 2615
    USA, 6188
Health insurance, Germany FR, 6120
Health policy, 6221
    Germany FR, 6226
    Spain, 6179, 6214
    USA, 6208-6209
Health services, 6211-6212, 6215, 6219, 6222, 6224
    Ethiopia, 6228
    Finland, 6223
    Netherlands, 6231
    United Kingdom, 6210, 6213
    USA, 6225, 6232
Heart diseases, 3189
    USA, 3198
Hegel, Georg Wilhelm Friedrich, 2099-2100,

5408
Heller, A., 881
Heredity, 3000
Heresies, Germany, 1873
Hermeneutics, 246, 251, 284, 336, 1247, 2041
Higher education, 2423, 2429, 2432, 2437, 2441, 2443, 2452, 2459, 2479, 2482
   Canada, 2439
   East Africa, 116
   Eastern Europe, 2456
   France, 2470, 2771, 5109
   German DR, 2453
   Germany FR, 2467
   India, 2455
   Japan, 2430, 2466, 2468
   Mexico, 2472
   North America, 2442
   Spain, 2458, 2465
   Sweden, 2470
   United Kingdom, 2436, 2470
   USA, 2425, 2445-2446, 2450, 2771, 5387
   USSR, 2450, 2454
   Venezuela, 2428
   Western Europe, 2442
   Yugoslavia, 2483
Hilferding, Rudolf, 5731
Hinduism, 1741, 5973
Historical analysis, 442, 450
Historicism, 334
History, 275, 1290, 1748, 2794, 2796, 2804, 2806, 2810, 2841
History of capitalism, 4444
   Germany, 4536, 4540
History of education, 2298
History of ideas, 1950
History of sociology, 37, 44, 56, 61, 69, 330, 480, 1973
   Bulgaria, 65
   Canada, 52
   France, 17
   Germany, 48, 259, 4375
   Germany FR, 57
   Hungary, 25
   Spain, 27
   USA, 13-14, 23-24, 38, 42, 58, 95, 1962
Hobbes, Thomas, 2590, 2874, 5734
Hofstee, E. W., 306
Homicide, 5830, 5982
   USA, 5839, 5855, 5871
Homosexuality, 3357, 3361, 3364, 3379, 3388
   Germany FR, 3382
   USA, 3377
Horkheimer, Max, 244
Hospital organization, 6233
Hospital services, 6229
Hospitals, 6216, 6220, 6230, 6257
   United Kingdom, 6217
Hours of work, 3269, 4906, 4924, 4960, 4963, 4967, 4985
   France, 4914
   USA, 4974

   USSR, 4971
Household, 2968
   Canada, 3519
   Mexico, 2943
Housewives, 2958, 2967, 4922
Housework, 1169, 4922
   USA, 4912
Housing, 3925
   Australia, 4297
   Canada, 3777
   developing countries, 587
   Eastern Europe, 4327
   France, 4245
   Guatemala, 1542
   Hungary, 1370, 4224
   India, 4393
   Ireland, 4216
   Spain, 4308
   United Kingdom, 4217, 4338
   USA, 3752, 4226, 4376, 4385, 4388
   USSR, 4327
Housing conditions, 4237
   Costa Rica, 4246
   France, 3070, 3823, 4195, 4363, 4786
   Hong Kong, 4407
   USA, 2375, 4247
Housing needs, 4372, 4400
   Africa, 4362
   Australia, 4290
   Turkey, 4206
   USA, 4273
   Yugoslavia, 4401
Housing policy, Korea R, 4355
   Nigeria, 4361
   United Kingdom, 4307, 4320-4321, 4328, 4332
   USA, 4196, 4265
   USSR, 4357
Hughes, Everett C., 268
Human biology, 2995, 2997-2998, 3001
Human ecology, 1285, 3939, 3962, 4479
Human geography, 437, 3942
   Latin America, 1383
Human nature, 2934, 2946, 2977
Human relations, 884
Human resources, 4709
   USSR, 4714
Human rights, 5517, 5521-5523, 5525
Human settlements, 3924, 3972-3973, 3975, 3977, 3980
   Israel, 3978
   Latin America, 3976
Humanization of work, 4920, 4945, 4952, 4976, 4990
   Germany FR, 4910, 4933, 4972, 4982
   USSR, 4984
Hunger, 5760
Husband, 3516
Hynam, Charles, 216
Identification, 935-936, 2657
Identity, 664, 672, 680, 682, 688, 691, 693, 706, 846, 1865, 1892, 2101, 2475,

3088, 3672
Ideology, 13, 1242-1244, 1247-1255,
    1257-1258, 1260-1264, 1266, 1290,
    1347, 1614, 1627, 1863, 1963,
    2030, 2066, 2098, 2284, 2535, 2977,
    3042, 3051, 3589, 3681, 4433, 4612,
    5422, 5468, 5735
  Germany FR, 3056
  Ghana, 5211
  Spain, 2378
Illegitimacy, Austria, 3521
  Israel, 3338
  United Kingdom, 3336
  USA, 3351
Illich, Ivan, 1123
Illiteracy, developed countries, 2513
  Latin America, 2514
  USA, 2510
Image, 1207
Imagination, 779, 807, 828
Imitation, 939
Immigrant acculturation, Canada, 3867
Immigrant assimilation, 3817, 3852, 3873
  Belgium, 3860
  Canada, 1705, 3840, 3867
  France, 3813, 3849
  Israel, 3674, 3869, 3872, 5695
  United Kingdom, 3821, 3856
  USA, 3505, 3683, 3696, 3844, 3850,
    3864, 3871, 3880-3881
Immigrants, Belgium, 3818
  Bolivia, 3255
  Canada, 3822
  France, 3823, 4195, 4731
  Israel, 3825-3826, 3843
  Japan, 3257
  Latin America, 3838
  Netherlands, 4864
  Portugal, 4798
  Spain, 1436
  United Kingdom, 3866
  USA, 1942, 3814, 3831, 3833, 3836
Immigration, Canada, 3863, 3875
  France, 3819
  Italy, 3877
  Saudi Arabia, 3845
  USA, 3774, 3841, 3848
Immigration law, France, 3868
  USA, 3837, 3878
Immigration policy, Canada, 3824
  United Kingdom, 2768
Imperialism, 2702, 5731, 5735
  USA, 5399
Impoverishment, 5764
In-group, 981, 1040, 1044
Incest, 3362, 3369
Incest taboo, 3367
Income, 3544, 4806
Income distribution, 2778, 3271, 4464, 4475,
    4486-4487, 4513, 4515
  Belgium, 4474
  Canada, 4503

France, 4508
Korea R, 4489
Latin America, 2335
Netherlands, 4500
USA, 1831, 4477, 4493, 4641, 5172, 5773
Incomes policy, Tanzania, 5270
Indicators, 592
Indigenous population, America, 3693
  Australia, 3680
  Brazil, 3143
  Canada, 3686
  Guatemala, 3660
  Mexico, 3667-3668, 3689
Individualism, 667, 678, 701, 712, 887, 4527,
    54300
  United Kingdom, 689
Individuality, 675, 691, 1303
Individuals, 659-660, 663, 665, 1616
Industrial development, 4643
  Peru, 2739
Industrial enterprises, 2190, 4636-4637
  United Kingdom, 4625, 4629
  USA, 4629
  USSR, 4627
Industrial plants, Germany FR, 5089
  Japan, 4956-4957
Industrial productivity, USSR, 4627
Industrial psychology, 4682, 4684, 4686
Industrial society, 1056, 1442, 2877, 2880,
    4577, 5740
Industrial sociology, 75, 4678-4679, 4687,
    4689, 4691-4692, 4990
  Germany FR, 4688
  South Africa, 4680
Industrial workers, 2495, 4991, 5087
  German DR, 5095
  Germany FR, 4950, 5089
  Hungary, 5099
  USSR, 5091
Industrialization, 3251, 4606, 4634, 4638,
    4645, 4762, 5085
  developing countries, 4630
  France, 4053
  Germany, 4540
  Italy, 3472
  Japan, 4011
  Latin America, 4427
  Peru, 4650
  Tanzania, 4639
  USA, 4641, 4647, 4929
Industry, 4626
Inequality, 2613
Infant mortality, 3206
  Australia, 3229
  Canada, 3220
  Congo, 3226
  Guatemala, 3221
  South Asia, 3224
Infertility, Upper Volta, 3272
Inflation, 4460, 4666
Informal groups, 900, 1013, 1016
Information, 185, 188, 190

Subject index

Information dissemination, 811, 2056
   China, 181
   France, 187
Information exchange, 178, 193, 1985
Information policy, 183
   Belgium, 194
   USA, 189
Information processing, 186, 195
Information sciences, 180, 196
   France, 191
Information sources, 184
Information systems, 192
Information technology, 179
Information theory, 603
Information users, 182, 374
Inheritance, 3103, 4506
Initiation rites, Southern Africa, 1847
Innovations, 1012, 1104, 2421, 4571, 4580, 4588-4589
   Italy, 2791
Institutionalization, 1451, 1458, 1489, 6235
Institutions, 642, 1171, 1442, 1493, 5535
Insurance, USA, 4670
Intellectual development, 2531-2532
Intellectuals, 267, 2742, 2748, 2750, 2755, 6015
   France, 1939
   Germany, 2737
   India, 2754
   Italy, 2732
   Portugal, 2752
   USA, 5237
   Yugoslavia, 2774
Intelligence, 810, 830, 840, 872
Intelligentsia, 2759, 2764
   developing countries, 2753
   Hungary, 2770
   USSR, 1576, 2731, 2735, 2751, 2758, 2760, 2762, 2767, 4102
Interdisciplinary research, 140, 199, 1047
   France, 139
Interest, 4667
Interest groups, 5605
   Italy, 5597
   Japan, 5606
   USA, 5607
Interethnic relations, 2452
   Brazil, 3741
   Canada, 3677, 3722
   Israel, 3730, 3787-3788
   Jamaica, 3748
   Malaysia, 3750
   Peru, 3791
   South Africa, 3756
   USA, 3766, 3773
   Zambia, 3742
Intergroup relations, 613, 960-962, 971, 973, 977, 981-982, 1203, 2019
   Caribbean, 969
Internal migrations, 2040, 3924, 3932
   Bangladesh, 3906
   Brazil, 3935, 4402

   Canada, 3913, 3926
   India, 3904, 3922
   Malaysia, 3908
   Mexico, 3885, 3931
   Papua-New Guinea, 3889
   South East Asia, 3923
   Syria, 3897
   Tunisia, 3902
   United Kingdom, 3886
   USA, 3887, 3901, 3907, 3910-3911, 3921, 3929, 3934, 3936
   Venezuela, 3928
International conflicts, 2648, 5736, 5738
International migrations, 2048, 3862
   Finland, 3858
   Latin America, 3815
International relations, 1212, 1714, 5721, 5723-5725, 5728
Internationalism, 5722, 5726-5727, 5729-5730
Interpersonal attraction, 902, 919-921, 924, 928-929, 932, 1134
Interpersonal bargaining, 952, 970
Interpersonal communication, 2037-2038, 2064, 3487, 3498
Interpersonal conflicts, 954
Interpersonal influence, 673, 937-938, 940, 3452
Interpersonal perception, 903, 906-907, 909, 1268, 1602
Interpersonal relations, 611, 885, 887-889, 891-892, 894, 896, 898-900, 1185
   Japan, 883
Interpretation, 378
Interviewers, 504, 513
Interviews, 505-508, 510-512, 515, 906, 2150
Islam, 1703-1704, 1706, 1708, 1711, 1714, 1724-1725, 1729, 1756, 1759, 1773, 1780, 1785, 2584, 3473, 5415-5416, 5478
   Africa, 1761
   Algeria, 1650
   Indonesia, 1742, 1783
   Iran, 2840
   Sudan, 1786
   USSR, 1312, 1710
   West Africa, 1791-1792
Jews, 85, 1753, 1767, 1771, 1775, 3763, 5807
   Canada, 1705, 1727, 1788, 1795
   France, 1709, 1736
   Morocco, 5665
   Tunisia, 5665
   United Kingdom, 1737, 1778
   USA, 1770, 1782, 1808, 3244
   USSR, 3827
   Yugoslavia, 1730
Job evaluation, 4765, 4774, 4780, 4783-4784
Job satisfaction, 1170, 4928, 4932, 4938-4940, 5320
   USA, 4978
Job seekers, 4737, 4757
Joint family, 3549
   USA, 3503
Joint management, 4551

Subject index

Journalists, 2137
Judaism, 1716, 1733, 1743, 1745-1746, 1749, 1772, 1775, 1777, 1781, 1789, 2059
   Israel, 1738
   USA, 1739-1740
Judiciary behaviour, USA, 5545
Jury, 755, 5548
Justice, 1654
Juvenile delinquency, 5852, 5859, 5866, 5887, 5913, 5933, 5944, 5948, 5955
   Canada, 5915
   Eastern Europe, 5949
   Germany FR, 5829
   Hungary, 5932
   Italy, 5837
   Spain, 5868
   USA, 5869, 5962, 5975, 5984, 5986
Kant, Emmanuel, 249
Kardelj, Edvard, 4117
Kibbutz, 5386
   Israel, 4623, 4632
Kinship, 3103, 3568, 4086
   Bangladesh, 3463
   China, 3465
   Greece, 3569
   India, 3492, 3550, 3793
   Japan, 3545, 3548
   Latin America, 4427
Knowledge, 283, 356, 1130, 1949, 1956-1957, 1999-2000
Labelling, 905, 911, 1566
   Japan, 5946
Labor disputes, USA, 5227
Labour, 715, 744, 746, 849, 1279, 4693-4694, 4696, 4699-4702, 4706-4707, 4715, 4719, 4725, 4729-4730
   German DR, 4695
   USSR, 4721
Labour contract, 4908, 4917, 4921, 4980
   German DR, 4986
Labour disputes, 5128, 5257, 5262, 5268, 5275, 5277-5278, 5280-5281
   France, 5255, 5282
   Germany FR, 5254
   Hong Kong, 5194
   India, 5253
   Italy, 5259-5260
   Turkey, 5285
   United Kingdom, 5264
   USA, 5305
Labour law, 5159-5160, 5163-5164
   Czechoslovakia, 5230
   Japan, 5139
   South Africa, 5161
   Sri Lanka, 5162
Labour market, 2452, 3734, 4710, 4713, 4720, 4722, 4727, 4772, 4776, 4781, 4975
   Argentina, 4735
   Austria, 2338
   Denmark, 4708
   Sudan, 3786
   Sweden, 5318
   United Kingdom, 4698
   USA, 3878, 3880, 4718, 4824
Labour migrations, 3892, 3895, 3898, 5252
   Asia, 3905
   Canada, 3888
   Europe, 3853
   Greece, 3900
   Middle East, 3905
   Southern Africa, 3914
   USA, 3909
   Yugoslavia, 3933, 4828
Labour mobility, 3472, 4711, 4728
   France, 4705
   Hong Kong, 4726
   Italy, 5166
   USA, 3936, 4718
Labour movements, 2720, 5247
   Brazil, 5181, 5226
   France, 5241
   Germany, 5218, 5246
   Latin America, 4712
   North Africa, 5222
   Panama, 5229
   United Kingdom, 5251
   USA, 5170
Labour policy, Colombia, 4723
   Mexico, 4723
Labour productivity, 4709, 4875, 4881, 4883, 4891-4892, 5111, 5184
Labour relations, 4771, 5128, 5131-5132, 5143, 5145-5146, 5250, 6082
   Africa, 5136
   Australia, 5149
   Brazil, 5141
   Eastern Europe, 5157
   France, 5129, 5147, 5155
   Germany FR, 5127, 5147, 5150
   India, 4893
   Ireland, 5126
   Italy, 5152
   Japan, 5138-5139, 5144
   Korea R, 5151
   Latin America, 5134
   Mexico, 5148
   Norway, 5153
   South Africa, 4680, 5156, 5161
   Tanzania, 5176
   United Kingdom, 5130, 5133, 5135, 5142, 5199
   USA, 5140, 5158
   USSR, 5137
   Western Europe, 5154
Labour supply, 3447, 4703
   France, 4697
Labour turnover, 5001, 5696
   USA, 4994
Lactation, 5772
Land reforms, Brazil, 4043
   China, 4179
   Costa Rica, 4157
   India, 4167

Subject index

Ireland, 4049
Japan, 4027
Latin America, 4082
Taiwan, 4179
Land tenure, Mexico, 3138
Peru, 4173, 4428
Spain, 4026
Land use, Australia, 4297
India, 4083, 4370
Nigeria, 4137
USA, 4108
Language, 529, 678, 1177, 1247, 1455, 1963, 2019-2020, 2034, 2072, 2082, 2086-2088, 2098-2100, 2103, 2106, 2110-2111, 2113, 2284, 5627
India, 2601
United Kingdom, 2096
Languages, 2071, 2078-2079, 2091, 2094, 2101, 2107, 2115, 2119, 3394
Africa, 2095
Caribbean, 2092
Guyana, 2085
Nigeria, 2073
North Africa, 1422
North America, 2080
Puerto Rico, 2081
Switzerland, 2105
USA, 1440, 2076
Latent structure analysis, 617-618
Latin America, 114
Laughter, 859
Law, 745, 1250, 1263, 1637, 1643, 1647-1648, 1651, 1653, 1657, 1661, 1664-1666, 1669-1671, 3473, 4462
Africa, 1668
developing countries, 1639
Europe, 1660
Israel, 1937, 3341
Japan, 1656
Latin America, 1660
Lawyers, 5125
Lazarsfeld, Paul, 408
Leaders, 1151
India, 5210
Leadership, 1139, 1143, 1145, 1147-1150, 1152-1155, 1182, 5168
Learned societies, China, 170
France, 171
Learning, 690, 773, 790, 794, 796-797, 803-804, 819, 827, 841, 2082, 2976
Legal codes, 1655
Legal systems, 1652, 1658
Morocco, 1649
Legislation, 1463
Legitimacy, 5420
Leipsius, Rainer, 57
Leisure, 3069, 5337-5338, 5340, 5343-5344, 5346, 5353
France, 5341
German DR, 5339
Spain, 5342
USSR, 5345

Leisure time, 5347-5351, 5355-5357
Germany FR, 5352
Spain, 5353
Leisure utilization, 5378
Europe, 5381
Israel, 5386
Leninism, 2848
Lévi-Strauss, Claude, 289
Levinas, Emile, 1611
Lexicology, 2008
Liberal professions, 5125
Librarians, USA, 203
Libraries, 5378
USA, 201
Life cycle, 3260
Life expectancy, Belgium, 3228
Life satisfaction, 3072
Life styles, 1300, 1373, 1387, 1402, 1589, 1895, 3112, 4660
Hungary, 1370, 4224
Japan, 1367
Life tables, 3222
USA, 3223
Life-long education, 2495, 2500, 2504-2505, 2516
Italy, 2498
Japan, 2517
USA, 2491
Likert scale, 623
Linguistics, 402, 559, 799, 2009, 2011-2012, 2026-2027
Canada, 2032
India, 2028
Literacy, 2488, 2499, 2518
Canada, 2507
Guadeloupe, 2506
India, 2511
Latin America, 2492
Spain, 2503
Literary criticism, 2241, 2256
Literature, 284, 772, 2242, 2254, 2256, 2258, 2979
Africa, 2259
Egypt, 2252
France, 897
India, 2253
Indonesia, 2257
Italy, 2260
United Kingdom, 2246
USSR, 1565
Local government, 2765, 4310
France, 4030, 5561
India, 4149, 4161
Japan, 5563, 5568
Sweden, 5564
United Kingdom, 5566
USA, 3701, 3991, 5298-5299, 5560, 5562, 5567
Lockouts, France, 5273
Germany FR, 5272
Italy, 5279
United Kingdom, 5269

Subject index

USA, 5286
Logic, 518-520, 523, 525
Loneliness, 890, 893, 897
Love, 922, 931, 3057
Lower class, Japan, 4300
Lukács, György, 2236, 2248
Lynd, Robert S., 209
Machiavel, Nicolas, 1986
Macro, 459
Madness, United Kingdom, 3200
Mafia, 5832
Magic, 1693, 1698
    France, 1696
Mail surveys, 509, 514
Majority groups, 1231
Malnutrition, 5759
Malthus, Thomas Robert, 316
Management, 2869, 3718, 4541, 4556, 4564-4565
    USSR, 2706
Managers, 4525, 4558, 5011, 5107, 5110, 5113-5114, 5121
    France, 5108-5109
    Germany FR, 5117
    Italy, 5124
    Japan, 5122
    Peru, 5123
    United Kingdom, 5118
    USA, 5119, 5123
Mandić, Oleg, 211
Mann, Fritz Karl, 218
Mannheim, Karl, 244, 334, 1998
Manpower, developing countries, 4704
    Europe, 4717
    Latin America, 4712
    Sudan, 4724
    USA, 4716
Manual workers, 5084
    Canada, 2680
Marcuse, Herbert, 273
Marginal people, Italy, 1508
Marginality, 1515, 1529, 1553, 1572, 3873
    Guatemala, 1542
    Malaysia, 1580
Marital conflict, 907, 3397
Marital life, 3417
Marital satisfaction, 3449
Marital separation, 3451
Marital status, 3415-3416
    Argentina, 3437
Market, 4664
    developing countries, 4663
Markovian processes, 610, 612, 614, 616, 4713
Marriage, 703, 933, 938, 2556, 3057, 3213, 3402-3403, 3405, 3419, 3423, 3430, 3440, 3452, 3568
    Asia, 3448
    Canada, 3436
    Czechoslovakia, 3432
    France, 3391, 5472
    India, 3483, 3486, 3793

Latin America, 3281
    Mexico, 3389
    Netherlands, 3400
    Pakistan, 3414
    Spain, 1936
    Syria, 3454
    United Kingdom, 2779
    USA, 3407
    Yugoslavia, 3434-3435
Marriage law, 3398
    Italy, 1888
Martin, Jean, 222
Marx, Karl, 254-255, 260, 275, 291-292, 300, 331, 383, 399, 1257, 1471, 1610, 1641, 1647, 1673, 1964, 2845, 4939, 5491
Marxism, 75, 243, 254, 256, 270, 272, 274, 278, 292, 295, 300, 304, 314, 325, 338, 728, 1107, 1247, 1262, 1647, 1669, 2241, 2568, 2654, 2670, 2801, 2807, 4191, 4692, 5462, 5501, 5517, 6075
    United Kingdom, 1249, 2803
    USA, 282
Masochism, 855
Mass behaviour, 1270, 1274
Mass communication, 2155, 2164, 2168, 2174, 2177, 2185, 2192, 2195, 2203-2204, 2213, 5343
    Ecuador, 2161
    Japan, 2138
Mass culture, 2265, 2391
Mass education, 3236
Mass media, 947, 1590, 2136, 2152, 2162, 2165, 2170, 2183-2184, 2190, 2198, 2203, 2206, 2208-2209, 5989
    Egypt, 2201
    German DR, 2172
    Germany FR, 2172, 2194
    Italy, 2171
    South Asia, 4324
    Spain, 2135
    USA, 2140, 2182
    USSR, 2173
Mass society, 1318, 2755
Mate selection, 3399, 3409, 3420, 3439, 3446
    Iran, 3441
    Spain, 3428
    USA, 3450
Materialism, 310
Mathematics, 2002
Matrix calculus, 521-522, 524
Mead, George H., 1964
Meaning, 2034, 2041, 2046, 2066
Measurement, 473, 475, 485, 487, 492
Media, 1343, 2068, 2141, 2166-2167
    Germany FR, 2143
    Latin America, 2144
    Nigeria, 2211
Medical care, 6184, 6191, 6198, 6206
    Australia, 6201
    Canada, 6199
    Spain, 6190

Subject index

United Kingdom, 6196
USA, 6180-6181, 6185
Medical personnel, 6198, 6241, 6243
Medical sociology, 3195, 6160, 6168-6169, 6173, 6175-6178
Medicine, 350, 6161, 6166
Cuba, 6165
Memory, 773, 804, 878
Men, 2961
USA, 2978
Mental deficiency, 3204
Mental diseases, 3182-3183, 3187, 3191, 3193, 6197
USA, 5874
Mental health, 2983, 6197, 6204-6205
Australia, 6200
USA, 6183, 6195
Mental hospitals, 6192, 6218
USA, 3782, 5882
Mental retardation, 3190
Sweden, 3197
USA, 3184Merton, Robert K., 157
Mestizos, 3770
USA, 3767
Methodology, 373, 381, 406-407, 409, 415, 427, 443, 453, 464, 491, 525, 2574, 5400
Metropolis, India, 4255
Middle class, 2657, 2660
Denmark, 2652
Egypt, 3484
Mexico, 2695
Peru, 3586
USA, 2685, 3529
Zambia, 2701
Zimbabwe, 2697
Middle management, United Kingdom, 5120
Middle range theory, 1062
Midwives, Taiwan, 6246
United Kingdom, 6235
USA, 6235
Migrants, Bolivia, 3811
Sudan, 3786
Migration policy, 3802
Western Europe, 4828
Migration research, Sweden, 3798
Migrations, 3551, 3794, 3800, 3803-3804, 3810
Argentina, 3809
Brazil, 3809
Canada, 3805, 3808
Europe, 4717
Latin America, 2722
Mali, 3795
Spain, 3796
Thailand, 3797
United Kingdom, 3806
West Africa, 3807
Militancy, 2542
Military, 5068, 5697, 5700, 5708-5709, 5715-5716, 5718
Black Africa, 5712

France, 5054, 5714
Germany FR, 5710
Israel, 5695
Switzerland, 5704
Syria, 3669
USA, 5702-5703, 5705, 5711, 5719
Military service, 5706
Military sociology, 5707, 5713
Germany FR, 5720
Millenarianism, 1694
Ministers of religion, Africa, 1834
Minority groups, 1017, 1020-1021, 1026
Hungary, 1024
USA, 1366, 3085, 3764
Mixed marriage, USA, 3431
Models, 342, 359, 379, 386, 399, 404
Modernization, 2065, 2843, 2857, 2860, 4603
Africa, 3273
developing countries, 2853
Indonesia, 1903
Israel, 3698
Japan, 2842
South Asia, 4324
Modes of production, 4424, 4577, 4603, 5087
India, 3492
Western Europe, 4591
Monasticism, developing countries, 1796
USA, 1810
Money, 3430, 4669
Montesquieu, Charles Louis de Secondat, 250
Moral development, 1635
Morality, 1232, 1620, 1628, 1634, 5678, 5811
USSR, 1608, 1621
Morals, 1219, 1536, 1618, 1623, 1632, 1909, 3390, 4670, 5213
Netherlands, 2151
Morbidity, Australia, 6201
Mortality, 3203, 3208-3209, 3213, 3219, 3222
Asia, 3227
Bangladesh, 3211
Far East, 3215
Kenya, 3207
USA, 3216, 3218
Moslems, Philippines, 1734
Mother, 3010, 3559, 4845
Motherhood, 3055
Japan, 3299
USA, 3299
Motivation to work, Italy, 4925
Motivational analysis, 2524
Motivations, 803, 815, 825, 853, 1271
Multilingualism, 2104
Multivariate analysis, 449, 467, 5659
Museums, 2223, 2230, 2233
Music, 2052, 2266-2268, 2270-2272
Hungary, 2269
Mysticism, 1882
Mythology, 1856-1857, 1862, 1866
Myths, 1206, 1701, 1863, 1872, 1874, 1879, 4700, 5853
Narcotics, 5811
Peru, 5794

USA, 5812, 5817
Nation, 1294, 1358
  USA, 1378
National consciousness, 2091, 5732
  USSR, 1382
National development, 2887, 2889
  Egypt, 2341
  Israel, 1738
National identity, Israel, 1321
  USA, 1366
National minorities, 3706, 5462
  USA, 3696
  USSR, 1335, 3657
National socialism, 5428
Nationalism, 429, 1686, 2101, 5458-5459, 5462
  Canada, 5446, 5451
  China, 1944
  Egypt, 5442
Natural law, 5734
Nature, 3968
Needs, 733, 777, 780-782, 817, 822, 838, 849-853, 857-858, 862, 876-877, 881-882, 4729
Neighbourhood, 1150, 4198, 4270, 4377
  USA, 4201, 4250
Nelson, Benjamin, 5725
Network analysis, 417, 426, 438, 614, 1066
New towns, 4271
  United Kingdom, 4207, 4229
Nobility, Spain, 2636
  United Kingdom, 2635
Noise, 3971
Nomadism, 3893
Nomads, Mauritania, 3918
Non-verbal communication, 2074, 2097, 2114
Nostalgia, 801
Novels, 2243, 2262
Nuclear energy, 1261, 4612
  France, 4581
Nuclear family, 3467
Nuclear weapons, 5741
Nuptiality, Mexico, 3433
Nursery schools, France, 2408
Nurses, 5059, 6238, 6257
  Canada, 5301
  France, 6240
  Spain, 6242
  USA, 5301
Nutrition, 5790-5791
Objectiveness, 341, 397-398
Observation, 476, 480, 499
Occupational achievement, 5031, 5067, 5078
Occupational choice, 3066, 3784, 5034, 5036, 6241, 6243
  France, 5054, 5062
  USA, 5048
Occupational life, 2952, 3531, 5063, 5066
Occupational mobility, 3413, 5057-5059, 5070
  Germany FR, 5051
  Israel, 3869
  USA, 5033, 5072

Occupational prestige, France, 5039
  India, 5074
  USSR, 5042
Occupational promotion, France, 4993
  Poland, 4997
Occupational qualification, 5031, 5037
  Canada, 5069
  Denmark, 5055
  France, 5079
  Latin America, 5028
  USA, 5076
Occupational roles, 2542, 5052, 5071
Occupational safety, 5023
Occupational segregation, 2948
Occupational sociology, 5020, 5023
  Spain, 6242
  Yugoslavia, 5027
Occupational status, 1829, 4938, 5029, 5038, 5049, 5073, 5513
  Germany FR, 5116
  Mexico, 4833
  USA, 5032, 5045
Occupational stratification, 5060, 5068, 5075
  Finland, 5050
  Portugal, 5061
  Sweden, 5044
  Trinidad and Tobago, 2736
Occupational structure, developing countries, 5041
  Germany FR, 5047
  Norway, 5064
Occupations, 4871, 5013-5014, 5016-5017, 5019, 5021, 5025-5026, 5034
  Israel, 5022
  USA, 3757, 4607, 4808
Office workers, 4938
Old age, 3068, 3072, 3074, 3077, 3082-3083, 3102-3103, 3105
  Spain, 3075
  United Kingdom, 3110
  USA, 3071
Older workers, 4825
  Australia, 4830
  France, 4868
  Japan, 4826, 4855
  USA, 4683
One-parent family, 3543
  Japan, 3525-3526
  USA, 3571
Opinion, 1228, 1231
Opinion change, 1241
Oral literature, 2240
Oral tradition, Africa, 2255
Organization, 977, 1086, 1088, 1102, 1116, 1122, 1130, 1133, 1449
Organization of research, 148, 162
  France, 139, 151, 161, 163
  Germany FR, 154
  Italy, 78, 153
Organizational analysis, 606, 1050-1052, 1056, 1062, 1066, 4528, 5939, 6254
Organizational behaviour, 45, 1075, 1090,

349

Subject index

1092-1093, 1098, 1101, 1103, 1106, 1110, 1115, 1117-1118, 1129, 1131, 4544, 6216
    USA, 1200, 5297
Organizational change, 1082-1083, 1089, 1094, 1104-1105, 1111, 1113-1114, 1120, 1124, 1126, 1128, 4564
    Sweden, 1078
Organizational research, 144, 1053, 1059, 1063-1065
Organizational size, 1112
Organizational theory, 1054-1055, 1057, 1060, 4545
Out-group, 981, 1040-1041
Parent-child relations, 2527, 2956, 3035, 3459, 3467, 3489, 3515, 3517-3518, 3523, 3532, 3537, 3555, 3561, 5662
    Egypt, 3484
    USA, 3468, 3477, 3485
Parent-teacher relations, 2545
Parenthood, 3527
Parents' education, 2556
Pareto, Vilfredo, 61, 257, 290, 293, 296, 381, 2756
Parish, France, 1823
    Italy, 1805
Park, Robert Ezra, 221
Parsons, Talcott, 98, 220, 224, 247, 277, 281, 294, 305, 313, 342, 404, 452, 816, 873, 2810
Participant observation, 489, 4936
Party identification, 5632, 5642, 5656
    Canada, 2680
Party members, Finland, 5050
Party systems, Australia, 5580
    Canada, 5580
Patients, 3202
Patriarchy, 3602
    India, 3626
Patriotism, 5452
Patten, Simon, 58
Peace, 5741
Peaceful coexistence, 5739
Peasantry, 1587, 4096, 4148, 4190, 5083
    France, 4028, 4041, 4093
    Italy, 4024
    Japan, 4027
    Korea R, 4094
    Malaysia, 4019
    Mexico, 4061, 4154
    Peru, 3481, 4066
    South Africa, 4036
    Spain, 4044, 4158
    USSR, 4068
    Yugoslavia, 4047
Peasants, 889, 3639, 3898, 4069
    Africa, 4097
    Caribbean, 4050
    China, 4142
    Costa Rica, 5624, 5657
    developing countries, 4141
    France, 4116

    Haiti, 4111
    Iran, 4057
    Latin America, 4014
    Mexico, 4038
    Poland, 4099
    Thailand, 4112
    Turkey, 4113
Peirce, Charles S., 2015
Pellizzi, Camillo, 212
Penal law, 1556, 1663, 5926, 5940
    German DR, 5519
    Nigeria, 1638
    USA, 1645
Penal sanctions, USA, 5828
Penitentiary system, 5842, 5956, 5972
    Algeria, 5918
    Belgium, 5990
    Canada, 5864, 5876, 5907
    Norway, 5921
    Spain, 5868
Perception, 795, 846, 2100, 2726
Perception of others, 696, 902, 910, 914, 1209, 2559
Performance, 784, 865, 1170, 2727, 5532
Performing arts, 2272, 5366
Periodicals, 44, 227, 230-232, 239
    Italy, 228
    USA, 3590
Personality, 660, 714, 716-718, 720, 722-723, 727, 729-733, 735-736, 738-739, 742, 745, 750-751, 754, 757, 761-763, 767, 852, 910, 1042, 1185, 1224, 1360, 1456, 1624, 1626, 2184, 2391, 2486, 4586-4587, 5630, 5641, 5660
Personality development, 666, 713, 715, 719, 721, 724-726, 728, 734, 737, 740-741, 743-744, 746-749, 752-753, 756, 758-760, 764-766, 768-770, 812, 1354, 1390, 1392, 1441, 1469, 1476, 1525, 2238, 2861, 4296, 4892, 5213, 5351, 5444
    German DR, 4695
Personality disorders, 1518
Personality measurement, 516-517
Personnel management, 4872-4873, 4878-4880, 4885, 4887-4888, 4890, 4895, 4897-4899, 4901-4902, 4905, 5128
    India, 4893
    USA, 5175
    USSR, 4884
Personnel selection, 4768, 4773, 4778
Persuasion, 2089, 2129, 2131
Phenomenology, 253, 255
Philosophy, 40, 265, 518, 633, 701, 1324, 1680, 3038
Phonetics, 2013
Photography, 195, 3469
Physical environment, 3957-3958, 3964
Physicians, 5059, 5066
    France, 6234, 6248
Piaget, Jean, 213, 833, 1956, 2299

350

Pilgrimages, France, 1839
Planning, 4674
Playing activities, 2046, 5362, 5364
Police, 2608, 5531, 5533, 5536, 5538-5540,
    5543, 5931
  Germany FR, 5529
  United Kingdom, 5985
  USA, 5529, 5537, 5541, 5924
  Western Europe, 5530
Political affiliation, 5636, 5649
Political attitudes, 5662
  India, 5647
  Sweden, 5659
  Venezuela, 5620
Political behaviour, 767, 1540, 1895, 1925,
    1930, 5548, 5630, 5641, 5666, 5750
  Brazil, 2786
  France, 4840, 5668
  Germany FR, 5625
Political coalitions, USA, 5677
Political communication, 5627, 5637
Political conflicts, 4464
Political corruption, 5621
Political culture, 5638, 5643, 5660
  Canada, 5653
  Germany, 5635
  Morocco, 5665
  Taiwan, 3716
  Tunisia, 5665
  USA, 5651
Political development, developing countries,
    5486
Political education, 2521, 2524
Political efficacy, 5658
Political elite, Indonesia, 5617
Political groups, 5585
Political ideologies, 1246, 5407, 5412, 5414,
    5417
  Nigeria, 5413
  United Kingdom, 5411
  USA, 5411
Political leadership, 5615
  Spain, 5618
Political life, 5694
  India, 5690
Political men, 723
  France, 5592, 5616
  Spain, 5618
Political opinion, Hungary, 5639
Political opposition, Tunisia, 5249
Political participation, 2152, 2209, 3034,
    4064, 5619, 5628, 5645
  Canada, 3592, 5623
  Costa Rica, 5624, 5657
  Denmark, 5652
  Norway, 5646
  Peru, 5631
  USA, 5648, 5651, 5661
Political parties, 5572, 5583, 5586-5587,
    5590-5591, 5594-5595
  Africa, 5570
  Black Africa, 5671

  Canada, 2611
  China, 5575
  France, 5573-5574, 5592
  Italy, 2732, 5593
  Latin America, 5588, 5691
  Spain, 5571
  United Kingdom, 5578
  USA, 5569, 5576, 5589
  USSR, 190, 2705, 5577, 5579, 5581-5582,
    5584, 6061-6062
Political philosophy, 263, 5408, 5410,
    5415-5416, 6000
Political power, 2605, 5418, 5421
  Italy, 5689
  United Kingdom, 5180
Political science, Yugoslavia, 5404
Political socialization, 823, 5629, 5640, 5650,
    5664
  Canada, 5633
  India, 5647
  Japan, 5644
  Spain, 5654
  Sweden, 5659
  USA, 5644, 5661
  USSR, 5669
Political society, 5503
Political sociology, 5396-5403, 5405-5406
Political systems, 2447, 5478, 5480,
    5483-5484, 5495, 5501, 5505, 5512,
    5521, 5583
  France, 5504
  Poland, 4997
  USSR, 5482, 5581
Political thought, Netherlands, 5409
Political trials, USA, 5686
Politicization, 5655, 5663
  Canada, 5634
Politics, 1925, 1930, 2039, 2660, 3593, 5539,
    5688, 5692, 5738
  France, 2236
  Italy, 5689
Polls, 494
Pollution, 3916
  USA, 3198, 3218
Pollution control, Japan, 5612
Polygamy, 3444
Polygyny, 3396, 3422
Poormen, Venezuela, 5781
Popper, Karl, 320, 329
Popular religion, USA, 1941
Population, 2894, 2901, 4436
  Burma, 2912
  France, 3128
  Latin America, 2940
  Spain, 2909
  USA, 2913
Population composition, 3175
  Yugoslavia, 3118
Population decline, Brazil, 3143
  Europe, 3123
  France, 3176
  Italy, 3136

USSR, 3124
Population density, Australia, 3126
Population distribution, 3144
    Malaysia, 3167
    Mexico, 3138
    USSR, 3147
Population distributions, USSR, 3146
Population dynamics, 3113, 3130, 3145, 3154, 3162
    Canada, 3155
    CMEA countries, 3177
    Iran, 3148
    Italy, 3131
    OECD countries, 3159
    USSR, 3121
Population education, India, 3295
Population growth, 3151, 3173-3174, 3396, 3617
    Cameroon, 3133
    Egypt, 3179
    India, 3168
    Peru, 3152
Population increase, Mexico, 3142
Population movement, 572, 3132, 3140, 3158
    Argentina, 3150
    Czechoslovakia, 3170
    developing countries, 3116
    Dominican Republic, 3153
    Europe, 2577
    Germany FR, 3122
    Israel, 3134
    Malaysia, 3139
    Pacific Islands FR, 3161
    Spain, 3114
    USA, 3141
    USSR, 3117, 3137
    Yemen, 3156
Population optimum, 3125
Population policy, 2908, 3288-3289, 3297, 3301, 3322, 3342
    Arab countries, 3345
    Australia, 3292
    Belgium, 3348-3349
    Bulgaria, 3313
    China, 3283
    Colombia, 3329
    Finland, 3311
    France, 3239
    Hungary, 3332, 3346
    India, 3317
    Italy, 3136
    Mexico, 3320
    Romania, 3324
    Singapore, 3298
    Uruguay, 3339
    USSR, 2911
Population projections, 2895
    Canada, 2896-2898
Porter, John, 225
Positivism, 246, 303, 312, 320, 329
Post-industrial society, 2822, 2890, 5688
    Netherlands, 2884

Poverty, 4073, 5764-5765, 5767-5768, 5771, 5783, 5785, 5789, 6053
    Africa, 5762
    Asia, 4512
    Belgium, 5763
    Canada, 4152
    France, 2785
    Haiti, 4111
    India, 4084, 4369
    Latin America, 5777, 5786
    Sierra Leone, 5776
    United Kingdom, 3110, 5775, 5787-5788
    USA, 5773, 5779-5780, 5793, 5841, 6113
Power, 1142, 5419
Pregnancy, France, 3536
Prehistory, India, 2802
Prejudice, 717, 1203, 1205, 1209
Premarital intercourse, 3375
Preschool education, 2403, 2417
Presidency, USA, 5532
Press, 2149, 2175-2176, 2179, 2193, 3963
    Italy, 2199
    Netherlands, 2151
    Spain, 2503
    United Kingdom, 6250
    USA, 2139
Prestige, 1134, 1137
Prevention of delinquency, 5938
    USA, 5883
Priests, Italy, 3860
Primary schools, Iran, 2405
    USA, 2419
Primitive religion, Zimbabwe, 1712
Prison, India, 5901
Prisoners, 702, 5831, 5881, 5895
    USA, 1154, 5843, 5882
Privacy, 685
Private education, France, 2326
Private schools, Germany FR, 2411
Probation system, 5029, 5979
    Canada, 5889
    USA, 5888
Problem solving, 789, 808, 831, 868, 4541, 6010
Producer cooperatives, 5320
Production, 4565
Production collectivities, 594, 4881, 5201, 5209, 5213, 5217
Productivity, 5330
Professionalism, 5018
Professionalization, 105, 5012, 5015, 5029, 6235
    Kenya, 5024
Professors, 2557, 4501
    USA, 2558
Proletariat, 2654
    France, 3536, 3562
Propaganda, 1223, 1269, 2126, 2128, 5463
Property, 4416, 4418-4420
    Nigeria, 3884
Prophecy, 1864
    Israel, 1881

Prostitution, 3353, 3360
   Germany FR, 3382
   India, 3721
   North America, 3381
Protestant churches, USA, 1924
Protestant ethics, 1887
Protestantism, 1748, 1750
   France, 1934, 5673
   United Kingdom, 1838
Protestants, 2975
   Canada, 3261
   France, 1731
Proudhon, P.-J., 280
Psychiatry, 1885, 6164, 6170-6171, 6174
   Canada, 6162
Psychoanalysis, 256, 279, 629, 632, 642, 655, 836, 983, 2809
Psycholinguistics, 2007, 2018
Psychologists, 80, 91, 94
Psychology, 627, 633, 636, 643, 649-650, 655, 1676, 1781
   Latin America, 637
   Peru, 625
Psychology of education, 825, 2299, 2311, 2544, 3354
Psychometrics, 646, 654
Psychosociology, 91, 94
Psychotherapy, 647
Public administration, 62, 1114, 5551, 5558-5559, 6085
   Hungary, 5554
Public education, Germany, 2361
Public health, Africa, 6194
   Spain, 6179
   United Kingdom, 6186, 6202
Public opinion, 494, 1219-1224, 1226-1227, 1230, 1232-1233, 1235-1237, 1239-1240, 2175, 3065, 4590, 4612, 5989
   Germany, 3763
   Hungary, 3332
   Netherlands, 4747
   USA, 3099
Public opinion research, 1229
Publishing, USA, 2178
Punishment, 5846, 5860-5861, 5892-5893, 5904-5905, 5917, 5934, 5940, 5994
   Europe, 5992
   France, 5914
   USA, 5872
Pupils, 1902
   India, 5647
Puritanism, 1905
Qualitative analysis, 422, 435, 440, 456, 463
Quality of life, 478, 877, 1507, 3003, 4479, 4482-4483, 4491, 4495, 4497, 4499, 4505, 4509-4510
   Belgium, 4476
   Caribbean, 4517
   Hong Kong, 4407
   Hungary, 4485
   USA, 2858, 4481, 4498, 4514, 4518

Questionnaires, 503
Race, 775, 3655, 3673, 3690
Race relations, 3718, 3736, 3754, 3775
   Brazil, 3739
   India, 3721
   New Zealand, 3761
   South Africa, 3717, 3747, 3758, 3765, 3776, 3783
   Trinidad and Tobago, 3729
   United Kingdom, 3755
   USA, 1378, 3723, 3727-3728, 3743, 3751, 3764, 3766, 3773
Racial attitudes, 3745
   South Africa, 3760
   USA, 3737, 3744, 3762, 3781
Racial conflicts, France, 3839
   United Kingdom, 3839
   USA, 3753
Racial discrimination, 3480, 3771, 3784, 3790, 5070
   Canada, 3777
   South Africa, 3785
   United Kingdom, 3733
   USA, 3719-3720, 3733, 3738, 3752, 3757, 3759, 3772, 3782, 4226, 5172, 5911
Racial prejudice, 2975, 3695, 3734, 3801
   South Africa, 1214, 1268, 3769
   USA, 3779
Racial segregation, Canada, 1788
   Sudan, 3786
   USA, 3724, 3728
Racism, 3726, 3732, 3789
   South Africa, 3780
   USA, 3774, 3792
Radicalism, 3064
   Germany FR, 5626
   Peru, 5667
   United Kingdom, 5622
Radio, Spain, 2169
Rape, 5853, 5885, 5919
   USA, 5911-5912
Rationalism, 252, 324
Rationality, 783, 813, 873, 1859, 2005
Rationalization, 2841
Readers, 1160, 2017, 2149
Reading, 772, 844
Rebellion, 1534
   Ireland, 1584
   United Kingdom, 1584
Recidivism, 5846
Recreation, 1152, 5375
Recruitment, Japan, 87
Recurrent education, 2497
Reference groups, 1039
Reference works, 197
Refugees, Laos, 3834
   Vietnam, 3696, 3846, 3859
Regional development, Latin America, 4192
Regional planning, USSR, 4322
   Vietnam, 4259
Regionalism, Canada, 5653
   Italy, 5457

Subject index

Spain, 5436
Western Europe, 5431
Regression analysis, 544, 557, 570, 584-585, 4481
Regulations, France, 1644
USA, 488
Relative deprivation, 2728
Reliability, 474
Religion, 1247, 1673, 1677-1678, 1681-1690, 1922, 5678
China, 1691, 1944
Japan, 4090
United Kingdom, 1718
USSR, 1910
Religiosity, 1886, 1889, 1897, 1900, 3088
Colombia, 1883
Indonesia, 1783, 1903
Mexico, 1898
Religious affiliation, 1912, 1915, 1938
Israel, 1937
USA, 3378
Religious authority, 1835
Religious behaviour, 502, 1676, 1884-1885, 1891, 1893-1895, 1902, 1904
Canada, 1901
Italy, 1899
Religious communities, 1806, 1813
Religious conversion, 1892
Religious doctrines, 1861
Religious education, 2527
Religious experience, 1860, 1865
Religious groups, 1801, 1813, 1821, 1826
Israel, 1825
Lebanon, 1804
Malaysia, 1817
USA, 1808
Religious history, 1674
Religious institutions, 1822
USA, 1829, 3720
Religious liberty, Italy, 1888
USA, 1217
Religious minorities, France, 1934
Switzerland, 1928
Religious movements, 1820, 1909, 1932-1933
Africa, 1940
Caribbean, 1920
Spain, 1936
USSR, 1911
Religious participation, Brazil, 1916
France, 1939
Italy, 1914
USA, 1924, 1942
Religious practice, 1917, 1925, 1930
France, 1935
Italy, 1899
Switzerland, 1913
USA, 2533
USSR, 1353, 1908, 1910
Religious protest, 1801
Religious revival, 1724, 1919
Japan, 1926
USA, 1923, 1929

Religious sciences, 1676
Religious symbolism, 2039
Africa, 1877
Remarriage, USA, 3429
Research, 135, 382, 5584
Western Europe, 113
Research and development, 141
Research centres, 145, 480, 1047
Belgium, 3530
Research financing, USA, 147
Research foundations, USA, 147
Research methods, 175, 338, 403, 408, 428, 445, 453-456, 466, 469-470, 763, 1401, 2311
Denmark, 5743
Research programmes, 159
Research strategy, 184, 424, 444
Research trends, 28, 114, 123
Brazil, 4075
Hungary, 126
India, 127
Mexico, 112
USA, 1454
USSR, 128
Research workers, 49, 86, 101, 178
Italy, 78
Spain, 83
Residential areas, 4086, 4384, 4391
Japan, 4395
Netherlands, 4285
Poland, 4368
USA, 4218
Residential mobility, 4249, 4284, 4311, 4340, 4367
Japan, 4389
USA, 4349, 4397
Residential segregation, 3090, 4202
Japan, 4335
USA, 4203, 4262, 4264, 4276, 4312-4314, 4326, 4358
Resistance to change, Libya, 2830
Responsibility, 1602, 1605, 1616, 1624, 1626, 1633, 3182
Rest, 5354
Retirement, 3069, 4995-4996, 5004, 5006-5007, 5011
United Kingdom, 5003
USA, 4739, 4999-5000
Return migrations, 1157, 3830
Israel, 3828
Malta, 3851
Spain, 3829
Tunisia, 3835
Turkey, 3876
Revolution, 2817-2818, 2826, 2828, 2837, 2848, 2856, 2865, 2867, 5735
Algeria, 2949
China, 2850
France, 2823, 5668
Iran, 2839
Revolutionary movements, 5609, 5611
Iraq, 2653

Subject index

Right to education, 5524
Rites, 1845-1846, 1854, 2046
 Papua New Guinea, 1848
Rites of passage, 1843
Rokkan, Stein, 446
Role, 703, 1156, 1158-1160, 1162-1163, 1165, 1167, 1170-1171, 2960, 3202, 5121
Role acquisition, 1039
Role conflicts, 1157, 1169, 5538, 5648
Role differentiation, 1161
Role distance, 1168
Role playing, 1166
Role set, 1164
Rousseau, Jean-Jacques, 2581
Ruling class, 2761
 Arab countries, 2749
 Italy, 2740
 Liberia, 2745
 Martinique, 3685
 Peru, 2739
Rural, 4185
Rural areas, 3108, 3497
 Canada, 4152
 Congo, 3981
 France, 4091, 6248
 India, 3295, 5074
 Mexico, 3433
 South Asia, 4054
 Spain, 5361, 6190
 USA, 4493, 4619, 6195
 USSR, 4120
Rural communities, Caribbean, 4050
 France, 4030, 4053
 Germany, 4132
 Ghana, 4156
 India, 4161
 Ireland, 4074
 Mediterranean countries, 4169
 USA, 2927, 4034
Rural development, 4033, 4040, 4064, 4073, 4079, 4081, 4107, 4188
 Africa, 4025, 4170
 Albania, 4060
 Australia, 4178
 Botswana, 4144
 Brazil, 4129
 China, 4103
 Colombia, 4067, 4184
 developing countries, 4078
 Eastern Europe, 4178
 Far East, 4020
 France, 4092, 4177
 India, 4013, 4046, 4062, 4076, 4130, 4138, 4149, 4159-4160
 Ivory Coast, 4063
 Latin America, 4178
 Mexico, 4616
 Nigeria, 4172
 Pakistan, 4162
 Philippines, 4042
 South Asia, 4110
 Taiwan, 4114
 Tanzania, 3259, 4032, 4128, 4174
 Uruguay, 3623, 4118
 USA, 2133, 4109, 4168
 USSR, 2538, 4166, 4615
 Yugoslavia, 4117
 Zaire, 3616
Rural environment, Germany, 2789
Rural life, 4029, 4101, 4171
 Brazil, 4080
 France, 4031, 4930
 Japan, 4017
 Tunisia, 4087
 United Kingdom, 4077
 USA, 4072
Rural migrations, 3919-3920, 3925, 3927, 3937
 Cameroon, 3133, 3890
 India, 3912
 Morocco, 3894
 Nigeria, 3884, 3896
 Turkey, 4113
 USA, 4264
 USSR, 3903
 Zambia, 3915
Rural population, 3145
 France, 3127
 India, 3115, 3295
 Turkey, 3149
 USSR, 3160, 3171-3172, 3178
Rural schools, France, 2407
Rural society, 4331
 China, 4136
 France, 2690, 4086, 4115, 4126, 5472
 India, 2766
 Italy, 3633
 Japan, 3548, 4089
 Nigeria, 4098
 Peru, 4055
 Spain, 4153
 United Kingdom, 4133
 USSR, 4121
 Vietnam, 4147
 Zaire, 4155
Rural sociology, 173, 177, 4033, 4134, 4145
 Brazil, 4075
 Germany, 2789
 Japan, 4135, 4164
Rural youth, 1491
Rural-urban, 1216, 3267, 4045, 4104, 4171
 China, 2850
 France, 4143
 India, 4370
 Indonesia, 4127
 Nigeria, 3268
 Switzerland, 4048
 USA, 4124
 USSR, 4125
Sacred, 1867
Saint-Simon, Claude-Henri de, 1376
Sales y Ferré, Manuel, 27
Sandwich courses, 5040
Satisfaction, 839, 842, 848, 870, 4246

Scale analysis, 619, 926, 1240
Scarcity, 5761, 5792
School administration, 2420-2422
School attendance, Italy, 1500
School environment, 1586
School segregation, 707
    USA, 681, 683, 2336, 2345, 2375, 2402
Schooling, 5078
    Canada, 2381
    United Kingdom, 3755
Schools, 2418
    United Kingdom, 2415
    USA, 2412
Schutz, Alfred, 694, 1326, 2810
Science, 148, 764, 1627, 1863, 1946, 1952, 1958, 1971, 1974, 1978, 1980, 1982-1983, 1985, 1987-1990, 1992, 1994-1996, 2001, 2003, 2006, 4673
    USSR, 1975
Science policy, 156, 160
    Netherlands, 150, 155
Scientific and technical progress, 148, 758, 781, 1355, 3047, 3151, 4534, 4569, 4572-4574, 4578, 4582, 4586-4587, 4590, 4593-4594, 4596, 4598, 4602, 4608, 4614, 4694, 4992, 5096
    Spain, 83, 1965
    USSR, 2762
Scientific co-operation, 164
    CMEA countries, 149
Scientific community, 152, 157-158
Scientists, 90
    USSR, 1297
Scientology, 1953
Seasonal migrations, Argentina, 3799
Second homes, France, 4253
Secondary education, Canada, 2416
    Senegal, 2404
Secondary schools, 2413
    USA, 2543
    USSR, 2409
Sects, 498, 1802, 1820, 1827, 1830
    Africa, 1763
    Latin America, 1797
    USA, 1797-1798, 1807, 1814, 1818, 1824, 1828
Secularization, 1921, 1931, 1974
Segregation, India, 1555
Self-attention, 677, 705, 711
Self-concept, 667-668, 670, 674, 682, 684, 695, 699-700, 703-704, 707, 710, 908, 1204, 3097, 5063
Self-esteem, 669-671, 681, 686-687, 697-698, 702, 709, 717, 3061
Self-evaluation, 673, 679, 690
Self-expression, 692, 708
Self-management, 4535, 4542, 4548-4549, 4552-4553, 6099
    Yugoslavia, 1077, 4085, 4414, 4550, 4563, 5271, 5312, 5316, 5404
Self-perception, 676, 696
Semantic differential, 2093

Semantics, 2014, 2024, 2031
Semiology, 2022, 2157
Semiotics, 2009-2010, 2015, 2017, 2020, 2023, 2030, 2033, 2041
    Poland, 2029
Sex, 460, 775, 2205, 2939, 2970, 2988, 5981
    United Kingdom, 5923
Sex differentiation, 669, 688, 944, 2945, 2951, 2953, 2965, 2974, 2976, 2990, 3211, 4463, 5067
    Costa Rica, 2931
    USA, 4716, 5562, 5983
Sex discrimination, 108, 1886, 2929, 2933, 2948, 2957, 2975, 4501, 5049, 5070
    India, 2922
    Netherlands, 2935
    USA, 2318, 2922, 2973, 3738
Sex distribution, 2923, 2954, 5850, 5962
    Israel, 5022
Sex equality, 1283, 2981
Sex roles, 1036, 1305, 1521, 2598, 2725, 2920, 2925, 2930, 2932, 2937-2938, 2942, 2950, 2952, 2955-2960, 2962-2964, 2969, 2971, 2974, 2979-2984, 2987, 2989, 2991-2993, 3050, 3395, 3505, 3523, 3583, 3636, 3639
    Cameroon, 2947
    Canada, 3592, 5623
    India, 1880
    Morocco, 1204
    Nigeria, 2947
    Sweden, 2966
    USA, 2921, 2924, 2936, 2941, 2944, 2978, 2986
Sexual behaviour, 945, 955, 3352, 3356, 3384, 3387, 6151
    USA, 3365, 3378
Sexual perversions, 3373, 3376
Sexuality, 2918, 3354-3355, 3358-3359, 3363, 3366, 3370-3372, 3374, 3380, 3383, 3385-3386
    France, 3368
Shamanism, Korea, 1695
    Korea R, 1697
Shop stewards, United Kingdom, 5231
Signs, 2015
Simmel, Georg, 301-302, 308
Simulation, 2170, 3399, 3440
Slavery, Africa, 2647
    Asia, 2647
    Brazil, 2640
    USA, 2631-2632, 2634, 2642
Sleep, 424, 821
Slums, 4377
    Bahamas, 4258
    Brazil, 4346
    Colombia, 4280
    India, 4330, 4369
    Latin America, 4405
    USA, 4247
    Venezuela, 4280

Small groups, 1000-1001, 1005-1006,
   1008-1012, 1014
Small towns, 4304, 4364
   France, 4092
   USA, 2111, 4283
Small-scale industry, Mexico, 4616
Smoking, 2123
Sociability, 886, 895, 1598
Social action, 757, 852, 999, 1561, 2235,
   6044, 6075, 6102
   United Kingdom, 5998
Social adaptation, 702, 1515, 1568
Social anthropology, 1277
Social biology, 6, 22, 1628
Social change, 227, 1417, 1468, 1658, 1785,
   2136, 2797, 2815, 2822, 2827,
   2832-2833, 2844, 2854-2856, 2859,
   2863-2864, 2868-2869, 2872, 3050,
   3240, 3597, 3974, 4410, 4605, 5706,
   5771, 5859
   Africa South of Sahara, 3253
   Arab countries, 2816
   Brazil, 2279, 2688
   Canada, 2849
   China, 2847
   Colombia, 2829
   Europe, 1660
   France, 4091
   Germany, 2789
   Germany FR, 2586
   India, 2393, 2637, 2824, 3483
   Indonesia, 1742
   Iran, 2840
   Iraq, 6045
   Japan, 2587
   Kuwait, 2862
   Latin America, 1660
   Mexico, 5549
   Poland, 1816
   South Africa, 2820
   Spain, 2834
   United Kingdom, 2882
   USA, 2858, 2871, 2883, 3622, 4619
   USSR, 2567, 3903
   Vietnam, 2893
Social classes, 822, 840, 935, 1085, 2284,
   2655, 2659, 2665-2666, 2674, 2681,
   2702, 2711, 2718, 2742, 3387, 3416,
   3563, 4454, 4457, 5281, 5450, 5728,
   5764, 5861, 6230
   Bangladesh, 2676
   Canada, 2671, 2673, 5653
   Denmark, 5479
   Europe, 2694
   France, 1935, 4697, 5668
   Ghana, 5211
   India, 2645-2646, 3721
   Iraq, 2653
   Mexico, 2687
   Nigeria, 3700
   South Africa, 3765
   Spain, 2668, 2700

United Kingdom, 2246, 2347, 2713
USA, 1378, 2658, 2662, 2713, 3744,
   5674, 5719
Yugoslavia, 2566
Social cognition, 1189
Social conditions, Canada, 1316, 1333
   Haiti, 1385
   South Africa, 1329
Social conformity, 1591
Social consciousness, 1225, 1447, 1505, 1523,
   1541, 1588, 1657, 2232, 3036
   Europe, 2694
   Germany FR, 5093
Social control, 874, 1084, 1137, 1446, 1454,
   1459, 1471, 1473-1474, 1484,
   1486-1487, 1492, 1505, 2086, 2219,
   2576, 4964, 5280-5281, 5421, 6039
   Canada, 1462
   Colombia, 4067
   France, 1450
   Norway, 5921
   Zimbabwe, 2362
Social determinism, 2568, 2575
Social development, 18, 193, 782, 1264,
   1384, 2575, 2819, 2825, 2831,
   2835-2836, 2838, 2845, 2851-2852,
   2861, 2866, 2870, 3044, 4191, 4614,
   5437
   Asia, 2846
   developing countries, 4575
   Greece, 3180
   Haiti, 2821
   USSR, 2409, 2675
Social differentiation, 1598, 2621, 2692, 5744
   Italy, 2604
   Kenya, 2596
   USA, 2616
Social disorganization, 5756
Social environment, 2418
Social equality, 2628
   USA, 2602
Social exchange, 2589
Social facts, 387
Social group work, 6138
Social history, 324, 1076, 2788, 2793, 2795,
   2797, 2801, 2807-2809, 2832, 5821
   Brazil, 5181
   Canada, 3519
   Colombia, 2829
   France, 118, 1844, 3012, 3127, 3368,
      5241, 5714
   Germany, 2737, 2789, 4132, 4266, 4754,
      5218
   Germany FR, 2799
   Guatemala, 3660
   India, 3721, 5838
   Italy, 2791
   Panama, 5229
   Portugal, 2805, 5061
   Southeast Asia, 2886
   Spain, 2700
   Sweden, 4745

United Kingdom, 2686, 2798, 2800, 2803, 5251
USA, 2790, 2792, 3552, 4813
USSR, 995
Social indicators, 186, 478, 530-532, 542-543, 550-551, 555, 559, 565, 567-568, 571-572, 574-575, 583, 587, 590, 593-595, 2778, 2875, 2907, 3059, 3516, 4227, 4246, 4365, 4376, 4483-4484, 4495, 4497, 4505, 4514, 5642, 5702
Germany FR, 597
USA, 545, 2602, 4518
Social inequality, 2608, 2614, 2619, 2623, 2625-2627, 4418, 4515, 5848
Belgium, 5763
China, 6095
France, 2356, 5196
Ghana, 2400
India, 2612, 2618
Nigeria, 2615
United Kingdom, 2594, 2599, 2630, 4217
USA, 2594, 2610, 5793, 6244
Social influence, 1448-1449, 1478, 1485, 3035
Social integration, 1498, 1507, 1522, 1537, 1550, 1587, 1593, 4236, 4578
Arab countries, 1081
USA, 1581
USSR, 1497, 1576
Social interaction, 929, 1028, 1234, 1501, 1512, 1527, 1533, 1535, 1544, 1554, 1583, 2116-2117, 3095, 3405
Social interest, 800
Social justice, 6000, 6042, 6048, 6072, 6098
Social legislation, Netherlands, 2935
United Kingdom, 6007
Social management, 1352, 1460, 4665, 6001, 6006, 6009, 6015, 6032-6033, 6051, 6056, 6069, 6079, 6081-6083, 6097, 6099, 6104-6105
Social medicine, 6163, 6167, 6172
Africa, 6194
Social mobility, 830, 837, 1632, 2778, 2781, 2784, 2864, 3282, 3559, 4949, 5484
Brazil, 2786
Canada, 3666
France, 2785
Germany, 2775
Germany FR, 2588
Hungary, 2777
Japan, 2783
Poland, 2777
Tunisia, 2776
Turkey, 3876
United Kingdom, 2779-2780, 2782
USA, 3429
USSR, 2343, 2787, 5081
Social movements, 332, 1132, 1141, 1432, 3656, 3706, 5599, 5601-5602, 5604, 5608, 5610, 5613-5614
Africa, 5603
Asia, 5603

China, 4142
Colombia, 1571
Italy, 5596
Japan, 5612
Spain, 3967, 5600
USA, 5598
Social networks, 986-987, 989-992, 995, 997, 999
Social norms, 1445, 1455, 1460-1461, 1463, 1465, 1475, 1481-1482, 1488, 1557, 5084
USA, 3552
Social order, 1983, 2590
Germany FR, 2563
Israel, 968
Social origin, 2448
Social participation, 1153, 1549, 1563
Italy, 1500
Japan, 1573
Social pathology, 5757
Social perception, 901, 904, 908, 912-913, 915
Social planning, 5217, 5996, 5999, 6022, 6024, 6028, 6052, 6073-6074, 6076, 6105
Germany FR, 6089
Greece, 6043
USA, 6094
USSR, 6071
Social policy, 4410, 6014, 6018-6022, 6035, 6039, 6046, 6050, 6053, 6055, 6077-6078, 6080, 6084-6085, 6096, 6101, 6119, 6122
China, 6095
Colombia, 6016
Czechoslovakia, 6070
Europe, 6049
Germany FR, 5997, 6086
India, 6059, 6092
Iraq, 6045
Switzerland, 6005
United Kingdom, 5775, 6026, 6064
USA, 5773, 6003, 6008, 6037, 6041, 6054, 6068
USSR, 6029, 6061-6062, 6067, 6090, 6103
Venezuela, 6063
Yugoslavia, 6047
Social problems, 1922, 3963, 5754, 6010, 6013, 6023, 6027, 6034, 6036, 6101
United Kingdom, 6038
USA, 6087
Social protest, 962, 1513, 1530, 1540, 2049, 6191
Canada, 1575
China, 1520
France, 1543, 1562
Sri Lanka, 3031
USA, 2477, 3031, 5598, 5703
Social psychology, 626, 628, 630, 634-635, 638, 640-641, 644-645, 648, 651-653, 656-657, 662, 809, 1562, 4005
Spain, 631

Social representations, 1206
Social research, 41, 159, 378, 440, 1539,
    5556, 5744, 5749
  Denmark, 5743
  USA, 488, 5751
Social science research, Peru, 122
Social sciences, 1, 11, 16, 18, 40, 46-47, 49,
    53-54, 62, 71, 105, 132, 135, 164, 168,
    196, 206, 270, 339, 341, 360, 398,
    406, 409, 432, 451, 492, 525, 701,
    6077
  China, 115
  East Africa, 116
  France, 151
  Latin America, 119, 202
  Mexico, 112
  United Kingdom, 5438
  USA, 147, 2178
  Western Europe, 113
Social security, 6109
  Andean countries, 6129
  Australia, 3457
  Bulgaria, 6114
  Canada, 6136
  Germany FR, 6117, 6137
  India, 6133
  Korea R, 3458
  Latin America, 5786, 6126
  USA, 6110, 6113
  Yugoslavia, 6130
Social services, 6254-6255, 6258
  Australia, 6252
  Canada, 6239
  Denmark, 6245
  Italy, 6247
  United Kingdom, 6253
  USA, 6244, 6249, 6251, 6259
Social status, 1036, 2723-2727, 2729, 3712,
    4381
  Australia, 6201
  Germany FR, 2730
  Iran, 3250
  USA, 2370, 3753
Social stratification, 1806, 2592, 2597-2598,
    2603, 2605, 2609, 2617, 2623, 2672,
    2919
  Canada, 2611, 3666, 3686, 3691
  Hong Kong, 2606
  India, 2601
  Japan, 3157
  Korea R, 4489
Social structure, 659, 826, 889, 2314,
    2560-2561, 2571, 2574, 2578-2580,
    2607, 4620
  China, 2569
  Eastern Europe, 2582
  Europe, 2577
  Germany FR, 2586, 2588
  Indonesia, 2573
  Italy, 2583
  Japan, 2587
  Spain, 1320

  USSR, 2567, 2585
  Western Europe, 446
  Yugoslavia, 2566
Social system, 468, 1260, 1652, 2562,
    2564-2565, 2570, 2572, 2576, 2581,
    2584, 2591, 2894, 3940, 4420, 6088
Social theory, 250, 6025, 6066, 6088, 6091
Social unrest, United Kingdom, 5755
Social work, 5783, 6140, 6142-6143, 6146,
    6148-6149, 6151-6153, 6155, 6157
  Germany FR, 6139
  Israel, 6156
  United Kingdom, 6040, 6154
  USA, 6141, 6144, 6158-6159
Social workers, 6236-6237, 6255
  United Kingdom, 5998, 6250, 6256
Socialism, 716, 1362, 1536, 2619, 2626, 4577,
    5423-5425, 5427, 5430, 5433, 5435,
    5437, 5443-5445, 5448-5450,
    5453-5454, 5456, 5460-5461
  China, 137
  developing countries, 5426
  Tanzania, 4639
Socialist countries, 1299, 1587, 2669, 3054,
    4119, 4423, 4435, 4539, 5424, 5510
  Africa, 2664
Socialist culture, 1324, 1338, 1354, 1360
Socialist society, 90, 396, 713, 719, 729, 739,
    753, 765-767, 777, 851, 858, 869,
    1222, 1258, 1270, 1274, 1283, 1292,
    1322, 1339-1340, 1347, 1352, 1358-
    1359, 1372, 1388, 1390, 1399-1400,
    1403, 1441, 1443, 1461, 1470, 1473,
    1482, 1498, 1505, 1616, 1657, 2226,
    2229, 2447, 2479, 2560, 2562, 2574,
    2691, 2717, 2759, 2764, 2859, 3016,
    3037, 3162, 3541-3542, 3546, 4422,
    4433, 4445, 4449, 4451, 4456-4457,
    4461, 4507, 4578, 4699, 4905, 5075,
    5086, 5105, 5317, 5347, 5356, 5471,
    5475, 5483, 5512, 5583, 5591, 5630,
    5733, 6015, 6019, 6069, 6081
  Eastern Europe, 4443
  USSR, 1382
Socialization, 715, 1308, 1445, 1502-1503,
    1506, 1511, 1525, 1532, 1552, 1567,
    1574, 1586, 1592, 1601, 1635, 2304,
    2312, 2932, 2993, 3024, 3459, 3484,
    3499, 5026, 5383
  Germany FR, 5710
  Japan, 1547
  Peru, 3025
  Puerto Rico, 1585
  USA, 1740
  USSR, 1565
Society, 519, 1319, 1331, 1336-1337, 1351,
    1371, 1376, 1398
  China, 1315
  Hungary, 1313, 1334, 1356
  India, 37, 1389
  Israel, 1288
  Spain, 1320

Subject index

Sociolinguistics, 1533, 2021, 2025, 2085
    India, 2016
Sociological analysis, 413
Sociologists, 76-77, 81, 85, 88-89, 91, 93-95, 97, 103-104, 106-109, 1013, 3673
    Arab countries, 2733
    Netherlands, 111
    USA, 98, 221
    Yugoslavia, 5027
Sociology, 2-3, 5, 8-9, 12, 15, 19-20, 26, 28-36, 41, 43, 50-51, 55, 59-60, 66-68, 70, 72, 75, 79, 82, 84, 92-93, 96, 100, 102-103, 110, 207, 231, 234, 236, 238, 241, 271, 323, 327-328, 370, 427, 445, 459, 1871, 2281, 2286, 4537, 4552, 6000
    Canada, 10, 121
    China, 137
    German DR, 172
    Germany, 129
    Germany FR, 133
    India, 127
    Israel, 3826
    Italy, 130
    Japan, 87, 136
    Netherlands, 131, 155
    South Africa, 1328
    USSR, 4, 146
    Yugoslavia, 117, 120, 124, 134
Sociology of art, 2220, 2228
Sociology of culture, 1278-1279
Sociology of development, 2873, 2888, 2891-2892
Sociology of education, 2282, 2286-2288, 2293, 2305, 2307-2310, 2313
    capitalist countries, 2297
    Germany FR, 2295
    Nigeria, 2292
Sociology of knowledge, 11, 244, 424, 444, 1945, 1947-1948, 1951, 1954-1955, 1959-1961, 1963-1964, 1967-1970, 1972-1973, 1975-1977, 1979-1981, 1984, 1986, 1990-1991, 1993, 1995, 1998, 2002, 2004-2005
    Spain, 1966
    USA, 1962
Sociology of law, 1640-1642, 1646, 1650, 1658-1659, 1662, 1666, 1963, 5125
Sociology of leisure, 5342
Sociology of literature, 7, 2243-2245, 2247-2251, 2261-2262
    Australia, 3680
Sociology of organizations, 1058, 1061
Sociology of religion, 1680, 1776, 1858, 1870-1871, 1875
    Germany FR, 1855
Sociology of science, 1997
Sociology of work, 232, 4601, 4676
    France, 4677, 4681, 4685
    Italy, 4681
    Japan, 4690
    USA, 2941

Sociometric relations, 926
Solidarity, 934
Sovereignty, 5733-5734
Soviet studies, 145
Space, 460, 468, 2045
Spatial distribution, 3974
Special education, 2522
    France, 2526
Speech, 457, 2068, 2070, 2077, 2090, 2102, 2108, 2116-2118
Sport, 1227, 5358, 5369-5370, 5373, 5380, 5383, 5388-5389, 5391, 5393-5394
    India, 1851
    United Kingdom, 5384
    USA, 5371, 5379, 5384, 5387
    USSR, 5359, 5390
Sportsmen, 5367
Standard of living, 4470, 4478, 4507, 5782
    Asia, 4512
    France, 3238
    Hungary, 4473
Standardization, 1479
State, 1647, 3083, 5019, 5476-5477, 5480-5481, 5485, 5487-5488, 5490-5491, 5493-5494, 5496-5497, 5500, 5502-5503, 5506-5507, 5510-5511, 5514, 5728, 6198
    Denmark, 5479
    developing countries, 5509
    Europe, 5492
    Latin America, 5516
    Western Europe, 4591
State capitalism, Germany FR, 133
State farms, USSR, 4016, 4615
Statistical analysis, 527, 534, 558, 562, 578-581, 591
Statistical data, 535
Statistical decision, 5681
Statistical models, 538-541, 547, 549, 560, 588
Statistics, 526, 528-529, 533, 552-554, 561, 573, 582
    Hungary, 548
Status congruency, 2728, 4391
Stereotypes, 4778
Stochastic models, 611, 613
Stouffer, Samuel A., 1216
Strikes, 5265, 5274, 5276
    Canada, 5284, 5295
    capitalist countries, 5266
    Denmark, 5267
    Ethiopia, 5283
    Germany FR, 5256
    Israel, 5261
    Tanzania, 5270
    United Kingdom, 5263
    Yugoslavia, 5271
Structural analysis, 430, 2833
Structural unemployment, 4738
Structuralism, 67-68, 243, 261, 289, 309
Student behaviour, 2422, 2449, 2451, 2457, 2475, 2950

Subject index

France, 2434
Germany FR, 2460, 2484
Greece, 2471
India, 2431
Italy, 2476
USA, 2424, 2477
Student movements, 2480
 USA, 2469
Students, 664, 775, 867, 1157, 1469, 1488, 1886, 1891, 2447-2448, 2473, 2475, 2486, 2559, 3375, 5357, 5952, 6241
 Brazil, 2462
 Canada, 2416, 5633
 China, 1944
 France, 2444 55, Germany FR, 2406
 India, 2474
 Japan, 372
 Puerto Rico, 1585
 South Africa, 1429, 3769
 United Kingdom, 372, 2435
 USA, 2986, 3781
 USSR, 1309, 2461, 2485
Sturzo, Luigi, 5410, 5522
Subculture, 1332
Suburban areas, 3109, 4003, 4311, 4366, 4381
 Japan, 4208
 USA, 3046, 4276, 4306, 4312
Suicide, 1168, 3217, 5870, 5896, 5922, 5930, 5952, 5973
 Argentina, 5886
 India, 5891
 USA, 5951
Superstition, 1693, 1869
Supervisors, 5111
 USA, 5112, 5175
Survey analysis, 405
Survey data, 462, 496
 United Kingdom, 497
Surveys, 363, 498-502
 USA, 495
Symbolic interaction, 685
Symbolism, 2039, 2045, 2052, 2063
 India, 1880
Symbols, 1544, 1583, 2035, 2047, 2049-2050, 2059, 2088, 2280, 3084
Systems analysis, 404, 416, 418-420, 423, 452
Taoism, 1713, 1754
 China, 1790
Taxonomy, 1891
Teacher recruitment, United Kingdom, 2553
Teacher training, Europe, 2539
 Germany FR, 2540
 Sweden, 2549
Teachers, 1469, 2542, 2554-2555, 2559, 5010
 Canada, 2547
 India, 2550
 Italy, 2541
 Peru, 2536
 USA, 2543
 USSR, 2538
Teaching, 1, 93, 103, 2451, 2486, 2544, 2552

 Europe, 6049
 Japan, 87
Teaching methods, 82, 92, 96, 445, 1871, 2286, 2548
Team work, 4906
Technical education, 2523
Technical schools, Germany FR, 2406
Technicians, 4016
Technological change, 3927, 4583, 4592, 4595, 4601, 4610, 4613, 4756
 China, 4576
 France, 4584
 USA, 4607
Technology, 1958, 4585, 4600, 4606, 4609, 4611, 4673
Technology transfer, 4571, 4597
 developing countries, 4570
Telecommunications, USA, 2133
Television, 829, 2145-2146, 2150, 2153-2154, 2158-2160, 2163, 2180, 2200, 2205, 2207, 3034
 Germany FR, 2188
 Mexico, 2197
 Spain, 2169
 USA, 2132, 2134, 2214
Terminology, 2903
Terrorism, 1495, 1510, 1558, 5938, 6010
Tertiary sector, 4620
Textbooks, 100, 233-241, 699, 980
Theatre, 2273-2274
 Latin America, 2276
 Poland, 2275
Theft, 5894, 5970
 Netherlands, 5937
 USA, 5858
Theology, 1675, 1679
Theory, 51, 247, 257, 262, 285, 294, 305, 319, 335, 356, 465, 788
Therapeutic groups, 1003-1004
Therapeutic relationship, 6203
Thesaurus, 208, 531
Thieves, Canada, 5929
Thinking, 798-799, 814, 845, 878, 2112
Thurnwald, Hilde, 226
Tillich, Paul, 1675
Time, 425, 431, 437, 447, 6233
Time budget, 1600, 4959-4960, 4970
 Costa Rica, 4962
 France, 4930, 4946
 Hungary, 4918
 Poland, 4915
 USA, 4929
 USSR, 4968, 4971, 4979
Tolerance, 1216, 2521, 3801
 USA, 1217
Top management, France, 5115
 USA, 4978
Topology, 604-605
Torture, 1499
Totalitarianism, 129
Touraine, Alain, 805, 5601
Tourism, 1506, 1917, 5363, 5365, 5368,

361

Subject index

5372, 5376-5377
Caribbean, 5382
Europe, 5381
Japan, 5392
Peru, 3791
Poland, 5385
South East Asia, 5395
Spain, 5361
Venezuela, 5360
Town planning, 4236, 4341, 4378
    Mexico, 4272
Towns, 2851, 4204, 4225, 4292, 4350, 4597
    Brazil, 2279
    Czechoslovakia, 4315
    France, 4295
    Germany FR, 4279, 4390
    India, 4369
    Iran, 4268
    Israel, 4230
    Japan, 4011, 4267, 4316, 4404
    Middle East, 4354, 4356
    USA, 2917, 4210, 4278, 4288
    USSR, 2173, 3165, 4263
Toynbee, Arnold, 2872
Trade unionism, 4516, 5184, 5187, 5247, 5493
    Brazil, 5239
    Europe, 5207
    France, 5190
    Germany, 5193
    Switzerland, 5171
    United Kingdom, 5190, 5243
    USA, 5172, 5205, 5212
Trade unions, 4860, 5168, 5174, 5179, 5185, 5198, 5200, 5228, 5244, 5250, 5540
    Brazil, 5188
    Canada, 4618, 5169, 5182, 5240
    Czechoslovakia, 5230
    France, 4832, 5155, 5196, 5225
    Germany FR, 5177, 5189, 5215
    Hong Kong, 5194
    India, 5210
    Italy, 5166-5167, 5173, 5186, 5235-5236
    Japan, 5214
    Mexico, 5203
    Norway, 5219
    Papua New Guinea, 5234
    Puerto Rico, 5197
    South Africa, 5204
    Spain, 5233
    Sweden, 5236
    Tanzania, 5176
    Tunisia, 5249
    United Kingdom, 5180, 5191-5192, 5199, 5202, 5216, 5224, 5238, 5248
    USA, 2923, 3759, 5175, 5178, 5183, 5192, 5206, 5208, 5223, 5227, 5237, 5245, 5297
Tradition, 974, 1596
    developing countries, 2853
    Israel, 3698
    Italy, 2791

Traditional culture, 1417
Traditional society, France, 974, 1667
    Spain, 2876
Traditionalism, 1595-1596
Training groups, 1002-1003, 1015
Transition from school to work, Italy, 2379
Travels, 5495
Triad, 1025
Tribalism, India, 3768, 3793
Tribes, India, 3715
Troeltsch, Ernst, 1776
Two-person games, 615
Typology, 372, 516, 5013, 5019, 5542
Underdevelopment, 2881
    Canada, 4152
    Italy, 2879
    Malaysia, 4019
    Paraguay, 2382
Underemployment, USA, 4742
Unemployed, 4734, 4746
    France, 4731
    Germany FR, 4761
    Netherlands, 4747
    Sweden, 4745
Unemployment, 4460, 4751, 4753, 4756, 5656
    France, 4758
    Germany, 4754
    Germany FR, 4827
    USA, 482, 4739
Unemployment insurance, United Kingdom, 6116
Universities, 89
    Austria, 2426
    developed countries, 2481
    France, 161, 2433, 5108
    Germany FR, 2478
    Japan, 2438
    USSR, 146
University management, 2427
    France, 2434
Unskilled workers, Germany FR, 4950
Urban areas, 2608, 2689, 3916
    Colombia, 4227
    United Kingdom, 5788
    USA, 4244, 4397
Urban communities, 4291
    USA, 4220
Urban concentration, Argentina, 4213
    Peru, 3152
Urban development, 4204, 4240, 4271, 4342, 4374, 4396
    Africa, 4334
    Australia, 4386
    developing countries, 4344
    Eastern Europe, 4319
    Ecuador, 4252
    India, 4303
    Latin America, 4192, 4252
    Nigeria, 4137
    South East Asia, 4301
    United Kingdom, 4257, 4261, 4317

USA, 4199-4200, 4269, 4323, 4333
USSR, 4211, 4239, 4296
Urban environment, 2062, 2915, 4274
Urban geography, 4231, 4282
Urban growth, 4383
    Algeria, 4347
    France, 4223, 4242
    India, 4360
    Italy, 4222, 4232
    Senegal, 4233
    Tunisia, 4294
Urban life, 590, 3217, 4251, 4394
    Japan, 4300
    United Kingdom, 5775, 6038
    USA, 4209, 4254
Urban planning, 4302, 4310, 4325, 4399, 4403, 4597
    Brazil, 4219
    Colombia, 4293
    France, 4305
    India, 4345
    USA, 4351, 4365
    USSR, 4235
Urban population, 3054, 3169
    Canada, 3155
    Eastern Europe, 4319
    France, 3135, 4295
    Italy, 3120
    Japan, 3157, 3166
    Sudan, 3129
    United Kingdom, 3866
    USA, 3119, 3164, 6188
    USSR, 2360, 3165
    Yugoslavia, 4387
Urban renewal, 4270, 4359
    Australia, 4297
    Europe, 4212
    France, 4193
    USA, 4228, 4234
Urban society, 1572, 3072, 4205, 4277
    France, 4343
    Germany, 4266
    Nigeria, 4339
    USA, 3351
Urban sociology, 4215, 4260, 4274, 4281, 4286, 4318, 4341, 4373, 4406, 4409
    France, 4287
    Germany, 4375
    USA, 4302
Urban space, 4221
    Brazil, 4380
    France, 4197
Urban structure, France, 4275
    USA, 4392
Urban transport, 4337
    France, 4243
    Ireland, 4298
Urbanism, 2264, 4194, 4214, 4238, 4348, 4398
    USA, 4289
    USSR, 4322
Urbanization, 4256, 4299, 4331

    Arab countries, 4336
    Brazil, 4402
    China, 4241
    Colombia, 4353
    developing countries, 4382
    Eastern Europe, 4329
    India, 4370
    Japan, 2842
    Korea R, 4355
    Latin America, 2722, 4371
    South Asia, 4324
    Spain, 4248
    Sudan, 3426
    USA, 4379
    USSR, 3117, 4309, 4408
    Vietnam, 4259
    West Africa, 4352
    Yugoslavia, 4387
Utopia, 1206, 1245-1246, 1256, 1259, 1262, 1265, 3589
Validity, 474, 491, 493
Value, 247, 1578-1579
Value judgment, 340, 345, 347, 401, 482
Value orientation, 516, 1444, 1453, 1469-1470, 1472, 1476, 1490-1491
    Japan, 1467
Value systems, 1443, 1447, 1452, 1456-1457, 1464, 1466, 1468, 1480, 1483, 1591, 1595, 1789, 2066, 2867, 3540, 4599, 4702, 5337, 5357, 5434
    Brazil, 1364
    India, 2766
    Switzerland, 1477
    USSR, 2706
Van Houten, Donald R., 1074
Variance analysis, 537, 546, 556, 576, 4480
Verbal behaviour, 2070, 2083, 2089, 2108, 2112, 2122, 3487
Verification, 390, 399
Vico, Giambattista, 662
Villages, 1625, 4119, 4131, 4150, 4186, 4292
    Algeria, 4037
    Bangladesh, 4035
    China, 4140
    Denmark, 4176
    France, 2278, 3511, 4106
    Hungary, 4095
    India, 1486, 1880, 2601, 4018, 4023, 4052, 4084
    Indonesia, 4146
    Israel, 3698
    Japan, 484, 2985, 4017, 4088, 4090, 4180-4183
    Mexico, 4061
    Netherlands, 4175
    Poland, 4105
    Tanzania, 4065, 4123
    Thailand, 3985
    United Kingdom, 4070
    USSR, 2396, 2538, 4015-4016, 4100, 4102, 4139, 4163, 4165-4166, 4187, 4189, 4239, 4615

Subject index

West Africa, 4059
Yugoslavia, 3998, 4004, 4085
Vincent, Paul, 214
Violence, 538, 947, 1275, 1516, 1521, 1524, 1548, 1556, 1560, 1564, 1577, 2198, 2207, 2431, 2817, 3508, 5388, 5496, 5977
   Colombia, 1571, 2829
   United Kingdom, 5384
   USA, 1509, 1526, 1528, 1582, 5384
Vocational education, 4748, 5077, 5080
   Hungary, 5046
Vocational guidance, USSR, 4987, 5042
Vocational interest, 6241
Vocational rehabilitation, USA, 5035
Vocational training, 5030, 5034
   France, 4993
   Italy, 5043
   USSR, 5065
Voluntary organizations, 1069, 1071
   Netherlands, 1070
Voluntary work, 4964
Voting behaviour, 5678, 5681, 5683
   Australia, 5672
   Canada, 2611, 2709
   France, 5673
   Italy, 5680
   Japan, 1573, 5675
   USA, 1923, 3994, 5674, 5679, 5685
Wach, J., 1835
Wage differentials, 4516
Wage rate, 4488, 4504, 5202
Wages, 4501, 4701, 5274
   Costa Rica, 2931
   USA, 5206, 5208, 5212
Wallerstein, Immanuel, 5725
War, 1889, 5737, 5740
Way of life, 186, 531, 719, 729, 858, 1283-1284, 1292-1293, 1299, 1303, 1306-1307, 1309, 1322, 1325, 1327, 1339-1340, 1347, 1350, 1352, 1355, 1357, 1359-1360, 1362, 1372, 1375, 1379-1381, 1384, 1386, 1388, 1390, 1392, 1396-1397, 1399-1401, 1403, 1411, 1443, 2226, 2323, 3037, 3954, 4572, 4662, 4699, 4951, 5098, 5391
   Mexico, 1281-1282
   Morocco, 1317
   USSR, 1291, 1297, 1305, 1312, 1314, 1335, 1353, 1369, 2760, 4068, 4801, 5489, 5515, 5582
Wealth, 4469, 4492
   Belgium, 4474
Weber, Max, 61, 242, 247, 249, 266, 286, 305, 318, 324, 337, 371, 397, 656, 880, 1138, 1686, 1835, 2309, 2579, 2806, 2810, 2841, 4441, 4455, 4687, 5403, 5421, 5590, 5594
Welfare, 2724, 4471-4472, 4480, 4484, 4494, 4502, 4511, 4513
   Italy, 3491
Welfare policy, United Kingdom, 6040

USA, 6004
USSR, 6058
Welfare state, 1069, 6011-6012, 6031, 6093
   Canada, 6060
   Germany FR, 5997
   Norway, 6057
   Sweden, 6017, 6065, 6100
   United Kingdom, 5995, 6030
   USA, 6002, 6060
Whites, 3734
   USA, 683, 3781
Widow, 3421
   Africa, 3418
Widowhood, 3390
   France, 3391
Wife, 1832, 3395, 3516, 5110
Wildcat strikes, USA, 5258
Witchcraft, 1693, 1699
   Colombia, 1883
   France, 1696
Witches, 1702
   Europe, 1692
Wittgenstein, Ludwig, 263, 1957, 2100
Women, 95, 152, 855, 2781, 2915, 2918-2919, 2928, 2952, 2961, 2994, 3076, 3097, 3187, 4871, 5025, 5796, 5827, 5845, 5895, 5963, 6226
   Algeria, 2949
   Caribbean, 2972
   Italy, 4831
   Japan, 2985, 3166
   Latin America, 2916, 2940
   Southern Africa, 1847
   USA, 2917, 2927, 4808, 4912, 5371
   USSR, 2926
Women's education, 3608, 3613
   Colombia, 3591
   France, 3624
   Hungary, 2142
   India, 3615
   Sierra Leone, 3256
Women's participation, 3645
   France, 3628
   Mexico, 3643
Women's promotion, 3597
   India, 3584
   USA, 3640
Women's rights, 3629
   Germany FR, 3646
   Greece, 3637
   USA, 3600
Women's status, 1305, 2598, 3416, 3574, 3580, 3582-3583, 3588, 3596, 3599, 3602, 3604, 3612, 3617, 3635-3636
   Afghanistan, 3581, 3644
   Arab countries, 3598
   Australia, 4810
   Canada, 3592
   Czechoslovakia, 3605, 3642, 3647
   developing countries, 3577
   EEC countries, 3606
   Egypt, 3603

France, 3610
Germany FR, 3575
Hungary, 4820
India, 3611, 3626, 4791
Iran, 3644
Ireland, 3620
Islam, 3578
Israel, 3711
Italy, 3595, 3633
Japan, 3609, 3630
Latin America, 3618
Morocco, 1649, 3578
Norway, 3607
Pakistan, 3631
Peru, 3586
Puerto Rico, 3576, 3619
Scandinavia, 4841
United Arab Emirates, 3641
Uruguay, 3623
USA, 3590, 3622, 3632
USSR, 3605, 4799
Yemen, 3621
Yemen PDR, 3627
Zaire, 3616
Work environment, 724, 1552, 4989, 5543
Work organization, 4876, 4886, 4889, 4903
France, 4882, 4900
Hungary, 4955
Italy, 4874
Workers, 740, 749, 2331, 3954, 4970, 5085-5086, 5096-5097, 5198, 5348, 5412
France, 4584, 5100-5101
Germany, 5821
Germany FR, 5093
USSR, 5081-5082, 5092, 5094, 6029
Workers committees, France, 5242
Zambia, 5195
Workers councils, 5220
Workers education, 2489, 2519
USSR, 2520
Yugoslavia, 2501
Workers participation, 5290, 5308-5309, 5313, 5316-5317, 5320, 5322, 5324, 5330-5331
Canada, 5323
China, 5315
Denmark, 5327, 5334
Europe, 5332, 5336
France, 5329
Germany FR, 5319, 5326, 5335
Malta, 5325
Netherlands, 5333
Peru, 5311
Sweden, 5307, 5318-5319
United Kingdom, 5328
USA, 5336
USSR, 5310, 5314
Yugoslavia, 5312

Working class, 1587, 1618, 1884, 2649-2650, 2663-2664, 2669-2670, 2682-2683, 2691-2692, 2714, 2720, 2890, 3594, 4949
Brazil, 2688
Canada, 2699, 2703
France, 2678, 3456
Hungary, 2684
Iran, 3230
Latin America, 2722
United Kingdom, 2686, 2715, 4698
USA, 2790, 3529, 4379, 5090
USSR, 1576, 2675, 2677, 2705-2706, 2712, 2721, 6090
Yugoslavia, 2357-2358
Working conditions, 692, 4491, 4499, 4573, 4608, 4693, 4894, 4911, 4916, 4928, 4936, 4943, 4963, 4981, 4988-4989, 4992, 5110
France, 4913, 4953
Germany FR, 4950
Hungary, 4955
Norway, 4941
Scandinavia, 4909
USSR, 4971, 4984
Working place, 4935, 4942, 4945
Working time, 4923, 4929, 4931, 4943, 4965, 4975, 4983
Writers, 2263
Young workers, 4734, 4863, 4951
Germany FR, 5089
Hungary, 4866
USSR, 4793, 4801, 4804
Youth, 838, 1226, 1287, 1306, 1308, 1453, 1464, 1470, 1893, 1919, 2179, 2274, 3036-3038, 3042-3044, 3047, 3051, 3053-3054, 3057-3059, 3062-3065, 4759, 5801, 5896
France, 3012
Germany FR, 3030, 3056
India, 2474
Israel, 1480, 3040
Japan, 1547
Spain, 5353
Taiwan, 3716
USA, 1480, 5803, 5813
USSR, 1608, 1908
Youth employment, Belgium, 4750
USA, 4733
Youth organizations, 3041, 3052
USSR, 3045
Youth unemployment, 4740-4741, 4748, 4752, 4760
France, 4744
Germany FR, 4761, 4763
Sweden, 4749
USA, 4743
Znanieckie, Florian, 285
Zoroastrianism, 1717

INDEX DES MATIÈRES

198, 232, 972, 974, 976, 978, 2624, 2929, 4776, 4781, 4876
Absentéisme 4934, 4998, 5005, 5009
   France, 5002
Accès à l'éducation
   Europe occidentale, 2332
Accidents 3217, 3856
Accomplissement 384, 812, 2289
Accroissement de population
   Mexique, 3142
Acculturation 1439
   Espagne, 1436
   Hawaï, 1425
Acculturation des immigrants
   Canada, 3867
Accumulation du capital 4436
Acquisition de connaissances 690, 773, 790, 794, 796-797, 803-804, 819, 827, 841, 2082, 2976
Acquisition de rôle 1039
Action 281, 297, 343, 786, 788-789, 805, 816, 853, 864, 1179, 1187, 1238, 1271, 2595
Action sociale 757, 852, 999, 1561, 2235, 6044, 6075, 6102
   Royaume-Uni, 5998
Actionalisme 281, 297
Activité militante 2542
Activité sociale *voir* Action sociale
Activités ludiques 2046, 5362, 5364
Adams, Henry Carter, 13
Adaptation sociale 702, 1515, 1568
Adhérents au parti
   Finlande, 5050
Administration coloniale 5565
Administration de l'enseignement 2346, 2348, 2354
Administration de la justice 5544, 5866
   États-Unis, 5546
   Inde, 5547
Administration locale 2765, 4310
   États-Unis, 3701, 3991, 5298-5299, 5560, 5562, 5567
   France, 4030, 5561
   Inde, 4149, 4161
   Japon, 5563, 5568
   Royaume-Uni, 5566
   Suède, 5564
Administration publique 62, 1114, 5551, 5558-5559, 6085
   Hongrie, 5554
Administration scolaire 2420
Adolescence 3032, 3048-3049, 3060
   Canada, 3018

Adolescents 686, 2289, 3033-3035, 3039, 3050
   Canada, 1462
   États-Unis, 3365
Adoption d'enfant 3480, 3499
   États-Unis, 3461
Adorno, Theodor W., 317, 319, 322, 2219
Affiliation politique 5636, 5649
Affiliation religieuse 1912, 1915, 1938
   États-Unis, 3378
   Israël, 1937
Âge 3005
Âge adulte 1532, 3066
Agression 942-945, 947, 949-951, 953, 955, 3971
Agressivité 941, 946, 948, 954, 956-957, 1560, 5111
Agriculteurs
   Canada, 1575
   URSS, 4039
   Yougoslavie, 4051, 4085, 4122
Agriculture 4621, 4894
   France, 4635
Agriexploitation
   Mexique, 4038
Agriexploitation collective
   URSS, 4633
   Yougoslavie, 4648
Aide à l'enfance 1169, 3468, 6111, 6122, 6155
   États-Unis, 6134
   Inde, 6123
Aide aux gens âgés 6106, 6112, 6115, 6124
   États-Unis, 6132
   France, 6108
   Pays-Bas, 6127
Aires culturelles
   États-Unis, 1295
   Mexique, 1302
Alcoolisme 842, 5795, 5802, 5804, 5807, 5814, 5816
   Allemagne, 5821
   États-Unis, 5803, 5813, 5822
   Royaume-Uni, 5819
   Suisse, 5826
Aliénation 889, 1151, 1514, 1536, 1539, 1578-1579, 1589, 1594, 3373, 4998, 5355
   Afrique du Sud, 1214
Alimentation 5758
   Tchécoslovaquie, 5774
Allaitement 5772
Allocations familiales 6119
   Canada, 6107
   États-Unis, 6121, 6128

Index des matières

France, 6125
Alphabétisation 2488, 2499, 2518
   Amérique latine, 2492
   Canada, 2507
   Espagne, 2503
   Guadeloupe, 2506
   Inde, 2511
Alphabétisation fonctionnelle
   Iran, 2493
Althusser, Louis, 383, 2659
Altruisme 911, 916, 918, 923, 927
Aménagement du temps de travail 4907
Aménagement urbain 4236, 4302, 4310, 4325, 4341, 4378, 4399, 4403, 4597
   Brésil, 4219
   Colombie, 4293
   États-Unis, 4351, 4365
   France, 4305
   Inde, 4345
   Mexique, 4272
   URSS, 4235
Amitié 917, 925, 930, 933, 997, 3103
Amour 922, 931, 3057
Analphabétisme
   Amérique latine, 2514
   États-Unis, 2510
   pays développés, 2513
Analyse causale 74
Analyse comparative 429, 446, 461, 1448, 2844
Analyse contextuelle 414
Analyse d'enquête 405
Analyse de contenu 432, 439, 450, 457, 471, 2077, 2151
Analyse de données 410-411, 433, 448, 465, 558
Analyse de groupe 983, 998
Analyse de motivation 2524
Analyse de régression 544, 557, 570, 584-585, 4481
Analyse de réseau 417, 426, 438, 614, 1066
Analyse de structure latente 617
Analyse de systèmes 404, 416, 418-420, 423, 452
Analyse de variance 537, 546, 556, 576, 4480
Analyse diachronique 601
Analyse différentielle 458
Analyse factorielle 536, 563-564, 577, 586
Analyse fonctionnelle 358
Analyse hiérarchique 619, 926, 1240
Analyse historique 442, 450
Analyse multivariée 449, 467, 5659
Analyse organisationnelle 606, 1050-1052, 1056, 1062, 1066, 4528, 5939, 6254
Analyse par cohorte 434, 3437
Analyse par grappe 421
Analyse qualitative 422, 435, 440, 456, 463
Analyse sociologique 413
Analyse statistique 527, 534, 558, 562, 578-581, 591
Analyse structurale 430, 2833
Analyse transculturelle 441, 640

Analyse transnationale 436, 2529, 5058
Anarchie 5466
Angoisse 676, 778, 823, 861, 2681
Animaux 2914
Animisme
   Taïwan, 1732
Anomie 1494, 1519, 4469
Anonymat 694
Anormal 1496
Anthropologie sociale 1277
Anthropologues 99
Antisémitisme 3731
   Allemagne, 3763
   États-Unis, 3725, 3735, 3778
   Royaume-Uni, 3749
Apartheid 3761
   Afrique du Sud, 3740
Appartenance au groupe 936, 1042, 1829
Apprentis 2523
Apprentissage 5056
Arbitrage 5288
   États-Unis, 5305
Arbitrage forcé 5292
Architecture 2264, 5365
Argent 3430, 4669
Aristocratie 2723
   États-Unis, 3314
   France, 5472
Armée 1037, 1634, 5717
   États-Unis, 5696, 5698
   Pays-Bas, 5701
Armes nucléaires 5741
Art 1862, 2217-2218, 2224, 2226, 2232, 2234-2235, 4585
   France, 2236
   Japan, 2231
Art populaire 2277
Articles 229, 231
Artistes 2227
Arts du spectacle 2272, 5366
Arts graphiques 2265
Arts libéraux
   Royaume-Uni, 2225
Ascétisme 1896
Asiles
   États-Unis, 6227
Aspirations 842, 847
Assimilation culturelle 1412
Assimilation des immigrants 3817, 3852, 3873
   Belgique, 3860
   Canada, 1705, 3840, 3867
   États-Unis, 3505, 3683, 3696, 3844, 3850, 3864, 3871, 3880
   France, 3813, 3849
   Israël, 3674, 3869, 3872, 5695
   Royaume-Uni, 3821, 3856
Associations 1067, 2542
   Espagne, 1072
   France, 1068
Assurance maladie
   Allemagne RF, 6120
Assurance-chômage

Royaume-Uni, 6116
Assurances
    États-Unis, 4670
Astrologie 1700
Athéisme 1876
Attentes 352, 774
Attention 824
Attention à soi 677, 705, 711
Attitude envers le travail 4790, 4859, 4919, 4926-4927, 4934, 4937, 4944, 4947, 4949, 4951, 4954, 4966, 4973, 4977, 4991, 5097
    États-Unis, 4961, 4969
    Japon, 4948, 4969
    Nouvelle-Zélande, 4958
    URSS, 4987
Attitudes 870, 1172-1173, 1176, 1178-1179, 1182-1185, 1189-1191, 1196-1197, 1199, 1237, 1577, 2090, 3415, 5112
    États-Unis, 3304
    Israël, 3040
    Japon, 5122
    Pays-Bas, 6178
Attitudes collectives 538
Attitudes politiques 5662
    Inde, 5647
    Suède, 5659
    Venezuela, 5620
Attitudes raciales 3745
    Afrique du Sud, 3760
    États-Unis, 3737, 3744, 3762, 3781
Attraction interpersonnelle 902, 919-921, 924, 928-929, 932, 1134
Authoritarisme
    États-Unis, 1215
Autogestion 4535, 4542, 4548-4549, 4552-4553, 6099
    Yougoslavie, 1077, 4085, 4414, 4550, 4563, 5271, 5312, 5316, 5404
Automation 2683
Automobiles
    États-Unis, 4619
Autoritarisme 1211, 1218, 2670, 5455
    Afrique du Sud, 1214, 3780
Autorité 680, 940, 1037, 1136, 1140, 3555, 5456
Autorités religieuses 1835
Avocats 5125
Avortement 3340
    États-Unis, 3299, 3304, 3306-3307, 3334
    France, 3308, 3318
    Inde, 3303
    Israël, 3341
    Japon, 3299
    Pays-Bas, 3293
    Philippines, 3309
    Thaïlande, 3327
Baisse de la fécondité 3236, 3291
    Costa Rica, 3233
    Sri Lanka, 3246
Bandes 1521
Banque de données

Royaume-Uni, 497
URSS, 200
Banques 4668
Banques de données
    Amérique latine, 202
Behaviorisme 223, 326
Bernstein 2282
Besoins 733, 777, 780-782, 817, 822, 838, 849-853, 857-858, 862, 876-877, 881-882, 4729
Besoins alimentaires 5778
    Inde, 2612
Besoins d'éducation 2372
Besoins de logement 4372, 4400
    Afrique, 4362
    Australie, 4290
    États-Unis, 4273
    Turquie, 4206
    Yougoslavie, 4401
Besoins fondamentaux 4762, 4766, 4782
    Kénya, 5770
    Singapour, 4755
    Tunisie, 5784
Bibliographies 2442, 4857
    Argentine, 3150
Bibliothécaires
    États-Unis, 203
Bibliothèques 5378
    États-Unis, 201
Bidonvilles 4377
    Amérique latine, 4405
    Bahamas, 4258
    Brésil, 4346
    Colombie, 4280
    États-Unis, 4247
    Inde, 4330, 4369
    Venezuela, 4280
Bien-être 2724, 4471-4472, 4480, 4484, 4494, 4502, 4511, 4513
    Italie, 3491
Biens culturels 2212
Bilinguisme 2084, 2109
    Afrique, 2259
    Belgique, 3699
    Canada, 2381
    Inde, 2120
    Tunisie, 2121
Biographies 219, 221, 223, 2954
    États-Unis, 215
Biologie humaine 2995, 2997-2998, 3001
Biologie sociale 6, 22, 1628
Blancs 3734
    États-Unis, 683, 3781
Blau, Peter M., 2589, 5060
Bonheur 848, 3006
Bouddhisme 658, 1707, 1723, 1726, 1764, 1766, 1774
    États-Unis, 1768
Bouddhsime
    Royaume-Uni, 1762
Bourdieu, Pierre, 2
Bourgeoisie 1757, 2698, 2723, 5084

Canada, 2708
France, 2690, 2707
Brahmanisme 1726, 1765
Brass, William, 3276
Braudel, Fernand, 2793
Bruit 3971
Budget temps 1600, 4959-4960, 4970
    Costa Rica, 4962
    États-Unis, 4929
    France, 4930, 4946
    Hongrie, 4918
    Pologne, 4915
    URSS, 4968, 4971, 4979
Bureaucratie 1076, 1091, 1096, 1099, 1107-1109, 1114, 1121, 1123, 1125, 1140, 5019, 5456, 5485
    Allemagne RF, 1073, 1080
    Asie du Sud, 1119
    Indonésie, 1100
    pays arabes, 1081
    Thaïlande, 1095, 1100
Bureaucratisation 1127, 1132
Burt, Cyril, 830
Buveurs 2473, 5798
Cadres 4525, 4558, 5011, 5107, 5110, 5113-5114, 5121
    Allemagne RF, 5117
    États-Unis, 5119, 5123
    France, 5108
    Italie, 5124
    Japon, 5122
    Pérou, 5123
    Royaume-Uni, 5118
Cadres moyens
    Royaume-Uni, 5120
Cadres supérieurs
    États-Unis, 4978
    France, 5115
Caillois, Roger, 807
Calcul matriciel 521-522, 524
Campagne électorale
    États-Unis, 5670, 5677
Cancer 3188, 3194-3196, 3203
Capitalisme 1211, 1262, 1513, 1769, 1905, 2043, 2793, 2878, 3047, 4425, 4429, 4448, 4454-4455, 4458-4459, 4462-4463, 4629, 4703
    Afrique méridionale, 4431
    Amérique latine, 4427
    Espagne, 4044
    pays en développement, 4439
    Royaume-Uni, 4441
Capitalisme d'État
    Allemagne RF, 133
Caractère 755
Carnaval 2280
Castells, Manuel, 4260, 4287, 4318
Castes
    Inde, 2633, 2637-2639, 2641, 2643-2646, 3550
Catastrophes 4205
Catholicisme 1680, 1751, 1755

Pays-Bas, 1722
Pologne, 1758
Catholiques
    Canada, 3261
    États-Unis, 1735
    Irlande, 3243
Causalité 350, 365, 368, 371, 566
Causes de décès 3217, 3219
    Canada, 3212
Célibat 3374
Censure
    États-Unis, 5526
Centres de recherche 145, 480, 1047
    Belgique, 3530
Chamanisme
    Corée, 1695
    Corée R, 1697
Chances d'éducation 2327, 2369, 2385, 3613
    Allemagne RF, 2383
    États-Unis, 2318, 2339, 2390
    Paraguay, 2401
Chances d'obtenir un emploi
    États-Unis, 2622, 2922, 2973, 3724, 4766, 4769
    Inde, 2922
Changement culturel 1419, 2174, 4595
    Afrique, 1431
    Asie du Sud-Est, 5395
    Chine, 1415
    Italie, 4024
    Japon, 1438
Changement d'attitude 937, 1174, 1177, 1188, 1193, 1195, 1198, 3050, 5950
Changement d'opinion 1241
Changement d'organisation 1082-1083, 1089, 1094, 1104-1105, 1111, 1113-1114, 1120, 1124, 1126, 1128, 4564
    Suède, 1078
Changement économique
    France, 1622
Changement social 227, 1417, 1468, 1658, 1785, 2136, 2797, 2815, 2822, 2827, 2832-2833, 2844, 2854-2856, 2859, 2863-2864, 2868-2869, 2872, 3050, 3240, 3597, 3974, 4410, 4605, 5706, 5771, 5859
    Afrique au sud du Sahara, 3253
    Afrique du Sud, 2820
    Allemagne, 2789
    Allemagne RF, 2586
    Amérique latine, 1660
    Brésil, 2279, 2688
    Canada, 2849
    Chine, 2847
    Colombie, 2829
    Espagne, 2834
    États-Unis, 2858, 2871, 2883, 3622, 4619
    Europe, 1660
    France, 4091
    Inde, 2393, 2637, 2824, 3483
    Indonésie, 1742
    Irak, 6045

Iran, 2840
Japon, 2587
Koweit, 2862
Mexique, 5549
pays arabes, 2816
Pologne, 1816
Royaume-Uni, 2882
URSS, 2567, 3903
Viet-Nam, 2893
Changement technologique 3927, 4583, 4592, 4595, 4601, 4610, 4613, 4756
Chine, 4576
États-Unis, 4607
France, 4584
Charisme 1135, 1138, 1141, 1803, 1826
Châtiment 5846, 5860-5861, 5892-5893, 5904-5905, 5917, 5934, 5940, 5994
États-Unis, 5872
Europe, 5992
France, 5914
Chercheurs 49, 86, 101, 178
Espagne, 83
Italie, 78
Choix 836
Choix collectif 1267, 1273
Choix d'une profession 3066, 3784, 5034, 5036, 6241, 6243
États-Unis, 5048
France, 5054, 5062
Choix du conjoint 3399, 3409, 3420, 3439, 3446
Espagne, 3428
États-Unis, 3450
Iran, 3441
Choix social *voir* Choix collectif
Chômage 4460, 4751, 4753, 4756, 5656
Allemagne, 4754
Allemagne RF, 4827
États-Unis, 482, 4739
France, 4758
Chômage déguisé
pays en développement, 4736
Chômage des jeunes 4740-4741, 4748, 4752, 4760
Allemagne RF, 4761, 4763
États-Unis, 4743
France, 4744
Suède, 4749
Chômage dġuisé
Argentine, 4735
Chomâge structurel 4738
Chômeurs 4734, 4746
Allemagne RF, 4761
France, 4731
Pays-Bas, 4747
Suède, 4745
Christianisme 658, 1617, 1720, 1728, 1744, 1747, 1752, 1757, 1760, 1769, 1776, 1779, 1784, 1787
Afrique, 1715, 1763
États-Unis, 1793
Europe, 1721

Japon, 1719, 1794
Taïwan, 1732
Zimbabwe, 1712
Cinéma 2156
Afrique, 2148
Allemagne, 2147
France, 2181, 2210
Royaume-Uni, 2189
Citations 199
Citoyenneté 3979
Canada, 3983
Civilisation
États-Unis, 1323, 1349
Maya, 1302
Royaume-Uni, 1301
Classe dirigeante 2761
Italie, 2740
Liberia, 2745
Martinique, 3685
pays arabes, 2749
Pérou, 2739
Classe inférieure
Japon, 4300
Classe moyenne 2657, 2660
Danemark, 2652
Égypte, 3484
États-Unis, 2685, 3529
Mexique, 2695
Pérou, 3586
Zambie, 2701
Zimbabwe, 2697
Classe ouvrière
Hongrie, 2684
Classe ouvrière 1587, 1618, 1884, 2649-2650, 2663-2664, 2669-2670, 2682-2683, 2691-2692, 2714, 2720, 2890, 3594, 4949
Amérique latine, 2722
Brésil, 2688
Canada, 2699, 2703
États-Unis, 2790, 3529, 4379, 5090
France, 2678, 3456
Iran, 3230
Royaume-Uni, 2686, 2715, 4698
URSS, 1576, 2675, 2677, 2705-2706, 2712, 2721, 6090
Yougoslavie, 2357
Classes sociales 822, 840, 935, 1085, 2284, 2655, 2659, 2665-2666, 2674, 2681, 2702, 2711, 2718, 2742, 3387, 3416, 3563, 4454, 4457, 5281, 5450, 5728, 5764, 5861, 6230
Afrique du Sud, 3765
Bangladesh, 2676
Canada, 2671, 2673, 5653
Danemark, 5479
Espagne, 2668, 2700
États-Unis, 1378, 2658, 2662, 2713, 3744, 5674, 5719
Europe, 2694
France, 1935, 4697, 5668
Ghana, 5211
Inde, 2645-2646, 3721

Index des matières

Irak, 2653
Mexique, 2687
Nigeria, 3700
Royaume-Uni, 2246, 2347, 2713
Yougoslavie, 2566
Classification 367, 382
Clergé 1833, 1836-1837, 3413
Royaume-Uni, 1838
Cléricalisme
France, 1890
Clubs 5378
Coalitions 967, 970
Coalitions politiques
États-Unis, 5677
Codes juridiques 1655
Coexistence pacifique 5739
Cognition 785, 791, 795, 809, 820, 826, 843, 860, 863, 871, 879, 1956, 2600, 3029
Cognition sociale 1189
Cohésion du groupe 903
Collectifs de production 594, 4881, 5201, 5209, 5213, 5217
Collectivisme 678
Collectivité 3984, 4003, 4007, 4012
Espagne, 2668
Collectivités rurales
Allemagne, 4132
Caraïbes, 4050
États-Unis, 2927, 4034
France, 4030, 4053
Ghana, 4156
Inde, 4161
Irlande, 4074
pays méditerranéens, 4169
Collectivités urbaines 4291
États-Unis, 4220
Colonialisme 2079
Comités d'entreprise
France, 5242
Zambie, 5195
Communauté scientifique 152, 157
Communautés religieuses 1806, 1813
Communication 183, 669, 892, 943, 1276, 1286, 1304, 1410, 2036, 2042-2044, 2050, 2053, 2055, 2057-2058, 2061-2062, 2065, 2067-2069, 2083, 4496
Allemagne RF, 5047
Italie, 2171
Communication dans l'entreprise 4519, 4543, 4551, 4554, 4559, 4566
Communication de masse 2155, 2164, 2168, 2174, 2177, 2185, 2192, 2195, 2203-2204, 2213, 5343
Équateur, 2161
Japon, 2138
Communication interpersonnelle 2037-2038, 2064, 3487, 3498
Communication non-verbale 2074, 2097, 2114
Communication politique 5627, 5637
Communisme 736, 759, 1253, 5429, 5439, 5447
URSS, 5440

Comportement 458, 1175, 1180-1181, 1186-1187, 1192, 1194, 1199, 2997, 3196
Comportement antisocial 1561
Comportement collectif 1271
France, 5282
Comportement de l'étudiant 2422, 2449, 2451, 2457, 2475, 2950
Allemagne RF, 2460, 2484
États-Unis, 2424, 2477
France, 2434
Grèce, 2471
Inde, 2431
Italie, 2476
Comportement de l'organisation 45, 1075, 1090, 1092-1093, 1098, 1101, 1103, 1106, 1110, 1115, 1117-1118, 1129, 1131, 4544, 6216
États-Unis, 1200, 5297
Comportement de masse 1270, 1274
Comportement du comsommateur 2130, 4652, 4655, 4659
Comportement du consommateur 4658
États-Unis, 4651
Norvège, 4656
Comportement du groupe 1030, 1033, 1035, 1166, 1191
Comportement économique 774, 4653
États-Unis, 4657
Comportement électoral 5678, 5681, 5683
Australie, 5672
Canada, 2611, 2709
États-Unis, 1923, 3994, 5674, 5679, 5685
France, 5673
Italie, 5680
Japon, 1573, 5675
Comportement judiciaire
États-Unis, 5545
Comportement politique 767, 1540, 1895, 1925, 1930, 5548, 5630, 5641, 5666, 5750
Allemagne RF, 5625
Brésil, 2786
France, 4840, 5668
Comportement religieux 502, 1676, 1884-1885, 1891, 1893-1895, 1902, 1904
Canada, 1901
Italie, 1899
Comportement sexuel 945, 955, 3352, 3356, 3384, 3387, 6151
États-Unis, 3365, 3378
Comportement verbal 2070, 2083, 2089, 2108, 2112, 2122, 3487
Composition de la population 3175
Yougoslavie, 3118
Comte, Auguste, 303, 1991
Concentration économique 4524
URSS, 4561
Concentration urbaine
Argentine, 4213
Pérou, 3152
Conception de soi 667-668, 670, 674, 682,

371

684, 695, 699-700, 703-704, 707, 710, 908, 1204, 3097, 5063
Concepts 360, 366, 370-371, 1351, 2617, 2733, 4470, 5421, 5459, 5628, 5655, 6075, 6082
Conceptualisation 1345
Concurrence 741, 4662, 4665
Condamnation pénale 3790, 5935, 5988
   États-Unis, 5880, 5890, 5911
Conditions de logement 4237
   Costa Rica, 4246
   États-Unis, 2375, 4247
   France, 3070, 3823, 4195, 4363, 4786
   Hong Kong, 4407
Conditions de travail 692, 4491, 4499, 4573, 4608, 4693, 4894, 4911, 4916, 4928, 4936, 4943, 4963, 4981, 4988-4989, 4992, 5110
   Allemagne RF, 4950
   France, 4913, 4953
   Hongrie, 4955
   Norvège, 4941
   Scandinavie, 4909
   URSS, 4971, 4984
Conditions sociales
   Afrique du Sud, 1329
   Canada, 1316, 1333
   Haïti, 1385
Conférences 175
Conflit conjugal 907, 3397
Conflits 963-964, 975, 980, 5280
Conflits de classe 2648, 2689
   Afrique du Sud, 2661
   États-Unis, 4124
   Malaisie, 3750
Conflits de rôles 1157, 1169, 5538, 5648
Conflits du travail 5128, 5257, 5262, 5268, 5275, 5277-5278, 5280
   Allemagne RF, 5254
   États-Unis, 5227, 5305
   France, 5255, 5282
   Hong Kong, 5194
   Inde, 5253
   Italie, 5259
   Royaume-Uni, 5264
   Turquie, 5285
Conflits internationaux 2648, 5736, 5738
Conflits interpersonnels 954
Conflits politiques 4464
Conflits raciaux
   États-Unis, 3753
   France, 3839
   Royaume-Uni, 3839
Conformité au groupe 1037
Conformité sociale 1591
Congé-éducation
   Canada, 5053
Congrégations 1837
Congrès 172-174, 177
   Amérique latine, 114
   Finlande, 176
   URSS, 176

Congruence du statut 2728, 4391
Conjoncture démographique 572, 3132, 3140, 3158
   Allemagne RF, 3122
   Argentine, 3150
   Espagne, 3114
   États-Unis, 3141
   Europe, 2577
   îles du Pacifique FR, 3161
   Israël, 3134
   Malaisie, 3139
   pays en développement, 3116
   République dominicaine, 3153
   Tchécoslovaquie, 3170
   URSS, 3117, 3137
   Yémen, 3156
Connaissance 283, 356, 1130, 1949, 1956-1957, 1999
Conscience collective 1269
Conscience de classe 2672
   Canada, 2680, 2709
Conscience nationale 2091, 5732
   URSS, 1382
Conscience sociale 1225, 1447, 1505, 1523, 1541, 1588, 1657, 2232, 3036
   Allemagne RF, 5093
   Europe, 2694
Conseils ouvriers 5220
Consensus 1234, 5420
Conservatisme 1318, 5434, 5438, 5455
   Allemagne RF, 5441
Consommation 58, 2125, 4654, 4656, 4659
Consommation culturelle 2160
Constitution 5499
   URSS, 5489, 5498, 5508, 5515
Contestation religieuse 1801
Contestation sociale 962, 1513, 1530, 1540, 2049, 6191
   Canada, 1575
   Chine, 1520
   États-Unis, 2477, 3031, 5598, 5703
   France, 1543, 1562
   Sri Lanka, 3031
Contraception 3302, 3310, 3315
   États-Unis, 3299
   France, 3321
   Japon, 3299
   Paraguay, 3323
   Yémen, 3156
Contrat de travail 4908, 4917, 4921, 4980
   RD allemande, 4986
Contre-culture 1296, 1308
Contremaîtres 5111
   États-Unis, 5112, 5175
Contrôle bureaucratique 1013, 1079, 1083-1085, 1087, 1097
Conventions collectives
   Autriche, 4838
   Hongrie, 5321
   Italie, 5173
   Royaume-Uni, 5238
Conversion religieuse 1892

Coopération scientifique 164
  pays du CAEM, 149
Coopératives
  Allemagne RF, 4546
  Bolivie, 4567
Coopératives agricoles 4649
  Canada, 4618
  Hongrie, 4646
  Israël, 4644
  Sierra Leone, 4426
  Turquie, 4617
Coopératives de production 5320
Corporatisme 5232
  Canada, 5221
Corrélation 566, 569, 584
Corruption politique 5621
Coup d'État 5693
Covariance 589, 596
Création artistique 2215-2216, 2222, 2229, 2238, 2254
Créativité 787, 792, 837, 847, 869, 2215
Crèches
  États-Unis, 2414
  Venezuela, 2410
Criminologie 237, 1375, 5847, 5854, 5862, 5879, 5910, 5953, 5957, 5959, 5964, 5967-5968, 5991, 5993
  Canada, 5867
Critique littéraire 2241, 2256
Croissance démographique 3151, 3173-3174, 3396, 3617
  Cameroun, 3133
  Égypte, 3179
  Inde, 3168
  Pérou, 3152
Croissance économique 4464, 4467
  Amérique latine, 5516
  Japon, 2395
Croissance urbaine 4383
  Algérie, 4347
  France, 4223, 4242
  Inde, 4360
  Italie, 4222, 4232
  Sénégal, 4233
  Tunisie, 4294
Croyance 704, 1173, 1225, 1238, 1700, 1854, 2628
Culin, Stewart, 3803
Cultes 1820, 1840-1842, 1849, 1853
  États-Unis, 1852
Culture 1244, 1280, 1285-1287, 1289, 1304, 1327, 1330, 1337, 1343-1345, 1368, 1377, 1395, 1403-1404, 1443, 1747, 1752, 2033, 2878, 4574, 4629, 5429
  Afrique, 1393
  Amérique latine, 1406
  Australie, 1394
  Brésil, 1364
  Chine, 1391
  États-Unis, 1323
  Hongrie, 1024
  Inde, 1389

Irlande, 1363
Italie, 2260
Japon, 2231
Mexique, 3689
Mongolie RP, 1341
URSS, 1346
Culture de classe 895
Culture de masse 2265, 2391
Culture et personnalité 1310
  Guadeloupe, 1361
  Martinique, 1361
Culture politique 5638, 5643, 5660
  Allemagne, 5635
  Canada, 5653
  États-Unis, 5651
  Maroc, 5665
  Taïwan, 3716
  Tunisie, 5665
Culture populaire
  Royaume-Uni, 4077
Culture socialiste 1324, 1338, 1354, 1360
Culture traditionnelle 1417
Curriculum 79, 84, 100, 102, 110, 533, 2535, 2546, 2551, 5746
  Canada, 2537
Cybernétique 452, 600, 602
Cycle de vie 3260
Däniken, Erich von, 312
Darwin, Charles, 245, 248
Débilité mentale 3204
Décentralisation
  Yougoslavie, 1077
Décision 835, 1034
Décision statistique 5681
Déduction 348
Délégués du personnel 5231
Délinquance 1671, 2951, 5827, 5840, 5851, 5863, 5897-5898, 5906, 5908-5909, 5927, 5941, 5945, 5963, 5981, 5989
  Australie, 5849
  États-Unis, 3094, 5841, 5865, 5924, 5936
  Japon, 5946
  RD allemande, 5969
  Royaume-Uni, 5923
  URSS, 5974
Délinquance juvénile 5852, 5859, 5866, 5887, 5913, 5933, 5944, 5948, 5955
  Allemagne RF, 5829
  Canada, 5915
  Espagne, 5868
  États-Unis, 5869, 5962, 5975, 5984, 5986
  Europe orientale, 5949
  Hongrie, 5932
  Italie, 5837
Délinquants 5845
  États-Unis, 5874
Délits 5833, 5848, 5856, 5884, 5902, 5931, 5939, 5943, 5945, 5954, 5960, 5977, 5987
  États-Unis, 5836, 5850, 5877, 5925, 5978, 5983
  Europe, 5992

Inde, 5838
Royaume-Uni, 5985
Demandeurs d'emploi 4737, 4757
Démocratie 76, 129, 5463-5465, 5467-5468, 5470-5471, 5473
Démocratisation 2432, 5721
Démographie 2901, 2903, 2905, 2910
Canada, 2899, 2902
Espagne, 2909
URSS, 2911
Densité de population
Australie, 3126
Déontologie 1612
États-Unis, 472
Dépeuplement
Brésil, 3143
Europe, 3123
France, 3176
Italie, 3136
URSS, 3124
Déscolarisation
Guinée-Bissau, 2329
Désintégration
Pologne, 3501
Désintégration familiale
Japon, 3573
Désorganisation sociale 5756
Despotisme 5469
Déterminisme social 2568, 2575
Développement agricole 4624, 4628
Irlande, 4640
Développement cognitif 776, 824, 833, 2035
Développement culturel 208, 1411, 1421, 2682, 5340
Italie, 2693
Développement de l'éducation
Autriche, 2338
Égypte, 2341
Développement de l'enfant 691, 827-828, 1574, 3007, 3011, 3015, 3022-3024, 3027, 3746
Inde, 3019
Pérou, 3025
Développement de la personnalité 666, 713, 715, 719, 721, 724-726, 728, 734, 737, 740-741, 743-744, 746-749, 752-753, 756, 758-760, 764-766, 768-770, 812, 1354, 1390, 1392, 1441, 1469, 1476, 1525, 2238, 2861, 4296, 4892, 5213, 5351, 5444
RD allemande, 4695
Développement des collectivités 3986, 3989, 4005, 4010, 4603
Belgique, 3996
Canada, 3805
États-Unis, 3988, 3992, 3995, 3999, 4001, 4009
France, 4002
Japon, 4011
Mexique, 3990
Nigeria, 4008
Philippines, 4000

Thaïlande, 3985
URSS, 4187
Venezuela, 5360
Yougoslavie, 3997-3998, 4004
Développement économique 3130, 3173, 3645, 4465, 5058
Canada, 4415
Chine, 2847
Espagne, 3796
Haïti, 2821
Iran, 3148
Développement économique et social 5772
Hongrie, 2875
Développement industriel 4643
Pérou, 2739
Développement intellectuel 2531
Développement moral 1635
Développement national 2887, 2889
Égypte, 2341
Israël, 1738
Développement politique
pays en développement, 5486
Développement régional
Amérique latine, 4192
Développement rural 4033, 4040, 4064, 4073, 4079, 4081, 4107, 4188
Afrique, 4025, 4170
Albanie, 4060
Amérique latine, 4178
Asie du Sud, 4110
Australie, 4178
Botswana, 4144
Brésil, 4129
Chine, 4103
Colombie, 4067, 4184
Côte d'Ivoire, 4063
États-Unis, 2133, 4109, 4168
Europe orientale, 4178
Extrême-Orient, 4020
France, 4092, 4177
Inde, 4013, 4046, 4062, 4076, 4130, 4138, 4149, 4159
Mexique, 4616
Nigeria, 4172
Pakistan, 4162
pays en développement, 4078
Philippines, 4042
Taïwan, 4114
Tanzanie, 3259, 4032, 4128, 4174
URSS, 2538, 4166, 4615
Uruguay, 3623, 4118
Yougoslavie, 4117
Zaïre, 3616
Développement social 18, 193, 782, 1264, 1384, 2575, 2819, 2825, 2831, 2835-2836, 2838, 2845, 2851-2852, 2861, 2866, 2870, 3044, 4191, 4614, 5437
Asie, 2846
Grèce, 3180
Haïti, 2821
pays en développement, 4575
URSS, 2409, 2675

Développement urbain 4204, 4240, 4271,
   4342, 4374, 4396
   Afrique, 4334
   Amérique latine, 4192, 4252
   Asie du Sud-Est, 4301
   Australie, 4386
   Équateur, 4252
   États-Unis, 4199-4200, 4269, 4323, 4333
   Europe orientale, 4319
   Inde, 4303
   Nigeria, 4137
   pays en développement, 4344
   Royaume-Uni, 4257, 4261, 4317
   URSS, 4211, 4239, 4296
Déviance 802, 905, 1493, 1504, 1517-1518,
   1531, 1538, 1545-1546, 1551, 1557,
   1559, 1566, 1569-1570, 1590, 1663,
   3695, 5666, 5697, 5811, 5981, 6010
Dialectes 2075
Dialectique 68, 255, 283, 301-302, 311, 323,
   328
Dictionnaires 204-207, 1857, 2300
Différence d'âge 3213
Différenciateur sémantique 2093
Différenciation de classes 2656
   Nigeria, 4098
Différenciation sexuelle 669, 688, 944, 2945,
   2951, 2953, 2965, 2974, 2976, 2990,
   3211, 4463, 5067
   Costa Rica, 2931
   États-Unis, 4716, 5562, 5983
Différenciation sociale 1598, 2621, 2692, 5744
   États-Unis, 2616
   Italie, 2604
   Kénya, 2596
Différentiation des rôles 1161
Diffusion de l'information 811, 2056
   Chine, 181
   France, 187
Diffusion de la culture
   Hongrie, 1434
Dimension de l'organisation 1112
Dimension de la famille 3475, 3544, 3553,
   3563, 4816
   Amérique latine, 5777
   Australie, 3457
   Corée R, 3458
   France, 3536
   Inde, 3344
   Irlande, 3476, 3572
Dimension du groupe 1022
Diplômés d'université 5067
   Espagne, 2463
   États-Unis, 2464, 4769
   pays socialistes, 2440
   Yougoslavie, 2487
Direction d'entreprise 4558, 4568
   États-Unis, 4560
Discrimination 1201
   États-Unis, 1200, 1208
Discrimination dans l'emploi 4772
   États-Unis, 4764, 4775, 4779

Discrimination raciale 3480, 3771, 3784,
   3790, 5070
   Afrique du Sud, 3785
   Canada, 3777
   États-Unis, 3719-3720, 3733, 3738, 3752,
      3757, 3759, 3772, 3782, 4226, 5172,
      5911
   Royaume-Uni, 3733
Discrimination sexuelle
   Inde, 2922
Discrimination sexuelle 108, 1886, 2929,
   2933, 2948, 2957, 2975, 4501, 5049,
   5070
   États-Unis, 2318, 2922, 2973, 3738
   Pays-Bas, 2935
Distance de rôle 1168
Divertissement 5366
Divination 1868
Division du travail 2593, 2600, 2629, 5071,
   5744, 6206
Divorce 3020, 3410, 3412-3413, 3442
   Amérique latine, 3408
   États-Unis, 3393, 3401, 3406, 3424, 3429
   France, 3427
   Tchécoslovaquie, 3453
   Yougoslavie, 3434
Doctrines religieuses 1861
Domination de classe
   Afrique, 2710
Données d'enquête 462, 496
   Royaume-Uni, 497
Données statistiques 535
Dot 3395, 3411
Droit 745, 1250, 1263, 1637, 1643,
   1647-1648, 1651, 1653, 1657, 1661,
   1664-1666, 1669-1671, 3473, 4462
   Afrique, 1668
   Amérique latine, 1660
   Europe, 1660
   Israël, 1937, 3341
   Japon, 1656
   pays en développement, 1639
Droit à l'éducation 5524
Droit civil
   États-Unis, 1636
Droit coutumier
   France, 1667
   Togo, 1672
Droit du travail 5159-5160, 5163
   Afrique du Sud, 5161
   Japon, 5139
   Sri Lanka, 5162
   Tchécoslovaquie, 5230
Droit matrimonial 3398
   Italie, 1888
Droit naturel 5734
Droit pénal 1556, 1663, 5926, 5940
   États-Unis, 1645
   Nigeria, 1638
   RD allemande, 5519
Droits de l'enfant 3008, 3028
Droits de l'homme 5517, 5521-5523, 5525

Droits de la femme 3629
    Allemagne RF, 3646
    États-Unis, 3600
    Grèce, 3637
Droits du citoyen
    États-Unis, 5520
    RD allemande, 5519
Déterminisme 287, 377
Duby, Georges, 1264
Durkheim, Émile, 44, 276, 291, 298, 307, 934, 1168, 1254, 1484, 1519, 1623, 1686, 1688, 4469, 4939, 5973
Dyade 921, 1018-1019, 2090, 2108, 2955
Dynamique culturelle
    Italie, 1424
Dynamique de groupe 985, 993
Dynamique de la population 3113, 3130, 3145, 3154, 3162
    Canada, 3155
    Iran, 3148
    Italie, 3131
    pays de l'OCDE, 3159
    pays du CAEM, 3177
    URSS, 3121
Ecclésiastiques 1832
    États-Unis, 1831
Échange d'information 178, 193, 1985
Échange social 2589
Échec 867
Échelle de Guttman 624
Échelle de Likert 623
Échelles d'attitude 620
Écodéveloppement 3940, 3961
École Chicago 268
École durkheimienne 330
École Frankfurt 259, 320
Écoles 2418
    États-Unis, 2412
    Royaume-Uni, 2415
Écoles maternelles
    France, 2408
Écoles primaires
    États-Unis, 2419
    Iran, 2405
Écoles privées
    Allemagne RF, 2411
Écoles rurales
    France, 2407
Écoles secondaires 2413
    États-Unis, 2543
    URSS, 2409
Écoles techniques
    Allemagne RF, 2406
Écologie 564, 3941, 3943, 3946, 3949-3951, 3953-3955, 3960
    Europe, 3956
    Pérou, 3664
Écologie humaine 1285, 3939, 3962, 4479
Économie de l'éducation 2306, 2454
    États-Unis, 2296
Économie de l'entreprise 4537
Économistes 76, 99

Écrivains 2263
Édition
    États-Unis, 2178
Éducation 205, 1623, 2283-2285, 2290, 2300-2304, 2312, 2314-2315, 2980, 5513
    Allemagne RF, 2294, 2334
    Canada, 3913
    Hongrie, 1024
    Tunisie, 2776
Éducation complémentaire
    Hongrie, 2509
Éducation de masse 3236
Éducation des adultes 2512, 2515
    Afrique occidentale, 2494
    États-Unis, 2490
    France, 2502
    Tanzanie, 2508
    Yougoslavie, 2501
Éducation des femmes 3608, 3613
    Colombie, 3591
    France, 3624
    Hongrie, 2142
    Inde, 3615
    Sierra Leone, 3256
Éducation des parents 2556
Éducation en matiére de population
    Inde, 3295
Éducation familiale 3540, 3547
    Hongrie, 1434
Éducation permanante
    Italie, 2498
    Japon, 2517
Éducation permanente 2495, 2500, 2504-2505, 2516
    États-Unis, 2491
Éducation politique 2521, 2524
Éducation préscolaire 2403, 2417
Éducation récurrente 2497
Éducation religieuse 2527
Éducation spéciale 2522
    France, 2526
Éducation syndicale 2489, 2519
    URSS, 2520
    Yougoslavie, 2501
Effet 369
Effets de groupe 560, 1038, 1045
Efficacité politique 5658
Égalitarisme 2620
Égalité de chances 2595, 2624, 3199
    États-Unis, 2339, 2622, 4766
    Europe occidentale, 2332
Égalité des sexes 1283, 2981
Égalité sociale 2628
    États-Unis, 2602
Église catholique 1800, 3712
    Amérique latine, 1819
    Brésil, 1907
    Canada, 1803
    États-Unis, 1811, 1815
    France, 1799
    Pologne, 1816

Église et État 1812, 1906, 1925, 1927, 1943
    Brésil, 1907
    Royaume-Uni, 1918
Églises protestantes
    États-Unis, 1924
Ego 658, 661, 666
Élections 5684
    Afrique noire, 5671
    Canada, 1671
    Royaume-Uni, 1671
Élèves 1902
    Inde, 5647
Élite 2733-2734, 2741, 2744, 2756, 2765, 5467
    Afrique, 2763
    Australie, 2757
    Canada, 2743
    États-Unis, 2747, 2757, 2771, 3991
    France, 2769, 2771, 4116
    Inde, 2766
    Israël, 2763
    Moyen-Orient, 2772
    Pakistan, 2746
    Philippines, 2773
    Royaume-Uni, 2768
    Trinité et Tobago, 2736
    Yougoslavie, 2738
Élite politique
    Indonésie, 5617
Émigrants
    Algérie, 3849
    Caraïbes, 3814
    Corée, 3257
    Europe, 3857
    Inde, 3836
    Italie, 3838, 3860
    Japon, 3255, 3881
    Maroc, 4864
    Mexique, 3833, 3865
    Portugal, 3873
    Yougoslavie, 3852
Émigration
    Afrique du Nord, 3819
    Chine, 3850
    Espagne, 3847
    États-Unis, 3879
    Grèce, 3871
    Italie, 3832, 4831
    Japon, 2048
    Pays-Bas, 3874
    Pologne, 3882
    Portugal, 3820
    Scandinavie, 3870
    Suède, 1409
    Tunisie, ;113835, 3861
    URSS, 3827
    Yémen, 3156
    Yougoslavie, 3854
Émotion 696, 793, 802, 818, 856
Emploi 3594, 4751, 4759, 4762
    Amérique latine, 5777
    Royaume-Uni, 3185

Singapour, 4755
Emploi des jeunes
    Belgique, 4750
    États-Unis, 4733
Employés 4927, 5105, 5187, 5198
    Finlande, 5106
    Hongrie, 4473
Employés de bureau 4938
Employeurs 5056
En-groupe 981, 1040, 1044
Endogamie 3445
    Royaume-Uni, 3438, 3443
    Soudan, 3426
Énergie 4605
Énergie nucléaire 1261, 4612
    France, 4581
Enfance 3013, 3021
    Canada, 3018
Enfants 384, 902, 904, 1280, 1448, 2068, 2109, 2207, 3009, 3016, 3020, 3540, 5338, 6230
    États-Unis, 2132, 2214
    France, 3012
    Tanzanie, 3014
    URSS, 1565
Enfants handicapés
    États-Unis, 3192
Engels, Friedrich, 260, 1641, 1673
Enquêtes 363, 498
    États-Unis, 495
Enquêtes par correspondance 509, 514
Enquêteurs 504, 513
Enseignants 1469, 2542, 2554-2555, 2559, 5010
    Canada, 2547
    États-Unis, 2543
    Inde, 2550
    Italie, 2541
    Pérou, 2536
    URSS, 2538
Enseignement 1, 93, 103, 2451, 2486, 2544, 2552
    Europe, 6049
    Japon, 87
Enseignement agricole
    États-Unis, 2525
Enseignement commercial 2528
Enseignement obligatoire
    France, 2356
Enseignement privé
    France, 2326
Enseignement professionnel 4748, 5077, 5080
    Hongrie, 5046
Enseignement public
    Allemagne, 2361
Enseignement secondaire
    Canada, 2416
    Sénégal, 2404
Enseignement supérieur 2423, 2429, 2432, 2437, 2441, 2443, 2452, 2459, 2479, 2482
    Afrique orientale, 116

Index des matières

Allemagne RF, 2467
Amérique du Nord, 2442
Canada, 2439
Espagne, 2458, 2465
États-Unis, 2425, 2445-2446, 2450, 2771, 5387
Europe occidentale, 2442
Europe orientale, 2456
France, 2470, 2771, 5109
Inde, 2455
Japon, 2430, 2466, 2468
Mexique, 2472
RD allemande, 2453
Royaume-Uni, 2436, 2470
Suède, 2470
URSS, 2450, 2454
Venezuela, 2428
Yougoslavie, 2483
Enseignement technique 2523
Entrepreneurs
    Allemagne, 4540
    Europe, 4527
Entreprises 4454, 4523, 4526, 4528, 4531-4534, 4544-4545, 4557, 4981, 5412
    Allemagne, 4536
    Chine, 4555
    France, 4521, 5108
    Italie, 4562
    Royaume-Uni, 4559
    URSS, 4530
Entreprises industrielles 2190, 4636
    États-Unis, 4629
    Royaume-Uni, 4625, 4629
    URSS, 4627
Entretiens 505-508, 510-512, 515, 906, 2150
Environnement 593, 649-650, 3000, 3109, 3938, 3941, 3944, 3949, 3952, 3959, 3963, 3965
    Espagne, 3947
    États-Unis, 3945
    Pays-Bas, 3948
Environnement physique 3957-3958, 3964
Épistémologie 263, 339, 353, 356, 363, 375, 381, 383, 388, 393, 1956, 1987, 4318
Épouse 1832, 3395, 3516, 5110
Équité *voir* Justice sociale
Ergonomie 4877, 4894, 4896, 4904, 4976
    Scandinavie, 4909
Esclavage
    Afrique, 2647
    Asie, 2647
    Brésil, 2640
    États-Unis, 2631-2632, 2634, 2642
Espace 460, 468, 2045
Espace urbain 4221
    Brésil, 4380
    France, 4197
Espacement des naissances
    Zaïre, 3294
Espérance de vie
    Belgique, 3228

Esthétique 2218-2219, 2239
    URSS, 2221, 2237
Estime de soi 669-671, 681, 686-687, 697-698, 702, 709, 717, 3061
Établissements humains 3924, 3972-3973, 3975, 3977, 3980
    Amérique latine, 3976
    Israël, 3978
État 1647, 3083, 5019, 5476-5477, 5480-5481, 5485, 5487-5488, 5490-5491, 5493-5494, 5496-5497, 5500, 5502-5503, 5506-5507, 5510-5511, 5514, 5728, 6198
    Amérique latine, 5516
    Danemark, 5479
    Europe, 5492
    Europe occidentale, 4591
    pays en développement, 5509
État providence 1069, 6011-6012, 6031, 6093
    Allemagne RF, 5997
    Canada, 6060
    États-Unis, 6002, 6060
    Norvège, 6057
    Royaume-Uni, 5995, 6030
    Suède, 6017, 6065, 6100
Éthique 49, 101, 498, 1235, 1457, 1603-1604, 1606-1607, 1609-1615, 1617, 1619, 1622, 1625, 1629-1630, 1661, 1677, 2806, 4583, 5737
    États-Unis, 1631
Éthique professionnelle *voir* Déontologie
Éthique protestante 1887
Ethnicité 697, 1021, 1771, 1782, 2019, 2924, 3652, 3672, 3674, 3678, 3681, 3683, 3690, 3712, 3871, 5651
    Canada, 3666, 3677, 3983
    États-Unis, 1378, 2140, 3665, 3675, 3682
    Inde, 3687
    Israël, 3711, 4644
    Italie, 3676
    Mexique, 2687
    Nigeria, 3700
    Pérou, 3664
    Royaume-Uni, 2096
    Sri Lanka, 3702
    Syrie, 3669
    Taïwan, 3716
Ethnocentrisme 1212
Ethnographie 1276-1277, 1613
Ethnopsychologie 799
Éthos 1627, 3672
Étiquetage 905, 911, 1566
    Japon, 5946
Étude de collectivité 478, 484, 490, 2794
    États-Unis, 486
Études soviétiques 145
Étudiants 664, 775, 867, 1157, 1469, 1488, 1886, 1891, 2447-2448, 2473, 2475, 2486, 2559, 3375, 5357, 5952, 6241
    Afrique du Sud, 1429, 3769
    Allemagne RF, 2406
    Brésil, 2462
    Canada, 2416, 5633

Index des matières

Chine, 1944
États-Unis, 2986, 3781
France, 2444
Inde, 2474
Japon, 372
Porto Rico, 1585
Royaume-Uni, 372, 2435
URSS, 1309, 2461, 2485
Étudiants étrangers 3855
Eugénisme 2999, 3726
Euthanasie 5950, 5980
Évaluation 135, 351, 354, 357, 374, 391-392, 394, 2315
Évaluation de soi 673, 679, 690
Évaluation des emplois 4765, 4774, 4780, 4783
Éventails des salaires 4516
Évolutionnisme 245, 248, 277, 1959
Examens
    États-Unis, 2355
Existentialisme 279
Exode des compétences 3812, 3816, 3855
    Inde, 3842
Exogamie 3394
    Royaume-Uni, 3438
Expérience religieuse 1860, 1865
Expérimentation 483, 488, 640, 1676
Explication 358, 402
Explication causale 343, 355, 377
Expression de soi 692, 708
Faim 5760
Faisceau de rôles 1164
Faits sociaux 387
Famille 104, 709, 725, 1161, 1164, 1502, 1683, 2136, 2906, 2961, 2968, 3021, 3057, 3282, 3455, 3462, 3469, 3471, 3473, 3482, 3502, 3520, 3524, 3530, 3538, 3564-3565, 3567-3568, 4594, 4610, 4753, 6119, 6157, 6230
    Asie, 3478
    Australie, 3490
    Autriche, 3521
    Brésil, 3534
    Canada, 3436, 3479, 3519, 6107
    Caraïbes, 3554
    Chine, 3465, 3558
    Égypte, 3484
    États-Unis, 1582, 3407, 3490, 3513, 3529, 3552, 3557
    France, 3368, 3456, 3562
    Inde, 3483, 3486
    Italie, 3466, 3491
    Japon, 3506
    Mexique, 3514, 4833
    Pérou, 3481
    URSS, 1621, 3496, 3566
Famille indivise 3549
    États-Unis, 3503
Famille monoparentale 3543
    États-Unis, 3571
    Japon, 3525
Famille nucléaire 3467

Famine, Sahel, 5769
Fanatisme 1213
Fascisme 5422
    Italie, 5432
Fécondité 1020, 2980, 3240, 3242, 3245, 3251, 3263, 3266-3267, 3269-3271, 3278-3280, 3282, 3447, 3528, 4110, 4811, 4845
    Afrique, 3234, 3273
    Afrique au sud du Sahara, 3253
    Allemagne RF, 3237, 3258
    Amérique latine, 3281
    Bolivie, 3255
    Canada, 3232, 3261
    Espagne, 3275
    États-Unis, 3235, 3244, 4812
    Fidji, 3285
    France, 3237-3238, 3254
    Inde, 3264, 3344
    Iran, 3230, 3250
    Irlande, 3243
    Japon, 3257
    Mexique, 3249
    Nigeria, 3231, 3268
    Pakistan, 3414
    pays de l'Ouest, 3247
    pays développés, 3277
    Sierra Leone, 3256
    Tanzanie, 3259
    Tchécoslovaquie, 3248
    Thaïlande, 3343, 3797
    Tunisie, 3276
Féminisme 3589, 3594, 3634
    Allemagne, 3614
    Espagne, 3601
    États-Unis, 3579, 3585, 3638
    France, 5225
    Italie, 3587, 3595
    Japon, 3625
Femmes 95, 152, 855, 2781, 2915, 2918-2919, 2928, 2952, 2961, 2994, 3076, 3097, 3187, 4871, 5025, 5796, 5827, 5845, 5895, 5963, 6226
    Afrique méridionale, 1847
    Algérie, 2949
    Amérique latine, 2916, 2940
    Caraïbes, 2972
    États-Unis, 2917, 2927, 4808, 4912, 5371
    Italie, 4831
    Japon, 2985, 3166
    URSS, 2926
Féodalisme 1264, 4432
    Pérou, 4428
Fermes
    Yougoslavie, 4622, 4648
Fermes collectives 1491, 4642
    URSS, 4039, 4631
Fermes d'État
    URSS, 4016, 4615
Fêtes 2063
    Argentine, 1850
    France, 1844, 2278

Index des matières

Inde, 1851
Feuerbach, Ludwig, 5490
Fiabilité 474
Fiamengo, Ante, 210, 217
Filles 3055
Films
    États-Unis, 2182, 2202
Financement de la recherche
    États-Unis, 147
Fisher, J. L., 309
Fitzhugh, George, 298
Foi 1859, 1876, 1878, 1912
Folie
    Royaume-Uni, 3200
Folklore 2278, 2281
    Brésil, 2279
Fonction publique
    Amérique latine, 5553
    États-Unis, 3719, 5557
    France, 5555
Fonctionnaires
    Allemagne RF, 5215
    Royaume-Uni, 5552
Fonctionnalisme 309, 333, 980
Fonctionnement du groupe 1048
Fondations de recherche
    États-Unis, 147
Formation complémentaire
    Royaume-Uni, 2496
Formation des enseignants
    Allemagne RF, 2540
    Europe, 2539
    Suède, 2549
Formation en alternance 5040
Formation professionnelle 5030, 5034
    France, 4993
    Italie, 5043
    URSS, 5065
Foucault, Michel, 258, 289, 1492, 1955, 1970, 5418, 5917
Foule 1268, 1275, 4367
    Inde, 1555
Franc-maçonnerie
    Espagne, 1809
Fréquentation scolaire
    Italie, 1500
Frère 3507
Freud, Sigmund, 257, 1845, 2590
Frustration 880
Futur 2812-2814, 2990
Futurologie 2811
Geertz, Clifford, 2808
Gellner, Ernest, 2605
Génétique 2996, 2999, 3002
Génocide 5873, 5976
Genre de vie 186, 531, 719, 729, 858, 1283-1284, 1292-1293, 1299, 1303, 1306-1307, 1309, 1322, 1325, 1327, 1339-1340, 1347, 1350, 1352, 1355, 1357, 1359-1360, 1362, 1372, 1375, 1379-1381, 1384, 1386, 1388, 1390, 1392, 1396-1397, 1399-1401, 1403, 1411, 1443, 2226, 2323, 3037, 3954, 4572, 4662, 4699, 4951, 5098, 5391
    Maroc, 1317
    Mexique, 1281
    URSS, 1291, 1297, 1305, 1312, 1314, 1335, 1353, 1369, 2760, 4068, 4801, 5489, 5515, 5582
Gens de maison 5104
    France, 5102
Géographie humaine 437, 3942
    Amérique latine, 1383
Géographie urbaine 4231, 4282
Gérontologie 3100, 3106, 3111
Gestion 2869, 3718, 4541, 4556, 4564
    URSS, 2706
Gestion d'entreprises 4524-4525, 4538, 4547, 5107, 5113
    Chine, 4555
Gestion du personnel 4872-4873, 4878-4880, 4885, 4887-4888, 4890, 4895, 4897-4899, 4901-4902, 4905, 5128
    États-Unis, 5175
    Inde, 4893
    URSS, 4884
Gestion sociale 1352, 1460, 4665, 6001, 6006, 6009, 6015, 6032-6033, 6051, 6056, 6069, 6079, 6081-6083, 6097, 6099, 6104
Gestion universitaire 2427
    France, 2434
Goffman, Erving, 1168
Goldmann, Lucien, 261, 1278, 2248
Gramsci, Antonio, 5450
Grèves 5265, 5274, 5276
    Allemagne RF, 5256
    Canada, 5284, 5295
    Danemark, 5267
    Éthiopie, 5283
    Israël, 5261
    pays capitalistes, 5266
    Royaume-Uni, 5263
    Tanzanie, 5270
    Yougoslavie, 5271
Grèves sauvages
    États-Unis, 5258
Grossesse
    France, 3536
Groupe familial 647, 2982, 3472, 3474, 3505, 3511, 3522, 3541-3542, 3546, 3560
    Afrique méridionale, 3914
    États-Unis, 3460
Groupes 984, 989, 1207, 4674
Groupes d'intérêt 5605
    États-Unis, 5607
    Italie, 5597
    Japon, 5606
Groupes de discussion 1007
Groupes de formation 1002-1003, 1015
Groupes de référence 1039
Groupes ethniques 3446, 3653, 3656, 3708
    Afrique occidentale, 3651
    Belgique, 3699

Index des matières

Canada, 3671, 3691, 3703, 3713
Cuba, 3681
États-Unis, 3659, 3705, 4203, 4276, 5562
Inde, 3709
Israël, 3698
Royaume-Uni, 3679
URSS, 3688
Groupes informels 900, 1013, 1016
Groupes majoritaires 1231
Groupes minoritaires 1017, 1020-1021, 1026
 États-Unis, 1366, 3085, 3764
 Hongrie, 1024
Groupes politiques 5585
Groupes religieux 1801, 1813, 1821, 1826
 États-Unis, 1808
 Israël, 1825
 Liban, 1804
 Malaisie, 1817
Groupes restreints 1000-1001, 1005-1006, 1008-1012, 1014
Groupes thérapeutiques 1003
Guérilla 5687
 Amérique latine, 5691
Guerre 1889, 5737, 5740
Gurvitch, Georges, 261
Habermas, Jürgen, 267, 288, 299, 304, 325, 335, 2546
Habitat
 Algérie, 3982
 Congo, 3981
Habitudes alimentaires 1598
Handicapés 3199
 Grèce, 3180
 Royaume-Uni, 3185
Hegel, Georg Wilhelm Friedrich, 2099-2100, 5408
Heller, A., 881
Hérédité 3000
Hérésies
 Allemagne, 1873
Héritage 3103, 4506
Herméneutique 246, 251, 284, 336, 1247, 2041
Heures de travail 3269, 4906, 4924, 4960, 4963, 4967, 4985
 États-Unis, 4974
 France, 4914
 URSS, 4971
Hilferding, Rudolf, 5731
Hindouisme 1741, 5973
Histoire 275, 1290, 1748, 2794, 2796, 2804, 2806, 2810, 2841
Histoire culturelle
 États-Unis, 1428
 Europe occidentale, 1416
Histoire de l'éducation 2298
Histoire de la sociologie 37, 44, 56, 61, 69, 330, 480, 1973
 Allemagne, 48, 259, 4375
 Allemagne RF, 57
 Bulgarie, 65
 Canada, 52

Espagne, 27
États-Unis, 13-14, 23-24, 38, 42, 58, 95, 1962
France, 17
Hongrie, 25
Histoire des idées 1950
Histoire du capitalisme 4444
 Allemagne, 4536, 4540
Histoire économique
 Canada, 4415
 Portugal, 2805
 Royaume-Uni, 2798, 2800
Histoire religieuse 1674
Histoire sociale 324, 1076, 2788, 2793, 2795, 2797, 2801, 2807-2809, 2832, 5821
 Allemagne, 2737, 2789, 4132, 4266, 4754, 5218
 Allemagne RF, 2799
 Asie du Sud-Est, 2886
 Brésil, 5181
 Canada, 3519
 Colombie, 2829
 Espagne, 2700
 États-Unis, 2790, 2792, 3552, 4813
 France, 118, 1844, 3012, 3127, 3368, 5241, 5714
 Guatemala, 3660
 Inde, 3721, 5838
 Italie, 2791
 Panama, 5229
 Portugal, 2805, 5061
 Royaume-Uni, 2686, 2798, 2800, 2803, 5251
 Suède, 4745
 URSS, 995
Historicisme 334
Hobbes, Thomas, 2590, 2874, 5734
Hofstee, E. W., 306
Homicide 5830, 5982
 États-Unis, 5839, 5855, 5871
Hommes 2961
 États-Unis, 2978
Hommes politiques 723
 Espagne, 5618
 France, 5592, 5616
Homosexualité 3357, 3361, 3364, 3379, 3388
 Allemagne RF, 3382
 États-Unis, 3377
Hôpitaux 6216, 6220, 6230, 6257
 Royaume-Uni, 6217
Hôpitaux psychiatriques 6192, 6218
 États-Unis, 3782, 5882
Horkheimer, Max, 244
Hors-groupe 981, 1040
Hughes, Everett C., 268
Humanisation du travail 4920, 4945, 4952, 4976, 4990
 Allemagne RF, 4910, 4933, 4972, 4982
 URSS, 4984
Hynam, Charles, 216
Identification 935-936, 2657
Identification au parti 5632, 5642, 5656

381

Index des matières

Canada, 2680
Identité 664, 672, 680, 682, 688, 691, 693, 706, 846, 1865, 1892, 2101, 2475, 3088, 3672
Identité culturelle 1418, 1430, 1432, 3706, 4570
   Afrique du Nord, 1413, 1422
   Afrique du Sud, 1429
   Belgique, 1433
   Brésil, 1916
Identité nationale
   États-Unis, 1366
   Israël, 1321
Idéologie 13, 1242-1244, 1247-1255, 1257-1258, 1260-1264, 1266, 1290, 1347, 1614, 1627, 1863, 1963, 2030, 2066, 2098, 2284, 2535, 2977, 3042, 3051, 3589, 3681, 4433, 4612, 5422, 5468, 5735
   Allemagne RF, 3056
   Espagne, 2378
   Ghana, 5211
Idéologies politiques 1246, 5407, 5412, 5414, 5417
   États-Unis, 5411
   Nigeria, 5413
   Royaume-Uni, 5411
Illégitimité
   Autriche, 3521
   États-Unis, 3351
   Israël, 3338
   Royaume-Uni, 3336
Illich, Ivan, 1123
Image 1207
Imagination 779, 807, 828
Imitation 939
Immigrants
   Amérique latine, 3838
   Belgique, 3818
   Bolivie, 3255
   Canada, 3822
   Espagne, 1436
   États-Unis, 1942, 3814, 3831, 3833, 3836
   France, 3823, 4195, 4731
   Israël, 3825-3826, 3843
   Japon, 3257
   Pays-Bas, 4864
   Portugal, 4798
   Royaume-Uni, 3866
Immigration
   Arabie saoudite, 3845
   Canada, 3863, 3875
   États-Unis, 3774, 3841, 3848
   France, 3819
   Italie, 3877
Impérialisme 2702, 5731, 5735
   États-Unis, 5399
Inceste 3362, 3369
Indicateurs 592
Indicateurs sociaux 186, 478, 530-532, 542-543, 550-551, 555, 559, 565, 567-568, 571-572, 574-575, 583, 587, 590, 593-595, 2778, 2875, 2907, 3059, 3516, 4227, 4246, 4365, 4376, 4483-4484, 4495, 4497, 4505, 4514, 5642, 5702
   Allemagne RF, 597
   États-Unis, 545, 2602, 4518
Indigenous population
   Guatemala, 3660
Individualisme 667, 678, 701, 712, 887, 4527, 5430
   Royaume-Uni, 689
Individualité 675, 691, 1303
Individus 659-660, 663, 665, 1616
Industrialisation 3251, 4606, 4634, 4638, 4645, 4762, 5085
   Allemagne, 4540
   Amérique latine, 4427
   États-Unis, 4641, 4647, 4929
   France, 4053
   Italie, 3472
   Japon, 4011
   pays en développement, 4630
   Pérou, 4650
   Tanzanie, 4639
Industrie 4626
Industrie culturelle 2167, 2191, 2212, 5355
   Hongrie, 2142
Inégalité 2613
Inégalité sociale 2608, 2614, 2619, 2623, 2625-2627, 4418, 4515, 5848
   Belgique, 5763
   Chine, 6095
   États-Unis, 2594, 2610, 5793, 6244
   France, 2356, 5196
   Ghana, 2400
   Inde, 2612, 2618
   Nigeria, 2615
   Royaume-Uni, 2594, 2599, 2630, 4217
Inférence causale 364, 380, 384
Infirmières 5059, 6238, 6257
   Canada, 5301
   Espagne, 6242
   États-Unis, 5301
   France, 6240
Inflation 4460, 4666
Influence du groupe 1026, 1043, 1174
Influence interpersonnelle 673, 937-938, 940, 3452
Influence sociale 1448-1449, 1478, 1485, 3035
Information 185, 188, 190
Informatique 166
Ingénieurs 1113
   Allemagne RF, 5116
Innovations 1012, 1104, 2421, 4571, 4580, 4588
   Italie, 2791
Institutionnalisation 1451, 1458, 1489, 6235
Institutions 642, 1171, 1442, 1493, 5535
Institutions religieuses 1822
   États-Unis, 1829, 3720
Intégration culturelle 1420, 1441
   Inde, 1437

Index des matières

Israël, 1426
Intégration de la collectivité
    Pérou, 4006
Intégration du groupe 1034
Intégration familiale 3077, 3470, 3493, 3500,
    3509, 3539, 3551, 3840
    Italie, 3488
Intégration sociale 1498, 1507, 1522, 1537,
    1550, 1587, 1593, 4236, 4578
    États-Unis, 1581
    pays arabes, 1081
    URSS, 1497, 1576
Intellectuels 267, 2742, 2748, 2750, 2755,
    6015
    Allemagne, 2737
    États-Unis, 5237
    France, 1939
    Inde, 2754
    Italie, 2732
    Portugal, 2752
    Yougoslavie, 2774
Intelligence 810, 830, 840, 872
Intelligentsia 2759, 2764
    Hongrie, 2770
    pays en développement, 2753
    URSS, 1576, 2731, 2735, 2751, 2758,
    2760, 2762, 2767, 4102
Interaction en groupe 899, 1027-1028,
    1031-1032, 1036
Interaction sociale 929, 1028, 1234, 1501,
    1512, 1527, 1533, 1535, 1544, 1554,
    1583, 2116-2117, 3095, 3405
Interaction symbolique 685
Intérêt 4667
Intérêt professionnel 6241
Intérêt social 800
Internationalisme 5722, 5726-5727, 5729
Interprétation 378
Invalidité 3186
Islam 1703-1704, 1706, 1708, 1711, 1714,
    1724-1725, 1729, 1756, 1759, 1773,
    1780, 1785, 2584, 3473, 5415-5416,
    5478
    Afrique, 1761
    Afrique occidentale, 1791
    Algérie, 1650
    Indonésie, 1742, 1783
    Iran, 2840
    Soudan, 1786
    URSS, 1312, 1710
Jeu de rôle 1166
Jeunes travailleurs 4734, 4863, 4951
    Allemagne RF, 5089
    Hongrie, 4866
    URSS, 4793, 4801, 4804
Jeunesse 838, 1226, 1287, 1306, 1308, 1453,
    1464, 1470, 1893, 1919, 2179, 2274,
    3036-3038, 3042-3044, 3047, 3051,
    3053-3054, 3057-3059, 3062-3065,
    4759, 5801, 5896
    Allemagne RF, 3030, 3056
    Espagne, 5353

    États-Unis, 1480, 5803, 5813
    France, 3012
    Inde, 2474
    Israël, 1480, 3040
    Japon, 1547
    Taïwan, 3716
    URSS, 1608, 1908
Jeunesse rurale 1491
Jeux 430
Jeux à deux personnes 615
Jeux d'argent
    États-Unis, 5374
Journalistes 2137
Judaïsme 1716, 1733, 1743, 1745-1746, 1749,
    1772, 1775, 1777, 1781, 1789, 2059
    États-Unis, 1739
    Israël, 1738
Jugement de valeur 340, 345, 347, 401, 482
Juifs 85, 1753, 1767, 1771, 1775, 3763, 5807
    Canada, 1705, 1727, 1788, 1795
    États-Unis, 1770, 1782, 1808, 3244
    France, 1709, 1736
    Maroc, 5665
    Royaume-Uni, 1737, 1778
    Tunisie, 5665
    URSS, 3827
    Yougoslavie, 1730
Jury 755, 5548
Justice 1654
Justice criminelle 5878, 5899-5900, 5916,
    5926, 5961, 5977
    États-Unis, 5857, 5875, 5903, 5920, 5928,
    5942, 5966, 5984
Justice sociale 6000, 6042, 6048, 6072, 6098
Kant, Emmanuel, 249
Kardelj, Edvard, 4117
Kibboutz 5386
    Israël, 4623, 4632
Langage 529, 678, 1177, 1247, 1455, 1963,
    2019-2020, 2034, 2072, 2082, 2086-
    2088, 2098-2100, 2103, 2106, 2110-
    2111, 2113, 2284, 5627
    Inde, 2601
    Royaume-Uni, 2096
Langues 2071, 2078-2079, 2091, 2094, 2101,
    2107, 2115, 2119, 3394
    Afrique, 2095
    Afrique du Nord, 1422
    Amérique du Nord, 2080
    Caraïbes, 2092
    États-Unis, 1440, 2076
    Guyane, 2085
    Nigeria, 2073
    Porto Rico, 2081
    Suisse, 2105
Lazarsfeld, Paul, 408
Leaders 1151
    Inde, 5210
Leaders charismatiques 1144
    Guyane, 1146
Leadership 1139, 1143, 1145, 1147-1150,
    1152-1155, 1182, 5168

Leadership politique 5615
    Espagne, 5618
Lecteurs 1160, 2017, 2149
Lecture 772, 844
Législation 1463
Législation sociale
    Pays-Bas, 2935
    Royaume-Uni, 6007
Légitimité 5420
Leipsius, Rainer, 57
Léninisme 2848
Lévi-Strauss, Claude, 289
Levinas, Emile, 1611
Lexicologie 2008
Liberté 377, 1537, 2571
    URSS, 5518
Liberté religieuse
    États-Unis, 1217
    Italie, 1888
Liberté surveillée 5029, 5979
    Canada, 5889
    États-Unis, 5888
Licenciement 5008
Lieu de travail 4935, 4942, 4945
Linguistique 402, 559, 799, 2009, 2011-2012, 2026
    Canada, 2032
    Inde, 2028
Littérature 284, 772, 2242, 2254, 2256, 2258, 2979
    Afrique, 2259
    Égypte, 2252
    France, 897
    Inde, 2253
    Indonésie, 2257
    Italie, 2260
    Royaume-Uni, 2246
    URSS, 1565
Littérature orale 2240
Lockouts
    Allemagne RF, 5272
    États-Unis, 5286
    France, 5273
    Italie, 5279
    Royaume-Uni, 5269
Logement 3925
    Australie, 4297
    Canada, 3777
    Espagne, 4308
    États-Unis, 3752, 4226, 4376, 4385, 4388
    Europe orientale, 4327
    France, 4245
    Guatémala, 1542
    Hongrie, 1370, 4224
    Inde, 4393
    Irlande, 4216
    pays en développement, 587
    Royaume-Uni, 4217, 4338
    URSS, 4327
Logique 518-520, 523, 525
Loi sur l'immigration
    États-Unis, 3837, 3878
    France, 3868
Loisir 3069, 5337-5338, 5340, 5343-5344, 5346, 5353
    Espagne, 5342
    France, 5341
    RD allemande, 5339
    URSS, 5345
Lukács
    György, 2236, 2248
Lutte anti-pollution
    Japon, 5612
Lutte de classes 314, 2716
    Afrique méridionale, 4431
    Amérique latine, 4014
    Brésil, 2462
    Colombie, 4067
    El Salvador, 2679
    Panama, 2667
Lynd, Robert S., 209
Machiavel, Nicolas, 1986
Macro 459
Mafia 5832
Magie 1693, 1698
    France, 1696
Main d'oeuvre
    Amérique latine, 4712
    États-Unis, 4716
    Europe, 4717
    pays en développement, 4704
    Soudan, 4724
Main d'oeuvre féminine 2956, 2992, 3447, 3559, 4790, 4795, 4797, 4802, 4806, 4811, 4814, 4816-4817, 4842-4843, 4845, 4849, 4852, 4854, 4856, 4860, 4870-4871, 4937, 5025, 5030, 5104
    Afrique occidentale, 4844
    Algérie, 4796
    Allemagne RF, 4827, 4829
    Argentine, 3437, 4848, 4869
    Asie du Sud, 4054
    Asie du Sud-Est, 4834
    Australie, 4810, 4821
    Autriche, 4838
    Bolivie, 4848
    Brésil, 4805
    Chine, 4789
    Égypte, 3603
    États-Unis, 3909, 4787-4789, 4803, 4808, 4812-4813, 4818, 4822-4823, 4835, 4839, 4846, 4859, 4862, 4938
    Europe, 4846
    France, 4832, 4840
    Guatémala, 4809
    Hongrie, 4820
    Inde, 3626, 4791-4792, 4858
    Israël, 4815
    Mexique, 4833
    Nigeria, 3231
    Paraguay, 4848
    Scandinavie, 4841
    Suède, 4789
    Suisse, 4800

Tchécoslovaquie, 4861
URSS, 4799
Malades 3202
Maladies 2989, 3201, 6184
    Iran, 3181
Maladies de coeur 3189
    États-Unis, 3198
Maladies mentales 3182-3183, 3187, 3191, 3193, 6197
    États-Unis, 5874
Malaise de la jeunesse
    États-Unis, 3031, 3046
    Sri Lanka, 3031
Malaise social
    Royaume-Uni, 5755
Malnutrition 5759
Malthus, Thomas Robert, 316
Mandić, Oleg, 211
Mann, Fritz Karl, 218
Mannheim, Karl, 244, 334, 1998
Manuels scolaires 100, 233-241, 699, 980
Marché 4664
    pays en développement, 4663
Marché du travail 2452, 3734, 4710, 4713, 4720, 4722, 4727, 4772, 4776, 4781, 4975
    Argentine, 4735
    Autriche, 2338
    Danemark, 4708
    États-Unis, 3878, 3880, 4718, 4824
    Royaume-Uni, 4698
    Soudan, 3786
    Suède, 5318
Marché financier 5276
Marcuse, Herbert, 273
Marginalité 1515, 1529, 1553, 1572, 3873
    Guatemala, 1542
    Malaisie, 1580
Marginaux
    Italie, 1508
Mari 3516
Mariage 703, 933, 938, 2556, 3057, 3213, 3402-3403, 3405, 3419, 3423, 3430, 3440, 3452, 3568
    Amérique latine, 3281
    Asie, 3448
    Canada, 3436
    Espagne, 1936
    États-Unis, 3407
    France, 3391, 5472
    Inde, 3483, 3486, 3793
    Mexique, 3389
    Pakistan, 3414
    Pays-Bas, 3400
    Royaume-Uni, 2779
    Syrie, 3454
    Tchécoslovaquie, 3432
    Yougoslavie, 3434
Mariage mixte
    États-Unis, 3431
Martin, Jean, 222
Marx, Karl, 254-255, 260, 275, 291-292, 300, 331, 383, 399, 1257, 1471, 1610, 1641, 1647, 1673, 1964, 2845, 4939, 5491
Marxisme 75, 243, 254, 256, 270, 272, 274, 278, 292, 295, 300, 304, 314, 325, 338, 728, 1107, 1247, 1262, 1647, 1669, 2241, 2568, 2654, 2670, 2801, 2807, 4191, 4692, 5462, 5501, 5517, 6075
    États-Unis, 282
    Royaume-Uni, 1249, 2803
Masochisme 855
Matérialisme 310
Maternité 3055
    États-Unis, 3299
    Japon, 3299
Mathématiques 2002
Mead, George H., 1964
Médecine 350, 6161, 6166
    Cuba, 6165
Médecine sociale 6163, 6167, 6172
    Afrique, 6194
Médecins 5059, 5066
    France, 6234, 6248
Mémoire 773, 804, 878
Ménage 2968
    Canada, 3519
    Mexique, 2943
Ménagères 2958, 2967, 4922
Mère 3010, 3559, 4845
Merton, Robert K., 157
Mesure 473, 475, 485, 487, 492
Mesure de la personnalité 516
Méthodes contraceptives
    France, 3300
Méthodes de recherche 175, 338, 403, 408, 428, 445, 453-456, 466, 469-470, 763, 1401, 2311
    Danemark, 5743
Méthodes pédagogiques 82, 92, 96, 445, 1871, 2286, 2548
Méthodologie 373, 381, 406-407, 409, 415, 427, 443, 453, 464, 491, 525, 2574, 5400
Métis 3770
    États-Unis, 3767
Métropole
    Inde, 4255
Migrants
    Bolivie, 3811
    Soudan, 3786
Migrations 3551, 3794, 3800, 3803-3804, 3810
    Afrique occidentale, 3807
    Amérique latine, 2722
    Argentine, 3809
    Brésil, 3809
    Canada, 3805, 3808
    Espagne, 3796
    Europe, 4717
    Mali, 3795
    Royaume-Uni, 3806
    Thaïlande, 3797
Migrations alternantes 3916

Australie, 3917
Belgique, 3891
Canada, 3883
États-Unis, 3899
Hongrie, 3930
Migrations de retour 1157, 3830
Espagne, 3829
Israël, 3828
Malte, 3851
Tunisie, 3835
Turquie, 3876
Migrations de travail 3892, 3895, 3898, 5252
Afrique méridionale, 3914
Asie, 3905
Canada, 3888
États-Unis, 3909
Europe, 3853
Grèce, 3900
Moyen-Orient, 3905
Yougoslavie, 3933, 4828
Migrations internationales 2048, 3862
Amérique latine, 3815
Finlande, 3858
Migrations internes 2040, 3924, 3932
Asie du Sud-Est, 3923
Bangladesh, 3906
Brésil, 3935, 4402
Canada, 3913, 3926
États-Unis, 3887, 3901, 3907, 3910-3911, 3921, 3929, 3934, 3936
Inde, 3904, 3922
Malaisie, 3908
Mexique, 3885, 3931
Papouasie-Nouvelle-Guinée, 3889
Royaume-Uni, 3886
Syrie, 3897
Tunisie, 3902
Venezuela, 3928
Migrations rurales 3919-3920, 3925, 3927, 3937
Cameroun, 3133, 3890
États-Unis, 4264
Inde, 3912
Maroc, 3894
Nigeria, 3884, 3896
Turquie, 4113
URSS, 3903
Zambie, 3915
Migrations saisonnières
Argentine, 3799
Milieu culturel 330
Milieu de travail 724, 1552, 4989, 5543
Milieu familial 840, 872, 1476, 1515, 2473, 3060, 3535
États-Unis, 5048
France, 5062
Milieu rural
Allemagne, 2789
Milieu scolaire 1586
Milieu social 2418
Milieu urbain 2062, 2915, 4274
Milieux d'affaires

Canada, 4522
Militaires 5068, 5697, 5700, 5708-5709, 5715-5716, 5718
Afrique noire, 5712
Allemagne RF, 5710
États-Unis, 5702-5703, 5705, 5711, 5719
France, 5054, 5714
Israël, 5695
Suisse, 5704
Syrie, 3669
Millénarisme 1694
Ministres du culte
Afrique, 1834
Minorités culturelles 1408
France, 1427
Minorités ethniques 3649, 3695
Australie, 3650
Canada, 1727, 3697, 3704
Chine, 2349
Espagne, 3684
États-Unis, 2076, 2390, 3648, 3661, 3663, 3665, 3694, 3707, 3714, 4397, 4477, 4498, 5638, 5931
Israël, 3654
Martinique, 3685
Pays-Bas, 3670, 3710
Roumanie, 3662
Surinam, 3658
Minorités nationales 3706, 5462
États-Unis, 3696
URSS, 1335, 3657
Minorités religieuses
France, 1934
Suisse, 1928
Mobilité de la main d'oeuvre 3472, 4711, 4728
États-Unis, 3936, 4718
France, 4705
Hong Kong, 4726
Italie, 5166
Mobilité géographique 3801
Mobilité professionnelle 3413, 5057-5059, 5070
Allemagne RF, 5051
États-Unis, 5033, 5072
Israël, 3869
Mobilité résidentielle 4249, 4284, 4311, 4340, 4367
États-Unis, 4349, 4397
Japon, 4389
Mobilité sociale 830, 837, 1632, 2778, 2781, 2784, 2864, 3282, 3559, 4949, 5484
Allemagne, 2775
Allemagne RF, 2588
Brésil, 2786
Canada, 3666
États-Unis, 3429
France, 2785
Hongrie, 2777
Japon, 2783
Pologne, 2777
Royaume-Uni, 2779-2780, 2782

Index des matières

Tunisie, 2776
Turquie, 3876
URSS, 2343, 2787, 5081
Mode 1597, 1601
Modèles 342, 359, 379, 386, 399, 404
Modèles culturels 1290
Modèles de congruité 1210
Modèles statistiques 538-541, 547, 549, 560, 588
Modèles stochastiques 611, 613
Modernisation 2065, 2843, 2857, 2860, 4603
    Afrique, 3273
    Asie du Sud, 4324
    Indonésie, 1903
    Israël, 3698
    Japon, 2842
    pays en développement, 2853
Modes de production 4424, 4577, 4603, 5087
    Europe occidentale, 4591
    Inde, 3492
Modes de vie 1300, 1373, 1387, 1402, 1589, 1895, 3112, 4660
    Hongrie, 1370, 4224
    Japon, 1367
Monachisme
    États-Unis, 1810
    pays en développement, 1796
Montesquieu, Charles Louis de Secondat, 250
Morale 1219, 1536, 1618, 1623, 1632, 1909, 3390, 4670, 5213
    Pays-Bas, 2151
Moralité 1232, 1620, 1628, 1634, 5678, 5811
    URSS, 1608, 1621
Morbidité
    Australie, 6201
Mort 1846, 3068, 3096, 3209, 3214, 3356, 3415, 6219
    Afrique, 3205
    États-Unis, 3210
    France, 3225
Mortalité 3203, 3208-3209, 3213, 3219, 3222
    Asie, 3227
    Bangladesh, 3211
    États-Unis, 3216, 3218
    Extrême-Orient, 3215
    Kénya, 3207
Mortalité infantile 3206
    Asie du Sud, 3224
    Australie, 3229
    Canada, 3220
    Congo, 3226
    Guatemala, 3221
Motivation au travail
    Italie, 4925
Motivations 803, 815, 825, 853, 1271
Motivations d'accomplissement 623, 775, 829, 834, 838, 874, 2727
Mouvements étudiants 2480
    États-Unis, 2469
Mouvements ouvriers 2720, 5247
    Afrique du Nord, 5222
    Allemagne, 5218, 5246

Amérique latine, 4712
Brésil, 5181, 5226
États-Unis, 5170
France, 5241
Panama, 5229
Royaume-Uni, 5251
Mouvements religieux 1820, 1909, 1932
    Afrique, 1940
    Caraïbes, 1920
    Espagne, 1936
    URSS, 1911
Mouvements révolutionnaires 5609, 5611
    Irak, 2653
Mouvements sociaux 332, 1132, 1141, 1432, 3656, 3706, 5599, 5601-5602, 5604, 5608, 5610, 5613
    Afrique, 5603
    Asie, 5603
    Chine, 4142
    Colombie, 1571
    Espagne, 3967, 5600
    États-Unis, 5598
    Italie, 5596
    Japon, 5612
Moyens de communication 1343, 2068, 2141, 2166
    Allemagne RF, 2143
    Amérique latine, 2144
    Nigeria, 2211
Moyens de communication de masse 947, 1590, 2136, 2152, 2162, 2165, 2170, 2183-2184, 2190, 2198, 2203, 2206, 2208-2209, 5989
    Allemagne RF, 2172, 2194
    Asie du Sud, 4324
    Égypte, 2201
    Espagne, 2135
    États-Unis, 2140, 2182
    Italie, 2171
    RD allemande, 2172
    URSS, 2173
Multilinguisme 2104
Musées 2223, 2230, 2233
Musique 2052, 2266-2268, 2270
    Hongrie, 2269
Musulmans
    Philippines, 1734
Mysticisme 1882
Mythes 1206, 1701, 1863, 1872, 1874, 1879, 4700, 5853
Mythologie 1856-1857, 1862, 1866
Naissance 3495
Nation 1294, 1358
    États-Unis, 1378
National-socialisme 5428
Nationalisme 429, 1686, 2101, 5458-5459, 5462
    Canada, 5446, 5451
    Chine, 1944
    Égypte, 5442
Nature 3968
Nature humaine 2934, 2946, 2977

Négociation collective 5026, 5287, 5290-5291, 5300, 5303
    Canada, 5295, 5301, 5306
    États-Unis, 5294, 5297-5299, 5301, 5304
    France, 5302
    Ghana, 5293
    Royaume-Uni, 5289
    Suède, 5296
Négociation interpersonnelle 952, 970
Négotiation 958, 966
Nelson, Benjamin, 5725
Niveau d'enseignement 2323
    Afrique du Sud, 3760
Niveau de culture 2331, 2357
    Italie, 2321
    URSS, 2360
    Yougoslavie, 2358
Niveau de vie 4470, 4478, 4507, 5782
    Asie, 4512
    France, 3238
    Hongrie, 4473
Noblesse
    Espagne, 2636
    Royaume-Uni, 2635
Noirs 697, 1289, 2473, 3549, 3673, 4377
    États-Unis, 681, 1942, 2139, 2425, 3450, 3504, 3692, 3701, 3737, 3753, 3781, 4306, 5371
Nomades
    Mauritanie, 3918
Nomadisme 3893
Normalisation 1479
Normes sociales 1445, 1455, 1460-1461, 1463, 1465, 1475, 1481-1482, 1488, 1557, 5084
    États-Unis, 3552
Nostalgie 801
Nuptialité
    Mexique, 3433
Nutrition 5790
Objectifs de l'éducation 2342, 2368
Objectivité 341, 397
Observation 476, 480, 499
Observation participante 489, 4936
Offre de main d'oeuvre 3447, 4703
    France, 4697
Opinion 1228, 1231
Opinion politique
    Hongrie, 5639
Opinion publique 494, 1219-1224, 1226-1227, 1230, 1232-1233, 1235-1237, 1239-1240, 2175, 3065, 4590, 4612, 5989
    Allemagne, 3763
    États-Unis, 3099
    Hongrie, 3332
    Pays-Bas, 4747
Opposition politique
    Tunisie, 5249
Optimum de peuplement 3125
Ordinateurs 165, 167-169, 471, 4676
Ordre social 1983, 2590
    Allemagne RF, 2563

Israël, 968
Organisation 977, 1086, 1088, 1102, 1116, 1122, 1130, 1133, 1449
Organisation de l'entreprise 4523, 4529
    Chine, 5315
Organisation de la recherche 148, 162
    Allemagne RF, 154
    France, 139, 151, 161, 163
    Italie, 78, 153
Organisation du travail 4876, 4886, 4889, 4903
    France, 4882, 4900
    Hongrie, 4955
    Italie, 4874
Organisation hospitalière 6233
Organisations complexes 1079
Organisations de jeunesse 3041, 3052
    URSS, 3045
Organisations patronales
    France, 5165
Organisations volontaires 1069, 1071
    Pays-Bas, 1070
Orientation aux valeurs 516, 1444, 1453, 1469-1470, 1472, 1476, 1490
    Japon, 1467
Orientation pédagogique
    États-Unis, 2370, 2986
Orientation professionnelle
    URSS, 4987, 5042
Origine sociale 2448
Ouvrages de référence 197
Ouvriers industriels 2495, 4991, 5087
    Allemagne RF, 4950, 5089
    Hongrie, 5099
    RD allemande, 5095
    URSS, 5091
Ouvriers non qualifiés
    Allemagne RF, 4950
Paix 5741
Parenté 3103, 3568, 4086
    Amérique latine, 4427
    Bangladesh, 3463
    Chine, 3465
    Grèce, 3569
    Inde, 3492, 3550, 3793
    Japon, 3545, 3548
Pareto, Vilfredo, 61, 257, 290, 293, 296, 381, 2756
Park, Robert Ezra, 221
Paroisse
    France, 1823
    Italie, 1805
Parole 457, 2068, 2070, 2077, 2090, 2102, 2108, 2116
Parsons, Talcott, 98, 220, 224, 247, 277, 281, 294, 305, 313, 342, 404, 452, 816, 873, 2810
Participation à la collectivité 3987, 3993
    États-Unis, 3991, 3994
Participation au groupe 1131
Participation des femmes 3645
    France, 3628

Mexique, 3643
Participation des travailleurs 4551, 5290,
    5308-5309, 5313, 5316-5317, 5320,
    5322, 5324, 5330
  Allemagne RF, 5319, 5326, 5335
  Canada, 5323
  Chine, 5315
  Danemark, 5327, 5334
  États-Unis, 5336
  Europe, 5332, 5336
  France, 5329
  Malte, 5325
  Pays-Bas, 5333
  Pérou, 5311
  Royaume-Uni, 5328
  Suède, 5307, 5318
  URSS, 5310, 5314
  Yougoslavie, 5312
Participation politique 2152, 2209, 3034,
    4064, 5619, 5628, 5645
  Canada, 3592, 5623
  Costa Rica, 5624, 5657
  Danemark, 5652
  États-Unis, 5648, 5651, 5661
  Norvège, 5646
  Pérou, 5631
Participation religieuse
  Brésil, 1916
  États-Unis, 1924, 1942
  France, 1939
  Italie, 1914
Participation sociale 1153, 1549, 1563
  Italie, 1500
  Japon, 1573
Partis politiques 5572, 5583, 5586-5587,
    5590-5591, 5594
  Afrique, 5570
  Afrique noire, 5671
  Amérique latine, 5588, 5691
  Canada, 2611
  Chine, 5575
  Espagne, 5571
  États-Unis, 5569, 5576, 5589
  France, 5573-5574, 5592
  Italie, 2732, 5593
  Royaume-Uni, 5578
  URSS, 190, 2705, 5577, 5579, 5581-5582,
    5584, 6061
Passage à la vie active
  Italie, 2379
Paternité-maternité 3527
Pathologie sociale 5757
Patriarcat 3602
  Inde, 3626
Patrimoine culturel 1421
  Palestine, 1407
  Suède, 1409
Patriotisme 5452
Patten
  Simon, 58
Paupérisation 5764
Pauvres

Venezuela, 5781
Pauvreté 4073, 5764-5765, 5767-5768, 5771,
    5783, 5785, 5789, 6053
  Afrique, 5762
  Amérique latine, 5777, 5786
  Asie, 4512
  Belgique, 5763
  Canada, 4152
  États-Unis, 5773, 5779-5780, 5793, 5841,
    6113
  France, 2785
  Haïti, 4111
  Inde, 4084, 4369
  Royaume-Uni, 3110, 5775, 5787
  Sierra Leone, 5776
Pays capitalistes 2651, 2741, 4460, 5477
Pays développés 3280
Pays en développement 123, 582, 1260, 2885,
    2889, 3173, 3271, 3291, 3617, 3927,
    4425, 5708, 5717
Pays socialistes 1299, 1587, 2669, 3054, 4119,
    4423, 4435, 4539, 5424, 5510
  Afrique, 2664
Paysannerie 1587, 4096, 4148, 4190, 5083
  Afrique du Sud, 4036
  Corée R, 4094
  Espagne, 4044, 4158
  France, 4028, 4041, 4093
  Italie, 4024
  Japon, 4027
  Malaisie, 4019
  Mexique, 4061, 4154
  Pérou, 3481, 4066
  URSS, 4068
  Yougoslavie, 4047
Paysans 889, 3639, 3898, 4069
  Afrique, 4097
  Amérique latine, 4014
  Caraïbes, 4050
  Chine, 4142
  Costa Rica, 5624, 5657
  France, 4116
  Haïti, 4111
  Iran, 4057
  Mexique, 4038
  pays en développement, 4141
  Pologne, 4099
  Thaïlande, 4112
  Turquie, 4113
Pêcheurs
  Royaume-Uni, 1143
Peine de mort 5844, 5958, 5971
  Allemagne RF, 5965
  États-Unis, 5834
Peirce
  Charles S., 2015
Pèlerinages
  France, 1839
Pellizzi
  Camillo, 212
Pensée 798-799, 814, 845, 878, 2112
Pensée économique 2004, 3968

Pensée politique
　Pays-Bas, 5409
Perception 795, 846, 2100, 2726
Perception d'autrui 696, 902, 910, 914, 1209, 2559
Perception de soi 676, 696
Perception interpersonnelle 903, 906-907, 909, 1268, 1602
Perception sociale 901, 904, 908, 912-913, 915
Père 3495
Performance 784, 865, 1170, 2727, 5532
Performance du groupe 1012, 1023, 1046-1047, 1147
Périodiques 44, 227, 230-232, 239
　États-Unis, 3590
　Italie, 228
Personnalité 660, 714, 716-718, 720, 722-723, 727, 729-733, 735-736, 738-739, 742, 745, 750-751, 754, 757, 761-763, 767, 852, 910, 1042, 1185, 1224, 1360, 1456, 1624, 1626, 2184, 2391, 2486, 4586-4587, 5630, 5641, 5660
Personnel médical 6198, 6241, 6243
Personnes âgées 839, 870, 1162, 3076, 3079-3080, 3084, 3088-3090, 3092, 3095, 3097, 3108-3109, 3111-3112, 3532, 3560, 5816, 5922, 5930, 5960
　Australie, 3087
　États-Unis, 2134, 3073, 3078, 3081, 3085-3086, 3091, 3094, 3098-3099, 3107, 3675
　France, 3070
Persuasion 2089, 2129, 2131
Perversions sexuelles 3373, 3376
Petite industrie
　Mexique, 4616
Petites villes 4304, 4364
　États-Unis, 2111, 4283
　France, 4092
Peur 771, 806, 2163, 3033, 5850, 5931, 5960
Phénoménologie 253, 255
Philosophie 40, 265, 518, 633, 701, 1324, 1680, 3038
Philosophie politique 263, 5408, 5410, 5415-5416, 6000
Phonétique 2013
Photographie 195, 3469
Piaget, Jean, 213, 833, 1956, 2299
Planification 4674
Planification de l'éducation
　Inde, 2389
　Indonésie, 2328
Planification de la famille 3291, 3296, 3329, 3331, 3544, 6118
　Allemagne RF, 3258
　Amérique latine, 3350
　Bangladesh, 3319
　Costa Rica, 4157
　Fidji, 3285
　Guatemala, 3290
　Inde, 3326, 3330, 3335, 3337, 3344

　Malaysie, 3312, 3328
　pays en développement, 3287
　Thaïlande, 3343
　Turquie, 3305
Planification régionale
　URSS, 4322
　Viet-Nam, 4259
Planification sociale 5217, 5996, 5999, 6022, 6024, 6028, 6052, 6073-6074, 6076, 6105
　Allemagne RF, 6089
　États-Unis, 6094
　Grèce, 6043
　URSS, 6071
Plein emploi 4732
Pluralisme culturel
　Canada, 1374
Police 2608, 5531, 5533, 5536, 5538-5540, 5543, 5931
　Allemagne RF, 5529
　États-Unis, 5529, 5537, 5541, 5924
　Europe occidentale, 5530
　Royaume-Uni, 5985
Politique 1925, 1930, 2039, 2660, 3593, 5539, 5688, 5692, 5738
　France, 2236
　Italie, 5689
Politique agricole 4628
Politique culturelle
　Argentine, 1423
　Espagne, 2169
Politique d'immigration
　Canada, 3824
　Royaume-Uni, 2768
Politique de bien-être
　États-Unis, 6004
　Royaume-Uni, 6040
　URSS, 6058
Politique de développement 3980, 4673
　Italie, 1424
Politique de la main d'œuvre *voir* Politique de l'emploi
Politique de l'éducation 2361
　Allemagne RF, 2319
　Amérique latine, 2335
　Brésil, 2387
　Chine, 2349
　Égypte, 2366
　États-Unis, 2367
　Ghana, 2392
　Royaume-Uni, 2367
　Sénégal, 2324, 2392
Politique de l'emploi 4767, 4943
　États-Unis, 4770
　France, 4777
　Philippines, 4782
Politique de l'information 183
　Belgique, 194
　États-Unis, 189
Politique démographique 2908, 3288-3289, 3297, 3301, 3322, 3342
　Australie, 3292

Index des matières

Belgique, 3348
Bulgarie, 3313
Chine, 3283
Colombie, 3329
Finlande, 3311
France, 3239
Hongrie, 3332, 3346
Inde, 3317
Italie, 3136
Mexique, 3320
pays arabes, 3345
Roumanie, 3324
Singapour, 3298
URSS, 2911
Uruguay, 3339
Politique des revenus
   Tanzanie, 5270
Politique du logement
   Corée R, 4355
   États-Unis, 4196, 4265
   Nigeria, 4361
   Royaume-Uni, 4307, 4320-4321, 4328, 4332
   URSS, 4357
Politique du travail
   Colombie, 4723
   Mexique, 4723
Politique économique 2716, 4671, 5534
   Chine, 4675
Politique énergétique
   pays en développement, 4575
Politique étrangère 5732
Politique familiale
   URSS, 6131, 6135
Politique gouvernementale 5528, 5534-5535, 5542
Politique migratoire 3802
   Europe occidentale, 4828
Politique sanitaire 6221
   Allemagne RF, 6226
   Espagne, 6179, 6214
   États-Unis, 6208
Politique scientifique 156, 160
   Pays-Bas, 150, 155
Politique sociale 4410, 6014, 6018-6022, 6035, 6039, 6046, 6050, 6053, 6055, 6077-6078, 6080, 6084-6085, 6096, 6101, 6119, 6122
   Allemagne RF, 5997, 6086
   Chine, 6095
   Colombie, 6016
   États-Unis, 5773, 6003, 6008, 6037, 6041, 6054, 6068
   Europe, 6049
   Inde, 6059, 6092
   Irak, 6045
   Royaume-Uni, 5775, 6026, 6064
   Suisse, 6005
   Tchécoslovaquie, 6070
   URSS, 6029, 6061-6062, 6067, 6090, 6103
   Venezuela, 6063
   Yougoslavie, 6047

Politisation 5655, 5663
   Canada, 5634
Pollution 3916
   États-Unis, 3198, 3218
Polygamie 3444
Polygynie 3396, 3422
Popper, Karl, 320, 329
Population 2894, 2901, 4436
   Amérique latine, 2940
   Birmanie, 2912
   Espagne, 2909
   États-Unis, 2913
   France, 3128
Population agricole 3163
Population indigène
   Amérique, 3693
   Australie, 3680
   Brésil, 3143
   Canada, 3686
   Mexique, 3667-3668, 3689
Population rurale 3145
   France, 3127
   Inde, 3115, 3295
   Turquie, 3149
   URSS, 3160, 3171-3172, 3178
Population urbaine 3054, 3169
   Canada, 3155
   États-Unis, 3119, 3164, 6188
   Europe orientale, 4319
   France, 3135, 4295
   Italie, 3120
   Japon, 3157, 3166
   Royaume-Uni, 3866
   Soudan, 3129
   URSS, 2360, 3165
   Yougoslavie, 4387
Porter, John, 225
Positivisme 246, 303, 312, 320, 329
Pouvoir 1142, 5419
Pouvoir de négociation 5071, 5202
Pouvoir économique 4672
Pouvoir politique 2605, 5418, 5421
   Italie, 5689
   Royaume-Uni, 5180
Pratique religieuse 1917, 1925, 1930
   États-Unis, 2533
   France, 1935
   Italie, 1899
   Suisse, 1913
   URSS, 1353, 1908, 1910
Préhistoire
   Inde, 2802
Préjugé 717, 1203, 1205, 1209
Préjugé racial 2975, 3695, 3734, 3801
   Afrique du Sud, 1214, 1268, 3769
   États-Unis, 3779
Présidence
   États-Unis, 5532
Presse 2149, 2175-2176, 2179, 2193, 3963
   Espagne, 2503
   États-Unis, 2139
   Italie, 2199

Index des matières

Pays-Bas, 2151
Royaume-Uni, 6250
Prestige 1134, 1137
Prestige professionnel
France, 5039
Inde, 5074
URSS, 5042
Prêtres
Italie, 3860
Prévention de la délinquance 5938
États-Unis, 5883
Prévisions 346, 352, 355, 361, 366, 376, 395-396, 2812
Prime enfance 2035
Prise de décision 188, 346, 552, 663, 811, 832, 854, 866, 875, 1001, 1009, 1033, 1117, 3417, 3452, 3985, 6184
Inde, 2766
Prison
Inde, 5901
Prisonniers 702, 5831, 5881, 5895
États-Unis, 1154, 5843, 5882
Privation relative 2728
Problèmes sociaux 1922, 3963, 5754, 6010, 6013, 6023, 6027, 6034, 6036, 6101
États-Unis, 6087
Royaume-Uni, 6038
Procès politiques
États-Unis, 5686
Processus markoviens 610, 612, 614, 616, 4713
Production 4565
Productivité 5330
Productivité du travail 4709, 4875, 4881, 4883, 4891-4892, 5111, 5184
Productivité industrielle
URSS, 4627
Professeurs 2557, 4501
États-Unis, 2558
Professionnalisation 105, 5012, 5015, 5029, 6235
Kénya, 5024
Professionnalisme 5018
Professions *voir aussi* Occupations 4871, 5013-5014, 5016-5017, 5019, 5021, 5025-5026, 5034
États-Unis, 3757, 4607, 4808
Israël, 5022
Professions libérales 5125
Professorat
États-Unis, 2534
Programmes de recherche 159
Progrès scientifique et technique 148, 758, 781, 1355, 3047, 3151, 4534, 4569, 4572-4574, 4578, 4582, 4586-4587, 4590, 4593-4594, 4596, 4598, 4602, 4608, 4614, 4694, 4992, 5096
Espagne, 83, 1965
URSS, 2762
Prohibition de l'inceste 3367
Projections démographiques 2895
Canada, 2896

Prolétariat 2654
France, 3536, 3562
Promotion de la femme 3597
États-Unis, 3640
Inde, 3584
Promotion professionnelle
France, 4993
Pologne, 4997
Propagande 1223, 1269, 2126, 2128, 5463
Prophétie 1864
Israël, 1881
Propriété 4416, 4418
Nigeria, 3884
Prostitution 3353, 3360
Allemagne RF, 3382
Amérique du Nord, 3381
Inde, 3721
Protection de l'environnement 2663, 3966, 3969
Espagne, 3967
Protection des données 412, 462
Protestantisme 1748, 1750
France, 1934, 5673
Royaume-Uni, 1838
Protestants 2975
Canada, 3261
France, 1731
Proudhon, P.-J., 280
Psychanalyse 256, 279, 629, 632, 642, 655, 836, 983, 2809
Psychiatrie 1885, 6164, 6170-6171, 6174
Canada, 6162
Psycholinguistique 2007, 2018
Psychologie 627, 633, 636, 643, 649-650, 655, 1676, 1781
Amérique latine, 637
Pérou, 625
Psychologie de l'éducation 825, 2299, 2311, 2544, 3354
Psychologie de l'enfant 639
Psychologie expérimentaux 424
Psychologie industrielle 4682, 4684, 4686
Psychologie sociale 626, 628, 630, 634-635, 638, 640-641, 644-645, 648, 651-653, 656-657, 662, 809, 1562, 4005
Espagne, 631
Psychologues 80, 91, 94
Psychométrie 646, 654
Psychosociologie 91, 94
Psychothérapie 647
Psychothérapie de groupe 988, 994, 996
Public 708, 1183
Publicité 2123-2125, 2127, 2130
Puériculture 3010, 3026, 3029, 5927
Philippines, 3017
Puritanisme 1905
Qualification professionnelle 5031, 5037
Amérique latine, 5028
Canada, 5069
Danemark, 5055
États-Unis, 5076
France, 5079

Qualité de la vie 478, 877, 1507, 3003, 4479, 4482-4483, 4491, 4495, 4497, 4499, 4505, 4509
  Belgique, 4476
  Caraïbes, 4517
  États-Unis, 2858, 4481, 4498, 4514, 4518
  Hong Kong, 4407
  Hongrie, 4485
Quartier 1150, 4198, 4270, 4377
  États-Unis, 4201, 4250
Questionnaires 503
Répartition par sexe 2923, 2954, 5850, 5962
Race 775, 3655, 3673, 3690
Racisme 3726, 3732, 3789
  Afrique du Sud, 3780
  États-Unis, 3774, 3792
Radicalisme 3064
  Allemagne RF, 5626
  Pérou, 5667
  Royaume-Uni, 5622
Radio
  Espagne, 2169
Radiodiffision
  Nigeria, 2186
Radiodiffusion 2187
  États-Unis, 2196
Rang de naissance 872, 3265
  Suisse, 3274
Rapports avant le mariage 3375
Rareté 5761, 5792
Rationalisation 2841
Rationalisme 252, 324
Rationalité 783, 813, 873, 1859, 2005
Réadaptation des handicapés 6187, 6192
  États-Unis, 5035, 6189, 6193
Réadaption des délinquents 5947
Réadaption professionnelle
  États-Unis, 5035
Rébellion 1534
  Irlande, 1584
  Royaume-Uni, 1584
Recensements
  États-Unis, 482
  Mauritanie, 3918
Recherche 135, 382, 5584
  Europe occidentale, 113
Recherche action 143
Recherche appliquée 138, 142
Recherche démographique 2904, 2906
  Afrique, 2900
Recherche empirique
  France, 17
Recherche en cours 132, 327
Recherche en sciences sociales
  Pérou, 122
Recherche et développement 141
Recherche interdisciplinaire 140, 199, 1047
  France, 139
Recherche organisationnelle 144, 1053, 1059, 1063
Recherche pédagogique 2289, 2291
Recherche sociale 41, 159, 378, 440, 1539, 5556, 5744, 5749
  Danemark, 5743
  États-Unis, 488, 5751
Recherche sur l'opinion publique 1229
Recherche sur la communication 2051, 2060
  Allemagne, 2043, 2176
  États-Unis, 2043, 2176
Recherche sur les migrations
  Suède, 3798
Récidivisme 5846
Reconstitution de la famille
  États-Unis, 3460
Récréation 1152, 5375
Recrutement
  Japon, 87
Recrutement des enseignants
  Royaume-Uni, 2553
Réformes administratives 5556
  Mexique, 5549
  Soudan, 5550
Réformes agraires 4096, 4191
  Mali, 4151
  Pérou, 2696, 4066, 4071
  Portugal, 4021-4022, 4058
  République dominicaine, 4056
Réformes de l'enseignement 2317, 2397
  Autriche, 2398
  Canada, 2352
  Grèce, 2316
  Hongrie, 2330
  Mali, 2374
Réformes foncières
  Amérique latine, 4082
  Brésil, 4043
  Chine, 4179
  Costa Rica, 4157
  Inde, 4167
  Irlande, 4049
  Japon, 4027
  Taïwan, 4179
Réfugiés
  RDP Lao, 3834
  Viet-Nam, 3696, 3846, 3859
Régimes fonciers
  Espagne, 4026
  Mexique, 3138
  Pérou, 4173, 4428
Régionalisme
  Canada, 5653
  Espagne, 5436
  Europe occidentale, 5431
  Italie, 5457
Règlement de conflits 959, 965-966, 968, 979, 1577
  Turquie, 5285
Réglementations
  États-Unis, 488
  France, 1644
Régulation des naissances 3284, 3333, 4852
  Afrique, 3234
  Chine, 3325
  États-Unis, 3314, 3347

Index des matières

pays en développement, 3286
Régulation sociale 874, 1084, 1137, 1446, 1454, 1459, 1471, 1473-1474, 1484, 1486-1487, 1492, 1505, 2086, 2219, 2576, 4964, 5280-5281, 5421, 6039
   Canada, 1462
   Colombie, 4067
   France, 1450
   Norvège, 5921
   Zimbabwe, 2362
Relation thérapeutique 6203
Relations culturelles 1410
   Canada, 1435
   Chine, 1414
   États-Unis, 1440
   URSS, 2758
Relations humaines 884
Relations industrielles 4771, 5128, 5131-5132, 5143, 5145-5146, 5250, 6082
   Afrique, 5136
   Afrique du Sud, 4680, 5156, 5161
   Allemagne RF, 5127, 5147, 5150
   Amérique latine, 5134
   Australie, 5149
   Brésil, 5141
   Corée R, 5151
   États-Unis, 5140, 5158
   Europe occidentale, 5154
   Europe orientale, 5157
   France, 5129, 5147, 5155
   Inde, 4893
   Irlande, 5126
   Italie, 5152
   Japon, 5138-5139, 5144
   Mexique, 5148
   Norvège, 5153
   Royaume-Uni, 5130, 5133, 5135, 5142, 5199
   Tanzanie, 5176
   URSS, 5137
Relations interethniques 2452
   Afrique du Sud, 3756
   Brésil, 3741
   Canada, 3677, 3722
   États-Unis, 3766, 3773
   Israël, 3730, 3787
   Jamaïque, 3748
   Malaisie, 3750
   Pérou, 3791
   Zambie, 3742
Relations intergroupes 613, 960-962, 971, 973, 977, 981-982, 1203, 2019
   Caraïbes, 969
Relations internationales 1212, 1714, 5721, 5723-5725, 5728
Relations interpersonnelles 611, 885, 887-889, 891-892, 894, 896, 898-900, 1185
   Japon, 883
Relations parents-enfants 2527, 2956, 3035, 3459, 3467, 3489, 3515, 3517-3518, 3523, 3532, 3537, 3555, 3561, 5662
   Égypte, 3484

   États-Unis, 3468, 3477, 3485
Relations parents-enseignants 2545
Relations raciales 3718, 3736, 3754, 3775
   Afrique du Sud, 3717, 3747, 3758, 3765, 3776, 3783
   Brésil, 3739
   États-Unis, 1378, 3723, 3727-3728, 3743, 3751, 3764, 3766, 3773
   Inde, 3721
   Nouvelle-Zélande, 3761
   Royaume-Uni, 3755
   Trinité et Tobago, 3729
Relations sociométriques 926
Religion 1247, 1673, 1677-1678, 1681-1690, 1922, 5678
   Chine, 1691, 1944
   Japon, 4090
   Royaume-Uni, 1718
   URSS, 1910
Religion populaire
   États-Unis, 1941
Religion primitive
   Zimbabwe, 1712
Religiosité 1886, 1889, 1897, 1900, 3088
   Colombie, 1883
   Indonésie, 1783, 1903
   Mexique, 1898
Remariage
   États-Unis, 3429
Rendement de l'éducation 2325, 2333, 3059
Rénovation urbaine 4270, 4359
   Australie, 4297
   États-Unis, 4228, 4234
   Europe, 4212
   France, 4193
Répartition de la population 3144
   Malaisie, 3167
   Mexique, 3138
   URSS, 3146
Répartition du revenu 2778, 3271, 4464, 4475, 4486-4487, 4513, 4515
   Amérique latine, 2335
   Belgique, 4474
   Canada, 4503
   Corée R, 4489
   États-Unis, 1831, 4477, 4493, 4641, 5172, 5773
   France, 4508
   Pays-Bas, 4500
Répartition par âge 3004, 5850, 5962
   URSS, 3137
Répartition par sexe
   Israël, 5022
Répartition spatiale 3974
Répertoire 77
Repos 5354
Représentations sociales 1206
Réseau de communication 2040, 2048, 2056, 2060
Réseaux sociaux 986-987, 989-992, 995, 997, 999
Résidences secondaires

Index des matières

France, 4253
Résistance au changement
   Libye, 2830
Résolution de problème 789, 808, 831, 868, 4541, 6010
Responsabilité 1602, 1605, 1616, 1624, 1626, 1633, 3182
Ressources humaines 4709
   URSS, 4714
Retard intellectuel 3190
   États-Unis, 3184
   Suède, 3197
Retraite 3069, 4995-4996, 5004, 5006-5007, 5011
   États-Unis, 4739, 4999
   Royaume-Uni, 5003
Réussite dans les études 2529
   États-Unis, 2533
Réussite professionnelle 5031, 5067, 5078
Réveil religieux 1724, 1919
   États-Unis, 1923, 1929
   Japon, 1926
Revenu 3544, 4806
Révolution 2817-2818, 2826, 2828, 2837, 2848, 2856, 2865, 2867, 5735
   Algérie, 2949
   Chine, 2850
   France, 2823, 5668
   Iran, 2839
Richesse 4469, 4492
   Belgique, 4474
Rire 859
Rites 1845-1846, 1854, 2046
   Papouasie-Nouvelle-Guinée, 1848
Rites d'initiation
   Afrique méridionale, 1847
Rites de passage 1843
Rokkan, Stein, 446
Rôle 703, 1156, 1158-1160, 1162-1163, 1165, 1167, 1170-1171, 2960, 3202, 5121
Rôles masculins et féminins 1036, 1305, 1521, 2598, 2725, 2920, 2925, 2930, 2932, 2937-2938, 2942, 2950, 2952, 2955-2960, 2962-2964, 2969, 2971, 2974, 2979-2984, 2987, 2989, 2991-2993, 3050, 3395, 3505, 3523, 3583, 3636, 3639
   Cameroun, 2947
   Canada, 3592, 5623
   États-Unis, 2921, 2924, 2936, 2941, 2944, 2978, 2986
   Inde, 1880
   Maroc, 1204
   Nigeria, 2947
   Suède, 2966
Rôles professionnels 2542, 5052, 5071
Romans 2243, 2262
Rotation de la main d'oeuvre 5001, 5696
   États-Unis, 4994
Rousseau, Jean-Jacques, 2581
Rural 4185
Rural-urbain 1216, 3267, 4045, 4104, 4171

Chine, 2850
États-Unis, 4124
France, 4143
Inde, 4370
Indonésie, 4127
Nigeria, 3268
Suisse, 4048
URSS, 4125
Sacré 1867
Sages-femmes
   États-Unis, 6235
   Royaume-Uni, 6235
   Taïwan, 6246
Saint-Simon, Claude-Henri de, 1376
Salaires 4501, 4701, 5274
   Costa Rica, 2931
   États-Unis, 5206, 5208, 5212
Sales y Ferré, Manuel, 27
Sanctions pénales
   États-Unis, 5828
Santé 4842, 5767, 6182, 6207
   États-Unis, 6188
   Nigeria, 2615
Santé mentale 2983, 6197, 6204
   Australie, 6200
   États-Unis, 6183, 6195
Santé publique
   Afrique, 6194
   Espagne, 6179
   Royaume-Uni, 6186, 6202
Satisfaction 839, 842, 848, 870, 4246
Satisfaction au travail 1170, 4928, 4932, 4938-4940, 5320
   États-Unis, 4978
Satisfaction conjugale 3449
Satisfaction de l'existence 3072
Schutz, Alfred, 694, 1326, 2810
Science 148, 764, 1627, 1863, 1946, 1952, 1958, 1971, 1974, 1978, 1980, 1982-1983, 1985, 1987-1990, 1992, 1994-1996, 2001, 2003, 2006, 4673
   URSS, 1975
Science économique 72, 2005, 4410, 4412, 4537, 4653
Science politique
   Yougoslavie, 5404
Sciences de l'information 180, 196
   France, 191
Sciences de la communication 2150
Sciences du comportement 21, 39, 45, 63-64, 73-74, 465, 4653, 5406
   États-Unis, 3692
Sciences économiques
   Yougoslavie, 4414
Sciences religieuses 1676
Sciences sociales 1, 11, 16, 18, 40, 46-47, 49, 53-54, 62, 71, 105, 132, 135, 164, 168, 196, 206, 270, 339, 341, 360, 398, 406, 409, 432, 451, 492, 525, 701, 6077
   Afrique orientale, 116
   Amérique latine, 119, 202

Index des matières

Chine, 115
États-Unis, 147, 2178
Europe occidentale, 113
France, 151
Mexique, 112
Royaume-Uni, 5438
Scientifiques 90
URSS, 1297
Scientologie 1953
Scolarité 5078
Canada, 2381
Royaume-Uni, 3755
Sectes 498, 1802, 1820, 1827, 1830
Afrique, 1763
Amérique latine, 1797
États-Unis, 1797-1798, 1807, 1814, 1818, 1824, 1828
Secteur tertiaire 4620
Sécularisation 1921, 1931, 1974
Sécurité d'emploi 4771
Sécurité du travail 5023
Sécurité sociale 6109
Allemagne RF, 6117, 6137
Amérique latine, 5786, 6126
Australie, 3457
Bulgarie, 6114
Canada, 6136
Corée R, 3458
États-Unis, 6110, 6113
Inde, 6133
pays andins, 6129
Yougoslavie, 6130
Ségrégation
Inde, 1555
Ségrégation professionnelle 2948
Ségrégation raciale
Canada, 1788
États-Unis, 3724, 3728
Soudan, 3786
Ségrégation résidentielle 3090, 4202
États-Unis, 4203, 4262, 4264, 4276, 4312-4314, 4326, 4358
Japon, 4335
Ségrégation scolaire 707
États-Unis, 681, 683, 2336, 2345, 2375, 2402
Sélection du personnel 4768, 4773, 4778
Sémantique 2014, 2024, 2031
Sémiologie 2022, 2157
Sémiotique 2009-2010, 2015, 2017, 2020, 2023, 2030, 2033, 2041
Pologne, 2029
Séparation conjugale 3451
Service militaire 5706
Services de santé 6211-6212, 6215, 6219, 6222, 6224
États-Unis, 6225, 6232
Éthiopie, 6228
Finlande, 6223
Pays-Bas, 6231
Royaume-Uni, 6210, 6213
Services hospitaliers 6229

Services sociaux 6254-6255, 6258
Australie, 6252
Canada, 6239
Danemark, 6245
États-Unis, 6244, 6249, 6251, 6259
Italie, 6247
Royaume-Uni, 6253
Sexe 460, 775, 2205, 2939, 2970, 2988, 5981
Royaume-Uni, 5923
Sexualité 2918, 3354-3355, 3358-3359, 3363, 3366, 3370-3372, 3374, 3380, 3383, 3385
France, 3368
Signes 2015
Signification 2034, 2041, 2046, 2066
Simmel, Georg, 301-302, 308
Simulation 2170, 3399, 3440
Situation de famille 3415
Argentine, 3437
Sociabilité 886, 895, 1598
Socialisation 715, 1308, 1445, 1502-1503, 1506, 1511, 1525, 1532, 1552, 1567, 1574, 1586, 1592, 1601, 1635, 2304, 2312, 2932, 2993, 3024, 3459, 3484, 3499, 5026, 5383
Allemagne RF, 5710
États-Unis, 1740
Japon, 1547
Pérou, 3025
Porto Rico, 1585
URSS, 1565
Socialisation politique 823, 5629, 5640, 5650, 5664
Canada, 5633
Espagne, 5654
États-Unis, 5644, 5661
Inde, 5647
Japon, 5644
Suède, 5659
URSS, 5669
Socialisme 716, 1362, 1536, 2619, 2626, 4577, 5423-5425, 5427, 5430, 5433, 5435, 5437, 5443-5445, 5448-5450, 5453-5454, 5456, 5460
Chine, 137
pays en développement, 5426
Tanzanie, 4639
Société 519, 1319, 1331, 1336-1337, 1351, 1371, 1376, 1398
Chine, 1315
Espagne, 1320
Hongrie, 1313, 1334, 1356
Inde, 37, 1389
Israël, 1288
Société bourgeoise 1269, 1412, 2877, 3968, 5463, 5470
Société capitaliste 2580, 4424, 4436, 4442, 4450
Société civile 2874, 2878
Société d'abondance 2054, 4490
Société de masse 1318, 2755
Société dualiste 2607

Société industrielle 1056, 1442, 2877, 2880, 4577, 5740
Société politique 5503
Société post-industrielle 2822, 2890, 5688
　Pays-Bas, 2884
Société rurale 4331
　Chine, 4136
　Espagne, 4153
　France, 2690, 4086, 4115, 4126, 5472
　Inde, 2766
　Italie, 3633
　Japon, 3548, 4089
　Nigeria, 4098
　Pérou, 4055
　Royaume-Uni, 4133
　URSS, 4121
　Viet-Nam, 4147
　Zaïre, 4155
Société socialiste 90, 396, 713, 719, 729, 739, 753, 765-767, 777, 851, 858, 869, 1222, 1258, 1270, 1274, 1283, 1292, 1322, 1339-1340, 1347, 1352, 1358-1359, 1372, 1388, 1390, 1399-1400, 1403, 1441, 1443, 1461, 1470, 1473, 1482, 1498, 1505, 1616, 1657, 2226, 2229, 2447, 2479, 2560, 2562, 2574, 2691, 2717, 2759, 2764, 2859, 3016, 3037, 3162, 3541-3542, 3546, 4422, 4433, 4445, 4449, 4451, 4456-4457, 4461, 4507, 4578, 4699, 4905, 5075, 5086, 5105, 5317, 5347, 5356, 5471, 5475, 5483, 5512, 5583, 5591, 5630, 5733, 6015, 6019, 6069, 6081
　Europe orientale, 4443
　URSS, 1382
Société traditionnelle
　Espagne, 2876
　France, 974, 1667
Société urbaine 1572, 3072, 4205, 4277
　Allemagne, 4266
　États-Unis, 3351
　France, 4343
　Nigeria, 4339
Sociétés savantes
　Chine, 170
　France, 171
Sociolinguistique 1533, 2021, 2025, 2085
　Inde, 2016
Sociologie 2-3, 5, 8-9, 12, 15, 19-20, 26, 28-36, 41, 43, 50-51, 55, 59-60, 66-68, 70, 72, 75, 79, 82, 84, 92-93, 96, 100, 102-103, 110, 207, 231, 234, 236, 238, 241, 271, 323, 327-328, 370, 427, 445, 459, 1871, 2281, 2286, 4537, 4552, 6000
　Afrique du Sud, 1328
　Allemagne, 129
　Allemagne RF, 133
　Canada, 10, 121
　Chine, 137
　Inde, 127
　Israël, 3826
　Italie, 130
　Japon, 87, 136
　Pays-Bas, 131, 155
　RD allemande, 172
　URSS, 4, 146
　Yougoslavie, 117, 120, 124, 134
Sociologie appliquée 142, 332, 5742, 5745-5748, 5750, 5752
　États-Unis, 5753
Sociologie bourgeoise 269, 287, 321, 975, 1640, 1968, 5615
　France, 125
Sociologie de l'art 2220, 2228
Sociologie de l'éducation 2282, 2286-2288, 2293, 2305, 2307-2310, 2313
　Allemagne RF, 2295
　Nigeria, 2292
　pays capitalistes, 2297
Sociologie de la connaissance 11, 244, 424, 444, 1945, 1947-1948, 1951, 1954-1955, 1959-1961, 1963-1964, 1967-1970, 1972-1973, 1975-1977, 1979-1981, 1984, 1986, 1990-1991, 1993, 1995, 1998, 2002, 2004
　Espagne, 1966
　États-Unis, 1962
Sociologie de la culture 1278
Sociologie de la littérature 7, 2243-2245, 2247-2251, 2261
　Australie, 3680
Sociologie de la profession 5020, 5023
　Espagne, 6242
　Yougoslavie, 5027
Sociologie de la religion 1680, 1776, 1858, 1870-1871, 1875
　Allemagne RF, 1855
Sociologie de la science 1997
Sociologie des loisirs 5342
Sociologie des organisations 1058, 1061
Sociologie du développement 2873, 2888, 2891
Sociologie du droit 1640-1642, 1646, 1650, 1658-1659, 1662, 1666, 1963, 5125
Sociologie du travail 232, 4601, 4676
　États-Unis, 2941
　France, 4677, 4681, 4685
　Italie, 4681
　Japon, 4690
Sociologie économique 4411, 4413
Sociologie électorale 5676
　Espagne, 5682
Sociologie industrielle 75, 4678-4679, 4687, 4689, 4691-4692, 4990
　Afrique du Sud, 4680
　Allemagne RF, 4688
Sociologie médicale 3195, 6160, 6168-6169, 6173, 6175
Sociologie militaire 5707, 5713
　Allemagne RF, 5720
Sociologie politique 5396-5403, 5405
Sociologie rurale 173, 177, 4033, 4134, 4145
　Allemagne, 2789

Index des matières

Brésil, 4075
Japon, 4135, 4164
Sociologie urbaine 4215, 4260, 4274, 4281, 4286, 4318, 4341, 4373, 4406, 4409
    Allemagne, 4375
    États-Unis, 4302
    France, 4287
Sociologues 76-77, 81, 85, 88-89, 91, 93-95, 97, 103-104, 106-109, 1013, 3673
    États-Unis, 98, 221
    pays arabes, 2733
    Pays-Bas, 111
    Yougoslavie, 5027
Soins médicaux 6184, 6191, 6198, 6206
    Australie, 6201
    Canada, 6199
    Espagne, 6190
    États-Unis, 6180-6181, 6185
    Royaume-Uni, 6196
Solidarité 934
Solidarité de groupe 1029, 1817
Solitude 890, 893, 897
Sommeil 424, 821
Sondages 494
Sorcellerie 1693, 1699
    Colombie, 1883
    France, 1696
Sorciers 1702
    Europe, 1692
Sources d'information 184
Sous-développement 2881
    Canada, 4152
    Italie, 2879
    Malaisie, 4019
    Paraguay, 2382
Sous-emploi
    États-Unis, 4742
Souveraineté 5733
Sport 1227, 5358, 5369-5370, 5373, 5380, 5383, 5388-5389, 5391, 5393
    États-Unis, 5371, 5379, 5384, 5387
    Inde, 1851
    Royaume-Uni, 5384
    URSS, 5359, 5390
Sportifs 5367
Statistique 526, 528-529, 533, 552-554, 561, 573, 582
    Hongrie, 548
Statut de la femme 1305, 2598, 3416, 3574, 3580, 3582-3583, 3588, 3596, 3599, 3602, 3604, 3612, 3617, 3635
    Afghanistan, 3581, 3644
    Allemagne RF, 3575
    Amérique latine, 3618
    Australie, 4810
    Canada, 3592
    Égypte, 3603
    Émirats Arabes Unis, 3641
    États-Unis, 3590, 3622, 3632
    France, 3610
    Hongrie, 4820
    Inde, 3611, 3626, 4791

Iran, 3644
Irlande, 3620
Islam, 3578
Israël, 3711
Italie, 3595, 3633
Japon, 3609, 3630
Maroc, 1649, 3578
Norvège, 3607
Pakistan, 3631
pays arabes, 3598
pays de la CEE, 3606
pays en développement, 3577
Pérou, 3586
Porto Rico, 3576, 3619
Scandinavie, 4841
Tchécoslovaquie, 3605, 3642, 3647
URSS, 3605, 4799
Uruguay, 3623
Yémen, 3621
Yémen RPD, 3627
Zaïre, 3616
Statut professionnel 1829, 4938, 5029, 5038, 5049, 5073, 5513
    Allemagne RF, 5116
    États-Unis, 5032, 5045
    Mexique, 4833
Statut social 1036, 2723-2727, 2729, 3712, 4381
    Allemagne RF, 2730
    Australie, 6201
    États-Unis, 2370, 3753
    Iran, 3250
Stéréotypes 4778
Stérilité
    Haute Volta, 3272
Stouffer, Samuel A., 1216
Stratégie de développement 2881
    Asie du Sud, 4054
Stratégie de recherche 184, 424, 444
Stratification professionnelle 5060, 5068, 5075
    Finlande, 5050
    Portugal, 5061
    Suède, 5044
    Trinité et Tobago, 2736
Stratification sociale 1806, 2592, 2597-2598, 2603, 2605, 2609, 2617, 2623, 2672, 2919
    Canada, 2611, 3666, 3686, 3691
    Corée R, 4489
    Hong Kong, 2606
    Inde, 2601
    Japon, 3157
Structuralisme 67-68, 243, 261, 289, 309
Structure de classe 2600, 2623, 2651, 2717
    Afrique du Sud, 2661
    Amérique centrale, 2719
    Europe orientale, 2582
    France, 2704
    Italie, 2693
    Pérou, 2696
    Royaume-Uni, 2630, 2780
Structure économique 4468

Structure professionnelle
　Allemagne RF, 5047
　Norvège, 5064
　pays en développement, 5041
Structure sociale 659, 826, 889, 2314,
　　2560-2561, 2571, 2574, 2578-2580,
　　2607, 4620
　Allemagne RF, 2586, 2588
　Chine, 2569
　Espagne, 1320
　Europe, 2577
　Europe occidentale, 446
　Europe orientale, 2582
　Indonésie, 2573
　Italie, 2583
　Japon, 2587
　URSS, 2567, 2585
　Yougoslavie, 2566
Structure urbaine
　États-Unis, 4392
　France, 4275
Stupéfiants 5811
　États-Unis, 5812, 5817
　Pérou, 5794
Sturzo, Luigi, 5410, 5522
Subculture 1332
Suicide 1168, 3217, 5870, 5896, 5922, 5930,
　　5952, 5973
　Argentine, 5886
　États-Unis, 5951
　Inde, 5891
Superstition 1693, 1869
Symboles 1544, 1583, 2035, 2047, 2049-2050,
　　2059, 2088, 2280, 3084
Symbolisme 2039, 2045, 2052, 2063
　Inde, 1880
Symbolisme religieux 2039
　Afrique, 1877
Syndicalisme 4516, 5184, 5187, 5247, 5493
　Allemagne, 5193
　Brésil, 5239
　États-Unis, 5172, 5205, 5212
　Europe, 5207
　France, 5190
　Royaume-Uni, 5190, 5243
　Suisse, 5171
Syndicats 4860, 5168, 5174, 5179, 5185,
　　5198, 5200, 5228, 5244, 5250, 5540
　Afrique du Sud, 5204
　Allemagne RF, 5177, 5189, 5215
　Brésil, 5188
　Canada, 4618, 5169, 5182, 5240
　Espagne, 5233
　États-Unis, 2923, 3759, 5175, 5178, 5183,
　　5192, 5206, 5208, 5223, 5227, 5237,
　　5245, 5297
　France, 4832, 5155, 5196, 5225
　Hong Kong, 5194
　Inde, 5210
　Italie, 5166-5167, 5173, 5186, 5235
　Japon, 5214
　Mexique, 5203

　Norvège, 5219
　Papouasie-Nouvelle-Guinée, 5234
　Porto Rico, 5197
　Royaume-Uni, 5180, 5191-5192, 5199,
　　5202, 5216, 5224, 5238, 5248
　Suède, 5236
　Tanzanie, 5176
　Tchécoslovaquie, 5230
　Tunisie, 5249
Système coopératif 4437
　Brésil, 4447, 4453
　Canada, 4452
　Colombie, 4438
　Italie, 4430
　Jordanie, 4434
　Portugal, 4440
　Royaume-Uni, 4421
　Sierra Leone, 4426
Système pénitentiaire 5842, 5956, 5972
　Algérie, 5918
　Belgique, 5990
　Canada, 5864, 5876, 5907
　Espagne, 5868
　Norvège, 5921
Système social 468, 1260, 1652, 2562,
　　2564-2565, 2570, 2572, 2576, 2581,
　　2584, 2591, 2894, 3940, 4420, 6088
Systèmes d'enseignement 2298, 2322, 2353,
　　5077
　Afrique, 2380
　Allemagne RF, 2359
　Australie, 2376
　Autriche, 2377
　Chine, 2363
　Corée R, 2371
　Danemark, 5055
　Espagne, 2320, 2378
　États-Unis, 2344, 2350, 2364
　Éthiopie, 2399
　France, 2373, 3624
　Ghana, 2400
　Inde, 2386, 2393
　Indonésie, 2351
　Japon, 2394
　Malaisie, 2337
　Nigeria, 2340
　Paraguay, 2382
　Pérou, 2384
　Royaume-Uni, 2096, 2347, 2365
　Tanzanie, 2388
　URSS, 2343, 2396
　Zimbabwe, 2362
Systèmes d'information 192
Systèmes de parti
　Australie, 5580
　Canada, 5580
Systèmes de valeur 1443, 1447, 1452,
　　1456-1457, 1464, 1466, 1468, 1480,
　　1483, 1591, 1595, 1789, 2066, 2867,
　　3540, 4599, 4702, 5337, 5357, 5434
　Brésil, 1364
　Inde, 2766

Suisse, 1477
URSS, 2706
Systèmes économiques 2584, 3422, 4417
Canada, 4415
Systèmes électoraux
États-Unis, 5527
Systèmes juridiques 1652, 1658
Maroc, 1649
Systèmes politiques 2447, 5478, 5480, 5483-5484, 5495, 5501, 5505, 5512, 5521, 5583
France, 5504
Pologne, 4997
URSS, 5482, 5581
Tables de mortalité 3222
États-Unis, 3223
Tâche du groupe 1032
Taoïsme 1713, 1754
Chine, 1790
Taux de fécondité
URSS, 3241
Taux de natalité
France, 3239
Japon, 3252
Taux de salaire 4488, 4504, 5202
Taxonomie 1891
Techniciens 4016
Techniques de prévision 344, 349, 362, 389, 400, 992, 3263, 3280, 3331, 5276
Technologie 1958, 4585, 4600, 4606, 4609, 4611, 4673
Technologie appropriée 4227, 4579, 4599, 4604
Technologie de l'information 179
Télécommunications
États-Unis, 2133
Télévision 829, 2145-2146, 2150, 2153-2154, 2158-2160, 2163, 2180, 2200, 2205, 2207, 3034
Allemagne RF, 2188
Espagne, 2169
États-Unis, 2132, 2134, 2214
Mexique, 2197
Temps 425, 431, 437, 447, 6233
Temps de loisir 5347-5351, 5355
Allemagne RF, 5352
Espagne, 5353
Temps de travail 4923, 4929, 4931, 4943, 4965, 4975, 4983
Tendances de recherche 28, 123
Amérique latine, 114
Brésil, 4075
États-Unis, 1454
Hongrie, 126
Inde, 127
Mexique, 112
URSS, 128
Terminologie 2903
Terrorisme 1495, 1510, 1558, 5938, 6010
Théâtre 2273
Amérique latine, 2276
Pologne, 2275

Théologie 1675, 1679
Théorie 51, 247, 257, 262, 285, 294, 305, 319, 335, 356, 465, 788
Théorie à moyenne portée 1062
Théorie critique 244, 267, 271, 299, 1248, 1947
Théorie de l'action 264, 315, 332, 337
Théorie de l'équilibre 507
Théorie de l'information 603
Théorie de l'organisation 1054-1055, 1057, 1060, 4545
Théorie des graphes 606
Théorie des jeux 2031
Théorie générale 342
Théorie générale des systèmes 598
Théorie sociale 250, 6025, 6066, 6088, 6091
Thésaurus 208, 531
Thurnwald, Hilde, 226
Tillich, Paul, 1675
Tolérance 1216, 2521, 3801
États-Unis, 1217
Topologie 604
Torture 1499
Totalitarisme 129
Touraine, Alain, 805, 5601
Tourisme 1506, 1917, 5363, 5365, 5368, 5372, 5376
Asie du Sud-Est, 5395
Caraïbes, 5382
Espagne, 5361
Europe, 5381
Japon, 5392
Pérou, 3791
Pologne, 5385
Venezuela, 5360
Toynbee, Arnold, 2872
Tradition 974, 1596
Israël, 3698
Italie, 2791
pays en développement, 2853
Tradition orale
Afrique, 2255
Traditionalisme 1595
Traitement de l'information 186, 195
Traitement des données 451
Transfert de technologie 4571, 4597
pays en développement, 4570
Transition démographique 2843
Transport urbain 4337
France, 4243
Irlande, 4298
Travail 715, 744, 746, 849, 1279, 4693-4694, 4696, 4699-4702, 4706-4707, 4715, 4719, 4725, 4729
RD allemande, 4695
URSS, 4721
Travail bénévole 4964
Travail d'équipe 4906
Travail des cas individuels 6145, 6147, 6150
Travail des enfants 4837, 4850, 4853
Inde, 4794, 4867
Travail forcé 2629

Index des matières

Travail ménager 1169, 4922
    États-Unis, 4912
Travail social 5783, 6140, 6142-6143, 6146, 6148-6149, 6151-6153, 6155, 6157
    Allemagne RF, 6139
    États-Unis, 6141, 6144, 6158
    Israël, 6156
    Royaume-Uni, 6040, 6154
Travail social des groupes 6138
Travail sur le terrain 477, 479, 481, 1277
    États-Unis, 472
Travailleurs 740, 749, 2331, 3954, 4970, 5085-5086, 5096-5097, 5198, 5348, 5412
    Allemagne, 5821
    Allemagne RF, 5093
    France, 4584, 5100
    URSS, 5081-5082, 5092, 5094, 6029
Travailleurs âgés 4825
    Australie, 4830
    États-Unis, 4683
    France, 4868
    Japon, 4826, 4855
Travailleurs agricoles 5083, 5098
    Tchécoslovaquie, 5088
    URSS, 3178
Travailleurs étrangers 2385, 4798, 4847, 4857
    Allemagne RF, 2383, 4851
    Canada, 3822
    Europe occidentale, 4807, 4824, 4828, 4836
    France, 3830, 3839, 4363, 4786, 4865
    pays de la CEE, 4785
    Pays-Bas, 4819, 4864
    Royaume-Uni, 3839
    Suisse, 4831
Travailleurs manuels 5084
    Canada, 2680
Travailleurs sociaux 6236-6237, 6255
    Royaume-Uni, 5998, 6250, 6256
Triade 1025
Tribalisme
    Inde, 3768, 3793
Tribus
    Inde, 3715
Troc
    pays en développement, 4446
Troeltsch, Ernst, 1776
Troubles de la personnalité 1518
Typologie 372, 516, 5013, 5019, 5542
Union consensuelle 3425
    États-Unis, 3404
    Norvège, 3392
Universités 89
    Allemagne RF, 2478
    Autriche, 2426
    France, 161, 2433, 5108
    Japon, 2438
    pays développés, 2481
    URSS, 146
Urbanisation 4256, 4299, 4331
    Afrique occidentale, 4352
    Amérique latine, 2722, 4371
    Asie du Sud, 4324
    Brésil, 4402
    Chine, 4241
    Colombie, 4353
    Corée R, 4355
    Espagne, 4248
    États-Unis, 4379
    Europe orientale, 4329
    Inde, 4370
    Japon, 2842
    pays arabes, 4336
    pays en développement, 4382
    Soudan, 3426
    URSS, 3117, 4309, 4408
    Viet-Nam, 4259
    Yougoslavie, 4387
Urbanisme 2264, 4194, 4214, 4238, 4348, 4398
    États-Unis, 4289
    URSS, 4322
Usage de stupéfiants 5796, 5801, 5805, 5818, 5820, 5824
    Allemagne RF, 5815
    Canada, 5806
    Espagne, 5809
    États-Unis, 5799, 5808, 5823
    France, 5800
    Mexique, 5806
    Pays-Bas, 5810
    URSS, 5797
Usage du tabac 2123
Usines
    Allemagne RF, 5089
    Japon, 4956
Utilisateurs d'information 182, 374
Utilisation des loisirs 5378
    Europe, 5381
    Israël, 5386
Utilisation des terres
    Australie, 4297
    États-Unis, 4108
    Inde, 4083, 4370
    Nigeria, 4137
Utopie 1206, 1245-1246, 1256, 1259, 1262, 1265, 3589
Valeur 247, 1578
Valeurs culturelles 1417
Valeurs de groupe 1044
Validité 474, 491, 493
Van Houten, Donald R., 1074
Vérification 390, 399
Veuvage 3390
    France, 3391
Veuve 3421
    Afrique, 3418
Vico, Giambattista, 662
Vie conjugale 3417
Vie économique 4466
Vie familiale 1548, 3464, 3487, 3497-3498, 3508, 3512, 3516, 3528, 3531, 3533, 3541-3542, 3556, 4870

Argentine, 3570
Brésil, 4080
Chine, 4140
États-Unis, 3504
Finlande, 3494
Royaume-Uni, 3510
Vie politique 5694
Inde, 5690
Vie privée 685
Vie professionnelle 2952, 3531, 5063, 5066
Vie quotidienne 1243, 1298, 1311, 1326, 1342, 1365, 1405, 1885, 2045, 2592
États-Unis, 1348
Vie rurale 4029, 4101, 4171
Brésil, 4080
États-Unis, 4072
France, 4031, 4930
Japon, 4017
Royaume-Uni, 4077
Tunisie, 4087
Vie urbaine 590, 3217, 4251, 4394
États-Unis, 4209, 4254
Japon, 4300
Royaume-Uni, 5775, 6038
Vieillesse 3068, 3072, 3074, 3077, 3082-3083, 3102-3103, 3105
Espagne, 3075
États-Unis, 3071
Royaume-Uni, 3110
Vieillissement 2064, 3069, 3093, 3096, 3101, 3104
Villages 1625, 4119, 4131, 4150, 4186, 4292
Afrique occidentale, 4059
Algérie, 4037
Bangladesh, 4035
Chine, 4140
Danemark, 4176
France, 2278, 3511, 4106
Hongrie, 4095
Inde, 1486, 1880, 2601, 4018, 4023, 4052, 4084
Indonésie, 4146
Israël, 3698
Japon, 484, 2985, 4017, 4088, 4090, 4180
Mexique, 4061
Pays-Bas, 4175
Pologne, 4105
Royaume-Uni, 4070
Tanzanie, 4065, 4123
Thaïlande, 3985
URSS, 2396, 2538, 4015-4016, 4100, 4102, 4139, 4163, 4165-4166, 4187, 4189, 4239, 4615
Yougoslavie, 3998, 4004, 4085
Villes 2851, 4204, 4225, 4292, 4350, 4597
Allemagne RF, 4279, 4390
Brésil, 2279
États-Unis, 2917, 4210, 4278, 4288
France, 4295

Inde, 4369
Iran, 4268
Israël, 4230
Japon, 4011, 4267, 4316, 4404
Moyen-Orient, 4354, 4356
Tchécoslovaquie, 4315
URSS, 2173, 3165, 4263
Villes nouvelles 4271
Royaume-Uni, 4207, 4229
Vincent, Paul, 214
Viol 5853, 5885, 5919
États-Unis, 5911
Violence 538, 947, 1275, 1516, 1521, 1524, 1548, 1556, 1560, 1564, 1577, 2198, 2207, 2431, 2817, 3508, 5388, 5496, 5977
Colombie, 1571, 2829
États-Unis, 1509, 1526, 1528, 1582, 5384
Royaume-Uni, 5384
Vol 5894, 5970
États-Unis, 5858
Pays-Bas, 5937
Voleurs
Canada, 5929
Voyages 5495
Wach, J., 1835
Wallerstein, Immanuel, 5725
Weber, Max, 61, 242, 247, 249, 266, 286, 305, 318, 324, 337, 371, 397, 656, 880, 1138, 1686, 1835, 2309, 2579, 2806, 2810, 2841, 4441, 4455, 4687, 5403, 5421, 5590, 5594
Wittgenstein, Ludwig, 263, 1957, 2100
Znaniecki, Florian, 285
Zones résidentielles 4086, 4384, 4391
États-Unis, 4218
Japon, 4395
Pays-Bas, 4285
Pologne, 4368
Zones rurales 3108, 3497
Asie du Sud, 4054
Canada, 4152
Congo, 3981
Espagne, 5361, 6190
États-Unis, 4493, 4619, 6195
France, 4091, 6248
Inde, 3295, 5074
Mexique, 3433
URSS, 4120
Zones suburbaines 3109, 4003, 4311, 4366, 4381
États-Unis, 3046, 4276, 4306, 4312
Japon, 4208
Zones urbaines 2608, 2689, 3916
Colombie, 4227
États-Unis, 4244, 4397
Royaume-Uni, 5788
Zoroastrisme 1717